Understanding Management

Richard L. Daft
Vanderbilt University

Dorothy Marcic
Columbia University

SOUTH-WESTERN
CENGAGE Learning

Australia • Brazil • Japan • Korea • Mexico • Singapore • Spain • United Kingdom • United States

Understanding Management, Eighth Edition
Richard L. Daft and Dorothy Marcic

Vice President of Editorial, Business: Jack W. Calhoun

Publisher: Erin Joyner

Executive Editor: Scott Person

Developmental Editor: Erin Guendelsberger

Senior Editorial Assistant: Ruth Belanger

Senior Marketing Communications Manager: Jim Overly

Marketing Manager: Jonathan Monahan

Marketing Coordinator: Julia Tucker

Director, Education Production: Barbara Fuller Jacobsen

Content Project Manager: Emily Nesheim

Media Editor: Rob Ellington

eBook Production Project Manager: Lynn Vagg

Manufacturing Planner: Ron Montgomery

Production Service: MPS Limited, a Macmillan Company

Senior Art Director: Tippy McIntosh

Cover and Internal Designer: Red Hangar Design, Ltd

Cover Image: ©ra2 studio, Shutterstock

Remember This icon: ©Francesco81, Shutterstock

Take Action icon: ©dencg, Shutterstock

Rights Acquisition Director: Audrey Pettengill

Rights Acquisition Specialist: Amber Hosea

Library of Congress Control Number: 2011940534

ISBN-13: 978-1-111-58024-7

ISBN-10: 1-111-58024-3

South-Western
5191 Natorp Boulevard
Mason, OH 45040
USA

Cengage Learning products are represented in Canada by Nelson Education, Ltd.

For your course and learning solutions, visit **www.cengage.com**

Purchase any of our products at your local college store or at our preferred online store **www.cengagebrain.com**

Printed in Canada
1 2 3 4 5 6 7 15 14 13 12 11

With deep appreciation to Dorothy,
the playwright and partner in my life,
and to my parents, who started my life
toward outcomes that I could not understand at the time
—RLD

In memory of
Carol Allen (1928–2010),
a management whiz, whose service and devotion
leave a lasting legacy,
and
Marcia Day (1928–2009),
an indomitable force in the arts
—DM

Preface

Innovative Management for a Changing World

Today's managers and organizations are being buffeted by massive and far-reaching social, technological, and economic changes. Any manager who believed in the myth of stability was rocked out of complacency when, one after another, large financial institutions in the United States began to fail; automakers filed for bankruptcy; the housing market collapsed; and a global economic recession took hold and wouldn't let go. Business schools, as well as managers and businesses, are still scrambling to cope with the aftermath, keep up with fast-changing events, and evaluate the impact this volatile period of history will have on organizations in the future. This edition of *Understanding Management* addresses themes and issues that are directly relevant to the current, fast-shifting business environment. We revised *Understanding Management* with a goal of helping current and future managers find innovative solutions to the problems that plague today's organizations—whether they are everyday challenges or once-in-a-lifetime crises. The world in which most students will work as managers is undergoing a tremendous upheaval. Ethical turmoil, the need for crisis management skills, e-business, economic recession and rampant unemployment, rapidly changing technologies, globalization, outsourcing, increasing government regulation, social media, global supply chains, the Wall Street meltdown, and other changes place demands on managers that go beyond the techniques and ideas traditionally taught in management courses. Managing today requires the full breadth of management skills and capabilities. This text provides comprehensive coverage of both traditional management skills and the new competencies needed in a turbulent environment characterized by economic turmoil, political confusion, and general uncertainty.

In the traditional world of work, management was to control and limit people, enforce rules and regulations, seek stability and efficiency, design a top-down hierarchy, and achieve bottom-line results. To spur innovation and achieve high performance, however, managers need different skills, particularly in today's tough economy that has caused suffering for many employees. They have to find ways to engage workers' hearts and minds as well as take advantage of their physical labor. The new workplace asks that managers focus on building trust, inspiring commitment, leading change, harnessing people's creativity and enthusiasm, finding shared visions and values, and sharing information and power. Teamwork, collaboration, participation, and learning are guiding principles that help managers and employees maneuver the difficult terrain of today's turbulent business environment. Managers focus on developing, not controlling, people to adapt to new technologies and extraordinary environmental shifts, and thus achieve high performance and total corporate effectiveness.

Our vision for the eighth edition of *Understanding Management* is to present the newest management ideas for turbulent times in a way that is interesting and valuable to students while retaining the best of traditional management thinking. To achieve this vision, we have included the most recent management concepts and research and have shown the contemporary application of management ideas in organizations. A short questionnaire at the beginning of each chapter draws students personally into the topic. A chapter feature for new managers, called the New Manager Self-Test, gives students a sense of what will be expected when they become managers. At the end of each major chapter section, we have added a Remember This feature that provides a quick review of the salient concepts and terms students should remember. The combination of established scholarship, new ideas, and real-life applications gives students a taste of the energy, challenge, and adventure inherent in the dynamic field of management. We and the South-Western/Cengage Learning staff have worked together to provide a textbook better than any other at capturing the excitement of organizational management.

We revised *Understanding Management* to provide a book of utmost quality that will create in students both respect for the changing field of management and confidence that they can understand and master it. The textual portion of this book has been enhanced through the engaging, easy-to-understand writing style and the many in-text examples, boxed items, and short exercises that make the concepts come alive for students. The graphic component has been enhanced with several new and revised exhibits and a new set of photo essays that illustrate specific management concepts. The well-chosen photographs provide vivid illustrations and intimate glimpses of management scenes, events, and people. The photos are combined with brief essays that explain how a specific management concept looks and feels. Both the textual and graphic portions of the textbook help students grasp the often abstract and distant world of management.

Focus on Innovation: New to the Eighth Edition

A primary focus for revising the eighth edition has been to relate management concepts and theories to events in today's turbulent environment by bringing in current issues that real-life managers face.

Learning Opportunities

The eighth edition includes several innovative pedagogical features to help students understand their own management capabilities and learn what it is like to manage in an organization today. Each chapter begins with an opening questionnaire that directly relates to the topic of the chapter. New Manager Self-Tests in each chapter provide further opportunity for students to understand their management abilities. These short feedback questionnaires give students insight into how they would function in the real world of management. Remember This bullet-point summaries at the end of each major chapter section give students a snapshot of the key points and concepts covered in that section. End-of-chapter questions have been carefully revised to encourage critical thinking and application of chapter concepts. End-of-chapter exercises, cases, and ethical dilemmas help students sharpen their diagnostic skills for management problem solving.

Chapter Content

Within each chapter, many topics have been added or expanded to address the current issues managers face.

Chapter 1 includes a discussion of some of the high-impact events and changes that have made innovative management so critical to the success of organizations today and into the future. This introductory chapter also talks about making the leap from being an individual contributor in the organization to becoming a new manager. The chapter continues with solid coverage of the historical development of management and organizations. It includes an expanded discussion of systems thinking and an updated discussion of the quantitative approach and how it has been applied in recent years. The chapter also examines contemporary management tools for turbulent times.

Chapter 2 contains an updated view of current issues related to the environment and corporate culture, including a discussion of how managers adapt their organizations to address changes or challenges in the external environment. The chapter also illustrates how managers shape a high-performance culture as an innovative response to a shifting environment.

Chapter 3 has been thoroughly updated and revised. This chapter takes a look at the shifting international landscape, including the growing clout of China, India, and Brazil, and what this means for managers around the world. The chapter includes a new discussion of economic interdependence, a new section on the China-ASEAN Free Trade Area, and a new discussion of the bottom of the pyramid concept. In addition, the complex issues surrounding globalization are discussed, including a consideration of the globalization backlash.

Chapter 4 makes the business case for incorporating ethical values in the organization. The chapter includes a new discussion of the state of ethical management today, the arguments surrounding the issue of executive compensation, and the role managers play in creating an ethical organization. The chapter also includes new descriptions of the virtue ethics and practical approaches to ethical decision making. It considers corporate social responsibility issues as well, including a new discussion of management responses to the rapidly growing *Green Movement*.

Chapter 5 provides a discussion of the overall planning and goal-setting process, including the use of strategy maps for aligning goals. A new section outlines the benefits and limitations of planning and goal setting. This chapter also takes a close look at crisis planning and how to use scenarios. The chapter continues with a focus on the basics of formulating and implementing strategy. The final section of the chapter provides an updated and more focused discussion of how managers effectively execute strategy.

Chapter 6 gives an overview of managerial decision making, including decision-making models, personal decision styles, and a revised discussion of biases that can cloud managers' judgment and lead to bad decisions. The final section looks at innovative group decision making and includes a new discussion of the need to act with speed when operating in a turbulent environment or facing a crisis situation.

Chapter 7 discusses basic principles of organizing and describes both traditional and contemporary organizational structures in detail. The chapter includes a discussion of the strengths and weaknesses associated with each structural approach.

Chapter 8 focuses on the critical role of managing change and innovation. The chapter includes a new discussion of disruptive innovation and reverse innovation as well as an expanded section on open innovation and crowdsourcing. This chapter provides information about product and technology changes as well as about changing people and culture, and it discusses techniques for effectively implementing change.

Chapter 9 has been thoroughly revised to reflect the shifting role of human resource management (HRM) in today's turbulent economic environment. The chapter includes an updated discussion of the strategic role of HRM in building human capital, expanded sections on the erosion of the social contract between employer and employee and the trend toward contingent employment, new information about legal issues and employee benefits, and a discussion of how social media are being used for HR activities. This chapter has also been revised and updated to reflect the most recent thinking on organizational diversity issues. The chapter looks at how diversity is changing the domestic and global workforce and includes a discussion of the traditional versus inclusive models for managing diversity.

Chapter 10 continues its solid coverage of the basics of understanding individual behavior, including personality, values and attitudes, perception, emotional intelligence, learning and problem-solving styles, and stress management. A new description of the importance of self-confidence and self-efficacy has been added, as well as a new discussion of positive and negative emotions and how emotions influence behavior in the workplace.

Chapter 11 has been enriched with new sections on authentic leadership, gender differences in leadership, and the importance of leaders discovering and honing their strengths. The chapter also includes a more focused discussion of task versus relationship leadership behaviors and an updated discussion of followership. The section on transformational leadership has been updated as well.

Chapter 12 covers the foundations of motivation and incorporates a new section on social learning theory as it relates to motivation. The chapter has been enriched as well with an updated and expanded treatment of employee engagement, a revised discussion of using incentives for motivation, and a refocused section on job design for motivation.

Chapter 13 begins with a discussion of how managers facilitate strategic conversations by directing everyone's attention to the vision, values, and goals of the organization. The chapter explores the foundations of good communication and includes an expanded section on gender differences in communication and an enriched discussion of nonverbal communication. A new section discusses communication technology in today's workplace, including the use of new forms of manager communication such as blogs and other social media.

Chapter 14 acknowledges that work teams are sometimes ineffective and explores the reasons for this, including problems such as free riders and lack of trust among team members. The chapter then looks at how to make teams effective, including a discussion of what makes an effective team leader. The chapter covers the types of teams and looks at effectively using technology in virtual teams. The chapter also contains a section on managing conflict, including a new explanation of task versus relationship conflict.

Chapter 15 provides an overview of financial and quality control, including Six Sigma, ISO certification, and a new application of the balanced scorecard, which views employee learning and growth as the foundation of high performance. The chapter also addresses current concerns about corporate governance, including new government regulations and requirements.

In addition to the topics listed above, this text integrates coverage of the Internet and new technology into the various topics covered in each and every chapter.

Organization

The chapter sequence in *Understanding Management* is organized around the management functions of planning, organizing, leading, and controlling. These four functions effectively encompass both management research and characteristics of the manager's job.

Part One introduces the world of management, including the nature of management, issues related to today's chaotic environment, historical perspectives on management, and the technology-driven workplace.

Part Two examines the environments of management and organizations. This section includes material on the business environment and corporate culture, the global environment, and ethics and social responsibility.

Part Three presents two chapters on planning, including organizational goal setting and planning and the decision-making process.

Part Four focuses on organizing processes. These chapters describe dimensions of structural design, the design alternatives managers can use to achieve strategic objectives, structural designs for promoting innovation and change, the design and use of the human resource function, and the ways managing diverse employees are significant to the organizing function.

Part Five is devoted to leadership. The section begins with a chapter on understanding individual behavior. This foundation paves the way for subsequent discussion of leadership, motivation of employees, communication, and team management.

Part Six describes the controlling function of management, including basic principles of total quality management, the design of control systems, and the difference between hierarchical and decentralized control.

Innovative Features

A major goal of this book is to offer better ways of using the textbook medium to convey management knowledge to the reader. To this end, the book includes several innovative features that draw students in and help them contemplate, absorb, and comprehend management concepts. South-Western has brought together a team of experts to create and coordinate color photographs, video cases, beautiful artwork, and supplemental materials for the best management textbook and package on the market.

Chapter Outline and Objectives. Each chapter begins with a clear statement of its learning objectives and an outline of its contents. These devices provide an overview of what is to come and can also be used by students to guide their study and test their understanding and retention of important points.

Are You Ready to Be a Manager? Questionnaire. This feature grabs student attention immediately, giving the student a chance to participate in the chapter content actively by completing a short questionnaire.

Take Action. At strategic places through the chapter, students are invited to "Take Action"—to complete a New Manager Self-Test or end-of-chapter activity that relates to the concepts being discussed.

New Manager Self-Test. Two New Manager Self-Tests in each chapter provide opportunities for self-assessment as a way for students to experience management issues in a personal way. The change from individual performer to new manager is dramatic, and these self-tests provide insight into what to expect and how students might perform in the world of the new manager.

Concept Connection Photo Essays. A key feature of the book is the use of photographs accompanied by detailed photo essay captions that enhance learning. Each caption highlights and illustrates one or more specific concepts from the text to reinforce student understanding of the concepts. Although the photos are beautiful to look at, they also convey the vividness, immediacy, and concreteness of management events in today's business world.

Contemporary Examples. Every chapter of the text contains several written examples of management incidents. They are placed at strategic points in the chapter and are designed to illustrate the application of concepts to specific companies. These in-text examples include small and mid-size businesses that students may start working with after graduation, well-known U.S. and international companies, and less well-known companies and not-for-profit organizations. These examples put students in touch with the real world of organizations so that they can appreciate the value of management concepts.

Spotlight On . . . Boxes. These features address specific topics straight from the field of management that are of special interest to students. They may describe a contemporary topic or problem that is relevant to chapter content, or they may contain a diagnostic questionnaire or a special example of how managers handle a problem. The boxes heighten student interest in the subject matter and provide an auxiliary view of management issues not typically available in textbooks.

Benchmarking Boxes. Each chapter contains a box that highlights some effective and productive technique or system developed by an outstanding manager or company.

Business Blooper. Although most of the book gives students insights into effective management behavior, forgetting common mistakes can be a real loss. Therefore, each chapter describes ineffective decisions and behaviors which have led to disastrous outcomes in companies.

Video Cases. Each chapter concludes with two video cases that illustrate the concepts presented in the text. The On the Job videos enhance the classroom experience by giving students the chance to hear from real-world business leaders so they can see the direct application of the management theories they have learned. Companies discussed include Camp Bow Wow, Barcelona, and Theo Chocolate. Each video case explores the issues covered in the video, allowing students to synthesize material they view. The video cases culminate with several questions that can be used to launch classroom discussion or can be assigned as homework. Suggested answers are provided in the Instructor's Manual. The Biz Flix videos add an element of interest to the classroom by allowing students to view clips from popular Hollywood movies, including *In Good Company, Friday Night Lights,* and *Failure to Launch.* Video cases and discussion questions are included to enhance classroom discussion, with suggested answers provided in the Instructor's Manual.

Exhibits. Several exhibits have been added or revised in the eighth edition to enhance student understanding. Many aspects of management are research based, and some concepts tend to be abstract and theoretical. The many exhibits throughout this book enhance students' awareness and understanding of these concepts. These exhibits consolidate key points, indicate relationships among concepts, and visually illustrate concepts. They also make effective use of color to enhance their imagery and appeal.

Remember This. At the end of each major section of a chapter is a Remember This bullet-point summary of the key concepts, ideas, and terms discussed in that section. The Remember This list gives students an easy way to review the salient points covered in the chapter.

Discussion Questions. Each chapter closes with discussion questions that will enable students to check their understanding of key issues, think beyond basic concepts, and determine areas that require further study.

End of Chapter Application Opportunities. End-of-chapter exercises called Self-Learning, Group Learning, Action Learning, and Ethical Dilemma provide opportunities for content application. Students can take self-tests, providing an opportunity to experience management issues in a personal way. These exercises take the form of questionnaires, scenarios, and activities, and many also provide an opportunity for students to work in teams. The exercises are tied into the chapters through the Take Action feature that refers students to the end-of-chapter exercises at the appropriate point in the chapter content.

Case for Critical Analysis. Also appearing at the end of each chapter is a brief but substantive case that offers an opportunity for student analysis and class discussion. Some of these cases are about companies whose names students will recognize; others are based on real management events, but the identities of companies and managers have been disguised. These cases allow students to sharpen their diagnostic skills for management problem solving.

Continuing Case. Located online in Appendix B, the Continuing Case is a running discussion of management topics appropriate to that part as experienced by Walmart. Focusing on one company allows students to follow the managers' and the organization's long-term problems and solutions in a sustained manner.

Supplementary Materials

Instructor's CD-ROM. Key instructor ancillaries (Instructor's Manual, Test Bank, ExamView, and PowerPoint slides) are provided on CD-ROM, giving instructors the ultimate tool for customizing lectures and presentations.

Instructor's Manual. Designed to provide support for instructors new to the course, as well as innovative materials for experienced professors, the Instructor's Manual includes Chapter Outlines, annotated learning objectives, Lecture Notes, and sample Lecture Outlines. Additionally, the Instructor's Manual includes answers and teaching notes to end-of-chapter materials, including the exercises and cases. This resource is available on the Instructor's Resource CD-ROM or on the companion Web site.

Test Bank. Scrutinized for accuracy, the Test Bank includes more than 3,000 multiple-choice, true/false, completion, short-answer, and essay questions. Page references are indicated for every question, and each question is also tagged based on AACSB guidelines and Bloom's Taxonomy. This resource is available on the Instructor's Resource CD-ROM or on the companion Web site.

ExamView. Available on the Instructor's Resource CD-ROM, ExamView contains all of the questions in the printed Test Bank. This program is easy-to-use test creation software. Instructors can add or edit questions, instructions, and answers, and select questions (randomly or numerically) by previewing them on screen. Instructors can also create and administer quizzes online, whether over the Internet, a local area network (LAN), or a wide area network (WAN).

PowerPoint Lecture Presentation. Available on the Instructor's Resource CD-ROM and the companion Web site, the PowerPoint Lecture Presentation enables instructors to customize their own multimedia classroom presentation. Containing an average of 27 slides per chapter, the package includes chapter outlines as well as exhibits from the text. Material is organized by chapter and can be modified or expanded for individual classroom use. PowerPoint slides are also easily printed to create customized Transparency Masters.

Reel to Real Video Package. Put management in action with this edition's new video package that includes both Biz Flix videos and new On the Job videos. Biz Flix film clips taken from popular Hollywood movies demonstrate management in familiar, memorable settings and are integrated with short printed Video Cases and discussion questions found at the end of each chapter. This edition's new On the Job videos illustrate management concepts at work within familiar companies, large and small. Students gain an insider's perspective on issues that businesses face as corresponding Video Cases and discussion questions reinforce concepts.

Text Companion Web Site. Access important teaching resources on this companion Web site. For your convenience, you can download electronic versions of the instructor supplements at the password-protected section of the site, including the Instructor's Manual, Test Bank, and PowerPoint presentations.

To access these additional course materials and companion resources, please visit www.cengagebrain.com. At the CengageBrain.com home page, search for the ISBN of your title (from the back cover of your book) using the search box at the top of the page. This will take you to the product page where free companion resources can be found.

MANAGEMENT CourseMate. Engaging, trackable, and affordable, the new MANAGEMENT CourseMate Web site offers a dynamic way to bring course concepts to life with interactive learning, study, and exam preparation tools that support this printed edition of the text. Watch student comprehension soar with all-new flash cards and engaging games, audio summaries, self assessments, streaming videos, and more in this textbook-specific Web site. A complete e-book provides you with the choice of an entire online learning experience. MANAGEMENT CourseMate goes beyond the book to deliver what you need!

CengageNOW. This robust, online course management system gives you more control in less time and delivers better student outcomes—NOW. CengageNOW for *Understanding Management*, Eighth Edition, includes teaching and learning resources organized around lecturing, creating assignments, grading, quizzing, and tracking student progress and performance. Flexible assignments, automatic grading, and a gradebook option provide more control while saving you valuable time. A Personalized Study diagnostic tool empowers students to master concepts, prepare for exams, and become more involved in class.

Aplia. Engage, prepare, and educate your students with this ideal online learning solution. Aplia's™ management solution ensures that students stay on top of their coursework with regularly scheduled homework assignments and automatic grading with detailed, immediate feedback on every question. Interactive teaching tools and content further increase engagement and understanding. Aplia™ assignments match the language, style, and structure of *Understanding Management*, Eighth Edition, allowing your students to apply what they learn in the text directly to their homework.

WebTutor™ for Blackboard® or WebCT®. Jumpstart your course with this interactive, Web-based, teaching and learning resource that is designed specifically for Daft/Marcic's *Understanding Management*, Eighth Edition. Easily blend, add, edit, reorganize, or delete content, including media assets, quizzing, Web links, discussion topics, interactive games and exercises, and more. These tools supplement the classroom experience and ensure that students leave with the resources they need to succeed in management today.

Acknowledgments

Richard L. Daft. Here at Vanderbilt, I want to extend special appreciation to my assistant, Barbara Haselton. Barbara provided excellent support and assistance on a variety of projects that gave me time to write. I also want to acknowledge an intellectual debt to my colleagues, Bruce Barry, Ray Friedman, Neta Moye, Rich Oliver, David Owens, Ranga Ramanujam, Bart Victor, and Tim Vogus. Thanks also to Deans Jim Bradford and Bill Christie, who have supported my writing projects and maintained a positive scholarly atmosphere in the school.

I want to acknowledge the love and contributions of my wife, Dorothy Marcic. Dorothy has been very supportive during this revision, as we share our lives together. I also want to acknowledge the love and support from my five daughters—Danielle, Amy, Roxanne, Solange, and Elizabeth—who make my life special during our precious time together. Thanks also to B. J. and Kaitlyn and Kaci and Matthew for their warmth and smiles that brighten my life, especially during our time together visiting interesting places.

—R.L.D.

Dorothy Marcic. There have been numerous people who have given time and support on this project, including my assistant, Allison Greer. Friends and colleagues who gave invaluable support include Patricia McGraw Romano, Bill Franzblau, Franky Grebacher, Georgia Sauer, Jane Faily, Lynn Lobban, Gail Phanuf, Peter Neamann, Victoria Marsick, Bob and Debby Rosenfeld, Nick Ritchie, Karen Streets-Anderson, Kathy Diaz, Andi Seals, Adrienne Corn, Mark and Maxine Rossman, Adrienne Ewing-Roush, Hillary Chapman, Mehr Mansuri, Annie Deardorff, Michael Heitzler, and Shidan Majidi. How can one do such a project without family love and support? My sister, Janet Mittelsteadt, is a true friend; my cousins Marilyn Nowak (a bright light), Michael Shoemaker (the genealogist who has helped me find my own roots), and Katherine Runde (who is so precious); my Aunt Babe, who is forever a link to the past. There is no way to imagine my life without my three beautiful daughters—Roxanne, Solange, and Elizabeth—who have taught me more than all my degrees combined. And, finally, my husband, Dick Daft, whose collaboration on this book is greatly satisfying.

—D.M.

A gratifying experience for us was working with the team of dedicated professionals at South-Western who were committed to the vision of producing the best management text ever. We are grateful to Scott Person, executive editor, whose interest, creative ideas, and assistance kept this book's spirit alive. Erin Guendelsberger, developmental editor, provided encouragement, superb project coordination, and excellent ideas that helped the team meet a demanding and sometimes arduous schedule. Emily Nesheim, content project manager, expertly managed the production phase and ensured that everyone working on the production process adhered to high standards of quality. Tippy McIntosh, art director, contributed her graphic arts skills to create a visually dynamic design. Ruth Belanger, senior editorial assistant, and Julia Tucker, marketing coordinator, skillfully pitched in to help keep the project on track. Joe Devine deserves a special thank-you for his layout expertise and commitment to producing an attractive, high-quality textbook. Additionally,

BJ Parker, Copyshop, USA, contributed the solid and well-researched Continuing Case, and Jane Woodside did an excellent job researching photos and writing new concept connections. Thanks also to media editor Rob Ellington, print buyer Ron Montgomery, and rights specialist Amber Hosea.

Another group of people who made a major contribution to this textbook are the management experts who provided advice, reviews, answers to questions, and suggestions for changes, insertions, and clarifications. We want to thank each of these colleagues for their valuable feedback and suggestions on the eighth edition:

Diane Bandow
Troy University

Paul Coakley
Community College of Baltimore County

Dawn Fairchild
Delta College

Jud Faurer
Metro State College of Denver

Wayne Gawlik
Joliet Junior College

Guy Lochiatto
Massachusetts Bay Community College

John Maslyn
Belmont University

Val Miskin
Washington State University

Gary Nichols
University of Central Florida

We would also like to continue to acknowledge those reviewers who have contributed comments, suggestions, and feedback on previous editions:

Larry Aaronson
Community College of Baltimore County

David C. Adams
Manhattanville College

David Alexander
Christian Brothers University

Erin M. Alexander
University of Houston–Clear Lake

Reginald L Audibert
California State University—Long Beach

Hal Babson
Columbus State Community College

Reuel Barksdale
Columbus State Community College

Gloria Bemben
Finger Lakes Community College

Pat Bernson
County College of Morris

Art Bethke
Northeast Louisiana University

Burrell A. Brown
California University of Pennsylvania

Paula Buchanan
Jacksonville State University

Thomas Butte
Humboldt State University

Peter Bycio
Xavier University, Ohio

Diane Caggiano
Fitchburg State College

Douglas E. Cathon
St. Augustine's College

Bruce Charnov
Hofstra University

Jim Ciminskie
Bay de Noc Community College

Paul Coakley
The Community College of Baltimore County

Gloria Cockerell
Collin College

Dan Connaughton
University of Florida

Bruce Conwers
Kaskaskia College

Jack Cox
Amberton University

Byron L. David
The City College of New York

Richard De Luca
William Paterson University

Robert DeDominic
Montana Tech

Linn Van Dyne
Michigan State University

John C. Edwards
East Carolina University

Mary Ann Edwards
College of Mount St. Joseph

Paul Ewell
Bridgewater College

Mary M. Fanning
College of Notre Dame of Maryland

Janice M. Feldbauer
Austin Community College

Merideth Ferguson
Baylor University

Daryl Fortin
Upper Iowa University

Karen Fritz
Bridgewater College

Michael P. Gagnon
New Hampshire Community Technical College

Wayne Gawlik
Joliet Junior College

Richard H. Gayor
Antelope Valley College

Dan Geeding
Xavier University, Ohio

James Genseal
Joliet Junior College

Peter Gibson
Becker College

Yezdi H. Godiwalla
University of Wisconsin—Whitewater

Carol R. Graham
Western Kentucky University

Gary Greene
Manatee Community College

James Halloran
Wesleyan College

Ken Harris
Indiana University Southeast

Paul Hayes
Coastal Carolina Community College

Dennis Heaton
Maharishi University of Management, Iowa

Stephen R. Hiatt
Catawba College

Jeffrey D. Hines
Davenport College

Bob Hoerber
Westminster College

Betty Hoge
Bridgewater College

James N. Holly
University of Wisconsin–Green Bay

Genelle Jacobson
Ridgewater College

C. Joy Jones
Ohio Valley College

Jody Jones
Oklahoma Christian University

Kathleen Jones
University of North Dakota

Sheryl Kae
Lynchburg College

David Kaiser
University of Minnesota

Jordan J. Kaplan
Long Island University

J. Michael Keenan
Western Michigan University

Jerry Kinard
Western Carolina University

Gloria Komer
Stark State College

Paula C. Kougl
Western Oregon University

Cynthia Krom
Mount St. Mary College

Sal Kukalis
California State University—Long Beach

Mukta Kulkarni
University of Texas–San Antonio

William B. Lamb
Millsaps College

Robert E. Ledman
Morehouse College

George Lehma
Bluffton College

Joyce LeMay
Bethel University

Cynthia Lengnick-Hall
University of Texas–San Antonio

Janet C. Luke
Georgia Baptist College of Nursing

Jenna Lundburg
Ithaca College

Walter J. MacMillan
Oral Roberts University

Myrna P. Mandell
California State University, Northridge

Daniel B. Marin
Louisiana State University

Michael Market
Jacksonville State University

Michael A. Mazzocco
University of Illinois

Wade McCutcheon
East Texas Baptist College

James C. McElroy
Iowa State University

Dennis W. Meyers
Texas State Technical College

Alan N. Miller
University of Nevada–Las Vegas

Irene A. Miller
Southern Illinois University

Tom Miller
Concordia University

W J Mitchell
Bladen Community College

James L. Moseley
Wayne State University

Micah Mukabi
Essex County College

David W. Murphy
Madisonville Community College

Nora Nurre
Upper Iowa University

Tomas J. Ogazon
St. Thomas University

Allen Oghenejbo
Mills College

John Okpara
Bloomsburg University

Linda Overstreet
Hillsborough Community College

Lori A. Peterson
Augsburg College

Ken Peterson
Metropolitan State University

Clifton D. Petty
Drury College

James I. Phillips
Northeastern State University

Michael Provitera
Barry University

Linda Putchinski
University of Central Florida

Abe Qastin
Lakeland College

Kenneth Radig
Medaille College

Gerald D. Ramsey
Indiana University Southeast

David Ransom
Hocking College

Holly Caldwell Ratwani
Bridgewater College

Barbara Redmond
Briar Cliff College

William Reisel
St. John's University–New York

Terry L. Riddle
Central Virginia Community College

Walter F. Rohrs
Wagner College

Meir Russ
University of Wisconsin–Green Bay

Marcy Satterwhite
Lake Land College

Don Schreiber
Baylor University

Kilmon Shin
Ferris State University

Daniel G. Spencer
University of Kansas

Gary Spokes
Pace University

M. Sprencz
David N. Meyers College

Shanths Srinivas
California State Polytechnic University, Pomona

Jeffrey Stauffer
Ventura College

William A. Stower
Seton Hall University

Peter Straus
Chico State

Mary Studer
Southwestern Michigan College

James Swenson
Moorhead State University, Minnesota

Thomas Sy
California State University—Long Beach

Irwin Talbot
St. Peter's College

Andrew Timothy
Lourdes College

Frank G. Titlow
St. Petersburg Junior College

John Todd
University of Arkansas

Kevin A. Van Dewark
Humphreys College

Philip Varca
University of Wyoming

Dennis L. Varin
Southern Oregon University

Gina Vega
Merrimack College

George S. Vozikis
University of Tulsa

Donna Waldron
Manchester Community College

Bruce C. Walker
Northeast Louisiana University

Peter Wachtel
Kean University

Noemy Watchel
Kean University

Mark Weber
University of Minnesota

Emilia S. Westney
Texas Tech University

Stan Williamson
Northeast Louisiana University

Alla L. Wilson
University of Wisconsin–Green Bay

Ignatius Yacomb
Loma Linda University

Imad Jim Zbib
Ramapo College of New Jersey

Nancy Zimmerman
Community College of Baltimore County, Catonsville

Vic Zimmerman
Pima Community College

About the Authors

Richard L. Daft, Ph.D., is the Brownlee O. Currey, Jr., Professor of Management in the Owen Graduate School of Management at Vanderbilt University. Professor Daft specializes in the study of organization theory and leadership. Dr. Daft is a Fellow of the Academy of Management and has served on the editorial boards of *Academy of Management Journal, Administrative Science Quarterly,* and *Journal of Management Education.* He was the associate editor-in-chief of *Organization Science* and served for three years as associate editor of *Administrative Science Quarterly*.

Professor Daft has authored or coauthored 13 books, including *The Executive and the Elephant: A Leader's Guide to Building Inner Excellence* (Jossey-Bass, 2010), *Organization Theory and Design* (South-Western, 2010), *The Leadership Experience* (South-Western, 2011), and *What to Study: Generating and Developing Research Questions* (Sage, 1982). He published *Fusion Leadership: Unlocking the Subtle Forces That Change People and Organizations* (Berrett-Koehler, 2000) with Robert Lengel. He has also authored dozens of scholarly articles, papers, and chapters. His work has been published in *Administrative Science Quarterly, Academy of Management Journal, Academy of Management Review, Strategic Management Journal, Journal of Management, Accounting Organizations* and *Society, Management Science, MIS Quarterly, California Management Review,* and *Organizational Behavior Teaching Review.* Professor Daft is also an active teacher and consultant. He has taught management, leadership, organizational change, organizational theory, and organizational behavior.

Professor Daft served as associate dean, produced for-profit theatrical productions, and helped manage a start-up enterprise. He has been involved in management development and consulting for many companies and government organizations, including the American Bankers Association, Bridgestone, Bell Canada, the Transportation Research Board, Nortel, TVA, Pratt & Whitney, State Farm Insurance, Tenneco, the United States Air Force, the United States Army, J. C. Bradford & Co., Central Parking System, Entergy, Bristol-Myers Squibb, First American National Bank, and the Vanderbilt University Medical Center.

Dorothy Marcic, Ed.D., MPH, is a professor at Columbia University and former faculty member at Vanderbilt University. Dr. Marcic is also a former Fulbright Scholar at the University of Economics in Prague and the Czech Management Center, where she taught courses and did research in leadership, organizational behavior, and cross-cultural management. She has taught courses at the Monterrey Institute of International Studies and has taught courses or given presentations at the Helsinki School of Economics, Slovenia Management Center, College of Trade in Bulgaria, City University of Slovakia, Landegg Institute in Switzerland, the Swedish Management Association, Technion University in Israel, and the London School of Economics. Other international work includes projects at the Autonomous University in Guadalajara, Mexico, and a training program for the World Health Organization in Guatemala. She has served on the boards of the Organizational Teaching Society, the Health Administration Section of the American Public Health Association, and the Journal of Applied Business Research.

Dr. Marcic has authored 12 books, including *Organizational Behavior: Experiences and Cases* (South-Western Publishing, 6th edition, 2001), *Management International* (West Publishing, 1984), *Women and Men in Organizations* (George Washington University, 1984), and *Managing with the Wisdom of Love: Uncovering Virtue in People and Organizations*

(Jossey-Bass, 1997), which was rated one of the top 10 business books of 1997 by *Management General.* Her most recent book is *Love Lift ME Higher (George Ronald).* In addition, she has had dozens of articles printed in such publications as *Journal of Management Development, International Quarterly of Community Health Education, Psychological Reports,* and *Executive Development.* She has recently been exploring how to use the arts in the teaching of leadership and has a new book, *RESPECT: Women and Popular Music* (Texere, 2002), which serves as the basis for the musical theater production *Respect: A Musical Journey of Women.* Her newest artistic endeavor is *SISTAS: The Musical.*

Professor Marcic has conducted hundreds of seminars on various business topics and consulted for executives at AT&T Bell Labs, the governor and cabinet of North Dakota, the U.S. Air Force, Slovak Management Association, Eurotel, Czech Ministry of Finance, the Cattaraugus Center, USAA Insurance, State Farm Insurance, and the Salt River–Pima Indian Tribe in Arizona.

Part 1 Introduction 2

Chapter 1 Innovative Management for a Changing World 5

Part 2 The Environment 52

Chapter 2 The Environment and Corporate Culture 55

Business Blooper
British Petroleum Oil Spill 57

Spotlight on Skills
Creating *Guanxi* in China 59

Spotlight on Skills
Zappos Shoes 71

Benchmarking
Netflix 80

Chapter 3 Managing in a Global Environment 91

Business Blooper
Aeroflot 99

Spotlight on Skills
How Well Do You Play The Culture Game? 107

Spotlight on Skills
Communication Skills Abroad 110

Benchmarking
Reality TV Afghanistan 119

Chapter 4 Managing Ethics and Social Responsibility 131

Benchmarking
Triodos Bank 137

Chapter 9

Managing Human Resources and Diversity 327

Part 5 Leading 392

Chapter 10

Understanding Individual Behavior 395

Chapter 13

Chapter 14

Chapter 15

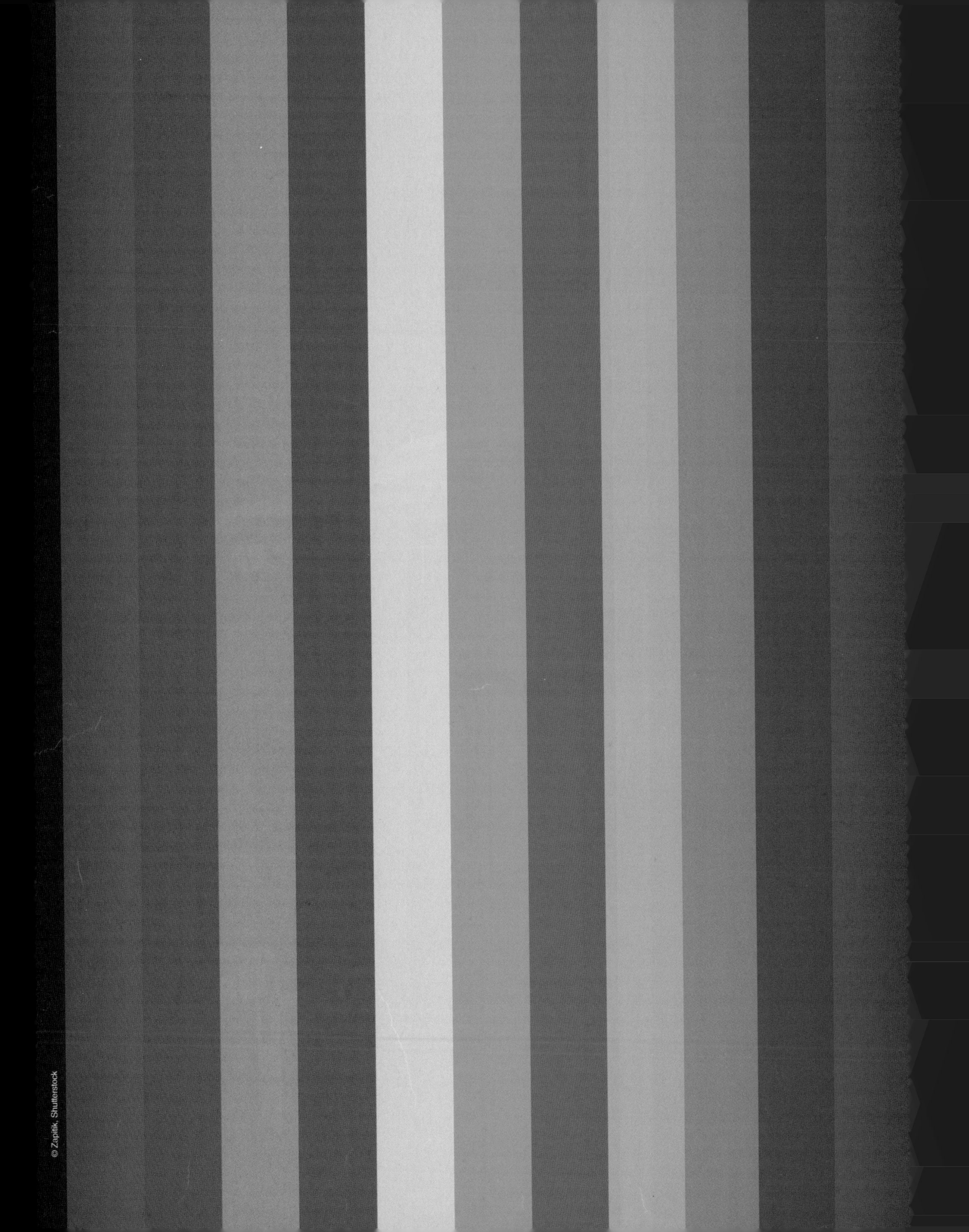

12:56
23 APR 2011 SAT
+25 °C
8:00AM
2 missed calls
10:30AM - 11:30AM
Conference hall

PART 1

Introduction 1

How do you define turbulence? Flying into gusty winds at 30,000 feet? A recent breakup? This month's cell phone bill?

For Sony Corp., turbulence is the recent data heist of more than 100 million PlayStation Network (PSN) user accounts, including stolen passwords, purchase histories, and possibly even credit card data.

The shocking news broke on April 26, 2011, when Sony's senior director of corporate communications issued a blog post saying that the online video game network suffered a massive security break-in. The attack occurred one week earlier, as cybercriminals successfully breached Sony's computer system, snatching private profiles and sensitive transaction information.

To prevent additional damage, Sony shut down its PlayStation and PC-based networks for nearly a month—a move that risked sending customers to Microsoft Xbox and Nintendo Wii. The crisis also prompted statements from Kazuo Hirai, Sony's PlayStation chief, who, with other top-level managers, offered a traditional heads-bowed Japanese apology. "We deeply apologize for the inconvenience we have caused," Hirai was quoted as saying.

Given the danger that lurks in the murky underworld of cybercrime, where hackers can breach even the firewalls of security fortresses like the Pentagon and Sony, today's multimedia managers must possess the ability to stay calm, be visible, and tell the truth—especially when facing worst-case scenarios.

Chapter Outline

Innovative Management for a Changing World

Learning Outcomes

After studying this chapter, you should be able to:

1. Explain the difference between efficiency and effectiveness, and discuss their importance for organizational performance.
2. Define ten roles that managers perform in organizations.
3. Appreciate the manager's role in small businesses and nonprofit organizations.
4. Understand the personal challenges involved in becoming a new manager.
5. Discuss turbulent forces that require a new workplace and the innovative management competencies needed to deal with today's environment.
6. Know the difference between the new-style and the old-style manager.
7. Understand how historical forces influence the practice of management.
8. Identify and explain major developments in the history of management thought.
9. Describe the major components of the classical and humanistic management perspectives.
10. Explain the major concepts of the contingency view and total quality management.

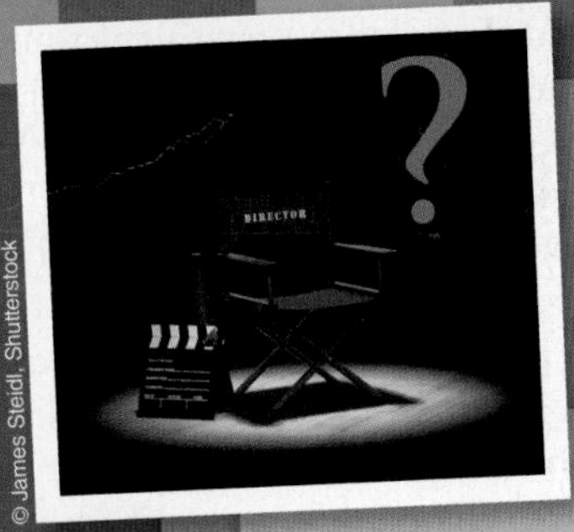

© James Steidl, Shutterstock

Are You Ready to Be a Manager?

Please circle your opinion below each of the following statements.

1 **I am good at multi-tasking.**

Mostly True — Mostly False

(See page 16, Adventures in Multitasking.)

2 **It's easy for me to relate to people both above me in status or position and also those lower.**

Mostly True — Mostly False

(See page 17, Being Caught in the Middle.)

3 **I can work well with frequent interruptions.**

Mostly True — Mostly False

(See page 17, Life on Speed Dial.)

4 **I like to be systematic when solving problems.**

Mostly True — Mostly False

(See page 29, Scientific Management.)

5 **I have a good understanding of other people's needs.**

Mostly True — Mostly False

(See page 34, Human Relations Movement.)

A person's first job can be one of the most exciting times of life, but few people get the experience and challenge of being a manager at the age of 16. Teresa Taylor, now chief operating officer at Qwest, feels that she got just that. Taylor considered herself lucky to be working as hostess at a local restaurant, but she was a bit stunned by the level of responsibility she had. "I was in charge of scheduling, and I was in charge of deciding who gets to go early, who gets to come in late, who gets to go on break, who doesn't, what stations should they be at," she says. It seemed like a lot of power for someone just entering the workforce, but Taylor soon realized she had to listen to the servers and try to meet their needs in order to keep things running smoothly. It was a valuable lesson she applied many times in future years, especially when she stepped into an official management role. "I had to take a step back and say, 'Well, I can't muscle my way through this. I can't do it all myself.'" Like most managers, Taylor found that the more her responsibilities grew, the more she had to listen to and rely on others to accomplish goals.[1]

Many new managers expect to have power, be in control, and be personally responsible for departmental outcomes. A big surprise for many people when they first become a manager is that they are much less in control of things than they expected. Managers depend on subordinates more than the reverse, and they are evaluated on the work of other people rather than on their own work. The nature of management is to motivate and coordinate others to cope with diverse and far-reaching challenges. Managers set up the systems and conditions that help other people perform well.

What makes a good manager? Go to the Group Learning, on page 44, that pertains to qualities and characteristics of effective versus ineffective managers.

In the past, many managers did exercise tight control over employees. But the field of management is undergoing a revolution that asks managers to do more with less, wholly engage employees, see change rather than stability as natural, and inspire vision and cultural values that allow people to create a truly collaborative and productive workplace. This textbook introduces and explains the process of management and the changing ways of thinking about the world that are critical for managers. By reviewing the actions of some successful and not-so-successful managers, you will learn the fundamentals of management. By the end of this chapter, you will already recognize some of the skills managers use to keep organizations on track, and you will begin to understand how managers can achieve astonishing results through people. By the end of this book, you will understand fundamental management skills for planning, organizing, leading, and controlling a department or an entire organization.

ConceptConnection

A business may develop from a founder's talent, but **good management** and vision can take it to the next level. Tattoo artists Ami James and Chris Núñez (pictured) started the business Miami Ink, which was the namesake of the TLC/Discovery reality television program that ran from 2005 until 2008. The partners pitched the concept for the show with a friend and turned their business into the most well-known tattoo design studio in the United States. Because TLC/Discovery owns the rights to the name Miami Ink, James and Núñez planned for life after reality TV by creating another Miami Beach tattoo studio, Love Hate Tattoo.

Why Innovative Management Matters

The day after Haiti was hit by a massive earthquake in January 2010, Facebook users around the globe were updating their statuses with the word *Haiti* at a rate of 1,500 times a minute. It was concrete evidence of the rapidly growing reach of Facebook, which started as a social networking site for college students.

Facebook's success can be attributed to its managers' effectiveness at innovation. Founder and CEO Mark Zuckerberg says he wants managers who aren't afraid to break things in order to

New Manager Self-Test

Manager Achievement Test

Rate each item below based on your orientation toward personal achievement. Read each item and check either Mostly True or Mostly False as you feel right now.

	MOSTLY TRUE <<<	>>> MOSTLY FALSE
1. I enjoy the feeling I get from mastering a new skill.	______	______
2. Working alone is typically better than working in a group.	______	______
3. I like the feeling I get from winning.	______	______
4. I like to develop my skills to a high level.	______	______
5. I rarely depend on anyone else to get things done.	______	______
6. I am frequently the most valuable contributor to a team.	______	______
7. I like competitive situations.	______	______
8. To get ahead, it is important to be viewed as a winner.	______	______

See It Online

Scoring and Interpretation: Give yourself 1 point for each Mostly True answer. In this case, a *low score* is better. A high score means a focus on personal achievement separate from others, which is ideal for a specialist or individual contributor. However, a manager is a generalist who gets things done through others. A desire to be a winner may cause you to compete with your people rather than develop their skills. As a manager, you will not succeed as a lone achiever who does not facilitate and coordinate others. If you checked three or fewer statements as Mostly True, your basic orientation is good. If you scored 6 or higher, your focus is on being an individual winner. You will want to shift your perspective to become an excellent manager.

make them better. Facebook's management team encourages a culture of fearlessness, helping the company win the top spot on *Fast Company*'s 2010 list of the world's 50 most innovative companies. Even during grim economic times, Facebook was increasing its engineering team, investing in new ideas, and pushing people to take risks for the future.[2]

Why does innovative management matter? Innovations in products, services, management systems, production processes, corporate values, and other aspects of the organization are what keep companies growing, changing, and thriving. Without innovation, no company can survive over the long run. In today's world, industries, technologies, economies, governments, and societies are in constant flux, and managers are responsible for helping their organizations navigate through the unpredictable with flexibility and innovation. The meltdown of the housing and finance industries in the United States and the resulting global financial crisis, volatile oil prices and a devastating oil spill on the Gulf Coast, sweeping government changes, natural disasters such as major earthquakes in Haiti and Chile, continuing threats of terrorism, massive problems for automakers from General Motors to Toyota, global health scares such as the H1N1 flu virus, and other recent events have confirmed for managers the folly of managing for stability. The growing clout and expertise of companies in developing countries, particularly China and India, also have many Western managers worried. In such a turbulent and hypercompetitive global environment, managers must help their companies innovate more—and more quickly—than ever.

People can learn to manage innovatively. Interestingly, some hard-nosed business executives have turned to a study of the Grateful Dead rock band for a lesson or two.

THE GRATEFUL DEAD

Who said that, "[in an information economy] the best way to raise demand for your product is to give it away"? Perhaps Jeff Bezos, founder of Amazon.com? Maybe Sergey Brin or Larry Page, cofounders of Google?

Actually, those words were written by Grateful Dead lyricist John Perry Barlow in a 1994 issue of *Wired* magazine, long before most people were even thinking about "Internet business models." The Dead were famous for allowing fans to tape their shows, giving up a major source of revenue in potential record sales but dramatically widening their fan base in the process—and those fans spent plenty of money on concert tickets, merchandise, and so forth, as well as records.

Far from being lackadaisical about their jobs, Dead members always treated the band as a business, incorporating early on and establishing a board of directors that included people from all levels of the organization. They pioneered numerous ideas and practices that were later embraced by corporations. One example was their decision to focus intensely on their most loyal fan base and find ways to create and deliver superior customer value. Even more interesting is how, in a pre-Facebook world, the band found ways to foster a "community of interest" that defied distance. Decades before the Internet and social networking sites, intense bonds of friendship and loyalty often developed among Deadheads living thousands of miles apart.

Barry Barnes, a business professor who lectures to business leaders about the Grateful Dead, says the band's ability to constantly think and behave innovatively is a lesson for today's managers. The band thrived for decades, through bad times as well as good. "If you're going to survive this economic downturn," Barnes says, "you better be able to turn on a dime. The Dead were exemplars."[3]

Innovation has become the new imperative, despite the need for companies to control costs in today's economy. In a January 2009 survey of corporate executives in Asia, North America, Europe, and Latin America, 76 percent agreed that "innovation is more important than cost reduction for long-term success."[4] Throughout this text, we will spotlight various companies that reflect managers' ability to think and act innovatively. In addition, Chapter 8 discusses innovation and change in detail. First, let's begin our exploration of the world of management by learning some basics about what it means to be a manager.

The Definition of Management

Every day, managers solve difficult problems, turn organizations around, and achieve astonishing performances. To be successful, every organization needs good managers.

What do managers actually do? The late famed management theorist Peter Drucker, often credited with creating the modern study of management, summed up the job of the manager by specifying five tasks.[5] In essence, managers set goals, organize activities, motivate and communicate, measure performance, and develop people. These five manager activities apply not only to top executives such as Mark Zuckerberg at Facebook, Steve Odland at Office Depot, or Ursula Burns at Xerox, but also to the manager of a restaurant in your hometown, the leader of an airport security team, a supervisor at a Web hosting service, or the director of sales and marketing for a local business.

Manager's activities fall into four core management functions: planning (setting goals and deciding activities), organizing (organizing activities and people), leading (motivating, communicating with, and developing people), and controlling (establishing targets and measuring performance). Depending on their job situation, managers perform numerous and varied tasks, but they all can be categorized under these four primary functions. Thus, our definition of management is as follows:

Management is the attainment of organizational goals in an effective and efficient manner through planning, organizing, leading, and controlling organizational resources. This definition holds two important ideas: (1) the four functions of planning, organizing, leading, and controlling, and (2) the attainment of organizational goals in an effective and efficient manner. Let's first take a look at the four primary management functions. Later in the chapter, we'll discuss organizational effectiveness and efficiency, as well as the multitude of skills managers use to successfully perform their jobs.

Exhibit 1.1 illustrates the process of how managers use resources to attain organizational goals through the functions of planning, organizing, leading, and controlling. Chapters of this book are devoted to the multiple activities and skills associated with each function, as well as to the environment, global competitiveness, and ethics that influence how managers perform these functions.

EXHIBIT 1.1

The Process of Management

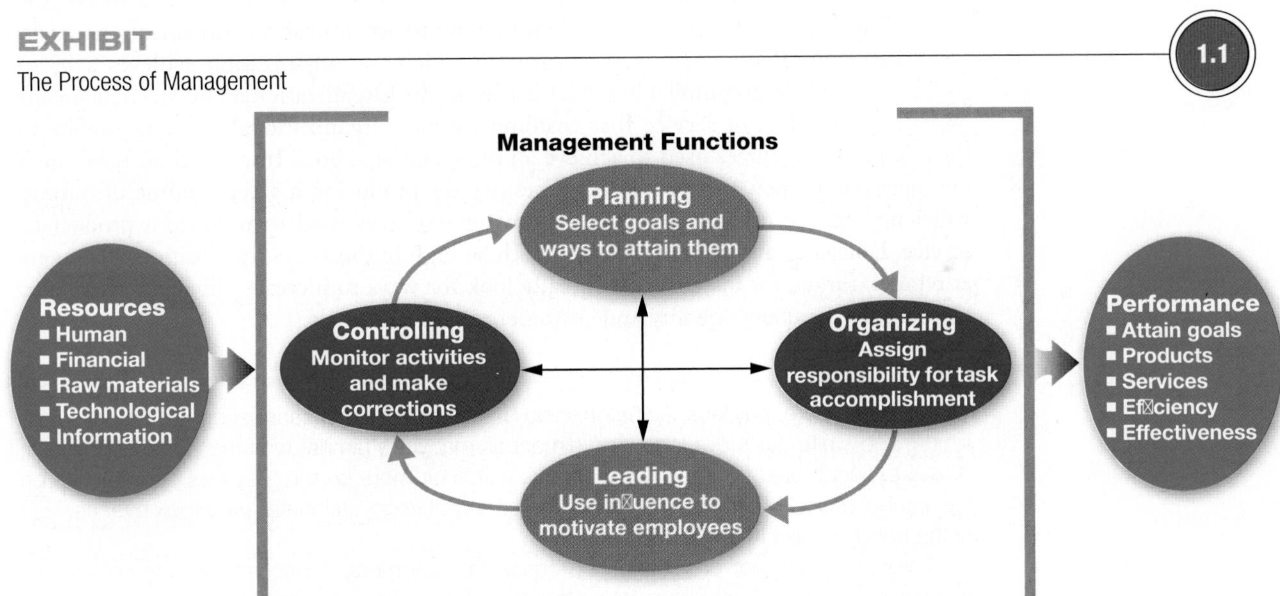

- Managers get things done by coordinating and motivating other people.
- Management often is a different experience from what people expect.
- Innovative management is critical in today's turbulent world.
- Facebook's success can be attributed to the effectiveness of its innovative managers.
- **Management** is defined as the attainment of organizational goals in an effective and efficient manner through planning, organizing, leading, and controlling organizational resources.

Organizational Performance

The second part of our definition of management is the attainment of organizational goals in an efficient and effective manner. Management is so important because organizations are so important. In an industrialized society where complex technologies dominate, organizations bring together knowledge, people, and raw materials to perform tasks no individual could do alone. Without organizations, how could technology be provided that enables us to share information around the world in an instant; electricity be produced from huge dams and nuclear power plants; and millions of songs, videos, and games be available for our entertainment at any time and place? Organizations pervade our society, and managers are responsible for seeing that resources are used wisely to attain organizational goals.

Our formal definition of an **organization** is a social entity that is goal directed and deliberately structured. *Social entity* means being made up of two or more people. *Goal directed* means designed to achieve some outcome, such as make a profit (Walmart), win pay increases for members (AFL-CIO), meet spiritual needs (United Methodist Church), or provide social satisfaction (college sorority). *Deliberately structured* means that tasks are divided and responsibility for their performance is assigned to organization members. This definition applies to all organizations, including both profit and nonprofit. Small, offbeat, and nonprofit organizations are more numerous than large, visible corporations—and just as important to society.

Based on our definition of management, the manager's responsibility is to coordinate resources in an effective and efficient manner to accomplish the organization's goals. Organizational **effectiveness** is the degree to which the organization achieves a *stated goal*, or succeeds in accomplishing what it tries to do. Organizational effectiveness means providing a product or service that customers value. Organizational **efficiency** refers to the amount of resources used to achieve an organizational goal. It is based on how much raw material, money, and people are necessary for producing a given volume of output. Efficiency can be calculated as the amount of resources used to produce a product or service. Efficiency and effectiveness can both be high in the same organization. Managers at retailer Target, for instance, continually look for ways to increase efficiency while also meeting the company's quality and customer satisfaction goals.

TARGET

Expect more, pay less. An astonishing 97 percent of Americans recognize Target's red-and-white bull's-eye logo, and almost as many are familiar with the slogan: "Pay less, expect more." "Sometimes we focus a little bit more on the 'pay less,' sometimes on the 'expect more,' but the guardrails are there," says Gregg Steinhafel, who took over as CEO of the trendy retailer in May 2008.

Target's slogan not only offers a promise to customers, it also reflects the company's emphasis on both effectiveness and efficiency. Target has an elite, secret team, called the "creative cabinet," made up of outsiders of various ages, interests, and nationalities who provide ideas and insights that keep the company on the cutting edge of consumer trends and who give their input regarding managers' strategic initiatives. Innovation, design, and quality are key goals, and managers focus on providing a fun store experience and a unique, exciting product line. At the same time, they keep a close eye on costs and operating efficiencies to keep prices low. "I talk a lot about gross margin rate and the key drivers to improve our metrics and performance," Steinhafel says. In its SuperTarget centers, the retailer is able to consistently underprice supermarkets on groceries by about 10 percent to 15 percent, and it comes very close to Walmart's rock-bottom prices.

In today's slow economy, Target, like other retailers, has had to adjust worker hours and look for other efficiencies, which has drawn unfavorable attention from worker advocacy groups. Managers have to walk a fine line to continue to meet their goals for both efficiency and effectiveness.[6]

All managers have to pay attention to costs, but severe cost cutting to improve efficiency can sometimes hurt organizational effectiveness. The ultimate responsibility of managers is to achieve high **performance**, which is the attainment of organizational goals by using resources in an efficient *and* effective manner. Consider what happened at music company EMI. Weak sales led managers to focus on financial efficiency, which successfully trimmed waste and boosted operating income. However, the efficiencies damaged the company's ability to recruit new artists, who are vital to record companies, and also led to internal turmoil that caused some long-time acts to leave the label. Thus, the company's overall performance suffered. Managers are struggling to find the right balance between efficiency and effectiveness to get EMI back on the right track.[7]

- An **organization** is a social entity that is goal directed and deliberately structured.
- Good management is important because organizations contribute so much to society.
- **Efficiency** pertains to the amount of resources—raw materials, money, and people—used to produce a desired volume of output.
- **Effectiveness** refers to the degree to which the organization achieves a stated goal.
- **Performance** is defined as the organization's ability to attain its goals by using resources in an efficient and effective manner.
- The marketing slogan for retailer Target reflects managers' concern with both keeping costs low (efficiency) and meeting customers' needs (effectiveness).

Management Skills

A manager's job is complex and multidimensional and, as we shall see throughout this book, requires a range of skills. Although some management theorists propose a long list of skills, the necessary skills for managing a department or an organization can be summarized in three categories: conceptual, human, and technical.[8] As illustrated in Exhibit 1.2, the application of these skills changes as managers move up in the organization. Although the degree of each skill necessary at different levels of an organization may vary, to perform effectively all managers must possess skills in each of these important areas.

Complete the Readiness for Management instrument, on p. 14, that pertains to how prepared you are to take on a management role. Reflect on the strength of your preferences among the skills, and the implications for you as a manager.

When Skills Fail

Everyone has flaws and weaknesses, and these shortcomings become most apparent under conditions of rapid change, uncertainty, or crisis.[9] Consider how Tony Hayward, a geologist by training, handled the BP Deepwater Horizon crisis in the Gulf of Mexico that ended his career as CEO and further damaged BP's reputation. Until the spring of 2010, Hayward had been praised for leading a successful turnaround at the oil giant. Yet, after an oil rig drilling a well for BP exploded, killing 11 workers and sending hundreds of millions of gallons of oil spewing into the Gulf of Mexico, Hayward faltered in his role as a crisis leader. His ill-advised comment that he wanted the crisis over as much as anyone because he "wanted his life back" showed an insensitivity and lack of diplomacy that roiled the public. One crisis expert, Robbie Vorhaus, says Hayward basically failed in the task of "becoming human" to people affected by the disaster, a failure that eventually led to calls for his ouster. Hayward resigned in July of 2010. "All of a sudden, you have

EXHIBIT 1.2

Relationship of Conceptual, Human, and Technical Skills to Management

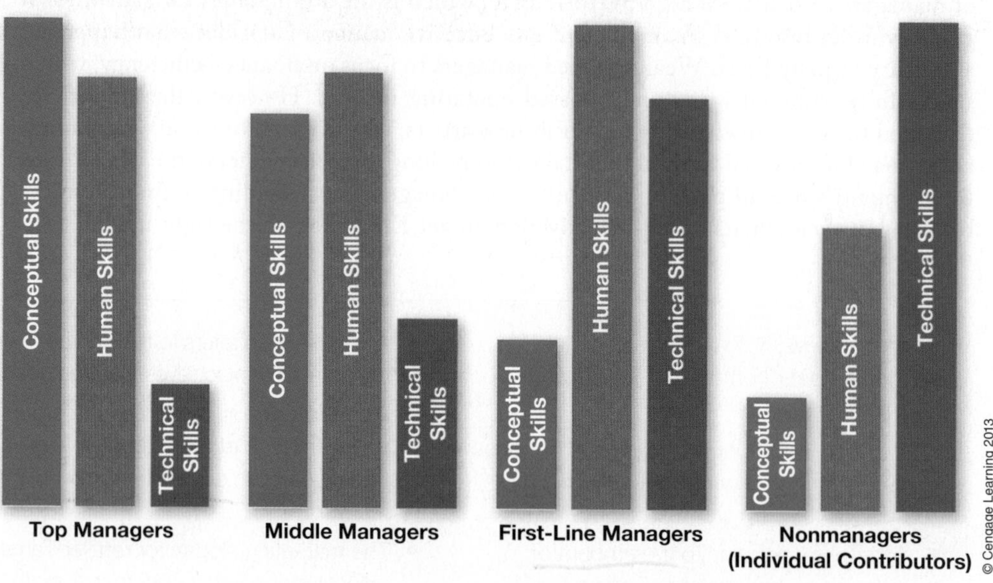

an event where you are now standing in the spotlight among shrimp fishermen and local politicians, and people who maybe make 20[,000] or 30,000 dollars a year," Vorhaus said. "A true leader needs to be able to come from the heart and make people feel that there is a connection."[10]

During turbulent times, managers really have to stay on their toes and apply all their skills and competencies in a way that benefits the organization and its stakeholders—employees, customers, investors, the community, and so forth. In recent years, numerous highly publicized examples have shown what happens when managers fail to effectively apply their skills to meet the demands of an uncertain, rapidly changing world. Ethical and financial scandals and the failure of companies in the finance and auto industries have left people cynical about business managers and even less willing to overlook mistakes. Sometimes a leader's ego can prevent the use of one's skills, as happened with Leslie Singer, described in the Business Blooper.

Crises and examples of corporate deceit and greed grab the headlines, but many more companies falter or fail less spectacularly. Managers fail to listen to customers, are unable to motivate employees, or can't build a cohesive team.

- Managers have complex jobs that require a range of abilities and skills, including conceptual, human, and technical.
- The two major reasons managers fail are poor communication and poor interpersonal skills.
- A manager's weaknesses become more apparent during stressful times of uncertainty, change, or crisis.

BUSINESS BLOOPER
Leslie Singer, Inc.

Designer par excellence Leslie Singer started her own accessory line, Leslie Singer, using imaginative psychedelic images that were inspired by the pattern-heavy models of Burberry. Her unique designs were noticed by designers and loved by consumers. She started to do trunk shows and got great response from boutiques across the country. Only problem: they saw her as very small and therefore placed tiny orders, maybe two dozen scarves each time. Big stores wouldn't even deal with her because of her size. Or else they'd ask her to redesign her collection to match the trend this year, something she felt compromised her artistic vision. Four years and $500,000 later, she "86'd" the business and went back to what she knew she could do successfully, branding and marketing, in her company HS Dominion. After much reflection, Singer realizes she did not do enough homework in high-volume fashion retail. "I never looked at the retailer side, at shows they buy, what the decision process is based on, who the gatekeepers are," she says. Because she had been so admired by her peers, she also sees that her overconfidence prevented her from doing the necessary legwork, as she assumed previous achievements would transform into the fashion world's open doors. "Not getting that was a crushing blow to my ego."

SOURCE: Malika Zouhali-Worrall, "Learning the Hard Way: Up to Her Neck in Small Orders," *INC Magazine*, October 2010, p, 70.

What Is It Like to Be a Manager?

Unless someone has actually performed managerial work, it is hard to understand exactly what managers do on an hour-by-hour, day-to-day basis. One answer to the question of what managers actually do to plan, organize, lead, and control was provided by Henry Mintzberg, who followed managers around and recorded all their activities.[11] He developed a description of managerial work that included three general characteristics and ten roles. These characteristics and roles, discussed in detail later in this section, have been supported by other research.[12]

How will you make the transition to a new manager's position? Complete the New Manager Self-Test on page 7, to see how prepared you are to step into a management role.

Researchers have also looked at what managers *like* to do. Both male and female managers across five different countries report that they most enjoy activities such as leading others, networking, and leading innovation. Activities managers like least include controlling subordinates, handling paperwork, and managing time pressures.[13] Many new managers, in particular, find the intense time pressures of management, the load of administrative paperwork, and the challenge of directing others to be quite stressful as they adjust to their new roles and responsibilities. Indeed, the initial leap into management can be one of the scariest moments in a person's career.

Making the Leap: Becoming a New Manager

Many people who are promoted into a manager position have little idea what the job actually entails and receive little training about how to handle their new role. It's no wonder that, among managers, first-line supervisors tend to experience the most job burnout and attrition.[14]

Organizations often promote the star performers—those who demonstrate individual expertise in their area of responsibility and have an ability to work well with

SPOTLIGHT ON SKILLS

What's Your Readiness for Management?

Welcome to the world of management. Are you ready for it? This questionnaire will help you see whether your priorities align with the demands placed on today's managers. Rate each of the following items based on what you think is the appropriate emphasis for that task to your success as a new manager of a department. Your task is to rate the top four priority items as "High Priority" and the other four as "Low Priority"; in other words, You will have four of the items rated high and four rated low.

	HIGH PRIORITY <<<	>>> LOW PRIORITY
1. Spend 50 percent or more of your time in the care and feeding of people.	______	______
2. Make sure people understand that you are in control of the department.	______	______
3. Use lunches to meet and network with peers in other departments.	______	______
4. Implement the changes you believe will improve department performance.	______	______
5. Spend as much time as possible talking with and listening to subordinates.	______	______
6. Make sure jobs get out on time.	______	______
7. Reach out to your boss to discuss her expectations for you and your department.	______	______
8. Make sure you set clear expectations and policies for your department.	______	______

Scoring and Interpretation: All eight items in the list may be important, but the odd-numbered items are considered more important than the even-numbered items for long-term success as a manager. If you checked three or four of the odd-numbered items, consider yourself ready for a management position. A successful new manager discovers that a lot of time has to be spent in the care and feeding of people, including direct reports and colleagues. People who fail in new management jobs often do so because they have poor working relationships or they misjudge management philosophy or cultural values. Developing good relationships in all directions is typically more important than holding on to old work skills or emphasizing control and task outcomes. Successful outcomes typically will occur when relationships are solid. After a year or so in a managerial role, successful people learn that more than half their time is spent networking and building relationships.

SOURCE: This questionnaire is adapted from research findings reported in Linda A. Hill, *Becoming a Manager: How New Managers Master the Challenges of Leadership*, 2nd ed. (Boston, MA: Harvard Business School Press, 2003); and John J. Gabarro, *The Dynamics of Taking Charge* (Boston, MA: Harvard Business School Press, 1987).

others—both to reward the individual and to build new talent into the managerial ranks. But making the shift from individual contributor to manager is often tricky. Dianne Baker, an expert nurse who was promoted to supervisor of an out-patient cardiac rehabilitation center, quickly found herself overwhelmed by the challenge of supervising former peers, keeping up with paperwork, and understanding financial and operational issues.[15] Baker's experience is duplicated every day as new managers struggle with the transition to their new jobs. Harvard professor Linda Hill followed a group of 19 managers over the first year of their managerial careers and found that one key to success is to recognize that becoming a manager involves more than learning a new set of skills. Rather, becoming a manager means a profound transformation in the way

EXHIBIT 1.3

Making the Leap from Individual Performer to Manager

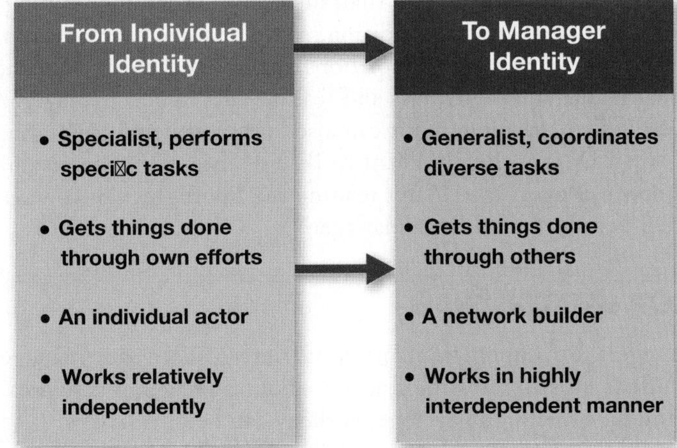

From Individual Identity
To Manager Identity
• Specialist, performs specific tasks
• Generalist, coordinates diverse tasks
• Gets things done through own efforts
• Gets things done through others
• An individual actor
• A network builder
• Works relatively independently
• Works in highly interdependent manner

SOURCE: Based on Exhibit 1.1, "Transformation of Identity," in Linda A. Hill, Becoming a Manager : Mastery of a New Identity, 2nd ed. (Boston, MA: Harvard Business School Press, 2003), p. 6.

people think of themselves, called *personal identity*, that includes letting go of deeply held attitudes and habits and learning new ways of thinking.[16] Exhibit 1.3 outlines the transformation from individual performer to manager.

Recall our earlier discussion of the role of manager as the person who builds systems rather than doing specific tasks. The individual performer is a specialist and a "doer." His mind is conditioned to think in terms of performing specific tasks and activities as expertly as possible. The manager, on the other hand, has to be a generalist and learn to coordinate a broad range of activities. Whereas the individual performer strongly identifies with her specific tasks, the manager has to identify with the broader organization and industry.

In addition, the individual performer gets things done mostly through his own efforts, and develops the habit of relying on self rather than others. The manager, though, gets things done through other people. Indeed, one of the most common mistakes new managers make is wanting to do all the work themselves rather than delegating to others and developing others' abilities.[17] For example, when Lisa Drakeman moved from a teaching job at Princeton to being CEO of a biotechnology start-up, she initially went to every meeting, interviewed every job candidate, and read every draft of clinical trial designs. She soon realized that she couldn't master every detail and that trying to do so would stall the company's growth. Although it was hard to step back, Drakeman eventually made the transition from doing individual tasks to managing and delegating to others.[18]

Another problem for many new managers is that they expect to have greater freedom to do what they think is best for the organization. In reality, though, managers find themselves hemmed in by interdependencies. Being a successful manager means thinking in terms of building teams and networks, becoming a motivator and organizer within a highly interdependent system of people and work. Although the distinctions may sound simple in the abstract, they are anything but. In essence, becoming a manager means becoming a new person and viewing oneself in a completely new way.

Can you make a personal transformation from individual performer to manager, accomplishing work by engaging and coordinating other people? Look back at your results on the "What's Your Readiness for Management?" questionnaire on page 14 to see how your priorities align with the demands placed on a manager.

Many new managers have to make the transformation in a "trial by fire," learning on the job as they go, but organizations are beginning to be more responsive to the need for new manager training. The cost to organizations of losing good employees who can't make the transition is greater than the cost of providing training to help new managers cope, learn, and grow. In addition, some of today's organizations use great care in selecting people for managerial positions, including ensuring that each candidate understands what management involves and really wants to be a manager. A career as a manager can be highly rewarding, but it can also be stressful and frustrating. The Spotlight on Skills titled Do You Really Want to Be a Manager? further examines some of the challenges new managers face. After reading the Spotlight, can you answer "yes" to the question "Do I really want to be a manager?"

Manager Activities

Most new managers are unprepared for the variety of activities managers routinely perform. One of the most interesting findings about managerial activities is how busy managers are and how hectic the average workday can be.

1

Adventures in Multitasking Managerial activity is characterized by variety, fragmentation, and brevity.[19] The widespread and voluminous nature of a manager's involvements leaves little time for quiet reflection. Mintzberg found that the average time a top executive spends on any one activity is less than nine minutes, and another study indicates that some first-line supervisors average one activity every 48 seconds![20]

Managers shift gears quickly. Significant crises are interspersed with trivial events in no predictable sequence. Every manager's job, though in most cases not as potentially dangerous, is similar in its diversity and fragmentation to that of U.S. Marine Corps officers managing the reconstruction efforts in Iraq. Consider the diverse events in a typical day for Capt. Sean Miller in Fallujah, Iraq:[21]

- Begins the day meeting with tribal sheiks and local officials to decide which projects to finance.
- Drives to a command center to check the status of a job that a contractor has left unfinished.
- Walks to a nearby school to discuss awards for students who recite passages from the Koran.
- Is interrupted by a handful of people who have come with questions or demands: One asks about a relative he says was detained several years ago; another pushes a contract for review into Miller's hands; a third is seeking work; and so on.
- Finally returns to the discussion of student awards.
- Agrees to a tour of the school, where a contractor explains his request for a $50,000 generator that Miller thinks can be obtained for $8,000.
- Checks the recently cleaned grounds at another school and finds that papers and other trash once again litter the area.
- Notices a man running a pipe from his roof and warns him against running his sewage to the school.
- Calms and directs his marines, some only in their upper teens, who grow as skittish as children and rush from the school building.
- Stops by a café to hear young men's complaints that they are asked to pay bribes to get a job on the police force.
- Near sunset, takes photos of a still-damaged cemetery door that contractors have been paid to repair.

SPOTLIGHT ON SKILLS

Do You Really Want to Be a Manager?

Is management for you? Becoming a manager is considered by most people to be a positive, forward-looking career move, and indeed life as a manager offers appealing aspects. However, it also holds many challenges, and not every person will be happy and fulfilled in a management position. Here are some of the issues would-be managers should consider before deciding they want to pursue a management career:

1. ***The increased workload.*** It isn't unusual for managers to work 70 to 80 hours per week, and some work even longer hours. A manager's job always starts before a shift and ends hours after the shift is over. When Ray Sarnacki was promoted to manager at an aerospace company, he found himself frustrated by the incessant travel, endless paperwork, and crowded meeting schedule. He eventually left the job and found happiness in a position earning about one-fifth of his peak managerial salary.
2. ***The challenge of supervising former peers.*** This issue can be one of the toughest for new managers. They frequently struggle to find the right approach, with some trying too hard to remain "one of the gang" and others asserting their authority too harshly. In almost all cases, the transition from a peer-to-peer relationship to a manager-to-subordinate one is challenging and stressful.
3. ***The headache of responsibility for other people.*** A lot of people get into management because they like the idea of having power, but the reality is that many managers feel overwhelmed by the responsibility of hiring, supervising, and disciplining others. New managers are often astonished at the amount of time it takes to handle "people problems." Kelly Cannell, who quit her job as a manager, puts it this way: "What's the big deal [about managing people]? The big deal is that people are human. … To be a good manager, you have to mentor them, listen to their problems, counsel them, and at the end of the day you still have your own work on your plate. …"
4. ***Being caught in the middle.*** Except for those in the top echelons, managers find themselves acting as a backstop, caught between upper management and the workforce. Even when managers disagree with the decisions of top executives, they are responsible for implementing them.

For some people, the frustrations of management aren't worth it. For others, management is a fulfilling and satisfying career choice and the emotional rewards can be great. One key to being happy as a manager may be carefully evaluating whether you can answer "yes" to the question "Do I really want to be a manager?"

SOURCES: Based on information in Henry Mintzberg, Managing (San Francisco: Berrett-Koehler, 2009); Erin White, "Learning to Be the Boss," *The Wall Street Journal*, November 21, 2005; Jared Sandberg, "Down Over Moving Up: Some New Bosses Find They Hate Their Jobs," *The Wall Street Journal*, July 27, 2005; Heath Row, "Is Management for Me? That Is the Question," Fast Company (February–March 1998), pp. 50–52; Timothy D. Schellhardt, "Want to Be a Manager? Many People Say No, Calling Job Miserable," *The Wall Street Journal*, April 4, 1997; and Matt Murray, "Managing Your Career—The Midcareer Crisis: Am I in This Business to Become a Manager?" *The Wall Street Journal*, July 25, 2000.

Life on Speed Dial The manager performs a great deal of work at an unrelenting pace.[22] Managers' work is fast paced and requires great energy. Most top executives routinely work at least 12 hours a day and spend 50 percent or more of their time traveling.[23] Calendars are often booked months in advance, but unexpected disturbances erupt every day. Mintzberg found that the majority of executives' meetings and other contacts are ad hoc, and even scheduled meetings are typically surrounded by other events such as quick phone calls, scanning of e-mail, or spontaneous encounters. During time away from the office, executives catch up on work-related reading, paperwork, phone calls, and e-mail. Technology, such as e-mail, text messaging, cell phones, and laptops, intensifies the pace. Brett Yormark, the National Basketball Association's youngest CEO (the New Jersey Nets), typically responds to about 60 messages before he even shaves and dresses for the day, and employees are accustomed to getting messages Yormark has zapped to them in the wee hours of the morning.[24]

The fast pace of a manager's job is illustrated by Heather Coin, a Cheesecake Factory manager. Coin arrives at work about 9:30 A.M. and checks the financials for how the restaurant performed the day before. Next comes a staff meeting and various personnel duties. Before and during the lunch shift, she's pitching in with whatever needs to be done—making salads in the kitchen, expediting the food, bussing the tables, or talking with guests. After lunch, from 3:00 to 4:30 P.M., Heather takes care of administrative duties, paperwork, or meetings with upper management, media, or community organizations. At 4:30, she holds a shift-change meeting to ensure a smooth transition from the day crew to the night crew. Throughout the day, Heather also mentors staff members, which she considers the most rewarding part of her job. After the evening rush, she usually heads for home about 10 P.M., the end of another 12½-hour day.[25]

Manager Roles

Mintzberg's observations and subsequent research indicate that diverse manager activities can be organized into 10 roles.[26] A **role** is a set of expectations for a manager's behavior. Exhibit 1.4 provides examples of each of the roles, divided into three conceptual

EXHIBIT 1.4
Ten Manager Roles

Category	Role	Activity
Informational	**Monitor**	Seek and receive information, scan periodicals and reports, maintain personal contacts.
	Disseminator	Forward information to other organization members; send memos and reports, make phone calls.
	Spokesperson	Transmit information to outsiders through speeches, reports, memos.
Interpersonal	**Figurehead**	Perform ceremonial and symbolic duties such as greeting visitors, signing legal documents.
	Leader	Direct and motivate subordinates; train, counsel, and communicate with subordinates.
	Liaison	Maintain information links both inside and outside organization; use e-mail, phone calls, meetings.
Decisional	**Entrepreneur**	Initiate improvement projects; identify new ideas, delegate idea responsibility to others.
	Disturbance handler	Take corrective action during disputes or crises; resolve conflicts among subordinates; adapt to environmental crises.
	Resource allocator	Decide who gets resources; schedule, budget, set priorities.
	Negotiator	Represent department during negotiation of union contracts, sales, purchases, budgets; represent departmental interests.

SOURCES: Adapted from Henry Mintzberg, The Nature of Managerial Work (New York: Harper & Row, 1973): 92–93; and Henry Mintzberg, "Managerial Work: Analysis from Observation," *Management Science* 18 (1971): B97–B110.

BENCHMARKING

Artisan Ice Cream

When Ben Van Leeuwen drove a Good humor truck in college, little did he know it would become the model for his new business venture, which he started two years after graduation. An admitted Foodie with a lifelong obsession with food, Ben was also obsessed with locally grown and sustainable ingredients. Wanting to get the right people on the bus (literally), he recruited his future wife, Laura O'Neill and his brother, Pete, to help him sell ultra-premium quality ice cream out of a truck in Brooklyn. From his college job, Ben had learned that funding a truck is a lot cheaper than a storefront.

Using a 60-page business plan he had completed in a college course, he was able to secure $80,000 in funding from family and friends. First, they bought a $5,000 truck on eBay and added a freezer, plumbing, a generator, and huge windows, plus chrome grilles and a butter-yellow coat of paint, to give the feel of old-fashioned ice cream. Ben's fiancée developed a handwritten menu. Total cost: $45,000.

Their next hurdle was finding a manufacturer. No supplier made ice cream in the quality they wanted. After months of tedious recipe testing, they found the formula but knew they did not have the capital to build a factory. Finally, they were able to get a contract in upstate New York with Mercer's Dairy, whose first run of 500 gallons cost $8,000.

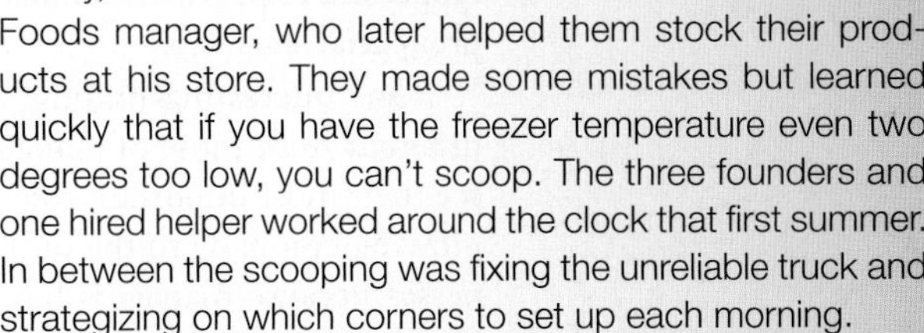

One day after Ben and Laura were married in summer of 2008, they drove their truck to a New York City street fair and sold 500 scoops. Fortuitously, one of them was to a Whole Foods manager, who later helped them stock their products at his store. They made some mistakes but learned quickly that if you have the freezer temperature even two degrees too low, you can't scoop. The three founders and one hired helper worked around the clock that first summer. In between the scooping was fixing the unreliable truck and strategizing on which corners to set up each morning.

Reaching out to social marketing, they managed to get one influential blogger, Gothamist, to give a great review, calling their product, "a taste of creamy ecstasy."

Revenues the first year were $425,000, with $125,000 of that profit. By 2009, they added two more trucks and sales soared to $900,000. Most of the profits have gone back into building the business. During the colder months, they've branched out into high-end coffee and pastries and have a goal of $2 in revenue. What a sweet life.

SOURCE: Kimberly Weisul, "Spurred by a passion for gourmet grub, Ben Van Leeuwen launched a fleet of truck offering a "taste of creamy ecstasy," *INC Magazine*, October 2010, p. 66.

categories: informational (managing by information), interpersonal (managing through people), and decisional (managing through action). Each role represents activities that managers undertake to ultimately accomplish the functions of planning, organizing, leading, and controlling. Although it is necessary to separate the components of the manager's job to understand the different roles and activities of a manager, it is important to remember that the real job of management cannot be practiced as a set of independent parts; all the roles interact in the real world of management.

Ben Van Leeuwen used both the Entreprenuerial role, as well as those of Spokesperson (through social media) and Resource Allocator in starting his premium ice-cream business, as described in the Benchmarking box.

- Becoming a new manager requires a shift in thinking from individual performer to an interdependent role of coordinating and developing others.
- Because of the interdependent nature of management, new managers often have less freedom and control than they expect to have.
- The job of a manager is highly diverse and fast paced.
- A **role** is a set of expectations for one's behavior.
- Managers at every level perform ten roles, which are grouped into informational roles, interpersonal roles, and decisional roles.

Managing in Small Businesses and Nonprofit Organizations

Small businesses are growing in importance. Hundreds of small businesses are opened every month, but the environment for small business today is highly complicated. Experts believe entrepreneurial ventures are crucial to global economic recovery, yet small companies can be particularly vulnerable in a turbulent environment. Small companies sometimes have difficulty developing the managerial dexterity to survive when conditions turn chaotic. Appendix A provides detailed information about managing in small businesses and entrepreneurial start-ups.

One interesting finding is that managers in small businesses tend to emphasize roles different from those of managers in large corporations. Managers in small companies often see their most important role as that of spokesperson because they must promote the small, growing company to the outside world. The entrepreneur role is also critical in small businesses because managers have to be innovative and help their organizations develop new ideas to remain competitive. Small-business managers tend to rate lower on the leader role and on information-processing roles compared with their counterparts in large corporations.

Nonprofit organizations also represent a major application of management talent. Organizations such as the Salvation Army, Nature Conservancy, Greater Chicago Food Depository, Girl Scouts, and Cleveland Orchestra all require excellent management. The functions of planning, organizing, leading, and controlling apply to nonprofits just as they do to business organizations, and managers in nonprofit organizations use similar skills and perform similar activities. The primary difference is that managers in businesses direct their activities toward earning money for the company, whereas managers in nonprofits direct their efforts toward generating some kind of social impact. The characteristics and needs of nonprofit organizations created by this distinction present unique challenges for managers.[27]

Financial resources for nonprofit organizations typically come from government appropriations, grants, and donations rather than from the sale of products or services to customers. In businesses, managers focus on improving the organization's products and services to increase sales revenues. In nonprofits, however, services are typically provided to nonpaying clients, and a major problem for many organizations is securing a steady stream of funds to continue operating. Nonprofit managers, committed to serving clients with limited resources, must focus on keeping organizational costs as low as possible.[28] Donors generally want their money to go directly to helping clients rather than for overhead costs. If nonprofit managers can't demonstrate a highly efficient use of resources, they might have a hard time securing additional donations or government appropriations. Although the Sarbanes-Oxley Act (the 2002 corporate governance reform law) doesn't apply to nonprofits, many are adopting its guidelines, striving for greater transparency and accountability, to boost credibility with constituents and be more competitive when seeking funding.[29]

In addition, because nonprofit organizations do not have a conventional *bottom line*, managers often struggle with the question of what constitutes results and effectiveness. It is easy to measure dollars and cents, but the metrics of success in nonprofits are much more ambiguous. Managers have to measure intangibles such as "improved public health," "a difference in the lives of the disenfranchised," or "increased appreciation for the arts." This intangible nature also makes it more difficult to gauge the performance of employees and managers. An added complication is that managers often depend on volunteers and donors who cannot be supervised and controlled in the same way a business manager deals with employees. Many people who move from the corporate world to a nonprofit are surprised to find that the work hours are often longer and the stress greater than in their previous management jobs.[30]

The roles defined by Mintzberg also apply to nonprofit managers, but these may differ somewhat. We might expect managers in nonprofit organizations to place more emphasis on the roles of spokesperson (to "sell" the organization to donors and the public), leader (to build a mission-driven community of employees and volunteers), and resource allocator (to distribute government resources or grant funds that are often assigned top-down).

Managers in all organizations—large corporations, small businesses, and nonprofit organizations—carefully integrate and adjust the management functions and roles to meet challenges within their own circumstances and keep their organizations healthy.

- Good management is just as important for small businesses and nonprofit organizations as it is for large corporations.
- Managers in these organizations adjust and integrate the various management functions, activities, and roles to meet the unique challenges they face.
- Managers in small businesses often see their most important roles as being a *spokesperson* for the business and acting as an *entrepreneur*.
- Managers in nonprofit organizations direct their efforts toward generating some kind of social impact rather than toward making money for the organization.
- Nonprofit organizations don't have a conventional bottom line, so managers often struggle with what constitutes effectiveness.

Innovative Management for the New Workplace

In recent years, the central theme being discussed in the field of management has been the pervasiveness of dramatic change in the workplace. Rapid environmental shifts are causing fundamental transformations that have a dramatic impact on the manager's job. These transformations are reflected in the transition to a new workplace, as illustrated in Exhibit 1.5.

Turbulent Forces

Dramatic advances in technology, globalization, shifting social values, changes in the workforce, and other environmental shifts have created a challenging environment for organizations. Perhaps the most pervasive change affecting organizations and management is technology. The Internet and electronic communication have transformed the way business is done and the way managers perform their jobs. Many organizations use digital technology to tie together employees and partners located worldwide. With new technology, it's easy for people to do their jobs from home or other locations outside company walls. In addition, many companies are shifting more and more chunks of what were once considered core functions to outside organizations via outsourcing, which requires coordination across organizations.

The pace of life for most people and organizations is high speed. People can work around the clock. Ideas, documents, music, personal information, and all types of data are constantly being zapped through cyberspace, and events in one part of the world can dramatically influence business all over the globe. In general, events in today's world are turbulent and unpredictable, with both small and large crises occurring on a more frequent basis.

EXHIBIT 1.5

The Transition to a New Workplace

	Managing the New Workplace	Managing the Old Workplace
Forces		
Technology	Digital	Mechanical
Focus	Global	Local, domestic markets
Workforce	Diverse	Homogenous
Pace	Change, speed	Stability, efficiency
Events	Turbulent, frequent crises	Calm, predictable
Characteristics		
Resources	Information, knowledge	Physical assets
Work	Flexible, virtual	Structured, localized
Workforce	Empowered employees	Loyal employees
Management Competencies		
Leadership	Dispersed, empowering	Autocratic
Doing Work	By teams	By individuals
Relationships	Collaboration	Conflict, competition
Design	Experimentation, learning	Top-down control

New Workplace Characteristics[31]

The *old workplace* was characterized by routine, specialized tasks, and standardized control procedures. Employees typically performed their jobs in one specific company facility, such as an automobile factory located in Detroit or an insurance agency located in Des Moines. Individuals concentrated on doing their own specific tasks, and managers were cautious about sharing knowledge and information across boundaries. The organization was coordinated and controlled through the vertical hierarchy, with decision-making authority residing with upper-level managers.

In the *new workplace*, by contrast, work is free flowing and flexible. Structures are flatter, and lower-level employees are empowered to make decisions based on widespread information and guided by the organization's mission and values.[32] Knowledge is widely shared, and people throughout the company keep in touch with a broad range of colleagues via advanced technology. The valued worker is one who learns quickly, shares knowledge, and is comfortable with risk, change, and ambiguity. People expect to work on a variety of projects and jobs throughout their careers rather than staying in one field or with one company.

In the new workplace, work is often virtual, with managers having to supervise and coordinate people who never actually "come to work" in the traditional sense.[33] Flexible hours, telecommuting, and virtual teams are increasingly popular ways of working that require new skills from managers. Teams may include outside contractors, suppliers, customers, competitors, and interim managers. **Interim managers**, or *contingent managers,* are managers who are not affiliated with a specific organization but work on a project-by-project basis or temporarily provide expertise to organizations in a specific area.[34] This approach enables a company to benefit from specialist skills without making a long-term commitment, and it provides flexibility for managers who like the challenge, variety, and learning that come from working in a wide range of organizations. One estimate is that the market for contingent managers will grow 90 percent over the next decade.[35]

©image100/Corbis

ConceptConnection

The recent recession has inspired more managers to give the **new workplace** a try. Driven by a need to cut costs, many companies have become more open to employees **telecommuting**. But even those employees who "come to work" are likely to find a changed workplace. According to the 2009 Alternative Workplace report, conducted by New Ways of Working, 40 percent of the companies surveyed expanded their nontraditional workplace programs between 2008 and 2010 in an effort to use office space more efficiently. One such innovation is the installation of *hot desks*, workstations that are used on an as-needed basis.

New Management Competencies

In the face of these transitions, managers rethink their approach to organizing, directing, and motivating employees. Instead of "management by keeping tabs," managers employ an empowering leadership style. When people are working at scattered locations, managers can't continually monitor behavior. In addition, they are sometimes coordinating the work of people who aren't under their direct control, such as those in partner organizations.

Success in the new workplace depends on collaboration across functions and hierarchical levels as well as with customers and other companies. Experimentation and learning are key values, and managers encourage people to share information and knowledge.

The shift to a new way of managing isn't easy for traditional managers who are accustomed to being "in charge," making all the decisions, and knowing where their subordinates are and what they're doing at every moment. Even many new managers have a hard time with today's flexible work environment. For example, managers of departments participating in Best Buy's Results-Only Work Environment program, which allows employees to work anywhere, anytime, as long as they complete assignments and meet goals, find it difficult to keep themselves from checking to see who's logged on to the company network.[36]

Even more changes and challenges are on the horizon for organizations and managers. This is an exciting and challenging time to be entering the field of management. Throughout this book, you will learn much more about the new workplace, about the new and dynamic roles managers are playing in the twenty-first century, and about how you can be an effective manager in a complex, ever-changing world.

Read the Ethical Dilemma, on page 45, that pertains to managing in the new workplace. Think about what you would do and why, to begin understanding how you will solve thorny management problems.

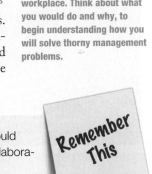

- Turbulent environmental forces have caused significant shifts in the workplace and the manager's job.
- In the old workplace, a manager's competency could include a command-and-control leadership style, and managers could focus on individual tasks and on standardizing procedures.
- In the new workplace, a manager's competency should include an empowering leadership style, and managers should focus on developing teamwork, collaboration, and learning.
- The new workplace often employs **interim managers**, managers who are not affiliated with any particular organization but work on a project-by-project basis or provide expertise to an organization in a specific area.

Innovative Management Thinking for a Changing World

All of the ideas and approaches discussed so far in this chapter go into the mix that makes up modern management. Dozens of ideas and techniques in current use can trace their roots to these historical perspectives.[37] In addition, innovative concepts continue to emerge to address management challenges in today's turbulent world.

Contemporary Management Tools

Managers tend to look for fresh ideas to help them cope during difficult times. For instance, consider that in 2002, surveys noted a dramatic increase in the variety of techniques and ideas managers were trying, reflecting the turbulence of the environment following the crash of the dot-coms, the 2001 terrorist attacks in the United States, and a series of corporate scandals such as Enron.[38] Similarly, recent challenges such as the tough economy and volatile stock market, environmental and organizational crises, lingering anxieties over war and terrorism, and public suspicion and skepticism resulting from the crisis on Wall Street have left today's executives searching for any management tool—new or old—that can help them get the most out of limited resources. The Spotlight on Skills titled Contemporary Management Tools lists a wide variety of ideas and techniques used by today's managers. Management idea life cycles have been growing shorter as the pace of change has increased. A study by professors at the University of Louisiana at Lafayette found that from the 1950s to the 1970s, it typically took more than a decade for interest in a popular management idea to peak. Now, the interval has shrunk to fewer than three years, and some trends come and go even faster.[39]

SELCO Solar Light Pvt. Ltd.

ConceptConnection

Energy engineer Harish Hande knew that in rural areas of his native India, there were silk workers who labored by kerosene lamp even though the fuel could potentially kill the worms. And there were rose pickers and midwives who needed a light source that left their hands free. To meet such needs, Hande used a ***jugaad*** mind-set and developed sustainable, affordable, solar-powered lighting systems for domestic and commercial use. Bangalore-based Selco Solar, the company Hande founded, has sold, installed, and serviced well over 100,000 modular solar systems since 1995. Says Hande, "If our product caters to a client's need, there's no way he won't buy it."

Managing the Technology-Driven Workplace

Three popular recent trends that have shown some staying power, as reflected in the Spotlight on Skills titled Contemporary Management Tools, are customer relationship management, outsourcing, and supply chain management. These techniques are related to the shift to a technology-driven workplace. Today, many employees perform much of their work on computers and may work in virtual teams, connected electronically to colleagues around the world. Even in factories that produce physical goods, machines have taken over much of the routine and uniform work, freeing workers to use more of their minds and abilities. Moreover, companies are using technology to keep in touch with customers and collaborate with other organizations on an unprecedented scale.

SPOTLIGHT ON SKILLS

Contemporary Management Tools

Over the history of management, many fashions and fads have appeared. Critics argue that new techniques may not represent permanent solutions. Others feel that managers adopt new techniques for continuous improvement in a fast-changing world.

In 1993, Bain and Company started a large research project to interview and survey thousands of corporate executives about the 25 most popular management tools and techniques. The list for 2009 and their usage rates are below. How many tools do you know? For more information on specific tools, visit the Bain website: www.bain.com/management_tools/home.asp.

Fashion. In the 2009 survey, benchmarking became the most popular tool for the first time in more than a decade, reflecting managers' concern with efficiency and cost cutting in a difficult economy. Three tools that ranked high in both use and satisfaction were *strategic planning*, *customer segmentation*, and *mission and vision statements*, tools that can guide managers thinking on strategic issues during times of rapid change.

Global. North American executives were using cost-cutting tools, especially downsizing, more than were managers in other parts of the world in 2008–2009. Latin American companies were the heaviest users of outsourcing. In the Asia-Pacific region, Chinese companies report the greatest use of *benchmarking*, *strategic planning*, *supply chain management*, and *total quality management*, whereas companies in India are more satisfied with *strategic alliances* and *collaborative innovation* than are other Asia-Pacific executives.

SOURCE: Darrell Rigby and Barbara Bilodeau, "Management Tools and Trends 2009," Copyright © 2009, Bain and Company, Inc., http://www.bain.com/management_tools/home.asp. Reprinted by permission.

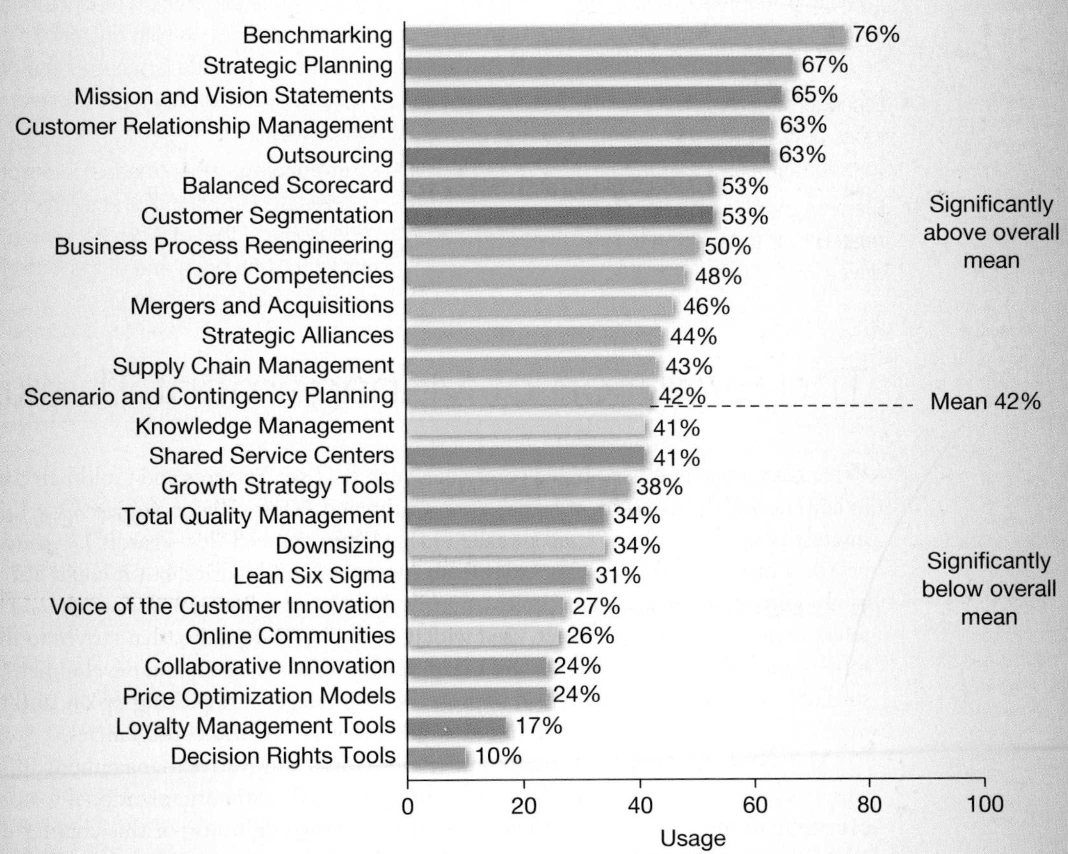

Customer Relationship Management One of today's most popular applications of technology is for customer relationship management. **Customer relationship management (CRM)** systems use the latest information technology to keep in close touch with customers and to collect and manage large amounts of customer data. These data can help employees and managers act on customer insights, make better decisions, and provide superior customer service.

There has been an explosion of interest in CRM. In the Spotlight on Skills titled Contemporary Management Tools, 63 percent of surveyed managers reported their companies used CRM in 2008, whereas only 35 percent of companies reported using this technique in 2000. Meeting customer needs and desires is a primary goal for organizations, and using CRM to give customers what they really want provides a tremendous boost to customer service and satisfaction.

Outsourcing Information technology has also contributed to the rapid growth of **outsourcing**, which means contracting out selected functions or activities to other organizations that can do the work more cost efficiently. The Bain survey indicates that the use of outsourcing increased as the economy declined. Outsourcing requires that managers not only be technologically savvy but that they learn to manage a complex web of relationships. These relationships might reach far beyond the boundaries of the physical organization; they are built through flexible e-links between a company and its employees, suppliers, partners, and customers.[40]

- Modern management is a lively mix of ideas and techniques from varied historical perspectives, but new concepts continue to emerge.
- Managers tend to look for innovative ideas and approaches particularly during turbulent times.
- Many of today's popular techniques are related to the transition to a technology-driven workplace.
- **Customer relationship management** systems use information technology to keep in close touch with customers, collect and manage large amounts of customer data, and provide superior customer value.
- **Outsourcing**, which means contracting out selected functions or activities to other organizations that can do the work more efficiently, has been one of the fastest-growing trends in recent years.

The Evolution of Management Thinking

What do managers at U.S.-based companies such as Cisco Systems and Goldman Sachs have in common with managers at India's Tata Group and Infosys Technologies? One thing is an interest in applying a new concept called jugaad (pronounced "joo-gaardh"). *Jugaad* perhaps will be a buzzword that quickly fades from managers' vocabularies, but it could also become as ubiquitous in management circles as terms such as *total quality* or *kaizen*. *Jugaad* basically refers to an innovation mind-set, used widely by Indian companies, that strives to meet customers' immediate needs quickly and inexpensively. With research and development budgets strained in today's economy, it's an approach U.S. managers are picking up on, and the term *jugaad* has been popping up in seminars, academia, and business consultancies.

Managers are always on the lookout for fresh ideas, innovative management approaches, and new tools and techniques. Management philosophies and organizational forms change over time to meet new needs. The questionnaire at the beginning of this chapter describes two differing philosophies about how people should be managed, and you will learn more about these ideas in this chapter.

If management is always changing, why does history matter to managers? The workplace of today is different from what it was 50 years ago—indeed, from what it was even

10 years ago. Yet today's managers find that some ideas and practices from the past are still highly relevant. For example, certain management practices that seem modern, such as open-book management or employee stock ownership, have actually been around for a long time. These techniques have repeatedly gained and lost popularity since the early twentieth century because of shifting historical forces.[41] A historical perspective provides a broader way of thinking, a way of searching for patterns and determining whether they recur across time periods. It is a way of learning from others' mistakes so as not to repeat them; learning from others' successes so as to repeat them in the appropriate situation; and most of all, learning to understand why things happen to improve our organizations in the future.

This part of the chapter provides a historical overview of the ideas, theories, and management philosophies that have contributed to making the workplace what it is today. The final section of the chapter looks at some recent trends and current approaches that build on this foundation of management understanding. This foundation illustrates that the value of studying management lies not in learning current facts and research but in developing a perspective that will facilitate the broad, long-term view needed for management success.

Management and Organization

Studying history doesn't mean merely arranging events in chronological order; it means developing an understanding of the impact of societal forces on organizations. Studying history is a way to achieve strategic thinking, see the big picture, and improve conceptual skills. Let's begin by examining how social, political, and economic forces have influenced organizations and the practice of management.[42]

Social forces refer to those aspects of a culture that guide and influence relationships among people. What do people value? What do people need? What are the standards of behavior among people? These forces shape what is known as the *social contract*, which refers to the unwritten, common rules and perceptions about relationships among people and between employees and management.

One social force is the changing attitudes, ideas, and values of Generation Y employees (sometimes called Millennials).[43] These young workers, the most educated generation in the history of the United States, grew up technologically adept and globally conscious. Unlike many workers of the past, they typically are not hesitant to question their superiors and challenge the status quo. They want a work environment that is challenging and supportive, with access to cutting-edge technology, opportunities to learn and further their careers and personal goals, and the power to make substantive decisions and changes in the workplace. In addition, Gen-Y workers have prompted a growing focus on work/life balance, reflected in trends such as telecommuting, flextime, shared jobs, and organization-sponsored sabbaticals.

Political forces refer to the influence of political and legal institutions on people and organizations. One significant political force is the increased role of government in business after the collapse of companies in the financial services sector and major problems in the auto industry. Some managers expect increasing government regulations in the coming years.[44] Political forces also include basic assumptions underlying the political system, such as the desirability of self-government, property rights, contract rights, the definition of justice, and the determination of innocence or guilt of a crime.

Economic forces pertain to the availability, production, and distribution of resources in a society. Governments, military agencies, churches, schools, and business organizations in every society require resources to achieve their goals, and economic forces influence the allocation of scarce resources. Companies in every industry have been affected by the recent financial crisis that was the worst since the Great Depression of the 1930s. Reduced consumer spending and tighter access to credit have curtailed growth and left companies scrambling to meet goals with limited resources. Although liquidity for large corporations showed an increase in early 2010, smaller companies continued to struggle to find funding.[45]

Another economic trend that affects managers worldwide is the growing economic power of countries such as China, India, and Brazil.[46]

Management practices and perspectives vary in response to these social, political, and economic forces in the larger society. Exhibit 1.6 illustrates the evolution of significant management perspectives over time. The timeline reflects the dominant time period for each approach, but elements of each are still used in today's organizations.[47]

- Managers are always on the lookout for new techniques and approaches to meet shifting organizational needs.
- Looking at history gives managers a broader perspective for interpreting and responding to current opportunities and problems.
- Management and organizations are shaped by forces in the larger society.
- **Social forces** are aspects of a society that guide and influence relationships among people, such as their values, needs, and standards of behavior.
- **Political forces** relate to the influence of political and legal institutions on people and organizations.
- The increased role of government in business is one example of a political force.
- **Economic forces** affect the availability, production, and distribution of a society's resources.

EXHIBIT 1.6
Management Perspectives over Time

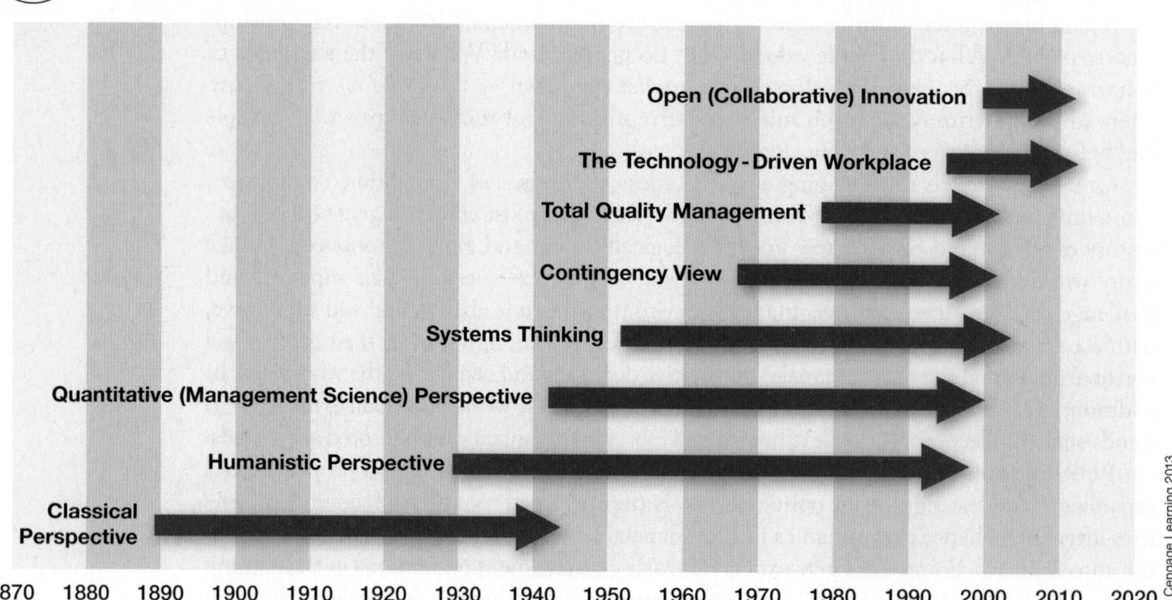

Classical Perspective

The practice of management can be traced to 3000 b.c., to the first government organizations developed by the Sumerians and Egyptians, but the formal study of management is relatively recent.[48] The early study of management as we know it today began with what is now called the **classical perspective**.

The classical perspective on management emerged during the nineteenth and early twentieth centuries. The factory system that began to appear in the 1800s posed challenges that earlier organizations had not encountered. Problems arose in tooling the plants, organizing managerial structure, training employees (many of them non-English-speaking immigrants), scheduling complex manufacturing operations, and dealing with increased labor dissatisfaction and resulting strikes.

These myriad new problems and the development of large, complex organizations demanded a new approach to coordination and control, and a "new sub-species of economic man—the salaried manager"[49]—was born. Between 1880 and 1920, the number of professional managers in the United States grew from 161,000 to more than 1 million.[50] These professional managers began developing and testing solutions to the mounting challenges of organizing, coordinating, and controlling large numbers of people and increasing worker productivity. Thus began the evolution of modern management with the classical perspective.

This perspective contains three subfields, each with a slightly different emphasis: scientific management, bureaucratic organizations, and administrative principles.[51]

Scientific Management

Scientific management emphasizes scientifically determined jobs and management practices as the way to improve efficiency and labor productivity. In the late 1800s, a young engineer, Frederick Winslow Taylor (1856–1915), proposed that workers "could be retooled like machines, their physical and mental gears recalibrated for better productivity."[52] Taylor insisted that improving productivity meant that management itself would have to change and, further, that the manner of change could be determined only by scientific study; hence, the label *scientific management* emerged. Taylor suggested that decisions based on rules of thumb and tradition be replaced with precise procedures developed after careful study of individual situations.[53]

The scientific management approach is illustrated by the unloading of iron from rail cars and reloading finished steel for the Bethlehem Steel plant in 1898. Taylor calculated that with correct movements, tools, and sequencing, each man was capable of loading 47.5 tons per day instead of the typical 12.5 tons. He also worked out an incentive system that paid each man $1.85 a day for meeting the new standard, an increase from the previous rate of $1.15. Productivity at Bethlehem Steel shot up overnight.

Although known as the *father of scientific management*, Taylor was not alone in this area. Henry Gantt, an associate of Taylor's, developed the *Gantt chart*—a bar graph that measures planned and completed work along each stage of production by time elapsed. Two other important pioneers in this area were the husband-and-wife team of Frank B. and Lillian M. Gilbreth. Frank B. Gilbreth (1868–1924) pioneered *time and motion study* and arrived at many of his management techniques independently of Taylor. He stressed efficiency and was known for his quest for the one best way to do work. Although Gilbreth is known for his early work with bricklayers, his work had great impact on medical surgery by drastically reducing the time patients spent on the operating table. Surgeons were able to save countless lives through the application of time and motion study. Lillian M. Gilbreth (1878–1972) was more interested in the human aspect of work. When her husband died at the age of 56, she had 12 children ages 2 to 19. The undaunted "first lady of management" went right on with her work. She presented a paper in place of her late husband, continued their seminars and consulting, lectured, and eventually became a professor at Purdue University.[54] She pioneered in the field of industrial psychology and made substantial contributions to human resource management.

Exhibit 1.7 shows the basic ideas of scientific management. To use this approach, managers should develop standard methods for doing each job, select workers with the appropriate abilities, train workers in the standard methods, support workers and eliminate interruptions, and provide wage incentives.

The ideas of scientific management that began with Taylor dramatically increased productivity across all industries, and they are still important today. Indeed, the idea of engineering work for greater productivity has enjoyed a renaissance in the retail industry.

EXHIBIT 1.7
Characteristics of Scientific Management

General Approach

- Developed standard method for performing each job
- Selected workers with appropriate abilities for each job
- Trained workers in standard methods
- Supported workers by planning their work and eliminating interruptions
- Provided wage incentives to workers for increased output

Contributions

- Demonstrated the importance of compensation for performance
- Initiated the careful study of tasks and jobs
- Demonstrated the importance of personnel selection and training

Criticisms

- Did not appreciate the social context of work and higher needs of workers
- Did not acknowledge variance among individuals
- Tended to regard workers as uninformed and ignored their ideas and suggestions

Supermarket chains such as Meijer Inc. and Hannaford, for example, use computerized labor waste elimination systems based on scientific management principles. The system breaks down tasks such as greeting a customer, working the register, scanning items, and so forth, into quantifiable units and devises standard times to complete each task. Executives say the computerized system has allowed them to staff stores more efficiently because people are routinely monitored by computer and are expected to meet the strict standards.[55]

A recent *Harvard Business Review* article discussing innovations that shaped modern management puts scientific management at the top of its list of 12 influential innovations. Indeed, the ideas of creating a system for maximum efficiency and organizing work for maximum productivity are deeply embedded in our organizations.[56] However, because scientific management ignores the social context and workers' needs, it can lead to increased conflict and clashes between managers and employees. The United Food and Commercial Workers Union, for instance, has filed a grievance against Meijer in connection with its cashier-performance system. Under such performance management systems, workers often feel exploited—a sharp contrast from the harmony and cooperation that Taylor and his followers had envisioned.

Bureaucratic Organizations

A systematic approach developed in Europe that looked at the organization as a whole is the **bureaucratic organizations** approach, a subfield within the classical perspective. Max Weber (1864–1920), a German theorist, introduced most of the concepts on bureaucratic organizations.[57]

During the late 1800s, many European organizations were managed on a personal, family-like basis. Employees were loyal to a single individual rather than to the organization or its mission. The dysfunctional consequence of this management practice was that resources were used to realize individual desires rather than organizational goals. Employees in effect owned the organization and used resources for their own gain rather than to serve customers. Weber envisioned organizations that would be managed on an impersonal, rational basis. This form of organization was called a *bureaucracy*.

SPOTLIGHT ON SKILLS

Are You a New-Style or an Old-Style Manager?

The following are various behaviors in which a manager may engage when relating to subordinates. Read each statement carefully and rate each one Mostly True or Mostly False to reflect the extent to which you would use that behavior.

	MOSTLY TRUE <<<	>>> MOSTLY FALSE
1. I feel I am the one responsible to set goals and deadlines for my subordinates.	_____	_____
2. I make sure there are adequate controls in place, so that my subordinates will do the job right.	_____	_____
3. I watch my subordinates closely, because it makes them work harder.	_____	_____
4. Every day I make sure I check with my subordinates to see if they need any help from me.	_____	_____
5. It is the manager's job to plan out work for subordinates.	_____	_____
6. If I see my subordinate's work quality is falling, I intervene immediately.	_____	_____
7. A good manager will have frequent meetings to keep up on what is happening.	_____	_____
8. The best managers aren't afraid to push their people to meet deadlines.	_____	_____

See It Online

Scoring and Interpretation: Add the total number of Mostly True answers and mark your score on the scale below. Theory X tends to be "old-style" management and Theory Y "new-style," because the styles are based on different assumptions about people. To learn more about these assumptions, you can refer to Exhibit 1.8 and review the assumptions related to Theory X and Theory Y. Strong Theory X assumptions are typically considered inappropriate for today's workplace. Where do you fit on the X–Y scale? Does your score reflect your perception of yourself as a current or future manager?

X–Y Scale

Theory X 10 5 0 Theory Y

Weber believed that an organization based on rational authority would be more efficient and adaptable to change, because continuity is related to formal structure and positions rather than to a particular person, who may leave or die. To Weber, rationality in organizations meant employee selection and advancement based not on whom you know, but rather on competence and technical qualifications, which are assessed by examination or according to training and experience. The organization relies on rules and written records for continuity. In addition, rules and procedures are impersonal and applied uniformly to all employees. A clear division of labor arises from distinct definitions of authority and responsibility, legitimized as official duties. Positions are organized in a hierarchy, with each position under the authority of a higher one. The manager depends not on her personality for successfully giving orders but on the legal power invested in the managerial position.

The term *bureaucracy* has taken on a negative meaning in today's organizations and is associated with endless rules and red tape. We have all been frustrated by waiting in long lines or following seemingly silly procedures. However, rules and other bureaucratic procedures provide a standard way of dealing with employees. Everyone gets equal treatment, and everyone knows what the rules are. This foundation enables many organizations to become extremely efficient. Consider United Parcel Service (UPS), sometimes called *Big Brown*.

UNITED PARCEL SERVICE (UPS)

UPS delivers more than 15 million packages every business day and is also a leader in air service, logistics, and global information services. The company operates in more than 200 countries and territories around the world.

Why has UPS been so successful? One important factor is the concept of bureaucracy. UPS operates according to strict rules and regulations. It teaches drivers an astounding 340 steps for how to correctly deliver a package—such as how to load the truck, how to fasten their seat belts, how to walk, and how to carry their keys. Specific safety rules apply to drivers, loaders, clerks, and managers. Strict dress codes are enforced—clean uniforms (called *browns*), every day, black or brown polished shoes with nonslip soles, no beards, no hair below the collar, no tattoos visible during deliveries, and so on. Before each shift, drivers conduct a "Z-scan," a Z-shaped inspection of the sides and front of their vehicles. Employees are asked to clean off their desks at the end of each day so they can start fresh the next morning. Managers are given copies of policy books with the expectation that they will use them regularly, and memos on various policies and rules circulate by the hundreds every day.

UPS has a well-defined division of labor. Each plant consists of specialized drivers, loaders, clerks, washers, sorters, and maintenance personnel. UPS thrives on written records, and it has been a leader in using new technology to enhance reliability and efficiency. All drivers have daily worksheets that specify performance goals and work output. Technical qualification is the criterion for hiring and promotion. The UPS policy book says the leader is expected to have the knowledge and capacity to justify the position of leadership. Favoritism is forbidden. The bureaucratic model works just fine at UPS, "the tightest ship in the shipping business."[58]

Administrative Principles

What would it be like for you to be a manager in a bureaucratic organization? Complete the Self-Learning instrument on page 43, to find out whether you would thrive in that type of environment.

Another major subfield within the classical perspective is known as the administrative principles approach. Whereas scientific management focused on the productivity of the individual worker, the **administrative principles** approach focused on the total organization. The major contributor to this approach was Henri Fayol (1841–1925), a French mining engineer who worked his way up to become head of a large mining group known as Comambault. Parts of Comambault survive today as a division of Usinor, a French government-owned metallurgical group. In his later years, Fayol wrote down his concepts on administration, based largely on his own management experiences.[59]

In his most significant work, *General and Industrial Management*, Fayol discussed 14 general principles of management, several of which are part of management philosophy today. For example:

- ***Unity of command.*** Each subordinate receives orders from one—and only one—superior.
- ***Division of work.*** Managerial work and technical work are amenable to specialization to produce more and better work with the same amount of effort.
- ***Unity of direction.*** Similar activities in an organization should be grouped together under one manager.
- ***Scalar chain.*** A chain of authority extends from the top to the bottom of the organization and should include every employee.

Fayol felt that these principles could be applied in any organizational setting. He also identified five basic functions or elements of management: *planning, organizing, commanding, coordinating*, and *controlling*. These functions underlie much of the general approach to today's management theory.

The overall classical perspective as an approach to management was very powerful and gave companies fundamental new skills for establishing high productivity and effective treatment of employees. Indeed, the United States surged ahead of the world in management techniques, and other countries, especially Japan, borrowed heavily from American ideas.

- The study of modern management began in the late nineteenth century with the **classical perspective**, which took a rational, scientific approach to management and sought to make organizations efficient operating machines.
- **Scientific management** is a subfield of the classical perspective that emphasizes scientifically determined changes in management practices as the solution to improving labor productivity.
- Frederick Winslow Taylor is known as the father of scientific management.
- Scientific management is considered one of the most significant innovations influencing modern management.
- Some supermarket chains are using computerized systems based on scientific management principles to schedule employees for maximum efficiency.
- Another subfield of the classical perspective is the **bureaucratic organizations** approach, which emphasizes management on an impersonal, rational basis through elements such as clearly defined authority and responsibility, formal record keeping, and separation of management and ownership.
- Max Weber introduced most of the concepts on bureaucratic organizations.
- **Administrative principles** is a subfield of the classical perspective that focuses on the total organization rather than the individual worker and delineates the management functions of planning, organizing, commanding, coordinating, and controlling.
- Henri Fayol, a major contributor to the administrative principles approach, outlined 14 general principles of management, several of which are a part of management philosophy today.

Humanistic Perspective

The **humanistic perspective** on management emphasized the importance of understanding human behaviors, needs, and attitudes in the workplace, as well as social interactions and group processes.[60] There are three primary subfields based on the humanistic perspective: the human relations movement, the human resources perspective, and the behavioral sciences approach.

Early Advocates

Two early advocates of a more humanistic approach were Mary Parker Follett and Chester Barnard. Mary Parker Follett (1868–1933) was trained in philosophy and political science at what was Radcliffe College. She applied herself in many fields, including social psychology and management. She wrote of the importance of common superordinate goals for reducing conflict in organizations.[61] Her work was popular with businesspeople of her day but was often overlooked by management scholars.[62] Follett's ideas served as a contrast to scientific management and are reemerging as applicable for modern managers dealing with rapid changes in today's global environment. Her approach to leadership stressed the importance of people rather than engineering techniques. She offered the pithy admonition, "Don't hug your blueprints," and analyzed the dynamics of management-organization interactions. Follett addressed issues that are timely today, such as ethics, power, and how to lead in a way that encourages employees to give their best. The concepts of *empowerment*, facilitating rather than controlling employees, and allowing employees to act depending on the authority of the situation opened new areas for theoretical study by Chester Barnard and others.[63]

National Archives

ConceptConnection

This 1914 photograph shows the initiation of a new arrival at a Nebraska planting camp. This initiation was not part of the formal rules and illustrates the significance of the **informal organization** described by Barnard. Social values and behaviors were powerful forces that could help or hurt the planting organization depending on how they were managed.

Chester I. Barnard (1886–1961) studied economics at Harvard but failed to receive a degree because he lacked a course in laboratory science. He went to work in the statistical department of AT&T and in 1927 became president of New Jersey Bell. One of Barnard's significant contributions was the concept of the informal organization. The *informal organization* occurs in all formal organizations and includes cliques and naturally occurring social groupings. Barnard argued that organizations are not machines and stressed that informal relationships are powerful forces that can help the organization if properly managed. Another significant contribution was the *acceptance theory of authority*, which states that people have free will and can choose whether to follow management orders. People typically follow orders because they perceive positive benefit to themselves, but they do have a choice. Managers should treat employees properly because their acceptance of authority may be critical to organization success in important situations.[64]

Human Relations Movement

The **human relations movement** was based on the idea that truly effective control comes from within the individual worker rather than from strict, authoritarian control.[65] This school of thought recognized and directly responded to social pressures for enlightened treatment of employees. The early work on industrial psychology and personnel selection received little attention because of the prominence of scientific management. Then a series of studies at a Chicago electric company, which came to be known as the **Hawthorne studies**, changed all that.

5 Beginning about 1895, a struggle developed between manufacturers of gas and electric lighting fixtures for control of the residential and industrial market.[66] By 1909, electric lighting had begun to win, but the increasingly efficient electric fixtures used less total power. The electric companies began a campaign to convince industrial users that they needed more light to get more productivity. When advertising did not work, the industry began using experimental tests to demonstrate their argument. Managers were skeptical about the results, so the Committee on Industrial Lighting (CIL) was set up to run the tests. To further add to the tests' credibility, Thomas Edison was made honorary chairman of the CIL. In one test location—the Hawthorne plant of the Western Electric Company—some interesting events occurred.

The major part of this work involved four experimental and three control groups. In all, five different tests were conducted. These pointed to the importance of factors *other* than illumination in affecting productivity. To more carefully examine these factors, numerous other experiments were conducted.[67] The results of the most famous study, the first Relay Assembly Test Room (RATR) experiment, were extremely controversial. Under the guidance of two Harvard professors, Elton Mayo and Fritz Roethlisberger, the RATR studies lasted nearly six years (May 10, 1927, to May 4, 1933) and involved 24 separate experimental periods. So many factors were changed and so many unforeseen factors uncontrolled that scholars disagree on the factors that truly contributed to the general increase in performance over that time period. Most early interpretations, however, agreed on one thing: Money was not the cause of the increased output.[68] It was believed that the factor that best explained increased output was *human relations*. Employees performed better when managers treated them in a positive manner. Recent reanalyses of the experiments have revealed

New Manager Self-Test

Evolution of Style

This questionnaire asks you to describe yourself. For each item, give the number "4" to the phrase that best describes you, "3" to the item that is next best, and on down to "1" for the item that is least like you.

1. My strongest skills are:
   _____ a. Analytical skills
   _____ b. Interpersonal skills
   _____ c. Political skills
   _____ d. Flair for drama
2. The best way to describe me is:
   _____ a. Technical expert
   _____ b. Good listener
   _____ c. Skilled negotiator
   _____ d. Inspirational leader
3. What has helped me the most to be successful is my ability to:
   _____ a. Make good decisions
   _____ b. Coach and develop people
   _____ c. Build strong alliances and a power base
   _____ d. Inspire and excite others
4. What people are most likely to notice about me is my:
   _____ a. Attention to detail
   _____ b. Concern for people
   _____ c. Ability to succeed in the face of conflict and opposition
   _____ d. Charisma
5. My most important leadership trait is:
   _____ a. Clear, logical thinking
   _____ b. Caring and support for others
   _____ c. Toughness and aggressiveness
   _____ d. Imagination and creativity
6. I am best described as:
   _____ a. An analyst
   _____ b. A humanist
   _____ c. A politician
   _____ d. A visionary

See It Online

Interpretation: New managers typically view their world through one or more mental frames of reference. (1) The *structural frame* of reference sees the organization as a machine that can be economically efficient and that provides a manager with formal authority to achieve goals. This manager frame became strong during the era of scientific management and bureaucratic administration. (2) The *human resource frame* sees the organization as people, with manager emphasis given to support, empowerment, and belonging. This manager frame gained importance with the rise of the humanistic perspective. (3) The *political frame* sees the organization as a competition for resources to achieve goals, with manager emphasis on negotiation and hallway coalition building. This frame reflects the need within systems theory to have all parts working together. (4) The *symbolic frame* of reference sees the organization as theater—a place to achieve dreams—with manager emphasis on symbols, vision, culture, and inspiration. This manager frame is important for learning organizations.

Which frame reflects your way of viewing the world? *The first two frames of reference—structural and human resource—are more important for new managers*. These two frames usually are mastered first. As new managers gain experience and move up the organization, they should acquire political skills and also learn to use symbols for communication. It is important for new managers not to be stuck for years in one way of viewing the organization because their progress may be limited. Many new managers evolve through and master each of the four frames as they become more skilled and experienced.

Scoring: Higher score represents your way of viewing the organization and will influence your management style. Compute your scores as follows:

ST = 1a + 2a + 3a + 4a + 5a + 6a = _______

HR = 1b + 2b + 3b + 4b + 5b + 6b = _______

PL = 1c + 2c + 3c + 4c + 5c + 6c = _______

SY = 1d + 2d + 3d + 4d + 5d + 6d = _______

SOURCE: From Roy G. Williams and Terrence E. Deal, *When Opposites Dance* (Davies Black, 2003). Used with permission.

that a number of factors were different for the workers involved, and some suggest that money may well have been the single most important factor.[69] An interview with one of the original participants revealed that just getting into the experimental group had meant a huge increase in income.[70]

These new data clearly show that money mattered a great deal at Hawthorne. In addition, worker productivity increased partly as a result of the increased feelings of importance and group pride employees felt by virtue of being selected for this important project.[71] One unintended contribution of the experiments was a rethinking of field research practices. Researchers and scholars realized that the researcher can influence the outcome of an experiment by being too closely involved with research subjects. This phenomenon has come to be known as the *Hawthorne effect* in research methodology. Subjects behaved differently because of the active participation of researchers in the Hawthorne experiments.[72]

Before reading on, take the New Manager Self-Test on page 35. This test will give you feedback about how your personal manager frame of reference relates to the human resources and other perspectives described in this chapter.

From a historical perspective, whether the studies were academically sound is of less importance than the fact that they stimulated an increased interest in looking at employees as more than extensions of production machinery. The interpretation that employees' output increased when managers treated them in a positive manner started a revolution in worker treatment for improving organizational productivity. Despite flawed methodology or inaccurate conclusions, the findings provided the impetus for the human relations movement. This approach shaped management theory and practice for well over a quarter-century, and the belief that human relations is the best approach for increasing productivity persists today.

Human Resources Perspective

The human relations movement initially espoused a *dairy farm* view of management—contented cows give more milk, so satisfied workers will give more work. Gradually, views with deeper content began to emerge. The **human resources perspective** maintained an interest in worker participation and considerate leadership but shifted the emphasis to consider the daily tasks that people perform. The human resources perspective combines prescriptions for design of job tasks with theories of motivation.[73] In the human resources view, jobs should be designed so that tasks are not perceived as dehumanizing or demeaning but instead allow workers to use their full potential. Two of the best-known contributors to the human resources perspective were Abraham Maslow and Douglas McGregor.

Abraham Maslow (1908–1970), a practicing psychologist, observed that his patients' problems usually stemmed from an inability to satisfy their needs. Thus, he generalized his work and suggested a hierarchy of needs. Maslow's hierarchy started with physiological needs and progressed to safety, belongingness, esteem, and finally, self-actualization needs. Chapter 16 discusses his ideas in more detail.

Look back at your scores on the questionnaire on new- versus old-style management as related to Theory X and Theory Y. How will your management assumptions about people fit into an organization today?

Douglas McGregor (1906–1964) had become frustrated with the early simplistic human relations notions while president of Antioch College in Ohio. He challenged both the classical perspective and the early human relations assumptions about human behavior. Based on his experiences as a manager and consultant, his training as a psychologist, and the work of Maslow, McGregor formulated his Theory X and Theory Y, which are explained in Exhibit 1.8.[74] McGregor believed that the classical perspective was based on Theory X assumptions about workers. He also felt that a slightly modified version of Theory X fit early human relations ideas. In other words, human relations ideas did not go far enough. McGregor proposed Theory Y as a more realistic view of workers for guiding management thinking.

The point of Theory Y is that organizations can take advantage of the imagination and intellect of all their employees. Employees will exercise self-control and will contribute to

EXHIBIT 1.8

Theory X and Theory Y

Assumptions of Theory X

- The average human being has an inherent dislike of work and will avoid it if possible.
- Because of the human characteristic of dislike for work, most people must be coerced, controlled, directed, or threatened with punishment to get them to put forth adequate effort toward the achievement of organizational objectives.
- The average human being prefers to be directed, wishes to avoid responsibility, has relatively little ambition, and wants security above all.

Assumptions of Theory Y

- The expenditure of physical and mental effort in work is as natural as play or rest. The average human being does not inherently dislike work.
- External control and the threat of punishment are not the only means for bringing about effort toward organizational objectives. A person will exercise self-direction and self-control in the service of objectives to which he or she is committed.
- The average human being learns, under proper conditions, not only to accept but to seek responsibility.
- The capacity to exercise a relatively high degree of imagination, ingenuity, and creativity in the solution of organizational problems is widely, not narrowly, distributed in the population.
- Under the conditions of modern industrial life, the intellectual potentialities of the average human being are only partially utilized.

SOURCE: Douglas McGregor, *The Human Side of Enterprise* (New York: McGraw-Hill, 1960), pp. 33–48.

organizational goals when given the opportunity. A few companies today still use Theory X management, but many are using Theory Y techniques. Consider how Cisco Systems applies Theory Y assumptions to tap into employee creativity and mind power.

CISCO SYSTEMS

Perhaps surprisingly for an innovative technology company, Cisco Systems started out as a typical hierarchical organization with a command-and-control mind-set. That all changed after the dot-com bubble burst in the early 2000s. Cisco's stock dropped 86 percent virtually overnight. CEO John Chambers believed the company needed a new approach to management if it was to survive. He knew collaboration and teamwork would be required to get the company growing again. In addition, Chambers thought employees would be more creative, more productive, and more committed to rebuilding the organization if they had more autonomy and fewer limitations. So, he essentially threw out the old structures and controls. Now, rather than having proposals and suggestions sent to top executives for approval, a network of councils and boards that cross functional, departmental, and hierarchical lines are empowered to launch new businesses. One board made up of volunteer self-identified "sports freaks" built a product called StadiumVision, which allows venue owners to push video and digital content such as advertising to fans in the stadium. Now a multibillion-dollar business, Stadium Vision came together in less than four months, without the CEO ever being involved in the decision.

Command and control is a thing of the past, Chambers asserts, with the future belonging to those companies that build leadership throughout the organization. The Theory Y approach helped Cisco emerge from the dot-com crisis more profitable than ever and the company has since outperformed many technology rivals.[75]

Behavioral Sciences Approach

The **behavioral sciences approach** uses scientific methods and draws from sociology, psychology, anthropology, economics, and other disciplines to develop theories about human behavior and interaction in an organizational setting. This approach can be seen in practically every organization. When a company such as Zappos.com conducts research to determine the best set of tests, interviews, and employee profiles to use when selecting new employees, it is using behavioral science techniques. When Best Buy electronics stores train new managers in the techniques of employee motivation, most of the theories and findings are rooted in behavioral science research.

One specific set of management techniques based in the behavioral sciences approach is *organization development* (OD). In the 1970s, organization development evolved as a separate field that applied the behavioral sciences to improve the organization's health and effectiveness through its ability to cope with change, improve internal relationships, and increase problem-solving capabilities.[76] The techniques and concepts of organization development have since been broadened and expanded to address the increasing complexity of organizations and the environment, and OD is still a vital approach for managers. OD will be discussed in detail in Chapter 8. Other concepts that grew out of the behavioral sciences approach include matrix organizations, self-managed teams, ideas about corporate culture, and management by wandering around. Indeed, the behavioral sciences approach has influenced the majority of tools, techniques, and approaches that managers have applied to organizations since the 1970s.

All the remaining chapters of this book contain research findings and management applications that can be attributed to the behavioral sciences approach.

- The **humanistic perspective** emphasized understanding human behavior, needs, and attitudes in the workplace.
- Mary Parker Follett and Chester Barnard were early advocates of a more humanistic approach to management.
- Follett emphasized worker participation and empowerment, shared goals, and facilitating rather than controlling employees. Barnard's contributions include the acceptance theory of authority.
- The **human relations movement** stresses the satisfaction of employees' basic needs as the key to increased productivity.
- The **Hawthorne studies** were important in shaping ideas concerning how managers should treat workers.
- The **human resources perspective** suggests that jobs should be designed to meet people's higher-level needs by allowing employees to use their full potential.
- The **behavioral sciences approach** draws from psychology, sociology, and other social sciences to develop theories about human behavior and interaction in an organizational setting.
- Many current management ideas and practices can be traced to the behavioral sciences approach.

Quantitative Perspective

World War II caused many management changes. The massive and complicated problems associated with modern global warfare presented managerial decision makers with the need for more sophisticated tools than ever before. The **quantitative perspective**, also referred to as *management science*, provided a way to address those problems. This view is distinguished for its application of mathematics, statistics, and other quantitative techniques to management decision making and problem solving. During World War II, groups of mathematicians, physicists, and other scientists were formed to solve military problems that frequently involved moving massive amounts of materials and large numbers of people quickly and efficiently. Managers soon saw how quantitative techniques could be applied to large-scale business firms.[77]

Recent Historical Trends

Despite recent heavy use of the quantitative approach by some managers, among the approaches we've discussed so far the humanistic perspective has remained most prevalent from the 1950s until today. The post–World War II period saw the rise of new concepts along with a continued strong interest in the human aspect of managing, such as team and group dynamics and other ideas that relate to the humanistic perspective. Three new concepts that appeared were systems thinking, the contingency view, and total quality management.

Systems Thinking

Systems thinking is the ability to see both the distinct elements of a system or situation and the complex and changing interaction among those elements. A **system** is a set of interrelated parts that function as a whole to achieve a common purpose.[78] **Subsystems** are parts of a system, such as an organization, that depend on one another. Changes in one part of the system (the organization) affect other parts. Managers need to understand the synergy of the whole organization, rather than just the separate elements, and to learn to reinforce or change whole-system patterns.[79] **Synergy** means that the whole is greater than the sum of its parts. The organization must be managed as a coordinated whole. Managers who understand subsystem interdependence and synergy are reluctant to make changes that do not recognize subsystem impact on the organization as a whole.

Many people have been trained to solve problems by breaking a complex system, such as an organization, into discrete parts and working to make each part perform as well as possible. However, the success of each piece does not add up to the success of the whole. In fact, sometimes changing one part

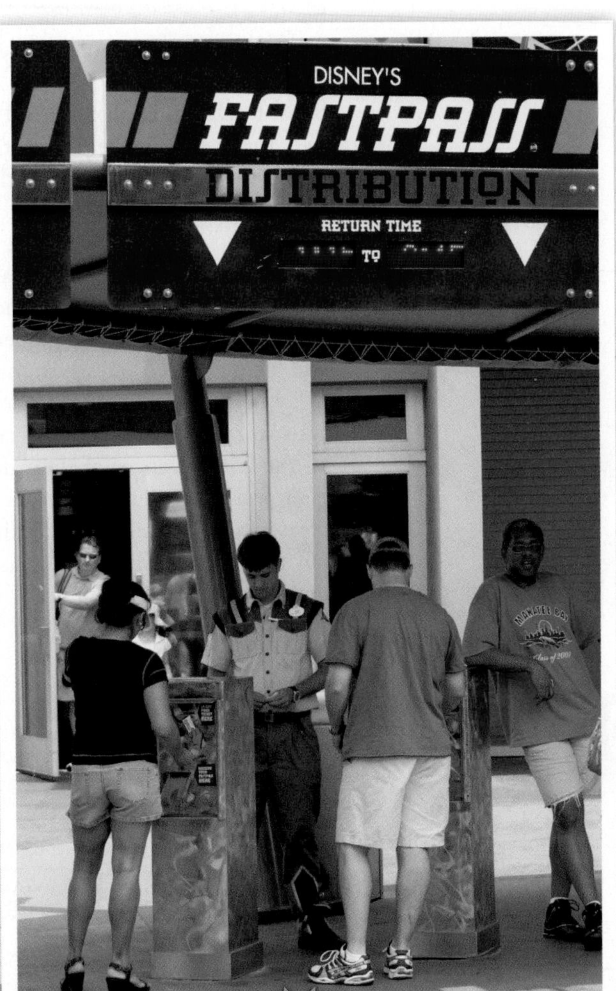

AP Photo/John Raoux

ConceptConnection

Standing in a long, snaking line with impatient children isn't a parent's idea of a good time. The Walt Disney Company used **quantitative techniques** to develop FASTPASS, a sophisticated computerized system that spares parents the ordeal for the most popular rides. Disney theme parks have machines that issue coupons with a return time that's been calculated based on the number of people standing in the actual line, the number who have already obtained passes, and each ride's capacity.

to make it better actually makes the whole system function less effectively. For example, a small city embarked on a road-building program to solve traffic congestion without whole-systems thinking. With new roads available, more people began moving to the suburbs. Rather than reduce congestion, the solution actually increased traffic congestion, delays, and pollution by enabling suburban sprawl.[80]

It is the *relationship* among the parts that form a whole system—whether a community, an automobile, a nonprofit agency, a human being, or a business organization—that matters. Systems thinking enables managers to look for patterns of movement over time and focus on the qualities of rhythm, flow, direction, shape, and networks of relationships that accomplish the performance of the whole. When managers can see the structures that underlie complex situations, they can facilitate improvement. But it requires a focus on the big picture.

An important element of systems thinking is to discern circles of causality. Peter Senge, author of *The Fifth Discipline*, argues that reality is made up of circles rather than straight lines. For example, Exhibit 1.9 shows circles of influence for increasing a retail firm's profits. The events in the circle on the left are caused by the decision to increase advertising; hence the retail firm adds to the advertising budget to aggressively promote its products. The advertising promotions increase sales, which increase profits, which provide money to further increase the advertising budget.

But another circle of causality is being influenced as well. The decision by marketing managers will have consequences for the operations department. As sales and profits increase, operations will be forced to stock up with greater inventory. Additional inventory will create a need for additional warehouse space. Building a new warehouse will cause a delay in stocking up. After the warehouse is built, new people will be hired, all of which adds to company costs, which will have a negative impact on profits. Thus, understanding all the consequences of their decisions via circles of causality enables company leaders to plan and allocate resources to warehousing as well as to advertising to ensure stable increases in sales and profits. Without understanding system causality, top managers would fail to understand why increasing advertising budgets could cause inventory delays and temporarily reduce profits.

1.9 EXHIBIT

Systems Thinking and Circles of Causality

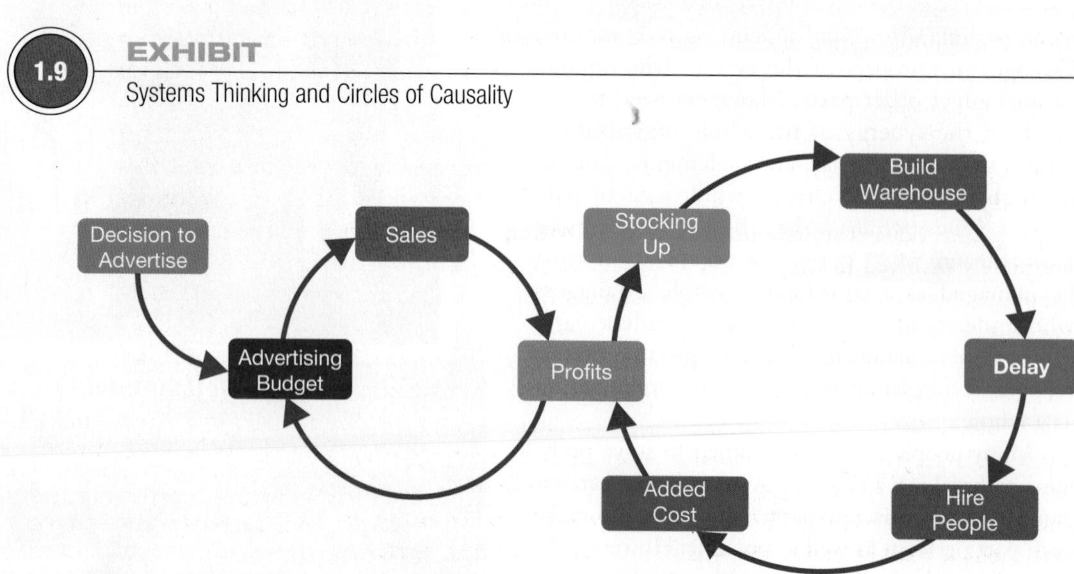

Contingency View

A second recent extension to management thinking is the **contingency view**. The classical perspective assumed a *universalist* view. Management concepts were thought to be universal; that is, whatever worked—management style, bureaucratic structure—in one organization would work in another. In business education, however, an alternative view exists. In this *case* view, each situation is believed to be unique. Principles are not universal, and one learns about management by experiencing a large number of case problem situations. Managers face the task of determining what methods will work in every new situation.

To integrate these views, the contingency view emerged.[81] Here neither of the other views is seen as entirely correct. Instead, certain contingencies, or variables, exist for helping management identify and understand situations. The contingency view tells us that what works in one setting might not work in another. Contingency means that one thing depends on other things, and a manager's response to a situation depends on identifying key contingencies in an organizational situation.

One important contingency, for example, is the industry in which the organization operates. The organizational structure that is effective for an Internet company such as Google would not be successful for a large auto manufacturer such as Ford. As well, a management-by-objectives (MBO) system that works well in a manufacturing firm might not be right for a school system. When managers learn to identify important patterns and characteristics of their organizations, they can then fit solutions to those characteristics.

Total Quality Management

The theme of quality is another concept that permeates current management thinking. The quality movement is strongly associated with Japanese companies, but these ideas emerged partly as a result of American influence after World War II. The ideas of W. Edwards Deming, known as the "father of the quality movement," were initially scoffed at in the United States, but the Japanese embraced his theories and modified them to help rebuild their industries into world powers.[82] Japanese companies achieved a significant departure from the American model by gradually shifting from an inspection-oriented approach to quality control toward an approach emphasizing employee involvement in the prevention of quality problems.[83]

During the 1980s and into the 1990s, **total quality management (TQM)**, which focuses on managing the total organization to deliver better quality to customers, moved to the forefront in helping U.S. managers deal with global competition. The approach infuses high-quality values throughout every activity within a company, with front-line workers intimately involved in the process. Four significant elements of quality management are employee involvement, focus on the customer, benchmarking, and continuous improvement, often referred to as *kaizen*.

Employee involvement means that achieving better quality requires companywide participation in quality control. All employees are *focused on the customer*; companies find out what customers want and try to meet their needs and expectations. *Benchmarking* refers to a process whereby companies find out how others do something better than they do and then try to imitate or improve on it. *Continuous improvement* is the implementation of small, incremental improvements in all areas of the organization on an ongoing basis. TQM is not a quick fix, but companies such as General Electric, Texas Instruments, Procter & Gamble, and DuPont achieved astonishing results in efficiency, quality, and customer satisfaction through total quality management.[84] TQM is still an important part of today's organizations, and managers consider benchmarking in particular a highly effective and satisfying management technique.[85]

Some of today's companies pursue highly ambitious quality goals to demonstrate their commitment to improving quality. For example, *Six Sigma,* popularized by Motorola and General Electric, specifies a goal of no more than 3.4 defects per million parts. However, the term also refers to a broad quality-control approach that emphasizes a disciplined and relentless pursuit of higher quality and lower costs. TQM will be discussed in detail in Chapter 15.

- The **quantitative perspective** uses mathematics, statistical techniques, and computer technology to facilitate management decision making, particularly for complex problems.
- The post–World War II period saw the rise of several new ideas that are a part of modern management.
- A **system** is a set of interrelated parts that function as a whole to achieve a common purpose. An organization is a system.
- **Systems thinking** means looking not just at discrete parts of an organizational situation but also at the continually changing interactions among the parts.
- When managers think systemically and understand subsystem interdependence and synergy, they can get a better handle on managing in a complex environment.
- **Subsystems** are parts of a system that depend on one another for their functioning.
- The concept of **synergy** says that the whole is greater than the sum of its parts. The organization must be managed as a whole.
- The **contingency view** tells managers that what works in one organizational situation might not work in others. Managers can identify important *contingencies* that help guide their decisions regarding the organization.
- The quality movement is associated with Japanese companies, but it emerged partly as a result of American influence after World War II.
- W. Edwards Deming is known as the "father of the quality movement."
- **Total quality management** focuses on managing the total organization to deliver quality to customers.
- Four significant elements of TQM are employee involvement, focus on the customer, benchmarking, and continuous improvement.

Discussion Questions

1. How do you feel about having a manager's responsibility in today's world characterized by uncertainty, ambiguity, and sudden changes or threats from the environment? Describe some skills and qualities that are important to managers under these conditions.
2. Assume you are a project manager at a biotechnology company, working with managers from research, production, and marketing on a major product modification. You notice that every memo you receive from the marketing manager has been copied to senior management. At every company function, he spends time talking to the big shots. You are also aware that sometimes when you and the other project members are slaving away over the project, he is playing golf with senior managers. What is your evaluation of his behavior? As project manager, what do you do?
3. Jeff Immelt of General Electric (GE) said that the most valuable thing he learned in business school was

that "there are 24 hours in a day, and you can use all of them." Do you agree or disagree? What are some of the advantages to this approach to being a manager? What are some of the drawbacks?

4. Why do some organizations seem to have a new CEO every year or two, whereas others have top leaders who stay with the company for many years (e.g., Jack Welch's 20 years as CEO at General Electric)? What factors about the manager or about the company might account for this difference?
5. Think about Toyota's highly publicized safety problems. One observer said that a goal of efficiency had taken precedence over a goal of quality within Toyota. Do you think managers can improve both efficiency and effectiveness simultaneously? Discuss. How do you think Toyota's leaders should respond to the safety situation?
6. You are a bright, hard-working entry-level manager who fully intends to rise up through the ranks. Your performance evaluation gives you high marks for your technical skills but low marks when it comes to people skills. Do you think people skills can be learned, or do you need to rethink your career path? If people skills can be learned, how would you go about it?
7. If managerial work is characterized by variety, fragmentation, and brevity, how do managers perform basic management functions such as planning, which would seem to require reflection and analysis?
8. How might the teaching of a management course be designed to help people make the transition from individual performer to manager in order to prepare them for the challenges they will face as new managers?
9. Why do you think Mary Parker Follett's ideas tended to be popular with business people of her day but were ignored by management scholars? Why are her ideas appreciated more today?
10. Why can an event such as the Hawthorne studies be a major turning point in the history of management even if the idea is later shown to be in error? Discuss.

Self-Learning

See It Online

Security or Autonomy[86]

Respond to each statement below based on whether you Mostly Agree or Mostly Disagree with it.

	Mostly Agree	Mostly Disagree
1. I value stability in my job.		
2. Rules, policies, and procedures generally frustrate me.		
3. I enjoy working for a firm that promotes employees based heavily on seniority.		
4. I'd prefer some kind of freelance job to working for the government.		
5. I'd be proud to work for the largest and most successful company in its field.		
6. Given a choice, I'd rather make $90,000 a year as a VP in a small company than $100,000 a year as a middle manager in a large company.		
7. I'd rather work directly for a single manager than on a team with shared responsibilities.		
8. I generally prefer to multitask and be involved in multiple projects.		
9. Good employee benefits are important to me.		
10. Rules are made to be broken.		

Scoring

Give yourself 1 point for each answer of "Mostly Agree" to the odd-numbered items and one point for each "Mostly Disagree" to the even-numbered items.

Interpretation

Your answers determine whether your preferences would fit with a bureaucratic organization. If your score is 8–10, a large, formal company would be compatible with your style and wishes. A score of 4–7 suggests you would receive modest satisfaction from working within a bureaucratic organization. A score of 1–3 suggests you would likely be frustrated by working in a large bureaucracy.

A large, bureaucratic organization provides security, benefits, and certainty compared to smaller or entrepreneurial firms where freedom and autonomy are greater. Do you want to optimize security or autonomy in your career? Would you be more satisfied in a large formal organization or in an organization that emphasizes a human resources perspective? Compare your scores with other students' scores and discuss any differences.

Group Learning

Your Best and Worst Managers

Step 1. By yourself, think of two managers you have had—the best and the worst. The managers could be anyone who served in an authority figure position over you, including an instructor, a boss at work, a manager of a student organization, a leader of a student group, a coach, a volunteer committee in a nonprofit organization, and so on. Think carefully about the specific behaviors that made each manager the best or worst and write down what the manager did.

The best manager I ever had did the following:

Was Fair, treated all of us as a team

No favorites or unequal treatment

The worst manager I ever had did the following:

Unfair, favorites

Did not Keep her word

Step 2. Divide into groups of four to six members. Share your experiences one person at a time. Write on the table below or on a whiteboard separate lists of "best" manager and "worst" manager behaviors.

	management principles followed or broken	skills evident or missing	lessons to be learned	advice you would give managers
The best managers				
The worst managers				

Step 3. Analyze the two lists. What themes or patterns characterize "best" and "worst" manager behaviors? What are the key differences between the two sets of behaviors?

Step 4. What lessons does your group learn from its analysis? What advice or "words of wisdom" would you give managers to help them be more effective?

Action Learning

1. Think about some time in your life where you were a leader or had some authority over others. It could have been on a school committee, or as camp counselor, youth coordinator in church/synagogue, yearbook/prom organizer, etc.
2. Either individually, or in a group of two to four, ask the following questions. If you are in a group, someone else can ask you the questions:
   a. Describe some incidents that went really well, where you handled a problem in a satisfying manner.
   b. List some examples when you did not handle problems in a positive manner.
   c. What were the differences between those two types of situations? Was it the type of person you dealt with, the level of your own supervision, the difficulty of the problem, and so on?

d. What can you learn about your own strengths and weaknesses and a manager from these situations?
e. What is your best strength as a manager? Can you find a theory in Chapter 1 that refers to that strength?
f. What would you do differently in any of the situations you described, if you had it to do over again?

3. Write a short (two- to three-page) paper, comparing situations you encountered. What are the deeper insights you have gained from reflection?
4. Your instructor may ask you to discuss your conclusions in groups, and to be prepared to share with them the whole class.

Ethical Dilemma

Can Management Afford to Look the Other Way?[87]

Harry Rull had been with Shellington Pharmaceuticals for 30 years. After a tour of duty in the various plants and seven years overseas, Harry was back at headquarters, looking forward to his new role as vice president of U.S. marketing.

Two weeks into his new job, Harry received some unsettling news about one of the managers under his supervision. Over casual lunch conversation, the director of human resources mentioned that Harry should expect a phone call about Roger Jacobs, manager of new product development. Jacobs had a history of being "pretty horrible" to his subordinates, she said, and one disgruntled employee asked to speak to someone in senior management. After lunch, Harry did some follow-up work. Jacobs's performance reviews had been stellar, but his personnel file also contained a large number of notes documenting charges of Jacobs's mistreatment of subordinates. The complaints ranged from "inappropriate and derogatory remarks" to subsequently dropped charges of sexual harassment. What was more disturbing was that the amount as well as the severity of complaints had increased with each of Jacobs's ten years with Shellington.

When Harry questioned the company president about the issue, he was told, "Yeah, he's had some problems, but you can't just replace someone with an eye for new products. You're a bottom-line guy; you understand why we let these things slide." Not sure how to handle the situation, Harry met briefly with Jacobs and reminded him to "keep the team's morale up." Just after the meeting, Sally Barton from Human Resources called to let him know that the problem she'd mentioned over lunch had been worked out. However, she warned, another employee had now come forward demanding that her complaints be addressed by senior management.

What Would You Do?

1. Ignore the problem. Jacobs's contributions to new product development are too valuable to risk losing him, and the problems over the past ten years have always worked themselves out anyway. No sense starting something that could make you look bad.
2. Launch a full-scale investigation of employee complaints about Jacobs, and make Jacobs aware that the documented history over the past ten years has put him on thin ice.
3. Meet with Jacobs and the employee to try to resolve the current issue, then start working with Sally Barton and other senior managers to develop stronger policies regarding sexual harassment and treatment of employees, including clear-cut procedures for handling complaints.

Case for Critical Analysis

Elektra Products, Inc.[88]

Barbara Russell, a manufacturing vice president, walked into the monthly companywide meeting with a light step and a hopefulness she hadn't felt in a long time. The company's new, dynamic CEO was going to announce a new era of employee involvement and empowerment at Elektra Products, an 80-year-old, publicly held company that had once been a leading manufacturer and retailer of electrical products and supplies. In recent years, the company had experienced a host of problems: market share was declining in the face of increased foreign and domestic competition; new product ideas were few and far between; departments such as manufacturing and sales barely spoke to one another; morale was at an all-time low, and many employees were actively seeking other jobs. Everyone needed a dose of hope.

Martin Griffin, who had been hired to revive the failing company, briskly opened the meeting with a challenge: "As we face increasing competition, we need new ideas, new energy, new spirit to make this company great. And the source for this change is you—each one of you." He then went on to explain that under the new empowerment campaign, employees would be getting more information about how the company was run and would be able to work with their fellow employees in new and creative ways. Martin proclaimed a new era of trust and cooperation at Elektra Products. Barbara felt the excitement stirring within her; but as she looked around the room, she saw many of the other employees, including her friend Simon, rolling their eyes. "Just another pile of corporate crap," Simon said later. "One minute they try downsizing, the next reengineering. Then they dabble in restructuring. Now Martin wants to push empowerment. Garbage like empowerment isn't a substitute for hard work and a little faith in the people who have been with this company for years. We made it great once, and we can do it again. Just get out of our way." Simon had been a manufacturing engineer with Elektra Products for more than 20 years. Barbara knew he was extremely loyal to the company, but he—and a lot of others like him—were going to be an obstacle to the empowerment efforts.

Top management assigned selected managers to several problem-solving teams to come up with ideas for implementing the empowerment campaign. Barbara loved her assignment as team leader of the manufacturing team, working on ideas to improve how retail stores got the merchandise they needed when they needed it. The team thrived, and trust blossomed among the members. They even spent nights and weekends working to complete their report. They were proud of their ideas, which they believed were innovative but easily achievable: Permit a manager to follow a product from design through sales to customers; allow salespeople to refund up to $500 worth of merchandise on the spot; make information available to salespeople about future products; and swap sales and manufacturing personnel for short periods to let them get to know one another's jobs.

When the team presented its report to department heads, Martin Griffin was enthusiastic. But shortly into the meeting he had to excuse himself because of a late-breaking deal with a major hardware store chain. With Martin absent, the department heads rapidly formed a wall of resistance. The director of human resources complained that the ideas for personnel changes would destroy the carefully crafted job categories that had just been completed. The finance department argued that allowing salespeople to make $500 refunds would create a gold mine for unethical customers and salespeople. The legal department warned that providing information to salespeople about future products would invite industrial spying.

The team members were stunned. As Barbara mulled over the latest turn of events, she considered her options: Keep her mouth shut; take a chance and confront Martin about her sincerity in making empowerment work; push slowly for reform and work for gradual support from the other teams; or look for another job and leave a company she really cared about. Barbara realized she was looking at no easy choices and no easy answers.

Questions

1. How might top management have done a better job changing Elektra Products into a new kind of organization? What might they do now to get the empowerment process back on track?
2. Can you think of ways Barbara could have avoided the problems her team faced in the meeting with department heads?
3. If you were Barbara Russell, what would you do now? Why?

aplia Aplia Highlights

Now use your Aplia homework to help you:

- Apply management theories in your life
- Assess your management skills
- Master management terms and concepts
- Apply your knowledge to real-world situations
- Analyze and solve challenging management problems

In order to take advantage of these elements, your instructor will need to have set up a course for your class within Aplia. Ask your instructor to contact his/her Cengage sales representative and Digital Solutions Manager to explore testing Aplia in your course this term.

Camp Bow Wow: Innovative Management for a Changing World

© Leremy, Shutterstock

Nearly everyone who has been to camp has vivid memories of the woodsy adventure. In particular, the sights and sounds of the great outdoors leave a lasting impression on campers. There are the cabins, the camp counselors, the campfire treats, the wide open spaces, the incessant barking of the furry four-legged camp goers—well, at least these are the sights and sounds for visitors of Camp Bow Wow, the fastest-growing doggie day-care center in the United States.

Founded little more than a decade ago by dog-lover Heidi Ganahl, Camp Bow Wow is a safe, happy place where people can take their pets when no one is home to care for them. For dog owners who work in the daytime, the Boulder, Colorado–based franchise offers premier doggie day-care services. For pets that need to stay a little longer, Camp Bow Wow has overnight boarding with spacious cabins and comfortable cots.

Every day, the experienced counselors at Camp Bow Wow supervise dozens of canine campers. Pooches receive plenty of personal attention, including grooming, outdoor exercise, food, baths, and medical support. For overprotective owners who worry their pups might get homesick while they are away, the camp's Live Camper Cams enable anytime viewing of pet play areas, using the Camp Bow Wow app for iPhone.

With more than 150 locations, Camp Bow Wow is one of the hottest franchise businesses in the nation. The pet-care service ranked No. 87 on *Entrepreneur* magazine's list of fastest-growing franchises in 2010, and the ranking is likely to go higher as new franchisees prepare for launch. Camp Bow Wow franchise owners receive three weeks of start-up training, and individual camps get corporate support in the form of co-op advertising, a grand opening, and ongoing field operations and evaluations.

Sue Ryan, a Camp Bow Wow franchisee from Colorado, knows the ins and outs of managing a doggie day camp. To help launch her business a few years ago, Ryan recruited experienced pet-care worker Candace Stathis, who came on as a camp counselor. Ryan soon recognized that Stathis was a star performer with a natural ability to work with clients and pets alike, and today Stathis serves as the camp's general manager. "Candace is good with the dogs, good with the customers, good with the employees, and she can manage the administrative part of the operation—she does a little bit of everything," Ryan said of her managerial top dog.

At Camp Bow Wow, store managers have distinct roles from camp counselors. Whereas counselors typically take care of dogs, answer phones, and book reservations, managers must know how to run all operations and manage people as well.

"What I do," said Stathis, "is make sure all the operational stuff goes off without a hitch—so, making sure that the dogs all get fed, that they get the meds when they're supposed to, that the staff is taking care of the dogs the way they are supposed to, and making sure that everybody is attentive to the pets. You're managing the dogs, but you're also managing the people."

To keep camp running as efficiently as possible, Stathis maintains a strict daily schedule for doggie baths, nail trimmings, feedings, and play time. Staying on schedule is no easy task, especially during the busy holidays and summer months—or whenever the pets get territorial. Stathis says that although dogs get in occasional tussles, all camp staff members are trained to handle such hairy situations. "It's part of the job; we are all really prepared to deal with it," says Stathis.

When it comes to keeping dogs happy at play, an ounce of prevention is worth a pound of cure. "We try to separate the dogs first and foremost by temperament, and then by size," says Stathis. "We put an even amount of dogs in the yards—say, a couple high-energy dogs with low-energy dogs—to try and balance the yards out." Other dog management strategies at Camp Bow Wow include the 15 to 1 dog-to-counselor ratio and the preliminary meet-and-greet, where pets are screened for vaccinations and spay and neuter status.

For franchise owner Sue Ryan, having competent management running the camp equals less worry and more personal relaxation—perhaps even more time to go on safari in Africa. For Candace Stathis, however, good management is simply about doing the work she loves. "I love the people, I love the dogs, and I wouldn't change anything for the world," Stathis says.

Discussion Questions

1. List the three broad management skill categories and explain which skills are needed most for each of the Camp Bow Wow leaders highlighted in the video.
2. Which activities at Camp Bow Wow require high efficiency? Which activities require high effectiveness?
3. List two activities that leaders at Camp Bow Wow perform daily, and identify which of the ten managerial roles discussed in the chapter figure prominently for each.

, Shutterstock

© VikaSuh, Shutterstock

In Good Company

A corporate takeover brings star advertising executive Dan Foreman (Dennis Quaid) a new boss who is half his age. Carter Duryea (Topher Grace), Dan's new boss, wants to prove his worth as the new marketing chief at *Sports America*, Waterman Publishing's flagship magazine. Carter applies his unique approaches while dating Dan's daughter, Alex (Scarlett Johansson).

Management Behavior This sequence starts with Carter Duryea entering Dan Foreman's office. It follows Foreman's interaction with Teddy K. (Malcolm McDowell), Globecom CEO, after Teddy K.'s speech. Carter Duryea enters while saying, "Oh, my God, Dan. Oh, my God." Mark Steckle (Clark Gregg) soon follows. The sequence ends with Carter asking, "Any ideas?" Dan Forman says, "One." The film cuts to the two of them arriving at Eugene Kalb's (Philip Baker Hall) office building.

What to Watch for and Ask Yourself

- Which management skills discussed in this chapter does Mark Steckle possess? Which does he lack?
- The sequence shows three people who represent different hierarchical levels in the company. Which hierarchical levels do you attribute to Carter Duryea, Dan Foreman, and Mark Steckle?
- Critique the behavior shown in the sequence. What are the positive and negative aspects of the behavior shown?

Endnotes

1. Teresa A. Taylor, "Everything on One Calendar, Please," (interview, "Corner Office" column) *The New York Times,* December 27, 2009.
2. Ellen McGirt, "1: Facebook," *Fast Company* (March 2010): 54–57, 110 (part of the section "The World's 50 Most Innovative Companies").
3. Joshua Green, "Management Secrets of the Grateful Dead," *The Atlantic* (March 2010): 64–67.
4. Darrell Rigby and Barbara Bilodeau, "Management Tools and Trends 2009," (Bain & Company, Inc., 2009), www.bain.com/management_tools/home.asp (accessed on March 10, 2010).
5. "What Do Managers Do?" *The Wall Street Journal Online*, http://guides.wsj.com/management/developing-a-leadership-style/what-do-managers-do/ (accessed August 11, 2010), article adapted from Alan Murray, *The Wall Street Journal Essential Guide to Management* (New York: Harper Business, 2010).
6. Jennifer Reingold, "Target's Inner Circle," *Fortune* (March 31, 2008): 74–86.
7. Aaron O. Patrick, "EMI Deal Hits a Sour Note," *The Wall Street Journal,* August 15, 2009.
8. Robert L. Katz, "Skills of an Effective Administrator," *Harvard Business Review* 52 (September–October 1974): 90–102.
9. Clinton O. Longenecker, Mitchell J. Neubert, and Laurence S. Fink, "Causes and Consequences of Managerial Failure in Rapidly Changing Organizations," *Business Horizons* 50 (2007): 145–155.
10. Paul Sonne, "The Gulf Oil Spill: Hayward Fell Short of Modern CEO Demands," *The Wall Street Journal*, July 26, 2010.
11. Henry Mintzberg, *Managing* (San Francisco: Berrett-Kohler Publishers, 2009); Mintzberg, *The Nature of Managerial Work* (New York: Harper & Row, 1973); and Mintzberg, "Rounding Out the Manager's Job," *Sloan Management Review* (Fall 1994): 11–26.
12. Robert E. Kaplan, "Trade Routes: The Manager's Network of Relationships," *Organizational Dynamics* (Spring 1984): 37–52; Rosemary Stewart, "The Nature of Management: A Problem for Management Education," *Journal of Management Studies* 21 (1984): 323–330; John P. Kotter, "What Effective General Managers Really Do," *Harvard Business Review* (November–December 1982): 156–167; and Morgan W. McCall, Jr., Ann M. Morrison, and Robert L. Hannan, "Studies of Managerial Work: Results and Methods," Technical Report No. 9, Center for Creative Leadership, Greensboro, NC, 1978.
13. Alison M. Konrad et al., "What Do Managers *Like* to Do? A Five-Country Study," *Group and Organizational Management* 26, no. 4 (December 2001): 401–433.
14. For a review of the problems faced by first-time managers, see Linda A. Hill, "Becoming the Boss," *Harvard Business Review* (January 2007): 49–56; Loren B. Belker and Gary S. Topchik, *The First-Time Manager: A Practical Guide to the Management of People*, 5th ed. (New York: AMACOM, 2005); J. W. Lorsch and P. F. Mathias, "When Professionals Have to Manage," *Harvard Business Review* (July–August 1987): 78–83; R. A. Webber, *Becoming a Courageous Manager: Overcoming Career Problems of New Managers* (Englewood Cliffs, NJ: Prentice Hall,

1991); D. E. Dougherty, *From Technical Professional to Corporate Manager: A Guide to Career Transition* (New York: Wiley, 1984); J. Falvey, "The Making of a Manager," *Sales and Marketing Management* (March 1989): 42–83; M. K. Badawy, *Developing Managerial Skills in Engineers and Scientists: Succeeding as a Technical Manager* (New York: Van Nostrand Reinhold, 1982); and M. London, *Developing Managers: A Guide to Motivating and Preparing People for Successful Managerial Careers* (San Francisco: Jossey-Bass, 1985).

15. Erin White, "Learning to Be the Boss; Trial and Error Is the Norm as New Managers Figure Out How to Relate to Former Peers," *The Wall Street Journal*, November 21, 2005.

16. This discussion is based on Linda A. Hill, *Becoming a Manager: How New Managers Master the Challenges of Leadership*, 2nd ed. (Boston, MA: Harvard Business School Press, 2003), pp. 6–8; and Hill, "Becoming the Boss."

17. See also "Boss's First Steps," sidebar in White, "Learning to Be the Boss"; and Belker and Topchik, *The First-Time Manager*.

18. Jeanne Whalen, "Chance Turns a Teacher into a CEO; Religion Lecturer Leaves Academic Path and Learns to Run a Biotech Start-Up" (Theory & Practice column), *The Wall Street Journal*, October 17, 2005.

19. Henry Mintzberg, *Managing*, pp. 17–41.

20. Ibid.

21. Based on Damien Cave, "A Tall Order for a Marine: Feeding the Hand That Bit You," *The New York Times*, December 30, 2007.

22. Mintzberg, *Managing*, pp. 17–41.

23. Carol Hymowitz, "Packed Calendars Rule," *The Asian Wall Street Journal,* June 16, 2009; and "The 18-Hour Day," *The Conference Board Review* (March–April 2008): 20.

24. Adam Shell, "CEO Profile: Casting a Giant (New Jersey) Net," *USA Today,* August 25, 2008; Matthew Boyle and Jia Lynn Yang, "All in a Day's Work," *Fortune* (March 20, 2006): 97–104.

25. Spielberg, "The Cheesecake Factory."

26. Mintzberg, *Managing*; Lance B. Kurke and Howard E. Aldrich, "Mintzberg Was Right!: A Replication and Extension of *The Nature of Managerial Work*," *Management Science* 29 (1983): 975–984; Cynthia M. Pavett and Alan W. Lau, "Managerial Work: The Influence of Hierarchical Level and Functional Specialty," *Academy of Management Journal* 26 (1983): 170–177; and Colin P. Hales, "What Do Managers Do? A Critical Review of the Evidence," *Journal of Management Studies* 23 (1986): 88–115.

27. This section is based on Peter F. Drucker, *Managing the Non-Profit Organization: Principles and Practices* (New York: HarperBusiness, 1992); and Thomas Wolf, *Managing a Nonprofit Organization* (New York: Fireside/Simon & Schuster, 1990).

28. Christine W. Letts, William P. Ryan, and Allen Grossman, *High Performance Nonprofit Organizations* (New York: Wiley & Sons, 1999), pp. 30–35.

29. Carol Hymowitz, "In Sarbanes-Oxley Era, Running a Nonprofit Is Only Getting Harder," *The Wall Street Journal*, June 21, 2005; and Bill Birchard, "Nonprofits by the Numbers," *CFO* (June 2005): 50–55.

30. Eilene Zimmerman, "Your True Calling Could Suit a Nonprofit," (interview, "Career Couch" column) *The New York Times,* April 6, 2008.

31. This section is based on "The New Organization: A Survey of the Company," *The Economist* (January 21, 2006); Harry G. Barkema, Joel A. C. Baum, and Elizabeth A. Mannix, "Management Challenges in a New Time," *Academy of Management Journal* 45, no. 5 (2002): 916–930; Michael Harvey and M. Ronald Buckley, "Assessing the 'Conventional Wisdoms' of Management for the 21st Century Organization," *Organizational Dynamics* 30, no. 4 (2002): 368–378; and Toby J. Tetenbaum, "Shifting Paradigms: From Newton to Chaos," *Organizational Dynamics* (Spring 1998): 21–32.

32. Caroline Ellis, "The Flattening Corporation," *MIT Sloan Management Review* (Summer 2003): 5.

33. Andrea Coombes, "Seeking Loyal, Devoted Workers? Let Them Stay Home," *The Wall Street Journal,* September 11, 2007; Christopher Rhoads and Sara Silver, "Working at Home Gets Easier," *The Wall Street Journal*, December 29, 2005; and Kelley Holland, "When Work Time Isn't Face Time," *The New York Times*, December 3, 2006.

34. Kerr Inkson, Angela Heising, and Denise M. Rousseau, "The Interim Manager: Prototype of the 21st Century Worker," *Human Relations* 54, no. 3 (2001): 259–284.

35. Estimate attributed to Jon Osborne, vice president of research at Staffing Industry Analysts, in "How to Become an Exec-for-Rent," *Fortune* (March 22, 2010): 41–42.

36. Holland, "When Work Time Isn't Face Time."

37. Thomas H. Davenport and Laurence Prusak, with Jim Wilson, *What's the Big Idea? Creating and Capitalizing on the Best Management Thinking* (Boston, MA: Harvard Business School Press, 2003); Theodore Kinni, "Have We Run out of Big Ideas?" *Across the Board* (March–April 2003): 16–21; Hamel, "The Why, What, and How of Management Innovation"; and Joyce Thompson Heames and Michael Harvey, "The Evolution of the Concept of the Executive from the 20th Century Manager to the 21st Century Global Leader," *Journal of Leadership and Organizational Studies* 13, no. 2 (2006): 29–41.

38. Darrell Rigby, "Management Tools Survey 2003: Usage Up as Companies Strive to Make Headway in Tough Times," *Strategy & Leadership* 31, no. 5 (2003): 4–11.

39. Study reported in Phred Dvorak, "Why Management Trends Quickly Fade Away ("Theory and Practice" column), *The Wall Street Journal*, June 26, 2006.

40. Andy Reinhardt, "From Gearhead to Grand High Pooh-Bah," *BusinessWeek* (August 28, 2000): 129–130.

41. Eric Abrahamson, "Management Fashion," *Academy of Management Review* 21, no. 1 (January 1996): 254–285. Also see "75 Years of Management Ideas and Practice," a supplement to the *Harvard Business Review* (September–October 19,97), for a broad overview of historical trends in management thinking.

42. Daniel A. Wren, *The Evolution of Management Thought*, 4th ed. (New York: Wiley, 1994).

43. Based on Stephanie Armour, "Generation Y: They've Arrived at Work with a New Attitude," *USA Today,* November 6, 2005, www.usatoday.com/money/workplace/2005-11-06-gen-y_x.htm (accessed November 10, 2005); and Marnie E. Green, "Beware and Prepare: The Government Workforce of the Future," *Public Personnel Management* (Winter 2000): 435ff.

44. Jena McGregor, "'There Is No More Normal,'" *BusinessWeek* (March 23 & 30, 2009): 30–34.

45. Michael Aneiro, "Credit Market Springs to Life," *The Wall Street Journal,* March 11, 2010.

46. Aziz Hannifa, "India, China Growth Dominates World Bank Meet," *India Abroad* (New York edition), November 2, 2007.
47. Robert Tell and Brian Kleiner, "Organizational Change Can Rescue Industry," *Industrial Management* (March–April 2009): 20–24.
48. Daniel A. Wren, "Management History: Issues and Ideas for Teaching and Research," *Journal of Management* 13 (1987): 339–350.
49. Business historian Alfred D. Chandler, Jr., quoted in Jerry Useem, "Entrepreneur of the Century," *Inc.* (20th Anniversary Issue, 1999): 159–174.
50. Useem, "Entrepreneur of the Century."
51. The following is based on Wren, *Evolution of Management Thought*, chapters 4, 5; and Claude S. George, Jr., *The History of Management Thought* (Englewood Cliffs, NJ: Prentice-Hall, 1968), chapter 4.
52. Cynthia Crossen, "Early Industry Expert Soon Realized a Staff Has Its Own Efficiency," *The Wall Street Journal*, November 6, 2006.
53. Alan Farnham, "The Man Who Changed Work Forever," *Fortune* (July 21, 1997): 114; Charles D. Wrege and Ann Marie Stoka, "Cooke Creates a Classic: The Story Behind F. W. Taylor's Principles of Scientific Management," *Academy of Management Review* (October 1978): 736–749; Robert Kanigel, *The One Best Way: Frederick Winslow Taylor and the Enigma of Efficiency* (New York: Viking, 1997); and "The X and Y Factors: What Goes Around Comes Around," special section in "The New Organisation: A Survey of the Company," *The Economist* (January 21–27, 2006): 17–18.
54. Wren, *Evolution of Management Thought*, 171; and George, *History of Management Thought*, pp. 103–104.
55. Vanessa O'Connell, "Stores Count Seconds to Trim Labor Costs," *The Wall Street Journal*, November 17, 2008.
56. Gary Hamel, "The Why, What, and How of Management Innovation," *Harvard Business Review* (February 2006): 72–84; Peter Coy, "Cog or Co-Worker?" *BusinessWeek* (August 20 & 27, 2007): 58–60.
57. Max Weber, *General Economic History*, trans. Frank H. Knight (London: Allen & Unwin, 1927); Max Weber, *The Protestant Ethic and the Spirit of Capitalism*, trans. Talcott Parsons (New York: Scribner, 1930); and Max Weber, *The Theory of Social and Economic Organizations*, ed. and trans. A. M. Henderson and Talcott Parsons (New York: Free Press, 1947).
58. Nadira A. Hira, "The Making of a UPS Driver," *Fortune* (November 12, 2007), 118–129; David J. Lynch, "Thanks to Its CEO, UPS Doesn't Just Deliver," *USA Today*, July 24, 2006, www.usatoday.com/money/companies/management/2006-07-23-ups_x.htm?tab1=t2 (accessed July 24, 2006); Kelly Barron, "Logistics in Brown," *Forbes* (January 10, 2000): 78–83; Scott Kirsner, "Venture Vérité: United Parcel Service," *Wired* (September 1999): 83–96; "UPS," *The Atlanta Journal and Constitution*, April 26, 1992; Kathy Goode, Betty Hahn, and Cindy Seibert, "United Parcel Service: The Brown Giant" (unpublished manuscript, Texas A&M University, 1981); and "About UPS," UPS corporate Web site, www.ups.com/content/corp/about/index.html?WT.svl=SubNav (accessed October 27, 2008).
59. Henri Fayol, *Industrial and General Administration*, trans. J. A. Coubrough (Geneva: International Management Institute, 1930); Henri Fayol, *General and Industrial Management*, trans. Constance Storrs (London: Pitman and Sons, 1949); and W. J. Arnold et al., *Business-Week, Milestones in Management* (New York: McGraw-Hill, vol. I, 1965; vol. II, 1966).
60. Gregory M. Bounds, Gregory H. Dobbins, and Oscar S. Fowler, *Management: A Total Quality Perspective* (Cincinnati, OH: South-Western Publishing, 1995), pp. 52–53.
61. Mary Parker Follett, *The New State: Group Organization: The Solution of Popular Government* (London: Longmans, Green, 1918); and Mary Parker Follett, *Creative Experience* (London: Longmans, Green, 1924).
62. Henry C. Metcalf and Lyndall Urwick, eds., *Dynamic Administration: The Collected Papers of Mary Parker Follett* (New York: Harper & Row, 1940); Arnold, *Business-Week, Milestones in Management.*
63. Follett, *The New State*; Metcalf and Urwick, *Dynamic Administration* (London: Sir Isaac Pitman, 1941).
64. William B. Wolf, *How to Understand Management: An Introduction to Chester I. Barnard* (Los Angeles: Lucas Brothers, 1968); and David D. Van Fleet, "The Need-Hierarchy and Theories of Authority," *Human Relations* 9 (Spring 1982): 111–118.
65. Curt Tausky, *Work Organizations: Major Theoretical Perspectives* (Itasca, IL: F. E. Peacock, 1978), p. 42.
66. Charles D. Wrege, "Solving Mayo's Mystery: The First Complete Account of the Origin of the Hawthorne Studies—The Forgotten Contributions of Charles E. Snow and Homer Hibarger," paper presented to the Management History Division of the Academy of Management (August 1976).
67. Ronald G. Greenwood, Alfred A. Bolton, and Regina A. Greenwood, "Hawthorne a Half Century Later: Relay Assembly Participants Remember," *Journal of Management* 9 (Fall/Winter 1983): 217–231.
68. F. J. Roethlisberger, W. J. Dickson, and H. A. Wright, *Management and the Worker* (Cambridge, MA: Harvard University Press, 1939).
69. H. M. Parson, "What Happened at Hawthorne?" *Science* 183 (1974): 922–932; John G. Adair, "The Hawthorne Effect: A Reconsideration of the Methodological Artifact," *Journal of Applied Psychology* 69, no. 2 (1984): 334–345; and Gordon Diaper, "The Hawthorne Effect: A Fresh Examination," *Educational Studies* 16, no. 3 (1990): 261–268.
70. R. G. Greenwood, A. A. Bolton, and R. A. Greenwood, "Hawthorne a Half Century Later," 219–221.
71. F. J. Roethlisberger and W. J. Dickson, *Management and the Worker.*
72. Ramon J. Aldag and Timothy M. Stearns, *Management*, 2nd ed. (Cincinnati, OH: South-Western Publishing, 1991), pp. 47–48.
73. Tausky, *Work Organizations: Major Theoretical Perspectives*, p. 55.
74. Douglas McGregor, *The Human Side of Enterprise* (New York: McGraw-Hill, 1960), pp. 16–18.
75. Jena McGregor, "'There Is No More Normal,'" *BusinessWeek* (March 23 & 30, 2009): 30–34; and Ellen McGirt, "Revolution in San Jose," *Fast Company* (January 2009): 88–94, 134–136.
76. Wendell L. French and Cecil H. Bell, Jr., "A History of Organizational Development," in Wendell L. French, Cecil H. Bell, Jr., and Robert A. Zawacki, *Organization Development and Transformation: Managing Effective Change* (Burr Ridge, IL: Irwin McGraw-Hill, 2000), pp. 20–42.
77. Mansel G. Blackford and K. Austin Kerr, *Business Enterprise in American History* (Boston: Houghton Mifflin, 1986), chapters 10, 11; and Alex Groner and the editors of *American Heritage* and

BusinessWeek, The American Heritage History of American Business and Industry (New York: American Heritage Publishing, 1972), Chapter 9.

78. Ludwig von Bertalanffy et al., "General Systems Theory: A New Approach to Unity of Science," *Human Biology* 23 (December 1951): 302–361; and Kenneth E. Boulding, "General Systems Theory—The Skeleton of Science," *Management Science* 2 (April 1956): 197–208.

79. This section is based on Peter M. Senge, *The Fifth Discipline: The Art and Practice of the Learning Organization* (New York: Doubleday, 1990); John D. Sterman, "Systems Dynamics Modeling: Tools for Learning in a Complex World," *California Management Review* 43, no. 4 (Summer 2001): 8–25; and Ron Zemke, "Systems Thinking," *Training* (February 2001): 40–46.

80. This example is cited in Sterman, "Systems Dynamics Modeling."

81. Fred Luthans, "The Contingency Theory of Management: A Path Out of the Jungle," *Business Horizons* 16 (June 1973): 62–72; and Fremont E. Kast and James E. Rosenzweig, *Contingency Views of Organization and Management* (Chicago: Science Research Associates, 1973).

82. Samuel Greengard, "25 Visionaries Who Shaped Today's Workplace," *Workforce* (January 1997): 50–59; and Ann Harrington, "The Big Ideas," *Fortune* (November 22, 1999): 152–154.

83. Mauro F. Guillen, "The Age of Eclecticism: Current Organizational Trends and the Evolution of Managerial Models," *Sloan Management Review* (Fall 1994): 75–86.

84. Jeremy Main, "How to Steal the Best Ideas Around," *Fortune* (October 19, 1992): 102–106.

85. Darrell Rigby and Barbara Bilodeau, "Management Tools and Trends 2009," Bain & Company, Inc., 2009, www.bain.com/management_tools/home.asp (accessed March 10, 2010).

86. Adapted from Don Hellriegel, Susan E. Jackson, and John W. Slocum, Jr., *Managing: A Competency-Based Approach* (Mason, OH: Thompson South-Western, 2008), p. 73.

87. Based on Doug Wallace, "A Talent for Mismanagement: What Would You Do?" *Business Ethics* 2 (November–December 1992): 3–4.

88. Based on Lawrence R. Rothstein, "The Empowerment Effort That Came Undone," *Harvard Business Review* (January–February 1995): 20–31.

12:56 PM
12:56
23 APR 2011 SAT
+25 °C
8:00AM
2 missed calls
10:30AM - 11:30AM

PART 2

2 The Environment

Amazon is known for having its nose in a book, but lately the dot-com giant has its head in a cloud.

The Seattle-based company got its start as a simple online bookstore, but with the recent introduction of Amazon Cloud, the retailer aims to become the global leader in cloud computing services.

With traditional computing, people store files and applications on their own hard drives. With cloud computing, everything is stored remotely on the servers of giant technology firms. The consumer's job is simple: Subscribe to the cloud service of your choice and compute from anywhere, with full access to all your stuff.

Apart from obvious privacy concerns, Amazon faces many challenges in becoming a global provider of cloud services. First, Amazon has to compete against major competitors within its task environment. For example, Google's cloud debut didn't lag far behind Amazon's. In addition, Apple's cloud service, built around iTunes and iPad, has the potential to make Amazon Cloud evaporate entirely.

Second, as a multinational company, Amazon is certain to encounter technological strain. Because Amazon operates in China, Japan, France, Germany, Canada, and the United Kingdom, the task of managing the world's files becomes herculean. This problem was on display recently when a worldwide Cloud promotion featuring Lady Gaga's *Born This Way* overloaded Amazon's servers. Music downloads died or were delayed, leaving global audiences cold. Such meltdowns are no small matter; in today's demanding got-to-have-it-now consumer culture, technical glitches are like rain on a parade. Indeed, they cast a very dark cloud over business.

Top Right: Aleksandar Bracinac/www.shutterstock.com Center: Haywiremedia/Shutterstock.com Bottom Right: Perov Stanislav/Shutterstock.com

Chapter Outline

The External Environment
- *General Environment*
- *Task Environment*

The Organization–Environment Relationship
- *Environmental Uncertainty*
- *Adapting to the Environment*

The Internal Environment: Corporate Culture
- *Symbols*
- *Stories*
- *Heroes*
- *Slogans*
- *Ceremonies*

Types of Culture
- *Adaptability Culture*
- *Achievement Culture*
- *Involvement Culture*
- *Consistency Culture*

Shaping Corporate Culture for Innovative Response
- *Managing the High-Performance Culture*
- *Cultural Leadership*

The Environment and Corporate Culture

Learning Outcomes

After studying this chapter, you should be able to:

1. Describe the general and task environments and the dimensions of each.
2. Explain the strategies managers use to help organizations adapt to an uncertain or turbulent environment.
3. Define corporate culture and give organizational examples.
4. Explain organizational symbols, stories, heroes, slogans, and ceremonies and their relationship to corporate culture.
5. Describe four types of cultures and how corporate culture relates to the environment.
6. Define a cultural leader and explain the tools a cultural leader uses to create a high-performance culture.

© James Steidl, Shutterstock

Are You Ready to Be a Manager?

Please circle your opinion below each of the following statements.

1 **I am good at dealing with business or school problems where I am able to keep a positive and personal touch.**

Mostly True — Mostly False

(See page 59, Creating Guanxi *in China.)*

2 **I am good at picking up what the values and norms are in a new campus club or other organization.**

Mostly True — Mostly False

(See page 70, The Internal Environment: Corporate Culture.)

3 **I fit well in an organizational culture that values creativity and risk taking or perhaps one that values achievement.**

Mostly True — Mostly False

(See page 74, Adaptability Culture and Achievement Culture.)

4 **I'd do best in a company that values stability and consistency.**

Mostly True — Mostly False

(See page 75, Consistency Culture.)

5 **I think I'd be really good in a company that promotes and rewards high performance.**

Mostly True — Mostly False

(See page 77, Managing the High-Performance Culture.)

Once upon a time, not so very long ago, a trip to the video store was a part of almost every young couple's weekend plans and an event eagerly anticipated by schoolchildren as the hours ticked by on a Friday afternoon. Blockbuster, the king of video rental, had faux movie lights, popcorn, and candy at the checkouts, and film posters on the walls. Shelves full of VHS (and later DVD) boxes beckoned, and it was a thrill to snap up the last copy of a hot new release. Now, the video store is going the way of the milkman as mail-order and video-on-demand services change how people rent and view movies. Blockbuster has closed hundreds of stores and is likely to file for bankruptcy. Meanwhile, Netflix, which offers movies by mail or via online streaming, expanded its customer base to more than 13 million and saw its stock price top $100 a share in early 2010. Blockbuster also offers mail order and streaming services, but the company was slow to respond to changes in the industry and stuck too long with its outdated business model of renting videos from large retail stores. Now, the growing popularity of Redbox, which rents movies for $1 a night out of vending machines conveniently located in supermarkets, could put the last nail in Blockbuster's coffin. CEO James Keyes conceded in March of 2010 that there was "substantial doubt about [Blockbuster's] ability to continue as a going concern."[1]

The environment in which companies operate is continually changing, sometimes quite rapidly, as Blockbuster learned, and managers have to be on their toes. Netflix was founded in 1997, but Blockbuster managers failed to pay attention. Even though sales at video stores began to decline, Blockbuster didn't start offering new options for renting movies until 2003. For organizations in all industries, environments are increasingly dynamic, requiring managers to be prepared to respond quickly to even subtle environmental shifts. This chapter explores in detail components of the external environment and how they affect the organization. The chapter also examines a major part of the organization's internal environment—corporate culture. Corporate culture is both shaped by the external environment and shapes how managers respond to changes in the external environment.

The External Environment

The tremendous and far-reaching changes occurring in today's world can be understood by defining and examining components of the external environment. The external **organizational environment** includes all elements existing outside the boundary of the organization that have the potential to affect the organization.[2] The environment includes competitors, resources, technology, and economic conditions that influence the organization. It does not include those events so far removed from the organization that their impact is not perceived.

The organization's external environment can be further conceptualized as having two components: general and task environments, as illustrated in Exhibit 2.1.[3] The **general environment** affects organizations indirectly. It includes social, economic, legal/political, international, natural, and technological factors that influence all organizations about equally. Changes in federal regulations or an economic recession are part of the organization's general environment. These events do not directly change day-to-day operations, but they do affect all organizations eventually. The **task environment** is closer to the organization and includes the sectors that conduct day-to-day transactions with the organization and directly influence its basic operations and performance. It is generally considered to include competitors, suppliers, customers, and the labor market. British Petroleum did not use technology as well as it could when it let profits determine levels of safety standards, even ignoring legal requirements, as shown in this chapter's Business Blooper.

The organization also has an **internal environment** that includes the elements within the organization's boundaries. The internal environment is composed of current employees,

BUSINESS BLOOPER
British Petroleum Oil Spill

After the worst oil spill in U.S. history, which started in April of 2010, then-CEO of British Petroleum (BP) Tony Hayward did not win any friends on Capitol Hill in June when he refused to provide details of the spill, and where he seemed nonchalant about the 760 "egregious willful" violations between 2007 and 2009 from the Occupational Safety and Health Administration. Two days after the hearing, he raised more ire with the news that he was off the Coast of England, watching his yacht perform in a race and having "rare private time with his son." This was at the same time some 60,000 barrels were still leaking each day in a disaster that had cost 11 lives so far. This was just a year after the explosion of a BP refinery in Texas, where 15 were killed and hundreds wounded. BP did not learn from its mistake and continued with a culture that ruthlessly cut costs and took dangerous shortcuts, often bulldozing subcontractors, such as Halliburton, who recommended more safety precautions in the designs. Mr. Hayward's yacht finished fourth out of 45.

SOURCES: Liz Robbins, "BP Chief Draw Outrage for Attending Yacht Race," *The New York Times*, June 20, 2010; and Joe Nocera, "BP Ignored Omens is Disaster," *The New York Times*, June 19, 2010.

management, and especially corporate culture, which define employee behavior in the internal environment and how well the organization will adapt to the external environment.

Exhibit 2.1 illustrates the relationship among the general, task, and internal environments. As an open system, the organization draws resources from the external environment and releases goods and services back to it. We will now discuss the two components of the external environment in more detail. Then we will discuss corporate culture, the key element in the internal environment. Other aspects of the internal environment, such as structure and technology, will be covered in later chapters of this book.

General Environment

The dimensions of the general environment influence the organization over time but often are not involved in day-to-day transactions with it. The dimensions of the general environment include international, technological, sociocultural, economic, legal-political, and natural.

EXHIBIT 2.1

Dimensions of the Organization's General, Task, and Internal Environments

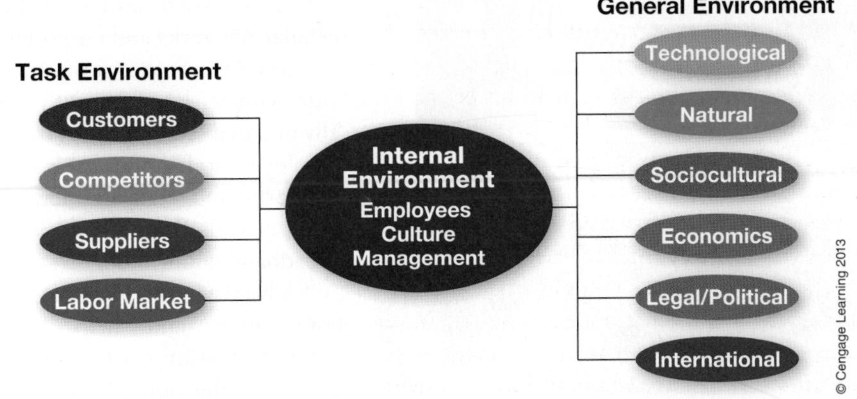

International The **international dimension** of the external environment represents events originating in foreign countries as well as opportunities for U.S. companies in other countries. The international environment provides new competitors, customers, and suppliers and shapes social, technological, and economic trends as well.

Today, every company has to compete on a global basis. The auto industry, for example, has experienced profound shifts as China recently emerged as the world's largest auto market. In response, car makers are moving international headquarters into China and designing features that appeal to the Chinese market, including bigger, limousine-like back seats, advanced entertainment systems, and light-colored interiors. These trends, inspired by the Chinese market, are reflected in models sold around the world.[4] For many other U.S. companies, such as Google, domestic markets have become saturated, and the only potential for growth lies overseas. Google's goal is to reach even the most far-flung corners of the globe by providing search results in more than 35 languages and a translation feature to users regardless of their native tongue.[5]

The global environment represents a complex, ever changing, and uneven playing field compared with the domestic environment. Managers who are used to thinking only about the domestic environment must learn new rules to remain competitive. When operating globally, managers have to consider legal, political, sociocultural, and economic factors not only in their home countries but in other countries as well. Global managers working in China, for example, recognize that their competitive success begins with their ability to build personal relationships and emotional bonds with their Chinese contacts. The Spotlight on Skills titled Creating *Guanxi* in China offers tips for creating successful business relationships in China.

Technological The **technological dimension** of the general environment includes scientific and technological advancements in a specific industry as well as in society at large. In recent years, this dimension created massive changes for organizations in all industries. Twenty years ago, many organizations didn't even use desktop computers. Today, computer networks, Internet access, handheld devices, videoconferencing capabilities, cell phones, and laptops are the minimum tools for doing business. A new generation of handhelds allows users to check their corporate e-mail, daily calendars, business contacts, and even customer orders from any location with a wireless network. Cell phones can now switch seamlessly between cellular networks and corporate WiFi connections. Some companies provide wireless key fobs with continually updated security codes that enable employees to log onto their corporate networks and securely view data or write e-mails from any device with a broadband connection.[6]

ROB KIM/Landov

ConceptConnection

Changes in the **technological dimension** of the environment have enabled H&R Block to expand its services as well as its marketing practices. In 2008, the company launched an ambitious, often whimsical social media campaign that included a Second Life island where avatars doled out tax advice. Because managers discovered customers were uncomfortable with spelling out their tax problems on Facebook and Twitter, Block changed its approach. It now uses those sites to direct customers to a Q&A Web page, *Get It Right*, where over 1,000 specially trained employees field questions.

Advances in technology drive competition and help innovative companies gain market share. They also have the potential to transform

SPOTLIGHT ON SKILLS

Creating *Guanxi* in China

With its low labor costs and huge potential market, China is luring thousands of U.S. companies in search of growth opportunities. Yet University of New Haven's Usha C. V. Haley recently found that only one-third of multinationals doing business in China have actually turned a profit. One reason Western businesses fall short of expectations, experts agree, is that they fail to grasp the centuries-old concept of *guanxi* that lies at the heart of Chinese culture.

At its simplest level, guanxi is a supportive, mutually beneficial connection between two people. Eventually, those personal relationships are linked together into a network, and it is through these networks that business gets done. Anyone considering doing business in China should keep in mind the following basic rules:

- ***Business is always personal.*** It is impossible to translate "don't take it so personally—it's only business" into Chinese. Western managers tend to believe that if they conclude a successful transaction, a good business relationship will follow. The development of a personal relationship is an added bonus, but not really necessary when it comes to getting things done. In the Chinese business world, however, a personal relationship must be in place before managers even consider entering a business transaction. Western managers doing business in China should cultivate personal relationships—both during and outside of business hours. Accept any and all social invitations—for drinks, a meal, or even a potentially embarrassing visit to a karaoke bar.
- ***Don't skip the small talk.*** Getting right down to business and bypassing the small talk during a meeting might feel like an efficient use of time to an American manager. To the Chinese, however, this approach neglects the all-important work of forging an emotional bond. Be aware that the real purpose of your initial meetings with potential business partners is to begin building a relationship, so keep your patience if the deal you are planning to discuss never even comes up.
- ***Remember that relationships are not short term.*** The work of establishing and nurturing guanxi relationships in China is never done. Western managers must put aside their usual focus on short-term results and recognize that it takes a long time for foreigners to be accepted into a guanxi network. Often, foreign companies must prove their trustworthiness and reliability over time. For example, firms that weathered the political instability that culminated in the 1989 student protests in Tiananmen Square found it much easier to do business afterward.
- ***Make contact frequently.*** Some experts recommend hiring ethnic Chinese staff members and then letting them do the heavy lifting of relationship-building. Others emphasize that Westerners themselves should put plenty of time and energy into forging links with Chinese contacts; those efforts will pay off because the contacts can smooth the way by tapping into their own guanxi networks. Whatever the strategy, contact should be frequent and personal. In addition, be sure to keep careful track of the contacts you make. In China, any and all relationships are bound to be important at some point in time.

SOURCES: Michelle Dammon Loyalka, "Before You Set Up Shop in China," part of the "Doing Business in China" special report, *BusinessWeek Online*, January 4, 2006, www.businessweek.com/smallbiz/content/jan2006/sb20060104_466114.htm (accessed January 6, 2006); Los Angeles Chinese Learning Center, "Chinese Business Culture," chinese-school.netfirms.com/guanxi.html; and Beijing British Embassy, "Golden Hints for Doing Business in China," http://chinese-school.netfirms.com/goldenhints.html.

consumer expectations of an entire industry. The amusement park industry, for example, has to continuously reinvest in spectacular, technologically advanced attractions to draw in younger, digitally savvy visitors. Disney invested $80 million in a makeover of its Adventure California theme park to respond to growing expectations for more dazzling attractions. Toy Story Mania essentially puts guests inside a video game and includes 56 giant screens programmed with 3-D animation from Pixar. Competitors, such as Universal Studios, are making similar investments in attractions to appeal to consumer demands for advanced technology.[7]

ConceptConnection

Shrewd home builders are responding to shifts in the **sociocultural dimension**. Aging baby boomers have been a mainstay of the housing market during the economic downturn, and what they want are smaller houses designed with features to help them stay in their own homes as long as possible. Pictured here is a 2009 AARP Livable Communities Award winner, the Green Lake Residence in Seattle, Washington, designed by Emory Baldwin of ZAI, Inc. The efficient, adaptable plan includes no-step entries and closets stacked on top of each other that can be converted into an elevator shaft if necessary.

Sociocultural The **sociocultural dimension** of the general environment represents the demographic characteristics as well as the norms, customs, and values of the general population. Important sociocultural characteristics are geographical distribution and population density, age, and education levels. Today's demographic profiles are the foundation of tomorrow's workforce and consumers. Forecasters see increased globalization of consumer markets and the labor supply, with increasing diversity both within organizations and consumer markets.[8] Consider the following key demographic trends in the United States:

1. As the U.S. population continues to age, organizations are rushing to create senior-friendly products and services. Currently, the U.S. population includes 78 million baby boomers, one-third of which will be 62 years old or older by 2013.[9] Organizations realize that it makes good business sense to create products and services for this aging population. One example is a Delta faucet that turns on and off when a user taps it anywhere on the spout or handle, making it convenient for customers who have a hard time gripping levers and knobs.[10]
2. The United States is experiencing the largest influx of immigrants in more than a century. The Hispanic population is expected to grow to 102.6 million, an increase of 188 percent since 2000, and it will make up about a quarter of the U.S. population by 2050. In this same time period, non-Hispanic whites will make up only about 50 percent of the population, down from 74 percent in 1995 and 69 percent in 2004.[11]
3. Members of Generation Y are flooding the workplace. To replace the 64 million skilled workers who will start retiring by the end of this decade, companies will be poised to attract Gen-Y workers if they offer competitive salaries, flat hierarchies, support networks, work–life balance, challenging work, and feedback on performance.[12]

Economic The **economic dimension** represents the general economic health of the country or region in which the organization operates. Consumer purchasing power, the unemployment rate, and interest rates are part of an organization's economic environment. Because organizations today are operating in a global environment, the economic dimension has become exceedingly complex and creates enormous uncertainty for managers. The global economic environment will be discussed in more detail in the next chapter.

In the last few years, the weakened U.S. economy has had a devastating impact on small business. In the first quarter of 2009, according to the Bureau of Labor Statistics, more than 400,000 businesses with fewer than 100 employees ceased operations, eliminating one million jobs.[13] When the construction industry collapsed, for instance, numerous small businesses could no longer survive. Knight-Celotext, the world's largest fiberboard maker, was taking in $115 million in revenue in 2006. By late 2008, revenue fell to $50 million and the company was sold in bankruptcy.[14] However, there remains a tremendous vitality in the small business sector of the economy. Small business and entrepreneurial start-ups will be discussed in detail in Appendix A.

Legal-Political The **legal-political dimension** includes government regulations at the local, state, and federal levels, as well as political activities designed to influence company behavior. The U.S. political system encourages capitalism, and the government tries not to overregulate business. However, government laws do specify rules of the game. The federal government influences organizations through the Occupational Safety and Health Administration (OSHA), Environmental Protection Agency (EPA), fair trade practices, libel statutes allowing lawsuits against business, consumer protection legislation, product safety requirements, import and export restrictions, and information and labeling requirements. Many organizations also have to contend with government and legal issues in other countries. The European Union (EU) adopted environmental and consumer protection rules that are costing American companies hundreds of millions of dollars a year. Companies such as Hewlett-Packard, Ford Motor Company, and General Electric have to pick up the bill for recycling the products they sell in the EU, for example.[15]

Managers must also recognize a variety of **pressure groups** that work within the legal-political framework to influence companies to behave in socially responsible ways. Wake Up Wal-Mart, a union-backed campaign group, drums up public awareness of Walmart's business practices to force the retailer to improve workers' wages and health-care benefits. The group's campaign director hopes smaller companies will then follow suit.[16] Other activists have boldly petitioned Home Depot, which introduced the Eco Options brand for its environmentally friendly products, to stop advertising on Fox News, whose hosts and commentators dismiss global warming as ludicrous.[17]

Natural In response to pressure from environmental advocates, organizations have become increasingly sensitive to the earth's diminishing natural resources and the environmental impact of their products and business practices. As a result, the natural dimension of the external environment is growing in importance. The **natural dimension** includes all elements that occur naturally on earth, including plants, animals, rocks, and natural resources such as air, water, and climate. Protection of the natural environment is emerging as a critical policy focus around the world. Governments are increasingly under pressure to explain their performance on pollution control and natural resource management. Nations with the best environmental performance, along with some comparison countries, are listed in Exhibit 2.2. Note that the top performer is Iceland, which gets most of its power from renewable sources—hydropower and geothermal energy.

The natural dimension is different from other sectors of the general environment because it has no voice of its own. Influence on managers to meet needs in the natural environment may come from other sectors, such as government regulation, consumer concerns, the media, competitors' actions, or even employees.[18] For example, environmental groups advocate various action and policy goals that include reduction and clean up of human-made pollution, development of renewable energy resources, reduction of greenhouse gases such as carbon dioxide, and sustainable use of scarce resources such as water, land, and air. The oil spill in the Gulf of Mexico in 2010 brought environmental issues to the forefront. Months after a BP-Transocean rig at the Deepwater Horizon oil well exploded, hundreds of thousands of gallons of oil were still flowing into open water

EXHIBIT 2.2

2010 Environmental Performance Index

Rank	Country	Score
1	Iceland	93.5
2	Switzerland	89.1
3	Costa Rica	86.4
4	Sweden	86.0
5	Norway	81.1
6	Mauritius	80.6
7	France	78.2
8	Austria	78.1
9	Cuba	78.1
10	Columbia	76.8
11	Malta	76.3
12	Finland	74.7
13	Slovakia	74.5
14	United Kingdom	74.2
15	New Zealand	73.4
43	Mexico	67.3
46	Canada	66.4
61	United States	63.5
99	Saudi Arabia	55.3
121	China	49.0
123	India	48.3
150	Iraq	41.0

SOURCE: 2010 Environmental Performance Index, Yale Center for Environmental Law and Policy, Yale University, http://epi.yale.edu; and Center for International Earth Science Information Network, Columbia University.

NOTE: The scores for each country are based on 25 performance indicators covering both environmental public health and ecosystem vitality, such as air pollution and greenhouse gas emissions.

each day, adding to the millions of gallons already contaminating the water and beaches along the coast in Louisiana, Mississippi, Alabama, and Florida, and threatening the region's fish, birds, turtles, and vegetation. "One of the last pristine, most biologically diverse coastal habitats in the country is about to get wiped out," said Felicia Coleman, who directs the Florida State University Coastal and Marine Laboratory. "And there's not much we can do about it." The effects of the devastating spill are likely to extend for dozens of years.[19]

- The **organizational environment**, consisting of both general and task environments, includes all elements existing outside the boundary of the organization that have the potential to affect the organization.
- The **general environment** indirectly influences all organizations within an industry and includes five dimensions.
- The **task environment** includes the sectors that conduct day-to-day transactions with the organization and directly influence its basic operations and performance.
- The **international dimension** of the external environment represents events originating in foreign countries as well as opportunities for U.S. companies in other countries.
- The **technological dimension** of the general environment includes scientific and technological advances in society.
- The **sociocultural dimension** includes demographic characteristics, norms, customs, and values of a population within which the organization operates.
- The **economic dimension** represents the general economic health of the country or region in which the organization operates.
- The **legal-political dimension** includes government regulations at the local, state, and federal levels, as well as political activities designed to influence company behavior.
- **Pressure groups** work within the legal-political framework to influence companies to behave in socially responsible ways.
- The **internal environment** includes elements within the organization's boundaries such as employees, management, and corporate culture.
- The **natural dimension** includes all elements that occur naturally on earth, including plants, animals, rocks, and natural resources such as air, water, and climate.

Task Environment

As described earlier, the task environment includes those sectors that have a direct working relationship with the organization, among them customers, competitors, suppliers, and the labor market.

Customers Those people and organizations in the environment that acquire goods or services from the organization are **customers**. As recipients of the organization's output, customers are important because they determine the organization's success. Patients are the customers of hospitals, students the customers of schools, and travelers the customers of airlines. Many companies are searching for ways to reach the coveted teen and youth market by tying marketing messages into online sites such as Twitter, MySpace, and Facebook. With high school and college students representing a $375 billion consumer spending market, it's serious business for managers at companies such as Target, Apple, Coca-Cola, and Disney.[20]

Customers today have greater power because of the Internet, which presents threats as well as opportunities for managers. Consider how Hulu is cashing in on a new way to provide television shows to viewers. Hulu is the second most popular destination for Internet video after YouTube in the United States and generated more than $100 million in advertising revenue in 2009. A joint venture owned by NBC Universal (General Electric), Fox Entertainment Group (News Corp.), and ABC, Inc. (Disney), Hulu offers free-to-watch episodes of popular TV shows such as *Glee, Lost*, or *Saturday Night Live*.[21] Cable industry executives have taken notice of TV viewers' shift to online viewing. Comcast,

Time Warner Cable, and other cable companies are going on the offensive and cannot afford to sit still. "We don't want to be alarmists," says Time Warner Cable CEO Glenn Britt, "but we really need to look at what consumers want."[22]

Competitors Specific competitive issues characterize each industry. Other organizations in the same industry or type of business that provide goods or services to the same set of customers are referred to as **competitors**. The recording industry differs from the steel industry and the pharmaceutical industry.

Competitive wars are being waged worldwide in all industries. UPS and FedEx are stiff competitors in overnight shipping, logistics management, and supply chain management. In a quest to claim e-commerce leadership for book sales, Walmart and Amazon regularly square off in price wars by offering the hottest, bestselling new books for just $10 each.[23] Internet jeweler Blue Nile clashes with Tiffany's, Zale's, and Kay's in a contest for leadership in the diamond ring market. Using its low overhead and strong purchasing power, Blue Nile sells diamond rings for 35 percent below most brick-and-mortar stores.[24]

Suppliers **Suppliers** provide the raw materials the organization uses to produce its output. A steel mill, for example, requires iron ore, machines, and financial resources. A candy bar manufacturer may use suppliers from around the globe for ingredients such as cocoa beans, sugar, and cream. Many multinational organizations rely on local suppliers for manufacturing their products in emerging markets such as Thailand, Malaysia, and Korea, but managers sometimes struggle to impose U.S. safety standards on foreign manufacturing processes. Imagine the problem managers at candy-maker Cadbury faced when they learned that a Beijing factory was using milk contaminated with minute traces of melamine in the production of Cadbury chocolates. Managers recalled all of the candy made in that plant and promptly investigated the source of the contamination—milk from a Chinese supplier. After further testing, the Cadbury's Beijing plant was found to be free of further contaminants. Managers, however, developed a heightened awareness of the risk of using local suppliers and boosted the number of tests for dangerous microbes and contaminants in the Beijing plant.[25]

The trend today is for companies to use fewer suppliers and try to build good relationships with them so that they will receive high-quality supplies, parts, and materials at lower prices. The relationship between manufacturers and suppliers has traditionally been an adversarial one, but managers are finding that cooperation is the key to saving money, maintaining quality, and speeding products to market.

Labor Market The **labor market** represents people in the environment who can be hired to work for the organization. Every organization needs a supply of trained, qualified personnel. Unions, employee associations, and the availability of certain classes of employees can influence the organization's labor market. Labor market forces affecting organizations right now include (1) the growing need for computer-literate knowledge workers; (2) the necessity for continuous investment in human resources through recruitment, education, and training to meet the competitive demands of the borderless world; and (3) the effects of international trading blocs, automation, outsourcing, and shifting facility locations on labor dislocations, creating unused labor pools in some areas and labor shortages in others.

Changes in these various sectors of the general and task environments can create tremendous challenges, especially for organizations operating in complex, rapidly changing industries. Nortel Networks, a Canadian company that also has offices in the United States, China, and the United Kingdom, is an example of an organization operating in a highly complex environment.

NORTEL NETWORKS

Nortel Networks is a global company that connects people to the information they need through advanced communication technologies. With customers in more than 150 countries, Nortel designs and installs new networks and upgrades, supports, and manages existing systems. Nortel's complex external environment, illustrated in Exhibit 2.3, directly influences its operations and performance. The Canadian-based company began in 1895 as a manufacturer of telephones and has reinvented itself many times to keep up with changes in the environment.

Today, Nortel's purpose is clear—to create a high-performance twenty-first-century communications company leveraging innovative technology that simplifies the complicated, hyper-connected world. To achieve this goal, Nortel adapts and responds to the uncertainty of the external environment. One response to the competitive environment was to spend billions to acquire data and voice networking companies, including Bay Networks (which makes Internet and data equipment), Cambrian Systems (a hot maker of optical technology), Periphonics (maker of voice-response systems), and Clarify (customer relationship management software). These companies brought Nortel top-notch technology, helping the company snatch customers away from rivals Cisco and Lucent Technologies. In addition, even during tough economic times, Nortel kept spending nearly 20 percent of its revenues on research and development to keep pace with changing technology.[26]

Remember This

- **Customers** are part of the task environment and include people and organizations that acquire goods or services from the organization.
- **Competitors** are organizations within the same industry or type of business that compete for the same set of customers.
- AT&T and Verizon are competitors in the telecommunications industry.
- **Suppliers** provide the raw materials the organization uses to produce its output.
- The **labor market** represents the people available for hire by the organization.

The Organization–Environment Relationship

Why do organizations care so much about factors in the external environment? The reason is that the environment creates uncertainty for organization managers, and they must respond by designing the organization to adapt to the environment.

Environmental Uncertainty

Uncertainty means that managers do not have sufficient information about environmental factors to understand and predict environmental needs and changes.[27] As indicated in Exhibit 2.4, environmental characteristics that influence uncertainty are the number of factors that affect the organization and the extent to which those factors change. A large multinational like Nortel Networks has thousands of factors in the external environment creating uncertainty for managers. When external factors change rapidly, the organization

Refer to your score on the questionnaire on page 68 to see how well you might adapt as a new manager in an uncertain environment.

EXHIBIT 2.3

The External Environment of Nortel

General Environment

Technological
- 3,750 issued U.S. patents
- Optical fiber networks
- Wireless technologies (4G)
- Carrier ethernet
- Secure networking

Natural
- Recycling initiatives in Brazil
- Reuse center in U.S. offices
- Teleworking for employees
- GreenCommute – "Best Workplace for Commuters"

Sociocultural
- Web surfers
- Opening new global markets
- Wireless lifestyles

Economic
- Worldwide economic slowdown
- Shifting access to credit and volatile interest rates

Legal/Political
- Canadian ownership
- Accounting and regulatory troubles
- Risk of terrorism
- Tough EU regulations
- NAFTA

International
- 40% of business outside U.S.
- Headquarters in Brampton, Ontario, Canada
- Competes in over 150 countries
- Joint ventures in Spain, Poland, and Israel

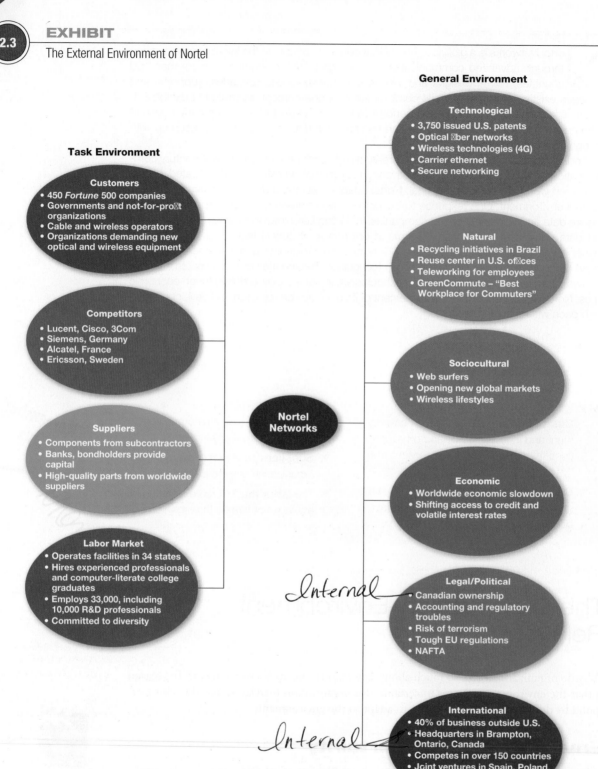

Task Environment

Customers
- 450 *Fortune* 500 companies
- Governments and not-for-profit organizations
- Cable and wireless operators
- Organizations demanding new optical and wireless equipment

Competitors
- Lucent, Cisco, 3Com
- Siemens, Germany
- Alcatel, France
- Ericsson, Sweden

Suppliers
- Components from subcontractors
- Banks, bondholders provide capital
- High-quality parts from worldwide suppliers

Labor Market
- Operates facilities in 34 states
- Hires experienced professionals and computer-literate college graduates
- Employs 33,000, including 10,000 R&D professionals
- Committed to diversity

Nortel Networks

SOURCES: "Chinese Ministry of Railways Chooses Nortel Mobile Network," *M2Presswire* (January 29, 2008); Nortel Web site, http:www.nortel.com (accessed May 12, 2010); J. Weber with A. Reinhardt and P. Burrows, "Racing Ahead at Nortel," *BusinessWeek* (November 8, 1999): 93–99; "Nortel's Waffling Continues: First Job Cuts, Then Product Lines, and Now the CEO," *Telephony* (May 21, 2001): 12; and M. Heinzl, "Nortel's Profits of $499 Million Exceeds Forecast," *The Wall Street Journal*, January 30, 2004.

EXHIBIT 2.4

The External Environment and Uncertainty

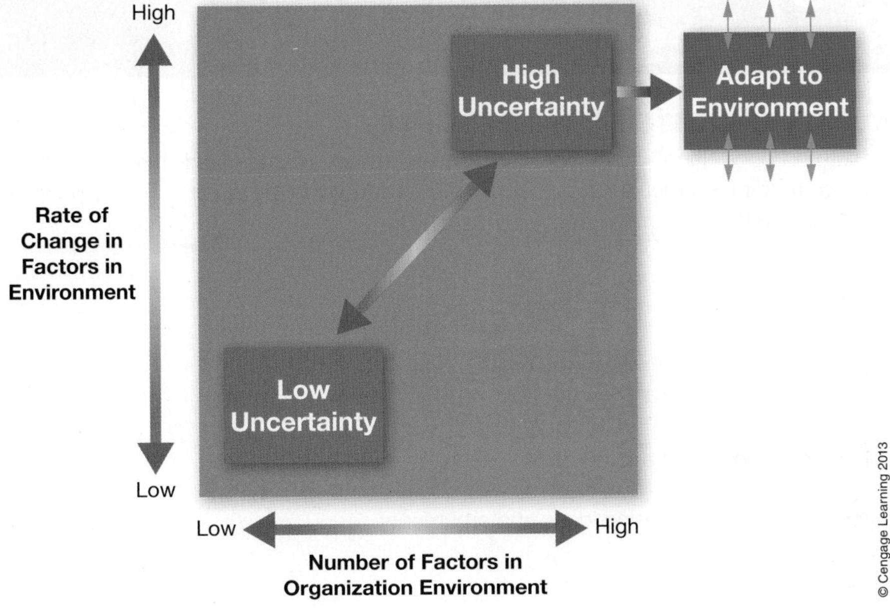

experiences high uncertainty; examples are telecommunications and aerospace firms, computer and electronics companies, and e-commerce organizations that sell products and services over the Internet. Companies have to make an effort to adapt to the rapid changes in the environment. When an organization deals with only a few external factors and these factors are relatively stable, such as those affecting soft-drink bottlers or food processors, managers experience low uncertainty and can devote less attention to external issues.

Adapting to the Environment

If an organization faces increased uncertainty with respect to competition, customers, suppliers, or government regulations, managers can use several strategies to adapt to these changes, including boundary-spanning roles, interorganizational partnerships, and mergers or joint ventures.

Boundary spanning is an increasingly important task in organizations because environmental shifts can happen quickly in today's world. Managers need good information about their competitors, customers, and other elements of the environment to make good decisions. Thus, the most successful companies involve everyone in boundary-spanning activities.

Read the Ethical Dilemma on page 84 that pertains to competitive intelligence. Do you have the courage to risk your job by challenging the boss's inappropriate use of confidential information?

Managers in partnering organizations are shifting from an adversarial orientation to a partnership orientation. The new paradigm, shown in Exhibit 2.5, is based on trust and the ability of partners to work out equitable solutions to conflicts so that everyone profits from the relationship. Managers work to reduce costs and add value to both sides rather than trying to get all the benefits for their own company. The new model is also characterized by a high level of information sharing, including e-business links for automatic ordering, payments, and other transactions. In addition, person-to-person interaction provides

New Manager Self-Test

Are You Fit for Managerial Uncertainty?

Do you approach uncertainty with an open mind? Think back to how you thought or behaved during a time of uncertainty when you were in a formal or informal leadership position. Please answer whether each of the following items was Mostly True or Mostly False in that circumstance.

	MOSTLY TRUE <<<	>>> MOSTLY FALSE
1. Enjoyed hearing about new ideas even when working toward a deadline.	______	______
2. Welcomed unusual viewpoints of others even if we were working under pressure.	______	______
3. Made it a point to attend industry trade shows and company events.	______	______
4. Specifically encouraged others to express opposing ideas and arguments.	______	______
5. Asked "dumb" questions.	______	______
6. Always offered comments on the meaning of data or issues.	______	______
7. Expressed a controversial opinion to bosses and peers.	______	______
8. Suggested ways of improving my and others' ways of doing things.	______	______

See It Online

Scoring and Interpretation: Give yourself 1 point for each item you marked as Mostly True. If you scored less than 5, you might want to start your career as a manager in a stable rather than unstable environment. A score of 5 or above suggests a higher level of mindfulness and a better fit for a new manager in an organization with an uncertain environment.

In an organization in a highly uncertain environment, everything seems to be changing. In that case, an important quality for a new manager is "mindfulness," which includes the qualities of being open-minded and an independent thinker. In a stable environment, a manager with a closed mind may perform okay because much work can be done in the same old way. In an uncertain environment, even a new manager needs to facilitate new thinking, new ideas, and new ways of working. A high score on the preceding items suggests higher mindfulness and a better fit with an uncertain environment.

SOURCE: These questions are based on ideas from R. L. Daft and R. M. Lengel, *Fusion Leadership* (San Francisco: Berrett Koehler, 2000): Chapter 4; B. Bass and B. Avolio, *Multifactor Leadership Questionnaire*, 2nd ed. (Menlo Park, CA: Mind Garden, Inc., 2004); and Karl E. Weick and Kathleen M. Sutcliffe, *Managing the Unexpected: Assuring High Performance in an Age of Complexity* (San Francisco: Jossey-Bass, 2001).

corrective feedback and solves problems. People from other companies may be on-site or participate in virtual teams to enable close coordination. Partners are frequently involved in one another's product design and production, and they are committed for the long term. It is not unusual for business partners to help one another, even outside of what is specified in the contract.[28]

A step beyond strategic partnerships is for companies to become involved in mergers or joint ventures to reduce environmental uncertainty. A **merger** occurs when two or

EXHIBIT 2.5

The Shift to a Partnership Paradigm

From Adversarial Orientation →	To Partnership Orientation
• Suspicion, competition, arm's length	• Trust, value added to both sides
• Price, efficiency, own profits	• Equity, fair dealing, everyone profits
• Information and feedback limited	• E-business links to share information and conduct digital transactions
• Lawsuits to resolve conflict	• Close coordination; virtual teams and people on-site
• Minimal involvement and up-front investment	• Involvement in partner's product design and production
• Short-term contracts	• Long-term contracts
• Contracts limit the relationship	• Business assistance goes beyond the contract

more organizations combine to become one. For example, Wells Fargo merged with Norwest Corporation and Wachovia Corporation to form the nation's fourth largest financial services corporation.

A **joint venture** involves a strategic alliance or program by two or more organizations. A joint venture typically occurs when a project is too complex, expensive, or uncertain for one firm to handle alone. Oprah Winfrey's Harpo Productions, Inc., formed a joint venture with Hearst Magazines to launch *O, The Oprah Magazine*.[29] Despite her popularity and success with her television show, Winfrey recognized the complexity and uncertainty involved in starting a new magazine. The combined resources and management talents of the partners contributed to the most successful start-up ever in the magazine publishing industry.

ConceptConnection

In May 2010, United Airlines Chairman, President, and CEO Glenn Tilton (left) and Continental Airlines Chairman, President, and CEO Jeff Smisek (right) announced the proposed $3 billion **merger** of their companies, resulting in the world's biggest airline. Two years earlier, Delta and Northwest merged, and Southwest and AirTran merged in September of 2010. Mergers are one strategy the industry is using to **adapt to a highly uncertain environment** full of uncontrollable external factors, such as 9/11, the credit crisis and recession, volatile fuel prices, the H1N1 flu scare, and a volcanic eruption in Iceland.

- When external factors change rapidly, the organization experiences high uncertainty.
- A **merger** occurs when two or more organizations combine to become one.
- A **joint venture** is a strategic alliance or program by two or more organizations.

The Internal Environment: Corporate Culture

The internal environment within which managers work includes corporate culture, production technology, organization structure, and physical facilities. Of these, corporate culture surfaces as extremely important to competitive advantage. The internal culture must fit the needs of the external environment and company strategy. When this fit occurs, highly committed employees create a high-performance organization that is tough to beat.[30]

Most people don't think about culture; it's just "how we do things around here" or "the way things are here." However, managers have to think about culture, because it typically plays a significant role in organizational success. The concept of culture has been of growing concern to managers since the 1980s as turbulence in the external environment has grown, often requiring new values and attitudes. Organizational culture has been defined and studied in many and varied ways. For the purposes of this chapter, we define **culture** as the set of key values, beliefs, understandings, and norms shared by members of an organization.[31] The concept of culture helps managers understand the hidden, complex aspects of organizational life. Culture is a pattern of shared values and assumptions about how things are done within the organization. This pattern is learned by members as they cope with external and internal problems, and taught to new members as the correct way to perceive, think, and feel.

Complete the Group Learning exercise on pages 82–83 that concerns identifying cultural norms.

Culture can be analyzed at two levels, as illustrated in Exhibit 2.6.[32] At the surface level are visible artifacts, which include things such as manner of dress, patterns of behavior, physical symbols, organizational ceremonies, and office layout. Visible artifacts are all the things one can see, hear, and observe by watching members of the organization. At a deeper, less obvious level are values and beliefs, which are not observable but can be discerned from how people explain and justify what they do. Members of the organization hold some values at a conscious level. These values can be interpreted from the stories, language, and symbols organization members use to represent them.

2.6 EXHIBIT

Levels of Corporate Culture

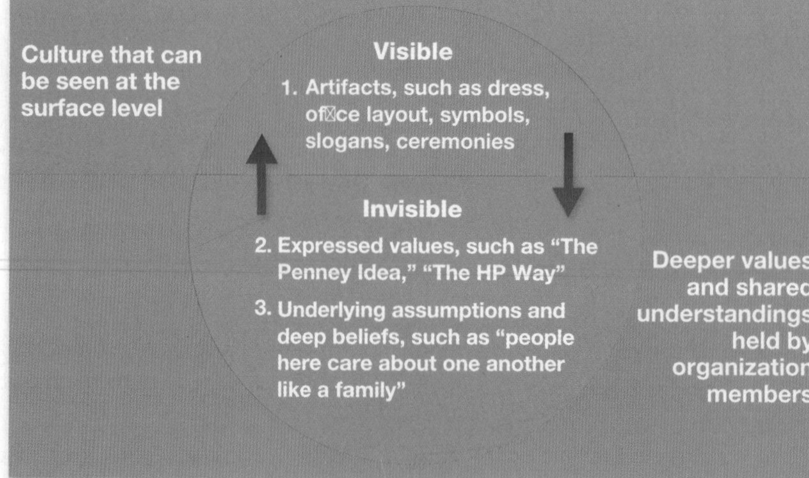

SPOTLIGHT ON SKILLS

Zappos Shoes

Zappos.com, an online retail site best known for its wide selection of shoes and its free shipping, boldly proclaims its unique culture in an offbeat set of ten core values, including "Create fun and a little weirdness." CEO Tony Hsieh believes these core values illustrate the company's innovative culture and demonstrate its ultimate business goal—*cultivating happiness.* Hsieh's management theory goes like this: If you create a work culture that fosters well-being, then good practices and (eventually) good profits will naturally flow out of the operation. So far, his theory is producing outstanding business results. The Zappos.com website is raking in $1 billion worth of annual gross merchandise sales, and employees widely report that their work is exciting and challenging. "We really buy into the idea that the better we treat each other, the better we'll all be able to treat our customers," says Rebecca Ratner, director of human resources.

One way the Zappos Family of companies perpetuates its unique culture is by hiring employees who will fit into the slightly wacky, drama-club atmosphere. After résumés have been reviewed in the standard way, potential employees go through a "culture interview" where they are asked unusual questions such as "How lucky are you in life?" Department managers know that people who consider themselves lucky are open-minded—one of the company's core values. The following table demonstrates other unique features of the Zappos Family culture.

Standard Interview Question
Zappos Family: How weird are you?
Typical Company: What are your strengths and weaknesses?

Hiring Bonus:
Zappos Family: New hires are offered $3,000 to refuse the job and go away. Those who stay (about 96 percent) are more committed and engaged thereafter.
Typical Company: Actual hiring bonus, which makes it hard to say "no" to a place where one may not fit in.

Atmosphere:
Zappos Family: Themed conference rooms including "Zen," "beach," and "superheroes."
Typical Company: Fluorescent lights, white walls.

Customer Service:
Zappos Family: Phone reps are trusted to connect with customers however they see fit.
Typical Company: Phone reps follow scripts, fill out call logs, and adhere to time limits.

Some values become so deeply embedded in a culture that members are no longer consciously aware of them. These basic, underlying assumptions and beliefs are the essence of culture and subconsciously guide behavior and decisions. In some organizations, a basic assumption might be that people are essentially lazy and will shirk their duties whenever possible; thus, employees are closely supervised and given little freedom, and colleagues are frequently suspicious of one another. More enlightened organizations operate on the basic assumption that people want to do a good job; in these organizations, employees are given more freedom and responsibility, and colleagues trust one another and work cooperatively. At the Zappos Family of companies, a culture of well-being and happiness has been instrumental in the growth of this successful online retailer.

The Zappos Family of companies has created a unique culture that is reflected in its core values. Fundamental values are demonstrated in organizations through symbols, stories, heroes, slogans, and ceremonies.

Symbols

A **symbol** is an object, act, or event that conveys meaning to others. Symbols can be considered a rich, nonverbal language that vibrantly conveys the organization's important values concerning how people relate to one another and interact with the environment.[33] For example, managers at a New York-based start-up that provides Internet solutions to local television broadcasters wanted a way to symbolize the company's unofficial mantra of "drilling

REUTERS/JP Moczulski

ConceptConnection

Toyota's handling of its 2010 recall crisis illustrates a paradox: A company can be a successful multinational but still not have a global corporate culture. Some observers characterize Toyota's **corporate culture** as parochial. They support this claim, in part, by pointing to the fact that President and CEO Akio Toyoda (pictured here painting an eye on a traditional Japanese doll) speaks only limited English, despite having earned his MBA in the United States. Critics attribute the company's reticence to go public once it realized there were quality problems to its deep roots in Japanese culture, which believes that airing dirty linen in public is impolite.

down to solve problems." They bought a dented old drill for $2 and dubbed it The Team Drill. Each month, the drill is presented to a different employee in recognition of exceptional work, and the employee personalizes the drill in some way before passing it on to the next winner.[34]

Stories

A **story** is a narrative based on true events and is repeated frequently and shared among organizational employees. Stories paint pictures that help symbolize the firm's vision and values and help employees personalize and absorb them.[35] A frequently told story at UPS concerns an employee who, without authorization, ordered an extra Boeing 737 to ensure timely delivery of a load of Christmas packages that had been left behind in the holiday rush. As the story goes, rather than punishing the worker, UPS rewarded his initiative. By telling this story, UPS workers communicate that the company stands behind its commitment to worker autonomy and customer service.[36]

Heroes

A **hero** is a figure who exemplifies the deeds, character, and attributes of a strong culture. Heroes are role models for employees to follow. Sometimes heroes are real, such as the security supervisor who once challenged IBM's chairman when she noticed he wasn't carrying the appropriate clearance identification to enter a security area.[37] Heroes show how to do the right thing in the organization. Companies with strong cultures take advantage of achievements to define heroes who uphold key values.

At 3M Corporation, top managers keep alive the image of heroes who developed projects that were killed by top management. One hero was a vice president who was fired earlier in his career for persisting with a new product even after his boss had told him, "That's a stupid idea. Stop!" After the worker was fired, he would not leave. He stayed in an unused office, working without a salary on the new product idea. Eventually he was rehired, the idea succeeded, and he was promoted to vice president. The lesson of this hero as a major element in 3M's culture is to persist at what you believe in.[38]

Slogans

A **slogan** is a phrase or sentence that succinctly expresses a key corporate value. Many companies use a slogan or saying to convey special meaning to employees. The Ritz-Carlton adopted the slogan, "Ladies and gentlemen taking care of ladies and gentlemen" to demonstrate its cultural commitment to take care of both employees and customers. "We're in the service business, and service comes only from people. Our promise is to take care of them, and provide a happy place for them to work," said General Manager Mark DeCocinis, who manages the Portman Hotel in Shanghai, recipient of the "Best Employer in Asia" award for three consecutive years.[39] Cultural values can also be discerned in written public statements, such as corporate mission statements or other formal statements that express the core values of the organization. The mission statement for Hallmark Cards, for example, emphasizes values of excellence, ethical and moral conduct in all relationships, business innovation, and corporate social responsibility.[40]

Ceremonies

A **ceremony** is a planned activity at a special event that is conducted for the benefit of an audience. Managers hold ceremonies to provide dramatic examples of company values. Ceremonies are special occasions that reinforce valued accomplishments, create a bond among people by allowing them to share an important event, and anoint and celebrate heroes.[41] In a ceremony to mark its 20th anniversary, Southwest Airlines rolled out a specialty plane it created called the "Lone Star One" that was designed like the Texas state flag to signify the company's start in Texas. Later, when the NBA chose Southwest Airlines as the league's official airline, Southwest launched another specialty plane, the "Slam Dunk One," designed in blue and orange with a large basketball painted toward the front of the plane. Today, ten specialty planes celebrate significant milestones in Southwest's history and demonstrate key cultural values.[42]

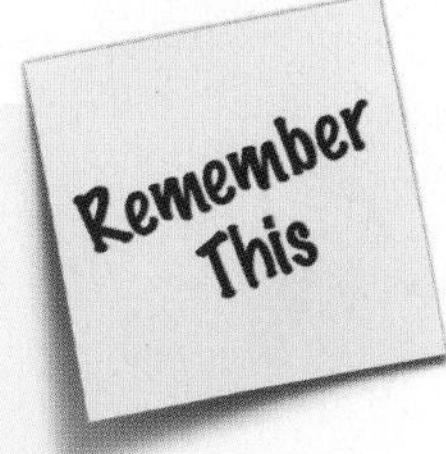

- Organizational **culture** is the set of key values, beliefs, understandings, and norms shared by members of an organization.
- A **symbol** is an object, act, or event that conveys meaning to others.
- A **story** is a narrative based on true events and is repeated frequently and shared among organizational employees.
- A **hero** is a figure who exemplifies the deeds, character, and attributes of a strong culture.
- A **slogan**, such as Disney's "The happiest place on earth," succinctly expresses a key corporate value.
- Managers hold **ceremonies**, planned activities at special events, to reinforce company values.

Types of Culture

A big influence on internal corporate culture is the external environment. Cultures can vary widely across organizations; however, organizations within the same industry often reveal similar cultural characteristics because they are operating in similar environments.[43] The internal culture should embody what it takes to succeed in the environment. If the external environment requires extraordinary customer service, the culture should encourage good service; if it calls for careful technical decision making, cultural values should reinforce managerial decision making.

In considering what cultural values are important for the organization, managers consider the external environment as well as the company's strategy and goals. Studies suggest that the right fit between culture, strategy, and the environment is associated with four categories or types of culture, as illustrated in Exhibit 2.7. These categories are based on

EXHIBIT 2.7

Four Types of Corporate Culture

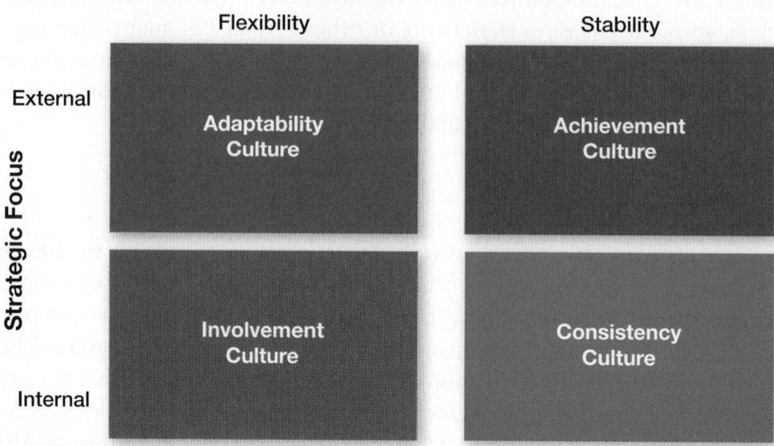

SOURCES: Based on D. R. Denison and A. K. Mishra, "Toward a Theory of Organizational Culture and Effectiveness," *Organization Science* 6, no. 2 (March–April 1995): 204–223; R. Hooijberg and F. Petrock, "On Cultural Change: Using the Competing Values Framework to Help Leaders Execute a Transformational Strategy," *Human Resource Management* 32, no.1 (1993): 29–50; and R. E. Quinn, *Beyond Rational Management: Mastering the Paradoxes and Competing Demands of High Performance* (San Francisco: Jossey-Bass, 1988).

two dimensions: (1) the extent to which the external environment requires flexibility or stability and (2) the extent to which a company's strategic focus is internal or external. The four categories associated with these differences are adaptability, achievement, involvement, and consistency.[44]

Adaptability Culture

3

The **adaptability culture** emerges in an environment that requires fast response and high-risk decision making. Managers encourage values that support the company's ability to rapidly detect, interpret, and translate signals from the environment into new behavior responses. Employees have autonomy to make decisions and act freely to meet new needs, and responsiveness to customers is highly valued. Managers also actively create change by encouraging and rewarding creativity, experimentation, and risk taking. Lush Cosmetics, a fast-growing maker of shampoos, lotions, and bath products made from fresh ingredients such as mangoes and avocados, provides a good example of an adaptability culture. A guiding motto at the company is "We reserve the right to make mistakes." Founder and CEO Mark Constantine is passionately devoted to change and encourages employees to break boundaries, experiment, and take risks. The company kills off one-third of its product line every year to offer new and offbeat products.[45] Other companies in the cosmetics industry, as well as those involved in electronics, e-commerce, and fashion, often use an adaptability culture because they must move quickly to respond to rapid changes in the environment.

Achievement Culture

The **achievement culture** is suited to organizations concerned with serving specific customers in the external environment but without the intense need for flexibility and rapid change. This results-oriented culture values competitiveness, aggressiveness, personal initiative, and willingness to work long and hard to achieve results. An emphasis on winning and achieving specific ambitious goals is the glue that holds the organization together.[46] Siebel Systems, now part of Oracle, thrived on an achievement culture. Professionalism and aggressiveness were core values at Siebel. Employees were forbidden to eat at their desks or to decorate with more than one or two personal photographs. People who succeeded at Siebel were those who were focused, competitive, and driven to win. Those who met stringent goals were richly rewarded; those who didn't were fired.[47]

Involvement Culture

The **involvement culture** emphasizes an internal focus on the involvement and participation of employees to adapt rapidly to changing needs from the environment. This culture places high value on meeting the needs of employees, and the organization may be characterized by a caring, family-like atmosphere. Managers emphasize values such as cooperation, consideration of both employees and customers, and avoiding status differences. Consider the involvement culture at Valero, which is partly responsible for helping the company become the top oil refinery in the United States.

VALERO

When Hurricane Katrina hit New Orleans in late August 2005, companies throughout the region set their disaster plans into action. But few matched the heroic efforts put forth by employees at Valero's St. Charles oil refinery. Just eight days after the storm, the St. Charles facility was up and running, while a competitor's plant across the road was weeks away from getting back online. During the same time period, St. Charles's disaster crew managed to locate every one of the plant's 570 employees.

Part of the credit goes to Valero's family-like, let's-get-it-done-together culture, which has given Valero a distinctive edge during an era of cutthroat global competition in the oil industry. As former CEO Bill Greehey transformed Valero, once primarily a natural-gas-pipeline company, into the nation's largest oil refinery business, he also instilled a culture where people care about one another and the company. Many of the refineries Valero bought were old and run-down. After buying a refinery, Greehey's first steps would be to assure people their jobs were secure, bring in new safety equipment, and promise employees that if they worked hard he would put them first, before shareholders and customers. Employees held up their end of the bargain, and so did Greehey.

Putting employees first has engendered amazing loyalty and dedication. When Greehey visited the St. Charles facility after Katrina, he was surprised to be greeted at a giant tent with a standing ovation. Even in the aftermath of a hurricane, employees had held to their tradition of throwing a plantwide barbecue lunch whenever top managers visit a plant. "Right now morale is so high in this refinery you can't get at it with a space shuttle," an electrical superintendent at St. Charles said. "Valero has been giving away gas, chain saws, putting up trailers for the employees. They've kept every employee paid. Other refineries shut down and stopped paying. What else can you ask?"[48]

Would you rather work in an organization with an adaptability, achievement, involvement, or consistency culture? Complete the New Manager Self-Test on page 76 to get an idea of what type of culture you would be most comfortable working in.

Some managers might think putting employees ahead of customers and shareholders is nice, but not very good for business. But at Valero, a strong involvement culture based on putting employees first has paid off in terms of high employee performance and rising market share, profits, and shareholder value.

Consistency Culture

The final category of culture, the **consistency culture**, uses an internal focus and a consistency orientation for a stable environment. Following the rules and being thrifty are valued, and the culture supports and rewards a methodical, rational, orderly way of doing things.

New Manager Self-Test

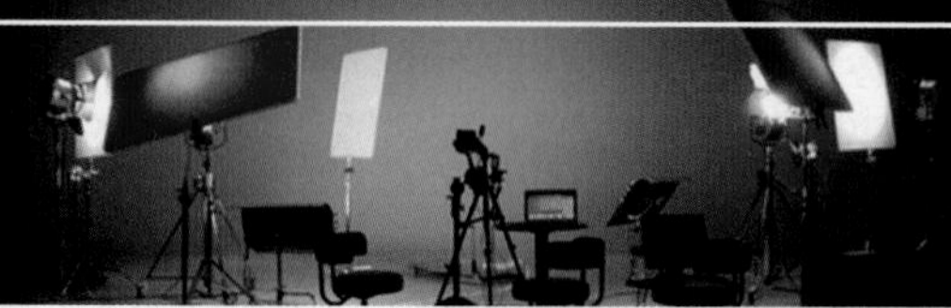

Culture Preference

The fit between a new manager and organizational culture can determine success and satisfaction. To understand your culture preference, rank the items below from 1 to 8 based on the strength of your preference (1 = strongest preference).

1. The organization is very personal, much like an extended family. 1 2 3 4 5 6 7 8
2. The organization is dynamic and changing, where people take risks. 1 2 3 4 5 6 7 8
3. The organization is achievement oriented, with the focus on competition and getting jobs done. 1 2 3 4 5 6 7 8
4. The organization is stable and structured, with clarity and established procedures. 1 2 3 4 5 6 7 8
5. Management style is characterized by teamwork and participation. 1 2 3 4 5 6 7 8
6. Management style is characterized by innovation and risk taking. 1 2 3 4 5 6 7 8
7. Management style is characterized by high performance demands and achievement. 1 2 3 4 5 6 7 8
8. Management style is characterized by security and predictability. 1 2 3 4 5 6 7 8

See It Online

Scoring and Interpretation: Each item pertains to one of the four types of culture in Exhibit 2.7. To compute your preference for each type of culture, add together the scores for each set of two items as follows:

Involvement culture—total for items 1, 5: ______

Adaptability culture—total for items 2, 6: ______

Achievement culture—total for items 3, 7: ______

Consistency culture—total for items 4, 8: ______

A lower score means a stronger culture preference. You will likely be more comfortable and more effective as a new manager in a corporate culture that is compatible with your personal preferences. A higher score means the culture would not fit your expectations, and you would have to change your style and preference to be comfortable. Review the text discussion of the four culture types. Do your cultural preference scores seem correct to you? Can you think of companies that fit your culture preference?

SOURCE: Adapted from Kim S. Cameron and Robert D. Quinn, *Diagnosing and Changing Organizational Culture* (Reading, MA: Addison-Wesley, 1999).

In today's fast-changing world, few companies operate in a stable environment, and most managers are shifting toward cultures that are more flexible and in tune with changes in the environment. However, one thriving company, Pacific Edge Software, successfully implemented elements of a consistency culture, ensuring that all its projects are on time and on budget. The husband-and-wife team of Lisa Hjorten and Scott Fuller implanted a culture of order, discipline, and control from the moment they founded the company. The emphasis on order and focus means employees can generally go home by 6:00 p.m. rather than working all night to finish an important project. Hjorten insists that the company's culture isn't rigid or uptight, just *careful*. Although sometimes being careful means being slow, so far Pacific Edge has managed to keep pace with the demands of the external environment.[49]

Each of these four categories of culture can be successful. In addition, organizations usually have values that fall into more than one category. The relative emphasis on various cultural values depends on the needs of the environment and the organization's focus. Managers are responsible for instilling the cultural values the organization needs to be successful in its environment.

- For the organization to be effective, corporate culture should be aligned with organizational strategy and the needs of the external environment.
- Organizations within the same industry often reveal similar cultural characteristics because they are operating in similar environments.
- The **adaptability culture** is characterized by values that support the company's ability to interpret and translate signals from the environment into new behavior responses.
- An **achievement culture** is a results-oriented culture that values competitiveness, personal initiative, and achievement.
- A culture that places high value on meeting the needs of employees and values cooperation and equality is an **involvement culture**.
- A **consistency culture** values and rewards a methodical, rational, orderly way of doing things.

Shaping Corporate Culture for Innovative Response

Research conducted by a Stanford University professor indicates that the one factor that increases a company's value the most is people and how they are treated.[50] In addition, surveys show that CEOs often cite organizational culture as their most important mechanism for attracting, motivating, and retaining talented employees, a capability considered the single best predictor of overall organizational excellence.[51] In a survey of Canadian senior executives, fully 82 percent believe a direct correlation exists between culture and financial performance.[52]

Corporate culture plays a key role in creating an organizational climate that enables learning and innovative responses to threats from the external environment, challenging new opportunities, or organizational crises. However, managers realize they can't focus all their effort on values; they also need a commitment to solid business performance.

Managing the High-Performance Culture

Companies that succeed in a turbulent world are those that pay careful attention to both cultural values *and* business performance. Cultural values can energize and motivate employees by appealing to higher ideals and unifying people around shared goals. In addition, values boost performance by shaping and guiding employee behavior, so that everyone's actions are aligned with strategic priorities.[53] Exhibit 2.8 illustrates four organizational outcomes based on the relative attention managers pay to cultural values and business

EXHIBIT 2.8

Combining Culture and Performance

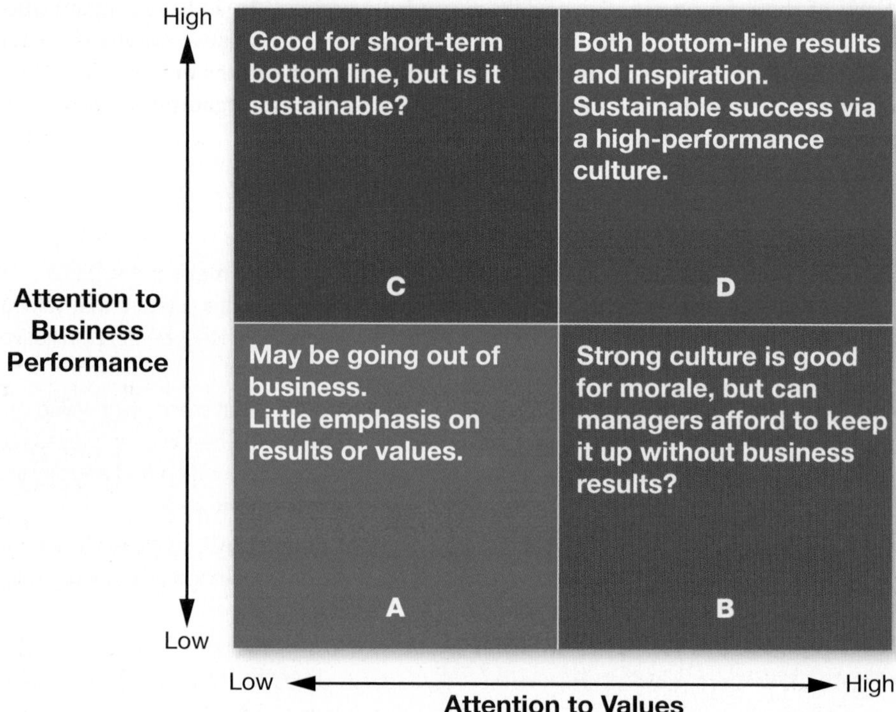

SOURCE: Adapted from Jeff Rosenthal and Mary Ann Masarech, "High-Performance Cultures: How Values Can Drive Business Results," *Journal of Organizational Excellence* (Spring 2003): 3–18.

performance.[54] A company in Quadrant A pays little attention to either values or business results and is unlikely to survive for long. Managers in Quadrant B organizations are highly focused on creating a strong cohesive culture, but they don't tie organizational values directly to goals and desired business results.

When cultural values aren't connected to business performance, they aren't likely to benefit the organization during hard times. The corporate culture at The LEGO Group headquarters in Billund, Denmark, nearly doomed the toymaker in the 1990s when sales plummeted as children turned away from traditional toys to video games. Imagination and creativity, not business performance, were what guided Lego. The attitude among employees was, "We're doing great stuff for kids—don't bother us with financial goals." New CEO Jørgen Vig Knudstorp upended the corporate culture with a new employee motto: "I am here to make money for the company." The shift to bottom-line results had a profound impact, and Lego has become one of the most successful companies in the toy industry.[55]

Quadrant C represents organizations that are focused primarily on bottom-line results and pay little attention to organizational values. This approach may be profitable in the short run, but the success is difficult to sustain over the long term because the "glue" that holds the organization together—that is, shared cultural values—is missing. Think about the numerous get-rich-quick goals of dot-com entrepreneurs. Thousands of companies that sprang up in the late 1990s were aimed primarily at fast growth and quick profits, with little effort to build a solid organization based on long-term mission and values. When the crash came, these companies failed. Those that survived were typically companies with strong cultural values that helped them weather the storm. For example, Amazon.com managers paid careful attention to organizational culture, as did smaller e-commerce companies like

Canada's Mediagrif Interactive Technologies, an online B2B brokerage that allows businesses to meet online and trade their goods.[56]

Finally, companies in Quadrant D put high emphasis on both culture and solid business performance as drivers of organizational success. Managers in these organizations align values with the company's day-to-day operations—hiring practices, performance management, budgeting, criteria for promotions and rewards, and so forth. A study of corporate values by Booz Allen Hamilton and the Aspen Institute found that managers in companies that report superior financial results typically put a high emphasis on values and link them directly to the way they run the organization.[57] A good example is the fast-growing Umpqua Bank, which expanded from 11 branches and $140 million in assets to 92 branches and $5 billion in assets over a period of nine years. At Umpqua, every element of the culture focuses on serving customers, and every aspect of operations reflects the cultural values. Consider training programs. To avoid the "it's not my job" attitude that infects many banks, managers devised the "universal associate" program, which trains every bank staffer in every task, so that a teller can take a mortgage application and a loan officer can process your checking account deposit. Employees are empowered to make their own decisions about how to satisfy customers, and branches have free reign to devise unique ways to coddle the clientele in their particular location. Umpqua also carefully measures and rewards the cultural values it wants to maintain. The bank's executive vice president of cultural enhancement devised a software program that measures how cultural values are connected to performance, which the bank calls "return on quality" (ROQ). The ROQ scores for each branch and department are posted every month, and they serve as the basis for determining incentives and rewards.[58]

Quadrant D organizations represent the **high-performance culture**, a culture that (1) is based on a solid organizational mission or purpose, (2) embodies shared adaptive values that guide decisions and business practices, and (3) encourages individual employee ownership of both bottom-line results and the organization's cultural backbone.[59] Reed Hastings has developed Netflix into a high-performing culture, as shown in this chapter's Benchmarking box.

One of the most important things managers do is create and influence organizational culture to meet strategic goals, because culture has a significant impact on performance. In *Corporate Culture and Performance*, Kotter and Heskett provided evidence that companies that intentionally managed cultural values outperformed similar companies that did not. Recent research validated that some elements of corporate culture are positively correlated with higher financial performance.[60] A good example is Caterpillar Inc. Caterpillar developed a cultural assessment process (CAP) to measure and manage how effectively the culture contributes to organizational effectiveness. The assessment gave top executives hard data documenting millions of dollars in savings attributed directly to cultural factors.[61]

Cultural Leadership

A primary way in which managers shape cultural norms and values to build a high-performance culture is through *cultural leadership*. Managers must *overcommunicate* to ensure that employees understand the new culture values, and they signal these values in actions as well as words.

A **cultural leader** defines and uses signals and symbols to influence corporate culture. Cultural leaders influence culture in two key areas:

1. ***The cultural leader articulates a vision for the organizational culture that employees can believe in.*** The leader defines and communicates central values that employees believe in and will rally around. Values are tied to a clear and compelling mission or core purpose.

BENCHMARKING

Netflix

Reed Hastings and his Netflix should have been run out of business. That is, if you believe stock analyst Michael Pachter, who called Netflix a "worthless piece of cr**" in 2005 and said it would be taken over by Walmart, Amazon, and Blockbuster. But Hastings, who sold his first company for $525 million when he was just 36, and who was ready for a life of leisure, was forced to pay a $40 late fee for one video and balked at the idea of paying a late fee greater than the cost of buying a new video. It bothered him so much, he started to think other people might be bothered too and would join a DVD club the same way they might join a health club, with monthly fees. No one thought the idea had any merit, that people would rent movies through the mail. "It was precisely because it was a contrarian idea that enabled us to get ahead of our competition," he said. When others started offering similar services, he lowered costs, speeded up DVD turnaround, and continued to improve the Netflix computer algorithm to make the experience more personal. He's got an offer out now to pay anyone $1 million who can improve on the algorithm. Who says geeks can't have fun?

But he wasn't content with just the mail-order part, or else he might have been trounced eventually by competition. When others say he can't do something, he uses it as motivation to work harder, to get his employees to be more creative. Pachter's quote, calling Netflix a "worthless piece of cr**," is hanging on the walls at the company today. Hastings is clearly achievement focused, as he loves thinking alongside the smartest people he can find. "For me, it's the thrill of making a contribution by solving hard problems," he says. Because of the hard-driving and risk-taking culture he's developed, Netflix is the leader in the movie-streaming business. He and his technical team started working on the possibility, but broadband width was too expensive and it took 16 hours to download one movie. Then YouTube came along in 2005, and they saw the beauty of streaming video. By 2009, 37 percent of Netflix users were streaming and that went up to 66 percent by the end of 2010. Most executives would balk at a strategy that cannibalized its own business, in this case the mail-in portion, but Hastings saw streaming as the future.

Don't think all this hard work against competition creates a cut-throat environment. Quite the opposite. Hastings works hard to keep the company culture one of trust and reliability within.

Not one to rest on laurels, he's on the watch for new competitors in services as yet to be thought of. On Facebook, for example, friends recommend movies, and that could mean millions of people might bypass Netflix altogether. But don't think he gets discouraged. This is just the kind of gut-wrenching, complicated problem that Hastings designed Netflix to solve. Bring it on, he beckons.

SOURCE: Michael Copeland, "Reed Hastings: Leader of the Pack," *Fortune* 162(9): 121–130.

2. ***The cultural leader heeds the day-to-day activities that reinforce the cultural vision.*** The leader makes sure that work procedures and reward systems match and reinforce the values. Actions speak louder than words, so cultural leaders "walk their talk."[62]

Managers widely communicate the cultural values through words and actions. Values statements that aren't reinforced by management behavior are meaningless or even harmful for employees and the organization. Whole Foods founder and CEO John Mackey wants his managers to place more value on creating "a better person, company, and world" than on pursuing personal financial gain. To demonstrate his personal commitment to this belief, he asked the board of directors to donate all his future stock options to the company's two foundations, the Animal Compassion Foundation and the Whole Planet Foundation.[63]

Cultural leaders also uphold their commitment to values during difficult times or crises, as illustrated by the example of Bill Greehey at Valero earlier in this chapter. On *Fortune* magazine's list of 100 Best Companies to Work For, Valero zoomed from Number 23 to Number 3 based on its treatment of employees following the devastating 2005 hurricanes. Despite the costs, Valero kept people on the payroll throughout the crisis, set up special booths to feed volunteers, and donated $1 million to the American Red Cross for hurricane relief efforts.[64] Upholding the cultural values helps organizations weather a crisis and come out stronger on the other side. Creating and maintaining a high-performance culture is not easy in today's turbulent environment and changing workplace, but through their words—and particularly their actions—cultural leaders let everyone in the organization know what really counts.

- Managers emphasize both values and business results to create a **high-performance culture**.
- Culture enables solid business performance through the alignment of motivated employees with the mission and goals of the company.
- Managers create and sustain adaptive high-performance cultures through cultural leadership.
- **Cultural leaders** define and articulate important values that are tied to a clear and compelling mission, which they communicate widely and uphold through their actions.

Discussion Questions

1. How can you prepare yourself to become an effective manager in an increasingly uncertain global business environment?
2. Would the task environment for a cellular phone company contain the same elements as that for a government welfare agency? Discuss.
3. What do you think are the most important forces in the external environment creating uncertainty for organizations today? Do the forces you identified typically arise in the task environment or the general environment?
4. Contemporary best-selling management books often argue that customers are the most important element in the external environment. Do you agree? In what company situations might this statement be untrue?
5. Why do you think many managers are surprised by environmental changes and hence are less able to help their organizations adapt?
6. Why are interorganizational partnerships so important for today's companies? What elements in the current environment might contribute to either an increase or a decrease in interorganizational collaboration? Discuss.
7. Many companies are "going green" or adopting environmentally friendly business strategies. Clorox, for example, now offers an eco-friendly household cleaner called Green Works. How do companies benefit from going green?
8. Cultural symbols are usually noticed through sight, sound, touch, and smell. For example, Abercrombie retail stores use music, attractive models, and fragrance to communicate elements of its retail store culture. Why are symbols important to a corporate culture?
9. Both China and India are rising economic powers. How might your approach to doing business with Communist China be different from your approach to doing business with India, the world's most populous democracy? In which country would you expect to encounter the most rules? The most bureaucracy?
10. General Electric is famous for firing the lowest-performing 10 percent of managers each year. With its strict no-layoff policy, Valero Energy believes people need to feel secure in their jobs to perform their best. Yet both are high-performing companies. How do you account for the success of such opposite philosophies?

Self-Learning

Working in an Adaptability Culture[65]

Think of a specific full-time job you have held. Please answer the following items according to your perception of the *managers above you* in that job. Circle a number on the 1–5 scale based on the extent to which you agree with each statement about the managers above you: 5 Strongly agree; 4 Agree; 3 Neither agree nor disagree; 2 Disagree; 1 Strongly disagree.

1. Good ideas got serious consideration from management above me.

   1 2 3 4 5

2. Management above me was interested in ideas and suggestions from people at my level in the organization.

   1 2 3 4 5

3. When suggestions were made to management above me, they received fair evaluation.

   1 2 3 4 5

4. Management did not expect me to challenge or change the status quo.

   1 2 3 4 5

5. Management specifically encouraged me to bring about improvements in my workplace.

   1 2 3 4 5

6. Management above me took action on recommendations made from people at my level.

   1 2 3 4 5

7. Management rewarded me for correcting problems.

   1 2 3 4 5

8. Management clearly expected me to improve work unit procedures and practices.

   1 2 3 4 5

9. I felt free to make recommendations to management above me to change existing practices.

   1 2 3 4 5

10. Good ideas did not get communicated upward because management above me was not very approachable.

    1 2 3 4 5

Scoring and Interpretation

To compute your score: Subtract each of your scores for items 4 and 10 from 6. Using your adjusted scores, add the numbers for all ten items to give you the total score. Divide that number by 10 to get your average score: ______.

An adaptability culture is shaped by the values and actions of top and middle managers. When managers actively encourage and welcome change initiatives from below, the organization will be infused with values for change. These ten items measure your management's openness to change. A typical average score for management openness to change is about 3. If your average score was 4 or higher, you worked in an organization that expressed strong cultural values of adaptation. If your average score was 2 or below, the culture was probably not an adaptability culture.

Thinking about this job, is the level of management openness to change correct for the organization? Why? Compare your scores to those of another student, and take turns describing what it was like working for the managers above your jobs. Do you sense a relationship between job satisfaction and your management's openness to change? What specific management characteristics and corporate values explain the openness scores in the two jobs?

Group Learning

Organizational Culture in the Classroom and Beyond

Step 1. Write down in the table below the norms that you believe to be operating in the following places: (1) in most of your courses, (2) in formal social groups such as fraternities and sororities, and (3) in student clubs or school-sponsored organizations. Use your personal experience in each place and consider the norms. Some norms are implicit, so you may have to think carefully to identify them. Other norms may be explicit. Make sure you list *norms* but not *practices*. The difference is that when a norm is broken, there is some negative reaction, or even punishment, whereas violating a practice carries no negative result.

List norm	Which group or organization is identified with this norm?	What is the negative result if norm is violated?

Step 2. After you have developed your lists, divide into groups of four to six students to discuss norms. Each student should share with the group the norms identified for each of the assigned places. Make a list of norms for each place and brainstorm any additional norms that you and fellow group members can think of.

Step 3. Try to group the norms by common themes, and give each group of norms a title. Decide as a group which norms are most important for regulating student behavior in each location. Use the table below.

Name of norm category	List norms in that category	Rate each norm from 1 to 5, with 1 being least important for regulating behavior and 5 most important.	Where does each norm originate? From environment, leader, or other?

Step 4. As a group, analyze the source or origin of each of the more important norms. Does the norm originate in the environment, from a leader, or elsewhere? Can you find any examples of norms that are expressed but not followed, which means that people do not "walk the talk" of the norms?

Step 5. What did you learn about cultural norms that exist in organizations and social groups? How is it helpful to make explicit those aspects of organization culture that are typically implicit? Who should be responsible for setting norms in your courses or in student social groups and organizations?

Action Learning

Answer the following questions yourself.

1. Think of a really good work situation you've had (or as member of a student organization) and a really bad one.
2. Consider the types of organization cultures listed in pages 73–77. Which culture was your best and which was your worst?
3. List aspects of culture that fit you or did not fit.
4. Can you learn anything from this about what you need in a workplace in order for you to operate at your best?

What was the name of the company or organization?	What type of culture was it? Refer to pages 73–77.	Which aspects fit you the best? Or, which aspects were the worst fit?
Best:		
Worst:		

As a group, discuss the following:

1. Were there similarities or differences in what the members found in terms of ideal cultures?
2. If you could design a very ideal culture for your group members, what would it look like?
3. What would the ideal culture look like for people who have different, even opposite, qualities?

Ethical Dilemma

Competitive Intelligence Predicament[66]

Miquel Vasquez was proud of his job as a new product manager for a biotechnology start-up, and he loved the high stakes and tough decisions that went along with the job. But as he sat in his den after a long day, he was troubled, struggling over what had happened earlier that day and the information he now possessed.

Just before lunch, Miquel's boss had handed him a stack of private strategic documents from their closest competitor. It was a competitive intelligence gold mine—product plans, pricing strategies, partnership agreements, and other documents, most clearly marked "proprietary and confidential." When Miquel asked where the documents came from, his boss told him with a touch of pride that he had taken them right off the competing firm's server. "I got into a private section of their intranet and downloaded everything that looked interesting," he said. Later, realizing Miquel was suspicious, the boss would say only that he had obtained "electronic access" via a colleague and had not personally broken any passwords. Maybe not, Miquel thought to himself, but this situation wouldn't pass the *60 Minutes* test. If word of this acquisition of a competitor's confidential data ever got out to the press, the company's reputation would be ruined.

Miquel didn't feel good about using these materials. He spent the afternoon searching for answers to his dilemma, but found no clear company policies or regulations that offered any guidance. His sense of fair play told him that to use the information was unethical, if not downright illegal. What bothered him even more was the knowledge that this kind of thing might happen again. Using this confidential information would certainly give him and his company a competitive advantage, but Miquel wasn't sure he wanted to work for a firm that would stoop to such tactics.

What Would You Do?

1. Go ahead and use the documents to the company's benefit, but make clear to your boss that you don't want him passing confidential information to you in the future. If he threatens to fire you, threaten to leak the news to the press.
2. Confront your boss privately and let him know you're uncomfortable with how the documents were obtained and what possession of them says about the company's culture. In addition to the question of the legality of using the information, point out that it is a public relations nightmare waiting to happen.
3. Talk to the company's legal counsel and contact the Society of Competitive Intelligence Professionals for guidance. Then, with their opinions and facts to back you up, go to your boss.

Case for Critical Analysis

Rio Grande Supply Company[67]

Jasper Hennings, president of Rio Grande Supply Company, knew full well that a company's top executives were largely responsible for determining a firm's corporate culture. That's why he took such personal pride in the culture of his Texas-based wholesale plumbing supply company. It didn't just pay lip service to the values it espoused: integrity, honesty, and a respect for each individual employee. His management team set a good example by living those principles. At least that's what he'd believed until the other day.

The importance Jasper attached to respecting each individual was apparent in the company's Internet use policy. It was abundantly clear that employees weren't to use Rio Grande's computers for anything but business-related activities. However, Jasper himself had vetoed the inclusion of what was becoming a standard provision in such policies that management had the right to access and review anything employees created, stored, sent, or received on company equipment. He cut short any talk of installing software filters that would prevent abuse of the corporate computer system. Still, the company reserved the right to take disciplinary action, including possible termination, and to press criminal charges if an employee were found to have violated the policy.

So how was he to square his cherished assumptions about his management team with what he'd just discovered? Henry Darger, his hard-working chief of operations and a member of his church, had summarily fired a female employee for having accessed another worker's e-mail surreptitiously. She hadn't taken her dismissal well. "Just ask Darger what he's up to when he shuts his office door," she snarled as she stormed out of Jasper's office. She made what Jasper hoped was an idle threat to hire a lawyer.

When Jasper asked Henry what the fired employee could possibly have meant, tears began to roll down the operations chief's face. He admitted that ever since a young nephew had committed suicide the year before and a business he'd helped his wife start had failed, he'd increasingly been seeking escape from his troubles by logging onto adult pornography sites. At first, he'd indulged at home, but of late he'd found himself spending hours at work visiting pornographic sites, the more explicit the better. Jasper was stunned. After a few speechless minutes, he told Henry to take the rest of the day off, go home, and think things over.

The president himself needed the afternoon to gather his wits. How should he handle this turn of events? On the one hand, Henry's immediate dismissal of the woman who'd tapped into another employee's e-mail when the operations chief was violating the Internet policy himself was hypocritical, to say the least. The person charged with enforcing that policy had to be held to the highest standards. On the other hand, Jasper knew that Rio Grande employees routinely used computers at their desks to check personal e-mail, do banking transactions, check the weather, or make vacation arrangements. The company had turned a blind eye because it didn't seem worth the effort of enforcing the hard-and-fast policy for such minor infractions. Besides, Henry was a valued, if clearly troubled, employee. Replacing him would be costly and difficult. If Jasper decided to keep him on, the president clearly had no choice but to cross the line and get involved in Henry's private life, and he would be treating Darger differently from the treatment the female employee received.

When he met with Henry again first thing in the morning, he needed to have a plan of action.

Questions

1. What environmental factors have helped to create the situation Jasper Hennings faces? What factors does Jasper need to consider when deciding on his course of action?
2. Analyze Rio Grande's culture. In addition to the expressed cultural values and beliefs, what other subconscious values and beliefs do you detect? Are conflicting values present? When values are in conflict, how would you decide which ones take precedence?
3. Assume you are Jasper. What are the first two action steps you would take to handle the Henry Darger situation? How would your role as a cultural leader influence your decision? What message will your solution send to the other managers and rank-and-file employees?

aplia Aplia Highlights

Now use your Aplia homework to help you:

- Apply management theories in your life
- Assess your management skills
- Master management terms and concepts
- Apply your knowledge to real-world situations
- Analyze and solve challenging management problems

In order to take advantage of these elements, your instructor will need to have set up a course for your class within Aplia. Ask your instructor to contact his/her Cengage sales representative and Digital Solutions Manager to explore testing Aplia in your course this term.

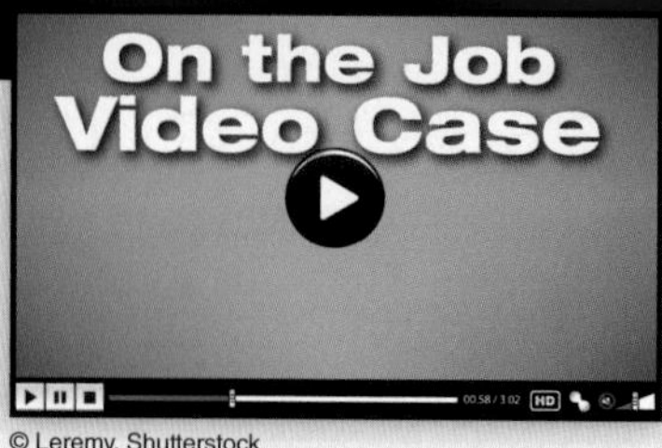

© Leremy, Shutterstock

Camp Bow Wow: The Environment and Corporate Culture

Founder stories play an important role in business. Andrew Carnegie's rise from a penniless immigrant to a captain of industry is one of the most famous rags-to-riches stories in American history. The tale of Bill Hewlett and Dave Packard starting HP in a garage has inspired a generation of Silicon Valley computer whizzes. More recently, Heidi Ganahl's launch of Camp Bow Wow has become a powerfully motivational story of triumph over tragedy.

Most people know Camp Bow Wow as a fun franchise that offers doggie day care for pet owners on the go. But the company's emergence from a single kennel in Denver, Colorado, to a $40 million franchise is as inspirational a story as any in business.

"After my husband died, I was struggling to find purpose in life and energy to get out of bed every day," said Heidi Ganahl in a recent interview about her popular camp for dogs. "I remember my dogs sitting there with tennis balls, dropping them at the base of the bed, like, 'Come on, get out of bed, life goes on, you have to keep moving, play ball'," the 44-year-old entrepreneur recalled.

When Ganahl and her first husband were in their mid-twenties, the dog-loving duo dreaded leaving pets at cold cramped clinics, and they dreamed of a better way to care for animals. The couple drew up plans for a dog-friendly kennel business and even began discussing a launch. Then, tragically, Ganahl's husband died on a Stearman WWII biplane joyride offered as a gift for his 25th birthday. Heidi's life went into a tailspin. Depressed and raising her child alone, Ganahl frittered away nearly $1 million received in a settlement, until her brother stepped in and urged her to launch the business she had envisioned with her husband. The intervention was magic, and Heidi's dogs gave her the extra motivation she needed to move forward. "I could not have started Camp Bow Wow if it wasn't for them," Ganahl says of her furry four-legged friends.

Heidi's life story has helped transform Camp Bow Wow into one of the fastest-growing franchises in the United States. The transition from a small family business to a national chain, however, required big changes in the company's culture. "As I've grown the company through the years with family and friends, and then getting to know the people who work for me and the franchisees who have come into the system, the focus had to shift from a family-based culture to a business-and-performance–oriented culture," Ganahl said. Her 2003 decision to turn Camp Bow Wow into a franchise was the right move. "Beginning to franchise wasn't something that I originally had in the plan, but it was the perfect fit for me because it allowed me to be the visionary and not handle the day-to-day operations," Ganahl said.

According to Camp Bow Wow's top dog, corporate culture has many elements: it can mean logos and branded material, a presence on the Internet, or even the relationships developed with customers and employees. But a key element of Camp Bow Wow's culture that doesn't exist in other franchises is the staff's deep emotional connection with animals. The connection is immediately apparent at Camp Bow Wow's corporate headquarters, where offices are bustling with employees and pets alike. "What we do is focus on what's important to us, and that's the animals," Ganahl said. "Whether it's the Foundation, our franchises, or our camp counselors, it all comes through in different ways, and it all goes back to the same thing: it's all about the pets. If we keep that focus and that commitment, I think our culture will be alive and well for a long time."

Discussion Questions

1. What aspects of Camp Bow Wow's corporate culture are visible and conscious? What aspects are invisible and unconscious?
2. Why did Camp Bow Wow have to change its culture when it became a national franchise?
3. What impact does Heidi Ganahl's story have on employees at Camp Bow Wow?

© Pedro Nogueira, Shutterstock

© VikaSuh, Shutterstock

Charlie Wilson's War

Democratic Congressman Charlie Wilson (Tom Hanks) from East Texas lives a reckless life that includes heavy drinking and chasing attractive women. The film focuses on the Afghanistan rebellion against the Soviet occupation in the 1980s. Wilson becomes the unlikely champion of the Afghan cause through his role in two major congressional committees that deal with foreign policy and covert operations. Houston socialite Joanne Herring (Julia Roberts) strongly urges the intervention. CIA agent Gust Avrakotos (Philip Seymour Hoffman) helps with some details.

Organizational Culture Observations This sequence appears early in the film after a scene showing the characters drinking and partying in a hot tub. It opens with a shot of the Capitol building. Congressman Charlie Wilson talks to his assistant Bonnie (Amy Adams) while walking to chambers for a vote. The sequence ends after Wilson enters the chambers. The film cuts to Wilson's office, where Larry Liddle (Peter Gerety) and his daughter Jane (Emily Blunt) wait for Wilson to arrive.

What to Watch for and Ask Yourself

- This chapter discussed organizational culture as having three levels of visibility. Visible artifacts are at the first level and are the easiest to see. Which visible artifacts did you observe in this sequence?
- Values appear at the next level of organizational culture. You can infer a culture's values from the behavior of organizational members. Which values appear in this sequence?
- Organizational members will unconsciously behave according to the basic assumptions of an organization's culture. You also infer these from observed behavior. Which basic assumptions appear in this sequence?

© Pedro Nogueira, Shutterstock

Endnotes

1. Josh Kosman, "Call It Block-Busted—Troubled Video Rental Chain Talks about Bankruptcy," *New York Post,* March 18, 2010; "Video Store Going the Way of the Milkman," *Herald,* March 7, 2010; Anthony Clark and Andrea Rumbaugh, "Did Netflix Kill the Video Store?" *Gainesville Sun,* June 3, 2010; and Darrell Smith, "Video Stores Fall Prey to the Web; More Outlets Are Closing Their Doors," *The Sacramento Bee,* April 23, 2010.
2. This section is based on Richard L. Daft, *Organization Theory and Design*, 10th ed. (Cincinnati, OH: South-Western, 2010), pp. 140–143.
3. L. J. Bourgeois, "Strategy and Environment: A Conceptual Integration," *Academy of Management Review* 5 (1980): 25–39.
4. Norihiko Shirouzu, "Chinese Inspire Car Makers' Designs," *The Wall Street Journal*, October 28, 2009.
5. Google Web site, www.google.com (accessed February 7, 2008).
6. Cliff Edwards, "Wherever You Go, You're on the Job," *BusinessWeek* (June 20, 2005): 87–90.
7. Brook Barnes, "Will Disney Keep Us Amused?" *The New York Times*, February 10, 2008.
8. William B. Johnston, "Global Work Force 2000: The New World Labor Market," *Harvard Business Review* (March–April 1991): 115–127.
9. Sara Lin, "Designing for the Senior Surge," *The Wall Street Journal,* April 25, 2008.
10. Ibid.
11. U.S. Census Bureau, "The Face of Our Population," *U.S. Census Bureau,* 2008, http://factfinder.census.gov/jsp/saff/SAFFInfo.jsp?_pageId=tp9_race_ethnicity (accessed January 28, 2008).
12. "You Raised Them, Now Manage Them," *Fortune* (May 28, 2007): 38–46.
13. Ian Mount, "And Seven Businesses That Did Not Survive," *The New York Times*, December 31, 2009.
14. Ibid.
15. Samuel Loewenberg, "Europe Gets Tougher on U.S. Companies," *The New York Times*, April 20, 2003.
16. Barney Gimbel, "Attack of the Wal-Martyrs," *Fortune* (December 11, 2006): 125.
17. Andrew Adam Newman, "Media Talk: Environmentalists Push, but Home Depot Refuses to Drop Ads on Fox News," *The New York Times*, July 30, 2007.
18. Dror Etzion, "Research on Organizations and the Natural Environment," *Journal of Management* 33 (August 2007): 637–654.
19. Elizabeth Weise and Doyle Rice, "Even the 'Best' Outcome Won't Be Good; The Oil Spill's Potential Toll Is Becoming Clear," *USA Today,* June 9, 2010.
20. Jessi Hempel, "The MySpace Generation," *BusinessWeek* (December 12, 2005): 86–94.

21. Daniel Ionescu, "Report: Hulu to Offer $10-per-Month Subscription," *PCWorld,* April 22, 2010, www.pcworld.com/article/194766/ (accessed July 12, 2010).
22. Brian Stetler and Brad Stone, "Successes (and Some Growing Pains) at Hulu," *The New York Times,* April 1, 2010; and Tom Lowry, "The Online TV Threat Has Cable Scrambling," *BusinessWeek* (April 13, 2009): 50.
23. Michael Bustillo and Jeffrey A. Trachtenberg, "Wal-Mart Strafes Amazon in Book War," *The Wall Street Journal,* October 16, 2009.
24. Gary Rivlin, "When Buying a Diamond Starts with a Mouse," *The New York Times*, January 7, 2007.
25. Aaron O. Patrick, Julie Jardon, Sky Canaves, and Jason Dean, "Food Giants Scrutinize Chinese Suppliers," *The Wall Street Journal,* September 30, 2008.
26. Nortel Web site, www.nortel.com/corporate/index.html (accessed February 2, 2008); and http://www.nortel.com/ (accessed July 10, 2010).
27. Robert B. Duncan, "Characteristics of Organizational Environment and Perceived Environmental Uncertainty," *Administrative Science Quarterly* 17 (1972): 313–327; and Daft, *Organization Theory and Design,* pp. 144–148.
28. Stephan M. Wagner and Roman Boutellier, "Capabilities for Managing a Portfolio of Supplier Relationships," *Business Horizons* (November–December 2002): 79–88; Peter Smith Ring and Andrew H. Van de Ven, "Developmental Processes of Corporate Interorganizational Relationships," *Academy of Management Review* 19 (1994): 90–118; Myron Magnet, "The New Golden Rule of Business," *Fortune* (February 21, 1994): 60–64; and Peter Grittner, "Four Elements of Successful Sourcing Strategies," *Management Review* (October 1996): 41–45.
29. Patricia Sellers, "The Business of Being Oprah," *Fortune* (April 1, 2002): 50–64.
30. Yoash Wiener, "Forms of Value Systems: A Focus on Organizational Effectiveness and Culture Change and Maintenance," *Academy of Management Review* 13 (1988): 534–545; V. Lynne Meek, "Organizational Culture: Origins and Weaknesses," *Organization Studies* 9 (1988): 453–473; John J. Sherwood, "Creating Work Cultures with Competitive Advantage," *Organizational Dynamics* (Winter 1988): 5–27; and Andrew D. Brown and Ken Starkey, "The Effect of Organizational Culture on Communication and Information," *Journal of Management Studies* 31, no. 6 (November 1994): 807–828.
31. Joanne Martin, *Organizational Culture: Mapping the Terrain* (Thousand Oaks, CA: Sage Publications, 2002); Ralph H. Kilmann, Mary J. Saxton, and Roy Serpa, "Issues in Understanding and Changing Culture," *California Management Review* 28 (Winter 1986): 87–94; and Linda Smircich, "Concepts of Culture and Organizational Analysis," *Administrative Science Quarterly* 28 (1983): 339–358.
32. Based on Edgar H. Schein, *Organizational Culture and Leadership*, 2nd ed. (San Francisco: Jossey-Bass, 1992): 3–27.
33. Michael G. Pratt and Anat Rafaeli, "Symbols as a Language of Organizational Relationships," *Research in Organizational Behavior* 23 (2001): 93–132.
34. Christine Canabou, "Here's the Drill," *Fast Company* (February 2001): 58.
35. Chip Jarnagin and John W. Slocum, Jr., "Creating Corporate Cultures through Mythopoetic Leadership," *Organizational Dynamics* 36, no. 3 (2007): 288–302.
36. Robert E. Quinn and Gretchen M. Spreitzer, "The Road to Empowerment: Seven Questions Every Leader Should Consider," *Organizational Dynamics* (Autumn 1997): 37–49.
37. Martin, *Organizational Culture*, pp. 71–72.
38. Terrence E. Deal and Allan A. Kennedy, *Corporate Cultures: The Rites and Rituals of Corporate Life* (Reading, MA: Addison-Wesley, 1982).
39. Arthur Yeung, "Setting People up for Success: How the Portman Ritz-Carlton Hotel Gets the Best from Its People," *Human Resource Management* 45, no. 2 (Summer 2006): 267–275.
40. Patricia Jones and Larry Kahaner, *Say It and Live It: 50 Corporate Mission Statements That Hit the Mark* (New York: Currency Doubleday, 1995).
41. Harrison M. Trice and Janice M. Beyer, "Studying Organizational Cultures through Rites and Ceremonials," *Academy of Management Review* 9 (1984): 653–669.
42. PRWeb, "Southwest Airlines Launches New NBA-Themed Specialty Airplane; Slam Dunk One Marks First Southwest Specialty Plane with a Partner in 17 Years," November 3, 2005, www.prweb.com/releases/2005/11/prweb306461.php (accessed February 7, 2008).
43. Jennifer A. Chatman and Karen A. Jehn, "Assessing the Relationship between Industry Characteristics and Organizational Culture: How Different Can You Be?" *Academy of Management Journal* 37, no. 3 (1994): 522–553.
44. This discussion is based on Paul McDonald and Jeffrey Gandz, "Getting Value from Shared Values," *Organizational Dynamics* 21, no. 3 (Winter 1992): 64–76; Daniel R. Denison and Aneil K. Mishra, "Toward a Theory of Organizational Culture and Effectiveness," *Organization Science* 6, no. 2 (March–April 1995): 204–223; and Richard L. Daft, *The Leadership Experience,* 3rd ed. (Cincinnati, OH: South-Western, 2005), pp. 570–573.
45. Lucas Conley, "Rinse and Repeat," *Fast Company* (July 2005): 76–77.
46. Robert Hooijberg and Frank Petrock, "On Cultural Change: Using the Competing Values Framework to Help Leaders Execute a Transformational Strategy," *Human Resource Management* 32, no. 1 (1993): 29–50.
47. Patrick Lencioni, "Make Your Values Mean Something," *Harvard Business Review* (July 2002): 113–117; and Melanie Warner, "Confessions of a Control Freak," *Fortune* (September 4, 2000): 130–140.
48. Janet Guyon, "The Soul of a Moneymaking Machine," *Fortune* (October 3, 2005): 113–120; Bill Leonard, "Taking Care of Their Own," *HR Magazine* (June 2006): 112–115; and Tim Young, "Rewarding Work," *HR Management,* Issue 3, October 3, 2006, http://www.hrmreport.com/article/Rewarding-work/ (accessed July 12, 2010).
49. Rekha Balu, "Pacific Edge Projects Itself," *Fast Company* (October 2000): 371–381.
50. Jeffrey Pfeffer, *The Human Equation: Building Profits by Putting People First* (Boston: Harvard Business School Press, 1998).
51. Jeremy Kahn, "What Makes a Company Great?" *Fortune* (October 26, 1998): 218; James C. Collins and Jerry I. Porras, *Built to Last: Successful Habits of Visionary Companies* (New York: HarperCollins, 1994); and James C. Collins, "Change Is Good—But First Know What Should Never Change," *Fortune* (May 29, 1995): 141.
52. Andrew Wahl, "Culture Shock," *Canadian Business* (October 10–23, 2005): 115–116.

53. Jennifer A. Chatman and Sandra Eunyoung Cha, "Leading by Leveraging Culture," *California Management Review* 45, no. 4 (Summer 2003): 20–34.

54. This section is based on Jeff Rosenthal and Mary Ann Masarech, "High-Performance Cultures: How Values Can Drive Business Results," *Journal of Organizational Excellence* (Spring 2003): 3–18.

55. Nelson D. Schwartz, "One Brick at a Time," *Fortune* (June 12, 2006): 45–46; and Nelson D. Schwartz, "Lego's Rebuilds Legacy," *International Herald Tribune* (September 5, 2009).

56. Katherine Mieszkowski, "Community Standards," *Fast Company* (September 2000): 368; Rosabeth Moss Kanter, "A More Perfect Union," *Inc.* (February 2001): 92–98; Raizel Robin, "Net Gains" segment of "E-Biz That Works," *Canadian Business* (October 14–October 26, 2003): 107.

57. Reggie Van Lee, Lisa Fabish, and Nancy McGaw, "The Value of Corporate Values: A Booz Allen Hamilton/Aspen Institute Survey," *Strategy + Business* 39 (Spring 2005): 52–65.

58. Lucas Conley, "Cultural Phenomenon," *Fast Company* (April 2005): 76–77.

59. Rosenthal and Masarech, "High-Performance Cultures."

60. John P. Kotter and James L. Heskett, *Corporate Culture and Performance* (New York: The Free Press, 1992); Eric Flamholtz and Rangapriya Kannan-Narasimhan, "Differential Impact of Cultural Elements on Financial Performance," *European Management Journal* 23, no. 1 (2005): 50–64. Also see J. M. Kouzes and B. Z. Posner, *The Leadership Challenge: How to Keep Getting Extraordinary Things Done in Organizations,* 3rd ed. (San Francisco: Jossey-Bass, 2002).

61. Micah R. Kee, "Corporate Culture Makes a Fiscal Difference," *Industrial Management* (November– December 2003): 16–20.

62. Rosenthal and Masarech, "High-Performance Cultures"; Lencioni, "Make Your Values Mean Something"; and Thomas J. Peters and Robert H. Waterman, Jr., *In Search of Excellence* (New York: Warner, 1988).

63. Jarnagin and Slocum, "Creating Corporate Cultures through Mythopoetic Leadership."

64. Guyon, "The Soul of a Moneymaking Machine"; and Geoff Colvin, "The 100 Best Companies to Work for in 2006," *Fortune* (January 23, 2006).

65. Based on S. J. Ashford, N. P. Rothbard, S. K. Piderit, and J. E. Dutton, "Out on a Limb: The Role of Context and Impression Management in Issue Selling," *Administrative Science Quarterly* 43 (1998): 23–57; and E. W. Morrison and C. C. Phelps, "Taking Charge at Work: Extrarole Efforts to Initiate Workplace Change," *Academy of Management Journal* 42 (1999): 403–419.

66. Adapted from Kent Weber, "Gold Mine or Fool's Gold?" *Business Ethics* (January–February 2001): 18.

67. Based on Willard P. Green, "Pornography at Work," *Business Ethics* (Summer 2003): 19; Patrick Marley, "Porn-Viewing Parole Agent Regains Job," *Milwaukee Journal Sentinel,* January 25, 2006; "Sample Internet Policies for Businesses and Organizations," *Websense,* www.websense-sales.com/internet-access-policy.html; and Art Lambert, "Technology in the Workplace: A Recipe for Legal Trouble," *Workforce Management,* February 14, 2005, http://www.workforce.com/archive/article/23/95/08.php (accessed July 12, 2010).

Chapter Outline

Managing in a Global Environment

Learning Outcomes

After studying this chapter, you should be able to:

1. Define globalization and explain how it is creating a borderless world for today's managers.
2. Describe various approaches businesses use to enter the international arena.
3. Discuss how the international landscape is changing, including the growing power of China, India, and Brazil.
4. Define international management and explain how it differs from the management of domestic business operations.
5. Indicate how dissimilarities in the economic, sociocultural, and legal-political environments throughout the world can affect business operations.
6. Discuss why cultural intelligence is necessary for managers working in foreign countries.
7. Describe how regional trading alliances are reshaping the international business environment.
8. Describe the globalization backlash and explain the bottom of the pyramid concept.

© James Steidl, Shutterstock

Are You Ready to Be a Manager?

Please circle your opinion below each of the following statements.

1 I consider myself to be a world citizen.

Mostly True — Mostly False

(See page 92, A Borderless World.)

2 I'm good at outsourcing (getting my little sister to do my chores, for example) and bartering, both skills important in international business.

Mostly True — Mostly False

(See page 96, Outsourcing.)

3 I work well individually and as part of a group.

Mostly True — Mostly False

(See page 105, Hofstede's Value Dimensions.)

4 When I am solving problems or developing plans, I can think in terms of both short-term and long-term goals.

Mostly True — Mostly False

(See page 106, Long-term vs. Short-term Orientation.)

5 I can easily move within other cultures and adapt to different behavioral norms.

Mostly True — Mostly False

(See page 112, Developing Cultural Intelligence.)

Many people think of Jaguar as a quintessentially British luxury car. Yet the automaker was actually owned by U.S.-based Ford Motor Company from 1989 until 2008, when it was sold to Tata Group, one of India's largest industrial conglomerates. Tata Motors sells Jaguars in prestigious markets, but it also makes the world's least expensive car, the tiny Nano, which sells in India for the equivalent of around US$2,500. Millions of families that could once afford only a motorbike for transportation are now driving Nanos. Tata plans to begin selling the Nano in Europe by 2013, and is eventually aiming for the U.S. market.[1]

Brazil, Russia, India, and China (often referred to as BRIC) as well as other emerging economies are growing rapidly as providers of both products and services to the United States, Canada, Europe, and other developed nations. At the same time, these regions are becoming major markets for the products and services of North American firms. For today's managers, the whole world is a source of business threats and opportunities. Even managers who spend their entire careers working in their hometown have to be aware of the international environment and probably interact with people from other cultures.

Every manager needs to think globally. The international dimension is an increasingly important part of the external environment discussed in this chapter, which introduces basic concepts about the global environment and international management. First, we provide an overview of today's borderless world and the stages of globalization companies typically pass through. We then touch on various strategies and techniques for entering the global arena and take a look at how emerging markets are reshaping the international business landscape. Next, we address the economic, legal-political, and sociocultural challenges companies encounter within the global business environment. This chapter also describes the impact of multinational corporations, looks at the role of trade agreements, and considers the globalization backlash.

A Borderless World

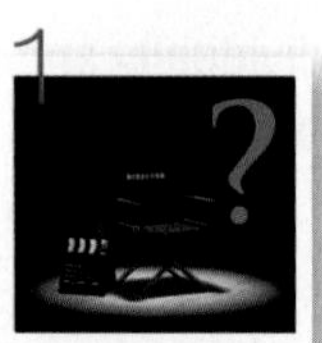

A manager's reality is that isolation from international forces is no longer possible. Consider that the FBI now ranks international cybercrime as one of its top priorities, because electronic boundaries between countries are virtually nonexistent. This openness has many positive aspects, but it also means hackers in one nation can steal secrets from companies in another or unleash viruses, worms, or other rogue programs to destroy the computer systems of corporations and governments around the world.[2] In addition to 61 attaché offices overseas, the FBI has opened cybercrime offices in at least four countries. One recent case involved eight major banks in the United States that were targeted by international hackers. A tip to the FBI enabled the banks to spot the attempted breaches and block them. The number of international cybercrime cases addressed by the FBI jumped from just a few in 2001 to more than 300 seven years later.[3]

Business, just like crime, has become a unified, global field. **Globalization** refers to the extent to which trade and investments, information, social and cultural ideas, and political cooperation flow between countries. One result is that countries, businesses, and people become increasingly interdependent. India-based Tata Consultancy Services gets more than half of its revenues from North America, while the U.S. firm IBM gets 65 percent of its tech services revenue from overseas, with sales in India growing 41 percent in one recent quarter. Increased demand and a sharp increase in the price of garlic in China caused the price of the herb to jump 70 percent in the United States between

New Manager Self-Test

Are You Ready To Work Internationally?

Are you ready to negotiate a sales contract with someone from another country? Companies large and small deal on a global basis. To what extent are you guilty of the behaviors below? Please answer each item as Mostly True or Mostly False for you.

ARE YOU TYPICALLY:	MOSTLY TRUE <<<	>>> MOSTLY FALSE
1. Impatient? Do you have a short attention span? Do you want to keep moving to the next topic?	______	______
2. A poor listener? Are you uncomfortable with silence? Does your mind think about what you want to say next?.	______	______
3. Argumentative? Do you enjoy arguing for its own sake?	______	______
4. Unfamiliar with cultural specifics in other countries? Do you have limited experience in other countries?	______	______
5. Short-term oriented? Do you place more emphasis on the short term than on the long term in your thinking and planning?	______	______
6. "All business"? Do you think that it is a waste of time getting to know someone personally before discussing business?	______	______
7. Legalistic to win your point? Do you hold others to an agreement regardless of changing circumstances?	______	______
8. Thinking "win/lose" when negotiating? Do you usually try to win a negotiation at the other's expense?	______	______

Scoring and Interpretation: American managers often display cross-cultural ignorance during business negotiations compared to counterparts in other countries. American habits can be disturbing, such as emphasizing areas of disagreement over agreement, spending little time understanding the views and interests of the other side, and adopting an adversarial attitude. Americans often like to leave a negotiation thinking they won, which can be embarrassing to the other side. For this quiz, a low score shows better international presence. If you answered Mostly True to three or fewer items, then consider yourself ready to assist with an international negotiation. If you scored six or more Mostly True responses, it is time to learn more about other national cultures before participating in international business deals. Try to develop greater focus on other people's needs and an appreciation for different viewpoints. Be open to compromise and develop empathy for people who are different from you.

SOURCE: Adapted from Cynthia Barnum and Natasha Wolniansky, "Why Americans Fail at Overseas Negotiations," *Management Review* (October 1989): 54–57.

2009 and 2010.[4] And although Japan's Honda gets 65 percent of its parts for the Accord from the United States or Canada and assembles the vehicle in Ohio, U.S.-based General Motors makes the Chevrolet HHR in Mexico with parts that come from all over the world.[5]

ConceptConnection

Today's companies compete in a **borderless world**. Procter & Gamble sales in Southeast Asia make up a rapidly growing percentage of the company's worldwide sales. These shoppers are purchasing P&G's diaper products, Pampers, in Malaysia.

Globalization has been on the rise since the 1970s, and most industrialized nations show a high degree of globalization today.[6] The KOF Swiss Economic Institute measures aspects of globalization and ranks countries on a globalization index. Exhibit 3.1 shows how selected countries ranked on the 2010 index (based on the year 2007) compared to their degree of globalization in the mid-1970s. Note that the United States is the least globalized of the countries shown in the exhibit. Among the 208 countries on the KOF Index, the United States ranks number 27. The 10 most globalized countries, according to the KOF Index, are Belgium, Austria, the Netherlands, Switzerland, Sweden, Denmark, Canada, Portugal, Finland, and Hungary.[7] In 1999, seven of the world's ten most valuable companies were based in the United States. By 2009, only four were U.S. based. Three were based in China, and one each in Brazil, Australia, and the United Kingdom.[8]

The difficulties and risks of a borderless world are matched by benefits and opportunities. Even small companies, for example, can locate different parts of the organization

EXHIBIT 3.1

Ranking of Six Countries on the Globalization Index

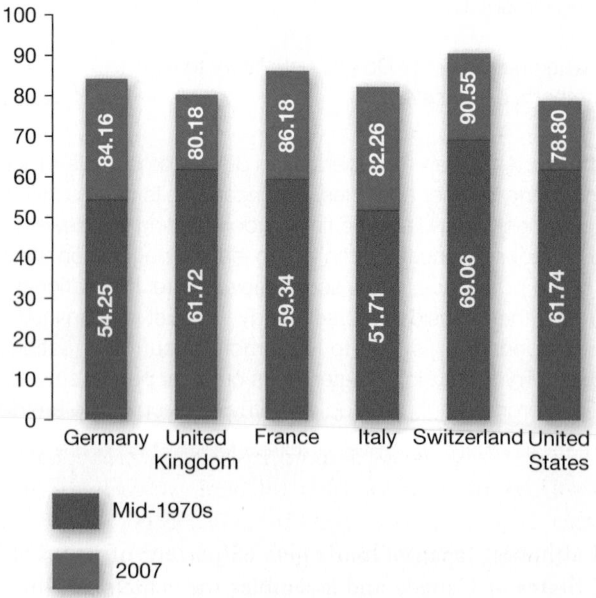

SOURCE: Based on "KOF Index of Globalization 2010," KOF Swiss Economic Institute Press Release (January 22, 2010), http://globalization.kof.ethz.ch/ (accessed on January 22, 2010); and "2010 KOF Index of Globalization Detailed Rankings, http://globalization.kof.ethz.ch/static/pdf/rankings_2010.pdf (accessed on April 5, 2010).

EXHIBIT 3.2

Four Stages of Globalization

	1. Domestic	2. International	3. Multinational	4. Global
Strategic Orientation	Domestically oriented	Export-oriented, multidomestic	Multinational	Global
Stage of Development	Initial foreign involvement	Competitive positioning	Explosion of international operations	Global
Cultural Sensitivity	Of little importance	Very important	Somewhat important	Critically important
Manager Assumptions	"One best way"	"Many good ways"	"The least-cost way"	"Many good ways"

SOURCE: Based on Nancy J. Adler, *International Dimensions of Organizational Behavior*, 4th ed. (Cincinnati, OH: South-Western, 2002), pp. 8–9.

wherever it makes the most business sense. Virtual connections enable close, rapid coordination among people working in different parts of the world, so it is no longer necessary to keep everything in one place. Organizations can go wherever they want to find the lowest costs or the best brainpower. Excel Foundry and Machine in Pekin, Illinois, makes parts for machinery used in heavy-construction and mining operations. President Doug Parsons uses a strategy of outsourcing the easily duplicated parts to contractors in China so that Excel can focus more money and energy on making higher-cost specialty products and innovating for the future.[9]

When managers think globally, the whole world is a source of ideas, resources, information, employees, and customers. Managers can move their companies into the international arena on a variety of levels, and organizations can be thought of as passing through four distinct stages as they become increasingly global. These stages are illustrated in Exhibit 3.2.

Complete the Self-Learning Exercise, on page 121, that pertains to your global management potential. How well do your knowledge and preferences reflect a global perspective?

- Today's companies and managers operate in a borderless world that provides both risks and opportunities.
- **Globalization** refers to the extent to which trade and investments, information, ideas, and political cooperation flow between countries.
- The most globalized countries according to one ranking are Belgium, Austria, the Netherlands, Switzerland, and Sweden.

Getting Started Internationally

Organizations have a couple of ways to become involved internationally. One is to seek cheaper resources such as materials or labor offshore, which is called *offshoring* or *global outsourcing*. Another is to develop markets for finished products or services outside their home countries, which may include exporting, licensing, and direct investing. Exporting is called a **market entry strategy** because it represents an alternative way to sell products and services in foreign markets. Exhibit 3.3 shows the strategies companies can use to engage in the international arena, either to acquire resources or to enter new markets.

EXHIBIT 3.3

Strategies for Entering the International Arena

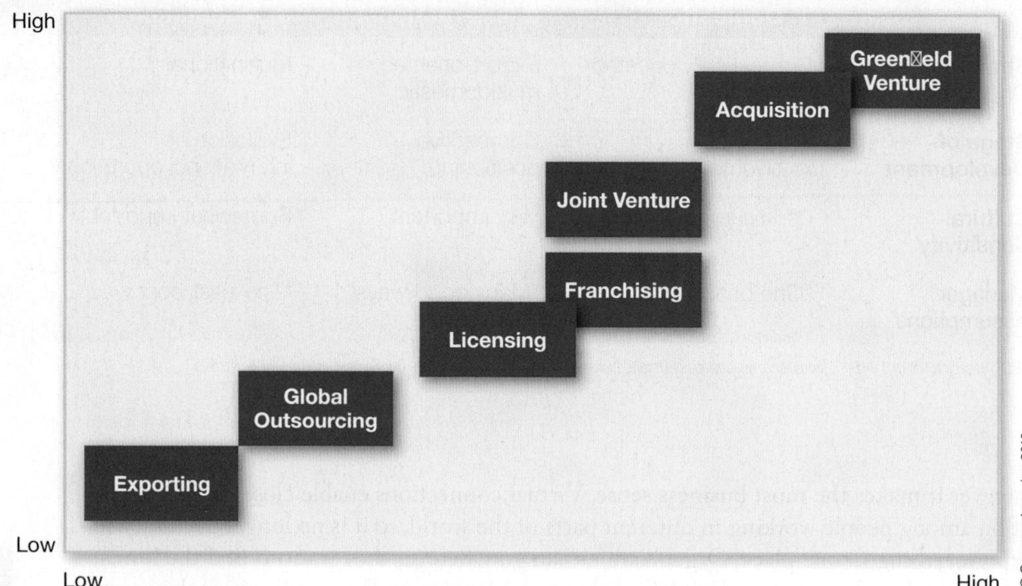

Exporting

With **exporting**, the company maintains its production facilities within the home nation and transfers its products for sale in foreign countries.[10] Exporting enables a company to market its products in other countries at modest resource cost and with limited risk. Exporting does entail numerous problems based on physical distances, government regulations, foreign currencies, and cultural differences, but it is less expensive than committing the firm's own capital to build plants in host countries. For example, Skooba Designs, a Rochester, New York, manufacturer of carrying cases for laptops, iPads, and other tools, exports to more than 30 countries. Although Skooba has to tailor its products somewhat to suit different tastes, the Rochester facility can easily handle production.[11]

A form of exporting to less-developed countries is called **countertrade**, which refers to the barter of products for products rather than the sale of products for currency. Many less-developed countries have products to exchange but have no foreign currency. Economists estimate that about 20 to 25 percent of world trade is countertrade.

Outsourcing

Global outsourcing, also called *offshoring*, means engaging in the international division of labor so that work activities can be done in countries with the cheapest sources of labor and supplies. Millions of low-level jobs such as textile manufacturing, call center operations, and credit card processing have been outsourced to low-wage countries in recent years. The Internet and plunging telecommunications costs are enabling companies to outsource more work and higher-level work as well, such as software development, accounting, or medical services. A patient might have an MRI (magnetic resonance imaging) test performed in Minneapolis and have it read by doctors in India.

The most recent trend is outsourcing core processes, which Joe McGrath, CEO of Unisys, refers to as the "natural next phase of the offshoring movement."[12] After the

Sarbanes-Oxley Act went into effect, Unisys had a hard time finding enough internal auditors in the United States, so managers outsourced their core auditing practice to China. Large pharmaceutical companies farm out much of their early-stage chemistry research to cheaper labs in China and India.[13] Many organizations even outsource aspects of innovation. One survey found that 65 percent of companies reported that part of their research and development takes place overseas.[14]

- Two major alternatives for engaging in the international arena are to seek cheaper resources via outsourcing and to develop markets outside the home country.
- **Global outsourcing**, sometimes called *offshoring*, means engaging in the international division of labor so as to obtain the cheapest sources of labor and supplies, regardless of country.
- **Market entry strategies** are various tactics managers use to enter foreign markets.
- **Exporting** is a market entry strategy in which a company maintains production facilities within its home country and transfers products for sale in foreign countries.
- One type of exporting is **countertrade**, the barter of products for other products rather than the sale of products for currency.

The Changing International Landscape

Many companies today are going straight to China or India as a first step into international business, either through outsourcing or by using various market entry strategies. China and India have been the world's fastest growing economies in recent years. In addition, Brazil is coming on strong as a major player in the international business landscape. From 2005 to 2008, IBM hired around 90,000 people in low-cost countries, primarily China, India, and Brazil.[15]

China Inc.

For the past several years, foreign companies have invested more in business in China than they spent anywhere else in the world. A market that was of little interest a decade ago has become the one place nearly every manager is thinking about. Beijing's announcement in June 2010 of a rise in the yuan's exchange rate will likely boost exports to that country.[16] So far, outsourcing has been the most widespread approach to international involvement in China. China manufactures an ever-growing percentage of the industrial and consumer products sold in the United States—and in other countries as well. China also beckons to U.S. companies as a major market. It has the largest mobile phone market in the world, for instance, with 687 million subscribers in late 2009, which is why Apple was willing to overcome all kinds of legal and regulatory hurdles to begin selling the iPhone there.[17]

Yet doing business in China has never been smooth and appears to be getting even tougher. New regulations and government policies are making life hard for foreign companies in all industries. A couple of years ago, for example, Chinese regulators blocked an acquisition bid by U.S.-based Coca-Cola for a local juice company, saying it would crowd out smaller companies and raise prices, even though the two combined companies held just a fifth of China's juice market.[18] For Internet companies such as Facebook, Twitter, eBay, and Google, China has been more a source of trouble and frustration than of new customers.[19] Google closed its Chinese site, Google.cn, in early 2010 because of government restrictions and censorship, although the company later renewed its license to provide limited services in China. "I am pro-China and I am for doing business in China, but I have some serious concerns about what has been happening in the last year," said an attorney with one U.S. law firm operating there.[20] Despite the problems, China is a market that foreign managers can't afford to ignore.

India, the Service Giant

India, second only to China in population, has taken a different path toward economic development. Whereas China is strong in manufacturing, India is a rising power in software design, services, and precision engineering. Nearly 50 percent of microchip engineering for Conexant Systems, a California-based company, is done in India.[21] Conexant makes the intricate brains behind Internet access for home computers and satellite-connection set-top boxes for televisions. Numerous companies are recognizing India as a major source of technological brainpower.

Although India is facing trying economic times, it is benefiting from the trend of outsourcing services. With its large English-speaking population, India has numerous companies offering services such as call-center operations, data processing, computer programming and technical support, accounting, and so forth. One index lists more than 900 business services companies in India that employ around 575,000 people.[22]

Brazil's Growing Clout

Brazil is another country that is increasingly gaining managers' attention.[23] Brazil's economy was projected to grow as much as 6 percent in 2010, and its stock market was rising even as those in most developed nations were falling. The country's economy, already the tenth largest in the world, is projected to move into fourth place by 2050. The recent choice of Rio de Janeiro to host the 2016 Summer Olympics is also an indication of Brazil's growing clout in the international arena.

Brazil has a young, vibrant population, the largest in Latin America, and a rapidly growing middle class eager to experience the finer things in life. Consumer spending represents about 60 percent of Brazil's economy. The Brazilian government has initiated major investments in the development of infrastructure such as highways, ports, and electricity projects, which is creating jobs as well as spurring the development of other businesses. In addition, Brazil announced a $22 billion investment in science and technology innovation in 2010, which has companies like IBM paying attention.

IBM

IBM Chief Executive Sam Palmisano recently spent nearly an hour talking with former Brazilian President Luiz Inácio Lula da Silva. Palmisano is searching the world for good places to set up "collaboratories," which will pair IBM researchers with experts from governments, universities, and other companies. So far, IBM has made deals for collaboratories in China, Saudi Arabia, Switzerland, Ireland, Taiwan, and India. Brazil is likely next on the list. To select a location, IBM takes into account a variety of factors, including available talent, government stability, corruption, and a country's commitment to technology investments. "Investments in innovation are critical," Palmisano says. "They can help Brazil and other countries, including the United States, realize an economic expansion."

Collaboration with outsiders all over the globe is a key part of IBM's research strategy. One partnership with China Telecom, for example, helps the communications giant understand customer desires and improve its services. For IBM, it opens a pathway to a huge market and provides a chance to try out new technologies using real-life data. The company sees equally important opportunities in Brazil as that country continues to pursue economic expansion.[24]

- Many companies are going straight to China or India as a first step into international business.
- Outsourcing is the most widespread involvement by foreign firms in these two countries.
- China is strong in manufacturing, whereas India is a major provider of services.
- Brazil, with its rapidly growing consumer market, is becoming a major player in the shifting international landscape.
- Rio de Janeiro's being selected to host the 2016 Summer Olympics is an indication of its growing clout in the international arena.
- Managers also look to China, India, and Brazil as sources of lower-cost technological brainpower.

The International Business Environment

International management is the management of business operations conducted in more than one country. The fundamental tasks of business management—including the financing, production, and distribution of products and services—do not change in any substantive way when a firm is transacting business across international borders. The basic management functions of planning, organizing, leading, and controlling are the same whether a company operates domestically or internationally. However, managers will experience greater difficulties and risks when performing these management functions on an international scale. Consider the following blunders:

- When U.S. chicken entrepreneur Frank Perdue translated a successful advertising slogan into Spanish, "It takes a tough man to make a tender chicken" came out as "It takes a virile man to make a chicken affectionate."[25]
- It took McDonald's more than a year to figure out that Hindus in India do not eat beef. The company's sales took off only after McDonald's started making its burgers sold in India out of lamb.[26]

BUSINESS BLOOPER

Aeroflot

Two incidents on Russia's Aeroflot Airlines suggest a lack of management oversight. The pilot of a jet taking off from London was chatting up passengers, when they noticed his speech was slurred. On another flight, a passenger got tired of the sloppy service he was receiving from two flight attendants, who had sampled from the liquor tray and were way over the legal limit. After more frustration dealing with the drunken attendants, he asked whether a sober employee would be able to serve him. Their response may indicate a need for customer service training: The two intoxicated crew members beat him up.

SOURCES: Lisa Monforton, "Flying High? You'll Be Grounded," *The Vancouver Sun*, March 21, 2009; and Adam Horowitz et al., "101 Dumbest Moments in Business," *Business 2.0* (January/February 2005): 103–112.

3.4 EXHIBIT

Key Factors in the International Environment

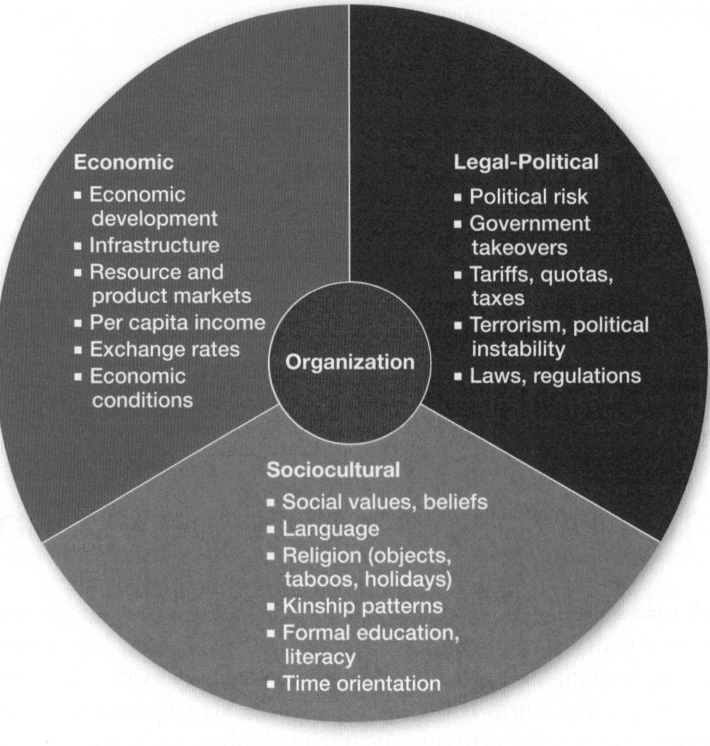

- In Africa, the labels on bottles show pictures of what is inside so illiterate shoppers can know what they're buying. When a baby-food company showed a picture of an infant on its label, the product didn't sell very well.[27]
- United Airlines discovered that even colors can doom a product. The airline handed out white carnations when it started flying from Hong Kong, only to discover that, to many Asians, such flowers represent death and bad luck.[28]

Some of these examples might seem humorous, but there's nothing funny about them to managers trying to operate in a highly competitive global environment. What should managers of emerging global companies look for to avoid obvious international mistakes? When they are comparing one country with another, the economic, legal-political, and sociocultural sectors present the greatest difficulties. Key factors to understand in the international environment are summarized in Exhibit 3.4.

- The basic management functions are the same in either a domestic or an international subsidiary, but managers will experience greater difficulties and risks when performing these functions internationally.
- **International management** means the management of business operations conducted in more than one country.
- When operating on an international basis, it is important for managers to give considerable thought to economic, legal-political, and sociocultural factors.

The Economic Environment

The economic environment represents the economic conditions in the country where the international organization operates. This part of the environment includes factors such as economic development and resource and product markets. In addition, factors such as inflation, interest rates, and economic growth are also part of the international economic environment.

Economic Development

Economic development differs widely among the countries and regions of the world. Countries can be categorized as either *developing* or *developed*. Developing countries are referred to as *less-developed countries (LDCs)*. The criterion traditionally used to classify countries as developed or developing is *per capita income*, which is the income generated by the nation's production of goods and services divided by total population. The developing countries have low per capita incomes. LDCs generally are located in Asia, Africa, and South America. In addition to Japan, developed countries are generally located in North America and Europe. Most international business firms are headquartered in the wealthier, economically advanced countries, but smart managers are investing heavily in Asia, Eastern Europe, Latin America, and Africa.[29] These companies face risks and challenges today, but they stand to reap huge benefits in the future.

Each year, the World Economic Forum analyzes data to gauge how companies are doing in the economic development race and releases its Global Competitiveness Report, which tallies numerous factors that contribute to an economy's competitiveness.[30] The report considers both hard data and perceptions of business leaders around the world and considers government policies, institutions, market size, the sophistication of financial markets, and other factors that drive productivity and thus enable sustained economic growth. Exhibit 3.5 shows the top ten countries in the overall ranking, along with several other countries for comparison. The United States fell out of first place in the 2009–2010 report. Note that highly developed countries typically rank higher in the competitiveness index. One important factor in gauging competitiveness is the country's **infrastructure**, that is, the physical facilities such as highways, airports, utilities, and telephone lines that support economic activities.

Resource and Product Markets

When operating in another country, managers must evaluate the market demand for their products and services. If market demand is high, managers may choose to export products to that country. To develop plants, however, resource markets for providing needed raw materials and labor must also be available. For example, the greatest challenge for McDonald's, which sells Big Macs on every continent except Antarctica, is to obtain supplies of everything from potatoes to hamburger buns to plastic straws. At the McDonald's in Cracow, the burgers come from a Polish plant, partly owned by Chicago-based OSI Industries; the onions come from Fresno, California; the buns come from a production and distribution center near Moscow; and the potatoes come from a plant in Aldrup, Germany.[31]

Economic Interdependence

One thing the recent financial crisis has made abundantly clear is how economically interconnected the world is. The crisis that began in the United States with the collapse of the

EXHIBIT 3.5

World Economic Forum Global Competitiveness Rankings 2009–2010

Country	Overall Ranking
Switzerland	1
United States	2
Singapore	3
Sweden	4
Denmark	5
Finland	6
Germany	7
Japan	8
Canada	9
Netherlands	10
Taiwan, China	12
China	29
Kuwait	39
South Africa	45
India	49
Brazil	56

SOURCE: The Global Competitiveness Report 2009–10, World Economic Forum, http://www.weforum.org/en/initiatives/gcp/Global%20Competitiveness%20Report/GlobalCompetitivnessReport (accessed March 17, 2010).

housing market and the failure, merger, and bailout of several large financial institutions rapidly spread to the rest of the world.

Although the recent crisis might seem atypical, savvy international managers realize that their companies will probably be buffeted by similar crises fairly regularly. Most students are familiar with the bursting of the dot-com bubble in the early part of this century, for example, which caused a severe drop in the stock market and affected companies around the globe. The Asian financial crisis of 1997–1998 similarly affected firms in North America, Europe, and other parts of the world. In 2010, Greece's inability to make payments on its debt sparked a panic that devalued the euro and threatened the stability of financial markets worldwide. The crisis dissipated somewhat when the European Union came up with a bailout fund for Greece and other debt-laden countries similar to the bailout fund used to save U.S. banks in 2008. However, concerns that EU leaders weren't united or aggressive enough in their efforts to stem the crisis continued to roil the markets and hurt the share prices of global corporations such as GE, Caterpillar, and Boeing. The U.S. stock market, for example, continued to plummet even after the EU approved the rescue fund, because of fears that many Western governments are living too much on borrowed money that will be difficult to repay.[32]

Recent financial woes have left a number of countries reeling, as reflected in a "misery index" created by a Moody's economist and illustrated in Exhibit 3.6. The misery index adds

EXHIBIT

How Countries Are Bearing the Economic Crisis: Misery Index, 2010 Compared to 2000

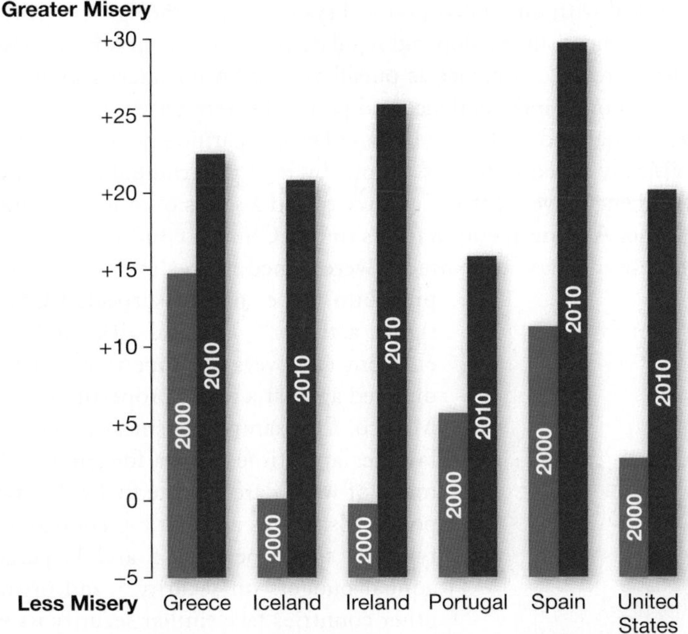

SOURCE: Based on "A New Definition of Misery," *The New York Times* (December 18, 2009), based on data from Moody's; http://www.nytimes.com/imagepages/2009/12/18/business/economy/20091219_CHARTS_GRAPHIC.html (accessed on December 19, 2009).

together a country's unemployment rate and the budget deficit as a percentage of gross domestic product (GDP). The estimated 2010 figures suggest significantly greater misery for almost every country, compared to the beginning of the century. Iceland and Ireland, two countries hit particularly hard by the recent economic crisis, had a negative misery index in 2000 but register high scores for misery in 2010. The United States went from a misery score of less than 5 in 2000 to about 21 in 2010.[33]

- Countries vary widely in terms of economic development and are classified as either developed countries or less-developed countries (LDCs).
- **Infrastructure** refers to a country's physical facilities such as highways, utilities, and airports that support economic activities.
- The United States recently fell out of first place on a ranking of global competitiveness.
- Managers who want to expand operations into another country evaluate the availability of raw materials and the market demand for their company's products and services.
- As recent financial crises in the United States and Europe show, countries are economically interconnected, and financial problems in one area of the world can rapidly spread around the globe.
- International business managers can expect their companies to be affected periodically by economic problems that cross geographical boundaries.

The Legal-Political Environment

Businesses must deal with unfamiliar political systems when they go international, as well as with more government supervision and regulation. Government officials and the general public often view foreign companies as outsiders or even intruders and are suspicious of their impact on economic independence and political sovereignty.

Political risk is defined as the risk of loss of assets, earning power, or managerial control due to politically based events or actions by host governments.[34] For example, National Security Agency investigators say they traced a series of online attacks on Google and dozens of other American corporations to two Chinese educational institutions with ties to the Chinese military. The attacks were aimed at stealing trade secrets and tapping into the e-mail of suspected Chinese human rights activists.[35] Political risk also includes government takeovers of property and acts of violence directed against a firm's properties or employees. In Mexico, for example, business executives and their families are prime targets for gangs of kidnappers, many of which are reportedly led by state and local police. Estimates are that big companies in Mexico typically spend between 5 and 15 percent of their annual budgets on security,[36] and organizations in other countries face similar security issues.

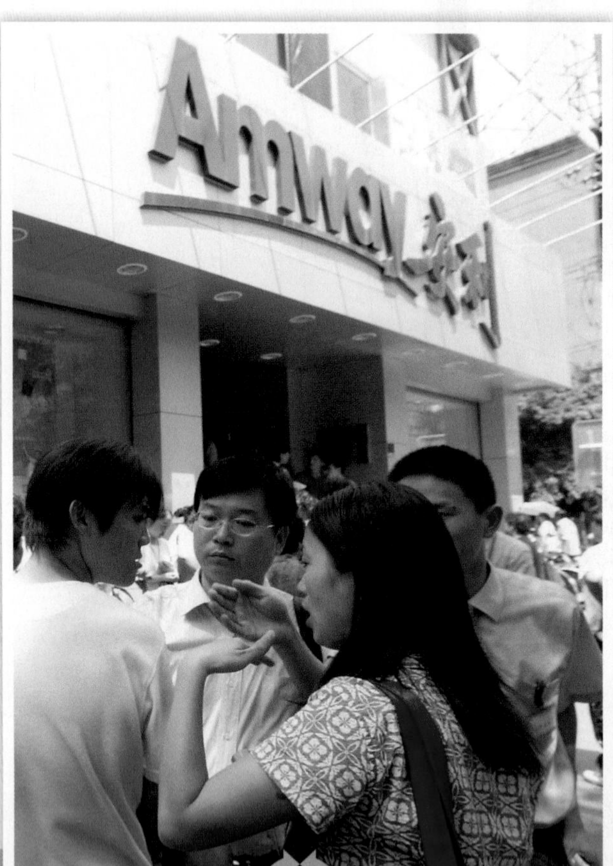

GOH CHAI HIN/AFP/Getty Images

ConceptConnection

In 2009, Amway realized $3 billion in revenue in China, making the country its top market. But the U.S.-based network marketing company had to spend years patiently negotiating China's **legal-political environment**. In 1998, the Chinese government closed down Amway operations because it suspected the company was either an illegal pyramid scheme or a sinister cult. Amway survived by cultivating relationships with government officials and by departing from its business model: for example, it ultimately opened over 200 retail stores, such as the one pictured here, to demonstrate its commitment. By 2006, the Chinese government once again allowed Amway to sell directly to consumers.

Another frequently cited problem for international companies is **political instability**, which includes riots, revolutions, civil disorders, and frequent changes in government. In recent decades, civil wars and large-scale violence occurred in the Ukraine, Kenya, Indonesia, Thailand, Sri Lanka (Ceylon), and Myanmar (Burma). China is highly vulnerable to periods of widespread public unrest due to the shifting political climate. The Middle East remains an area of extreme instability as the United States pursues a difficult and protracted reconstruction following the Iraqi war. U.S. firms or companies linked to the United States often are subject to major threats in countries characterized by political instability.

Differing laws and regulations also make doing business a challenge for international firms. Host governments have myriad laws concerning libel statutes, consumer protection, information and labeling, employment and safety, and wages. International companies must learn these rules and regulations and abide by them. In India, with its volatile mix of religions and ethnic politics, for example, government has the right to impose "reasonable restrictions" on free speech to maintain public order. Internet companies such as Yahoo, Facebook, and Twitter are required by law to comply with requests to take down content considered incendiary or else face fines and jail sentences.[37]

- Complicated legal and political forces can create huge risks for international managers and organizations.
- **Political risk** refers to a company's risk of loss of assets, earning power, or managerial control due to politically based events or actions by host governments.
- **Political instability** includes events such as riots, revolutions, or government upheavals that can affect the operations of an international company.
- Companies such as Google doing business in China have experienced the effects of political risk and political instability.
- Managers must understand and follow the differing laws and regulations in the various countries where they do business.

The Sociocultural Environment

A nation's culture includes the shared knowledge, beliefs, and values as well as the common modes of behavior and ways of thinking among members of a society. Cultural factors can sometimes be more perplexing than political and economic factors when working or living in a foreign country. Take the quiz in this chapter's Spotlight on Skills titled How Well Do You Play the Culture Game? to see how much you know about cross-cultural communication and etiquette.

Social Values

Many U.S. managers fail to realize that the values and behaviors that typically govern how business is done in the United States don't translate to the rest of the world. One way managers can get a handle on local cultures is to understand differences in social values.

Hofstede's Value Dimensions In research that included 116,000 IBM employees in 40 countries, Geert Hofstede identified four dimensions of national value systems that influence organizational and employee working relationships.[38] Examples of how countries rate on the four dimensions are shown in Exhibit 3.7.

1. ***Power distance.*** High **power distance** means that people accept inequality in power among institutions, organizations, and people. Low power distance means that people expect equality in power. Countries that value high power distance are Malaysia, the Philippines, and Panama. Countries that value low power distance are Denmark, Austria, and Israel.
2. ***Uncertainty avoidance.*** High **uncertainty avoidance** means that members of a society feel uncomfortable with uncertainty and ambiguity and thus support beliefs that promise certainty and conformity. Low uncertainty avoidance means that people have high tolerance for the unstructured, the unclear, and the unpredictable. High uncertainty avoidance countries include Greece, Portugal, and Uruguay. Countries with low uncertainty avoidance values are Singapore and Jamaica.
3. ***Individualism and collectivism.*** **Individualism** reflects a value for a loosely knit social framework in which individuals are expected to take care of themselves. **Collectivism** means a preference for a tightly knit social framework in which individuals look after one another and organizations protect their members'

EXHIBIT 3.7

Rank Orderings of Ten Countries along Four Dimensions of National Value Systems

Country	Power Distance[a]	Uncertainty Avoidance[b]	Individualism[c]	Masculinity[d]
Australia	7	7	2	5
Costa Rica	8 (tie)	2 (tie)	10	9
France	3	2 (tie)	4	7
West Germany	8 (tie)	5	5	3
India	2	9	6	6
Japan	5	1	7	1
Mexico	1	4	8	2
Sweden	10	10	3	10
Thailand	4	6	9	8
United States	6	8	1	4

a 1 = highest power distance
10 = lowest power distance

b 1 = highest uncertainty avoidance
10 = lowest uncertainty avoidance

c 1 = highest individualism
10 = lowest individualism

d 1 = highest masculinity
10 = lowest masculinity

SOURCES: Dorothy Marcic, *Organizational Behavior and Cases*, 4th ed. (St. Paul, MN: West, 1995). Based on two books by Geert Hofstede: Culture's Consequences (London: Sage Publications, 1984) and *Cultures and Organizations: Software of the Mind* (New York: McGraw-Hill, 1991).

interests. Countries with individualist values include the United States, Canada, Great Britain, and Australia. Countries with collectivist values are Guatemala, Ecuador, and China.

Read the Ethical Dilemma, on page 123, that pertains to social and cultural differences.

4. ***Masculinity/femininity.*** **Masculinity** stands for preference for achievement, heroism, assertiveness, work centrality (with resultant high stress), and material success. **Femininity** reflects the values of relationships, cooperation, group decision making, and quality of life. Societies with strong masculine values are Japan, Austria, Mexico, and Germany. Countries with feminine values are Sweden, Norway, Denmark, and France. Both men and women subscribe to the dominant value in masculine and feminine cultures.

Hofstede and his colleagues later identified a fifth dimension, long-term orientation versus short-term orientation. The **long-term orientation**, found in China and other Asian countries, includes a greater concern for the future and highly values thrift and perseverance. A **short-term orientation**, found in Russia and West Africa, is more concerned with the past and the present and places a high value on tradition and meeting social obligations.[39] Researchers continue to explore and expand on Hofstede's findings. For example, in the last 25 years, more than 1,400 articles and numerous books were published on individualism and collectivism alone.[40]

GLOBE Project Value Dimensions Recent research by the Global Leadership and Organizational Behavior Effectiveness (GLOBE) Project extends Hofstede's

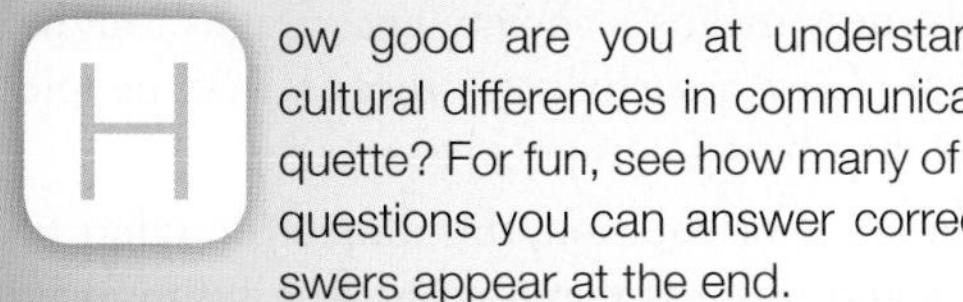

How Well Do You Play the Culture Game?

How good are you at understanding cross-cultural differences in communication and etiquette? For fun, see how many of the following questions you can answer correctly. The answers appear at the end.

1. You want to do business with a Greek company, but the representative insists on examining every detail of your proposal for several hours. This time-consuming detail means that the Greek representative:
   a. Doesn't trust the accuracy of your proposal.
   b. Is being polite, and really doesn't want to go ahead with the deal.
   c. Is signaling you to consider a more reasonable offer, but doesn't want to ask directly.
   d. Is uncomfortable with detailed proposals and would prefer a simple handshake.
   e. Is showing good manners and respect to you and your proposal.
2. Male guests in many Latin American countries often give their visitors an *abrazzo* when greeting them. An *abrazzo* is:
   a. A light kiss on the nose.
   b. A special gift, usually wine or food.
   c. Clapping hands in the air as the visitor approaches.
   d. A strong embrace, or kiss with hand on shoulder.
   e. A firm two-handed handshake, lasting almost one minute.
3. Japanese clients visit you at your office for a major meeting. Where should the top Japanese official be seated?
   a. Closest to the door
   b. As close to the middle of the room as possible
   c. Anywhere in the room; seating location isn't important to Japanese businesspeople
   d. Somewhere away from the door with a piece of artwork behind him or her
   e. Always beside rather than facing the host
4. One of the most universal gestures is:
   a. A pat on the back (congratulations).
   b. A smile (happiness or politeness).
   c. Scratching your chin (thinking).
   d. Closing your eyes (boredom).
   e. Arm up, shaking back and forth (waving).
5. While visiting a German client, you compliment the client on his beautiful pen set. What will probably happen?
   a. The client will insist very strongly that you take it.
   b. The client will tell you where to buy such a pen set at a good price.
   c. The client will accept the compliment and get on with business.
   d. The client will probably get upset that you aren't paying attention to the business at hand.
   e. The client will totally ignore the comment.
6. Managers from which country are least likely to tolerate someone being 5 minutes late for an appointment?
   a. United States
   b. Australia
   c. Brazil
   d. Sweden
   e. Saudi Arabia
7. In which of the following countries are office arrangements *not* usually an indicator of the person's status?
   a. United Kingdom
   b. Germany
   c. Saudi Arabia
   d. China
   e. United States
8. In many Asian cultures, a direct order such as "Get me the AmEx report" is most likely to be given by:
   a. Senior management to most subordinates.
   b. A junior employee to a peer.
   c. Senior management only to very junior employees.
   d. Junior employees to outsiders.
   e. None of the above
9. In the United States, scratching one's head usually means that the person is confused or skeptical. In Russia, it means:
   a. "You're crazy!"
   b. "I am listening carefully."
   c. "I want to get to know you better."
   d. "I'm confused or skeptical."
   e. None of the above
10. A polite way to give your business card to a Japanese businessperson is:
    a. Casually, after several hours of getting to know the person.
    b. When first meeting, presenting your card with both hands.
    c. At the very end of the first meeting.
    d. Casually during the meeting, with the information down to show humility.
    e. Never; it is considered rude in Japan to give business cards.

SOURCES: Steven L. McShane and Mary Ann Von Glinow, *Organizational Behavior: Emerging Realities for the Workplace Revolution*, 3rd ed. (New York: McGraw-Hill/Irwin, 2004); "Cross-Cultural Communication Game," developed by Steven L. McShane, based on material in R. Axtell, *Gestures: The Do's and Taboos of Body Language around the World* (New York: Wiley, 1991); R. Mead, *Cross-Cultural Management Communication* (Chichester, UK: Wiley, 1990), Chapter 7;and J. V. Thill and C. L. Bovée, *Excellence in Business Communication* (New York: McGraw-Hill, 1995), Chapter 17.

Answers
1. e; 2. d; 3. d; 4. b; 5. c; 6. d; 7. c; 8. c; 9. d; 10. b

assessment and offers a broader understanding for today's managers. The GLOBE Project used data collected from 18,000 managers in 62 countries to identify nine dimensions that explain cultural differences. In addition to the ones identified by Hofstede, the GLOBE project identifies the following characteristics:[41]

1. ***Assertiveness.*** A high value on assertiveness means a society encourages toughness, assertiveness, and competitiveness. Low assertiveness means that people value tenderness and concern for others over being competitive.
2. ***Future orientation.*** Similar to Hofstede's time orientation, this dimension refers to the extent to which a society encourages and rewards planning for the future over short-term results and quick gratification.
3. ***Gender differentiation.*** This dimension refers to the extent to which a society maximizes gender role differences. In countries with low gender differentiation, such as Denmark, women typically have higher status and a stronger role in decision making. Countries with high gender differentiation accord men higher social, political, and economic status.
4. ***Performance orientation.*** A society with a high performance orientation places high emphasis on performance and rewards people for performance improvements and excellence. A low performance orientation means people pay less attention to performance and more attention to loyalty, belonging, and background.
5. ***Humane orientation.*** The final dimension refers to the degree to which a society encourages and rewards people for being fair, altruistic, generous, and caring. A country high on humane orientation places high value on helping others and being kind. A country low on this orientation expects people to take care of themselves. Self-enhancement and gratification are of high importance.

Exhibit 3.8 gives examples of how some countries rank on these GLOBE dimensions. These dimensions give managers an added tool for identifying and managing cultural

3.8 EXHIBIT

Examples of Country Rankings on Selected GLOBE Value Dimensions

Dimension	Low	Medium	High
Assertiveness	Sweden Switzerland Japan	Egypt Iceland France	Spain United States Germany (former East)
Future Orientation	Russia Italy Kuwait	Slovenia Australia India	Denmark Canada Singapore
Gender Differentiation	Sweden Denmark Poland	Italy Brazil Netherlands	South Korea Egypt China
Performance Orientation	Russia Greece Venezuela	Israel England Japan	United States Taiwan Hong Kong
Humane Orientation	Germany France Singapore	New Zealand Sweden United States	Indonesia Egypt Iceland

SOURCE: Mansour Javidan and Robert J. House, "Cultural Acumen for the Global Manager: Lessons from Project GLOBE," *Organizational Dynamics* 29, no. 4 (2001): 289–305, with permission from Elsevier.

differences. Social values greatly influence organizational functioning and management styles. Consider the difficulty that managers encountered when implementing self-directed work teams in Mexico. As shown in Exhibit 3.7, Mexico is characterized by very high power distance and a relatively low tolerance for uncertainty, characteristics that often conflict with the American concept of teamwork, which emphasizes shared power and authority, with team members working on a variety of problems without formal guidelines, rules, and structure. Many workers in Mexico, as well as in France and Mediterranean countries, expect organizations to be hierarchical. In Russia, people are good at working in groups and like competing as a team rather than on an individual basis. Organizations in Germany and other central European countries typically strive to be impersonal, well-oiled machines. Effective management styles differ in each country, depending on cultural characteristics.[42]

- Hofstede's sociocultural value dimensions measure power distance, uncertainty avoidance, individualism–collectivism, and masculinity–femininity.
- **Power distance** is the degree to which people accept inequality in power among institutions, organizations, and people.
- **Uncertainty avoidance** is characterized by people's intolerance for uncertainty and ambiguity and the resulting support for beliefs that promise certainty and conformity.
- **Individualism** refers to a preference for a loosely knit social framework in which individuals are expected to take care of themselves.
- **Collectivism** refers to a preference for a tightly knit social framework in which individuals look after one another and organizations protect their members' interests.
- **Masculinity** is a cultural preference for achievement, heroism, assertiveness, work centrality, and material success.
- **Femininity** is a cultural preference for relationships, cooperation, group decision making, and quality of life.
- Hofstede later identified another dimension: **long-term orientation**, which reflects a greater concern for the future and a high value on thrift and perseverance, versus **short-term orientation**, which reflects a concern with the past and present and a high value on meeting current obligations.
- Value dimensions recently identified by Project GLOBE are assertiveness, future orientation, gender differentiation, performance orientation, and humane orientation.

Communication Differences

People from some cultures tend to pay more attention to the social context (social setting, nonverbal behavior, social status) of their verbal communication than Americans do. For example, American managers working in China have discovered that social context is considerably more important in that culture, and they need to learn to suppress their impatience and devote the time necessary to establish personal and social relationships.

Exhibit 3.9 indicates how the emphasis on social context varies among countries. In a **high-context culture**, people are sensitive to circumstances surrounding social exchanges. People use communication primarily to build personal social relationships; meaning is derived from context—setting, status, and nonverbal behavior—more than from explicit words; relationships and trust are more important than business; and the welfare and harmony of the group are valued. In a **low-context culture**, people use communication primarily to exchange facts and information; meaning is derived primarily from words; business transactions are more important than building relationships and trust; and individual welfare and achievement are more important than the group.[43]

SPOTLIGHT ON SKILLS

Communication Skills Abroad

No country can be isolated from the rest of the world. This means managers in today's business world need language skills and must also know how to communicate when cultures have different standards and norms. When this is not the case, mistakes are made—mistakes which could have been avoided. When managers are prepared and trained for cross-cultural interactions, studies show their productivity increases by 30 percent.

The manager's attitude is perhaps the most important factor in success. Those who go abroad with a sense of wonder about the new culture are better off than those with a judgmental view that implies, "If it is different, then my culture must be better." Such evaluations lead to an "us versus them" approach, which never sits well with the locals. Seeing differences as new and interesting by *appreciating* rather than *evaluating* cultural differences is more productive than being critical. One of the keys to cultural adaptation is open-mindedness, being able to respect other points of view.

Although every culture has its own way of communicating, here are some basic principles to follow in international business relations:

1. Always show respect and listen carefully. Don't be in a hurry to finish the "business." Many cultures value the social component of these interactions.
2. Try to gain an appreciation for the differences between Hofstede's "masculine" and "feminine" cultures. American masculine business behaviors include high achievement and acquisition of material goods and efficiency, whereas more-feminine cultures value relationships, leisure time with family, and developing a sense of community. Don't mistake this more feminine approach with lack of motivation. Similarly, cultures that value "being" and inner spiritual development, rather than compulsively "doing," are not necessarily inferior.
3. Try hard not to feel that your way is best. This can come across as arrogance and rubs salt in deep wounds in some lesser-developed countries.
4. Emphasize points of agreement.
5. When there are disagreements, check on the perceived definitions of words. Often there may be a huge or subtle shade of meaning that is causing the problem. Two people may both actually be trying to say the same thing.
6. Save face and "give" face as well, for this can be a way of showing honor to others.
7. Don't go alone. Take someone who knows the culture or language better than you do. If the discussion is in English and the others "know" the language, you might be surprised how much they miss. Often taking an excellent translator along is a good investment.
8. Don't assume the other country views leadership the same way that you do. In many other cultures, "empowerment" seems more like anarchy and the result of an ineffectual manager.
9. Don't lose your temper.
10. Don't embarrass anyone in front of others. Even if you "meant it as a joke," it likely won't be taken that way.
11. Avoid clique building and try to interact with the locals as much as possible. Often, Americans tend to hang together in packs or tribes, which is not welcoming to the locals.
12. Be aware that most Asian countries are "high-context cultures" based on a complicated system of relationships and moral codes (some of which may not mesh with your own morals), whereas the United States is "low-context," meaning people are more direct and rely on legal codes.
13. Leave the common American task-oriented, fast-paced style at home. Effective transfer of skills to other cultures requires patient nonjudgment. Hasty criticisms of foreign ideas only serves to shut people down and close the door to meaningful interactions.
14. However, be aware that some countries, such as Israel, are even more fast paced, and people there get impatient with American "small talk."
15. Also be sensitive to the difference between the North American low-context culture, where employees are encouraged to be self-reliant, and high-context cultures (much of Asia, Africa, South America), where workers expect warmly supportive relationships with their American supervisors and coworkers.
16. If you travel to the increasingly visited "out-of-the-way" locations, learn to tolerate unpredictability and go without what you may consider basic amenities. Avoid complaining to business clients about poor phone service, lack of hot (or any, for that matter) water, erratic availability of electricity, or unsavory food. Just remember, you are a guest and should act graciously as such.

SOURCES: Pranee Chitakomkijsil, "Intercultural Communication Challenges and Multinational Organizational Communication," *International Journal of Organizational Innovation* 3, no. 2 (Fall 2010): 6–21; and "Competency of Intercultural Management," *The Jakarta Post*, March 11, 2009.

EXHIBIT 3.9

High-Context and Low-Context Cultures

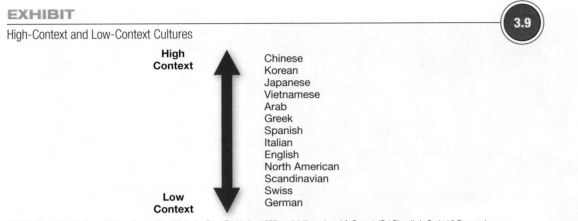

High Context	Chinese
	Korean
	Japanese
	Vietnamese
	Arab
	Greek
	Spanish
	Italian
	English
	North American
	Scandinavian
	Swiss
Low Context	German

SOURCE: Edward T. Hall, *Beyond Culture* (Garden City, NY: Anchor Press/Doubleday, 1976); and J. Kennedy and A. Everest, "Put Diversity in Context," *Personnel Journal* (September 1991): 50–54.

To understand how differences in cultural context affect communications, consider the U.S. expression "The squeaky wheel gets the oil." It means that the loudest person will get the most attention, and attention is assumed to be favorable. Equivalent sayings in China and Japan are "Quacking ducks get shot," and "The nail that sticks up gets hammered down," respectively. Standing out as an individual in these cultures merits unfavorable attention. Consider what happened after China's Lenovo Group acquired IBM's PC business. In meetings and conference calls, Western executives were frustrated by their Chinese counterparts' reluctance to speak up, whereas the Chinese managers were irritated by the Americans propensity to "just talk and talk," as one vice president of human resources put it.[44]

Refer to your score on the New Manager Self-Test on page 93, which will give you some insight into whether you lean toward low-context or high-context communications. A higher score indicates low-context behavior, which would clash when trying to do business in a high-context culture.

High-context cultures include Asian and Arab countries. Low-context cultures tend to be American and Northern European. Even within North America, cultural subgroups vary in the extent to which context counts, explaining why differences among groups can hinder successful communication. White females, Native Americans, and African Americans all tend to prefer higher context communication than do white males. A high-context interaction requires more time because a relationship has to be developed, and trust and friendship must be established. Furthermore, most male managers and most people doing the hiring in organizations are from low-context cultures, which conflicts with people entering the organization from a background in a higher context culture.

Other Cultural Characteristics

Other cultural characteristics that influence international organizations are language, religion, social organization, education, and attitudes. Some countries, such as India, are characterized by *linguistic pluralism*, meaning that several languages exist there. Other countries rely heavily on spoken versus written language. Religion includes sacred objects, philosophical attitudes toward life, taboos, and rituals. Social organization includes such matters as status systems, kinship and families, social institutions, and opportunities for social mobility. Education influences the literacy level, the availability of qualified employees, and the predominance of primary or secondary degrees.

Attitudes toward achievement, work, and people can all affect organizational productivity. For example, one study found that the prevalent American attitude that treats employees as a resource to be used (an *instrumental* attitude toward people) can be a strong impediment to business success in countries where people are valued as an end in

Kiyoshi Ota/Getty Images

ConceptConnection

Pictured at a traditional Japanese ceremony is Hiroshi Mikitani (second from right), Rakuten Inc.'s founder and CEO. Tokyo-based Rakuten is an Internet group that includes Rakuten Marketplace, a flourishing e-commerce site. In keeping with Rakuten's ambitious global expansion plans, Mikitani announced that all board meetings, strategy discussions, and weekly employee gatherings will be in English, the most commonly used language in international business. As Rakuten expands, managers from Japan's **high-context culture**, where communication is used to build relationships, must not only become proficient in a foreign language but also learn to communicate effectively with managers from **low-context cultures**, where communication is used primarily to conduct business.

themselves rather than as a means to an end (a *humanistic* attitude). U.S. companies sometimes use instrumental human resource policies that conflict with local humanistic values.[45] Attitudes toward time can also be quite different in different parts of the world. One U.S. executive newly working in Dubai was shocked when a group of executives with more experience in the region arrived at a meeting several hours late. In Arab cultures, time has more fluidity, and schedules are much more flexible than in the clock-driven world of corporate America.[46]

Ethnocentrism, which refers to a natural tendency of people to regard their own culture as superior and to downgrade or dismiss other cultural values, can be found in all countries. Strong ethnocentric attitudes within a country make it difficult for foreign firms to operate there. American managers are regularly accused of an ethnocentric attitude that assumes the American way is the best way.

Developing Cultural Intelligence

Before reading the next, find out your CQ (cultural intelligence) by answering the items in the New Manager Self-Test, on page 113. Your answers will indicate your level of cultural intelligence and help you relate to the concepts that follow.

Managers will be most successful in foreign assignments if they are culturally flexible and able to adapt easily to new situations and ways of doing things. In other words, managers working internationally need cultural intelligence. **Cultural intelligence (CQ)** refers to a person's ability to use reasoning and observation skills to interpret unfamiliar gestures and situations and devise appropriate behavioral responses.[47] Consider what Pat McGovern does whenever he travels to a foreign country. McGovern is the founder and CEO of IDG, a technology publishing and research firm in Massachusetts that owns magazines such as *CIO* and *Computerworld*. IDG operates in 85 countries and gets 80 percent of profits from outside the United States. When McGovern goes to a country for the first time, he spends the weekend just wandering around observing people. By watching how people in a foreign country behave, McGovern says he gets a sense of the culture—how fast people walk, how much they gesture, what they wear, how the treat one another.[48] McGovern believes you can be in sync anywhere if you pay attention.

5

Cultural intelligence includes three components that work together: cognitive, emotional, and physical.[49] The cognitive component involves a person's observational and learning skills and the ability to pick up on clues to understanding. The emotional aspect concerns one's self-confidence and self-motivation. A manager has to believe in his or her ability to understand and assimilate into a different culture. Difficulties and setbacks are triggers to work harder, not a cause to give up. Working in a foreign environment is stressful, and most managers in foreign assignments face a period of homesickness, loneliness, and culture shock from being suddenly immersed in a culture with completely different languages, foods, values, beliefs, and ways of doing things. **Culture shock** refers to the frustration and anxiety that result from constantly being subjected to strange and unfamiliar

New Manager Self-Test

Are You Culturally Intelligent?

The job of a manager demands a lot, and before long your activities will include situations that will test your knowledge and capacity for dealing with people from other national cultures. Are you ready? To find out, think about your experiences in other countries or with people from other countries. To what extent does each of the following statements characterize your behavior? Please answer each of the following items as Mostly True or Mostly False for you.

	MOSTLY TRUE <<<	>>> MOSTLY FALSE
1. I plan how I'm going to relate to people from a different culture before I meet them.	______	______
2. I understand the religious beliefs of other cultures.	______	______
3. I understand the rules for nonverbal behavior in other cultures.	______	______
4. I seek out opportunities to interact with people from different cultures.	______	______
5. I can handle the stresses of living in a different culture with relative ease.	______	______
6. I am confident that I can befriend locals in a culture that is unfamiliar to me.	______	______
7. I change my speech style (e.g., accent, tone) when a cross-cultural interaction requires it.	______	______
8. I alter my facial expressions and gestures as needed to facilitate a cross-cultural interaction.	______	______
9. I am quick to change the way I behave when a cross-cultural encounter seems to require it.	______	______

See It Online

Scoring and Interpretation: Each item pertains to some aspect of cultural intelligence. Items 1–3 pertain to the head (*cognitive CQ* subscale); items 4–6, to the heart (*emotional CQ* subscale); and items 7–9, to behavior (*physical CQ* subscale). If you have sufficient international experience and CQ to have answered Mostly True to two of three items for each subscale, or six of nine for all the items, then consider yourself at a high level of CQ for a new manager. If you scored one or fewer Mostly True on each subscale or three or fewer for all nine items, it is time to learn more about other national cultures. Hone your observational skills and learn to pick up on clues about how people from a different country respond to various situations.

SOURCES: Based on P. Christopher Earley and Elaine Mosakowski, "Cultural Intelligence," *Harvard Business Review* (October 2004): 139–146; Soon Ang et al., "Cultural Intelligence: Its Measurement and Effects on Cultural Judgment and Decision Making, Cultural Adaptation and Task Performance," *Management and Organization Review* 3 (2007): 335–371.

cues about what to do and how to do it. A person with high CQ is able to move quickly through this initial period of culture shock.

The third component of CQ, the physical, refers to a person's ability to shift his or her speech patterns, expressions, and body language to be in tune with people from a different culture. Most managers aren't equally strong in all three areas, but maximizing cultural

Go to the Group Learning, on pages 121–122, that pertains to exposure to entrepreneurial conditions around the world.

intelligence requires that they draw upon all three facets. In a sense, CQ requires that the head, heart, and body work in concert.

High CQ also requires that a manager be open and receptive to new ideas and approaches. For example, the Dutch have to learn English, German, and French, as well as Dutch, to interact and trade with their economically dominant neighbors. English Canadians must not only be well versed in American culture and politics, but they also have to consider the views and ideas of French Canadians, who, in turn, must learn to think like North Americans, members of a global French community, Canadians, and Quebecois.[50] People in the United States who have grown up without this kind of language and cultural diversity typically have more difficulties with foreign assignments, but willing managers from any country can learn to open their minds and appreciate other viewpoints.

- A **high-context culture** is one in which people use communication to build personal relationships.
- In a **low-context culture**, people use communication primarily to exchange facts and information.
- The United States is a low-context culture. China is an example of a high-context culture.
- Managers working internationally should guard against **ethnocentrism**, which is the natural tendency among people to regard their own culture as superior to others.
- Managers who develop cultural intelligence are more successful in international assignments.
- **Cultural intelligence (CQ)** refers to a person's ability to use reasoning and observation to interpret culturally unfamiliar situations and know how to respond appropriately.
- Managers working in foreign countries often experience **culture shock**, feelings of confusion, disorientation, and anxiety that result from being constantly confronted with unfamiliar cues about how to behave.

International Trade Alliances

One of the most visible changes in the international business environment in recent years has been the development of regional trading alliances and international trade agreements.

GATT and the World Trade Organization

The General Agreement on Tariffs and Trade (GATT), signed by 23 nations in 1947, started as a set of rules to ensure nondiscrimination, clear procedures, the negotiation of disputes, and the participation of lesser-developed countries in international trade.[51] GATT sponsored eight rounds of international trade negotiations aimed at reducing trade restrictions. The 1986 to 1994 Uruguay Round (the first to be named for a developing country) involved 125 countries and cut more tariffs than ever before. In addition to lowering tariffs 30 percent from the previous level, it boldly moved the world closer to global free trade by calling for the establishment of the World Trade Organization (WTO).

The WTO represents the maturation of GATT into a permanent global institution that can monitor international trade and has legal authority to arbitrate disputes on some 400 trade issues. As of July 2008, 153 countries, including China, Vietnam, and Ukraine, were members of the WTO. As a permanent membership organization, the WTO is bringing greater trade liberalization in goods, information, technological developments, and services; stronger enforcement of rules and regulations; and greater power to resolve disputes among trading partners.

European Union

An alliance begun in 1957 to improve economic and social conditions among its members, the European Economic Community has evolved into the 27-nation European Union (EU) illustrated in Exhibit 3.10. The biggest expansion came in 2004, when the EU welcomed ten new members from central and eastern Europe.[52]

The goal of the EU is to create a powerful single market system for Europe's millions of consumers, allowing people, goods, and services to move freely. The increased competition and economies of scale within Europe enable companies to grow large and efficient, becoming more competitive in the United States and other world markets.

Another aspect of significance to countries operating globally is the introduction of the euro. Sixteen member states of the EU have adopted the **euro**, a single European currency that replaced national currencies in Austria, Belgium, Cyprus, Finland, France, Germany, Greece, Ireland, Italy, Luxembourg, Malta, the Netherlands, Portugal, Slovakia, Slovenia, and Spain.[53] The implications of a single European currency are enormous, within as well as outside Europe. Because it potentially replaces up to 27 European domestic currencies, the

EXHIBIT 3.10

The Nations of the European Union

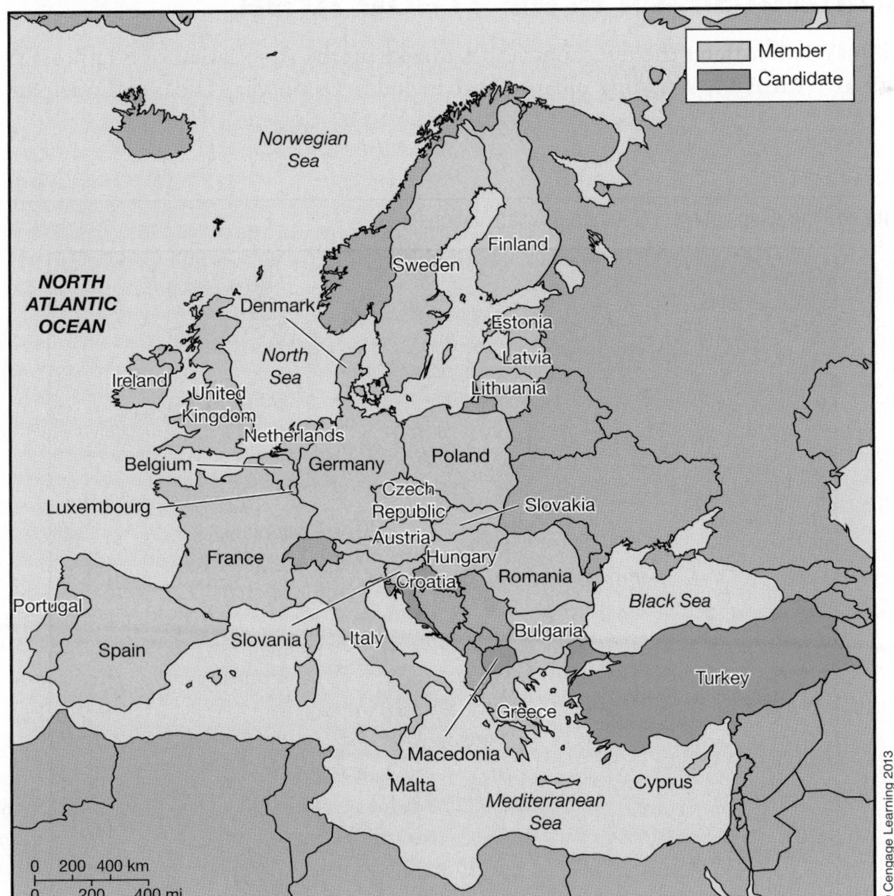

euro will affect legal contracts, financial management, sales and marketing tactics, manufacturing, distribution, payroll, pensions, training, taxes, and information management systems.

North American Free Trade Agreement (NAFTA)

The North American Free Trade Agreement (NAFTA), which went into effect on January 1, 1994, merged the United States, Canada, and Mexico into a single market. Intended to spur growth and investment, increase exports, and expand jobs in all three nations, NAFTA broke down tariffs and trade restrictions over a 15-year-period in a number of key areas. Thus, by 2008, virtually all U.S. industrial exports into Canada and Mexico were duty free.

Over the first decade of NAFTA, U.S. trade with Mexico increased more than threefold, while trade with Canada also rose dramatically.[54] Significantly, NAFTA spurred the entry of small businesses into the global arena. Jeff Victor, general manager of Treatment Products, Ltd., which makes car cleaners and waxes, credits NAFTA for his surging export volume. Prior to the pact, Mexican tariffs as high as 20 percent made it impossible for the Chicago-based company to expand its presence south of the border.[55]

However, opinions over the benefits of NAFTA appear to be as divided as they were when talks began, with some people calling it a spectacular success and others referring to it as a dismal failure.[56] Although NAFTA has not lived up to its grand expectations, experts stress that it increased trade, investment, and income and continues to enable companies in all three countries to compete more effectively with rival Asian and European firms.[57]

China–ASEAN Free Trade Area

Exhibit 3.11 illustrates the ten countries that make up the Association of Southeast Asian Nations (ASEAN), a trading alliance that includes Cambodia, Laos, and Vietnam. In

3.11 EXHIBIT

China and the Association of Southeast Asian Nations

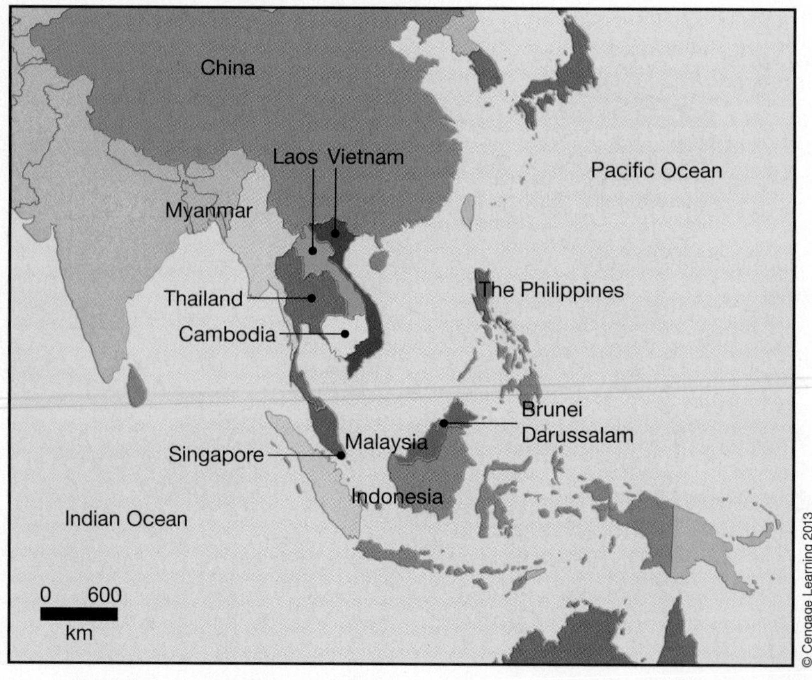

January of 2010, China joined with these ten countries to form the China–ASEAN Free Trade Area, the world's third largest free-trade area behind the EU and NAFTA.[58] This new free trade area, encompassing 1.9 billion people and $45 trillion in trade, will remove all tariffs between China and ASEAN member countries by 2015, with China, Indonesia, Thailand, the Philippines, Malaysia, Singapore, and Brunei expected to remove all tariffs in 2010. Trade between China and the ASEAN nations has soared to more than $190 billion annually, making China ASEAN's third largest trading partner behind Japan and the EU (the United States is the fourth largest, with more than $180 billion in trade).[59]

- Regional trading alliances and international trade agreements are significantly shaping global business.
- The World Trade Organization is a permanent membership organization that monitors trade and has authority to arbitrate disputes among 153 member countries.
- Three important regional trade agreements are the European Union (EU), the North American Free Trade Agreement (NAFTA), and the China-ASEAN Free Trade Area.
- The **euro** is a single European currency that has replaced the currencies of 16 EU member nations.

International Issues

The Globalization Backlash

The size and power of multinationals, combined with the growth of free trade agreements, has sparked a backlash over globalization. In a *Fortune* magazine poll, 68 percent of Americans say other countries benefit the most from free trade, and a 2010 survey by *The Wall Street Journal* and NBC News found that 53 percent of Americans surveyed said free trade has actually hurt the United States. That figure is up from 46 percent in 2007 and 32 percent in 1999. The sentiment is reflected in other countries such as Germany, France, and even India. "For some reason, everyone thinks they are the loser," said former U.S. trade representative Mickey Kantor.[60]

In the United States, the primary concern is the loss of jobs as companies expand their offshoring activities by exporting more and more work overseas. The transfer of jobs such as making shoes, clothing, and toys began decades ago. Today, services and knowledge work are rapidly moving to developing countries. An analyst at Forrester Research Inc. predicts

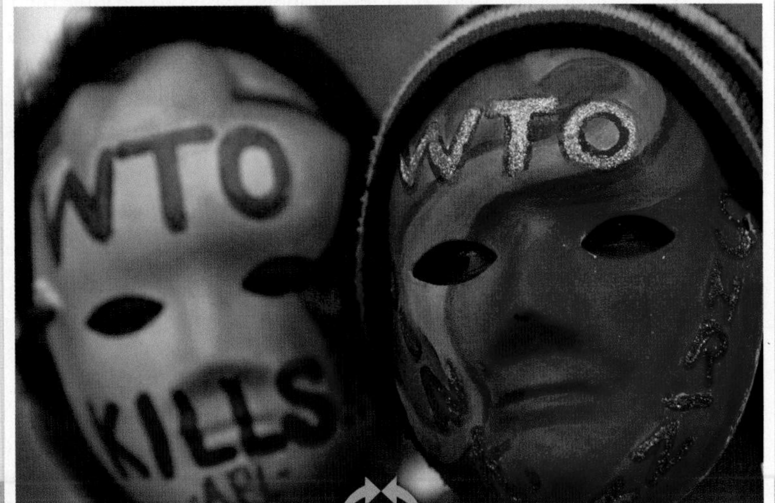

AP Photo/Mike Alquinto

ConceptConnection

As the world becomes more interconnected, a **globalization backlash** has developed. On November 30, 2009, the tenth anniversary of the first anti–World Trade Organization (WTO) protests that took place in Seattle, Filipino activists rallied at the Mendiola Bridge in Manila. On the same day, 153 members assembled in Geneva for the 7th WTO Ministerial Meeting. WTO opponents claim the organization benefits large corporations while harming farmers, workers, and others. In the process, they say, the global institution subverts the cause of economic, social, and environmental justice.

that at least 3.3 million mostly white-collar jobs and $136 billion in wages will shift from the United States to low-wage countries by 2015.[61] Many American shoppers say they'd be willing to pay higher prices to keep down foreign competition.[62]

Business leaders, meanwhile, insist that economic benefits flow back to the U.S. economy in the form of lower prices, expanded markets, and increased profits that can fund innovation.[63] Some American companies are clearly benefiting from free trade. When Kalexsyn, a small chemistry research company in Kalamazoo, Michigan, couldn't get contracts with major U.S. pharmaceutical companies that were sending work to India and China, the owners found that European companies were eager to outsource chemical research to the United States.[64] Yet the anti-globalization fervor is just getting hotter—and is not likely to dissipate anytime soon. In the end, it is not whether globalization is good or bad, but how business and government managers can work together to ensure that the advantages of a global world are fully and fairly shared.

Serving the Bottom of the Pyramid

Although large, multinational organizations are accused of many negative contributions to society, they also have the resources needed to do good things in the world. One approach that combines business with social responsibility is referred to as *serving the bottom of the pyramid.*

The **bottom of the pyramid (BOP)** concept proposes that corporations can alleviate poverty and other social ills, as well as make significant profits, by selling to the world's poorest people. The term *bottom of the pyramid* refers to the more than 4 billion people who make up the lowest level of the world's economic "pyramid" as defined by per capita income. These people earn less than US$1,500 a year, with about one-fourth of them earning less than a dollar a day.[65] Traditionally, these people haven't been served by most large businesses because products and services are too expensive, inaccessible, and not suited to their needs. A number of leading companies are changing that by adopting BOP business models geared to serving the poorest of the world's consumers. Nokia, for instance, has captured 40 percent of the global cell phone handset market, and 66 percent of the market in Africa, by making phones that are affordable to people in places like Lagos and Calcutta who earn just a few dollars a day.[66] Although the BOP concept has gained significant attention recently, the basic idea is nothing new. Here's an example of a company that has been practicing bottom of the pyramid activities for more than a hundred years.

UNILEVER/ HINDUSTAN LEVER

The World Health Organization estimates that diarrhea-related illnesses kill more than 1.8 million people a year. One way to prevent the spread of these diseases is better hand-washing, and marketing managers for Lifebuoy soap are trying to make sure people know that fact.

British soap maker Lever Brothers (now the global organization Unilever) introduced Lifebuoy to India more than a century ago, promoting it as the enemy of dirt and disease. The basic approach today is the same. Several years ago, the company's India subsidiary, Hindustan Lever Limited, introduced a campaign called *Swasthya Chetna* (Glowing Health), sending Lifebuoy teams into rural villages with a "glo-germ kit" to show people that even clean-looking hands can carry dangerous germs—and that soap-washed hands don't.

Sales of Lifebuoy have risen sharply since the campaign, aided by the introduction of a smaller-size bar that costs five rupees (about 12 cents). Just as importantly, says Hindustan Lever's chairman Harish Manwani, the campaign has reached around 80 million of the rural poor with education about how to prevent needless deaths.[67]

BENCHMARKING

Reality TV Afghanistan

Anna Elliot first visited Afghanistan in 2007 as a Hampshire College student, when she went to visit her international-aid-worker father. She saw dignified and gracious people who were trying desperately to overcome the ravages of a protracted war, with shortages in electricity, health care, and jobs. How could she help? she wondered. Why not start a Donald Trump–like reality business competition? Why not, indeed?

As part of her undergraduate design-your-own major, she traveled back to Kabul and got local sponsors for "Dream & Achieve," first broadcast in 2008, with the goal of inspiring and educating people to lift the country out of poverty by starting socially responsible businesses. That first year, the finalists included a sustainable fish farmer, a milk refrigeration venture, a rice miller, saffron growers and apricot dryers. Each of the 20 runners-up got $5,000 worth of business development services, including plane tickets and mobile phones. Economics student Sohaila Vahidi won third place with a cotton-growing plan as an alternative to growing opium. Her prize: a $10,000 scholarship. Second place and a $10,000 business start-up grant went to Maryam Al Ahmadi for her company to employ refugees and widows to make artisan pickles and jams. First prize of $20,000 went to Faivulhaq Moshkani, who has already used the money to start a plastics recycling company.

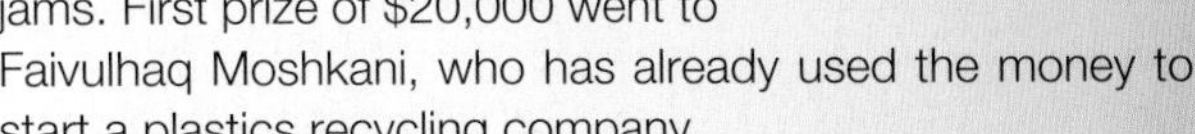

"Dream & Achieve" captured 7 million viewers that first season. Anna feels she's accomplished her dream of a business reality show that looks at more than merely money in judging its winners. Elliot's new dream is to replicate "Dream & Achieve" around the world. Her business plan and the pilot series won her a $60,000 grant from the Echoing Green Foundation in New York.

Maybe she'll help more budding entrepreneurs around the world build socially responsible businesses like Ben & Jerry's or the Body Shop.

SOURCE: Lora Kolodny, "Bringing Reality TV Business Competition to Afghanistan," *The New York Times*, June 30, 2010, http://boss.blogs.nytimes.com/2010/07/01/social-entrepreneur-idol-do-good-reality-tv-in-afghanistan/#more-19643.

College student Anna Elliot found her own way to serve the bottom of the pyramid in Afghanistan, as shown in the Benchmarking box.

Numerous other companies are pushing strongly into emerging markets by offering products tailored to the poor. The British candy maker Cadbury, for instance, hopes to capture millions of new customers by offering chocolates that sell for a few pennies. Procter & Gamble has initiated educational efforts to get people in developing countries to use diapers and feminine hygiene products that sell at low prices.[68] Proponents of bottom of the pyramid thinking believe multinational corporations can contribute to positive lasting change when the profit motive goes hand in hand with the desire to make a contribution to humankind.

- The increasing size and power of multinational corporations and the growth of free trade agreements has sparked a globalization backlash.
- Multinational corporations have the resources to reach and serve the world's poorest people, who cannot afford the typical products and services offered by big companies.
- The **bottom of the pyramid (BOP)** concept proposes that corporations can alleviate poverty and other social ills, as well as make significant profits, by selling to the world's poor.

As a means of learning across borders, here is a poem that addresses cultural differences.

An Asian View of Cultural Difference

Eastern Perspective	Western Perspective
We live in time.	You live in space.
We are always at rest.	You are always on the move.
We are passive.	You are aggressive.
We like to contemplate.	You like to act.
We accept the world as it is.	You try to change the world according to your blueprint.
We live in peace with nature.	You try to impose your will in her.
Religion is our first love.	Technology is your passion.
We delight to think about the meaning of life.	You delight in physics.
We believe in freedom of silence.	You believe in freedom of speech.
We lapse into meditation.	You strive for articulation.
We marry first, then love.	You love first, then marry.
Our marriage is the beginning of a love affair.	Your marriage is the happy end of a romance.
It is an indissoluble bond.	It is a contract.
Our love is mute.	Your love is vocal.
We try to conceal it from the world.	You delight in showing it to others.
Self-denial is the secret to our survival.	Self-assertiveness is the key to your success.
We are taught from the cradle to want less and less.	You are urged every day to want more and more.
We glorify austerity and renunciation.	You emphasize gracious living and enjoyment.
In the sunset years of life we renounce the world and prepare for the hereafter.	You retire to enjoy the fruits of your labor.

SOURCE: Dr. Mai Van Trang, Indochinese Materials Center.

Discussion Questions

1. What specifically would the experience of living and working in another country contribute to your skills and effectiveness as a manager in your own country?
2. Do you think it is realistic that bottom of the pyramid business practices can have a positive effect on poverty and other social problems in developing countries? Discuss.
3. What do you think is your strongest component of cultural intelligence? Your weakest? How would you go about shoring up your weaknesses?
4. What opportunities are available to you and your classmates to increase your cultural intelligence and your ability to function in another country?
5. What steps could a company take to avoid making product design and marketing mistakes when introducing new consumer products into Brazil?
6. Why do you think many people are so frightened by globalization? Based on what is occurring in the world today, do you expect the globalization backlash to grow stronger or weaker over the next decade?
7. Two U.S. companies are competing to take over a large factory in the Czech Republic. One delegation tours the facility and asks questions about how the plant might be run more efficiently. The other delegation focuses on ways to improve working conditions and produce a better product. Which delegation do you think is more

likely to succeed with the plant? Why? What information would you want to collect to decide whether to acquire the plant for your company?

8. Which style of communicating do you think would be most beneficial to the long-term success of a U.S. company operating internationally—high-context or low-context communications? Why?
9. How might the social value of low versus high power distance influence how you would lead and motivate employees? What about the value of low versus high performance orientation?

Self-Learning

Rate Your Global Management Potential[69]

A global environment requires that managers learn to deal effectively with people and ideas from a variety of cultures. How well prepared are you to be a global manager? Read the following statements and circle the number on the response scale that most closely reflects how well the statement describes you.

Good Description 10 9 8 7 6 5 4 3 2 1 Poor Description

1. I reach out to people from different cultures.
   10 9 8 7 6 5 4 3 2 1
2. I frequently attend seminars and lectures about other cultures or international topics.
   10 9 8 7 6 5 4 3 2 1
3. I believe female expatriates can be equally as effective as male expatriates.
   10 9 8 7 6 5 4 3 2 1
4. I have a basic knowledge about several countries in addition to my native country.
   10 9 8 7 6 5 4 3 2 1
5. I have good listening and empathy skills.
   10 9 8 7 6 5 4 3 2 1
6. I have spent more than two weeks traveling or working in another country.
   10 9 8 7 6 5 4 3 2 1
7. I easily adapt to the different work ethics of students from other cultures when we are involved in a team project.
   10 9 8 7 6 5 4 3 2 1
8. I can speak a foreign language.
   10 9 8 7 6 5 4 3 2 1
9. I know which countries tend to cluster into similar sociocultural and economic groupings.
   10 9 8 7 6 5 4 3 2 1
10. I feel capable of assessing different cultures on the basis of power distance, uncertainty avoidance, individualism, and masculinity.
    10 9 8 7 6 5 4 3 2 1

Total Score: __________

Scoring and Interpretation

Add up the total points for the ten items. If you scored 81–100 points, you have a great capacity for developing good global management skills. A score of 61–80 points indicates that you have potential but may lack skills in certain areas, such as language or foreign experience. A score of 60 or less means you need to do some serious work to improve your potential for global management. Regardless of your total score, go back over each item and make a plan of action to increase scores of less than 5 on any item.

Group Learning

Global Entrepreneurship IQ

Complete the instrument below. Your instructor will give you the correct answers later.

1. Which country is the best place to launch a new business?
   a. Great Britain
   b. United States
   c. Canada
   d. Denmark
   e. Germany
2. In which location is it the most expensive to start a business?
   a. France
   b. Netherlands

   c. Japan
   d. Austria
   e. Hong Kong
3. In which place will it take you about 694 days to finish the bureaucratic and government red tape in order to get permission to open your business?
   a. Surinam
   b. Tasmania
   c. Ghana
   d. Zimbabwe
   e. Russia
4. Which country has the highest fees for entrepreneurial licenses at 500 percent of the average annual per capita income? Which charges the least?
   a. Nigeria
   b. Zimbabwe
   c. Canada
   d. United States
   e. Russia
   f. Ukraine
5. Which country has made the most progress in reducing red tape for entrepreneurs?
   a. Indonesia
   b. France
   c. India
   d. China
   e. Samoa
6. Where is the largest percentage of women starting new businesses?
   a. Norway
   b. United States
   c. Peru
   d. Argentina
   e. Sweden
7. Which two countries have the most job growth due to early-stage entrepreneurs? (Choose two out of five.)
   a. Turkey
   b. Iceland
   c. Ireland
   d. Israel
   e. India
8. Which two countries have the most innovation for early-stage entrepreneurs?
   a. Italy
   b. Brazil
   c. Peru
   d. China
   e. Chile
9. Identify three of the top four countries where the working-age population sees positive opportunities for starting a business in the area where they live.
   a. Ireland
   b. Spain
   c. Chile
   d. Iceland
   e. United States
   f. Argentina
   g. Denmark
10. In which two countries do people feel they started their own businesses because of a lack of decent jobs?
    a. Netherlands
    b. Chile
    c. Iceland
    d. Denmark
    e. Argentina

SOURCES: L. Jeff May, "By the Numbers/Global Entrepreneurship," *The Wall Street Journal*, November 15, 2010; and Donna J. Kelley, Niels Bosma, and Jose Ernesto Amoros, 2010 Global Report, Global Entrepreneurship Research Association, 2011.

Action Learning

Try Being a Minority

1. Singly, or in groups of no more than two, find a place to be a minority, such as a wedding for people of a different culture or religion, a cultural fair for a different culture, a church that is very different from what you've experienced (including worship houses of other racial, national, or ethnic groups), a home for the elderly, etc. Do *not* choose something dangerous like a biker bar or inner-city club.
2. Go to the place or event and make an effort to talk to at least five people.
3. Write up your experiences in a short paper, answering the following question:
   a. How did it feel to be different?
   b. How did people treat you? Is that how you react to someone who is a minority in a situation?
   c. What are the difficulties in being a member of a minority group?
   d. What skills do you need in such a situation?
   e. Do you see minorities any differently now than you did before this Action Learning?
4. Be prepared to discuss your experiences and conclusions in class.

SOURCE: Adapted from Renate R. Mai-Dalton, "Becoming a Minority," *Organizational Behavior Teaching Review* 9, no. 3: 1984–1985.

Ethical Dilemma

AH Biotech[70]

Dr. Abraham Hassan knew he couldn't put off the decision any longer. AH Biotech, the Bound Brook, New Jersey-based company started up by this psychiatrist-turned-entrepreneur, had developed a novel drug that seemed to promise long-term relief from panic attacks. If it gained FDA approval, it would be the company's first product. It was now time for large-scale clinical trials. But where should AH Biotech conduct those tests?

David Berger, who headed up research and development, was certain he already knew the answer to that question: Albania. "Look, doing these trials in Albania will be quicker, easier, and a lot cheaper than doing them in the States," he pointed out. "What's not to like?"

Dr. Hassan had to concede Berger's arguments were sound. If they did trials in the United States, AH Biotech would spend considerable time and money advertising for patients and then finding physicians who'd be willing to serve as clinical trial investigators. Rounding up U.S. doctors prepared to take on that job was getting increasingly difficult. They just didn't want to take time out of their busy practices to do the testing, not to mention all the recordkeeping such a study entailed.

In Albania, it was an entirely different story. It was one of the poorest Eastern European countries, if not *the* poorest, with a just barely functioning health-care system. Albanian physicians and patients would practically arrive at AH Biotech's doorstep asking to take part. Physicians there could earn much better money as clinical investigators for a U.S. company than they could actually practicing medicine, and patients saw signing up as test subjects as their best chance for receiving any treatment at all, let alone cutting-edge Western medicine. All of these factors meant that the company could count on realizing at least a 25 percent savings, maybe more, by running the tests overseas.

What's not to like? As the Egyptian-born CEO of a start-up biotech company with investors and employees hoping for its first marketable drug, there was absolutely nothing not to like. It was when he thought like a U.S.-trained physician that he felt qualms. If he used U.S. test subjects, he knew they'd likely continue to receive the drug until it was approved. At that point, most would have insurance that covered most of the cost of their prescriptions. But he already knew it wasn't going to make any sense to market the drug in a poor country like Albania, so when the study was over, he'd have to cut off treatment. Sure, he conceded, panic attacks weren't usually fatal. But he knew how debilitating these sudden bouts of feeling completely terrified were—the pounding heart, chest pain, choking sensation, and nausea. The severity and unpredictability of these attacks often made a normal life all but impossible. How could he offer people dramatic relief and then snatch it away?

What Would You Do?

1. Do the clinical trials in Albania. You'll be able to bring the drug to market faster and cheaper, which will be good for AH Biotech's employees and investors and good for the millions of people who suffer from anxiety attacks.
2. Do the clinical trials in the United States. Even though it will certainly be more expensive and time-consuming, you'll feel as if you're living up to the part of the Hippocratic Oath that instructed you to "prescribe regimens for the good of my patients according to my ability and my judgment and never do harm to anyone."
3. Do the clinical trials in Albania, and if the drug is approved, use part of the profits to set up a compassionate use program in Albania, even though setting up a distribution system and training doctors to administer the drug, monitor patients for adverse effects, and track results will entail considerable expense.

Case for Critical Analysis

Shui Fabrics[71]

Ray Betzell, general manager for the past five years of a joint venture between Ohio-based Rocky River Industries and Shanghai Fabric Ltd., was feeling caught in the middle these days.

As he looked out over Shanghai's modern gleaming skyline from his corner office, Ray knew his Chinese deputy general manager, Chiu Wai, couldn't be more pleased with the way things were going. Ten years ago, Rocky River had launched Shui Fabrics, a 50–50 joint venture between the U.S. textile manufacturer and the Chinese company, to produce dye and coat fabric for sale to both Chinese and international sportswear manufacturers. After many obstacles, considerable red tape, and several money-losing years, the joint venture was fulfilling Chiu Wai's expectations—and those of the local government and party officials who were keeping careful tabs on the enterprise—much more quickly than he'd anticipated. By providing jobs to close to 3,000 people, Shui was making a real contribution to the local economy. Job creation was no small accomplishment in a country where outside experts estimated that the actual (as opposed to the official) unemployment rate routinely hovered at 20 percent.

From Chiu Wai's point of view, Shui was generating just the right level of profit—not too little and, just as importantly, not too much. With so many U.S.–Chinese joint ventures still operating in the red, Chiu Wai saw no reason Ray's American bosses shouldn't be more than satisfied with their 5 percent annual return on investment. But those earnings weren't going to land him in hot water with local authorities, many of whom still viewed profits made by Western companies on Chinese soil as just one more instance of exploitation in a long history of foreign attempts at domination.

See It Online

If Chiu Wai had been eavesdropping on the conversation Ray had just had with Rocky River president Paul Danvers, the Chinese manager would have certainly been dismayed. Ray, who'd thoroughly enjoyed his time in China, was painfully aware of the quiet frustration in his boss's voice as it traveled over the phone lines from the other side of the world. To be sure, Paul conceded, Shui had cut Rocky River's labor costs, given the company access to the potentially huge Chinese market, and helped inoculate the firm against the uncertainty surrounding the periodic, often contentious U.S.–Chinese textile trade negotiations. Current U.S. tariffs and quotas could change at any time.

"But a 5 percent ROI [return on investment] is just pathetic," Paul complained. "And we've been stuck there for three years now. At this point, I'd expected to be looking at something more on the order of 20 percent." He pointed out that greater efficiency plus incorporating more sophisticated technology would allow Shui to reduce its workforce substantially and put it on the road to a more acceptable ROI. "I'm well aware of the fact that the Chinese work for a fraction of what we'd have to pay American workers, and I do appreciate the pressure the government is putting on you guys. But still, it doesn't make any sense for us to hire more workers than we would in a comparable U.S. plant."

After an uncomfortable silence, during which Ray tried and failed to picture broaching the subject of possible layoffs to his Chinese counterparts, he heard Paul ask the question he'd been dreading: "I'm beginning to think it's time to pull the plug on Shui. Is there any way you can see to turn this around, Ray, or should we start thinking about other options? Staying in China is a given, but there has to be a better way to do it."

Questions

1. How would you characterize the main economic, legal-political, and sociocultural differences influencing the relationship between the partners in Shui Fabrics? What GLOBE Project dimensions would help you understand the differences in Chinese and American perspectives illustrated in the case?
2. How would you define Shui's core problem? Are sociocultural differences the main underlying cause of this problem? Why or why not? How would you handle the conflict with your boss back in the United States?
3. If you were Ray Betzell, what other options to the 50–50 joint venture would you consider for manufacturing textiles in China? Make the argument that one of these options is more likely to meet Rocky River's expectations than the partnership already in place.

aplia Aplia Highlights

Now use your Aplia homework to help you:

- Apply management theories in your life
- Assess your management skills
- Master management terms and concepts
- Apply your knowledge to real-world situations
- Analyze and solve challenging management problems

In order to take advantage of these elements, your instructor will need to have set up a course for your class within Aplia. Ask your instructor to contact his/her Cengage sales representative and Digital Solutions Manager to explore testing Aplia in your course this term.

© Leremy, Shutterstock

Holden Outerwear: Managing in a Global Environment

Where can snowboarding enthusiasts find apparel that is fashionable around the globe, whether the destination is Vancouver's Cypress Mountain, Switzerland's Saas-Fee, or Loveland, Colorado? Today's style-minded boarders buy their snow duds from Mikey LeBlanc, a snowboard professional who founded Holden Outerwear in 2002 to inject fashion into the sport. In just one decade, Holden's independent do-it-yourself ethic has hit slopes worldwide, from Japan and Norway, to France and Canada.

Holden is a brand with attitude. First, the company's namesake association with Holden Caulfield, the angst-fueled antihero of J. D. Salinger's *The Catcher in the Rye*, is a symbol not lost on today's youth. Next, Holden jackets and pants, with their street-wear cuts borrowed from skate culture and the global fashion industry, represent a rejection of the "Michelin Man look" so common among skiers. "Fashion definitely figures in to Holden—that's where we look for inspiration," LeBlanc says of his brand's distinct style. "A lot of our competitors look inside our industry for inspiration. We've always looked outside, whether it was stores, current trends in fashion, or to our friends." Not only do Holden jackets make a statement, but they also may be good for the planet. Holden fabrics are made from hemp, recycled plastic, and bamboo, and finished garments ship in biodegradable bags that reduce waste while keeping products free of dust.

Although Holden boasts followers throughout Asia, Europe, and North America, LeBlanc's team manages business operations from the sports-apparel Mecca of Portland, Oregon, home to such iconic brands as Nike, Columbia, and Nau. To serve stores in the United States and Canada, Holden maintains an in-house sales team led by a company sales manager. Overseas marketing, however, is handled through partnerships with outside distributors.

Like so many other American brands, Holden apparel is "made in China." LeBlanc explains that while he would like to manufacture lines in the United States, government regulations, labor costs, and high corporate tax rates are too heavy a burden. "If we were to produce garments in the United States, our prices would be doubled," LeBlanc says. "It's really hard to beat the price coming out of China." Domestic costs are not the only reason Holden produces outerwear in Asian factories: availability of materials is another factor. "A lot of the goods are located there—fabrics, buttons, and snaps," LeBlanc says. "If we were to make a garment in the United States, we would still have to bring the pieces in from Asia." In addition to the tricky economics of domestic production, garment making requires skilled laborers, and LeBlanc says that the United States lacks a manufacturing base to do the job. "It's really hard to find workers in the United States who know how to take garments and do all the things you need when producing a technical garment."

Finally, for any company that sources materials and labor overseas, shipping is a vital, ongoing concern. In the early years, LeBlanc used nearly a dozen shippers to transport garments from China to warehouses in the United States and Canada. To increase efficiency and reduce costs, LeBlanc found a way to coordinate overseas factories through a single distribution hub in China. Now Holden's transport is carried out through just two shipping companies.

The behind-the-scenes management at Holden is paying off. Yet for small companies that have mastered the making, moving, and marketing of goods, scheduling can be the difference between success and failure. "You want to be on time—that's the biggest thing," LeBlanc says. "When I talk to my retailers and ask what is the most important thing, the answer is time. The most important thing you can do is have your product in stores on your in-date." He adds that you have to see things from the retailer's perspective: customers shop retail stores looking for products, and if they can't find them, they'll walk away—perhaps permanently.

Holden Outerwear may have an independent spirit, but LeBlanc has no interest in missing the delivery dates of his retail customers. After all, helping snowboarders suit up for the world's most challenging courses is a team effort, not a solo performance by a heroic recluse in a Salinger novel.

Discussion Questions

1. Which stage of globalization characterizes Holden Outerwear's international involvement?
2. Identify Holden's primary approach to entering the international market. What are the benefits of this entry strategy?
3. What are the challenges of international management for leaders at Holden?

Lost in Translation

Jet lag conspires with culture shock to force the meeting of Charlotte (Scarlett Johansson) and Bob Harris (Bill Murray). Neither can sleep after their Tokyo arrival. They meet in their luxury hotel's bar, forging an enduring relationship as they experience Tokyo's wonders, strangeness, and complexity. Based on director Sophia Coppola's Academy Award–winning screenplay, this film was shot entirely on location in Japan. It offers extraordinary views of various parts of Japanese culture that are not available without visiting.

Cross-Cultural Observations This sequence is an edited composite taken from different parts of *Lost in Translation*. It shows selected aspects of Tokyo and Kyoto, Japan. Charlotte has her first experience with the complex, busy Tokyo train system. She later takes the train to Kyoto, Japan's original capital city for more than ten centuries.

What to Watch for and Ask Yourself

- While watching this scene, pretend you have arrived in Tokyo and are experiencing what you are seeing. Do you understand everything you see?
- Is Charlotte bewildered by her experiences? Is she experiencing some culture shock?
- What aspects of Japanese culture appear in this scene? What do you see as important values of Japanese culture?

Endnotes

1. Phil Patton, "A Tata Nano Takes Manhattan," *The New York Times,* February 14, 2010.
2. Lolita C. Baldor, "FBI Sends More Agents Abroad to Shield U.S. from Cybercrime; Foreign Hackers Stepping up Their Attacks," *South Florida Sun-Sentinel,* December 10, 2009; and Cassell Bryan-Low, "Criminal Network: To Catch Crooks in Cyberspace, FBI Goes Global," *The Wall Street Journal*, November 21, 2006.
3. Baldor, "FBI Sends More Agents Abroad."
4. Steve Hamm, "IBM vs. Tata: Which Is More American?" *BusinessWeek* (May 5, 2008): 28; Erik Heinrich, "China's Garlic Bubble Hits the U.S.," *Fortune* (March 22, 2010): 18.
5. Chris Woodyard, "The American Car," *USA Today,* February 17, 2009.
6. "KOF Index of Globalization 2010," press release, KOF Swiss Economic Institute (January 22, 2010), http://globalization.kof.ethz.ch/ (accessed January 22, 2010).
7. Ibid. Note: The 2010 KOF analysis of globalization dimensions is based on the year 2007.
8. Ibid.
9. Ted C. Fishman, "Half a World Away, An Entrepreneur Grapples with (and Profits from) China's Boom," special section in "How China Will Change Your Business," *Inc.* (March 2005): 70–84.
10. Jean Kerr, "Export Strategies," *Small Business Reports* (May 1989): 20–25.
11. Kate Milani, "Three Best Ways to Export," *The Wall Street Journal Online,* March 15, 2010, http://online.wsj.com/article/SB10001424052748703909804575123783077762888.html?KEYWORDS=kate+milani (accessed March 17, 2010).
12. Jennifer Pellet, "The New Logic of Outsourcing: The Next Generation of Offshoring—Innovating and Engineering—Is at Hand (Roundtable)," *Chief Executive* (September 2007): 36–41.
13. Alison Stein Wellner, "Turning the Tables," *Inc.* (May 2006): 55–59.
14. Pellet, "The New Logic of Outsourcing."
15. Steve Hamm, "International Isn't Just IBM's First Name," *BusinessWeek* (January 28, 2008): 36–40.
16. Jason Dean, "The Yuan: Multinationals May Gain from Yuan; But China's Exporters Could See Profits Crimped," *The Wall Street Journal Europe,* June 21, 2010.
17. Loretta Chao, Lorraine Luk, and Aaron Back, "Sales of iPhone in China Set Under 3-Year Accord," *The*

Wall Street Journal, August 31, 2009; and Loretta Chao, Juliet Ye, and Yukari Iwatani Kane, "Apple, Facing Competition, Readies iPhone for Launch in Giant China Market," *The Wall Street Journal,* August 28, 2009.

18. Andrew Browne and Jason Dean, "Business Sours on China," *The Wall Street Journal,* March 17, 2010.
19. David Barboza and Brad Stone, "A Nation That Trips up Many," *The New York Times,* January 16, 2010.
20. Attorney Fraser Mendel of Schwabe, Williamson & Wyatt, quoted in Browne and Dean, "Business Sours on China."
21. James Flanigan, "Now, High-Tech Work Is Going Abroad," *The New York Times*, November 17, 2005.
22. W. Michael Cox and Richard Alm, "China and India: Two Paths to Economic Power," *Economic Letter*, Federal Reserve Bank of Dallas, August 2008, www.dallasfed.org/research/eclett/2008/el0808.html (accessed July 14, 2010).
23. This section is based on Paulo Prada, "For Brazil, It's Finally Tomorrow," *The Wall Street Journal,* March 29, 2010; Melanie Eversley, "Brazil's Olympian Growth," *USA Today,* October 5, 2009; Liam Denning, "Are Cracks Forming in the BRICs?" *The Wall Street Journal,* February 16, 2010; and David Thomas, "Brazil to Lead the BRIC Economies in 2009," The Creative Leadership Forum, January 7, 2009, www.thecreativeleadershipforum.com/creativity-matters-blog/2009/1/7/brazil-to-lead-the-bric-economies-in-2009.html (accessed March 17, 2010).
24. Steve Hamm, "Big Blue's Global Lab," *BusinessWeek* (September 7, 2009): 41–45.
25. Cited in Gary Ferraro, *Cultural Anthropology: An Applied Perspective*, 3rd ed. (Belmont, CA: West/Wadsworth, 1998), p. 68.
26. Jim Holt, "Gone Global?" *Management Review* (March 2000): 13.
27. Ibid.
28. "Slogans Often Lose Something in Translation," *The New Mexican*, July 3, 1994.
29. Louis S. Richman, "Global Growth Is on a Tear," in *International Business 97/98, Annual Editions*, ed. Fred Maidment (Guilford, CT: Dushkin Publishing Group, 1997), pp. 6–11.
30. "The Global Competitiveness Report 2009–2010," World Economic Forum, www.weforum.org/issues/global-competitiveness (accessed March 17, 2010).
31. Andrew E. Serwer, "McDonald's Conquers the World," *Fortune* (October 17, 1994): 103–116.
32. M. Walker, C. Forelle, and D. Gauthier-Villars, "Europe Bailout Lifts Gloom," *The Wall Street Journal*, May 11, 2010; and G. Bowley and C. Hauser, "Stocks Plunge on Fears of a Spreading European Crisis," *The New York Times,* May 21, 2010.
33. "A New Definition of Misery," *The New York Times*, December 18, 2009 (based on data from *Moody's*), www.nytimes.com/imagepages/2009/12/18/business/economy/20091219_CHARTS_GRAPHIC.html (accessed December 19, 2009).
34. Ian Bremmer, "Managing Risk in an Unstable World," *Harvard Business Review* (June 2005): 51–60; and Mark Fitzpatrick, "The Definition and Assessment of Political Risk in International Business: A Review of the Literature," *Academy of Management Review* 8 (1983): 249–254.
35. John Markoff and David Barboza, "Inquiry Is Said to Link Attack on Google to Chinese Schools," *The New York Times,* February 19, 2010.
36. Kevin Sullivan, "Kidnapping Is Growth Industry in Mexico; Businessmen Targeted in Climate of Routine Ransoms, Police Corruption," *The Washington Post*, September 17, 2002.
37. Amol Sharma and Jessica E. Vascellaro, "Google and India Test the Limits of Liberty," *The Wall Street Journal,* January 4, 2010.
38. Geert Hofstede, *Culture's Consequences: International Differences in Work-Related Values* (Beverly Hills, CA: Sage, 1980); G. Hofstede, "The Interaction between National and Organizational Value Systems," *Journal of Management Studies* 22 (1985): 347–357; and G. Hofstede, *Cultures and Organizations: Software of the Mind* (revised and expanded 2nd ed.) (New York: McGraw-Hill, 2005).
39. Geert Hofstede, "Cultural Constraints in Management Theory," *Academy of Management Executive* 7 (1993): 81–94; and G. Hofstede and M. H. Bond, "The Confucian Connection: From Cultural Roots to Economic Growth," *Organizational Dynamics* 16 (1988): 4–21.
40. For an overview of the research and publications related to Hofstede's dimensions, see "Retrospective: *Culture's Consequences*," a collection of articles focusing on Hofstede's work, in *The Academy of Management Executive* 18, no. 1 (February 2004): 72–93. See also Michele J. Gelfand et al., "Individualism and Collectivism," in *Culture, Leadership and Organizations: The Globe Study of 62 Societies,* R. J. House et al., eds. (Thousand Oaks, CA: Sage, 2004).
41. Mansour Javidan et al., "In the Eye of the Beholder: Cross-Cultural Lessons from Project GLOBE," *Academy of Management Perspectives* (February 2006): 67–90; Robert J. House et al., eds., *Culture, Leadership, and Organizations: The GLOBE Study of 62 Societies* (Thousand Oaks, CA: Sage Publications, 2004); M. Javidan and R. J. House, "Cultural Acumen for the Global Manager: Lessons from Project GLOBE," *Organizational Dynamics* 29, no. 4 (2001): 289–305; and R. J. House et al., "Understanding Cultures and Implicit Leadership

Theories Across the Globe: An Introduction to Project GLOBE," *Journal of World Business* 37 (2002): 3–10.

42. Chantell E. Nicholls, Henry W. Lane, and Mauricio Brehm Brechu, "Taking Self-Managed Teams to Mexico," *Academy of Management Executive* 13, no. 2 (1999): 15–27; Carl F. Fey and Daniel R. Denison, "Organizational Culture and Effectiveness: Can American Theory Be Applied in Russia?" *Organization Science* 14, no. 6 (November–December 2003): 686–706; Ellen F. Jackofsky, John W. Slocum, Jr., and Sara J. McQuaid, "Cultural Values and the CEO: Alluring Companions?" *Academy of Management Executive* 2 (1988): 39–49.
43. J. Kennedy and A. Everest, "Put Diversity in Context," *Personnel Journal* (September 1991): 50–54.
44. Jane Spencer, "Lenovo Goes Global, But Not without Strife," *The Wall Street Journal,* November 4, 2008.
45. Terence Jackson, "The Management of People across Cultures: Valuing People Differently," *Human Resource Management* 41, no. 4 (Winter 2002): 455–475.
46. Emily Flitter, "Faux Pas: Time Runs Differently in the Emirates," *The Wall Street Journal Online,* April 16, 2008, www.wsjonline.com/article/SB120776365272902197.html (accessed April 18, 2008).
47. The discussion of cultural intelligence is based on P. Christopher Earley and Elaine Mosakowski, "Cultural Intelligence," *Harvard Business Review* (October 2004): 139; Ilan Alon and James M. Higgins, "Global Leadership Success through Emotional and Cultural Intelligence," *Business Horizons* 48 (2005): 501–512; P. C. Earley and Soon Ang, *Cultural Intelligence: Individual Actions Across Cultures* (Stanford, CA: Stanford Business Books); and David C. Thomas and Kerr Inkson, *Cultural Intelligence* (San Francisco: Berrett-Koehler, 2004).
48. Pat McGovern, "How to Be a Local, Anywhere," *Inc.* (April 2007): 113–114.
49. These components are from Earley and Mosakowski, "Cultural Intelligence."
50. Karl Moore, "Great Global Managers," *Across the Board* (May–June 2003): 40–43.
51. This discussion is based on "For Richer, for Poorer," *The Economist* (December 1993): 66; Richard Harmsen, "The Uruguay Round: A Boon for the World Economy," *Finance & Development* (March 1995): 24–26; Salil S. Pitroda, "From GATT to WTO: The Institutionalization of World Trade," *Harvard International Review* (Spring 1995): 46–47, 66–67; and World Trade Organization Web site, www.wto.org (accessed February 11, 2008).
52. EUROPA Web site, "The History of the European Union," http://europa.eu/about-eu/eu-history/index_en.htm (accessed July 14, 2010).
53. European Commission Economic and Financial Affairs Web site, http://ec.europa.eu/economy_finance/euro/index_en.htm (accessed March 18, 2010).
54. Tapan Munroe, "NAFTA Still a Work in Progress," *Knight Ridder/Tribune News Service,* January 9, 2004; and J. S. McClenahan, "NAFTA Works," *IW* (January 10, 2000): 5–6.
55. Amy Barrett, "It's a Small (Business) World," *BusinessWeek* (April 17, 1995): 96–101.
56. Eric Alterman, "A Spectacular Success?" *The Nation* (February 2, 2004): 10; Jeff Faux, "NAFTA at 10: Where Do We Go From Here?" *The Nation* (February 2, 2004): 11; Geri Smith and Cristina Lindblad, "Mexico: Was NAFTA Worth It? A Tale of What Free Trade Can and Cannot Do," *BusinessWeek* (December 22, 2003): 66; Jeffrey Sparshott, "NAFTA Gets Mixed Reviews," *The Washington Times,* December 18, 2003; and Munroe, "NAFTA Still a Work in Progress."
57. Munroe, "NAFTA Still a Work in Progress"; Sparshott, "NAFTA Gets Mixed Reviews" and Amy Borrus, "A Free-Trade Milestone, with Many More Miles to Go," *BusinessWeek* (August 24, 1992): 30–31.
58. This section is based on Lu Jianren, "A New Asian Alliance," *Beijing Review* (January 21, 2010): 14; and Liz Gooch, "Asia Free-Trade Zone Raises Hopes, and Some Fears About China," *The New York Times,* January 1, 2010.
59. Association of Southeast Asian Nations Web site, www.aseansec.org/stat/Table20.pdf (accessed March 18, 2010).
60. Sara Murray and Douglas Belkin, "Americans Sour on Trade: Majority Say Free-Trade Pacts Have Hurt U.S.," *The Wall Street Journal*, October 4, 2010; and Nina Easton, "Make the World Go Away," *Fortune* (February 4, 2008): 105–108.
61. Jyoti Thottam, "Is Your Job Going Abroad?" *Time* (March 1, 2004): 26–36.
62. Easton, "Make the World Go Away."
63. Michael Schroeder and Timothy Aeppel, "Skilled Workers Sway Politicians with Fervor against Free Trade," *The Wall Street Journal*, December 10, 2003.
64. Alison Stein Wellner, "Turning the Tables," *Inc.* (May 2006): 55–59.
65. C. K. Prahalad and S. L. Hart, "The Fortune at the Bottom of the Pyramid," *Strategy + Business* 26 (2002): 54–67; Scott Johnson, "SC Johnson Builds Business at the Base of the Pyramid," *Global Business and Organizational Excellence* (September–October, 2007): 6–17; and José Antonio Rosa, Madhubalan Viswanathan, and Julie A. Ruth, "Global Business: Emerging Lessons," *The Wall Street Journal,* October 20, 2008.

66. Moon Ihlwan and Nandini Lakshman, "Mad Dash for the Low End," *BusinessWeek* (February 18, 2008): 30.

67. Rob Walker, "Cleaning Up," *New York Times Magazine* (June 10, 2007): 20.

68. Sonya Misquitta, "Cadbury Redefines Cheap Luxury," *The Wall Street Journal,* June 8, 2009; Leslie Wayne, "P&G Sees the World As Its Client," *The New York Times,* December 12, 2009.

69. Based in part on "How Well Do You Exhibit Good Intercultural Management Skills?" in John W. Newstrom and Keith Davis, *Organizational Behavior: Human Behavior at Work* (Boston, MA: McGraw-Hill Irwin, 2002), pp. 415–416.

70. Based on Gina Kolata, "Companies Facing Ethical Issue As Drugs Are Tested Overseas," *The New York Times*, March 5, 2004; and Julie Schmit, "Costs, Regulations Move More Drug Tests Outside USA," *USA Today*, June 16, 2005.

71. Based on Katherine Xin and Vladimir Pucik, "Trouble in Paradise," *Harvard Business Review* (August 2003): 27–35; Lillian McClanaghan and Rosalie Tung, "Summary of 'Negotiating and Building Effective Working Relationships with People in China,'" presentation by Sidney Rittenberg, Pacific Region Forum on Business and Management Communication, Simon Fraser University, Harbour Centre, Vancouver, B.C., March 21, 1991, www.cic.sfu.ca/forum/rittenbe.html; and Charles Wolfe, Jr., "China's Rising Unemployment Challenge," Rand Corporation Web page, www.rand.org/commentary/070704AWSJ.html.

Chapter Outline

Managing Ethics and Social Responsibility

Learning Outcomes

After studying this chapter, you should be able to:

1. Define ethics and explain how ethical behavior relates to behavior governed by law and free choice.
2. Discuss why ethics is important for managers, and identify recent events that call for a renewed commitment to ethical management.
3. Explain the utilitarian, individualism, moral-rights, justice, virtue ethics, and practical approaches for making ethical decisions.
4. Describe the factors that shape a manager's ethical decision making, including levels of moral development.
5. Identify important stakeholders for an organization and discuss how managers balance the interests of various stakeholders.
6. Explain the philosophy of sustainability and why organizations are embracing it.
7. Define corporate social responsibility and how to evaluate it along economic, legal, ethical, and discretionary criteria.
8. Discuss how ethical organizations are created through ethical leadership and organizational structures and systems.

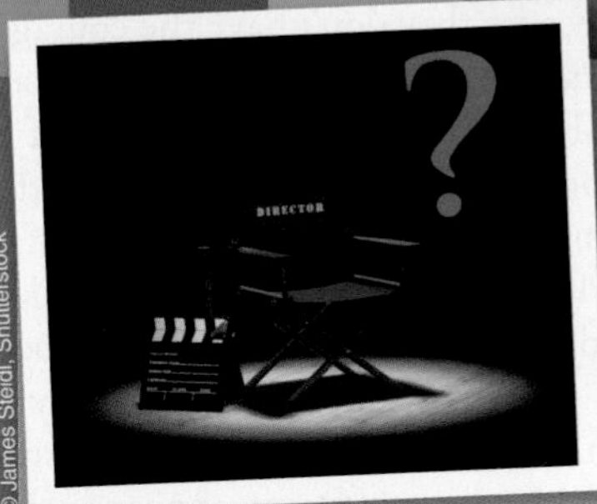

© James Steidl, Shutterstock

Are You Ready to Be a Manager?

Please circle your opinion below each of the following statements.

1 I always strive to do the "right thing," even when it is difficult and I might suffer negative consequences.

Mostly True | Mostly False

(See page 133, Will You Be a Courageous Manager? and page 153, Whistle-Blowing.)

2 Even if something is legal, I still maintain it is important to make moral decisions.

Mostly True | Mostly False

(See page 132, What is Managerial Ethics?)

3 When I am faced with a difficult decision, I try to make sure all parties involved are dealt with fairly, rather than merely trying to "win" or gain the most.

Mostly True | Mostly False

(See page 141, Manager Ethical Choices.)

4 When there is a right and wrong moral dilemma, I don't act just based on what people will find out, or what they will think of me, but rather look to a moral or spiritual principal to follow.

Mostly True | Mostly False

(See page 141, Manager Ethical Choices.)

5 I am a tireless recycler, and I want to work with a company that values the environment.

Mostly True | Mostly False

(See page 147, The Green Movement.)

1 What does courage have to do with a chapter on ethics? If you read articles about the collapse of the housing market in the United States, the fall of financial icons such as Lehman Brothers and Bear Stearns, or the implosion of early twenty-first-century high-flyers like WorldCom and Enron, it soon becomes apparent. There were not only plenty of managers in these organizations behaving unethically, but also plenty of managers who thought the behavior was wrong but lacked the courage to challenge their superiors or call attention to the misdeeds.

Unfortunately, many managers slide into unethical or even illegal behavior simply because they don't have the courage to stand up and do the right thing. At WorldCom, for example, controller David Myers admits he "didn't think it was the right thing to do" when CEO Bernard Ebbers and Chief Financial Officer Scott Sullivan asked him to reclassify some expenses that would boost the company's earnings for the quarter. Myers pushed his misgivings aside because he didn't want to oppose his superiors. After that first mistake, Myers had to keep making—and asking his subordinates to make—increasingly irregular adjustments to try to get things back on track.[1]

Lack of courage isn't the only problem, of course. Managers and organizations engage in unethical behavior for any number of reasons such as personal ego, greed, or pressures to increase profits or appear successful. Interviews with people in the mortgage wholesale industry, for example, revealed that many wholesalers (who work for banks and buy loan applications from independent mortgage brokers) operated from pure greed. They frequently altered documents, coached brokers on how to skirt the rules, and even offered bribes and sexual favors to generate more loans and thus more profits. In the educational field, administrators at some law schools in the United States have been accused of channeling lower-scoring applicants into part-time programs and using other tricks to improve their institution's scores on *U.S. News and World Report*'s widely read law-school rankings.[2] And at American Apparel, CEO Dov Charney allegedly ordered his accountants to inflate figures on the company's balance sheet so the private company would appear more successful when it was seeking outside investment.[3]

This chapter expands on the ideas about environment, corporate culture, and the international environment discussed in Chapter 3. We first focus on the topic of ethical values, which builds on the idea of corporate culture. We look at the current ethical climate in corporate America, examine fundamental approaches that can help managers think through difficult ethical issues, and consider various factors that influence how managers make ethical choices. Understanding these ideas will help you build a solid foundation on which to base future decision making. We also examine organizational relationships to the external environment as reflected in corporate social responsibility. The final section of the chapter describes how managers build an ethical organization, using codes of ethics and other organizational policies, structures, and systems.

What Is Managerial Ethics?

2 Ethics is difficult to define in a precise way. In a general sense, **ethics** is the code of moral principles and values that governs the behaviors of a person or group with respect to what is right or wrong. Ethics sets standards as to what is good or bad in conduct and decision making.[4] An ethical issue is present in a situation when the actions of a person or organization may harm or benefit others.[5] Yet ethical issues can sometimes be exceedingly complex. People may hold widely divergent views about the most ethically appropriate or inappropriate actions related to a situation.[6]

Consider the issue of competitive intelligence. Green Project Inc., a small ink-cartridge reseller, has filed suit against Seiko Epson, saying the larger company sent an investigator

New Manager Self-Test

Will You Be a Courageous Manager?

It probably won't happen right away, but soon enough in your duties as a new manager you will be confronted with a situation that will test the strength of your moral beliefs or your sense of justice. Are you ready? To find out, think about times when you were part of a student or work group. To what extent does each of the following statements characterize your behavior? Please answer each of the following items as Mostly True or Mostly False for you.

	MOSTLY TRUE <<<	>>> MOSTLY FALSE
1. I risked substantial personal loss to achieve the vision.	______	______
2. I took personal risks to defend my beliefs.	______	______
3. I would say no to inappropriate things, even if I had a lot to lose.	______	______
4. My significant actions were linked to higher values.	______	______
5. I easily acted against the opinions and approval of others.	______	______
6. I quickly told people the truth as I saw it, even when it was negative.	______	______
7. I spoke out against group or organizational injustice.	______	______
8. I acted according to my conscience, even if I could have lost stature.	______	______

See It Online

Scoring and Interpretation: Each of these items pertains to some aspect of displaying courage in a group situation, which often reflects a person's level of moral development. Count the number of checks for Mostly True. If you scored 5 or more, congratulations! That behavior would enable you to become a courageous manager about moral issues. A score below 4 indicates that you may avoid difficult issues or have not been in situations that challenged your moral courage.

Study the specific items for which you scored Mostly True and Mostly False to learn more about your specific strengths and weaknesses. Think about what influences your moral behavior and decisions, such as need for success or approval. Study the behavior of others you consider to be moral individuals. How might you increase your courage as a new manager?

pretending to be a customer to snoop around the company. Green Project says the tactic constitutes trespassing and theft of trade secrets. The laws regarding information gathering aren't clear cut, and neither are opinions regarding the ethics of such tactics. What do you think? Whereas some people think any form of corporate spying is wrong, others think it is an acceptable way of learning about the competition.[7] Managers frequently face situations in which it is difficult to determine what is right. In addition, they might be torn between their misgivings and their sense of duty to their bosses and the organization. Sometimes, managers want to take a stand but don't have the backbone to go against others, don't want to bring unfavorable attention to themselves, or don't want to risk their jobs.

Ethics can be more clearly understood when compared with behaviors governed by law and by free choice. Exhibit 4.1 illustrates that human behavior falls into three

EXHIBIT 4.1

Three Domains of Human Action

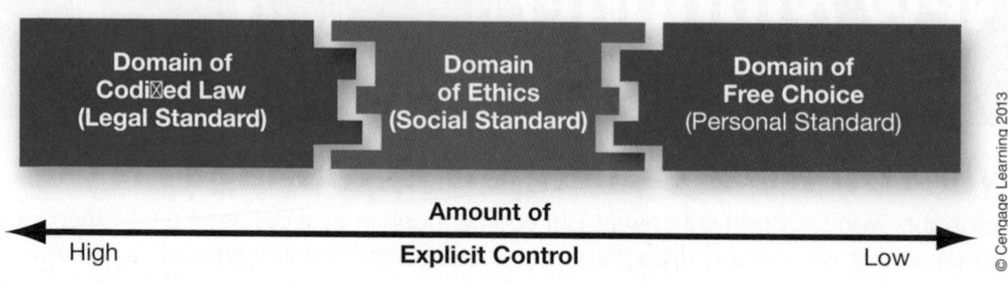

categories. The first is codified law, in which values and standards are written into the legal system and enforceable in the courts. In this area, lawmakers set rules that people and corporations must follow in a certain way, such as obtaining licenses for cars, paying corporate taxes, or following other local, state, and national laws. Managers at Swiss banking giant UBS, for example, are serving jail sentences for their role in helping clients cheat on their taxes, and Goldman Sachs is paying a $550 million fine to settle a Securities and Exchange Commission lawsuit charging the firm misled and defrauded investors.[8] The domain of free choice is at the opposite end of the scale and pertains to behavior about which the law has no say and for which an individual or organization enjoys complete freedom.

Between these domains lies the area of ethics. This domain has no specific laws, yet it does have standards of conduct based on shared principles and values about moral conduct that guide an individual or company. Consider that Anne Chinoda, top executive at Florida Blood Centers, is under pressure to resign because she took a $71,000 pay increase just months before she laid off 42 employees. Chinoda didn't break any laws, but nonprofit experts and the local community agree that the move was a violation of Chinoda's ethical responsibilities. Many nonprofits have frozen or even cut the salaries of top management to reduce costs during the recession, and Chinoda's salary was already higher than most others in the industry.[9]

Many companies and individuals get into trouble with the simplified view that decisions are governed by either law or free choice. This view leads people to mistakenly assume that if it's not illegal, it must be ethical, as if there were no third domain.[10] A better option is to recognize the domain of ethics and accept moral values as a powerful force for good that can regulate behaviors both inside and outside organizations.

AP Photo/Charles Dharapak

ConceptConnection

Goldman Sachs CEO Lloyd Blankfein (center) was on the hot seat as he defended the firm's role in creating Abacus, a mortgage-backed fund allegedly designed to fail. Although Goldman bet against the fund as a way to hedge against a weakening housing market, its trading side facilitated sales of Abacus to institutional customers. This maneuver helped Goldman weather the financial crisis but raised serious questions about its **managerial ethics**. Blankfein said the firm's trading side is simply "a machine that lets people buy and sell what they want to buy and sell." Despite this defense, in 2010, Goldman agreed to pay $550 million to settle federal claims that it misled investors.

- Managers face many pressures that can sometimes tempt them to engage in unethical behaviors.
- **Ethics** is the code of moral principles and values that governs the behaviors of a person or group with respect to what is right or wrong.
- Just because managers aren't breaking the law doesn't necessarily mean they are being ethical.
- An ethical issue is present in any situation when the actions of an individual or organization may harm or benefit others.
- Managers sometimes need courage to stand up and do the right thing.

Ethical Management Today

Every decade seems to experience its share of scoundrels, but the pervasiveness of ethical lapses during the first decade of this century has been astounding. A survey of 20,000 people in 19 countries, conducted by market research firm GfK for *The Wall Street Journal*, found that 55 percent of respondents believe cheating in business is more common today than it was ten years ago.[11] Although public confidence in business managers in particular is at an all-time low, politics, sports, and nonprofit organizations have also been affected. Sports star Tiger Woods fell from grace in a sordid sex scandal, and his agent and managers were later accused of helping arrange liaisons and covering up his activities. Britain's Parliament is embroiled in an explosive scandal related to politicians' expenses, with members of all parties allegedly finding myriad ways to bilk the system.[12] And EduCap Inc., a U.S. student-loan charity, has been accused of charging excessive interest on loans and providing lavish perks for managers, including use of the organization's private jet for weekend getaways.[13]

In the business world, the names of once-revered corporations have become synonymous with greed, deceit, irresponsibility, and lack of moral conscience: AIG, Lehman Brothers, Enron, Bear Stearns, Countrywide, WorldCom. It is no wonder a recent poll found that 76 percent of people surveyed say corporate America's moral compass is "pointing in the wrong direction." Sixty-nine percent say executives rarely consider the public good in making decisions, and a whopping 94 percent say executives make decisions based primarily on advancing their own careers.[14] One company is trying to be a role model for ethical business practices, as shown in this chapter's Benchmarking box.

Managers carry a tremendous responsibility for setting the ethical climate in an organization and can act as role models for others.[15] Managers are responsible for seeing that resources are used to serve the interests of stakeholders, including shareholders, employees, customers, and the broader society. Unfortunately, in recent years, too many managers have pursued their own self-interest at the expense of the very people they are supposed to serve. Exhibit 4.2 details various ways organizations sometimes behave unethically toward customers, employees, and other stakeholders.[16]

In the United States, the recent crisis in the housing and finance industries has brought the topic of ethical management to the forefront. Legal experts and government watchdogs continue sorting out how much of the crisis can be attributed to activities that were actually illegal, but—the question of legality aside—the whole episode reflects a failure of

EXHIBIT 4.2

Examples of Unethical and Illegal Organizational Behavior

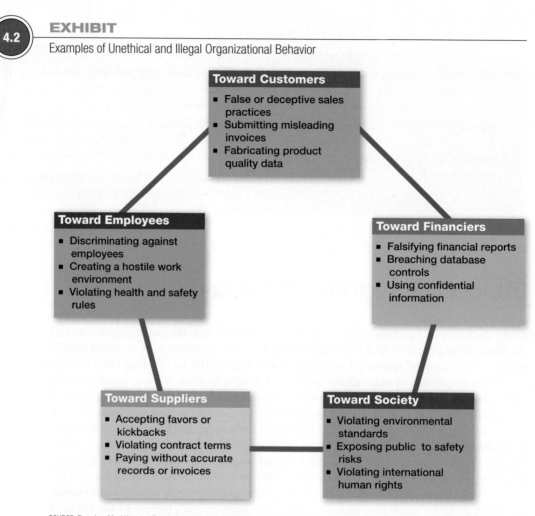

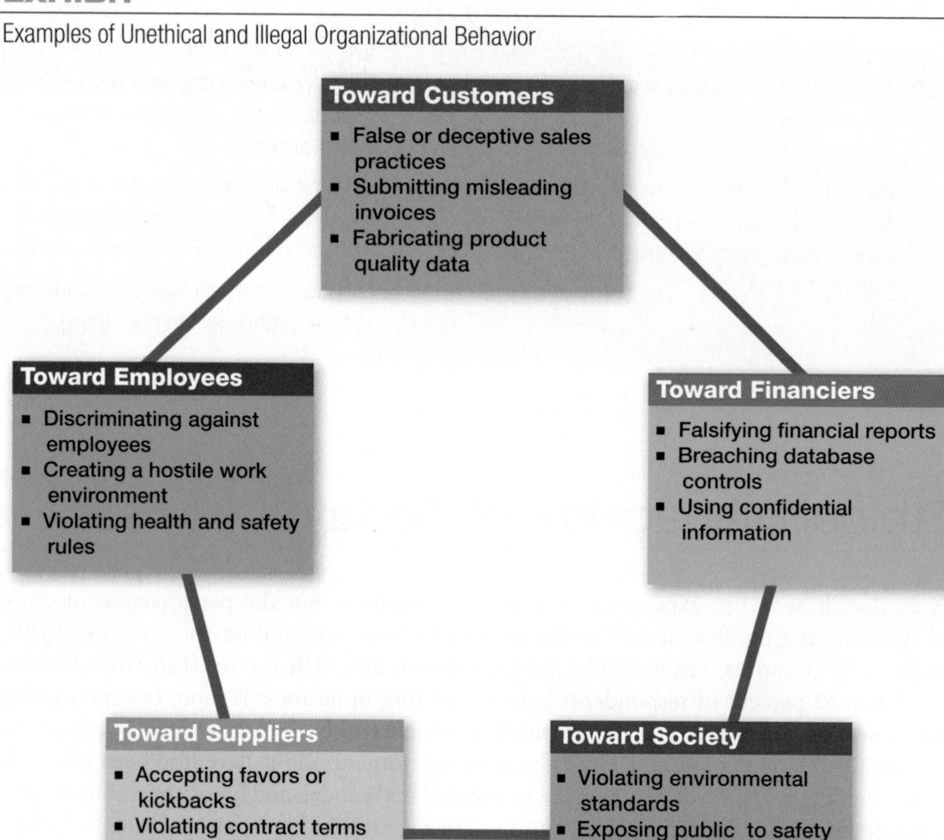

Toward Customers
False or deceptive sales practices
Submitting misleading invoices
Fabricating product quality data
Toward Employees
Discriminating against employees
Creating a hostile work environment
Violating health and safety rules
Toward Financiers
Falsifying financial reports
Breaching database controls
Using confidential information
Toward Suppliers
Accepting favors or kickbacks
Violating contract terms
Paying without accurate records or invoices
Toward Society
Violating environmental standards
Exposing public to safety risks
Violating international human rights

SOURCE: Based on Muel Kaptein, "Developing a Measure of Unethical Behavior in the Workplace: A Stakeholder Perspective," *Journal of Management* 34, no. 5 (October 2008): 978–1008.

responsible and ethical management. For instance, mortgage loan originators frequently made loans to people who obviously could not afford the home they were purchasing or the payments on the loan, simply for the purpose of generating loan volume—thus grabbing as much of the pie as they could, with little concern for who might be hurt in the process. Similarly, executives at companies that securitized and insured the loans grabbed at the pie too. AIG, for instance, paid around $165 million in bonuses—with one executive receiving $6.4 million and six others receiving more than $4 million each—even after the company reported the largest quarterly loss in history and had accepted a $170 billion bailout from the U.S. government.[17]

Executive compensation has become a hot-button issue. Consider that between 1993 and 2007, Richard Fuld, the CEO who steered Lehman Brothers straight into bankruptcy, took home nearly half a billion dollars in total compensation.[18] In 2008, the pay of CEOs at large U.S. corporations averaged 344 times what the average employee was paid. That compares to about 40 times the average worker's pay two decades earlier.[19] In contrast, Whole Foods has a rule that no one in the company can make more than 19 times what the average team member is paid.[20] The question of whether it is ethical for

BENCHMARKING

Triodos Bank

What's a "Marxist anarchist" to do in the current global financial crisis? Especially if he wants to be radical? Why, start a bank, of course. "I realized you could really change things when you were changing the flow of money," says Peter Blom, currently CEO of the Netherlands's Triodos Bank, which began in 1980 with Blom as one of the founding five employees. It has become the model for what a bank can do and how to sustain itself even in the midst of a global financial meltdown.

The Dutch bank now has branches in four countries and only lends to companies that will benefit society and the environment, fair-traded businesses, organic farms, and community health clinics. It won't give money for nuclear energy, environmental hazards, or weapons, or anything the bank sees as "unsustainable." As a result, the bank has flourished. During the Great Recession, it grew by 15 percent, and its operating profit rose by 50 percent from a year earlier. "People are looking for simple business models they can trust," says a Harvard professor Simon Zadek. "People running banks like Triodos are not in it to become billionaires, so at the very gut level, people know the bank isn't taking unnecessary risks with their money." Part of their secret is open information through what they call the "Black box," meaning any registered investor can track any of the bank's 9,000 loan recipients. The *Financial Times* and the World Bank named Triodos "Sustainable Bank of the Year" in 2009.

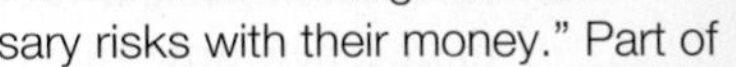

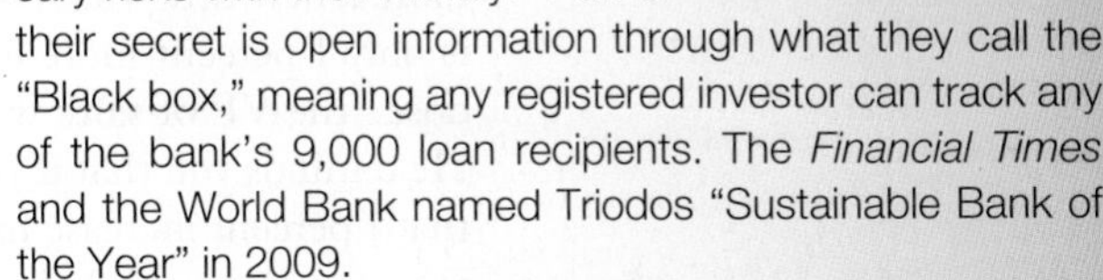

Still, Zadek says world finance is still dominated by "impatient funds trading on short-term margins and young, spotty traders." So in 2009, Triodos joined up with ten other values-minded banks to start the Global Alliance for Banking on Values. After the financial crisis, one investor moved more of his funds to Triodos. "They only invest in real companies that do real things and not imaginary businesses."

SOURCE: Danielle Sacks, "Opening the Black box," *Fast Company* (April 2010): 48.

© Kuzmik, Shutterstock

managers to rake in huge sums of money compared to other employees is of growing concern, and in general the widespread ethical lapses of the past decade have put managers under increasing scrutiny.

- Managers are ethically responsible for seeing that organizational resources are used to serve the interests of stakeholders, including shareholders, employees, customers, and the broader society.
- Unethical managers seek to serve their own needs and interests at the expense of stakeholders.
- Confidence in business managers and leaders in all walks of life is at an all-time low.
- One hot-button ethical issue concerns excessive executive compensation.

Ethical Dilemmas: What Would You Do?

Ethics is always about making decisions, and some issues are difficult to resolve. Although most companies have codes of ethics that specify expected behavior, disagreements and dilemmas about what is appropriate often occur. An **ethical dilemma** arises in a situation concerning right or wrong when values are in conflict.[21] Right and wrong cannot be clearly identified.

The individual who must make an ethical choice in an organization is the *moral agent*.[22] Here are some dilemmas that a manager in an organization might face. Think about how you would handle them:

1. Your company requires a terrorist watch list screening for all new customers, which takes approximately 24 hours from the time an order is placed. You can close a lucrative deal with a potential long-term customer if you agree to ship the products overnight, even though that means the required watch list screening will have to be done after the fact.[23]
2. As a sales manager for a major pharmaceuticals company, you've been asked to promote a new drug that costs $2,500 per dose. You've read the reports saying the drug is only 1 percent more effective than an alternate drug that costs less than $625 per dose. The VP of sales wants you to aggressively promote the $2,500-per-dose drug. He reminds you that if you don't, lives could be lost that might have been saved with that 1 percent increase in the drug's effectiveness.
3. Your company is hoping to build a new overseas manufacturing plant. You could save about $5 million by not installing standard pollution-control equipment that is required in the United States. The plant will employ many local workers in a poor country where jobs are scarce. Your research shows that pollutants from the factory could potentially damage the local fishing industry. Yet building the factory with the pollution-control equipment will likely make the plant too expensive to build.[24]
4. You have been collaborating with a fellow manager on an important project. One afternoon, you walk into his office a bit earlier than scheduled and see sexually explicit images on his computer screen. The company has a zero-tolerance sexual harassment policy as well as strict guidelines regarding personal use of the Internet. However, your colleague was in his own office and not bothering anyone else.[25]

These kinds of dilemmas and issues fall squarely in the domain of ethics. How would you handle each of the above situations? Now consider the following hypothetical dilemma, which scientists are using to study human morality.[26]

- A runaway trolley is heading down the tracks toward five unsuspecting people. You're standing near a switch that will divert the trolley onto a siding, but there is a single workman on the siding who cannot be warned in time to escape and will almost certainly be killed. Would you throw the switch?
- Now, what if the workman were standing on a bridge over the tracks and you would have to push him off the bridge to stop the trolley with his body in order to save the five unsuspecting people? (Assume his body is large enough to stop the trolley and yours is not.) Would you push the man, even though he will almost certainly be killed?

These dilemmas show how complex questions of ethics and morality can sometimes be. In *Time* magazine's readers' poll, 97 percent of respondents said they could throw the switch (which would almost certainly lead to the death of the workman), but only 42 percent said they could actually push the man to his death.[27]

- Ethics is about making choices.
- Most managers encounter ethical dilemmas that are tough to resolve.
- An **ethical dilemma** is a situation in which all alternative choices or behaviors have potentially negative consequences. Right and wrong cannot be clearly distinguished.

Criteria for Ethical Decision Making

Most ethical dilemmas involve a conflict between the needs of the part and the whole—the individual versus the organization, or the organization versus society as a whole. For example, should a company perform surveillance on managers' nonworkplace conduct, which might benefit the organization as a whole but would reduce the individual freedom of employees? Or should products that fail to meet tough Food and Drug Administration (FDA) standards be exported to other countries where government standards are lower, benefiting the company but potentially harming world citizens? Sometimes ethical decisions entail a conflict between two groups. For example, should the potential for local health problems resulting from a company's effluents take precedence over the jobs it creates as the town's leading employer?

Managers faced with these kinds of tough ethical choices often benefit from a normative strategy—one based on norms and values—to guide their decision making. Normative ethics uses several approaches to describe values for guiding ethical decision making. Six approaches that are relevant to managers are the utilitarian approach, individualism approach, moral-rights approach, justice approach, virtue ethics approach, and practical approach.[28]

Utilitarian Approach The **utilitarian approach**, espoused by the nineteenth-century philosophers Jeremy Bentham and John Stuart Mill, holds that moral behavior produces the greatest good for the greatest number. Under this approach, a decision maker is expected to consider the effect of each decision alternative on all parties and select the one that optimizes the benefits for the greatest number of people. In the trolley dilemma earlier in this chapter, for instance, the utilitarian approach would hold that it would be moral to push one person to his death in order to save five. The utilitarian ethic is cited as the basis for the recent trend among companies to monitor employee use of the Internet and police personal habits such as alcohol and tobacco consumption, because such behavior affects the entire workplace.[29]

Individualism Approach The **individualism approach** contends that acts are moral when they promote the individual's best long-term interests.[30] In theory, with everyone pursuing self-direction, the greater good is ultimately served because people learn to accommodate each other in their own long-term interest. Individualism is believed to lead to honesty and integrity because that works best in the long run. Lying and cheating for immediate self-interest just causes business associates to lie and cheat in return. Thus, proponents say, individualism ultimately leads to behavior toward others that fits standards of behavior people want toward themselves.[31] However, because individualism is easily misinterpreted to support immediate self-gain, it is not popular in the highly organized and group-oriented society of today.

Moral-Rights Approach The **moral-rights approach** asserts that human beings have fundamental rights and liberties that cannot be taken away by an individual's decision. Thus, an ethically correct decision is one that best maintains the rights of those affected by it. To make ethical decisions, managers need to avoid interfering with the fundamental rights of others, such as the right to privacy, the right of free consent, or the right to freedom of speech. Performing experimental treatments on unconscious trauma patients, for example, might be construed to violate the right to free consent. A decision to monitor employees' nonwork activities violates the right to privacy. The right of free speech would support whistle-blowers who call attention to illegal or inappropriate actions within a company.

Justice Approach The **justice approach** holds that moral decisions must be based on standards of equity, fairness, and impartiality. Three types of justice are of concern to managers. **Distributive justice** requires that different treatment of people not be based on arbitrary characteristics. For example, men and women should not receive different salaries if they have the same qualifications and are performing the same job. **Procedural justice** requires that rules be administered fairly. Rules should be clearly stated and consistently and impartially enforced. **Compensatory justice** argues that individuals should be compensated for the cost of their injuries by the party responsible. The justice approach is closest to the thinking underlying the domain of law in Exhibit 4.1 because it assumes that justice is applied through rules and regulations. Managers are expected to define attributes on which different treatment of employees is acceptable.

Virtue Ethics Approach Rather than relying on rules or the consequences of an action to determine the appropriate ethical decision, the **virtue ethics approach** says that moral behavior stems from personal virtues.[32] That is, if a manager develops good character traits such as compassion, generosity, or courage, and learns to overcome negative traits such as greed or anger, he or she will make ethical decisions naturally as a result of being a virtuous person. This approach dates back to ancient Greek philosophy, particularly the thinking of Plato and Aristotle. To make ethical choices, the manager behaves in a way that does not violate personal virtues. According to virtue ethics, managers can develop not only their ability to do the right thing but also their motivation to do right rather than wrong. Warren Buffett, for example, has been recognized as a highly ethical manager who does the right thing because of his personal character.

WARREN BUFFETT, BERKSHIRE HATHAWAY

Berkshire Hathaway and Warren Buffett haven't escaped the fallout from the recent economic crisis. The year 2008 was Buffett's worst year in business in four decades, with his holding company reporting a 62 percent drop in net income. In his early 2009 letter to shareholders, Buffett accepted the blame for some of the declines but also pointed a finger at unnamed, unethical CEOs who left the credit market and stock market in shambles.

What makes Buffett one of corporate America's best leaders is not his investing ability, but his ethical leadership. The two are, in a sense, tied together. Buffett always looks at a company's "intrinsic business value" rather than just at the stock price. He is known for his commitment to sound ethics and transparency in disclosing mistakes or failures. At annual meetings, he and his partner answer shareholder questions for more than four hours. Although Wall Street pressures boards to fire CEOs who don't produce short-term results, Buffett has a long record of retaining the CEOs of his companies. As for bending the rules, his advice to employees of Salomon Brothers when it was embroiled in a scandal with the U.S. Treasury Department seems apt for today's climate: "You don't need to play outside the lines," Buffett says. "You can make a lot of money hitting the ball down the middle."

Buffett takes a modest salary and leads a modest lifestyle. He lives in the same house he bought for $31,500 in 1956, drives an old car, and eats simple meals at inexpensive restaurants. "I do not want to live like a king," Buffett says. "I just love to invest."[33]

Practical Approach The approaches discussed so far presume to determine what is "right" or good in a moral sense. However, as has been mentioned, ethical issues are frequently not clear cut and there are disagreements over what is the ethical choice. The **practical approach** sidesteps debates about what is right, good, or just and bases decisions on prevailing standards of the profession and the larger society, taking the interests of all stakeholders into account.[34] A decision would be considered ethical if it were one that would be considered acceptable by the professional community, one the manager would not hesitate to publicize on the evening news, and one that a person would typically feel comfortable explaining to family and friends. Using the practical approach, managers may combine elements of the utilitarian, moral-rights, justice, and virtue ethics approaches in their thinking and decision making.

Remember This

- Most ethical dilemmas involve a conflict between the interests of different groups or between the needs of the individual versus the needs of the organization.
- Managers can use various approaches based on norms and values to help them make ethical decisions.
- The **utilitarian approach** to ethical decision making says that the ethical choice is the one that produces the greatest good for the greatest number.
- The **individualism approach** suggests that actions are ethical when they promote the individual's best long-term interests, because with everyone pursuing self-interest, the greater good is ultimately served.
- The individualism approach is not considered appropriate today because it is easily misused to support one's personal gain at the expense of others.
- Some managers rely on a **moral rights approach**, which holds that ethical decisions are those that best maintain the fundamental rights of the people affected by them.
- The **justice approach** says that ethical decisions must be based on standards of equity, fairness, and impartiality.
- **Distributive justice** requires that different treatment of individuals not be based on arbitrary characteristics.
- **Procedural justice** holds that rules should be clearly stated and consistently and impartially enforced.
- **Compensatory justice** argues that individuals should be compensated for the cost of their injuries by the party responsible, and individuals should not be held responsible for matters over which they have no control.
- The **virtue ethics approach** says that moral behavior stems from personal virtues. If a manager develops good character traits and learns to overcome negative traits, he or she will make ethical decisions based on personal virtue.
- Today's managers also use the **practical approach**, which sidesteps debates about what is right, good, or just, and bases decisions on prevailing standards of the profession and the larger society, taking the interests of all stakeholders into account.

Manager Ethical Choices

3

A number of factors influence a manager's ability to make ethical decisions. Individuals bring specific personality and behavioral traits to the job. Personal needs, family influence, and religious background all shape a manager's value system. Specific

Chris Crisman

ConceptConnection

Edna Ruth Byler started what eventually became the Mennonite nonprofit retail chain Ten Thousand Villages in 1946 because she felt Puerto Rican embroiderers were being unjustly compensated. The company reflects Byler's **postconventional level of moral development**. Ten Thousand Villages is committed to paying artisans a fair wage for the home items, accessories, and gifts sold in 200 stores in the United States and Canada. In comparison to the 1 to 5 cents of every retail dollar that typically goes to artisans, Ten Thousand Villages craftspeople receive 21 cents. Pictured here is store manager Darlene DeLaPaz.

personality characteristics, such as ego strength, self-confidence, and a strong sense of independence, may enable managers to make ethical choices despite personal risks.

One important personal trait is the stage of moral development.[35] A simplified version of one model of personal moral development is shown in Exhibit 4.3.

At the *preconventional level*, individuals are concerned with external rewards and punishments and obey authority to avoid detrimental personal consequences. In an organizational context, this level may be associated with managers who use an autocratic or coercive leadership style, with employees oriented toward dependable accomplishment of specific tasks.

At level two, called the *conventional level*, people learn to conform to the expectations of good behavior as defined by colleagues, family, friends, and society. Meeting social and interpersonal obligations is important. Work group collaboration is the preferred manner for accomplishment of organizational goals, and managers use a leadership style that encourages interpersonal relationships and cooperation.

At the *postconventional*, or *principled* level, individuals are guided by an internal set of values based on universal principles of justice and right and will even disobey rules or laws that violate these principles. Internal values become more important than the expectations of significant others. The Spotlight on Ethics titled How to Challenge the Boss on Ethical Issues gives some tips for how postconventional managers can effectively challenge their superiors concerning questionable ethical matters. One example of the postconventional or principled approach comes from World War II. When the *USS Indianapolis* sank after being torpedoed, one Navy pilot disobeyed orders and risked his life to save men who were being picked off by sharks. The pilot was operating from the highest level of moral development in attempting the rescue despite a direct order from superiors. When managers operate from this highest level of development, they use transformative, or servant, leadership, focusing on the needs of followers and encouraging others to think for themselves and to engage in higher levels of moral reasoning. Employees are empowered and given opportunities for constructive participation in governance of the organization.

Review your responses to the questionnaire toward the beginning of this chapter, which will give you some insight into your own level of manager courage, which is related to moral development. As a new manager, strive for a high level of personal moral development. You can test yours by completing the New Manager Self-Test on page 145.

The great majority of managers operate at level two, meaning their ethical thought and behavior is greatly influenced by their superiors, colleagues, and other significant people in the organization or industry. A few have not advanced beyond level one. Only about 20 percent of American adults reach the level-three postconventional stage of moral development. People at level three are able to act in an independent, ethical manner regardless of expectations from others inside or outside the organization. Managers at level three of moral development will make ethical decisions whatever the organizational consequences for them.

EXHIBIT 4.3

Three Levels of Personal Moral Development

Level 1 Preconventional	Level 2 Conventional	Level 3 Postconventional
Follows rules to avoid punishment. Acts in own interest. Obedience for its own sake.	Lives up to expectations of others. Fulfills duties and obligations of social system. Upholds laws.	Follows self-chosen principles of justice and right. Aware that people hold different values and seeks creative solutions to ethical dilemmas. Balances concern for individual with concern for common good.
Self-Interest	Societal Expectations	Internal Values

Leader Style:	Autocratic/coercive	Guiding/encouraging, team oriented	Transforming, or servant leadership
Employee Behavior:	Task accomplishment	Work group collaboration	Empowered employees, full participation

SOURCE: Based on L. Kohlberg, "Moral Stages and Moralization: The Cognitive-Developmental Approach," in *Moral Development and Behavior: Theory, Research, and Social Issues*, ed. T. Lickona (New York: Holt, Rinehart, and Winston, 1976), pp. 31–53; and Jill W. Graham, "Leadership, Moral Development and Citizenship Behavior," *Business Ethics Quarterly* 5, no. 1 (January 1995): 43–54.

- Personality characteristics, family influence, religious background, and other factors influence a manager's ability to make ethical choices.
- One important factor is whether a manager is at a preconventional, conventional, or postconventional level of moral development.
- Most managers operate at a *conventional level*, conforming to standards of behavior expected by society.
- Only about 20 percent of adults reach the *postconventional level* and are able to act in an independent, ethical manner regardless of the expectations of others.

What Is Corporate Social Responsibility?

Now let's turn to the issue of corporate social responsibility. In one sense, the concept of social responsibility, like ethics, is easy to understand: It means distinguishing right from wrong and doing right. It means being a good corporate citizen. The formal definition of **corporate social responsibility (CSR)** is management's obligation to make choices and take actions that will contribute to the welfare and interests of society as well as the organization.[36]

As straightforward as this definition seems, CSR can be a difficult concept to grasp because different people have different beliefs as to which actions improve society's welfare.[37] To make matters worse, social responsibility covers a range of issues, many of which are

SPOTLIGHT ON ETHICS

How to Challenge the Boss on Ethical Issues

Many of today's top executives put a renewed emphasis on ethics in light of serious ethical lapses that tarnished the reputations and hurt the performance of previously respected and successful companies. Yet keeping an organization in ethical line is an ongoing challenge, and it requires that people at all levels be willing to stand up for what they think is right. Challenging the boss or other senior leaders on potentially unethical behaviors is particularly unnerving for most people. Here are some tips for talking to the boss about an ethically questionable decision or action. Following these guidelines can increase the odds that you'll be heard and your opinions will be seriously considered.

- ***Do your research.*** Marshall any facts and figures that support your position on the issue at hand, and develop an alternative policy or course of action that you can suggest at the appropriate time. Prepare succinct answers to any questions you anticipate being asked about your plan.
- ***Begin the meeting by giving your boss the floor.*** Make sure you really do understand what the decision or policy is and the reasons behind it. Ask open-ended questions, and listen actively, showing through both your responses and your body language that you're seriously listening and trying to understand the other person's position. In particular, seek out information about what the senior manager sees as the decision or policy's benefits as well as any potential downside. It'll give you information you can use later to highlight how your plan can produce similar benefits while avoiding the potential disadvantages.
- ***Pay attention to your word choice and demeanor.*** No matter how strongly you feel about the matter, don't rant and rave about it. You're more likely to be heard if you remain calm, objective, and professional. Try to disagree without making it personal. Avoid phrases such as "you're wrong," "you can't," "you should," or "how could you?" to prevent triggering the other person's automatic defense mechanisms.
- ***Take care how you suggest your alternative solution.*** You can introduce your plan with phrases such as "Here's another way to look at this" or "What would you think about …?" Check for your superior's reactions by both explicitly asking for feedback and being sensitive to body language clues. Point out the potential negative consequences of implementing decisions that might be construed as unethical by customers, shareholders, suppliers, or the public.
- ***Be patient.*** Don't demand a resolution on the spot. During your conversation, you may realize that your plan needs some work, or your boss might just need time to digest the information and opinions you've presented. It's often a good idea to ask for a follow-up meeting.

If the decision or action being considered is clearly unethical or potentially illegal, and this meeting doesn't provide a quick resolution, you might have to take your concerns to higher levels or even blow the whistle to someone outside the organization who can make sure the organization stays in line. However, most managers don't want to take actions that will harm the organization, its people, or the community. In many cases, questionable ethical issues can be resolved by open and honest communication. That, however, requires that people have the courage—and develop the skills—to confront their superiors in a calm and rational way.

SOURCE: Kevin Daley, "How to Disagree: Go Up Against Your Boss or a Senior Executive and Live to Tell the Tale," *T&D* (April 2004); Diane Moore, "How to Disagree with Your Boss—and Keep Your Job," *Toronto Star*, November 12, 2003; "How to Disagree with Your Boss," *WikiHow*, http://wiki.ehow.com/Disagree-With-Your-Boss; and "How to Confront Your Boss Constructively," *The Buzz* (October 23–29, 1996).

ambiguous with respect to right or wrong. If a bank deposits the money from a trust fund into a low-interest account for 90 days, from which it makes a substantial profit, is it being a responsible corporate citizen? How about two companies engaging in intense competition? Is it socially responsible for the stronger corporation to drive the weaker one into bankruptcy or a forced merger? Or consider General Motors, Kmart, Lehman Brothers, and the numerous other companies that have declared bankruptcy in recent years—which is perfectly legal—to avoid mounting financial obligations to suppliers, labor unions, or competitors. These examples contain moral, legal, and economic considerations that make socially responsible behavior hard to define.

New Manager Self-Test

Self and Others

Leaders differ in how they view human nature and the tactics they use to get things done through others. Answer the items below based on how you view yourself and others. Think carefully about each one, and be honest about what you feel inside. Please answer whether each item below is Mostly True or Mostly False for you.

	MOSTLY TRUE <<<	>>> MOSTLY FALSE
1. I prefer not to depend on anyone else to get things done.	______	______
2. I appreciate that I am a special person.	______	______
3. I help orient new people even though it is not required.	______	______
4. I like to be the center of attention.	______	______
5. I am always ready to lend a helping hand to those around me.	______	______
6. I tend to see my coworkers as competitors.	______	______
7. I am quick to see and point out others' mistakes.	______	______
8. I frequently interrupt someone to make my point.	______	______
9. I often have to admit that people around me are not very competent.	______	______

See It Online

Scoring and Interpretation: This scale is about orientation toward self versus others. A high score suggests you could be ego centered, and may come across to others as something of an obnoxious person. To compute your score, give yourself 1 point for each Mostly False answer to items 3 and 5, and 1 point for each Mostly True answer to items 1, 2, 4, 6, 7, 8, and 9. A score of 7 to 9 points suggests a self-oriented person who might take the *individualism approach* to the extreme or function at the *preconventional level 1* of moral development (Exhibit 4.3). A score from 4 to 6 points suggests a balance between self and others. A score from 0 to 3 points would indicate an "other" orientation associated with a *utilitarian* or *moral-rights approach* and *level 2* or *level 3 moral development*, suggesting little likelihood of coming across as obnoxious.

Organizational Stakeholders

One reason for the difficulty understanding and applying CSR is that managers must confront the question "Responsibility to whom?" Recall from Chapter 2 that the organization's environment consists of several sectors in both the task and general environment. From a social responsibility perspective, enlightened organizations view the internal and external environment as a variety of stakeholders.

A **stakeholder** is any group within or outside the organization that has a stake in the organization's performance. Each stakeholder has a different criterion of responsiveness because it has a different interest in the organization.[38] For example, Walmart uses aggressive bargaining tactics with suppliers so that it is able to provide low prices for customers. Some stakeholders see this type of corporate behavior as responsible because it benefits customers and forces suppliers to be more efficient. Others, however, argue that the aggressive tactics are unethical and socially irresponsible because they force U.S. manufacturers to lay off workers, close factories, and outsource from low-wage countries. One supplier said clothing is being sold so cheaply at Walmart that many U.S. companies could not compete even if they paid their employees nothing.[39]

Exhibit 4.4 illustrates important stakeholders for Monsanto. Most organizations are influenced by a similar variety of stakeholder groups. Investors and shareholders, employees, customers, and suppliers are considered primary stakeholders, without whom the organization cannot survive. Investors, shareholders, and suppliers' interests are served by managerial efficiency—that is, use of resources to achieve profits. Employees expect work satisfaction, pay, and good supervision. Customers are concerned with decisions about the quality, safety, and availability of goods and services. When any primary stakeholder group becomes seriously dissatisfied, the organization's viability is threatened.[40]

Other important stakeholders are the government and the community, which have become increasingly important in recent years. Most corporations exist only under the proper charter and licenses and operate within the limits of safety laws, environmental protection requirements, antitrust regulations, antibribery legislation, and other laws and regulations in the government sector. Government regulations affecting business are increasing

4.4 EXHIBIT

Major Stakeholders Relevant to Monsanto Company

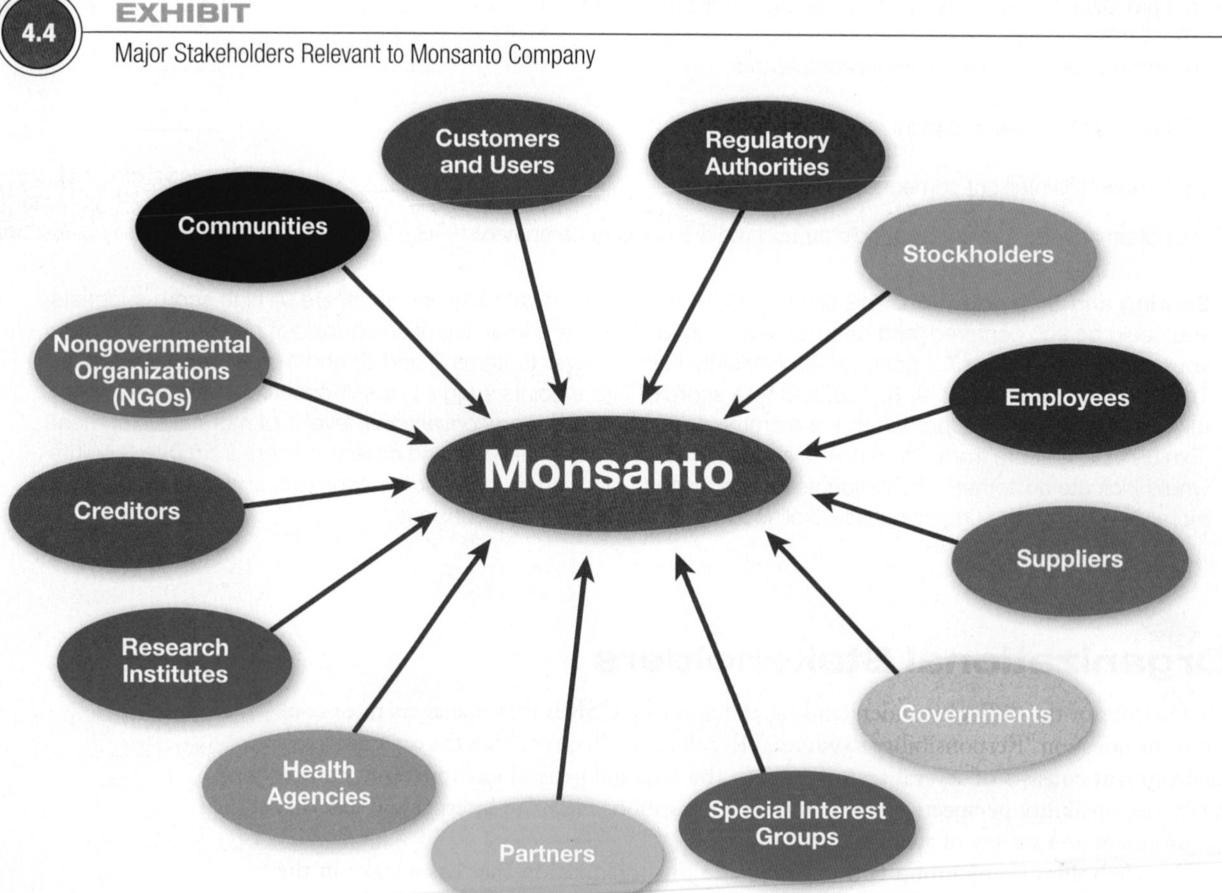

SOURCES: Based on information in D. Wheeler, B. Colbert, and R. E. Freeman, "Focusing on Value: Reconciling Corporate Social Responsibility, Sustainability, and a Stakeholder Approach in a Networked World," *Journal of General Management* 28, no. 3 (Spring 2003): 1–28; and J. E. Post, L. E. Preston, and S. Sachs, "Managing the Extended Enterprise: The New Stakeholder View," *California Management Review* 45, no. 1 (Fall 2002): 6–28.

because of recent events. The community includes local government, the natural and physical environments, and the quality of life provided for residents. Special interest groups, still another stakeholder, may include trade associations, political action committees, professional associations, and consumerists. One special interest group of particular importance today is the Green movement.

The Green Movement

5

The year was 2004, and Jeffrey Immelt, CEO of General Electric, had just presented a plan for a "green" business initiative to 35 top GE executives. They voted it down. But Immelt, in a rare move, overruled them, and Ecoimagination was born. Today, GE's Ecoimagination is one of the world's most widely recognized corporate green programs. It has led to cost savings of well over $100 million, has cut GE's greenhouse gas emissions by 30 percent, and has added 80 new products and services, including energy-efficient MRIs, locomotives, and light bulbs, that are generating billions in annual revenue.[41]

"Going green" has become a new business imperative, driven by shifting social attitudes, new governmental policies, climate changes, and the information technology that quickly spreads news of a corporation's negative impact on the environment. Nike is still struggling with ethical issues related to sweatshop labor in its contract factories, but the company is getting high marks for its reinvention of the shoe design process to create less waste and introduce less toxic material into the environment.[42] Walmart has become a surprise darling of the Green movement with its implementation of an energy-efficient trucking fleet, its growing use of green materials in buildings, and its zero waste initiative that

SPOTLIGHT ON ETHICS

Interface

If you were looking for an industry to blame for the destruction of our natural environment, the carpet business would rank right up there—massive consumption of fossil fuels, heavy use of water, and tons of debris going into landfills. But several years ago, Ray Anderson had a different vision: What if his company, Interface, Inc., could be a model of environmental sustainability? People thought he was crazy—a carpet company a paragon of corporate environmental virtue?

Anderson bucked the conventional thinking and declared that Interface would eliminate its environmental footprint by 2020—and make money in the process. After the initial shock, customers and employees became inspired by the idea. Investors took a little longer to "see the green light," but growing sales proved Anderson was onto something. Today, Interface is a leader in the industry, as well as a leader in environmental sustainability. Between 1994 and 2008, the company cut its use of fossil fuels by 45 percent and its water and landfill use by 80 percent. Sales in the last quarter before the economic slump hit were almost $300 million. The recent downturn has hurt Interface, and leaders have been forced to make some tough business decisions, including laying off 500 people and closing manufacturing operations in Belleville, Ontario.

However, Anderson points out that staying focused on environmental goals helped Interface weather the last downturn. When the industry lost 37 percent in sales between 2001 and 2004, Interface lost only about half that percentage, thanks to its focus on sustainability.

Anderson sums up the ultimate goal of sustainability this way: "Take nothing, waste nothing, do no harm, and do very, very well by doing good." Today, even companies that have typically paid little attention to the Green movement are grappling with issues related to sustainability, partly because of the growing clout of environmentalists and a shift in public attitudes. A survey of 6,000 global consumers in the fall of 2008 found that 87 percent believe it is their "duty" to contribute to a better environment. Another study found that MBA students would forgo an average of $13,700 in compensation to work for a company that had a good reputation for environmental sustainability.

SOURCES: Sharda Prashad, "The Value Chain," *Canadian Business* (February 17–March 2, 2009): 65–69; Marjorie Kelly, "Not Just for Profit," *Strategy + Business*, February 24, 2009, www.strategy-business.com/article/09105 (accessed May 19, 2010); Edelman survey, reported in Kauffeld et al., "Green Is a Strategy."; Reported in Kate O'Sullivan, "Virtue Rewarded," *CFO* (October 2006): 47–52.

AP Photo/Beth Hall

ConceptConnection

Walmart has become a corporate leader in the **Green movement**, upgrading its trucking fleet to be more environmentally friendly, meeting stringent environmental goals, and asking suppliers to do the same. Organizations such as consumer products giant P&G are following Walmart's lead and developing **sustainability** scorecards to rate how effective their own suppliers are at producing environmentally sustainable products. The companies then factor the results into their purchasing decisions, along with more traditional considerations such as price, quality, and service.

aims to eliminate all the company's landfill waste by 2025. In addition, Walmart is pushing these initiatives down to suppliers, which could have a tremendous impact.[43]

These and other corporations are embracing an idea called *sustainability* or *sustainable development.* **Sustainability** refers to economic development that generates wealth and meets the needs of the current generation while saving the environment so future generations can meet their needs as well.[44] With a philosophy of sustainability, managers weave environmental and social concerns into every strategic decision, revise policies and procedures to support sustainability efforts, and measure their progress toward sustainability goals. One of the most ardent, and perhaps unlikely, advocates of sustainability is a carpet manufacturer.

- **Corporate social responsibility** refers to the obligation of organizational managers to make choices and take actions that will enhance the welfare and interests of society as well as the organization.
- Different stakeholders have different interests in the organization and thus different criteria for social responsiveness.
- The term **stakeholder** refers to any group within or outside the organization that has a stake in the organization's performance.
- Shareholders, employees, customers, and suppliers are considered primary stakeholders without whom the organization could not survive.
- Government, the community, and special interest groups are also important stakeholders.
- The *Green movement* is a special interest group of particular importance today.
- **Sustainability** refers to economic development that generates wealth and meets the needs of the current population while preserving the environment for the needs of future generations.
- In one survey, 87 percent of people said they think it is their duty to contribute to a better natural environment.
- Companies such as General Electric, Nike, Walmart, and Interface are getting high marks for their commitment to sustainability.

Evaluating Corporate Social Responsibility

A model for evaluating corporate social performance is presented in Exhibit 4.5. The model indicates that total corporate social responsibility can be divided into four primary criteria: economic, legal, ethical, and discretionary responsibilities.[45] These four criteria fit together to form the whole of a company's social responsiveness.

EXHIBIT 4.5

Criteria of Corporate Social Performance

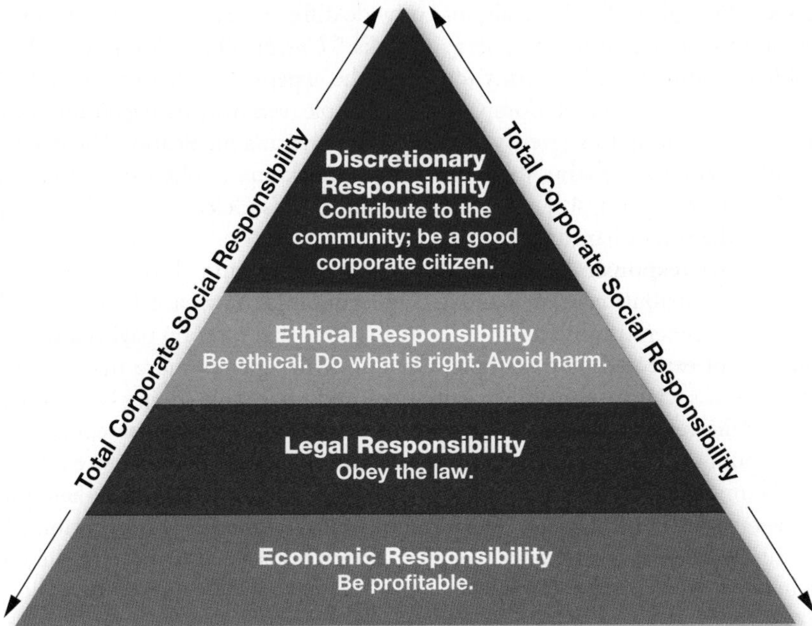

SOURCES: Based on Archie B. Carroll, "A Three-Dimensional Conceptual Model of Corporate Performance," *Academy of Management Review* 4 (1979): 499; A. B. Carroll, "The Pyramid of Corporate Social Responsibility: Toward the Moral Management of Corporate Stakeholders," *Business Horizons* 34 (July–August 1991): 42; and Mark S. Schwartz and Archie B. Carroll, "Corporate Social Responsibility: A Three-Domain Approach," *Business Ethics Quarterly* 13, no. 4 (2003): 503–530.

The first criterion of social responsibility is *economic responsibility*. The business institution is, above all, the basic economic unit of society. Its responsibility is to produce the goods and services that society wants and to maximize profits for its owners and shareholders. Economic responsibility, carried to the extreme, is called the *profit-maximizing view*, advocated by Nobel economist Milton Friedman. This view argues that the corporation should be operated on a profit-oriented basis, with its sole mission to increase its profits as long as it stays within the rules of the game.[46] The purely profit-maximizing view is no longer considered an adequate criterion of performance in Canada, the United States, and Europe. This approach means that economic gain is the only social responsibility and can lead companies into trouble, as recent events in the mortgage and finance industries have clearly shown.

Legal responsibility defines what society deems as important with respect to appropriate corporate behavior.[47] That is, businesses are expected to fulfill their economic goals within the framework of legal requirements imposed by local town councils, state legislators, and federal regulatory agencies. Examples of illegal acts by corporations include corporate fraud, intentionally selling defective goods, performing unnecessary repairs or procedures, deliberately misleading consumers, and billing clients for work not done. Organizations that knowingly break the law are poor performers in this category. Siemens, for example, paid a whopping $1.6 billion in fines after being convicted of violating German and U.S. antibribery laws. Manager Reinhard Siekaczek oversaw an annual "bribery budget" of about $50 million that was used to pay off corrupt officials and help the firm win contracts around the world.[48]

Read the Ethical Dilemma, on page 158, that pertains to legal and ethical responsibilities.

Ethical responsibility includes behaviors that are not necessarily codified into law and may not serve the corporation's direct economic interests. As described earlier in this chapter, to be *ethical*, organization decision makers should act with equity, fairness, and impartiality, respect the rights of individuals, and provide different treatment of individuals only when relevant to the organization's goals and tasks.[49] *Unethical* behavior occurs when decisions enable an individual or company to gain at the expense of other people or society as a whole. Managers at Merck & Company, for example, seriously damaged the company's reputation by continuing to aggressively market the arthritis medication Vioxx even after they had information suggesting there were heart attack and stroke risks associated with the drug. Merck was facing stiff competition from Pfizer's Celebrex and chose to pursue profits even at the risk of harming patients.

Discretionary responsibility is purely voluntary and is guided by a company's desire to make social contributions not mandated by economics, law, or ethics. Discretionary activities include generous philanthropic contributions that offer no payback to the company and are not expected. For example, General Mills spends more than 5 percent of pretax profits on social responsibility initiatives and charitable giving.[50] Another good illustration of discretionary behavior occurred when Emigrant Savings deposited $1,000 into the accounts of nearly 1,000 customers living in areas hit hardest by Hurricane Katrina.[51] Numerous U.S. corporations sent generous donations of money and goods to earthquake-ravaged Haiti. Discretionary responsibility is the highest criterion of social responsibility because it goes beyond societal expectations to contribute to the community's welfare.

- The model for evaluating a company's social performance uses four criteria: economic, legal, ethical, and discretionary.
- Companies may get into trouble when they use economic criteria as their only measure of responsibility, sometimes called the *profit-maximizing* view.
- **Discretionary responsibility** is purely voluntary and is guided by the organization's desire to make social contributions not mandated by economics, laws, or ethics.
- Corporations that sent generous donations to Haiti following the devastating earthquake were practicing discretionary responsibility.

Managing Company Ethics and Social Responsibility

An expert on the topic of ethics said, "Management is responsible for creating and sustaining conditions in which people are likely to behave themselves."[52] Exhibit 4.6 illustrates ways in which managers create and support an ethical organization. One of the most important steps managers can take is to practice ethical leadership. *Ethical leadership* means that managers are honest and trustworthy, fair in their dealings with employees and customers, and behave ethically in both their personal and professional lives. In response to recent ethical violations and critics of management education saying MBA stands for "Me Before Anyone,"[53] some business schools and students are taking a fresh look at how future managers are trained.

HARVARD BUSINESS SCHOOL, COLUMBIA BUSINESS SCHOOL, YALE SCHOOL OF MANAGEMENT

Some members of the 2009 graduating class of Harvard Business School did something unusual. They signed a voluntary student-led pledge saying that the goal of a business manager is to "serve the greater good" and promising that they will act responsibly and ethically and refrain from advancing their "own narrow ambitions" at the expense of others.

At Harvard and other business schools, there has been an explosion of interest in ethics classes and activities that focus on personal and corporate responsibility. Many students, as well as educators, are recognizing a need to give future managers a deeper understanding of how to practice ethical leadership rather than just how to make money. At Columbia Business School, which requires an ethics course, students formed a popular Leadership and Ethics Board that sponsors lectures and other activities. Yale School of Management developed sessions in its core curriculum related to the recent crisis and worked with the Aspen Institute to create a curriculum aimed at teaching business students how to act on their values at work. About 55 business schools are using all or part of the curriculum in pilot programs. "There is a feeling that we want our lives to mean something more and to run organizations for the greater good," said Max Anderson, one of the organizers of Harvard's pledge. "No one wants to have their future criticized as a place filled with unethical behaviors."[54]

Changing how future managers are trained could be one key to solving the ethics deficit pervading organizations. Managers and first-line supervisors are important role models for ethical behavior, and they strongly influence the ethical climate in the organization by adhering to high ethical standards in their own behavior and decisions. Moreover, managers are proactive in influencing employees to embody and reflect ethical values.[55]

Managers can also implement organizational mechanisms to help employees and the company stay on an ethical footing. Some of the primary ones are codes of ethics, ethical structures, and measures to protect whistle-blowers.

Code of Ethics

A **code of ethics** is a formal statement of the company's values concerning ethics and social issues; it communicates to employees what the company stands for. Codes of ethics tend to

EXHIBIT 4.6

Building an Ethical Organization

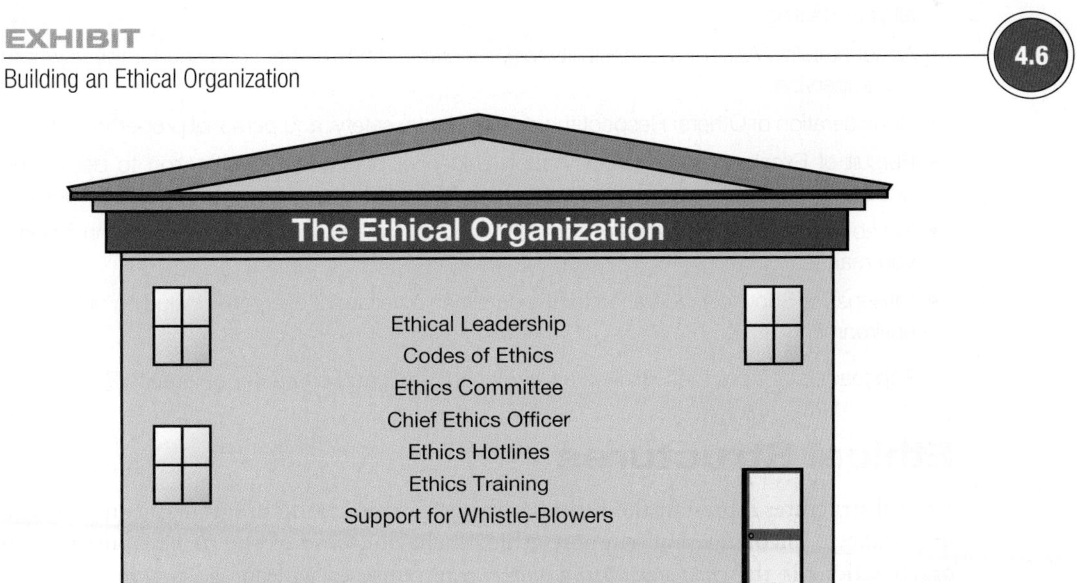

SOURCE: Adapted from Linda Klebe Treviño, Laura Pincus Hartman, and Michael Brown, "Moral Person and Moral Manager," *California Management Review* 42, no. 4 (Summer 2000): 128–142.

exist in two types: principle-based statements and policy-based statements. *Principle-based statements* are designed to affect corporate culture; they define fundamental values and contain general language about company responsibilities, quality of products, and treatment of employees. General statements of principle are often called *corporate credos*. One good example is Johnson & Johnson's "The Credo." Available in 36 languages, the Credo has guided Johnson & Johnson's managers for more than 60 years in making decisions that honor the company's responsibilities to employees, customers, the community, and stockholders.

Policy-based statements generally outline the procedures to be used in specific ethical situations. These situations include marketing practices, conflicts of interest, observance of laws, proprietary information, political gifts, and equal opportunities. Examples of policy-based statements are Boeing's "Business Conduct Guidelines," Chemical Bank's "Code of Ethics," GTE's "Code of Business Ethics" and "Anti-Trust and Conflict of Interest Guidelines," and Norton's "Norton Policy on Business Ethics."[56]

Codes of ethics state the values or behaviors expected and those that will not be tolerated. When top management supports and enforces these codes, including rewards for compliance and discipline for violation, ethics codes can boost a company's ethical climate.[57] At Granite Construction, top management commitment to honoring and enforcing its Code of Conduct is one reason the company was named one of the "World's Most Ethical Companies" for 2010 by the Ethisphere Institute.

GRANITE CONSTRUCTION

The construction industry isn't always a shining beacon of ethical and socially responsible behavior, and Granite Construction has experienced its share of troubles over the years. However, Granite's Code of Conduct has helped the company maintain a highly ethical culture in a tough industry. The code includes eight core values that are intended to guide employees in how they treat one another, how they deal with customers, and how they respond to other stakeholders. Here are the eight values and some highlights:

- Honesty: Be candid and nondeceptive in communication and conduct.
- Integrity: Have the courage to contend boldly for that which is right and reject firmly that which is wrong.
- Fairness: Be reasonable, open-minded, impartial, even-handed, and non-discriminatory in all your dealings.
- Accountability: Accept responsibility for your own actions or inactions and for those whom you supervise.
- Consideration of Others: Respect the dignity, rights, safety, and personal property of others.
- Pursuit of Excellence: Consistently apply diligence, perseverance, attention to detail, and good work habits to ensure quality projects, quality products, and excellent customer service.
- Reliability: Only make realistic commitments and follow through on the commitments you make.
- Citizenship: Show consideration for the safety and welfare of everyone, including our natural environment.

Top leaders refer to these values as "the heart, soul, and character of Granite."[58]

Ethical Structures

Ethical structures represent the various systems, positions, and programs a company can undertake to encourage and support ethical behavior. One of the newest positions in organizations is the *chief accounting officer*, a response to widespread financial wrongdoing in recent years. These high-level executives handle reporting and compliance, ensure due diligence, and work with outside auditors.[59] An **ethics committee** is a group of executives appointed to oversee company ethics. The committee provides rulings on questionable ethical issues and assumes responsibility for disciplining wrongdoers. Motorola's Ethics Compliance Committee, for instance, is charged with interpreting, clarifying, and communicating the company's code of ethics and with adjudicating suspected code violations.

Many companies set up ethics offices with full-time staff to ensure that ethical standards are an integral part of company operations. These offices are headed by a **chief ethics officer**, a company executive who oversees all aspects of ethics and legal compliance, including establishing and broadly communicating standards, ethics training, dealing with exceptions or problems, and advising senior managers in the ethical and compliance aspects of decisions.[60] The title of *chief ethics officer* was almost unheard of a decade ago, but highly publicized ethical and legal problems in recent years sparked a growing demand for these ethics specialists. The Ethics and Compliance Officers Association, a trade group, reports that membership soared 70 percent, to more than 1,260 companies, in the five years following the collapse of Enron due to financial wrongdoing.[61] Most ethics offices also work as counseling centers to help employees resolve difficult ethical issues. A toll-free confidential *ethics hotline* allows employees to report questionable behavior as well as seek guidance concerning ethical dilemmas.

Ethics training programs also help employees deal with ethical questions and translate the values stated in a code of ethics into everyday behavior.[62] Training programs are an important supplement to a written code of ethics. General Electric implemented a strong compliance and ethics training program for all 320,000 employees worldwide. Much of the training is conducted online, with employees able to test themselves on how they would handle thorny ethical issues. In addition, small group meetings give people a chance to ask questions and discuss ethical dilemmas or questionable actions. Every quarter, each of GE's business units reports to headquarters the percentage of division employees who completed training sessions and the percentage that have read and signed off on the company's ethics guide, "Spirit and Letter."[63] At McMurray Publishing Company in Phoenix, all employees attend a *weekly* meeting on workplace ethics, where they discuss how to handle ethical dilemmas and how to resolve conflicting values.[64]

Complete the Self Learning Exercise, on pages 156–157, that pertains to ethical work environments.

Whistle-Blowing

Employee disclosure of illegal, unethical, or illegitimate practices on the employer's part is called **whistle-blowing**.[65] No organization can rely exclusively on codes of conduct and ethical structures to prevent all unethical behavior. Holding organizations accountable depends to some degree on individuals who are willing to blow the whistle if they detect illegal, dangerous, or unethical activities. Whistle-blowers often report wrongdoing to outsiders, such as regulatory agencies, senators, or newspaper reporters. Some firms have instituted innovative programs and confidential hotlines to encourage and support internal whistle-blowing. For this practice to be an effective ethical safeguard, however, companies must view whistle-blowing as a benefit to the company and make dedicated efforts to protect whistle-blowers.[66] PricewaterhouseCoopers conducted a Global Economic Crime survey and reported that the two most effective investments in ethics programs are internal auditing and support of whistle-blowers.[67] Countrywide did not support its whistle blowers, as shown in the Business Bloopers Box. As a result, both the company and the former CEO paid dearly.

Without effective protective measures, whistle-blowers suffer. They can lose their jobs, be ostracized by coworkers, or be transferred to lower-level positions. Matthew Lee, a former senior vice president in Lehman Brothers's accounting division, for example, lost his job just weeks after he raised concerns about how the firm was masking risks by temporarily "parking" $50 billion in risky loan assets off its balance sheet. Lawrence McDonald, a former Lehman trader who has written a book about the giant firm's collapse, says Lehman routinely sacked or sidelined whistle-blowers, which allowed the company to continue its risky and unethical behavior.[68]

BUSINESS BLOOPER

Countrywide

Countrywide's CEO Angelo Mozilo's desperation to be Number One led to a race to the bottom as the mortgage crisis spun out of control and he was unwilling to give up any of his control. Mortgage delinquency rates more than doubled to 24 percent, and Countrywide was sold to Bank of America, with its value shrunk from $25 billion to $4 billion. Mozilo was arrested for fraud and settled out of court by paying a fine of $67.5 million.

Not long after, the wrongful termination suit of Michael Winston from Countrywide began. As a new executive, Winston learned of the company's growth strategy: "Fund' em," even if the loan was going to a person with no job. "Fund 'em," he was told. He expressed his concerns about this anything-goes strategy in writing. His next "mistake" was when he refused to misrepresent the company's financial situation to Moody's Investors Service, Inc., the famous ratings agency. Soon his budget was frozen, and he was uninvited to meetings and finally fired. He sued the company, which hired huge law firms with outsized budgets and brought in witnesses such as Mozilo. The jury was not impressed. "When plain ordinary citizens see the evidence and hear the facts, the are repulsed by what these people did," said one member. "There was an air of arrogance about them." The jury awarded Winston $3.8 million in damages.

SOURCES: Bethany MacLean and Joe Nocera, *All the Devils Are Here: The Hidden History of the Financial Crisis* (Portfolio Hardcover, 2010); and Gretchen Morgenson, How a Whistle-Blower Conquered Countrywide, *The New York Times*, February 20, 2011.

Unfortunately, many managers still look on whistle-blowers as disgruntled employees who aren't good team players. Yet to maintain high ethical standards, organizations need people who are willing to point out wrongdoing. Managers can be trained to view whistle-blowing as a benefit rather than a threat, and systems can be set up to effectively protect employees who report illegal or unethical activities.

The Business Case for Ethics and Social Responsibility

Most managers now realize that paying attention to ethics and social responsibility is as important a business issue as paying attention to costs, profits, and growth. For one thing, in today's information age, bad behavior is increasingly hard to hide, and "out-behaving the competition" can provide a real competitive advantage.[69]

Naturally, the relationship of a corporation's ethics and social responsibility to its financial performance concerns both managers and management scholars and has generated a lively debate.[70] One concern of managers is whether good citizenship will hurt performance—after all, ethics programs and social responsibility cost money. Hundreds of studies have been undertaken to determine whether heightened ethical and social responsiveness increases or decreases a company's financial performance. Studies have provided varying results, but they have generally found a positive relationship between ethical and socially responsible behavior and firm financial performance.[71] For example, a study of the financial performance of large U.S. corporations considered "best corporate citizens" found that they enjoy both superior reputations and superior financial performance.[72] Similarly, Governance Metrics International, an independent corporate governance ratings agency in New York, reports that the stocks of companies run on more selfless principles perform better than those run in a self-serving manner.[73] Although results from these studies are not proof, they do provide an indication that use of resources for ethics and social responsibility does not hurt companies.[74]

Companies are also making an effort to measure the nonfinancial factors that create value. Researchers found, for example, that people prefer to work for companies that demonstrate a high level of ethics and social responsibility; thus, these organizations can attract and retain high-quality employees.[75] Customers pay attention too. A study by Walker Research indicates that, price and quality being equal, two-thirds of customers say they would switch brands to do business with a company that is ethical and socially responsible.[76] Another series of experiments by Remi Trudel and June Cotte of the University of Western Ontario's Ivey School of Business found that consumers were willing to pay slightly more for products they were told had been made using high ethical standards.[77]

Enlightened managers realize that integrity and trust are essential elements in sustaining successful and profitable business relationships with an increasingly connected and well-informed web of employees, customers, suppliers, and partners. Although doing the right thing might not always be profitable in the short run, many managers believe it can provide a competitive advantage by developing a level of trust that money can't buy.

Eaton Corporation

ConceptConnection

Gen-Yers throughout the world expect a serious commitment to sustainability from their employers. For example, one study found that over 95 percent want to work for an organization that goes beyond merely complying with existing environmental legislation. Cleveland-based Eaton Corporation, a diversified power management company, prominently features its commitment to sustainability on its career Web page and at career fairs, such as the one pictured here, in order to **attract high-quality employees**. "It's actually helped us in acquiring top talent at a lot of top universities," says Joel Wolfsberger, Eaton vice president for environment, health, and safety.

- Managers are role models. One of the most important ways managers create ethical and socially responsible organizations is by practicing ethical leadership.
- Some students at Harvard Business School sign a pledge promising to act responsibly and ethically as managers.
- MBA students are leading the way toward a new approach to training managers that emphasizes personal ethics and social responsibility.
- A **code of ethics** is a formal statement of the organization's values regarding ethics and social issues.
- An **ethics committee** is a group of executives charged with overseeing company ethics by ruling on questionable issues and disciplining violators.
- Some organizations have ethics offices headed by a **chief ethics officer**, a manager who oversees all aspects of ethics and legal compliance.
- **Ethics training** is used to help employees deal with ethical questions and translate the values stated in a code of ethics into everyday behavior.
- Managers who want ethical organizations support **whistle-blowing**, the disclosure by employees of unethical, illegitimate, or illegal practices by the organization.
- Companies that are ethical and socially responsible perform as well as—and often better than—those that are not socially responsible.

Discussion Questions

1. Dr. Martin Luther King, Jr., said, "As long as there is poverty in the world, I can never be rich. . . . As long as diseases are rampant, I can never be healthy. . . . I can never be what I ought to be until you are what you ought to be." Discuss whether this quote would apply to corporations as well as individuals.
2. What various stakeholder groups did oil giant BP have to respond to in regard to the massive 2010 oil spill in the Gulf of Mexico? From what you know about the BP oil spill, how would you evaluate BP executives' behavior in terms of corporate social responsibility?
3. Imagine yourself in a situation of being encouraged by colleagues to inflate your expense account. What factors do you think would influence your choice? Explain.
4. Is it socially responsible for organizations to undertake political activity or join with others in a trade association to influence the government? Discuss.
5. Managers at some banks and mortgage companies have argued that providing subprime mortgages was based on their desire to give poor people a chance to participate in the American dream of home ownership. What is your opinion of this explanation in terms of ethics and social responsibility?
6. A noted business executive said, "A company's first obligation is to be profitable. Unprofitable enterprises can't afford to be socially responsible." Discuss why you agree or disagree with this statement.
7. Do you believe it is ethical for organizational managers to try to get access to and scrutinize Facebook pages of employees or job applicants? Discuss.
8. Which do you think would be more effective for shaping long-term ethical behavior in an organization: a written code of ethics combined with ethics training, or strong ethical leadership? Which would have more impact on you? Why?
9. Lincoln Electric considers customers and employees to be more important stakeholders than its shareholders. Is it appropriate for management to define some stakeholders as more important than others? Should all stakeholders be considered equal?
10. The chapter refers to a survey that shows that many people think cheating is more common today than it was a decade ago. Do you think cheating is really more common, or does it just seem so? Why?

Self-Learning

Ethical Work Climates[78]

Think of an organization for which you were employed. Answer the following items twice: The first time, circle the number that best describes the way things actually were. The second time, answer the items based on your beliefs about the ideal level to meet the needs of both individuals and the organization.

Disagree ① ② ③ ④ ⑤ **Agree**

See It Online

1. What was best for everyone in the company was the major consideration there.

   1 2 3 4 5

2. Our major concern was always what was best for the other person.

   1 2 3 4 5

3. People were expected to comply with the law and professional standards over and above other considerations.

   1 2 3 4 5

4. In the company, the first consideration was whether a decision violated any law.

   1 2 3 4 5

5. It was very important to follow the company's rules and procedures there.

   1 2 3 4 5

6. People in the company strictly obeyed the company policies.

   1 2 3 4 5

7. In the company, people were mostly out for themselves.

   1 2 3 4 5

8. People were expected to do anything to further the company's interests, regardless of the consequences.

   1 2 3 4 5

9. In the company, people were guided by their own personal ethics.

   1 2 3 4 5

10. Each person in the company decided for himself or herself what was right and wrong.

    1 2 3 4 5

Scoring and Interpretation

Subtract each of your scores for items 7 and 8 from the number 6. Then, add up your score for all ten items: Actual = ________. Ideal = ________. These items measure the dimensions of an organization's ethical climate. Items 1 and 2 measure caring for people; items 3 and 4 measure lawfulness; items 5 and 6 measure adherence to rules; items 7 and 8 measure emphasis on financial and company performance; and items 9 and 10 measure individual independence. A total score above 40 indicates a highly positive ethical climate. A score from 30 to 40 indicates above-average ethical climate. A score from 20 to 30 indicates a below-average ethical climate, and a score below 20 indicates a poor ethical climate. How far from your ideal score was the actual score for your organization? What does that difference mean to you?

Go back over the items and think about changes that you could have made to improve the ethical climate in the organization. Discuss with other students what you could do as a manager to improve ethics in future companies for which you work.

Group Learning

Current Events of an Unethical Type[79]

Step 1. Prior to meeting as a group, each person finds two newspaper or magazine articles from the past several months relating to someone violating business ethics or potentially violating the law regarding business practices.

Step 2. Summarize the key points of the articles you found.

Step 3. Meet as a group. Each person in turn shares key points from articles with group members.

Step 4. Identify similar themes across the unethical incidents reported in the articles. What was the source or underlying cause of the unethical behavior? What was the hoped-for outcome? Was an individual or group involved? Can you identify similar conditions of any kind across incidents? Did the accused seem repentant or defensive? Write the common themes in a list on a sheet of paper or whiteboard.

Step 5. What could you do as a manager to prevent such unethical behavior in your organization? What could you do to fix this kind of problem after it occurred in your organization?

Step 6. Report your findings to the class if asked to do so by your instructor.

Action Learning

1. Write down at least three times when you were presented with an ethical dilemma, such as the opportunity to cheat on a test or a paper, being undercharged for something at a store or restaurant, being given "free" food by your friend who was an employee there, taking office supplies home from a workplace, using work time for personal activities, etc.
2. As a group of three to six people, choose three of the examples from the group to analyze.

Describe the ethical dilemma	What did you do?	What should you have done?	What ethical principal was involved?
1.			
2.			
3.			

3. Each person in the group responds to this: Think of a time when someone behaved *unethically* toward you, and fill out the table below.

Describe unethical behavior	How did you react to unethical behavior?	How did it impact your relationship with that person?	What would have been ethical behavior by the other person?

4. In your group, discuss behaviors and consequences in your dilemmas and situations.
5. Why is it important to be ethical?

Ethical Dilemma

Should We Go Beyond the Law?[80]

Nathan Rosillo stared out his office window at the lazy curves and lush, green, flower-lined banks of the Dutch Valley River. He'd grown up near here, and he envisioned the day his children would enjoy the river as he had as a child. But now his own company might make that a risky proposition.

Nathan is a key product developer at Chem-Tech Corporation, an industry leader. Despite its competitive position, Chem-Tech experienced several quarters of dismal financial performance. Nathan and his team developed a new lubricant product that the company sees as the turning point in its declining fortunes. Top executives are thrilled that they can produce the new product at a significant cost savings because of recent changes in environmental regulations. Regulatory agencies loosened requirements on reducing and recycling wastes, which means Chem-Tech can now release waste directly into the Dutch Valley River.

Nathan is as eager as anyone to see Chem-Tech survive this economic downturn, but he doesn't think this route is the way to do it. He expressed his opposition regarding the waste dumping to both the plant manager and his direct supervisor, Martin Feldman. Martin has always supported Nathan, but this time was different. The plant manager too turned a deaf ear. "We're meeting government standards," he'd said. "It's up to them to protect the water. It's up to us to make a profit and stay in business."

Frustrated and confused, Nathan turned away from the window, his prime office view mocking his inability to protect the river he loved. He knew the manufacturing vice president was visiting the plant next week. Maybe if he talked with her, she would agree that the decision to dump waste materials in the river was ethically and socially irresponsible. But if she didn't, he would be skating on thin ice. His supervisor had already accused him of not being a team player. Maybe he should just be a passive bystander—after all, the company wasn't breaking any laws.

What Would You Do?

1. Talk to the manufacturing vice president and emphasize the responsibility Chem-Tech has, as an industry leader, to set an example. Present her with a recommendation that Chem-Tech participate in voluntary pollution reduction as a marketing tool, positioning itself as the environmentally friendly choice.
2. Mind your own business and just do your job. The company isn't breaking any laws, and if Chem-Tech's economic situation doesn't improve, a lot of people will be thrown out of work.
3. Call the local environmental advocacy group and get them to stage a protest of the company.

Case for Critical Analysis

Empress Luxury Lines[81]

From what computer technician Kevin Pfeiffer just told him, it looked to Antonio Melendez as if top management at Empress Luxury Lines had finally found a way to fund the computer system upgrade he'd been requesting ever since he'd taken the job two years ago.

It all began innocently enough, Kevin said. When he reported to the luxury cruise line's corporate headquarters, his supervisor Phil Bailey informed him that the computer system had been hit by a power surge during the fierce thunderstorms that rolled through southern Florida the night before. "Check out the damage, and report directly back to me," Phil instructed.

When Kevin delivered what he thought would be good news—the damaged underground wires and computer circuits could be repaired to the tune of about $15,000—he couldn't understand why Phil looked so deflated. "Go out to the reception area. I've got to call Roger," Phil snapped, referring to Empress's CFO—and Antonio's boss. In a few minutes, Phil called Kevin back into the office and instructed him to dig up nearly all the underground wire and cable and then haul it all off before the insurance adjustor appeared. If Kevin carried out Phil's orders, he knew the costs would balloon astronomically to about a half-million dollars, a tidy sum that would go a long way toward covering the costs of a computer system upgrade, as Phil pointed out.

Kevin took a deep breath and refused, even though as a new hire he was still on probation. When Antonio congratulated Kevin on his integrity, the technician shook his head. "Didn't really matter," he said. "On my way back to my cubicle, Matt passed me on his way to do the deed."

Antonio could guess at the motivation behind the scam. During the 1990s, Empress increased its fleet of ships in response to the healthy demand for its luxury cruises during the stock market bubble. But the bubble burst, the nation was traumatized by September 11, and some of the vacationers who did venture onto cruises were felled by an outbreak of the Norwalk virus. Bookings fell off precipitously. To top it all off, the 2005 hurricanes hit, forcing Empress to write piles of refund checks for their Caribbean and Gulf cruises while coping with steep increases in fuel costs. Seriously sagging earnings explained why Antonio's requests for that system upgrade went unheeded.

He could also guess at the likely consequences if he chose to do the right thing. Since taking the job, he'd heard rumors that Empress successfully defrauded insurance companies before he arrived.

He dismissed them at the time, but now he wasn't so sure. No confidential mechanism was in place for employees to report wrongdoing internally, and no protections were available for whistle-blowers. Shaken, Antonio wasn't feeling at all confident that, even if he bypassed the CFO, he would find upper-level management all that eager to thwart the scheme. He had a hunch that the person most likely to be penalized was the whistle-blower.

"I debated about just calling the insurance company," Kevin said, "but I decided to come to you first." So what should Antonio do? Should he advise Kevin to go ahead and report Empress to the insurance company? Or should he treat Kevin's communication as confidential and deal with the situation himself, in effect putting only his own job in jeopardy? And really, considering the high degree of personal risk and the low probability that the problem would actually be addressed, should he just sweep the problem under the rug?

Questions

1. When determining what his obligations are to his subordinate, Kevin Pfeiffer, what decision would Antonio Melendez most likely reach if he applied the utilitarian approach to decision making? What conclusions would probably result if he employed the individualism approach?
2. Put yourself in Antonio's position and decide realistically what you would do. Is your response at a preconventional, conventional, or postconventional level of moral development? How do you feel about your response?
3. If Antonio or Kevin were fired because he reported Empress's fraud, would he be justified in removing all traces of his employment at the cruise line from his résumés so he don't have to explain to a prospective employer why he was fired? Why or why not?

aplia Aplia Highlights

Now use your Aplia homework to help you:

- Apply management theories in your life
- Assess your management skills
- Master management terms and concepts
- Apply your knowledge to real-world situations
- Analyze and solve challenging management problems

In order to take advantage of these elements, your instructor will need to have set up a course for your class within Aplia. Ask your instructor to contact his/her Cengage sales representative and Digital Solutions Manager to explore testing Aplia in your course this term.

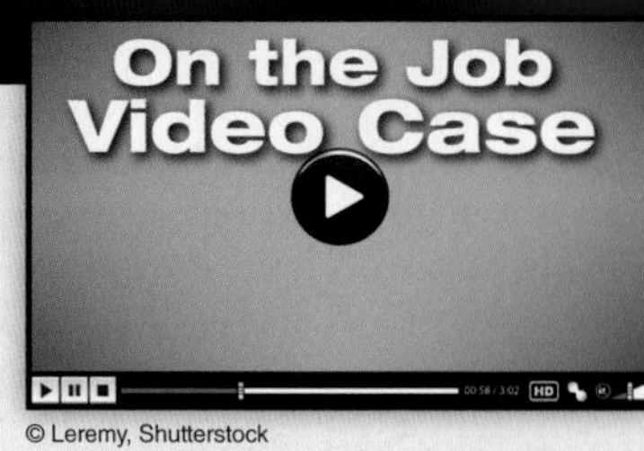

© Leremy, Shutterstock

Theo Chocolate: Managing Ethics and Social Responsibility

As a boy growing up in Philadelphia, just hours from Hershey, Pennsylvania, confectioner Joe Whinney fell in love with chocolate. Halloween was sheer bliss for the youngster, and Whinney recalls often getting lost in thought while munching on a chocolate bar.

When he grew older, Whinney got an opportunity to visit cocoa bean farms in the rainforests of Central America, while serving as a volunteer for a conservation program. The experience was life changing.

Propelled by his combined love of chocolate and the environment, Whinney dreamed of building the first organic fair trade chocolate factory in the United States. In 1994 he pioneered the import of organic cocoa beans to the United States, and in 2006 Whinney's Theo Chocolate company became the first and only sustainable chocolate maker in the nation.

Unlike U.S. chocolate manufacturers who deliver sweets in high volume, Theo's award winning chocolate is produced in small batches. The company's "bean-to-bar" production method uses cocoa beans grown without pesticides and without harm to the environment or farmers. The result is a creamy delectable milk chocolate bar that is as good for the ecosystem as it is for the palate.

Like other social entrepreneurs, Joe Whinney exudes a sense of mission in everything he does. "After my experience in Central America," says Whinney, "I saw that social and environmental degradation were really business problems, and I wanted to help save the world by making chocolate." The chocolate maker's objective is to operate a business that is profitable, ethical, and good for the environment. "Our business ethic," says Whinney, "is informed by our belief that all life on the planet is interconnected. We need consumers to be healthy and well, our farmers to be healthy and well, and the entire planet to be healthy and well in order for us to be successful and profitable."

Organic farming and fair trade are important to Whinney. In Theo Chocolate's world, *organic* means that the cocoa beans are naturally grown and harvested in ways that preserve habitats and the balance of the ecosystem. *Fair trade* is an economic concept that ensures equity between buyers and growers in developing nations, as well as fair treatment of workers. Theo Chocolate is proud of its status as a certified fair trade company. "Fair trade certification is important for us to build trust with our consumers, so that we do what we say we are going to do," says Whinney.

Since fair trade certification is important in preventing companies from exaggerating their green credibility, Theo chose IMO Fair for Life to be its accountability certification program. "What's great about Fair for Life is that it is a certification that ensures the economic and social integrity of our entire supply chain, from the cocoa farmers that we work with all the way through to our own factory operations," remarked Whinney.

Debra Music, a fellow chocoholic and the vice president of sales and marketing at Theo, says the company is an example of "enlightened capitalism." Music expresses pride in being the only fair-trade-certified bean-to-bar chocolate factory in the United States. "We're trying to define the intersection of artisan world-class chocolate making with sustainable practices," Music says. "Simply put, I like to say it's about doing good while doing well."

While Theo Chocolate is finding good success in the organic foods industry, perhaps the most exciting thing for "Theonistas" is that the company is being hailed as a voice for change. Employees say they have gained a loyal following for their efforts in the developing world, and business success has opened up new opportunities for sharing their vision of a better world.

Discussion Questions

1. What practices at Theo Chocolate embody the concept of *sustainability*?
2. What does Vice President Debra Music mean when she says that Theo is a "triple bottom line" company? How is this different from any other company?
3. What does the term *fair trade* mean to the leaders at Theo? What happens if fair trade goals conflict with a company's primary responsibility to be profitable?

© Pedro Nogueira, Shutterstock

© VikaSuh, Shutterstock

The Emperor's Club

William Hundert (Kevin Kline), a professor at the exclusive Saint Benedict's Academy for Boys, believes in teaching his students about living a principled life. He also wants them to learn his beloved classical literature. A new student, Sedgewick Bell (Emile Hirsch), challenges Hundert's principled ways. Bell's behavior during the 73rd annual Mr. Julius Caesar Contest causes Hundert to suspect that Bell leads a less than principled life, a suspicion confirmed years later during a reenactment of the competition.

Ethics and Ethical Behavior Mr. Hundert is the honored guest of his former student Sedgewick Bell (Joel Gretsch) at Bell's estate. Depaak Mehta (Rahul Khanna), Bell, and Louis Masoudi (Patrick Dempsey) compete in a reenactment of the Julius Caesar competition. Bell wins the competition, but Hundert notices that Bell is wearing an earpiece. Earlier in the film, Hundert had suspected that young Bell wore an earpiece during the competition, but Headmaster Woodbridge (Edward Herrmann) urged him to ignore his suspicion.

This scene appears at the end of the film. It is an edited version of the competition reenactment. Bell announced his candidacy for the U.S. Senate just before he spoke with Hundert in the bathroom. In his announcement, he carefully described his commitment to specific values he would pursue if elected.

What to Watch for and Ask Yourself

1. Does William Hundert describe a specific type of life that one should lead? If so, what are its elements?
2. Does Sedgewick Bell lead that type of life? Is he committed to any specific view or theory of ethics?
3. What consequences or effects do you predict for Sedgewick Bell because of the way he chooses to live his life?

© Pedro Nogueira, Shutterstock

Endnotes

1. This example comes from Susan Pulliam, "Crossing the Line: At Center of Fraud, WorldCom Official Sees Life Unravel," *The Wall Street Journal*, March 24, 2005; and S. Pulliam, "Over the Line: A Staffer Ordered to Commit Fraud Balked, Then Caved," *The Wall Street Journal*, June 23, 2003.
2. Mara Der Hovanesian, "Sex, Lies, and Mortgage Deals," *BusinessWeek* (November 24, 2009): 71–74; Amir Efrati, "Law School Rankings Reviewed to Deter 'Gaming,'" *The Wall Street Journal*, August 26, 2008.
3. Nicholas Casey, "Corporate News: Ex-American Apparel Accountant Sues; Plaintiff Claims He Was Fired after Refusing to Inflate Balance-Sheet Figures," *The Wall Street Journal*, November 12, 2008.
4. Gordon F. Shea, *Practical Ethics* (New York: American Management Association, 1988); and Linda K. Treviño, "Ethical Decision Making in Organizations: A Person-Situation Interactionist Model," *Academy of Management Review* 11 (1986): 601–617.
5. Thomas M. Jones, "Ethical Decision Making by Individuals in Organizations: An Issue-Contingent Model," *Academy of Management Review* 16 (1991): 366–395.
6. Shelby D. Hunt and Jared M. Hansen, "Understanding Ethical Diversity in Organizations," *Organizational Dynamics* 36, no 2 (2007): 202–216.
7. Justin Scheck, "Accusations of Snooping in Ink-Cartridge Dispute," *The Wall Street Journal Online*, August 11, 2009, http://online.wsj.com/article/SB124995836273921661.html (accessed August 14, 2009).
8. Katharina Bart, "UBS Lays Out Employee Ethics Code," *The Wall Street Journal Online*, January 12, 2010, http://online.wsj.com/article/SB10001424052748704586504574653901865050062.html (accessed January 15, 2010); and Louise Story, "Goldman Employee Denies S.E.C. Fraud Accusations," *The New York Times*, July 20, 2010.
9. Dan Tracy, "Blood-Bank Chief's Pay Raised to $605,000: 13% Bump Came Before 42 Job Cuts," *Orlando Sentinel*, February 17, 2010.
10. Rushworth M. Kidder, "The Three Great Domains of Human Action," *Christian Science Monitor*, January 30, 1990.
11. Adam Cohen, "Who Cheats? Our Survey on Deceit," *The Wall Street Journal*, June 27, 2008.

12. Alistair MacDonald and Stephen Fidler, "School for Scandal," *The Wall Street Journal*, May 16–17, 2009.

13. CBS News reports, as discussed in Deborah L. Rhode and Amada K. Packet, "Ethics and Nonprofits," *Stanford Social Innovation Review* 7, no. 3 (Summer 2009): 29–35.

14. Marist College Institute for Public Opinion and Knights of Columbus survey, results reported in Kevin Turner, "Corporate Execs: Nobody Trusts Us; U.S. Lacks Confidence in Business Ethics, Poll Says," *Florida Times Union*, February 27, 2009.

15. Gary R. Weaver, Linda Klebe Treviño, and Bradley Agle, "'Somebody I Look Up To:' Ethical Role Models in Organizations," *Organizational Dynamics* 34, no. 4 (2005): 313–330.

16. These measures of unethical behavior are from Muel Kaptein, "Developing a Measure of Unethical Behavior in the Workplace: A Stakeholder Perspective," *Journal of Management* 34, no. 5 (October 2008): 978–1008.

17. Jackie Calmes and Louise Story, "AIG Bonus Outcry Builds: Troubled Insurance Giant Gave out More Millions Last Week," *Pittsburgh Post Gazette*, March 18, 2009; Graham Bowley, "Wall Street '09 Bonuses Increase 17% to $20 Billion," *The New York Times*, February 24, 2010; and Adam Shell, "Despite Recession, Average Wall Street Bonus Leaps 25%; About $20.3 Billion Distributed in 2009," *USA Today*, February 24, 2010.

18. Nicholas D. Kristof, "Lehman CEO Fuld Takes the Prize; Need a Job? $17,000 an Hour; No Success Required," *The Gazette*, September 19, 2008; Paul Goodsell, "Are CEOs Worth Their Salt? *Omaha World-Herald*, October 5, 2008.

19. Reported in Kristof, "Lehman CEO Fuld Takes the Prize"; and Chuck Collins, "Rein in Runaway CEO Pay," *McClatchy-Tribune News Service*, February 3, 2009.

20. Nick Paumgarten, "Food Fighter: The Whole Foods CEO vs. His Customers" (Profiles column), *The New Yorker* (January 4, 2010): 36.

21. Linda K. Treviño and Katherine A. Nelson, *Managing Business Ethics: Straight Talk about How to Do It Right* (New York: John Wiley & Sons, Inc. 1995), p. 4.

22. Jones, "Ethical Decision Making by Individuals in Organizations."

23. Based on a question from a General Electric employee ethics guide, reported in Kathryn Kranhold, "U.S. Firms Raise Ethics Focus," *The Wall Street Journal*, November 28, 2005.

24. Based on information in Constance E. Bagley, "The Ethical Leader's Decision Tree," *Harvard Business Review* (February 2003): 18–19.

25. Based on information in Vadim Liberman, "Scoring on the Job," *Across the Board* (November–December 2003): 46–50.

26. From Jeffrey Kluger, "What Makes Us Moral? *Time* (December 3, 2007): 54–60.

27. "The Morality Quiz," *Time*, www.time.com/time/specials/2007/article/0,28804,1685055_1685076_1686619,00.html (accessed February 19, 2008).

28. This discussion is based on Gerald F. Cavanagh, Dennis J. Moberg, and Manuel Velasquez, "The Ethics of Organizational Politics," *Academy of Management Review* 6 (1981): 363–374; Justin G. Longenecker, Joseph A. McKinney, and Carlos W. Moore, "Egoism and Independence: Entrepreneurial Ethics," *Organizational Dynamics* (Winter 1988): 64–72; Carolyn Wiley, "The ABCs of Business Ethics: Definitions, Philosophies, and Implementation," *IM* (February 1995): 22–27; and Mark Mallinger, "Decisive Decision Making: An Exercise Using Ethical Frameworks," *Journal of Management Education* (August 1997): 411–417.

29. Michael J. McCarthy, "Now the Boss Knows Where You're Clicking," and "Virtual Morality: A New Workplace Quandary," *The Wall Street Journal*, October 21, 1999; and Jeffrey L. Seglin, "Who's Snooping on You?" *Business 2.0* (August 8, 2000): 202–203.

30. John Kekes, "Self-Direction: The Core of Ethical Individualism," in *Organizations and Ethical Individualism*, ed. Konstanian Kolenda (New York: Praeger, 1988), pp. 1–18.

31. Tad Tulega, *Beyond the Bottom Line* (New York: Penguin Books, 1987).

32. Simone de Colle and Patricia H. Werhane, "Moral Motivation across Ethical Theories: What Can We Learn for Designing Corporate Ethics Programs?" *Journal of Business Ethics* 81 (2008): 751–764; Aristotle, *Nichomachean Ethics*, translated by T. Irving (Indianapolis, IN: Hackett Publishing 1999); and Rosalind Hursthouse, *On Virtue Ethics* (Oxford: Oxford University Press, 2001).

33. Bill George, "The Master Gives It Back" and "Truly Authentic Leadership" segments in "Special Report: America's Best Leaders," *U.S. News & World Report* (October 30, 2006): 50–87; and David Segal, "In Letter, Buffett Accepts Blame and Faults Others," *The New York Times*, March 1, 2009.

34. Bill Lynn, *"Ethics,"* Practical Ethics.Web site, www.practicalethics.net/ethics.html (accessed March 23, 2010); Richard E. Thompson, "So, Greed's Not Good after All," *Trustee* (January 2003): 28; and Dennis F. Thompson, *"What Is Practical Ethics?"* Harvard University Edmond J. Safra Foundation Center for Ethics Web site, www.ethics.harvard.edu/the-center/what-is-practical-ethics (accessed March 23, 2010).

35. L. Kohlberg, "Moral Stages and Moralization: The Cognitive-Developmental Approach," in *Moral Development and Behavior: Theory, Research, and Social*

Issues, ed. T. Lickona (New York: Holt, Rinehart & Winston, 1976), pp. 31–83; L. Kohlberg, "Stage and Sequence: The Cognitive- Developmental Approach to Socialization," in *Handbook of Socialization Theory and Research,* ed. D. A. Goslin (Chicago: Rand McNally, 1969); Linda K. Treviño, Gary R. Weaver, and Scott J. Reynolds, "Behavioral Ethics in Organizations: A Review, *Journal of Management* 32, no 6 (December 2006): 951–990; and Jill W. Graham, "Leadership, Moral Development, and Citizenship Behavior," *Business Ethics Quarterly* 5, no. 1 (January 1995): 43–54.

36. Eugene W. Szwajkowski, "The Myths and Realities of Research on Organizational Misconduct," in *Research in Corporate Social Performance and Policy,* ed. James E. Post (Greenwich, CT: JAI Press, 1986), 9:103–122; and Keith Davis, William C. Frederick, and Robert L. Blostrom, *Business and Society: Concepts and Policy Issues* (New York: McGraw-Hill, 1979).

37. Douglas S. Sherwin, "The Ethical Roots of the Business System," *Harvard Business Review* 61 (November–December 1983): 183–192.

38. Nancy C. Roberts and Paula J. King, "The Stakeholder Audit Goes Public," *Organizational Dynamics* (Winter 1989): 63–79; Thomas Donaldson and Lee E. Preston, "The Stakeholder Theory of the Corporation: Concepts, Evidence, and Implications," *Academy of Management Review* 20, no. 1 (1995): 65–91; and Jeffrey S. Harrison and Caron H. St. John, "Managing and Partnering with External Stakeholders," *Academy of Management Executive* 10, no. 2 (1996): 46–60.

39. Clay Chandler, "The Great Wal-Mart of China," *Fortune* (July 25, 2005): 104–116; and Charles Fishman, "The Wal-Mart You Don't Know—Why Low Prices Have a High Cost," *Fast Company* (December 2003): 68–80.

40. Max B. E. Clarkson, "A Stakeholder Framework for Analyzing and Evaluating Corporate Social Performance," *Academy of Management Review* 20, no. 1 (1995): 92–117.

41. Rich Kauffeld, Abhishek Malhotra, and Susan Higgins, "Green Is a Strategy," *Strategy + Business* (December 21, 2009).

42. Eugenia Levenson, "Citizen Nike," *Fortune* (November 14, 2008): 165–170.

43. Ann Zimmerman, "Retailer's Image Moves From Demon to Darling," *The Wall Street Journal Online,* July 16, 2009, http://online.wsj.com/article/SB124770244854748495.html (accessed July 24, 2009); Samuel Fromartz, "The Mini-Cases: 5 Companies, 5 Strategies, 5 Transformations," *MIT Sloan Management Review* (Fall 2009): 41–45; and Ram Nidumolu, C. K. Prahalad, and M. R. Rangaswami, "Why Sustainability Is Now the Key Driver of Innovation," *Harvard Business Review* (September 2009): 57–64.

44. This definition is based on Marc J. Epstein and Marie-Josée Roy, "Improving Sustainability Performance: Specifying, Implementing and Measuring Key Principles," *Journal of General Management* 29, no. 1 (Autumn 2003): 15–31; World Commission on Economic Development, *Our Common Future* (Oxford: Oxford University Press, 1987); and Marc Gunther, "Tree Huggers, Soy Lovers, and Profits," *Fortune* (June 23, 2003): 98–104.

45. Mark S. Schwartz and Archie B. Carroll, "Corporate Social Responsibility: A Three-Domain Approach," *Business Ethics Quarterly* 13, no. 4 (2003): 503–530; and Archie B. Carroll, "A Three-Dimensional Conceptual Model of Corporate Performance," *Academy of Management Review* 4 (1979): 497–505. For a discussion of various models for evaluating corporate social performance, also see Diane L. Swanson, "Addressing a Theoretical Problem by Reorienting the Corporate Social Performance Model," *Academy of Management Review* 20, no. 1 (1995): 43–64.

46. Milton Friedman, *Capitalism and Freedom* (Chicago: University of Chicago Press, 1962), p. 133; and Milton Friedman and Rose Friedman, *Free to Choose* (New York: Harcourt Brace Jovanovich, 1979).

47. Eugene W. Szwajkowski, "Organizational Illegality: Theoretical Integration and Illustrative Application," *Academy of Management Review* 10 (1985): 558–567.

48. Siri Schubert and T. Christian Miller, "Where Bribery Was Just a Line Item," *The New York Times,* December 21, 2008.

49. David J. Fritzsche and Helmut Becker, "Linking Management Behavior to Ethical Philosophy—An Empirical Investigation," *Academy of Management Journal* 27 (1984): 165–175.

50. O'Sullivan, "Virtue Rewarded."

51. Katie Hafner and Claudi H. Deutsch, "When Good Will Is Also Good Business," *The New York Times,* September 14, 2005.

52. Saul W. Gellerman, "Managing Ethics from the Top Down," *Sloan Management Review* (Winter 1989): 73–79.

53. Attributed to Philip Delves Broughton in David A. Kaplan, "MBAs Get Schooled in Ethics," *Fortune* (October 26, 2009): 27–28.

54. Leslie Wayne, "A Promise to Be Ethical in an Era of Temptation," *The New York Times* May 30, 2009; and Kelley Holland, "Is It Time to Retrain B-Schools?" *The New York Times,* March 15, 2009.

55. Michael E. Brown and Linda K. Treviño, "Ethical Leadership: A Review and Future Directions," *The Leadership Quarterly* 17 (2006): 595–616; Weaver et al., "'Somebody I Look Up To'"; and L. K. Treviño, G. R. Weaver, David G. Gibson, and Barbara Ley Toffler, "Managing Ethics and Legal Compliance:

What Works and What Hurts?" *California Management Review* 41, no. 2 (Winter 1999): 131–151.

56. Treviño et al., *Managing Ethics and Legal Compliance.*

57. K. Matthew Gilley, Chris Robertson, and Tim Mazur, "The Bottom-Line Benefits of Ethics Code Commitment," *Business Horizons,* vol. 53 (January–February 2010): 31–37; Joseph L. Badaracco and Allen P. Webb, "Business Ethics: A View from the Trenches," *California Management Review* 37, no. 2 (Winter 1995): 8–28; and Ronald B. Morgan, "Self- and Co-Worker Perceptions of Ethics and Their Relationships to Leadership and Salary," *Academy of Management Journal* 36, no. 1 (February 1993): 200–214.

58. Granite Construction Company Code of Conduct, www.graniteconstruction.com/about-us/codeofconduct.cfm (accessed March 26, 2010); and "Granite Construction Named One of the 2010 'World's Most Ethical Companies,'" *Business Wire* (March 22, 2010).

59. Cheryl Rosen, "A Measure of Success? Ethics after Enron," *Business Ethics* (Summer 2006): 22–26.

60. Alan Yuspeh, "Do the Right Thing," *CIO* (August 1, 2000): 56–58.

61. Reported in Rosen, "A Measure of Success? Ethics after Enron."

62. Beverly Geber, "The Right and Wrong of Ethics Offices," *Training* (October 1995): 102–118.

63. Kranhold, "U.S. Firms Raise Ethics Focus"; "Our Actions: GE 2005 Citizenship Report," General Electric Company, 2005.

64. Amy Zipkin, "Getting Religion on Corporate Ethics," *The New York Times*, October 18, 2000.

65. Marcia Parmarlee Miceli and Janet P. Near, "The Relationship among Beliefs, Organizational Positions, and Whistle-Blowing Status: A Discriminant Analysis," *Academy of Management Journal* 27 (1984): 687–705; and Michael T. Rehg, Marcia P. Miceli, Janet P. Near, and James R. Van Scotter, "Antecedents and Outcomes of Retaliation Against Whistleblowers: Gender Differences and Power Relationships," *Organization Science* 19, no. 2 (March–April 2008): 221–240.

66. Eugene Garaventa, "*An Enemy of the People* by Henrik Ibsen: The Politics of Whistle-Blowing," *Journal of Management Inquiry* 3, no. 4 (December 1994): 369–374; Marcia P. Miceli and Janet P. Near, "Whistleblowing: Reaping the Benefits," *Academy of Management Executive* 8, no. 3 (1994): 65–74.

67. Reported in Rosen, "A Measure of Success? Ethics after Enron."

68. Christine Seib and Alexandra Frean, "Lehman Whistleblower Lost Job Month After Speaking Out," *The Times,* March 17, 2010.

69. Richard McGill Murphy, "Why Doing Good Is Good For Business," *Fortune* (February 8, 2010): 90–95.

70. Homer H. Johnson, "Does It Pay to Be Good? Social Responsibility and Financial Performance," *Business Horizons* (November–December 2003): 34–40; Jennifer J. Griffin and John F. Mahon, "The Corporate Social Performance and Corporate Financial Performance Debate: Twenty-Five Years of Incomparable Research," *Business and Society* 36, no. 1 (March 1997): 5–31; Bernadette M. Ruf, Krishnamurty Muralidar, Robert M. Brown, Jay J. Janney, and Karen Paul, "An Empirical Investigation of the Relationship between Change in Corporate Social Performance and Financial Performance: A Stakeholder Theory Perspective," *Journal of Business Ethics* 32, no. 2 (July 2001): 143ff; Philip L. Cochran and Robert A. Wood, "Corporate Social Responsibility and Financial Performance," *Academy of Management Journal* 27 (1984): 42–56.

71. Heli Wang, Jaepil Choi, and Jiatao Li, "Too Little or Too Much? Untangling the Relationship between Corporate Philanthropy and Firm Financial Performance," *Organization Science* 19, no. 1 (January–February 2008): 143–159; Philip L. Cochran, "The Evolution of Corporate Social Responsibility," *Business Horizons* 50 (2007): 449–454; Paul C. Godfrey, "The Relationship between Corporate Philanthropy and Shareholder Wealth: A Risk Management Perspective," *Academy of Management Review* 30, no. 4 (2005): 777–798; Oliver Falck and Stephan Heblich, "Corporate Social Responsibility: Doing Well by Doing Good," *Business Horizons* 50 (2007): 247–254; J. A. Pearce II and J. P. Doh, "The High Impact of Collaborative Social Initiatives"; Curtis C. Verschoor and Elizabeth A. Murphy, "The Financial Performance of Large U.S. Firms and Those with Global Prominence: How Do the Best Corporate Citizens Rate?" *Business and Society Review* 107, no. 3 (Fall 2002): 371–381; Johnson, "Does It Pay to Be Good?"; Dale Kurschner, "5 Ways Ethical Business Creates Fatter Profits," *Business Ethics* (March–April 1996): 20–23.

72. Verschoor and Murphy, "The Financial Performance of Large U.S. Firms."

73. Phred Dvorak, "Finding the Best Measure of 'Corporate Citizenship,'" *The Wall Street Journal*, July 2, 2007.

74. Jean B. McGuire, Alison Sundgren, and Thomas Schneeweis, "Corporate Social Responsibility and Firm Financial Performance," *Academy of Management Journal* 31 (1988): 854–872; and Falck and Heblich, Corporate Social Responsibility: Doing Well by Doing Good."

75. Daniel W. Greening and Daniel B. Turban, "Corporate Social Performance as a Competitive Advantage in Attracting a Quality Workforce," *Business and Society* 39, no. 3 (September 2000): 254; and O'Sullivan, "Virtue Rewarded."

76. "The Socially Correct Corporate Business," in Leslie Holstrom and Simon Brady, "The Changing Face of Global Business," *Fortune* (July 24, 2000): S1–S38.

77. Remi Trudel and June Cotte, "Does Being Ethical Pay?" *The Wall Street Journal*, May 12, 2008.

78. Based on Bart Victor and John B. Cullen, "The Organizational Bases of Ethical Work Climates," *Administrative Science Quarterly* 33 (1988): 101–125.

79. Adapted from Richard L. Daft and Dorothy Marcic, *Understanding Management* (Mason, OH: South-Western, 2008), 134.

80. Adapted from Janet Q. Evans, "What Do You Do: What If Polluting Is Legal?" *Business Ethics* (Fall 2002): 20.

81. Based on Don Soeken, "On Witnessing a Fraud," *Business Ethics* (Summer 2004): 14; Amy Tao, "Have Cruise Lines Weathered the Storm?" *BusinessWeek Online,* September 11, 2003, www.businessweek.com/bwdaily/dnflash/sep2003/nf20030911_6693_db014.htm; and Joan Dubinsky, "A Word to the Whistle-Blower," *Workforce* (July 2002): 28.

12:56
23 APR 2011 SAT
+25 °C
8:00AM
2 missed calls
10:30AM - 11:30AM
Conference hall

PART 3

Planning

3

The future of mobile computing has arrived. Touchscreen tablets are flooding the market, and Motorola, Samsung, Apple, and HP are in a heated competition to win today's on-the-go consumer.

Yet all eyes are on Apple and its trailblazing iPad 2. Users say the device is the ultimate multimedia platform for consuming movies, music, books, and games, and 15 million units sold in a single year.

To keep pace with the top-selling gadget, developers of competing tablets need to find out how Apple delivers iPad's stunning quality and price advantages. Because Apple is famously tight-lipped, however, managers look to supply-chain researchers to discover what's inside iPad's sleek outer casing.

Thanks to "gadget teardown" research published by IHS iSuppli, designers of the Motorola Xoom, Samsung Galaxy Tab, and HP TouchPad get a good look at iPad's electronics. With iPad teardowns, researchers literally crack open the gadget to reveal the internals, giving outsiders a peek at Apple's entire bill of materials, including part numbers, suppliers, and all components—GPS chips, flash memory, touchscreens, and more.

There's method to the madness. If gadget makers can assess the market leader's advantages and align their own brands with strategic opportunities, they will be better positioned to stake a claim in the coming tablet universe.

Chapter Outline

Managerial Planning and Goal Setting

Learning Outcomes

After studying this chapter, you should be able to:

1. Define goals and plans and explain the relationship between them.
2. Explain the concept of organizational mission and how it influences goal setting and planning.
3. Describe the types of goals an organization should have and how managers use strategy maps to align goals.
4. Define the characteristics of effective goals.
5. Discuss the benefits and limitations of planning.
6. Describe and explain the importance of contingency planning, scenario building, and crisis planning for today's managers.
7. Identify innovative planning approaches managers use in a fast-changing environment.
8. Define the components of strategic management and discuss the levels of strategy.
9. Describe the strategic management process and SWOT analysis.
10. Discuss organizational dimensions managers use to execute strategy.

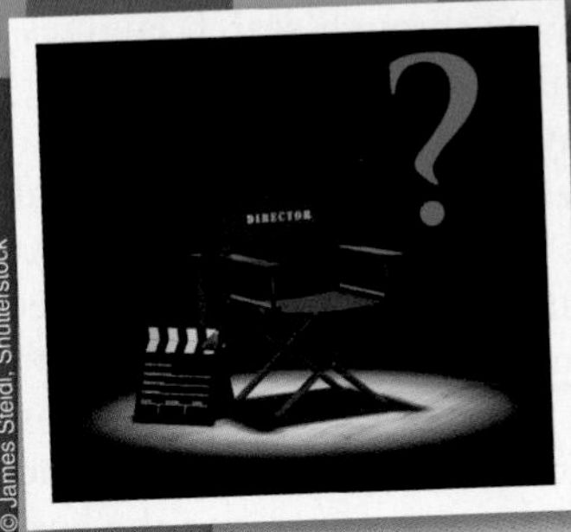

© James Steidl, Shutterstock

Are You Ready to Be a Manager?

Please circle your opinion below each of the following statements.

1 I have a specific goal, or mission, I want to achieve in the next 5 to10 years.

Mostly True Mostly False

(See page 173, Organizational Mission.)

2 I have figured out what I need to do to achieve the goal in #1, above. In other words, I have come up with a workable strategy to help me reach my dreams.

Mostly True Mostly False

(See page 174, Goals and Plans.)

3 I have a good understanding of appropriate use of social media regarding my professional life.

Mostly True Mostly False

(See page 178, Is a Tweet Just a Tweet?)

4 I develop goals for my studying, my work, and my life. These goals help me stay focused and motivated and help me figure out how to allocate my time and money.

Mostly True Mostly False

(See page 177, Benefits and Limitations of Planning.)

5 I have honestly assessed my strengths and weaknesses, and I have looked for ways to utilize my strengths in the most effective way possible.

Mostly True Mostly False

(See page 190, SWOT Analysis.)

Apple Inc. used to be a personal computer manufacturer. The company still makes computers, but today Apple is better known for the iPhone, the iPod, the iPad, and the iTunes music service, which sells music over the Internet. In 2008, Apple surpassed Walmart as the largest seller of music. Now Apple managers are planning for an overhaul that will push the company even further into the business of selling entertainment. For one thing, rather than requiring that consumers use Apple software and download songs from Apple's virtual store onto a specific device, the new approach would let people buy and listen to music through a Web browser. That means iTunes could sell music through search engines and other Websites, and people could access their purchases from anywhere as long as they're connected to the Internet. Moreover, insiders say Apple is planning to add a television subscription service within the next couple of years, making the company a direct competitor with cable and satellite companies such as Comcast and DirecTV.[1] At the time this was written, Apple's plans were still not public, and managers remained tight-lipped as they continued evaluating various goals and options.

One of the primary responsibilities of managers is to set goals for where the organization should go in the future and plan how to get it there. Managers at Apple decided some years ago to move into the business of selling music online, and now they are planning to extend the company's reach in entertainment.

In some organizations, typically small ones, planning is informal. In others, managers follow a well-defined planning framework. The company establishes a basic mission and periodically develops formal goals and plans for carrying it out. Large organizations such as Royal Dutch/Shell, IBM, and United Way undertake a comprehensive planning exercise each year—reviewing their missions, goals, and plans to meet environmental changes or the expectations of important stakeholders such as the community, owners, or customers.

Of the four management functions—planning, organizing, leading, and controlling, described in Chapter 1, planning is considered the most fundamental. Everything else stems from planning. Yet planning also is the most controversial management function. How do managers plan for the future in a constantly changing environment? The economic, political, and social turmoil of recent years has sparked a renewed interest in organizational planning, particularly planning for crises and unexpected events, yet it also has some managers questioning whether planning is even worthwhile in a world that is in constant flux. Planning cannot read an uncertain future. Planning cannot tame a turbulent environment. A statement by General Colin Powell, former U.S. Secretary of State, offers a warning for managers: "No battle plan survives contact with the enemy."[2] Does that mean it is useless for managers to make plans? Of course not. No plan can be perfect, but without plans and goals, organizations and employees flounder. However, good managers understand that plans should grow and change to meet shifting conditions.

As a new manager, what approach will you take to goal setting and planning? Complete the New Manager Self-Test, on page 171, to get some insight into your planning approach from the way you study as a student.

In this chapter, we explore the process of planning and consider how managers develop effective plans. Special attention is given to goal setting, for that is where planning starts. Then, we discuss the various types of plans managers use to help the organization achieve those goals. We also take a look at planning approaches that help managers deal with uncertainty, such as contingency planning, scenario building, and crisis planning. Next, we examine new approaches to planning that emphasize the involvement of employees, and sometimes other stakeholders, in strategic thinking and execution. Finally, we look at strategic planning in depth and examine a number of strategic options managers can use in a competitive environment. In Chapter 6, we look at management decision making. Appropriate decision-making techniques are crucial to selecting the organization's goals, plans, and strategic options.

New Manager Self-Test

Your Approach to Studying

Your approach to studying may be a predictor of your planning approach as a new manager. Answer the items below as they apply to your study behavior. Please answer whether each item below is Mostly True or Mostly False for you.

	MOSTLY TRUE <<<	>>> MOSTLY FALSE
1. Before I tackle an assignment, I try to work out the reasoning behind it.	______	______
2. When I am reading, I stop occasionally to reflect on what I am trying to get out of it.	______	______
3. When I finish my work, I check it through to see whether it really meets the assignment.	______	______
4. Now and then, I stand back from my studying to think generally how successfully it is going.	______	______
5. I frequently focus on the facts and details because I do not see the overall picture.	______	______
6. I write down as much as possible during lectures because I often am not sure what is really important.	______	______
7. I try to relate ideas to other topics or courses whenever possible.	______	______
8. When I am working on a topic, I try to see in my own mind how all the ideas fit together.	______	______
9. It is important to me to see the bigger picture within which a new concept fits.	______	______

See It Online

Scoring and Interpretation: Give yourself 1 point for each item you marked as Mostly True except items 5 and 6. For items 5 and 6, give yourself 1 point for each one you marked Mostly False. An important part of a new manager's job is to plan ahead, which involves grasping the bigger picture. The items above measure *metacognitive awareness*, which means the ability to step back and see the bigger picture of one's own learning activities. This same approach enables a manager to step back and see the big picture required for effective planning, monitoring, and evaluating an organization. If you scored 3 or fewer points, you may be caught up in the details of current activities. A score of 7 or above suggests that you see yourself in a bigger picture, which is an approach to studying that very well may reflect a successful planning aptitude.

SOURCES: Adapted from Kristin Backhaus and Joshua P. Liff, "Cognitive Styles and Approaches to Studying in Management Education," *Journal of Management Education* 31 (August 2007): 445–466; and A. Duff, "Learning Styles Measurement: The Revised Approaches to Studying Inventory (RASI)," *Bristol Business School Teaching and Research Review* 3 (2000).

Overview of the Goal-Setting and Planning Process

A **goal** is a desired future state that the organization attempts to realize.[3] Goals are important because organizations exist for a purpose, and goals define and state that purpose. A **plan** is a blueprint for goal achievement and specifies the necessary resource allocations, schedules, tasks, and other actions. Goals specify future ends; plans specify today's means. The concept of **planning** usually incorporates both ideas; it means determining the organization's goals and defining the means for achieving them.[4]

The planning process starts with a formal mission that defines the basic purpose of the organization, especially for external audiences. The mission is the basis for the strategic (company) level of goals and plans. Top managers are typically responsible for establishing *strategic* goals and plans that reflect a commitment to both organizational efficiency and effectiveness, as described in Chapter 1.

Tactical goals and plans are the responsibility of middle managers, such as the heads of major divisions or functional units. A division manager will formulate tactical plans that focus on the major actions the division must take to fulfill its part in the strategic plan set by top management.

The Organizational Planning Process

The overall planning process, illustrated in Exhibit 5.1, prevents managers from thinking merely in terms of day-to-day activities. The process begins when managers develop the overall plan for the organization by clearly defining mission and strategic (company-level) goals. Second, they translate the plan into action, which includes defining tactical plans and objectives, developing a strategy map to align goals, formulating contingency and scenario plans, and identifying intelligence teams to analyze major competitive issues. Third, managers lay out the operational factors needed to achieve goals. This involves devising operational goals and plans, selecting the measures and targets that will be used to determine whether things are on track, and identifying stretch goals and crisis plans that might have to be put into action. Tools for executing the plan include management by objectives, performance dashboards, single-use plans, and decentralized responsibility. Finally, managers periodically review plans to learn from results and shift plans as needed, starting a new planning cycle.

- Planning is the most fundamental of the four management functions.
- A **goal** is a desired future state that the organization wants to realize.
- **Planning** is the act of determining goals and defining the means for achieving them.
- A **plan** is a blueprint specifying the resource allocations, schedules, and other actions necessary for attaining goals.
- Planning helps managers think toward the future rather than thinking merely in terms of day-to-day activities.

Goal-Setting in Organizations

Setting goals starts with top managers. The overall planning process begins with a mission statement and goals for the organization as a whole.

EXHIBIT 5.1

The Organizational Planning Process

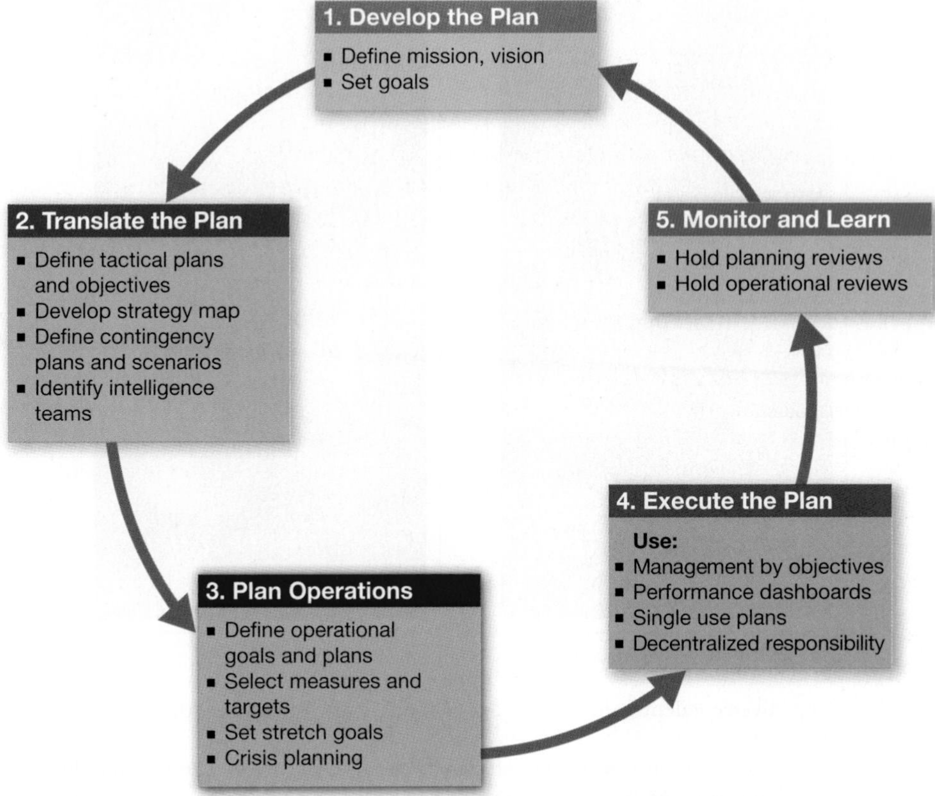

SOURCE: Based on Robert S. Kaplan and David P. Norton, "Mastering the Management System," *Harvard Business Review* (January 2008): 63–77.

Organizational Mission

At the top of the goal hierarchy is the **mission**—the organization's reason for existence. The mission describes the organization's values, aspirations, and reason for being. A well-defined mission is the basis for development of all subsequent goals and plans. Without a clear mission, goals and plans may be developed haphazardly and not take the organization in the direction it needs to go. One of the defining attributes of successful companies such as Apple, Johnson & Johnson, Southwest Airlines, and Walmart is that they have a clear mission that guides decisions and actions.

The formal **mission statement** is a broadly stated definition of purpose that distinguishes the organization from others of a similar type. A well-designed mission statement can enhance employee motivation and organizational performance.[5] The content of a mission statement often focuses on the market and customers and identifies desired fields of endeavor. Some mission statements describe company characteristics such as corporate values, product quality, location of facilities, and attitude toward employees. The mission statement of DaVita Inc. is shown in Exhibit 5.2. Such short, straightforward mission statements describe basic business activities and purposes as well as the values that guide the company. Another example of this type of mission statement is that of State Farm Insurance:

> State Farm's mission is to help people manage the risks of everyday life, recover from the unexpected, and realize their dreams.
>
> We are people who make it our business to be like a good neighbor; who built a premier company by selling and keeping promises through our marketing partnership;

EXHIBIT 5.2

Mission Statement for DaVita Inc.

SOURCE: © 2009 DaVita Inc. All rights reserved.

who bring diverse talents and experiences to our work of serving the State Farm customer.

Our success is built on a foundation of shared values—quality service and relationships, mutual trust, integrity, and financial strength.[6]

Because of mission statements such as those of DaVita and State Farm, employees as well as customers, suppliers, and stockholders know the company's stated purpose and values.

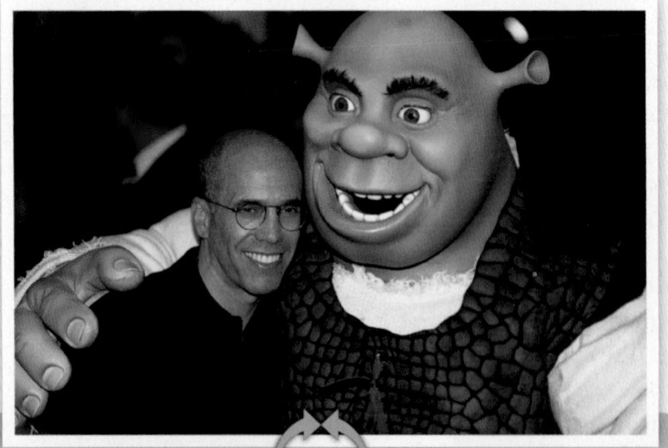

AP Photo/Rob Griffith

ConceptConnection

Walt Disney used to say, "I make movies for children and the child in all of us." DreamWorks, according to CEO Jeffrey Katzenberg, "makes movies for adults and the adult that exists in every child." That subtle difference in wording provides the key to the studio's sense of **mission** and the way it sets itself apart. Starting with *Shrek* in 2001, a film where the villain tortured the Gingerbread Man by dipping him into a glass of milk, DreamWorks has produced feature-length animated films aimed at appealing equally to adults and children by being irreverent and a little subversive.

Goals and Plans

Strategic goals, sometimes called *official goals*, are broad statements describing where the organization wants to be in the future. These goals pertain to the organization as a whole rather than to specific divisions or departments.

Strategic plans define the action steps by which the company intends to attain strategic goals. The strategic plan is the blueprint that defines the organizational activities and resource allocations—in the form of cash, personnel, space, and facilities—required for meeting these targets. Strategic planning tends to be long term and may define organizational action steps from two to five years in the future. The purpose of strategic plans is to turn organizational goals into realities within that time period. Managers at General Motors are working to define a new strategic plan to get the automaker back on track after years of decline that eventually landed the company in bankruptcy.

GENERAL MOTORS

In the 1920s, Alfred P. Sloan formulated a strategic goal of innovation that set GM on course to become the world's largest automaker. By offering "a car for every purse and purpose," GM surpassed Ford in 1932 and owned 50 percent of the U.S. auto market by the late 1950s.

Flash forward to 2009, though, and the storied automaker was bankrupt and struggling to survive, practically begging people to buy its vehicles. The high cost of offering a multiplicity of brands started to cause problems for GM in the 1970s, largely due to spikes in oil prices and growing competition from foreign automakers. Instead of crafting a focused plan, however, managers began a juggling act, with some pushing for strategic goals of innovation and others for goals of cost control. GM spent billions to explore innovative ideas such as hybrid technology (begun in the 1970s), the Saturn small-car company in the 1980s, and the EV1 electric vehicle in the 1990s, but then failed to provide the projects with adequate funding because they cost too much or weren't providing enough immediate profit.

New managers, led by former CEO Ed Whitacre, Jr., and Stephen Girsky, vice president in charge of corporate strategy, made plans to focus on just four core brands (Chevrolet, Cadillac, Buick, and GMC) to try to save the once-renowned automaker. Although cost cutting has been a necessity, focused innovation is the core of the strategic plan. One strategic goal is to boost U.S. market share to 20 percent over the next couple of years. Plans to reach the goal include getting new vehicles to market faster, reinvigorating the Chevrolet division, increasing GM's lineup of fuel-efficient small cars, and introducing an extended-range electric vehicle for 2011.[7]

General Motors is a huge company and has numerous other strategic goals and plans, but managers are trying to make sure goals are clear and focused so that resources can be directed appropriately.

After strategic goals are formulated, the next step is to define **tactical goals**, which are the results that major divisions and departments within the organization intend to achieve. These goals apply to middle management and describe what major subunits must do for the organization to achieve its overall goals.

Tactical plans are designed to help execute the major strategic plans and to accomplish a specific part of the company's strategy.[8] Tactical plans typically have a shorter time horizon than strategic plans—over the next year or so. The word *tactical* originally comes from the military. In a business or nonprofit organization, tactical plans define what major departments and organizational subunits will do to implement the organization's strategic plan. For example, one tactical goal for GM's Chevrolet division is to enhance the reputation of GM's most important brand (Chevrolet accounts for about 70 percent of GM's U.S. sales). Tactical plans include buying ads on Web sites where people go to price Toyotas or Hondas, showcasing Chevys at Little League baseball games and other sporting events, and letting people test-drive Chevys at auto shows. In *Consumer Reports's* annual brand survey released January 2010, Chevy had moved from ninth to fourth place, indicating that the division is achieving its tactical goals, which will help GM achieve the strategic goal of increasing U.S. market share to 20 percent.[9] Tactical goals and plans help top managers implement their overall strategic plan. Normally, it is the middle manager's job to take the broad strategic plan and identify specific tactical plans, as James Campbell, the new head of the Chevrolet division, did at GM.

Go to the Self-Learning, on page 199, that pertains to developing action plans for accomplishing strategic goals.

The results expected from departments, work groups, and individuals are the **operational goals**. They are precise and measurable. "Process 150 sales applications each week," "Achieve 90 percent of deliveries on time," "Reduce overtime by 10 percent next month," and "Develop two new online courses in accounting" are examples of operational goals. Chevrolet's marketing department might have an operational goal of increasing customer showroom visits by 10 percent by year end, and its transportation department an operational goal of improving on-time delivery of Chevrolet cars and trucks to dealers by 20 percent.

Operational plans are developed at the lower levels of the organization to specify action steps toward achieving operational goals and to support tactical plans. The operational plan is the department manager's tool for daily and weekly operations. Goals are stated in quantitative terms, and the department plan describes how goals will be achieved. Operational planning specifies plans for department managers, supervisors, and individual employees. Schedules are an important component of operational planning. Schedules define precise time frames for the completion of each operational goal required for the organization's tactical and strategic goals. Operational planning also must be coordinated with the budget because resources must be allocated for desired activities.

- Planning starts with the organization's purpose or reason for existence, which is called its **mission**.
- A **mission statement** is a broadly stated definition of the organization's basic business scope and operations that distinguishes it from similar types of organizations.
- Goals begin with broad strategic goals, followed by more specific tactical goals and then operational goals.
- Plans are defined similarly, with strategic, tactical, and operational plans used to achieve the goals.
- **Strategic goals** are broad statements about where the organization wants to be in the future and pertain to the organization as a whole rather than to specific divisions or departments.
- **Strategic plans** are the action steps by which an organization intends to attain strategic goals.
- The outcomes that major divisions and departments must achieve for the organization to reach its overall goals are called **tactical goals**.
- **Tactical plans** are designed to help execute major strategic plans and to accomplish a specific part of the company's strategy.
- **Operational goals** are specific, measurable results that are expected from departments, work groups, and individuals.
- **Operational plans** specify the action steps toward achieving operational goals and support tactical activities.
- Managers at General Motors have defined new strategic, tactical, and operational goals and plans as part of their turnaround efforts.
- Goals and plans have to be in alignment so that they are consistent and mutually supportive.

Operational Planning

Managers use operational goals to direct employees and resources toward achieving specific outcomes that enable the organization to perform efficiently and effectively. One consideration is how to establish effective goals. Then managers use a number of planning approaches, including management by objectives, single-use plans, and standing plans.

Criteria for Effective Goals

Research has identified certain factors, listed in Exhibit 5.3, that characterize effective goals. First and foremost, goals must be *specific and measurable.* When possible, operational goals should be expressed in quantitative terms, such as increasing profits by 2 percent, having zero incomplete sales order forms, or increasing average teacher effectiveness ratings from 3.5 to 3.7. Not all goals can be expressed in numerical terms, but vague goals have

EXHIBIT 5.3

Characteristics of Effective Goal Setting

Goal Characteristics
• Specific and measurable
• Defined time period
• Cover key result areas
• Challenging but realistic
• Linked to rewards

little motivating power for employees. By necessity, goals are qualitative as well as quantitative. The important point is that the goals be precisely defined and allow for measurable progress. Effective goals also have a *defined time period* that specifies the date on which goal attainment will be measured. School administrators might set a deadline for improving teacher effectiveness ratings, for instance, at the end of the 2012 school term. When a goal involves a two- to three-year time horizon, setting specific dates for achieving parts of it is a good way to keep people on track toward the goal.

Goals should *cover key result areas.* Goals cannot be set for every aspect of employee behavior or organizational performance; if they were, their sheer number would render them meaningless. Instead, managers establish goals based on the idea of *choice and clarity.* A few carefully chosen, clear, and direct goals can more powerfully focus organizational attention, energy, and resources.[10] Managers should set goals that are *challenging but realistic.* When goals are unrealistic, they set employees up for failure and lead to a decrease in employee morale. However, if goals are too easy, employees may not feel motivated. Goals should also be *linked to rewards.* The ultimate impact of goals depends on the extent to which salary increases, promotions, and awards are based on goal achievement. Employees pay attention to what gets noticed and rewarded in the organization.[11]

Many companies are discovering a need to develop standing plans regarding the use of social media, as discussed in the Spotlight on Skills titled Is a Tweet Just a Tweet?

Benefits and Limitations of Planning

Some managers believe planning ahead is necessary to accomplish anything, whereas others think planning limits personal and organizational performance. Both opinions have merit because planning can have both advantages and disadvantages.

Research indicates that planning generally positively affects a company's performance.[12] Here are some reasons why:[13]

- ***Goals and plans provide a source of motivation and commitment.*** Planning can reduce uncertainty for employees and clarify what they should accomplish. Lack of a clear goal hampers motivation because people don't understand what they're working toward.
- ***Goals and plans guide resource allocation.*** Planning helps managers decide where they need to allocate resources, such as employees, money, and equipment. At Netflix, for example, a goal of offering more video online rather than in DVD format means allocating more funds for Internet movie rights and spending more of managers' time developing alliances with other companies.[14]

SPOTLIGHT ON SKILLS

Is a Tweet Just a Tweet?

If any organization should be security conscious, it is the U.S. Department of Defense. Yet in 2010, the DoD officially made it acceptable to access sites such as Twitter, Facebook, and MySpace from the department's unclassified computer network. "People who are coming into the military take all of this for granted," said Price Floyd, the Pentagon's "social media czar." "They can't imagine a world where one didn't have access to these sorts of sites."

Managers in all types of organizations are learning that trying to keep employees off social media sites is not realistic and that, in fact, social networking can bring benefits to the organization. However, companies need social media policies as a way to limit the risks of online roaming. Every company will differ in terms of what is acceptable, but here are some guidelines for developing an effective social media policy:

- **Keep it short and to the point, and make sure employees see it often.** People aren't going to read a long, weighty document. Most social media policies have no more than ten bullet points. Post the policy in conspicuous places, and consider having it pop up on users' screens when they log on.
- **Define the boundaries of acceptable use.** Employees need to know clearly the lines they can't cross. Most policies emphasize that employees must avoid the following:
  - Engaging in illegal activity
  - Sharing confidential or proprietary information
  - Harassing or spreading gossip about others
  - Talking negatively about the company, coworkers, customers, competitors, or suppliers
  - Wasting work time
- **Stipulate any requirements.** Some companies require that any mention of the employer by name needs management approval. Others require that online social networking be limited to breaks or other specific times of the workday.
- **Tie the policy to other company policies.** The social media policy needs to be tied to the company's sexual harassment policy, code of ethics, and other policies governing employee behavior.
- **Make clear that employee use of social media may be monitored.** Getting signed or implied employee consent regarding monitoring the workplace use of social media is crucial to avoid charges of violations of privacy.

Managers say their biggest concerns regarding employee use of social media are leaks of confidential information and damage to the company's reputation. However, nearly half of all companies surveyed in 2009 had not developed social media policies. A clear policy can help managers balance the risks and benefits of employee social networking.

SOURCES: Based on "Twitter Is the Latest Electronic Tool with Pros and Cons," *HR Focus* (August 2009): 8; Gene Connors, "10 Social Media Commandments for Employers," *Workforce Management Online*, February 2010, www.thesocialworkplace.com/2010/03/09/10-social-media-commandments-for-employers-workforce-management/ (accessed May 21, 2010); "Social Media Policy Balances Web 2.0 with Security," *U.S. Fed News Service* (March 5, 2010); and Tamara Schweitzer, "Do You Need a Social Media Policy?" *Inc.com*, January 25, 2010, www.inc.com/articles/2010/01/need-a-social-media-policy.html (accessed May 21, 2010).

- ***Goals and plans are a guide to action.*** Planning focuses attention on specific targets and directs employee efforts toward important outcomes. Planning helps managers and other employees know what actions they need to take to achieve the goal.
- ***Goals and plans set a standard of performance.*** Because planning and goal setting define desired outcomes, they also establish performance criteria so managers can measure whether things are on or off track. Goals and plans provide a standard of assessment.

Despite these benefits, some researchers also think planning can hurt organizational performance in some ways.[15] Thus, managers should understand the limitations to planning, particularly when the organization is operating in a turbulent environment:

- ***Goals and plans can create a false sense of certainty.*** Having a plan can give managers a false sense that they know what the future will be like. However, all planning is based on assumptions, and managers can't know what the future holds for their industry or for their competitors, suppliers, and customers.

- ***Goals and plans may cause rigidity in a turbulent environment.*** A related problem is that planning can lock the organization into specific goals, plans, and time frames, which may no longer be appropriate. Managing under conditions of change and uncertainty requires a degree of flexibility. Managers who believe in "staying the course" will often stick with a faulty plan even when conditions change dramatically.
- ***Goals and plans can get in the way of intuition and creativity.*** Success often comes from creativity and intuition, which can be hampered by too much routine planning. For example, during the process of setting goals in the MBO process described earlier, employees might play it safe to achieve objectives rather than offer creative ideas. Similarly, managers sometimes squelch creative ideas from employees that do not fit with predetermined action plans.[16]

In the case of Johnson & Johnson, plans got in the way of ethical behaviors, as shown in this chapter's Business Blooper box.

- Managers formulate goals that are specific and measurable, cover key result areas, are challenging but realistic, have a defined time period, and are linked to rewards.
- Benefits of planning and goal setting include serving as a source of motivation, determining resource allocation, providing a guide to action, and setting a standard for performance measurement.
- Limitations of planning and goal setting include the potential to create a false sense of certainty, create rigidity that hinders response to a turbulent environment, and get in the way of creativity and intuition.

Planning for a Turbulent Environment

Considering the limitations to planning, what are managers to do? One way managers can gain benefits from planning and control its limitations is by using innovative planning approaches that are in tune with today's turbulent environment. Three approaches that help brace the organization for unexpected—even unimaginable—events are contingency planning, building scenarios, and crisis planning.

BUSINESS BLOOPER

Johnson & Johnson

Rather than spend time devising strategic plans, Johnson & Johnson executives got involved in an elaborate scheme to pay 20 percent kickbacks on medical devices to doctors in Greece, paid bribes to Polish doctors who sat on hospital committees and ordered their equipment, and bribed Romanian doctors who prescribed their drugs. Top managers spent endless time debating how they could bring these illegal behaviors into compliance with the law. The admission by Johnson & Johnson included the information that they had let the government know of their own illegal activity in 2007, which led the Justice Department on a wide investigation in the health industry. Johnson & Johnson's agreement to pay $70 million in fines is the first victory. At least they did the right thing, in the end. No doubt the executives themselves are taking their own antacid brand, Rolaids, but hopefully not the ones that were recalled along with 50 other products during the past year.

SOURCE: Gardiner Harris, "Johnson & Johnson Settles Bribery Complaint for $70 Million in Fines, *The New York Times*, April 9, 2010.

Contingency Planning

When organizations are operating in a highly uncertain environment or dealing with long time horizons, sometimes planning can seem like a waste of time. Indeed, inflexible plans may hinder rather than help an organization's performance in the face of rapid technological, social, economic, or other environmental change. In these cases, managers can develop multiple future alternatives to help them form more adaptive plans.

Contingency plans define company responses to be taken in the case of emergencies, setbacks, or unexpected conditions. To develop contingency plans, managers identify important factors in the environment, such as possible economic downturns, declining markets, increases in cost of supplies, new technological developments, or safety accidents. Managers then forecast a range of alternative responses to the most likely high-impact contingencies, focusing on the worst case.[17] For example, if sales fall 20 percent and prices drop 8 percent, what will the company do? Managers can develop contingency plans that might include layoffs, emergency budgets, new sales efforts, or new markets. A real-life example comes from FedEx, which has to cope with some kind of unexpected disruption to its service somewhere in the world on a daily basis. In one recent year alone, managers activated contingency plans related to more than two dozen tropical storms, an air traffic controller strike in France, and a blackout in Los Angeles. The company also has contingency plans in place for events such as labor strikes, social upheavals in foreign countries, or incidents of terrorism.[18]

Scenario Building

An extension of contingency planning is a forecasting technique known as scenario building.[19] **Scenario building** involves looking at current trends and discontinuities and visualizing future possibilities. Rather than looking only at history and thinking about what has been, managers think about what *could be*. The events that cause the most damage to companies are those that no one even conceived of. In today's tumultuous world, traditional planning can't help managers cope with the many shifting and complex variables that can affect their organizations.

Managers can't predict the future, but they can rehearse a framework within which future events can be managed. With scenario building, a broad base of managers mentally rehearses different scenarios based on anticipating varied changes that could affect the organization. Scenarios are like stories that offer alternative vivid pictures of what the future will be like and how managers will respond. Typically, two to five scenarios are developed for each set of factors,

Robert Giroux/Getty Images News/Getty Images

ConceptConnection

During 2009, Mike Claver, State Farm Insurance Company's emergency management superintendent, oversaw the company's exceptionally thorough H1N1 **contingency planning**. In addition to coordinating with area agencies, Claver tested the company's ability to function should managers have to ask employees to work at home during an outbreak. More than 1,000 people, about 10 percent of the workforce at the Bloomington, Illinois, headquarters, logged into the company computer network from their homes one August day. Managers used the results of the dry run to fine-tune contingency plans.

ranging from the most optimistic to the most pessimistic view. Scenario building forces managers to mentally rehearse what they would do if their best-laid plans collapse.

Crisis Planning

As a new manager, get in the mind-set of scenario planning. Go to www.shell.com/scenarios, where Shell Oil publishes the outline of its annual scenario planning exercise. You might also want to do an Internet search and enter "national intelligence agency scenarios" to find links to reports of global trends and scenario planning done by various organizations.

Surveys of companies' use of management techniques reveal that the use of contingency and scenario planning surged after the September 11, 2001, terrorist attacks in the United States. Although their popularity waned for several years, these approaches have made a comeback due to increasing environmental turbulence and the recent global financial crisis. A *McKinsey Quarterly* survey, for example, found that 50 percent of respondents said scenario planning was playing a bigger role in planning or was newly added to the planning process in 2009 as compared to the previous year, reflecting managers' growing concern with managing uncertainty.[20] Some firms also engage in *crisis planning* to enable them to cope with unexpected events that are so sudden and devastating that they have the potential to destroy the organization if managers aren't prepared with a quick and appropriate response.

Crises have become integral features of organizations in today's world. Consider events such as the massive BP oil spill in the Gulf of Mexico; shooting rampages at Fort Hood in Texas, Virginia Tech University, and the American Civic Association in Binghamton, New York; deaths from listeriosis linked to tainted meat from Canada's Maple Leaf Foods; the explosion at the Massey Energy coal mine near Charleston, West Virginia; or the attempted New York Times Square bombing in the spring of 2010. Although crises may vary, a carefully thought-out and coordinated plan can be used to respond to any disaster. In addition, crisis planning reduces the incidence of trouble, much like putting a good lock on a door reduces burglaries.[21] BP, for instance, has been sharply criticized for a lack of planning that probably contributed to the Gulf oil spill disaster. Exhibit 5.4 outlines two essential stages of crisis planning.[22]

- ***Crisis Prevention.*** The *crisis prevention* stage involves activities managers undertake to try to prevent crises from occurring and to detect warning signs of potential crises. A critical part of the prevention stage is building open, trusting relationships with key stakeholders such as employees, customers, suppliers, governments, unions, and the community. By developing favorable relationships, managers can often prevent crises from happening and respond more effectively to

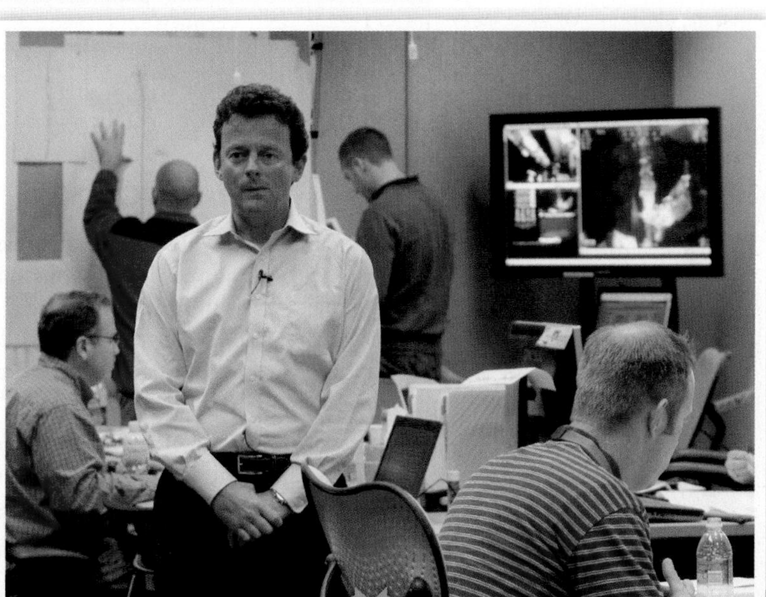

AP Photo/POOL, Pat Sullivan

ConceptConnection

After the Deepwater Horizon oil rig that was drilling a well for BP exploded in the Gulf of Mexico, Rep. Henry Waxman observed that "a striking feature of the incident is the apparent lack of an adequate plan to contain the spreading environmental damage." Former BP CEO Tony Hayward, pictured here, admitted Waxman was right. Because BP saw a deep-water leak as highly unlikely and touted the Deepwater Horizon as one of the world's most technologically advanced drilling platforms, it had no specific **crisis plan** for an uncontrolled blowout. Hayward confessed, "What is undoubtedly true is that we did not have the tools you would want in your toolkit."

EXHIBIT

Essential Stages of Crisis Planning

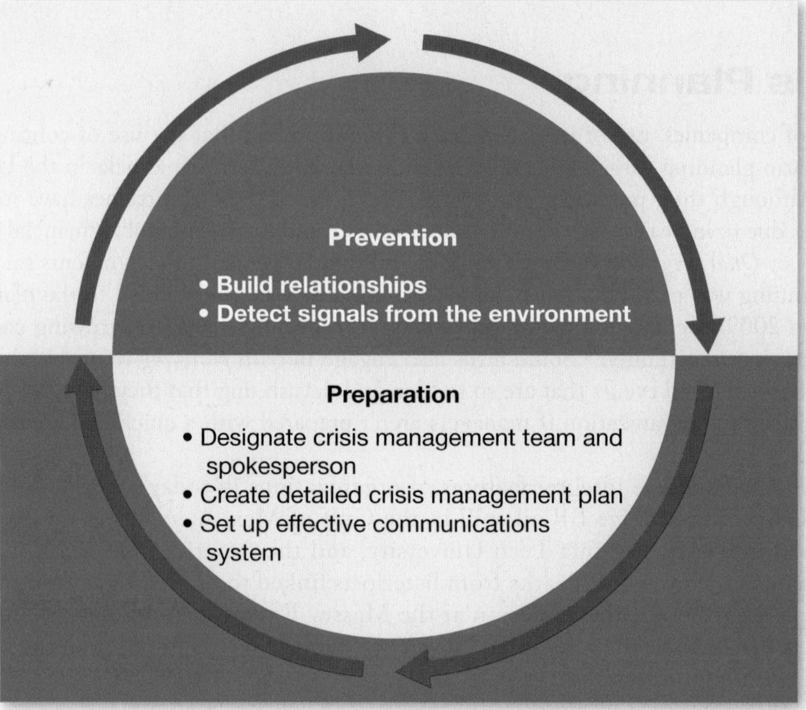

SOURCE: Based on information in W. Timothy Coombs, *Ongoing Crisis Communication: Planning, Managing, and Responding* (Thousand Oaks, CA: Sage Publications, 1999).

those that cannot be avoided. For example, organizations that have open, trusting relationships with employees and unions may avoid crippling labor strikes. Coca-Cola suffered a major crisis in Europe because it failed to respond quickly to reports of "foul-smelling" Coke in Belgium. A former CEO observed that every problem the company has faced in recent years "can be traced to a singular cause: We neglected our relationships."[23]

- ***Crisis Preparation.*** The *crisis preparation* stage includes all the detailed planning to handle a crisis when it occurs. Three steps in the preparation stage are (1) designating a crisis management team and spokesperson, (2) creating a detailed crisis management plan, and (3) setting up an effective communications system. The crisis management team, for example, is a cross-functional group of people who are designated to swing into action if a crisis occurs. The organization should also designate a spokesperson to be the voice of the company during the crisis.[24] The crisis management plan (CMP) is a detailed, written plan that specifies the steps to be taken, and by whom, if a crisis occurs. The CMP should include the steps for dealing with various types of crises, such as natural disasters like fires or earthquakes, normal accidents like economic crises or industrial accidents, and abnormal events such as product tampering or acts of terrorism.[25] A key point is that a crisis management plan should be a living, changing document that is regularly reviewed, practiced, and updated as needed.

- Managers use innovative planning approaches to cope with today's turbulent environment.
- **Contingency planning** identifies important factors in the environment and defines a range of alternative responses to be taken in the case of emergencies, setbacks, or unexpected conditions.
- With **scenario building**, managers look at trends and discontinuities and imagine possible alternative futures to build a framework within which unexpected future events can be managed.
- Scenarios are alternative vivid pictures of what the future might be like.
- Many companies increased their use contingency and scenario planning in 2009 because of the financial crisis and volatile economic conditions.
- Crisis planning involves the two major stages of prevention and preparation.

Innovative Approaches to Planning

The process of planning changes over time, like other aspects of managing, to be more in tune with shifts in the environment and employee attitudes. A fresh approach to planning is to involve everyone in the organization, and sometimes outside stakeholders as well, in the planning process. The evolution to a new approach began with a shift to **decentralized planning**, which means that planning experts work with managers in major divisions or departments to develop their own goals and plans. Managers throughout the company come up with their own creative solutions to problems and become more committed to following through on the plans. As the environment became even more volatile, top executives saw the benefits of pushing decentralized planning even further by having planning experts work directly with line managers and front-line employees to develop dynamic plans that meet fast-changing needs.

Go to the Ethical Dilemma, on page 200, that pertains to potential problems with innovative planning approaches.

In a complex and competitive business environment, strategic thinking and execution become the expectation of every employee.[26] Planning comes alive when employees are involved in setting goals and determining the means to reach them. Here are some guidelines for innovative planning.

Set Stretch Goals for Excellence

Stretch goals are reasonable yet highly ambitious goals that are so clear, compelling, and imaginative that they fire up employees and engender excellence. Stretch goals are typically so far beyond the current levels that people have to be innovative to find ways to reach them. An extension of the stretch goal is the *big hairy audacious goal,* or *BHAG*. The phrase was first proposed by James Collins and Jerry Porras in their 1996 article entitled "Building Your Company's Vision."[27] Since then, it has evolved to a term used to describe any goal that is so big, inspiring, and outside the prevailing paradigm that it hits people in the gut and shifts their thinking. At the same time, however, goals must be seen as achievable or employees will be discouraged and demotivated, and some might resort to extreme or unethical measures to meet the targets.[28]

Stretch goals and BHAGs have become extremely important because things move fast. A company that focuses on gradual, incremental improvements in products, processes, or systems will be left behind. Managers can use these goals to compel employees to think in new ways that can lead to bold, innovative breakthroughs. Motorola used stretch goals to achieve *Six Sigma* quality, which has now become the standard for numerous companies. Managers first set a goal of a tenfold increase in quality over a two-year period. After this goal was met, they set a new stretch goal of a hundredfold improvement over a four-year period.[29]

- Approaches to planning change with the times. In many companies today, planning is decentralized.
- **Decentralized planning** means that top executives or planning experts work with managers in major divisions or departments to develop their own goals and plans.
- **Stretch goals** are reasonable yet highly ambitious and compelling goals that energize people and inspire excellence.
- Motorola used stretch goals to achieve *Six Sigma* quality.

Thinking Strategically

How important is strategic management? It largely determines which organizations succeed and which ones struggle. Differences in the strategies managers chose and how effectively they executed them help explain why consumer electronics retailer Best Buy is thriving and Circuit City is dead, how Facebook has taken a firm lead over MySpace in social networking, and why Apple is beating Microsoft in the world of mobile computing.

Every company is concerned with strategy. Executives for the "American Idol" television show shifted their strategy as viewership began to decline for the popular series after eight seasons. The ninth season strategy was to add Ellen DeGeneres as a judge, bring back the top 24 semifinals format, and focus more on talented people with high aspirations and less on bizarre and obviously untalented contestants being humiliated by the judges. In the fast-food industry, McDonald's has succeeded with a new strategy of adding the McCafé line of hot and iced coffee drinks and offering more products for health-conscious consumers. The chain recently struck a deal in New Zealand to use the Weight Watchers logo on several of its lower-calorie meal options.[30]

Strategic blunders can hurt a company. Kodak still hasn't recovered from managers' failure to plan for the rapid rise of digital photography. Between 2001 and 2005, Kodak's earnings dropped about 60 percent as interest in film photography tanked, and the company has never caught up in digital. At e-commerce pioneer eBay, managers are struggling to find the right strategy after several years of slowing growth and profits. So far, the company's shift away from online auctions toward fixed prices and retail items has had limited success and has alienated many previously loyal eBay sellers.[31]

Managers at eBay, McDonald's, Kodak, and Microsoft are all involved in strategic management. They look for ways to respond to competitors, cope with difficult environmental challenges, meet changing customer needs, and effectively use available resources. Strategic management has taken on greater importance in today's environment because managers are responsible for positioning their organizations for success in a world that is constantly changing.

Earlier in this chapter, an overview of the types of goals and plans that organizations use was presented. Now, we explore strategic management, which is one specific type of planning. First, we define the components of strategic management and discuss the

New Manager Self-Test

Your Approach to Studying, Part 2

Your approach to studying may reveal whether you have the ability to think strategically. Answer the items below as they apply to your study behavior. Please answer whether each item below is Mostly True or Mostly False for you.

	MOSTLY TRUE <<<	>>> MOSTLY FALSE
1. One way or another, I manage to obtain whatever books and materials I need for studying.	_____	_____
2. I make sure I find study conditions that let me do my work easily.	_____	_____
3. I put effort into making sure I have the most important details at my fingertips.	_____	_____
4. When I read an article or book, I try to work out for myself what is being said.	_____	_____
5. I know what I want to get out of this course and I am determined to achieve it.	_____	_____
6. When I am working on a new topic, I try to see in my mind how the ideas fit together.	_____	_____
7. It is important to me to follow the argument and see the reasoning behind something.	_____	_____
8. I look at the evidence carefully and then try to reach my own conclusions about things I am studying.	_____	_____
9. When I am reading, I think how the ideas fit in with previous material.	_____	_____

See It Online

Scoring and Interpretation: The items above represent a *strategic approach* to studying. Strategy means knowing your desired outcomes, how to acquire factual knowledge, thinking clearly about tactics and cause-effect relationships, and implementing behaviors that will achieve the desired outcomes. Give yourself 1 point for each item you marked as Mostly True. If you scored 3 or lower, you probably are not using a strategic approach to studying. A score of 6 or above suggests a strategic approach to studying that will likely translate into strategic management ability as a new manager.

SOURCES: Adapted from Kristin Backhaus and Joshua P. Liff, "Cognitive Styles and Approaches to Studying in Management Education," *Journal of Management Education*, 31 (August 2007): 445–466, and A. Duff, "Learning Styles Measurement: The Revised Approaches to Studying Inventory," *Bristol Business School Teaching and Research Review* 3 (2000).

purposes and levels of strategy. Then, we examine several models of strategy formulation at the corporate, business, and functional levels. We also look at some new trends in strategy for today's environment. Finally, we discuss the tools managers use to execute their strategic plans.

What does it mean to think strategically? Strategic thinking means to take the long-term view and to see the big picture, including the organization and the competitive

Complete the New Manager Self-Test, on page 185, to get some idea about your strategic thinking ability.

environment, and consider how they fit together. Strategic thinking is important for both businesses and nonprofit organizations. In for-profit firms, strategic planning typically pertains to competitive actions in the marketplace. In nonprofit organizations such as the American Red Cross or The Salvation Army, strategic planning pertains to events in the external environment.

Research has shown that strategic thinking and planning positively affect a firm's performance and financial success.[32] Most managers are aware of the importance of strategic planning, as evidenced by a *McKinsey Quarterly* survey. Of responding executives whose companies had no formal strategic planning process, 51 percent said they were dissatisfied with the company's development of strategy, compared to only 20 percent of those at companies that had a formal planning process.[33] CEOs at successful companies make strategic thinking and planning a top management priority. For an organization to succeed, the CEO must be actively involved in making the tough choices and trade-offs that define and support strategy.[34] However, senior executives at today's leading companies want middle- and lower-level managers to think strategically as well. Understanding the strategy concept and the levels of strategy is an important start toward strategic thinking.

- To think strategically means to take the long-term view and see the big picture.
- Managers in all types of organizations, including businesses, nonprofit organizations, and government agencies, have to think about how the organization fits in the environment.

What Is Strategic Management?

Strategic management refers to the set of decisions and actions used to formulate and execute strategies that will provide a competitively superior fit between the organization and its environment so as to achieve organizational goals.[35] Managers ask questions such as the following: What changes and trends are occurring in the competitive environment? Who are our competitors and what are their strengths and weaknesses? Who are our customers? What products or services should we offer and how can we offer them most efficiently? What does the future hold for our industry, and how can we change the rules of the game? Answers to these questions help managers make choices about how to position their organizations in the environment with respect to rival companies.[36] Superior organizational performance is not a matter of luck. It is determined by the choices that managers make. Trinity College leaders asked themselves these questions and came up with a solution that led them to rounding success, as described in this chapter's Benchmarking box.

Purpose of Strategy

The first step in strategic management is to define an explicit **strategy**, which is the plan of action that describes resource allocation and activities for dealing with the environment, achieving a competitive advantage, and attaining the organization's goals. **Competitive advantage** refers to what sets the organization apart from others and provides it with a distinctive edge for meeting customer or client needs in the marketplace. The essence of formulating strategy is choosing how the organization will be different.[37] Managers make decisions about whether the company will perform different activities or will execute similar activities differently than its rivals do. Strategy necessarily changes over time to fit

BENCHMARKING

Trinity College Squash Team

Trinity College was in trouble. It could no longer stand with its competitors, Amherst and Williams, mostly because it was located in one of Hartford's blighted and crime-ridden neighborhoods. New college president Evan Dobelle realized he had to fix the surroundings and started a $225 million urban-renewal project, which included building new schools and a performing arts center. Knowing this would all take years, Dobelle tried to think of another way to enhance Trinity's brand in the meantime. Sports. But the kind of money it took to move the basketball team out of its Division III status was more than they could afford. Why not squash, where they at least had already played Harvard and Yale? If they could rustle some feathers there, it could make big news.

Dobelle called in the squash coach, Paul Assaiante. What would it take for Trinity to compete with the Ivy League? Without hesitation, the experienced coach replied, "Recruit foreign players." In the 15 years since that meeting, Assaiante has scoured the globe for players. What he knew back then was that the United States isn't particularly good at squash, but other countries are, and there are excellent players who would love to get an education at a top U.S. university. Currently, Trinity has players from India, South Africa, Colombia, Malaysia, Jamaica and El Salvador.

© Kuzmik, Shutterstock

Trinity's strategy to focus on squash over other sports had paid off. The NESCAC allows Trinity to give 71 yearly spots (allocated as they wish) to athletes who might not otherwise be admitted. A large portion of those go for squash. Because of the tracking of worldwide sports on the Internet, it is easier for Assaiante to follow top squash high-schoolers around the world. In the intervening years since that conversation, Trinity has won 13 consecutive national championships and has not lost a single match to another school. At over 240 matches and counting, this is the longest winning streak in college sports. Not bad from a college on the wrong side of the tracks, is it?

SOURCE: Paul Wachter, "Squashing the Ivies," *New York Times Magazine*, (February 20, 2011): 37–39.

environmental conditions, but to remain competitive, companies develop strategies that focus on core competencies, provide synergy, and create value for customers.

Exploit Core Competence A company's **core competence** is something the organization does especially well in comparison to its competitors. A core competence represents a competitive advantage because the company acquires expertise that competitors do not have. A core competence may be in the area of superior research and development, expert technological know-how, process efficiency, or exceptional customer service.[38] Managers at companies such as Walmart, Southwest Airlines, and Dollar General, for example, focus on a core competence of operational efficiency that enables them to keep costs low. Gaylord Hotels, which has large hotel and conference centers in several states as well as the Opryland complex near Nashville, Tennessee, thrives based on a strategy of superior service for large group meetings.[39] Robinson Helicopter succeeds through superior technological know-how for building small, two-seater helicopters used for everything from police patrols in Los Angeles to herding cattle in Australia.[40] In each case, leaders identified what their company does especially well and built strategy around it.

Build Synergy When organizational parts interact to produce a joint effect that is greater than the sum of the parts acting alone, **synergy** occurs. The organization may attain a special advantage with respect to cost, market power, technology, or management skill. When properly managed, synergy can create additional value with existing resources, providing a big boost to the bottom line.[41] Synergy was the motivation for PepsiCo to buy Frito-Lay for instance, and for Oracle to buy Sun Microsystems. Oracle's purchase of Sun gives the software company a giant hardware business, enabling Oracle to provide corporations with most of the technology they need in a single package.[42]

Synergy can also be obtained by good relationships between organizations. For example, the Disney Channel invites magazines such as *J-14*, *Twist*, and *Popstar* to visit the sets of shows such as *Hannah Montana* and *JONAS*, gives reporters access for interviews and photo shoots, and provides brief videos for the magazines to post on their Web sites. The synergy keeps preteen interest booming for both the television shows and the magazines.[43]

Deliver Value Delivering value to the customer is at the heart of strategy. Value can be defined as the combination of benefits received and costs paid. Managers help their companies create value by devising strategies that exploit core competencies and attain synergy. To compete with the rising clout of satellite television, for example, cable companies such as Time Warner Cable and Comcast offer *value packages* that provide a combination of basic cable, digital premium channels, video-on-demand, high-speed Internet, and digital phone service for a reduced cost.

Consider how Acer Inc. has become the world's second-largest computer maker with a strategy based on exploiting core competencies, building synergy, and providing value to customers.

ACER INC.

In 2004, Acer owned less than 5 percent of the global personal computer market, compared to Hewlett-Packard's 15 percent and Dell's nearly 20 percent. Six years later, the Taiwan-based company had surpassed Dell and was closing in on HP. How did it happen? Managers, led by CEO Gianfranco Lanci, used a strategy based on exploiting the company's core competencies of lean operations and speedy response to shifting consumer trends.

Acer has a bare-bones cost structure. Unlike rival companies, it sells only through retailers, and the company outsources all manufacturing and assembly to a network of partners. That has helped keep overhead expenses for Acer at about 8 percent of sales, compared to around 14 to 15 percent for rival companies. Cost savings are passed on to consumers, with a high-quality ultrathin laptop selling for around $650, compared to $1,800 for a similar HP model and $2,000 for Dell's ultrathin. Moreover, Acer managers saw the trend toward smaller devices and moved faster than rivals to introduce a wide selection of inexpensive netbooks.

Now, Acer is pushing into new territory to fuel growth, introducing its first smartphone in 2009, with plans to add six or seven new models in 2010. It's one of the fastest-growing sectors in the industry. With Acer's low cost structure, it can give consumers high quality smartphones at lower cost and still see profit margins in the range of 15 to 20 percent.[44]

- **Strategic management** refers to the set of decisions and actions used to formulate and implement strategies that will provide a competitively superior fit between the organization and its environment so as to achieve organizational goals.
- A **strategy** is the plan of action that describes resource allocation and activities for dealing with the environment, achieving a competitive advantage, and attaining goals.
- **Competitive advantage** refers to what sets the organization apart from others and provides it with a distinctive edge in the marketplace.
- Managers strive to develop strategies that focus on core competencies, create synergy, and deliver value.
- A **core competence** is something that the organization does particularly well in comparison to others.
- The Taiwan-based computer maker Acer Inc. focuses on a core competence of operational efficiency.
- **Synergy** exists when the organization's parts interact to produce a joint effect that is greater than the sum of the parts acting alone.
- Oracle bought Sun Microsystems to gain synergy by being able to provide customers with most of the technology they need in a single package.
- The heart of strategy is to deliver value to customers.

The Strategic Management Process

The overall strategic management process is illustrated in Exhibit 5.5. It begins when executives evaluate their current position with respect to mission, goals, and strategies. They then scan the organization's internal and external environments and identify strategic factors that might require change. Managers at BP didn't have to look far to see a need for change after a giant drilling rig exploded and sank in April 2010, killing 11 crew members and spilling massive amounts of oil into the Gulf of Mexico. BP's strategy has been based on being a leader in pushing the frontiers of the oil industry, such as drilling the world's deepest wells, scouting for oil in the Arctic, and other aggressive efforts. The strategy was successful. BP steadily increased production and overtook Royal Dutch Shell PLC in market capitalization in January of 2010.[45] A few months later, though, disaster struck, presenting a crisis that will be tough for BP to weather and requiring a new approach to strategy for the oil giant. BP will have to evaluate whether its strategy fits the environment and its own capabilities.

For all organizations, internal or external events sometimes indicate a need to redefine the mission or goals or to formulate a new strategy at either the corporate, business, or functional level. The final stage in the strategic management process outlined in Exhibit 5.5 is execution of the new strategy.

Strategy Formulation Versus Execution

Strategy formulation includes the planning and decision making that lead to the establishment of the firm's goals and the development of a specific strategic plan.[46] **Strategy formulation** may include assessing the external environment and internal problems and integrating the results into goals and strategy. This process is in contrast to

EXHIBIT 5.5

The Strategic Management Process

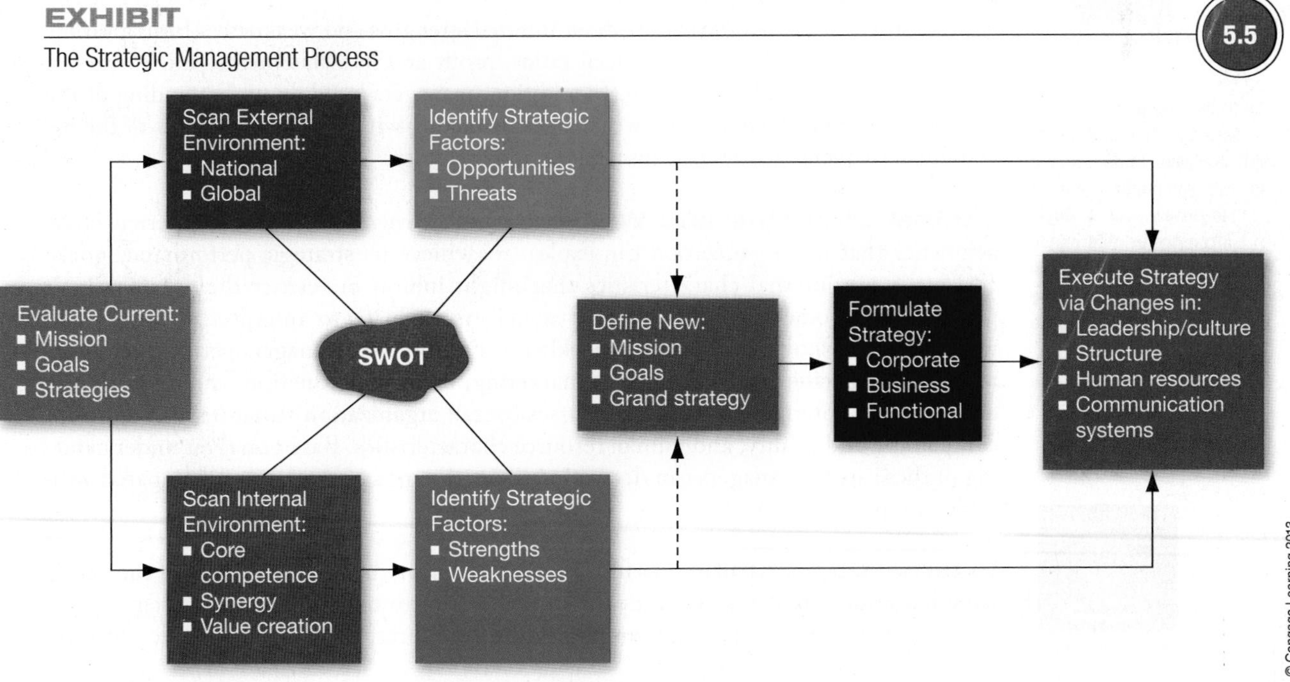

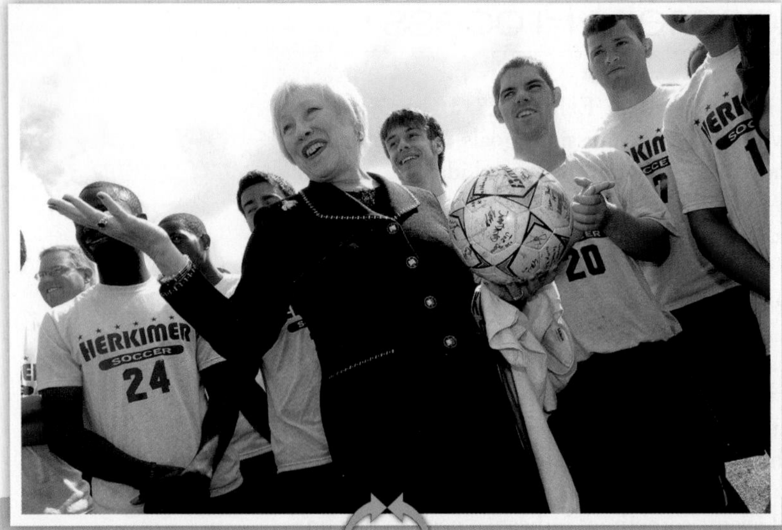

AP Photo/ Steve Jacobs

ConceptConnection

State University of New York (SUNY) Chancellor Nancy L. Zimpher toured all 64 SUNY campuses—including Herkimer County Community College, shown here—as she began overseeing the process of **formulating a new strategy** for the system. The effort was precipitated by the $450 million in state funding cuts SUNY experienced over a two-year period as New York tried to cope with a daunting budget deficit resulting from the recession. A key part of the new strategy involves finding ways to translate theoretical knowledge into tangible economic benefits, a point Zimpher hopes will convince legislators that any further budget cuts would only hurt the state's economy.

strategy execution, which is the use of managerial and organizational tools to direct resources toward accomplishing strategic results.[47] Strategy execution is the administration and implementation of the strategic plan. Managers may use persuasion, new equipment, changes in organization structure, or a revised reward system to ensure that employees and resources are used to make formulated strategy a reality.

SWOT Analysis

SWOT analysis includes a careful assessment of strengths, weaknesses, opportunities, and threats that affect organizational performance. Managers obtain external information about opportunities and threats from a variety of sources, including customers, government reports, professional journals, suppliers, bankers, friends in other organizations, consultants, or association meetings. Many firms contract with special scanning organizations to provide them with newspaper clippings, Internet research, and analyses of relevant domestic and global trends. Others hire competitive intelligence professionals to scope out competitors, as we discussed in Chapter 2, and use intelligence teams, as described earlier in this chapter.

Go to the Group Learning, on page 199, that pertains to SWOT analysis. Before reading further, you might also want to review your strategic strengths as determined by your responses to the questionnaire at the beginning of this chapter.

Executives acquire information about internal strengths and weaknesses from a variety of reports, including budgets, financial ratios, profit and loss statements, and surveys of employee attitudes and satisfaction. In addition, managers build an understanding of the company's internal strengths and weaknesses by talking with people at all levels of the hierarchy in frequent face-to-face discussions and meetings.

Internal Strengths and Weaknesses *Strengths* are positive internal characteristics that the organization can exploit to achieve its strategic performance goals. *Weaknesses* are internal characteristics that might inhibit or restrict the organization's performance. Some examples of what managers evaluate to interpret strengths and weaknesses are shown in the audit checklist in Exhibit 5.6. Managers perform an internal audit of specific functions such as marketing, finance, production, and research and development. Internal analysis also assesses overall organization structure, management competence and quality, and human resource characteristics. Based on their understanding of these areas, managers can determine their strengths or weaknesses compared with other companies.

5

External Opportunities and Threats *Threats* are characteristics of the external environment that may prevent the organization from achieving its strategic goals. One threat to Microsoft, for example, is the proliferation of cheap or free software

EXHIBIT 5.6

Audit Checklist for Analyzing Organizational Strengths and Weaknesses

Management and Organization	Marketing	Human Resources
Management quality Staff quality Degree of centralization Organization charts Planning, information, control systems	Distribution channels Market share Advertising efficiency Customer satisfaction Product quality Service reputation Sales force turnover	Employee experience, education Union status Turnover, absenteeism Work satisfaction Grievances
Finance	**Production**	**Research and Development**
Profit margin Debt-equity ratio Inventory ratio Return on investment Credit rating	Plant location Machinery obsolescence Purchasing system Quality control Productivity/efficiency	Basic applied research Laboratory capabilities Research programs New-product innovations Technology innovations

available over the Internet.[48] *Opportunities* are characteristics of the external environment that have the potential to help the organization achieve or exceed its strategic goals. The U.S. auto manufacturers have an unprecedented opportunity to steal customers from Toyota because of the quality, safety, and public relations problems that company is experiencing. Managers are searching for ways to take advantage of the opportunity without alienating consumers by trashing the beleaguered number one automaker. Fortunately for General Motors, top managers had approved an advertising campaign boasting "May the Best Car Win" six months before Toyota's problems came to light.[49]

Managers evaluate the external environment based on the ten sectors described in Chapter 2. The task environment sectors are the most relevant to strategic behavior and include the behavior of competitors, customers, suppliers, and the labor supply. The general environment contains those sectors that have an indirect influence on the organization but nevertheless must be understood and incorporated into strategic behavior. The general environment includes technological developments, the economy, legal-political and international events, the natural environment, and sociocultural changes. Additional areas that might reveal opportunities or threats include pressure groups, interest groups, creditors, and potentially competitive industries.

Social networking company Facebook provides an example of how managers can use SWOT analysis in formulating an appropriate strategy.

So far, Facebook's strategy is working, but the company continues to face threats related to privacy and safety concerns. Zuckerberg keeps adding seasoned executives to his team to help the company cope with the complexity of the environment and try to avoid serious blunders.

SPOTLIGHT ON SKILLS

Facebook, Inc.

Whatever happened to MySpace? Just a few years ago, it was tops in online social networking, but Facebook is now by far the market leader with about 400 million users compared to MySpace's 100 million. Facebook grew rapidly in the first four years after 23-year-old Mark Zuckerberg founded it while still a student at Harvard University. To keep it growing, the young CEO made some strategic decisions that can be understood by looking at the company's strengths, weaknesses, opportunities, and threats.

Facebook's *strengths* include technological know-how and an aggressive and innovative culture. The company negotiated a major partnership with Microsoft, which invested millions of dollars in the site, brokers banner ads for the company, and created tools that make it easy to create links between Windows applications and Facebook's network. In 2009, the company got additional funding for expansion from an Internet investment group and also began making enough money to cover its costs. The primary *weakness* is a lack of management expertise to help the company meet the challenges of rapid growth. In addition, Zuckerberg has a reputation in the industry as an arrogant and standoffish manager, which could damage Facebook's reputation and its chances of successful partnerships.

The biggest *threats* to the company are related to issues of privacy, online safety, and copyright infringements. Since Facebook opened the site to third-party developers, it has gotten into hot water with companies such as Hasbro and Mattel for online versions of popular games. The company has been accused of arrogance for not adding a button that could alert police to pedophiles and other online predators. *Opportunities* abound to expand the company's operations internationally and to take advantage of Facebook's popularity to introduce features that can command higher Web advertising rates and bring in more revenue.

What does SWOT analysis suggest for Facebook? Zuckerberg has cemented Facebook's popularity by making it a place for outside companies to provide services to members. That means people who might be working to develop the next hot social networking site are working for Facebook instead. Non-Internet companies have also created Facebook pages and applications to reach Facebook's vast customer base. Even the White House has a Facebook page. Organizations can experience a sort of viral popularity as word spreads among millions of members. The company has launched several international sites (around 70 percent of users are outside the United States) and was reportedly gearing up for launch in China by the end of 2010.

To implement the growth strategy, Zuckerberg has brought in executives with more management experience than himself, such as Sheryl Sandberg, formerly of Google, as chief operating officer, and David Ebersman, longtime chief financial officer of Genentech, as CFO. These managers have the traditional skills Facebook needs to execute the strategy both in the United States and internationally.

SOURCE: Randall Stross, "Getting Older Without Getting Old," *The New York Times*, March 7, 2010; Benny Evangelista, "Facebook Reportedly Gearing Up for China Launch Before Year's End," *San Francisco Chronicle*, April 3, 2010; "Facebook's Latest Fracas: Your Privacy vs. Its Profit," *The Washington Post*, April 4, 2010; David Kirkpatrick, "Facebook's Plan to Hook up the World," *Fortune* (June 11, 2007): 127–130; Rebecca Camber, "Arrogant Facebook Failing to Tackle Paedophile Threat," *Daily Mail*, April 9, 2010; and Vauhini Vara, "Facebook CEO Seeks Help As Site Suffers Growing Pains," *The Wall Street Journal*, March 5, 2008.

- **Strategy formulation** is the stage of strategic management that includes the planning and decision making that lead to the establishment of the organization's goals and a specific strategic plan.
- Managers often start with a **SWOT analysis**, an audit or careful examination of *strengths*, *weaknesses*, *opportunities*, and *threats* that affect organizational performance.
- The proliferation of free software over the Internet is a *threat* to Microsoft. Toyota's safety problems have provided an unexpected *opportunity* for U.S. automakers.
- **Strategy execution** is the stage of strategic management that involves the use of managerial and organizational tools to direct resources toward achieving strategic outcomes.

Formulating Business-Level Strategy

Now we turn to strategy formulation within the strategic business unit, in which the concern is how to compete. A popular and effective model for formulating strategy is Porter's competitive forces and strategies. Michael E. Porter studied a number of business organizations and proposed that business-level strategies are the result of five competitive forces in the company's environment.[50] More recently, Porter examined the impact of the Internet on business-level strategy.[51] Web-based technology is influencing industries in both positive and negative ways, and understanding this impact is essential for managers to accurately analyze their competitive environments and design appropriate strategic actions.

Porter's Five Competitive Forces

Exhibit 5.7 illustrates the competitive forces that exist in a company's environment and indicates some ways Internet technology is affecting each area. These forces help determine a company's position vis-à-vis competitors in the industry environment. Although such a model might be used on a corporate level, most large companies have separate business

EXHIBIT 5.7

Porter's Five Forces Affecting Industry Competition

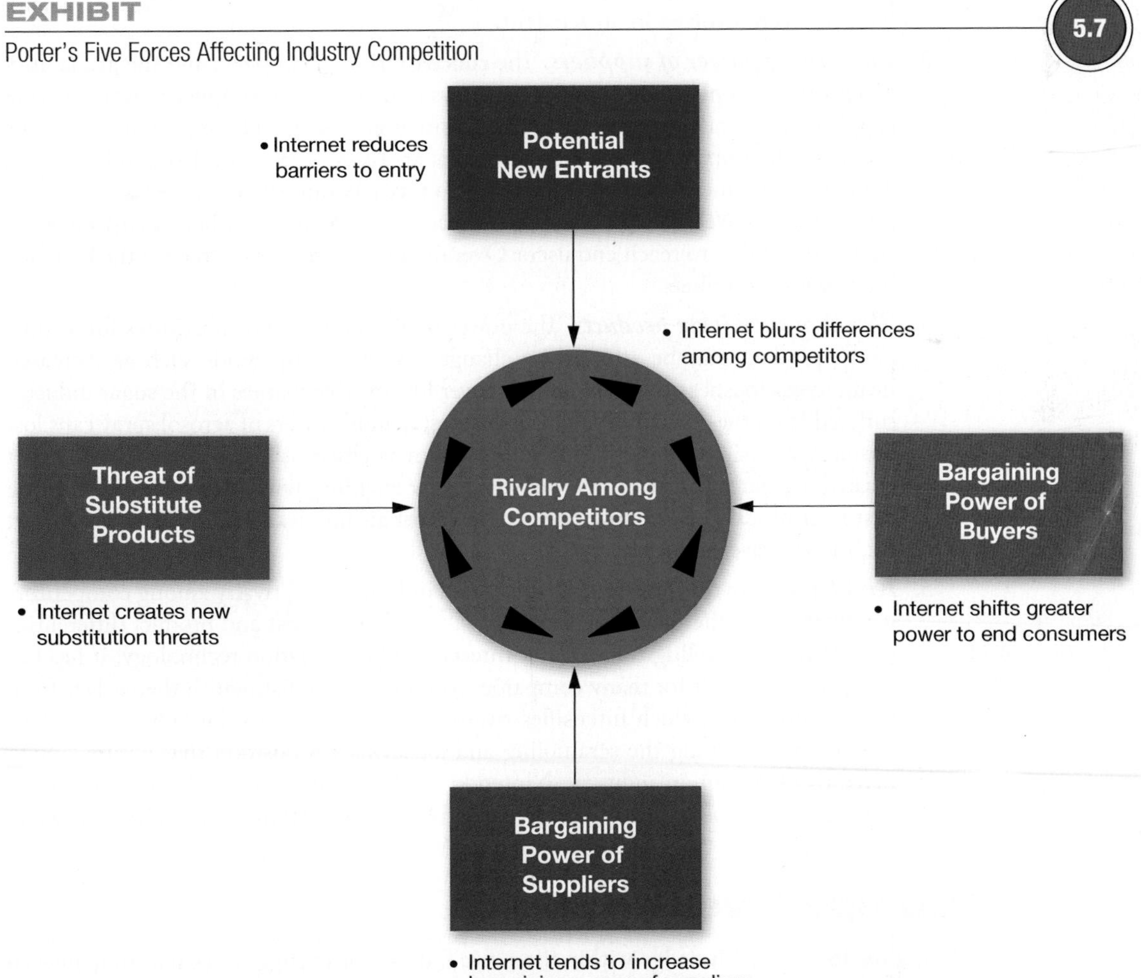

SOURCES: Based on Michael E. Porter, *Competitive Strategy: Techniques for Analyzing Industries and Competitors* (New York: Free Press, 1980); and Michael E. Porter, "Strategy and the Internet," *Harvard Business Review* (March 2001): 63–78.

lines and do an industry analysis for each line of business or SBU. Mars, Inc., for example, operates in six business segments: chocolate (Snickers); pet care (Pedigree); gum and confections (Juicy Fruit); food (Uncle Ben's); drinks (Flavia); and symbioscience (veterinary care, plant care). Competitive forces for the chocolate division would be different from those for the symbioscience division, so managers would do a competitive analysis for each business segment, looking at Porter's five forces.

1. ***Potential new entrants.*** Capital requirements and economies of scale are examples of two potential barriers to entry that can keep out new competitors. It is far more costly to enter the automobile industry, for instance, than to start a specialized mail-order business. In general, Internet technology has made it much easier for new companies to enter an industry by curtailing the need for such organizational elements as an established sales force, physical assets such as buildings and machinery, or access to existing supplier and sales channels.
2. ***Bargaining power of buyers.*** Informed customers become empowered customers. The Internet provides easy access to a wide array of information about products, services, and competitors, thereby greatly increasing the bargaining power of end consumers. For example, a customer shopping for a car can gather extensive information about various options, such as wholesale prices for new cars or average value for used vehicles, detailed specifications, repair records, and even whether a used car has ever been involved in an accident.
3. ***Bargaining power of suppliers.*** The concentration of suppliers and the availability of substitute suppliers are significant factors in determining supplier power. The sole supplier of engines to a manufacturer of small airplanes will have great power, for example. The impact of the Internet in this area can be both positive and negative. That is, procurement over the Web tends to give a company greater power over suppliers, but the Web also gives suppliers access to a greater number of customers, as well as the ability to reach end users. Overall, the Internet tends to raise the bargaining power of suppliers.
4. ***Threat of substitute products.*** The power of alternatives and substitutes for a company's product may be affected by changes in cost or in trends such as increased health consciousness that will deflect buyer loyalty. Companies in the sugar industry suffered from the growth of sugar substitutes; manufacturers of aerosol spray cans lost business as environmentally conscious consumers chose other products. The Internet created a greater threat of new substitutes by enabling new approaches to meeting customer needs. For example, offers of low-cost airline tickets over the Internet hurt traditional travel agencies.
5. ***Rivalry among competitors.*** As illustrated in Exhibit 5.7, rivalry among competitors is influenced by the preceding four forces, as well as by cost and product differentiation. With the leveling force of the Internet and information technology, it has become more difficult for many companies to find ways to distinguish themselves from their competitors, which intensifies rivalry. Porter referred to the "advertising slugfest" when describing the scrambling and jockeying for position that occurs among fierce rivals within an industry. Nintendo and Sony are fighting for control of the video game console industry, and Pepsi and Coke are battling it out in the cola wars.

Competitive Strategies

In finding its competitive edge within these five forces, Porter suggests that a company can adopt one of three strategies: differentiation, cost leadership, or focus. The organizational characteristics typically associated with each strategy are summarized in Exhibit 5.8.

EXHIBIT 5.8

Organizational Characteristics of Porter's Competitive Strategies

Strategy	Organizational Characteristics
Differentiation	Acts in a flexible, loosely knit way, with strong coordination among departments
	Strong capability in basic research
	Creative flair, thinks "out of the box"
	Strong marketing abilities
	Rewards employee innovation
	Corporate reputation for quality or technological leadership
Cost Leadership	Strong central authority; tight cost controls
	Maintains standard operating procedures
	Easy-to-use manufacturing technologies
	Highly efficient procurement and distribution systems
	Close supervision, finite employee empowerment
Focus	Frequent, detailed control reports
	May use combination of above policies directed at particular strategic target
	Values and rewards flexibility and customer intimacy
	Measures cost of providing service and maintaining customer loyalty
	Pushes empowerment to employees with customer contact

SOURCES: Based on Michael E. Porter, *Competitive Strategy: Techniques for Analyzing Industries and Competitors* (New York: The Free Press: 1980); Michael Treacy and Fred Wiersema, "How Market Leaders Keep Their Edge," *Fortune* (February 6, 1995): 88–98; and Michael A. Hitt, R. Duane Ireland, and Robert E. Hoskisson, *Strategic Management* (St. Paul, MN: West, 1995), p. 100–113.

Strategy Execution

The final step in the strategic management process is strategy execution—how strategy is implemented or put into action. Many companies have file drawers full of winning strategies, but they still struggle to succeed. Why? Practicing managers remind us that "strategy is easy, but execution is hard."[52] Indeed, many strategy experts agree that execution is the most important, yet the most difficult, part of strategic management.[53]

No matter how brilliant the formulated strategy, the organization will not benefit if it is not skillfully executed. One key to effective strategy execution is *alignment*, so that all aspects of the organization are in congruence with the strategy and every department and individual's efforts are coordinated toward accomplishing strategic goals. Alignment basically means that everyone is moving in the same direction.[54] Recall our discussion of strategy maps from the previous chapter. Just as managers make sure goals are in alignment, they check that all aspects of the organization are coordinated to be supportive of the strategies designed to achieve those goals.

One reason strategy execution is so tough is that organizational barriers may exist that hinder the implementation process. Exhibit 5.9 lists six *silent killers of strategy* that managers may not be aware of.[55] When they recognize these barriers, managers can work to overcome them by altering and fine-tuning various aspects of the organization to support strategic

EXHIBIT 5.9
Six Silent Killers of Strategy

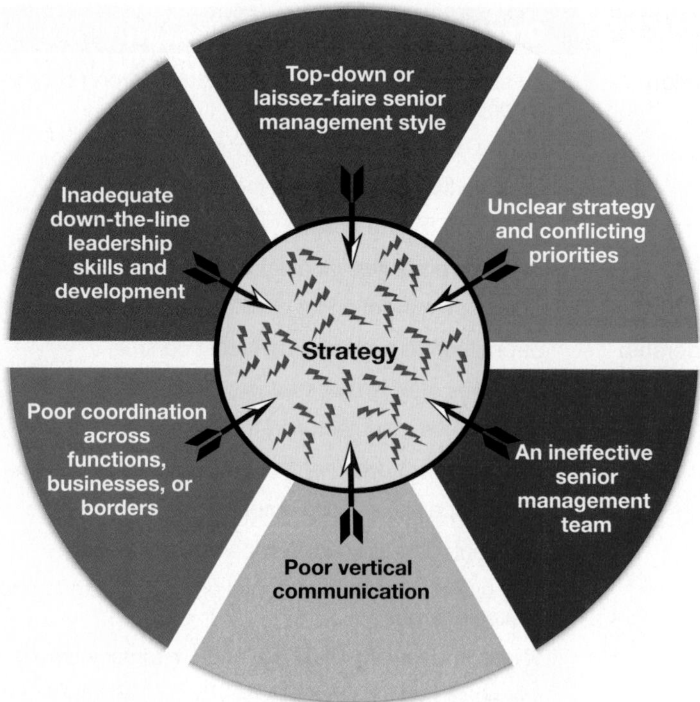

SOURCE: Based on M. Beer and R. A. Eisenstat, "The Silent Killers of Strategy Implementation and Learning," *MIT Sloan Management Review* 41, no. 4 (Summer 2000), pp. 29–41.

efforts. Exhibit 5.10 illustrates the primary tools managers use to solve the problem of poor strategy execution: visible leadership, clear roles and accountability, candid communication, and appropriate human resource practices.[56]

- ***Visible leadership.*** The primary key to successful strategy execution is good leadership. *Leadership* is the ability to influence people to adopt the new behaviors needed for putting the strategy into action. Kathleen Taylor, chief operating officer of Four Seasons Hotels and Resorts, visits up to 30 hotels each year to talk with hotel managers, department heads, and employees.[57] Leaders actively use persuasion, motivation techniques, and cultural values that support the new strategy. They might make speeches to employees, build coalitions of people who support the new strategic direction, and persuade middle managers to go along with their vision for the company. Most importantly, they lead by example.[58]
- ***Clear roles and accountability.*** People need to understand how their individual actions can contribute to achieving the strategy. Trying to execute a strategy that conflicts with structural design, particularly in relation to managers' roles, authority, and accountability, is a top obstacle to putting strategy into action.[59] To execute strategy effectively, top executives clearly define roles and delegate authority to individuals and teams who are accountable for results. This is part of Michael Dell's plan to execute a new strategy to get Dell Computer back on track. When he returned as CEO, one of Dell's first moves was to implement a new management structure that makes managers of each division accountable for meeting financial targets and gives them broad authority for how to reach them.[60]

EXHIBIT 5.10

Tools for Putting Strategy into Action

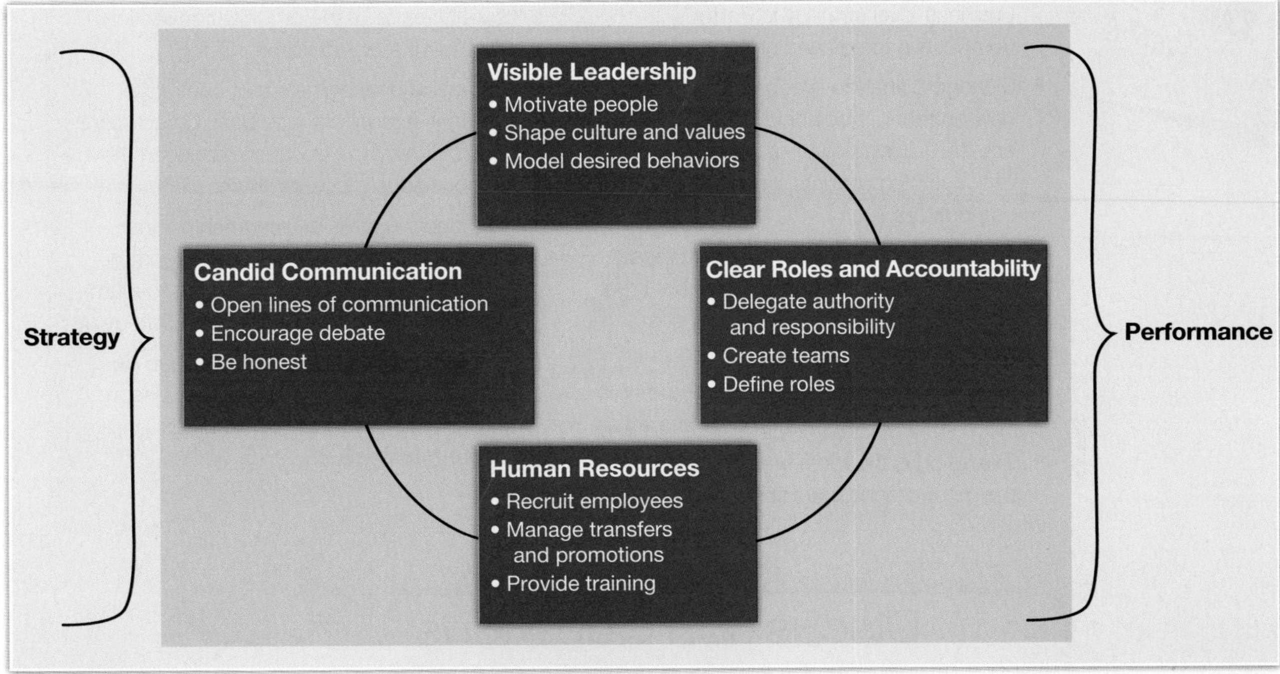

SOURCES: Based on Jay R. Galbraith and Robert K. Kazanjian. *Strategy Implementation: Structure, Systems, and Process* 2nd ed. (Cincinnati, OH: South-Western, Cengage Learning, 1986); Lawrence G. Hrebiniak, *Making Strategy Work: Leading Effective Execution and Change* (Upper Saddle River, N. J.: Wharton School Publishing/Pearson Education Inc., 2005); and Eric Beaudan, "Creative Execution," *Ivey Business Journal* (March–April 2010), http://www.iveybusinessjournal.com/article.asp?intArticle_ID=891 (accessed March 26, 2010).

- ***Candid Communication.*** Managers openly and avidly promote their strategic ideas, but they also listen to others and encourage disagreement and debate. They create a culture based on openness and honesty, which encourages teamwork and collaboration across hierarchical and departmental boundaries. Effective strategy execution also requires candid communication with shareholders, customers, and other stakeholders. Sergey Brin and Larry Page, the founders of Google, take turns writing a direct and open letter to shareholders each year. The original letter written for the initial public offering (IPO) makes clear that Google wouldn't try to "smooth out" its quarterly results, as some publicly traded companies do.[61]
- ***Appropriate human resource practices.*** The organization's *human resources* are its employees. The human resource function recruits, selects, trains, compensates, transfers, promotes, and lays off employees to achieve strategic goals. Managers make sure human resource practices are aligned with the strategy. JCPenney hired a team of in-house designers to support its strategy of becoming a stylish alternative to more expensive department stores such as Macy's, for example.[62] Longo Toyota of El Monte, California, recruits a highly diverse workforce to create a competitive advantage in selling cars and trucks. The staff speaks more than 30 languages and dialects, which gives Longo a lead because research shows that minorities prefer to buy a vehicle from someone who speaks their language and understands their culture.[63] Training employees is also important because it helps people understand the purpose and importance of the strategy, overcome resistance, and develop the necessary skills and behaviors to implement the strategy.

- A popular model for formulating business-level strategy is Porter's competitive forces and strategies.
- Managers analyze five forces: potential new entrants, bargaining power of buyers, bargaining power of suppliers, threat of substitute products, and rivalry among competitors.
- To find a competitive edge within these forces, managers adopt one of the three types of strategy: differentiation, cost leadership, or focus.
- Even the most creative strategies have no value if they cannot be translated into action.
- Execution is the most important, but also the most difficult, part of strategy.
- One key to effective execution is making sure all parts of the organization are in alignment to support the strategy.
- Organizational barriers that can hinder strategy execution have been called *silent killers of strategy* because managers have to consciously look for them.
- Managers use visible leadership, clear roles and accountability, candid communication, and appropriate human resource practices to effectively execute strategy.
- JCPenney hired a team of in-house designers to support its strategy of becoming a stylish alternative to more expensive department stores.

Discussion Questions

1. Write a brief mission statement for a local business with which you are familiar. How might having a clear, written mission statement benefit a small organization?
2. What strategic plans could the college or university at which you are taking this management course adopt to compete for students in the marketplace? Would these plans depend on the school's goals?
3. One of the benefits of a strategy map is that goals and how they are linked can be clearly communicated to everyone in the organization. Does a minimum wage maintenance worker in a hospital really need to understand any goals beyond keeping the place clean? Discuss.
4. A new business venture must develop a comprehensive business plan to borrow money to get started. Companies such as FedEx, Nike, and Rolm Corporation say they did not follow the original plan closely. Does that mean that developing the plan was a waste of time for these eventually successful companies?
5. How do you think planning in today's organizations compares to planning 25 years ago? Do you think planning becomes more important or less important in a world where everything is changing quickly and crises are a regular part of organizational life? Why?
6. Assume Southern University decides to (1) raise its admission standards and (2) initiate a business fair to which local townspeople will be invited. What types of plans might it use to carry out these two activities?
7. Some people say an organization could never be "prepared" for a disaster such as the massacre at Virginia Tech, which left 33 people dead, or the huge BP oil spill in the Gulf of Mexico. Discuss the potential value of crisis planning in situations like these, even if the situations are difficult to plan for.
8. Based on your knowledge of the following companies, how effective would you say any one of the following acquisitions were in terms of creating synergy: The purchase of MySpace by News Corporation (owner of Fox Broadcasting)? PepsiCo's purchase of Frito-Lay? Ebay's purchase of PayPal? Luby's purchase of Fuddruckers? InBev's acquisition of Budweiser?
9. You are a middle manager helping to implement a new corporate cost-cutting strategy, and you're meeting skepticism, resistance, and in some cases, outright hostility from your subordinates. In what ways might you or the company have been able to avoid this situation? Where do you go from here?
10. Perform a SWOT analysis for the school or university you attend. Do you think university administrators consider the same factors when devising their strategy?
11. Using Porter's competitive strategies, how would you describe the strategies of Walmart, Macy's, and Target?

Self-Learning

Business School Ranking

The dean of the business school at a major university in your state has contacted students in your class to develop a plan for improving its national ranking among business schools. The school recently dropped ten places in the rankings, and the dean wants to restore the school's perceived luster. The dean provided the following list of variables on which the national ranking is based.

- Written assessment by deans from peer institutions on a scale of 1 to 5
- Written assessment by recruiters on a scale of 1 to 5
- Average GPA of incoming students
- Acceptance rate of student applications (a lower percentage is better)
- Average starting salary of the school's most recent graduates
- Percentage of graduates employed on the date of graduation
- Percentage of graduates employed three months after graduation
- Average SAT (for the undergraduate program) and GMAT (for the MBA program) scores for entering students

The business school has a goal of improving its ranking by ten places in two years. Brainstorm ideas and develop a ten-point action plan that will list the steps the dean can take to achieve this goal. To develop the plan, think carefully about actions the school might take to improve its ranking on any or all of the measured variables listed above.

After writing down your ideas to develop a plan, meet with a partner to share ideas and discuss the most helpful action steps that will be part of the action plan recommended to the business school dean.

Group Learning

SWOT Analysis[64]

Step 1. In a group of three to five students, select a local eating establishment for a SWOT analysis. This could be a restaurant, an ice-cream store, or a bakery with which your group is familiar.

Step 2. Write a statement of what you perceive to be the business's current strategy.

Step 3. What do you perceive to be the key strengths and weaknesses of this business from a customer's perspective? Make one list for strengths and another list for weaknesses.

Step 4. What do you perceive to be potential opportunities and threats for this business? Make one list for opportunities and another for threats.

Step 5. If the store manager or owner is available, interview the person for his or her perception of strategy strengths, weaknesses, opportunities, and threats. Add new items to your lists.

Step 6. Use your SWOT analysis findings to set a goal of where this business could be in two years in terms of growth, size, new offerings, or expanded customer base. What steps do you recommend to achieve this goal?

Step 7. How did your SWOT analysis help you determine the goal and how to accomplish it during the next two years? What did you learn from this exercise?

Name of the local restaurant, café, or so forth:

Questions to ask	Answers
Key strengths from customer point of view	
Key weaknesses from customer point of view	
Potential opportunities	
Potential threats	
Results of manager interview, if available	
Using your analysis, where do you think this business could be in two years?	
What steps would you recommend for the business to achieve what you have just proposed?	
What did you learn from this exercise?	

Action Learning

1. Think back to some of the courses you have taken in college or graduate school.
2. List the one in which you feel you did the best and got the best grade, and the one in which you did the worst.
   a. Best b. Worst
3. What did you do differently in the two classes? Fill out the table below:

	Study strategies and other behaviors that helped	**Strategies and behaviors that did not help**
Name of course		
Best:		
Worst:		

4. What were the differences in what you did in the best course versus the worst one?
5. List down lessons you can learn that will help you in future courses:
   a.
   b.
   c.
   d.
   e.
   f.

Ethical Dilemma

Inspire Learning Corporation[65]

When the idea first occurred to her, it seemed like such a win–win situation. Now she wasn't so sure.

Marge Brygay was a hard-working sales rep for Inspire Learning Corporation, a company intent on becoming the top educational software provider in five years. That newly adopted strategic goal translated into an ambitious million-dollar sales target for each of Inspire's sales reps. At the beginning of the fiscal year, her share of the sales department's operational goal seemed entirely reasonable to Marge. She believed in Inspire's products. The company had developed innovative, highly regarded math, language, science, and social studies programs for the K–12 market. What set the software apart was a foundation in truly cutting-edge research. Marge had seen for herself how Inspire programs could engage whole classrooms of normally unmotivated kids; the significant rise in test scores on those increasingly important standardized tests bore out her subjective impressions.

But now, just days before the end of the year, Marge's sales were $1,000 short of her million-dollar goal. The sale that would have put her comfortably over the top fell through due to last-minute cuts in one large school system's budget. At first, she was nearly overwhelmed with frustration, but then it occurred to her that if she contributed $1,000 to Central High, the inner-city high school in her territory probably most in need of what she had for sale, they could purchase the software and put her over the top.

Her scheme would certainly benefit Central High students. Achieving her sales goal would make Inspire happy, and it wouldn't do her any harm, either professionally or financially. Making the goal would earn her a $10,000 bonus check that would come in handy when the time came to write out that first tuition check for her oldest child, who had just been accepted to a well-known, private university.

Initially, it seemed like the perfect solution all the way around. The more she thought about it, however, the more it didn't quite sit well with her conscience. Time was running out. She needed to decide what to do.

What Would You Do?

1. Donate the $1,000 to Central High, and consider the $10,000 bonus a good return on your gift.
2. Accept the fact you didn't quite make your sales goal this year. Figure out ways to work smarter next year to increase the odds of achieving your target.
3. Don't make the donation, but investigate whether any other ways were available to help Central High raise the funds that would allow them to purchase the much-needed educational software.

Case for Critical Analysis

Nielsen Media Research[66]

David Calhoun left a job he loved as a star executive at General Electric to step into a mess as CEO of the A. C. Nielsen Corporation. His immediate challenge: the media research unit, which is under heavy fire from television clients such as NBC and CBS for chronic delays in reporting television ratings. Nielsen held a conference call with major clients, acknowledging the delays and promising to do better, but the following Monday, the company again failed to report any ratings at all for the previous day. Nielson was not delivering data to customers as promised.

What's the big deal? Calhoun and Chief of Research Susan Whiting know that about $70 billion a year in advertising revenues for the television industry depends on Nielsen ratings. Viewers might think TV networks are in the business of providing entertainment, but management's primary goal is providing eyeballs for advertisers. When television managers and advertisers don't get timely, accurate data from Nielsen, they're shooting in the dark with decisions about how to allocate resources. Daily meetings at some companies are scheduled based on getting the information from Nielsen when promised. "There is so much revenue involved over which we have no quality control," said Alan Wurtzel, president of research for NBC. "We don't just use this data for analytical purposes. This is the currency of the business."

Calhoun and other top managers are analyzing what went wrong at Nielsen. Originated in 1923 to perform surveys of the production of industrial equipment, Nielsen became a household name when it launched its television ratings system in 1950. More than 60 years later, Nielsen still functions as a near-monopoly in the ratings business. Yet the company could be facing a serious threat from cable and satellite companies that are working on a way to get set-top boxes to provide real-time TV viewing data to rival Nielsen's.

Managers see several factors involved in the problems at Nielsen, but the biggest one is that the amount of data the company processes doubled in a year, overloading computer servers and straining the company's human systems. The increase has come both because of changes in how people are watching television, such as over the Internet and other digital devices, and in the amount of information networks want. As the television business gets cut into thinner slices, clients need even more precise data to make good decisions. Nielsen is pursuing a strategy it calls "Anytime, Anywhere Media Measurement" to stay relevant and address new competition, but it has to get its quality problems fixed quickly.

Clients understand the strain, but they have little sympathy. They want to know why Nielsen managers didn't anticipate the spike in data demands and plan accordingly.

Questions

1. Where do you think the problems lie at Nielsen? For example, are they primarily with the company's strategic goals and plans, tactical goals and plans, or operational goals and plans? With alignment of goals and plans?
2. Do you think developing a strategy map would be a good idea for Nielsen? Why or why not?
3. If you were David Calhoun, what kind of planning processes might you implement right now to fix this problem?

aplia Aplia Highlights

Now use your Aplia homework to help you:

- Apply management theories in your life
- Assess your management skills
- Master management terms and concepts
- Apply your knowledge to real-world situations
- Analyze and solve challenging management problems

In order to take advantage of these elements, your instructor will need to have set up a course for your class within Aplia. Ask your instructor to contact his/her Cengage sales representative and Digital Solutions Manager to explore testing Aplia in your course this term.

Modern Shed: Managerial Planning and Goal Setting

© Leremy, Shutterstock

In 2003, builder Ryan Smith was restoring an old home in Washington when a client marveled at the small work shed he set up for the project. The customer admired the compact portable structure, and it dawned on Smith that the kit could be decked out with modern features and used for studio spaces, home offices, guesthouses, and more. Smith ran with the idea and launched his own start-up business, Modern Shed. Today his company designs stylish prefabricated backyard dwellings for nearly any purpose.

To make the best use of limited resources, Modern Shed hires outside contractors to help produce its small paneled sheds. Because the company doesn't have an in-house marketing and sales department, Smith outsources the firm's marketing planning to Seattle consultant Scott Pearl, a real estate veteran who serves as the company's go-to guy for sales. "Scott has always been interested in the real estate market—he's a natural to work with," Ryan Smith said of his marketing partner.

But planning and goal setting can be a real challenge for the small Seattle-based company. As a new product concept that lacks a well-established market, Modern Shed finds itself in uncharted territory. Until recently, the company had few clear sales objectives. "When I joined with Modern Shed," Pearl recalls, "they didn't have any sales goals because they were still primarily selling through their Web site and through their dwell ad. So we had to start somewhere." Fortunately for Modern Shed, Pearl is an experienced marketer who thinks outside the box and has little trouble generating fresh ideas.

After being hired on as a consultant, Pearl began analyzing the company's local ads to see what product types were selling. He noted that Modern Shed was popular with people who wanted small backyard offices and studio spaces, and he determined that selling two 10 ft. × 12 ft. structures per month would be an effective first sales goal. As expected, he was able to achieve that goal in a timely manner.

Today Pearl is looking to expand the company's sales goals. Instead of focusing only on Modern Shed's small structures, Pearl has added sales targets for the company's larger, more profitable sheds. According to the marketing consultant, Modern Shed's larger dwellings need to represent 25 percent of all products sold—a stretch for the young firm.

With a new stretch goal in place for the company's larger dwellings, Pearl has begun creating a plan for how to achieve his higher target. In recent months, Pearl has narrowed down consumer segments, and he believes he has identified a perfect customer for the larger sheds: dual-income families that use nannies and au pairs to manage the home. Because Modern Shed manufactures a 12 ft. × 16 ft. dwelling with a bathroom and comfortable living quarters, Pearl believes he can pitch the shed as a "nanny solution" for Seattle's well-to-do families. Using information gathered from local title companies, Pearl discovered that his new residential target customer tends to live in upscale neighborhoods with mid-century modern architecture. Once Pearl's marketing plan is finalized, Modern Shed's sales teams will be ready to contact customers by direct mail, telesales, and personal sales appointments.

Pearl's marketing plan appears to be a good next step toward achieving Modern Shed's top-level strategic goals. "Modern Shed has been really popular with folks who are doing backyard offices, studios, and guestrooms, but the potential in the residential arena is a once-in-a-lifetime opportunity," Pearl says. According to the Seattle marketer, the economic recession actually works in the company's favor. "Because the downturn in the economy has been so severe, we're now seeing finished lot prices in the Northwest as low as $15,000 per lot, which is unheard of," Pearl said. "One of the reasons I'm driving this now is that we may not in our lifetimes see land at the price it is today."

Given the present state of the economy, Modern Shed's low-cost living solutions could catch on quickly, especially in Seattle, where starter houses can average $300,000. "We might be able to bring finished lot and house product to market for under $200,000, which would be unbelievable," Pearl says. For certain, if the plan works out, Modern Shed's little living spaces could become the next big thing.

Discussion Questions

1. What level of planning and goal setting does marketer Scott Pearl perform for Modern Shed?
2. Do Scott Pearl's goals meet the criteria of effective goal setting as discussed in the chapter? Explain.
3. What are some of the ways in which Scott Pearl's plans and goals benefit Modern Shed as an organization? Are there potential downsides to such planning?

Inside Man

New York City detective Keith Frazier (Denzel Washington) leads an effort to remove Dalton Russell (Clive Owen) and his armed gang from the Manhattan Trust Bank building. Complexities set in when bank chairman Arthur Case (Christopher Plummer) seeks the help of power broker Madeline White (Jodie Foster) to prevent the thieves from getting a particular safe deposit box. This fast-paced action film goes in many directions to reach its unexpected ending.

Planning This scene starts as Captain John Darius (Willem Dafoe) approaches the diner. Detectives Keith Frazier and Bill Mitchell (Chiwetlel Ejiofor) leave the diner to join Captain Darius. The scene ends after the three men enter the New York Police Department command post after Captain Darius says, "Your call." The film cuts to Madeline White and Arthur Case walking along a river.

What to Watch for and Ask Yourself

- Does this scene show strategic or tactical planning?
- What pieces of the planning type does it specifically show? Give examples from the scene.
- Do you expect this plan to succeed? Why or why not?

Endnotes

1. Ethan Smith and Yukari Iwatani Kane, "Apple Plots Reboot of iTunes for Web," *The Wall Street Journal,* December 10, 2009; and Sam Schechner and Yukari Iwatani Kane, "Corporate News: Apple TV Proposal Gets Some Nibbles," *The Asian Wall Street Journal,* December 23, 2009.
2. Quoted in Oren Harari, "Good/Bad News about Strategy," *Management Review* (July 1995): 29–31.
3. Amitai Etzioni, *Modern Organizations* (Englewood Cliffs, NJ: Prentice Hall, 1984), p. 6.
4. Ibid.
5. Mary Klemm, Stuart Sanderson, and George Luffman, "Mission Statements: Selling Corporate Values to Employees," *Long-Range Planning* 24, no. 3 (1991): 73–78; John A. Pearce II and Fred David, "Corporate Mission Statements: The Bottom Line," *Academy of Management Executive* (1987): 109–116; Jerome H. Want, "Corporate Mission: The Intangible Contributor to Performance," *Management Review* (August 1986): 46–50; and Forest R. David and Fred R. David, "It's Time to Redraft Your Mission Statement," *Journal of Business Strategy* (January–February 2003): 11–14.
6. "Tennessee News and Notes from State Farm," State Farm Mutual Automobile Insurance Company, 2004.
7. Micheline Maynard, "With Eye on Profits, G.M. Began Missing on Innovation," *The New York Times,* December 6, 2008; John D. Stoll, Kevin Helliker, and Neal E. Boudette, "A Saga of Decline and Denial," *The Wall Street Journal,* June 2, 2009; David Welch, "GM: His Way or the Highway," *BusinessWeek* (October 5, 2009): 62; Sharon Terlep, "General Motors Bolsters Leadership Ranks," *The Wall Street Journal,* February 23, 2010; and General Motors Web site, www.gmreinvention.com/?evar24=Reinvent_Sitelet (accessed March 31, 2010).
8. Paul Meising and Joseph Wolfe, "The Art and Science of Planning at the Business Unit Level," *Management Science* 31 (1985): 773–781.
9. David Welch, "The Man with the Toughest Job at GM," *BusinessWeek* (March 1, 2010): 54.
10. Sayan Chatterjee, "Core Objectives: Clarity in Designing Strategy," *California Management Review* 47, no. 2 (Winter 2005): 33–49.
11. Edwin A. Locke, Gary P. Latham, and Miriam Erez, "The Determinants of Goal Commitment," *Academy of Management Review* 13 (1988): 23–39.
12. C. Chet Miller and Laura B. Cardinal, "Strategic Planning and Firm Performance: A Synthesis of More Than Two Decades of Research," *Academy of Management Journal* 37, no. 6 (1994): 1649–1685.
13. These are based on E. A. Locke and G. P. Latham, *A Theory of Goal Setting & Task Performance* (Englewood Cliffs, N. J.: Prentice Hall, 1990); Richard L. Daft and Richard M. Steers, *Organizations: A Micro/Macro Approach* (Glenview, IL: Scott, Foresman, 1986), pp. 319–321; Herbert A. Simon, "On the Concept of Organizational Goals," *Administrative Science Quarterly* 9 (1964): 1–22; and Charles B. Saunders and Francis D. Tuggel, "Corporate Goals," *Journal of General Management* 5 (1980): 3–13
14. Nick Wingfield, "Netflix Boss Plots Life After the DVD," *The Wall Street Journal,* June 23, 2009.

15. These are based on Henry Mintzberg, *The Rise and Fall of Strategic Planning* (New York: The Free Press, 1994); H. Mintzberg, "Rethinking Strategic Planning, Part I: Pitfalls and Fallacies," *Long Range Planning* 27 (1994): 12–21; and H. Mintzberg, "The Pitfalls of Strategic Planning," *California Management Review* 36 (1993): 32–47.
16. Roth, "Is Management by Objectives Obsolete?"
17. Curtis W. Roney, "Planning for Strategic Contingencies," *Business Horizons* (March–April 2003): 35–42; and "Corporate Planning: Drafting a Blueprint for Success," *Small Business Report* (August 1987): 40–44.
18. Ellen Florian Kratz, "For FedEx, It Was Time to Deliver," *Fortune* (October 3, 2005): 83–84.
19. This section is based on Steven Schnaars and Paschalina Ziamou, "The Essentials of Scenario Writing," *Business Horizons* (July–August 2001): 25–31; Peter Cornelius, Alexander Van de Putte, and Mattia Romani, "Three Decades of Scenario Planning in Shell," *California Management Review* 48, no. 1 (Fall 2005); Audrey Schriefer and Michael Sales, "Creating Strategic Advantage with Dynamic Scenarios," *Strategy & Leadership* 34, no. 3 (2006): 31–42; William J. Worthington, Jamie D. Collins, and Michael A. Hitt, "Beyond Risk Mitigation: Enhancing Corporate Innovation with Scenario Planning," *Business Horizons* 52 (2009): 441–450; and Gill Ringland, "Innovation: Scenarios of Alternative Futures Can Discover New Opportunities for Creativity," *Strategy & Leadership* 36, no. 5 (2008): 22–27.
20. Bain & Company Management Tools and Trends Survey, reported in Darrell Rigby and Barbara Bilodeau, "A Narrowing Focus on Preparedness," *Harvard Business Review* (July–August 2007): 21–22; Worthington et al., "Beyond Risk Mitigation"; Tuna, "Pendulum Is Swinging Back on 'Scenario Planning'"; and "Strategic Planning in a Crisis: A *McKinsey Quarterly* Survey," *The McKinsey Quarterly: The Online Journal of McKinsey & Co.,* April 2009, www.mckinseyquarterly.com (accessed April 20, 2009).
21. Ian Mitroff with Gus Anagnos, *Managing Crises Before They Happen* (New York: AMACOM, 2001); Ian Mitroff and Murat C. Alpaslan, "Preparing for Evil," *Harvard Business Review* (April 2003): 109–115.
22. This discussion is based largely on W. Timothy Coombs, *Ongoing Crisis Communication: Planning, Managing, and Responding* (Thousand Oaks, CA: Sage Publications, 1999).
23. Ian I. Mitroff, "Crisis Leadership," *Executive Excellence* (August 2001): 19; Andy Bowen, "Crisis Procedures that Stand the Test of Time," *Public Relations Tactics* (August 2001): 16.
24. Christine Pearson, "A Blueprint for Crisis Management," *Ivey Business Journal* (January–February 2002): 69–73.
25. See Mitroff and Alpaslan, "Preparing for Evil," for a discussion of the "wheel of crises" outlining the many different kinds of crises organizations may face.
26. Harari, "Good/Bad News about Strategy."
27. James C. Collins and Jerry I. Porras, "Building Your Company's Vision," *Harvard Business Review* (September–October 1996): 65–77.
28. Steven Kerr and Steffan Landauer, "Using Stretch Goals to Promote Organizational Effectiveness and Personal Growth: General Electric and Goldman Sachs," *Academy of Management Executive* 18, no. 4 (November 2004): 134–138; and Lisa D. Ordóñez, Maurice E. Schweitzer, Adam D. Galinsky, and Max H. Bazerman, "Goals Gone Wild: The Systematic Side Effects of Overprescribing Goal Setting," *Academy of Management Perspectives* (February 2009): 6–16.
29. See Kenneth R. Thompson, Wayne A. Hockwarter, and Nicholas J. Mathys, "Stretch Targets: What Makes Them Effective?" *Academy of Management Executive* 11, no. 3 (August 1997): 48.
30. Edward Wyatt, "For 'Idol,' More Hope and Less Humiliation," *The New York Times,* January 13, 2009; Paul Lilley, "Weight Watchers Reveals New Partner: McDonald's," *Virginian-Pilot,* March 4, 2010.
31. William M. Bulkeley, "SofterView; Kodak Sharpens Digital Focus on Its Best Customers: Women," *The Wall Street Journal*, July 6, 2005; Geoffrey A. Fowler, "Auctions Fade in eBay's Bid for Growth," *The Wall Street Journal*, May 26, 2009.
32. Chet Miller and Laura B. Cardinal, "Strategic Planning and Firm Performance: A Synthesis of More Than Two Decades of Research," *Academy of Management Journal* 37, no. 6 (1994): 1649–1665.
33. Renée Dye and Olivier Sibony, "How to Improve Strategic Planning," *McKinsey Quarterly*, no. 3 (2007).
34. Keith H. Hammonds, "Michael Porter's Big Ideas," *Fast Company* (March 2001): 150–156.
35. John E. Prescott, "Environments As Moderators of the Relationship between Strategy and Performance," *Academy of Management Journal* 29 (1986): 329–346; John A. Pearce II and Richard B. Robinson, Jr., *Strategic Management: Strategy, Formulation, and Implementation,* 2nd ed. (Homewood, IL: Irwin, 1985); and David J. Teece, "Economic Analysis and Strategic Management," *California Management Review* 26 (Spring 1984): 87–110.
36. Jack Welch, "It's All in the Sauce," excerpt from his book, *Winning*, in *Fortune* (April 18, 2005): 138–144; and Constantinos Markides, "Strategic Innovation," *Sloan Management Review* (Spring 1997): 9–23.
37. Michael E. Porter, "What Is Strategy?" *Harvard Business Review* (November–December 1996): 61–78.
38. Arthur A. Thompson, Jr., and A. J. Strickland III, *Strategic Management: Concepts and Cases,* 6th ed. (Homewood, IL: Irwin, 1992); and Briance Mascarenhas, Alok Baveja, and Mamnoon Jamil, "Dynamics of Core Competencies in Leading Multinational Companies," *California Management Review* 40, no. 4 (Summer 1998): 117–132.
39. "Gaylord Says Hotels Prosper by Becoming Destinations," *The Tennessean*, July 24, 2005.
40. Chris Woodyard, "Big Dreams for Small Choppers Paid Off," *USA Today*, September 11, 2005.
41. Michael Goold and Andrew Campbell, "Desperately Seeking Synergy," *Harvard Business Review* (September–October 1998): 131–143.
42. Ashlee Vance, "Oracle Elbows Its Way into a Crowded Fight; With Close of Sun Deal, It Hopes to Beat Out Rivals Offering One-Stop Shops," *International Herald Tribune,* January 28, 2010.
43. Elizabeth Olson, "OMG! Cute Boys, Kissing Tips and Lots of Pics, As Magazines Find a Niche," *The New York Times*, May 28, 2007.
44. Bruce Einhorn, "Acer's Game-Changing PC Offensive," *BusinessWeek* (April 20, 2009): 65; Charmian Kok and Ting-I Tsai, "Acer Makes China Push from Taiwan; PC Maker's Chief Expects Best Gains in New Markets, Including Brazil, As Aims

to Surpass H-P," *The Wall Street Journal,* April 1, 2010; and "Experience Will Propel Acer to Top of Smartphone Market by 2013," *Gulf News,* January 22, 2010.

45. Guy Chazan, "BP's Worsening Spill Crisis Undermines CEO's Reforms," *The Wall Street Journal*, May 3, 2010.

46. Milton Leontiades, "The Confusing Words of Business Policy," *Academy of Management Review* 7 (1982): 45–48.

47. Lawrence G. Hrebiniak and William F. Joyce, *Implementing Strategy* (New York: Macmillan, 1984).

48. Peter Burrows, "Microsoft Defends Its Empire" *BusinessWeek* (July 6, 2009): 28–33.

49. David Welch, Keith Naughton, and Burt Helm, "Detroit's Big Chance," *Bloomberg BusinessWeek* (February 22, 2010): 38–44.

50. Michael E. Porter, "The Five Competitive Forces That Shape Strategy," *Harvard Business Review* (January 2008): 79–93; Michael E. Porter, *Competitive Strategy* (New York: Free Press, 1980), pp. 36–46; Danny Miller, "Relating Porter's Business Strategies to Environment and Structure: Analysis and Performance Implementations," *Academy of Management Journal* 31 (1988): 280–308; and Michael E. Porter, "From Competitive Advantage to Corporate Strategy," *Harvard Business Review* (May–June 1987): 43–59.

51. Michael E. Porter, "Strategy and the Internet," *Harvard Business Review* (March 2001): 63–78.

52. Quote from Gary Getz, Chris Jones, and Pierre Loewe, "Migration Management: An Approach for Improving Strategy Implementation," *Strategy & Leadership* 37, no. 6 (2009): 18–24.

53. Lawrence G. Hrebiniak, "Obstacles to Effective Strategy Implementation," *Organizational Dynamics* 35, no. 1 (2006): 12–31; Eric M. Olson, Stanley F. Slater, and G. Tomas M. Hult, "The Importance of Structure and Process to Strategy Implementation," *Business Horizons* 48 (2005): 47–54; L. J. Bourgeois III and David R. Brodwin, "Strategic Implementation: Five Approaches to an Elusive Phenomenon," *Strategic Management Journal* 5 (1984): 241–264; Anil K. Gupta and V. Govindarajan, "Business Unit Strategy, Managerial Characteristics, and Business Unit Effectiveness at Strategy Implementation," *Academy of Management Journal* (1984): 25–41; and Jeffrey G. Covin, Dennis P. Slevin, and Randall L. Schultz, "Implementing Strategic Missions: Effective Strategic, Structural, and Tactical Choices," *Journal of Management Studies* 31, no. 4 (1994): 481–505.

54. Riaz Khadem, "Alignment and Follow-Up: Steps to Strategy Execution," *Journal of Business Strategy* 29, no. 6 (2008): 29–35; and Olson, Slater, and Hult, "The Importance of Structure and Process to Strategy Implementation."

55. M. Beer and R. A. Eisenstat, "The Silent Killers of Strategy Implementation and Learning," *MIT Sloan Management Review* 41, no. 4 (Summer 2000): 29–41.

56. This discussion is based on Eric Beaudan, "Creative Execution," *Ivey Business Journal,* March–April 2010, www.iveybusinessjournal.com/topics/leadership/creative-execution (accessed March 26, 2010); Jay R. Galbraith and Robert K. Kazanjian, *Strategy Implementation: Structure, Systems and Process,* 2nd ed. (St. Paul, MN: West, 1986); Victoria L. Crittenden and William F. Crittenden, "Building a Capable Organization: The Eight Levers of Strategy Implementation," *Business Horizons* 51 (2008): 301–309; Paul C. Nutt, "Selecting Tactics to Implement Strategic Plans," *Strategic Management Journal* 10 (1989): 145–161; and Lawrence G. Hrebiniak, *Making Strategy Work: Leading Effective Execution and Change* (Upper Saddle River, NJ: Wharton School Publishing/Pearson Education Inc., 2005).

57. Beaudan, "Creative Execution."

58. Crittenden and Crittenden, "Building a Capable Organization."

59. Survey results reported in Hrebiniak, "Obstacles to Effective Strategy Implementation."

60. Cliff Edwards, "Dell's Do-Over," *BusinessWeek* (October 26, 2009): 36–40.

61. Beaudan, "Creative Execution."

62. Rachel Dodes, "Showdown on 34th Street," *The Wall Street Journal,* August 1, 2009.

63. Obasi Akan, Richard S. Allen, Marilyn M. Helms, and Samuel A. Spralls III, "Critical Tactics for Implementing Porter's Generic Strategies," *Journal of Business Strategy* 27, no. 1 (2006): 43–53.

64. Adapted from Richard L. Daft and Dorothy Marcic, *Understanding Management* (Mason, OH: South-Western, 2008), pp. 177–178.

65. Based on Shel Horowitz, "Should Mary Buy Her Own Bonus?" *Business Ethics* (Summer 2005): 34.

66. Based on Bill Carter, "Nielsen Tells TV Clients It Is Working on Ending Delays in Ratings," *The New York Times*, February 9, 2008; Richard Siklos, "Made to Measure," *Fortune* (March 3, 2008): 68–74; and Louise Story, "Nielsen Tests Limits of Wider Tracking," *International Herald Tribune*, February 28, 2008.

Chapter Outline

Managerial Decision Making

Learning Outcomes

After studying this chapter, you should be able to:

1. Explain why decision making is an important component of good management.
2. Discuss the difference between programmed and nonprogrammed decisions and the decision characteristics of certainty and uncertainty.
3. Describe the ideal, rational model of decision making and the political model of decision making.
4. Explain the process by which managers actually make decisions in the real world.
5. Identify the six steps used in managerial decision making.
6. Describe four personal decision styles used by managers, and explain the biases that frequently cause managers to make bad decisions.
7. Identify and explain techniques for innovative group decision making.

© James Steidl, Shutterstock

Are You Ready to Be a Manager?

Please circle your opinion below each of the following statements.

1 I am good at making decisions both when there is certainty and when there is uncertainty, and I make both kinds of decisions, not automatically, but with thought and weighing of possible outcomes.

Mostly True — Mostly False

(See page 210, Programmed and Nonprogrammed Decisions.)

2 When conditions are difficult and priorities conflicting, sometimes you have to make a decision based on "this is the best we can do" and you have to abandon the idea of getting all the needs met.

Mostly True — Mostly False

(See page 215, Bounded Rationality and Satisficing.)

3 I trust my intuition, or gut instincts, to help me perceive what is really going in the decision-making process.

Mostly True — Mostly False

(See page 216, Intuition.)

4 I am good at building a coalition or helping build consensus around a problem and its solution.

Mostly True — Mostly False

(See page 218, The Political Model.)

5 I try to avoid making bad decisions by not letting myself (a) justify past decisions I made so I won't look bad now; (b) be overconfident; (c) try to keep things the way they are, or the status quo; (d) be influenced by emotions or (e) be swayed by initial impressions rather than dig deeper for more evidence.

Mostly True — Mostly False

(See page 226, Why Do Managers Make Bad Decisions?)

With the advantage of hindsight, it seems like a no-brainer. Your auto company has learned that accelerator pedals are sticking on some models, causing cars to accelerate out of control. People have died as a result of accidents allegedly caused by the problem. It might be costly, but issue a recall *now*. Investigations reveal, though, that Toyota managers dragged their feet on the decision, possibly further endangering drivers. In the spring of 2010, the U.S. National Highway Traffic Safety Administration (NHTSA) levied a record fine of $16.4 million after documents showed Toyota managers knew of the defect at least four months before they publicly acknowledged it and recalled millions of vehicles.[1] Toyota managers then faced another tough decision: accept the penalty, which might be construed as an admission of wrongdoing, or fight it at the cost of more bad publicity.[2]

Welcome to the world of managerial decision making. Managers often are referred to as *decision makers,* and every organization grows, prospers, or fails as a result of decisions made by its managers. Yet decision making, particularly in relation to complex problems such as those faced by Toyota in recent years, is not always easy. There are charges that Toyota executives ignored safety concerns and failed to live up to their legal and ethical responsibilities, as defined in Chapter 4. However, managers can sometimes make the wrong decision even when their intentions are right. Managers frequently must make decisions amid ever-changing factors, unclear information, and conflicting points of view.

The business world is full of evidence of both good and bad decisions. Apple Inc., which seemed all but dead in the mid-1990s, became the world's most admired company on *Fortune* magazine's list for three years in a row (2008–2010) based on decision making by former CEO Steve Jobs and other top managers. No longer just a maker of computers, Apple Inc. is now in the music player business, the cell phone business, and the retailing business, among others. On the other hand, Maytag's decision to introduce the Neptune Drying Center was a complete flop. The $1,200 product was hyped as a breakthrough in laundry, but the six-foot-tall Drying Center wouldn't fit into most people's existing laundry rooms. Or consider the decision of Timex managers to replace the classic tag line, "It takes a licking and keeps on ticking," with the bland "Life is ticking." The desire to modernize their company's image led Timex managers to ditch one of the most recognizable advertising slogans in the world in favor of a lame and rather depressing new one (they have since modified the line to "Keeps on ticking").[3]

Good decision making is a vital part of good management because decisions determine how the organization solves problems, allocates resources, and accomplishes its goals. This chapter describes decision making in detail. First, we examine decision characteristics. Then we look at decision-making models and the steps executives should take when making important decisions. The chapter also explores some biases that can cause managers to make bad decisions. Finally, we examine some techniques for innovative group decision making in today's fast-changing environment. See the New Manager Self-Test on page 209 to understand your own strengths.

Types of Decisions and Problems

A **decision** is a choice made from available alternatives. For example, an accounting manager's selection among Colin, Tasha, and Carlos for the position of junior auditor is a decision. Many people assume that making a choice is the major part of decision making, but it is only a part.

New Manager Self-Test

How Do You Make Decisions?

Most of us make decisions automatically and without realizing that people have diverse decision-making behaviors, which they bring to management positions.[4] Think back to how you make decisions in your personal, student, or work life, especially where other people are involved. Please answer whether each of the following items is Mostly True or Mostly False for you.

	MOSTLY TRUE <<<	>>> MOSTLY FALSE
1. I like to decide quickly and move on to the next thing.	_____	_____
2. I would use my authority to make the decision if certain I were right.	_____	_____
3. I appreciate decisiveness.	_____	_____
4. There is usually one correct solution to a problem.	_____	_____
5. I identify everyone who needs to be involved in the decision.	_____	_____
6. I explicitly seek conflicting perspectives.	_____	_____
7. I use discussion strategies to reach a solution.	_____	_____
8. I look for different meanings when faced with a great deal of data.	_____	_____
9. I take time to reason things through and use systematic logic.	_____	_____

See It Online

Scoring and Interpretation: All nine items in the list reflect appropriate decision-making behavior, but items 1–4 are more typical of new managers. Items 5–8 are typical of successful senior manager decision making. Item 9 is considered part of good decision making at all levels. If you checked Mostly True for three or four of items 1–4 and 9, consider yourself typical of a new manager. If you checked Mostly True for three or four of items 5–8 and 9, you are using behavior consistent with top managers. If you checked a similar number of both sets of items, your behavior is probably flexible and balanced.

New managers typically use a different decision behavior than seasoned executives. The decision behavior of a successful CEO may be almost the opposite of a first-level supervisor. The difference is due partly to the types of decisions and partly to learning what works at each level. New managers often start out with a more directive, decisive, command-oriented behavior and gradually move toward more openness, diversity of viewpoints, and interactions with others as they move up the hierarchy.

Decision making is the process of identifying problems and opportunities and then resolving them. Decision making involves effort both before and after the actual choice. Thus, the decision as to whether to select Colin, Tasha, or Carlos requires the accounting manager to ascertain whether a new junior auditor is needed, determine the availability of potential job candidates, interview candidates to acquire necessary information, select one candidate, and follow up with the socialization of the new employee into the organization to ensure the decision's success.

Programmed and Nonprogrammed Decisions

Management decisions typically fall into one of two categories: programmed and nonprogrammed. **Programmed decisions** involve situations that have occurred often enough to enable decision rules to be developed and applied in the future.[5] Programmed decisions are made in response to recurring organizational problems. The decision to reorder paper and other office supplies when inventories drop to a certain level is a programmed decision. Other programmed decisions concern the types of skills required to fill certain jobs, the reorder point for manufacturing inventory, exception reporting for expenditures 10 percent or more over budget, and selection of freight routes for product deliveries. Once managers formulate decision rules, subordinates and others can make the decision, freeing managers for other tasks.

Go to the Ethical Dilemma, on pages 235–236, that pertains to making nonprogrammed decisions.

Nonprogrammed decisions are made in response to situations that are unique, are poorly defined and largely unstructured, and have important consequences for the organization. The decision regarding a recall at Toyota is an example of a nonprogrammed decision. Another good example comes from the financial services industry.

JPMORGAN CHASE AND BEAR STEARNS

The call came just before Jamie Dimon was leaving to celebrate his 52nd birthday at a Greek restaurant with his wife and oldest daughter. He poked his head into a conference room where senior managers were meeting and said casually, "I got a call from someone else who wants us to consider buying their company." The call, it turns out, was from Bear Stearns, teetering on the brink of collapse. As the only major bank whose managers had made the decision to aggressively cut back the firm's exposure to risky subprime mortgages, JPMorgan was one of the few places Bear's managers could turn to for help.

It was Thursday, March 13, 2008, and something had to be done by the time the Asian financial markets opened on Sunday night. At 11:00 P.M. on Thursday, Dimon sent a team to the Bear Stearns offices, where they were joined by teams from both the Federal Reserve and the Securities and Exchange Commission. Two thousand JPMorgan people spent the weekend poring over Bear's books and evaluating the situation. Dimon told them to cut the firm into pieces and report to him every three hours with a sense of their value. "We had literally 48 hours to do what normally takes a month," Dimon says.

Dimon spent the weekend on the phone and in meetings with Treasury and Fed officials, other JPMorgan executives and board members, and top managers from Bear Stearns. Despite working round the clock and having thousands of people analyzing the pros and cons, it was impossible for Dimon to have complete information about what acquiring Bear Stearns would mean for his company. Some of his colleagues thought the deal would be a disaster. Other advisers saw it as an opportunity. Hearing his team's concerns over the amount of risky mortgage assets in Bear's portfolio, Dimon called off talks on Sunday morning to do further analysis. Eventually, he had to make a gut decision, with the interests of JPMorgan shareholders paramount in his mind. By the end of the weekend, JPMorgan had made a final offer to buy parts of the once-thriving financial giant for $2 a share, an offer Bear Stearns managers might not have liked, yet had little alternative but to accept. (The offer was later revised to more than $10 a share.)[6]

Jamie Dimon's decision turned out to enhance both his own and his company's reputation. JPMorgan's business declined along with the economy, but its market share in retail banking continued to rise. The company's assets and market value were the highest in the industry during the first six months of 2009, and Dimon was being called "the world's most important banker."[7]

Many nonprogrammed decisions, such as the one at JPMorgan, are related to strategic planning, because uncertainty is great and decisions are complex. Decisions to acquire a company, build a new factory, develop a new product or service, enter a new geographical market, or relocate headquarters to another city are all nonprogrammed decisions.

Facing Certainty and Uncertainty

One primary difference between programmed and nonprogrammed decisions relates to the degree of certainty or uncertainty that managers deal with in making the decision. In a perfect world, managers would have all the information necessary for making decisions. In reality, however, some things are unknowable; thus, some decisions will fail to solve the problem or attain the desired outcome. Managers try to obtain information about decision alternatives that will reduce decision uncertainty. Every decision situation can be organized on a scale according to the availability of information and the possibility of failure. The four positions on the scale are certainty, risk, uncertainty, and ambiguity, as illustrated in Exhibit 6.1. Whereas programmed decisions can be made in situations involving certainty, many situations that managers deal with every day involve at least some degree of uncertainty and require nonprogrammed decision making.

Certainty **Certainty** means that all the information the decision maker needs is fully available.[8] Managers have information on operating conditions, resource costs, or constraints and each course of action and possible outcome. For example, if a company considers a $10,000 investment in new equipment that it knows for certain will yield $4,000 in cost savings per year over the next five years, managers can calculate a before-tax rate of return of about 40 percent. If managers compare this investment with one that will yield only $3,000 per year in cost savings, they can confidently select the 40 percent return. However, few decisions are certain in the real world. Most contain risk or uncertainty.

Risk **Risk** means that a decision has clear-cut goals and that good information is available, but the future outcomes associated with each alternative are subject to chance. However, enough information is available to allow the probability of a successful outcome for each alternative to be estimated.[9] Statistical analysis might be used to calculate the probabilities

EXHIBIT 6.1

Conditions That Affect the Possibility of Decision Failure

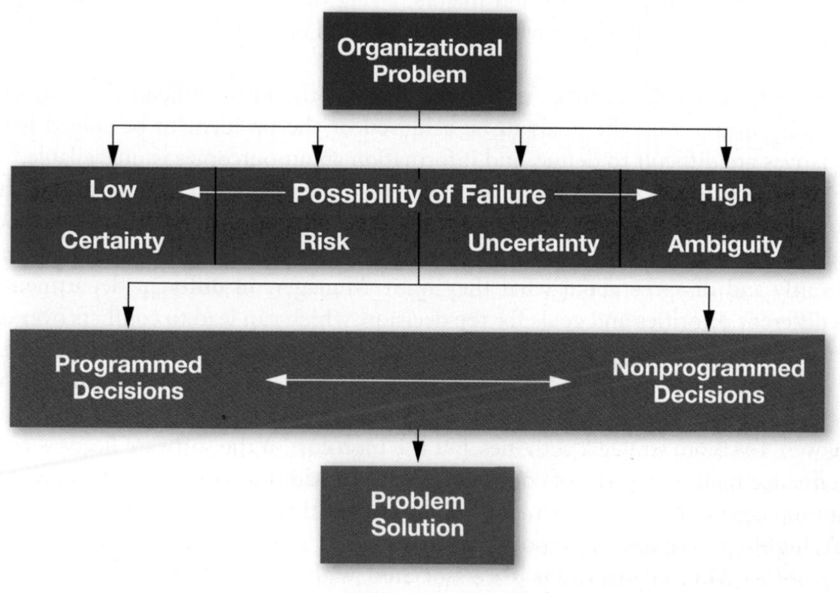

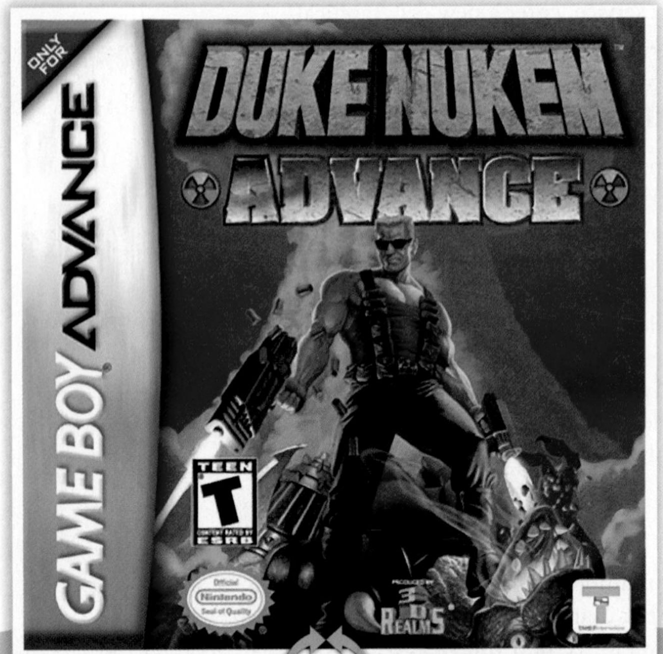

ConceptConnection

George Broussard and Scott Miller revolutionized the videogame world with the phenomenally successful *Duke Nukem* series in 1996. Naturally, they planned to make a sequel, *Duke Nukem Forever.* But Broussard's elusive quest to make the new version the most awe-inspiring game of all time resulted in an **ambiguous decision situation** for the development team. The closest the project came to having a goal was Broussard's pronouncement that it would be released "when it's done." By 2010, the game—called *Duke Nukem Taking Forever* by some—was still not finished, the original team had been laid off, and the game's fate was uncertain.

of success or failure. The measure of risk captures the possibility that future events will render the alternative unsuccessful. For example, to make restaurant location decisions, McDonald's can analyze potential customer demographics, traffic patterns, supply logistics, and the local competition, and can come up with reasonably good forecasts of how successful a restaurant will be in each possible location.[10]

Uncertainty **Uncertainty** means that managers know which goals they wish to achieve, but information about alternatives and future events is incomplete. Factors that may affect a decision, such as price, production costs, volume, or future interest rates, are difficult to analyze and predict. Managers may have to make assumptions they will use to forge the decision, even though it will be wrong if the assumptions are incorrect. Former U.S. Treasury Secretary Robert Rubin defined uncertainty as a situation in which even a good decision might produce a bad outcome.[11] Managers face uncertainty every day. Many problems have no clear-cut solution, but managers rely on creativity, judgment, intuition, and experience to craft a response. Nonprofit organizations as well as businesses face uncertainty. Berea College, a small liberal arts college in Kentucky, charges no tuition to its low-income students and gets 80 percent of its budget from its endowment. When the stock market plummeted, the endowment lost a third of its value. President Larry Shinn and other managers had to evaluate alternatives such as the possibility of charging tuition for the first time since 1892, cutting departments and majors, laying off employees, and increasing enrollment, with no clear evidence of which solution would be best.[12]

Ambiguity and Conflict **Ambiguity** is by far the most difficult decision situation. Ambiguity means that the goals to be achieved or the problem to be solved is unclear, alternatives are difficult to define, and information about outcomes is unavailable.[13] Ambiguity is what students would feel if an instructor created student groups, told each group to complete a project, but gave the groups no topic, direction, or guidelines whatsoever. In some situations, managers involved in a decision create ambiguity because they see things differently and disagree about what they want. Managers in different departments often have different priorities and goals for the decision, which can lead to conflicts over decision alternatives. For example, at Rockford Health System, the decision about implementing a new self-service benefits system wasn't clear cut. Human resources (HR) managers wanted the system, which would allow employees to manage their own benefits and free up HR employees for more strategic activities, but the high cost of the software licenses conflicted with finance managers' goals of controlling costs. In addition, if HR got the new system, it meant managers in other departments might not get their projects approved.[14]

A highly ambiguous situation can create what is sometimes called a *wicked decision problem.* Wicked decisions are associated with conflicts over goals and decision

BENCHMARKING

CollegeHumor

"Funny is not enough," spouts 29 year-old CollegeHumor CEO Ricky Van Veen, when talking about the company's "family recipe" for producing comedy videos that usually go viral. It's not only about being funny. It has to be *viral* funny. "They're about identity creation. You send the video to your friends to say something about yourself. You're saying, 'I get this. Do you get it?'" When he was only 18, Van Veen launched CollegeHumor with his friend Josh Abramson (now company president) at an Internet-company launch party with millionaires in their twenties. "I want to do this," Van Veen told himself, so he started the company right there, at the party, on his laptop.

In the early days, the site was a bare-bones place for college students to post funny stories and revealing photos. After this Phase One, in 2006, Barry Diller bought a majority share of the parent company's site, taking a shine to Van Veen. After the acquisition, Van Veen and his three partners changed the site to one of original videos, some of which were episodes in an ongoing series. That was Phase Two. Now they are creating Phase Three, a new kind of content that viewers might not even know they like yet. Previously, there were three "containers" for entertainment: a 22- or 44-minute TV show or a feature film. Van Veen says that now the decision facing CollegeHumor is, are they going to make a 30-minute short to sell to iTunes or should they make 3-minute shorts in five episodes? Creators now must decide not only what to put in the container, but they have to make the container as well.

Ultimately, Van Veen wants to transform what is already a profitable website into a sort of mini-network that would draw revenue from branded content, advertising, and sponsorships, letting the Internet be more like the airwaves and get subscribers from various social network sites. Still, not everything is completely new. Van Veen recently watched some retro-style promo slides for their new programs. He loved them. "They look just like old-time broadcast TV," he said. Whatever happened to that, by the way?

SOURCE: Adam Sternbergh, "The Stunt Man," *New York Magazine* (December 20–27, 2010): 103–105.

© Kuzmik, Shutterstock

alternatives, rapidly changing circumstances, fuzzy information, unclear links among decision elements, and the inability to evaluate whether a proposed solution will work. For wicked problems, there often is no "right" answer.[15] Managers have a difficult time coming to grips with the issues and must conjure up reasonable scenarios in the absence of clear information. The decision for JPMorgan Chase to buy parts of Bear Stearns would be considered a wicked decision. CollegeHumor is operating in an ambiguous decision-making environment, where they are creating new categories of humor, as described in the Benchmarking Box.

Remember This

- Good decision making is a vital part of good management, but decision making is not easy.
- **Decision making** is the process of identifying problems and opportunities and then resolving them.
- A **decision** is a choice made from available alternatives.
- A **programmed decision** is one made in response to a situation that has occurred often enough to enable managers to develop decision rules that can be applied in the future.
- A **nonprogrammed decision** is one made in response to a situation that is unique, is poorly defined and largely unstructured, and has important consequences for the organization.
- Decisions differ according to the amount of certainty, risk, uncertainty, or ambiguity in the situation.

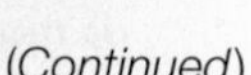
(*Continued*)

- **Certainty** is a situation in which all the information the decision maker needs is fully available.
- **Risk** means that a decision has clear-cut goals and good information is available, but the future outcomes associated with each alternative are subject to chance.
- **Uncertainty** occurs when managers know which goals they want to achieve, but information about alternatives and future events is incomplete.
- **Ambiguity** is a condition in which the goals to be achieved or the problem to be solved is unclear, alternatives are difficult to define, and information about outcomes is unavailable.
- Highly ambiguous circumstances can create a wicked decision problem, the most difficult decision situation managers face.

Decision-Making Models

The approach managers use to make decisions usually falls into one of three types—the classical model, the administrative model, or the political model. The choice of model depends on the manager's personal preference, whether the decision is programmed or nonprogrammed, and the degree of uncertainty associated with the decision.

The Ideal, Rational Model

The **classical model** of decision making is based on rational economic assumptions and manager beliefs about what ideal decision making should be. This model has arisen within the management literature because managers are expected to make decisions that are economically sensible and in the organization's best economic interests. The four assumptions underlying this model are as follows:

1. The decision maker operates to accomplish goals that are known and agreed on. Problems are precisely formulated and defined.
2. The decision maker strives for conditions of certainty, gathering complete information. All alternatives and the potential results of each are calculated.
3. Criteria for evaluating alternatives are known. The decision maker selects the alternative that will maximize the economic return to the organization.
4. The decision maker is rational and uses logic to assign values, order preferences, evaluate alternatives, and make the decision that will maximize the attainment of organizational goals.

The classical model of decision making is considered to be **normative**, which means it defines how a decision maker *should* make decisions. It does not describe how managers actually make decisions so much as it provides guidelines on how to reach an ideal outcome for the organization. The ideal, rational approach of the classical model is often unattainable by real people in real organizations, but the model has value because it helps decision makers be more rational and not rely entirely on personal preference in making decisions. Indeed, a global survey by McKinsey & Company found that when managers incorporate thoughtful analysis into decision making, they get better results. Studying the responses of more than 2,000 executives regarding how their companies made a specific decision,

McKinsey concluded that techniques such as detailed analysis, risk assessment, financial models, and considering comparable situations typically contribute to better financial and operational outcomes.[16]

The classical model is most useful when applied to programmed decisions and to decisions characterized by certainty or risk, because relevant information is available and probabilities can be calculated. For example, new analytical software programs automate many programmed decisions, such as freezing the account of a customer who has failed to make payments, determining the cell phone service plan that is most appropriate for a particular customer, or sorting insurance claims so that cases are handled most efficiently.[17]

Airlines use automated systems to optimize seat pricing, flight scheduling, and crew assignment decisions. Imagine being an airline manager during and after the five-day ban on European flights due to a cloud of volcanic ash caused by an eruption under Iceland's EyjafjallajÖkull glacier. The nightmare would have been compounded if airlines didn't have computerized systems to help managers make decisions about where to assign planes and crew members as they struggled to get nearly 10 million stranded passengers to their destinations.[18] Alaska Airlines has been using such analysis on its own since 1980, when Mount St. Helens erupted near the airline's home base and crippled the company for days. A team of aviation and weather experts developed computer models to predict the trajectory of volcanic ash and often enabled flights to work around it. The airline encounters volcanic ash in Alaska every couple of years. One unbendable rule is that planes never take off, fly, or land in ash, but Ken Williams, the airline's fleet captain, says collaboration and scientific, data-based analysis enables the flexibility needed to work around ash in many instances.[19]

The growth of quantitative decision techniques that use computers has expanded the use of the classical approach. Quantitative techniques include tools such as decision trees, payoff matrices, break-even analysis, linear programming, forecasting, and operations research models.

How Managers Actually Make Decisions

Another approach to decision making, called the **administrative model**, is considered to be **descriptive**, meaning that it describes how managers actually make decisions in complex situations rather than dictating how they *should* make decisions according to a theoretical ideal. The administrative model recognizes the human and environmental limitations that affect the degree to which managers can pursue a rational decision-making process. In difficult situations, such as those characterized by nonprogrammed decisions, uncertainty, and ambiguity, managers are typically unable to make economically rational decisions even if they want to.[20]

Bounded Rationality and Satisficing The administrative model of decision making is based on the work of Herbert A. Simon. Simon proposed two concepts that were instrumental in shaping the administrative model: bounded rationality and satisficing. **Bounded rationality** means that people have limits, or boundaries, on how rational they can be. Organizations are incredibly complex, and managers have the time and ability to process only a limited amount of information with which to make decisions.[21] Because managers do not have the time or cognitive ability to process complete information about complex decisions, they must satisfice. **Satisficing** means that decision makers choose the first solution alternative that satisfies minimal decision criteria. Rather than pursuing all alternatives to identify the single solution that will maximize economic returns, managers will opt for the first solution that appears to solve the problem, even if better solutions are presumed to exist. The decision maker cannot justify the time and expense of obtaining complete information.[22]

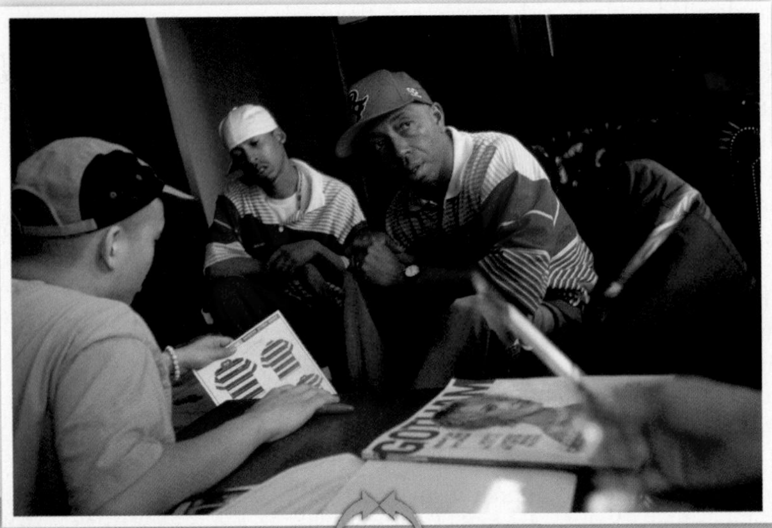
James Leynse/Corbis

ConceptConnection

"Lots of people hear what I'm doing and think, 'That's a crazy idea!'" says Russell Simmons. The successful entrepreneur, who heads the New York–based media firm Rush Communications, has relied on his **intuition** to build a half-billion dollar empire on one profitable "crazy idea" after another. It all began with his belief that he could go mainstream with the vibrant rap music he heard in African American neighborhoods. In 1983, he started the pioneering hip-hop Def Jam record label, launching the careers of Beastie Boys, LL Cool J, and Run-DMC, among others. He's since moved on to successful ventures in fashion, media, consumer products, and finance.

Managers sometimes generate alternatives for complex problems only until they find one they believe will work. For example, managers at MySpace faced a tough decision regarding how to contend with fast-growing rival Facebook. When Facebook matched the former market leader in monthly U.S. visitors for the first time, MySpace leaders began searching for a way to regain a competitive edge. Uncertain of how best to turn things around, they satisficed with a quick decision to lay off about a third of the workforce in order to become more efficient and team oriented. Managers believed this quick restructuring would provide some breathing room to consider further changes to enhance operations.[23]

The administrative model relies on assumptions different from those of the classical model and focuses on organizational factors that influence individual decisions. According to the administrative model:

1. Decision goals often are vague, conflicting, and lack consensus among managers. Managers often are unaware of problems or opportunities that exist in the organization.
2. Rational procedures are not always used, and when they are, they are confined to a simplistic view of the problem that does not capture the complexity of real organizational events.
3. Managers' searches for alternatives are limited because of human, information, and resource constraints.
4. Most managers settle for a satisficing rather than a maximizing solution, partly because they have limited information and partly because they have only vague criteria for what constitutes a maximizing solution.

3

Intuition Another aspect of administrative decision making is intuition. **Intuition** represents a quick apprehension of a decision situation based on past experience but without conscious thought.[24] Intuitive decision making is not arbitrary or irrational, because it is based on years of practice and hands-on experience that enable managers to quickly identify solutions without going through painstaking computations. In today's fast-paced business environment, intuition plays an increasingly important role in decision making. Numerous studies have found that effective managers use a combination of rational analysis and intuition in making complex decisions under time pressure.[25] Mel Kiper and his wife Kim use Mel's football intuition to keep their draft empire successful, as shown in the Spotlight on Skills titled Mel Kiper and the NFL Draft.

Psychologists and neuroscientists have studied how people make good decisions using their intuition under extreme time pressure and uncertainty.[26] Good intuitive decision

SPOTLIGHT ON SKILLS

Mel Kiper and the NFL Draft

Mel Kiper, Jr., began working at ESPN in 1984, before either one of them were the household names they are now. And Mel may be a football draft genius and the person who pioneered the concept of a draft expert, but it is his wife, Kim Kiper, who has turned that talent into a successful family business. As a high school student hoping to become a football scout, Mel gave reports to Baltimore Orioles executive, Ernie Acorsi, who told him he should be selling the information. But it took until college, when Mel watched dozens of Baltimore Orioles games on satellite dish in his family's backyard, for that idea to take hold. With an uncanny ability to spot talent, Mel was encouraged and helped by his father to start a college draft report service. Mel placed one ad in a football publication and got 130 orders. When Dad died, Mom took over the business side, working late into the night, copying customer information on individual cards and completing the accounting by hand.

After Mel and Kim got married (during football season, no less), Kim quit her job in pharmaceutical sales and worked with Mel, soon realizing they were in a crisis. "That was the beginning of the end," says Kim, because at that time things were changing in draft publications. So she started by creating a computerized customer database and buying an automated postage machine, ultimately transforming Mel Kiper Enterprises into a sprawling home business. Their workday started at 8 A.M., with Mel spending hours on the phone (pre-Internet) getting team statistics, doing radio spots at night to promote his draft guides, and then both of them working until 3 A.M. laying out the publications. From the beginning, he's provided the information and she runs the business. There's no overlap. Once a year, Mel spends two days on ESPN during draft picks, with barely time for a bathroom break. Kim and their 14-year-old daughter say no one could live with the intense Mel from TV. "At home, he's so easy," says Kim. "Every time you see him on TV, he looks like he's going to bite someone's head off." But even at home, no one will watch games with him, because he sits in his study changing channels with a crazy frenzy. Kim is a casual sports fan, but she prefers to lay out sports information to watching and following games. This suits Mel just fine. "You think I want a wife who knows football? That would drive me crazy."

SOURCES: Liz Farmer, "The Business of Being NFL Draft Analyst Mel Kiper," *Daily Record*, April 19, 2010; and Judy Battista, "A Mom-and-Pop Draft Empire," *The New York Times*, April 24, 2009.

making is based on an ability to recognize patterns at lightning speed. When people have a depth of experience and knowledge in a particular area, the right decision often comes quickly and effortlessly as a recognition of information that has been largely forgotten by the conscious mind. For example, firefighters make decisions by recognizing what is typical or abnormal about a fire, based on their experiences. This ability can also be seen among soldiers in Iraq who have been responsible for stopping many roadside bomb attacks based on gut feelings. High-tech gear designed to detect improvised explosive devices, or IEDs, is merely a supplement rather than a replacement for the ability of the human brain to sense danger and act on it. Soldiers with experience in Iraq subconsciously know when something doesn't look or feel right. It might be a rock that wasn't there yesterday, a piece of concrete that looks too symmetrical, odd patterns of behavior, or just a different feeling of tension in the air.[27] Similarly, in the business world, managers continuously perceive and process information that they may not consciously be aware of, and their base of knowledge and experience helps them make decisions that may be characterized by uncertainty and ambiguity.

However, intuitive decisions don't always work out, and managers should take care to apply intuition under the right circumstances and in the right way rather than considering it a magical technique for making important decisions.[28] Managers may walk a fine line between two extremes: on the one hand, making arbitrary decisions without careful study; and on the other, relying obsessively on rational analysis. One is not better than the other, and managers need to take a balanced approach by considering both rationality and intuition as important components of effective decision making.[29]

Do you tend to analyze things or rely on gut feelings when it comes to making an important decision? Complete the New Manager Self-Test on page 218 to find out your predominant approach.

New Manager Self-Test

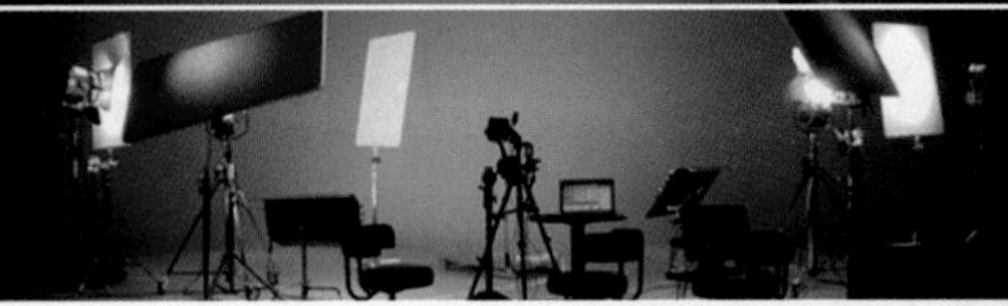

Making Important Decisions

How do you make important personal decisions? To find out, think about a time when you made an important career decision or made a large purchase or investment. To what extent does each of the terms below describe how you reached the final decision? Please check five terms below that best describe how you made your final choice.

1. Logic ______
2. Inner knowing ______
3. Data ______
4. Felt sense ______
5. Facts ______
6. Instincts ______
7. Concepts ______
8. Hunch ______
9. Reason ______
10. Feelings ______

Scoring and Interpretation: The odd-numbered items pertain to a linear decision style and the even-numbered items pertain to a nonlinear decision approach. Linear means using logical *rationality* to make decisions; nonlinear means using primarily *intuition* to make decisions. Of the five terms you chose, how many represent rationality versus intuition? If all five are either linear or nonlinear, then that is clearly your dominant decision approach. If four terms are either linear or nonlinear, then that approach would be considered your preference. Rationality approach means a preference for the *rational model* of decision making as described in the text. Intuition approach suggests a preference for the *satisficing* and *intuition* models.

SOURCE: Charles M. Vance, Kevin S. Groves, Yongsun Paik, and Herb Kindler, "Understanding and Measuring Linear-Nonlinear Thinking Style for Enhanced Management Education and Professional Practice" *Academy of Management Learning & Education* 6, no. 2 (2007): 167–185.

The Political Model

The third model of decision making is useful for making nonprogrammed decisions when conditions are uncertain, information is limited, and there are manager conflicts about what goals to pursue or what course of action to take. Most organizational decisions involve many managers who are pursuing different goals, and they have to talk with one another to share information and reach an agreement. Managers often engage in coalition building for making complex organizational decisions.[30] A **coalition** is an informal alliance among managers who support a specific goal. *Coalition building* is the process of forming alliances among managers. In other words, a manager who supports a specific alternative, such as increasing the corporation's growth by acquiring another company, talks informally to other executives and tries to persuade them to support the decision. Without a coalition, a powerful individual or group could derail the decision-making process. Coalition building gives several managers an opportunity to contribute to decision making, enhancing their commitment to the alternative that is ultimately adopted. Results from the global survey by McKinsey & Company mentioned earlier suggest that informal coalition building is associated with faster implementation of decisions because managers have developed consensus about which action to pursue.[31]

The political model closely resembles the real environment in which most managers and decision makers operate. For example, interviews with CEOs in high-tech industries found that they strived to use some type of rational process in making decisions, but the way they actually decided things was through a complex interaction with other managers, subordinates, environmental factors, and organizational events.[32] Decisions are complex and involve many people, information is often ambiguous, and disagreement and conflict over problems and solutions are normal. The political model begins with four basic assumptions:

1. Organizations are made up of groups with diverse interests, goals, and values. Managers disagree about problem priorities and may not understand or share the goals and interests of other managers.
2. Information is ambiguous and incomplete. The attempt to be rational is limited by the complexity of many problems as well as personal and organizational constraints.
3. Managers do not have the time, resources, or mental capacity to identify all dimensions of the problem and process all relevant information. Managers talk to each other and exchange viewpoints to gather information and reduce ambiguity.
4. Managers engage in the push and pull of debate to decide goals and discuss alternatives. Decisions are the result of bargaining and discussion among coalition members.

Google's decision to abandon its China-based search engine, Google.cn, provides an example of the political model. Google opened the site in 2006, agreeing to the censorship requirements of the Chinese government. However, when the 2008 Summer Olympics in Beijing were over, some managers felt that China increased its Web censoring and began interfering more and more with company operations. Cofounder Sergey Brin began pushing for the company to stop censoring its search engine results, whereas CEO Eric Schmidt and other executives believed Google should stay the course in China. Managers engaged in discussion and debate regarding which direction to take. Eventually they reached the decision to abandon the policy of censoring results, and Google withdrew from the world's largest Internet market in the spring of 2010. Company managers later decided to seek renewal of Google's license to operate in China.[33]

The key dimensions of the classical, administrative, and political models are listed in Exhibit 6.2. Research into decision-making procedures found rational, classical procedures to be associated with high performance for organizations in stable environments. However, administrative and political decision-making procedures and intuition have been associated with high performance in unstable environments in which decisions must be made rapidly and under more difficult conditions.[34]

EXHIBIT 6.2

Characteristics of Classical, Administrative, and Political Decision-Making Models

Classical Model	Administrative Model	Political Model
Clear-cut problem and goals	Vague problem and goals	Pluralistic; conflicting goals
Condition of certainty	Condition of uncertainty	Condition of uncertainty or ambiguity
Full information about alternatives and their outcomes	Limited information about alternatives and their outcomes	Inconsistent viewpoints; ambiguous information
Rational choice by individual for maximizing outcomes	Satisficing choice for resolving problem using intuition	Bargaining and discussion among coalition members

- The ideal, rational approach to decision making, called the **classical model**, is based on the assumption that managers should make logical decisions that are economically sensible and in the organization's best economic interests.
- The classical model is **normative**, meaning that it defines how a manager *should* make logical decisions and provides guidelines for reaching an ideal outcome.
- Software programs based on the classical model are being applied to programmed decisions, such as how to schedule airline crews or how to process insurance claims most efficiently.
- The **administrative model** includes the concepts of *bounded rationality* and *satisficing* and describes how managers make decisions in situations that are characterized by uncertainty and ambiguity.
- The administrative model is **descriptive**, an approach that describes how managers actually make decisions rather than how they should make decisions according to a theoretical model.
- **Bounded rationality** means that people have the time and cognitive ability to process only a limited amount of information on which to base decisions.
- **Satisficing** means choosing the first alternative that satisfies minimal decision criteria, regardless of whether better solutions are presumed to exist.
- **Intuition** is an aspect of administrative decision making that refers to a quick comprehension of a decision situation based on past experience but without conscious thought.
- Soldiers in Iraq have been known to detect roadside bombs using their intuition.
- The political model takes into consideration that many decisions require debate, discussion, and coalition building.
- A **coalition** is an informal alliance among managers who support a specific goal or solution.
- Google managers used the political model to make the decision to withdraw from China.

Decision-Making Steps

Whether a decision is programmed or nonprogrammed, and regardless of managers' choice of the classical, administrative, or political model of decision making, six steps typically are associated with effective decision processes. These steps are summarized in Exhibit 6.3.

Recognition of Decision Requirement

Managers confront a decision requirement in the form of either a problem or an opportunity. A **problem** occurs when organizational accomplishment is less than established goals. Some aspect of performance is unsatisfactory. An **opportunity** exists when managers see potential accomplishment that exceeds specified current goals. Managers see the possibility of enhancing performance beyond current levels.

Awareness of a problem or opportunity is the first step in the decision sequence and requires surveillance of the internal and external environment for issues that merit executive attention.[35] This process resembles the military concept of gathering intelligence. Managers scan the world around them to determine whether the organization is satisfactorily progressing toward its goals.

EXHIBIT 6.3

Six Steps in the Managerial Decision-Making Process

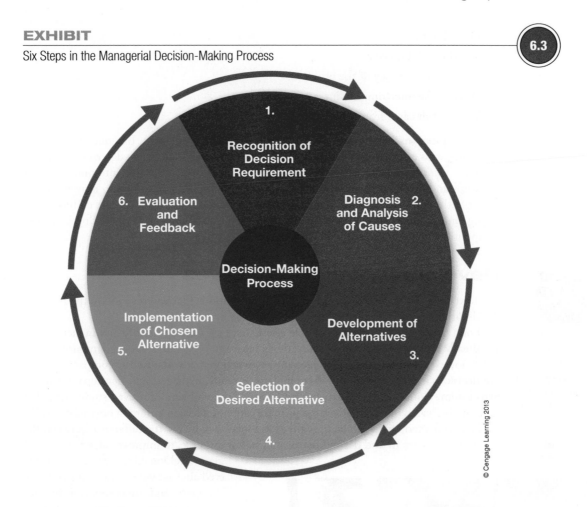

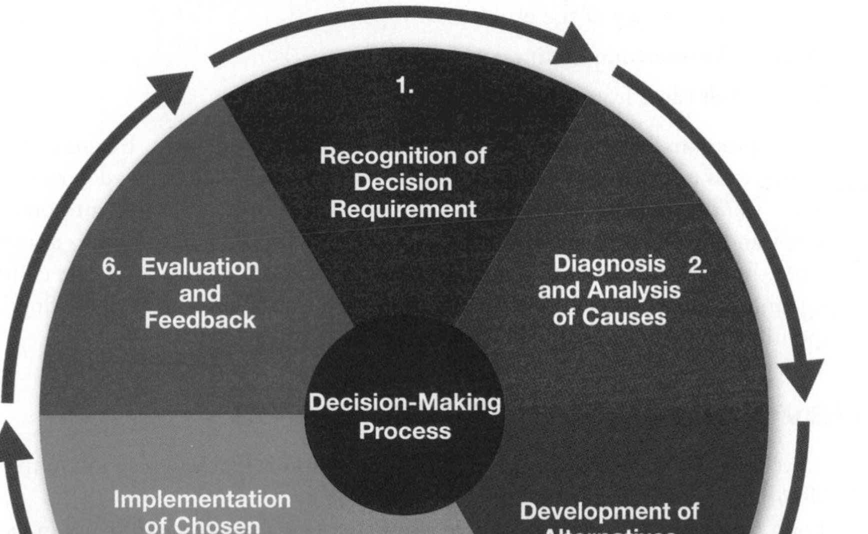

Some information comes from periodic financial reports, performance reports, and other sources that are designed to discover problems before they become too serious. Managers also take advantage of informal sources. They talk to other managers, gather opinions on how things are going, and seek advice on which problems should be tackled or which opportunities embraced.[36] Recognizing decision requirements is difficult because it often means integrating bits and pieces of information in novel ways. For example, the failure of U.S. intelligence leaders to recognize the imminent threat of Al Qaeda prior to the September 11, 2001, terrorist attacks has been attributed partly to the lack of systems that could help leaders put together myriad snippets of information that pointed to the problem.[37]

Diagnosis and Analysis of Causes

Once a problem or opportunity comes to a manager's attention, the understanding of the situation should be refined. **Diagnosis** is the step in the decision-making process in which managers analyze underlying causal factors associated with the decision situation.

Kepner and Tregoe, who conducted extensive studies of manager decision making, recommend that managers ask a series of questions to specify underlying causes, including the following:

- What is the state of disequilibrium affecting us?
- When did it occur?
- Where did it occur?

- How did it occur?
- To whom did it occur?
- What is the urgency of the problem?
- What is the interconnectedness of events?
- What result came from which activity?[38]

Such questions help specify what actually happened and why. Imagine the complicated diagnosis executives at General Motors have been conducting to determine how the company went from being "Microsoft and Apple and Toyota all rolled into one" to being bankrupt and owned primarily by the U.S. government. They have had to examine every aspect of the company, including management and labor practices, corporate culture, marketing, and products, as well as elements of the external environment, including increased competition, changing consumer tastes, and volatile oil prices.[39]

Development of Alternatives

The Group Learning, on pages 234–235, will give you a chance to practice a new approach to decision making that focuses on desired outcomes rather than looking at the cause of problems.

The next stage is to generate possible alternative solutions that will respond to the needs of the situation and correct the underlying causes.

For a programmed decision, feasible alternatives are easy to identify and in fact usually are already available within the organization's rules and procedures. Nonprogrammed decisions, however, require developing new courses of action that will meet the company's needs. For decisions made under conditions of high uncertainty, managers may develop only one or two custom solutions that will satisfice for handling the problem. However, studies find that limiting the search for alternatives is a primary cause of decision failure in organizations.[40]

Decision alternatives can be thought of as tools for reducing the difference between the organization's current and desired performance. For example, to improve sales at fast-food giant McDonald's, executives considered alternatives such as using mystery shoppers and unannounced inspections to improve quality and service, motivating demoralized franchisees to get them to invest in new equipment and programs, taking R&D out of the test kitchen and encouraging franchisees to help come up with successful new menu items, and closing some stores to avoid cannibalizing its own sales.[41]

Courtesy of Red Door Interactive

ConceptConnection

Reid Carr, founder and CEO of San Diego–based Red Door Interactive, Inc., a firm that manages clients' online presence, involves his staff throughout the decision-making process. Carr believes that when **developing, selecting, and implementing alternatives**, managers should "decide slowly and collaboratively so that you have the best plan produced by those who are tasked with execution. Then, let them execute." Red Door's annual "Start, Stop, and Keep" survey is one way Carr gathers feedback. It asks employees to suggest which internal processes and practices should be introduced, discontinued, or continued.

Selection of Desired Alternative

Once feasible alternatives are developed, one must be selected. In this stage, managers try to select the most promising of several alternative courses of action. The best alternative is one in which the solution best fits the overall goals and values of the organization and achieves the desired results using the fewest resources.[42] Managers want to select the choice with the least amount of risk and uncertainty. Because some risk is inherent for most non-programmed decisions, managers try to gauge prospects for success. They might rely on their intuition and experience to estimate whether a given course of action is likely to succeed. Basing choices on overall goals and values can also effectively guide the selection of alternatives.

Choosing among alternatives also depends on managers' personality factors and willingness to accept risk and uncertainty. **Risk propensity** is the willingness to undertake risk with the opportunity of gaining an increased payoff. At drug maker Novartis, for example, researchers have been trying to convince CEO Daniel L. Vasella to give the go-ahead for an experimental vaccine for Alzheimer's disease. The potential payoff is huge, but Vasella thinks the risks are too high. He prefers to focus research on smaller, narrowly defined groups of patients, often suffering from rare diseases that are well understood scientifically but that desperately need new drugs. For Vasella, investing in a drug for Alzheimer's before the disease is better understood is wasting time and money.[43] The level of risk a manager is willing to accept will influence the analysis of cost and benefits to be derived from any decision. Consider the situations in Exhibit 6.4. In each situation, which alternative would you choose? A person with a low risk propensity would tend to take ensured moderate returns by going for a tie score, building a domestic plant, or pursuing a career as a physician. A risk taker would go for the victory, build a plant in a foreign country, or embark on an acting career.

Implementation of Chosen Alternative

The **implementation** stage involves the use of managerial, administrative, and persuasive abilities to ensure that the chosen alternative is carried out. This step is similar to the idea of strategy execution described in Chapter 5. The ultimate success of the

EXHIBIT 6.4

Decision Alternatives with Different Levels of Risk

In each of the following situations, which alternative would you choose?	
You're the coach of a college football team and in the final seconds of a game with the team's archrival, you face a choice:	1. Choose a play that has a 95 percent chance of producing a tie score OR 2. Go for a play that has a 30 percent chance of leading to victory but will lead to certain defeat if it fails.
As president of a Canadian manufacturing company, you face a decision about building a new factory. You can:	1. Build a plant in Canada that has a 90 percent chance of producing a modest return on investment OR 2. Build a plant in a foreign country that has an unstable political history. This alternative has a 40 percent chance of failing, but the returns will be enormous if it succeeds.
It's your senior year and it is time to decide your next move. Here are the alternatives you're considering:	1. Go to medical school and become a physician, a career in which you are 80 percent likely to succeed OR 2. Follow your dreams and be an actor, even though the opportunity for success is only around 20 percent.

chosen alternative depends on whether it can be translated into action.[44] Sometimes an alternative never becomes reality because managers lack the resources or energy needed to make things happen. Implementation may require discussion with people affected by the decision. Communication, motivation, and leadership skills must be used to see that the decision is carried out. When employees see that managers follow up on their decisions by tracking implementation success, they are more committed to positive action.[45]

Evaluation and Feedback

In the evaluation stage of the decision process, decision makers gather information that tells them how well the decision was implemented and whether it was effective in achieving its goals. Feedback is important because decision making is an ongoing process. Decision making is not completed when a manager or board of directors votes yes or no. Feedback provides decision makers with information that can precipitate a new decision cycle. The decision may fail, thus generating a new analysis of the problem, evaluation of alternatives, and selection of a new alternative. Many big problems are solved by trying several alternatives in sequence, each providing modest improvement. Feedback is the part of monitoring that assesses whether a new decision needs to be made.

To illustrate the overall decision-making process, including evaluation and feedback, consider the decision to introduce a new smartphone at Motorola illustrated in the Spotlight on Skills titled Motorola.

Motorola's decision illustrates all the decision steps, and the process ultimately ended in success. Strategic decisions always contain some risk, but feedback and follow-up can help get companies back on track. By learning from their decision mistakes, managers can turn problems into opportunities.

SPOTLIGHT ON SKILLS

Motorola

When Sanjay Jha took the job as co-chief executive of Motorola, he found the company in a mess. The pioneer of cell phones and maker of formerly hot models such as the Razr had been struggling for years to come up with another hit.

Analyzing and diagnosing what went wrong, Jha and other executives realized that the company's engineering talent was strong, but a dysfunctional management culture had caused Motorola to miss the consumer shift toward wanting phones that do nearly everything a computer can do, such as Apple's iPhone.

Managers considered various alternatives for the operating systems, microprocessors, and radio chips that would be the core of the new line of handsets. For the operating system, for instance, Jha and his team made the tough decision to cut the entire line of phones using Nokia's Symbian system, as well as phones using several other systems, and focus the company's energies totally on developing phones using Google's Android. One manager recalls the day Jha said, "Burn the ships and focus on Android." Implementation meant reassigning project managers and pouring resources into developing the new phone. Thousands of smaller decisions had to be made to find the right combination between design and performance. Verizon Wireless introduced Motorola's Droid smartphone in the fall of 2009, and soon afterward T-Mobile began selling a Motorola phone it calls the CLIQ.

Evaluation and feedback is ongoing, which recently yielded the improved Motorola Droid X, considered equal to the iPhone. One analyst put it this way: "If they hadn't delivered something like this, they'd be out of business."

SOURCE: Saul Hansell, "Strategy of New Chief at Motorola Appears Poised to Pay Off," *The New York Times*, October 29, 2009; and David Pogue, "Big Phone, Big Screen, Big Pleasure," *The New York Times*, June 30, 2010, www.nytimes.com/2010/07/01/technology/personaltech/01pogue.html (accessed June 30, 2010).

- Managers face the need to make a decision when they either confront a problem or see an opportunity.
- A **problem** is a situation in which organizational accomplishments have failed to meet established goals.
- An **opportunity** is a situation in which managers see potential organizational accomplishments that exceed current goals.
- The decision-making process typically involves six steps: recognition of the need for a decision, diagnosing causes, developing alternatives, selecting an alternative, implementing the alternative, and evaluating decision effectiveness.
- **Diagnosis** is the step in which managers analyze underlying causal factors associated with the decision situation.
- Selection of an alternative depends partly on managers' **risk propensity**, or their willingness to undertake risk with the opportunity of gaining an increased payoff.
- The **implementation** step involves using managerial, administrative, and persuasive abilities to translate the chosen alternative into action.

Personal Decision Framework

Imagine you were a manager at Motorola, Google, a local movie theater, or the public library. How would you go about making important decisions that might shape the future of your department or company? So far we have discussed a number of factors that affect how managers make decisions. For example, decisions may be programmed or nonprogrammed, situations are characterized by various levels of uncertainty, and managers may use the classical, administrative, or political model of decision making. In addition, the decision-making process follows six recognized steps.

However, not all managers go about making decisions in the same way. In fact, significant differences distinguish the ways in which individual managers may approach problems and make decisions concerning them. These differences can be explained by the concept of personal **decision styles**. Exhibit 6.5 illustrates the role of personal style in the decision-making process. Personal decision style refers to distinctions among people with respect to how they evaluate problems, generate alternatives, and make choices. Research has identified four major decision styles: directive, analytical, conceptual, and behavioral.[46]

1. The *directive style* is used by people who prefer simple, clear-cut solutions to problems. Managers who use this style often make decisions quickly because they do not like to deal with a lot of information and may consider only one or two alternatives. People who prefer the directive style generally are efficient and rational and prefer to rely on existing rules or procedures for making decisions.
2. Managers with an *analytical style* like to consider complex solutions based on as much data as they can gather. These individuals carefully consider alternatives and often base their decisions on objective, rational data from management control systems and other sources. They search for the best possible decision based on the information available.
3. People who tend toward a *conceptual style* also like to consider a broad amount of information. However, they are more socially oriented than those with an analytical style and like to talk to others about the problem and possible alternatives for solving it. Managers using a conceptual style consider many broad alternatives, rely on information from both people and systems, and like to solve problems creatively.

6.5 EXHIBIT
Personal Decision Framework

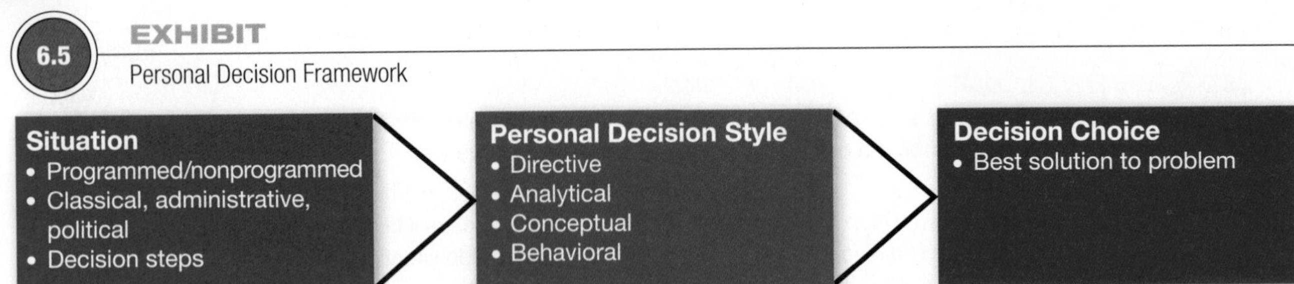

SOURCES: Based on A. J. Rowe, J. D. Boulgaides, and M. R. McGrath, *Managerial Decision Making* (Chicago: Science Research Associates, 1984); and Alan J. Rowe and Richard O. Mason, *Managing with Style: A Guide to Understanding, Assessing, and Improving Your Decision Making* (San Francisco: Jossey-Bass, 1987).

4. The *behavioral style* is often the style adopted by managers having a deep concern for others as individuals. Managers using this style like to talk to people one-on-one, understand their feelings about the problem, and consider the effect of a given decision on them. People with a behavioral style usually are concerned with the personal development of others and may make decisions that help others achieve their goals.

To learn more about how you make decisions, go to the Self-Learning, on pages 233–234, that evaluates your personal decision style.

Many managers have a dominant decision style. For example, U.S. President Barack Obama's decision to increase troop strength in Afghanistan reflects his primarily conceptual style of decision making. The President held ten meetings with key military decision makers in a decision process that has been called "intense, methodical, earnest, and at times deeply frustrating." Obama requested detailed reports, asked numerous questions, and showed an almost insatiable need for information. One participant described him as a cross "between a college professor and a gentle cross-examiner."[47]

However, managers frequently use several different styles or a combination of styles in making the varied decisions they confront daily. A manager might use a directive style for determining which company to use for office supplies, yet shift to a more conceptual style when handling an interdepartmental conflict. The most effective managers are able to shift among styles as needed to meet the situation. Being aware of one's dominant decision style can help a manager avoid making critical mistakes when his or her usual style may be inappropriate to the problem at hand.

- A manager's personal decision style influences how he or she makes decisions.
- **Decision styles** are differences among people with respect to how they perceive problems and make choices.
- Four major decision styles are directive, analytical, conceptual, and behavioral.
- U.S. President Barack Obama uses a primarily conceptual style of decision making.
- Most experienced managers use a variety of styles depending on the decision situation.

5 Why Do Managers Make Bad Decisions?

Managers are faced with a relentless demand for decisions, from solving minor problems to implementing major strategic changes. Even the best manager will make mistakes, but managers can increase their percentage of good decisions by understanding some of the factors that cause people to make bad ones. Most bad decisions are errors in judgment that originate in the human mind's limited capacity and in the natural biases managers display during decision making. Awareness of the following six biases can help managers make more enlightened choices:[48]

1. ***Being influenced by initial impressions.*** When considering decisions, the mind often gives disproportionate weight to the first information it receives. These initial impressions, statistics, or estimates act as an anchor to our subsequent thoughts and judgments. Anchors can be as simple as a random comment by a colleague or a statistic read in a newspaper. Past events and trends also act as anchors. For example, in business, managers frequently look at the previous year's sales when estimating sales for the coming year. Giving too much weight to the past can lead to poor forecasts and misguided decisions.
2. ***Justifying past decisions.*** Many managers fall into the trap of making choices that justify their past decisions, even if those decisions no longer seem valid. Consider managers who invest tremendous time and energy into improving the performance of a problem employee whom they now realize should never have been hired in the first place. Another example is when a manager continues to pour money into a failing project, hoping to turn things around. One study of product development found that managers who initiate a new product are much more likely to continue funding it despite evidence that it is failing.[49] People don't like to make mistakes, so they continue to support a flawed decision in an effort to justify or correct the past.
3. ***Seeing what you want to see.*** People frequently look for information that supports their existing instinct or point of view and avoid information that contradicts it.

   This bias affects where managers look for information, as well as how they interpret the information they find. People tend to give too much weight to supporting information and too little to information that conflicts with their established viewpoints. For example, NBC quickly agreed to the International Olympic Committee's request of $2 billion for the television rights to the 2010 Winter Games and 2012 Summer Games. (Fox had offered $1.3 billion, and ESPN had proposed a revenue share.) NBC had acquired the rights to every Olympics from 2000 to 2008, and managers didn't want to risk losing the franchise, so they based their decision on previous information and failed to look closely at the new situation. Unfortunately, with the slump in advertising brought about by the recession, the network lost an estimated $200 million on the Winter Games. One observer suggested that NBC managers let their hearts rule their heads.[50] It is important for managers to be honest with themselves about their motives and to examine all the evidence with equal rigor. Having a devil's advocate is also a good way to avoid seeing only what you want to see.
4. ***Perpetuating the status quo.*** Managers may base decisions on what has worked in the past and fail to explore new options, dig for additional information, or investigate new technologies. For example, General Motors stuck with its strategic decision to offer a multitude of brands long after there was clear evidence that trying to cover the whole range of the auto market was paving the way to disaster. The strategy started to fray in the 1970s with increased competition from Japanese automakers and spikes in oil prices. Yet, as late as February 2008, managers were saying that talk about killing brands was "not a thoughtful discussion." Only bankruptcy and a forced restructuring finally pushed managers to cut GM's brands from eight down to four.[51]
5. ***Being influenced by emotions.*** If you've ever made a decision when you were angry, upset, or ecstatically happy, you might already know the danger of being influenced by emotions. Unfortunately, some managers let their emotions influence their decisions on a regular basis. There is some evidence that when people make poor

SPOTLIGHT ON SKILLS

Evidence-Based Management

At a time when decision making is so important, many managers do not know how to make a good choice among alternatives. Using evidence-based decision making can help. Evidence-based decision making simply means a commitment exists to make more informed and intelligent decisions based on the best available facts and evidence. It means being aware of our biases and seeking and examining evidence with rigor. Managers practice evidence-based decision making by being careful and thoughtful rather than carelessly relying on assumptions, past experience, rules of thumb, or intuition.

Here are some ideas for applying evidence-based decision making:

- ***Demand Evidence.*** Educate people throughout the organization to use data and facts to the extent possible to inform their decisions. Many manager problems are uncertain, and hard facts and data aren't available, but by always asking for evidence, managers can avoid relying on faulty assumptions. Managers at one computer company kept blaming the marketing staff for the trouble the company had selling their products in retail stores. Then, members of the senior team posed as mystery shoppers and tried to buy the company's computers. They kept encountering sales clerks that tried to dissuade them from purchasing the firm's products, citing the excessive price, clunky appearance, and poor customer service. Real-world observations told them something that was very different from what they assumed.
- ***Practice the Five Whys.*** One simple way to get people to think more broadly and deeply about problems rather than going with a superficial understanding and a first response is called the Five Whys. For every problem, managers ask "Why?" not just once, but five times. The first *why* generally produces a superficial explanation for the problem, and each subsequent *why* probes deeper into the causes of the problem and potential solutions.
- ***Do a Postmortem Review.*** A technique many companies have adopted from the U.S. Army to encourage examination of the evidence and continuous learning is the after-action review. After implementation of any significant decision, managers evaluate what worked, what didn't, and how to do things better. Many problems are solved by trial and error. For example, postmortem reviews of decisions regarding attacks from roadside bombs in Iraq led soldiers to suggest implementation of an overall counterinsurgency strategy rather than relying so much on technology.
- ***Balance Decisiveness and Humility.*** The best decision makers have a healthy appreciation for what they don't know. They're always questioning and encouraging others to question their knowledge and assumptions. They foster a culture of inquiry, observation, and experimentation.

SOURCES: Based on Jeffrey Pfeffer and Robert I. Sutton, "Evidence-Based Management," *Harvard Business Review* (January 2006): 62–74; Rosemary Stewart, *Evidence-based Decision Making* (Abingdon, UK: Radcliffe Publishing, 2002); Joshua Klayman, Richard P. Larrick, and Chip Heath, "Organizational Repairs," *Across the Board* (February 2000): 26–31; and Peter Eisler, Blake Morrison, and Tom Vanden Brook, "Strategy That's Making Iraq Safer Was Snubbed for Years," *USA Today*, December 19, 2007.

As a new manager, be aware of biases that can cloud your judgment and lead to bad decisions. The Spotlight on Skills above describes a new way of thinking about decision making that can help you avoid decision traps.

decisions under the influence of strong emotions (such as firing off an angry e-mail message), they tend to continue to make poor decisions because it becomes part of the mind's blueprint for how to behave.[52] Another finding is that doctors make less effective decisions when they feel emotions of like or dislike for a patient. If they like a patient, they are less likely to prescribe a painful procedure. If they feel dislike, they may blame the patient for the condition and provide less treatment.[53] An objective emotion-free approach seems to lead to better decisions.

6. ***Overconfidence.*** Most people overestimate their ability to predict uncertain outcomes. For example, when people are asked to define quantities about which they have little direct knowledge ("What was Walmart's 2010 revenue?" or "What was the market value of Google as of March 14, 2011?"), they overestimate their accuracy. Similarly, many managers have unrealistic expectations of their ability to understand the risks and

BUSINESS BLOOPER

J. Crew

When J. Crew CEO Millard Drexler let the board know he was putting the company up for sale, it must have slipped his mind that he was supposed to conduct an auction of sorts, to get the highest bidder for shareholders. Instead, he made a behind-closed-doors, clouded-in-secrecy $3 billion deal with TPG and Leonard Green & Partners, the private equity firms. Shareholders were not impressed and took Drexler to court, because the required "go-shop" had actually become a "no-shop." One wonders why the three (out of seven) academics (from Dartmouth, Babson, and Boston College) on the Leonard Green & Partners board were not paying more attention—and whether they'd be open to being used as a case study by their students.

SOURCE: Bob Cox, Lisa Lee, and Una Galani, "J. Crew Shows What Not to Do," *The New York Times*, February 4, 2011.

make the right choice. Consider how overconfidence in blowout preventer technology contributed to the disastrous BP oil spill off the Gulf Coast. If the crew of the Deepwater Horizon oil rig lost control of a well and a blowout occurred, a fail-safe device called a blind shear ram was supposed to slice through the drill pipe and seal off the well. But when this disastrous event actually happened, the technology failed. Based on previous incidents, BP and Transocean managers had decided to use just one blind shear ram in the blowout preventer, even though some other rigs were already using two. Overconfidence that they understood and could manage the risks of deep sea drilling caused managers to make numerous poor decisions that led to disaster, and overconfidence meant that executives weren't prepared to deal with a huge deep-sea oil spill.[54]

If any of the decision makers involved in the J. Crew buyout had asked the five whys, they probably would have avoided going to court, as described in this chapter's Business Blooper.

- Being aware of biases that cloud judgment helps managers avoid decision traps and make better decisions.
- Biases to watch out for include being influenced by initial impressions, trying to correct or justify past flawed decisions, seeing only what you want to see, perpetuating the status quo, being influenced by emotions, and being overconfident.

Innovative Group Decision Making

The ability to make fast, widely supported, high-quality decisions on a frequent basis is a critical skill in today's fast-moving organizations.[55] Does this mean managers should make the majority of decisions on their own? No. The rapid pace of the business environment calls for just the opposite—that is, for people throughout the organization to be involved in decision making and have the information, skills, and freedom they need to respond immediately to problems and questions.

Managers do make some decisions as individuals, but decision makers more often are part of a group. Indeed, major decisions in the business world rarely are made entirely by a single manager.

Start with Brainstorming

Brainstorming uses a face-to-face interactive group to spontaneously suggest a wide range of alternatives for decision making. The keys to effective brainstorming are that people can build on one another's ideas; all ideas are acceptable, no matter how crazy they seem; and criticism and evaluation are not allowed. The goal is to generate as many ideas as possible. Brainstorming has been found to be highly effective for quickly generating a wide range of alternate solutions to a problem, but it does have some drawbacks.[56] For one thing, people in a group often want to conform to what others are saying. Some may be concerned about pleasing the boss or impressing colleagues. In addition, many creative people simply have social inhibitions that limit their participation in a group session or make it difficult to come up with ideas in a group setting. In fact, one study found that when four people are asked to "brainstorm" individually, they typically come up with twice as many ideas as a group of four brainstorming together.

One recent approach, electronic brainstorming, takes advantage of the group approach while overcoming some disadvantages. **Electronic brainstorming**, sometimes called *brainwriting*, brings people together in an interactive group over a computer network.[57] One member writes an idea, another reads it and adds other ideas, and so on. Studies show that electronic brainstorming generates about 40 percent more ideas than individuals brainstorming alone, and 25 to 200 percent more ideas than regular brainstorming groups, depending on group size.[58] Why? Because the process is anonymous, the sky's the limit in terms of what people feel free to say. People can write down their ideas immediately, avoiding the possibility that a good idea might slip away while the person is waiting for a chance to speak in a face-to-face group. Social inhibitions and concerns are avoided, which typically allows for a broader range of participation. Another advantage is that electronic brainstorming can potentially be done with groups made up of employees from around the world, further increasing the diversity of alternatives.

Engage in Rigorous Debate

An important key to better decision making is to encourage a rigorous debate of the issue at hand. Good managers recognize that constructive conflict based on divergent points of view can bring a problem into focus, clarify people's ideas, stimulate creative thinking, limit the role of bias, create a broader understanding of issues and alternatives, and improve decision quality.[59] Chuck Knight, the former CEO of Emerson Electric, always sparked heated debates during strategic planning meetings. Knight believed rigorous debate gave people a clearer picture of the competitive landscape and forced managers to look at all sides of an issue, helping them reach better decisions.[60]

Stimulating rigorous debate can be done in several ways. One way is by ensuring that the group is diverse in terms of age and gender, functional area of expertise, hierarchical level, and experience with the business. Some groups assign a **devil's advocate**, who has the role of challenging the assumptions and assertions made by the group.[61] The devil's advocate may force the group to rethink its approach to the problem and avoid reaching premature conclusions. Jeffrey McKeever, CEO of MicroAge, often plays the devil's advocate, changing his position in the middle of a debate to ensure that other executives don't just go along with his opinions.[62]

Another approach is to have group members develop as many alternatives as they can as quickly as they can.[63] It allows the team to work with multiple alternatives and encourages people to advocate ideas they might not prefer simply to encourage debate. Still another way to encourage constructive conflict is to use a technique called **point–counterpoint**, which breaks a decision-making group into two subgroups and assigns them different, often competing, responsibilities.[64] The groups then develop and exchange proposals and discuss and debate the various options until they arrive at a common set of understandings and recommendations.

Avoid Groupthink

It is important for managers to remember that some disagreement and conflict is much healthier than blind agreement. Pressures for conformity exist in almost any group, and particularly when people in a group like one another they tend to avoid anything that might create disharmony. **Groupthink** refers to the tendency of people in groups to suppress contrary opinions.[65] When people slip into groupthink, the desire for harmony outweighs concerns over decision quality. Group members emphasize maintaining unity rather than realistically challenging problems and alternatives. People censor their personal opinions and are reluctant to criticize the opinions of others.

Author and scholar Jerry Harvey coined the related term *Abilene paradox* to illustrate the hidden pressures for conformity that can exist in groups.[66] Harvey tells the story of how members of his extended family sat sweltering on the porch in 104-degree heat in a small town about 50 miles from Abilene, Texas. When someone suggested driving to a café in Abilene, everyone went along with the idea, even though the car was not air conditioned. Everyone was miserable and returned home exhausted and irritable. Later, all the people admitted that they hadn't wanted to make the trip and had thought it was a ridiculous idea. They only went because they all thought the others wanted to go.

Know When to Bail

In a fast-paced environment, good managers encourage risk taking and learning from mistakes, but they also aren't hesitant to pull the plug on something that isn't working. Research has found that managers and organizations often continue to invest time and money in a solution despite strong evidence that it is not appropriate. This tendency is referred to as **escalating commitment**. Managers might block or distort negative information because they don't want to be responsible for a bad decision, or they might simply refuse to accept that their solution is wrong.[67] A study in Europe verified that even highly successful managers often miss or ignore warning signals because they become committed to a decision and believe if they persevere it will pay off.[68] As companies face increasing competition, complexity, and change, it is important that managers don't get so attached to their own ideas that they're unwilling to recognize when to move on. According to Stanford University professor Robert Sutton, the key to successful creative decision making is to "fail early, fail often, and pull the plug early."[69]

Daniel Acker/Bloomberg / Getty Images

ConceptConnection

When automobile customers of DuPont paint stopped submitting production schedules, DuPont's then CEO and chairman Chad Holliday got a wake-up call: he realized the 2008 credit crisis would have far-reaching consequences for his company. Holliday knew he must **act with speed**. He immediately activated DuPont's **crisis management** plan. Over the next six weeks, managers explained the crisis and its potential effects to all 60,000 employees and revised 2008 and early 2009 financial goals. By the end of the year, 4,000 contractors had been laid off to cut costs. DuPont returned to profitability by the fourth quarter of 2009.

Act with Speed

Today's accelerated pace of business means that some decisions have to be made incredibly fast. Just a couple of decades ago, managers could take weeks or even months to make the type of decisions that now must be made in hours or minutes if the company wants to keep pace with competitors.[70] The time frame has compressed for even major decisions such as mergers and acquisitions, the development of new products, and changes in structure or strategy. Ursula Burns made the biggest acquisition in Xerox's history, buying Affiliated Computer Services for $6.4 billion, just weeks after she took over as CEO of the giant company. At General Motors, speeding up decision making was one of the key goals of former CEO Ed Whitacre, Jr. He ended the regular Friday sessions where teams presented plans, charts, financial projections, and tons of data to top executives, instead pushing decision making down to the managers of various divisions. Accelerated decision making enabled GM to pull the plug on a new Buick sport utility vehicle just eight days after it was announced. Feedback from potential customers, bloggers, and Twitter users said the design was "hideous," and GM quickly made the decision to go back to the drawing board.[71]

Don't Ignore a Crisis

One area where speed is particularly crucial is when the organization faces a crisis. Managers are under tremendous pressure to get a team together quickly to assess the situation and step forward with a response. For example, two prankster employees at a Domino's Pizza franchise posted a YouTube video of the two fouling a pizza on the way to delivery. In what has been referred to as one of the quickest responses ever to a corporate crisis, Domino's managers tracked down and fired the employees, filed charges against them, and issued an online apology within the space of a few days.[72] Johnson & Johnson had to react quickly to potentially damaging news from the Food and Drug Administration that acetaminophen, the pain ingredient in J&J's Tylenol, poses a risk of overdose and resulting liver damage.[73]

Managers should expect and plan for crises, as described in Chapter 5. In addition, some suggestions for making effective decisions under the pressure of crisis include these:

- Keep emotions and ego in check so they don't impede judgment.
- Face the reality of the situation, no matter how unpleasant.
- Consider the big picture and context, as well as potentially far-reaching consequences.
- Focus on the desired outcome.
- Take quick action based on ever-evolving information.[74]

- Most decisions within organizations are made as part of a group.
- **Brainstorming** is a technique that uses a face-to-face group to spontaneously suggest a broad range of alternatives for making a decision.
- **Electronic brainstorming** brings people together in an interactive group over a computer network rather than meeting face-to-face.
- A **devil's advocate** is a person who is assigned the role of challenging the assumptions and assertions made by the group to prevent premature consensus.
- A group decision-making technique that breaks people into subgroups and assigns them to express competing points of view regarding the decision is called **point–counterpoint**.
- **Groupthink** refers to the tendency of people in groups to suppress contrary opinions in a desire for harmony.
- **Escalating commitment** refers to continuing to invest time and money in a decision solution despite evidence that it is failing.
- Using group decision making helps organizations act quickly in a fast-changing environment.
- General Motors pulled the plug on a new Buick SUV project just eight days after it was announced because feedback from potential customers pronounced the design "hideous."
- Managers have to make decisions incredibly quickly when facing a crisis such as the BP oil spill in 2010.

Discussion Questions

1. You are a busy partner in a legal firm, and an experienced administrative assistant complains of continued headaches, drowsiness, dry throat, and occasional spells of fatigue and flu. She tells you she believes air quality in the building is bad and would like something to be done. How would you respond?
2. Why do you think decision making is considered a fundamental part of management effectiveness?
3. Explain the difference between risk and ambiguity. How might decision making differ for a risky versus an "ambiguous" situation?
4. Analyze three decisions you made over the past six months. Which of these were programmed and which were nonprogrammed? Which model—the classical, administrative, or political—best describes the approach you took to make each decision?
5. What opportunities and potential problems are posed by the formation of more than one coalition within an organization, each one advocating a different direction or alternative? What steps can you take as a manager to make sure that dueling coalitions result in constructive discussion rather than dissension?
6. Can you think of a bad decision from your own school or work experience or from the recent business or political news that was made in an effort to correct or justify a past decision? As a new manager, how might you resist the urge to choose a decision alternative based on the idea that it might correct or validate a previous decision?
7. As a new, entry-level manager, how important is it to find ways to compensate for your relative lack of experience when trying to determine which alternative before you is most likely to succeed? What are some ways you can meet this challenge?
8. List some possible advantages and disadvantages to using computer technology for managerial decision making.
9. Do you think intuition is a valid approach to making decisions in an organization? Why or why not? How might intuition be combined with a rational decision approach?
10. What do you think is your dominant decision style? Is your style compatible with group techniques such as brainstorming and engaging in rigorous debate? Discuss.

Self-Learning

What's Your Personal Decision Style?[75]

Read each of the following items and circle the answer that best describes you. Think about how you typically act in a work or school situation and mark the answer that first comes to mind. There are no right or wrong answers.

1. **In performing my job or class work, I look for**
   a. Practical results
   b. The best solution
   c. Creative approaches or ideas
   d. Good working conditions
2. **I enjoy jobs that**
   a. Are technical and well-defined
   b. Have a lot of variety
   c. Allow me to be independent and creative
   d. Involve working closely with others
3. **The people I most enjoy working with are**
   a. Energetic and ambitious
   b. Capable and organized
   c. Open to new ideas
   d. Agreeable and trusting
4. **When I have a problem, I usually**
   a. Rely on what has worked in the past
   b. Apply careful analysis
   c. Consider a variety of creative approaches
   d. Seek consensus with others
5. **I am especially good at**
   a. Remembering dates and facts
   b. Solving complex problems
   c. Seeing many possible solutions
   d. Getting along with others

6. **When I don't have much time, I**
   a. Make decisions and act quickly
   b. Follow established plans or priorities
   c. Take my time and refuse to be pressured
   d. Ask others for guidance and support
7. **In social situations, I generally**
   a. Talk to others
   b. Think about what's being discussed

c. Observe
d. Listen to the conversation

8. Other people consider me
a. Aggressive
b. Disciplined
c. Creative
d. Supportive

9. What I dislike most is
a. Not being in control
b. Doing boring work
c. Following rules
d. Being rejected by others

10. The decisions I make are usually
a. Direct and practical
b. Systematic or abstract
c. Broad and flexible
d. Sensitive to others' needs

Scoring and Interpretation

These items rate your personal decision style, as described in the text and listed in Exhibit 6.5.

Count the number of *a* answers. They provide your *directive* score.

Count the number of *b* answers for your *analytical* score.

The number of *c* answers is your *conceptual* score.

The number of *d* answers is your *behavioral* score.

What is your dominant decision style? Are you surprised, or does this result reflect the style you thought you used most often?

Group Learning

A New Approach to Making Decisions[76]

Managers are typically effective at focusing on problems and diagnosing what is wrong and how to fix it when they have to make a decision. The typical questions managers might ask themselves include these: What is the problem here? What is the cause of this problem? Why do I have this problem? What alternatives do I have? What is the best alternative? How do I implement this alternative?

There is a novel approach to decision-making, called *outcome-directed thinking*, that some managers have learned to use. It focuses on future outcomes and possibilities rather than on the causes of the problem. People tend to feel more positive emotions, have more creative ideas, and experience more optimism about solving a problem when they focus on desired future outcomes rather than on who or what caused the problem.

Step 1 Think of a problem you have in your life right now for which something is not what you would like it to be. It could be any problem you are having at school, home, or work that you would like to solve. Write a few words below that summarize the problem:

____

____

____

____

Step 2. Now write brief answers to the following questions:

A. What do I really want instead of this problem? (Your answer equals your desired future outcome.)

____

____

____

____

B. How will I know when I have achieved this future outcome? (What will I see, hear, and feel?)

____

____

____

____

C. What resources do I need to pursue this future outcome?

____

____

____

____

D. What is the first step I can take to achieve this outcome?

____

____

____

____

Step 3. In a group of three to five students, take turns sharing your answers to the above four questions. In addition, share what you are feeling about your solution to the problem. For example, do you feel that you have created a beginning solution that you feel responsible to implement? In addition, share how you think your decision-making process compares in creativity and effectiveness in focusing on problem causes rather than focusing on desired outcomes.

Action Learning

1. Think about two times when you made decisions, one that had a positive outcome and one that did not turn out so well.
2. Fill out the table below.

What decision did you have to make?	Decision #1 (positive outcome)	Decision #2 (negative outcome)
Was the decision programmed or nonprogrammed?		
Was there certainty or uncertainty?		
Did you use your intuition?		
Did you build a coalition?		
Did you engage in any bad decision behaviors, such as defending previous decisions, being too emotional, unduly influenced by initial impressions, and so on?		
Did you explore different alternatives?		
Did you use evidence-based thinking?		
Did you consult a devil's advocate?		

3. What differences do you see in the two decision-making situations?
4. What can you learn from this on how to make decisions more effectively in the future?

Ethical Dilemma

The No-Show Consultant[77]

Jeffrey Moses was facing one of the toughest decisions of his short career as a manager with International Consulting. Andrew Carpenter, one of his best consultants, was clearly in trouble, and his problems were affecting his work. International Consulting designs, installs, and implements complex back-office software systems for companies all over the world. About half the consultants work out of the main office, and the rest, including Carpenter, work primarily from home.

This Monday morning, Moses had gotten an irate call from a major New York client saying Andrew Carpenter never showed up at the company's headquarters, where the client had been expecting his new computer system to go live for the first time. In calling around to other customers on the East Coast, trying to locate the missing consultant, Moses heard other stories. Carpenter had also missed a few other appointments—all on Monday mornings—but no one had felt the need to report it because he had called to reschedule. In addition, he had practically come to blows with an employee who had challenged him about the capabilities of the new system, and he had inexplicably walked out of one customer's office in the middle of the day, without a word to anyone. Another client reported that the last time he had seen Carpenter, the consultant appeared to have a serious hangover. Most of the clients liked Carpenter, but they were concerned that his behavior was increasingly erratic. One client suggested that she would prefer to work with someone else. As for the major New York customer, he preferred that Andrew, rather than a new consultant, finish the project, but they were also demanding that International eat half the $250,000 consultant's fee.

After Moses finally located Carpenter by calling his next-door neighbor, Andrew confessed that he'd had a "lost weekend" and been too drunk to get on the plane. He then told Moses that his wife had left and taken their two-year-old son with her. He admitted that he had been drinking a little more than usual lately but insisted that he was getting himself under control and promised no more problems. "I'm really not an alcoholic or anything," he said. "I've just been upset about Brenda leaving, and I let it get out of hand this weekend." Moses told Carpenter that if he would get to New York and complete the project, all would be forgiven.

Now, however, he wondered whether he should really just let things slide. Moses talked to Carpenter's team leader about the situation and was told that the leader was aware of his recent problems but thought everything would smooth itself over. "Consultants with his knowledge, level of skill, and willingness to travel are hard to find. He's well liked among all the customers; he'll get his act together." However, when Moses discussed the problem with Carolyn Walter, vice president of operations, she argued that Carpenter should be dismissed. "You're under no obligation to keep him just because you said you would," she pointed out. "This was a major screw-up, and it's perfectly legal to fire someone for absenteeism. Your calls to customers should make it clear that this situation was not a one-time thing. Get rid of him now before things get worse. If you think eating half that $250,000 fee hurts now, just think what could happen if this behavior continues."

What Would You Do?

1. Give him a month's notice and terminate. He's known as a good consultant, so he probably won't have any trouble finding a new job, and you'll avoid any further problems associated with his emotional difficulties and his possible alcohol problem.
2. Let it slide. Missing the New York appointment is Carpenter's first big mistake. He says he is getting things under control, and you believe he should be given a chance to get himself back on track.
3. Let Carpenter know that you care about what he's going through, but insist that he take a short paid leave and get counseling to deal with his emotional difficulties and evaluate the seriousness of his problems with alcohol. If the alcohol abuse continues, require him to attend a treatment program or find another job.

Case for Critical Analysis

A Manager's Dilemma: Who Gets the Project?[78]

"It seemed like a real ego booster when I got to take over my boss's job during his vacation," thought Dave Peterson. "Now I'm not so sure. Both Seamus and Jeremy really want to be in charge of this new project. I have to decide between them, and I will still have to work with them as a peer after this is all over."

Background

CMT is a leading innovator in the telecommunications industry. Rapid growth and persistence in the face of early company setbacks have generated a culture based on problem solving and meeting customer expectations. The primary guidelines directing action are "If you see a problem that needs to be fixed, it becomes your problem" and "Do what you have to do to satisfy the customer." This environment has led to frequent conflicts and job stress but also provided opportunities for job enrichment and advancement. Additional company characteristics follow:

- *History*: ten years old, telecommunications industry, rapid growth, $50 million in annual revenue
- *Culture*: innovative, encourages individual initiative, respect for technical expertise, conflict accepted as part of company life

Dave is the manager of customer software support. His department provides support to customers and field staff when software problems occur. Dave worked as a systems analyst in customer software support prior to his promotion to manager. He and his staff have considerable experience with CMT's products and many contacts with CMT's software developers.

Seamus is in charge of the technical publications department, which provides technical and user manuals and other materials for customers and CMT field staff. These manuals detail the technical operations of CMT Corporation's equipment and software. Seamus and his staff work closely with designers and have a good reputation for translating terminology into more user-friendly materials that can be understood by those without engineering training.

Jeremy Olson manages the software training department. This department offers courses that explain CMT Corporation's software products, and trains customers and company employees on the proper use of the products. The software training department utilizes documentation generated by the technical publications department for its training courses. Jeremy and his staff members are especially good at designing courses that communicate technical information in a way that customers can readily understand. Course design and presentation are particularly important due to the high degree of modularity of CMT software.

The New Project

A new hardware product is under development, with associated software. Because of the low target price for the product and the need for inexpensive training, CMT's sales department requested that a CD-ROM self-study course be developed for customers of the new product. At this time, CMT Corporation has not yet begun using CD-ROM technology for training.

Both Seamus and Jeremy have been lobbying heavily to be allowed to develop the new course. Seamus argued that he and his staff had superior technical expertise because of their close working relationship with engineers during the development of technical manuals for the new product. In addition, some of his staff has previously developed CD-ROM presentations.

Jeremy noted that the primary purpose of the course is to train employees and customers in a situation where there are no company consultants or trainers available to answer questions. Thus, he argued, the presentation of the material and the pedagogy used are critical for the success of the CD-ROM. Both managers presented their respective cases to their supervisor, Henry Mathews, the director of software support.

During the next two months, the lobbying intensified and the level of conflict escalated to the point where both Jeremy and Seamus openly declared that the other department simply "lacked the needed skills to get the job done"; each said that if the project were not assigned to his department, it would surely fail. Both managers had approached Dave, asking for his support.

The culture at CMT accepts conflict that is based on doing the best job for the customer. In spite of this, Dave feels that the conflict between Seamus and Jeremy has gotten out of hand. If it goes on much longer, Dave feels the conflict might spill over into other areas where all three departments need to cooperate.

The Decision

Henry took a two-week vacation, and when he left on Friday, he put Dave temporarily in charge of the entire unit. The following Monday, both Seamus and Jeremy informed Dave that a decision on the new project had to be made right away. The purchase order for the filming equipment had to be placed immediately in order for it to arrive in time. They, of course, disagreed on the type of equipment that should be used, so a decision had to be made as to the long-term assignment of the project. Furthermore, the project was now behind schedule given the needed development time based on the projected product release date.

Dave realized that how he handled this decision would reflect on his management competencies and possibly influence his opportunity for advancement. "I know if I assign this project to either Seamus or Jeremy, someone is going to be very upset," Dave pondered, "and I don't know if I can get these two to talk to each other, let alone agree on a compromise. The only thing I do know is that I have to make a decision on this before Henry returns."

Questions

1. Describe aspects of the political decision-making model that are evident in this case.
2. What examples of bounded rationality can you identify in the case?
3. If you were Dave Peterson, what decision would you make? Explain how you arrived at this decision.

aplia Aplia Highlights

Now use your Aplia homework to help you:

- Apply management theories in your life
- Assess your management skills
- Master management terms and concepts
- Apply your knowledge to real-world situations
- Analyze and solve challenging management problems

In order to take advantage of these elements, your instructor will need to have set up a course for your class within Aplia. Ask your instructor to contact his/her Cengage sales representative and Digital Solutions Manager to explore testing Aplia in your course this term.

© Leremy, Shutterstock

Plant Fantasies: Managerial Decision Making

Teresa Carleo considered a career in cooking after a boss once passed her up for a promotion. But when her husband urged against it, the New York resident instead launched a landscaping business and began searching for opportunities to beautify the Big Apple. Today, Carleo's business, Plant Fantasies, is the gardener for such well-known city properties as the Trump Organization, John Jay College, and Jack Resnick & Sons. My niche is owners and developers in the real estate industry," Carleo says of her landscaping business.

Although the opportunity to serve New York's rich and famous may sound exciting, pleasing the Donald Trumps of the world is a challenging task. Fortunately, Carleo is no mere apprentice when it comes to high-class service. "The decision to start the business was exciting, but the determination to stay with the business was excruciating," Carleo says of her demanding job. Carleo's patience has been a virtue, however, as wealthy New York City property owners pay top dollar for healthy shrubs and fragrant flowers. Installation fees at Plant Fantasies begin at $1,200, and high-end exterior landscapes can cost customers up to $600,000. With well over 100 clients, Plant Fantasies is able to generate nearly $5 million in annual revenues.

In New York City, where appearances matter, real estate owners have little tolerance for wilting plants or lagging service. Carleo's attention to detail is evident in all of her installations—most notably her rooftop gardens. Gardens come carefully constructed with a drainage layer, waterproof protective membrane, biodegradable coconut mat, soil, and lush foliage. Each installation requires close collaboration between architects, floral designers, landscape workers, and even code inspectors. Once a garden is built, landscape teams keep a watchful eye to make sure weeds are pulled and shrubs are manicured. The same care and attention is displayed in other company services, including holiday decorations and Christmas trees. Whether it's placing wreaths or planting gardens, fancy flora is what Plant Fantasies does best.

In landscaping, success often boils down to big decisions over little details. "It's my role as a business owner to give suggestions and ideas—they're looking to me for that," Carleo says. "They don't know about plants and flowers, but they might know that they like the color red." Whereas some decisions involve plant colors and types, others involve complex negotiation with people, such as when Plant Fantasies builds designs created by outside landscape architects. "It's easier when we are the landscape designers because we are picking the plant material. We have a sense of what we want to do, and we have faith in our design and choices," says Carleo. "But when you're working with landscape architects, they could come up with something that we don't even really agree with."

Despite Carleo's confidence in her own decision making, the Plant Fantasies owner understands the benefits of empowering others. "More and more, as I'm trying to grow the company, I'm trying to get my team to be more independent of me. I don't want to know every single thing." Regardless of who makes decisions, Carleo expects all her employees to share her high standards for quality: "I want them to take care of it, but I want them to take care of it the way I would take care of it myself. And that's hard, because not everybody is the same."

Discussion Questions

1. Did Plant Fantasies owner Teresa Carleo follow the rational decision-making process to launch Plant Fantasies? Explain.
2. List an example of a programmed decision at Plant Fantasies. Identify a nonprogrammed decision at Plant Fantasies.
3. How might managers at Plant Fantasies conduct the final evaluation stage of the decision-making process when installing a new garden for a client?

© VikaSuh, Shutterstock

Failure to Launch

Meet Tripp (Matthew McConaughey), 35 years old, nice car, loves sailing, and lives in a nice home—his parents' house. Tripp's attachment to his family usually annoys any woman with whom he becomes serious. Mother Sue (Kathy Bates) and father Al (Terry Bradshaw) hire Paula (Sarah Jessica Parker). She specializes in detaching people like Tripp from their families. The term *failure to launch* refers to the failure to move out of the family home at an earlier age.

The Bird Problem: Fast Decision Making! This fast-moving sequence begins with the sound of a bird chirping as it perches on a tree limb. Kit (Zooey Deschanel) and Ace (Justin Bartha) have waited patiently for the bird' s arrival. This bird has annoyed Kit for many days. Ace believes that Kit only pumped the shotgun twice. The sequence ends after the bird leaves the house. The film continues with Kit and Ace embracing and then cuts to a baseball game.

What to Watch for and Ask Yourself

- Does "the bird problem" present Kit and Ace with a programmed or nonprogrammed decision? What features of their decision problem led to your choice?
- Assess the degree of certainty or uncertainty that Kit and Ace face in this decision problem. What factors set the degree of certainty or uncertainty?
- Review the earlier section describing the decision-making steps. Which of those steps appears in "the bird problem?" Note the examples of each step that you see.

© Pedro Nogueira, Shutterstock

Endnotes

1. Micheline Maynard, "Toyota Delayed a U.S. Recall, Documents Show," *The New York Times,* April 12, 2010.
2. Ken Thomas, "Toyota Mulling $16 Million Decision," *The Ledger,* April 6, 2010.
3. Michael V. Copeland, "Stuck in the Spin Cycle," *Business 2.0* (May 2005): 74–75; Adam Horowitz, Mark Athitakis, Mark Lasswell, and Owen Thomas, "101 Dumbest Moments in Business," *Business 2.0* (January–February 2004): 72–81.
4. See Kenneth R. Brousseau, Michael L. Driver, Gary Hourihan, and Rikard Larsson, "The Seasoned Executive's Decision Making Style," *Harvard Business Review* (February 2006): 110ff, for a discussion of how decision-making behavior evolves as managers progress in their careers.
5. Herbert A. Simon, *The New Science of Management Decision* (Englewood Cliffs, NJ: Prentice Hall, 1977), p. 47.
6. Duff McDonald, "The Banker Who Saved Wall Street; How JPMorgan Chase CEO Jamie Dimon Bailed out Bear Stearns and the Federal Government and Lived to Turn a Profit," *Newsweek* (September 21, 2009); and Kate Kelly, "Inside the Fall of Bear Stearns," *The Wall Street Journal,* May 9–10, 2009 (excerpted from K. Kelly, *Street Fighters: The Last 72 Hours of Bear Stearns, the Toughest Firm on Wall Street* (Portfolio/Penguin 2009).
7. McDonald, "The Banker Who Saved Wall Street."
8. Samuel Eilon, "Structuring Unstructured Decisions," *Omega* 13 (1985): 369–377; and Max H. Bazerman, *Judgment in Managerial Decision Making* (New York: Wiley, 1986).
9. James G. March and Zur Shapira, "Managerial Perspectives on Risk and Risk Taking," *Management Science* 33 (1987): 1404–1418; and Inga Skromme Baird and Howard Thomas, "Toward a Contingency Model of Strategic Risk Taking," *Academy of Management Review* 10 (1985): 230–243.
10. Hugh Courtney, "Decision-Driven Scenarios for Assessing Four Levels of Uncertainty," *Strategy & Leadership* 31, no. 1 (2003): 14–22.
11. Reported in David Leonhardt, "This Fed Chief May Yet Get a Honeymoon," *The New York Times,* August 23, 2006.
12. David A. Kaplan, "Berea College's Dilemma," *Fortune* (May 3, 2010): 40.
13. Michael Masuch and Perry LaPotin, "Beyond Garbage Cans: An AI Model of Organizational Choice," *Administrative Science Quarterly* 34 (1989): 38–67; and Richard L. Daft and Robert H. Lengel, "Organizational Information Requirements, Media Richness and Structural Design," *Management Science* 32 (1986): 554–571.
14. Ben Worthen, "Cost Cutting Versus Innovation: Reconcilable Difference," *CIO* (October 1, 2004): 89–94.
15. Peter C. Cairo, David L. Dotlich, and Stephen H. Rhinesmith, "Embracing Ambiguity," *The Conference Board Review* (Summer 2009): 56–61; John C. Camillus, "Strategy as a Wicked Problem," *Harvard Business Review* (May 2008): 98–106; and Richard O. Mason and Ian I. Mitroff, *Challenging Strategic Planning Assumptions* (New York: Wiley Interscience, 1981).
16. "How Companies Make Good Decisions: McKinsey Global Survey Results," *The McKinsey Quarterly,* January 2009, www.mckinseyquarterly.com (accessed February 3, 2009).
17. Thomas H. Davenport and Jeanne G. Harris, "Automated Decision Making Comes of Age," *MIT Sloan Management Review* (Summer 2005): 83–89; and Stacie McCullough, "On the Front Lines," *CIO* (October 15, 1999): 78–81.

18. Dan Milmo, Ian Sample, and Sam Jones, "Volcano Chaos: How the Battle for the Skies Ended in Victory for Airlines," *The Guardian,* April 22, 2010; and Daniel Michaels, Sara Schaefer Munox, and Bruce Orwall, "Airlines Rush to Move Millions," *The Wall Street Journal Europe,* April 22, 2010.
19. Scott McCartney, "The Middle Seat: How One Airline Skirts the Ash Cloud," *The Wall Street Journal,* April 22, 2010.
20. Herbert A. Simon, *The New Science of Management Decision* (New York: Harper & Row, 1960), pp. 5–6; and Amitai Etzioni, "Humble Decision Making," *Harvard Business Review* (July–August 1989): 122–126.
21. James G. March and Herbert A. Simon, *Organizations* (New York: Wiley, 1958).
22. Herbert A. Simon, *Models of Man* (New York: Wiley, 1957), pp. 196–205; and Herbert A. Simon, *Administrative Behavior,* 2nd ed. (New York: Free Press, 1957).
23. Emily Steel, "MySpace Slashes Jobs As Growth Slows Down," *The Wall Street Journal,* June 17, 2009.
24. Weston H. Agor, "The Logic of Intuition: How Top Executives Make Important Decisions," *Organizational Dynamics* 14 (Winter 1986): 5–18; and Herbert A. Simon, "Making Management Decisions: The Role of Intuition and Emotion," *Academy of Management Executive* 1 (1987): 57–64. For a recent review of research, see Erik Dane and Michael G. Pratt, "Exploring Intuition and Its Role in Managerial Decision Making," *Academy of Management Review* 32, no. 1 (2007): 33–54.
25. Jaana Woiceshyn, "Lessons from 'Good Minds': How CEOs Use Intuition, Analysis, and Guiding Principles to Make Strategic Decisions," *Long Range Planning* 42 (2009): 298–319.
26. See Gary Klein, *Intuition at Work: Why Developing Your Gut Instincts Will Make You Better at What You Do* (New York: Doubleday, 2002); Kurt Matzler, Franz Bailom, and Todd A. Mooradian, "Intuitive Decision Making," *MIT Sloan Management Review* 49, no. 1 (Fall 2007): 13–15; Malcolm Gladwell, *Blink: The Power of Thinking without Thinking* (New York: Little Brown, 2005); and Sharon Begley, "Follow Your Intuition: The Unconscious You May Be the Wiser Half," *The Wall Street Journal*, August 30, 2002.
27. Benedict Carey, "Hunches Prove to Be Valuable Assets in Battle," *The New York Times,* July 28, 2009.
28. C. Chet Miller and R. Duane Ireland, "Intuition in Strategic Decision Making: Friend or Foe in the Fast-Paced 21st Century?" *Academy of Management Executive* 19, no. 1 (2005): 19–30; and Eric Bonabeau, "Don't Trust Your Gut," *Harvard Business Review* (May 2003): 116ff.
29. Eugene Sadler-Smith and Erella Shefy, "The Intuitive Executive: Understanding and Applying 'Gut Feel' in Decision Making," *Academy of Management Executive* 18, no. 4 (2004): 76–91; Simon, "Making Management Decisions," and Ann Langley, "Between 'Paralysis by Analysis' and 'Extinction by Instinct,'" *Sloan Management Review* (Spring 1995): 63–76.
30. This discussion is based on Stephen Friedman and James K. Sebenius, "Organizational Transformation: The Quiet Role of Coalitional Leadership," *Ivey Business Journal* (January–February 2009): 1ff; Gerald R. Ferris, Darren C. Treadway, Pamela L. Perrewé, Robyn L. Brouer, Ceasar Douglas, and Sean Lux, "Political Skill in Organizations," *Journal of Management* (June 2007): 290–320; and William B. Stevenson, Jon L. Pierce, and Lyman W. Porter, "The Concept of 'Coalition' in Organization Theory and Research," *Academy of Management Review* 10 (1985): 256–268.
31. "How Companies Make Good Decisions."
32. George T. Doran and Jack Gunn, "Decision Making in High-Tech Firms: Perspectives of Three Executives," *Business Horizons* (November– December 2002): 7–16.
33. Jessica E. Vascellaro, "Brin Led Google to Quit China," *The Wall Street Journal,* March 25, 2010.
34. James W. Fredrickson, "Effects of Decision Motive and Organizational Performance Level on Strategic Decision Processes," *Academy of Management Journal* 28 (1985): 821–843; James W. Fredrickson, "The Comprehensiveness of Strategic Decision Processes: Extension, Observations, Future Directions," *Academy of Management Journal* 27 (1984): 445–466; James W. Dean, Jr., and Mark P. Sharfman, "Procedural Rationality in the Strategic Decision-Making Process," *Journal of Management Studies* 30, no. 4 (July 1993): 587–610; Nandini Rajagopalan, Abdul M. A. Rasheed, and Deepak K. Datta, "Strategic Decision Processes: Critical Review and Future Directions," *Journal of Management* 19, no. 2 (1993): 349–384; and Paul J. H. Schoemaker, "Strategic Decisions in Organizations: Rational and Behavioral Views," *Journal of Management Studies* 30, no. 1 (January 1993): 107–129.
35. Marjorie A. Lyles and Howard Thomas, "Strategic Problem Formulation: Biases and Assumptions Embedded in Alternative Decision-Making Models," *Journal of Management Studies* 25 (1988): 131–145; and Susan E. Jackson and Jane E. Dutton, "Discerning Threats and Opportunities," *Administrative Science Quarterly* 33 (1988): 370–387.
36. Richard L. Daft, Juhani Sormumen, and Don Parks, "Chief Executive Scanning, Environmental Characteristics, and Company Performance: An Empirical Study" (unpublished manuscript, Texas A&M University, 1988).
37. Jena McGregor, "Gospels of Failure," *Fast Company* (February 2005): 62–67.
38. C. Kepner and B. Tregoe, *The Rational Manager* (New York: McGraw-Hill, 1965).
39. John D. Stoll, Kevin Helliker, and Neil E. Boudette, "A Saga of Decline and Denial," *The Wall Street Journal,* June 2, 2009.
40. Paul C. Nutt, "Expanding the Search for Alternatives during Strategic Decision Making," *Academy of Management Executive* 18, no. 4 (2004): 13–28; and P. C. Nutt, "Surprising But True: Half the Decisions in Organizations Fail," *Academy of Management Executive* 13, no. 4 (1999): 75–90.
41. Pallavi Gogoi and Michael Arndt, "Hamburger Hell," *BusinessWeek* (March 3, 2003): 104.
42. Peter Mayer, "A Surprisingly Simple Way to Make Better Decisions," *Executive Female* (March–April 1995): 13–14; and Ralph L. Keeney, "Creativity in Decision Making with Value-Focused Thinking," *Sloan Management Review* (Summer 1994): 33–41.
43. Kerry Capell, "Novartis: Radically Remaking Its Drug Business," *BusinessWeek* (June 22, 2009): 30–35.
44. Mark McNeilly, "Gathering Information for Strategic Decisions, Routinely," *Strategy & Leadership* 30, no. 5 (2002): 29–34.
45. Ibid.
46. Based on A. J. Rowe, J. D. Boulgaides, and M. R. McGrath, *Managerial Decision Making* (Chicago: Science Research Associates, 1984); and Alan J. Rowe and Richard O. Mason, *Managing with Style: A Guide to Understanding, Assessing, and Improving Your Decision Making* (San Francisco: Jossey-Bass, 1987).
47. Peter Baker, "How Obama's Afghanistan War Plan Came to Be," *International Herald Tribune,* December 7, 2009; and Ron Walters, "Afghanistan: The Big Decision," *The Washington Informer,* December 10–16, 2009.
48. This section is based on John S. Hammond, Ralph L. Keeney, and Howard Raiffa, *Smart Choices: A Practical Guide to Making*

Better Decisions (Boston: Harvard Business School Press, 1999); Max H. Bazerman and Dolly Chugh, "Decisions without Blinders," *Harvard Business Review* (January 2006): 88–97; J. S. Hammond, R. L. Keeney, and H. Raiffa, "The Hidden Traps in Decision Making," *Harvard Business Review* (September– October 1998): 47–58; Oren Harari, "The Thomas Lawson Syndrome," *Management Review* (February 1994): 58–61; Dan Ariely, "Q&A: Why Good CIOs Make Bad Decisions," *CIO* (May 1, 2003): 83–87; Leigh Buchanan, "How to Take Risks in a Time of Anxiety," *Inc.* (May 2003): 76–81; and Max H. Bazerman, *Judgment in Managerial Decision Making,* 5th ed. (New York: John Wiley & Sons, 2002).

49. J. B. Schmidt and R. J. Calantone, "Escalation of Commitment during New Product Development," *Journal of the Academy of Marketing Science* 30, no. 2 (2002): 103–118
50. Richard Sandomir, "NBC Haunted by Its Knockout Bid for the Games," *The New York Times,* January 20, 2010.
51. Stoll et al. "A Saga of Decline and Denial."
52. Dan Ariely, "The Long-Term Effects of Short-Term Emotions," *Harvard Business Review* (January-February 2010): 38.
53. Example from Jerome Groopman, *How Doctors Think* (New York: Houghton Mifflin, 2007).
54. Ben Casselman and Guy Chazan, "Disaster Plans Lacking at Deep Rigs," *The Wall Street Journal,* May 18, 2010; and David Barstow, Laura Dodd, James Glanz, Stephanie Saul, and Ian Urbina, "Regulators Failed to Address Risks in Oil Rig Fail-Safe Device," *The New York Times,* June 20, 2010, www.nytimes.com/2010/06/21/us/21blowout.html (accessed July 7, 2010).
55. Kathleen M. Eisenhardt, "Strategy As Strategic Decision Making," *Sloan Management Review* (Spring 1999): 65–72.
56. Josh Hyatt, "Where the Best—and Worst—Ideas Come From" (a brief synopsis of "Idea Generation and the Quality of the Best Idea" by Karen Girotra, Christian Terwiesch, and Karl T. Ulrich), *MIT Sloan Management Review* (Summer 2008): 11–12; and Robert C. Litchfield, "Brainstorming Reconsidered: A Goal-Based View," *Academy of Management Review* 33, no. 3 (2008): 649–668.
57. R. B. Gallupe, W. H. Cooper, M. L. Grise, and L. M. Bastianutti, "Blocking Electronic Brainstorms," *Journal of Applied Psychology* z (1994): 77–86; R. B. Gallupe and W. H. Cooper, "Brainstorming Electronically," *Sloan Management Review* (Fall 1993): 27–36; and Alison Stein Wellner, "A Perfect Brainstorm," *Inc.* (October 2003): 31–35.
58. Wellner, "A Perfect Brainstorm"; Gallupe and Cooper, "Brainstorming Electronically."
59. Sydney Finkelstein, "Think Again: Good Leaders, Bad Decisions," *Leadership Excellence* (June 2009): 7; "Flaws in Strategic Decision Making: McKinsey Global Survey Results," *The McKinsey Quarterly,* January 2009, www.mckinsey.com/Flaws_in_strategic_decision_making_McKinsey_Global_Survey_Results_2284; Michael A. Roberto, "Making Difficult Decisions in Turbulent Times," *Ivey Business Journal* (May–June 2003): 1–7; Eisenhardt, "Strategy As Strategic Decision Making"; and David A. Garvin and Michael A. Roberto, "What You Don't Know about Making Decisions," *Harvard Business Review* (September 2001): 108–116.
60. Roberto, "Making Difficult Decisions in Turbulent Times."
61. David M. Schweiger and William R. Sandberg, "The Utilization of Individual Capabilities in Group Approaches to Strategic Decision Making," *Strategic Management Journal* 10 (1989): 31–43; "Avoiding Disasters," sidebar in Paul B. Carroll and Chunka Mui, "7 Ways to Fail Big," *Harvard Business Review* (September 2008): 82–91; and "The Devil's Advocate," *Small Business Report* (December 1987): 38–41.
62. Doran and Gunn, "Decision Making in High-Tech Firms."
63. Eisenhardt, "Strategy As Strategic Decision Making."
64. Garvin and Roberto, "What You Don't Know about Making Decisions."
65. Irving L. Janis, *Groupthink: Psychological Studies of Policy Decisions and Fiascoes,* 2nd ed. (Boston: Houghton Mifflin, 1982).
66. Jerry B. Harvey, "The Abilene Paradox: The Management of Agreement," *Organizational Dynamics* (Summer 1988): 17–43.
67. S. Trevis Certo, Brian L. Connelly, and Laszlo Tihanyi, "Managers and Their Not-So-Rational Decisions," *Business Horizons* 51 (2008): 113–119.
68. Hans Wissema, "Driving through Red Lights; How Warning Signals Are Missed or Ignored," *Long Range Planning* 35 (2002): 521–539.
69. Ibid.
70. Jay Stuller, "The Need for Speed," *The Conference Board Review* (Fall 2009): 34–41; Paul Barsch, "As Decision-Making Windows Shrink," *The Conference Board Review* (Fall 2009): 39.
71. Geoff Colvin, "C-Suite Strategies: Ursula Burns," *Fortune* (May 3, 2010): 96–102; Sharon Terlep, "GM's Plodding Culture Vexes Its Impatient CEO," *The Wall Street Journal,* April 7, 2010; and Stuller, "The Need for Speed."
72. Reported in Stuller, "The Need for Speed."
73. Vanessa O'Connell and Shirley S. Wang, "J&J Acts Fast on Tylenol," *The Wall Street Journal,* July 9, 2009.
74. Ken Naglewski, "Are You Ready to Make Effective Decisions When Disaster Strikes? Strategies for Crisis Decision-Making," *Journal of Private Equity* (Spring 2006): 45–51.
75. Adapted from Rowe and Richard O. Mason, *Managing with Style,* pp. 40–41.
76. This approach to decision-making was developed by Robert P. Bostrom and Victoria K. Clawson of Bostrom and Associates, Columbia, Missouri, and this exercise is based on a write-up appearing in *Inside USAA,* the company newsletter of USAA (September 11, 1996), pp. 8–10; and Victoria K. Clawson and Robert P. Bostrom, "Research-Driven Facilitation Training for Computer-Supported Environments," *Group Decision and Negotiation* 5 (1996): 7–29.
77. Based on information in Jeffrey L. Seglin, "The Savior Complex," *Inc.* (February 1999): 67–69; and Nora Johnson, "'He's Been Beating Me,' She Confided," *Business Ethics* (Summer 2001): 21.
78. D. Polly and P. Weber, "A Manager's Dilemma: Who Gets the Project?" in J. K. Benson, ed., *Journal of Critical Incidents* (2008): 1, 15–17, as edited and presented in D. Hellriegel and J. Slocum, *Organizational Behavior,* 13th ed. (Cincinnati, OH: South-Western/Cengage), pp. 441–442. Presented to and accepted by the Society for Case Research. All rights reserved to SCR. *This case was prepared by the authors and is intended to be used as a basis for class discussion. The views represented here are those of the case authors and do not necessarily reflect the views of the Society for Case Research. The authors' views are based on their professional judgment. The names of the organization, individuals, and location have been disguised to preserve the organization's anonymity. Used with permission.*

12:56
23 APR 2011 SAT
+25 °C
8:00AM
2 missed calls
PART
4

Organizing

4

Netflix is an entertainment industry innovator. When DVD technology first hit the market, software designer Reed Hastings mailed discs to himself to see whether they would ship safely. Hastings liked the result, and today the computer whiz's DVD movie delivery service is tops.

Prior to Netflix, film rentals were slow and inconvenient. Today Netflix customers browse film listings online and receive new releases and old classics overnight—with no late fees.

Strategic organizing is key to Netflix's success. Delivering 2 million DVDs to customers daily would be impossible without the retailer's strategically located distribution centers. Netflix operates a single warehouse in Sunnyvale, California, and 100 smaller distribution centers around the country. The smaller centers manage a constant flow of incoming movie returns and outgoing orders, allowing for same-day processing. The purpose of rapid turnaround is to eliminate the need for additional warehouse storage, as Netflix DVDs are kept in customers' homes.

Innovative materials handling is another vital aspect of Netflix's business. Netflix distribution centers feature state-of-the-art automation, such as "stuffer machines" that place DVDs in mailers. In addition, each DVD receives its own UPC code, enabling instant tracking by computer.

But big changes lie ahead for movie distribution. Just as DVDs replaced videocassettes, on-demand digital streaming will eventually make DVDs obsolete. Even now, Netflix customers have the option to stream programs to their TVs using Xbox, Wii, PS3, and other Internet-enabled devices.

As the entertainment industry transitions to digitally distributed media, Netflix will be out in front to guide the way forward. A decade ago, Netflix carried only DVDs; a decade from now, the only DVDs at Netflix will be those hanging on the walls of corporate offices as mementos of the company's early history.

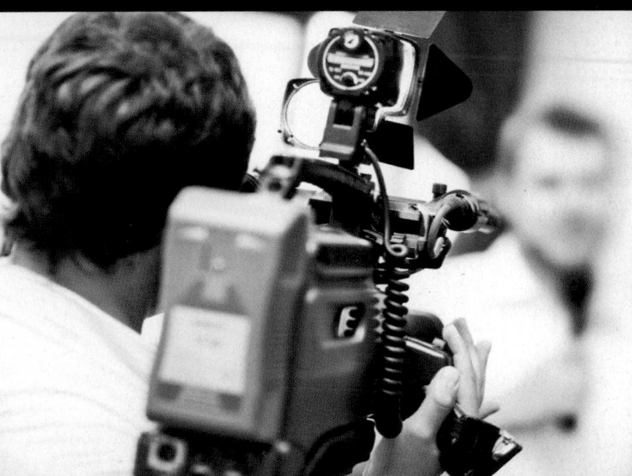

Chapter Outline

Designing Adaptive Organizations

Learning Outcomes

After studying this chapter, you should be able to:

1. Discuss the fundamental characteristics of organizing, including concepts such as work specialization, chain of command, span of management, and centralization versus decentralization.
2. Describe functional and divisional approaches to structure.
3. Explain the matrix approach to structure and its application to both domestic and international organizations.
4. Describe the contemporary team and virtual network structures and why they are being adopted by organizations.
5. Explain why organizations need coordination across departments and hierarchical levels, and describe mechanisms for achieving coordination.
6. Identify how structure can be used to achieve an organization's strategic goals.
7. Define production technology (manufacturing, service, and digital) and explain how it influences organization structure.

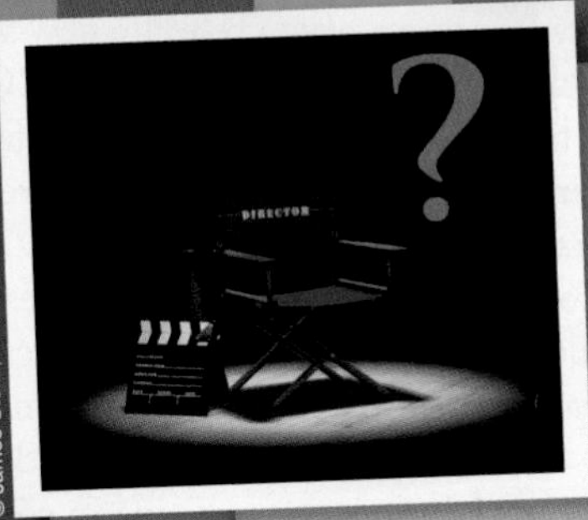

Are You Ready to Be a Manager?

Please circle your opinion below each of the following statements.

1 I am comfortable taking on any authority that is given to me.

Mostly True — Mostly False

(See page 249, Authority, Responsibility, and Delegation.)

2 I am able to delegate tasks to other people; In other words, I do not hold on with tight control or distrust of others.

Mostly True — Mostly False

(See page 252, How to Delegate.)

3 I can work in both an organization that is highly centralized and one that is decentralized with power and authority coming more from smaller units than from top management.

Mostly True — Mostly False

(See page 254, Centralization and Decentralization.)

4 I am a good team player; I work well in groups.

Mostly True — Mostly False

(See page 262, Team Approach.)

5 I can be a productive member of a virtual work group, one that never or rarely has any face-time.

Mostly True — Mostly False

(See page 263, The Virtual Network Approach.)

Dell Computer recently went through two major restructurings in the space of a year, and each time there were several executives who left the company. In some cases, positions were eliminated, but in others the managers chose to leave the organization.[1] Why? A manager's work is influenced by how the company is organized, and when reorganization occurs, some people find that they no longer feel comfortable or effective working in the revised structure. New managers in particular are typically more comfortable and more effective working in an organization system that is compatible with their leadership beliefs.

All organizations wrestle with the question of structural design, and reorganization often is necessary to reflect a new strategy, changing market conditions, or innovative technology. At Dell, for example, CEO Michael Dell is trying to transform the company from a built-to-order computer manufacturer into a provider of a wide range of products and services. To give managers more responsibility and flexibility to respond quickly to customers, he restructured the company into four customer divisions: consumers, large corporations, small and mid-sized businesses, and educational and government agencies. A part of the second restructuring was to create a communication solutions division that will focus specifically on products such as mobile phones and other portable devices.[2]

Managers have to understand and learn to work within a variety of structural configurations. In recent years, many companies have realigned departmental groupings, chains of command, and horizontal coordination mechanisms to attain new strategic goals or to cope with a turbulent environment. Managers at Hachette Filipacchi Media U.S., which owns magazines such as *Elle* and *Woman's Day*, created brand officer positions to increase horizontal coordination across departments and make sure everyone from editorial to event marketing is in the information loop. Wyeth Pharmaceuticals, now part of Pfizer, outsourced its entire clinical testing operation for new drugs to Accenture's Health and Life Sciences Practice in order to improve quality, efficiency, and speed of innovation. And the United States Army added its own aviation division to perform air surveillance in Iraq and Afghanistan. The Army had previously relied totally on surveillance from the Air Force, but resources were limited and had to be assigned by top officers at headquarters, causing delays and poor coordination with battlefield needs. The Army's new unit is on call for commanders in the field and fits with the Army's goal of being more responsive to the needs of smaller combat units in direct conflict with adversaries.[3] Each of these organizations is using fundamental concepts of organizing.

Organizing is the deployment of organizational resources to achieve strategic goals. The deployment of resources is reflected in the organization's division of labor into specific departments and jobs, formal lines of authority, and mechanisms for coordinating diverse organization tasks.

Organizing is important because it follows from strategy—the topic of Part 3. Strategy defines *what* to do; organizing defines *how* to do it. Structure is a powerful tool for reaching strategic goals, and a strategy's success often is determined by its fit with organizational structure. Part 4 explains the variety of organizing principles and concepts used by managers. This chapter covers fundamental concepts that apply to all organizations and departments, including organizing the vertical structure and using mechanisms for horizontal coordination. Chapter 7 discusses how organizations can be structured to facilitate innovation and change. Chapter 9 consider how to use human resources to the best advantage within the organization's structure.

Organizing the Vertical Structure

The organizing process leads to the creation of organization structure, which defines how tasks are divided and resources deployed. **Organization structure** is defined as (1) the set of formal tasks assigned to individuals and departments; (2) formal reporting relationships, including lines of authority, decision responsibility, number of hierarchical levels, and span of managers' control; and (3) the design of systems to ensure effective coordination of employees across departments.[4] Ensuring coordination across departments is just as critical as defining the departments to begin with. Without effective coordination systems, no structure is complete.

The set of formal tasks and formal reporting relationships provides a framework for vertical control of the organization. The characteristics of vertical structure are portrayed in the **organization chart**, which is the visual representation of an organization's structure.

A sample organization chart for a water bottling plant is illustrated in Exhibit 7.1. The plant has four major departments—accounting, human resources, production, and marketing. The organization chart delineates the chain of command, indicates departmental tasks and how they fit together, and provides order and logic for the organization. Every employee has an appointed task, line of authority, and decision responsibility. The following sections discuss several important features of vertical structure in more detail.

Work Specialization

Organizations perform a wide variety of tasks. A fundamental principle is that work can be performed more efficiently if employees are allowed to specialize.[5] **Work specialization**, sometimes called *division of labor*, is the degree to which organizational tasks are subdivided into separate jobs. Work specialization in Exhibit 7.1 is illustrated by the separation of production tasks into bottling, quality control, and maintenance. Employees within each department

EXHIBIT 7.1

Organization Chart for a Water Bottling Plant

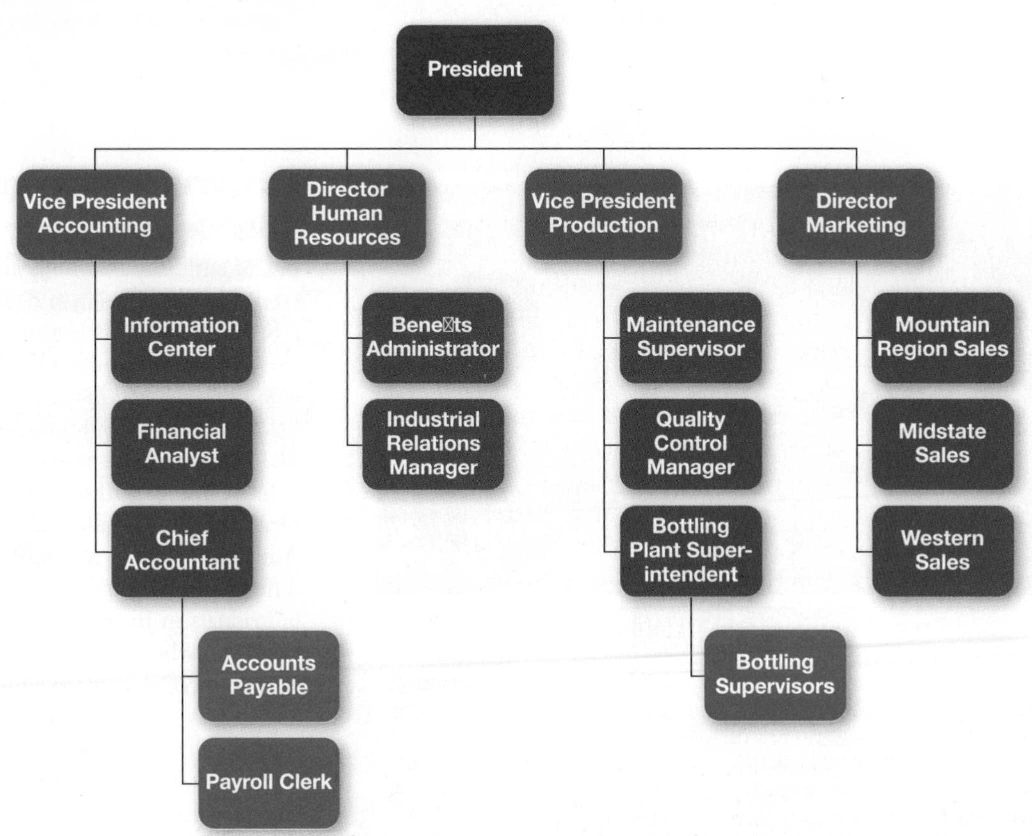

perform only the tasks relevant to their specialized function. When work specialization is extensive, employees specialize in a single task. Jobs tend to be small, but they can be performed efficiently. Work specialization is readily visible on an automobile assembly line, where each employee performs the same task over and over again. It would not be efficient to have a single employee build the entire automobile or even perform a large number of unrelated jobs.

Despite the apparent advantages of specialization, many organizations are moving away from this principle. With too much specialization, employees are isolated and do only a single, boring job. In addition, too much specialization creates separation and hinders the coordination that is essential for organizations to be effective. Many companies are implementing teams and other mechanisms that enhance coordination and provide greater challenge for employees.

- Managers in every organization face the question about how to organize for maximum efficiency and effectiveness.
- **Organizing** refers to the deployment of organizational resources to achieve strategic goals.
- Dell Inc. has undergone several rounds of reorganizing as managers search for the right organization structure to meet new goals.
- **Organization structure** is defined as the framework in which the organization defines how tasks are divided, resources are deployed, and departments are coordinated.
- An **organization chart** is the visual representation of an organization's structure.
- Fundamental characteristics of vertical organization structure include work specialization, chain of command, span of management, and centralization and decentralization.
- **Work specialization**, sometimes called *division of labor*, is the degree to which organizational tasks are subdivided into individual jobs.

Chain of Command

The **chain of command** is an unbroken line of authority that links all employees in an organization and shows who reports to whom. It is associated with two underlying principles. *Unity of command* means that each employee is held accountable to only one supervisor. The *scalar principle* refers to a clearly defined line of authority in the organization that includes all employees. Authority and responsibility for different tasks should be distinct. All individuals in the organization should know to whom they report as well as the successive management levels all the way to the top. In Exhibit 7.1, the payroll clerk reports to the chief accountant, who in turn reports to the vice president, who in turn reports to the company president.

AP Photo/ M.Lakshman

ConceptConnection

Cognizant Technology Solutions Corporation, a U.S.-based outsourcing firm, has an unusual **chain of command** referred to as "two in a box." Originally, project managers supervised company staff in India while themselves living in the United States, where most customers were located. Because spanning that many time zones was difficult, chief operating officer Francisco D'Souza (now CEO, pictured second from right) implemented a solution: Assign two managers to each project, one in India and one at the client's site. Each is equally responsible for the project's success. The model works because it enhances the company's customer responsiveness, even though it violates the principle of **unity of command**.

New Manager Self-Test

What Are Your Leadership Beliefs?

The fit between a new manager and the organization is often based on personal beliefs about the role of leaders. Things work best when organization design matches a new manager's beliefs about his or her leadership role.

Think about the extent to which each statement reflects your beliefs about a leader's role in an organization. Mark as Mostly True the four statements that are *most* true for you, and mark as Mostly False the four that are *least* true for you.

	MOSTLY TRUE <<<	>>> MOSTLY FALSE
1. A leader should take charge of the group or organization.	______	______
2. The major tasks of a leader are to make and communicate decisions.	______	______
3. Group and organization members should be loyal to designated leaders.	______	______
4. The responsibility for taking risks lies with the leaders.	______	______
5. Leaders should foster member discussions about the future.	______	______
6. Successful leaders make everyone's learning their highest priority.	______	______
7. An organization should always be changing the way it does things, to adapt to a changing world.	______	______
8. Everyone in an organization should be responsible for accomplishing organizational goals.	______	______

See It Online

Scoring and Interpretation: Each item pertains to one of two subscales of *leadership beliefs*. Items 1–4 reflect *position-based* leadership beliefs. This is the belief that the most competent and loyal people are placed in positions of leadership, where they assume responsibility and authority for the group or organization. Items 5–8 reflect *nonhierarchical* leadership beliefs. This belief is that the group or organization faces a complex system of adaptive challenges, and leaders see their job as facilitating (1) the flow of information among members and (2) their full engagement to respond to those challenges. The subscale for which you checked more items Mostly True may reveal your personal beliefs about position-based versus nonhierarchical leadership.

Position-based beliefs typically work for managers in a traditional vertical hierarchy or mechanistic organization. Nonhierarchical beliefs typically work for managers engaged with horizontal organizing or organic organizations, such as managing teams, projects, and networks.

SOURCE: This questionnaire is based on Richard M. Wielkiewicz, "The Leadership Attitudes and Beliefs Scale: An Instrument for Evaluating College Students' Thinking About Leadership and Organizations," *Journal of College Student Development* 41 (May–June 2000): 335–346.

Authority, Responsibility, and Delegation The chain of command illustrates the authority structure of the organization. **Authority** is the formal and legitimate right of a manager to make decisions, issue orders, and allocate resources to achieve organizationally desired outcomes. Authority is distinguished by three characteristics:[6]

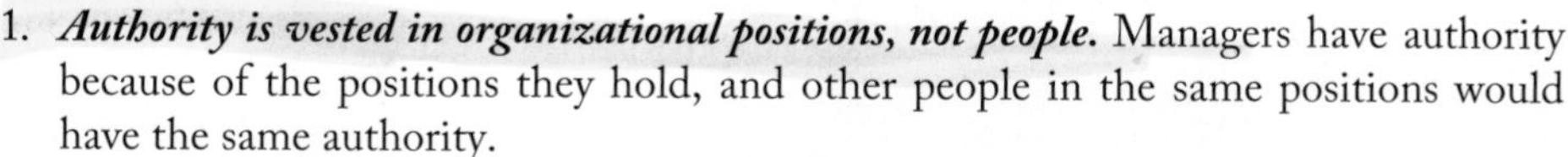

1. ***Authority is vested in organizational positions, not people.*** Managers have authority because of the positions they hold, and other people in the same positions would have the same authority.

2. ***Authority flows down the vertical hierarchy.*** Positions at the top of the hierarchy are vested with more formal authority than are positions at the bottom.
3. ***Authority is accepted by subordinates.*** Although authority flows top-down, subordinates comply because they believe that managers have a legitimate right to issue orders. The *acceptance theory of authority* argues that a manager has authority only if subordinates choose to accept his or her commands. If subordinates refuse to obey because the order is outside their zone of acceptance, a manager's authority disappears.[7]

In order to look at your own attitudes about authority and responsibility, take the New Manager Self-Test about leadership beliefs.

Responsibility is the flip side of the authority coin. **Responsibility** is the duty to perform the task or activity as assigned. Typically, managers are assigned authority commensurate with responsibility. When managers have responsibility for task outcomes but have little authority, the job is possible but difficult. These managers rely on persuasion and luck. When managers have authority exceeding responsibility, they may become tyrants, using authority toward frivolous outcomes.[8]

Accountability is the mechanism through which authority and responsibility are brought into alignment. **Accountability** means that the people with authority and responsibility are subject to reporting and justifying task outcomes to those above them in the chain of command.[9] For organizations to function well, everyone needs to know what they are accountable for and accept the responsibility and authority for performing it.

Another important concept related to authority is delegation.[10] **Delegation** is the process managers use to transfer authority and responsibility to positions below them in the hierarchy. Most organizations today encourage managers to delegate authority to the lowest possible level to provide maximum flexibility to meet customer needs and adapt to shifts in the environment. Consider how managers at the Walt Disney Company used delegation to revive the company's once-famous animation studio.

WALT DISNEY ANIMATION STUDIO

When Bob Iger, CEO of the Walt Disney Company, reached a deal to buy Pixar, some people worried that bringing the successful animation company into Disney's bureaucracy could mean the end of Pixar's flexible, innovative approach—and maybe the end of its string of box-office hits. After all, one of the founders of Pixar, John Lasseter, had earlier been fired from Disney. But Iger took a different approach to the merger. Instead of trying to integrate Pixar into Disney, he gave Pixar's top managers (Lasseter and cofounder Ed Catmull) full control of Walt Disney Animation Studios.

Lasseter and Catmull quickly began implementing changes to transform Disney Animation from "an executive-led studio" to a "filmmaker-led studio," as Lasseter puts it. Previously at Disney, there were layers of executives telling animators what to do, which had squelched creativity and produced a dispirited organization that had lost some of its top employees and left the rest demoralized and unmotivated. Lasseter and Catmull changed the top-down development process by delegating decision-making regarding story ideas, the direction of projects, and other matters to the creative team. For many employees, it was a dream come true.

It turned out to be a blessing for Disney as well. When Catmull and Lasseter arrived, the studio was working on *Bolt.* After delegating decision-making authority to the team, the two issued a challenge: Finish the project in 18 months instead of the four years it normally takes for a computer-generated animation film. The team didn't make it quite that quickly, but *Bolt* came out less than two years later to rave reviews, grossed roughly $280 million worldwide, and was nominated for the best animated feature film in 2009 (it lost to Pixar's *WALL-E*). According to director and team leader Chris Williams, everyone involved had "a feeling this was the beginning of a whole new era for Disney. . . . I have never seen people work so hard or complain so little."[11]

As illustrated by the example of Walt Disney Animation Studios, delegating decision making to lower-level managers and employees can be highly motivating and improve speed, flexibility, and creativity. However, many managers find delegation difficult. When managers can't delegate, they undermine the role of their subordinates and prevent people from doing their jobs effectively. Techniques for effective delegation are discussed in the Spotlight on Skills titled How to Delegate.

Line and Staff Authority An important distinction in many organizations is between line authority and staff authority, reflecting whether managers work in line or staff departments in the organization's structure. *Line departments* perform tasks that reflect the organization's primary goal and mission. In a software company, line departments make and sell the product. In an Internet-based company, line departments would be those that develop and manage online offerings and sales. *Staff departments* include all those that provide specialized skills in support of line departments. Staff departments have an advisory relationship with line departments and typically include marketing, labor relations, research, accounting, and human resources.

Line authority means that people in management positions have formal authority to direct and control immediate subordinates. **Staff authority** is narrower and includes the right to advise, recommend, and counsel in the staff specialists' areas of expertise. Staff authority is a communication relationship; staff specialists advise managers in technical areas. For example, the finance department of a manufacturing firm would have staff authority to coordinate with line departments about which accounting forms to use to facilitate equipment purchases and standardize payroll services.

To understand the importance of the chain of command and clear lines of authority, responsibility, and delegation, consider the BP-Transocean Deepwater Horizon oil rig explosion in the Gulf of Mexico that killed 11 crewmembers and set off an environmental disaster. Activities were so loosely organized that no one seemed to know who was in charge or what their level of authority and responsibility was. When the explosion occurred, confusion reigned. Twenty-three-year-old Andrea Fleytas issued a mayday (distress signal) over the radio when she realized no one else had done so, but she was chastised for overstepping her authority. One manager says he didn't call for help because he wasn't sure he had authorization to do so. Still another said he tried to call to shore but was told the order needed to come from someone else. Crewmembers knew the emergency shutdown needed to be triggered, but there was confusion over who had the authority to give the OK. As fire spread, several minutes passed before people got directions to evacuate. Again, an alarmed Fleytas turned on the public address system and announced that the crew was abandoning the rig. "The scene was very chaotic," said worker Carlos Ramos. "There was no chain of command. Nobody in charge." In the aftermath of the explosion and oil spill, several federal agencies are also on the hot seat because of loose oversight and confusion over responsibility that led to delays and disagreements that prolonged the suffering of local communities.[12]

Go to the Ethical Dilemma, on page 282, that pertains to issues of authority, responsibility, and delegation.

Span of Management

The **span of management** is the number of employees reporting to a supervisor. Sometimes called the *span of control*, this characteristic of structure determines how closely a supervisor can monitor subordinates. Traditional views of organization design recommended a span of management of about 7 to 10 subordinates per manager. However, many lean organizations today have spans of management as high as 30, 40, and even higher. At the PepsiCo, Inc., Gamesa cookie operation in Mexico, for instance, employees are trained to keep production running smoothly and are rewarded for quality,

SPOTLIGHT ON SKILLS

How to Delegate

The attempt by top management to decentralize decision making often gets bogged down because middle managers are unable to delegate. Managers may cling tightly to their decision-making and task responsibilities. Failure to delegate occurs for a number of reasons: Managers are most comfortable making familiar decisions; they feel they will lose personal status by delegating tasks; they believe they can do a better job themselves; or they have an aversion to risk—they will not take a chance on delegating because performance responsibility ultimately rests with them.

Yet decentralization offers an organization many advantages. Decisions are made at the right level, lower-level employees are motivated, and employees have the opportunity to develop decision-making skills. Overcoming barriers to delegation in order to gain these advantages is a major challenge. The following approaches can help each manager delegate more effectively:

1. ***Delegate the whole task.*** A manager should delegate an entire task to one person rather than dividing it among several people. This type of delegation gives the individual complete responsibility and increases his or her initiative while giving the manager some control over the results.
2. ***Select the right person***. Not all employees have the same capabilities and degree of motivation. Managers must match talent to task if delegation is to be effective. They should identify subordinates who made independent decisions in the past and show a desire for more responsibility.
3. ***Ensure that authority equals responsibility***. Merely assigning a task is not effective delegation. Managers often load subordinates with increased responsibility but do not extend their decision-making range. In addition to having responsibility for completing a task, the worker must be given the authority to make decisions about how best to do the job.
4. ***Give thorough instruction.*** Successful delegation includes information on what, when, why, where, who, and how. The subordinate must clearly understand the task and the expected results. It is a good idea to write down all provisions discussed, including required resources and when and how the results will be reported.
5. ***Maintain feedback.*** Feedback means keeping open lines of communication with the subordinate to answer questions and provide advice, but without exerting too much control. Open lines of communication make it easier to trust subordinates. Feedback keeps the subordinate on the right track.
6. ***Evaluate and reward performance.*** Once the task is completed, the manager should evaluate results, not methods. When results do not meet expectations, the manager must assess the consequences. When they do meet expectations, the manager should reward employees for a job well done, with praise, financial rewards when appropriate, and delegation of future assignments.

Are You a Positive Delegator?

Positive delegation is the way an organization implements decentralization. Do you help or hinder the decentralization process? If you answer "yes" to more than three of the following items, you may have a problem delegating:

- I tend to be a perfectionist.
- My boss expects me to know all the details of my job.
- I don't have the time to explain clearly and concisely how a task should be accomplished.
- I often end up doing tasks myself.
- My subordinates typically are not as committed as I am.
- I get upset when other people don't do the task right.
- I really enjoy doing the details of my job to the best of my ability.
- I like to be in control of task outcomes.

SOURCES: Thomas R. Horton, "Delegation and Team Building: No Solo Acts Please," *Management Review* (September 1992): 58–61; Andrew E. Schwartz, "The Why, What, and to Whom of Delegation," *Management Solutions* (June 1987): 31–38; "Delegation," *Small Business Report* (June 1986): 38–43; and Russell Wild, "Clone Yourself," *Working Woman* (May 2000): 79–80.

teamwork, and productivity. Teams are so productive and efficient that Gamesa factories operate with around 56 subordinates per manager.[13] Research over the past 40 or so years shows that span of management varies widely and that several factors influence the span.[14] Generally, when supervisors must be closely involved with subordinates, the span should be small, and when supervisors need little involvement with subordinates, it can be large. The following list describes the factors that are associated with less supervisor involvement and thus larger spans of control.

1. Work performed by subordinates is stable and routine.
2. Subordinates perform similar work tasks.
3. Subordinates are concentrated in a single location.
4. Subordinates are highly trained and need little direction in performing tasks.
5. Rules and procedures defining task activities are available.
6. Support systems and personnel are available for the manager.
7. Little time is required in nonsupervisory activities such as coordination with other departments or planning.
8. Managers' personal preferences and styles favor a large span.

The average span of control used in an organization determines whether the structure is tall or flat. A **tall structure** has an overall narrow span and more hierarchical levels. A **flat structure** has a wide span, is horizontally dispersed, and has fewer hierarchical levels.

Having too many hierarchical levels and narrow spans of control is a common structural problem for organizations. In a recent survey conducted for The Conference Board, 72 percent of managers surveyed said they believed their organizations had too many levels of management.[15] The result may be that routine decisions are made too high in the organization, which pulls higher-level executives away from important long-range strategic issues and limits the creativity, innovativeness, and accountability of lower-level managers.[16] The trend in recent years has been toward wider spans of control as a way to facilitate delegation.[17] Exhibit 7.2 illustrates how an international metals company was reorganized. The multilevel set of managers shown in panel *a* was replaced with 10 operating managers and 9 staff specialists reporting directly to the CEO, as shown in panel *b*. The CEO welcomed this wide span of 19 management subordinates because it fit his style; his management team was top quality and needed little supervision; and they were all located on the same floor of an office building.

EXHIBIT 7.2

Reorganization to Increase Span of Management for President of an International Metals Company

Centralization and Decentralization

Centralization and decentralization pertain to the hierarchical level at which decisions are made. **Centralization** means that decision authority is located near the top of the organization. With **decentralization**, decision authority is pushed downward to lower organization levels. Organizations may have to experiment to find the correct hierarchical level at which to make decisions. For example, most large school systems are highly centralized. However, a study by William Ouchi found that three large urban school systems that shifted to a decentralized structure, giving school principals and teachers more control over staffing, scheduling, and teaching methods and materials, performed better and more efficiently than centralized systems of similar size.[18] In Los Angeles, Mayor Antonio Villaraigosa is trying to turn the struggling public school system around by pushing authority down to principals rather than having all major decisions made at the district level. The initiative currently affects only ten schools where parents and teachers voted to participate, but leaders hope to expand it quickly once positive results are evident. One teacher said that before the change, "every year there would be a new top-down reform fed to us from the district. It was as if the system were set up to be unresponsive."[19]

In the United States and Canada, the trend over the past 30 years has been toward greater decentralization of organizations. Decentralization is believed to relieve the burden on top managers, make greater use of employees' skills and abilities, ensure that decisions are made close to the action by well-informed people, and permit more rapid response to external changes. Stanley McChrystal, former commander of U.S. and NATO forces in Afghanistan, once said, "I learned . . . that any complex task is best approached by flattening hierarchies. It gets everybody feeling like they're in the inner circle, so that they develop a sense of ownership."[20] Nearly a decade of fighting a complex, decentralized enemy has pushed the U.S. armed forces to decentralize as well. The U.S. Army recently implemented its Starfish Program to train leaders to think, act, and operate in a decentralized fashion. The program is based on ideas in Ori Brafman and Rod Beckstrom's *The Starfish and the Spider*, which makes the case that decentralized "starfish" are less vulnerable to attack than centralized "spiders."[21]

However, not every organization should decentralize all decisions. Managers should diagnose the organizational situation and select the decision-making level that will best meet the organization's needs. Factors that typically influence centralization versus decentralization are as follows:

1. ***Greater change and uncertainty in the environment are usually associated with decentralization.*** A good example of how decentralization can help cope with rapid change and uncertainty occurred following Hurricane Katrina. Mississippi Power restored power in just 12 days, thanks largely to a decentralized management system that empowered people at the electrical substations to make rapid on-the-spot decisions.[22]
2. ***The amount of centralization or decentralization should fit the firm's strategy.*** Top executives at New York City Transit are decentralizing the subway system to let managers of individual subway lines make almost every decision about what happens on the tracks, in the trains, and in the stations. Decentralization fits the strategy of responding faster and more directly to customer complaints or other problems.[23] Taking the opposite approach, to compete better with Kohl's and Macy's, managers at JCPenney centralized product planning and buying operations, enabling the company to get more fashionable merchandise to stores quickly and at lower prices. Yahoo! also recentralized some of its operations and divisions to leverage the company's capabilities across business units and give Yahoo! products a more consistent appearance.[24]

3. ***In times of crisis or risk of company failure, authority may be centralized at the top.*** When Honda could not get agreement among divisions about new car models, President Nobuhiko Kawamoto made the decision himself.[25]

- The **chain of command** is an unbroken line of authority that links all individuals in the organization and specifies who reports to whom.
- **Authority** is the formal and legitimate right of a manager to make decisions, issue orders, and allocate resources to achieve outcomes desired by the organization.
- **Responsibility** is the flip side of the authority coin; it refers to the duty to perform the task or activity one has been assigned.
- **Accountability** means that people with authority and responsibility are subject to reporting and justifying task outcomes to those above them in the chain of command.
- When managers transfer authority and responsibility to positions below them in the hierarchy, it is called **delegation**.
- Managers may have **line authority**, which refers to the formal power to direct and control immediate subordinates, or **staff authority**, which refers to the right to advise, counsel, and recommend in the manager's area of expertise.
- **Span of management**, sometimes called *span of control*, refers to the number of employees reporting to a supervisor.
- A **tall structure** is characterized by an overall narrow span of management and a relatively large number of hierarchical levels.
- A **flat structure** is characterized by an overall broad span of management and relatively few hierarchical levels.
- The trend is toward broader spans of management and greater decentralization.
- **Decentralization** means that decision authority is pushed down to lower organization levels.
- **Centralization** means that decision authority is located near top organization levels.

Departmentalization

Another fundamental characteristic of organization structure is **departmentalization**, which is the basis for grouping positions into departments and departments into the total organization. Managers make choices about how to use the chain of command to group people together to perform their work. Five approaches to structural design reflect different uses of the chain of command in departmentalization, as illustrated in Exhibit 7.3. The functional, divisional, and matrix are traditional approaches that rely on the chain of command to define departmental groupings and reporting relationships along the hierarchy. Two innovative approaches are the use of teams and virtual networks, which have emerged to meet changing organizational needs in a turbulent global environment. Sometimes departments or even larger units do not have adequate accountability, as was discussed earlier in this chapter, which was the problem at French automaker Renault, described in this chapter's Business Blooper.

The basic difference among structures illustrated in Exhibit 7.3 is the way in which employees are departmentalized and the persons to whom they report.[26] Each structural approach is described in detail in the following sections.

EXHIBIT 7.3

Five Approaches to Structural Design

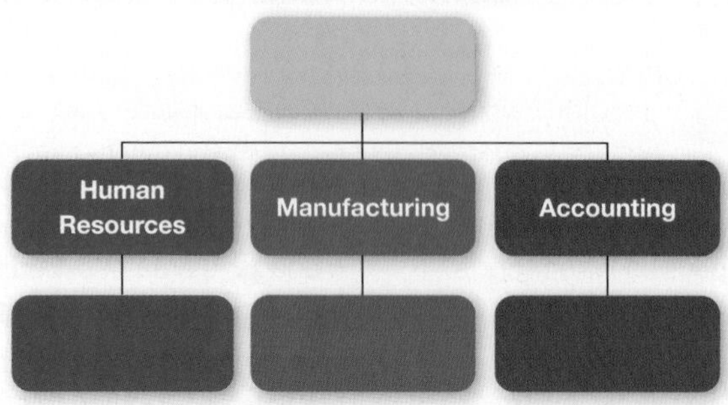

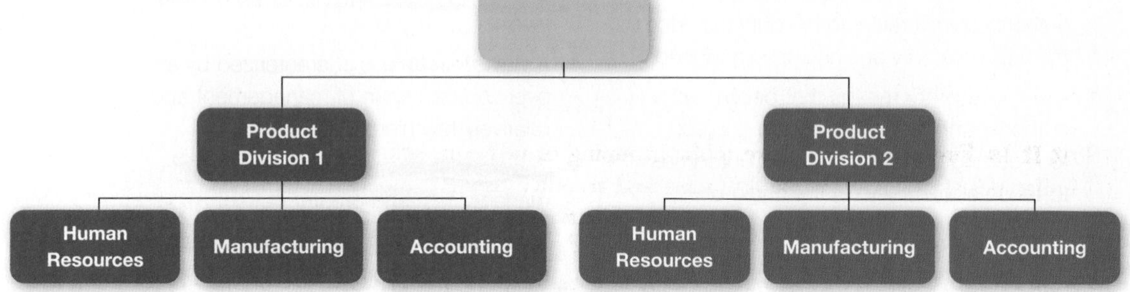

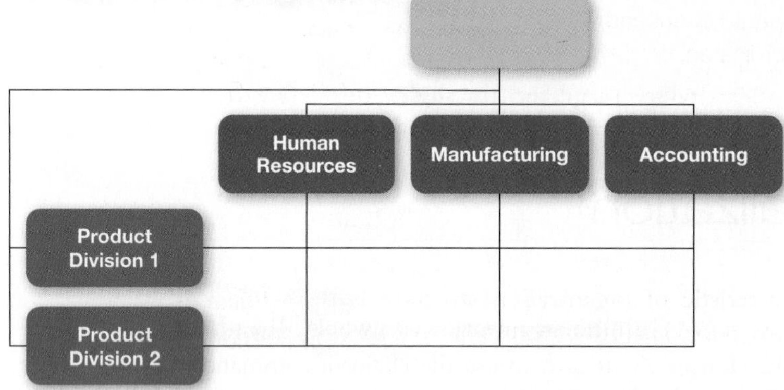

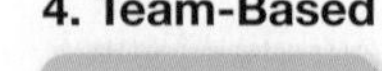

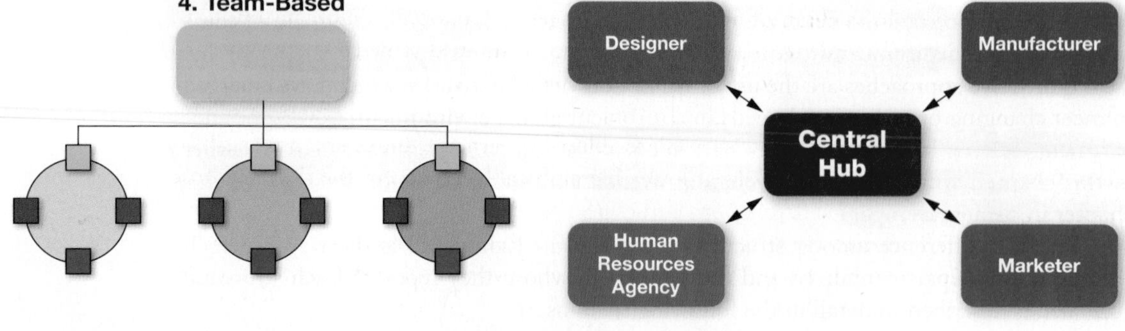

BUSINESS BLOOPER

Renault

What if you accused three employees of being corporate spies trying to sell company secrets to the likes of China and then, after firing them, discovered they weren't spies at all? Plus now you'd offended the innocent Chinese. The case fell apart when French police could not find the Swiss bank accounts into which the three men were accused of funneling the money. Instead, the authorities uncovered evidence that pointed to a scheme designed to defraud the company. Now Renault is paying purportedly $15.9 million euros to the wrongly accused non-spies, and it has dismissed its CEO and six others believed to be part of the fraud. Internal and external audits found the French automaker had "a chain of failures" in the unjust accusations and faulted "the supervision and control of the activities of the management of the company's security department." The local workers' union said the blunders weren't from just a few managers, but more widespread, and would not result in any changes "without an overhaul of the function and structure of management at every level."

SOURCE: David Jolly, "An Upheaval at Renault after 'Failures' in a Spy Case," *The New York Times*, April 12, 2011.

Vertical Functional Approach

What It Is **Functional structure** is the grouping of positions into departments based on similar skills, expertise, work activities, and resource use. A functional structure can be thought of as departmentalization by organizational resources, because each type of functional activity—accounting, human resources, engineering, and manufacturing—represents specific resources for performing the organization's task. People, facilities, and other resources representing a common function are grouped into a single department. One example is Blue Bell Creameries, which relies on in-depth expertise in its various functional departments to produce high-quality ice creams for a limited regional market. The quality-control department, for example, tests all incoming ingredients and ensures that only the best go into Blue Bell's ice cream. Quality inspectors also test outgoing products and, because of their years of experience, can detect the slightest deviation from expected quality. Blue Bell also has functional departments such as sales, production, maintenance, distribution, research and development, and finance.[27]

How It Works Refer to Exhibit 7.1, on page 247, for an example of a functional structure. The major departments under the president are groupings of similar expertise and resources, such as accounting, human resources, production, and marketing. Each of the functional departments is concerned with the organization as a whole. The marketing department is responsible for all sales and marketing, for example, and the accounting department handles financial issues for the entire company.

The functional structure is a strong vertical design. Information flows up and down the vertical hierarchy, and the chain of command converges at the top of the organization. In a functional structure, people within a department communicate primarily with others in the same department to coordinate work and accomplish tasks or implement decisions that are passed down the hierarchy. Managers and employees are compatible because of similar training and expertise. Typically, rules and procedures govern the duties and responsibilities of each employee, and employees at lower hierarchical levels accept the right of those higher in the hierarchy to make decisions and issue orders. Rajeev Goyal understands hierarchy and chain of command in an unusual way and, as a result, has been responsible for the dramatic increase in funding for the Peace Corps despite overall congressional cutbacks, as shown in the Benchmarking box.

BENCHMARKING

Peace Corps

Thirty-one year-old Rajeev Goyal looks like a college student. He grew up on Long Island, New York, graduated from Brown University in pre-med, and served as a volunteer to the Peace Corps from 2001 to 2003 in Nepal, which is very similar to his immigrant parents' country, India. He was sent to teach English in a village of fewer than 600 people. But Rajeev couldn't help but notice how much time people spent hauling water, often three times a day, making arduous trips. So he consulted engineers and studied hydraulic pumps, piping, and filtration systems. He flew back to Long Island and raised US$18,000 from his father's doctor friends. He had to organize labor and find tools, both in his village and those nearby. He learned who were the villages' informal leaders, the ones he needed to get onboard because then everyone else would follow. He called his mission "the village well-route," or the path to success. Rajeev succeeded in enlisting 540 people in several villages to volunteer, and after many challenges, finally got water pumped into the village.

Back in the United States, the Peace Corps was slipping in the public's mind and in funding. It was at half its 1966 levels despite an increase in applications post 9/11. Kevin Quigley, head of the Peace Corps Organization, saw that the vast community of former volunteers had become too passive. "You have to get organized," he said. They hired Rajeev to help them. Rajeev realized that the U.S. Congress is structured not unlike an Indian or Nepalese village, with a caste system to navigate. He had to find the equivalent of a "village well-route." This turned out to be the hallways in congressional buildings, the hearing rooms, and the coffee shops where people hung out, where he just might be able to meet a member of Congress. "He just picked off Democrats and Republicans one by one," said Sam Farr (D–Calif.). "I don't know lobbyists who are that persistent." Rajeev's methods might rankle some, but he has gotten more money for the Peace Corps than anyone thought possible. "I've been in Congress for 17 years, and always lobbying for the Peace Corps, but I've never been as effective as I have in the last two sessions," Farr said. "And I would attribute that to Rajeev."

Rajeev learned from a colleague in Nepal that individuals are more important than the system, and you have to work through the people with authority. "His [Rajeev's colleague's] style is to go directly to the most powerful person and ask what he wants," Rajeev said. At first this was hard to do in Washington, until Rajeev got a book with color photographs of all members of the House and the Senate. He recognized someone at the airport, another person at Starbucks, someone else at Le Pain Quotidien, and he would just start conversations with these people. He went to committee hearings, so he could talk during breaks to officials. He was told this routine was called "bird-dogging" and that most lobbyists don't do this. He read everyone's background and history, so he had something to talk about when he ran into a member of Congress. In two days recently, he saw 15 senators without an appointment. When Diane Feinstein said the economic climate was not good to ask for increases, he told her that compared to the $5.5 billion military budget, what he was asking for—$46 million—was "dust," and she said she'd look at his proposal. And then she approved it. Rajeev takes it all philosophically. "People believe that in order to be in politics, you have to be a politician. That's not true. You can be the lowest villager and still be involved."

SOURCE: Peter Hessler, "Village Voice," *The New Yorker* (December 20 & 27, 2010): 100–109.

Divisional Approach

What It Is In contrast to the functional approach, in which people are grouped by common skills and resources, the **divisional structure** occurs when departments are grouped together based on similar organizational outputs. The divisional structure is sometimes called a *product structure*, *program structure*, or *self-contained unit structure*. Each of these terms means essentially the same thing: Diverse departments are brought together to produce a single organizational output, whether it is a product, a program, or service to a single customer.

Most large corporations have separate divisions that perform different tasks, use different technologies, or serve different customers. When a huge organization produces products for different markets, the divisional structure works because each division is an autonomous business. For example, Sony Corporation includes divisions such as Sony Pictures Entertainment, Sony Disc & Digital Solutions, Sony Financial Holdings, and Sony Ericsson Mobile Communications, among others.[28] United Technologies Corporation (UTC), which is among the 50 largest U.S. industrial firms, has numerous divisions, including Carrier (air conditioners and heating), Otis (elevators and escalators), Pratt & Whitney (aircraft engines), and Sikorsky (helicopters).[29]

How It Works Functional and divisional structures are illustrated in Exhibit 7.4. In the divisional structure, divisions are created as self-contained units with separate functional departments for each division. For example, in Exhibit 7.4, each functional department resource needed to produce the product is assigned to each division. Whereas in a functional structure, all research-and-development (R&D) engineers are grouped together and work on all products, in a divisional structure

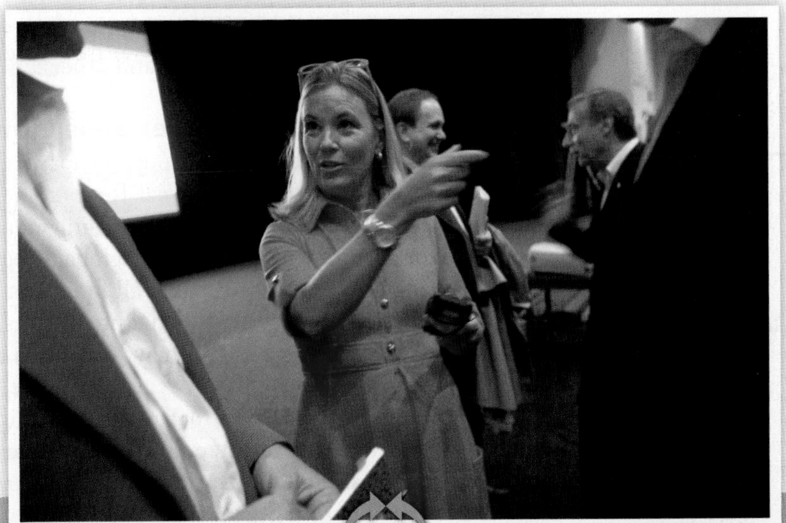

Librado Romero/The New York Times

ConceptConnection

Mary Berner started her job as chief executive of Reader's Digest Association by realigning its business units. She broke up the book and magazine units and reorganized them along consumer interests. This revised **divisional structure** created ad-friendly clusters of consumer interests such as the Food and Entertaining unit, which includes magazines *Every Day with Rachel Ray* and *Taste of Home* along with Allrecipes.com.

EXHIBIT 7.4

Functional versus Divisional Structures

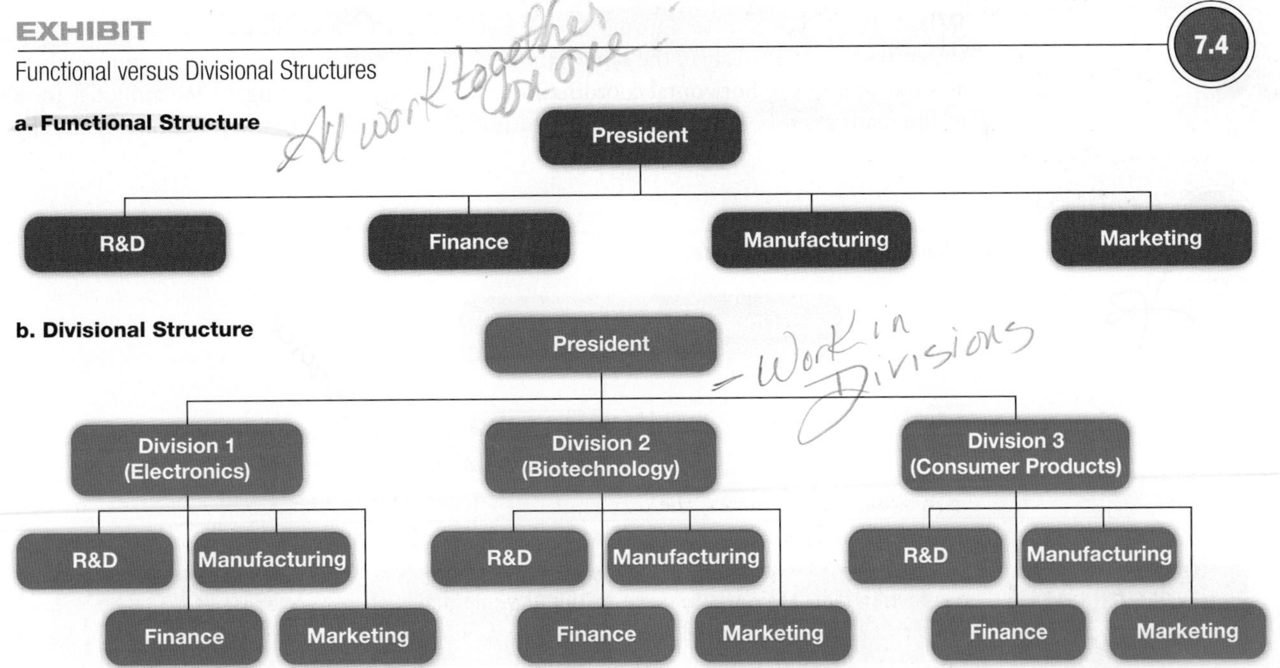

separate R&D departments are created within each division. Each department is smaller and focuses on a single product line or customer segment. Departments are duplicated across product lines.

The primary difference between divisional and functional structures is that the chain of command from each function converges lower in the hierarchy. In a divisional structure, differences of opinion among R&D, marketing, manufacturing, and finance would be resolved at the divisional level rather than by the president. Thus, the divisional structure encourages decentralization. Decision making is pushed down at least one level in the hierarchy, freeing the president and other top managers for strategic planning.

Geographic- or Customer-Based Divisions An alternative for assigning divisional responsibility is to group company activities by geographic region or customer group. For example, the Internal Revenue Service shifted to a structure focused on four distinct taxpayer (customer) groups: individuals, small businesses, corporations, and non-profit or government agencies.[30] A global geographic structure is illustrated in Exhibit 7.5. In a geographic-based structure, all functions in a specific country or region report to the same division manager. The structure focuses company activities on local market conditions. Competitive advantage may come from the production or sale of a product or service adapted to a given country or region. Colgate-Palmolive Company operates in 200 countries and is organized into four regional divisions: North America, Europe-South Pacific, Latin America, and Greater Asia-Africa.[31] The geographic structure works for Colgate because personal care products often have to be tailored to cultural values and local customs.

Large nonprofit organizations such as the United Way, National Council of YMCAs, Habitat for Humanity International, and the Girl Scouts of the USA also frequently use a type of geographical structure, with a central headquarters and semiautonomous local units. The national organization provides brand recognition, coordinates fund-raising services, and handles some shared administrative functions, while day-to-day control and decision making are decentralized to local or regional units.[32]

Matrix Approach

What It Is The **matrix approach** combines aspects of both functional and divisional structures simultaneously in the same part of the organization. The matrix structure evolved as a way to improve horizontal coordination and information sharing.[33] One unique feature of the matrix is that it has dual lines of authority. In Exhibit 7.6, the functional hierarchy

7.5 EXHIBIT

Geographic-Based Global Organization Structure

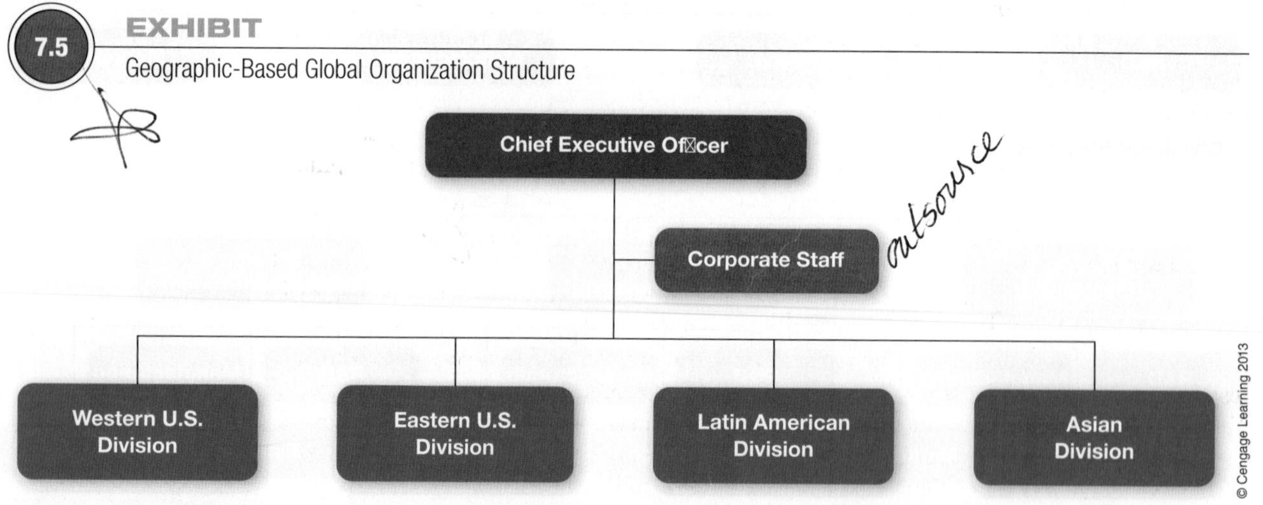

EXHIBIT 7.6

Dual-Authority Structure in a Matrix Organization

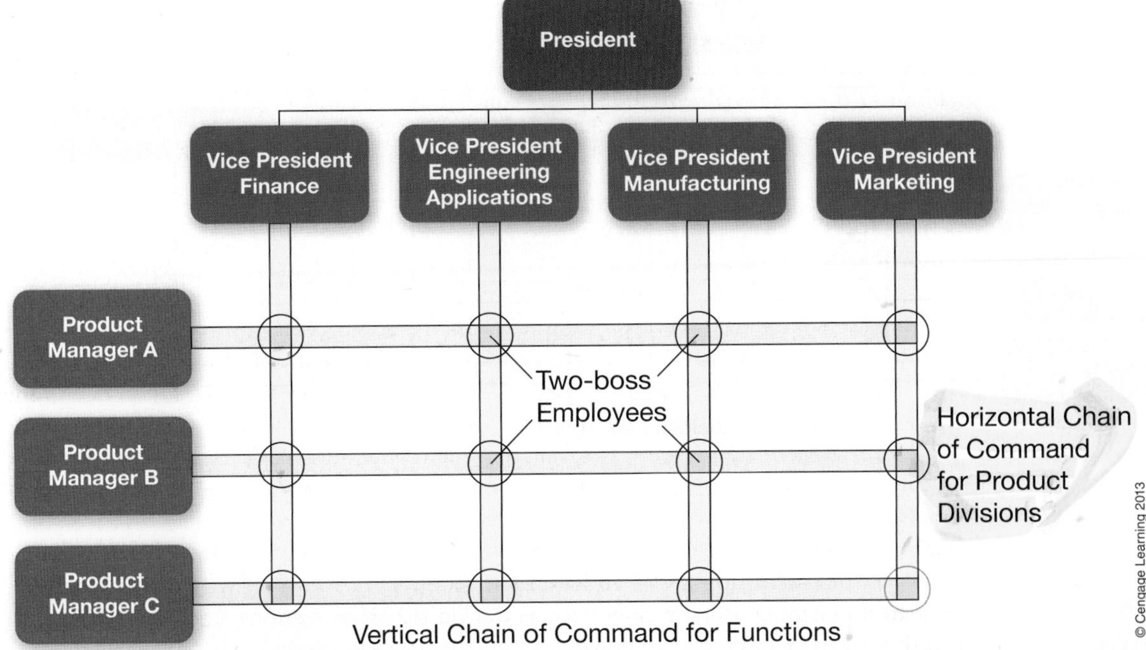

of authority runs vertically, and the divisional hierarchy of authority runs horizontally. The vertical structure provides traditional control within functional departments, and the horizontal structure provides coordination across departments. The matrix structure therefore supports a formal chain of command for both functional (vertical) and divisional (horizontal) relationships. As a result of this dual structure, some employees actually report to two supervisors simultaneously.

How It Works The dual lines of authority make the matrix unique. To see how the matrix works, consider the global matrix structure illustrated in Exhibit 7.7. The two lines of authority are geographic and product. The geographic boss in Germany coordinates all subsidiaries in Germany, and the plastics products boss coordinates the manufacturing and sale of plastics products around the world. Managers of local subsidiary companies in Germany would report to two superiors, both the country boss and the product boss. The dual authority structure violates the unity-of-command concept described earlier in this chapter, but is necessary to give equal emphasis to both functional and divisional lines of authority. Dual lines of authority can be confusing, but after managers learn to use this structure, the matrix provides excellent coordination simultaneously for each geographic region and each product line.

The success of the matrix structure depends on the abilities of people in key matrix roles. **Two-boss employees**, those who report to two supervisors simultaneously, must resolve conflicting demands from the matrix bosses. They must work with senior managers to reach joint decisions. They need excellent human relations skills with which to confront managers and resolve conflicts. The **matrix boss** is the product or functional boss, who is responsible for one side of the matrix. The top leader is responsible for the entire matrix. The **top leader** oversees both the product and functional chains of command. His or her responsibility is to maintain a power balance between the two sides of the matrix. If disputes arise between them, the problem will be kicked upstairs to the top leader.

EXHIBIT 7.7
Global Matrix Structure

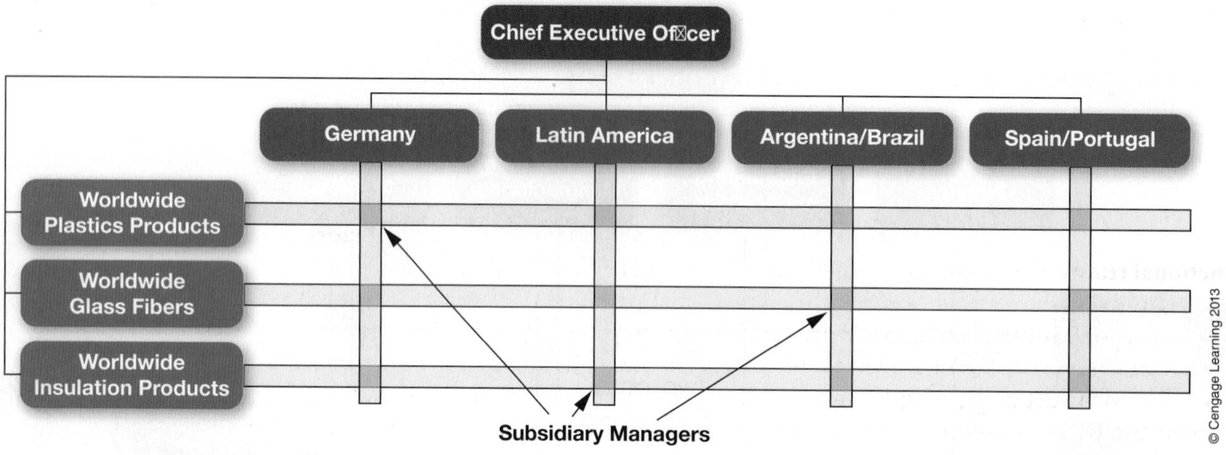

- **Departmentalization** is the basis for grouping individual positions into departments and departments into the total organization.
- Three traditional approaches to departmentalization are functional, divisional, and matrix.
- A **functional structure** groups employees into departments based on similar skills, tasks, and use of resources.
- The **divisional structure** groups employees and departments based on similar organizational outputs (products or services), such that each division has a mix of functional skills and tasks.
- An alternative approach to divisional structure is to group employees and departments based on geographic region or customer group.
- Colgate-Palmolive is structured into four geographic divisions.
- The **matrix approach** uses both functional and divisional chains of command simultaneously in the same part of the organization.
- In a matrix structure, some employees, called **two-boss employees**, report to two supervisors simultaneously.
- A **matrix boss** is a functional or product supervisor responsible for one side of the matrix.
- In a matrix structure, the **top leader** is the overseer of both the product and the functional chains of command and is responsible for the entire matrix.

Team Approach

What It Is Probably the most widespread trend in departmentalization in recent years has been the implementation of team concepts. The vertical chain of command is a powerful means of control, but passing all decisions up the hierarchy takes too long and keeps responsibility at the top. The team approach gives managers a way to delegate authority, push responsibility to lower levels, and be more flexible and responsive in a complex and competitive global environment. For example, teams are part of the strategy used by the Federal Bureau of Investigation (FBI) to combat terrorism. The FBI, like other organizations, must find ways to operate with limited resources. After the September 11, 2001, terrorist attacks in the United States, managers realized they couldn't fully staff offices around the globe and knew they needed to find better ways to use existing resources. One innovation was the creation of Flying Squads, which are teams of volunteer agents and support staff from various offices who are ready to spring into action when minimally staffed FBI offices around the world request assistance.[34] Chapter 14 will discuss teams in detail.

How It Works One approach to using teams in organizations is through **cross-functional teams**, which consist of employees from various functional departments who are responsible to meet as a team and resolve mutual problems. Team members typically still report to their functional departments, but they also report to the team, one member of whom may be the leader. Cross-functional teams are used to provide needed horizontal coordination to complement an existing divisional or functional structure. A frequent use of cross-functional teams is for change projects, such as new product or service innovation.

The second approach is to use **permanent teams**, groups of employees who are organized in a way similar to a formal department. Each team brings together employees from all functional areas, focused on a specific task or project, such as parts supply and logistics for an automobile plant. Emphasis is on horizontal communication and information sharing because representatives from all functions are coordinating their work and skills to complete a specific organizational task. Authority is pushed down to lower levels, and front-line employees are often given the freedom to make decisions and take action on their own. Team members may share or rotate team leadership. With a **team-based structure**, the entire organization is made up of horizontal teams that coordinate their work and work directly with customers to accomplish the organization's goals. At Whole Foods Market, a team structure is considered a major contributor to the company's success. Each Whole Foods store is made up of eight or so self-directed teams that oversee departments such as fresh produce, prepared foods, dairy, or checkout. Teams are responsible for all key operating decisions, such as product selection, pricing, ordering, hiring, and in-store promotions, and they are accountable for their performance.[35]

The Virtual Network Approach

What It Is The most recent approach to departmentalization extends the idea of horizontal coordination and collaboration beyond the boundaries of the organization. In a variety of industries, vertically integrated, hierarchical organizations are giving way to loosely interconnected groups of companies with permeable boundaries.[36] *Outsourcing*, which means farming out certain activities, such as manufacturing or credit processing, has become a significant trend. Hitachi once made all its own televisions with Hitachi-made components, but the company is now outsourcing manufacturing and getting key components from outside suppliers. The pharmaceuticals company Pfizer is using an innovative approach that lets some employees pass off certain parts of their jobs to an outsourcing firm in India with a click of a button. Rather than shifting entire functions to contractors, this "personal outsourcing" approach allows people to shift only certain tedious and time-consuming tasks to be handled by the outsourcing partner while they focus on higher-value work.[37]

Some organizations take this networking approach to the extreme to create an innovative structure. The **virtual network structure** means that the firm subcontracts most of its major functions to separate companies and coordinates their activities from a small headquarters organization.[38] Randy and Nicola Wilburn run real estate, consulting, design, and baby food businesses out of their home by contracting with freelance professionals around the world to write promotional materials, design logos, update Web sites, handle legal paperwork, and perform numerous other activities and functions.[39]

How It Works The organization may be viewed as a central hub surrounded by a network of outside specialists, sometimes spread all over the world, as illustrated in Exhibit 7.8. Rather than being housed under one roof, services such as accounting, design, manufacturing, and distribution are outsourced to separate organizations that are connected electronically to the central office.[40] Networked computer systems, collaborative software, and the Internet enable organizations to exchange data and information so rapidly and smoothly that a loosely connected network of suppliers, manufacturers, assemblers, and distributors can look and act like one seamless company.

The idea behind networks is that a company can concentrate on what it does best and contract out other activities to companies with distinctive competence in those specific areas, which enables a company to do more with less.[41] The "heart-healthy" food company Smart Balance has been able to innovate and expand rapidly by using a virtual network approach, as shown in the Spotlight on Skills titled Smart Balance.

With a network structure such as that used at Smart Balance, it is difficult to answer the question "Where is the organization?" in traditional terms. The different organizational parts are drawn together contractually and coordinated electronically, creating a new form of organization. Much like building blocks, parts of the network can be added or taken away to meet changing needs.[42]

A similar approach to networking is called the **modular approach**, in which a manufacturing company uses outside suppliers to provide entire chunks of a product, which are then assembled into a final product by a handful of workers. The modular approach hands off responsibility for engineering and production of entire sections of a product, such as

7.8 **EXHIBIT**

Network Approach to Departmentalization

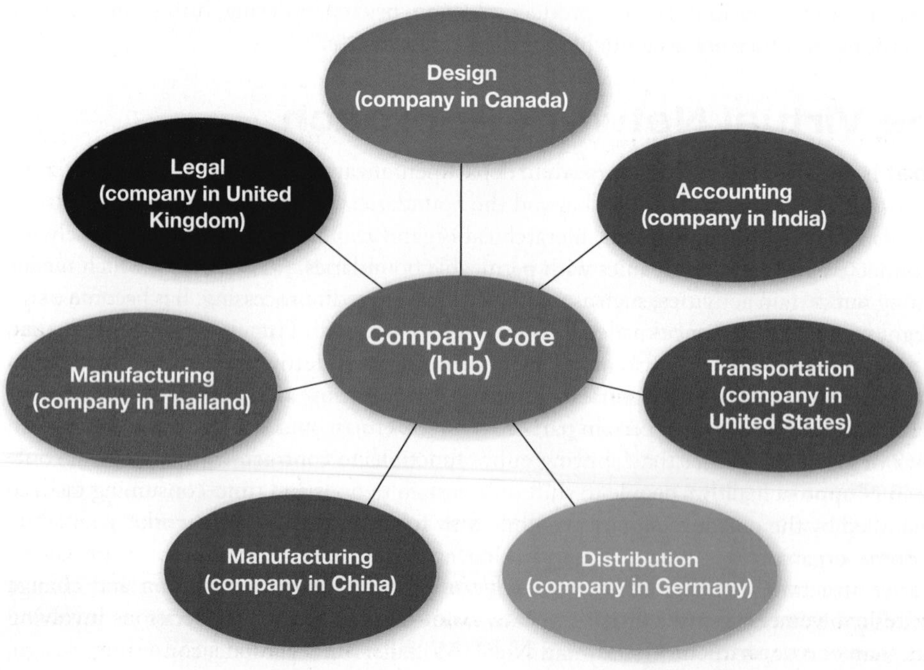

SPOTLIGHT ON SKILLS

Smart Balance

Smart Balance has about 67 employees, but nearly 400 people are working for the company. Smart Balance started by making a buttery spread and now has a line of spreads, all-natural peanut butter, nutrient-enhanced milk, cheese, sour cream, popcorn, and other products. Managers credit the virtual network approach for helping the company innovate and expand rapidly.

Smart Balance keeps product development and marketing in-house, but uses contractors to do just about everything else, including manufacturing, distribution, sales, information technology services, and research and testing. The way the company got into the milk business shows how the network structure increases speed and flexibility. Peter Dray, vice president of product development, was able to get the help he needed to perfect the product from contractors. Outside scientists and research and development consultants worked on the formula. The company contracted with a dairy processor to do tests and trial production runs. An outside laboratory assessed nutritional claims, and another company managed consumer taste tests.

Each morning, full-time employees and virtual workers exchange a flurry of e-mail messages and phone calls to update each other on what took place the day before and what needs to happen today. Executives spend much of their time managing relationships. Twice a year they hold all-company meetings that include permanent staff and contractors. Information is shared widely, and managers make a point of recognizing the contributions of contractors to the company's success, which helps create a sense of unity and commitment.

SOURCES: Joann S. Lublin, "Smart Balance Keeps Tight Focus on Creativity" (Theory & Practice column), *The Wall Street Journal*, June 8, 2009; and Rebecca Reisner, "A Smart Balance of Staff and Contractors," *BusinessWeek Online*, June 16, 2009, www.businessweek.com/managing/content/jun2009/ca20090616_217232.htm (accessed April 30, 2010).

a Volkswagen automobile or a Boeing airplane, to outside suppliers. Suppliers design a module, making some of the parts themselves and subcontracting others. These modules are delivered right to the assembly line, where a handful of employees bolt them together into a finished vehicle.[43]

Advantages and Disadvantages of Each Structure

Each of these approaches to departmentalization—functional, divisional, matrix, team, and network—has strengths and weaknesses. The major advantages and disadvantages of each are listed in Exhibit 7.9.

Functional Approach Grouping employees by common task permits economies of scale and efficient resource use. For example, at American Airlines, all information technology (IT) people work in the same large department. They have the expertise and skills to handle almost any IT problem for the organization. Large, functionally based departments enhance the development of in-depth skills because people work on a variety of related problems and are associated with other experts within their own department. Because the chain of command converges at the top, the functional structure also offers a way to centralize decision making and provide unified direction from top managers. The primary disadvantages reflect barriers that exist across departments. Because people are separated into distinct departments, communication and coordination across functions are often poor, causing a slow response to environmental changes. Innovation and change require involvement of several departments. Another problem is that decisions involving more than one department may pile up at the top of the organization and be delayed.

EXHIBIT 7.9

Structural Advantages and Disadvantages

Structural Approach	Advantages	Disadvantages
Functional	Efficient use of resources; economies of scale In-depth skill specialization and development Top manager direction and control	Poor communication across functional departments Slow response to external changes; lagging innovation Decisions concentrated at top of hierarchy, creating delay
Divisional	Fast response, flexibility in unstable environment Fosters concern for customer needs Excellent coordination across functional departments	Duplication of resources across divisions Less technical depth and specialization Poor coordination across divisions
Matrix	More efficient use of resources than single hierarchy Flexibility, adaptability to changing environment Interdisciplinary cooperation, expertise available to all divisions	Frustration and confusion from dual chain of command High conflict between two sides of the matrix Many meetings, more discussion than action
Team	Reduced barriers among departments, increased compromise Shorter response time, quicker decisions Better morale, enthusiasm from employee involvement	Dual loyalties and conflict Time and resources spent on meetings Unplanned decentralization
Virtual Network	Can draw on expertise worldwide Highly flexible and responsive Reduced overhead costs	Lack of control; weak boundaries Greater demands on managers Weaker employee loyalty

Divisional Approach By dividing employees and resources along divisional lines, the organization will be flexible and responsive to change because each unit is small and tuned in to its environment. By having employees working on a single product line, the concern for customers' needs is high. Coordination across functional departments is better because employees are grouped together in a single location and committed to one product line. Great coordination exists within divisions; however, coordination *across* divisions is often poor. Problems occurred at Hewlett-Packard, for example, when autonomous divisions went in opposite directions. The software produced in one division did not fit the hardware produced in another. Thus, the divisional structure was realigned to establish adequate coordination across divisions. Another major disadvantage is duplication of resources and the high cost of running separate divisions. Instead of a single research department in which all research people use a single facility, each division may have its own research facility. The organization loses efficiency and economies of scale. In addition, the small size of departments within each division may result in a lack of technical specialization, expertise, and training.

Matrix Approach The matrix structure is controversial because of the dual chain of command. However, the matrix can be highly effective in a complex, rapidly changing environment in which the organization needs to be flexible, innovative, and adaptable.[44] The conflict and frequent meetings generated by the matrix allow new issues to be raised and resolved. The matrix structure makes efficient use of human resources because specialists can be transferred from one division to another. The major problem is the confusion and frustration caused by the dual chain of command. Matrix bosses and two-boss employees have difficulty with the dual reporting relationships. The matrix structure also can generate high conflict because it pits divisional against functional goals in a domestic structure, or product line versus country goals in a global structure. Rivalry between the two sides of the matrix can be exceedingly difficult for two-boss employees to manage. This problem leads to the third disadvantage: time lost to meetings and discussions devoted to resolving this conflict. Often the matrix structure leads to more discussion than action because different goals and points of view are being addressed. Managers may spend a great deal of time coordinating meetings and assignments, which takes time away from core work activities.[45]

Team Approach The team approach breaks down barriers across departments and improves coordination and cooperation. Team members know one another's problems and compromise rather than blindly pursue their own goals. The team concept also enables the organization to more quickly adapt to customer requests and environmental changes and speeds decision making because decisions need not go to the top of the hierarchy for approval. Another big advantage is the morale boost. Employees are typically enthusiastic about their involvement in bigger projects rather than narrow departmental tasks. At video games company Ubisoft, for example, each studio is set up so that teams of employees and managers work collaboratively to develop new games. Employees don't make a lot of money, but they're motivated by the freedom they have to propose new ideas and put them into action.[46]

Yet the team approach has disadvantages as well. Employees may be enthusiastic about team participation, but they may also experience conflicts and dual loyalties. A cross-functional team may make different work demands on members than do their department managers, and members who participate in more than one team must resolve these conflicts. A large amount of time is devoted to meetings, thus increasing coordination time. Unless the organization truly needs teams to coordinate complex projects and adapt to the environment, it will lose production efficiency with them. Finally, the team approach may cause too much decentralization. Senior department managers who traditionally made decisions might feel left out when a team moves ahead on its own. Team members often do not see the big picture of the corporation and may make decisions that are good for their group but bad for the organization as a whole.

Virtual Network Approach The biggest advantages to a virtual network approach are flexibility and competitiveness on a global scale. The extreme flexibility of a network approach is illustrated by today's "war on terrorism." Most experts agree that the primary reason the insurgency is so difficult to fight is that it is a far-flung collection of groups that share a specific mission, but are free to act on their own. "Attack any single part of it, and the rest carries on largely untouched," wrote one journalist after talking with U.S. and Iraqi officials. "It cannot be decapitated because the insurgency, for the most part, has no head."[47] One response of the United States and its allies is to organize into networks to quickly change course, put new people in place as needed, and respond to situations and challenges as they emerge.[48]

Similarly, today's business organizations can benefit from a flexible network approach that lets them shift resources and respond quickly. A network organization can draw on resources and expertise worldwide to achieve the best quality and price and can sell its products and services worldwide. Flexibility comes from the ability to hire whatever services are needed and to change a few months later without constraints from owning plants, equipment, and facilities. The organization can continually redefine itself to fit new product and market opportunities. This structure is perhaps the leanest of all organization forms because little supervision is required. Large teams of staff specialists and administrators are not needed. A network organization may have only two or three levels of hierarchy, compared with ten or more in traditional organizations.[49]

One of the major disadvantages is lack of hands-on control.[50] Managers do not have all operations under one roof and must rely on contracts, coordination, negotiation, and electronic linkages to hold things together. Each partner in the network necessarily acts in its own self-interest. The weak and ambiguous boundaries create higher uncertainty and greater demands on managers for defining shared goals, coordinating activities, managing relationships, and keeping people focused and motivated. Finally, in this type of organization, employee loyalty can weaken. Employees might feel they can be replaced by contract services. A cohesive corporate culture is less likely to develop, and turnover tends to be higher because emotional commitment between organization and employee is fragile.

- Popular contemporary approaches to departmentalization include team and virtual network structures.
- To be more responsive in the fight against terrorism, the FBI created Flying Squad teams that spring into action when minimally staffed offices request assistance.
- A **cross-functional team** is a group of employees from various functional departments that meet as a team to resolve mutual problems.
- A **permanent team** is a group of employees from all functional areas permanently assigned to focus on a specific task or activity.
- A **team-based structure** is one in which the entire organization is made up of horizontal teams that coordinate their activities and work directly with customers to accomplish organizational goals.
- Whole Foods Market uses a team-based structure.
- With a **virtual network structure**, the organization subcontracts most of its major functions to separate companies and coordinates their activities from a small headquarters organization.
- The **modular approach** is one in which a manufacturing company uses outside suppliers to provide large chunks of a product such as an automobile, which are then assembled into a final product by a few employees.
- Each approach to departmentalization has distinct advantages and disadvantages.

Organizing for Horizontal Coordination

One reason for the growing use of teams and networks is that many companies are recognizing the limits of traditional vertical organization structures in a fast-shifting environment. In general, the trend is toward breaking down barriers between departments, and many companies are moving toward horizontal structures based on work processes rather than departmental functions.[51] However, regardless of the type of structure, every organization needs mechanisms for horizontal integration and coordination. The structure of an organization is not complete without designing the horizontal as well as the vertical dimensions of structure.[52]

The Need for Coordination

As organizations grow and evolve, two things happen. First, new positions and departments are added to deal with factors in the external environment or with new strategic needs. For example, U.S. President Barack Obama added a *chief of cybersecurity* position to better protect the nation's computer networks against spies, criminals, and terrorists.[53] Ace Hardware is adding a *customer coordinator* position in each of its 4,600 U.S. stores, to implement a strategic decision to improve customer focus and service. The coordinator observes customers during heavy traffic periods, analyzing their body language to determine whether they are browsers, "mission shoppers" with no time for small talk, or serious do-it-yourselfers embarking on a project. Then, the coordinator radios sales staff so that the right expert is there to offer service.[54] As companies add positions and departments to meet changing needs, they grow more complex, with hundreds of positions and departments performing incredibly diverse activities.

Second, senior managers have to find a way to tie all these departments together. The formal chain of command and the supervision it provides is effective, but it is not enough. The organization needs systems to process information and enable communication among people in different departments and at different levels. **Coordination** refers to the quality of collaboration across departments. Without coordination, a company's left hand will not act in concert with its right hand, causing problems and conflicts. Coordination is required regardless of whether the organization has a functional, divisional, or team structure. Employees identify with their immediate department or team, taking its interest to heart, and they may not want to compromise with other units for the good of the organization as a whole.

The dangers of poor coordination are reflected in what Lee Iacocca said about Chrysler Corporation in the 1980s:

> What I found at Chrysler were 35 vice presidents, each with his own turf. . . . I couldn't believe, for example, that the guy running engineering departments wasn't in constant touch with his counterpart in manufacturing. But that's how it was. Everybody worked independently. I took one look at that system and I almost threw up. That's when I knew I was in really deep trouble.
>
> I'd call in a guy from engineering, and he'd stand there dumbfounded when I'd explain to him that we had a design problem or some other hitch in the engineering-manufacturing relationship. He might have the ability to invent a brilliant piece of engineering that would save us a lot of money. He might come up with a terrific new design. There was only one problem: He didn't know that the manufacturing people couldn't build it. Why? Because he had never talked to them about it. Nobody at Chrysler seemed to understand that interaction among the different functions in a company is absolutely critical. People in engineering and manufacturing almost have to be sleeping together. These guys weren't even flirting![55]

The problem of coordination is amplified in the international arena, because organizational units are differentiated not only by goals and work activities but also by geographical distance, time differences, cultural values, and perhaps language. How can managers ensure that needed coordination will take place in their company, both domestically and globally? Coordination is the outcome of information and cooperation. Managers can design systems and structures to promote horizontal coordination, as illustrated by the following example.

TOTAL ATTORNEYS

Ed Scanlan started Total Attorneys, a Chicago-based company that provides software and services to small law firms, with just a few people who worked closely together to write code, fix problems, or launch new products and services. As the company grew, though, managers implemented a functional structure to increase efficiency. Projects were broken down into sequential parts, and designers, coders, quality assurance testers, and other specialists worked in separate departments. Designers rarely interacted with developers, and people in functions such as accounting or customer service had little contact with those in production.

Eventually, the functional approach began to cause problems. Breaking projects down into sequential stages that moved from one department to another slowed product development down so much that clients' needs had sometimes changed by the time the product was completed. Scanlan realized his company of 180 people was getting less done than the original team of four or five people had accomplished. He solved the problem by creating small, cross-functional teams to increase horizontal coordination. Now, designers, coders, and quality-assurance testers work closely together on a project. Large jobs are broken into mini-projects with short deadlines. Call center representatives were moved to the same floor as software developers to enhance communication, and sometimes reps serve on development teams.[56]

Total Attorneys' vertical functional structure worked fine for a while, but when client needs began to change rapidly, it was too slow and cumbersome. Exhibit 7.10 illustrates the evolution of organizational structures, with a growing emphasis on horizontal coordination. Although the vertical functional structure is effective in stable environments, it does not provide the horizontal coordination needed in times of rapid change. Innovations such as cross-functional teams, task forces, and project managers work within the vertical structure but provide a means to increase horizontal communication and cooperation. The next stage involves reengineering to structure the organization into teams working on horizontal processes. **Reengineering** refers to the radical redesign of business processes to achieve dramatic improvements in cost, quality, service, and speed. Because the focus of reengineering is on process rather than function, reengineering generally leads to a shift away from a strong vertical structure to one emphasizing stronger horizontal coordination. The vertical hierarchy is flattened, with perhaps only a few senior executives in traditional support functions such as finance and human resources.

Task Forces, Teams, and Project Management

A **task force** is a temporary team or committee designed to solve a short-term problem involving several departments.[57] Task force members represent their departments and share information that enables coordination. For example, the Shawmut National Corporation

EXHIBIT 7.10

Evolution of Organization Structures

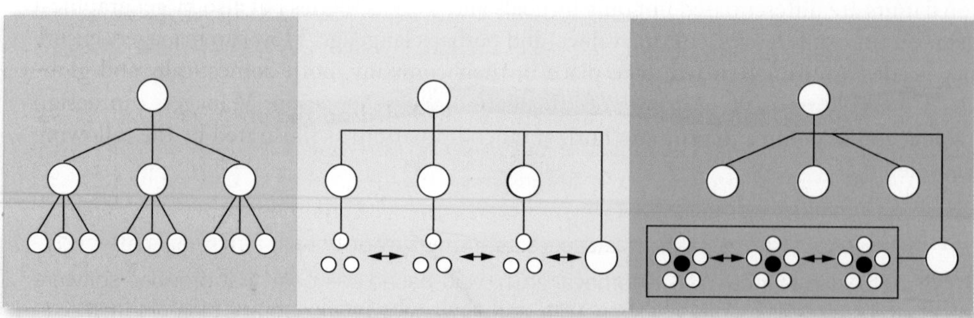

created a task force in human resources to consolidate all employment services into a single area. The task force looked at job banks, referral programs, employment procedures, and applicant tracking systems; found ways to perform these functions for all Shawmut's divisions in one human resource department; and then disbanded.[58] In addition to creating task forces, companies also set up *cross-functional teams,* such as those at Total Attorneys, described earlier. A cross-functional team furthers horizontal coordination because participants from several departments meet regularly to solve ongoing problems of common interest.[59] This team is similar to a task force except that it works with continuing rather than temporary problems and might exist for several years. Team members think in terms of working together for the good of the whole rather than just for their own department.

Companies also use project managers to increase coordination among functional departments. A **project manager** is a person who is responsible for coordinating the activities of several departments for the completion of a specific project.[60] Project managers might also have titles such as product manager, integrator, program manager, or process owner. Project managers are critical today because many organizations are continually reinventing themselves, creating flexible structures, and working on projects with an ever-changing assortment of people and organizations.[61] Project managers might work on several different projects at one time and might have to move in and out of new projects at a moment's notice.

Alli Harvey/WireImage/Getty Images

ConceptConnection

The SciFi Channel had outgrown its brand image. Managers assembled a **task force** to create a new image that better represented the network's fantasy programming and appealed to a broader audience, especially women. After reviewing more than 300 names, the task force settled on *Syfy* because, said president David Howe, "It's changing your name without changing your name." It also chose a logo (pictured) with softer, warmer-looking letters and created a short film, chockfull of special effects, to introduce the new name, logo, and slogan (*Imagine Greater*) to advertisers. It worked: the number of *Syfy* female viewers has grown substantially.

The distinctive feature of the project manager position is that the person is not a member of one of the departments being coordinated. Project managers are located outside of the departments and have responsibility for coordinating several departments to achieve desired project outcomes. General Mills, Procter & Gamble, and General Foods all use product managers to coordinate their product lines. A manager is assigned to each line, such as Cheerios, Bisquick, and Hamburger Helper. Product managers set budget goals, marketing targets, and strategies, and obtain the cooperation from advertising, production, and sales personnel needed for implementing product strategy.

In some organizations, project managers are included on the organization chart, as illustrated in Exhibit 7.11. The project manager is drawn to one side of the chart to indicate authority over the project, but not over the people assigned to it. Dashed lines to the project manager indicate responsibility for coordination and communication with assigned team members, but department managers retain line authority over functional employees. Project managers need excellent people skills. They use expertise and persuasion to achieve coordination among various departments, and their jobs involve getting people together, listening, building trust, confronting problems, and resolving conflicts and disputes in the best interest of the project and the organization.

As a potential new manager, check out your authority role models by completing the New Manager Self-Test on page 272.

New Manager Self-Test

Authority Role Models

An organization's structure is based on authority. Expectations about authority for a new manager are often based on experiences in your first authority figures and role models—Mom and Dad. To understand your authority role models, please answer each of the following items as Mostly True or Mostly False for you. Think about each statement as it applies to the parent or parents who made primary decisions about raising you.

	MOSTLY TRUE <<<	>>> MOSTLY FALSE
1. My parent(s) believed that children should get their way in the family as often as the parents do.	______	______
2. When a family policy was established, my parent(s) discussed the reasoning behind it with the children.	______	______
3. My parent(s) believed it was for my own good if I were made to conform to what they thought was right.	______	______
4. My parent(s) felt we children should make up our own minds about what we wanted to do, even if they did not agree with us.	______	______
5. My parent(s) directed my activities through reasoning and discussion.	______	______
6. My parent(s) were clear about who was the boss in the family.	______	______
7. My parent(s) allowed me to decide most things for myself without a lot of direction.	______	______
8. My parent(s) took the children's opinions into consideration when making family decisions.	______	______
9. If I didn't meet parental rules and expectations, I could expect to be punished.	______	______

See It Online

Scoring and Interpretation: Each question pertains to one of three subscales of **parental authority**. Items 1, 4, and 7 reflect *permissive* parental authority; items 2, 5, and 8 indicate *flexible* authority; and items 3, 6, and 9 indicate *authoritarian* parental authority. The subscale for which you checked more items Mostly True may reveal personal expectations from your early role models that shape your comfort with authority as a new manager. *Authoritarian* expectations typically would fit in a traditional vertical structure with fixed rules and a clear hierarchy of authority (mechanistic organization characteristics). *Flexible* authority expectations typically would fit with horizontal organizing, such as managing teams, projects, and reengineering (organic organization characteristics). Because most organizations thrive on structure, *permissive* expectations may be insufficient to enforce accountability under any structure. How do you think your childhood role models affect your authority expectations? Remember, this questionnaire is just a guide, because your current expectations about authority may not directly reflect your childhood experiences.

SOURCE: Adapted from John R. Buri, "Parental Authority Questionnaire," *Journal of Personality and Social Assessment* 57 (1991): 110–119.

EXHIBIT 7.11

Example of Project Manager Relationships to Other Departments

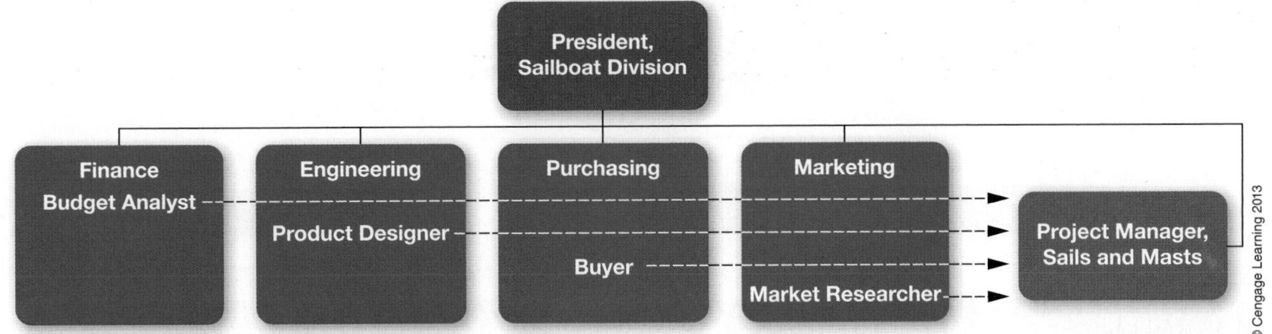

- In addition to the vertical structure, every organization needs mechanisms for horizontal integration and coordination.
- **Coordination** refers to the quality of collaboration across departments and divisions.
- As organizations grow, they add new positions, departments, and hierarchical levels, which leads to greater coordination problems.
- U.S. President Barack Obama added a *chief of cybersecurity* position, charged with protecting the nation's computer networks against spies, criminals, and terrorists.
- Mechanisms for increasing horizontal coordination include task forces, teams, and project managers.
- A **task force** is a temporary team or committee formed to solve a specific short-term problem involving several departments.
- A **project manager** is a person responsible for coordinating the activities of several departments for the completion of a specific project.
- Companies often shift to a more horizontal approach after going through **reengineering**, which refers to the radical redesign of business processes to achieve dramatic improvements in cost, quality, service, and speed.

Factors Shaping Structure

Vertical hierarchies continue to thrive because they often provide important benefits for organizations. However, in today's environment, organizations with stronger horizontal designs typically perform better.[62] How do managers know whether to design a structure that emphasizes the formal, vertical hierarchy or one with an emphasis on horizontal communication and collaboration? The answer lies in the organization's strategic goals and the nature of its technology. Exhibit 7.12 illustrates that forces affecting organization structure come from both outside and inside the organization. External strategic needs, such as environmental conditions, strategic direction, and organizational goals, create top-down pressure for designing the organization in such a way as to fit the environment and accomplish strategic goals. Structural decisions also take into consideration pressures from the bottom-up—that is from the technology and work processes that are performed to produce the organization's products and services.

EXHIBIT 7.12

Factors Affecting Organization Structure

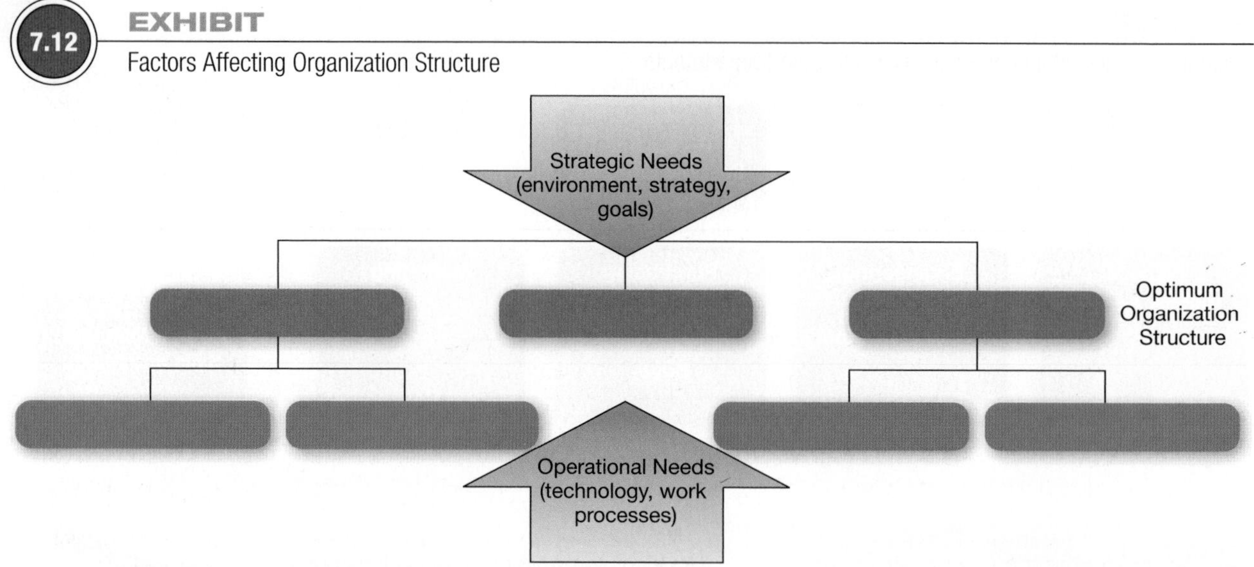

SOURCE: Based on David A. Nadler and Michael L. Tushman, with Mark B. Nadler, *Competing by Design: The Power of Organizational Architecture* (New York: Oxford University Press, 1997), p. 54.

Structure Follows Strategy

Go to the Self-Learning, on page 280, that pertains to organic versus mechanistic structure.

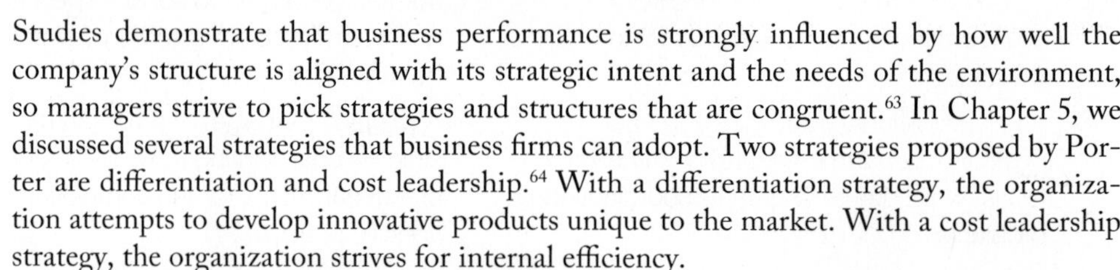

Studies demonstrate that business performance is strongly influenced by how well the company's structure is aligned with its strategic intent and the needs of the environment, so managers strive to pick strategies and structures that are congruent.[63] In Chapter 5, we discussed several strategies that business firms can adopt. Two strategies proposed by Porter are differentiation and cost leadership.[64] With a differentiation strategy, the organization attempts to develop innovative products unique to the market. With a cost leadership strategy, the organization strives for internal efficiency.

Typically, strategic goals of cost efficiency occur in more stable environments, whereas goals of innovation and flexibility occur in more uncertain environments. The terms *mechanistic* and *organic* can be used to explain structural responses to strategy and the environment.[65] Goals of efficiency and a stable environment are associated with a mechanistic system. This type of organization typically has a rigid, vertical, centralized structure, with most decisions made at the top. The organization is highly specialized and characterized by rules, procedures, and a clear hierarchy of authority. With goals of innovation and a rapidly changing environment, however, the organization tends to be much looser, free-flowing, and adaptive, using an organic system. The structure is more horizontal, and decision-making authority is decentralized. People at lower levels have more responsibility and authority for solving problems, enabling the organization to be more fluid and adaptable to changes.[66]

The Group Learning, on page 281, will give you a chance to practice organizing to meet strategic needs.

Exhibit 7.13 shows a simplified continuum that illustrates how different structural approaches are associated with strategy and the environment. The pure functional structure is appropriate for achieving internal efficiency goals in a stable environment. The vertical functional structure uses task specialization and a strict chain of command to gain efficient use of scarce resources, but it does not enable the organization to be flexible or innovative. In contrast, horizontal teams are appropriate when the primary goal is innovation and the organization needs flexibility to cope with an uncertain environment. Each team is small and able to be responsive, and has the people and resources necessary for performing its task. The flexible horizontal structure enables organizations to differentiate themselves and respond quickly to the demands of a shifting environment, but at the expense of efficient resource use.

EXHIBIT 7.13

Relationship of Structural Approach to Strategy and the Environment

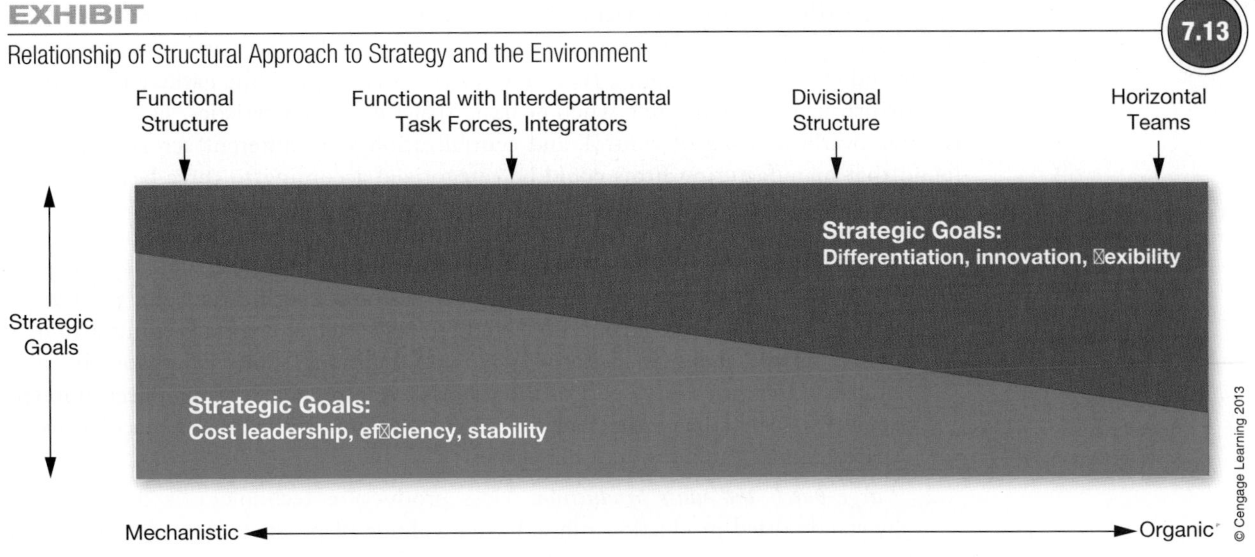

Exhibit 7.13 also illustrates how other forms of structure represent intermediate steps on the organization's path to efficiency or innovation. The functional structure with cross-functional teams and project managers provides greater coordination and flexibility than the pure functional structure. The divisional structure promotes differentiation because each division can focus on specific products and customers, although divisions tend to be larger and less flexible than small teams. Exhibit 7.13 does not include all possible structures, but it illustrates how structures can be used to facilitate the organization's strategic goals.

- Contingency factors of strategic goals, environment, and technology influence the correct structural approach.
- A mechanistic, vertical structure is appropriate for a cost leadership strategy, which typically occurs in a stable environment.
- An organic, horizontal approach is needed for a differentiation strategy and when the organization needs flexibility to cope with an uncertain environment.

Structure Fits the Technology

Technology includes the knowledge, tools, techniques, and activities used to transform organizational inputs into outputs.[67] Technology includes machinery, employee skills, and work procedures. A useful way to think about technology is as "production activities." The production activities may be to produce Web site content, steel castings, television programs, or computer software. Technologies vary between manufacturing and service organizations. In addition, new digital technology has an impact on structure.

Woodward's Manufacturing Technology The most influential research into the relationship between manufacturing technology and organization structure was conducted by Joan Woodward, a British industrial sociologist.[68] She gathered data from 100 British firms to determine whether basic structural characteristics, such as administrative overhead, span of control, and centralization were different across firms. She found that manufacturing firms could be categorized according to three basic types of production technology:

1. ***Small-batch and unit production.*** **Small-batch production** firms produce goods in batches of one or a few products designed to customer specification. This technology also is used to make large, one-of-a-kind products such as computer-controlled machines. Small-batch manufacturing is close to traditional skilled-craft work, because human beings are a large part of the process. Examples of items produced through small-batch manufacturing include custom clothing, special-order machine tools, space capsules, satellites, and submarines.
2. ***Large-batch and mass production.*** **Mass production** technology is distinguished by standardized production runs. A large volume of products is produced, and all customers receive the same product. Standard products go into inventory for sale as customers need them. This technology makes greater use of machines than does small-batch production. Machines are designed to do most of the physical work, and employees complement the machinery. Examples of mass production are automobile assembly lines and the large-batch techniques used to produce tobacco products and textiles.
3. ***Continuous process production.*** In **continuous process production**, the entire workflow is mechanized in a sophisticated and complex form of production technology. Because the process runs continuously, it has no starting and stopping. Human operators are not part of actual production because machinery does all of the work. Human operators simply read dials, fix machines that break down, and manage the production process. Examples of continuous process technologies are chemical plants, distilleries, petroleum refineries, and nuclear power plants.

The difference among the three manufacturing technologies is called **technical complexity**. Technical complexity is the degree to which machinery is involved in the production to the exclusion of people. With a complex technology, employees are hardly needed except to monitor the machines.

The structural characteristics associated with each type of manufacturing technology are illustrated in Exhibit 7.14. Note that centralization is high for mass production technology and low for small-batch and continuous process. Unlike small-batch and continuous process production, standardized mass-production machinery requires centralized decision making and well-defined rules and procedures. The administrative ratio and the percentage of indirect labor required also increase with technological complexity. Because the production process is nonroutine, closer supervision is needed. More indirect labor in the form of maintenance people is required because of the machinery's complexity; thus, the indirect–direct labor ratio is high. Span of control for first-line supervisors is greatest for mass production. On an assembly line, jobs are so routinized that a supervisor can handle an average of 48 employees. The number of employees per supervisor in small-batch and continuous process production is lower because closer supervision is needed. Overall, small-batch and continuous process firms have somewhat loose, flexible structures (organic), and mass production firms have tight vertical structures (mechanistic).

Woodward found that the relationship between structure and technology was directly related to company performance. Low-performing firms tended to deviate from

EXHIBIT 7.14

Relationship between Manufacturing Technology and Organization Structure

	Manufacturing Technology		
	Small Batch	Mass Production	Continuous Process
Technical Complexity of Production Technology	Low	Medium	High
Structural Characteristics:			
Centralization	Low	High	Low
Top administrator ratio	Low	Medium	High
Indirect/direct labor ratio	1/9	1/4	1/1
Supervisor span of control	23	48	15
Communication:			
Written (vertical)	Low	High	Low
Verbal (horizontal)	High	Low	High
Overall structure	Organic	Mechanistic	Organic

SOURCE: Based on Joan Woodward, *Industrial Organizations: Theory and Practice* (London: Oxford University Press, 1965).

the preferred structural form, often adopting a structure appropriate for another type of technology. High-performing organizations had characteristics similar to those listed in Exhibit 7.14.

Service Technology Examples of service organizations include consulting companies, law firms, brokerage houses, airlines, hotels, advertising companies, amusement parks, and educational organizations. In addition, service technology characterizes many departments in large corporations, even manufacturing firms. In a manufacturing company such as Ford Motor Company, the legal, human resources, finance, and market research departments all provide service. Thus, the structure and design of these departments reflect their own service technology rather than the manufacturing plant's technology. **Service technology** can be defined as follows:

1. ***Intangible output.*** The output of a service firm is intangible. Services are perishable and, unlike physical products, cannot be stored in inventory. The service is either consumed immediately or lost forever. Manufactured products are produced at one point in time and can be stored until sold at another time.
2. ***Direct contact with customers.*** Employees and customers interact directly to provide and purchase the service. Production and consumption are simultaneous. Service firm employees have direct contact with customers. In a manufacturing firm, technical employees are separated from customers, and hence no direct interactions occur.[69]

One distinct feature of service technology that directly influences structure is the need for employees to be close to the customer.[70] Structural characteristics are similar to those for continuous manufacturing technology, shown in Exhibit 7.14. Service firms tend to be flexible, informal, and decentralized. Horizontal communication is high because employees must share information and resources to serve customers and solve problems. Services also are dispersed; hence each unit is often small and located geographically close to customers. For example, banks, hotels, fast-food franchises, and doctors' offices disperse their facilities into regional and local offices to provide faster and better service to customers.

Some services can be broken down into explicit steps, so that employees can follow set rules and procedures. For example, McDonald's has standard procedures for serving customers, and Marriott has standard procedures for cleaning hotel rooms. When services can be standardized, a tight centralized structure can be effective, but service firms in general tend to be more organic, flexible, and decentralized.

Digital Technology **Digital technology** is characterized by use of the Internet and other digital processes to conduct or support business online. Organizations such as Amazon.com, Google, Facebook, and Priceline.com are all examples of firms based on digital technology. In addition, most large companies such as General Electric, Walgreens, and Ford Motor Company use digital technology to conduct transactions with suppliers and partners.

Like service firms, organizations based on digital technology tend to be flexible and decentralized. Horizontal communication and collaboration are typically high, and these companies may frequently be involved in virtual network arrangements. Digital technology is driving the move toward horizontal forms that link customers, suppliers, and partners into the organizational network, with everyone working together as if they were one organization. People may use electronic connections to link themselves together into teams. For example, an employee may send an e-mail to people both within and outside the organization who can help with a particular customer problem and quickly form a virtual team to develop a solution. In other words, digital technology encourages *boundarylessness*, where information and work activities flow freely among various organizational participants. Centralization is low, and employees are empowered to work in teams to meet fast-changing needs. Verbal and electronic communication is high, both up and down as well as across the organization, because up-to-the minute information is essential. In the digital world, advantage comes from seeing first and moving fastest, which requires extraordinary openness and flexibility.[71]

Hiroko Masuike/The New York Times/Redux Pictures

ConceptConnection

Cisco Systems Inc. redesigned its organization structure to fit its **digital technology**—not surprising as it designs and produces the equipment that makes social networking tools such as blogs and teleconferencing possible. Instead of a command-and-control organization, Cisco today is **decentralized and collaborative**. A network of councils and boards—spanning functions, departments, and even countries—is authorized to launch new products and initiatives. Although CEO John Chambers admits that shedding his old command-and-control ways was difficult, he acknowledges that executives operating collaboratively are making better decisions than the ones he would have made alone.

- Types of technologies include manufacturing, service, and digital.
- **Small-batch production** is a type of manufacturing technology that involves the production of goods in batches of one or a few products designed to customer specification.
- **Mass production** is characterized by long production runs to manufacture a large volume of products with the same specifications.
- **Continuous process production** involves mechanization of the entire workflow and nonstop production, such as in chemical plants or petroleum refineries.
- Small batch and continuous process technologies are associated with a more flexible horizontal structure, whereas a tighter vertical structure is appropriate for mass production.
- Manufacturing technologies differ in terms of **technical complexity**, which refers to the degree to which complex machinery is involved in the production process to the exclusion of people.
- **Service technology** is characterized by intangible outputs and direct contact between employees and customers.
- Examples of service firms include banks, hotels, and fast-food restaurants.
- **Digital technology** is characterized by use of the Internet and other digital processes to conduct or support business operations.
- Service technologies tend to have more flexible horizontal structures, as do organizations based on digital technology.

Discussion Questions

1. Sandra Holt, manager of Electronics Assembly, asked Hector Cruz, her senior technician, to handle things in the department while Sandra worked on the budget. She needed peace and quiet for at least a week to complete her figures. After ten days, Sandra discovered that Hector had hired a senior secretary, not realizing that Sandra had promised interviews to two other people. Evaluate Sandra's approach to delegation.
2. Most organizations have been making greater use of teams in recent years. What factors might account for this trend?
3. An organizational consultant was heard to say, "Some aspect of functional structure appears in every organization." Do you agree? Explain.
4. The divisional structure is often considered almost the opposite of a functional structure. Do you agree? Briefly explain the major differences in these two approaches to departmentalization.
5. Some people argue that the matrix structure should be adopted only as a last resort because the dual chains of command can create more problems than they solve. Discuss. Do you agree or disagree? Why?
6. What is the virtual network approach to structure? Is the use of authority and responsibility different compared with other forms of departmentalization? Explain.
7. The Hay Group published a report that some managers have personalities suited to horizontal relationships such as project management that achieve results with little formal authority. Other managers are more suited to operating roles with much formal authority in a vertical structure. In what type of structure—functional, matrix, team, or virtual network—do you believe your personality would best fit? Which structure would be the most challenging for you? Give your reasons.
8. Experts say that organizations are becoming increasingly decentralized, with authority, decision-making responsibility, and accountability being pushed farther down into the organization. How will this trend affect what will be asked of you as a new manager?

9. The chapter suggested that structure should be designed to fit strategy. Some theorists argue that strategy should be designed to fit the organization's structure. With which theory do you agree? Explain.

10. Would you expect the structure of a company such as Facebook that operates almost entirely online to differ from the structure of a bricks-and-mortar company such as AT&T that uses the Internet for some things, such as customer service and business-to-business transactions? Why or why not?

Self-Learning

Organic Versus Mechanistic Organization Structure

Interview an employee at your university, such as a department head or secretary. Have the employee answer the following 13 items about his or her job and organizational conditions. Then, answer the same set of items for a job you have held.

Disagree Strongly ① ② ③ ④ ⑤ Agree Strongly

1. Your work would be considered routine.

   1 2 3 4 5

See It Online

2. A clearly known way is established to do the major tasks you encounter.

   1 2 3 4 5

3. Your work has high variety and frequent exceptions.

   1 2 3 4 5

4. Communications from above consist of information and advice rather than instructions and directions.

   1 2 3 4 5

5. You have the support of peers and your supervisor to do your job well.

   1 2 3 4 5

6. You seldom exchange ideas or information with people doing other kinds of jobs.

   1 2 3 4 5

7. Decisions relevant to your work are made above you and passed down.

   1 2 3 4 5

8. People at your level frequently have to figure out for themselves what their jobs are for the day.

   1 2 3 4 5

9. Lines of authority are clear and precisely defined.

   1 2 3 4 5

10. Leadership tends to be democratic rather than autocratic in style.

    1 2 3 4 5

11. Job descriptions are written and up to date for each job.

    1 2 3 4 5

12. People understand each other's jobs and often do different tasks.

    1 2 3 4 5

13. A manual of policies and procedures is available to use when a problem arises.

    1 2 3 4 5

Scoring and Interpretation

To obtain the total score, subtract the scores for items 1, 2, 6, 7, 9, 11, and 13 from the number 6 and total the adjusted scores.

Total Score, employee: __________

Total Score, you: __________

Compare the total score for a place you have worked to the score of the university employee you interviewed. A total score of 52 or above suggests that you or the other respondent is working in an organic organization. The score reflects a loose, flexible structure that is often associated with uncertain environments and small-batch or service technology. People working in this structure feel empowered. Many organizations today are moving in the direction of flexible structures and empowerment.

A score of 26 or below suggests a mechanistic structure. This structure uses traditional control and functional specialization, which often occurs in a certain environment, a stable organization, and routine or mass-production technology. People in this structure may feel controlled and constrained.

Discuss the pros and cons of organic versus mechanistic structure. Does the structure of the employee you interviewed fit the nature of the organization's environment, strategic goals, and technology? How about the structure for your own workplace? How might you redesign the structure to make the work organization more effective?

Group Learning

Family Business

Step 1. In groups of three to five students, assume you are a consulting team to a family business. The family has used an inheritance to acquire a medium-sized pharmaceutical company. Last year sales were down 10 percent from the previous year. Indeed, business has declined over the past three years, even though the pharmaceutical industry has been growing. The family that acquired the business seeks your help.

Step 2. Your task as a group is to rank the priority of the departmental functions in the order of importance for assigning additional resources to improve business in the future.

Step 3. Individually, rank the following ten functions in order of importance, and note your reasons:

Distribution
Manufacturing
Market research
New-product development
Human resources
Product promotion
Quality assurance
Sales
Legal and governmental affairs
Office of the controller

Step 4. As a group, discuss the order of importance for the ten functions, sharing your reasons for how functional priority should relate to the company's strategic needs.

Step 5. How does the group's reasoning and ranking differ from your original thinking?

Step 6. What did you learn about organization structure and design from this exercise?

SOURCE: Adapted by Dorothy Marcic from "Organizing," in Donald D. White and H. William Vroman, eds., *Action in Organizations*, 2nd ed. (Boston: Allyn & Bacon), p. 154.

Action Learning

Team Skills

1. Think of three times you have been a member of a work team, with varying levels of success. Complete the table below.

	Team 1	Team 2	Teams 3
Was there any formal authority in the team? How did that work?			
What was the informal structure?			
How was work divided? What was their specialization?			
Did anyone delegate? How did that work out?			
Over the course of time, did the team get better or did it deteriorate? Why?			

2. Can you see any patterns in the success of the team and some of the characteristics you have identified?
3. Based on what you have learned, how would you recommend structuring a work team?

Ethical Dilemma

A Matter of Delegation[72]

Tom Harrington loved his job as an assistant quality control officer for Rockingham Toys. After six months of unemployment, he was anxious to make a good impression on his boss, Frank Golopolus. One of his new responsibilities was ensuring that new product lines met federal safety guidelines. Rockingham had made several manufacturing changes over the past year. Golopolus and the rest of the quality-control team had been working 60-hour weeks to troubleshoot the new production process.

Harrington was aware of numerous changes in product safety guidelines that he knew would affect the new Rockingham toys. Golopolus was also aware of the guidelines, but he was taking no action to implement them. Harrington wasn't sure whether his boss expected him to implement the new procedures. The ultimate responsibility was his boss's, and Harrington was concerned about moving ahead on his own. To cover for his boss, he continued to avoid the questions he received from the factory floor, but he was beginning to wonder whether Rockingham would have time to make changes with the Christmas season rapidly approaching.

Harrington felt loyalty to Golopolus for giving him a job and didn't want to alienate him by interfering. However, he was beginning to worry what might happen if he didn't act. Rockingham had a fine product safety reputation and was rarely challenged on matters of quality. Should he question Golopolus about implementing the new safety guidelines?

What Would You Do?

1. Prepare a memo to Golopolus, summarizing the new safety guidelines that affect the Rockingham product line and requesting his authorization for implementation.
2. Mind your own business. Golopolus hasn't said anything about the new guidelines, and you don't want to overstep your authority. You've been unemployed and need this job.
3. Send copies of the reports anonymously to the operations manager, who is the boss of Golopolus.

Case for Critical Analysis

FMB&T[73]

Marshall Pinkard, president and CEO of FMB&T, a growing California-based regional commercial and consumer retail bank, clicked on an e-mail from Ayishia Coles. Ayishia was the bright, hardworking, self-confident woman who'd recently come on board as the bank's executive vice president and chief information officer. The fact that the person in Coles's position in the company's traditional vertical organization now reported directly to him and was a full-fledged member of the executive committee reflected FMB&T's recognition of just how important information technology was to all aspects of its increasingly competitive business. The successful, leading-edge banks were the ones using information technology not only to operate efficiently but also to help them focus more effectively on customer needs. Marshall settled back to read what he expected would be a report on how she was settling in. He was sadly mistaken.

After a few months on the job, Ayishia Coles was frustrated. What she needed from him, she wrote, was a clear statement of her responsibilities and authority. The way Ayishia saw it, the relationship between information technology (IT) and the bank's other business units was muddled, often causing considerable confusion, friction, and inefficiency. Typically someone from retail banking or marketing, for example, came to her department with a poorly defined problem, such as how to link up checking account records with investment records, and they always expected a solution the same day. What made the situation even more vexing was that more often than not, the problem crossed organizational lines. She found that, generally, the more work units the problem affected, the less likely it was that any single unit took responsibility for defining exactly what they wanted IT to do. Who exactly was supposed to be getting all these units together and coordinating requests? When she tried to step into the breach and act as a facilitator, unit managers usually didn't welcome her efforts.

Despite the vagueness of their requests, the work units still expected IT to come up with a solution—and come up with it quickly. All these expectations seemed almost calculated to drive the methodical IT folks mad. Before taking on a problem, they wanted to make sure they thoroughly understood all of its dimensions so that the solution would fit seamlessly into the existing systems. This coordination took time that other parts of the bank weren't willing to give IT.

In addition, Ayishia knew the IT staff was increasingly feeling underused. The staff wanted to identify opportunities for dazzling new IT developments to contribute to business strategies, but it found itself limited to applications work. Ayishia's greatest concern was the president of a large regional branch who was actively campaigning to locate decentralized IT departments in each large branch under branch authority so that work would be completed faster to meet branch needs. He said it would be better to let work units coordinate their own IT departments rather than run everything through corporate IT. Under that scenario, Ayishia Coles's department could end up one-half its current size.

Marshall leaned back in his high-backed executive chair and sighed. At the very least, he needed to clarify Ayishia's authority and responsibilities as she had asked him to do. But he recognized that the new vice president was talking about a much larger can of worms. Was it time to rethink the bank's entire organizational structure?

Questions

1. What are the main organizational causes of the frustration that Ayishia Coles feels?
2. If you were Marshall Pinkard, how would you address both Ayishia's request for clarification about her authority and responsibilities and the underlying problems her e-mail brings to his attention? Can the problems be addressed with minor adjustments, or would you need to consider a drastic overhaul of the bank's organizational structure? What environmental and technological factors would influence your decision?
3. Sketch a general chart for the type of organization that you think would work best for IT at FMB&T.

aplia Aplia Highlights

Now use your Aplia homework to help you:

- Apply management theories in your life
- Assess your management skills
- Master management terms and concepts
- Apply your knowledge to real-world situations
- Analyze and solve challenging management problems

In order to take advantage of these elements, your instructor will need to have set up a course for your class within Aplia. Ask your instructor to contact his/her Cengage sales representative and Digital Solutions Manager to explore testing Aplia in your course this term.

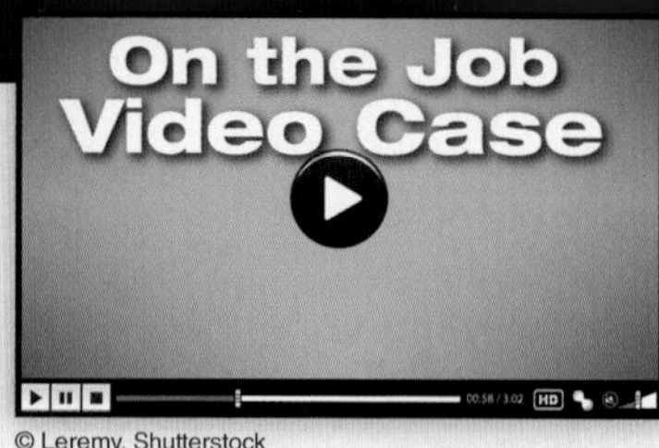

© Leremy, Shutterstock

Modern Shed: Designing Adaptive Organizations

If anyone knows about structural designs that are sturdy, contemporary, and adaptive, it's Ryan Smith, the owner and founder of Modern Shed, a small Seattle company that builds modernized space-saving dwellings.

Smith's interest in building things began in childhood while playing with a favorite plywood train set. His early fascination matured into an architectural career, and Smith quickly established a reputation as a skillful builder with an eye for stylish home design and renovation.

But in 2003, Smith stumbled upon a very little big idea: after setting up a small temporary work shed while working on a home restoration project, a client remarked that he really liked Smith's tiny work shelter. A light bulb went on inside Smith's creative mind, and the enterprising builder determined that the kit could be decked out with modern living features and sold for a range of uses. Today he builds small paneled dwellings for use as studio spaces, home offices, pool houses, project sheds, guesthouses, and more.

Like his stylish sheds, Smith's company is built to be adaptive, scalable, and suited to the needs of the environment. Modern Shed counts only 12 to 14 full time employees in the firm's Seattle office. However, at times the company's output rivals that of a large builder, which is achieved through collaboration with outside sales reps and a dealer network comprised of 35 independent contractors across the United States.

According to Smith, partnering with outside specialists was the most efficient, effective, and flexible way to run a startup company. "If you need to create a business organization, and you bring it all in house," says Smith, "you need to have the accounting position, the organizing position, the person who is going to answer the phones, and the people who are going to make the things—and you just can't do that when you start a company. It doesn't make sense."

One partner who helps boost Modern Shed's output is Scott Pearl, a marketing consultant who also lives in Seattle. Pearl's background is in real estate, where he worked on multimillion-dollar projects before starting his own marketing consultant firm. In light of the recent crash of the real estate market, Pearl is excited to be managing many of Modern Shed's sales and marketing functions. According to Pearl, Modern Shed is one of the few building concepts thriving in today's depressed housing market. "Modern Shed has positioned itself so that we're insulated from what's going on in the general marketplace," the marketer states.

Smith's dealer network is made up of dozens of such partners who specialize in everything from materials and construction to sales and office processes. The partners connect regularly to discuss projects and plans. "On a monthly basis we'll have conference calls with the reps and the dealers about new products, new promotions, changes in pricing, and new opportunities for them in terms of their marketing," Pearl remarks. "It's very lean and unstructured because all those folks are independent contractors."

What impresses Scott Pearl most about Modern Shed is the organization's ability to respond quickly to the needs of the market. "We were recently approached by a nationally recognized home-and-garden expert who wanted us to create an entirely new product line of Modern Shed," says Pearl. "The fact that Ryan can just drop everything and focus on this, get the team focused on it, and actually come up with a brand new product in under eight weeks is phenomenal. It could not be done unless the organization was nimble like we are."

Small, flexible, responsive—these are the qualities that have enabled Modern Shed to thrive even during an economic recession. According to Smith, the logical process of building sheds from smaller scale structures to larger ones is a metaphor for how modern organizations should be built. "You can use the analogy for organizations and people as well as structures," Smith states. "If you go too big you don't understand it; you have to start small."

As for Scott Pearl, he doesn't expect to become an employee of Modern Shed. Nevertheless, the marketing consultant considers himself an important part of Modern Shed's organization and success.

Discussion Questions

1. Which of the five approaches to structural design is used at Modern Shed, and how are the company's departments organized and coordinated?
2. What are the advantages and disadvantages of Modern Shed's organizational structure?
3. How did Ryan Smith determine whether his company needed a mechanistic structure with a formal vertical hierarchy or an organic one involving free-flowing partnerships?

Rendition

U.S. government operatives suddenly whisk Anwar el-Ibrahimi (Omar Metwally) from his flight from Cape Town, South Africa, after it arrives in Washington, D.C. He is a suspected terrorist whom the government sends to North Africa for torture and interrogation (extraordinary rendition). Douglas Freeman (Jake Gyllenhaal), a CIA analyst, becomes involved. He reacts negatively to the torture techniques and urges El-Ibrahimi's release. The story has other complications in the form of El-Ibrahimi's pregnant wife at home, who desperately works for her husband's safe return.

Organizational Structure This scene opens with a night shot of the Washington monument. It follows a discussion between Kahlid (Moa Khouas) and Hamadi (Hassam Ghancy), the leader of the terrorist bomb group. Congressional aide Alan Smith's (Peter Sarsgaard) voice-over asks, "She called you?" The scene ends after Senator Hawkins (Alan Arkin) tells Alan to back off. The film cuts to a panning shot of a market area and Douglas Freeman drinking.

Alan Smith's question, "She called you?" refers to Corrine Whitman (Meryl Streep), head of U.S. intelligence. She authorized the extraordinary rendition of El-Ibrahimi. Alan Smith, earlier in the film, pressed her for El-Ibrahimi's release and his return to the United States. Whitman lied about El-Ibrahimi's existence. This scene does not explicitly discuss organizational structure, but you can infer several aspects of structure from the scene.

What to Watch for and Ask Yourself

- What formal tasks does this scene imply? What reporting relationships does it show?
- Can you sense the division of labor represented by Senator Hawkins and Alan Smith? Corrine Whitman does not appear in this scene but is also part of a division of labor.
- Does the scene show line authority or staff authority? Does it imply a functional or divisional structure? Give some examples from the scene.

Endnotes

1. Ben Charney and Justin Scheck, "Dell Elevates Insiders in Strategy Change," *The Wall Street Journal,* January 2, 2009; Cliff Edwards, "Dell's Do-Over," *BusinessWeek* (October 26, 2009): 36–40; and Justin Scheck, "Dell Reorganizes, Creating New Mobile Device Division," *The Wall Street Journal,* December 5, 2009.
2. Edwards, "Dell's Do-Over"; and Scheck, "Dell Reorganizes."
3. Russell Adams, "Hachette to Break Through 'Silos' As It Restructures Women's Magazines" *The Wall Street Journal,* March 2, 2009; Pete Engardio with Michael Arndt and Dean Foust, "The Future of Outsourcing," *BusinessWeek* (January 30, 2006): 50–58; and Thom Shanker, "Edging Away from Air Force, Army Adds Air Unit," *The New York Times,* June 22, 2008.
4. John Child, *Organization: A Guide to Problems and Practice*, 2nd ed. (London: Harper & Row, 1984).
5. Adam Smith, *The Wealth of Nations* (New York: Modern Library, 1937).
6. This discussion is based on A. J. Grimes, "Authority, Power, Influence, and Social Control: A Theoretical Synthesis," *Academy of Management Review* 3 (1978): 724–735; and W. Graham Astley and Paramjit S. Sachdeva, "Structural Sources of Intraorganizational Power: A Theoretical Synthesis," *Academy of Management Review* 9 (1984): 104–113.
7. C. I. Barnard, *The Functions of the Executive* (Cambridge, MA: Harvard University Press, 1938).
8. Thomas A. Stewart, "CEOs See Clout Shifting," *Fortune* (November 6, 1989): 66.
9. Michael G. O'Loughlin, "What Is Bureaucratic Accountability and How Can We Measure It?" *Administration & Society* 22, no. 3 (November 1990): 275–302; and Brian Dive, "When Is an Organization Too Flat?" *Across the Board* (July–August 2003): 20–23.
10. Carrie R. Leana, "Predictors and Consequences of Delegation," *Academy of Management Journal* 29 (1986): 754–774.

11. Peter Sanders, "Disney Learns Lessons from Pixar," *The Wall Street Journal,* October 27, 2008; Gaby Wood, "Review: Cover Story: The Genius Shaping the Future of the Movies," *The Observer,* January 18, 2009; and Colin Hunter, "Being Beaten by WALL-E an Honour," *Waterloo Region Record,* February 26, 2009. The Chris Williams quote is from Martin Knelman, "Bolt from the Blue Took Canadian to Oscars," *Toronto Star,* February 25, 2009.
12. Ian Urbina, "In Gulf, It Was Unclear Who Was in Charge of Oil Rig," *The New York Times,* June 5, 2010; and Douglas A. Blackmon, Vanessa O'Connell, Alexandra Berzon, and Ana Campoy, "There Was 'Nobody in Charge,'" *The Wall Street Journal,* May 27, 2010.
13. George Anders, "Overseeing More Employees—With Fewer Managers" (Theory & Practice column), *The Wall Street Journal,* March 24, 2008.
14. Barbara Davison, "Management Span of Control: How Wide Is Too Wide?" *Journal of Business Strategy* 24, no. 4 (2003): 22–29; Paul D. Collins and Frank Hull, "Technology and Span of Control: Woodward Revisited," *Journal of Management Studies* 23 (March 1986): 143–164; David D. Van Fleet and Arthur G. Bedeian, "A History of the Span of Management," *Academy of Management Review* 2 (1977): 356–372; and C. W. Barkdull, "Span of Control—A Method of Evaluation," *Michigan Business Review* 15 (May 1963): 25–32.
15. Brian Dive, "Hierarchies for Flow and Profit," *Strategy + Business,* August 26, 2008, www.strategy-business.com/article/08315 (accessed May 25, 2010).
16. Dive, "Hierarchies for Flow and Profit"; and Gary Neilson, Bruce A. Pasternack, and Decio Mendes, "The Four Bases of Organizational DNA," *Strategy + Business*, Issue 33 (December 10, 2003): 48–57.
17. Anders, "Overseeing More Employees"; Barbara Davison, "Management Span of Control"; Brian Dive, "When Is an Organization Too Flat?"; Brian Dumaine, "What the Leaders of Tomorrow See," *Fortune* (July 3, 1989): 48–62; and Raghuram G. Rajan and Julie Wulf, "The Flattening Firm: Evidence from Panel Data on the Changing Nature of Corporate Hierarchies," working paper, reported in Caroline Ellis, "The Flattening Corporation," *MIT Sloan Management Review* (Summer 2003): 5.
18. William G. Ouchi, "Power to the Principals: Decentralization in Three Large School Districts," *Organization Science* 17, no. 2 (March–April 2006): 298–307.
19. Gabriel Kahn, "Los Angeles Sets School-Rescue Program," *The Wall Street Journal,* September 2, 2008.
20. Quoted in Robert D. Kaplan, "Man Versus Afghanistan," *The Atlantic* (April 2010): 60–71.
21. Gen. Martin E. Dempsey, "The Army's Starfish Program and an Emphasis on Decentralization," Official Army Web site, April 26, 2010, www.army.mil/-news/2010/04/26/37979-the-armys-starfish-program-and-an-emphasis-on-decentralization/ (accessed August 30, 2010); and Bruce E. DeFeyter, "The Lion, the Starfish, and the Spider: Hitting Terrorists Where It Hurts," *Special Warfare* (March–April 2010): 26.
22. Dennis Cauchon, "The Little Company That Could," *USA Today*, October 9, 2005, www.usatoday.com/money/companies/management/2005-10-09-mississippi-power-usat_x.htm.
23. William Newman, "Management of Subways to Be Split," *The New York Times*, December 6, 2007.
24. Penney example reported in Ann Zimmerman, "Home Depot Learns to Go Local," *The Wall Street Journal,* October 7, 2008; Jessica E. Vascellaro, "Yahoo CEO Set to Install Top-Down Management," *The Wall Street Journal*, February 29, 2009.
25. Clay Chandler and Paul Ingrassia, "Just As U.S. Firms Try Japanese Management, Honda Is Centralizing," *The Wall Street Journal*, April 11, 1991.
26. The following discussion of structural alternatives draws from Jay R. Galbraith, *Designing Complex Organizations* (Reading, MA: Addison-Wesley, 1973); Jay R. Galbraith, *Organization Design* (Reading, MA: Addison-Wesley, 1977); Jay R. Galbraith, *Designing Dynamic Organizations* (New York: AMACOM, 2002); Robert Duncan, "What Is the Right Organization Structure?" *Organizational Dynamics* (Winter 1979): 59–80; N. Anand and Richard L. Daft, "What Is the Right Organization Design?" *Organizational Dynamics* 36, no. 4 (2007): 329–344; and J. McCann and Jay R. Galbraith, "Interdepartmental Relations," in *Handbook of Organizational Design*, ed. P. Nystrom and W. Starbuck (New York: Oxford University Press, 1981), pp. 60–84.
27. Based on the story of Blue Bell Creameries in Richard L. Daft, *Organization Theory and Design,* 9th ed. (Mason, OH: South- Western, 2007), p. 103.
28. Richard Siklos, "Sony; Lost in Transformation," *Fortune* (July 6, 2009): 68–74; and Sony Corp. Web site, "Sony Group Organizational Chart Summary," www.sony.net/SonyInfo/CorporateInfo/Data/organization.html (accessed April 29, 2010).
29. Anand and Daft, "What Is the Right Organization Design?"
30. Eliza Newlin Carney, "Calm in the Storm," *Government Executive* (October 2003): 57–63; and the Internal Revenue Service Web site, www.irs.gov (accessed April 20, 2004).

31. Robert J. Kramer, *Organizing for Global Competitiveness: The Geographic Design* (New York: The Conference Board, 1993), pp. 29–31; Christopher Tkaczyk, "100 Best Companies to Work For: Colgate-Palmolive," *Fortune* (May 3, 2010): 39; and "*Colgate-Palmolive Company 2009 Annual Report,*" Colgate- Palmolive Company Web site, www.colgate.com/app/Colgate/US/Corp/Annual-Reports/2009/Financial-Highlights/Growth-Highlights-Of-Five-Divisions.cvsp (accessed April 28, 2010).
32. Maisie O'Flanagan and Lynn K. Taliento, "Nonprofits: Ensuring That Bigger Is Better," *McKinsey Quarterly*, no. 2 (2004): 112ff.
33. The discussion of matrix structure is based on S. H. Appelbaum, D. Nadeau, and M. Cyr, "Performance Evaluation in a Matrix Organization: A Case Study," *Industrial and Commercial Training* 40, no. 5 (2008): 236–241; T. Sy and S. Cote, "Emotional Intelligence: A Key Ability to Succeed in the Matrix Organization," *Journal of Management Development* 23, no. 5 (2004): 439; L. R. Burns, "Matrix Management in Hospitals: Testing Theories of Matrix Structure and Development," *Administrative Science Quarterly* 34 (1989): 349–368; Carol Hymowitz, "Managers Suddenly Have to Answer to a Crowd of Bosses," *The Wall Street Journal*, August 12, 2003; and Stanley M. Davis and Paul R. Lawrence, *Matrix* (Reading, MA: Addison-Wesley, 1977).
34. Dan Carrison, "Borrowing Expertise from the FBI," *Industrial Management* (May–June 2009): 23–26.
35. Gary Hamel, "Break Free," *Fortune* (October 1, 2007): 119–126, excerpted from Gary Hamel, *The Future of Management* (Boston: Harvard Business School Press, 2007); and Nick Paumgarten, "Food Fighter: The Whole Foods CEO vs. His Customers" (Profiles column), *The New Yorker* (January 4, 2010): 36.
36. Melissa A. Schilling and H. Kevin Steensma, "The Use of Modular Organizational Forms: An Industry-Level Analysis," *Academy of Management Journal*, 44, no. 6 (December 2001): 1149–1169.
37. Yuzo Yamaguchi and Daisuke Wakabayashi, "Hitachi to Outsource TV Manufacture," *The Wall Street Journal Online,* July 10, 2009, http://online.wsj.com/article/SB124714255400717925.html (accessed July 17, 2009); and Jena McGregor, "The Chore Goes Offshore," *BusinessWeek* (March 23 & 30, 2009): 50–51.
38. Raymond E. Miles and Charles C. Snow, "The New Network Firm: A Spherical Structure Built on a Human Investment Philosophy," *Organizational Dynamics* (Spring 1995): 5–18; and Raymond E. Miles, Charles C. Snow, John A. Matthews, Grant Miles, and Henry J. Coleman, Jr., "Organizing in the Knowledge Age: Anticipating the Cellular Form," *Academy of Management Executive* 11, no. 4 (1997): 7–24.
39. Pete Engardio, "Mom-and-Pop Multinationals," *BusinessWeek* (July 14 & 21, 2008): 77–78.
40. Raymond E. Miles and Charles C. Snow, "Organizations: New Concepts for New Forms," *California Management Review* 28 (Spring 1986): 62–73; and John W. Wilson and Judith H. Dobrzynski, "And Now, the Post-Industrial Corporation," *BusinessWeek* (March 3, 1986): 64–74.
41. N. Anand, "Modular, Virtual, and Hollow Forms of Organization Design," working paper, London Business School (2000); Don Tapscott, "Rethinking Strategy in a Networked World," *Strategy + Business*, issue 24 (Third Quarter 2001): 34–41.
42. Gregory G. Dess, Abdul M. A. Rasheed, Kevin J. McLaughlin, and Richard L. Priem, "The New Corporate Architecture," *Academy of Management Executive* 9, no. 3 (1995): 7–20.
43. Kathleen Kerwin, "GM: Modular Plants Won't Be a Snap," *BusinessWeek* (November 9, 1998): 168, 172.
44. Robert C. Ford and W. Alan Randolph, "Cross-Functional Structures: A Review and Integration of Matrix Organization and Project Management," *Journal of Management* 18, no. 2 (1992): 267–294; and T. Sy and L. S. D'Annunzio, "Challenges and Strategies of Matrix Organizations: Top-Level and Mid-Level Managers' Perspectives," *Human Resources Planning* 28, no. 1 (2005): 39–48.
45. These disadvantages are based on Michael Goold and Andrew Campbell, "Making Matrix Structures Work: Creating Clarity on Unit Roles and Responsibilities," *European Management Journal* 21, no. 3 (June 2003): 351–363; and Sy and D'Annunzio, "Challenges and Strategies of Matrix Organizations."
46. Geoff Keighley, "Massively Multinational Player," *Business 2.0* (September 2005): 64–66.
47. Dexter Filkins, "Profusion of Rebel Groups Helps Them Survive in Iraq," *The New York Times*, December 2, 2005, www.nytimes.com/2005/12/02/international/middleeast/02insurgency.html (accessed August 30, 2010).
48. Scott Shane and Neil A. Lewis, "At Sept. 11 Trial, Tale of Missteps and Mismanagement," *The New York Times*, March 31, 2006, www.nytimes.com/2006/03/31/us/nationalspecial3/31plot.html (accessed August 30, 2010).
49. Raymond E. Miles, "Adapting to Technology and Competition: A New Industrial Relations System for the Twenty-First Century," *California Management Review* (Winter 1989): 9–28; and Miles and Snow, "The New Network Firm."
50. These disadvantages are based on Cecily A. Raiborn, Janet B. Butler, and Marc F. Massoud, "Outsourcing

Support Functions: Identifying and Managing the Good, the Bad, and the Ugly," *Business Horizons* 52 (2009): 347–356; Dess et al., "The New Corporate Architecture"; Anand and Daft, "What Is the Right Organization Design?"; Henry W. Chesbrough and David J. Teece, "Organizing for Innovation: When Is Virtual Virtuous?" *The Innovative Entrepreneur* (August 2002): 127–134; N. Anand, "Modular, Virtual, and Hollow Forms of Organization Design"; and M. Lynne Markus, Brook Manville, and Carole E. Agres, "What Makes a Virtual Organization Work?" *Sloan Management Review* (Fall 2000): 13–26.

51. Laurie P. O'Leary, "Curing the Monday Blues: A U.S. Navy Guide for Structuring Cross-Functional Teams," *National Productivity Review* (Spring 1996): 43–51; and Alan Hurwitz, "Organizational Structures for the 'New World Order,'" *Business Horizons* (May–June 1996): 5–14.
52. Jay Galbraith, Diane Downey, and Amy Kates, "Processes and Lateral Capability," *Designing Dynamic Organizations*, (New York: AMACOM, 2002) chapter 4.
53. Siobhan Gorman and Yochi J. Dreazen, "Obama to Create 'Cyber Czar' Job," *The Wall Street Journal*, May 29, 2009.
54. Aili McConnon, "Ace Hardware (#10): Calling the Right Play for Each Customer," *BusinessWeek* (March 3, 2008): 50.
55. Lee Iacocca with William Novak, *Iacocca: An Autobiography* (New York: Phantom Books, 1984), pp. 152–153.
56. Darren Dahl, "Strategy: Managing Fast, Flexible, and Full of Team Spirit," *Inc.* (May 2009): 95–97.
57. William J. Altier, "Task Forces: An Effective Management Tool," *Management Review* (February 1987): 52–57.
58. "Task Forces Tackle Consolidation of Employment Services," *Shawmut News*, Shawmut National Corporation, May 3, 1989.
59. Henry Mintzberg, *The Structure of Organizations* (Englewood Cliffs, NJ: Prentice Hall, 1979).
60. Paul R. Lawrence and Jay W. Lorsch, "New Managerial Job: The Integrator," *Harvard Business Review* (November– December 1967): 142–151.
61. Ronald N. Ashkenas and Suzanne C. Francis, "Integration Managers: Special Leaders for Special Times," *Harvard Business Review* (November–December 2000): 108–116.
62. Harold J. Leavitt, "Why Hierarchies Thrive," *Harvard Business Review* (March 2003): 96–102, provides a discussion of the benefits and problems of hierarchies. See Timothy Galpin, Rod Hilpirt, and Bruce Evans, "The Connected Enterprise: Beyond Division of Labor," *Journal of Business Strategy* 28, no. 2 (2007): 38–47, for a discussion of the advantages of horizontal over vertical designs.
63. Eric M. Olson, Stanley F. Slater, and G. Tomas M. Hult, "The Importance of Structure and Process to Strategy Implementation," *Business Horizons* 48 (2005): 47–54; and Dale E. Zand, "Strategic Renewal: How an Organization Realigned Structure with Strategy," *Strategy & Leadership* 37, no. 3 (2009): 23–28.
64. Michael E. Porter, *Competitive Strategy* (New York: Free Press, 1980), pp. 36–46.
65. Tom Burns and G. M. Stalker, *The Management of Innovation* (London: Tavistock, 1961).
66. John A. Coutright, Gail T. Fairhurst, and L. Edna Rogers, "Interaction Patterns in Organic and Mechanistic Systems," *Academy of Management Journal* 32 (1989): 773–802.
67. For more on technology and structure, see Denise M. Rousseau and Robert A. Cooke, "Technology and Structure: The Concrete, Abstract, and Activity Systems of Organizations," *Journal of Management* 10 (1984): 345–361; Charles Perrow, "A Framework for the Comparative Analysis of Organizations," *American Sociological Review* 32 (1967): 194–208; and Denise M. Rousseau, "Assessment of Technology in Organizations: Closed versus Open Systems Approaches," *Academy of Management Review* 4 (1979): 531–542.
68. Joan Woodward, *Industrial Organizations: Theory and Practice* (London: Oxford University Press, 1965); and Joan Woodward, *Management and Technology* (London: Her Majesty's Stationery Office, 1958).
69. Peter K. Mills and Thomas Kurk, "A Preliminary Investigation into the Influence of Customer-Firm Interface on Information Processing and Task Activity in Service Organizations," *Journal of Management* 12 (1986): 91–104; Peter K. Mills and Dennis J. Moberg, "Perspectives on the Technology of Service Operations," *Academy of Management Review* 7 (1982): 467–478; and Roger W. Schmenner, "How Can Service Businesses Survive and Prosper?" *Sloan Management Review* 27 (Spring 1986): 21–32.
70. Richard B. Chase and David A. Tansik, "The Customer Contact Model for Organization Design," *Management Science* 29 (1983): 1037–1050; and Gregory B. Northcraft and Richard B. Chase, "Managing Service Demand at the Point of Delivery," *Academy of Management Review* 10 (1985): 66–75.
71. Thomas A. Stewart, "Three Rules for Managing in the Real-Time Economy," *Fortune* (May 1, 2000): 333–334.

72. Based on Doug Wallace, "The Man Who Knew Too Much," *Business Ethics* 2 (March–April 1993): 7–8.
73. Based on Perry Glasser, "In CIOs We Trust," *CIO Enterprise* (June 15, 1999): 34–44; Stephanie Overby, "What Really Matters: Staying in the Game," *CIO Magazine* (October 1, 2004): 68–69, 72–76; and Alenka Grealish, "Banking Trends in 2005 That Will Make A Difference," *Bank Systems & Technology*, December 14, 2004, www.banktech.com/story/news/showArticle.jhtml?articleID=55301770 (accessed August 30, 2010).

Chapter Outline

Top Left: © Robnroll, Shutterstock   Top Right: © James Steidl, Shutterstock

Managing Change and Innovation

Learning Outcomes

After studying this chapter, you should be able to:

1. Define organizational change and explain the forces driving innovation and change in today's organizations.
2. Identify the three innovation strategies managers implement for changing products and technologies.
3. Explain the value of creativity, idea incubators, horizontal linkages, open innovation, idea champions, and new-venture teams for innovation.
4. Discuss why changes in people and culture are critical to any change process.
5. Define organization development (OD) and large-group interventions.
6. Explain the OD stages of unfreezing, changing, and refreezing.
7. Identify sources of resistance to change.
8. Explain force-field analysis and other implementation tactics that can be used to overcome resistance.

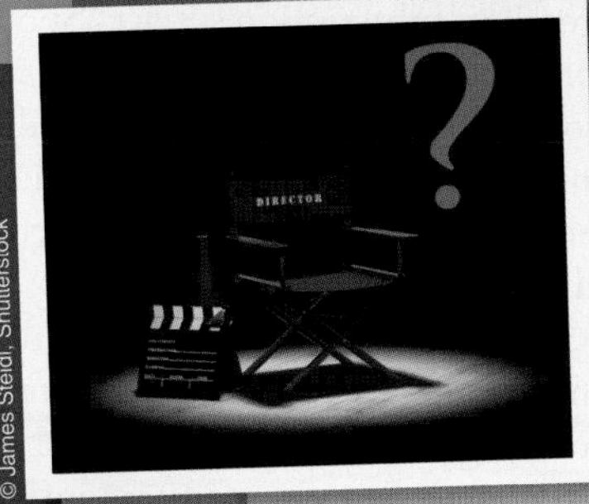

© James Steidl, Shutterstock

Are You Ready to Be a Manager?

Please circle your opinion below each of the following statements.

1 I am open to new ideas or ways of doing things.

Mostly True | Mostly False

(See page 292, Innovation and the Changing Workplace.)

2 I come up with novel ways to look at situations or solve problems.

Mostly True | Mostly False

(See page 295, Exploration.)

3 I am curious and persistent in solving problems.

Mostly True | Mostly False

(See page 295, Exploration.)

4 I have an easy time working with other people when trying to figure a new way of getting something done.

Mostly True | Mostly False

(See page 298, Cooperation.)

5 I love to learn, experiment, and take risks and appreciate it when I have the autonomy to do so.

Mostly True | Mostly False

(See page 302, Entrepreneurship.)

Apple's iPod and iTunes revolutionized the music industry, but Apple has some stiff competition looming on the horizon. In fact, one writer suggested that Spotify, the European streaming music service expected to launch in the United States in 2010, "leaves iTunes looking very dated . . . and increasingly unnecessary." Spotify seemed to come out of nowhere to land at Number 15 on *Fast Company*'s list of "The World's Most Innovative Companies 2010." Since the company was started in Sweden in October 2008, Spotify's free service that pulls music "out of the cloud" has been used by more than 7 million people across Europe. Increasing numbers of customers are also signing up for the company's premium subscription service. Spotify's entry into the United States has been slowed due to complex negotiations with music industry executives, but managers aren't giving up on the world's largest music market easily. Spotify continues to add innovative features, such as one that allows integration with Facebook and Twitter, that could make Spotify the music service to beat. "These guys are good, smart, and focused," said an executive at Broadcast Music, Inc.[1]

Companies might still be struggling through a tough economy, but smart managers know they can't let innovation take a back seat. Winning companies are continually innovating in both large and small ways. Google runs 50 to 200 online experiments at any given time. The company intentionally puts out imperfect or unfinished products to test the response and get ideas for how to perfect them.[2] Chinese car and battery manufacturer BYD Auto beat other automakers to market with the first plug-in hybrid and is likely to do the same with its all-electric full-size E6, which BYD managers hope to sell in the United States by the end of 2010.[3] General Electric developed a pocket-size ultrasound device that lets primary care doctors make diagnoses on site that once required referral to a specialist.[4]

If organizations don't successfully change and innovate, they die. Consider that just 71 of the companies on *Fortune* magazine's first list of America's 500 largest corporations, compiled in 1955, survived the next half-century.[5] Every organization sometimes faces the need to change swiftly and dramatically to cope with a changing environment. LEGO Group, the Swedish company known for its brightly colored toy bricks, was near bankruptcy in 2004, but has become one of the most successful companies in the toy industry by responding to changes in how kids play. LEGO has introduced video games, a virtual reality system, and toys and games tied to popular Hollywood movies.[6]

In this chapter, we look at how organizations can be designed to respond to the environment through internal change and development. First, we look at two key aspects of change in organizations: introducing new products and technologies, and changing people and culture. Then we examine how managers implement change, including overcoming resistance.

Innovation and the Changing Workplace

1

Organizational change is defined as the adoption of a new idea or behavior by an organization.[7] Sometimes change and innovation are spurred by forces outside the organization, such as when a powerful customer demands annual price cuts, when a key supplier goes out of business, or when new government regulations go into effect. Managers in finance companies had to revise credit card procedures and marketing practices due to requirements of the Credit Card Accountability, Responsibility, and Disclosure (CARD) Act, signed into law in 2010 as part of government efforts to reform the U.S. financial system. Some financial firms, in response to public outrage over the excesses that contributed to the Wall Street meltdown, have created new structures and systems designed to look for and challenge signs of excessive greed, overly aggressive risk taking, or double-dealing.[8] In the European Union, banks have to make changes to adjust to a pay cap legislated by the European Parliament that will limit bankers' short-term risk taking. In China, organizations are under pressure from the government to increase wages to help workers cope with rising food costs.[9] These outside forces compel managers to look for greater efficiencies in operations and other changes to keep their organizations profitable. Other times, managers within the company want to initiate major changes, such as forming employee-participation teams, introducing new products, or instituting new training systems, but they don't know how to make the changes successful.

Disruptive innovation is becoming a goal for companies that want to remain competitive on a global basis. **Disruptive innovation** refers to innovations in products, services, or processes that radically change an industry's rules of the game for producers and consumers. CDs all but wiped out the phonograph industry, and now iPods and streaming music are threatening the same fate for CDs. Digital cameras appear to be eliminating the photographic film industry. Starbucks's approach to selling a meaningful experience instead of just a cup of coffee was a disruptive innovation in the food and beverage industry. Many disruptive innovations come from small entrepreneurial firms, and some observers think companies in emerging markets such as China and India will produce a great percentage of such innovations in the coming years.[10] In addition, Western firms are increasingly using an approach referred to as *trickle-up innovation* or *reverse innovation*. Rather than innovating in affluent countries and transferring products to emerging markets, companies such as General Electric, Microsoft, Xerox, and Nokia are now creating innovative low-cost products for emerging markets and then quickly and inexpensively repackaging them for sale in developed countries. General Electric created a $1,000 handheld electrocardiogram (ECG) machine for sale in China and India, for example, and now sells it as the Mac 800 in the United States, at a cost 80 percent less than other machines with similar capabilities.[11]

However, change—especially major change—is not easy, and many organizations struggle with changing successfully. In some cases, employees don't have the desire or motivation to come up with new ideas, or their ideas never get heard by managers who could put them into practice. In other cases, managers learn about good ideas but have trouble getting cooperation from employees for implementation. Successful change requires that organizations be capable of both creating and implementing ideas, which means the organization must learn to be *ambidextrous*.

An **ambidextrous approach** means incorporating structures and processes that are appropriate for both the creative impulse and for the systematic implementation of innovations. For example, a loose, flexible structure and greater employee freedom are excellent for the creation and initiation of ideas; however, these same conditions often make it difficult to implement a change because employees are less likely to comply. Or, as one scholar put it, companies "that are healthy enough to consider innovation are also hearty enough to resist change."[12] With an ambidextrous approach, managers encourage flexibility and freedom to innovate and propose new ideas with creative departments, venture teams, and other mechanisms we will discuss in this chapter, but they use a more rigid, centralized, and standardized approach for implementing innovations.[13] For example, Tatsuo Higuchi, president of Oksuka Pharmaceutical Company, insists that the firm's research labs "put a high value on weird people" in order to get the kind of creative spirit willing to try new things. In the department that manufactures drugs, however, where routine and precision are important, the emphasis is on following standard rules and procedures.[14] Organizations must embrace many types of change. Businesses must develop improved production technologies, create new products and services desired in the marketplace, implement new administrative systems, and upgrade employees' skills. In the following section, we discuss technology and product changes, which typically rely on new ideas that bubble up from lower levels of the organization.

- Every organization must change and innovate to survive.
- **Organizational change** is defined as the adoption of a new idea or behavior by an organization.
- **Disruptive innovation** refers to innovations in products, services, or processes that radically change competition in an industry, such as the advent of CDs or digital cameras.
- An **ambidextrous approach** means incorporating structures and processes that are appropriate for both the creative impulse and the systematic implementation of innovations.

Changing *Things*: New Products and Technologies

Introducing new products and technologies is a vital area for innovation. A **product change** is a change in the organization's product or service outputs. Product and service innovation is the primary way in which organizations adapt to changes in markets, technology, and competition.[15] Examples of new products include Apple's iPad, the Chevy Volt from General Motors, and the Flip lightweight handheld video camera from Pure Digital Technologies (now owned by Cisco Systems). The introduction of video streams by Hulu is an example of a service innovation, as is the launch of *e-file*, which allows online filing of tax returns to the U.S. Internal Revenue Service (IRS). Product changes are related to changes in the technology of the organization. A **technology change** is a change in the organization's production process—how the organization does its work. Technology changes are designed to make the production of a product or service more efficient. Hammond's Candies saves hundreds of thousands of dollars a year by implementing technology changes suggested by employees. One example was tweaking a machine gear that reduced the number of employees needed on an assembly line from five to four. Another idea was a new way to package candy canes that would protect them from getting broken while enroute to stores.[16] Other examples of technology change include the introduction of efficiency-boosting winglets on aircraft at Southwest Airlines, the adoption of automatic mail-sorting machines by the U.S. Postal Service, and the use of biosimulation software to run virtual tests on new drugs at Johnson & Johnson Pharmaceutical Research and Development.

Joerg koch/Ddp/Getty Images

ConceptConnection

Every four years, the International Federation of Association Football commissions a new World Cup soccer ball. For the 2010 match, Adidas spent years designing a smooth, almost perfectly round ball that incorporated a "Grip 'n' Groove" **innovation** intended to ensure consistent performance. The company claims the resulting Jabulani (Zulu for "celebrate") is "the most innovative ball ever made." English player David James calls the **new product** "rubbish." James and other players complained the ball moved unpredictably. Time will tell. No one liked the now-iconic black-and-white World Cup ball Adidas introduced in 1970 either.

Three critical innovation strategies for changing products and technologies are illustrated in Exhibit 8.1.[17] The first strategy, *exploration*, involves designing the organization to encourage creativity

EXHIBIT 8.1

Three Innovative Strategies for New Products and Technologies

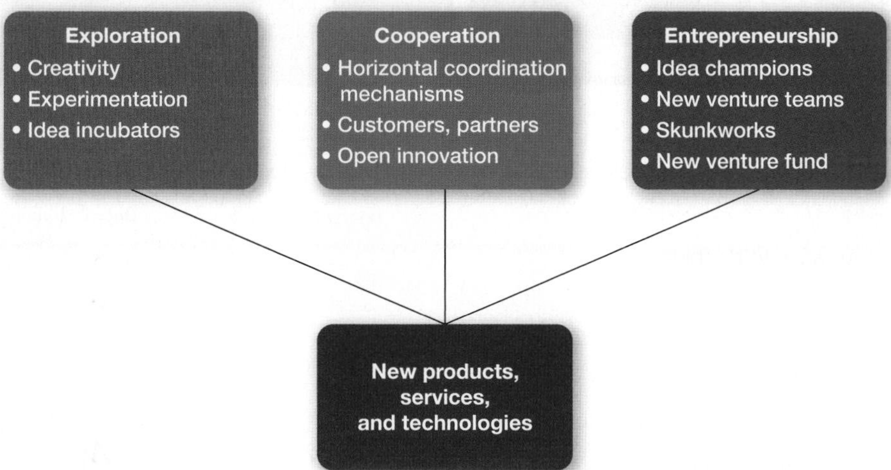

SOURCES: Based on Patrick Reinmoeller and Nicole van Baardwijk, "The Link Between Diversity and Resilience," *MIT Sloan Management Review* (Summer 2005), pp. 61–65.

and the initiation of new ideas. The strategy of *cooperation* refers to creating conditions and systems to facilitate internal and external coordination and knowledge sharing. Finally, *entrepreneurship* means that managers put in place processes and structures to ensure that new ideas are carried forward for acceptance and implementation.

Exploration

Exploration is the stage where ideas for new products and technologies are born. Managers design the organization for exploration by establishing conditions that encourage creativity and allow new ideas to spring forth. **Creativity** refers to the generation of novel ideas that might meet perceived needs or respond to opportunities for the organization.[18] People noted for their creativity include Edwin Land, who invented the Polaroid camera, and Swiss engineer George de Mestral, who created Velcro after noticing the tiny hooks on the burrs caught on his wool socks. These people saw unique and creative opportunities in a familiar situation. Stanford University's Technology Ventures program recently sponsored a contest challenging people to come up with creative uses for everyday objects, such as rubber bands. Ignacio Donoso Olive, a computer science student in Ecuador, connected bands to form an elastic hem around the mesh canopies that are hung over beds at night to combat malaria. The elastic band helps prevent the canopies, usually tucked under mattresses, from slipping loose and giving deadly entrance to mosquitoes.[19]

Characteristics of highly creative people are illustrated in the left-hand column of Exhibit 8.2. Creative people often are known for originality, open-mindedness, curiosity, a focused approach to problem solving, persistence, a relaxed and playful attitude, and receptivity to new ideas.[20] Creativity can also be designed into organizations. Companies or departments within companies can be organized to be creative and initiate ideas for change. Most companies want more highly creative employees and often seek to hire creative individuals. However, the individual is only part of the story, and each of us has some potential for creativity. Managers are responsible for creating a work environment that allows creativity to flourish.[21]

New Manager Self-Test

Are You Innovative?

Think about your current life. Indicate whether each item below is Mostly True or Mostly False for you.

	MOSTLY TRUE <<<	>>> MOSTLY FALSE
1. I am always seeking new ways to do things.	______	______
2. I consider myself creative and original in my thinking and behavior.	______	______
3. I rarely trust new gadgets until I see whether they work for people around me.	______	______
4. In a group or at work, I am often skeptical of new ideas.	______	______
5. I typically buy new foods, gear, and other innovations before other people do.	______	______
6. I like to spend time trying out new things.	______	______
7. My behavior influences others to try new things.	______	______
8. Among my coworkers, I will be one of the first to try out a new idea or method.	______	______

See It Online

Scoring and Interpretation: *Personal Innovativeness* reflects the awareness of the need to innovate and a readiness to try new things. Innovativeness is also thought of as the degree to which a person adopts innovations earlier than other people in the peer group. Innovativeness is considered a positive characteristic for people in many companies where individuals and organizations are faced with a constant need to change.

To compute your score on the Personal Innovativeness scale, add the number of Mostly True answers to items 1, 2, 5, 6, 7, and 8 above and the Mostly False answers to items 3 and 4 for your score. A score of 6 to 8 indicates that you are very innovative and likely are one of the first people to adopt changes. A score of 4 to 5 would suggest that you are average or slightly above average in innovativeness compared to others. A score of 0 to 3 means that you might prefer the tried and true and hence are not excited about new ideas or innovations. As a new manager, a high score suggests you will emphasize innovation and change. A low score suggests you may prefer stability and established methods.

SOURCES: Based on H. Thomas Hurt, Katherine Joseph, and Chester D. Cook, "Scales for the Measurement of Innovativeness," *Human Communication Research* 4, no. 1 (1977): 58–65, and John E. Ettlie and Robert D. O'Keefe, "Innovative Attitudes, Values, and Intentions in Organizations," *Journal of Management Studies* 19, no. 2 (1982): 163–182.

The characteristics of creative organizations correspond to those of individuals, as illustrated in the right-hand column of Exhibit 8.2. Creative organizations are loosely structured. People find themselves in a situation of ambiguity, assignments are vague, territories overlap, tasks are loosely defined, and much work is done through teams. Managers in creative companies embrace risk and experimentation. They involve employees in a varied range of projects so that people are not stuck in the rhythm of routine

EXHIBIT 8.2

Characteristics of Creative People and Organizations

The Creative Individual	The Creative Organization or Department
1. Conceptual fluency Open-mindedness	1. Open channels of communication Contact with outside sources Overlapping territories; cross-pollination of ideas across disciplines Suggestion systems, brainstorming, freewheeling discussions
2. Originality	2. Assigning nonspecialists to problems Eccentricity allowed Hiring outside your comfort zone
3. Less authority Independence Self-confidence	3. Decentralization, loosely defined positions, loose control Acceptance of mistakes; rewarding risk-taking People encouraged to challenge their bosses
4. Playfulness Undisciplined exploration Curiosity	4. Freedom to choose and pursue problems Not a tight ship, playful culture, doing the impractical Freedom to discuss ideas; long time horizon
5. Persistence Commitment Focused approach	5. Resources allocated to creative personnel and projects without immediate payoff Reward system encourages innovation Absolution of peripheral responsibilities

SOURCES: Based on Gary A. Steiner, ed., *The Creative Organization* (Chicago: University of Chicago Press, 1965): 16–18; Rosabeth Moss Kanter, "The Middle Manager as Innovator," *Harvard Business Review* (July–August 1982): 104–105; James Brian Quinn, "Managing Innovation: Controlled Chaos," *Harvard Business Review* (May–June 1985): 73–84; Robert I. Sutton, "The Weird Rules of Creativity," *Harvard Business Review* (September 2001): 94–103; and Bridget Finn, "Playbook: Brainstorming for Better Brainstorming," *Business* 2.0 (April 2005), 109–114.

jobs, and they drive out the fear of making mistakes that can inhibit creative thinking.[22] At West Paw Design, a manufacturer of pet toys and accessories, managers decided to get everyone involved in coming up with new products, as described in the Spotlight on Skills titled West Paw Design.

A company doesn't have to make toys to encourage the kind of fun and experimentation that West Paw's design competition creates. Consider the London Probation Area, whose thousands of employees work with criminal offenders. The agency's creative approach to innovation was recognized at the CQI London Excellence awards. One project, for example, invited staff to participate in a "Dragon's Den" exercise modeled on the popular BBC television show.[23] Creative organizations in any field of endeavor are those that have an internal culture of playfulness, freedom, challenge, and grass-roots participation.[24] Exhibit 8.3 shows the world's top ten innovative companies from the 2010 lists in *BusinessWeek* and *Fast Company*.

Go to the Self-Learning, on page 317, that pertains to creativity in organizations.

Another popular way to encourage new ideas within the organization is the **idea incubator**. An idea incubator provides a safe harbor where ideas from employees throughout the company can be developed without interference from company bureaucracy or politics.[25] Yahoo started an offsite incubator called "Brickhouse" to speed up development of ideas and be more competitive with Google. Located in a hip section of San Francisco, the idea incubator gets about 200 ideas submitted each month and a panel sorts out the top five to ten. "The goal is to take the idea, develop it, and make sure it's seen by senior management quickly," says Salim Ismail, head of Brickhouse.[26]

SPOTLIGHT ON SKILLS

West Paw Design

One of West Paw Design's hot new dog toys might have been dreamed up in the accounting department. That's because once a year everyone in the company, from salespeople to production workers, to the company president, spends an afternoon designing and producing prototypes for new products. Seth Partain, West Paw's production manager, came up with the idea after the company's R&D team hit a collective creative roadblock. Facing stiff competition from other companies, president Spencer Williams quickly jumped on board, set some ground rules, and let the fun begin.

At the end of the day, all employees vote by secret ballot to choose the winner, and the team responsible receives a small gift card and the Golden Hairball statue. One winner that became a hit product was the Eco Bed, a stuffed dog bed made out of recycled materials. Many prototypes never make it into production, but managers are careful to focus on the positive qualities of each and every contest entry. Williams points out that it isn't just about looking for products the company can sell right now, but about gathering creative ideas that might be used down the road for other products. Cheryl Grisso, an accountant, says she now dreams up new products on a regular basis. "Other companies just want you to do your job," says Grisso. "This competition has given me the chance to offer my opinions."

SOURCE: Nadine Heintz, "Managing: Employee Creativity Unleashed. How to Turn Anyone into a Designer," *Inc.* (June 2009): 101–102.

- A **product change** is a change in the organization's products or services, such as the Apple iPad or the Chevrolet Volt.
- **Technology change** refers to a change in production processes—how the organization does its work.
- *Exploration* involves designing the organization to encourage creativity and the initiation of new ideas.
- **Creativity** is the generation of novel ideas that may meet perceived needs or respond to opportunities for the organization.
- West Paw Design uses special techniques to awaken creativity in its employees.
- An **idea incubator** is an organizational program that provides a safe harbor where employees can generate and develop ideas without interference from company bureaucracy or politics.

Cooperation

4

Another important aspect of innovation is providing mechanisms for both internal and external coordination. Ideas for product and technology innovations typically originate at lower levels of the organization and have to flow horizontally across departments. In addition, people and organizations outside the firm can be rich sources of innovative ideas. Lack of innovation is widely recognized as one of the biggest problems facing today's businesses. Consider that 72 percent of top executives surveyed by *BusinessWeek* and the Boston Consulting Group reported that innovation is a top priority, yet almost half said they are dissatisfied with their results in that area.[27] Thus, many companies are undergoing a transformation in the way they find and use new ideas, focusing on improving both internal and external coordination.

EXHIBIT 8.3

The World's Most Innovative Companies 2010

Rank	*Fast Company* List	*BusinessWeek* List
1	Facebook	Apple
2	Amazon	Google
3	Apple	Microsoft
4	Google	IBM
5	Huawei	Toyota
6	First Solar	Amazon
7	PG&E	LG Electronics
8	Novartis	BYD Auto
9	Walmart	General Electric
10	Hewlett-Packard	Sony

SOURCES: "The World's 50 Most Innovative Companies," *Fast Company* (March 2010), pp. 52–97; and "The 50 Most Innovative Companies 2010," *Bloomberg BusinessWeek Online*, http://bwnt.businessweek.com/interactive_reports/innovative_companies_2010 (accessed May 5, 2010).

Internal Coordination Successful innovation requires expertise from several departments simultaneously, and failed innovation is often the result of failed cooperation.[28] Consider the partner at a large accounting firm who was leading a team of 50 experts to develop new services. After a year of effort, they'd come up with few ideas, and the ones they had produced weren't successful. What went wrong? The leader had divided the team into three separate groups so that researchers would come up with ideas, then hand them off to technical specialists, who in turn passed them along to marketers. Because the groups were working in isolation, much time and energy was spent on ideas that didn't meet technical specialists' criteria or that the marketers knew wouldn't work commercially.[29] "Innovation is a team sport," says Drew Boyd, a businessman who speaks about innovation to other companies. Ed Catmull, president of Pixar Animation Studios and Disney Animation Studios, agrees. "Creativity involves a large number of people from different disciplines working together," Catmull says of his companies' innovation processes.[30]

Companies that successfully innovate usually have the following characteristics:

1. People in marketing have a good understanding of customer needs.
2. Technical specialists are aware of recent technological developments and make effective use of new technology.
3. Members from key departments—research, manufacturing, marketing—cooperate in the development of the new product or service.[31]

One approach to successful innovation is called the **horizontal linkage model**, which is illustrated in the center circle of Exhibit 8.4.[32] The model shows that the research, manufacturing, and sales and marketing departments within an organization simultaneously contribute to new products and technologies. People from these departments meet frequently in teams and task forces to share ideas and solve problems. Research people inform marketing of new technical developments to learn whether they will be useful to customers. Marketing people pass customer complaints to research to use in the design of new products and to manufacturing people to develop new ideas for improving production speed and quality. Manufacturing informs other departments whether a product idea can be manufactured within cost limits.

EXHIBIT 8.4

Coordination Model for Innovation

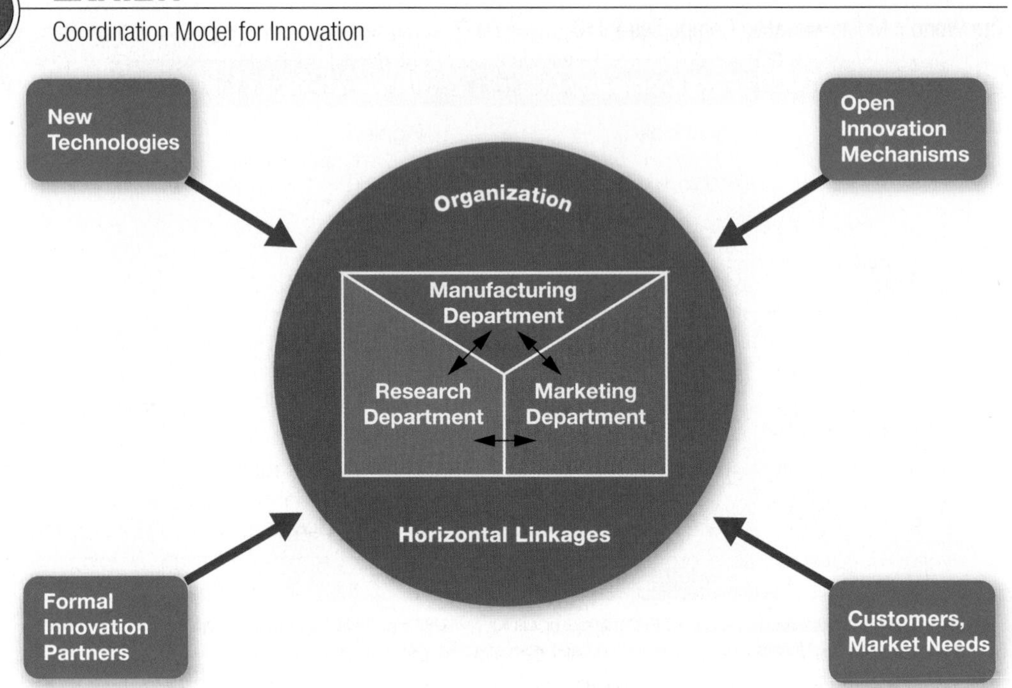

The horizontal linkage model is increasingly important in today's high-pressure business environment that requires rapidly developing and commercializing products and services. This kind of teamwork is similar to a rugby match wherein players run together, passing the ball back and forth as they move downfield.[33] Speed is emerging as a pivotal strategic weapon in the global marketplace for a wide variety of industries.[34] Many companies now do most of their concept testing online, which allows them to know within hours if an idea has merit. At the Spanish apparel chain Zara, sales managers continually monitor sales at every store around the world so they can let designers know which products are hits and which ones are flops. Best sellers can be restocked in just a couple of days, and new designs arrive at stores every two weeks.[35] Some companies use fast-cycle teams to deliver products and services faster than competitors, giving them a significant strategic advantage. A **fast-cycle team** is a multifunctional, and sometimes multinational, team that works under

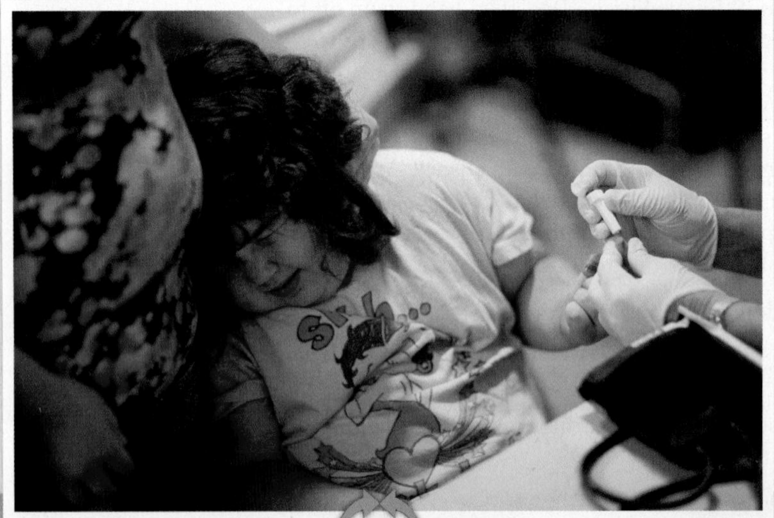

Bloomberg/Contributor/Getty Images

ConceptConnection

In 2010, Harvard University's Catalyst Linkages Program, an online hub for cross-disciplinary scientific work, announced a yearlong trial of an **open innovation** approach to medical research. Working with InnoCentive, a company that conducts open innovation contests, Catalyst sponsored its first "Prize for Innovation" competition—a call for questions and ideas related to juvenile diabetes research. It was open to 200,000 members of the InnoCentive network plus the Harvard community—faculty, students, administrators, and staff. Those with the ideas that showed the most promise to spark innovative research directions and collaborations were eligible for cash prizes ranging from $2,500 to $10,000.

BENCHMARKING

Twitter's Jack Dorsey

As an 8-year-old boy in St. Louis, Jack Dorsey was obsessed with maps—city maps, transit maps, maps in magazines—all of which papered his bedroom walls, and he was fascinated with taxis, police cars, and locomotives. He got his first computer that year and started designing his own maps graphic program. Teaching himself to program so he could make small dots to represent buses and trains, he spent his days listening to police frequencies and then plotting ambulances or fire trucks as they moved toward an accident, a fire, or the hospital. Later on, as a skilled teenage programmer, he developed his own strangely poetic outlook on the precise city grid and how it worked.

When he got a job as a programmer at Odeo, a San Francisco–based software start-up, he suggested a program that would solve the problem of taxis finding the people who need them, where a person would send a simple text message to anyone who wanted to receive it. Odeo Chief Evan Williams loved the idea and made Dorsey head CEO of a new company called Twitter, whose minimalism (tweets are confined to 140 characters) reflects Dorsey's own precision, his own terseness, and asceticism. Five years later, Twitter has taken social media by storm and has 200 million users. But Dorsey has remained out of the limelight. No one knows he earlier pursued a career in botanical illustration and later on, one as a massage therapist, and more recently studied fashion design. It's because Dorsey sees himself as a craftsman, someone with an idea for a service, not an idea to start a company. And back then he didn't like management, nor was he good at it, which has a lot to do with why he was ousted from Twitter as CEO (he remains Chair of the Board).

© Kuzmik, Shutterstock

His new passion is his latest company, Square, where anyone can accept credit card payments by downloading an app, attaching a plastic square to a mobile phone or tablet, and finally swiping the card through the slot. In the same way that Twitter allowed anyone to be a pundit, Square allows anyone to be a merchant. Dorsey has a heartland optimism that is infectious and that sees good in democracy, common good and human potential. All of his works, he says, are designed to make society work more humanely and efficiently. "My role as an observer and technologist," he says, "is to show everything that's happening in the world in real time and get us to that data immediately, so we can change our lives even faster, with better knowledge."

SOURCE: David Kirkpatrick, "Twitter Was Act One," *Vanity Fair*, April 2011, pp. 170–173, 198.

stringent timelines and is provided with high levels of resources and empowerment to accomplish an accelerated product development project.[36]

External Coordination Exhibit 8.4 also illustrates that organizations look outside their boundaries to find and develop new ideas. Engineers and researchers stay aware of new technological developments. Marketing personnel pay attention to shifting market conditions and customer needs. Some organizations build formal strategic partnerships such as alliances and joint ventures to improve innovation success. Twitter's Jack Dorsey was always looking outside himself to see how data could help people lead different lives, as described in this chapter's Benchmarking box.

Today's most successful companies include customers, strategic partners, suppliers, and other outsiders directly in the product and service development process. One of the hottest trends is *open innovation*.[37] In the past, most businesses generated their own ideas in-house and then developed, manufactured, marketed, and distributed them, a closed innovation approach. Today, however, forward-looking companies are trying a different method. **Open innovation** means extending the search for and commercialization of new ideas beyond the boundaries of the organization and even beyond the boundaries of the industry.

Some of the best-selling products from consumer products company Procter & Gamble, including the Swiffer SweeperVac, Olay Regenerist, and Mr. Clean Magic Eraser, were developed in whole or in part by someone outside the company. P&G, which gets more than 50 percent of its innovation from outside company walls, solicits solutions to various scientific or product development challenges and also accepts unsolicited ideas.[38] Eli Lilly and Company set the standard in the pharmaceuticals industry in the 1990s with its "research without walls" approach. Lilly developed a network of external partners in biotechnology, academia, and other fields to provide ideas for innovation.[39] IBM has opened its R&D labs to customers and other outsiders and holds online Innovation Jams that often attract as many as 150,000 employees, customers, partners, and academics.[40]

The Internet has made it possible for companies to tap into ideas from around the world and let hundreds of thousands of people contribute to the innovation process, which is why some approaches to open innovation are referred to as *crowdsourcing*. One company that has taken crowdsourcing to the extreme is online T-shirt retailer Threadless, now owned by skinnyCorp. Threadless sponsors design competitions on an online social network, where people socialize, blog, and discuss ideas. Members submit T-shirt designs by the hundreds each week and then vote on which ones they like best. Managers also built a Web site that lets Twitter followers suggest their favorite tweets for consideration as T-shirt slogans. In the first five months, the Twitter experiment attracted 100,000 submission and 3.5 million votes, resulting in new designs that provided hundreds of thousands of dollars in additional revenue.[41]

Companies such as Threadless, IBM, and Procter & Gamble are at the forefront of a movement to drastically rethink innovation. In line with the new way of thinking we discussed in Chapter 1, which sees partnership and collaboration as more important than independence and competition, the boundaries between an organization and its environment are becoming porous, with ideas flowing back and forth among different people and organizations around the world.

- Successful product and service innovation depends on cooperation, both within the organization and with customers and others outside the organization.
- Using a **horizontal linkage model** means that several departments, such as marketing, research, and manufacturing, work closely together to develop new products.
- A **fast-cycle team** is a multifunctional team that is empowered with autonomy and high levels of resources to speed an important new product or service to market.
- Some companies, such as Eli Lilly and Procter & Gamble, extend the search for innovative ideas beyond the boundaries of the organization—a process called **open innovation**.
- *Crowdsourcing*, an open innovation approach used by Threadless and other companies, taps into ideas from around the world and lets thousands or hundreds of thousands of people participate in the innovation process, usually via the Internet.

Entrepreneurship

5

The third aspect of product and technology innovation is creating mechanisms to make sure new ideas are carried forward, accepted, and implemented. Managers can directly influence whether entrepreneurship flourishes in the organization by expressing support of entrepreneurial activities, giving employees a degree of autonomy, and rewarding learning and risk taking.[42] One important factor is fostering idea champions. The formal definition of an **idea champion** is a person who sees the need for and champions productive change within the organization.

Remember: Change does not occur by itself. Personal energy and effort are required to successfully promote a new idea. When Texas Instruments studied 50 of its new-product introductions, a surprising fact emerged: Without exception, every new product that failed lacked a zealous champion. In contrast, most of the new products that succeeded had a champion. Managers made an immediate decision: No new product would be approved unless someone championed it. Similarly, at SRI International, a contract research and development firm, managers use the saying "No champion, no product, no exception."[43] Research confirms that successful new ideas are generally those that are backed by someone who believes in the idea wholeheartedly and is determined to convince others of its value.[44]

Sometimes a new idea is rejected by top managers, but champions are passionately committed to a new idea or product despite rejection by others. For example, Robert Vincent was fired twice by two different division managers at a semiconductor company. Both times, he convinced the president and chairman of the board to reinstate him to continue working on his idea for an airbag sensor that measures acceleration and deceleration. He couldn't get approval for research funding, so Vincent pushed to finish another project in half the time and used the savings to support the new product development.[45]

Championing an idea successfully requires roles in organizations, as illustrated in Exhibit 8.5. Sometimes a single person may play two or more of these roles, but successful innovation in most companies involves the interplay of different people, each adopting one role. The *inventor* comes up with a new idea and understands its technical value but has neither the ability nor the interest to promote it for acceptance within the organization. The *champion* believes in the idea, confronts the organizational realities of costs and benefits, and gains the political and financial support needed to bring it to reality. The *sponsor* is a high-level manager who approves the idea, protects it, and removes major organizational barriers to acceptance. The *critic* counterbalances the zeal of the champion by challenging the concept and providing a reality test against hard-nosed criteria. The critic prevents people in the other roles from adopting a bad idea.[46]

Are you an idea champion for changes or new ideas you believe in? To find out, complete the New Manager Self-Test on page 304.

Another way to facilitate entrepreneurship is through a **new-venture team**. A new-venture team is a unit separate from the rest of the organization that is responsible for developing and initiating a major innovation.[47] New-venture teams give free rein to members' creativity because their separate facilities and location unleash people from the restrictions imposed by organizational rules and procedures. These teams typically are small, loosely structured, and flexible, reflecting the characteristics of creative organizations described

EXHIBIT 8.5

Four Roles in Organizational Change

Inventor	Champion	Sponsor	Critic
Develops and understands technical aspects of idea Does not know how to win support for the idea or make a business of it	Believes in idea Visualizes benefits Confronts organizational realities of cost, benefits Obtains financial and political support Overcomes obstacles	High-level manager who removes organizational barriers Approves and protects idea within organization	Provides reality test Looks for shortcomings Defines hard-nosed criteria that idea must pass

SOURCES: Based on Harold L. Angle and Andrew H. Van de Ven, "Suggestions for Managing the Innovation Journey," *in Research in the Management of Innovation: The Minnesota Studies*, ed. A. H. Van de Ven, H. L. Angle, and Marshall Scott Poole (Cambridge, MA: Ballinger/Harper & Row, 1989); and Jay R. Galbraith, "Designing the Innovating Organization," *Organizational Dynamics* (Winter 1982): 5–25.

New Manager Self-Test

Taking Charge of Change

As a new manager, do you have what it takes to be an idea champion? Will you initiate change? Think of a job you held for a period of time. Answer the following items according to your behaviors and perspective on that job. Please answer whether each item is Mostly True or Mostly False for you.

	MOSTLY TRUE <<<	>>> MOSTLY FALSE
1. I often tried to adopt improved procedures for doing my job.	______	______
2. I felt a personal sense of responsibility to bring about change in my workplace.	______	______
3. I often tried to institute new work methods that were more effective for the company.	______	______
4. I often tried to change organizational rules or policies that were nonproductive or counterproductive.	______	______
5. It was up to me to bring about improvement in my workplace.	______	______
6. I often made constructive suggestions for improving how things operated.	______	______
7. I often tried to implement new ideas for pressing organizational problems.	______	______
8. I often tried to introduce new structures, technologies, or approaches to improve efficiency.	______	______

See It Online

Scoring and Interpretation: An important part of a new manager's job is to facilitate improvements through innovation and change. Will you be a champion for change? Your answers to the items may indicate the extent to which you have a natural inclination toward taking charge of change. Not everyone thrives in a position of initiating change, but as a new manager, initiating change within the first six months will enhance your impact.

Give yourself 1 point for each item you marked as Mostly True. If you scored 4 or less, you may not have been flexing your change muscles on the job and may need to become more active at taking charge of change. Moreover, you may need to be in a more favorable change situation. Research indicates that jobs with open-minded management, where change is believed likely to succeed and be rewarded, increase a person's initiative. So the organization in which you are a new manager plus your own inclination will influence your initiation of change. A score of 5 or more suggests a positive level of previous change initiation behavior and solid preparation for a new manager role as an idea champion.

SOURCE: Based on Elizabeth W. Morrison and Corey C. Phelps, "Taking Charge at Work: Extrarole Efforts to Initiate Workplace Change," *Academy of Management Journal* 42 (1999): 403–419.

in Exhibit 8.2. One good example is Nestlé's Nespresso venture, which developed a line of high-quality coffees packaged in individual capsules for use in specially designed coffee machines. The team found itself hampered by the large company's rules, structures, and regulations. In addition, the project faced resistance from managers who feared the new premium line would hurt the existing Nescafé brand. Top managers moved the Nespresso business outside the existing structure so it could thrive with an entrepreneurial culture and promote innovative ideas.[48]

One variation of a new-venture team is called a **skunkworks**.[49] A skunkworks is a separate small, informal, highly autonomous, and often secretive group that focuses on breakthrough ideas for the business. The original skunkworks, which still exists, was created by Lockheed Martin more than 50 years ago. The essence of a skunkworks is that highly talented people are given the time and freedom to let creativity reign.[50] The laser printer was invented by a Xerox researcher who was transferred to a skunkworks, the Xerox Palo Alto Research Center (PARC), after his ideas about using lasers were stifled within the company for being "too impractical and expensive."[51] Adam Gryglak, the chief diesel engineer at Ford Motor Company, transferred the team developing Ford's new diesel engine to a skunkworks so the team could develop the innovative engine quickly and protect Ford's hold on the lucrative market for contractor grade pickups. He knew it would be impossible for the team to meet the tight deadline for the all-new engine while working within the rigid atmosphere of the larger organization. The engine would be the first of its kind to use state-of-the-art antipollution technology that will meet new federal regulations, have the best fuel economy in its category, and need no significant maintenance for 300,000 miles. Gryglak moved the team off campus, named the project Scorpion, and developed a logo featuring a menacing mechanical scorpion-like creature (meant to keep the bosses from interfering). The bosses had a hard time of it, but they forced themselves to leave the team alone, which enabled it to get the job done right on time.[52]

A related idea is the **new-venture fund**, which provides resources from which individuals and groups can draw to develop new ideas, products, or businesses. At Pitney Bowes, for example, the New Business Opportunity (NBO) program provides funding for teams to explore potentially lucrative but unproven ideas. The NBO program is intended to generate a pipeline of new businesses for the mail and document management services company. Similarly, Royal Dutch Shell puts 10 percent of its R&D budget into the GameChanger program, which provides seed money for innovation projects that are highly ambitious, radical, or long term and would get lost in the larger product development system.[53] With these programs, the support and assistance of senior managers are often just as important as the funding.[54]

Go to the Ethical Dilemma, on page 319, that pertains to structural change.

- *Entrepreneurship* means developing an internal culture, philosophy, and structure that encourages entrepreneurial activity and produces a higher-than-average number of innovations.
- An **idea champion** is a person who sees the need for change and is passionately committed to making it happen.
- One structural mechanism that promotes entrepreneurship is the **new-venture team**, which is a unit separate from the mainstream organization that is responsible for initiating and developing innovations.
- A variation is a **skunkworks**, a separate informal, highly autonomous, and often secretive group that focuses on breakthrough ideas.
- Lockheed Martin created the original skunkworks more than 50 years ago.
- A **new-venture fund** provides financial resources from which individuals or teams can draw to develop new ideas, products, or businesses.

Changing People and Culture

All successful changes involve changes in people and culture as well. Changes in people and culture pertain to how employees think—changes in mind-set. **People change** concerns just a few employees, such as sending a handful of middle managers to a training course to improve their leadership skills. **Culture change** pertains to the organization as a whole, such as when the IRS shifted its basic mind-set from an organization focused on collection and compliance to one dedicated to informing, educating, and serving customers (taxpayers).[55] Large-scale culture change is not easy. Indeed, managers routinely report that changing people and culture is their most difficult job.[56] Two specific tools that can smooth the process are training and development programs and organization development (OD).

Training and Development

Training is one of the most frequently used approaches to changing people's mind-sets. A company might offer training programs to large blocks of employees on subjects such as teamwork, diversity, emotional intelligence, quality circles, communication skills, or participative management.

Successful companies want to provide training and development opportunities for everyone, but they might particularly emphasize training and development for managers, with the idea that the behavior and attitudes of managers will influence people throughout the organization and lead to culture change. A number of Silicon Valley companies, including Intel, Advanced Micro Devices (AMD), and Sun Microsystems, regularly send managers to the Growth and Leadership Center (GLC), where they learn to use emotional intelligence to build better relationships. Nick Kepler, director of technology development at AMD, was surprised to learn how his emotionless approach to work was intimidating people and destroying the rapport needed to shift to a culture based on collaborative teamwork.[57]

Organization Development

Organization development (OD) is a planned, systematic process of change that uses behavioral science knowledge and techniques to improve an organization's health and effectiveness through its ability to adapt to the environment, improve internal relationships, and increase learning and problem-solving capabilities.[58] OD focuses on the human and social aspects of the organization and works to change attitudes and relationships among employees, helping to strengthen the organization's capacity for adaptation and renewal.[59]

OD can help managers address at least three types of current problems:[60]

1. ***Mergers/acquisitions.*** The disappointing financial results of many mergers and acquisitions are caused by the failure of executives to determine whether the administrative style and corporate culture of the two companies fit. Executives may concentrate on potential synergies in technology, products, marketing, and control systems, but fail to recognize that two firms may have widely different values, beliefs, and practices. These differences create stress and anxiety for employees, and these negative emotions affect future performance. Cultural differences should be evaluated during the acquisition process, and OD experts can be used to smooth the integration of two firms.
2. ***Organizational decline/revitalization.*** Organizations undergoing a period of decline and revitalization experience a variety of problems, including a low level of trust, lack of innovation, high turnover, and high levels of conflict and stress. The period of transition requires opposite behaviors, including confronting stress, creating open

communication, and fostering creative innovation to emerge with high levels of productivity. OD techniques can contribute greatly to cultural revitalization by managing conflicts, fostering commitment, and facilitating communication.

3. ***Conflict management.*** Conflict can occur at any time and place within a healthy organization. For example, a product team for the introduction of a new software package was formed at a computer company. Made up of strong-willed individuals, the team made little progress because members could not agree on project goals. At a manufacturing firm, salespeople promised customers delivery dates that were in conflict with shop supervisor priorities for assembling customer orders. In a publishing company, two managers disliked each other intensely. They argued at meetings, lobbied politically against each other, and hurt the achievement of both departments. Organization development efforts can help resolve these kinds of conflicts as well as conflicts related to growing diversity and the global nature of today's organizations.

Organization development can be used to solve the types of problems just described and many others. However, to be truly valuable to companies and employees, organization development practitioners go beyond looking at ways to settle specific problems. Instead, they become involved in broader issues that contribute to improving organizational life, such as encouraging a sense of community, pushing for an organizational climate of openness and trust, and making sure the company provides employees with opportunities for personal growth and development.[61]

OD Activities OD consultants use a variety of specialized techniques to help meet OD goals. Three of the most popular and effective are the following:

1. ***Team-building activities.*** **Team building** enhances the cohesiveness and success of organizational groups and teams. For example, a series of OD exercises can be used with members of cross-departmental teams to help them learn to act and function as a team. An OD expert can work with team members to increase their communication skills, facilitate their ability to confront one another, and help them accept common goals.
2. ***Survey-feedback activities.*** **Survey feedback** begins with a questionnaire distributed to employees on values, climate, participation, leadership, and group cohesion within their organization. After the survey is completed, an OD consultant meets with groups of employees to provide feedback about their responses and the problems identified. Employees are engaged in problem solving based on the data.
3. ***Large-group interventions.*** In recent years, the need for bringing about fundamental organizational change in today's

Spencer Platt/Getty Images News/Getty Images

ConceptConnection

Google managers rely on **survey feedback** to make sure they're providing the environment and benefits employees value. But Google doesn't stop there. In addition to the annual survey, managers solicit feedback on an ongoing basis through various innovative **organization development** tools. One example is the TGIF (Thank goodness it's Friday) meeting held each week. Managers share the latest news, and employees ask questions and offer opinions about matters ranging from product decisions to human resource policies. Those unable to attend in person can participate online.

complex, fast-changing world prompted a growing interest in applications of OD techniques to large-group settings.[62] The **large-group intervention** approach brings together participants from all parts of the organization—often including key stakeholders from outside the organization as well—to discuss problems or opportunities and plan for change. A large-group intervention might involve 50 to 500 people and last several days. The idea is to include everyone who has a stake in the change, gather perspectives from all parts of the system, and enable people to create a collective future through sustained, guided dialogue.

Large-group interventions reflect a significant shift in the approach to organizational change from earlier OD concepts and approaches. Exhibit 8.6 lists the primary differences between the traditional OD model and the large-scale intervention model of organizational change.[63] In the newer approach, the focus is on the entire system, which takes into account the organization's interaction with its environment. The source of information for discussion is expanded to include customers, suppliers, community members, even competitors, and this information is shared widely so that everyone has the same picture of the organization and its environment. The acceleration of change when the entire system is involved can be remarkable. In addition, learning occurs across all parts of the organization simultaneously rather than in individuals, small groups, or business units. The result is that the large-group approach offers greater possibilities for fundamental, radical transformation of the entire culture, whereas the traditional approach creates incremental change in a few individuals or small groups at a time.

- Often, a manager's toughest job is changing people and culture.
- **People change** refers to a change in the attitudes and behaviors of a few employees.
- **Culture change** is a major shift in the norms, values, and mind-set of the entire organization.
- **Organization development (OD)** is a planned, systematic process of change that uses behavioral science techniques to improve an organization's health and effectiveness through its ability to cope with environmental changes, improve internal relationships, and increase learning and problem-solving capabilities.
- OD can help managers with the task of blending corporate cultures following mergers and acquisitions, as well as with many other people-related problems.
- **Team building** is an OD intervention that enhances cohesiveness by helping groups of people learn to work together as a team.
- With **survey feedback**, OD change agents survey employees to gather their opinions regarding corporate values, leadership, participation, cohesiveness, and other aspects of the organization, then meet with small groups to share the results and brainstorm solutions to problems identified by the results.
- **Large-group intervention** is an OD approach that brings together people from different parts of the organization (and often including outside stakeholders) to discuss problems or opportunities and plan for change.

OD Steps Organization development experts acknowledge that changes in corporate culture and human behavior are tough to accomplish and require major effort. The theory underlying OD proposes three distinct stages for achieving behavioral and attitudinal change: (1) unfreezing, (2) changing, and (3) refreezing.[64]

EXHIBIT 8.6

OD Approaches to Culture Change

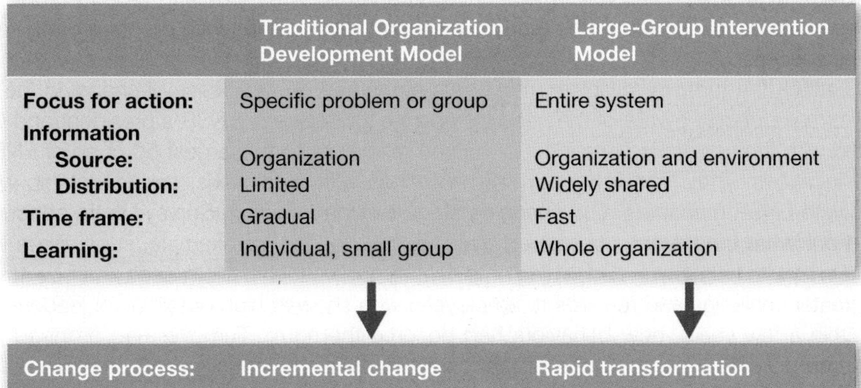

	Traditional Organization Development Model	Large-Group Intervention Model
Focus for action:	Specific problem or group	Entire system
Information		
Source:	Organization	Organization and environment
Distribution:	Limited	Widely shared
Time frame:	Gradual	Fast
Learning:	Individual, small group	Whole organization
Change process:	Incremental change	Rapid transformation

SOURCE: Adapted from Barbara Benedict Bunker and Billie T. Alban, "Conclusion: What Makes Large Group Interventions Effective?" *Journal of Applied Behavioral Science* 28, no. 4 (December 1992): 579–591.

The first stage, **unfreezing**, makes people throughout the organization aware of problems and the need for change. This stage creates the motivation for people to change their attitudes and behaviors. Unfreezing may begin when managers present information that shows discrepancies between desired behaviors or performance and the current state of affairs. In addition, managers need to establish a sense of urgency to unfreeze people and create an openness and willingness to change. The unfreezing stage is often associated with *diagnosis*, which uses an outside expert called a *change agent*. The **change agent** is an OD specialist who performs a systematic diagnosis of the organization and identifies work-related problems. He or she gathers and analyzes data through personal interviews, questionnaires, and observations of meetings. The diagnosis helps determine the extent of organizational problems and helps unfreeze managers by making them aware of problems in their behavior.

The second stage, **changing**, occurs when individuals experiment with new behavior and learn new skills to be used in the workplace. This process is sometimes known as intervention, during which the change agent implements a specific plan for training managers and employees. The changing stage might involve a number of specific steps.[65] For example, managers put together a coalition of people with the will and power to guide the change, create a vision for change that everyone can believe in, and widely communicate the vision and plans for change throughout the company. In addition, successful change involves using emotion as well as logic to persuade people and empowering employees to act on the plan and accomplish the desired changes.

The third stage, **refreezing**, occurs when individuals acquire new attitudes or values and are rewarded for them by the organization. The impact of new behaviors is evaluated and reinforced. The change agent supplies new data that show positive changes in performance. Managers may provide updated data to employees that demonstrate positive changes in individual and organizational performance. Top executives celebrate successes and reward positive behavioral changes. At this stage, changes are institutionalized in the organizational culture so that employees begin to view the changes as a normal, integral part of how the organization operates. Employees may also participate in refresher courses to maintain and reinforce the new behaviors.

The process of unfreezing–changing–refreezing can be illustrated by efforts of managers at ENSR to create a high-performance, employee-focused culture.

ENSR

When top executives at ENSR began hearing that high employee turnover was hurting the company's relationships with clients, they knew something had to be done. ENSR is a full-service environmental services firm with around 3,000 employees in 90 locations around the world. Long-term relationships with clients are the key to ENSR's success.

To attack the turnover problem, managers embarked on a process of changing the culture. To make people aware of the need for change (unfreezing), ENSR's president and CEO traveled with the senior vice president of human resources to the largest 50 or so of ENSR's global locations. They held town hall–style meetings with employees, and leadership workshops with ENSR managers. The *changing* stage included training. Surveys were conducted to find out what employees considered their primary needs. For example, supervisors were trained in how to help lower-performing employees improve their performance and how to provide greater challenge and rewards to employees who showed high potential for leadership.

Within a few years, new behaviors had become the norm. Turnover had dropped from 22 percent to only 9 percent, one of the lowest rates in the industry, and employees were recognized and rewarded for meeting high individual and collective goals (refreezing). ENSR continues to attract high-quality employees to fill job openings, which helps to keep the high-performance culture alive.[66]

- OD practitioners recommend a three-stage approach for changing people's attitudes and behavior.
- **Unfreezing** is the stage in which people are made aware of problems and the need for change.
- Unfreezing requires diagnosing problems, which uses a **change agent**—an OD specialist who contracts with an organization to help managers facilitate change.
- **Changing** is the "intervention" stage of OD, when change agents teach people new behaviors and skills and guide them in using them in the workplace.
- At the **refreezing** stage, people have incorporated new values, attitudes, and behaviors into their everyday work and the changes become institutionalized in the culture.

Implementing Change

The final step to be managed in the change process is *implementation*. A new, creative idea will not benefit the organization until it is in place and being used fully. One frustration for managers is that employees often seem to resist change for no apparent reason. To effectively manage the implementation process, managers should be aware of the reasons people resist change and use techniques to enlist employee cooperation. Major, corporate-wide changes can be particularly challenging, as discussed in the Spotlight on Skills titled Making Change Stick.

Need for Change

Many people are not willing to change unless they perceive a problem or a crisis. A crisis or strong need for change lowers resistance. The shifting relationship between General Motors (GM) and the United Auto Workers (UAW) provides a good example. GM managers' efforts to build a more collaborative relationship typically met with resistance from UAW leaders until bankruptcy proved the urgent need for working more closely together. Today, the UAW owns 17.5 percent of GM's stock—the union wanted cash for the money GM owed

SPOTLIGHT ON SKILLS

Making Change Stick

Employees are not always receptive to change. A combination of factors can lead to rejection of, or even outright rebellion against, management's "new and better ideas." Consider what happened when managers at Lands' End, Inc., of Dodgeville, Wisconsin, tried to implement a sweeping overhaul incorporating many of today's management trends—teams, 401(k) plans, peer reviews, and the elimination of guards and time clocks. Despite managers' best efforts, employees balked. They had liked the old family-like atmosphere and uncomplicated work environment, and they considered the new requirement for regular meetings a nuisance. "We spent so much time in meetings that we were getting away from the basic stuff of taking care of business," says one employee. Even a much-ballyhooed new mission statement seemed "pushy." One long-time employee complained, "We don't need anything hanging over our heads telling us to do something we're already doing."

Confusion and frustration reigned at Lands' End and was reflected in an earnings drop of 17 percent. Eventually, a new CEO initiated a return to the familiar "Lands' End way" of doing things. Teams were disbanded, and many of the once-promising initiatives were shelved as workers embraced what was familiar.

The inability of people to adapt to change is not new. Neither is the failure of management to sufficiently lay the groundwork to prepare employees for change. Harvard professor John P. Kotter established an eight-step plan for implementing change that can provide a greater potential for successful transformation of a company:

1. Establish a sense of urgency through careful examination of the market and identification of opportunities and potential crises.
2. Form a powerful coalition of managers able to lead the change.
3. Create a vision to direct the change and the strategies for achieving that vision.
4. Communicate the vision throughout the organization.
5. Empower others to act on the vision by removing barriers, changing systems, and encouraging risk taking.
6. Plan for and celebrate visible, short-term performance improvements.
7. Consolidate improvements, reassess changes, and make necessary adjustments in the new programs.
8. Articulate the relationship between new behaviors and organizational success.

Major change efforts can be messy and full of surprises, but following these guidelines can break down resistance and mean the difference between success and failure.

SOURCES: Gregory A. Patterson, "Lands' End Kicks out Modern New Managers, Rejecting a Makeover," *The Wall Street Journal,* April 3, 1995; and John P. Kotter, "Leading Changes: Why Transformation Efforts Fail," *Harvard Business Review* (March–April 1995): 59–67.

it but gave in for the sake of the whole enterprise. In addition, the crisis convinced the UAW to pledge not to strike before 2015, ceding leverage at the bargaining table and giving GM a better chance to survive.[67] Sometimes, though, there is no obvious crisis. Many organizational problems are subtle, so managers have to recognize and then make others aware of the need for change.[68] A **need for change** is a disparity between existing and desired performance levels.

Resistance to Change

Getting others to understand the need for change is the first step in implementation. Yet most changes will encounter some degree of resistance. Idea champions often discover that other employees are unenthusiastic about their new ideas. Members of a new-venture group may be surprised when managers in the regular organization do not support or approve their innovations. Managers and employees not involved in an innovation often seem to prefer the status quo. People resist change for several reasons, and understanding them can help managers implement change more effectively.

Self-Interest People typically resist a change they believe conflicts with their self-interests. A proposed change in job design, structure, or technology may increase employees' workload,

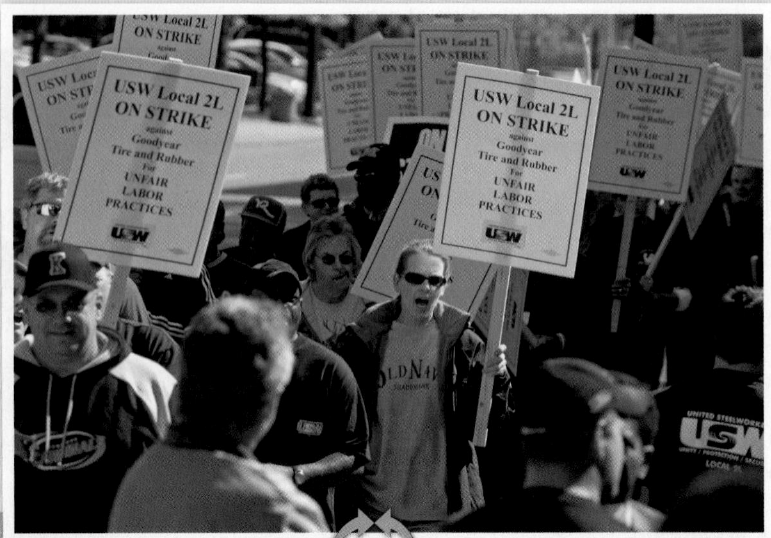

AP Photo/Mark Duncan

ConceptConnection

Fear of job loss is one of the biggest reasons for **resistance to change**. Managers at Goodyear Tire & Rubber Company decided the company needed to outsource some of its private label business to compete with low-cost foreign producers. Unfortunately, the change would lead to plant closings in the United States. After having made major concessions several years earlier to help the ailing tire manufacturer, United Steelworkers Union (USW) members were strongly opposed to further job losses. Despite months of talks, the two sides failed to reach an agreement and 15,000 USW members went on strike.

for example, or cause a real or perceived loss of power, prestige, pay, or benefits. *The fear of personal loss is perhaps the biggest obstacle to organizational change.*[69] Consider what is happening at Anheuser-Busch, which was acquired by the Belgian company InBev. The lavish executive suites at Anheuser-Busch headquarters have been demolished in favor of an open floor plan that has staff members and executives working side-by-side. Managers accustomed to flying first class or on company planes are now required to fly coach. It has become a competition to get a company-provided BlackBerry, as InBev has dramatically cut the number it will provide for employees. Free beer is a thing of the past, and complimentary tickets to sporting events are few and far between. Once the envy of others in the industry because of their lavish perks, Anheuser-Busch employees are resisting the new managers' wide-ranging changes because they feel they are losing both financially and in terms of status.[70]

Lack of Understanding and Trust Employees often distrust the intentions behind a change or do not understand the intended purpose of a change. If previous working relationships with an idea champion have been negative, resistance may occur. When CareFusion Corporation was spun off as a subsidiary of Cardinal Health, CEO David L. Schlotterbeck and other top executives wanted to implement new values of collaboration and teamwork, but lower-level managers were initially suspicious of their intentions. Only when they saw that top leaders were fully committed to the values and honored them in their own behavior did others begin to support the changes.[71]

Uncertainty *Uncertainty* is the lack of information about future events. It represents a fear of the unknown. Uncertainty is especially threatening for employees who have a low tolerance for change and fear anything out of the ordinary. They do not know how a change will affect them and worry about whether they will be able to meet the demands of a new procedure or technology.[72] For example, employees at one mail-order company resisted the introduction of teams because they were comfortable with their working environment and uncertain about how the implementation of teams would alter it. People had developed good collaborative working relationships informally, and they didn't see the need for being forced to work in teams.

Different Assessments and Goals Another reason for resistance to change is that people who will be affected by an innovation may assess the situation differently from an idea champion or new-venture group. Critics frequently voice legitimate disagreements over the proposed benefits of a change. Managers in each department pursue different goals, and an innovation may detract from performance and goal achievement for some departments. For example, if marketing gets the new product it wants for customers, the cost of manufacturing may increase, and the manufacturing superintendent thus will resist. Resistance may call attention to problems with the innovation. At a consumer products company in Racine, Wisconsin, middle managers resisted the introduction of a new employee program that turned out to be a bad idea. The managers truly believed that the program would do more harm than good.[73]

These reasons for resistance are legitimate in the eyes of employees affected by the change. Managers should not ignore resistance, but instead should diagnose the reasons and design strategies to gain acceptance by users.[74] Strategies for overcoming resistance to change typically involve two approaches: the analysis of resistance through the force-field technique and the use of selective implementation tactics to overcome resistance.

The Group Learning on pages 317–318 will give you an idea of how difficult it can sometimes be for people to change.

Force-Field Analysis

Force-field analysis grew from the work of Kurt Lewin, who proposed that change was a result of the competition between *driving* and *restraining forces*.[75] Driving forces can be thought of as problems or opportunities that provide motivation for change within the organization. Restraining forces are the various barriers to change, such as a lack of resources, resistance from middle managers, or inadequate employee skills. When a change is introduced, management should analyze both the forces that drive change (problems and opportunities) as well as the forces that resist it (barriers to change). By selectively removing forces that restrain change, the driving forces will be strong enough to enable implementation, as illustrated by the move from A to B in Exhibit 8.7. As barriers are reduced or removed, behavior will shift to incorporate the desired changes.

Just-in-time (JIT) inventory control systems schedule materials to arrive at a company just as they are needed on the production line. In an Ohio manufacturing company, management's analysis showed that the driving forces (opportunities) associated with the implementation of JIT were (1) the large cost savings from reduced inventories, (2) savings from needing fewer workers to handle the inventory, and (3) a quicker, more competitive market response for the company. Restraining forces (barriers) discovered by managers were (1) a freight system that was too slow to deliver inventory on time, (2) a facility layout that emphasized inventory maintenance over new deliveries, (3) worker skills inappropriate for handling rapid inventory deployment, and (4) union resistance to loss of jobs. The driving forces were not sufficient to overcome the restraining forces.

To shift the behavior to JIT, managers attacked the barriers. An analysis of the freight system showed that delivery by truck provided the flexibility and quickness needed to schedule inventory arrival at a specific time each day. The problem with facility layout was met by adding four new loading docks. Inappropriate worker skills were attacked with a

EXHIBIT 8.7

Using Force-Field Analysis to Change from Traditional to Just-in-Time Inventory System

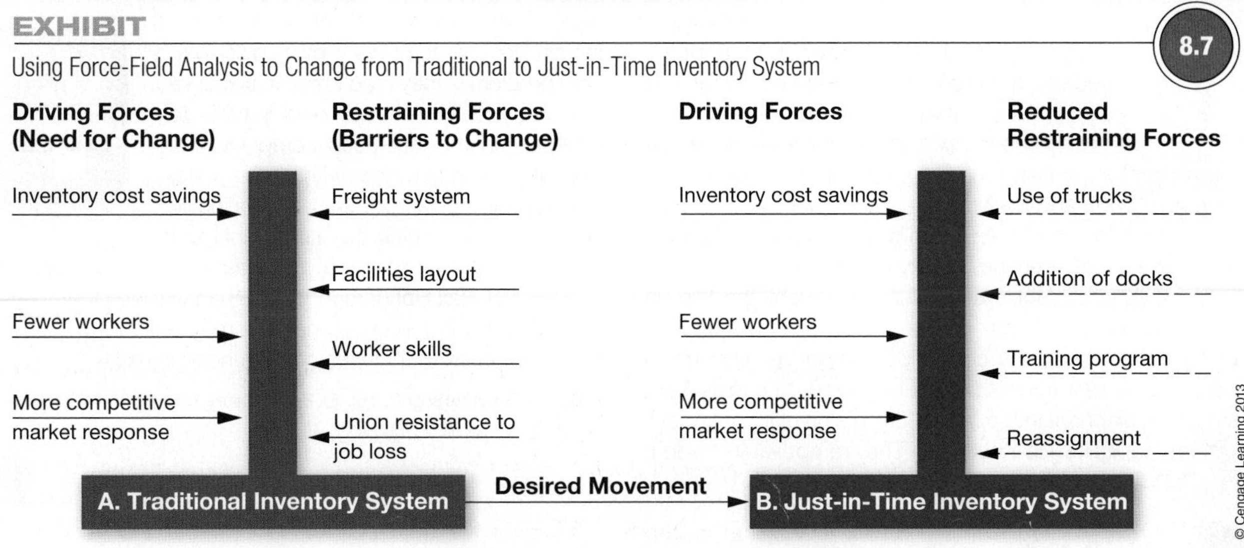

training program to instruct workers in JIT methods and in assembling products with uninspected parts. Union resistance was overcome by agreeing to reassign workers no longer needed for maintaining inventory to jobs in another plant. With the restraining forces reduced, the driving forces were sufficient to allow the JIT system to be implemented.

Cisco Systems needed to do a force-field analysis or some other change tactic when they bought out Flip videos. Because they did not handle the change process effectively, Flip had a sad demise, as described in this chapter's Business Blooper.

Implementation Tactics

The other approach to managing implementation is to adopt specific tactics to overcome resistance. Researchers have studied various methods for dealing with resistance to change. The following five tactics, summarized in Exhibit 8.8, have proven successful.[76]

Communication and Education *Communication* and *education* are used when solid information about the change is needed by users and others who may resist implementation. Education is especially important when the change involves new technical knowledge or users are unfamiliar with the idea. Canadian Airlines International spent a year and a half preparing and training employees before changing its entire reservations, airport, cargo, and financial systems as part of a new "Service Quality" strategy. Smooth implementation resulted from this intensive training and communications effort, which involved 50,000 tasks, 12,000 people, and 26 classrooms around the world.[77] Managers should also remember that implementing change requires speaking to people's hearts (touching their feelings) as well as to their minds (communicating facts). Emotion is a key component in persuading and influencing others. People are much more likely to change their behavior when they both understand the rational reasons for doing so and see a picture of change that influences their feelings.[78]

Participation *Participation* involves users and potential resisters in designing the change. This approach is time consuming, but it pays off because users understand and become committed to the change. At Learning Point Associates, which needed to change dramatically to meet new challenges, the change team drew up a comprehensive road map

BUSINESS BLOOPER

Flip

Perhaps the greatest tech start-up story of the decade, the Flip video camera crashed as fast as it initially soared. Started by some scrappy entrepreneurs in a small office above a department store in San Francisco, the Flip emerged on the market in 2007 and became the camcorder leader almost overnight. Within two years, 2 million units were sold. With a balance sheet seeming to salivate for consumer goods, network-service giant Cisco Systems bought the Flip, in an exuberant grab to be part of the consumer economy. But the giant company could not change fast enough to adapt to the new kind of market it entered. "It's really hard to turn an elephant into a horse. Cisco's an elephant," says venture capitalist Mo Koyfman. "They're not wired to do it themselves, so they do it by acquisition." Only problem is they didn't "do" it. Because of a combination of their own inability to change and the increased competition of innovative smartphones, within four years, the Flip has gone from start-up darling to defunct. "I don't think there's an analyst on the planet who thought that Flip was a good acquisition," said analyst Alex Henderson. "Cisco had this idea that they wanted to be in the consumer's home network, but they had a grand vision that was not grounded in reality."

SOURCE: Sam Grobart and Evelyn M. Busli, "For Flip Video Camera, Four Years from Hot Start-Up to Obsolete, *The New York Times*, April 13, 2011, pp. B1, B8.

EXHIBIT 8.8

Tactics for Overcoming Resistance to Change

Approach	When to Use
Communication, education	• Change is technical. • Users need accurate information and analysis to understand change.
Participation	• Users need to feel involved. • Design requires information from others. • Users have power to resist.
Negotiation	• Group has power over implementation. • Group will lose out in the change.
Coercion	• A crisis exists. • Initiators clearly have power. • Other implementation techniques have failed.
Top management support	• Change involves multiple departments or reallocation of resources. • Users doubt legitimacy of change.

SOURCE: Based on J. P. Kotter and L.A. Schlesinger, "Choosing Strategies for Change," *Harvard Business Review* 57 (March–April 1979): 106–114.

for transformation, but had trouble getting the support of most managers. The managers argued that they hadn't been consulted about the plans and didn't feel compelled to participate in implementing them.[79] Research studies have shown that proactively engaging front-line employees in upfront planning and decision making about changes that affect their work results in much smoother implementation.[80] Participation also helps managers determine potential problems and understand the differences in perceptions of change among employees.

Negotiation Negotiation is a more formal means of achieving cooperation. *Negotiation* uses formal bargaining to win acceptance and approval of a desired change. For example, if the marketing department fears losing power if a new management structure is implemented, top managers may negotiate with marketing to reach a resolution. Companies that have strong unions frequently must formally negotiate change with the unions. The change may become part of the union contract reflecting the agreement of both parties.

Coercion *Coercion* means that managers use formal power to force employees to change. Resisters are told to accept the change or lose rewards or even their jobs. In most cases, this approach should not be used because employees feel like victims, are angry at change managers, and may even sabotage the changes. However, coercion may be necessary in crisis situations when a rapid response is urgent. For example, at Chrysler Group, new CEO Sergio Marchionne reassigned or terminated several top managers who didn't agree with his changes for returning Chrysler to profitability after it emerged from bankruptcy protection.[81]

Top Management Support One survey found that 80 percent of companies that are successful innovators have top executives who frequently reinforce the importance of innovation both verbally and symbolically.[82] The visible support of top management helps overcome resistance to change. For instance, one of the primary correlates of the success of new business ventures is the strong support of top managers, which gives the project legitimacy.[83] *Top management support* symbolizes to all employees that the change is important for the organization. Recall from the example earlier in the text how the CEO of ENSR traveled to sites all over the world to talk with employees about the changes and why they were needed. Top management support is especially important when a change involves multiple departments or when resources are being reallocated among departments. Without top management support, changes can get bogged down in squabbling among departments. Moreover, when change agents fail to enlist the support of top executives, these leaders can inadvertently undercut the change project by issuing contradictory orders.

Managers can soften resistance and facilitate change and innovation by using smart techniques. By communicating with employees, providing training, and closely involving employees in the change process, managers can smooth implementation. In addition, change agents should never underestimate the importance of top management support for any change effort to succeed.

- A **need for change** is a disparity between actual and desired performance.
- When managers see a need, they want to make changes to fill it, but they may be frustrated because employees seem to have a resistance to change for no apparent reason.
- Many people aren't willing to change unless they perceive a crisis.
- There are many legitimate reasons why people resist change, such as self-interest, uncertainty, or lack of trust.
- **Force-field analysis** is a technique for determining which forces drive a proposed change and which forces restrain it.
- Driving forces are problems or opportunities that provide motivation to change. Restraining forces are barriers such as a lack of resources or inadequate employee skills.
- The support of top executives is crucial to the successful implementation of a change. In addition, managers use a variety of techniques to smooth the implementation process.

Discussion Questions

1. Times of shared crisis, such as the September 11, 2001, terrorist attack on the World Trade Center or the Gulf Coast hurricanes in 2005, can induce many companies that have been bitter rivals to put their competitive spirit aside and focus on cooperation and courtesy. Do you believe this type of change will be a lasting one? Discuss.
2. A manager of an international chemical company said that few new products in her company were successful. What would you advise the manager to do to help increase the company's success rate?
3. As a manager, how would you deal with resistance to change when you suspect employees' fears of job loss are well founded?
4. How might businesses use the Internet to identify customer needs through open innovation? What do you see as the major advantages and disadvantages of the open innovation approach?
5. To tap into the experience of battle-tested soldiers, the U.S. Army recently began encouraging personnel from all ranks to go online and collaboratively rewrite some of the Army's field manuals in a Wikipedia-like fashion. When the rank and file showed little interest, one retired colonel suggested top leaders should make soldiers participate. Does coercion seem like a good way to implement this type of change? Discuss.

6. Analyze the driving and restraining forces of a change you would like to make in your life. Do you believe understanding force-field analysis can help you more effectively implement a significant change in your own behavior?
7. Which role or roles—the inventor, champion, sponsor, or critic—would you most like to play in the innovation process? Why do you think idea champions are so essential to the initiation of change? Could they be equally important for implementation?
8. You are a manager, and you believe the expense reimbursement system for salespeople is far too slow, taking weeks instead of days. How would you go about convincing other managers that this problem needs to be addressed?
9. Do the underlying values of organization development differ from assumptions associated with other types of change? Discuss.
10. How do large-group interventions differ from OD techniques such as team building and survey feedback?

Self-Learning

Is Your Company Creative?[84]

An effective way to assess the creative climate of an organization for which you have worked is to fill out the following questionnaire. Answer each item based on your work experience in that firm. Discuss the results with members of your group, and talk about whether changing the firm along the dimensions in the items would make it more creative.

Instructions: Answer each of the following items using the 5-point scale (*Note:* No rating of 4 is used):

(0) We never do this.

(1) We rarely do this.

(2) We sometimes do this.

(3) We frequently do this.

(5) We always do this.

1. We are encouraged to seek help anywhere inside or outside the organization with new ideas for our work unit.

   0 1 2 3 5

2. Assistance is provided to develop ideas into proposals for management review.

   0 1 2 3 5

3. Our performance reviews encourage risky, creative efforts, ideas, and actions.

   0 1 2 3 5

4. We are encouraged to fill our minds with new information by attending professional meetings and trade fairs, visiting customers, and so on.

   0 1 2 3 5

5. Our meetings are designed to allow people to freewheel, brainstorm, and generate ideas.

   0 1 2 3 5

6. All members contribute ideas during meetings.

   0 1 2 3 5

7. Meetings often involve much spontaneity and humor.

   0 1 2 3 5

8. We discuss how company structure and our actions help or spoil creativity within our work unit.

   0 1 2 3 5

9. During meetings, the chair is rotated among members.

   0 1 2 3 5

10. Everyone in the work unit receives training in creativity techniques and maintaining a creative climate.

    0 1 2 3 5

Scoring and Interpretation

Add your total score for all ten items: ________

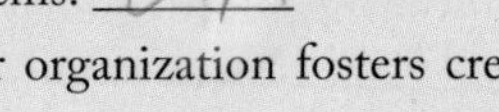

To measure how effectively your organization fosters creativity, use the following scale:

Highly effective: 35–50, Moderately effective: 20–34, Moderately ineffective: 10–19, Ineffective: 0–9.

Group Learning

Are You Ready to Implement Personal Change?[85]

Step 1. Think about a specific behavior change—for example, stopping smoking, scheduling regular exercise, learning a new skill, adopting a healthier diet, dropping a bad habit—you have considered making in your life. With that specific behavior or habit in mind, carefully answer each item in the following table as Mostly True or Mostly False for you.

	Mostly True	Mostly False
1. To be honest, my problem is not so bad that it needs changing.	______	______
2. The behavior may be a fault, but it is nothing that I really need to change.	______	______
3. I am aware of the issue, but I am fine with it.	______	______
4. I have been thinking that I would like to change that behavior.	______	______
5. I wish I knew more about how to solve that problem.	______	______
6. I would like to understand better that behavior to start changing it.	______	______
7. I am actually doing something about it right now.	______	______
8. I am really starting to change, but I am not there yet.	______	______
9. I am in the process of changing, but I want to be more consistent.	______	______
10. I have already completed the change, and I do not plan to backslide.	______	______
11. The change has become part of my day, and I feel it if I do not stay with it.	______	______
12. The new behavior is now a part of my life, and I do not think about it anymore.	______	______

Step 2. Scoring and Interpretation: The items above pertain to a person's stage of readiness to implement a personal change. Each of the four stages is measured by three items in the scale. Give yourself 1 point for each item marked Mostly True.

I. Pre-contemplation: Items 1, 2, 3. Score ________

II. Contemplation: Items 4, 5, 6. Score ________

III. Action: Items 7, 8, 9. Score ________

IV. Maintenance: Items 10, 11, 12. Score ________

You will probably find that you have a higher score for one of the stages, which means you are in that stage for your specific change. If you have the same score for two adjacent stages, then you are probably transitioning from one stage to the next. What does your score imply about your likelihood of success in making the change?

Step 3. In groups of three to five students, take turns describing your desired change and the meaning of the stage you are in. Compare notes and discuss progress on each person's change.

Step 4. Discuss the answers to the following questions as a group:

How likely is it that you will implement your desired change successfully? Why? To implement a personal change, how important is it to feel a strong need for change? Can you identify driving and restraining forces for the personal changes in your group? Which implementation tactics from this chapter would help your group members make the change? Why do you think so?

Action Learning

1. Think about two times you had to go through a change. It might have been in your worklife, as a student, in your family, or with friends. Try to choose two situations that ended differently. In other words, one had a positive outcome in the long-term, and the other one did not have a positive outcome. Thinking about these two times of change, fill in the table below.

	Situation 1: (positive outcome):	Situation 2: (not a positive outcome)
Factors in the situation		
Were you happy with the way things were before the change?		
What was the cause of the change?		
What was your initial reaction to the change?		
Did you find any ways to cope with the change or find something positive? Explain.		

(Continued)

	Situation 1: (positive outcome):	Situation 2: (not a positive outcome)
How did authority figures communicate with you? How did authority figures handle the situation in general?		
Was there support from other people?		
What was the long-term outcome?		

2. Can you see differences in the way the two situations unfolded in terms of other people's behaviors?
3. Were there differences in your behaviors in the two situations? Why?
4. What would you do differently, if you could go back?
5. What new insights do you now have about going through change?

Ethical Dilemma

Crowdsourcing[86]

Last year, when Ai-Lan Nguyen told her friend Greg Barnwell that Off the Hook Tees, based in Asheville, North Carolina, was going to experiment with crowdsourcing, he warned her she wouldn't like the results. Now, as she was about to walk into a meeting called to decide whether to adopt this new business model, she was afraid her friend had been right.

Crowdsourcing uses the Internet to invite anyone, professionals and amateurs alike, to perform tasks such as product design that employees usually perform. In exchange, contributors receive recognition—but little or no pay. Ai-Lan, as vice president of operations for Off the Hook, a company specializing in witty T-shirts aimed at young adults, upheld the values of founder Chris Woodhouse, who like Ai-Lan was a graphic artist. Before he sold the company, the founder always insisted that T-shirts be well designed by top-notch graphic artists to make sure each screen print was a work of art. Those graphic artists reported to Ai-Lan.

During the past 18 months, Off the Hook's sales stagnated for the first time in its history. The crowdsourcing experiment was the latest in a series of attempts to jump-start sales growth. Last spring, Off the Hook issued its first open call for T-shirt designs and then posted the entries on the Web so people could vote for their favorites. The top five vote getters were handed over to the in-house designers, who tweaked the submissions until they met the company's usual quality standards.

When CEO Rob Taylor first announced the company's foray into crowdsourcing, Ai-Lan found herself reassuring the designers that their positions were not in jeopardy. Now Ai-Lan was all but certain she would have to go back on her word. Not only had the crowdsourced tees sold well, but Rob had put a handful of winning designs directly into production, bypassing the design department altogether. Customers didn't notice the difference.

Ai-Lan concluded that Rob was ready to adopt some form of the Web-based crowdsourcing because it made T-shirt design more responsive to consumer desires. Practically speaking, it reduced the uncertainty that surrounded new designs, and it dramatically lowered costs. The people who won the competitions were delighted with the exposure it gave them.

However, when Ai-Lan looked at the crowdsourced shirts with her graphic artist's eye, she felt that the designs were competent, but none achieved the aesthetic standards attained by her in-house designers. Crowdsourcing essentially replaced training and expertise with public opinion. That made the artist in her uncomfortable.

More distressing, it was beginning to look as if Greg had been right when he'd told her that his working definition of crowdsourcing was "a billion amateurs want your job." It was easy to see that if Off the Hook adopted crowdsourcing, she would be handing out pink slips to most of her design people, long-time employees whose work she admired. "Sure, crowdsourcing costs the company less, but what about the human cost?" Greg asked.

What future course should Ai-Lan argue for at the meeting? And what personal decisions does she face if Off the Hook decides to put the crowd completely in charge when it comes to T-shirt design?

What Would You Do?

1. Go to the meeting and argue for abandoning crowdsourcing for now in favor of maintaining the artistic integrity and values that Off the Hook has always stood for.
2. Accept the reality that because Off the Hook's CEO Rob Taylor strongly favors crowdsourcing, it's a fait accompli. Be a team player and help work out the details of the new design approach. Prepare to lay off graphic designers as needed.
3. Accept the fact that converting Off the Hook to a crowdsourcing business model is inevitable, but because it violates your own personal values, start looking for a new job elsewhere.

Case for Critical Analysis

Southern Discomfort[87]

Jim Malesckowski remembers the call of two weeks ago as if he just put down the telephone receiver. "I just read your analysis and I want you to get down to Mexico right away," Jack Ripon, his boss and chief executive officer, had blurted in his ear. "You know we can't make the plant in Oconomo work anymore—the costs are just too high. So go down there, check out what our operational costs would be if we move, and report back to me in a week."

At that moment, Jim felt as if a knife had been stuck in his side, just below the rib cage. As president of the Wisconsin Specialty Products Division of Lamprey, Inc., he knew quite well the challenge of dealing with high-cost labor in a third-generation, unionized U.S. manufacturing plant. And although he had done the analysis that led to his boss's knee-jerk response, the call still stunned him. There were 520 people who made a living at Lamprey's Oconomo facility, and if it closed, most of them wouldn't have a journeyman's prayer of finding another job in the town of 9,000 people.

Instead of the $16-per-hour average wage paid at the Oconomo plant, the wages paid to the Mexican workers—who lived in a town without sanitation and with an unbelievably toxic effluent from industrial pollution—would amount to about $1.60 an hour on average. That would be a savings of nearly $15 million a year for Lamprey, to be offset in part by increased costs for training, transportation, and other matters.

After two days of talking with Mexican government representatives and managers of other companies in the town, Jim had enough information to develop a set of comparative figures of production and shipping costs. On the way home, he started to outline the report, knowing full well that unless some miracle occurred, he would be ushering in a blizzard of pink slips for people he had come to appreciate.

The plant in Oconomo had been in operation since 1921, making special apparel for persons suffering injuries and other medical conditions. Jim had often talked with employees who would recount stories about their fathers or grandfathers working in the same Lamprey company plant—the last of the original manufacturing operations in town.

But friendship aside, competitors had already edged past Lamprey in terms of price and were dangerously close to overtaking it in product quality. Although both Jim and the plant manager had tried to convince the union to accept lower wages, union leaders resisted. In fact, on one occasion when Jim and the plant manager tried to discuss a cell manufacturing approach, which would cross-train employees to perform up to three different jobs, local union leaders could barely restrain their anger. Yet probing beyond the fray, Jim sensed the fear that lurked under the union reps' gruff exterior. He sensed their vulnerability, but could not break through the reactionary bark that protected it.

A week has now passed, and Jim has just submitted his report to his boss. Although he didn't specifically bring up the point, it was apparent that Lamprey could put its investment dollars in a bank and receive a better return than what its Oconomo operation is currently producing.

See It Online

Tomorrow, he'll discuss the report with the CEO. Jim doesn't want to be responsible for the plant's dismantling, an act he personally believes would be wrong as long as there's a chance its costs can be lowered. "But Ripon's right," he said to himself. "The costs are too high, the union's unwilling to cooperate, and the company needs to make a better return on its investment if it's to continue at all. It sounds right but feels wrong. What should I do?"

Questions

1. What forces for change are evident at the Oconomo plant?
2. What is the primary type of change needed—changing "things" or changing the "people and culture?" Can the Wisconsin plant be saved by changing things alone, by changing people and culture, or must both be changed? Explain your answer.
3. What do you think is the major underlying cause of the union leaders' resistance to change? If you were Jim Malesckowski, what implementation tactics would you use to try to convince union members to change to save the Wisconsin plant?

© Leremy, Shutterstock

Holden Outerwear: Managing Change and Innovation

Although many apparel manufacturers dream of setting trends in the world of fashion, Holden Outerwear is the ultimate fashion innovator. Founded in 2002 by professional snowboarder Mikey LeBlanc, the Portland, Oregon, sports-apparel maker has given traditional baggy outerwear a complete style makeover. Unlike ski-apparel brands that focus on utility at the expense of looking good, Holden believes technical garments can look cool. "What I love most about Holden is that they take cues from fashion and they're not looking at what everyone else in the outerwear market is doing," says Nikki Brush, design and development manager at Holden.

For Mikey LeBlanc, Holden is the perfect vehicle for expressing his two favorite interests, snowboarding and urban wear. When the pro boarder is not out taming the mountain, he's somewhere talking about his company's approach to design. "We brought an element of old world tailoring to our stuff, so we deal with paper patterns and fit, and we work with the shape of a garment—that was new to the industry," LeBlanc says. Most outerwear brands focus on keeping skiers warm and dry, not on fashion. Not so with Holden. "We were the first to bring a couple different fits," LeBlanc adds. "We had a standard fit and a skinny fit on our pants, for example."

Soon after Holden launched, the company was heralded as the new and improved outerwear maker because of its attention to detail. "We use a lot of genuine leather, a lot of wool, and things that weren't found in outerwear," LeBlanc says. Holden pants and jackets possess unique features like leather-covered snaps, leather shoulders, and urban-style snaps and stitching. LeBlanc and his design teams keep a close eye on runway brands like Marc Jacobs and G-Star, as Holden is always looking to bring new elements of style to the slopes. "It's all about bringing that element of fashion design instead of technical design to outerwear," says Holden's founder. "We've been labeled as the brand that pushes the style portion of technical outerwear."

As a trained designer, Nikki Brush relishes the innovative aspects of working at Holden. "I have a pretty solid background in development and designs, so I get excited about technology, whether it's working with the fabric mill or a garment manufacturer," Brush says. In particular, the designer enjoys taking a standard industry garment and doing it differently, as with Holden's use of denim. "I think our denim is very exciting. Most companies are working in cheap nylons that are printed to look like denim, but we are not." Unlike brands that substitute faux materials, Brush works with true cotton twill, which is first cut for style and then laminated with waterproofing. "It performs on the mountain as high performance outerwear, but looks like jeans," Brush says.

By far Holden's greatest innovation has been the creation of a new eco-friendly fabric. In 2005, LeBlanc and a business partner had an idea to make a natural-fiber waterproof breathable fabric, which didn't yet exist. So the partners pioneered it. In addition to being technically durable, the new garment material was hailed as an environmental breakthrough.

Today Holden has the attention of everyone in its industry. Retailers wait anxiously to see LeBlanc's newest collections, and competitors from Burton and Salomon, to Bonfire and Walmart borrow heavily from Holden's collections. LeBlanc doesn't worry too much about the rampant plagiarism that goes on in his industry. As the pro boarder sees it, imitation is the highest form of flattery. Plus, Holden's business is based on finding the next big thing. When it comes to style, Holden is the leader, never the follower.

Discussion Questions

1. Identify the type of change that Holden's leaders are managing on a daily basis.
2. Is Holden's creative approach to outerwear an example of *disruptive innovation?* Why or why not?
3. What resistance has Holden encountered while introducing innovative garment designs?

© VikaSuh, Shutterstock

Field of Dreams

Ray Kinsella (Kevin Costner) hears a voice while working in his Iowa cornfield that says, "If you build it, he will come." Ray concludes that "he" is the legendary "Shoeless Joe" Jackson (Ray Liotta), a 1919 Chicago White Sox player suspended for supposedly taking part in "throwing" the 1919 World Series. With the support of his wife, Annie (Amy Madigan), Ray jeopardizes his farm by replacing some cornfields with a modern baseball diamond. Shoeless Joe soon arrives, followed by the rest of the suspended players. This charming fantasy film, based on W. P. Kinsellas's novel *Shoeless Joe*, shows the rewards of pursuing a dream.

Forces for Change This scene is part of the "People Will Come" sequence toward the end of the film. By this time in the story, Ray has met Terrence Mann (James Earl Jones), and they have traveled together from Boston to Minnesota to find A. W. "Moonlight" Graham (Burt Lancaster). At this point, the three are at Ray's Iowa farm.

This scene follows Mark's (Timothy Busfield) arrival to discuss the foreclosure of Ray and Annie's mortgage. Mark, who is Annie's brother, cannot see the players on the field. Karin (Gaby Hoffman), Ray and Annie's daughter, has proposed that people will come to Iowa City and buy tickets to watch a baseball game. Mark does not understand her proposal. The film continues to its end.

What to Watch for and Ask Yourself

- Who is the target of change in this scene?
- What are the forces for change? Are the forces for change internal or external to the change target?
- Does the scene show the role of leadership in organizational change? If it does, who is the leader? What does this person do to get desired change?

© Pedro Nogueira, Shutterstock

Endnotes

1. Shane Richmond, "Spotify Steals a Big March on iTunes," *The Daily Telegraph*, April 29, 2010; Tim Bradshaw, "Spotify Hopes Major Upgrade Will Wean Users Off iTunes," *Financial Times*, April 27, 2010; Alex Pham, Todd Martens, and Mark Milian, "Internet: Spotify CEO Looks before Leap to U.S.," *The Los Angeles Times*, March 19, 2010; and "The World's 50 Most Innovative Companies," *Fast Company* (March 2010): 52–97.
2. Erik Brynjolfsson and Michael Schrage, "The New, Faster Face of Innovation; Thanks to Technology, Change Has Never Been So Easy or So Cheap," *The Wall Street Journal*, August 17, 2009; and Vindu Goel, "Why Google Pulls the Plug," *The New York Times*, February 15, 2009.
3. "The World's 50 Most Innovative Companies," *Fast Company* (March 2010): 52–97.
4. Ibid.
5. Reported in "90 Years in Business," *The Conference Board Review* (September–October 2006): 30–39.
6. Nelson D. Schwartz, "Lego's Rebuilds Legacy," *International Herald Tribune*, September 5, 2009.
7. Richard L. Daft, "Bureaucratic vs. Nonbureaucratic Structure in the Process of Innovation and Change," in Samuel B. Bacharach, ed., *Perspectives in Organizational Sociology: Theory and Research* (Greenwich, CT: JAI Press, 1982), pp. 129–166.
8. David Lieberman, "Goldman Sachs Creates Standards Committee," *USA Today*, May 9, 2010, www.usatoday.com/money/industries/banking/2010-05-07-goldman-business-practices_N.htm (accessed on May 10, 2010); and "Another View: Full Speed Ahead on Banking Reforms," *San Gabriel Valley Tribune*, February 25, 2010.
9. Liz Alderman, "Cap on Bank Bonuses Clears Hurdle in Europe," *The New York Times*, July 7, 2010; Keith Bracsher, "Newest Export Out of China: Inflation Fears," *The New York Times*, April 16, 2004, www.nytimes.com/2004/04/16/business/newest-export-out-of-china-inflation-fears.html (accessed August 30, 2010).
10. David W. Norton, and B. Joseph Pine II, "Unique Experiences: Disruptive Innovations Offer Customers More 'Time Well Spent,'" *Strategy & Leadership* 37, no. 6 (2009): 4; and "The Power to Disrupt," *The Economist* (April 17, 2010): 16.
11. Daniel McGinn, "Cheap, Cheap, Cheap," *Newsweek.com*, January 21, 2010, www.newsweek.com/2010/01/20/cheap-cheap-cheap.html (accessed September 3, 2010); and Reena Jana, "Inspiration from Emerging Economies," *BusinessWeek* (March 23 & 30, 2009): 38–41.
12. C. Brooke Dobni, "The Innovation Blueprint," *Business Horizons* (2006): 329–339.
13. For more information on the ambidextrous approach, see R. Duncan, "The Ambidextrous Organization: Designing Dual Structures for Innovation," in R. H. Killman, L. R. Pondy, and D. Sleven, eds., *The Management of Organization* (New York: North Holland), pp. 167–188; S. Raisch, J. Birkinshaw, G. Probst, and M. L. Tushman, "Organizational Ambidexterity: Balancing Exploitation and Exploration for Sustained

Performance," *Organization Science* 20, no. 4 (July–August 2009), pp. 685–695; Sebastian Raisch and Julian Birkinshaw, "Organizational Ambidexterity: Antecedents, Outcomes, and Moderators," *Journal of Management* 34, no 3 (June 2008), pp. 375–409; Charles A. O'Reilly III and Michael L. Tushman, "The Ambidextrous Organization," *Harvard Business Review* (April 2004), pp. 74–81; Duane Ireland and Justin W. Webb, "Crossing the Great Divide of Strategic Entrepreneurship: Transitioning between Exploration and Exploitation," *Business Horizons* 52 (2009): 469–479; and Sebastian Raisch, "Balanced Structures: Designing Organizations for Profitable Growth," *Long Range Planning* 41 (2008): 483–508.

14. Peter Landers, "Back to Basics: With Dry Pipelines, Big Drug Makers Stock Up in Japan," *The Wall Street Journal,* November 24, 2003.

15. Glenn Rifkin, "Competing through Innovation: The Case of Broderbund," *Strategy + Business* 11 (Second Quarter 1998): 48–58; and Deborah Dougherty and Cynthia Hardy, "Sustained Product Innovation in Large, Mature Organizations: Overcoming Innovation-to-Organization Problems," *Academy of Management Journal* 39, no. 5 (1996): 1120–1153.

16. Teri Evans, "Entrepreneurs Seek to Elicit Workers' Ideas—Contests with Cash Prizes and Other Rewards Stimulate Innovation in Hard Times," *The Wall Street Journal,* December 22, 2009.

17. Adapted from Patrick Reinmoeller and Nicole van Baardwijk, "The Link between Diversity and Resilience," *MIT Sloan Management Review* (Summer 2005): 61–65.

18. Teresa M. Amabile, "Motivating Creativity in Organizations: On Doing What You Love and Loving What You Do," *California Management Review* 40, no. 1 (Fall 1997): 39–58; Brian Leavy, "Creativity: The New Imperative," *Journal of General Management* 28, no. 1 (Autumn 2002): 70–85; and Timothy A. Matherly and Ronald E. Goldsmith, "The Two Faces of Creativity," *Business Horizons* (September–October 1985): 8.

19. Lee Gomes, "Our Columnist Judges a Brainstorming Bee, and Meets a Genius," *The Wall Street Journal,* March 5, 2008.

20. Gordon Vessels, "The Creative Process: An Open-Systems Conceptualization," *Journal of Creative Behavior* 16 (1982): 185–196.

21. Robert J. Sternberg, Linda A. O'Hara, and Todd I. Lubart, "Creativity as Investment," *California Management Review* 40, no. 1 (Fall 1997): 8–21; Amabile, "Motivating Creativity in Organizations"; Leavy, "Creativity: The New Imperative"; and Ken Lizotte, "A Creative State of Mind," *Management Review* (May 1998): 15–17.

22. James Brian Quinn, "Managing Innovation: Controlled Chaos," *Harvard Business Review* 63 (May–June 1985): 73–84; Howard H. Stevenson and David E. Gumpert, "The Heart of Entrepreneurship," *Harvard Business Review* 63 (March–April 1985): 85–94; Marsha Sinetar, "Entrepreneurs, Chaos, and Creativity—Can Creative People Really Survive Large Company Structure?" *Sloan Management Review* 6 (Winter 1985): 57–62; Constantine Andriopoulos, "Six Paradoxes in Managing Creativity: An Embracing Act," *Long Range Planning* 36 (2003): 375–388; and Michael Laff, "Roots of Innovation," *T&D* (July 2009): 35–39.

23. Vincent Desmond, "How a Systematic Approach to Innovation Can Bring Radical Improvements to Organisations by Liberating the Staff," *Industrial and Commercial Training* 41, no. 6 (2009): 321–325.

24. Cynthia Browne, "Jest for Success," *Moonbeams* (August 1989): 3–5; and Rosabeth Moss Kanter, *The Change Masters* (New York: Simon and Schuster, 1983).

25. Sherry Eng, "Hatching Schemes," *The Industry Standard* (November 27– December 4, 2000): 174–175.

26. Reena Jana, "Brickhouse: Yahoo's Hot Little Incubator," *IN* (November 2007): 14.

27. Jena McGregor et al., "The World's Most Innovative Companies," *BusinessWeek* (April 24, 2006): 62ff.

28. James I. Cash, Jr., Michael J. Earl, and Robert Morison, "Teaming up to Crack Innovation and Enterprise Integration," *Harvard Business Review* (November 2008): 90–100; Barry Jaruzelski, Kevin Dehoff, and Rakesh Bordia, "Money Isn't Everything," *Strategy + Business*, no. 41 (December 5, 2005): 54–67; William L. Shanklin and John K. Ryans, Jr., "Organizing for High-Tech Marketing," *Harvard Business Review* 62 (November–December 1984): 164–171; and Arnold O. Putnam, "A Redesign for Engineering," *Harvard Business Review* 63 (May–June 1985): 139–144.

29. Rob Cross, Andrew Hargadon, Salvatore Parise, and Robert J. Thomas, "Business Insight (A Special Report); Together We Innovate: How Can Companies Come up with New Ideas? By Getting Employees Working with One Another," *The Wall Street Journal*, September 15, 2007.

30. Janet Rae-DuPree, "Teamwork, the True Mother of Invention," *The New York Times,* December 7, 2008.

31. Andrew H. Van de Ven, "Central Problems in the Management of Innovation," *Management Science* 32 (1986): 590–607; Richard L. Daft, *Organization Theory and Design* (Mason, OH: South-Western 2010), pp. 424–425; and Science Policy Research Unit, University of Sussex, *Success and Failure in Industrial Innovation* (London: Centre for the Study of Industrial Innovation, 1972).

32. Daft, *Organization Theory and Design.*

33. Brian Dumaine, "How Managers Can Succeed through Speed," *Fortune* (February 13, 1989): 54–59; and George Stalk, Jr., "Time—The Next Source of Competitive Advantage," *Harvard Business Review* (July–August 1988): 41–51.

34. Erik Brynjolfsson and Michael Schrage, "The New, Faster Face of Innovation," *The Wall Street Journal Online,* August 17, 2009, http://online.wsj.com/article/SB10001424052970204830304574130820184260340.html (accessed August 21, 2009); Steve Hamm, with Ian Rowley, "Speed Demons," *BusinessWeek* (March 27, 2006): 68–76; and John A. Pearce II, "Speed Merchants," *Organizational Dynamics* 30, no. 3 (2002): 191–205.

35. Kerry Capell, "Zara Thrives by Breaking All the Rules," *BusinessWeek* (October 20, 2008): 66; and Cecilie Rohwedder and Keith Johnson, "Pace-Setting Zara Seeks More Speed to Fight Its Rising Cheap-Chic Rivals," *The Wall Street Journal,* February 20, 2008.

36. V. K. Narayanan, Frank L. Douglas, Brock Guernsey, and John Charnes, "How Top Management Steers Fast Cycle Teams to Success," *Strategy & Leadership* 30, no. 3 (2002): 19–27.

37. The discussion of open innovation is based on Henry Chesbrough, "The Era of Open Innovation," *MIT Sloan Management Review* (Spring 2003): 35–41; Julian Birkinshaw and Susan A. Hill, "Corporate Venturing Units: Vehicles for Strategic Success in the New Europe," *Organizational Dynamics* 34, no. 3 (2005): 247–257; Amy Muller and Liisa Välikangas, "Extending the Boundary of Corporate Innovation," *Strategy & Leadership* 30, no. 3 (2002): 4–9; Navi Radjou, "Networked Innovation Drives Profits," *Industrial Management* (January–February 2005): 14–21; Darrell Rigby and Barbara Bilodeau, "The Bain 2005 Management Tool Survey," *Strategy & Leadership* 33, no. 4 (2005): 4–12; Ian Mount, "The Return of the Lone Inventor," *FSB (Fortune Small Business)* (March 2005): 18; McGregor et al., "The World's Most Innovative

Companies;" and Henry Chesbrough, "The Logic of Open Innovation: Managing Intellectual Property," *California Management Review* 45, no. 3 (Spring 2003): 33–58.

38. A. G. Lafley and Ram Charan, *The Game Changer: How You Can Drive Revenue and Profit Growth with Innovation* (New York: Crown Business, 2008); Larry Huston and Nabil Sakkab, "Connect and Develop; Inside Procter & Gamble's New Model for Innovation," *Harvard Business Review* (March 2006): 58–66; and G. Gil Cloyd, "P&G's Secret: Innovating Innovation," *Industry Week* (December 2004): 26–34.

39. Lawrence Owne, Charles Goldwasser, Kristi Choate, and Amy Blitz, "Collaborative Innovation throughout the Extended Enterprise," *Strategy & Leadership* 36, no. 1 (2008): 39–45.

40. Steve Lohr, "The Crowd Is Wise (When It's Focused)," *The New York Times,* July 19, 2009; S. Lohr, "The Corporate Lab As Ringmaster," *The New York Times,* August 16, 2009; and Steve Hamm, "Big Blue's Global Lab," *BusinessWeek* (September 7, 2009): 41–45.

41. Max Chafkin, "The Customer Is the Company," *Inc.* (June 2008): 88–96; and Max Chafkin, "5 Ways to Actually Make Money on Twitter," *Inc.* (December 2009–January 2010): 96–101.

42. Daniel T. Holt, Matthew W. Rutherford, and Gretchen R. Clohessy, "Corporate Entrepreneurship: An Empirical Look at Individual Characteristics, Context, and Process," *Journal of Leadership and Organizational Studies* 13, no. 4 (2007): 40–54.

43. Curtis R. Carlson and William W. Wilmot, *Innovation: The Five Disciplines for Creating What Customers Want* (New York: Crown Business, 2006).

44. Robert I. Sutton, "The Weird Rules of Creativity," *Harvard Business Review* (September 2001): 94–103; and Julian Birkinshaw and Michael Mol, "How Management Innovation Happens," *MIT Sloan Management Review* (Summer 2006): 81–88.

45. Jane M. Howell, "The Right Stuff: Identifying and Developing Effective Champions of Innovation," *Academy of Management Executive* 19, no. 2 (2005): 108–119.

46. Harold L. Angle and Andrew H. Van de Ven, "Suggestions for Managing the Innovation Journey," in A. H. Van de Ven, H. L. Angle, and Marshall Scott Poole, eds., *Research in the Management of Innovation: The Minnesota Studies* (Cambridge, MA: Ballinger/ Harper & Row, 1989).

47. C. K. Bart, "New Venture Units: Use Them Wisely to Manage Innovation," *Sloan Management Review* (Summer 1988): 35–43; Michael Tushman and David Nadler, "Organizing for Innovation," *California Management Review* 28 (Spring 1986): 74–92; Peter F. Drucker, *Innovation and Entrepreneurship* (New York: Harper & Row, 1985); and Henry W. Chesbrough, "Making Sense of Corporate Venture Capital, *Harvard Business Review* 80, no. 3 (March 2002): 90–99.

48. Raisch, "Balanced Structures."

49. Christopher Hoenig, "Skunk Works Secrets," *CIO* (July 1, 2000): 74–76; and Tom Peters and Nancy Austin, *A Passion for Excellence: The Leadership Difference* (New York: Random House, 1985).

50. Hoenig, "Skunk Works Secrets."

51. Sutton, "The Weird Rules of Creativity."

52. David Kiley, "Putting Ford on Fast-Forward," *BusinessWeek* (October 26, 2009): 56–57.

53. David Dobson, "Integrated Innovation at Pitney Bowes," *Strategy + Business Online,* October 26, 2009, www.strategy-business.com/article/09404b?gko=f9661 (accessed December 30, 2009); and Cash et al., "Teaming up to Crack Innovation and Enterprise Integration."

54. Robert C. Wolcott and Michael J. Lippitz, "The Four Models of Corporate Entrepreneurship," *MIT Sloan Management Review* (Fall 2007): 75–82.

55. E. H. Schein, "Organizational Culture," *American Psychologist* 45 (February 1990): 109–119; Eliza Newlin Carney, "Calm in the Storm," *Government Executive* (October 2003): 57–63.

56. Rosabeth Moss Kanter, "Execution: The Un-Idea," sidebar in Art Kleiner, "Our 10 Most Enduring Ideas," *Strategy + Business* no. 41 (December 12, 2005): 36–41.

57. Michelle Conlin, "Tough Love for Techie Souls," *BusinessWeek* (November 29, 1999): 164–170.

58. M. Sashkin and W. W. Burke, "Organization Development in the 1980s," *General Management* 13 (1987): 393–417; and Richard Beckhard, "What Is Organization Development?" in Wendell L. French, Cecil H. Bell, Jr., and Robert A. Zawacki, eds., *Organization Development and Transformation: Managing Effective Change* (Burr Ridge, IL: Irwin McGraw-Hill, 2000), pp. 16–19.

59. Wendell L. French and Cecil H. Bell, Jr., "A History of Organization Development," in French, Bell, and Zawacki, eds., *Organization Development and Transformation,* pp. 20–42; and Christopher G. Worley and Ann E. Feyerherm, "Reflections on the Future of Organization Development," *The Journal of Applied Behavioral Science* 39, no. 1 (March 2003): 97–115.

60. Paul F. Buller, "For Successful Strategic Change: Blend OD Practices with Strategic Management," *Organizational Dynamics* (Winter 1988): 42–55; Robert M. Fulmer and Roderick Gilkey, "Blending Corporate Families: Management and Organization Development in a Postmerger Environment," *The Academy of Management Executive* 2 (1988): 275–283; and Worley and Feyerherm, "Reflections on the Future of Organization Development."

61. W. Warner Burke, "The New Agenda for Organization Development," *Organizational Dynamics* (Summer 1997): 7–19.

62. This discussion is based on Kathleen D. Dannemiller and Robert W. Jacobs, "Changing the Way Organizations Change: A Revolution of Common Sense," *The Journal of Applied Behavioral Science* 28, no. 4 (December 1992): 480–498; and Barbara Benedict Bunker and Billie T. Alban, "Conclusion: What Makes Large Group Interventions Effective?" *The Journal of Applied Behavioral Science* 28, no. 4 (December 1992): 570–591.

63. Bunker and Alban, "Conclusion: What Makes Large Group Interventions Effective?"

64. Kurt Lewin, "Frontiers in Group Dynamics: Concepts, Method, and Reality in Social Science," *Human Relations* 1 (1947): 5–41; and E. F. Huse and T. G. Cummings, *Organization Development and Change*, 3rd ed. (St. Paul, MN: West, 1985).

65. Based on John Kotter's eight-step model of planned change, which is described in John P. Kotter, *Leading Change* (Boston: Harvard Business School Press, 1996), pp. 20–25, and John Kotter, "Leading Change: Why Transformation Efforts Fail," *Harvard Business Review* (March–April, 1995): 59–67.

66. Based on Bob Kelleher, "Employee Engagement Carries ENSR Through Organizational Challenges and Economic Turmoil," *Global Business and Organizational Excellence* 28, no. 3 (March–April 2009): 6–19.

67. Paul Ingrassia, "GM Gets a Second Chance," *The Wall Street Journal Europe,* July 10, 2009; and "Ford to Seek Same No-Strike Vow from UAW as GM and Chrysler Obtained," *National Post,* June 18, 2009.

68. Kotter, *Leading Change*, pp. 20–25; and "Leading Change: Why Transformation Efforts Fail."

69. J. P. Kotter and L. A. Schlesinger, "Choosing Strategies for Change," *Harvard Business Review* 57 (March–April 1979): 106–114.

70. David Kesmodel and Suzanne Vranica, "Unease Brewing at Anheuser as New Owners Slash Costs," *The Wall Street Journal,* April 29, 2009.

71. Joann S. Lublin, "Theory & Practice: Firm Offers Blueprint for Makeover in a Spinoff," *The Wall Street Journal,* June 29, 2009.

72. G. Zaltman and Robert B. Duncan, *Strategies for Planned Change* (New York: Wiley Interscience, 1977).

73. Leonard M. Apcar, "Middle Managers and Supervisors Resist Moves to More Participatory Management," *The Wall Street Journal*, September 16, 1985.

74. Dorothy Leonard-Barton and Isabelle Deschamps, "Managerial Influence in the Implementation of New Technology," *Management Science* 34 (1988): 1252–1265.

75. Kurt Lewin, *Field Theory in Social Science: Selected Theoretical Papers* (New York: Harper & Brothers, 1951).

76. Paul C. Nutt, "Tactics of Implementation," *Academy of Management Journal* 29 (1986): 230–261; Kotter and Schlesinger, "Choosing Strategies for Change"; R. L. Daft and S. Becker, *Innovation in Organizations: Innovation Adoption in School Organizations* (New York: Elsevier, 1978); and R. Beckhard, *Organization Development: Strategies and Models* (Reading, MA: Addison-Wesley, 1969).

77. Rob Muller, "Training for Change," *Canadian Business Review* (Spring 1995): 16–19.

78. Gerard H. Seijts and Grace O'Farrell, "Engage the Heart: Appealing to the Emotions Facilitates Change," *Ivey Business Journal* (January–February 2003): 1–5; John P. Kotter and Dan S. Cohen, *The Heart of Change: Real-Life Stories of How People Change Their Organizations* (Boston: Harvard Business School Press, 2002); and Shaul Fox and Yair Amichai Hamburger, "The Power of Emotional Appeals in Promoting Organizational Change Programs," *Academy of Management Executive* 15, no. 4 (2001): 84–95.

79. Gina Burkhardt and Diane Gerard, "People: The Lever for Changing the Business Model at Learning Point Associates," *Journal of Organizational Excellence* (Autumn 2006): 31–43.

80. Henry Hornstein, "Using a Change Management Approach to Implement IT Programs," *Ivey Business Journal* (January–February 2008); Philip H. Mirvis, Amy L. Sales, and Edward J. Hackett, "The Implementation and Adoption of New Technology in Organizations: The Impact on Work, People, and Culture," *Human Resource Management* 30 (Spring 1991): 113–139; Arthur E. Wallach, "System Changes Begin in the Training Department," *Personnel Journal* 58 (1979): 846–848, 872; and Paul R. Lawrence, "How to Deal with Resistance to Change," *Harvard Business Review* 47 (January–February 1969): 4–12, 166–176.

81. Kate Linebaugh and Jeff Bennett, "Marchionne Upends Chrysler's Ways: CEO Decries Detroit's 'Fanatical' Focus on Market Share," *The Wall Street Journal,* January 12, 2010.

82. Strategos survey results, reported in Pierre Loewe and Jennifer Dominiquini, "Overcoming the Barriers to Effective Innovation, *Strategy & Leadership* 34, no. 1 (2006): 24–31.

83. Donald F. Kuratko, Jeffrey G. Covin, and Robert P. Garrett, "Corporate Venturing: Insights from Actual Performance," *Business Horizons* 52 (2009): 459–467.

84. Adapted from Edward Glassman, *Creativity Handbook: Idea Triggers and Sparks That Work* (Chapel Hill, NC: LCS Press, 1990). Used by permission.

85. Based on Eileen A. McConnaughy, James O. Prochaska, and Wayne F. Velicer, "Stages of Change in Psychotherapy: Measurement and Sample Profiles," *Psychotherapy: Theory, Research and Practice* 20, no. 3 (1983): 368–375.

86. Based on Paul Boutin, "Crowdsourcing: Consumers As Creators," *BusinessWeek Online,* July 13, 2006, www.businessweek.com/innovate/content/jul2006/id20060713_755844.htm (accessed August 30, 2010); Jeff Howe, "The Rise of Crowdsourcing," *Wired,* June 2006, www.wired.com/wired/archive/14.06/crowds.html (accessed August 30, 2010); and Jeff Howe, Crowdsourcing blog, www.crowdsourcing.com (accessed August 30, 2010).

87. Doug Wallace, "What Would You Do?" Business Ethics (March/April 1996): 52–53. Copyright 1996 by New Mountain Media LLC. Reproduced with permission of New Mountain Media LLC.

Chapter Outline

Managing Human Resources and Diversity

Learning Outcomes

After studying this chapter, you should be able to:

1. Explain the strategic role of human resource management.
2. Explain what the changing social contract between organizations and employees means for workers and human resource managers.
3. Show how organizations determine their future staffing needs through human resource planning.
4. Describe how organizations develop an effective workforce through training and performance appraisal.
5. Understand the pervasive demographic changes occurring in the domestic and global marketplace and how corporations are responding.
6. Recognize the complex attitudes, opinions, and issues that employees bring to the workplace, including prejudice, discrimination, stereotypes, and ethnocentrism.
7. Recognize the factors that affect women's opportunities, including the glass ceiling, the opt-out trend, and the female advantage.
8. Explain the five steps in developing cultural competence in the workplace.

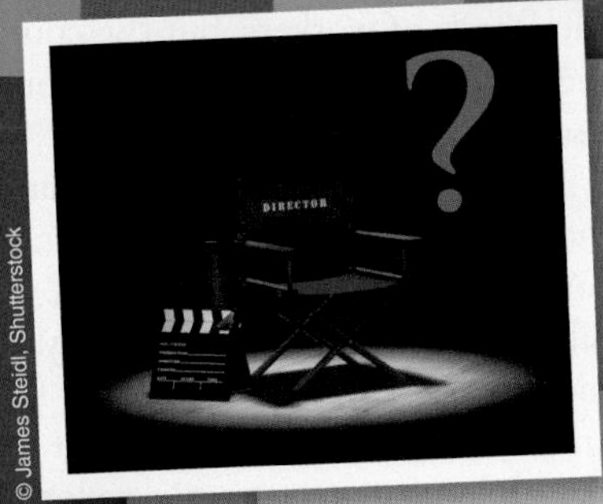

© James Steidl, Shutterstock

Are You Ready to Be a Manager?

Please circle your opinion below each of the following statements.

1 **I see a company's employees as an asset to be respected and developed.**

Mostly True — Mostly False

(See page 329, The Strategic Approach.)

2 **I want to be part of an organization that works to become an employer of choice, one that people looking for jobs would flock to.**

Mostly True — Mostly False

(See page 337, Becoming an Employer of Choice.)

3 **I know how important it is to behave and dress professionally in a job interview.**

Mostly True — Mostly False

(See page 345, Interview.)

4 **It is easy for me to relate to people from different ethic backgrounds, social classes or religions.**

Mostly True — Mostly False

(See page 357, Diversity in the United States.)

5 **I think companies should make it easier for people to get their jobs done if they have disabilities, a religious dress code, or child-care needs.**

Mostly True — Mostly False

(See page 376, Accommodating Special Needs.)

The year 2009 was a tough time to be looking for a job. On one Monday morning in January 2009 alone, companies announced more than 75,000 job cuts. That came on the heels of millions of job cuts the previous year, particular in the beleaguered financial services and auto industries, and the job slashes continued into 2010. Yet, even as companies were handing out pink slips, human resource managers were busy looking for people with different skills to fill other jobs. Boeing, for instance, cut 3,000 jobs in the first four months of 2009, mostly in the commercial airplanes division, but at the same time managers were hiring new employees to fill slots in the defense unit. IBM also laid off thousands of workers, but the company opened a new consulting unit and began recruiting people who had a combination of technical skills and expertise in areas such as health care and government.[1]

Hiring and keeping high-quality employees with the right set of skills is one of the most urgent concerns for today's organizations.[2] Employees give a company its primary source of competitive advantage, so even in an economic downturn smart managers make talent management a top priority. The term **human resource management (HRM)** refers to the design and application of formal systems in an organization to ensure the effective and efficient use of human talent to accomplish organizational goals.[3] This includes activities undertaken to attract, develop, and maintain an effective workforce. Managers have to find the right people, place them in positions where they can be most effective, and develop them so they contribute to company success.

Human resource management has shed its old "personnel" image and gained recognition as a vital player in corporate strategy.[4] "Many organizations are looking for their HR leader to be able to understand in great detail the business and the challenges of the business," says Fran Luisi of Charleston Partners, a search firm that specializes in HR managers.[5] Increasingly, large corporations are outsourcing routine HR administrative activities, freeing HRM staff from time-consuming paperwork and enabling them to take on more strategic responsibilities.[6] The growing clout of the HR function is reflected in the fact that current and former HR managers are increasingly being sought to fill board seats as outside directors at other companies. Hot-button issues such as executive compensation, changing government regulations, and the frequency of mergers and acquisitions make human resource management a critical skill for both business and nonprofit organizations.[7]

All managers need to be skilled in the basics of human resource management. With today's flatter organizations, managers throughout the organization play an active role in recruiting and selecting the right employees, developing effective training programs, designing appropriate compensation systems, and creating effective performance appraisal procedures. HRM professionals act to guide and assist line managers in managing human resources to achieve the organization's strategic goals.

The Strategic Role of HRM Is to Drive Organizational Performance

How a company manages talent may be the single most important factor in sustained competitive success. Today's best human resources departments not only support strategic objectives but also actively pursue an ongoing, integrated plan for furthering the organization's performance.[8] Research has found that effective human resource management and the alignment of HR strategies with the organization's strategic direction has a positive impact on performance, including higher employee productivity and stronger financial results.[9]

The Strategic Approach

The strategic approach to human resource management recognizes three key elements. First, all managers are involved in human resource management. Second, employees are viewed as assets. No strategy can be effectively implemented without the right people to put it into action. Employees, not buildings and machinery, give a company its competitive edge. Third, human resource management is a matching process, integrating the organization's strategy and goals with the correct approach to managing human capital.[10] In companies that take a strategic approach, HR managers are key players on the executive team and play a pivotal role in driving performance. At retailer Target, for example, the formal mission of the human resources department is to "drive company performance by building a fast, fun, and friendly team committed to excellence." To fulfill the mission, HR managers are directly involved in building a culture that distinguishes Target from other retailers, finding the right people to fit the culture, and then creating training programs, compensation, and other mechanisms to develop and retain high-quality employees.[11] Some current strategic issues of particular concern to managers include the following:

- Right people to become more competitive on a global basis
- Right people for improving quality, innovation, and customer service
- Right people to retain during mergers and acquisitions
- Right people to apply new information technology for e-business

All of these strategic decisions determine a company's need for skills and employees.

This chapter examines the three primary goals of HRM, as illustrated in Exhibit 9.1. HRM activities and goals do not take place inside a vacuum but within the context of issues and factors affecting the entire organization, such as globalization, changing technology, a growing need for rapid innovation, quick shifts in

EXHIBIT 9.1

Strategic Human Resource Management

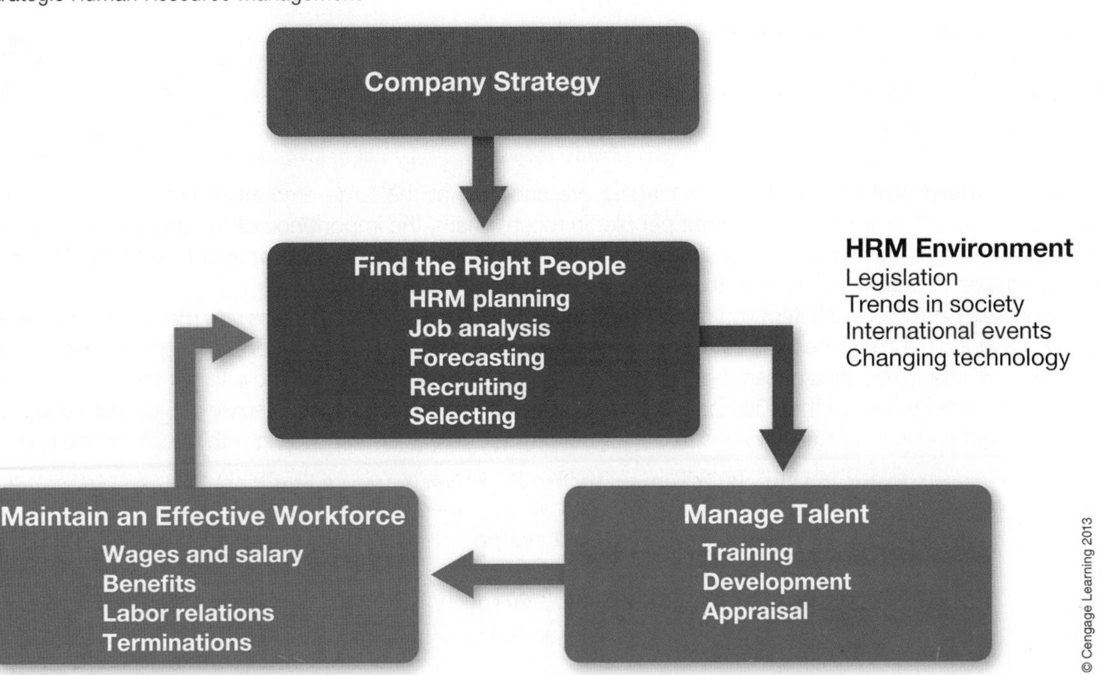

New Manager Self-Test

Getting the Right People on the Bus

As a new manager, how much emphasis will you give to getting the right people on your team? How much emphasis on people is needed? Find out by answering the following questions, based on your expectations and beliefs for handling the people part of your management job. Please answer whether each item is Mostly True or Mostly False for you.

	MOSTLY TRUE <<<	>>> MOSTLY FALSE
1. I will readily fire someone who isn't working out for the interests of the organization.	_____	_____
2. Selecting the right people for a winning business team is as important to me as it is to a winning sports team.	_____	_____
3. I expect to spend 40 to 60 percent of my management time on issues such as recruiting, developing, and placing people.	_____	_____
4. I will paint a realistic picture of negative job aspects that will help scare off the wrong people for the job.	_____	_____
5. My priority as a manager is first to hire the right people, second to put people in the right positions, and third to then decide strategy and vision.	_____	_____
6. With the right people on my team, problems of motivation and supervision will largely go away.	_____	_____
7. I expect that hiring the right people is a lengthy and arduous process.	_____	_____
8. I view firing someone as helping them find the place where they belong to find fulfillment.	_____	_____

See It Online

Scoring and Interpretation: Most new managers are shocked at the large amount of time, effort, and skill required to recruit, place, and retain the right people. In recent years, the importance of "getting the right people on the bus" has been described in popular business books such as *Good to Great* and *Execution*. The right people can make an organization great; the wrong people can be catastrophic.

Give yourself 1 point for each item you marked as Mostly True. If you scored 4 or less you may be in for a shock as a new manager. People issues will take up most of your time, and if you don't handle people correctly, your effectiveness will suffer. You should learn how to get the right people on the bus and how to get the wrong people off the bus. The faster you learn these lessons, the better a new manager you will be. A score of 5 or more suggests you have the right understanding and expectations for becoming a manager and dealing with people on the bus.

SOURCE: Based on ideas presented in Jim Collins, *Good to Great: Why Some Companies Make the Leap … and Others Don't* (New York: Harper Business, 2001); James Collins, *Good to Great*; Larry Bossidy et al, *Execution* (New York: Crown Business, 2002).

markets and the external environment, societal trends, government regulations, and changes in the organization's culture, structure, strategy, and goals.

The three broad HRM activities outlined in Exhibit 9.1 are to find the right people, manage talent so people achieve their potential, and maintain the workforce over the long term.[12] Achieving these goals requires skills in planning, recruiting, training, performance appraisal, wage and salary administration, benefit programs, and even termination.

Building Human Capital to Drive Performance

Today, more than ever, strategic decisions are related to human resource considerations. In many companies, especially those that rely more on employee information, creativity, knowledge, and service rather than on production machinery, success depends on the ability to manage *human capital*.[13] **Human capital** refers to the economic value of the combined knowledge, experience, skills, and capabilities of employees.[14] To build human capital, HRM develops strategies for finding the best talent, enhancing their skills and knowledge with training programs and opportunities for personal and professional development, and providing compensation and benefits that support the sharing of knowledge and appropriately reward people for their contributions to the organization.

The importance of human capital for business results is illustrated in Exhibit 9.2. The exhibit shows a portion of a framework developed by Accenture and used by software and services company SAP. SAP needed a way to evaluate and revise its human capital

EXHIBIT 9.2

The Role and Value of Human Capital Investments

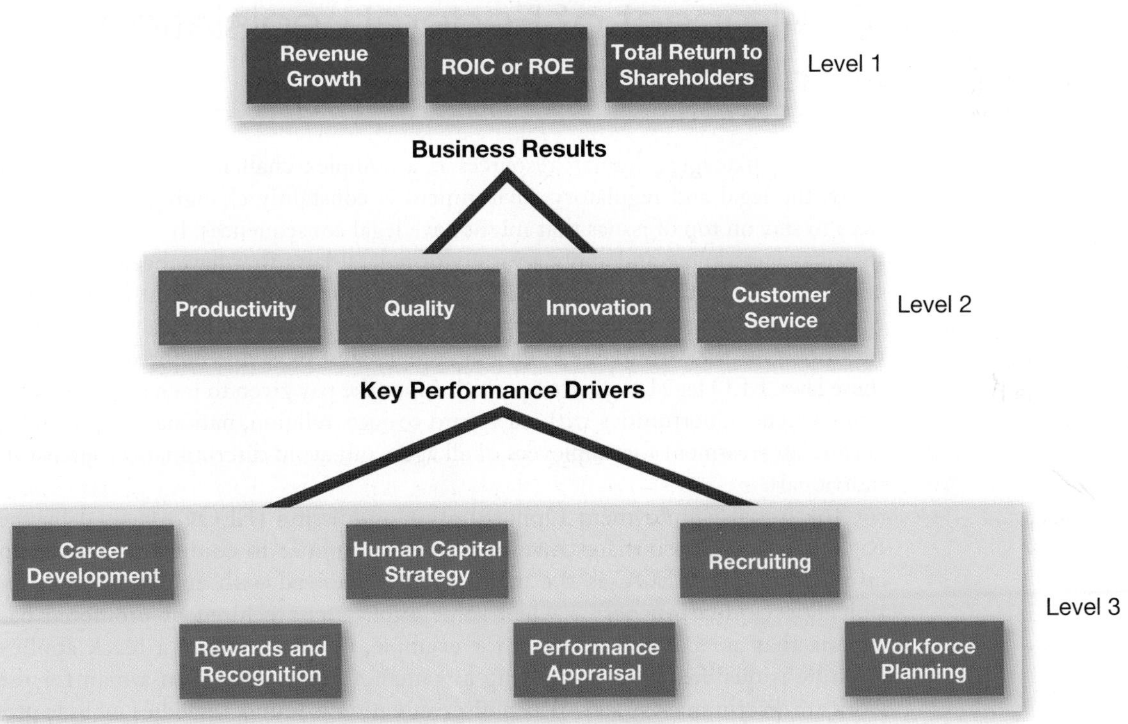

SOURCE: Adapted from Susan Cantrell, James M. Benton, Terry Laudal, and Robert J. Thomas, "Measuring the Value of Human Capital Investments: The SAP Case," *Strategy & Leadership* 34, no. 2 (2006): 43–52.

processes to shift to a new strategy that called for stronger customer focus and greater individual employee accountability. The idea is to show how investments in human capital contribute to stronger organizational performance and better financial results. The framework begins at the bottom (level 3) by assessing internal processes such as workforce planning, career development, performance appraisal, and so forth. Managers use these activities to increase human capital capabilities that drive higher performance in key areas such as innovation or customer service (level 2). Improvements in key performance areas, in turn, lead to improved business results (level 1).[15]

- **Human resource management (HRM)** refers to the design and application of formal systems to ensure the effective and efficient use of human talent to accomplish organizational goals.
- HRM includes activities undertaken to attract, select, develop, and maintain an effective workforce.
- Human resource managers are vital players in corporate strategy because no strategy can be effective without the right people to put it into action.
- The formal mission of the human resources department at Target is to "drive company performance by building a fast, fun, and friendly team committed to excellence."
- **Human capital** refers to the economic value of the combined knowledge, experience, skills, and capabilities of employees.

The Impact of Federal Legislation on HRM

Effectively managing human resources is a complex challenge for managers. For one thing, the legal and regulatory environment is constantly changing, and HR managers have to stay on top of issues that might have legal consequences. It is critically important that managers know and apply a variety of federal laws that have been passed to ensure equal employment opportunity (EEO). Some of the most significant legislation and executive orders are summarized in Exhibit 9.3. The point of the laws is to stop discriminatory practices that are unfair to specific groups and to define enforcement agencies for these laws. EEO legislation attempts to balance the pay given to men and women; provide employment opportunities without regard to race, religion, national origin, and gender; ensure fair treatment for employees of all ages; and avoid discrimination against disabled individuals.

The Equal Employment Opportunity Commission (EEOC) created by the Civil Rights Act of 1964 initiates investigations in response to complaints concerning discrimination. The EEOC is the major agency involved with employment discrimination. **Discrimination** occurs when some applicants are hired or promoted based on criteria that are not job relevant; for example, refusing to hire a black applicant for a job he is qualified to fill or paying a woman a lower wage than a man for the same work are discriminatory acts. When discrimination is found, remedies include providing back pay and taking affirmative action. **Affirmative action** requires that an employer take positive steps to guarantee equal employment opportunities for people within protected groups. An affirmative action plan is a formal document that can be reviewed by

EXHIBIT 9.3

Major Federal Laws Related to Human Resource Management

Federal Law	Year	Provisions
Equal Opportunity/ Discrimination Laws		
Civil Rights Act	1991	Provides for possible compensatory and punitive damages plus traditional back pay for cases of intentional discrimination brought under title VII of the 1964 Civil Rights Act. Shifts the burden of proof to the employer.
Americans with Disabilities Act	1990	Prohibits discrimination against qualified individuals by employers on the basis of disability and demands that "reasonable accommodations" be provided for the disabled to allow performance of duties.
Vocational Rehabilitation Act	1973	Prohibits discrimination based on physical or mental disability and requires that employees be informed about affirmative action plans.
Age Discrimination in Employment Act (ADEA)	1967 (amended 1978, 1986)	Prohibits age discrimination and restricts mandatory retirement.
Civil Rights Act, Title VII	1964	Prohibits discrimination in employment on the basis of race, religion, color, sex, or national origin.
Compensation/ Benefits Laws		
Health Insurance Portability Accountability Act (HIPPA)	1996	Allows employees to switch health insurance plans when changing jobs and get the new coverage regardless of preexisting health conditions; prohibits group plans from dropping a sick employee.
Family and Medical Leave Act	1993	Requires employers to provide up to 12 weeks unpaid leave for childbirth, adoption, or family emergencies.
Equal Pay Act	1963	Prohibits sex differences in pay for substantially equal work.
Health/Safety Laws		
Patient Protection and Affordable Care Act	2010	Imposes a fee on firms with 50 or more employees if the government subsidizes their employees' health care coverage.
Consolidated Omnibus Budget Reconciliation Act (COBRA)	1985	Requires continued health insurance coverage (paid by employee) following termination.
Occupational Safety and Health Act (OSHA)	1970	Establishes mandatory safety and health standards in organizations.

employees and enforcement agencies. The goal of organizational affirmative action is to reduce or eliminate internal inequities among affected employee groups.

Failure to comply with equal employment opportunity legislation can result in substantial fines and penalties for employers. Suits for discriminatory practices can cover a broad range of employee complaints. One issue of growing concern is *sexual harassment,* which is also a violation of Title VII of the Civil Rights Act. The EEOC guidelines specify that

As a new manager, you may need to keep detailed records that document compliance with federal laws and regulations. Complete the test in the Spotlight on Skills box, on page 335, to see whether you have a natural orientation toward systematic record keeping.

behavior such as unwelcome advances, requests for sexual favors, and other verbal and physical conduct of a sexual nature becomes sexual harassment when submission to the conduct is tied to continued employment or advancement or when the behavior creates an intimidating, hostile, or offensive work environment.[16] Sexual harassment will be discussed in more detail later in this chapter.

Exhibit 9.3 also lists major federal laws related to compensation and benefits, and health and safety issues. This is only a sampling of the federal laws that HR managers must know and understand. In addition, many states and municipalities have their own laws that relate to human resource issues. The scope of human resource legislation is increasing at federal, state, and municipal levels. For example, the U.S. health-care overhaul bill passed in 2010 is expected to impose a $2,000 per employee fee on organizations if the government subsidizes their employees' health-care coverage.[17] Legislative issues influence HR managers' work on a daily basis.

- HR managers have to understand and apply a variety of federal laws that prohibit discrimination, establish safety standards, or require organizations to provide certain benefits.
- **Discrimination** means the hiring or promoting of applicants based on criteria that are not job relevant.
- **Affirmative action** requires that employers take positive steps to guarantee equal employment opportunities for people within protected groups.

The Changing Nature of Careers

Another current issue is the changing nature of careers and a shift in the relationship between employers and employees.

The Changing Social Contract

In the old social contract between organization and employee, the employee could contribute ability, education, loyalty, and commitment and expect in return that the company would provide wages and benefits, work, advancement, and training throughout the employee's working life. But volatile changes in the environment have disrupted this contract. Consider the following list found on a bulletin board at a company undergoing major restructuring:

- We can't promise you how long we'll be in business.
- We can't promise you that we won't be acquired.
- We can't promise that there'll be room for promotion.
- We can't promise that your job will exist when you reach retirement age.
- We can't promise that the money will be available for your pension.
- We can't expect your undying loyalty, and we aren't even sure we want it.[18]

SPOTLIGHT ON SKILLS

What Is Your HR Work Orientation?

As a new manager, what is your orientation concerning day-to-day work issues? To find out, think about your preferences for the questions below. Check "a" or "b" for each item, depending on which one is accurate for you. There are no right or wrong answers.

1. The work elements I prefer are
   _____ a. administrative.
   _____ b. conceptualizing.
2. The work elements I prefer are
   _____ a. creative.
   _____ b. organizing.
3. My mode of living is
   _____ a. conventional.
   _____ b. original.
4. The most important quality to me is
   _____ a. how something looks (form).
   _____ b. how well it works (function).
5. I like to work with
   _____ a. a practical person.
   _____ b. an idea person.
6. I am more
   _____ a. idealistic.
   _____ b. realistic.
7. For weekend activities, I prefer to
   _____ a. plan in advance.
   _____ b. be free to do what I want.
8. A daily work routine for me is
   _____ a. painful.
   _____ b. comfortable.

Scoring and Interpretation: The HR department typically is responsible for monitoring compliance with federal laws, and it provides detailed and specific employee procedures and records for an organization. Every new manager is involved in HR activities for his or her direct reports, which involves systematic record keeping, awareness of applicable laws, and follow-through. For your HR work orientation, score 1 point for each "a" answer for items 1, 3, 5, 7 and 1 point for each "b" answer for items 2, 4, 6, 8.

New managers with a high score (7 or 8) for HR work orientation tend to be practical, organized, good at record keeping, and meet commitments on time. New managers with a low score (1 or 2) on HR work orientation tend to be more free-spirited, creative, and conceptual. These managers tend to think out of the box and may dislike the organization, routine, and legal record keeping required for efficient HR management. If your score is midrange (3 to 6), you may do well with HR work if you put your mind to it, but HR may not be your area of greatest strength.

Downsizing, outsourcing, rightsizing, and restructuring have led to the elimination of many positions in organizations. Employees who are left may feel little stability. The recent downturn has accelerated the erosion of the old social contract. Two mainstays for many companies until recently—employer-subsidized retirement benefits and employer-paid health care—are in serious decline. One survey found that the number of employers offering health-care benefits declined from 69 percent in 2000 to 60 percent in 2009. Those that do offer coverage are increasing employees' share of the expense. As for retirement benefits, only about 20 percent of employees are covered by traditional pension plans today, and during the recession many companies suspended their contributions to employee 401(k) plans. Moreover, many organizations that cut benefits say they don't intend to restore them.[19]

These changes and the list in the above paragraph reflect a primarily negative view of the new employer–employee relationship, but there are positive aspects as well. Many people, particularly younger employees, like the expectation of responsibility and mobility embedded in the new social contract. Everyone is expected to be a self-motivated worker who is continuously acquiring new skills and demonstrating value to the organization. Most younger employees don't even think in terms of a career with one company.

Exhibit 9.4 lists some elements of the new social contract. The new contract is based on the concept of employability rather than lifetime employment. Individuals are responsible for developing their own skills and abilities, understanding their employer's business needs, and demonstrating their value to the organization. The employer, in turn, invests in creative training and development opportunities so that people will be more employable when the company no longer needs their services. This means offering challenging work assignments, opportunities to participate in decision making, and access to information and resources. In addition, an important challenge for HRM is revising performance evaluation, compensation, and other practices to be compatible with the new social contract. For example, with the tough economy in recent years, companies have had to lay off thousands of experienced employees. Many organizations, including KPMG, IBM, and Lockheed Martin, have set up "alumni social networks" so that people who have to be let go can keep in touch with colleagues and the industry. The Web sites post industry news, job leads, health insurance deals, or other valuable information. Alumni social networks benefit the company by keeping managers in touch with qualified workers who might be recruited back when needed, and they benefit former employees by giving them access to information, contacts, and job leads they might otherwise not have. Microsoft's network, for instance, posts job ads free for any company looking to recruit from the 10,000 or so former Microsoft employees who use the site.[20]

The new social contract can benefit both employees and organizations. However, some companies take the new approach as an excuse to treat people as economic factors to be used when needed and then let go. This attitude hurts morale, employee commitment, and organizational performance. Studies in both the United States and China, for example, have found lower employee and firm performance and decreased commitment in companies where the interaction between employer and employee is treated as an

9.4 EXHIBIT

The Changing Social Contract

	New Contract	Old Contract
Employee	• Employability; personal responsibility • Partner in business improvement • Learning; skill development	• Job security • A cog in the machine • Knowing
Employer	• Creative development opportunities • Lateral career moves; incentive compensation • Challenging assignments • Information and resources; decision-making authority	• Standard training programs • Traditional compensation package • Routine jobs • Limited information

SOURCES: Based on Louisa Wah, "The New Workplace Paradox," *Management Review* (January 1998): 7; and Douglas T. Hall and Jonathan E. Moss, "The New Protean Career Contract: Helping Organizations and Employees Adapt," *Organizational Dynamics* (Winter 1998): 22–37.

BUSINESS BLOOPER

Walmart

Imagine getting a minimum-wage job at Walmart, and a temporary one at that. It is the day after Thanksgiving, often the heaviest retail day of the year. You are standing, ready to greet all the enthusiastic customers. Instead, you get trampled to death. This happened to Jdimytai Damour at a Walmart on Long Island in 2008. Walmart spent $2 million fighting OSHA's $7,000 fine, causing federal employees to spend more than 4,700 hours in legal work. Walmart put nationwide crowd-control plans into effect the following year but still objected to the judge's ruling that they should have realized the dangers and put those changes into effect prior to the fatal accident. In March 2011, Judge Covette Rooney upheld the fine, concluding that "unruly crowds the day after Thanksgiving were a recognized hazard and that there were feasible means to control that hazard." Walmart fought the fine because they said that OSHA wanted to define "crowd trampling" as an occupational hazard retailers are responsible to prevent.

SOURCE: Steven Greenhouse, "Judge Upholds $7000 Fine in Trampling at Walmart," *The New York Times*, March 26, 2011.

economic exchange rather than a genuine human and social relationship.[21] Part of the old social contract, backed up by laws, was that the workplace would be safe. Walmart and OSHA had some legal dispute about this after an employee was trampled to death, as described in this chapter's Business Blooper.

Innovations in HRM

The rapid change and uncertainty in today's business environment bring significant new challenges for human resource management. Some important issues are becoming an employer of choice, addressing the needs of temporary employees and part-time workers, and acknowledging growing employee demands for work/life balance.

Becoming an Employer of Choice The old social contract may be broken for good, but today's best companies recognize the importance of treating people right and thinking for the long term rather than looking for quick fixes based on an economic exchange relationship with employees. At Southwest Airlines, for example, managers do monthly check-ins with all nonunion employees to talk about their career goals and progress. Even as many organizations were cutting investments in employee development, Southwest hired full-time "talent development managers" for every department to help line managers appropriately coach and guide employees.[22]

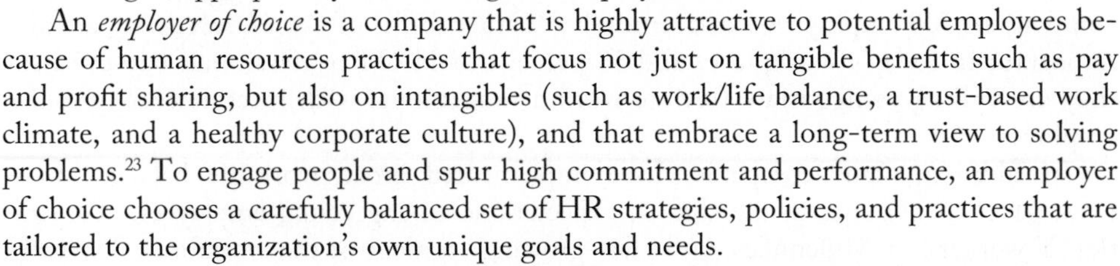

An *employer of choice* is a company that is highly attractive to potential employees because of human resources practices that focus not just on tangible benefits such as pay and profit sharing, but also on intangibles (such as work/life balance, a trust-based work climate, and a healthy corporate culture), and that embrace a long-term view to solving problems.[23] To engage people and spur high commitment and performance, an employer of choice chooses a carefully balanced set of HR strategies, policies, and practices that are tailored to the organization's own unique goals and needs.

Using Temporary and Part-Time Employees Contingent workers are becoming a larger part of the workforce in both the United States and Europe. **Contingent workers** are people who work for an organization, but not on a permanent or full-time

Rod Lamkey Jr.

ConceptConnection

LIST Innovative Solutions's **flexible scheduling** program works. The Herndon, Virginia-based software development company has enjoyed a 95 percent employee retention rate over the last 16 years. Inspired by her own experience as a harried parent, CEO and company founder Katie Sleep instituted a policy that allows her employees to decide when and where they work. Katie Stumpf (pictured), LIST human resources director and a mother of young children, achieves a **work/life balance** by going to the office when she needs to put in some "face time" and working at home on self-directed projects.

basis.[24] In 2005, approximately 26 percent of the U.S. workforce was made up of contingent workers, including temporary placements, independent contractors, freelancers, and part-time employees.[25] That percentage has likely swelled since then because of the huge numbers of people laid off from permanent jobs during the recession that followed the 2008 financial crisis. The number of "involuntary part-timers," for example, has doubled since the recession began.[26] People in temporary jobs do everything from data entry, to project management, to becoming the interim CEO. A related trend is the use of temporary teams. Some are made up entirely of people who are hired on a project-by-project basis. Many companies depend on part-time or temporary employees to maintain flexibility and keep costs low.[27]

Although in the past most temporary workers were in clerical and manufacturing positions, in recent years demand has grown for contingent professionals such as accountants and financial analysts, interim managers, information technology specialists, product managers, and even lawyers and health-care workers. Sydney Reiner, who loves the freedom and flexibility of contingent work, has had five assignments in five years as an interim chief marketing officer, including a stint with Godiva Chocolatier in Japan.[28]

Promoting Work/Life Balance Initiatives that enable people to lead a balanced life are a critical part of many organizations' retention strategies. Particularly today, when some companies can't afford pay raises for valued employees, managers are offering people more flexible scheduling or more control over their assignments as rewards.[29] One approach is to let employees work part of the time from home or another remote location. **Telecommuting** means using computers and telecommunications equipment to do work without going to an office. According to the Office of Personnel Management, more than 100,000 employees of the federal government work from home at least one day a week. At Aspect Software, about 28 percent of the company's 1,700 employees work remotely.[30] Other forms of *flexible scheduling* are also important in today's workplace, and 55 percent of HRM professionals surveyed say they are willing to negotiate flexible work arrangements with interviewees and new employees.[31]

In addition, many companies have implemented broad work/life balance initiatives, partly in response to the shift in expectations among young employees.[32] Generation Y workers, or Millennials, are a fast-growing segment of the workforce. Typically, Gen-Y employees work smart and work hard on the job, but they refuse to let work be their whole life. Unlike their parents, who placed a high priority on career, Gen-Y workers expect the job to accommodate their personal lives.[33]

- The new social contract between employers and employees is based on the notion of employability and personal responsibility rather than lifelong employment by an organization.
- **Contingent workers** are people who work for an organization, but not on a permanent or full-time basis, including temporary placements, independent contractors, freelancers, and part-time employees.
- **Telecommuting** means using computers and telecommunications equipment to perform work from home or another remote location.
- About 28 percent of Aspect Software's 1,700 employees telecommute at least part of the time.

Finding the Right People

Now let's turn to the three broad goals of HRM: finding, developing, and maintaining an effective workforce. The first step in finding the right people is human resource planning, in which managers or HRM professionals predict the need for new employees based on the types of vacancies that exist, as illustrated in Exhibit 9.5. The second step is to use recruiting procedures to communicate with potential applicants. The third step is to select from the applicants those persons believed to be the best potential contributors to the organization. Finally, the new employee is welcomed into the organization.

Underlying the organization's effort to attract employees is a matching model. With the **matching model**, the organization and the individual attempt to match the needs, interests,

EXHIBIT 9.5

Attracting an Effective Workforce

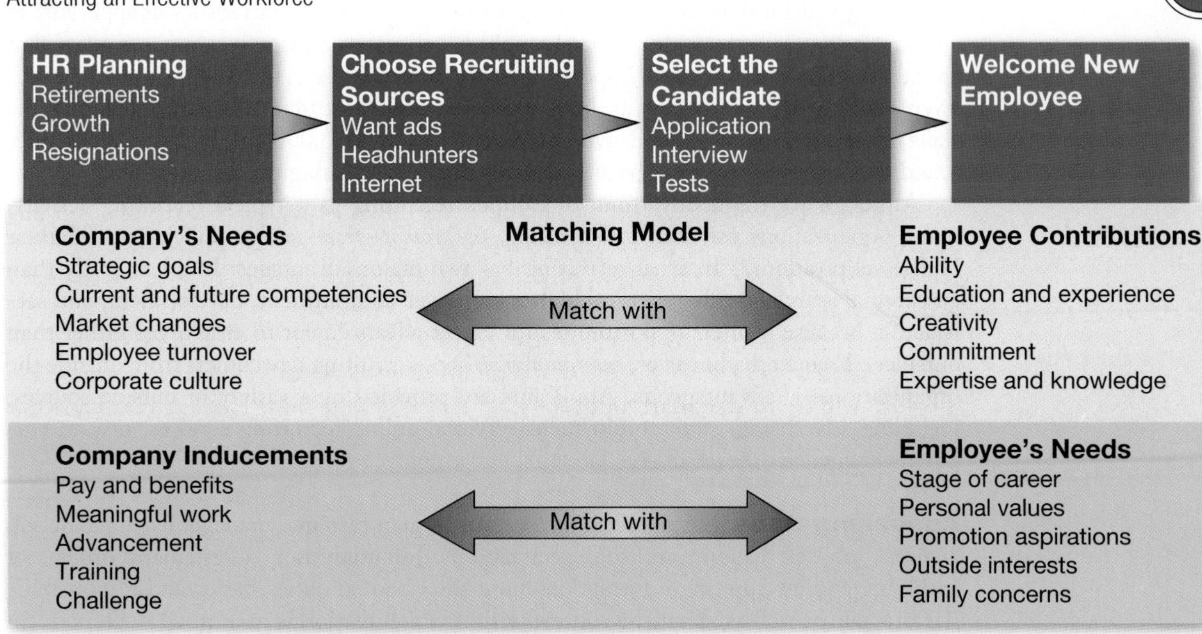

and values that they offer each other.[34] For example, a small software developer might require long hours from creative, technically skilled employees. In return, it can offer freedom from bureaucracy, tolerance of idiosyncrasies, and potentially high pay. A large manufacturer can offer employment security and stability, but it might have more rules and regulations and require greater skills for "getting approval from the higher-ups." The individual who would thrive working for the software developer might feel stymied and unhappy working for a large manufacturer. Both the company and the employee are interested in finding a good match.

Human Resource Planning

Human resource planning is the forecasting of human resource needs and the projected matching of individuals with expected vacancies. Human resource planning begins with several questions:

- What new technologies are emerging, and how will these affect the work system?
- What is the volume of the business likely to be in the next five to ten years?
- What is the turnover rate, and how much, if any, is avoidable?

The responses to these questions are used to formulate specific questions pertaining to HR activities, such as the following:

- What types of engineers will we need and how many?
- How many administrative personnel will we need to support the additional engineers?
- Can we use temporary, part-time, or virtual workers to handle some tasks?[35]

By anticipating future human resource needs, the organization can prepare itself to meet competitive challenges more effectively than organizations that react to problems only as they arise.

Recruiting

Recruiting is defined as "activities or practices that define the characteristics of applicants to whom selection procedures are ultimately applied."[36] Today, recruiting is sometimes referred to as *talent acquisition* to reflect the importance of the human factor in the organization's success.[37] Even when unemployment rates are high, companies often have trouble finding people with the skills the organization needs. A survey by Manpower Inc. of 33,000 employers in 23 countries found that 40 percent reported having difficulty finding and hiring the desired talent.[38]

Although we frequently think of campus recruiting as a typical recruiting activity, many organizations use *internal recruiting,* or *promote-from-within* policies, to fill their high-level positions.[39] Internal recruiting has two major advantages: It is less costly than an external search, and it generates higher employee commitment, development, and satisfaction because it offers opportunities for career advancement to employees rather than outsiders. Frequently, however, *external recruiting*—recruiting newcomers from outside the organization—is advantageous. Applicants are provided by a variety of outside sources, including advertising, state employment services, online recruiting services, private employment agencies *(headhunters),* job fairs, and employee referrals.

Assessing Jobs Basic building blocks of human resource management include job analysis, job descriptions, and job specifications. **Job analysis** is a systematic process of gathering and interpreting information about the essential duties, tasks, and responsibilities of a job, as well as about the context within which the job is performed.[38] To perform job analysis, managers or specialists ask about work activities and work flow, the degree of supervision given and received in the job, knowledge and skills needed, performance standards, working conditions, and so forth. The manager then prepares a written **job**

description, which is a clear and concise summary of the specific tasks, duties, and responsibilities, and **job specifications**, which outline the knowledge, skills, education, physical abilities, and other characteristics needed to adequately perform the job.

Job analysis helps organizations recruit the right kind of people and match them to appropriate jobs. For example, to enhance internal recruiting, Sara Lee Corporation identified six functional areas and 24 significant skills that it wants its finance executives to develop, as illustrated in Exhibit 9.6. Managers are tracked on their development and moved into other positions to help them acquire the needed skills.[41]

Realistic Job Previews Job analysis also enhances recruiting effectiveness by enabling the creation of **realistic job previews**. A realistic job preview (RJP) gives applicants all pertinent and realistic information—positive and negative—about the job and the organization.[42] RJPs contribute to greater employee satisfaction and lower turnover because they facilitate matching individuals, jobs, and organizations. Individuals have a better basis on which to determine their suitability to the organization and "self-select" into or out of positions based on full information.

Legal Considerations Managers must ensure that their recruiting practices conform to the law. As discussed earlier in this chapter, equal employment opportunity (EEO) laws stipulate that recruiting and hiring decisions cannot discriminate on the basis of race, national origin, religion, or gender. The Americans with Disabilities Act underscored the need for well-written job descriptions and specifications that accurately reflect the mental and physical dimensions of jobs so that people with disabilities will not be discriminated against. *Affirmative action* refers to the use of goals, timetables, or other methods in

EXHIBIT 9.6

Sara Lee's Required Skills for Finance Executives

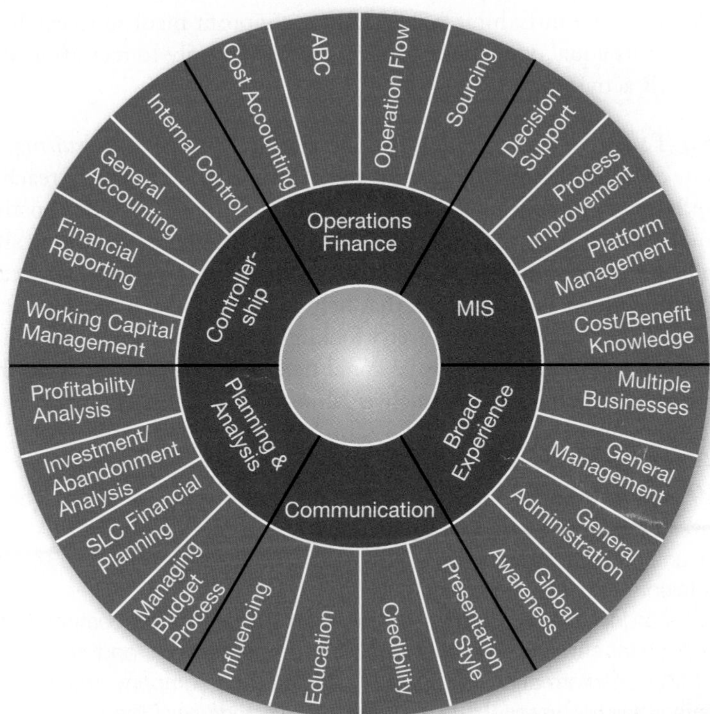

SOURCE: Reprinted with permission from *CFO*, October 1, 1998. Visit our website at www.cfo.com. © CFO Publishing LLC. All Rights Reserved. Foster Printing Service: 866-879-9144, www.marketingreprints.com. License #13921.

EXHIBIT 9.7

PAIRE's Recruitment and Hiring Policy

PAIRE

I. PAIRE's policy of equal employment is aimed at, and committed to, building and maintaining a diverse workforce with high standards and expectations for excellence. State and federal laws continue to require a commitment to equal employment opportunity and a workplace that is free from any form of unlawful discrimination. As an equal opportunity employer PAIRE will endeavor to select the best qualified individuals based on job-related qualifications, regardless of such factors as race, sex, color, age, ancestry, citizenship, pregnancy, religion, national origin, marital status, parental status, sexual orientation, political affiliation, physical or mental disability or medical condition (as defined under state law), status as a disabled veteran or Vietnam-era veteran, when the individual is otherwise qualified or on any other basis prohibited by federal, state or local law.

II. This policy defines PAIRE's commitment to providing equal opportunity in all phases of employment including, but not limited to the following:

A. Recruiting and soliciting for employment
B. Hiring, placement, promotion, transfer and demotion
C. Employment training or selection for training
D. Rate of pay, compensation, and benefits
E. Termination of employment

SOURCE: Palo Alto Institute for Research & Education, http://www.paire.org/hr/documents/Recruiting-and-Hiring-Policy.pdf (accessed June 1, 2010). Reprinted by permission of PAIRE Inc.

recruiting to promote the hiring, development, and retention of protected groups. Most large organizations try to comply with affirmative action and EEO guidelines. A portion of the recruitment and hiring policy of the Palo Alto Institute for Research & Education (PAIRE) is shown in Exhibit 9.7. PAIRE, a nonprofit medical research organization, makes clear that its equal opportunity policy applies not only to recruiting and hiring but also to other HR activities.

E-cruiting Today, much recruiting is done via the Internet.[43] *E-cruiting*, or recruiting job applicants online, dramatically extends the organization's recruiting reach, offering access to a wider pool of applicants and saving time and money. Besides posting job openings on company Web sites, many organizations use commercial recruiting sites where job seekers can post their résumés and companies can search for qualified applicants. In addition, new online services have emerged that help managers search for "passive candidates," people who are highly qualified and aren't looking for jobs but might be the best fit for a company's opening. For example, professional networking leader LinkedIn has become a significant threat to the big job sites such as Monster and CareerBuilder.

LINKEDIN

LinkedIn started in 2003 as an online networking site for business managers and other professionals to broaden their base of contacts, pursue job opportunities, develop sales leads, and so forth. HR recruiters quickly saw the site's potential as a source for locating high-quality talent.

Individuals can join LinkedIn and get a basic account for free, but companies that purchase a corporate account can post job openings, search the network, and contact users directly with offers. EMC, an information management and storage company, routinely uses LinkedIn to recruit potential employees. U.S. Cellular corporate recruiter Elise Bannon says she used to spend up to $4 million a year posting jobs and screening résumés through job sites such as Monster, CareerBuilder, and HotJobs. Now, U.S. Cellular pays a $60,000 annual fee to LinkedIn and gets access to more than 42 million members around the world. Using the site helped the company find the right person to fill an important position in 30 days rather than the six months it typically takes to fill that job. "Finding passive candidates—that's our sweet spot," says David Hahn, LinkedIn's director of product management.[44]

Using social media has given HR managers a new method to find the right talent and fill jobs quickly. Even Twitter is being used for recruiting. A legal recruiter received an e-mail one morning from a client needing 40 lawyers immediately for a temporary project. She sent a "tweet" to her followers, who sent it to others. The recruiter filled every position by lunchtime.[45]

Innovations in Recruiting Organizations look for ways to enhance their recruiting success, such as using Twitter, LinkedIn, and other social media, as just discussed. Managers are always searching for innovative approaches to recruit the right people. One highly effective method is getting referrals from current employees. Many organizations offer cash awards to employees who submit names of people who subsequently accept employment, because referral by current employees is one of the cheapest and most reliable methods of external recruiting.[46] Social media has also enhanced this means of recruiting because people can search their networks for contacts with the right training or skills. About half of the 21 new employees hired by Chicago-based Total Attorneys during a six-week period in 2009 came from employee referrals, and half of those were located using a social networking search. "This is beyond the HR department," said Total Attorney's CEO Ed Scanlan. "All employees should be talent recruiters."[47]

Companies use a number of other approaches to find the right talent. One technique is to search among the membership of relevant trade groups, such as at trade shows, meetings, and on the associations' Web sites.[48] Some organizations turn to nontraditional sources to find dedicated employees, particularly in a tight labor market or when the organization needs specific types of workers. When Walker Harris couldn't find workers for his ice company, Harris Ice, he began hiring former prison inmates, many of whom have turned out to be reliable, loyal employees.[49] Companies such as Walmart, General Electric, and PepsiCo that were facing a shortage of young talent in the management ranks discovered a gold mine among junior military officers. These young leaders bring a maturity to the job, honed by their experience leading people in critical missions that involve life and death. "They're ready to go from Plan A to Plan B to Plan C without missing a beat," says René Brooks, who runs a recruiting firm.[50]

Here's how managers at I Love Rewards, a small company that advises organizations that want to implement online employee benefits and performance-based rewards programs, met their challenge of finding the right people.

I LOVE REWARDS

When managers at I Love Rewards, with only 38 employees in Wellesley, Massachusetts, and Toronto, Canada, received 1,200 applications for just nine job openings, they were overwhelmed by the challenge of finding the right people among all the potentially wrong ones. Just the thought of reading through all the résumés was daunting for the small team.

Their creative answer to the problem? A sort of speed dating screening process. First, the company sent an e-mail to all applicants thanking them for their interest and inviting them to an open house at the Toronto office. Only 400 applicants showed up, so that means 800 people "self-selected" out right up front. At the open house, the first floor was set up as an area where job candidates and employees could mingle informally. Upstairs was the speed dating area, where each prospect had a one-on-one contact with the employees for five minutes. Within that space of time, people were able to ask a few questions and get a pretty good sense of whether the applicant would be a good fit with the culture.

By the end of the evening, the team had narrowed 400 applicants down to the 68 most promising candidates, who were further screened and called back for individual and group interviews. The process worked so well that I Love Rewards now uses Open House events as its primary recruiting strategy. When the company wanted to fill 20 new positions in the spring of 2010, it didn't ask for résumés; instead, it scheduled two open houses and let the speed dating begin.[51]

- Finding the right people starts with **human resource planning**, which refers to the forecasting of human resource needs and the projected matching of individuals with anticipated job vacancies.
- The **matching model** is a human resources approach in which the organization and the individual attempt to match each other's needs, interests, and values.
- **Recruiting** refers to activities or practices that define the desired characteristics of applicants for specific jobs.
- Many of today's organizations recruit online, including the use of social media such as Twitter, LinkedIn, and Facebook.
- **Job analysis** is the systematic process of gathering and interpreting information about the essential duties, tasks, and responsibilities of a job.
- Managers prepare a **job description** for each open position, which is a concise summary of the specific tasks and responsibilities of that job.
- **Job specification** outlines the knowledge, skills, education, physical abilities, and other characteristics needed to adequately perform a specific job.
- Managers use **realistic job previews** in recruiting to give applicants all pertinent and realistic information, both positive and negative, about a job and the organization.
- Getting referrals from current employees is one of the least expensive and most effective ways to find good people for open job positions.
- I Love Rewards used a "speed dating" type of screening process when it received 1,200 applications for nine open positions.

Selecting

The next step for managers is to select desired employees from the pool of recruited applicants. In the **selection** process, employers assess applicants' characteristics in an attempt to determine the "fit" between the job and applicant characteristics. Several selection devices are used for assessing applicant qualifications. The most frequently used are the application form, interview, employment test, and assessment center. In general, the greater the skill requirements and work demands of an open position, the greater the number and variety of selection tools the organization will use.[52] Human resource professionals may use a combination of devices to get an idea of a candidate's potential performance.

TAKE ACTION

Refer to the New Manager Self-Test on page 330 to test your own preparation as a new manager for recruiting and selecting the right people for your team. Do you have what it takes?

Application Form The **application form** is used to collect information about the applicant's education, previous job experience, and other background characteristics. Research shows that biographical information inventories can validly predict future job success.[53]

One pitfall to be avoided is the inclusion of questions that are irrelevant to job success. In line with affirmative action, the application form should not ask questions that will create an adverse impact on protected groups unless the questions are clearly related to the job.[54] For example, employers should not ask whether the applicant rents or owns his or her own home because (1) an applicant's response might adversely affect his or her chances at the job, (2) minorities and women may be less likely to own a home, and (3) home ownership is probably unrelated to job performance. By contrast, the CPA exam is relevant to job performance in a CPA firm; thus, it is appropriate to ask whether an applicant for employment has passed the CPA exam, even if only one-half of all female or minority applicants have done so versus nine-tenths of male applicants.

Interview The *interview* is used as a selection technique in almost every job category in nearly every organization. It is another area where the organization can get into legal trouble if the interviewer asks questions that violate EEO guidelines. Exhibit 9.8 lists some examples of appropriate and inappropriate interview questions.

3

There is some evidence that the typical interview is not generally a good predictor of job performance. One estimate is that conventional interviews have a 0.2 correlation with predicting a successful hire.[55] People can improve their chances of having a successful

EXHIBIT 9.8

Employment Applications and Interviews: What Can You Ask?

Category	Okay to Ask	Inappropriate or Illegal to Ask
National origin	• The applicant's name • If applicant has ever worked under a different name	• The origin of applicant's name • Applicant's ancestry/ethnicity
Race	• Nothing	• Race or color of skin
Disabilities	• Whether applicant has any disabilities that might inhibit performance of job	• If applicant has any physical or mental defects • If applicant has ever filed workers' compensation claim
Age	• If applicant is over 18	• Applicant's age • When applicant graduated from high school
Religion	• Nothing	• Applicant's religious affiliation • What religious holidays applicant observes
Criminal record	• If applicant has ever been convicted of a crime	• If applicant has ever been arrested
Marital/family status	• Nothing	• Marital status, number of children or planned children • Childcare arrangements
Education and experience	• Where applicant went to school • Prior work experience	• When applicant graduated • Hobbies
Citizenship	• If applicant has a legal right to work in the United States	• If applicant is a citizen of another country

SOURCES: Based on "Appropriate and Inappropriate Interview Questions," in George Bohlander, Scott Snell, and Arthur Sherman, *Managing Human Resources*, 12th ed. (Cincinnati, OH: South-Western, 2001): 207; and "Guidelines to Lawful and Unlawful Preemployment Inquiries," Appendix E, in Robert L. Mathis and John H. Jackson, *Human Resource Management*, 2nd ed. (Cincinnati, OH: South-Western, 2002), 189–190.

SPOTLIGHT ON SKILLS

Top Interview Blunders; *Hint:* Don't Bring a Date

Have you ever jogged to a job interview and shown up soaked in sweat? How about called your mom in the middle of the interview to let her know it was going well? Most of us haven't committed such serious faux pas, but many of us have experienced a job interview where everything seems to be going well but then takes a drastic turn for the worse. According to CareerBuilder.com, most interview blunders fall into five key categories:

1. ***Communication Skills*** Managers often cite poor communication skills, such as inappropriate body language, talking too much or too little, not making eye contact, or using profanity or street slang. Here are some extreme examples:
   - "She kept telling me her personal problems."
   - "A job seeker gestured with his hands so much that he sat on them to stop it."
2. ***Performance*** Professionalism during the interview plays an important part in the hiring decision for most managers. Consider these candidates who were unprepared, distracted, or a little *too* comfortable:
   - "The candidate showed up with a box of doughnuts and ate them during the interview."
   - "When asked by the hiring manager if he had any questions, the candidate replied by telling a knock-knock joke."
   - "The person was dancing during the interview. He kept saying things like, 'I love life!' and 'Oh, yeah!' "
3. ***Attitude*** People who show arrogance and disrespect toward the interviewer are a huge turn-off. Would you hire these candidates?
   - "When asked where she saw herself in five years, the candidate replied, 'How am I supposed to know—isn't that your job?'"
   - "He asked me to speed up the interview because he had a lunch date."
4. ***Appearance*** In most cases, people should wear traditional, professional attire for an interview. Proper grooming, cleanliness, and good manners are also essential. These candidates clearly didn't understand this:
   - "A candidate for a manager position showed up in a low-cut blouse that revealed a panther tattoo on her breast."
   - "The applicant chewed bubble gum and blew bubbles."
   - "He showed up in jeans and a T-shirt, with dirty fingernails, and he looked like he just woke up."
5. ***Honesty*** Candidates who lie or give the impression that they are dishonest don't get a callback. Consider these smooth moves:
   - "The job seeker asked to use the hiring manager's phone. She proceeded to fake a coughing fit as she called in sick to her boss."
   - "After being complimented on his choice of college and the GPA he achieved, the candidate replied, 'I'm glad that got your attention. I didn't really go there.'"

These examples are humorous, but even the most practiced job seeker can make mistakes. Focusing on proper etiquette in these five areas can increase the chances of a successful interview.

SOURCES: CareerBuilder.com, as reported in "Job Interview Dos and Don'ts; Hint: Don't Be a Slob, Don't Eat, and Dress Appropriately," *Pittsburgh Post-Gazette,* February 14, 2004; "Avoid These Interview Blunders," *USA Today,* 138, no. 2771 (August 2009); Joann S. Lublin, "The New Job Is in the Details," *The Wall Street Journal,* January 5, 2010; "Interview Blunders Can Close Door on Job Opportunities," *New Pittsburgh Courier,* April 16, 2003; "The Lighter Side: Interview Blunders," *CPA Client Bulletin,* May 1999; and Rachel Warbington, "Interview Blunders Undermine Job Search," *Women in Business* (September–October 2000): 10.

interview by understanding some common pet peeves that trigger a negative response from interviewers, as outlined in the Spotlight on Skills titled Top Interview Blunders; *Hint:* Don't Bring a Date.

Today's managers use a variety of interview approaches to get a more reliable picture of a candidate's suitability for the job. **Structured interviews** use a set of standardized questions that are asked of every applicant so comparisons can easily be made. These may include *biographical interviews* that ask about the person's life and work experiences, *behavioral interviews* that ask people to describe how they have performed a certain task or handled a particular problem, and *situational interviews* that require people to describe how they might handle a hypothetical situation. **Nondirective interviews** allow the applicant a great deal of freedom in determining the course of the conversation, with the interviewer taking care not to influence the person's remarks. The interviewer asks broad, open-ended questions and permits the applicant to talk freely with minimal interruption. Nondirective interviews may bring to light information, attitudes, and behavioral characteristics that might be concealed when answering structured questions.

Some organizations put candidates through a series of interviews, each one conducted by a different person and each one probing a different aspect of the candidate. Others use **panel interviews**, in which the candidate meets with several interviewers who take turns asking questions.[56] At Boston Consulting Group, for instance, six applicants per job opening are given first-round interviews with two BCG consultants. About half go on to a second round, where they are interviewed by three or four consultants.[57] Some organizations also supplement traditional interviewing information with *computer-based interviews*. This type of interview typically requires a candidate to answer a series of multiple-choice questions tailored to the specific job. The answers are compared to an ideal profile or to a profile developed on the basis of other candidates.

Employment Test Organizations use many types of employment tests to assess candidates on various factors considered important for the job to be performed. **Employment tests** may include cognitive ability tests, physical ability tests, personality inventories, and other assessments. *Cognitive ability tests* measure an applicant's thinking, reasoning, verbal, and mathematical abilities. *Physical ability tests* that measure qualities such as strength, energy, and endurance may be used for jobs such as delivery drivers who must lift heavy packages, electric line workers who must climb ladders and carry equipment, and other positions that involve physical tasks. It is essential that these tests only assess cognitive and physical skills that are job related, to avoid violating laws against discrimination.

Many companies also use various types of *personality tests* to assess such characteristics as openness to learning, agreeableness, responsibility, creativity, and emotional stability. In addition, companies look for personality characteristics that match the needs of the particular job, so there is a good fit. One company found that people who score high in traits such as assertiveness and extroversion typically make good salespeople, so they looked for those traits in testing candidates for new positions.[58] By one estimate, 80 percent of midsize and large companies use personality and ability tests for either preemployment screening or new-employee orientation.[59] In today's era of ethical scandals, some companies also use tests to assess a person's honesty and integrity. Another unusual type of test, called a *brain teaser*, is being used by companies that put a premium on innovativeness and problem solving. The answers aren't as important as how the applicant goes about solving the problem. See how you do answering the brain teasers in Exhibit 9.9.

Assessment Center First developed by psychologists at AT&T, assessment centers are typically used to select individuals with high potential for managerial careers.[60] **Assessment centers** present a series of managerial situations to groups of applicants over a two- or three-day period. One technique is the *in-basket simulation,* which requires the applicant to play the role of a manager who must decide how to respond to ten memos in his or her in-basket within a two-hour period. Panels of two or three trained judges observe the applicant's decisions and assess the extent to which they reflect interpersonal, communication, and problem-solving skills. At one Michigan auto parts plant, applicants for plant manager

EXHIBIT 9.9

Try Your Hand at Some Interview Brain Teasers

How would you answer the following questions in a job interview?

1. How would you weigh a jet plane without using scales?
2. Why are manhole covers round?
3. How many golf balls can fit inside a standard school bus?
4. How much should you charge to wash all the windows in Seattle?
5. You're shrunk and trapped in a blender that will turn on in 60 seconds. What do you do?

Answers: There might be many solutions to these questions. Here are some that interviewers consider good answers:

1. Fly it onto an aircraft carrier or other ship big enough to hold it. Paint a mark on the hull of the ship showing the water level. Then remove the jet. The ship will rise in the water. Now load the ship with items of known weight (100 lb. bales of cotton, for instance) until it sinks to exactly the line you painted on the hull. The total weight of the items will equal the weight of the jet.
2. A square cover might fall into its hole. If you hold a square manhole cover vertically and turn it a little, it will fall easily into the hole. In contrast, a round cover with a slight recess in the center can never fall in, no matter how it is held.
3. About 500,000, assuming the bus is 50 balls high, 50 balls wide, and 200 balls long.
4. Assuming 10,000 city blocks, 600 windows per block, five minutes per window, and a rate of $20 per hour, about $10 million.
5. Use the measurement marks on the side of the container to climb out.

SOURCES: Similar questions are used at companies such as Microsoft, Google, and eBay. Reported in Michael Kaplan, "Job Interview Brainteasers," *Business 2.0* (September 2007): 35–37; and William Poundstone, "Impossible Questions," *Across the Board* (September–October 2003): 44–48.

go through four-hour "day-in-the-life" simulations in which they have to juggle memos, phone calls, and employee or job problems.[61]

Some organizations use this technique for front-line employees as well, by administering **work sample tests**, which require an applicant to complete simulated tasks that are a part of the desired job. A communications firm in the United Kingdom, for example, asked candidates for the position of customer assistant to participate in simulated exercises with customers to assess their listening skills, customer sensitivity, and ability to cope under pressure.[62] The city of Miami Beach has used work sample tests for a variety of jobs, including plumbers, planners, and accountants.[63]

Online Checks One of the newest ways of gauging whether a candidate is right for the company is by seeing what the person has to say about him- or herself on blogs and social networking sites. Recent college graduates looking for jobs have found doors closed to them because of risqué or teasing photos or vivid comments about drinking, drug use, or sexual exploits. Recruiters from more than two dozen companies told career counselors at New York University, for example, that if an applicant's online presentation raises red flags, the person isn't likely to even get an interview.[64] Companies today are not only interested in a candidate's educational and work qualifications, but also in personal characteristics and values that fit with the organization's culture. One recruiter said the open admission of excessive drinking and so forth makes managers question the applicant's maturity and judgment. HR managers may also search online for criminal records, credit history, and other indications of the candidate's honesty, integrity, and stability.[65]

- **Selection** is the process of assessing the skills, abilities, and other attributes of applicants in an attempt to determine the fit between the job and each applicant's characteristics.
- The **application form** is a selection device that collects information about the applicant's education, previous work experience, and other background characteristics.
- A **structured interview** uses a set of standardized questions that are asked of every applicant, so comparisons can easily be made.
- In a **nondirective interview**, the interviewer asks broad, open-ended questions and permits the applicant to talk freely with minimal interruption, in an attempt to bring to light information, attitudes, and behavioral characteristics that might be concealed when answering structured questions.
- A **panel interview** is an interview in which the candidate meets with several interviewers who take turns asking questions.
- Boston Consulting Group uses panel interviews when hiring new consultants.
- **Employment tests** assess candidates on various factors considered important for the job to be performed; they include cognitive ability tests, physical ability tests, and personality tests.
- An **assessment center** is used to select individuals with high managerial potential based on their performance on a series of simulated managerial tasks.
- Managers may administer **work sample tests** to applicants for front-line positions to evaluate their performance in completing simulated tasks that are a part of the job.
- One way in which HR managers gauge an applicant's suitability for an open position is by checking what the applicant says on his or her blog or social networking page.

Managing Talent

Following selection, the next goal of HRM is to develop employees into an effective workforce. Key development activities include training and performance appraisal.

Training and Development

Training and development programs represent a planned effort by an organization to facilitate employees' learning of job-related skills and behaviors.[66] *Training* magazine's "Industry Report" shows that organizations spent some $52.2 billion on formal training programs in 2009, a decrease of nearly $4 billion from the previous year, reflecting that many companies have cut training due to the slow economy.[67] Training conducted by an instructor in a classroom was the most popular method of training reported in the 2009 "Industry Report," but some organizations reported using online training, social networking, and mobile training methods.[68]

Development is sometimes distinguished from the general term *training*. Training is typically used to refer to teaching people how to perform tasks related to their present jobs, whereas development means teaching people broader skills that are not only useful in their present jobs but also prepare them for greater responsibilities in future jobs. IBM has created an innovative development program to expand managers' potential for global leadership.

IBM

Julie Lockwood works as a supply chain manager for IBM in Boulder, Colorado, but she recently spent four weeks in Ghana, helping fledgling businesses there make their operations more efficient and professional. Lockwood was one the select few chosen to participate in IBM's Corporate Service Corps, which sends teams to developing countries to work with nonprofit organizations, entrepreneurs, and small businesses. It sounds like corporate philanthropy, but IBM devised the program as a development exercise for high-potential managers.

The program stretches participants beyond their comfort zone in numerous ways. Simply adapting to another culture, particularly in a developing country, is the first learning experience. Many participants work with nonprofits, where the measure of accomplishment isn't as clear as in a business. Others are working with tiny businesses that are as different from the huge corporation they came from as night and day. Most are working on projects that are outside their normal job area. And all have to learn to accomplish things collaboratively—not just by issuing orders.

More than 5,500 IBM employees applied for the new development program, and top executives had to narrow it down to 600 people who demonstrated the greatest leadership potential. After their overseas stints, participants go through intensive debriefings to discuss what they learned and help the company's HR executives create the next development opportunities for them.[69]

On-the-Job Training The most common type of training is on-the-job training. In **on-the-job training (OJT)**, an experienced employee is asked to take a new employee "under his or her wing" and show the newcomer how to perform job duties. OJT has many advantages, such as few out-of-pocket costs for training facilities, materials, or instructor fees and easy transfer of learning back to the job. When implemented well, OJT is considered the fastest and most effective means of facilitating learning in the workplace.[70] One type of on-the-job training involves moving people to various types of jobs within the organization, where they work with experienced employees to learn different tasks. This *cross-training* may place an employee in a new position for as short a time as a few hours or for as long as a year, enabling the individual to develop new skills and giving the organization greater flexibility. General Electric uses cross-training to build leadership talent. Each year, GE hires 15 to 25 junior officers fresh out of the military for its Junior Officer Leadership Program, then rotates each person through a variety of jobs in a particular division, such as GE Oil & Gas.[71]

Corporate Universities Another popular approach to training and development is the corporate university. A **corporate university** is an in-house training and education facility that offers broad-based learning opportunities for employees—and frequently for customers, suppliers, and strategic partners as well—throughout their careers.[72] One well-known corporate university is Hamburger University, McDonald's worldwide management training center, which has been in existence for more than 40 years. Numerous other companies, including FedEx, General Electric, Intel, Harley-Davidson, and Capital One, pump millions of dollars into corporate universities to continually build human capital.[73] Employees at Caterpillar attend courses at Caterpillar University, which combines e-training, classroom sessions, and hands-on training activities. The U.S. Department of Defense runs Defense Acquisition University to provide ongoing training to 129,000 military and civilian workers in acquisitions, technology, and logistics. And Procter & Gamble has different "colleges" at every hierarchical level that hold regular career education programs.[74]

Promotion from Within Another way to further employee development is through promotion from within, which helps companies retain and develop valuable people. Promotions provide more challenging assignments, prescribe new responsibilities, and help employees grow by expanding and developing their abilities. The Peebles Hydro Hotel in Scotland is passionate about promoting from within as a way to retain good people and give them opportunities for growth. A maid has been promoted to head housekeeper, a wine waitress to restaurant head, and a student worker to deputy manager. The hotel also provides ongoing training in all areas. These techniques, combined with a commitment to job flexibility, helped the hotel retain high-quality workers at a time when others in the tourism and hospitality industry were suffering from a shortage of skilled labor. Staff members with 10, 15, or even 20 years of service aren't uncommon at Hydro.[75]

Mentoring and Coaching For many management and professional jobs, traditional on-the-job training is supplemented or replaced by mentoring and coaching. With **mentoring**, an experienced employee guides and supports a newcomer or less-experienced employee. Mentors typically offer counsel regarding how to network and advance in the company in addition to guiding the employee in developing his or her skills and abilities. **Coaching** is a method of directing, instructing, and training a person, with the goal to develop specific management skills. Coaching usually applies to higher-level managers who want to develop their personal competencies. For instance, a coach might observe a senior executive in action and provide feedback about how the executive can improve his or her interaction skills. Managers can also discuss difficult situations as they arise, with the coach helping them work through various alternative scenarios for dealing with the situation.[76]

Performance Appraisal

Performance appraisal comprises the steps of observing and assessing employee performance, recording the assessment, and providing feedback to the employee. During performance appraisal, skillful managers give feedback and praise concerning the acceptable elements of the employee's performance. They also describe performance areas that need improvement. Employees can use this information to change their job performance. Unfortunately, only three in ten employees in a recent survey believe their companies' performance review system actually helps to improve performance, indicating a need for improved methods of appraisal and feedback.[77]

Generally, HRM professionals concentrate on two things to make performance appraisal a positive force in their organizations: (1) the accurate assessment of performance through the development and application of assessment systems such as rating scales, and (2) training managers to effectively use the performance appraisal interview so managers can provide feedback that will reinforce good performance and motivate employee development. Current thinking is that performance appraisal should be ongoing, not something that is done once a year as part of a consideration of raises.

Assessing Performance Accurately Jobs are multidimensional and performance thus may be multidimensional as well. A recent trend in performance appraisal is called **360-degree feedback**, a process that uses multiple raters, including self-rating, as a way to increase awareness of strengths and weaknesses and guide employee development. Members of the appraisal group may include supervisors, coworkers, and customers, as well as the individual, thus providing appraisal of the employee from a variety of perspectives.[78] Some companies are using social networking–style systems to make 360-degree performance feedback a dynamic, ongoing process. One software program from Rypple, for example, lets people post short Twitter-style questions about their performance of a particular task and get feedback from managers, peers, or anyone else the user selects. Another system from Accenture has employees post photos, status updates, and two or three weekly goals that can be viewed, followed, and assessed by colleagues.[79]

Another alternative performance-evaluation method is the *performance review ranking system*.[80] This method is increasingly coming under fire because it essentially evaluates employees by pitting them against one another. As most commonly used, a manager evaluates his or her direct reports relative to one another and categorizes each on a scale, such as A = outstanding performance (20%), B = high-middle performance (70%), or C = in need of improvement (10%). Some companies routinely fire those managers falling in the bottom 10 percent of the ranking. Proponents say the technique provides an effective way to assess performance and offer guidance for employee development. But critics of these systems, sometimes called *rank and yank,* argue that they are based on subjective judgments, produce skewed results, and discriminate against employees who are "different" from the mainstream. One study found that forced rankings that include firing the bottom 5 or 10 percent can lead to a dramatic improvement in organizational performance in the short term, but the benefits dissipate over several years as people become focused on competing with one another rather than improving the business.[81] Many companies are building more flexibility into the performance review ranking system, and some are abandoning it altogether.[82]

Performance Evaluation Errors Although we would like to believe that every manager assesses employees' performance in a careful and bias-free manner, researchers have identified several rating problems.[83] One of the most dangerous is **stereotyping,** which occurs when a rater places an employee into a class or category based on one or a few traits or characteristics—for example, stereotyping an older worker as slower and more difficult to train. Another rating error is the **halo effect,** in which a manager gives an employee the same rating on all dimensions, even if his or her performance is good on some dimensions and poor on others.

One approach to overcome performance evaluation errors is to use a behavior-based rating technique, such as the behaviorally anchored rating scale. The **behaviorally anchored rating scale (BARS)** is developed from critical incidents pertaining to job performance. Each job performance scale is anchored with specific behavioral statements that describe varying degrees of performance. By relating employee performance to specific incidents, raters can more accurately evaluate an employee's performance.[84]

9.10 EXHIBIT

Example of a Behaviorally Anchored Rating Scale

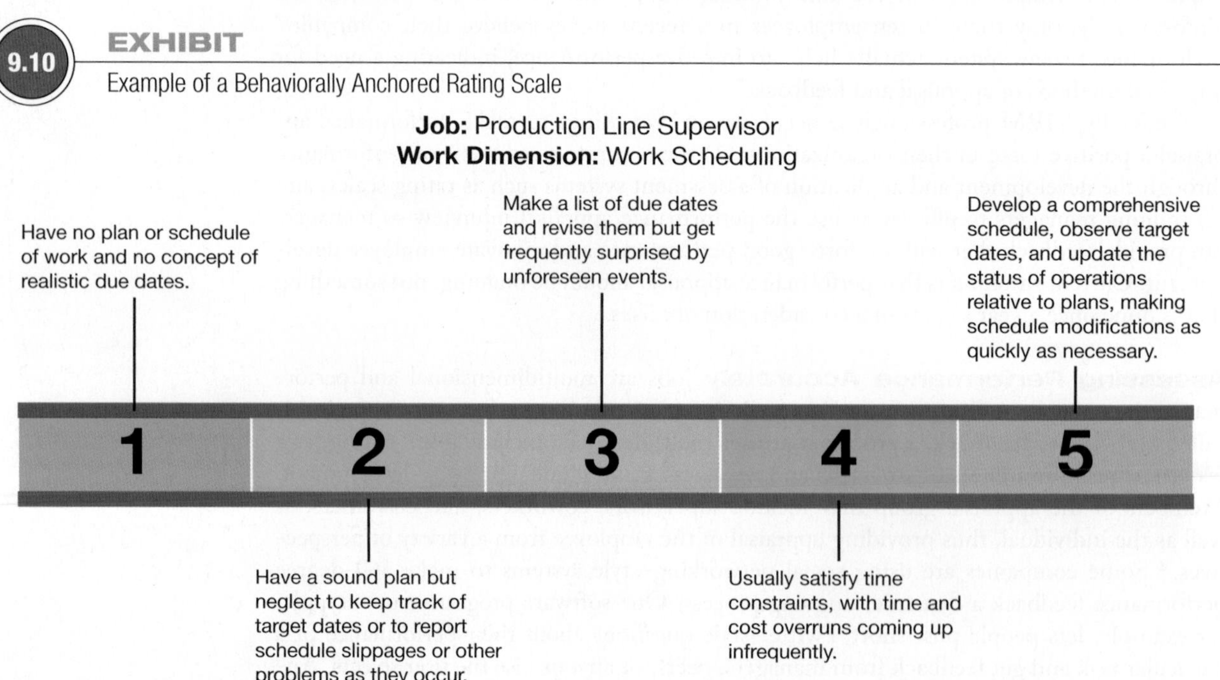
Job: Production Line Supervisor
Work Dimension: Work Scheduling
Have no plan or schedule of work and no concept of realistic due dates.
Make a list of due dates and revise them but get frequently surprised by unforeseen events.
Develop a comprehensive schedule, observe target dates, and update the status of operations relative to plans, making schedule modifications as quickly as necessary.
1
2
3
4
5
Have a sound plan but neglect to keep track of target dates or to report schedule slippages or other problems as they occur.
Usually satisfy time constraints, with time and cost overruns coming up infrequently.

SOURCES: Based on J. P. Campbell, M. D. Dunnette, R. D. Arvey, and L. V. Hellervik, "The Development and Evaluation of Behaviorally Based Rating Scales," *Journal of Applied Psychology* 57 (1973): 15–22; and Francine Alexander, "Performance Appraisals," *Small Business Reports* (March 1989): 20–29.

Exhibit 9.10 illustrates the BARS method for evaluating a production line supervisor. The production supervisor's job can be broken down into several dimensions, such as equipment maintenance, employee training, or work scheduling. A behaviorally anchored rating scale should be developed for each dimension. The dimension in Exhibit 9.10 is work scheduling. Good performance is represented by a 4 or 5 on the scale, and unacceptable performance, by a 1 or 2. If a production supervisor's job has eight dimensions, the total performance evaluation will be the sum of the scores for each of eight scales.

Remember This

- Training typically refers to teaching people skills needed in their current job, whereas development refers to teaching people broader career skills.
- The most common method of training is **on-the-job-training (OJT)**, in which an experienced employee is asked to teach a new employee how to perform job duties.
- A **corporate university** is an in-house training and development facility that offers broad-based learning opportunities for employees.
- One corporate university is McDonald's worldwide management training center, called Hamburger University.
- **Mentoring** refers to when an experienced employee or manager guides and supports a newcomer or less-experienced employee.
- **Coaching** is a method of directing, instructing, and training a person, with the goal of developing specific management skills.
- **Performance appraisal** is the process of observing and evaluating an employee's performance, recording the assessment, and providing feedback.
- A recent trend is **360-degree feedback**, which uses multiple raters, including self-rating, to appraise employee performance and guide development.
- Performance review ranking systems are increasingly being criticized because they tend to pit employees against one another rather than promoting cooperation and teamwork.
- **Stereotyping** is a performance evaluation error that occurs when a manager places an employee into a class or category based on one or a few traits or characteristics.
- The **halo effect** occurs when a manager gives an employee the same rating on all dimensions of the job even though performance may be good on some dimensions and poor on others.
- One way to overcome evaluation errors is to use a **behaviorally anchored rating scale**, which is a performance evaluation technique that relates an employee's performance to specific job-related incidents.

Maintaining an Effective Workforce

Now we turn to the topic of how managers and HRM professionals maintain a workforce that has been recruited and developed. Maintenance of the current workforce involves compensation, wage and salary systems, benefits, and occasional terminations.

Compensation

The term **compensation** refers to (1) all monetary payments and (2) all goods or commodities used in lieu of money to reward employees.[85] An organization's compensation structure includes wages and salaries and benefits such as health insurance, paid vacations, or employee fitness centers. Developing an effective compensation system is an important part of human resource management because it helps to attract and retain talented workers. In addition, a company's compensation system has an impact on strategic performance.[86] Human resource managers design the pay and benefits systems to fit company strategy and to provide compensation equity.

Wage and Salary Systems Ideally, management's strategy for the organization should be a critical determinant of the features and operations of the pay system.[87] For example, managers may have the goal of maintaining or improving profitability or market share by stimulating employee performance. Thus, they should design and use a merit pay system rather than a system based on other criteria such as seniority.

The most common approach to employee compensation is *job-based pay,* which means linking compensation to the specific tasks an employee performs. However, these systems present several problems. For one thing, job-based pay may fail to reward the type of learning behavior needed for the organization to adapt and survive in a turbulent environment. In addition, these systems reinforce an emphasis on organizational hierarchy and centralized decision making and control, which are inconsistent with the growing emphasis on employee participation and increased responsibility.[88]

Skill-based pay systems are becoming increasingly popular in both large and small companies, including Sherwin-Williams, Au Bon Pain, and Quaker Oats. Employees with higher skill levels receive higher pay than those with lower skill levels. At the Quaker Oats pet food plant in Topeka, Kansas, for example, employees might start at something like $8.75 per hour but reach a top hourly rate of $14.50 when they master a series of skills.[89] Also called *competency-based pay,* skill-based pay systems encourage people to develop their skills and competencies, thus making them more valuable to the organization as well as more employable if they leave their current jobs.

Compensation Equity Whether the organization uses job-based pay or skill-based pay, good managers strive to maintain a sense of fairness and equity within the pay structure and thereby fortify employee morale. **Job evaluation** refers to the process of determining the value or worth of jobs within an organization through an examination of job content. Job evaluation techniques enable managers to compare similar and dissimilar jobs and to determine internally equitable pay rates—that is, pay rates that employees believe are fair compared with those for other jobs in the organization.

Organizations also want to make sure their pay rates are fair compared to other companies. HRM managers may obtain **wage and salary surveys** that show what other organizations pay incumbents in jobs that match a sample of "key" jobs selected by the organization. These surveys are available from a number of sources, including the U.S. Bureau of Labor Statistics National Compensation Survey.

Pay for Performance Many of today's organizations develop compensation plans based on a *pay-for-performance standard* to raise productivity and cut labor costs in a competitive global environment. **Pay for performance**, also called *incentive pay*, means tying at least part of compensation to employee effort and performance, whether it be through merit-based pay, bonuses, team incentives, or various gain-sharing or profit-sharing plans. Data show that, although growth in base wages has slowed in many industries, the use of pay for performance has steadily increased since the early 1990s, with approximately 70 percent of companies now offering some form of incentive pay.[90] With pay for performance, incentives are aligned with the behaviors needed to help the organization achieve its strategic goals. Employees have an incentive to make the company more efficient and profitable because if goals are not met, no bonuses are paid.

However, recent years have shown the potential dangers of misdirected pay-for-performance plans. Alan Blinder, Princeton professor of economics and public affairs, points out that a fundamental cause of the 2008–2009 financial crisis in the United States was the "perverse go-for-broke incentives" that rewarded people for taking excessive risks with other people's money.[91] During the financial meltdown, it became clear that people at every level of the financial system were getting rewarded for short-term performance—if things went wrong down the line, it was someone else's problem. Then it all came crashing down. Managers can take care to create pay-for-performance plans that align with the long-term interests of the organization, shareholders, and the broader society.

Benefits

An effective compensation package requires more than money. Although salary is an important component, it is only a part. Equally important are the benefits offered by the organization.

Some benefits are required by law, such as Social Security, unemployment compensation, and workers' compensation. Other types of benefits, such as health insurance, vacations, and things such as on-site day care or educational reimbursements are not required by law but are provided by organizations to maintain an effective workforce. Many organizations offer *cafeteria-plan benefits packages* that allow employees to select the benefits of greatest value to them.[92] Others use surveys to determine which combination of fixed benefits is most desirable. The benefits packages provided by large companies attempt to meet the needs of all employees.

However, during the recent recession, employers cut many of the benefits not required by law, and most say they don't plan to restore them to pre-recession levels. "Those days are gone. Benefits across the board are no longer sacred cows," says Tim Prichard, head of BridgeStreet Consulting, a benefits administration consulting firm.[93] Although new U.S. legislation requires that every American have minimal health insurance coverage by 2014, employer-sponsored plans are getting skimpier, more expensive, and less available. Verizon, AT&T, and Caterpillar are among the companies that have conducted internal analyses to see how much they could save by dropping employer-sponsored coverage and paying the $2,000 per employee fine that will be imposed under the new law. AT&T found that it could save a whopping $1.8 billion![94] HR managers are working to study the law and advise executives on their responsibilities and options so the organization can be compliant and avoid penalties.

Rightsizing the Organization

In some cases, organizations have more people than they need and have to let some employees go. **Rightsizing** refers to intentionally reducing the company's workforce to the point where the number of employees is deemed to be right for the company's current situation. Also called *downsizing*, planned reductions in the size of the workforce are a reality for many of today's companies. According to statistics from the U.S. Department of Labor, organizations laid off more than 700,000 workers in the first quarter of 2009, and nearly as many in the second quarter. The primary reason cited by companies for mass layoffs was "business demand factors," such as slack work because of decreased demand for products.[95] In September 2010, the unemployment rate in the United States was still hovering at around 9.6 percent.

As the term *rightsizing* implies, the goal is to make the company stronger and more competitive by aligning the size of the workforce with the company's current needs. However, some researchers have found that massive cuts often fail to achieve the intended benefits and in some cases significantly harm the organization.[96] Unless HRM departments

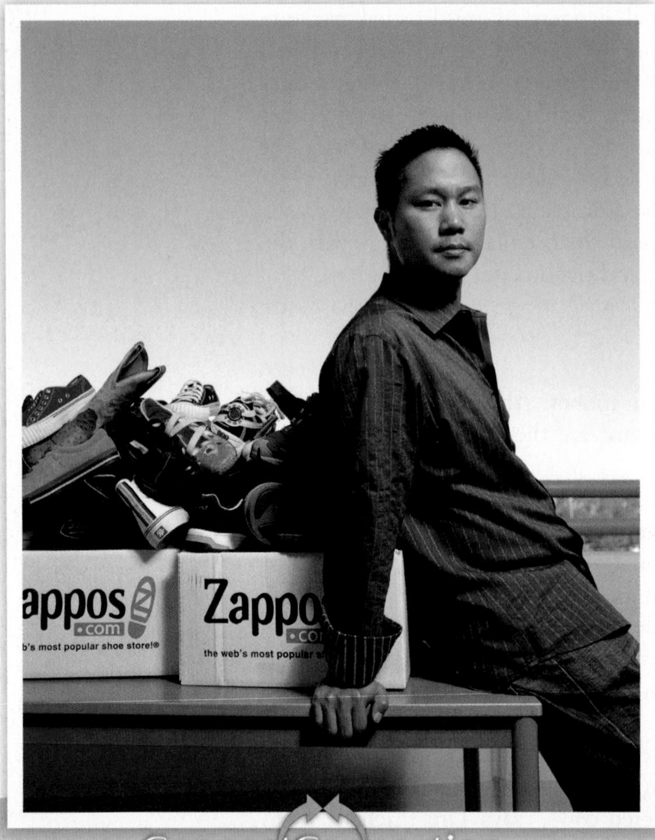

Brad Swonetz/Redux

ConceptConnection

Not many companies got *positive* press for how they managed **downsizing** during the 2008 financial crisis, but Zappos.com did. CEO Tony Hsieh used e-mail and blogs to get the news out quickly and detail the generous benefits Zappos offered: ample severance pay based on length of service, six months of paid health insurance, and the 40 percent employee discount continued through the holiday season. "Let's take care of our employees who got us this far," said Hsieh.

effectively and humanely manage the rightsizing process, layoffs can lead to decreased morale and performance. Managers can smooth the process by regularly communicating with employees and providing them with as much information as possible, providing assistance to workers who will lose their jobs, and using training and development to help address the emotional needs of remaining employees and enable them to cope with new or additional responsibilities.[97]

Termination

Despite the best efforts of line managers and HRM professionals, the organization will lose employees. Some will retire, others will depart voluntarily for other jobs, and still others will be forced out through mergers and cutbacks or for poor performance.

The value of termination for maintaining an effective workforce is twofold. First, employees who are poor performers can be dismissed. Productive employees often resent disruptive, low-performing employees who are allowed to stay with the company and receive pay and benefits comparable to theirs. Second, managers can use exit interviews as a valuable HR tool, regardless of whether the employee leaves voluntarily or is forced out. An **exit interview** is an interview conducted with departing employees to determine why they are leaving. Of companies surveyed by the Society for Human Resource Management, 68 percent say they either routinely or occasionally conduct formal exit interviews.[98] The value of the exit interview is to provide an inexpensive way to learn about pockets of dissatisfaction within the organization and hence find ways to reduce future turnover.[99] As John Donahoe, president and CEO of eBay, put it, "When people are leaving, they're often in a very reflective state and … they're also just stunningly direct, because it's like they have nothing to lose." One thing Donahoe learned from conducting exit interviews at eBay was that mid-level executives were unclear about their responsibility and authority, so he has reorganized to clarify lines of decision-making responsibility and authority.[100] The oil services giant Schlumberger includes an exit interview as part of a full-scale investigation of every departure, with the results posted online so managers all around the company can get insight into problems.[101]

However, in some cases, employees who leave voluntarily are reluctant to air uncomfortable complaints or discuss their real reasons for leaving. Companies such as T-Mobile, Campbell Soup, and Conair found that having people complete an online exit questionnaire yields more open and honest information. When people have negative things to say about managers or the company, the online format is a chance to speak their mind without having to do it in a face-to-face meeting.[102]

- **Compensation** refers to all monetary payments and all nonmonetary goods or benefits used to reward employees.
- Managers strive to maintain fairness and equity in the pay system.
- **Job evaluation** is the process of determining the value of jobs within an organization through an examination of job content.
- **Wage and salary surveys** show what other organizations pay incumbents in jobs that match a sample of key jobs selected by the organization.
- **Pay for performance,** also called incentive pay, means tying at least a portion of compensation to employee effort and performance.
- Benefits make up a large portion of labor costs in the United States.
- During the recession, many organizations have cut benefits that are not required by law.
- **Rightsizing,** also called downsizing, refers to intentionally reducing the company's workforce to the point where the number of employees is deemed right for the company's current situation.
- If not managed effectively and humanely, rightsizing can lead to decreased morale and performance.
- An **exit interview** is an interview conducted with departing employees to determine reasons for their departure and learn about potential problems in the organization.
- Campbell Soup Company lets people complete an online exit questionnaire so they can freely express their complaints or ideas without having to be face-to-face with a manager.

The Changing Workplace

When Brenda Thomson, the director of diversity and leadership education at the Las Vegas MGM Mirage, steps into one of the company's hotel lobbies, she closes her eyes and listens. "It's amazing all the different languages I can hear just standing in the lobbies of any of our hotels," she says. "Our guests come from all over the world, and it really makes us realize the importance of reflecting that diversity in our workplace."[103] The diversity Thomson sees in the lobbies of the MGM Mirage hotels is a small reflection of the cultural diversity in the larger domestic and global workplaces.

Diversity in the United States

Today's U.S. corporations reflect the country's image as a melting pot, but with a difference. In the past, the United States was a place where people of different national origins, ethnicities, races, and religions came together and blended to resemble one another. Opportunities for advancement were limited to those workers who easily fit into the mainstream of the larger culture. Some immigrants chose desperate measures to fit in, such as abandoning their native languages, changing their last names, and sacrificing their own unique cultures. In essence, everyone in the workplace was encouraged to share similar beliefs, values, and lifestyles despite differences in gender, race, and ethnicity.[104]

Now organizations recognize that everyone is not the same and that the differences people bring to the workplace are valuable.[105] Rather than expecting all employees to adopt

SPOTLIGHT ON SKILLS

CNN en Español

Trying to entice more Hispanic viewers in the United States, CNN's Spanish-language branch is adding new programs, new sets, a spiffy new studio in Miami, and a new logo. Vanished is the usual repetitive half-hour news block, and introduced is the magazine-style programming reinforcing its new slogan, "Live the News."

Though CNN en Español boasts that it broadcasts from "Alaska to Patagonia," the new focus will help North American operations. Partly resulting from 2010 census data showing the U.S. Hispanic population has grown by 40 percent in ten years, CNN wants to reach more of that 50 million population base. The network is thinking strategically, because some estimates show the Latin population doubling again by mid-century.

New programs include a personal investment show called "CNN Dinero," a late-night "Conclusiones" with a news wrap-up, and three hours of news in the morning. CNN en Español's general manager and VP for Hispanic strategy Cynthia Hudson refers to the "aspirational" tone of Spanish-language TV. Perhaps the best example of that upward mobility is their own Ismael Cala, who has his own Larry King–like interview show and who became TV-savvy as a Cuban defector living in Toronto, where he found an abandoned TV and was instantly mesmerized by Oprah and her interviewing style. He says, "At first I had no idea who she was. But as I became a regular viewer, I not only trained my ear to hearing English but also came to appreciate what a skillful interviewer she is. I learned a lot more from watching Oprah than just vocabulary." Aspirational, indeed.

SOURCE: Larry Rohter, "CNN's Latin Sister Looks to Capture a Booming Market," *The New York Times*, March 13, 2011.

similar attitudes and values, managers are learning that these differences enable their companies to compete globally and to tap into rich sources of new talent. Although diversity in North America has been a reality for some time, genuine efforts to accept and *manage* diverse people began only in recent years. Exhibit 9.11 lists some interesting milestones in the history of corporate diversity.

Diversity in corporate America has become a key topic in part because of the vast changes occurring in today's workplace. The following statistics illustrate how the workplace is changing and challenging front-line managers who are trying to build cohesive teams:

- ***Three-generation workforce.*** Today's workforce is in a state of flux as a blend of three generations present new management challenges. Baby boomers, heading to retirement in increasing numbers, share a "corporate memory" that is invaluable to organizations. Gen-Yers, sometimes called Millennials, are characterized as ambitious, lacking loyalty to one organization, and eager for quick success. Gen Xers, the generation in the middle, struggle with reduced guarantees about their financial futures and job security.[106] This type of age diversity creates a challenge for the manager trying to unify a team behind a common vision.
- ***Aging workers.*** Baby boomers continue to affect the workplace as this massive group of workers progresses through its life stages. A baby boomer turns 60 every seven seconds, continuously bumping up the average age of the workforce. In addition, the number of workers between the ages of 65 and 74 is predicted to soar by 83.4 percent between 2006 and 2016.[107] In 1986, the median age of the U.S. labor force was 35.4 years. It increased to 40.8 years in 2006 and will increase to 42.1 years in 2016.[108]
- ***Growth in Hispanic and Asian workers.*** The greatest increase in employment will occur with Asians and Hispanics. In fact, the number of Hispanics in the U.S. workforce is expected to increase by 7.3 million between 2008 and 2018, and Hispanics will make up 17.6 percent of the workforce by 2018.[109] CNN is trying to capitalize on the growing Hispanic population, as described in the Spotlight on Skills titled CNN en Español.

EXHIBIT 9.11

Milestones in the History of Corporate Diversity

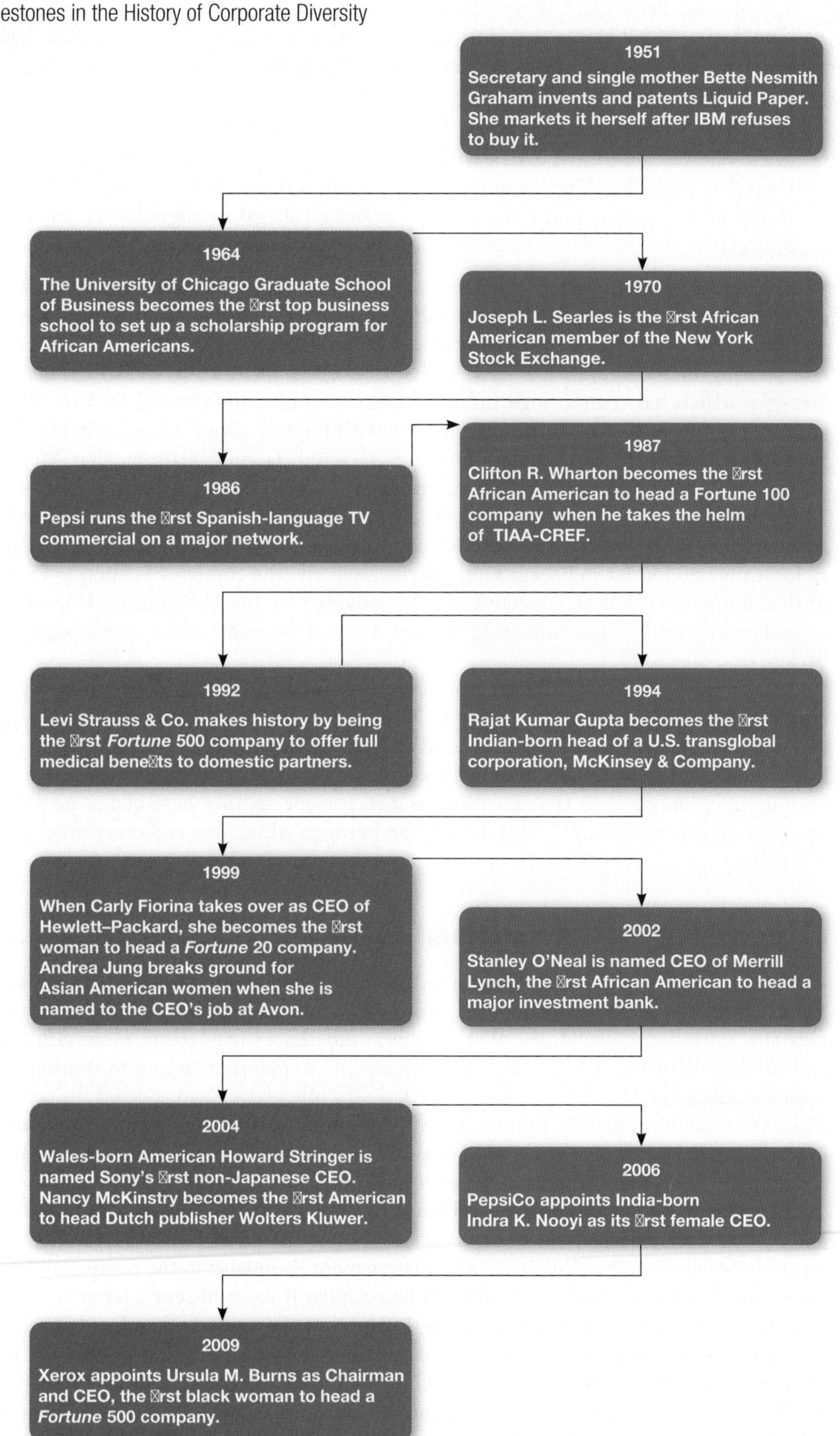

1951
Secretary and single mother Bette Nesmith Graham invents and patents Liquid Paper. She markets it herself after IBM refuses to buy it.
1964
The University of Chicago Graduate School of Business becomes the first top business school to set up a scholarship program for African Americans.
1970
Joseph L. Searles is the first African American member of the New York Stock Exchange.
1986
Pepsi runs the first Spanish-language TV commercial on a major network.
1987
Clifton R. Wharton becomes the first African American to head a Fortune 100 company when he takes the helm of TIAA-CREF.
1992
Levi Strauss & Co. makes history by being the first *Fortune* 500 company to offer full medical benefits to domestic partners.
1994
Rajat Kumar Gupta becomes the first Indian-born head of a U.S. transglobal corporation, McKinsey & Company.
1999
When Carly Fiorina takes over as CEO of Hewlett–Packard, she becomes the first woman to head a *Fortune* 20 company. Andrea Jung breaks ground for Asian American women when she is named to the CEO's job at Avon.
2002
Stanley O'Neal is named CEO of Merrill Lynch, the first African American to head a major investment bank.
2004
Wales-born American Howard Stringer is named Sony's first non-Japanese CEO. Nancy McKinstry becomes the first American to head Dutch publisher Wolters Kluwer.
2006
PepsiCo appoints India-born Indra K. Nooyi as its first female CEO.
2009
Xerox appoints Ursula M. Burns as Chairman and CEO, the first black woman to head a *Fortune* 500 company.

SOURCES: "Spotlight on Diversity," special advertising section, *MBA Jungle* (March–April 2003): 58–61; and Xerox corporate Web site, http://www.news.xerox.com.

- ***Women outnumbering men.*** Women now outnumber men in many job applications and in some fields.[110] Yet fewer than 16 percent of top corporate officers are females. Companies with a higher percentage of female senior officers, such as PepsiCo, which is led by CEO Indra Nooyi, and Xerox, headed by CEO Ursula Burns, have programs that help women prepare for these powerful senior jobs.[111]
- ***Growth in foreign-born population.*** Between 1980 and 2008, about 29 million immigrants entered the United States, with nearly a third of those estimated to be unauthorized. Although illegal immigration slowed significantly in 2008 and 2009, largely due to the poor economy and fewer job opportunities, illegal immigration is still a hot-button issue and an area of tremendous challenge for some managers.[112]

The ability of organizations to manage diversity has not kept pace with these demographic trends. For example, many law-abiding managers in organizations that depend on immigrant workers feel they are in a no-win situation. Mohawk Industries, a carpet and flooring manufacturer, has most of its production facilities in Whitfield County, Georgia, which has seen a huge influx of Latino immigrants (from 2,000 in 1990 to around 30,000 in 2010), and the company's workforce is about 40 percent Hispanic. Former employees of the company filed a class-action lawsuit charging that Mohawk knowingly hired undocumented aliens in order to depress wages for the rest of the hourly workers. The company settled the suit out of court, but managers admitted no wrongdoing and insist that they check out prospective employees as diligently as possible. If they go too far in background checks, they say, the company is open to charges of discrimination. Indeed, Mohawk was investigated by the U.S. Justice Department several years ago for discriminating against Latinos by conducting overly aggressive background checks.[113]

Other demographic shifts have also created significant challenges for minority and female employees, as well as for managers. Progress for women and minorities in both pay and leadership roles has stalled or regressed at many U.S. corporations, as reflected in these statistics: 75 percent of 357 global senior executives report that their companies have one or no minorities among their top executives, and 56 percent say they have one or no women among their top executives.[114] And the pay gap between white men and every other group still exists.[115]

Diversity on a Global Scale

Implications of an increasingly diverse workforce are not limited to the United States. For example, the aging of the population is a global phenomenon. In addition, for organizations operating globally, social and cultural differences may create more difficulties and conflicts than any other source. For instance, U.S. managers trying to transfer their diversity policies and practices to European divisions often haven't considered the complex social and cultural systems in Europe. Even the meaning of diversity presents problems. In many European languages, the closest word implies separation rather than the inclusion sought by U.S. diversity programs.[116]

Foreign firms doing business in the United States face similar challenges understanding and dealing with diversity issues. For example, Japanese leaders at Toyota Motor Company seriously bungled the handling of a sexual harassment complaint in the company's North American division, leading to a lawsuit. When Sayaka Kobayashi sent a letter to Dennis Cuneo, senior vice president of Toyota North America, saying she had endured months of romantic and sexual advances from her boss, Cuneo told her he would discuss the issue with the boss, Hideaki Otaka. However, Cuneo allegedly said that he didn't want to offend the man (a cultural norm), so he planned to say it was Kobayashi's boyfriend who was upset about the overtures. The in-text example below lists some interesting tips for foreign managers working in the United States, to help them understand and relate to Americans. Do you agree that these statements provide a good introduction to American culture for a non-native?

National cultures are intangible, pervasive, and difficult to comprehend. However, it is imperative that managers learn to understand local cultures and deal with them effectively.[117] One way of bridging the gap between cultures is by tapping into the linguistic and cultural skills of employees who understand local markets. Jenny Ming, a 19-year Gap veteran and founding team member of Old Navy, was promoted to president in 2004. Born in China's southern Guangdong province, Ming's understanding of Asian markets have poised her to navigate cultural differences as Old Navy expands into growing Asian markets.[118]

A GUIDE FOR EXPATRIATE MANAGERS IN AMERICA

Although each person is different, individuals from a specific country typically share certain values and attitudes. Managers planning to move to a foreign country can learn about these broad value patterns to help them adjust to working and living abroad. The following characteristics are often used to help foreign managers understand what Americans are like.

1. ***Americans are informal.*** They tend to treat everyone alike, even when individuals differ significantly in age or social status.
2. ***Americans are direct and decisive.*** To some foreigners, this behavior may seem abrupt or even rude. Typically, Americans don't "beat around the bush," which means they don't talk around things but get right to the point. They quickly define a problem and decide on the course of action they believe is most likely to get the desired results.
3. ***Americans love facts.*** They value statistics, data, and information in any form.
4. ***Americans are competitive.*** They like to keep score, whether at work or play. Americans like to win, and they don't tolerate failure well. Some foreigners might think Americans are aggressive or overbearing. For example, Americans are not at all shy about selling themselves. In fact, it's expected.
5. ***Americans believe in work.*** For many, commitment to work and career comes first. In general, Americans rarely take time off, even if a family member is ill. They don't believe in long vacations—even corporation presidents often take only two weeks, if that.
6. ***Americans are independent and individualistic.*** They place a high value on freedom and believe that people can control their own destinies.
7. ***Americans are questioners.*** They ask a lot of questions, even of someone they have just met. Some of these questions may seem pointless ("How ya doin'?") or personal ("What kind of work do you do?").
8. ***Americans dislike silence.*** They would rather talk about the weather than deal with silence in a conversation.
9. ***Americans value punctuality.*** They keep appointment calendars and live according to schedules and clocks.
10. ***Americans pay close attention to appearances.*** They take note of designer clothing and good grooming. They may in fact seem obsessed with bathing, eliminating body odors, and wearing clean clothes.

How many of these statements do you agree with? Discuss them with your friends and classmates, including people from different countries and members of different subcultural groups from the United States.[119]

- The U.S. workforce is being transformed by a three-generation workforce, aging baby boomers, growth in Hispanic and Asian workers, an increasing number of women employees, and growth of the foreign-born population.
- Forward-thinking organizations are taking steps to attract and retain a workforce that reflects the cultural diversity of the population.
- Salaries and advancement opportunities for women and minorities have stalled in many U.S. organizations.
- To succeed in the global marketplace, managers need to understand other cultures and deal with them effectively.

Managing Diversity

Now let's explore the expanding definition of *diversity* and consider the dividends of cultivating a diverse workforce.

What Is Diversity?

Diversity is defined as all the ways in which people differ.[120] Diversity wasn't always defined this broadly. Decades ago, many companies defined diversity in terms of race, gender, age, lifestyle, and disability. That focus helped create awareness, change mind-sets, and create new opportunities for many. Today, companies are embracing a more inclusive definition of diversity that recognizes a spectrum of differences that influence how employees approach work, interact with each other, derive satisfaction from their work, and define who they are as people in the workplace.[121]

Exhibit 9.12 illustrates the difference between the traditional model and the inclusive model of diversity. The dimensions of diversity shown in the traditional model include inborn differences that are immediately observable such as race, gender, age, and physical ability. However, the inclusive model of diversity includes *all* of the ways in which employees differ, including aspects of diversity that can be acquired or changed throughout one's lifetime. These dimensions may have less impact than those included only in the traditional model but nevertheless affect a person's self-definition and worldview and the way the person is viewed by others. Many organizational leaders embrace this more inclusive definition of diversity. "Diversity has to be looked at in its broadest sense," said Wally Parker, former CEO of KeySpan Energy (now National Grid). "To me, it's all about recognizing, respecting, and supporting individuals regardless of what makes up that individuality. So, yes, that's race, gender and sexual orientation. But it's also introverted and extroverted, ethnic backgrounds, cultural upbringing, all those things."[122]

A diverse workforce poses unique challenges. Employees with different backgrounds bring different opinions and ideas. Conflict, anxiety, and misunderstandings may increase. Embracing these differences and using them to improve company performance can be challenging. **Managing diversity**, a key management skill in today's global economy, means creating a climate in which the potential advantages of diversity for organizational or group performance are maximized, while the potential disadvantages are minimized.[123]

Dividends of Workplace Diversity

Corporations that build strong, diverse organizations reap numerous dividends, as described here:[124]

EXHIBIT 9.12

Traditional vs. Inclusive Models of Diversity

SOURCE: Adapted from Anthony Oshiotse and Richard O'Leary, "Corning Creates an Inclusive Culture to Drive Technology Innovation and Performance," Wiley InterScience, *Global Business and Organizational Excellence*, 26 no. 3 (March/April 2007): 7–21.

- ***Better use of employee talent.*** Companies with the best talent are the ones with the best competitive advantage. Attracting a diverse workforce is not enough; companies must also provide career opportunities and advancement for minority and women employees to retain them.
- ***Increased understanding of the marketplace.*** A diverse workforce is better able to anticipate and respond to changing consumer needs. Ford Motor Company realized it could reach its business objectives only if it created a workforce that reflected the multicultural face of the country. So it assembled a workforce made up of 25 percent minorities (18.4% are African American) to foster a culture of inclusion, winning it a spot on *Black Enterprise's* "40 Best Companies for Diversity."[125]
- ***Enhanced breadth of understanding in leadership positions.*** Homogeneous top management teams tend to be myopic in their perspectives. According to Niall FitzGerald of Unilever, "It is important for any business operating in an increasingly complex and rapidly changing environment to deploy a broad range of talents. That provides a breadth of understanding of the world and environment and a fusion of the very best values and different perspectives which make up that world."[126]
- ***Increased quality of team problem solving.*** Teams with diverse backgrounds bring different perspectives to a discussion that result in more creative ideas and solutions.[127] Although a large percent of Ernst & Young's senior leadership is still male, the company is taking steps to create a more diverse leadership team because it's better for business. "We know you get better solutions when you put a diverse team at the table. People come from different backgrounds, and they have different frames of reference. When you put these people together, you get the best solution for our clients," says Billie Williamson, director of flexibility and gender equity strategy at Ernst & Young.[128]
- ***Reduced costs associated with high turnover, absenteeism, and lawsuits.*** Companies that foster a diverse workforce reduce turnover, absenteeism, and the risk of lawsuits. Because family responsibilities contribute to turnover and absenteeism, many companies now offer child-care and elder-care benefits, flexible work arrangements, telecommuting, and part-time employment to accommodate employee responsibilities at home.

Discrimination lawsuits are also a costly side effect of a discriminatory work environment. A racial harassment suit against Lockheed Martin Corporation cost the company $2.5 million, the largest individual racial-discrimination payment obtained by the Equal Employment Opportunity Commission.[129]

The most successful companies appreciate the importance of diversity and know that their biggest asset is their people. Savvy enterprises such as MetLife, featured below, also know that a diverse workforce drives innovation—and that, in turn, drives business.

METLIFE, INC.

MetLife, Inc., the largest life insurer in the United States, believes that its talented, diverse employees are instrumental to its global business success. "If you're going to compete as a global insurance company, you have to do it through creativity in your products and an understanding of your customers," says Roger Taylor, MetLife's vice president of strategic staffing. "Diversity—in people, products, and processes—makes that happen."

As more companies recognize that a workforce representing different backgrounds offers a competitive edge, competition for minority candidates has become increasingly intense. To find and attract a diverse slate of candidates, MetLife has consulted with outside experts such as CareerBuilder.com to identify the best diversity candidates for every position, in every location in the company. CareerBuilder is the nation's largest online job site, with over 5.5 million ethnically diverse and 12 million female visitors each month.

According to Jason Ferrar, vice president of corporate marketing at CareerBuilder.com, MetLife is able to recruit a diverse workforce through creative strategies. First, it partners with CareerBuilders.com's 110 diversity partner sites, such as BET and Univision, and also uses targeted e-mail campaigns and advertising to reach a diverse workforce. Through these innovative strategies, MetLife is ensured a diverse slate of candidates for every position. These novel recruitment strategies help MetLife maintain its leadership position. "We're in a global competitive environment, and we need the ability to be innovative," says Taylor. "Diversity gives us a competitive edge."[130]

- **Diversity** is defined as all the ways in which employees differ.
- The definition of diversity has been broadened in recent years to be more inclusive and recognize a wide spectrum of characteristics.
- **Managing diversity**, which means creating a climate in which the potential advantages of diversity for organizational performance are maximized while the potential disadvantages are minimized, is a key management skill today.
- Corporations that recruit and retain a diverse workforce reap numerous benefits, including improved team problem solving and increased understanding of the marketplace.

Factors Shaping Personal Bias

To reap the benefits of diversity described above, organizations are seeking managers who will serve as catalysts in the workplace to reduce barriers and eliminate obstacles for disadvantaged people. To successfully manage a diverse workgroup and create a positive, productive environment for all employees, managers need to start with an understanding of the complex attitudes, opinions, and issues that already exist in the workplace or that employees bring into the workplace. These include several factors that shape personal bias: prejudice, discrimination, stereotypes, and ethnocentrism.

Prejudice, Discrimination, and Stereotypes

Prejudice is the tendency to view people who are different as being deficient. If someone acts out their prejudicial attitudes toward people who are the targets of their prejudice, discrimination has occurred.[131] Paying a woman less than a man for the same work is gender discrimination. Mistreating people because they have a different ethnicity is ethnic discrimination. Although blatant discrimination is not as widespread as in the past, bias in the workplace often shows up in subtle ways: a lack of choice assignments, the disregard by a subordinate of a minority manager's directions, or the ignoring of comments made by women and minorities at meetings. A survey by Korn Ferry International found that 59 percent of minority managers surveyed had observed a racially motivated double standard in the delegation of assignments.[132] Their perceptions are supported by a study that showed minority managers spend more time in the "bullpen" waiting for their chance—and then have to prove themselves over and over again with each new assignment. Minority employees typically feel that they have to put in longer hours and extra effort to achieve the same status as their white colleagues. "It's not enough to be as good as the next person," says African-American Bruce Gordon, president of Bell Atlantic's enterprise group. "We have to be better."[133]

A major component of prejudice is **stereotypes**, rigid, exaggerated, irrational beliefs associated with a particular group of people.[134] To be successful managing diversity, managers have to eliminate harmful stereotypes from their thinking, shedding any biases that negatively affect the workplace. Managers can learn to *value differences,* which means they recognize cultural differences and see these differences with an appreciative attitude. To facilitate this attitude, managers can learn about cultural patterns and typical beliefs of groups to help understand why people act the way they do. It helps to understand the difference between these two ways of thinking, most notably that stereotyping is a barrier to diversity, but valuing cultural differences facilitates diversity. These two different ways of thinking are described below and illustrated in Exhibit 9.13.[135]

- ***Stereotypes are often based on folklore, media portrayals, and other unreliable sources of information.*** In contrast, legitimate cultural differences are backed up by systematic research of real differences.
- ***Stereotypes contain negative connotations.*** On the other hand, managers who value diversity view differences as potentially positive or neutral. For example, the observation that Asian males

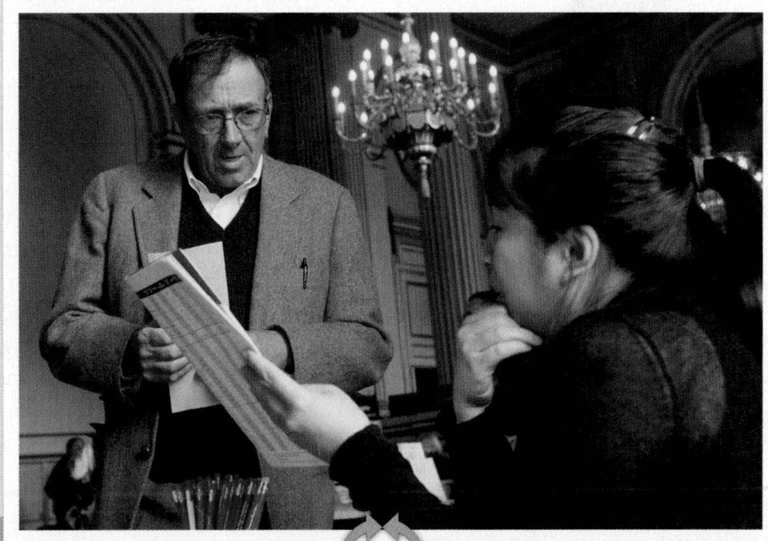

Justin Sullivan/ Getty Images News /Getty Images

ConceptConnection

Age discrimination has made a difficult situation even more trying for older workers who lost jobs during the recent recession. In May 2010, for instance, the average duration of unemployment for older job seekers, such as Larry Visakowitz (pictured at a job fair for veterans), climbed to 44.2 weeks. That's 11 weeks longer than the national average. **Stereotypes** that plague older job seekers include the beliefs that they are more expensive, harder to train, more likely to leave, and less productive, adaptable, and technologically adept.

EXHIBIT 9.13

Difference between Stereotyping and Valuing Cultural Differences

Stereotyping	Valuing Cultural Differences
Is based on false assumptions, anecdotal evidence, or impressions without any direct experience with a group	Is based on cultural differences verified by scientific research methods
Assigns negative traits to members of a group	Views cultural differences as positive or neutral
Assumes that all members of a group have the same characteristics	Does not assume that all individuals within a group have the same characteristics
Example: Suzuko Akoi is an Asian; therefore, she is not aggressive by white, male standards.	Example: As a group, Asians tend to be less aggressive than white, male Americans.

SOURCE: Adapted from Taylor Cox, Jr., and Ruby L. Beale, *Developing Competency to Manage Diversity: Readings Cases and Activities* (San Francisco: Berrett-Koehler Publishers, Inc., 1997).

are typically less aggressive does not imply they are inferior or superior to white males—it simply means that there is a difference.

- ***Stereotypes assume that all members of a group have the same characteristics.*** Managers who value diversity recognize that individuals within a group of people may or may not share the same characteristics of the group.[136]

How tolerant are you of people who are different from you? Complete the Self-Learning test on pages 380–381 to assess your tolerance for diversity.

Not only should managers rid themselves of stereotypical thinking, they should also recognize the stereotype threat that may jeopardize the performance of at-risk employees. **Stereotype threat** describes the psychological experience of a person who, when engaged in a task, is aware of a stereotype about his or her identity group suggesting that he or she will not perform well on that task.[137] Suppose you are a member of a minority group presenting complicated market research results to your management team and are anxious about making a good impression. Assume that some members of your audience have a negative stereotype about your identity group. As you ponder this, your anxiety skyrockets and your confidence is shaken. Understandably, your presentation suffers because you are distracted by worries and self-doubt as you invest energy in overcoming the stereotype. The feelings you are experiencing are called *stereotype threat.*

People most affected by stereotype threat are those we consider as disadvantaged in the workplace due to negative stereotypes—racial and ethnic minorities, members of lower socioeconomic classes, women, older people, gay and lesbian individuals, and people with disabilities. Although anxiety about performing a task may be normal, people with stereotype threat feel an extra scrutiny and worry that their failure will reflect not only on themselves as individuals, but on the larger group to which they belong. As Beyoncé Knowles said, "It's like you have something to prove, and you don't want to mess it up and be a negative reflection on black women."[138]

Ethnocentrism

Ethnocentrism is one roadblock for managers trying to recognize, welcome, and encourage differences among people so they can develop their unique talents and be effective organizational members. **Ethnocentrism** is the belief that one's own group and subculture are inherently superior to other groups and cultures. Ethnocentrism makes it difficult to value diversity. Viewing one's own culture as the best culture is a natural tendency among most people. Moreover, the business world still tends to reflect the values, behaviors, and assumptions based on the experiences of a rather homogeneous, white, middle-class, male workforce. Indeed, most theories of management presume that workers share similar values, beliefs, motivations, and attitudes about work and life in general. These theories presume that one set of behaviors best helps an organization to be productive and effective and therefore should be adopted by all employees.[139]

Ethnocentric viewpoints and a standard set of cultural practices produce a **monoculture**, a culture that accepts only one way of doing things and one set of values and beliefs, which can cause problems for minority employees. People of color, women, gay people, the disabled, the elderly, and other diverse employees may feel undue pressure to conform, may be victims of stereotyping attitudes, and may be presumed deficient because they are different. White, heterosexual men, many of whom do not fit the notion of the "ideal" employee, may also feel uncomfortable with the monoculture and resent stereotypes that label white males as racists and sexists. Valuing diversity means ensuring that *all* people are given equal opportunities in the workplace.[140]

The goal for organizations seeking cultural diversity is pluralism rather than a monoculture and ethnorelativism rather than ethnocentrism. **Ethnorelativism** is the belief that groups and subcultures are inherently equal. **Pluralism** means that an organization accommodates several subcultures. Movement toward pluralism seeks to fully integrate into the organization the employees who otherwise would feel isolated and ignored. To promote pluralism in its Mountain View corporate headquarters, chefs at Google's corporate cafeteria ensure that its menu accommodates the different tastes of its ethnically diverse workforce, as shown in the Benchmarking box.

BENCHMARKING

Google

Employees in Google's corporate headquarters come from all corners of the world, but they feel a little closer to home when they see familiar foods from their homeland on the cafeteria menu. With a goal of satisfying a diverse, ethnically varied palate, Google's first food guru and chef, Charlie Ayers, designed menus that reflected his eclectic tastes yet also met the needs of an increasingly diverse workforce. He created his own dishes, searched all types of restaurants for new recipes, and often got some of his best ideas from foreign-born employees. For example, a Filipino accountant offered a recipe for chicken *adobo*, a popular dish from her native country. Scattered around the Googleplex are cafes specializing in Southwestern, Italian, California-Mediterranean, and vegetarian cuisines. And because more and more Googlers originally hail from Asia, employees can find sushi at the Japanese-themed Pacific Café or Thai red curry beef at the East Meets West Café.

Google believes food can be a tool for supporting an inclusive workplace. The array of menu options gives people a chance to try new things and learn more about their coworkers. And Google knows that when people need a little comfort and familiarity, nothing takes the edge off of working in a foreign country like eating food that reminds you of home.

Jim Carlton, "Dig In," *The Wall Street Journal,* November 14, 2005; Tony DiRomualdo, "Is Google's Cafeteria a Competitive Weapon?" *Wisconsin Technology Network,* August 30, 2005, http://wistechnology.com/article.php?id=2190 (accessed August 31, 2005); Marc Ramirez, "Tray Chic: At Work, Cool Cafeterias, Imaginative Menus," *The Seattle Times,* November 21, 2005, http://seattletimes.nwsource.com/html/living/2002634266_cafes21.html?pageid=display-in-thenews.module&pageregion=itnbody (accessed November 22, 2005).

- The tendency to view people who are different as being deficient is called **prejudice**.
- Discrimination occurs when someone acts out their prejudicial attitudes toward people who are the targets of their prejudice.
- A rigid, exaggerated, irrational belief associated with a particular group of people is called a **stereotype**.
- **Stereotype threat** occurs when a person who, when engaged in a task, is aware of a stereotype about his or her identity group suggesting that he or she will not perform well on that task.
- Ethnocentrism is the belief that one's own group is inherently superior to other groups.
- A culture that accepts only one way of doing things and one set of values and beliefs is called a **monoculture**.
- **Ethnorelativism** is the belief that groups and subcultures are inherently equal.
- **Pluralism** describes an environment in which the organization accommodates several subcultures, including employees who would otherwise feel isolated and ignored.

Factors Affecting Women's Careers

Progressive organizations realize the business advantage of hiring, retaining, and promoting women in the workplace. In fact, research shows that companies with several senior-level women outperform those without senior-level women both financially and organizationally.

Despite substantial gains in the workplace in recent decades, many women find their career goals are still unattainable or difficult to achieve. In addition, men as a group still have the benefit of higher wages and faster promotions. In the United States in 2005, for example, women employed full-time earned 81 cents for every dollar that men earned.[141] Walmart, the world's largest retailer, struggled to rebound after seven women filed a class-action suit on behalf of all women working for the company in 2001. They complained of a general pattern of discrimination in pay and promotions. Six years before the lawsuit, a law firm found widespread gender disparities in pay and promotion at Walmart and Sam's Club stores and urged the company to take basic steps. In response to the report and the lawsuit, Walmart has taken steps to reduce the disparity occurring in the promotion and pay of women and men. In fact, Walmart has told its 50,000 managers to promote more women and minorities, with 15 percent of managers' bonuses tied to achieving diversity goals. Women now hold 46 percent of assistant store manager positions, up from 40 percent five years ago.[142]

Both the glass ceiling and the decision to "opt out" of a high-pressure career have an impact on women's advancement opportunities and pay. Yet women are sometimes favored in leadership roles for demonstrating behaviors and attitudes that help them succeed in the workplace, a factor called "the female advantage."

Glass Ceiling

The **glass ceiling** is an invisible barrier that separates women from top management positions. They can look up through the ceiling and see top management, but prevailing attitudes and stereotypes are invisible obstacles to their own advancement. This barrier also impedes the career progress of minorities.

In addition, women and minorities are often excluded from informal manager networks and often don't get access to the type of general and line management experience that is required for moving to the top.[143] Research suggests the existence of *glass walls* that serve as invisible barriers to important lateral movement within the organization. Glass walls, like exclusion from manager networks, bar experience in areas such as line supervision that would enable women and minorities to advance vertically.[144]

Evidence that the glass ceiling persists is the distribution of women and minorities, who are clustered at the bottom levels of the corporate hierarchy. Among minority groups, women have made the biggest strides in recent years, but they still represent only 15.7 percent of corporate officers in America's 500 largest companies, up from 12.5 percent in 2000 and 8.7 percent in 1995.[145] In 2007, just seven companies, or 1 percent, among the *Fortune* 500 companies had female CEOs.[146] And both male and female African Americans and Hispanics continue to hold only a small percentage of all management positions in the United States.[147]

Women and minorities also make less money. As shown in Exhibit 9.14, African American men earn about 22 percent less, white women 24 percent less, and Hispanic men 37 percent less than white males. Minority women fare even worse, with African American women earning 35 percent less and Hispanic women 46 percent less than white males.[148]

Another sensitive issue related to the glass ceiling is homosexuals in the workplace. Many gay men and lesbians believe they will not be accepted as they are and risk losing their jobs or their chances for advancement. Gay employees of color are particularly hesitant to disclose their sexual orientation at work because by doing so they risk a double dose of discrimination.[149] Although some examples of openly gay corporate leaders can be found, such as David Geffen, cofounder of DreamWorks SKG, and Ford Vice Chairman Allan D. Gilmour, most managers still believe staying in the closet is the only way they can succeed at work. Thus, gays and lesbians often fabricate heterosexual identities to keep their jobs or avoid running into the glass ceiling they see other employees encounter.

Opt-Out Trend

Some women never hit the glass ceiling because they choose to get off the fast track long before it comes into view. In recent years, an ongoing discussion concerns something referred to as the *opt-out trend*. In a survey of nearly 2,500 women and 653 men, 37 percent

EXHIBIT 9.14

The Wage Gap

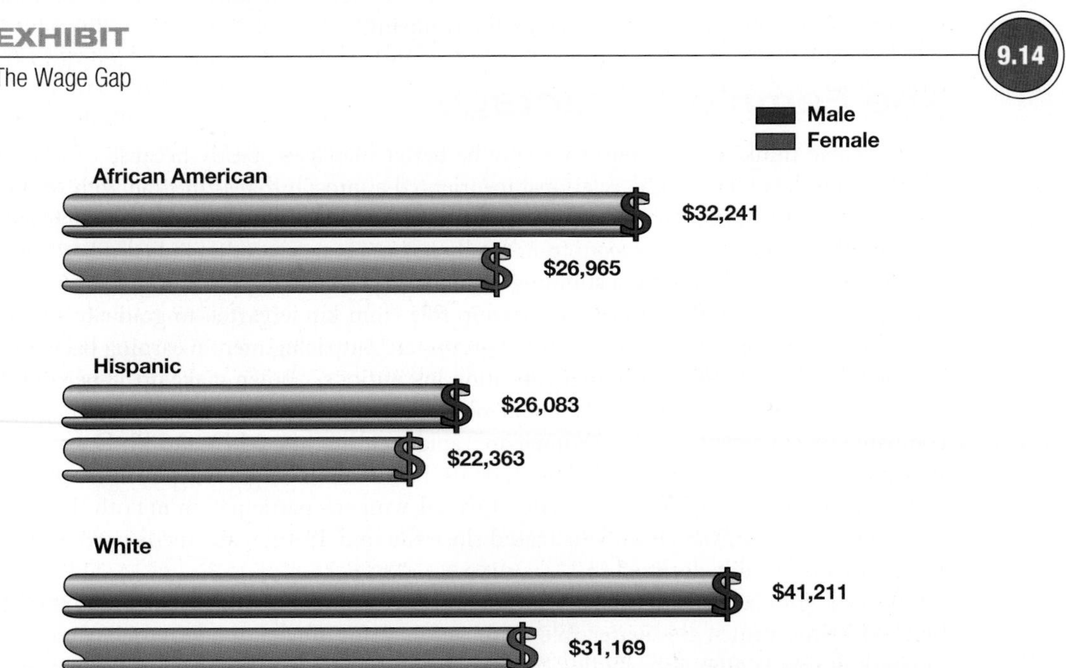

SOURCE: "2006 Median Annual Earnings by Race and Sex," U.S. Census Bureau, Current Population Survey, 2007 Annual Social and Economic Supplement, http://www.infoplease.com/us/census/median-earnings-by-race-2006.html.

of highly qualified women report that they voluntarily left the workforce at some point in their careers, compared to only 24 percent of similarly qualified men.[150]

Quite a debate rages over the reasons for the larger number of women who drop out of mainstream careers. Opt-out proponents say women are deciding that corporate success isn't worth the price in terms of reduced family and personal time, greater stress, and negative health effects.[151] For example, Marge Magner left her job as CEO of Citigroup's Global Consumer Group after suffering both the death of her mother and a personal life-changing accident in the same year. In evaluating her reasons, Magner said she realized that "life is about everything, not just the work." Some organizations are trying to create work environments that help women balance the stress of both work and family. PricewaterhouseCoopers developed its Full Circle Mentoring program to help retain talented women who want a family as well as a career. This innovative program allows men and women to leave the firm for up to five years and devote themselves to full-time parenting. After five years, they can rejoin the firm. This program helps women, in particular, feel they don't have to choose between their families or the company in an "all or nothing" decision.[152]

What judgmental beliefs or attitudes do you have that influence your feelings about men's and women's roles in the workplace? Complete the New Manager Self-Test, on page 371, to see how prepared you are to put stereotypes aside so you can manage effectively.

One school of thought says women don't want corporate power and status in the same way that men do, and clawing one's way up the corporate ladder has become less appealing. Yet critics argue that this view is just another way to blame women themselves for the dearth of female managers at higher levels.[153] Vanessa Castagna, for example, left JCPenney, after decades with the company, not because she wanted more family or personal time but because she kept getting passed over for top jobs.[154] Although some women are voluntarily leaving the fast track, many more genuinely want to move up the corporate ladder but find their paths blocked. In a survey by Catalyst of executive women, 55 percent said they aspire to senior leadership levels.[155] In addition, a survey of 103 women voluntarily leaving executive jobs in *Fortune* 1000 companies found that corporate culture was cited as the No. 1 reason for leaving.[156] The greatest disadvantages of women leaders stem largely from prejudicial attitudes and a heavily male-oriented corporate culture.[157] Some years ago, when Procter & Gamble asked the female executives it considered "regretted losses" (that is, high performers the company wanted to retain) why they left their jobs, the most common answer was that they didn't feel valued by the company.[158]

The Female Advantage

Some people think women might actually be better managers, partly because of a more collaborative, less hierarchical, relationship-oriented approach that is in tune with today's global and multicultural environment.[159] As attitudes and values change with changing generations, the qualities women seem to naturally possess may lead to a gradual role reversal in organizations. For example, a stunning gender reversal is taking place in U.S. education, with girls taking over almost every leadership role from kindergarten to graduate school. In addition, women of all races and ethnic groups are outpacing men in earning bachelor's and master's degrees. In most higher education institutions, women make up 58 percent of enrolled students.[160] Among 25- to 29-year-olds, 32 percent of women have college degrees, compared to 27 percent of men. Women are rapidly closing the M.D. and Ph.D. gap, and they make up about half of all U.S. law students, half of all undergraduate business majors, and about 30 percent of MBA candidates. Overall, women's participation in both the labor force and civic affairs has steadily increased since the mid-1950s, while men's participation has slowly but steadily declined.[161]

According to James Gabarino, an author and professor of human development at Cornell University, women are "better able to deliver in terms of what modern society requires of people—paying attention, abiding by rules, being verbally competent, and dealing with interpersonal relationships in offices."[162] His observation is supported by the fact that female managers are typically rated higher by subordinates on interpersonal skills as well

New Manager Self-Test

Are You Tuned In to Gender Differences?

How much do you know about gender differences in behavior? Please answer whether each item below is true or false. Answer all questions before looking at the answers at the bottom of the page.

	TRUE <<<	>>> FALSE
1. Men control the content of conversation, and they work harder to keep conversations going.	______	______
2. Women use less personal space than men.	______	______
3. A male speaker is listened to more carefully than a female speaker, even when they make an identical presentation.	______	______
4. In the classroom, male students receive more reprimands and criticism.	______	______
5. Men are more likely to interrupt women than to interrupt other men.	______	______
6. Female managers communicate with more emotional openness and drama than male managers.	______	______
7. Women are more likely to answer questions not addressed to them.	______	______
8. In general, men smile more than women do.	______	______
9. Both male and female direct reports see female managers as better communicators than male managers.	______	______
10. In a classroom, teachers are more likely to give verbal praise to female students.	______	______

See It Online

Scoring and Interpretation: Check your answers below. If you scored seven or more correctly, consider yourself perceptive and observant about gender behavior. If you scored three or fewer, you may want to tune in to the gender dynamics you are missing.

SOURCE: Myra Sadker and Joyce Kaser, *The Communications Gender Gap* (Washington, DC: Mid-Atlantic Center for Sex Equity, 1984). Reprinted by permission.

Answers

1. False (Men control content, women work harder.) 2. True; 3. True; 4. True; 5. True; 6. False (Managers of both sexes communicate about the same way.); 7. False; 8. False (Women smile more.); 9. True; 10. False.

as on factors such as task behavior, communication, ability to motivate others, and goal accomplishment.[163] Recent research found a correlation between balanced gender composition in companies (that is, roughly equal male and female representation) and higher organizational performance. Moreover, a study by Catalyst indicates that organizations with the highest percentage of women in top management financially outperform, by about 35 percent, those with the lowest percentage of women in higher-level jobs.[164]

- Companies that promote women to senior-level positions outperform those without women in these positions, both financially and organizationally.
- The **glass ceiling,** an invisible barrier that separates women from top management positions, impedes women's career growth.
- Proponents of the opt-out trend say some women choose to leave the workforce because they decide success isn't worth it in terms of reduced family and personal time, greater stress, and negative health effects.
- Critics say the opt-out trend is just a way to blame women for the scarcity of female top managers, and they argue that organizations must change.
- Women are likely to be more collaborative, less hierarchical, and more relationship-oriented than men, qualities that prepare them to succeed in today's multicultural work environment.

Cultural Competence

A corporate culture, as discussed in Chapter 2, is defined by the values, beliefs, understandings, and norms shared by members of the organization. Although some corporate cultures foster diversity, many managers struggle to create a culture that values and nurtures the organization's diverse employees. Managers who have made strategic decisions to foster diversity need a plan that moves the corporate culture toward one that reduces obstacles for disadvantaged employees. A successful diversity plan leads to a workforce that demonstrates *cultural competence* in the long run. **Cultural competence** is the ability to interact effectively with people of different cultures.[165]

Exhibit 9.15 illustrates the five-step process for implementing a diversity plan.[166] These steps create cultural competence among employees by helping them better understand, communicate with, and successfully interact with diverse coworkers.

9.15 EXHIBIT

Five Steps to Develop Diversity

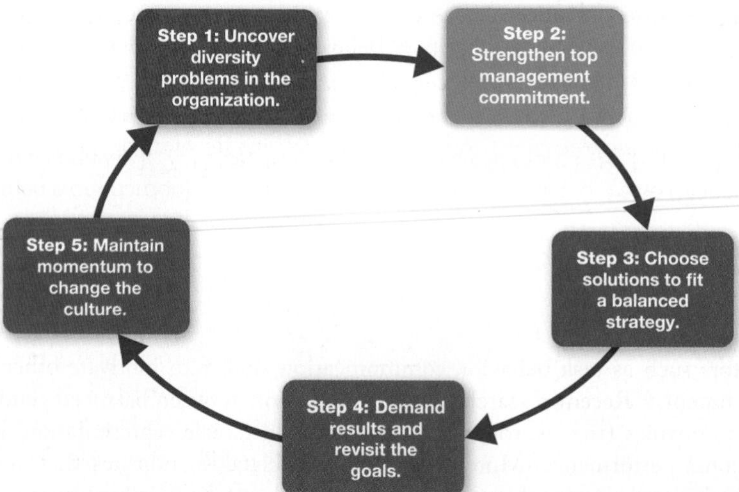

SOURCE: Based on Ann M. Morrison, *The New Leaders: Guidelines on Leadership Diversity in America* (San Francisco: Jossey-Bass Publishers, 1992), p. 160.

Step 1: Uncover diversity problems in the organization. Most doctors can't make a medical diagnosis without first examining the patient. Similarly, organizations cannot assess their progress toward cultural competence without first investigating where the culture is right now. A *cultural audit* is a tool that identifies problems or areas needing improvement in a corporation's culture. The cultural audit is completed by employees who answer the following types of questions: How do promotion rates compare? Is there pay disparity between managers in the same pay grade? Does a glass ceiling limit the advancement of women and minorities? Answers to these questions help managers assess the cultural competence of the organization and focus their diversity efforts on specific problems.

Step 2: Strengthen top management commitment. The most important component of a successful diversity strategy is management commitment, leadership, and support.[167] Some of the ways that top managers demonstrate their support of diversity efforts are by allocating time and money to diversity activities, supporting the recommendations of problem-solving task forces, and communicating the commitment to diversity through speeches and vision and mission statements. Committed top managers also make diversity a priority by setting an example for others to follow.

Step 3: Choose solutions to fit a balanced strategy. The best solutions to diversity problems are those that address the organization's most pressing problems uncovered during Step 1. To be most effective, solutions should be presented in a balanced strategy and address three factors: education, enforcement, and exposure. *Education* may include new training programs that improve awareness and diversity skills. *Enforcement* means providing incentives for employees who demonstrate new behaviors and disciplinary action for those who violate diversity standards. A good example is Denny's restaurants. After facing discrimination lawsuits in the early 1990s, Denny's rebounded with a multifaceted diversity program that included 25 percent discretionary bonuses to all senior managers who significantly improved their record of hiring and promoting minority workers.[168] *Exposure* involves exposing traditional managers to nontraditional peers to help break down stereotypical beliefs. For example, a company might team a white male manager with a female African American manager.

Step 4: Demand results and revisit the goals. The simple rule "what doesn't get measured doesn't get done" applies to diversity efforts. Diversity performance should be measured by numerical goals to ensure solutions are being implemented successfully. Numerical goals demonstrate that diversity is tied to business objectives. Examples of numerical goals might include tracking the salaries, rates of promotion, and managerial positions for women and minorities. But these personnel statistics don't completely measure an organization's progress toward cultural competence. Other measures might include productivity and profitability tied to diversity efforts, employee opinions about their coworkers, and an assessment of the corporation's ability to provide a satisfying work environment for all employees.[169]

Step 5: Maintain momentum to change the culture. Success with any of the previous four steps is a powerful motivator for continuing diversity efforts. Corporations should use these successes as fuel to move forward and to provide leverage for more progress.

- **Cultural competence** is the ability to interact effectively with people of different cultures.
- When a corporate culture embraces diversity and fosters an environment where all people thrive, the organization has achieved cultural competence.
- The five steps toward cultural competence include identifying diversity problems, strengthening top management commitment, choosing solutions, demanding results, and maintaining momentum.

Diversity Initiatives and Programs

Read the Ethical Dilemma, on page 383, that pertains to accommodating the religious practices of employees. Think about how you would handle this challenging management situation.

Today's managers choose from a variety of solutions that create cultural competence. As described in Step 3 of Exhibit 9.15, organizations may develop initiatives and programs that address their unique diversity problems. These initiatives may include: (1) changing structures and policies, (2) focusing on diversity recruiting, (3) establishing mentor relationships, (4) accommodating special needs; and (5) offering training and education.

Changing Structures and Policies

Many policies within organizations originally were designed to fit the stereotypical male employee. Now leading companies are changing structures and policies to facilitate and support diversity. Most large organizations have formal policies against racism and gender discrimination, as well as structured grievance procedures and complaint review processes. Companies are also developing policies to support the recruitment and career advancement of diverse employees. Many have staff dedicated exclusively to encouraging diversity. Increasingly, organizations such as Procter & Gamble, Ernst & Young, and Allstate Insurance are tying managers' bonuses and promotions to how well they diversify the workforce. Exhibit 9.16 illustrates some of the most common diversity initiatives.

Some leading financial and accounting consultants, such as Deloitte, have taken aggressive steps to change their policies and structures to create a women-friendly workplace.

DELOITTE

In the 1990s, Deloitte was known for its rigid and stodgy workplace. But changes in the environment created a crisis for the organization. Deloitte's clients had started requesting more female consultants on project teams, because mixed teams present better results than pure male teams. Yet only 7 percent of Deloitte's partners, principals, or directors were women, and the company was having a tough time recruiting and retaining women.

Talented, well-educated women who were interested in consulting were not attracted to a culture that was not family friendly. Deloitte responded to this crisis through a number of innovative initiatives. First, it implemented several programs designed to help its 38,000 U.S. employees manage family problems and balance work and family life. One such program, called Mass Career Customization, allows employees to "dial up or dial down" their careers, depending on life circumstances. Employees can scale up or back in areas of workload, location, schedule, and roles. Through these changes and hundreds more like it, Deloitte transformed its culture from a sexist boys' club to a revolutionary, pro-women company where managers go the extra mile to nurture women's careers.

Today, Deloitte's diversity record is impressive: 46 percent of all employees are women, 33 percent of all staff are minorities, and 19 percent of its partners are women.[170]

Expanding Recruitment Efforts

For many organizations, a new approach to recruitment means making better use of formal recruiting strategies, offering internship programs to give people opportunities, and developing creative ways to draw on previously unused labor markets. Nationwide's Scholars Program brings in Hispanic and African American college students for a three-year program that includes summer internships and yearlong mentoring.[171] Marathon Petroleum created a six-point recruiting strategy to increase diversity, including (1) recruiting corporate-wide and cross-functionally, (2) building relationships with first- and second-tiered schools to recruit minority students, (3) offering internships for racial and ethnic minorities, (4) offering minority scholarships, (5) establishing informal mentoring programs, and (6) forming affiliations with minority organizations.[172]

EXHIBIT 9.16

The Most Common Diversity Initiatives: Percentage of *Fortune* 1000 Respondents

SOURCE: Adapted from data in "Impact of Diversity Initiatives on the Bottom Line: A SHRM Survey of the *Fortune* 1000," pp. S12–S14, in *Fortune*, special advertising section, "Keeping Your Edge: Managing a Diverse Corporate Culture," produced in association with the Society for Human Resource Management, http://www.fortune.com/sections.

Establishing Mentor Relationships

The successful advancement of diverse group members means that organizations must find ways to eliminate the glass ceiling. One of the most successful structures to accomplish this goal is the mentoring relationship. A **mentor** is a higher-ranking organizational member who is committed to providing upward mobility and support to a protégé's professional career.[173] Mentoring provides minorities and women with direct training and inside information on the norms and expectations of the organization. A mentor also acts as a friend or counselor, enabling the employee to feel more confident and capable. Joseph Cleveland has made a point of helping young African Americans navigate the corporate maze in his career at General Electric and Lockheed Martin. For Pamela Blow-Mitchell, Cleveland's mentoring changed the course of her career and enabled her to seize opportunities she might otherwise have missed. "He kind of dunked down deep in the organization to initiate a conversation with someone that he saw potential in," said Mitchell. "At the time, I could not see the range of opportunities, but I trusted his advice."[174]

One researcher who studied the career progress of high-potential minorities found that those who advance the furthest all share one characteristic—a strong mentor or network of mentors who nurtured their professional development.[175] However, research also indicates that minorities, as well as women, are much less likely than white men to develop mentoring relationships.[176] Women and minorities might not seek mentors because they feel that job competency should be enough to succeed, or they might feel uncomfortable seeking out a mentor when most of the senior executives are white males. Women might fear that initiating a mentoring relationship could be misunderstood as a romantic overture, whereas male mentors may think of women as mothers, wives, or sisters rather than as executive material. Cross-race mentoring relationships sometimes leave both parties uncomfortable, but the mentoring of minority employees must often be across race because of the low number of minorities in upper-level positions. The few minorities and women who have reached the upper ranks often are overwhelmed with mentoring requests from people like themselves, and they may feel uncomfortable in highly visible minority–minority or female–female mentoring relationships, which isolate them from the white male status quo.

The solution is for organizations to overcome some of the barriers to mentor relationships between white males and minorities. When organizations can institutionalize the value of white males actively seeking women and minority protégés, the benefits will mean that women and minorities will be steered into pivotal jobs and positions critical to advancement. Mentoring programs also are consistent with the Civil Rights Act of 1991 that requires the diversification of middle and upper management.

Accommodating Special Needs

5

Many people have special needs of which top managers may be unaware. For example, if numerous people entering the organization at the lower level are single parents, the company can reassess job scheduling and opportunities for child care. If a substantial labor pool is non-English–speaking, training materials and information packets can be provided in another language, or the organization can provide English language classes.

In many families today, both parents work, which means that the company can provide structures to deal with child care, maternity or paternity leave, flexible work schedules, telecommuting or home-based employment, and perhaps part-time employment or seasonal hours that reflect the school year. The key to attracting and keeping elderly or disabled workers may include long-term-care insurance and special health or life insurance benefits. Alternative work scheduling also may be important for these groups of workers. Organizations struggling with generational diversity must find ways to meet the needs of workers at different ages and places in the life cycle.[177] Pitney Bowes created the Life Balance Resources program to help employees in different generations cope with life cycle issues, such as helping Generation Y workers find their first apartments or cars, assisting Generation X employees in locating child care or getting home loans, helping baby boomers plan for retirement, and aiding older workers in researching insurance and long-term care options.[178]

Another issue for U.S. companies is that racial/ethnic minorities and immigrants have often had fewer educational opportunities than other groups. Some companies work with high schools to provide fundamental skills in literacy and math, or they provide these programs within the company to upgrade employees to appropriate educational levels. The movement toward providing educational services for employees can be expected to increase for immigrants and the economically disadvantaged in the years to come.

Providing Diversity Skills Training

Most of today's organizations provide special training, called **diversity training**, to help people identify their own cultural boundaries, prejudices, and stereotypes and develop the skills for managing and working in a diverse workplace. By some estimates, about $80 billion has been invested in corporate diversity programs over the past ten years, much of it spent on training.[179] Working or living within a multicultural context requires a person to use interaction skills that transcend the skills typically effective when dealing with others from one's own in-group.[180]

The first step is typically *diversity awareness training* to make employees aware of the assumptions they make and to increase people's sensitivity and openness to those who are different from them. A basic aim of awareness training is to help people recognize that hidden and overt biases direct their thinking about specific individuals and groups. If people can come away from a training session recognizing that they prejudge people and that this tendency needs to be consciously addressed in communications with and treatment of others, an important goal of diversity awareness training has been reached.

The next step is *diversity skills training* to help people learn how to communicate and work effectively in a diverse environment. Rather than just attempting to increase employees' understanding and sensitivity, this training gives people concrete skills they can use in everyday situations, such as how to handle conflict in a constructive manner or how to modify nonverbal communication such as body language and facial expression.[181] Verizon Communications uses an online training tool where managers can tap into various diversity scenarios that might occur in the workplace and see how they can manage them in an appropriate way.[182] In addition to online training, companies may also use classroom sessions, experiential exercises, videotapes or DVDs, and outside consulting firms that help organizations with diversity management issues.

Increasing Awareness of Sexual Harassment

Although psychological closeness between men and women in the workplace may be a positive experience, sexual harassment is not. Sexual harassment is illegal. As a form of sexual discrimination, sexual harassment in the workplace is a violation of Title VII of the 1964 Civil Rights Act. Sexual harassment in the classroom is a violation of Title VIII of the Education Amendment of 1972. Many companies offer sexual harassment awareness programs that create awareness of what defines sexual harassment and the legal ramifications of violations. The following list categorizes various forms of sexual harassment as defined by one university:

- ***Generalized.*** This form involves sexual remarks and actions that are not intended to lead to sexual activity but that are directed toward a coworker based solely on gender and reflect on the entire group.
- ***Inappropriate/offensive.*** Though not sexually threatening, it causes discomfort in a coworker, whose reaction in avoiding the harasser may limit his or her freedom and ability to function in the workplace.
- ***Solicitation with promise of reward.*** This action treads a fine line as an attempt to "purchase" sex, with the potential for criminal prosecution.
- ***Coercion with threat of punishment.*** The harasser coerces a coworker into sexual activity by using the threat of power (through recommendations, grades, promotions, and so on) to jeopardize the victim's career.
- ***Sexual crimes and misdemeanors.*** The highest level of sexual harassment, these acts would, if reported to the police, be considered felony crimes and misdemeanors.[183]

Statistics in Canada indicate that between 40 and 70 percent of women and about 5 percent of men have been sexually harassed at work.[184] The situation in the United States is just as dire. Over a ten-year period, the Equal Employment Opportunity Commission shows a 150 percent increase in the number of sexual harassment cases filed annually.[185] About 10 percent of those were filed by males. The Supreme Court held that same-sex harassment as well as harassment of men by female coworkers is just as illegal as the harassment of women by men. In the suit that prompted the court's decision, a male oil-rig worker claimed he was singled out by other members of the all-male crew for crude sex play, unwanted touching, and threats of rape.[186] A growing number of men are urging recognition that sexual harassment is not just a woman's problem.[187]

- Many organizations have expanded their recruitment efforts to attract minority candidates.
- A **mentor** is a higher-ranking senior member of the organization who is committed to providing upward mobility and support to a protégé's professional career.
- **Diversity training** is designed to educate employees about the importance of diversity, make people aware of their own biases, and teach them skills for communicating and working in a diverse workplace.
- To eliminate sexual harassment, companies may offer sexual harassment awareness programs that define harassment and the legal ramifications of harassment.

New Diversity Initiatives

In responding to a survey by the Society for Human Resource Management, 91 percent of companies believe that diversity initiatives help maintain a competitive advantage. Some specific benefits they cited include improving employee morale, decreasing interpersonal conflict, facilitating progress in new markets, and increasing the organization's creativity.[188] In addition to the ideas already discussed, two new approaches to diversity management—multicultural teams and employee networks—have arisen in response to the rapid change and complexity of the twenty-first–century organization.

Multicultural Teams

Companies have long known that putting together teams made up of members from different functional areas results in better problem solving and decision making. Now, they are recognizing that **multicultural teams**—teams made up of members from diverse national, racial, ethnic, and cultural backgrounds—provide even greater potential for enhanced creativity, innovation, and value in today's global marketplace.[189] Research indicates that diverse teams generate more and better alternatives to problems and produce more creative solutions than homogeneous teams.[190] A team made up of people with different perspectives, backgrounds, and cultural values creates a healthy mix of ideas and leads to greater creativity and better decisions.

Despite their many advantages,[191] multicultural teams are more difficult to manage because of the increased potential for miscommunication and misunderstanding. Multicultural teams typically have more difficulty learning to communicate and work together smoothly, but with effective cross-cultural training and good management, teams can learn to work well together.[192] One management team videotaped its meetings so members could see how their body language reflects cultural differences. An American manager remarked, "I couldn't believe how even my physical movements dominated the table, while Ron [a Filipino American] . . . actually worked his way off-camera within the first five minutes."[193]

Employee Network Groups

Employee network groups are based on social identity, such as gender or race, and are organized by employees to focus on concerns of employees from that group.[194] Network groups pursue a variety of activities, such as meetings to educate top managers, mentoring programs, networking events, training sessions and skills seminars, minority intern programs, and community volunteer activities. These activities give people a chance to meet, interact with, and develop social and professional ties to others throughout the organization, which may include key decision makers. Network groups are a powerful way to reduce social isolation for women and minorities, help these employees be more effective, and enable members to achieve greater career advancement. A recent study confirms that network groups can be important tools for helping organizations retain managerial-level minority employees.[195] For example, Best Buy's Julie Gilbert launched a women's leadership forum, known as WOLF, to get more women involved in solving core business problems and to pull front-line employees into the top ranks. Gilbert's WOLF teams choose a project, create a solution, and then implement the ideas in stores within three months. The result is that recruitment of female regional sales managers at Best Buy is up 100 percent over the previous year, and turnover among women managers has dropped almost 10 percentage points.[196]

An important characteristic of network groups is that they are created informally by employees, not the organization, and membership is voluntary. Employee networks for minorities who have faced barriers to advancement in organizations, including African Americans, Hispanics, American Indians, Asian Americans, women, gays and lesbians, and disabled employees, show tremendous growth. Even managers who once thought of minority networks as "gripe groups" are now seeing them as essential to organizational success because they help to retain minority employees, enhance diversity efforts, and spark new ideas that can benefit the organization.[197] At Kraft Foods, networks are considered critical to the success of multicultural teams because they build awareness and acceptance of cultural differences and help people feel more comfortable working together.[198] In general, female and minority employees who participate in a network group feel more pride about their work and are more optimistic about their careers than those who do not have the support of a network.[199]

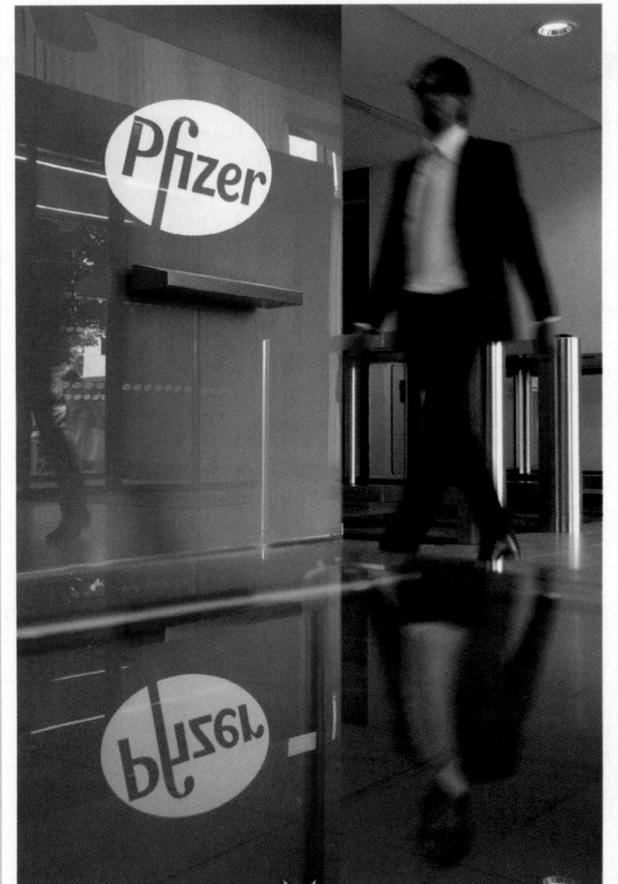

Michele Tantussi/Bloomberg/Getty Images

ConceptConnection

The Pfizer African American Leadership Network (PAALN), a colleague resource group, shows how **cross-race mentoring** can benefit both parties. PAALN recently recruited David Simmons, a white executive who had rapidly advanced in the organization, to be its sponsor. Not surprisingly, Simmons helps PAALN members overcome hurdles as they seek upper-level positions. However, the sponsorship experience has also changed Simmons's perspective. A PAALN member pointed out that "'for someone that looks like a Ken doll, you may be getting doors opened that you don't even realize simply because of the way you look.'" Admits the PAALN sponsor, "It kind of stopped me in my tracks."

- **Multicultural teams** are made up of members from diverse national, racial, ethnic, and cultural backgrounds.
- Multicultural teams provide greater potential for enhanced creativity, innovation, and value in today's global marketplace.
- **Employee network groups** are based on social identity, such as gender or race, and are organized by employees to focus on concerns of employees from that group.

Discussion Questions

1. Assume it is the year 2020. In your company, central planning has given way to front-line decision making, and bureaucracy has given way to teamwork. Shop floor workers use handheld devices and robots. A labor shortage currently affects many job openings, and the few applicants you do attract lack skills to work in teams, make their own production decisions, or use sophisticated technology. As vice president of human resource management since 2008, what should you have done to prepare for this situation?
2. Which selection criteria (personal interview, employment test, assessment center) do you think would be most valuable for predicting effective job performance for a college professor? For an assembly-line worker in a manufacturing plant? Discuss.
3. How do you think the growing use of telecommuters, temporary and part-time workers, and virtual teams affects human resource management? How can managers improve recruiting and retention of these employees?
4. One human resource manager recently got a thank-you note on her iPhone that said "Thx 4 the Iview! Wud ♥ to wrk 4 u☺ " The manager had liked the candidate's interview, but after getting the note, she put him in the reject pile. Do you think it was fair for the manager to automatically reject the candidate? Should "textspeak" be considered acceptable workplace communication? Discuss.
5. As a manager, how would you draw up a telecommuting contract with a new employee? Include considerations such as job description, compensation and benefits, performance measures, training, and grounds for dismissal.
6. Is it wise for managers to evaluate a candidate's postings on social networking sites such as Facebook as grounds for rejection before even interviewing a promising candidate? Is it fair? Discuss.
7. Explain how a manager's personal biases and stereotypes may affect an organization's success in creating a workplace that is culturally competent.
8. Shelley Willingham-Hinton, president of the National Organization for Diversity in Sales and Marketing, was quoted in the chapter as saying, "Our country's consumer base is so varied. I can't think of how a company can succeed without having that kind of diversity with their employees." Why should corporations have workforces that mirror the country's diverse consumer base?
9. Evaluate your own experiences so far with people from other backgrounds. How well do you think those experiences prepared you to understand the unique needs and dilemmas of a diverse workforce?
10. What is the glass ceiling, and why do you think it has proven to be such a barrier to women and minorities?
11. Why do you think a large number of women are *opting out* of corporate management? Discuss whether this trend is likely to continue over the next ten years.
12. How can organizations strike a balance between respecting and meeting the needs of a diverse workforce and shaping a high-performance corporate culture where shared values contribute to the accomplishment of strategic goals?

Self-Learning

How Tolerant Are You?

For each of the following questions, circle the answer that best describes you.

1. Most of your friends
   a. are very similar to you.
   b. are very different from you and from each other.
   c. are like you in some respects but different in others.
2. When someone does something you disapprove of, you
   a. break off the relationship.
   b. tell how you feel but keep in touch.
   c. tell yourself it matters little and behave as you always have.

3. Which virtue is most important to you?
   a. Kindness
   b. Objectivity
   c. Obedience
4. When it comes to beliefs, you
   a. do all you can to make others see things the same way you do.

b. actively advance your point of view but stop short of argument.
c. keep your feelings to yourself.

5. Would you hire a person who has had emotional problems?
   a. No
   b. Yes, provided the person shows evidence of complete recovery
   c. Yes, if the person is suitable for the job
6. Do you voluntarily read material that supports views different from your own?
   a. Never
   b. Sometimes
   c. Often
7. You react to old people with
   a. patience.
   b. annoyance.
   c. sometimes a, sometimes b.
8. Do you agree with the statement, "What is right and wrong depends upon the time, place, and circumstance"?
   a. Strongly agree
   b. Agree to a point
   c. Strongly disagree
9. Would you marry someone from a different race?
   a. Yes
   b. No
   c. Probably not
10. If someone in your family were homosexual, you would
    a. view this as a problem and try to change the person to a heterosexual orientation.
    b. accept the person as a homosexual with no change in feelings or treatment.
    c. avoid or reject the person.
11. You react to little children with
    a. patience.
    b. annoyance.
    c. sometimes a, sometimes b.
12. Other people's personal habits annoy you
    a. often.
    b. not at all.
    c. only if extreme.
13. If you stay in a household run differently from yours (cleanliness, manners, meals, and other customs), you
    a. adapt readily.
    b. quickly become uncomfortable and irritated.
    c. adjust for a while, but not for long.
14. Which statement do you agree with most?
    a. We should avoid judging others because no one can fully understand the motives of another person.
    b. People are responsible for their actions and have to accept the consequences.
    c. Both motives and actions are important when considering questions of right and wrong.

Scoring and Interpretation

Circle your score for each of the answers and total the scores:

1. a = 4; b = 0; c = 2
2. a = 4; b = 2; c = 0
3. a = 0; b = 2; c = 4
4. a = 4; b = 2; c = 0
5. a = 4; b = 2; c = 0
6. a = 4; b = 2; c = 0
7. a = 0; b = 4; c = 2
8. a = 0; b = 2; c = 4
9. a = 0; b = 4; c = 2
10. a = 2; b = 0; c = 4
11. a = 0; b = 4; c = 2
12. a = 4; b = 0; c = 2
13. a = 0; b = 4; c = 2
14. a = 0; b = 4; c = 2

Total Score

0–14: If you score 14 or below, you are a very tolerant person and dealing with diversity comes easily to you.

15–28: You are basically a tolerant person and others think of you as tolerant. In general, diversity presents few problems for you; you may be broad-minded in some areas and have less tolerant ideas in other areas of life, such as attitudes toward older people or male–female social roles.

29–42: You are less tolerant than most people and should work on developing greater tolerance of people different from you. Your low tolerance level could affect your business or personal relationships.

43–56: You have a very low tolerance for diversity. The only people you are likely to respect are those with beliefs similar to your own. You reflect a level of intolerance that could cause difficulties in today's multicultural business environment.

SOURCE: Adapted from the Tolerance Scale by Maria Heiselman, Naomi Miller, and Bob Schlorman, Northern Kentucky University, 1982. In George Manning, Kent Curtis, and Steve McMillen, *Building Community: The Human Side of Work* (Cincinnati, OH: Thomson Executive Press, 1996): 272–277.

Group Learning

An Ancient Tale

1. Read the Introduction and Case Study and answer the questions.
2. In groups of three or four, discuss your answers.
3. Groups report to the whole class, and the instructor leads a discussion on the issues raised.

Introduction

To understand, analyze, and improve organizations, we must carefully think through the issue of who is responsible for what activities in different organizational settings. Often we hold responsible someone who has no control over the outcome, or we fail to teach or train someone who could make the vital difference.

To explore this issue, the following exercise could be conducted on either an individual or group basis. It provides an opportunity to see how different individuals assign responsibility for an event. It is also a good opportunity to discuss the concept of organizational boundaries (What is the organization? Who is in or out? etc.)

Case Study

You should read the short story and respond quickly to the first three questions. Then take a little more time on questions 4 through 6. The results, criteria, and implications could then be discussed in groups.

Long ago in an ancient kingdom, there lived a princess who was very young and very beautiful. The princess, recently married, lived in a large and luxurious castle with her husband, a powerful and wealthy lord. The young princess was not content, however, to sit and eat strawberries by herself while her husband took frequent and long journeys to neighboring kingdoms. She felt neglected and soon became quite unhappy. One day, while she was alone in the castle gardens, a handsome vagabond rode out of the forest bordering the castle. He spied the beautiful princess, quickly won her heart, and carried her away with him.

Following a day of dalliance, the young princess found herself ruthlessly abandoned by the vagabond. She then discovered that the only way back to the castle led through the bewitched forest of the wicked sorcerer. Fearing to venture into the forest alone, she sought out her kind and wise godfather. She explained her plight, begged forgiveness of the godfather, and asked his assistance in returning home before her husband returned. The godfather, however, surprised and shocked at her behavior, refused forgiveness and denied her any assistance. Discouraged but still determined, the princess disguised her identity and sought the help of the most noble of all the kingdom's knights. After hearing the sad story, the knight pledged his unfailing aid—for a modest fee. But, alas, the princess had no money, and the knight rode away to save other damsels.

The beautiful princess had no one else from whom she might seek help, and decided to brave the great peril alone. She followed the safest path she knew, but when she was almost through the forest, the wicked sorcerer spied her and caused her to be devoured by the fire-breathing dragon.

1. Who was inside the organization and who was outside? Where were the boundaries?
2. Who is most responsible for the death of the beautiful princess?
3. Who is next most responsible? Least responsible?
4. What is your criterion for the above decisions?
5. What interventions would you suggest to prevent a recurrence?
6. What are the implications for *organizational development and change?*

Character	Most Responsible	Next Most Responsible	Least Responsible
Princess			
Husband			
Vagabond			
Godfather			
Knight			
Sorcerer			

Check one character in each column.

SOURCE: Adapted from J. B. Ritchie and Paul Thompson. Reprinted with permission from *Organization and People: Readings, Cases and Exercises in Organizational Behavior.* Copyright 1980 by West Publishing, pp. 68–70. All rights reserved, in Dorothy Marcic, *Organizational Behavior: Experiences and Cases,* 4/e, pp. 378–379.

Action Learning

Interview Questions

1. Meet with four or five people who have recently gone through job interviews. Ask them what questions they were asked, and list those down on a sheet of paper. Note whether the same questions were asked to more than one of these people, that is, how many people were asked that type of question? Find out which questions they found uncomfortable or invasive, and ask them how they responded to those questions.
2. Your instructor may ask you to form groups of three to five people. If so, come up with a composite list of questions. Refer to Exhibit 9.8 to see which of the questions should not have been asked.
3. How did people answer difficult questions?
4. List effective and ineffective ways to answer the difficult or illegal questions.
5. Be prepared to make a presentation to the entire class.
6. The instructor may lead a discussion about appropriate interview questions and how to respond to them.

Ethical Dilemma

Sunset Prayers[200]

Frank Piechowski, plant manager for a Minnesota North Woods Appliance Corporation refrigerator plant, just received his instructions from the vice president for manufacturing. He was to hire 40 more temporary workers through Twin Cities Staffing, the local labor agency North Woods used. Frank already knew from past experience that most, if not all, of the new hires available to work the assembly line would be Muslim Somali refugees, people who had immigrated to Minnesota from their war-torn native country en masse over the past 15 years.

North Woods, like all appliance manufacturers, was trying to survive in a highly competitive, mature industry. Appliance companies were competing mainly on price. The entrance of large chains such as Best Buy and Home Depot only intensified the price wars, not to mention that consumers could easily do comparison shopping before leaving home by logging on to the Internet. The pressure to keep production costs low was considerable.

That's where the Somali workers came in. In an effort to keep labor costs low, North Woods was relying more and more on temporary workers rather than increasing the ranks of permanent employees. Frank was quite pleased with the Somalis already at work on the assembly line. Although few in number, they were responsible, hard-working, and willing to work for the wages he could afford to pay.

It was the first time this son of Polish immigrants had ever come into contact with Muslims, but so far it had gone well. Frank had established a good working relationship with the Somalis' spokesperson, Halima Adan, who explained that unlike most Western faiths, Islamic religious practices were inextricably woven into everyday life. So together, they worked out ways to accommodate Muslim customs. Frank authorized changes in the plant's cafeteria menu so the Somali workers had more options that conformed to their dietary restrictions, and he allowed women to wear traditional clothing as long as they weren't violating safety standards.

After learning that the Somalis would need to perform at least some of the ceremonial washing and prayers they were required to do five times a day during work hours, the plant manager set aside a quiet, clean room where they could observe their 15-minute rituals during their breaks and at sunset. The Maghrib sunset prayers that second-shift workers had to perform were disruptive to a smooth workflow. Compared to their midday and afternoon rituals, the Muslim faithful had considerably less leeway as to when they said the sunset prayers, and of course the sun set at a slightly different time each day. But so far, they'd all coped.

But what was he going to do about the sunset prayers with an influx of 40 Somali workers that would dramatically increase the number of people who would need to leave the line to pray? Was it time to modify his policy? He knew that Title VII of the Civil Right Act required that he make "reasonable" accommodations to his employees' religious practices unless doing so would impose an "undue hardship" on the employer. Had he reached the point where the accommodations Halima Adan would probably request crossed the line from reasonable to unreasonable? But if he changed his policy, did he risk alienating his workforce?

What Would You Do?

1. Continue the current policy that leaves it up to the Muslim workers as to when they leave the assembly line to perform their sunset rituals.
2. Try to hire the fewest possible Muslim workers so the work line will be efficient on second shift.
3. Ask the Muslim workers to delay their sunset prayers until a regularly scheduled break occurs, pointing out that North Woods is primarily a place of business, not a house of worship.

Case for Critical Analysis

Commonwealth Worldwide Chauffeured Transportation[201]

Dawson Rutter started a limousine company so he'd have a nice place to work—but not have to work very hard. Rutter was content to keep the company small and play golf several times a week. Six years later, though, after being offered what he considered a paltry figure from a larger company that wanted to acquire Commonwealth, Rutter realized he needed to do more to build value in the business. He envisioned transforming his local driver's service into a company with international reach and a level of customer service that would set new benchmarks in the industry.

From his previous experience driving taxis and limos for other companies, Rutter knew what his priority would be in building his business: "Other companies are metal-centric—mostly about the cars," he says. "We are flesh-centric. We are about people." To provide the best customer experience meant Commonwealth had to provide a level and consistency of service above and beyond what was offered by other companies. At the time, Commonwealth had few professional or management employees, with Rutter handling most duties, including sales and marketing. He started his transformation by recruiting a top-notch sales manager, who steadily began building the client base. Commonwealth expanded into New York City and snagged accounts from some of the choicest hotels. Some guests liked the service so well they retained Commonwealth for their own companies. But more customers led to more challenges. It was one thing to provide boutique service with a small, locally focused company serving 40 or so customers, but providing it to 4,000 clients around the world was a different matter.

In the limo business, 90 percent of staff members have direct contact with clients, but Rutter knew his primary focus had to be the drivers. Finding workers wasn't a problem; with the slowing economy, there were plenty of people who needed jobs. But driver jobs typically attract poorly educated, unskilled, and itinerant workers. How could Rutter build a squadron of organized, professional, fastidious employees dedicated to the business and committed to a mission of exceptional customer service?

Questions

1. What types of employees would you suggest Dawson Rutter add to his company next? Why?
2. Which of the three broad HRM activities (finding people, managing talent, or maintaining the workforce) would you invest in most heavily in order to begin building the human capital Commonwealth needs? Discuss.
3. Suggest at least one idea for training, one for performance evaluation, and one for compensation that might be used to develop and maintain a committed corps of limo drivers.

Barcelona Restaurant Group: Managing Human Resources

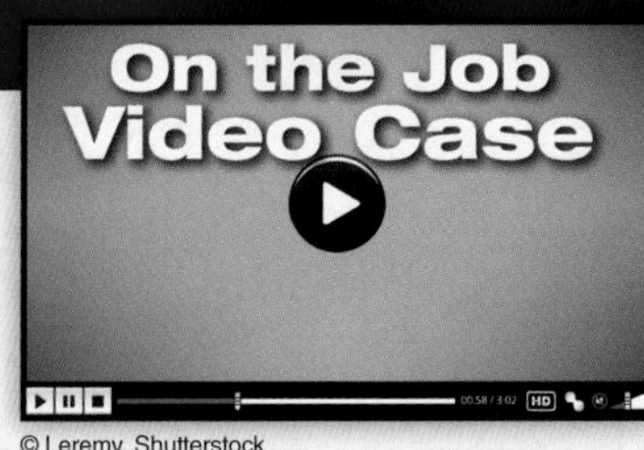

© Leremy, Shutterstock

The restaurant business is always in flux, with workers coming and going in a revolving-door fashion. This is true even of high-end concepts like Barcelona Restaurant Group, a collection of seven wine and tapas bars located in Connecticut and Atlanta, Georgia.

At Barcelona, life is all about authentic cuisine, exceptional service, and a great time. The restaurant group offers eclectic Spanish cuisine with an authentic ambience that recalls a neighborhood eatery in Milan or Rio de Janeiro. At Barcelona, wait staff are friendly, and chefs are known to create personalized dishes that impress regulars. Barcelona's flavorful tapas are infused with olive oil, lemon, and smoky paprika, and the comprehensive wine list features top vintages from Spain, Portugal, and vineyards around the world.

It takes the right mix of people to deliver this upscale culinary experience, and that's a job for Barcelona COO Scott Lawton. "Human resources is one of the most important things we do in our business," says Lawton. "This is a transient business, so people are constantly moving. The minute you stop looking for talent, you're actually sliding backwards—so we're always hiring."

For anyone who has waited tables, restaurant turnover is a familiar experience. Cooks, servers, and bussers have short careers in most establishments; managers typically stick around longer. But Barcelona has exceptionally high standards for service, and this requires letting go employees who aren't up to snuff. "In the three years I've worked here, only one or two managers have quit," Lawton states. "However, we've turned over probably 60 to 70 percent of all management in the past three years, and that's because we were not afraid to let people go. We demand a certain level of quality, and we're continuously raising the bar on our expectations."

With so much talent revolving through the organization, Lawton integrates recruitment into daily operations. The restaurant keeps want ads running at all times, and managers conduct interviews each and every day. The process is highly strategic. According to Barcelona's operations chief, smart restaurant managers can hire their way out of problems simply by selecting the right people. "We can train people all day," Lawton states, "but we can't train happy people with good attitudes—we can't train that into people." Lawton instructs managers to hire the right people with the right work attitudes.

Judging an applicant's work attitudes is no easy task, however. To ensure that Barcelona finds the right employees, Lawton uses a three-stage recruitment process. First, leaders conduct 20-minute interviews with dozens of candidates. Next, applicants are sent on "a shop"—an assignment during which candidates spend $100 dollars at a Barcelona restaurant and write an essay about the event. For applicants who survive the first two stages of the selection process, there is one final assessment: "the trail." At Barcelona, the trail acts as a kind of test drive in which job candidates command the floor, interact with wait staff and customers, and demonstrate job skills. Approximately one-fourth of the candidates who go on a trail can expect to be hired.

At the end of the day, according to Scott Lawton, people either possess the necessary intelligence and skills to run a restaurant or they don't. The industry doesn't have much time for learning curves, and the success or failure of any establishment depends on the performance of competent, self-motivated employees. No one knows this more than Lawton. "For any company that is involved in customer service," states the restaurant veteran, "the most important thing you can do is have the right people in front of your customers."

Discussion Questions

1. List the three main activities of human resource management (HRM) and identify which activity is examined at length in the video.
2. Of the various steps in Barcelona's employee selection process, the job interview is the most brief. Do you agree with the company's approach to interviewing? Why or why not?
3. Identify Barcelona's three-stage process for matching job applicants with its organizational objectives, and explain how each stage reveals the fit between job applicants and the needs of the restaurant.

© VikaSuh, Shutterstock

Played

Ray Burns (Mick Rossi) does prison time for a crime he did not commit. After his release, he focuses on getting even with his enemies. This fast-moving film peers deeply into London's criminal world, which includes some crooked London police, especially Detective Brice (Vinnie Jones). The film's unusual ending reviews all major parts of the plot.

Recruitment These scenes begin with a close-up of a photograph of an ape that Riley (Patrick Bergin) carefully examines. We follow Detective Brice's order to Riley to kill the person who will not give them money. Riley shoots him in a pub. The scenes end after Ray Burns accepts Riley's offer. He walks away saying, "All right. Let's rock and roll, man. All right. Thanks, Riley." Riley says, "Thank you, Ray." The film cuts to Terry (Trevor Nugent) talking to Nikki (Meridith Ostrom) before Ray's arrival.

What to Watch for and Ask Yourself

- This chapter emphasized a strategic approach to human resource management. Detective Brice outlines a strategy in the opening of these scenes for the job he describes to Riley. What are the key parts of that strategy? What are the human resource implications of the strategy?
- Riley's next step is to recruit Ray Burns. Which recruitment guidelines and activities does he follow? Give examples from that portion of the film scenes.
- Does Riley give Ray a "realistic job preview"? Use examples from the film scenes to support your answer.

Endnotes

1. Catherine Rampell, with Jack Healy, "Layoffs Spread to More Sectors of the Economy," *The New York Times,* January 26, 2009; and Cari Tuna, "Theory & Practice: Many Companies Hire as They Fire; As Employers Adapt to Changing Terrain, Different Skill Sets Are Required," *The Wall Street Journal,* May 11, 2009.
2. Results of a McKinsey Consulting survey, reported in Leigh Branham, "Planning to Become an Employer of Choice," *Journal of Organizational Excellence* (Summer 2005): 57–68.
3. Robert L. Mathis and John H. Jackson, *Human Resource Management: Essential Perspectives,* 2nd ed. (Cincinnati, OH: South-Western Publishing, 2002), p. 1.
4. See James C. Wimbush, "Spotlight on Human Resource Management," *Business Horizons* 48 (2005): 463–467; Jonathan Tompkins, "Strategic Human Resources Management in Government: Unresolved Issues," *Public Personnel Management* (Spring 2002): 95–110; Noel M. Tichy, Charles J. Fombrun, and Mary Anne Devanna, "Strategic Human Resource Management," *Sloan Management Review* 23 (Winter 1982): 47–61; Cynthia A. Lengnick-Hall and Mark L. Lengnick-Hall, "Strategic Human Resources Management: A Review of the Literature and a Proposed Typology," *Academy of Management Review* 13 (July 1988): 454–470; and Eugene B. McGregor, *Strategic Management of Human Knowledge, Skills, and Abilities* (San Francisco: Jossey-Bass, 1991).
5. Quoted in Erin White, "HR Departments Get New Star Power at Some Firms; Business Executives Now Tapped to Lead As Job Is Rethought," (Theory & Practice column) *The Wall Street Journal,* June 23, 2008.
6. Edward E. Lawler III, "HR on Top," *Strategy + Business,* no. 35 (Second Quarter 2004): 21–25; and Jim Rendon, "Ten Things Human Resources Won't Tell You," *The Wall Street Journal Online,* April 19, 2010, http://online.wsj.com/article/SB10001424052702303491304575188023801379324.html (accessed April 19, 2010).
7. Joann S. Lublin, "HR Executives Suddenly Get Hot," (Theory & Practice column) *The Wall Street Journal,* December 14, 2009.
8. P. Wright, G. McMahan, and A. McWilliams, "Human Resources and Sustained Competitive Advantage: A Resource-Based Perspective," *International Journal of Human Resource Management* 5 (1994): 301–326; and Tompkins, "Strategic Human Resource Management in Government."
9. Liza Castro Christiansen and Malcolm Higgs, "How the Alignment of Business Strategy and HR Strategy Can Impact Performance," *Journal of General Management* 33, no. 4 (Summer 2008): 13–33; Seema Sanghi, "Building Competencies," *Industrial Management* (May–June 2009): 14–17; B. Becker and M. Huselid, "High Performance Work Systems and Firm Performance: A Synthesis of Research and Managerial Implications," *Research in Personnel and Human Resources Management* 16 (1998): 53–101; S. Ramlall, "Measuring Human Resource Management's Effectiveness in Improving Performance," *Human Resource Planning* 26 (2003): 51; Mark A. Huselid, Susan E. Jackson, and Randall S. Schuler, "Technical and Strategic Human Resource Management Effectiveness as Determinants of Firm Performance," *Academy of Management Journal* 40, no. 1 (1997): 171–188; and John T. Delaney and Mark A. Huselid, "The Impact of Human Resource Management Practices on Perceptions of Organizational Performance," *Academy of Management Journal* 39, no. 4 (1996): 949–969.
10. James N. Baron and David M. Kreps, "Consistent Human Resource Practices," *California Management Review* 41, no. 3 (Spring 1999): 29–53.

11. Sunil J. Ramlall, "Strategic HR Management Creates Value at Target," *Journal of Organizational Excellence* (Spring 2006): 57–62.
12. Cynthia D. Fisher, "Current and Recurrent Challenges in HRM," *Journal of Management* 15 (1989): 157–180.
13. Floyd Kemske, "HR 2008: A Forecast Based on Our Exclusive Study," *Workforce* (January 1998): 46–60.
14. This definition and discussion is based on George Bohlander, Scott Snell, and Arthur Sherman, *Managing Human Resources,* 12th ed. (Cincinnati, OH: South-Western, 2001), pp. 13–15; and Harry Scarbrough, "Recipe for Success," *People Management* (January 23, 2003): 22–25.
15. Susan Cantrell, James M. Benton, Terry Laudal, and Robert J. Thomas, "Measuring the Value of Human Capital Investments: The SAP Case," *Strategy & Leadership* 34, no. 2 (2006): 43–52.
16. Section 1604.1 of the EEOC Guidelines based on the Civil Rights Act of 1964, Title VII.
17. "What's in Health Care Bill? Take a Dose," *CBS News.com,* March 19, 2010, www.cbsnews.com/stories/2010/03/19/politics/main6314410.shtml (accessed June 1, 2010).
18. Reported in D. T. Hall and P. H. Mirvis, "The New Protean Career: Psychological Success and the Path with a Heart," in D. T. Hall & Associates, *The Career is Dead—Long Live the Career: A Relational Approach to Careers* (San Francisco: Jossey-Bass, 1995), pp. 15–45.
19. Phred Dvorak and Scott Thurm, "Slump Prods Firms to Seek New Compact with Workers," *The Wall Street Journal,* October 20, 2009.
20. Stephen Baker, "You're Fired—But Stay in Touch," *Business-Week* (May 4, 2009): 54–55.
21. A. S. Tsui, J. L. Pearce, L. W. Porter, and A. M. Tripoli, "Alternative Approaches to the Employee-Organization Relationship: Does Investment in Employees Pay Off?" *Academy of Management Journal* 40 (1997): 1089–1121; and D. Wang, A. S. Tsui, Y. Zhang, and L. Ma, "Employment Relationships and Firm Performance: Evidence from an Emerging Economy," *Journal of Organizational Behavior* 24 (2003): 511–535.
22. Jena McGregor, "The Midyear Review's Sudden Impact," *BusinessWeek* (July 6, 2009): 50–52; and Sarah Needleman, "Businesses Mount Efforts to Retain Valued Employees," *The Wall Street Journal,* November 16, 2009.
23. Based on Branham, "Planning to Become an Employer of Choice."
24. This discussion is based on Peter Coy, Michelle Conlin, and Moira Herbst, "The Disposable Worker," *Bloomberg BusinessWeek* (January 18, 2010): 33–39; Kris Maher, "More People Pushed into Part-Time Work Force," *The Wall Street Journal*, March 8, 2008; Marshall Goldsmith, "The Contingent Workforce," *BusinessWeek,* May 23, 2007, www.businessweek.com/careers/content/may2007/ca20070523_580432.htm (accessed April 8, 2008); and John Tagliabue, "Europe No Longer Shuns Part-Time and Temporary Jobs," *The New York Times*, May 11, 2006.
25. Estimate from the Iowa Policy Project, reported in Coy et al., "The Disposable Worker."
26. Ibid.
27. Thomas Frank, "TSA Struggles to Reduce Persistent Turnover," *USA Today*, February 25, 2008.
28. Coy et al., "The Disposable Worker."
29. Needleman, "Businesses Mount Efforts to Retain Valued Employees."
30. Stephen Barr, "Working from Home a Work in Progress," *The Washington Post*, June 19, 2007.
31. Ellen Gragg, "Are Telecommuting and Flextime Dead?" *Office Solutions* (January/February 2006): 28.
32. John Challenger, "There Is No Future for the Workplace," *Public Management* (February 1999): 20–23; Susan Caminiti, "Work-Life," *Fortune* (September 19, 2005): S1–S17.
33. Stephanie Armour, "Generation Y: They've Arrived at Work with a New Attitude," *USA Today*, November 6, 2005, www.usatoday.com/money/workplace/2005-11-06-gen-y_x.htm (accessed November 6, 2005); Ellyn Spragins, "The Talent Pool," *FSB* (October 2005): 92–101; and Caminiti, "Work-Life."
34. James G. March and Herbert A. Simon, *Organizations* (New York: Wiley, 1958).
35. Dennis J. Kravetz, *The Human Resources Revolution* (San Francisco: Jossey-Bass, 1989).
36. J. W. Boudreau and S. L. Rynes, "Role of Recruitment in Staffing Utility Analysis," *Journal of Applied Psychology* 70 (1985): 354–366.
37. Megan Santosus, "The Human Capital Factor," *CFO-IT* (Fall 2005): 26–27.
38. Reported in Robert E. Ployhart, "Staffing in the 21st Century: New Challenges and Strategic Opportunities," *Journal of Management* 32, no. 6 (December 2006): 868–897.
39. Brian Dumaine, "The New Art of Hiring Smart," *Fortune* (August 17, 1987): 78–81.
40. This discussion is based on Mathis and Jackson, *Human Resource Management*, Chapter 4, pp. 49–60.
41. Victoria Griffith, "When Only Internal Expertise Will Do," *CFO* (October 1998): 95–96, 102.
42. J. P. Wanous, *Organizational Entry* (Reading, MA: Addison-Wesley, 1980).
43. Samuel Greengard, "Technology Finally Advances HR," *Workforce* (January 2000): 38–41; and Scott Hays, "Hiring on the Web," *Workforce* (August 1999): 77–84.
44. Matthew Boyle, "Enough to Make Monster Tremble," *BusinessWeek* (July 6, 2009): 43–45; Stephanie Armour, "Networking Takes Giant Strides Online," *USA Today*, March 11, 2007, www.usatoday.com/money/industries/technology/2007-03-11-networking_N.htm (accessed March 12, 2007); and Thomas Lee, "Social Networking Goes to Work," *South Florida Sun-Sentinel,* January 19, 2009.
45. Boyle, "Enough to Make Monster Tremble."
46. Kathryn Tyler, "Employees Can Help Recruit New Talent," *HR Magazine* (September 1996): 57–60.
47. Julie Weed, "Referrals on Facebook Ease Strain of Job Search," *International Herald Tribune,* June 1, 2009.
48. Sarah E. Needleman, "If You Want to Stand Out, Join the Crowd," *The Wall Street Journal*, August 14, 2007.
49. Ron Stodghill, "Soul on Ice," *FSB* (October 2005): 129–134.
50. Brian O'Keefe, "Battle-Tested: How a Decade of War Has Created a New Generation of Elite Business Leaders," *Fortune* (March 22, 2010): 108–118.
51. Emily Maltby, "To Find Best Hires, Firms Become Creative–'Speed Dating' Interviews and Personality Tests Help Winnow Deep Applicant Pools, Improve Matches," *The Wall Street Journal,* November 17, 2009; and "I Love Rewards Launches Largest Recruiting Round in Company History," *Canada NewsWire,* March 22, 2010.
52. Wimbush, "Spotlight on Human Resource Management."

53. Paul W. Thayer, "Somethings Old, Somethings New," *Personnel Psychology* 30, no. 4 (Winter 1977): 513–524.
54. J. Ledvinka, *Federal Regulation of Personnel and Human Resource Management* (Boston: Kent, 1982); and *Civil Rights Act,* Title VII, Section 2000e *et seq., U.S. Code* 42 (1964).
55. Reported in Stephanie Clifford, "The New Science of Hiring," *Inc.* (August 2006): 90–98.
56. Bohlander et al., *Managing Human Resources*, p. 202.
57. Sarah E. Needleman, "Lifting the Curtain on the Hiring Process," *The Wall Street Journal,* January 26, 2010.
58. Susan Greco, "Sales & Marketing: He Can Close, but How Is His Interpersonal Sensitivity? Testing Sales Recruits," *Inc.* (March 2009): 96–98.
59. Reported in Toddi Gutner, "Applicants' Personalities Put to the Test," *The Wall Street Journal,* August 26, 2008.
60. "Assessment Centers: Identifying Leadership through Testing," *Small Business Report* (June 1987): 22–24; and W. C. Byham, "Assessment Centers for Spotting Future Managers," *Harvard Business Review* (July–August 1970): 150–167.
61. Erin White, "Walking a Mile in Another's Shoes—Employers Champion Tests of Job Candidates to Gauge Skills at 'Real World' Tasks" (Theory & Practice column), *The Wall Street Journal*, January 16, 2006.
62. Mike Thatcher, "'Front-line' Staff Selected by Assessment Center," *Personnel Management* (November 1993): 83.
63. Example cited in George Bohlander and Scott Snell, *Managing Human Resources,* 15th ed. (Cincinnati, OH: South-Western, 2010), p. 276.
64. Alan Finder, "For Some, Online Persona Undermines a Résumé," *The New York Times*, June 11, 2006.
65. Rendon, "Ten Things Human Resources Won't Tell You."
66. Bernard Keys and Joseph Wolfe, "Management Education and Development: Current Issues and Emerging Trends," *Journal of Management* 14 (1988): 205–229.
67. "2009 Training Industry Report," *Training* (October–November 2009): 32–36.
68. "2009 Training Industry Report"; and Marjorie Derven, "Social Networking: A Force for Development?" *T&D* (July 2009): 58–63.
69. Claudia H. Deutsch, "Volunteering Abroad to Climb at IBM," *The New York Times,* March 26, 2008.
70. William J. Rothwell and H. C. Kazanas, *Improving On-the-Job Training: How to Establish and Operate a Comprehensive OJT Program* (San Francisco: Jossey-Bass, 1994).
71. O'Keefe, "Battle-Tested."
72. Jeanne C. Meister, "The Brave New World of Corporate Education," *The Chronicle of Higher Education* (February 9, 2001): B10; and Meryl Davids Landau, "Corporate Universities Crack Open Their Doors," *The Journal of Business Strategy* (May–June 2000): 18–23.
73. Meister, "The Brave New World of Corporate Education"; Edward E. Gordon, "Bridging the Gap," *Training* (September 2003): 30; and John Byrne, "The Search for the Young and Gifted," *BusinessWeek* (October 4, 1999): 108–116.
74. Doug Bartholomew, "Taking the E-Train," *Industry Week* (June 2005): 34–37; Joel Schettler, "Defense Acquisition University: Weapons of Mass Instruction," *Training* (February 2003): 20–27; Roger O. Crockett, "How P&G Finds—and Keeps—a Prized Workforce, *BusinessWeek* (April 20, 2009): 55.
75. Jim Dow, "Spa Attraction," *People Management* (May 29, 2003): 34–35.
76. See C. H. Deutsch, "A New Kind of Whistle-Blower: Company Refines Principles of Coaching and Teamwork," *The New York Times*, May 7, 1999; and B. Filipczak, "The Executive Coach: Helper or Healer?" *Training* (March 1998): 30–36.
77. Survey by HR consulting firm Watson Wyatt, reported in Kelley Holland, "Performance Reviews: Many Need Improvement," *The New York Times*, September 10, 2006.
78. Walter W. Tornow, "Editor's Note: Introduction to Special Issue on 360-Degree Feedback," *Human Resource Management* 32, no. 2–3 (Summer–Fall 1993): 211–219; and Brian O'Reilly, "360 Feedback Can Change Your Life," *Fortune* (October 17, 1994): 93–100.
79. Jena McGregor, "Job Review in 140 Keystrokes," *BusinessWeek* (March 23 & 30, 2009): 58.
80. This discussion is based on Dick Grote, "Forced Ranking: Behind the Scenes," *Across the Board* (November–December 2002): 40–45; Matthew Boyle, "Performance Reviews: Perilous Curves Ahead," *Fortune* (May 28, 2001): 187–188; Carol Hymowitz, "Ranking Systems Gain Popularity but Have Many Staffers Riled," *The Wall Street Journal*, May 15, 2001; and Kris Frieswick, "Truth and Consequences," *CFO* (June 2001): 56–63."
81. Reported in Jena McGregor, "The Struggle to Measure Performance," *BusinessWeek* (January 9, 2006): 26.
82. Ibid.
83. V. R. Buzzotta, "Improve Your Performance Appraisals," *Management Review* (August 1988): 40–43; and H. J. Bernardin and R. W. Beatty, *Performance Appraisal: Assessing Human Behavior at Work* (Boston: Kent, 1984).
84. Bernardin and Beatty, *Performance Appraisal.*
85. Richard I. Henderson, *Compensation Management: Rewarding Performance*, 4th ed. (Reston, VA: Reston, 1985).
86. L. R. Gomez-Mejia, "Structure and Process Diversification, Compensation Strategy, and Firm Performance," *Strategic Management Journal* 13 (1992): 381–397; and E. Montemayor, "Congruence between Pay Policy and Competitive Strategy in High-Performing Firms," *Journal of Management* 22, no. 6 (1996): 889–908.
87. Renée F. Broderick and George T. Milkovich, "Pay Planning, Organization Strategy, Structure and 'Fit': A Prescriptive Model of Pay," paper presented at the 45th Annual Meeting of the Academy of Management, San Diego (August 1985).
88. E. F. Lawler, III, *Strategic Pay: Aligning Organizational Strategies and Pay Systems* (San Francisco: Jossey-Bass, 1990); and R. J. Greene, "Person-Focused Pay: Should It Replace Job-Based Pay?" *Compensation and Benefits Management* 9, no. 4 (1993): 46–55.
89. L. Wiener, "No New Skills? No Raise," *U.S. News and World Report* (October 26, 1992): 78.
90. Data from Hewitt Associates, Bureau of Labor Statistics, reported in Michelle Conlin and Peter Coy, with Ann Therese Palmer and Gabrielle Saveri, "The Wild New Workforce," *BusinessWeek* (December 6, 1999): 39–44; and Amy Joyce, "The Bonus Question; Some Managers Still Strive to Reward Merit," *The Washington Post,* November 13, 2005.
91. Alan S. Blinder, "Crazy Compensation and the Crisis," *The Wall Street Journal*, May 28, 2009.
92. Robert S. Catapano-Friedman, "Cafeteria Plans: New Menu for the '90s," *Management Review* (November 1991): 25–29.
93. Joe Walker, "Even with a Recovery, Job Perks May Not Return," *The Wall Street Journal Online,* April 5, 2010, http://online.wsj.com/article/SB10001424052702304017404575165854181296256.html (accessed April 10, 2010).

94. Diane Stafford, "Health Plans to Take Some Hits Under New Insurance Reforms," *Buffalo News,* May 30, 2010; John C. Goodman, "Goodbye, Employer-Sponsored Insurance," *The Wall Street Journal,* May 21, 2010.

95. Table A, "Selected Measures of Extended Layoff Activity," in "Extended Mass Layoffs—First Quarter 2010," Bureau of Labor Statistics, U.S. Department of Labor, www.bls.gov/mls/ (accessed June 8, 2010).

96. James R. Morris, Wayne F. Cascio, and Clifford Young, "Downsizing after All These Years: Questions and Answers about Who Did It, How Many Did It, and Who Benefited from It," *Organizational Dynamics* (Winter 1999): 78–86; William McKinley, Carol M. Sanchez, and Allen G. Schick, "Organizational Downsizing: Constraining, Cloning, Learning," *Academy of Management Executive* 9, no. 3 (1995): 32–42; and Brett C. Luthans and Steven M. Sommer, "The Impact of Downsizing on Workplace Attitudes," *Group and Organization Management* 2, no. 1 (1999): 46–70.

97. Effective downsizing techniques are discussed in detail in Bob Nelson, "The Care of the Un-Downsized," *Training and Development* (April 1997): 40–43; Shari Caudron, "Teaching Downsizing Survivors How to Thrive," *Personnel Journal* (January 1996): 38; Joel Brockner, "Managing the Effects of Layoffs on Survivors," *California Management Review* (Winter 1992): 9–28; and Kim S. Cameron, "Strategies for Successful Organizational Downsizing," *Human Resource Management* 33, no. 2 (Summer 1994): 189–211.

98. Society for Human Resource Management 2006 Talent Management Survey Report, reported in "Formal Findings," *The Wall Street Journal*, June 4, 2007.

99. Scott Westcott, "Goodbye and Good Luck," *Inc.* (April 2006): 40–42.

100. Adam Bryant, "There's No Need to Bat .900," (Corner Office column, an interview with John Donahoe), *The New York Times,* April 5, 2009.

101. Nanette Byrnes, "Star Search," *BusinessWeek* (October 10,2005): 68–78.

102. Mike Brewster, "No Exit," *Fast Company* (April 2005): 93.

103. Caminiti, "The Diversity Factor."

104. M. Fine, F. Johnson, and M. S. Ryan, "Cultural Diversity in the Workforce," *Public Personnel Management* 19 (1990): 305–319.

105. Taylor H. Cox, "Managing Cultural Diversity: Implications for Organizational Competitiveness," *Academy of Management Executive* 5, no. 3 (1991): 45–56; and Faye Rice, "How to Make Diversity Pay," *Fortune* (August 8, 1994): 78–86.

106. FreshMinds Work 2.0 Survey, *Management Today* (March, 2008): 42–46.

107. "Projected Growth in Labor Force Participation of Seniors, 2006–2016," U.S. Department of Labor, Bureau of Labor Statistics, July 31, 2008, www.bls.gov/opub/ted/2008/jul/wk4/art04.htm (accessed September 20, 2010).

108. "Spotlight on Statistics: Older Workers," U.S. Department of Labor, Bureau of Labor Statistics, July 2008, www.bls.gov/spotlight/2008/older_workers/ (accessed September 20, 2010).

109. "Employment Projections: 2008–2018 Summary," U.S. Department of Labor, Bureau of Labor Statistics, December 10, 2009, www.bls.gov/news.release/ecopro.nr0.htm (accessed September 21, 2010).

110. Reported in Del Jones, "Stock Soars: 2009 Was Great for Female CEOs' Companies," *USAToday,* December 29, 2009, www.usatoday.com/money/companies/management/2009-12-29-female-ceos-2009-results_N.htm (accessed December 29, 2009).

111. Nanette Byrnes, Roger O. Crockett, and Jena McGregor, "An Historic Succession at Xerox," *BusinessWeek* (June 8, 2009): 18ff.

112. Michael Hoefer, Nancy Rytina, and Bryan C. Baker, "Estimates of the Unauthorized Immigrant Population Residing in the United States: January 2009," Department of Homeland Security, Office of Immigration Statistics (January 2010), www.dhs.gov/xlibrary/assets/statistics/publications/ois_ill_pe_2009.pdf (accessed July 30, 2010).

113. Cynthia Tucker, "Illegal, But Eventually Invaluable," *The Atlanta Journal-Constitution,* June 20, 2010; and Christopher Helman and Susan Radlauer, "Labor Pains," part of a special report on "Immigration," *Forbes* (June 28, 2010): 26–28.

114. Joseph Daniel McCool, "Diversity Pledges Ring Hollow," *Business Week,* February 5, 2008, www.businessweek.com/managing/content/feb2008/ca2008025_080192.htm (accessed March 11, 2008).

115. Carol Hymowitz, "On Diversity, America Isn't Putting Its Money Where Its Mouth Is" (In the Lead column), *The Wall Street Journal*, February 25, 2008.

116. Helen Bloom, "Can the U.S. Export Diversity?" *Across the Board* (March/April 2002): 47–51.

117. Richard L. Daft, *The Leadership Experience* (Cincinnati, OH: Cengage Learning, 2008), p. 340.

118. Sheree R. Curry, "Fighting the Glass Ceiling: Why Asian Americans Don't Have More Positions at the Top," *Chief Executive* (January– February 2006): 30.

119. Winston Fletcher, "The American Way of Work," *Management Today* (August 1, 2005): 46; "What Are Americans Like?" in Stephen P. Robbins and Mary Coulter, *Management*, 8th ed. (Upper Saddle River, NJ: Pearson Prentice Hall, 2005); Exhibit 4-6, as adapted from M. Ernest, ed., *Predeparture Orientation Handbook: For Foreign Students and Scholars Planning to Study in the United States* (Washington, DC: U.S. Information Agency, Bureau of Cultural Affairs, 1984), pp. 103–105; Amanda Bennett, "American Culture Is Often a Puzzle for Foreign Managers in the U.S.," *The Wall Street Journal*, February 12, 1986; "Don't Think Our Way's the Only Way," *The Pryor Report* (February 1988): 9; and B. Wattenberg, "The Attitudes Behind American Exceptionalism," *U.S. News and World Report* (August 7, 1989): 25.

120. Michael L. Wheeler, "Diversity: Business Rationale and Strategies," *The Conference Board,* Report No. 1130-95-RR, 1995, p. 25.

121. Anthony Oshiotse and Richard O'Leary, "Corning Creates an Inclusive Culture to Drive Technology Innovation and Performance," Wiley InterScience, *Global Business and Organizational Excellence*, 26 no. 3 (March/April 2007): 10.

122. "When CEOs Drive Diversity, Everybody Wins," *Chief Executive*, July, 2005, www.chiefexecutive.net/ME2/dirmod.asp?sid=&nm=&type=Publishing&mod=Publications%3A%3AArticle&mid=8F3A7027421841978F18BE895F87F791&tier=4&id=201D3B11B9D4419893E78DDA4B7ACDC8 (accessed September 21, 2010).

123. Taylor Cox, Jr., and Ruby L. Beale, *Developing Competency to Manage Diversity* (San Francisco: Berrett-Koehler Publishers, Inc., 1997), p. 2.

124. Robinson and Dechant, "Building a Business Case for Diversity."

125. Sonie Alleyne and Nicole Marie Richardson, "The 40 Best Companies for Diversity," *Black Enterprise* 36, no. 12 (July 2006): 15.

126. Robinson and Dechant, "Building a Business Case for Diversity."

127. Ibid.

128. Quoted in Carol Hymowitz, "Coaching Men on Mentoring Women Is Ernst & Young Partner's Mission," *The Wall Street Journal Online,* June 14, 2007, http://online.wsj.com/article/SB118167178575132768-search.html (accessed July 9, 2007).

129. Kris Maher, "Lockheed Settles Racial-Discrimination Suit," *The Wall Street Journal,* January 3, 2008.
130. "The Power of Diversity," special advertisement for CareerBuilder.com, *Fortune* (March 17, 2008): 118.
131. Norma Carr-Ruffino, *Managing Diversity: People Skills for a Multicultural Workplace* (Tucson, AZ: Thomson Executive Press, 1996), p. 92.
132. Roy Harris, "The Illusion of Inclusion," *CFO* (May 2001): 42–50.
133. Stephanie N. Mehta, "What Minority Employees Really Want," *Fortune* (June 10, 2000): 181–186.
134. Carr-Ruffino, *Managing Diversity: People Skills for a Multicultural Workplace,* pp. 98–99.
135. Cox and Beale, "Developing Competency to Manage Diversity," p. 79.
136. Ibid., pp. 80–81.
137. Loriann Roberson and Carol T. Kulik, "Stereotype Threat at Work," *Academy of Management Perspectives* 21, no. 2 (May 2007): 25–27.
138. Ibid., 26.
139. Robert Doktor, Rosalie Tung, and Mary Ann von Glinow, "Future Directions for Management Theory Development," *Academy of Management Review* 16 (1991): 362–365; and Mary Munter, "Cross-Cultural Communication for Managers," *Business Horizons* (May–June 1993): 69–78.
140. Renee Blank and Sandra Slipp, "The White Male: An Endangered Species?" *Management Review* (September 1994): 27–32; Michael S. Kimmel, "What Do Men Want?" *Harvard Business Review* (November–December 1993): 50–63; and Sharon Nelton, "Nurturing Diversity," *Nation's Business* (June 1995): 25–27.
141. Alice H. Eagly and Linda L. Carli, "Leadership," *Harvard Business Review* (September, 2007): 64.
142. Steven Greenhouse, "Report Warned Wal-Mart of Risks before Bias Suit," *The New York Times,* June 3, 2010, www.nytimes.com/2010/06/04/business/04lawsuit.html (accessed June 4, 2010).
143. Sheila Wellington, Marcia Brumit Kropf, and Paulette R. Gerkovich, "What's Holding Women Back?" *Harvard Business Review* (June 2003): 18–19.
144. Julie Amparano Lopez, "Study Says Women Face Glass Walls As Well As Ceilings," *The Wall Street Journal,* March 3, 1992; Ida L. Castro, "Q: Should Women Be Worried about the Glass Ceiling in the Workplace?" *Insight* (February 10, 1997): 24–27; Debra E. Meyerson and Joyce K. Fletcher, "A Modest Manifesto for Shattering the Glass Ceiling," *Harvard Business Review* (January– February 2000): 127–136; Wellington et al., "What's Holding Women Back?"; and Annie Finnigan, "Different Strokes," *Working Woman* (April 2001): 42–48.
145. Catalyst survey results reported in Jason Forsythe, "Winning with Diversity," *The New York Times Magazine* (March 28, 2004): 65–72.
146. Eagly and Carli, "Leadership."
147. Jory Des Jardins, "I Am Woman (I Think)," *Fast Company* (May 2005): 25–26; Lisa Belkin, "The Opt-Out Revolution," *The New York Times Magazine* (October 26, 2003): 43–47, 58; Finnigan, "Different Strokes"; and Meyerson and Fletcher, "A Modest Manifesto for Shattering the Glass Ceiling."
148. Statistics from the U.S. Census Bureau, Current Population Survey, 2004 Annual Social and Economic Supplement, as reported in "2003 Median Annual Earnings by Race and Sex," http://www .infoplease.com/ipa/A0197814 .html; and "The Economics of Gender and Race: Examining the Wage Gap in the United States," The Feminist Majority Foundation Choices Campus Campaign, http://www.feministcampus.org.
149. Cliff Edwards, "Coming Out in Corporate America," *BusinessWeek* (December 15, 2003): 64–72; Belle Rose Ragins, John M. Cornwell, and Janice S. Miller, "Heterosexism in the Workplace: Do Race and Gender Matter?" *Group & Organization Management* 28, no. 1 (March 2003): 45–74.
150. Sylvia Ann Hewlett and Carolyn Buck Luce, "Off-Ramps and On-Ramps: Keeping Talented Women on the Road to Success," *Harvard Business Review* (March 2005): 43–54.
151. Belkin, "The Opt-Out Revolution."
152. Jennifer N. Demirdjian, "Mentors Help New Moms Transition Back to Work at Pricewaterhouse-Coopers," *Global Business and Organizational Excellence* (January/February, 2009): 28.
153. C. J. Prince, "Media Myths: The Truth about the Opt-Out Hype," *NAFE Magazine* (Second Quarter 2004): 14–18; Patricia Sellers, "Power: Do Women Really Want It?" *Fortune* (October 13, 2003): 80–100.
154. Jia Lynn Yang, "Goodbye to All That," *Fortune* (November 14, 2005): 169–170.
155. Sheila Wellington et al. "What's Holding Women Back?"
156. The Leader's Edge/Executive Women Research 2002 survey, reported in "Why Women Leave," *Executive Female* (Summer 2003): 4.
157. Barbara Reinhold, "Smashing Glass Ceilings: Why Women Still Find It Tough to Advance to the Executive Suite," *Journal of Organizational Excellence* (Summer 2005): 43–55; Des Jardins, "I Am Woman (I Think)"; and Alice H. Eagly and Linda L. Carli, "The Female Leadership Advantage: An Evaluation of the Evidence," *The Leadership Quarterly* 14 (2003): 807–834.
158. Claudia H. Deutsch, "Behind the Exodus of Executive Women: Boredom," *USA Today,* May 2, 2005.
159. Eagly and Carli, "The Female Leadership Advantage"; Reinhold, "Smashing Glass Ceilings"; Sally Helgesen, *The Female Advantage: Women's Ways of Leadership* (New York: Doubleday Currency, 1990); Rochelle Sharpe, "As Leaders, Women Rule: New Studies Find that Female Managers Outshine Their Male Counterparts in Almost Every Measure," *Business week* (November 20, 2000): 5ff; and Del Jones, "2003: Year of the Woman Among the Fortune 500?" *USAToday*, December 30, 2003.
160. Tamar Lewin, "At Colleges, Women Are Leaving Men in the Dust," *The New York Times Online,* July 9, 2006, www.nytimes.com/2006/07/09/education/09college.html?_r=1&scp=1&sq=at%20 colleges,%20women%20are%20leaving%20men%20in%20the%20 dust&st=cse&oref=slogin (accessed March 13, 2008).
161. Michelle Conlin, "The New Gender Gap," and Michelle Conlin, "A Better Education Equals Higher Pay," *BusinessWeek* (May 26, 2003): 74–82.
162. Quoted in Conlin, "The New Gender Gap."
163. Kathryn M. Bartol, David C. Martin, and Julie A. Kromkowski, "Leadership and the Glass Ceiling: Gender and Ethnic Group Influences on Leader Behaviors at Middle and Executive Managerial Levels," *The Journal of Leadership and Organizational Studies* 9, no. 3 (2003): 8–19; Bernard M. Bass and Bruce J. Avolio, "Shatter the Glass Ceiling: Women May Make Better Managers," *Human Resource Management* 33, no. 4 (Winter 1994): 549–560; and Sharpe, "As Leaders, Women Rule."
164. Dwight D. Frink, Robert K. Robinson, Brian Reithel, Michelle M. Arthur, Anthony P. Ammeter, Gerald R. Ferris, David M. Kaplan, and Hubert S. Morrisette, "Gender Demography and Organization Performance: A Two-Study Investigation with Convergence," *Group & Organization Management* 28, no. 1

(March 2003): 127–147; Catalyst research project cited in Reinhold, "Smashing Glass Ceilings."

165. Mercedes Martin and Billy Vaughn "Cultural & Global Competence; Cultural Competence: The Nuts & Bolts of Diversity & Inclusion," *Strategic Diversity & Inclusion Management* (2007): 31–36.

166. Ann M. Morrison, *The New Leaders: Guidelines on Leadership Diversity in America* (San Francisco: Jossey-Bass Publishers, 1992), p. 235.

167. Wheeler, "Diversity: Business and Strategies."

168. Alleyne and Richardson, "The 40 Best Companies for Diversity," 100.

169. Morrison, "*The New Leaders*."

170. Susan Adams, "Making a Female-Friendly Workplace," *Forbes*, April 26, 2010, http://www.forbes.com/forbes/2010/0426/human-capital-deloitte-antoinette-leatherberry-womens-initiative-work.html (accessed July 5, 2010); Melanie Trottman, "A Helping Hand," *The Wall Street Journal*, November 14, 2005; and Lahle Wolfe, "Deloitte's Network for Women Bridges the Gender Gap by Helping Men, Too," *About.com: Women in Business*, http://womeninbusiness.about .com/od/networking/a/deloitte-networ.htm (accessed July 8, 2010).

171. Finnigan, "Different Strokes."

172. "Diversity in an Affiliated Company," cited in Vanessa J. Weaver, "Winning with Diversity," *Business Week* (September 10, 2001).

173. Trottman, "A Helping Hand"; B. Ragins, "Barriers to Mentoring: The Female Manager's Dilemma," *Human Relations* 42, no. 1 (1989): 1–22; and Belle Rose Ragins, Bickley Townsend, and Mary Mattis, "Gender Gap in the Executive Suite: CEOs and Female Executives Report on Breaking the Glass Ceiling," *Academy of Management Executive* 12, no. 1 (1998): 28–42.

174. Trottman, "A Helping Hand."

175. David A. Thomas, "The Truth about Mentoring Minorities—Race Matters," *Harvard Business Review* (April 2001): 99–107.

176. Mary Zey, "A Mentor for All," *Personnel Journal* (January 1988): 46–51.

177. Joanne Sujansky, "Lead a Multi-Generational Workforce," *The Business Journal of Tri-Cities, Tennessee–Virginia* (February 2004): 21–23.

178. "Keeping Your Edge: Managing a Diverse Corporate Culture," special advertising section, *Fortune* (June 3, 2001).

179. Kimberly L. Allers, "Won't It Be Grand When We Don't Need Diversity Lists?" *Fortune* (August 22, 2005): 101.

180. J. Black and M. Mendenhall, "Cross-Cultural Training Effectiveness: A Review and a Theoretical Framework for Future Research," *Academy of Management Review* 15 (1990): 113–136.

181. Laura Egodigwe, "Back to Class," *The Wall Street Journal*, November 14, 2005.

182. Lee Smith, "Closing the Gap," *Fortune* (November 14, 2005): 211–218.

183. "Sexual Harassment: Vanderbilt University Policy" (Nashville, TN: Vanderbilt University, 1993).

184. Rachel Thompson, "Sexual Harassment: It Doesn't Go with the Territory," *Horizons* 15, no. 3 (Winter 2002): 22–26.

185. Statistics reported in Jim Mulligan and Norman Foy, "Not in My Company: Preventing Sexual Harassment," *Industrial Management* (September/October 2003): 26–29; also see *EEOC Charge Complaints*, http://www.eeoc.gov.

186. Jack Corcoran, "Of Nice and Men," *Success* (June 1998): 65–67.

187. Barbara Carton, "At Jenny Craig, Men Are Ones Who Claim Sex Discrimination," *The Wall Street Journal*, November 29, 1994.

188. "Impact of Diversity Initiatives on the Bottom Line: A SHRM Survey of the *Fortune* 1000," in "Keeping Your Edge: Managing a Diverse Corporate Culture," special advertising section produced in association with the Society for Human Resource Management, *Fortune* (June 3, 2001): S12–S14.

189. Joseph J. Distefano and Martha L. Maznevski, "Creating Value with Diverse Teams in Global Management," *Organizational Dynamics* 29, no. 1 (Summer 2000): 45–63; and Finnigan, "Different Strokes."

190. W. E. Watson, K. Kumar, and L. K. Michaelsen, "Cultural Diversity's Impact on Interaction Process and Performance: Comparing Homogeneous and Diverse Task Groups," *Academy of Management Journal* 36 (1993): 590–602; Robinson and Dechant, "Building a Business Case for Diversity"; and D. A. Thomas and R. J. Ely, "Making Differences Matter: A New Paradigm for Managing Diversity," *Harvard Business Review* (September–October 1996): 79–90.

191. See Distefano and Maznevski, "Creating Value with Diverse Teams" for a discussion of the advantages of multicultural teams.

192. W.E. Watson et al., "Cultural Diversity's Impact on Interaction Process and Performance."

193. Distefano and Maznevski, "Creating Value with Diverse Teams."

194. This definition and discussion is based on Raymond A. Friedman, "Employee Network Groups: Self-Help Strategy for Women and Minorities," *Performance Improvement Quarterly* 12, no. 1 (1999): 148–163.

195. Raymond A. Friedman and Brooks Holtom, "The Effects of Network Groups on Minority Employee Turnover Intentions," *Human Resource Management* 41, no. 4 (Winter 2002): 405–421.

196. Diane Brady and Jena McGregor, "What Works in Women's Networks," *BusinessWeek* (June 18, 2007): 58.

197. Elizabeth Wasserman, "A Race for Profits," *MBA Jungle* (March–April 2003): 40–41.

198. Finnigan, "Different Strokes."

199. Raymond A. Friedman, Melinda Kane, and Daniel B. Cornfield, "Social Support and Career Optimism: Examining the Effectiveness of Network Groups among Black Managers," *Human Relations* 51, no. 9 (1998): 1155–1177.

200. Based on Rob Johnson, "30 Muslim Workers Fired for Praying on Job at Dell," *The Tennessean*, March 10, 2005; Anayat Durrani, "Religious Accommodation for Muslim Employees," *Workforce.com*, www.workforce.com/archive/feature/religious-accommodation-muslim-employees/index.php (accessed September 21, 2010); "Questions and Answers about Employer Responsibilities Concerning the Employment of Muslims, Arabs, South Asians, and Sikhs," The U.S. Equal Employment Opportunity Commission, http://www.eeoc .gov/facts/backlash-employer.html (accessed September 20, 2010); and "2006 Household Appliance Industry Outlook," U.S. Department of Commerce, International Trade Administration, www.ita .doc.gov/td/ocg/outlook06_appliances.pdf (accessed September 21, 2010).

201. Based on Leigh Buchanan, "What's Wrong with This Picture? Nothing!" Inc. Magazine (June 2007): 98–105.

PART 5

Leading

5

Wikis, Facebook, and Twitter began as social media fads, but they have since found a place in corporate boardrooms, marketing campaigns, and team collaboration toolboxes. Given their advanced communication features, it's not surprising that social media often double as powerful tools for business.

If current demand for mobile devices is any indication, the next trend in digital communication may take the form of an app. So who's cooking up the next killer app for social media? Mark Zuckerberg? Andrew Mason? Would you believe … Ashton?

Yes, Hollywood hipster Ashton Kutcher, one of the most "followed" celebrities on Twitter, has teamed up with Twitter-app designer UberMedia to revolutionize social surfing. Ashton wants to help people navigate the oceans of social data streaming across the Internet, and he intends to be their guide.

Kutcher's new app, A.Plus, begins with familiar Twitter features. But it proceeds to offer eight content channels, a three-pane layout, and a links previewer for easy browsing. With A.Plus, users receive Kutcher's daily tweet stream and a channel selector that organizes Kutcher-chosen content by topic.

The goal of A.Plus is to enable fans to see what Ashton finds interesting on the Web and to follow along in real time. The interface could become standard for sorting large amounts of social data, both in noncommercial and commercial settings.

Considering Kutcher's 7 million Twitter followers, UberMedia has good reason to believe A.Plus will be an instant hit. CEO Bill Gross said the firm was "excited to help Ashton create his very own Twitter client." Kutcher told the press his social media surfing device would "enhance the discovery process of the real-time Web."

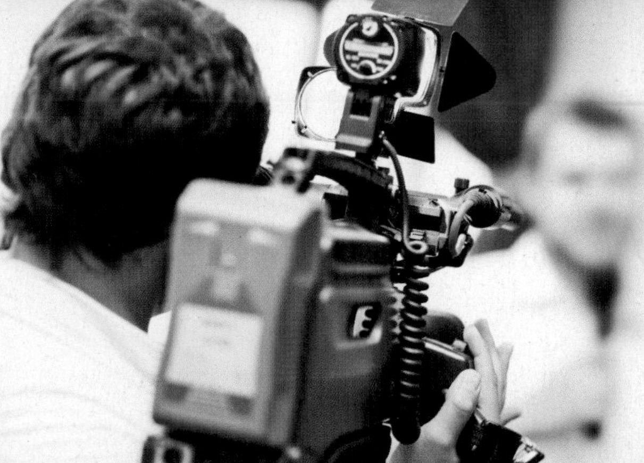

Top Right: Credit to come Center: Haywiremedia/Shutterstock.com Bottom Right: Perov Stanislav/Shutterstock.com

Chapter Outline

Top Left: © Robnroll, Shutterstock   Top Right: © James Steidl, Shutterstock

Understanding Individual Behavior

Learning Outcomes

After studying this chapter, you should be able to:

1. Define attitudes and explain their relationship to personality, perception, and behavior.
2. Discuss the importance of work-related attitudes.
3. Define major personality traits and describe how personality can influence workplace attitudes and behaviors.
4. Identify positive and negative emotions and describe how emotions affect behavior.
5. Define the four components of emotional intelligence and explain why they are important for today's managers.
6. Explain how people learn in general and in terms of individual learning styles.
7. Discuss the effects of stress and identify ways individuals and organizations can manage stress to improve employee health, satisfaction, and productivity.

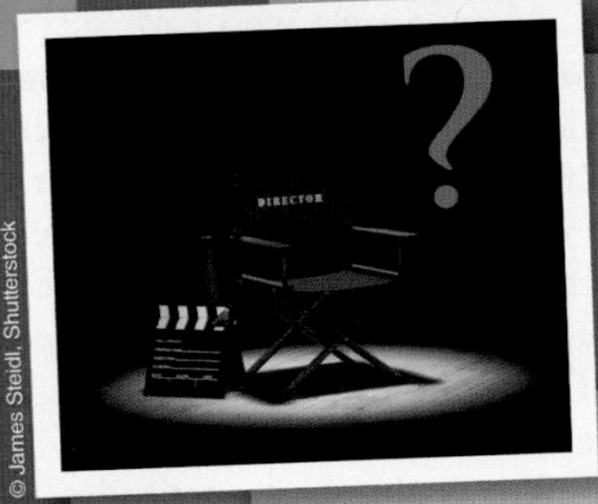

© James Steidl, Shutterstock

Are You Ready to Be a Manager?

Please circle your opinion below each of the following statements.

1 **If I try something and it fails, I don't give up, but instead keep trying.**

Mostly True   Mostly False

(See page 396, Self-Efficacy.)

2 **Any job or work I take on, I always try to find ways to enjoy the work.**

Mostly True   Mostly False

(See page 400, Job Satisfaction.)

3 **Everyone has prejudices and stereotypes, and I try to become aware of my own, so that they don't get in the way of positive relationships.**

Mostly True   Mostly False

(See page 404, Perceptual Distortions.)

4 **I am aware of my personality strengths and I try not to judge people on their "goodness" as being similar to my own personality.**

Mostly True   Mostly False

(See page 408, Personality and Behavior.)

5 **When I go through tough times, I try to understand what I can learn from the difficulties.**

Mostly True   Mostly False

(See page 421, Learning Styles.)

When a small London publishing house released a book about an 11-year-old wizard on June 26, 1997, no one had any idea it would launch a global phenomenon and create the world's first billionaire author. After all, J. K. Rowling's manuscript for *Harry Potter and the Philosopher's Stone* had been rejected by 12 publishers before Bloomsbury bought it for the equivalent of US$4,000. A decade or so and six books later, the Harry Potter series had been translated into 67 languages and sold more than 400 million copies. In her commencement speech to the 2008 graduating class at Harvard University, Rowling recounted how setbacks and rejection had made her stronger.[1]

Many people who have accomplished great outcomes, like Rowling, give credit to their previous failures for driving them to succeed. At the same time, there are many talented individuals who experience one defeat and never try again.[2] What makes the difference? Psychologists suggest it comes down to a characteristic called *self-efficacy*. It is one of the many ways in which individuals differ, along with their personality traits, attitudes, emotions, and values. **Self-efficacy** is an individual's strong belief that he or she can successfully accomplish a specific task or outcome.[3] Self-efficacy is one dimension of **self-confidence**, which refers to general assurance in one's own ideas, judgment, and capabilities.

Personality traits, attitudes, values, and characteristics such as self-confidence and self-efficacy influence how people behave, including how they handle work situations and relate to others. Managers' individual characteristics can profoundly affect the workplace and influence employee motivation, morale, and job performance. Equally important is managers' ability to understand others. Insight into why people behave the way they do is a part of good management. People bring their individual differences to work each day, and these differences influence how they interpret assignments, whether they like to be told what to do, how they handle challenges, and how they interact with others.

Differences among people can make a manager's job exceedingly challenging, which means all managers need to understand the basic principles of organizational behavior—that is, the way individuals and groups tend to act in organizations. By increasing their understanding of individual differences, managers can learn how to get the best out of each employee and more effectively lead people through workplace challenges. This chapter provides a broad overview of how individuals differ along the dimensions of attitudes, personality, perception, emotions, learning, and responses to stress.

Organizational Behavior

Organizational behavior, commonly called OB, is an interdisciplinary field dedicated to the study of human attitudes, behavior, and performance in organizations. OB draws concepts from many disciplines, including psychology, sociology, cultural anthropology, industrial engineering, economics, ethics, and vocational counseling, as well as the discipline of management. The concepts and principles of organizational behavior are important to managers because in every organization human beings ultimately make the decisions that determine how the organization acquires and uses resources. Those people may cooperate with, compete with, support, or undermine one another. Their beliefs and feelings about themselves, their coworkers, and the organization shape what they do and how well they do it. People can distract the organization from its strategy by engaging in conflict and misunderstandings, or they can pool their diverse talents and perspectives to accomplish much more as a group than they could ever do as individuals.

New Manager Self-Test

Are You Self-Confident?

Self-confidence is the foundation for many important behaviors of a new manager. To learn something about your level of self-confidence, answer the following questions. Please answer whether each item is Mostly True or Mostly False for you.

	MOSTLY TRUE <<<	>>> MOSTLY FALSE
1. I have lots of confidence in my decisions.	_____	_____
2. I would like to change some things about myself.	_____	_____
3. I am satisfied with my appearance and personality.	_____	_____
4. I would be nervous about meeting important people.	_____	_____
5. I come across as a positive person.	_____	_____
6. I sometimes think of myself as a failure.	_____	_____
7. I am able to do things as well as most people.	_____	_____
8. I find it difficult to believe nice things someone says about me.	_____	_____

See It Online

Scoring and Interpretation: Many good things come from self-confidence. How self-confident are you? Give yourself 1 point for each *odd-numbered* item above marked as Mostly True and 1 point for each *even-numbered* item marked Mostly False. If you scored 3 or less, your self-confidence may not be very high. You might want to practice new behavior in problematic areas to develop greater confidence. A score of 6 or above suggests a high level of self-confidence and a solid foundation on which to begin your career as a new manager.

If a new manager lacks self-confidence, he or she is more likely to avoid difficult decisions and confrontations and may tend to overcontrol subordinates, which is called micromanaging. A lack of self-confidence also leads to less sharing of information and less time hiring and developing capable people. Self-confident managers, by contrast, can more easily delegate responsibility, take risks, give credit to others, confront problems, and assert themselves for the good of their team.

Organizational citizenship refers to the tendency of people to help one another and put in extra effort that goes beyond job requirements to contribute to the organization's success. An employee demonstrates organizational citizenship by being helpful to coworkers and customers, doing extra work when necessary, and looking for ways to improve products and procedures. These behaviors enhance the organization's performance and contribute to positive relationships both within the organization and with customers. Managers can encourage organizational citizenship by applying their knowledge of human behavior, such as selecting people with positive attitudes, managing different personalities, putting people in jobs where they can thrive, and enabling employees to cope with and learn from workplace challenges.[4]

- All managers need to understand basic principles of **organizational behavior (OB)**, an interdisciplinary field dedicated to the study of how individuals and groups tend to act in organizations.
- OB involves the study of human attitudes, personality, emotions, and other individual characteristics and how these influence behavior and performance.
- **Self-efficacy** is an individual's strong belief that he or she can successfully accomplish a specific task or outcome.
- J. K. Rowling demonstrated self-efficacy with her belief that she could successfully publish her first book about Harry Potter despite repeated rejections.
- Self-efficacy is related to **self-confidence**, which means general assurance in one's own ideas, judgment, and capabilities.
- **Organizational citizenship** refers to work behavior that goes beyond job requirements and contributes as needed to the organization's success.

Attitudes

Most students have probably heard the expression that someone "has an attitude problem," which means some consistent quality about the person affects his or her behavior in a negative way. An employee with an attitude problem might be hard to get along with, might constantly gripe and cause problems, and might persistently resist new ideas. We all seem to know intuitively what an attitude is, but we do not consciously think about how strongly attitudes affect our behavior. Defined formally, an **attitude** is an evaluation—either positive or negative—that predisposes a person to act in a certain way. Understanding employee attitudes is important to managers because attitudes determine how people perceive the work environment, interact with others, and behave on the job. Emerging research is revealing the importance of positive attitudes to both individual and organizational success. For example, studies have found that the characteristic most common to top executives is an optimistic attitude. People rise to the top because they have the ability to see opportunities where others see problems and can instill in others a sense of hope and possibility for the future.[5]

Managers strive to develop and reinforce positive attitudes among all employees, because happy, positive people are healthier, more effective, and more productive.[6] Some companies, such as David's Bridal, the nation's largest bridal store chain, are applying scientific research to improve employee attitudes—and sales performance, as you'll see in the Spotlight on Skills titled David's Bridal.

As the Spotlight on Skills shows, sometimes negative attitudes can result from characteristics of the job such as a high stress level, but managers can find ways to help people have better attitudes. Managers should pay attention to negative attitudes because they can be both the result of underlying problems in the workplace as well as a contributor to forthcoming problems.[7]

Components of Attitudes

One important step for managers is recognizing and understanding the *components* of attitudes, which is particularly important when attempting to change attitudes.

Behavioral scientists consider attitudes to have three components: cognitions (thoughts), affect (feelings), and behavior.[8] The cognitive component of an attitude includes the beliefs, opinions, and information the person has about the object of the attitude, such as knowledge of what a job entails and opinions about personal abilities. The affective component is the person's emotions or feelings about the object of the attitude, such as enjoying or hating

SPOTLIGHT ON SKILLS

David's Bridal

Planning a wedding can be one of the most joyful experiences in a woman's life—and one of the most nerve-wracking. The salespeople at David's Bridal, a 267-store chain owned by Federated Department Stores, bear the brunt of these intense emotions. For many, dealing with those emotions can be overwhelming and exhausting, translating into negative attitudes and impatience with already stressed customers.

Managers turned to new research on happiness to help employees cope and develop more positive attitudes. In a pilot training program based on the work of psychologist Martin Seligman, salespeople were taught how to feel more cheerful with techniques such as "emotion regulation," "impulse control," and "learned optimism." These techniques enable salespeople to be calm and centered with harried, indecisive brides-to-be, which helps customers stay calm and centered as well. The constructive behavior translates into better sales, meaning employees make better commissions, which in turn contributes to more positive attitudes toward the job.

Jeffrey Zaslow, "Pursuits: Happiness, Inc.," *The Wall Street Journal*, March 18, 2006.

a job. The behavioral component of an attitude is the person's intention to behave toward the object of the attitude in a certain way. Exhibit 10.1 illustrates the three components of a positive attitude toward one's job. The cognitive element is the conscious thought that "my job is interesting and challenging." The affective element is the feeling that "I love this

EXHIBIT 10.1

Components of an Attitude

Cognitive...thoughts...
"My job is interesting."
Affective...feelings...
"I love my job."
Behavioral...intention to act...
"I'm going to get to work early with a smile on my face."
Attitude: Job Satisfaction

job." These elements, in turn, are related to the behavioral component—an employee might arrive at work early because he or she is happy with the job.

The emotional (affective) component is often the stronger factor in affecting behavior, so managers should be aware of situations that involve strong feelings. However, as a general rule, changing just one component—cognitions, affect, or behavior—can contribute to an overall change in attitude. Suppose a manager concludes that some employees have the attitude that the manager should make all the decisions affecting the department, but the manager prefers that employees assume more decision-making responsibility. To change the underlying attitude, the manager would consider whether to educate employees about the areas in which they can make good decisions (changing the cognitive component); build enthusiasm with pep talks about the satisfaction of employee empowerment (changing the affective component); or simply insist that employees make their own decisions (behavioral component), with the expectation that, once they experience the advantages of decision-making authority, they will begin to like it.

High-Performance Work Attitudes

The attitudes of most interest to managers are those related to work, especially attitudes that influence how well people perform on the job. Two attitudes that might relate to high performance are satisfaction with one's job and commitment to the organization.

Job Satisfaction A positive attitude toward one's job is called **job satisfaction**. In general, people experience this attitude when their work matches their needs and interests, when working conditions and rewards (such as pay) are satisfactory, when they like their coworkers, and when they have positive relationships with supervisors. You can take the quiz in Exhibit 10.2 to better understand some of the factors that contribute to job satisfaction. Gary and Ruth Namie believe workplace bullying is responsible for lower job satisfaction, as shown in the Spotlight on Skills titled Workplace Bullying and Trauma Institute.

EXHIBIT 10.2

Rate Your Job Satisfaction

Think of a job—either a current or previous job—that was important to you, and then answer the following questions with respect to how satisfied you were with that job. Please answer the six questions with a number 1–5 that reflects the extent of your satisfaction.

1 = Very dissatisfied	3 = Neutral	5 = Very satisfied
2 = Dissatisfied	4 = Satisfied	

1. Overall, how satisfied are you with your job?	1	2	3	4	5
2. How satisfied are you with the opportunities to learn new things?	1	2	3	4	5
3. How satisfied are you with your boss?	1	2	3	4	5
4. How satisfied are you with the people in your work group?	1	2	3	4	5
5. How satisfied are you with the amount of pay you receive?	1	2	3	4	5
6. How satisfied are you with the advancement you are making in the organization?	1	2	3	4	5

Scoring and Interpretation: Add up your responses to the six questions to obtain your total score: ________. The questions represent various aspects of satisfaction that an employee may experience on a job. If your score is 24 or above, you probably feel satisfied with the job. If your score is 12 or below, you probably do not feel satisfied. What is your level of performance in your job, and is your performance related to your level of satisfaction?

SOURCES: These questions were adapted from Daniel R. Denison, *Corporate Culture and Organizational Effectiveness* (New York: John Wiley, 1990); and John D. Cook, Susan J. Hepworth, Toby D. Wall, and Peter B. Warr, *The Experience of Work: A Compendium and Review of 249 Measures and their Use* (San Diego, CA: Academic Press, 1981).

SPOTLIGHT ON SKILLS

Workplace Bullying and Trauma Institute

When Dr. Ruth Namie found herself with a debilitating boss at the Health Maintenance Organization she worked at in 1995, she decided to take action. "Sheila" tormented Ruth, using typical bullying tactics of berating her in front of colleagues, being disruptive to her work, starting rumors, and screaming. Attorneys told her there was no legislation to protect her, so Dr. Ruth and her husband, University of Southern California management professor Gary Namie, took this on as their white whale. They started the Workplace Bullying and Trauma Institute and eventually helped El Paso, Texas, declare October 17, 2011, as the first ever Freedom from Workplace Bullies Week. As such, Gary has become the champion of employees worn down by their boss's hysteria.

© Bata Zivanovic, Shutterstock

People are getting interested. The Conference Board says that workplace satisfaction has gone from 61 percent in 1987 to 41 percent in 2010, and the Namies think increased bullying is part of the reason. Gary quit academia and spends his time trying to rid the workplace of bullies. The fact that so many people are signing up for his programs shows they are hitting a need. It seems lots of people want to get rid of bullies.

SOURCE: Spencer Morgan, "The Office Bully Mogul," *Bloomberg Businessweek*, (November1–7, 2010, pp. 1–3.

Many managers believe job satisfaction is important because they think satisfied employees will do better work. In fact, research shows that the link between satisfaction and performance is generally small and is influenced by other factors.[9] For example, the importance of satisfaction varies according to the amount of control the employee has; an employee doing routine tasks may produce about the same output no matter how he or she feels about the job. Managers of today's knowledge workers, however, often rely on job satisfaction to keep motivation and enthusiasm high. They can't afford to lose talented, highly skilled employees. Regrettably, a 2009 survey by the Conference Board found that only 45 percent of U.S. employees say they are satisfied at work, the lowest satisfaction level in the survey's history.[10]

Managers create the environment that determines whether employees have positive or negative attitudes toward their jobs.[11] A related attitude is organizational commitment.

Organizational Commitment **Organizational commitment** refers to an employee's loyalty to and engagement with the organization. An employee with a high degree of organizational commitment is likely to say *we* when talking about the company. Such a person likes being a part of the organization and tries to contribute to its success. This attitude is illustrated by an incident at the A.W. Chesterton Company, a manufacturer of mechanical seals and pumps. When two Chesterton pumps that supply water on Navy ship *USS John F. Kennedy* failed on a Saturday night just before the ship's

Bill Pugliano/Getty Images

ConceptConnection

Just how has the recession affected **job satisfaction**? It depends on which pollsters you ask. On one hand, the 2009 Conference Board survey reported only 45 percent of those surveyed were satisfied with their work, the lowest level in 20 years. But the 2009 Yahoo! Hot Jobs Survey found that job satisfaction was "solid," with 83 percent reporting that they were "very satisfied" or "satisfied," up from 77 percent at the recession's start. Liz Bywater, Bywater Consulting Group president, speculated that with unemployment hovering around 10 percent, many employees, such as this GM assembly plant worker, "are just glad to have a job."

scheduled departure, the team that produces the seals swung into action. Two members worked through the night to make new seals and deliver them to be installed before the ship left port.[12]

Most managers want to enjoy the benefits of loyal, committed employees, including low turnover and employee willingness to do more than the job's basic requirements. Results of a Towers Perrin study of more than 360,000 employees from 40 companies around the world indicate that companies with highly committed employees perform better.[13] Alarmingly, though, another recent survey suggests that commitment levels around the world are relatively low. Only one-fifth of the respondents were categorized as fully engaged, that is, reflecting a high level of commitment. In the United States, the percentage classified as fully engaged was 29 percent, compared to 54 percent in Mexico, 37 in percent in Brazil, and 36 percent in India. Countries where employees reflect similar or lower levels of commitment than the United States include Canada at 23 percent, Spain at 19 percent, Germany at 17 percent, China at 16 percent, the United Kingdom at 14 percent, France at 12 percent, and Japan at only 3 percent.[14]

Trust in management decisions and integrity is one important component of organizational commitment.[15] Unfortunately, in recent years many employees in the United States have lost that trust. Only 20 percent of people surveyed by Leadership IQ, a leadership training organization, said they strongly trust their top management, with 36 percent reporting a moderate trust level and 44 percent saying they either do not trust or strongly distrust their bosses.[16] In addition, the survey confirms that trust relates to organizational commitment. According to the study, about 32 percent of an employee's desire to stay with a company or leave depends on trust in management. Sadly, most of us don't need a poll to tell us that the level of trust in business and government leaders is dismal. From the Enron debacle to the scads of Wall Street managers and traders rewarded for unethical behavior with large bonuses, there are numerous reasons why people mistrust organizational leadership.

Managers can promote stronger organizational commitment by being honest and trustworthy in their business dealings, keeping employees informed, giving them a say in decisions, providing the necessary training and other resources that enable them to succeed, treating them fairly, and offering rewards they value. "People in leadership positions simply have not done a good job of earning trust," says Doug Harward, president of Training Industry, Inc. "Employees have a right to expect that their managers are trustworthy and that they will create stable organizations. Too many of our leaders have violated that trust."[17]

Conflicts among Attitudes

Sometimes a person may discover that his or her own attitudes conflict with one another or are not reflected in behavior. For example, a person's high level of organizational commitment might conflict with a commitment to family members. If employees routinely work evenings and weekends, their long hours and dedication to the job might conflict with their belief that family ties are important. This conflict can create a state of **cognitive dissonance**, a psychological discomfort that occurs when individuals recognize inconsistencies in their own attitudes and behaviors.[18] The theory of cognitive dissonance, developed by social psychologist Leon Festinger in the 1950s, says that people want to behave in accordance with their attitudes and usually will take corrective action to alleviate the dissonance and achieve balance.

In the case of working overtime, people who can control their hours might restructure responsibilities so that they have time for both work and family. In contrast, those who are unable to restructure workloads might develop an unfavorable attitude toward the employer, reducing their organizational commitment. They might resolve their dissonance by saying they would like to spend more time with their kids but their unreasonable employer demands that they work too many hours.

- An **attitude** is a cognitive and affective evaluation that predisposes a person to act in a certain way.
- Attitudes have a cognitive component, an affective component, and a behavioral component.
- David's Bridal, a chain of bridal stores, trains employees in how to keep a positive attitude.
- A positive attitude toward one's job is called **job satisfaction**.
- Some surveys surveys suggest that job satisfaction levels are at an all-time low.
- **Organizational commitment** refers to loyalty to and engagement with one's work organization.
- A survey found that 32 percent of an employee's desire to stay with a company or leave depends on the employee's trust in management.
- **Cognitive dissonance** is a psychological discomfort that occurs when two attitudes or an attitude and a behavior are perceived to be in conflict.

Perception

Another critical aspect of understanding behavior is perception. **Perception** is the cognitive process people use to make sense out of the environment by selecting, organizing, and interpreting information from the environment. Because of individual differences in attitudes, personality, values, interests, and so forth, people often "see" the same thing in different ways. A class that is boring to one student might be fascinating to another. One student might perceive an assignment to be challenging and stimulating, whereas another might find it a silly waste of time.

We can think of perception as a step-by-step process, as shown in Exhibit 10.3. First, we observe information (sensory data) from the environment through our senses: taste, smell, hearing, sight, and touch. Next, our mind screens the data and will select only the items we will process further. Third, we organize the selected data into meaningful patterns for interpretation and response. Most differences in perception among people at work are related to how they select and organize sensory data. You can experience differences in perceptual organization by looking at the visuals in Exhibit 10.4. What do you see in part a of Exhibit 10.4? Most people see this as a dog, but others see only a series of unrelated ink blots. Some people will see the figure in part b as a beautiful young woman, whereas others will see an old one. Now look at part c. How many blocks do you see—six or seven? Some people have to turn the figure upside down before they can see seven blocks. These visuals illustrate how complex perception is.

EXHIBIT 

The Perception Process

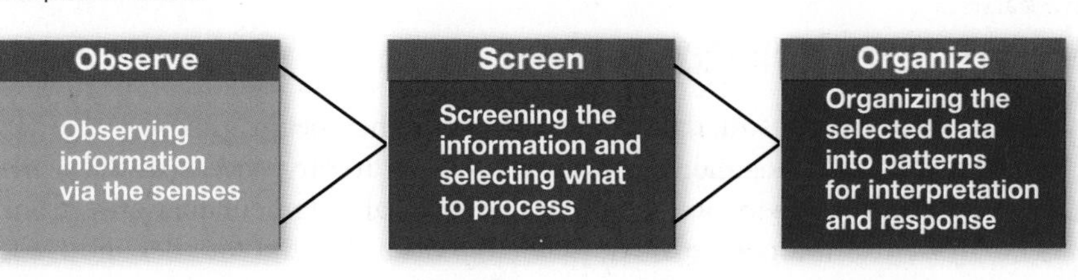

EXHIBIT 10.4
Perception—What Do You See?

a. Do you see the dog?

b. Old woman or young woman?

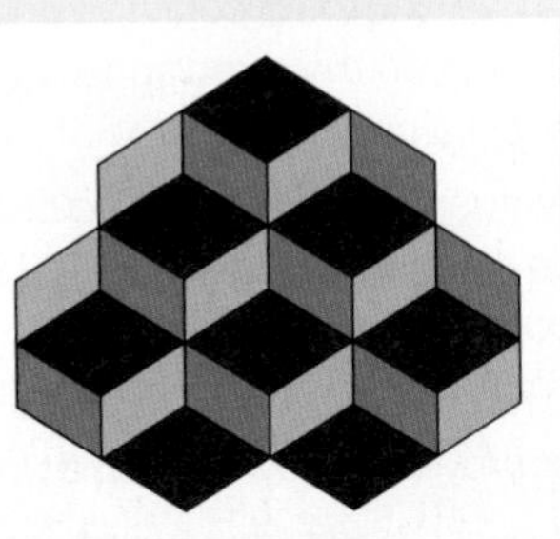
c. How many blocks?

Perceptual Selectivity

We are bombarded by so much sensory data that it is impossible to process it all. Thus, we tune in to some things and tune out others. **Perceptual selectivity** is the process by which individuals subconsciously screen and select the various objects and stimuli that vie for their attention.

People typically focus on stimuli that satisfy their needs and that are consistent with their attitudes, values, and personality. For example, employees who need positive feedback to feel good about themselves might pick up on positive statements made by a supervisor but tune out most negative comments. A supervisor could use this understanding to tailor feedback in a positive way to help the employee improve work performance. The influence of needs has been studied in laboratory experiments and found to have a strong impact on what people perceive.[19]

Characteristics of the stimuli themselves also affect perceptual selectivity. People tend to notice stimuli that stand out against other stimuli or that are more intense than surrounding stimuli. Examples would be a loud noise in a quiet room or a bright red dress at a party where most women are wearing basic black. People also tend to notice things that are familiar to them, such as a familiar voice in a crowd, as well as things that are new or different from their previous experiences. In addition, *primacy* and *recency* are important to perceptual selectivity. People pay relatively greater attention to sensory data that occur toward the beginning of an event or toward the end. Primacy supports the old truism that first impressions really do count, whether it be on a job interview, meeting a date's parents, or participating in a new social group. Recency reflects the reality that the last impression might be a lasting impression. For example, Malaysian Airlines discovered its value in building customer loyalty. A woman traveling with a 9-month-old might find the flight itself an exhausting blur, but one such traveler enthusiastically told people for years how Malaysian Airlines flight attendants helped her with baggage collection and ground transportation.[20]

3

Perceptual Distortions

Once people select the sensory data to be perceived, they begin grouping the data into recognizable patterns (perceptual organization). Of particular concern in the work environment are **perceptual distortions**, errors in perceptual judgment that arise from inaccuracies in any part of the perceptual process. American Apparel founder and CEO Dov

Charney may have his own perceptual distortions; where he sees his own "bad boy" behaviors as role-modeling freedom. At the same time, others file lawsuits against him and the company for behaviors that seem narcissistic and destructive, as shown in this chapter's Business Blooper.

One common perceptual error is **stereotyping**, the tendency to assign an individual to a group or broad category (e.g., female, black, elderly; or male, white, disabled) and then to attribute widely held generalizations about the group to the individual. Thus, someone meets a new colleague, sees he is in a wheelchair, assigns him to the category "physically disabled," and attributes to this colleague generalizations she believes about people with disabilities, which may include a belief that he is less able than other coworkers. However, the person's inability to walk should not be seen as indicative of lesser abilities in other areas. Stereotyping prevents people from truly knowing those they classify in this way. In addition, negative stereotypes prevent talented people from advancing in an organization and fully contributing their talents to the organization's success.

The **halo effect** occurs when the perceiver develops an overall impression of a person or situation based on one characteristic, either favorable or unfavorable. In other words, a halo blinds the perceiver to other characteristics that should be used in generating a more complete assessment. The halo effect can play a significant role in performance appraisal, as we discussed in Chapter 9. For example, a person with an outstanding attendance record may be assessed as responsible, industrious, and highly productive; another person with less than average attendance may be assessed as a poor performer. Either assessment may be true, but it is the manager's job to be sure the assessment is based on complete information about all job-related characteristics and not just his or her preferences for good attendance.

Projection is the tendency of perceivers to see their own personal traits in other people; that is, they project their own needs, feelings, values, and attitudes onto their judgment of others. A manager who is achievement oriented might assume that subordinates are as

BUSINESS BLOOPER

American Apparel

Once the darling of Wall Street and fashionistas, American Apparel lost $86 million in 2010 and is on the verge of collapse. Deloitte & Touche, its accounting firm, resigned, noting "Materials weaknesses in internal control over financial reporting." Stockholders have filed class-action lawsuits, citing mismanagement. Stock prices plummeted from $15 in 2007 to 78 cents in 2011.

Founder and CEO, Dov Charney was once glamorized for his bad-boy lifestyle, but it has lately gotten him into trouble. Though he sees himself more like the X-rated comedian Lenny Bruce, who was legally curtailed, his high jinks have spawned a series of lawsuits. Charney might aspire to a life like Hugh Hefner's—he lives in a 20-room mansion and has many employees (mostly young women) as roommates—he's had much more backlash than Hefner. Although the company had revenues of $201 million in 2005, it also has the first of its sexual harassment suits, filed by three former employees. The following year, another former employee filed charges . . . and five more did so in 2011. As a result, the Equal Opportunity Commission determined that female employees were systematically harassed at American Apparel. At the height of his popularity, Charney perhaps brought on his own ultimate decline. He performed unprintable acts in front a reporter for the now defunct magazine, *Jane.* Even is own father said, "He's not great at tact."

A number of advisors have suggested Charney step aside and move into a more creative role, but he's not enthusiastic. "I'm supposed to hire all these clowns, like they know better," he said, later throwing a rival's shoe against his office wall.

SOURCE: Laura M. Holson, "He's Only Just Begun to Fight," *The New York Times*, April 14, 2011.

EXHIBIT 10.5 How Accurate Is Your Perception?

Think about a job you have held or a project you have worked on in class or a volunteer organization. With respect to data or information coming to you, rate whether each statement below is Mostly True or Mostly False for you.

	Mostly True	Mostly False
1. I look for inconsistencies and seek explanations for them.	______	______
2. I generate multiple explanations for available information.	______	______
3. I check for omissions, distortions, or exaggerations in available information.	______	______
4. I make it a point to distinguish facts from opinions.	______	______
5. I stay conscious of my own style of approaching problems and how this might affect the way I process information.	______	______
6. I am well aware of my own biases and values that influence the way I see people.	______	______

Scoring and Interpretation: Your total score is the number of Mostly True answers to all six questions. A score of five or above suggests that you are conscious of and make attempts to remove distortions from your perceptual process. A score of three or four indicates that you make solid effort, and a score of one or two suggests that you take perception for granted. Look at any individual items where you have marked Mostly False to get an idea of where you might have perceptual weaknesses. What can you do to improve your perceptual process?

SOURCE: Adapted from Patricia M. Fandt, *Management Skills: Practice and Experience* (Minneapolis, MN: West Publishing, 1994), pp. 210–211.

well. This assumption might cause the manager to restructure jobs to be less routine and more challenging, without regard for employees' actual satisfaction.

Perceptual defense is the tendency of perceivers to protect themselves against ideas, objects, or people that are threatening. People perceive things that are satisfying and pleasant but tend to disregard things that are disturbing and unpleasant. In essence, people develop blind spots in the perceptual process so that negative sensory data do not hurt them. How accurate is your perception? Answering the questions in Exhibit 10.5 will give you an idea of whether you allow perceptual distortions to cloud your judgment.

- **Perception** is the cognitive process people use to make sense out of the environment by selecting, organizing, and interpreting information.
- People often see the same thing in different ways.
- **Perceptual selectivity** is the process by which individuals screen and select the various stimuli that vie for their attention.
- People tend to pay relatively greater attention to sensory data that occur toward the beginning of an event, so first impressions really do count.
- The concept of *recency* suggests that people also pay relatively greater attention to data that occur at the end of an event.
- **Perceptual distortions** are errors in perceptual judgment that result from inaccuracies in any part of the perceptual process.
- **Stereotyping** refers to the tendency to assign an individual to a group or broad category and then attribute generalizations about the group to the individual.
- The **halo effect** occurs when a perceiver develops an overall impression of a person or situation based on one characteristic, either favorable or unfavorable.
- The tendency to see one's own personal traits in other people is called **projection.**
- **Perceptual defense** is the tendency of individuals to protect themselves by disregarding ideas, objects, or people that are threatening to them.

Attributions

Among the judgments people make as part of the perceptual process are attributions. **Attributions** are judgments about what caused a person's behavior—something about the person or something about the situation. People make attributions as an attempt to understand why others behave as they do. An *internal attribution* says characteristics of the person led to the behavior. ("Susan missed the deadline because she's careless and lazy.") An *external attribution* says something about the situation caused the person's behavior. ("Susan missed the deadline because she couldn't get the information she needed in a timely manner.") Understanding attributions is important because attributions influence how a manager will handle a situation. In the case of the missed deadline, a manager who blames it on the employee's personality will view Susan as the problem and might give her unfavorable performance reviews and less attention and support. In contrast, a manager who blames the behavior on the situation might try to prevent such situations in the future, such as by improving horizontal communication mechanisms so people get the information they need in a timely way.

Social scientists have studied the attributions people make and identified three factors that influence whether an attribution will be external or internal.[21] These three factors are illustrated in Exhibit 10.6.

1. ***Distinctiveness.*** The behavior is unusual for that person (in contrast to a person displaying the same kind of behavior in many situations). If the behavior is distinctive, the perceiver probably will make an *external* attribution.
2. ***Consistency.*** The person being observed has a history of behaving in the same way. People generally make *internal* attributions about consistent behavior.

EXHIBIT 10.6

Factors Influencing Whether Attributions Are Internal or External

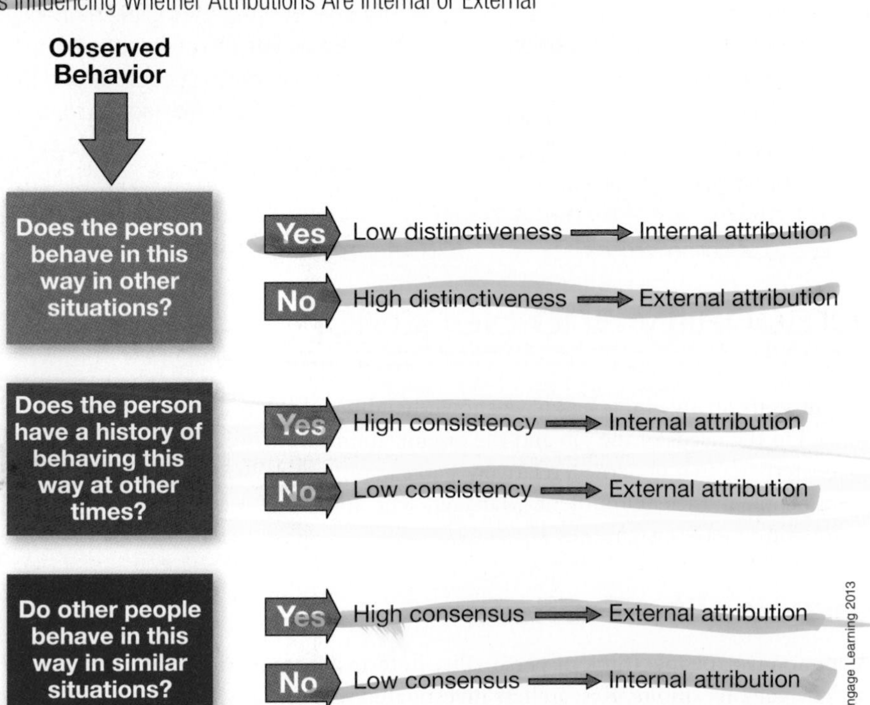

3. ***Consensus.*** Other people tend to respond to similar situations in the same way. A person who has observed others handle similar situations in the same way will likely make an *external* attribution; that is, it will seem that the situation produces the type of behavior observed.

In addition to these general rules, people tend to have biases that they apply when making attributions. When evaluating others, we tend to underestimate the influence of external factors and overestimate the influence of internal factors. This tendency is called the **fundamental attribution error**. Consider the case of someone being promoted to CEO. Employees, outsiders, and the media generally focus on the characteristics of the person that allowed him or her to achieve the promotion. In reality, however, the selection of that person might have been heavily influenced by external factors, such as business conditions creating a need for someone with a strong financial or marketing background at that particular time.

Another bias that distorts attributions involves attributions we make about our own behavior. People tend to overestimate the contribution of internal factors to their successes and overestimate the contribution of external factors to their failures. This tendency, called the **self-serving bias**, means people give themselves too much credit for what they do well and give external forces too much blame when they fail. Thus, if your manager says you don't communicate well enough, and you think your manager doesn't listen well enough, the truth may actually lie somewhere in between.

- **Attributions** are judgments about what caused a person's behavior—either characteristics of the person or of the situation.
- An internal attribution says characteristics of the individual caused the person to behave in a certain way, whereas an external attribution places the cause on aspects of the situation.
- Factors that influence whether an attribution will be internal or external are distinctiveness, consistency, and consensus.
- The **fundamental attribution error** is a tendency to underestimate the influence of external factors on another person's behavior and to overestimate the influence of internal factors.
- The **self-serving bias** is the tendency to overestimate the contribution of internal factors to one's successes and the contribution of external factors to one's failures.

Personality and Behavior

4

In recent years, many employers have shown heightened interest in matching people's personalities to the needs of the job and the organization. An individual's **personality** is the set of characteristics that underlie a relatively stable pattern of behavior in response to ideas, objects, or people in the environment. Managers who appreciate the ways their employees' personalities differ have insight into what kinds of leadership behavior will be most influential.

Personality Traits

In common use, people think of personality in terms of traits, the fairly consistent characteristics a person exhibits. Researchers investigated whether any traits stand up to scientific scrutiny. Although investigators examined thousands of traits over the years, their findings fit into five general dimensions that describe personality. These dimensions, often called the "Big Five" personality factors, are illustrated in Exhibit 10.7.[22] Each factor may contain a wide range of specific traits. The **Big Five personality factors** describe an individual's extroversion, agreeableness, conscientiousness, emotional stability, and openness to experience:

1. ***Extroversion.*** The degree to which a person is outgoing, sociable, assertive, and comfortable with interpersonal relationships.
2. ***Agreeableness.*** The degree to which a person is able to get along with others by being good-natured, likable, cooperative, forgiving, understanding, and trusting.
3. ***Conscientiousness.*** The degree to which a person is focused on a few goals, thus behaving in ways that are responsible, dependable, persistent, and achievement oriented.
4. ***Emotional stability.*** The degree to which a person is calm, enthusiastic, and self-confident, rather than tense, depressed, moody, or insecure.
5. ***Openness to experience.*** The degree to which a person has a broad range of interests and is imaginative, creative, artistically sensitive, and willing to consider new ideas.

Jeff Greenberg / Alamy

ConceptConnection

Marriott carefully screens candidates for critical customer service positions, such as this reservations and front desk clerk at a Cleveland, Ohio, Marriott Residence Inn. One important way managers determine whether people have the "right stuff" is through **personality testing**. During the application process, candidates answer a series of questions about their beliefs, attitudes, work habits, and how they might handle situations, enabling Marriott to identify people with interests and motivations that are compatible with company values. As managers reevaluate Marriott's mission and goals, the test evolves. Some fear personality tests have too much influence, determining not just who gets hired, but who gets an interview in the first place.

As illustrated in the exhibit, these factors represent a continuum. That is, a person may have a low, moderate, or high degree of each quality. Answer the questions in Exhibit 10.7 to see where you fall on the Big Five scale for each of the factors. Having a moderate to high degree of each of the Big Five personality factors is considered desirable for a wide range of employees, but this isn't always a key to success. For example, having an outgoing, sociable personality (extroversion) is considered desirable for managers, but many successful top executives, including Bill Gates, Charles Schwab, and Steven Spielberg, are introverts, people who become drained by social encounters and need time alone to reflect and recharge their batteries. One study found that four in ten top executives test out to be introverts.[23] Thus, the quality of extroversion is not as significant as is often presumed. Traits of agreeableness, on the other hand, seem to be particularly important in today's collaborative organizations. The days are over when a hard-driving manager can run roughshod over others to earn a promotion. Companies want managers who work smoothly with others and get help from lots of people inside and outside the organization. Executive search firm Korn/Ferry International examined data from millions of manager profiles since the early

EXHIBIT 10.7

The Big Five Personality Traits

Each individual's collection of personality traits is different; it is what makes us unique. But, although each *collection* of traits varies, we all share many common traits. The following phrases describe various traits and behaviors. Rate how accurately each statement describes you, based on a scale of 1 to 5, with 1 being very inaccurate and 5 very accurate. Describe yourself as you are now, not as you wish to be. There are no right or wrong answers.

1 2 3 4 5

Very Inaccurate Very Accurate

Extroversion					
I am usually the life of the party.	1	2	3	4	5
I feel comfortable around people.	1	2	3	4	5
I am talkative.	1	2	3	4	5

Neuroticism (Low Emotional Stability)					
I often feel critical of myself.	1	2	3	4	5
I often envy others.	1	2	3	4	5
I am temperamental.	1	2	3	4	5

Agreeableness					
I am kind and sympathetic.	1	2	3	4	5
I have a good word for everyone.	1	2	3	4	5
I never insult people.	1	2	3	4	5

Openness to New Experiences					
I am imaginative.	1	2	3	4	5
I prefer to vote for liberal political candidates.	1	2	3	4	5
I really like art.	1	2	3	4	5

Conscientiousness					
I am systematic and efficient.	1	2	3	4	5
I pay attention to details.	1	2	3	4	5
I am always prepared for class.	1	2	3	4	5

Which are your most prominent traits? For fun and discussion, compare your responses with those of classmates.

2000s and found that the most successful executives today are team-oriented leaders who gather information and work collaboratively with many different people.[24]

One recent book argues that the secret to success in work and in life is *likability.* We all know we're more willing to do something for someone we like than for someone we don't, whether it is a teammate, a neighbor, a professor, or a supervisor. Managers can increase their likability by developing traits of agreeableness, including being friendly and cooperative, understanding other people in a genuine way, and striving to make people feel positive about themselves.[25]

Many companies, including JCPenney, DuPont, Toys "R" Us, and the Union Pacific Railroad, use personality testing to hire, evaluate, or promote employees. Surveys indicate that at least 30 percent of organizations use some kind of personality testing for hiring.[26] However, despite the growing use of personality tests, there is so far little hard evidence showing them to be valid predictors of job success. Some companies, like Acxiom Corporation, a global marketing firm, use testing instead as a way to help employees better understand themselves and others.

ACXIOM CORPORATION

Dana Lund wears blue every day when she goes to work. No, it's not a uniform, just a blue badge that tells her coworkers Lund is a "planner," one of four personality and behavioral styles measured by the test the 24-year-old took when she joined the company. Almost every employee at Acxiom completes the Birkman Method personality assessment, a 45-minute test that asks a series of questions designed to determine the individual's work style and typical behavior characteristics. The results are plotted on a four-square matrix attached to a color. Each individual is identified as a green (communicator), a red (problem solver), a yellow (detailed scheduler), or a blue (planner), and employees wear badges proclaiming their dominant style.

"We see the assessment as an opportunity for our professionals to better understand themselves," says the company's human resources training and development leader. Lund agrees. She learned that she performs best by planning a task step-by-step and having time to think and reflect. When working with someone who is a "communicator," she says, she knows to provide a lot of information; if a teammate is a "detailed scheduler," she knows to be very specific. The test, Lund says, "helped me learn how to interact better with work teams and to leverage my strengths in the workplace."[27]

Attitudes and Behaviors Influenced by Personality

An individual's personality influences his or her work-related attitudes and behaviors. As a new manager, you will have to manage people with a wide variety of personality characteristics. The Spotlight on Skills titled Bridging the Personality Gap discusses how managers can cope with the challenge of bridging personality differences. Four areas related to personality that are of particular interest to managers are locus of control, authoritarianism, Machiavellianism, and problem-solving styles.

Locus of Control Individuals differ in terms of what they tend to accredit as the cause of their success or failure. **Locus of control** refers to how people perceive the cause of life events—whether they place the primary responsibility within themselves or on outside forces.[28] Some people believe that their own actions strongly influence what happens to them. They feel in control of their own fate. These individuals have a high *internal* locus of control. Other people believe that events in their lives occur because of chance, luck, or outside people and events. They feel more like pawns of their fate. These individuals have a high *external* locus of control.

Research on locus of control shows real differences in behavior across a wide range of settings. People with an internal locus of control are easier to motivate because they believe the rewards are the result of their behavior. They are better able to handle complex information and problem solving, are more achievement oriented, but are also more independent and therefore more difficult to manage. By contrast, people with an external locus of control are harder to motivate, less involved in their jobs, more likely to blame others when faced with a poor performance evaluation, but more compliant and conforming and therefore easier to manage.[29]

Do you believe luck plays an important role in your life, or do you feel that you control your own fate? To find out more about your locus of control, read the instructions and complete the questionnaire in Exhibit 10.8.

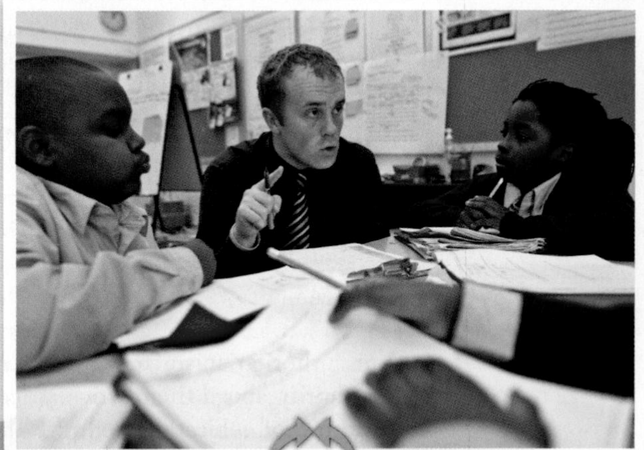

Fred R. Conrad/The New York Times/Redux Pictures

ConceptConnection

Teach for America sends recent college graduates, such as Dan Cosgrove, pictured here, to teach for two years in low-income schools throughout the United States. What does Teach for America look for when reviewing approximately 35,000 applications for only 4,100 positions? Founder and CEO Wendy Kopp says a high **internal locus of control** is at the top of her list. Those are the candidates who, when faced with a challenge, respond with optimism and resolve. Says Kopp, "They have the instinct to figure out what they can control and to own it, rather than to blame everyone else in the system."

Authoritarianism **Authoritarianism** is the belief that power and status differences should exist within the organization.[30] Individuals high

SPOTLIGHT ON SKILLS

Bridging the Personality Gap

Personality differences among employees make the life of a new manager interesting—and sometimes exasperating. Consultant Deborah Hildebrand took a lighthearted look at this issue by comparing the manager to a ringmaster at the circus. Here are a few of the "performers" managers encounter:

- ***The Lion Tamer.*** These people are fiercely independent and like to be in control. They are willing to tackle the biggest, toughest projects but aren't typically good team players. The manager can give lion tamers some freedom, but must be sure they understand who is ultimately in charge. Lion tamers crave recognition. Praising them for their accomplishments is a sure way to keep them motivated and prevent them from acting out to draw attention to themselves.
- ***The Clown.*** Everybody loves him (or her), but the clown tends to goof off a little too much, as well as disrupt the work of others. Keeping this person focused is the key to keeping him or her productive. A little micromanaging can be a good thing with a clown. It's also good to put clowns in jobs where socializing is a key to productivity and success.
- ***Sideshow Performers.*** These are the knife throwers, fire eaters, and sword swallowers. They have unique strengths and skills but tend to get overwhelmed with broad projects. These folks are expert team members because they like to combine their talents with others to make up a whole. Don't ask a sideshow performer to do a lion tamer's job.

This list is intended to be humorous, but in the real world of management, working with different personalities isn't always a laughing matter. Differences at work can create an innovative environment but also lead to stress, conflict, and bad feelings. Managers can learn to work more effectively with different personality types by following some simple tips.

1. ***Understand your own personality and how you react to others.*** Try to avoid judging people based on limited knowledge. Realize that everyone has many facets to his or her personality.
2. ***Treat everyone with respect.*** People like to be accepted and appreciated for who they are. Even if you find someone's personality grating, remain professional and keep your frustration and irritation to yourself.
3. ***When leading a team or group, make sure everyone has an equal chance to participate.*** Don't let the outgoing members dominate the scene.
4. ***Remember that everyone wants to fit in.*** No matter their personalities, people typically take on behavior patterns that are the norm for their environment. Managers can create norms that keep everyone focused on positive interactions and high performance.

SOURCES: Based on Deborah S. Hildebrand, "Managing Different Personalities," *Suite101.com*, June 25, 2007, www.suite101.com/content/managing-different-personalities-a24620 (accessed September 20, 2010); Jamie Walters and Sarah Fenson, "Building Rapport with Different Personalities," *Inc.com*, March 2000, www.inc.com/articles/2000/03/17713.html (accessed September 20, 2010); Tim Millett, "Learning to Work with Different Personality Types," *Ezine Articles*, http://ezinearticles.com/?Learning-To-Work-With-Different-Personality-Types&id=725606 (accessed September 20, 2010); and Carol Ritberter, "Understanding Personality: The Secret to Managing People," *Dream Manifesto*, March 6, 2007, http://www.dreammanifesto.com/understanding-personality-the-secret-of-managing-people.html (accessed April 17, 2008).

in authoritarianism tend to be concerned with power and toughness, obey recognized authority above them, stick to conventional values, critically judge others, and oppose the use of subjective feelings. The degree to which managers possess authoritarianism will influence how they wield and share power. The degree to which employees possess authoritarianism will influence how they react to their managers. If a manager and employees differ in their degree of authoritarianism, the manager may have difficulty leading effectively. The trend toward empowerment and shifts in expectations among younger employees for more equitable relationships contribute to a decline in strict authoritarianism in many organizations.

Machiavellianism Another personality dimension that is helpful in understanding work behavior is **Machiavellianism**, which is characterized by the acquisition of

EXHIBIT 10.8

Measuring Locus of Control

Your Locus of Control

This questionnaire is designed to measure locus-of-control beliefs. For each of these 10 questions, indicate the extent to which you agree or disagree using the following scale:

1 = Strongly disagree	4 = Neither disagree nor Agree	7 = Strongly agree
2 = Disagree	5 = Slightly agree	
3 = Slightly disagree	6 = Agree	

1. When I get what I want, it is usually because I worked hard for it.	1	2	3	4	5	6	7
2. When I make plans, I am almost certain to make them work.	1	2	3	4	5	6	7
3. I prefer games involving some luck over games requiring pure skill.	1	2	3	4	5	6	7
4. I can learn almost anything if I set my mind to it.	1	2	3	4	5	6	7
5. My major accomplishments are entirely due to my hard work and ability.	1	2	3	4	5	6	7
6. I usually don't set goals because I have a hard time following through on them.	1	2	3	4	5	6	7
7. Competition discourages excellence.	1	2	3	4	5	6	7
8. Often people get ahead just by being lucky.	1	2	3	4	5	6	7
9. On any sort of exam or competition, I like to know how well I do relative to everyone else.	1	2	3	4	5	6	7
10. It's pointless to keep working on something that's too difficult for me.	1	2	3	4	5	6	7

Scoring and Interpretation

To determine your score, reverse the values you selected for questions 3, 6, 7, 8, and 10 (1 = 7, 2 = 6, 3 = 5, 4 = 4, 5 = 3, 6 = 2, 7 = 1). For example, if you strongly disagree with the statement in question 3, you would have given it a value of 1. Change this value to a 7. Reverse the scores in a similar manner for questions 6, 7, 8, and 10. Now add the point values for all ten questions together.

Your score ________

Researchers using this questionnaire in a study of college students found a mean of 51.8 for men and 52.2 for women, with a standard deviation of 6 for each. The higher your score on this questionnaire, the more you tend to believe that you are generally responsible for what happens to you; in other words, higher scores are associated with internal locus of control. Low scores are associated with external locus of control. Scoring low indicates that you tend to believe that forces beyond your control, such as powerful other people, fate, or chance, are responsible for what happens to you.

SOURCES: Adapted from J. M. Burger, *Personality: Theory and Research* (Belmont, CA: Wadsworth, 1986): 400–401, cited in D. Hellriegel, J. W. Slocum, Jr., and R. W. Woodman, *Organizational Behavior*, 6th ed. (St. Paul, MN: West, 1992): 97–100. Original source: D. L. Paulhus,"Sphere-Specific Measures of Perceived Control," *Journal of Personality and Social Psychology*, 44, 1253–1265.

power and the manipulation of other people for purely personal gain. Machiavellianism is named after Niccolo Machiavelli, a sixteenth-century author who wrote *The Prince*, a book for noblemen of the day on how to acquire and use power.[31] Psychologists developed instruments to measure a person's Machiavellianism (Mach) orientation.[32] Research shows that high Machs are predisposed to being pragmatic, capable of lying to achieve personal goals, more likely to win in win–lose situations, and more likely to persuade than be persuaded.[33]

Different situations may require people who demonstrate one or the other type of behavior. In loosely structured situations, high Machs actively take control, while low Machs accept the direction given by others. Low Machs thrive in highly structured situations, while high Machs perform in a detached, disinterested way. High Machs are particularly good in jobs that require bargaining skills or that involve substantial rewards for winning.[34]

- **Personality** is the set of characteristics that underlie a relatively stable pattern of behavior in response to ideas, objects, or people in the environment.
- Acxiom Corporation uses personality tests to help employees better understand themselves and their colleagues and develop more effective working relationships.
- The **Big Five personality factors** are dimensions that describe an individual's extroversion, agreeableness, conscientiousness, emotional stability, and openness to experience.
- **Locus of control** defines whether an individual places the primary responsibility for his successes and failures within himself or on outside forces.
- **Authoritarianism** is the belief that power and status differences should exist within an organization.
- A person high in authoritarianism is typically concerned with power and status, obeys established authority, and sticks to conventional values.
- **Machiavellianism** refers to a tendency to direct one's behavior toward the acquisition of power and the manipulation of other people for personal gain.

Problem-Solving Styles and the Myers-Briggs Type Indicator Managers also need to realize that individuals solve problems and make decisions in different ways. One approach to understanding problem-solving styles grew out of the work of psychologist Carl Jung. Jung believed differences resulted from our preferences in how we go about gathering and evaluating information.[35] According to Jung, gathering information and evaluating information are separate activities. People gather information either by *sensation* or *intuition*, but not by both simultaneously. Sensation-type people would rather work with known facts and hard data and prefer routine and order in gathering information. Intuitive-type people would rather look for possibilities than work with facts and prefer solving new problems and using abstract concepts.

Evaluating information involves making judgments about the information a person has gathered. People evaluate information by *thinking* or *feeling*. These represent the extremes in orientation. Thinking-type individuals base their judgments on impersonal analysis, using reason and logic rather than personal values or emotional aspects of the situation. Feeling-type individuals base their judgments more on personal feelings such as harmony and tend to make decisions that result in approval from others.

According to Jung, only one of the four functions—sensation, intuition, thinking, or feeling—is dominant in an individual. However, the dominant function usually is backed up by one of the functions from the other set of paired opposites. Exhibit 10.9 shows the four problem-solving styles that result from these matchups, as well as occupations that people with each style tend to prefer.

Two additional sets of paired opposites not directly related to problem solving are *introversion–extroversion* and *judging–perceiving*. Introverts gain energy by focusing on personal thoughts and feelings, whereas extroverts gain energy from being around others and interacting with others. On the judging versus perceiving dimension, people with a judging preference like certainty and closure and tend to make decisions quickly based on available data. Perceiving people, on the other hand, enjoy ambiguity, dislike deadlines, and may change their minds several times as they gather large amounts of data and information to make decisions.

A widely used test that measures how people differ on all four of Jung's sets of paired opposites is the **Myers-Briggs Type Indicator (MBTI)™** assessment. The MBTI™

EXHIBIT 10.9

Four Problem-Solving Styles

Personal Style	Action Tendencies	Likely Occupations
Sensation-Thinking	• Emphasizes details, facts, certainty • Is a decisive, applied thinker • Focuses on short-term, realistic goals • Develops rules and regulations for judging performance	• Accounting • Production • Computer programming • Market research • Engineering
Intuitive-Thinking	• Prefers dealing with theoretical or technical problems • Is a creative, progressive, perceptive thinker • Focuses on possibilities using impersonal analysis • Is able to consider a number of options and problems simultaneously	• Systems design • Systems analysis • Law • Middle/top management • Teaching business, economics
Sensation-Feeling	• Shows concern for current, real-life human problems • Is pragmatic, analytical, methodical, and conscientious • Emphasizes detailed facts about people rather than tasks • Focuses on structuring organizations for the benefit of people	• Directing supervisor • Counseling • Negotiating • Selling • Interviewing
Intuitive-Feeling	• Avoids specifics • Is charismatic, participative, people oriented, and helpful • Focuses on general views, broad themes, and feelings • Decentralizes decision making, develops few rules and regulations	• Public relations • Advertising • Human Resources • Politics • Customer service

assessment measures a person's preferences for introversion versus extroversion, sensation versus intuition, thinking versus feeling, and judging versus perceiving. The various combinations of these four preferences result in 16 unique personality types.

Each of the 16 different personality types can have positive and negative consequences for behavior. Based on the limited research that has been done, the two preferences that seem to be most strongly associated with effective management in a variety of organizations and industries are thinking and judging.[36] However, people with other preferences can also be good managers. One advantage of understanding your natural preferences is to maximize your innate strengths and abilities. Dow Chemical executive Kurt Swogger believes the MBTI™ assessment can help put people in the right jobs—where they will be happiest and make the strongest contribution to the organization.

Go to the Self-Learning, on pages 428–430, that pertains to evaluating your personality type.

DOW CHEMICAL

When Kurt Swogger arrived at Dow Chemical's plastics business, it took anywhere from 6 to 15 years to launch a new product—and the unit hadn't launched a single one for 3 years. Ten years later, a new product launch took just 2 to 4 years, and Swogger's R&D team was launching hit after hit.

What changed? "The biggest obstacle to launching great new products was not having the right people in the right jobs," says Swogger (now vice president of Performance Plastics & Chemicals Business Development for Dow). Swogger began reassigning people based on his intuition and experience, distinguishing pure inventors from those who could add value later in the game and still others who were best at marketing the new products. He says he was right-on about 60 percent of the time. If someone didn't work out after six months, Swogger would put him or her in another assignment.

Seeking a better way to determine people's strengths, Swogger began using the Myers–Briggs Type Indicator (MBTI)™ instrument and noting which types would be best suited to each stage of the product development and launch cycles. After administering the test to current and former Dow plastics employees, he found some startling results. When Swogger came on board, the match between the right personality type and the right role was only 29 percent. Ten years later, the rate had jumped to 93 percent. Swogger's next step was to administer the MBTI™ assessment to new hires, so he could immediately assign people to jobs that matched their natural thinking and problem-solving styles, leading to happier employees and higher organizational performance.[37]

Other organizations also use the MBTI™ assessment, with 89 of the *Fortune* 100 companies recently reporting that they use the test in hiring and promotion decisions.[38] Putting the right people in the right jobs is a vital skill for managers, whether they do it based on intuition and experience or by using various personality tests.

Person–Job Fit

An important responsibility of managers is to try to match employee and job characteristics so that work is done by people who are well suited to do it. The extent to which a person's ability and personality match the requirements of a job is called **person–job fit**. When managers achieve person–job fit, employees are more likely to contribute and have higher levels of job satisfaction and commitment.[39] The importance of person–job fit became apparent during the dot-com heyday of the late 1990s. People who rushed to Internet companies in hopes of finding a new challenge—or making a quick buck—found themselves floundering in jobs for which they were unsuited. One manager recruited by a leading executive search firm lasted less than two hours at his new job. The search firm, a division of Russell Reynolds Associates, later developed a "Web Factor" diagnostic to help determine whether people have the right personality for dot-com jobs, including characteristics such as a tolerance for risk and uncertainty, an obsession with learning, and a willingness to do whatever needs doing, regardless of job title.[40]

CANDICE C. CUSIC/MCT /Landov

ConceptConnection

Instant Technology, a technology staffing provider, is growing by leaps and bounds. Here, national accounting manager Amanda Morris is tallying the firm's latest victory at its Chicago headquarters. One key to the firm's success is its 2–1 approach: Instant Technology sends just two candidates for each opening. Employees use social network searches to gain insights into both the applicant's character and the client organization's culture. Thus, the screening process helps ensure **person–job** and **person–environment fit**. "It has allowed us to better match clients with candidates in a cultural way," says founder, president, and CEO Rona Borre.

A related concern is *person–environment fit*, which looks not only at whether the person and job are suited to one another but also at how well the individual will fit in the overall organizational environment. An employee who is by nature strongly authoritarian, for example, would have a hard time in an organization such as W.L. Gore &

Associates, which has few rules, no hierarchy, no fixed or assigned authority, and no bosses. Many of today's organizations pay attention to person–environment fit from the beginning of the recruitment process. Texas Instruments's Web site includes an area called Fit Check that evaluates personality types anonymously and gives a prospective job candidate the chance to evaluate whether he or she would be a good match with the company.[41]

- Four problem-solving styles are sensation-thinking, intuitive-thinking, sensation-feeling, and intuitive-feeling.
- The **Myers–Briggs Type Indicator (MBTI)™** assessment measures a person's preference for introversion versus extroversion, sensation versus intuition, thinking versus feeling, and judging versus perceiving.
- **Person–job fit** refers to the extent to which a person's ability and personality match the requirements of a job.
- One manager at Dow Chemical's plastics division used the MBTI™ assessment to help match people with the jobs where they could be most effective.

Emotions

Managers might like to think people come to work and conduct their jobs in a logical and rational manner, leaving their emotions at home or tucked safely in the car until it's time to go home for the day. Yet people cannot be separated from their emotions, and wise managers know organizations suffer when they fail to pay attention to how employees' emotions affect productivity and the work environment.[42] Managers can increase their effectiveness by understanding positive and negative emotions and developing emotional intelligence.

Positive and Negative Emotions

Although the term is somewhat difficult to define in a precise way, an **emotion** can be thought of as a mental state that arises spontaneously within a person, based on interaction with the environment rather than through conscious effort, and is often accompanied by physiological changes or sensations. People can experience a wide range of emotions at work, such as happiness, anger, fear, or relief, and these affect their workplace attitudes and behaviors. Researchers have been attempting to understand emotions for thousands of years, and scientific debate continues about how to categorize emotions.[43] One model that is useful for managers, shown in Exhibit 10.10, distinguishes the major positive and negative emotions. Negative emotions are sparked when a person becomes frustrated in trying to achieve his or her goals, whereas positive emotions are triggered when people are on track toward achieving goals.

Consider the breakup of a romantic relationship. If you wanted the relationship to continue, the breakup might trigger emotions of sadness or perhaps even anger. If, on the other hand, your goal was to get out of a relationship you no longer wanted, the breakup would likely cause a feeling of relief and perhaps even happiness. Similarly, an employee who fails to get a pay raise or is reprimanded by a supervisor would likely experience negative emotions such as sadness, anger, or anxiety, whereas a person who gets a promotion would experience feelings of pride and happiness. Thus, emotions can be understood as being determined by whether people are getting their needs and goals met.

EXHIBIT 10.10
Positive and Negative Emotions

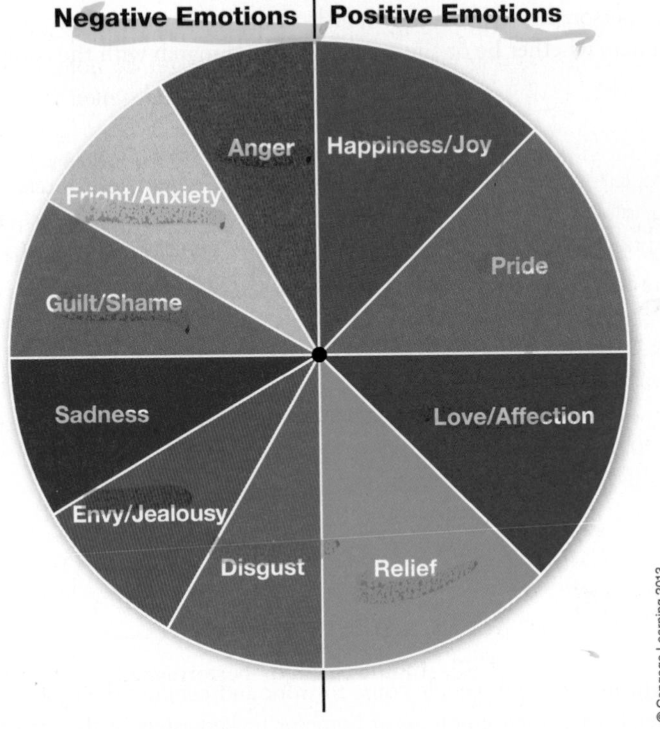

Managers can influence whether people experience primarily positive or negative emotions at work. For one thing, the emotional state of the manager influences the entire team or department. Most of us realize that we can "catch" emotions from others. If we're around someone who is happy and enthusiastic, the positive emotions rub off on us. On the other hand, someone who is sad and angry can bring us down. This *emotional contagion*[44] means that managers who express positive emotions such as happiness, enthusiasm, and appreciation trigger positive emotions in employees. Research suggests that nearly all human beings are subject to emotional contagion and will automatically and unconsciously start feeling and displaying the same emotions as those around them.[45] When managers have to give negative feedback, they can point out things the employee does well or express concern and a willingness to help rather than being angry and unconstructive in their feedback. Good managers pay attention to people's emotions, because positive emotions are typically linked to higher productivity and greater effectiveness. A *Gallup Management Journal* survey found that managers, especially front-line supervisors, have a lot to do with whether employees have positive or negative emotions associated with their work lives.[46]

Emotional Intelligence

In recent years, research in the area of *emotional intelligence* has shown that managers who are in touch with their own feelings and the feelings of others can enhance employee and organizational performance. Emotional intelligence (EQ) includes four basic components:[47]

1. ***Self-awareness.*** The basis for all the other components; being aware of what you are feeling. People who are in touch with their feelings are better able to guide

their own lives and actions. A high degree of self-awareness means you can accurately assess your own strengths and limitations and have a healthy sense of self-confidence.

2. ***Self-management.*** The ability to control disruptive or harmful emotions and balance one's moods so that worry, anxiety, fear, or anger do not cloud thinking and get in the way of what needs to be done. People who are skilled at self-management remain optimistic and hopeful despite setbacks and obstacles. This ability is crucial for pursuing long-term goals. MetLife found that applicants who failed the regular sales aptitude test but scored high on optimism made 21 percent more sales in their first year and 57 percent more in their second year than those who passed the sales test but scored high on pessimism.[48] Theatrical Producer Eric Krebs has learned self-management skills are essential to continued success, as shown in the Benchmarking box.
3. ***Social awareness.*** The ability to understand others and practice *empathy*, which means being able to put yourself in someone else's shoes, to recognize what others are feeling without them needing to tell you. People with social awareness are capable of understanding divergent points of view and interacting effectively with many different types of people.
4. ***Relationship management.*** The ability to connect to others, build positive relationships, respond to the emotions of others, and influence others. People with relationship management skills know how to listen and communicate clearly, and they treat others with compassion and respect.

Complete the New Manager Self-Test on page 420 to assess your own level of emotional intelligence. You might also want to refer back to the questionnaire related to self-confidence at the beginning of this chapter. Self-confidence strongly influences a new manager's EQ.

Studies show a positive relationship between job performance and high levels of emotional intelligence in a variety of jobs. Numerous organizations, including the U.S. Air Force and Canada Life, use EQ tests to measure things such as self-awareness, ability to empathize, and capacity to build positive relationships.[49] Altera Corporation uses "empathy

BENCHMARKING

Eric Krebs

One of the most important lessons Eric Krebs has learned in his years as an Off-Broadway producer is: Don't anger easily. In the sometimes ego-filled theater world, that is very useful advice.

Recently he got an e-mail that showed what can happen if you let your emotions take charge. Krebs was involved with producing a play at one of the university theaters in New York. Someone doing the scheduling double-booked, so Professor X showed up for class and found his space already taken. Rather than look around for alternate accommodations, the professor sent an angry e-mail, declaring the situation "utterly inconsiderate," saying the students had been "tossed to the wind," and cc'ing the e-mail to six other people. Krebs noted the problem could have been solved much more quietly and directly by communicating in a less volatile fashion and with only the main person involved. As a result of this e-mail, six extra people had the chance to get worked up from the prickly e-mail.

Krebs has had many chances to practice his own advice. Starting out as a poet and then playwright, he found it difficult for his work to get onstage, so he "temporarily" decided to become a producer of his own works. As a result, he became the founder (and producing director for 14 years) of the George Street Playhouse in New Brunswick, New Jersey, and now works regularly as an admired producer in New York and elsewhere.

Krebs says his mantra these days is: "I'm too tired to get angry. Get over it. Life is short. Let's just figure out how to solve the problem."

SOURCE: Eric Krebs, personal interview, April, 2011.

New Manager Self-Test

What's Your EQ?

Understanding yourself and others is a major part of new manager's job. To learn about your insights into self and others, answer each item below as Mostly True or Mostly False for you.

	MOSTLY TRUE <<<	>>> MOSTLY FALSE
1. I am aware of sensations and emotions within my body.	_____	_____
2. I am slow to react to others' slights or negative actions toward me.	_____	_____
3. I can tell my friends' moods from their behavior.	_____	_____
4. I am good at building consensus among others.	_____	_____
5. I have a good sense of why I have certain feelings.	_____	_____
6. I calm down right away if upset and am quick to forgive.	_____	_____
7. I often sense the impact of my words or behavior on others.	_____	_____
8. Other people are happier when I am around.	_____	_____

See It Online

Scoring and Interpretation: The categories of emotional intelligence are below. Give yourself one point for each item marked Mostly True.

Self-Awareness: Items 1, 5

Self-Management: Items 2, 6,

Social Awareness: Items 3, 7

Relationship Management: Items 4, 8

These are the four dimensions of EQ described in the text. If you scored 2 on a dimension, you probably do well on it. If you scored 0 on a dimension, you may want to work on that aspect of your EQ before becoming a manager. The important thing as a manager is to know and guide yourself, to understand the emotional state of others, and to guide your relationships in a positive direction.

coaches" to help its salespeople develop greater social awareness and see things from their customers' point of view.[50] EQ seems to be particularly important for jobs such as sales that require a high degree of social interaction. It is also critical for managers, who are responsible for influencing others and building positive attitudes and relationships in the organization.

Managers with low emotional intelligence can undermine employee morale and harm the organization. Consider that 44 percent of people surveyed by the Employment Law Alliance say they have worked for a manager that they considered an abusive bully.[51] Growing concerns over workplace bullying have prompted enlightened companies to take action that helps managers develop greater emotional intelligence, such as by honing their self-awareness. Lars Dalgaard, founder and CEO of software company SuccessFactors, says he never realized he acted like a jerk until a leadership coach helped him see that he ran roughshod over people's feelings. Now, Dalgaard makes a conscious effort to build good relationships with employees and help others be more emotionally intelligent as well. SuccessFactors, which has an official "no jerks" rule, has twice been voted one of the best places to work in the San Francisco Bay area.[52]

- An **emotion** is a mental state that arises spontaneously rather than through conscious effort and is often accompanied by physiological changes.
- People experience both positive emotions of happiness, pride, love, and relief, as well as negative emotions of anger, anxiety, guilt, sadness, envy, and disgust.
- The concept of *emotional contagion* suggests that people can catch emotions from those around them, so good managers try to express positive emotions at work.
- Emotional intelligence includes the components of self-awareness, self-management, social awareness, and relationship management.

Learning

5

Years of schooling have conditioned many of us to think that learning is something students do in response to teachers in a classroom. With this view, in the managerial world of time deadlines and concrete action, learning seems remote—even irrelevant. However, successful managers and effective employees need specific knowledge and skills as well as the ability to adapt to changes in the world around them. That is, they have to learn. **Learning** is a change in behavior or performance that occurs as the result of experience. Two individuals who undergo similar experiences—for example, a business transfer to a foreign country—probably will differ in how they adapt their behaviors to (that is, learn from) the experience. In other words, each person learns in a different way.

The Learning Process

One model of the learning process, shown in Exhibit 10.11, depicts learning as a four-stage cycle.[53] First, a person encounters a concrete experience. This event is followed by thinking and reflective observation, which leads to abstract conceptualization and, in turn, to active experimentation. The results of the experimentation generate new experiences, and the cycle repeats. The arrows in the model indicate that this process is a recurring cycle. People continually test their conceptualizations and adapt them as a result of their personal reflections and observations about their experiences.

Learning Styles

Individuals develop personal learning styles that vary in terms of how much they emphasize each stage of the learning cycle. These differences occur because the learning process is directed by individual needs and goals. For example, an engineer might place greater emphasis on abstract concepts, while a salesperson might emphasize concrete experiences. Because of these preferences, personal learning styles typically have strong and weak points.

EXHIBIT 10.11

The Experiential Learning Cycle

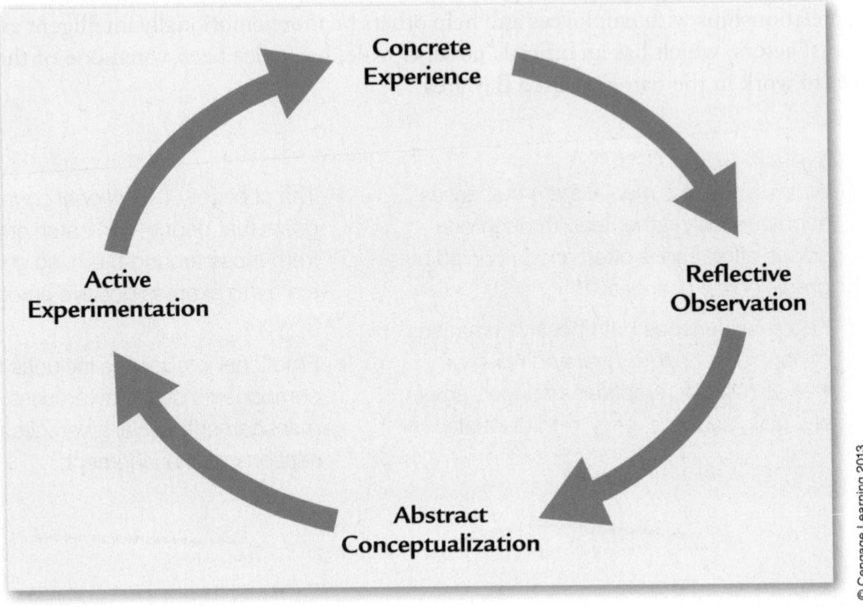

Questionnaires can assess a person's strong and weak points as a learner by measuring the relative emphasis the person places on each of the four learning stages shown in Exhibit 10.11: concrete experience, reflective observation, abstract conceptualization, and active experimentation. Some people have a tendency to overemphasize one stage of the learning process or to avoid some aspects of learning. Not many people have totally balanced profiles, but the key to effective learning is competence in each of the four stages when it is needed.

Researchers have identified four fundamental learning styles, outlined in Exhibit 10.12, labeled Diverger, Assimilator, Converger, and Accommodator. Each style combines elements of the four stages of the learning cycle.[54] The exhibit lists some questions that can help you understand your dominant learning abilities and identifies some occupations you might enjoy based on your dominant style. For example, people whose dominant style is Accommodator are often drawn to sales and marketing. Those with a primarily Diverger style might enjoy human resource management.

- **Learning** is a change in behavior or performance that occurs as the result of experience.
- Learning can be thought of as a four-stage cycle that includes concrete experience, reflective observation, abstract conceptualization, and active experimentation.
- Individuals tend to emphasize each stage of the learning cycle to varying degrees, depending on their personal learning style.
- Four learning styles are diverger, assimilator, converger, and accommodator.

EXHIBIT 10.12

What's Your Learning Style?

Learning Style Type	Dominant Learning Abilities	Is This Your Style?	You Might Be Good At:
Diverger	• Concrete experience • Reflective observation	• Are you good at generating ideas, seeing a situation from multiple perspectives, and being aware of meaning and value? • Are you interested in people, culture, and the arts?	• Human resource management • Counseling • Organization development specialist
Assimilator	• Abstract conceptualization • Reflective observation	• Are you good at inductive reasoning, creating theoretical models, and combining disparate observations into an integrated explanation? • Do you tend to be less concerned with people than ideas and abstract concepts?	• Research • Strategic planning
Converger	• Abstract conceptualization • Active experimentation	• Are you good at making decisions, the practical application of ideas, and hypothetical deductive reasoning? • Do you prefer dealing with technical tasks rather than interpersonal issues?	• Engineering
Accommodator	• Concrete experience • Active experimentation	• Are you good at implementing decisions, carrying out plans, and getting involved in new experiences? • Do you tend to be at ease with people but are sometimes seen as impatient or pushy?	• Marketing • Sales

Stress and Stress Management

Now let's turn our attention to a problem every manager will likely encounter at some time in his or her career: workplace stress. Formally defined, **stress** is an individual's physiological and emotional response to external stimuli that place physical or psychological demands on the individual and create uncertainty and lack of personal control when important outcomes are at stake.[55] These stimuli, called *stressors,* produce some combination of frustration (the inability to achieve a goal, such as the inability to meet a deadline because of inadequate resources) and anxiety (such as the fear of being disciplined for not meeting deadlines).

In recent years, financial worries and massive job cuts have upped the stress level in almost every organization. Managers have found themselves dealing with a workforce that is frightened, nervous, and unsure about the future.[56] The number of employees who are irritable, insulting, or discourteous has grown as people cope with the stress of job uncertainty, overwhelming debt, tighter access to credit, and increased workloads due to downsizing. In a 2009 survey, nearly half of U.S. workers responding reported experiencing yelling and verbal abuse on the job, and another study found that 2 to 3 percent of people admit to pushing, slapping, or hitting someone at work.[57] In addition, the stress caused by economic worries is contributing to health problems such as ulcers, severe depression, and heart attacks.[58]

Stress isn't always negative. People's responses to stressors vary according to their personalities, the resources available to help them cope, and the context in which the stress occurs. When the level of stress is low relative to a person's coping resources, stress can be a positive force, stimulating desirable change and achievement. However, too much stress is associated with many negative consequences, including sleep disturbances, drug and alcohol abuse, headaches, ulcers, high blood pressure, and heart disease. People who are experiencing the ill effects of too much stress may become irritable or withdraw from interactions with their coworkers, take excess time off, and have more health problems. In the United States, an estimated 1 million people each day don't show up for work because of stress.[59] Similarly, a survey in the United Kingdom found that 68 percent of nonmanual workers and 42 percent of manual workers reported missing work because of stress-related illness.[60] Just as big a problem for organizations as absenteeism is *presenteeism*, which refers to people who go to work but are too stressed and distracted to be productive.[61] Clearly, too much stress is harmful to employees as well as to companies.

Type A and Type B Behavior

Researchers observed that some people seem to be more vulnerable than others to the ill effects of stress. From studies of stress-related heart disease, they categorized people as having behavior patterns called Type A and Type B.[62] The **Type A behavior** pattern includes extreme competitiveness, impatience, aggressiveness, and devotion to work. In contrast, people with a **Type B behavior** pattern exhibit less of these behaviors. They consequently experience less conflict with other people and a more balanced, relaxed lifestyle. Type A people tend to experience more stress-related illness than Type B people.

Most Type A individuals are high-energy people and may seek positions of power and responsibility. By pacing themselves and learning control and intelligent use of their natural high-energy tendencies, Type A individuals can be powerful forces for innovation and leadership within their organizations. However, many Type A personalities cause stress-related problems for themselves, and sometimes for those around them. Type B individuals typically live with less stress unless they are in high-stress situations. A number of factors can cause stress in the workplace, even for people who are not naturally prone to high stress.

Causes of Work Stress

Go to the Ethical Dilemma, on pages 431–432, that pertains to organizational sources of stress.

Even prior to recent economic difficulties, workplace stress has been skyrocketing worldwide for some years. The World Congress on Health and Safety at Work presented studies suggesting that job-related stress may be as big a danger to the world's people as chemical and biological hazards.[63] The number of people in the United States who say they are overworked grew from 28 to 44 percent over a four-year period, and one-third of Americans between the ages of 25 and 39 say they feel burned out by their jobs. Surveys in Canada consistently peg work as the top source of stress for people in that country. In India, growing numbers of young software professionals and call-center workers are falling prey to depression, anxiety, and other mental illnesses because of increasing workplace stress.[64] And in France, companies did some serious soul searching after the notes of three engineers who committed suicide within five months implied that workplace stress was a major factor in their decision to end their lives.[65] "Work conditions can cause mental illness," says psychologist Rodney L. Lowman. "If we put healthy, well-adjusted people in the right foxhole with guns blaring at them, the likelihood of them experiencing depression and anxiety is very high."[66]

Most people have a general idea of what a stressful job is like: difficult, uncomfortable, exhausting, even frightening. Managers can better cope with their own stress and establish ways for the organization to help employees cope if they define the conditions that tend to produce work stress. One way to identify work stressors is to think about stress caused by the demands of job tasks and stress caused by interpersonal pressures and conflicts.

- ***Task demands*** are stressors arising from the tasks required of a person holding a particular job. Some kinds of decisions are inherently stressful: those made under time pressure, those that have serious consequences, and those that must be made with incomplete information. For example, emergency room doctors are under tremendous stress as a result of the task demands of their jobs. They regularly have to make quick decisions, based on limited information, that may determine whether a patient lives or dies. Almost all jobs, especially those of managers, have some level of stress associated with task demands. Task demands also sometimes cause stress because of **role ambiguity**, which means that people are unclear about what task behaviors are expected of them.
- ***Interpersonal demands*** are stressors associated with relationships in the organization. Although in some cases interpersonal relationships can alleviate stress, they also can be a source of stress when the group puts pressure on an individual or when conflicts arise between individuals. Managers can resolve many conflicts using techniques that will be discussed in Chapter 14. **Role conflict** occurs when an individual perceives incompatible demands from others. Managers often feel role conflict because the demands of their superiors conflict with those of the employees in their department. They may be expected to support employees and provide them with opportunities to experiment and be creative, while at the same time top executives are demanding a consistent level of output that leaves little time for creativity and experimentation.

Innovative Responses to Stress Management

Organizations that want to challenge their employees and stay competitive will never be stress-free, but healthy workplaces promote the physical and emotional well-being of their employees. Managers have direct control over many of the things that cause people stress, including their own behavior. Exhibit 10.13 lists some of the top things managers do to cause excessive and unnecessary stress.

In addition to avoiding the behaviors that cause unnecessary stress for employees, good managers in today's high-pressure environment are proactive in identifying when people are suffering from too much stress. At Pitney Bowes, managers and front-line supervisors are trained to look for signs of employee distress that might not be obvious—and might not even be work related. "People bring all sorts of demons to work . . . that they shouldn't think they can solve on their own," says Michele Coleman Mayes, senior vice president and general counsel. Pitney Bowes has a company physician, as well as a program offering referrals to counselors. When managers notice that someone seems to be having difficulty, they talk to the individual, listen empathetically, and encourage the person to get help. Most of all, managers don't let people who are suffering remain isolated.[67]

A variety of techniques can help individuals manage stress. Among the most basic strategies are those that help people stay healthy: exercising regularly, getting plenty of rest,

EXHIBIT 10.13
How Managers Create Stress for Employees

Working for a bad boss is a major cause of workplace stress. Here are some things bad bosses do to create stress for their subordinates:

1. Impose unreasonable demands and overwhelming workloads.
2. Don't let people have a say in how they do their work.
3. Create perpetual doubt about how well employees are performing.
4. Refuse to get involved in conflicts between employees; let them work it out.
5. Fail to give people credit for their contributions and achievements.
6. Keep people guessing about what is expected of them.
7. Bully and harass people to keep them on their toes.
8. Don't allow people to form a community; tell them work isn't a social club.

SOURCES: Based on "Getting the Least from Your Staff," sidebar in Don Mills, "Running on High Octane or Burning out Big Time?" *National Post*, April 8, 2006; Donna Callea, "Workers Feeling the Burn; Employee Burnout a New Challenge to Productive, Morale, Experts Say," *News Journal*, March 27, 2006; and Joe Humphreys, "Stress Will Be Main Cause of Workplace Illness by 2020," *Irish Times*, July 27, 2005.

and eating a healthful diet. Although individuals can pursue stress management strategies on their own, today's enlightened companies support healthy habits to help people manage stress and be more productive. Stress costs businesses billions of dollars a year in absenteeism, lower productivity, staff turnover, accidents, and higher health insurance and workers' compensation costs.[68] Taking care of employees has become a business as well as an ethical priority. In Britain, employers are required to meet certain minimal conditions to manage workplace stress, such as ensuring that employees are not exposed to a poor physical work environment, have the necessary skills and training to meet their job requirements, and are given a chance to offer input into the way their work is done.[69]

Helping employees manage stress can sometimes be as simple as encouraging people to take regular breaks and vacations. Consider that more than a third of U.S. employees surveyed by the Families and Work Institute don't take their full allotment of vacation time.[70] Here are some proactive approaches managers are taking to combat the growing stress level in today's workplace:

- Some companies have designated *quiet rooms* or meditation centers where employees can take short, calming breaks at any time they feel the need.[71] The time off is a valuable investment when it allows employees to approach their work with renewed energy and a fresh perspective.
- Wellness programs provide access to nutrition counseling and exercise facilities. A worldwide study of wellness programs conducted by the Canadian government found that for each dollar spent, the company gets from $1.95 to $3.75 return payback from benefits.[72]
- Training programs and conferences can help people identify stress and teach them coping mechanisms. Training managers to recognize warning signs is critical.
- Manager intervention is a growing trend in enlightened companies. At Boston Consulting Group, for instance, the boss steps in if he or she sees someone working too hard or displaying signs of excessive stress. Mark Ostermann says, "It was a great feeling [to have the boss provide support]. I didn't have to complain to anyone. They were proactive in contacting me."[73]
- Broad work–life balance initiatives may include flexible work options such as telecommuting and flexible hours, as well as benefits such as onsite child care or elder care,

fitness centers, and personal services such as pickup and delivery of dry cleaning. *Daily flextime* is considered by many employees to be the most effective work–life practice, which means giving employees the freedom to vary their hours as needed, such as leaving early to take an elderly parent shopping or taking time off to attend a child's school play.[74]

The study of organizational behavior reminds managers that employees are *human* resources with human needs. By acknowledging the personal aspects of employees' lives, these various initiatives communicate that managers and the organization care about employees. In addition, managers' attitudes make a tremendous difference in whether employees are stressed out and unhappy or relaxed, energetic, and productive.

- **Stress** is a physiological and emotional response to stimuli that place physical or psychological demands on an individual and create uncertainty and lack of personal control when important outcomes are at stake.
- Stress can sometimes be a positive force, but too much stress is harmful to individuals and the organizations where they work.
- The behavior pattern referred to as **Type A behavior** is characterized by extreme competitiveness, impatience, aggressiveness, and devotion to work.
- **Type B behavior** is a behavior pattern that reflects few of the Type A characteristics and includes a more balanced, relaxed approach to life.
- Type A managers can be powerful forces for innovation and change, but they can also create high stress for themselves and others.
- Work stress can be caused by both task demands and interpersonal demands.
- **Role ambiguity** refers to uncertainty about what behaviors are expected of a person in a particular role.
- **Role conflict** refers to incompatible demands of different roles, such as the demands of a manager's superiors conflicting with those of the manager's subordinates.
- Managers have direct control over many of the things that cause stress for employees.

Discussion Questions

1. As a manager, how might you deal with an employee who is always displaying negative emotions that affect the rest of the team? How might you use an understanding of attribution theory and emotional contagion to help you decide what to do?
2. In what ways might the cognitive and affective components of attitude influence the behavior of employees who are faced with learning an entirely new set of computer-related skills to retain their jobs at a manufacturing facility?
3. The chapter suggests that optimism is an important characteristic for a manager, yet some employees complain that optimistic managers cause them significant stress because they expect their subordinates to meet unreasonable goals or expectations. How might an employee deal with a perpetually optimistic manager?
4. How might a manager be able to use an understanding of perceptual selectivity and perceptual organization to communicate more effectively with subordinates?

5. In the Big Five personality factors, extroversion is considered a "good" quality to have. Why might introversion be an equally positive quality?
6. Surveys by the Conference Board show that job satisfaction has declined from 61 percent of people surveyed in 1987 to 45 percent in 2009, and one workplace analyst has said a high level of dissatisfaction is "the new normal." What are some factors that might explain this decline in satisfaction levels? Do you think it is possible for managers to reverse the trend? Discuss.
7. Which of the four components of emotional intelligence do you consider most important to an effective manager in today's world? Why?
8. How might understanding whether an employee has an internal or an external locus of control help a manager better communicate with, motivate, and lead the employee?
9. You are a manager, and you realize that one of your employees repeatedly teases coworkers born in another country, saying that they come from a backward country with pagan beliefs. How would you decide whether it's necessary to respond to the situation? If you decide to intervene, what would your response be?
10. Review Exhibit 10.12. Which learning style best characterizes you? How can you use this understanding to improve your learning ability? To improve your management skills?
11. Why do you think workplace stress is skyrocketing? Do you think it is a trend that will continue? Explain the reasons for your answer. Do you think it is the responsibility of managers and organizations to help employees manage stress? Why or why not?

Self-Learning

Personality Assessment: Jung's Typology[75]

See It Online

For each of the following items, circle either "a" or "b". In some cases, both "a" and "b" may apply to you. You should decide which is more like you, even if it is only slightly more true.

1. I would rather
   a. solve a new and complicated problem.
   b. work on something that I have done before.
2. I like to
   a. work alone in a quiet place.
   b. be where "the action" is.
3. I want a boss who
   a. establishes and applies criteria in decisions.
   b. considers individual needs and makes exceptions.
4. When I work on a project, I
   a. like to finish it and get some closure.
   b. often leave it open for possible change.
5. When making a decision, the most important considerations are
   a. rational thoughts, ideas, and data.
   b. people's feelings and values.
6. On a project, I tend to
   a. think it over and over before deciding how to proceed.
   b. start working on it right away, thinking about it as I go along.
7. When working on a project, I prefer to
   a. maintain as much control as possible.
   b. explore various options.
8. In my work, I prefer to
   a. work on several projects at a time and learn as much as possible about each one.
   b. have one project that is challenging and keeps me busy.
9. I often
   a. make lists and plans whenever I start something and may hate to seriously alter my plans.
   b. avoid plans and just let things progress as I work on them.
10. When discussing a problem with colleagues, it is easy for me
    a. to see "the big picture."
    b. to grasp the specifics of the situation.
11. When the phone rings in my office or at home, I usually
    a. consider it an interruption.
    b. don't mind answering it.
12. The word that describes me better is
    a. analytical.
    b. empathetic.
13. When I am working on an assignment, I tend to
    a. work steadily and consistently.
    b. work in bursts of energy with "downtime" in between.
14. When I listen to someone talk on a subject, I usually try to
    a. relate it to my own experience and see whether it fits.
    b. assess and analyze the message.
15. When I come up with new ideas, I generally
    a. "go for it."
    b. like to contemplate the ideas some more.
16. When working on a project, I prefer to
    a. narrow the scope so it is clearly defined.
    b. broaden the scope to include related aspects.
17. When I read something, I usually
    a. confine my thoughts to what is written there.

b. read between the lines and relate the words to other ideas.

18. When I have to make a decision in a hurry, I often
    a. feel uncomfortable and wish I had more information.
    b. am able to do so with available data.

19. In a meeting, I tend to
    a. continue formulating my ideas as I talk about them.
    b. speak out only after I have carefully thought the issue through.

20. In work, I prefer spending a great deal of time on issues of
    a. ideas.
    b. people.

21. In meetings, I am most often annoyed with people who
    a. come up with many sketchy ideas.
    b. lengthen the meeting with many practical details.

22. I tend to be
    a. a morning person.
    b. a night owl.

23. My style in preparing for a meeting is
    a. to be willing to go in and be responsive.
    b. to be fully prepared and sketch an outline of the meeting.

24. In meetings, I would prefer for people to
    a. display a fuller range of emotions.
    b. be more task-oriented.

25. I would rather work for an organization where
    a. my job was intellectually stimulating.
    b. I was committed to its goals and mission.

26. On weekends, I tend to
    a. plan what I will do.
    b. just see what happens and decide as I go along.

27. I am more
    a. outgoing.
    b. contemplative.

28. I would rather work for a boss who is
    a. full of new ideas.
    b. practical.

In the following, choose the word in each pair that appeals to you more:

29. a. Social b. Theoretical
30. a. Ingenuity b. Practicality
31. a. Organized b. Adaptable
32. a. Active b. Concentration

Scoring and Interpretation

Count 1 point for each of the following items that you circled in the inventory.

	Score for I (Introversion)	Score for E (Extroversion)	Score for S (Sensing)	Score for N (Intuition)
	2a	2b	1b	1a
	6a	6b	10b	10a
	11a	11b	13a	13b
	15b	15a	16a	16b
	19b	19a	17a	17b
	22a	22b	21a	21b
	27b	27a	28b	28a
	32b	32a	30b	30a
Totals	______	______	______	______

Circle the one with more points: I or E

(If tied on I/E, don't count #11)

Circle the one with more points: S or N

(If tied on S/N, don't count #16)

	Score for T (Thinking)	Score for F (Feeling)	Score for J (Judging)	Score for P (Perceiving)
	3a	3b	4a	4b
	5a	5b	7a	7b
	12a	12b	8b	8a
	14b	14a	9a	9b
	20a	20b	18b	18a
	24b	24a	23b	23a
	25a	25b	26a	26b
	29b	29a	31a	31b
Totals	______	______	______	______

Circle the one with more points:
T or F
(If tied on T/F, don't count #24)

Circle the one with more points:
J or P
(If tied on J/P, don't count #23)

Your Score Is: I or E __E__ S or N __N__ T or F __T__ J or P __J__

Your type is __ENTJ__ (example: INTJ; ESFP; etc.)

Characteristics Frequently Associated with Each Type

The scores above measure variables similar to the Myers-Briggs Type Indicator (MBTI)™ assessment based on the work of psychologist Carl Jung. The MBTI™ assessment, which was described in the chapter text, identifies four dimensions and 16 different "types." The dominant characteristics associated with each type are shown below. Remember that no one is a pure type; however, each individual has preferences for introversion versus extroversion, sensing versus intuition, thinking versus feeling, and judging versus perceiving. Read the description of your type as determined by your scores in the survey. Do you believe the description fits your personality?

Characteristics associated with each type

ISTJ: Organizer, trustworthy, responsible, good trustee or inspector.

ISFJ: Quiet, conscientious, devoted, handles detail, good conservator.

INFJ: Perseveres, inspirational, quiet caring for others, good counselor.

INTJ: Independent thinker, skeptical, theory, competence, good scientist.

ISTP: Cool, observant, easy-going, good craftsperson.

ISFP: Warm, sensitive, team player, avoids conflict, good artist.

INFP: Idealistic, strong values, likes learning, good at noble service.

INTP: Designer, logical, conceptual, likes challenges, good architect.

ESTP: Spontaneous, gregarious, good at problem solving and promoting.

ESFP: Sociable, generous, makes things fun, good as entertainer.

ENFP: Imaginative, enthusiastic, starts projects, good champion.

ENTP: Resourceful, stimulating, dislikes routine, tests limits, good.

ESTJ: Order, structure, practical, good administrator or supervisor.

ESFJ: People skills, harmonizer, popular, does things for people, good host.

ENFJ: Charismatic, persuasive, fluent presenter, sociable, active, good teacher.

ENTJ: Visionary planner, takes charge, hearty speaker, natural leader.

Group Learning

Attribution Theory and Personality Role Play[76]

Step 1. Read the following background information: You are the new distribution manager for French Grains Bakery. Five drivers report to you that deliver French Grains baked goods to grocery stores in the metropolitan area. The drivers are expected to complete the Delivery Report to keep track of actual deliveries and any changes that occur. The Delivery Report is a key element in inventory control and provides the data for French Grains's invoicing of grocery stores. Errors become excessive when drivers fail to complete the report each day, especially when store managers request additional or different breads and baked goods when the driver arrives. As a result, French Grains may not be paid for several loaves of bread a day for each mistake in the Delivery Report. The result is lost revenue and poor inventory control.

One of the drivers accounts for about 60 percent of the errors in the Delivery Reports. This driver is a nice person and is generally reliable, but he is sometimes late for work. His major problem is that he falls behind in his paperwork. A second driver accounts for about 30 percent of the errors, and a third driver for about 10 percent of the errors. The other two drivers turn in virtually error-free Delivery Reports.

Step 2. Divide into groups of four to six students. As a group, discuss why you think one driver makes so many mistakes. Then, one person volunteers to play the role of the new Distribution Manager and another person plays the role of the driver who accounts for 60 percent of the errors in the delivery reports.

Step 3. The new distribution manager should act the role as if his or her personality is high on "thinking" and low on "feeling," or as if he or she is high on "authoritarianism." You have called the driver into your office to talk to him about doing a more complete and accurate job with the Delivery Report. Make some notes below about how you will go about correcting this problem as a thinking-oriented or authoritarian leader. Exactly what will you say and how will you get the driver to listen and change his behavior?

Step 4. Now, start the role play between the distribution manager and the driver. Other group members act as observers.

Step 5. After the role play is completed, the observers give feedback on what worked and did not work with respect to the thinking or authoritarian personality style of giving feedback. How effective was it?

Step 6. Repeat steps 3 through 5, with other students volunteering to be the distribution manager and driver. This time the manager should act as if his or her personality is strongly "feeling" or nonauthoritarian. Was this personality style more or less effective for correcting the problem?

Step 7. The instructor can ask students to volunteer to play the role of the distribution manager and the driver in front of the class. Different students might take turns playing the role of distribution manager, emphasizing a different personality trait each time. The instructor can ask other students for feedback on the leader's effectiveness and about which approach seems more effective for correcting this situation, and why.

Step 8. The instructor will lead a discussion on attribution theory and personality types and how these relate to good work behaviors.

Action Learning

1. On your own, complete the following table, making assessments of your family members according to the Myers-Briggs Type Indicator™. Include some notes on why you have chosen each type for that particular person.
2. Talk over these assessments with at least one person in your family, and try to listen to that other person's opinions, changing any of your own assessments as you think is necessary.
3. In class, in groups of 3 or 4, share your results and talk about why you think each person is a certain type and whether you changed any assessments after the discussion with a family member. Also talk about how the combination of personality types has impacted your family.
4. Your instructor may choose to have you write a paper on your assessments.

	Introvert or Extravert?	Sensing or Intuition?	Thinking or Feeling?	Perceptive or Judging?
Mother				
Father				
Sibling				
Sibling				
Other				
Other				
Other				

Ethical Dilemma

Should I Fudge the Numbers?[77]

Sara MacIntosh recently joined MicroPhone, a large telecommunications company, to take over the implementation of a massive customer service training project. The program was created by Kristin Cole, head of human resources and Sara's new boss. According to the grapevine, Kristin was hoping this project alone would give her the "star quality" she needed to earn a coveted promotion. Industry competition was heating up, and MicroPhone's strategy called for being the best at customer service, which meant having the most highly trained people in the industry, especially those who worked directly with customers. Kristin's new training program called for an average of one full week of intense customer service training for each of 3,000 people and had a price tag of about $40 million.

Kristin put together a team of overworked staffers to develop the training program, but now she needed someone well qualified and dedicated to manage and implement the project. Sara, with eight years of experience, a long list of accomplishments, and advanced degrees in finance and organizational behavior, seemed perfect for the job. However, during a thorough review of the proposal, Sara discovered some assumptions built into the formulas that raised red flags. She approached Dan Sotal, the team's coordinator, about her concerns, but the more Dan tried to explain how the financial projections were derived, the more Sara realized that Kristin's proposal was seriously flawed. No matter how she tried to work them out, the most that could be squeezed out of the $40 million budget was 20 hours of training per person, not the 40 hours everyone expected for such a high price tag.

Sara knew that although the proposal had been largely developed before she came on board, it would bear her signature. As she carefully described the problems with the proposal to Kristin and outlined the potentially devastating consequences, Kristin impatiently tapped her pencil. Finally, she stood up, leaned forward, and interrupted Sara, quietly saying, "Sara, make the numbers work so that it adds up to 40 hours and stays within the $40 million budget."

Sara glanced up and replied, "I don't think it can be done unless we either change the number of employees who are to be trained or the cost figure."

Kristin's smile froze on her face and her eyes began to snap as she again interrupted. "I don't think you understand what I'm saying. We have too much at stake here. *Make the previous numbers work.*" Stunned, Sara belatedly began to realize that Kristin was ordering her to fudge the numbers. She felt an anxiety attack coming on as she wondered what she should do.

What Would You Do?

1. Make the previous numbers work. Kristin and the entire team have put massive amounts of time into the project, and they all expect you to be a team player. You don't want to let them down. Besides, this project is a great opportunity for you in a highly visible position.
2. Stick to your principles and refuse to fudge the numbers. Tell Kristin you will work overtime to help develop an alternate proposal that stays within the budget by providing more training to employees who work directly with customers and fewer training hours for those who don't have direct customer contact.
3. Go to the team and tell them what you've been asked to do. If they refuse to support you, threaten to reveal the true numbers to the CEO and board members.

Case for Critical Analysis

Reflex Systems

As the plane took off from the L.A. airport for Chicago and home, Henry Rankin tried to unwind, something that didn't come naturally to the Reflex Systems software engineer. He needed time to think, and the flight from Los Angeles was a welcome relief. He had gone to L.A. to help two members of his project team solve technical glitches in software. Rankin had been pushing himself and his team hard for three months now, and he didn't know when they would get a break. Rankin was responsible for the technical implementation of the new customer relationship management software being installed for western and eastern sales offices in L.A. and Chicago. The software was badly needed to improve follow-up sales for his company, Reflex Systems. Reflex sold exercise equipment to high schools and colleges through a national force of 310 salespeople. Reflex also sold products to small and medium-sized businesses for recreation centers.

Rankin knew CEO Mike Frazer saw the new CRM software as the answer to one of the exercise equipment manufacturer's most persistent problems. Even though Reflex's low prices generated healthy sales, follow-up service was spotty. Consequently, getting repeat business from customers—high schools, colleges, and corporate recreation centers—was an uphill battle. Excited by the prospect of finally removing this major roadblock, Frazer ordered the CRM software installed in just ten weeks, a goal Rankin privately thought was unrealistic. He also felt the project budget wasn't adequate. Rankin thought about meeting the next day with his three Chicago team members and about the status update he would give his boss, Nicole Dyer, the senior vice president for Information Technology. Rankin remembered that Dyer had scheduled ten weeks for the CRM project. He had always been a top performer by driving himself hard and had been in his management position three years now. He was good with technology but was frustrated when members of his five-person team didn't seem as committed. Dyer had told him last week that she didn't feel a sense of urgency from his team. How could she think that? Rankin had requested that team members work evenings and weekends because the budget was too tight to fill a vacant position. They agreed to put in the hours, although they didn't seem enthusiastic.

Still, Frazer was the boss, so if he wanted the job done in ten weeks, Rankin would do everything in his power to deliver, even if it meant the entire team worked nights and weekends. He wasn't asking any more of his subordinates than he was asking of himself, as he frequently reminded them when they came to him with bloodshot eyes and complained about the hours. Rankin thought back to a flight one month ago when he had returned to Chicago from L.A. Sally Phillips had sat next to him. Phillips was on one of five members on Rankin's team and had told him she had an offer from a well-known competitor. The money was less, but she was interested in the quality of life aspect of the company. Phillips had asked for feedback on how she was doing and about her career prospects at Reflex. Rankin had said he didn't want her to leave, but what more could he say? She got along well with people, but she wasn't as technically gifted as some on the team. Rankin needed her help to finish the project and he'd told her so. Two weeks later, though, she had turned in her letter of resignation, and now the team was shorthanded. Rankin was also aware that his own possible promotion in two years, when Nicole Dyer was eligible for retirement, depended on his success with this project. He would just take up the slack himself. He loved studying, analyzing, and solving technical problems when he could get time alone.

Henry Rankin knew that Nicole Dyer had noticed a lack of commitment on the part of the team members. He wondered whether she had discussed the team's performance with Frazer as well. Rankin hadn't noticed any other problems, but he recalled his partner on the project, Sam Matheny, saying that two Chicago team members, Bob Finley and Lynne Johnston, were avoiding each other. How did Sam know that? Matheny was in charge of nontechnical sales implementation of the CRM project, which meant training salespeople, redesigning sales procedures, updating customer records, and so forth. Rankin had called Finley and Johnston to his office and said he expected them to get along for the good of the project. Finley said he had overreacted to Johnston from lack of sleep and wondered when the project would be over. Rankin wasn't certain because of all the problems with both software and hardware, but he'd said the project shouldn't last more than another month.

As the plane taxied to the gate, an exhausted Rankin couldn't quell his growing fears that as the deadline fast approached, the project team was crumbling. How could he meet that deadline? As the plane taxied to the gate at Chicago, Rankin wondered about the project's success. Was there more to managing this team than working hard and pushing others hard? Even he was tired. Maybe he would ask his wife when he got home. He hadn't seen her or the kids for a week, but they had not complained.

Questions

1. What personality and behavior characteristics does Henry Rankin exhibit? Do you think these traits contribute to a good person–job fit for him? If you were an executive coach hired to help Rankin be a better manager, what would you say to him? Why?
2. Does Rankin display type A or type B behavior? What are the causes of stress for his team?
3. If you were Rankin, how would you have handled your team members (Sally Phillips, Bob Finley, and Lynne Johnston)? Be specific. What insights or behaviors would make Rankin a better manager?

aplia Aplia Highlights

Now use your Aplia homework to help you:

- Apply management theories in your life
- Assess your management skills
- Master management terms and concepts
- Apply your knowledge to real-world situations
- Analyze and solve challenging management problems

In order to take advantage of these elements, your instructor will need to have set up a course for your class within Aplia. Ask your instructor to contact his/her Cengage sales representative and Digital Solutions Manager to explore testing Aplia in your course this term.

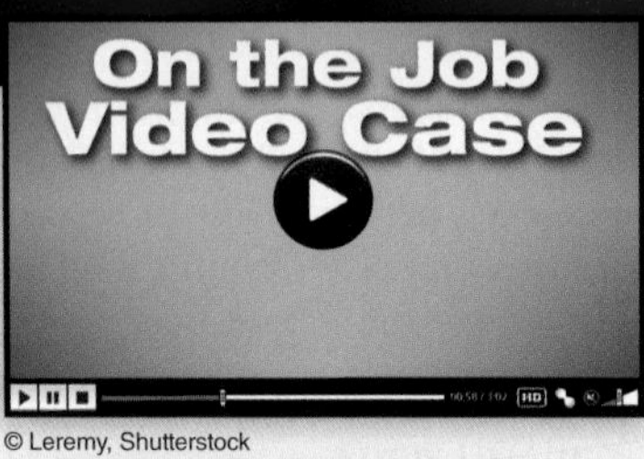

© Leremy, Shutterstock

Mitchell Gold + Bob Williams: Understanding Individual Behavior

When Information Technology (IT) Manager Kim Clay began answering phones as a consumer inquiry representative for Mitchell Gold + Bob Williams (MG+BW), she was not particularly self-confident, nor was she certain about the direction of her career. "When I first started working here, I definitely wouldn't say that confidence was something I exuded," Clay says of her early days at the furniture company. Clay took the position because the company was near to her apartment, and she also liked interacting with people. "In Consumer Inquiry, I would answer the phone and tell people about our furniture and where they could find it," she recalls.

Although Clay's start at MG+BW was uneventful, coworkers noted her positive work attitudes. "Kim was someone you could really rely on and trust—she was a great communicator," says Dan Gauthreaux, vice president of human resources. "You knew that if Kim was given an assignment or project, or needed to follow up with this customer or expedite something, she would make it happen."

Clay soon moved on to the Customer Care department, where she dealt with customer issues at the retail level. Her good-natured personality was popular not only with customers but also with coworkers who frequented her cubicle to get help with computer issues. "It seemed that when people had problems with their computers, they typically came to me and asked for help," Clay remembers.

In many organizations, hidden talents often remain hidden. But at Mitchell Gold + Bob Williams, management pushes employees to discover their talents and seize new opportunities. In this case, MG+BW managers recognized Clay's knack for computers, and they came to her to discuss a new idea: a computer help desk. "We decided to create the help desk, which we never had before," Clay states. "Since everybody was coming to me with computer questions, it seemed a good fit for me." Although Clay lacked formal computer training, she was willing to put herself out there and see where the opportunity might lead. "I felt like it was a big challenge to move from customer care to technology. I had never done anything with computers before, so I was really excited to try it," she says.

Today Kim Clay is the IT manager for the entire BG+BW organization. Her positive work attitudes have made her an up-and-coming leader over a high-tech process. At MG+BW, all new furniture pieces begin with a production ticket generated from a computer enterprise resource planning (ERP) system. As items move through the process, computers track development all the way to final shipping and invoicing. Clay oversees the computerized system from end to end. "It's a constantly changing field, and we have to stay on top of it to keep the business competitive," Clay states. "We have to know the new technology that's out there and incorporate it into our business as quickly as we can."

Although Clay's rise through the ranks was no surprise to those who saw her early potential, few could have predicted the career path she made for herself at MG+BW. Vice President Dan Gauthreaux, who recognized Clay's work ethic and organizational commitment early on, never imagined she would become a top manager over technology. But as Gauthreaux is quick to add, MG+BW seeks maximum development for all its employees. "There is a tolerance for letting folks expand and develop on their own," Gauthreaux says of the company's approach to human resources. "We're the kind of company that, whomever Kim reports to, they're not going to let her step off that ledge and not be successful." He adds that personal development is a learning partnership between the employee and the organization: "Employees are encouraged to push themselves, but we've created a culture where we're not going to let each other fail. There's a sense that your success is my success."

Discussion Questions

1. Which component of attitudes does Vice President Dan Gauthreaux express when he says, "I think you can learn from any job you do and try to make the best of it"?
2. How did Kim Clay's organizational citizenship behavior lead to the creation of a new computer help desk at MG+BW?
3. What role did management play in fostering Kim Clay's high organizational commitment? In what ways does this commitment benefit the organization?

© VikaSuh, Shutterstock

Because I Said So

Meet Daphne Wilder (Diane Keaton)—your typical meddling, overprotective, and divorced mother of three daughters. Two of her three beautiful daughters have married. That leaves Millie (Mandy Moore) as the focus of Daphne's undivided attention and compulsive behavior to find Millie a mate. Daphne places some online advertising, screens the applicants, and submits those she approves to Millie. Along the way, Daphne meets Joe (Stephen Collins), the father of one applicant. Romance emerges, and the film comes to a delightful, though expected, conclusion.

Personality Assessment This scene starts after Daphne answers her cell phone and says the person has the wrong number. It follows the frantic rearrangement of the sofa, which ends up in the same place it started. The film cuts to Millie and Jason (Tom Everett Scott) dining at his place.

What to Watch for and Ask Yourself

- Which Big Five personality traits best describe Daphne? Give examples of behavior from the film scene to support your observations.
- Which Big Five personality traits best describe Millie? Give examples of behavior from the film scene to support your observations.
- Review the discussion of emotional intelligence earlier in this chapter. Assess both Daphne and Millie on the four parts of emotional intelligence.

Endnotes

1. "There's Life (and a Living) after Rejection," *The Independent on Sunday,* January 6, 2008; Amy Ellis Nutt, "Harry Potter's Disappearing Act," *Newhouse News Service* (April 23, 2007): 1; and Tom Muha, "Achieving Happiness: Setbacks Can Make Us Stronger," *The Capital,* May 31, 2009.
2. Muha, "Achieving Happiness"; and Melinda Beck, "If at First You Don't Succeed, You're in Excellent Company," *The Wall Street Journal,* April 29, 2008.
3. M. E. Gist, "Self-Efficacy: Implications for Organizational Behavior and Human Resource Management," *Academy of Management Review* (July 1987): 47; and Arthur Bandura, "Self-efficacy," in V. S. Ramachaudran, ed., *Encyclopedia of Human Behavior,* vol. 4 (New York: Academic Press, 1994): pp. 71–81.
4. See Michael West, "Hope Springs," *People Management* (October 2005): 38ff; and Mark C. Bolino, William H. Turnley, and James M. Bloodgood, "Citizenship Behaviors and the Creation of Social Capital in Organizations," *Academy of Management Review* 27, no. 4 (2002): 505–522.
5. Reported in Del Jones, "Optimism Puts Rose-Colored Tint in Glasses of Top Execs; Or Do They Just Have a Feeble Grip on Reality?" *USA Today*, December 15, 2005.
6. Jerry Krueger and Emily Killham, "At Work, Feeling Good Matters," *Gallup Management Journal*, December 8, 2005,http://gmj.gallup.com/content/20311/work-feeling-goodmatters.aspx (accessed September 17, 2010).
7. John W. Newstrom and Keith Davis, *Organizational Behavior: Human Behavior at Work,* 11th ed. (Burr Ridge, IL: McGraw-Hill Irwin, 2002): Chapter 9.
8. S. J. Breckler, "Empirical Validation of Affect, Behavior, and Cognition as Distinct Components of Attitude," *Journal of Personality and Social Psychology* (May 1984): 1191–1205; and J. M. Olson and M. P. Zanna, "Attitudes and Attitude Change," *Annual Review of Psychology* 44 (1993): 117–154.
9. M. T. Iaffaldano and P. M. Muchinsky, "Job Satisfaction and Job Performance: A Meta-Analysis," *Psychological Bulletin* (March 1985): 251–273; C. Ostroff, "The Relationship between Satisfaction, Attitudes, and Performance: An Organizational Level Analysis," *Journal of Applied Psychology* (December 1992): 963–974; and M. M. Petty, G. W. McGee, and J. W. Cavender, "A Meta-Analysis of the Relationship between Individual Job Satisfaction and Individual Performance," *Academy of Management Review* (October 1984): 712–721.
10. Conference Board survey, reported in "Job Satisfaction in U.S. Hits All-Time Low," *News for You* (February 17, 2010): 4.
11. Tony Schwartz, "The Greatest Sources of Satisfaction in the Workplace Are Internal and Emotional," *Fast Company* (November 2000): 398–402.
12. William C. Symonds, "Where Paternalism Equals Good Business," *BusinessWeek* (July 20, 1998): 16E4, 16E6.
13. Towers Perrin survey reported in "Employee Engagement," TowersWatson.com. www.towersperrin.com/tp/showhtml.jsp?url=global/service-areas/research-and-surveys/employee-research/ee-engagement.htm&country=global (accessed September 17, 2010).
14. "Closing the Engagement Gap: A Road Map for Driving Superior Business Performance," *Towers Perrin Global*

Workforce Study 2007–2008, www.towersperrin.com/tp/getwebcachedoc?webc=HRS/USA/2008/200803/GWS_Global_Report20072008_31208.pdf (accessed September 20, 2010).

15. W. Chan Kin and Renée Mauborgne, "Fair Process: Managing in the Knowledge Economy," *Harvard Business Review* (January 2003): 127–136.
16. Leadership IQ survey, reported in "Many Employees Don't Trust Their Boss," *Machine Design* (September 2007): 2.
17. Quoted in Paul Harris, "Leadership: Role Models Earn Trust and Profits," *T&D* (March 2010): 47.
18. For a discussion of cognitive dissonance theory, see Leon A. Festinger, *Theory of Cognitive Dissonance* (Stanford, CA: Stanford University Press, 1957).
19. J. A. Deutsch, W. G. Young, and T. J. Kalogeris, "The Stomach Signals Satiety," *Science* (April 1978): 22–33.
20. Richard B. Chase and Sriram Dasu, "Want to Perfect Your Company's Service? Use Behavioral Science," *Harvard Business Review* (June 2001): 79–84.
21. H. H. Kelley, "Attribution in Social Interaction," in E. Jones et al., eds., *Attribution: Perceiving the Causes of Behavior* (Morristown, NJ: General Learning Press, 1972).
22. See J. M. Digman, "Personality Structure: Emergence of the Five-Factor Model," *Annual Review of Psychology* 41 (1990): 417–440; M. R. Barrick and M. K. Mount, "Autonomy As a Moderator of the Relationships between the Big Five Personality Dimensions and Job Performance," *Journal of Applied Psychology* (February 1993): 111–118; and J. S. Wiggins and A. L. Pincus, "Personality: Structure and Assessment," *Annual Review of Psychology* 43 (1992): 473–504.
23. Del Jones, "Not All Successful CEOs Are Extroverts," *USA Today*, June 6, 2006, www.usatoday.com/money/companies/management/2006-06-06-shy-ceo-usat_x.htm (accessed September 20, 2010).
24. Reported in Christopher Palmeri, "Putting Managers to the Test," *BusinessWeek* (November 20, 2006): 82.
25. Tim Sanders, *The Likeability Factor: How to Boost Your L-Factor and Achieve the Life of Your Dreams* (New York: Crown, 2005).
26. Lisa Takeuchi Cullen, "SATs for J-O-B-S," *Time* (April 3, 2006): 89.
27. Toddi Gutner, "Applicants' Personalities Put to the Test," *The Wall Street Journal,* August 26, 2008.
28. Julian B. Rotter, "Generalized Expectancies for Internal versus External Control of Reinforcement," *Psychological Monographs* 80, no. 609 (1966); and J. B. Rotter, "Internal versus External Control of Reinforcement: A Case History," *American Psychologist* 45, no. 4 (April 1990):489–493.
29. See P. E. Spector, "Behavior in Organizations as a Function of Employee's Locus of Control," *Psychological Bulletin* (May 1982): 482–497.
30. T. W. Adorno, E. Frenkel-Brunswick, D. J. Levinson, and R. N. Sanford, *The Authoritarian Personality* (New York: Harper & Row, 1950).
31. Niccolo Machiavelli, *The Prince,* trans. George Bull (Middlesex: Penguin, 1961).
32. Richard Christie and Florence Geis, *Studies in Machiavellianism* (New York: Academic Press, 1970).
33. R. G. Vleeming, "Machiavellianism: A Preliminary Review," *Psychological Reports* (February 1979): 295–310.
34. Christie and Geis, *Studies in Machiavellianism.*
35. Carl Jung, *Psychological Types* (London: Routledge and Kegan Paul, 1923).
36. Mary H. McCaulley, "Research on the MBTI™ and Leadership: Taking the Critical First Step," keynote address, The Myers–Briggs Type Indicator and Leadership: An International Research Conference (January 12–14, 1994).
37. Alison Overhold, "Are You a Polyolefin Optimizer? Take This Quiz!" *Fast Company* (April 2004): 37.
38. Reported in Cullen, "SATs for J-O-B-S."
39. Charles A. O'Reilly III, Jennifer Chatman, and David F. Caldwell, "People and Organizational Culture: A Profile Comparison Approach to Assessing Person-Organization Fit," *Academy of Management Journal* 34, no. 3 (1991): 487–516.
40. Anna Muoio, "Should I Go .Com?" *Fast Company* (July 2000): 164–172.
41. Michelle Leder, "Is That Your Final Answer?" *Working Woman* (December–January 2001): 18.
42. Michael Kinsman, "Businesses Can Suffer If Workers' Emotions Not Dealt With" (an interview with Mel Fugate), *The San Diego Union-Tribune*, December 17, 2006; and Mel Fugate, Angelo J. Kinicki, and Gregory E. Prussia, "Employee Coping with Organizational Change: An Examination of Alternative Theoretical Perspectives and Models," *Personnel Psychology* 61, no. 1 (Spring 2008): 1–36.
43. "Emotion," *The Free Dictionary*, www.thefreedictionary.com/Emotions (accessed June 15, 2010); and "Motivation and Emotion," *Psychology 101* (AllPsych Online),http://allpsych.com/psychology101/emotion.html (accessed June 15, 2010).
44. E. Hatfield, J. T. Cacioppo, and R. L. Rapson, *Emotional Contagion* (New York: Cambridge University Press, 1994).
45. Robert I. Sutton, "Are You Being a Jerk? Again?" *BusinessWeek* (August 25, 2008): 52.
46. Krueger and Killham, "At Work, Feeling Good Matters."
47. Daniel Goleman, "Leadership That Gets Results," *Harvard Business Review* (March–April 2000): 79–90; and Daniel Goleman, *Emotional Intelligence: Why It Can Matter More Than IQ* (New York: Bantam Books, 1995).
48. Alan Farnham, "Are You Smart Enough to Keep Your Job?" *Fortune* (January 15, 1996): 34–47.
49. Hendrie Weisinger, *Emotional Intelligence at Work* (San Francisco: Jossey-Bass, 2000); D. C. McClelland, "Identifying Competencies with Behavioral-Event Interviews," *Psychological Science* (Spring 1999): 331–339; Daniel Goleman, "Leadership That Gets Results," *Harvard Business Review* (March–April 2000): 78–90; D. Goleman, *Working with Emotional Intelligence* (New York: Bantam Books, 1999); and Lorie Parch, "Testing . . . 1,2,3," *Working Woman* (October 1997): 74–78.
50. Cliff Edwards, "Death of a Pushy Salesman," *BusinessWeek* (July 3, 2006): 108–109.
51. Reported in Cari Tuna, "Lawyers and Employers Take the Fight to 'Workplace Bullies'" (Theory & Practice column), *The Wall Street Journal,* August 4, 2008.
52. Sue Shellenbarger, "To Combat an Office Tyrant, Look at the Roots," *The Wall Street Journal,* April 28, 2010; and Ed Frauenheim, "Pulling No Punches," *Workforce Management* (October 6, 2008): 1.
53. David A. Kolb, "Management and the Learning Process," *California Management Review* 18, no. 3 (Spring 1976): 21–31.

54. See David. A. Kolb, I. M. Rubin, and J. M. McIntyre, *Organizational Psychology: An Experimental Approach*, 3rd ed. (Englewood Cliffs, NJ: Prentice Hall, 1984): 27–54.

55. T. A. Beehr and R. S. Bhagat, *Human Stress and Cognition in Organizations: An Integrated Perspective* (New York: Wiley, 1985); and Bruce Cryer, Rollin McCraty, and Doc Childre, "Pull the Plug on Stress," *Harvard Business Review* (July 2003): 102–107.

56. Anita Bruzzese, "Wall Street Woes, Election Add to Workplace Stress," *Gannett News Service* (September 29, 2008).

57. "Desk Rage Rising," *Office Solutions* (January 2009): 9; and Carol Hymowitz, "Bosses Have to Learn How to Confront Troubled Employees," *The Wall Street Journal,* April 23, 2007.

58. Jeannine Aversa, "Stress over Debt Taking Toll on Health," *USA Today,* June 9, 2008, www.usatoday.com/news/health/2008-06-09-debt-stress_N.htm (accessed June 10, 2008).

59. Reported in Brian Nadel, "The Price of Pressure," special advertising feature, *Fortune* (December 11, 2006): 143–146.

60. Health and Safety Authority survey, reported in Joe Humphreys, "Stress Will Be Main Cause of Workplace Illness by 2020," *Irish Times*, July 27, 2005.

61. Don Mills, "Running on High Octane or Burning out Big Time? Stress Flunkies," *National Post*, April 8, 2006.

62. M. Friedman and R. Rosenman, *Type A Behavior and Your Heart* (New York: Knopf, 1974).

63. Reported in "Work Stress Is Costly," *Morning Call*, October 18, 2005.

64. Families and Work Institute survey, reported in "Reworking Work," *Time* (July 25, 2005): 50–55; Spherion survey, reported in Donna Callea, "Workers Feeling the Burn: Employee Burnout a New Challenge to Productivity, Morale, Experts Say," *News Journal*, March 27, 2006; Mills, "Running on High Octane or Burning out Big Time?"; Vani Doraisamy, "Young Techies Swell the Ranks of the Depressed," *The Hindu*, October 11, 2005.

65. Jenna Goudreau, "Dispatches from the War on Stress," *BusinessWeek* (August 6, 2007): 74–75.

66. Quoted in Elizabeth Bernstein, "When a Co-Worker Is Stressed Out," *The Wall Street Journal*, August 26, 2008.

67. Hymowitz, "Bosses Have to Learn How to Confront Troubled Employees."

68. Claire Sykes, "Say Yes to Less Stress," *Office Solutions* (July-August 2003): 26; and Andrea Higbie, "Quick Lessons in the Fine Old Art of Unwinding," *The New York Times*, February 25, 2001.

69. Donalee Moulton, "Buckling under the Pressure," *OH & S Canada* 19, no. 8 (December 2003): 36.

70. Rosabeth Moss Kanter, "Balancing Work and Life," *Knight-Ridder Tribune News Service,* April 8, 2005.

71. Leslie Gross Klass, "Quiet Time at Work Helps Employee Stress," *Johnson City Press*, January 28, 2001.

72. Moulton, "Buckling under the Pressure."

73. Goudreau, "Dispatches from the War on Stress."

74. David T. Gordon, "Balancing Act," *CIO* (October 15, 2001): 58–62.

75. From Dorothy Marcic, *Organizational Behavior,* 4th ed. (Mason OH: South-Western, Cengage Learning, 1995). Reproduced by permission.

76. Based on K. J. Keleman, J. E. Garcia, and K. J. Lovelace, *Management Incidents: Role Plays for Management Development* (Dubuque, IA: Kendall Hunt Publishing Company, 1990): 69–72.

77. Adapted from Doug Wallace, "Fudge the Numbers or Leave," *Business Ethics* (May–June 1996): 58–59. Copyright © 1996 by New Mountain Media LLC. Reproduced with permission of New Mountain Media LLC.

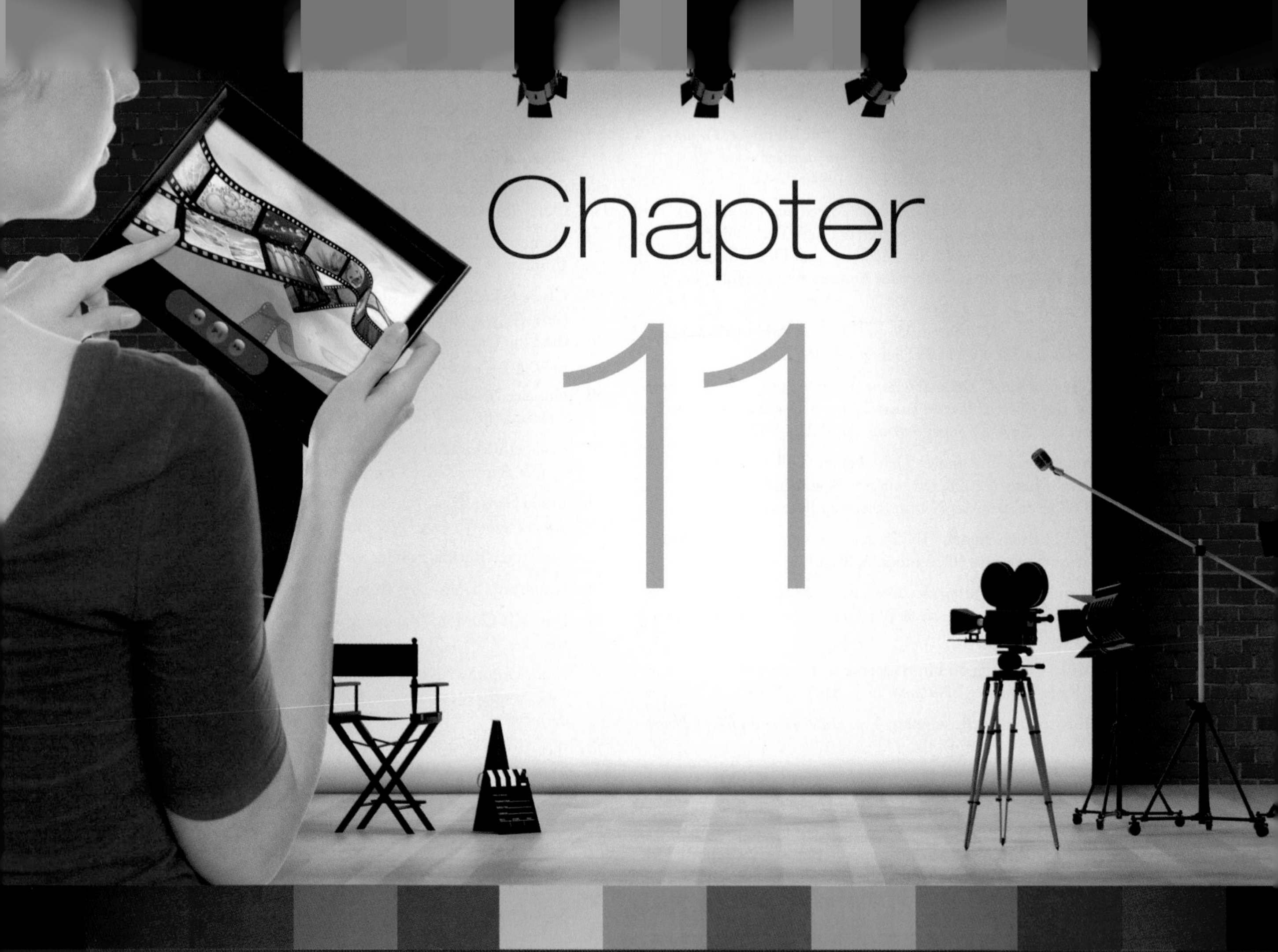

Chapter 11

Chapter Outline

Leadership

Learning Outcomes

After studying this chapter, you should be able to:

1. Define leadership and explain its importance for organizations.
2. Describe how leadership is changing in today's organizations, including Level 5 leadership, servant leadership, and authentic leadership.
3. Discuss how women's style of leading is typically different from men's.
4. Identify personal characteristics associated with effective leaders.
5. Define task-oriented behavior and people-oriented behavior and explain how these categories are used to evaluate and adapt leadership style.
6. Describe the situational model of leadership and its application to subordinate participation.
7. Discuss how leadership fits the organizational situation and how organizational characteristics can substitute for leadership behaviors.
8. Describe transformational leadership and when it should be used.
9. Explain how followership is related to effective leadership.
10. Identify sources of leader power and the tactics leaders use to influence others.

© James Steidl, Shutterstock

Are You Ready to Be a Manager?

Please circle your opinion below each of the following statements.

1 **I am able to get people enthused about an idea and to take action.**

Mostly True — Mostly False

(See page 440, Nature of Leadership, and page 459, Charismatic and Visionary Leadership.)

2 **I am aware of becoming egotistical and work hard to remain more humble.**

Mostly True — Mostly False

(See page 442, Level 5 Leadership.)

3 **I can focus on the task to be done, when it is required, but I also have the ability to work on relationships and making sure peoples' needs are addressed.**

Mostly True — Mostly False

(See page 452, Task versus People, and page 454, Contingency Approaches.)

4 **When I am working with a leader, I make sure I bring my critical thinking skills so that I am not merely a passive follower.**

Mostly True — Mostly False

(See page 462, Followership.)

5 **When am working with a group, I am able to get things done through the strength of the relationships and my expertise, rather than relying on authoritarian methods.**

Mostly True — Mostly False

(See page 465, Personal Power.)

Qi Lu grew up in a rural village in China with no electricity or running water. Today, he is president of Microsoft's online services division. How did he get there? Not from personal ambition, say former colleagues at Yahoo. "He shunned the limelight," said Tim Cadogan, now CEO of OpenX, "but he was considered one of the stars." Lu rose through the ranks at Yahoo and got the job at Microsoft, based not on aggressiveness and pursuit of personal advancement, but rather because of his sheer intellectual abilities and his commitment to go above and beyond the call of duty to accomplish organizational goals. Lu is an excellent example of a new kind of leader for today's collaborative world, a leader who quietly builds strong teams and organizations rather than touting his own abilities and accomplishments.[1]

In the previous chapter, we explored differences in attitudes and personality that affect behavior. Some of the most important attitudes for the organization's success are those of its leaders, because leader attitudes and behaviors play a critical role in shaping employee attitudes and performance. In this chapter, we define leadership and explore how managers develop leadership qualities. We look at some important leadership approaches for contemporary organizations, as well as examine trait, behavioral, and contingency theories of leadership effectiveness, discuss charismatic and transformational leadership, explore the role of followership, and consider how leaders use power and influence to get things done. Chapters 12 through 14 will look in detail at many of the functions of leadership, including employee motivation, communication, and encouraging teamwork.

The Nature of Leadership

In most situations, a team, military unit, department, or volunteer group is only as good as its leader. Yet there are as many variations among leaders as there are among other individuals, and many different styles of leadership can be effective.

So, what does it mean to be a leader? Among all the ideas and writings about leadership, three aspects stand out—people, influence, and goals. Leadership occurs among people, involves the use of influence, and is used to attain goals.[2] *Influence* means that the relationship among people is not passive. Moreover, influence is designed to achieve some end or goal. Thus, **leadership**, as defined here, is the ability to influence people toward the attainment of goals. This definition captures the idea that leaders are involved with other people in the achievement of goals. Leadership is reciprocal, occurring *among* people.[3] Leadership is a "people" activity, distinct from administrative paper shuffling or problem-solving activities. Role models for leadership can come from wide and varied sources, as shown in the Spotlight on Skills titled Seven—or Six—Leadership Habits of SpongeBob SquarePants.

- The attitudes and behaviors of leaders shape the conditions that determine how well employees can do their jobs; thus, leaders play a tremendous role in the organization's success.
- **Leadership** is the ability to influence people toward the attainment of organizational goals.
- Many different styles of leadership can be effective.

SPOTLIGHT ON SKILLS

Seven—or Six—Leadership Habits of SpongeBob SquarePants

A new leader is emerging. He lives with his pet snail, Gary, in a pineapple at the bottom of the ocean and adores his fry-cook job at the Krusty Krab. He's the son of two round sea sponges. SpongeBob seems to get into trouble a lot. In fact, that is his gift. He hangs out with his starfish pal, Patrick, and his thrill-seeking friend, Sandy Cheeks, a squirrel. SpongeBob has had some harrowing experiences and has learned important leadership skills:

1. ***Be resilient.*** Today it's all about the globalization and learning multicultural skills. When SpongeBob is marooned in a frightening abyss, he is forced to find his willpower and resources to learn a new dialect, find some chow, and maneuver his way back to Bikini Bottom. (Episode: "Rock Bottom")
2. ***Recruit the finest.*** When he learns that his superhero friends and crimefighters, Mermaid Man and Barnacle Boy, have been relegated to a nursing home, SpongeBob convinces them to come out of retirement to fulfill their destinies: warding off evildoers from Goo Lagoon. (Episode: "Mermaid Man and Barnacle Man")
3. ***No resting on laurels.*** SpongeBob is in a rut, but a good one. After becoming employee of the month 26 times straight, he feels himself at risk of losing the title. He compulsively strives to outcook, outclean, and outwork rival Squidward. "Having pride in your work," says SpongeBob, "is the only thing that makes it all worthwhile." (Episode: "Employee of the Month")
4. ***Innovate and innovate.*** Good leaders are those that follow the rules, whereas great leaders change them. SpongeBob suggests multicolored "pretty parties," which are rejected by management. Undaunted, he sets out on his own, becoming a wild success. Showing cool business savvy, he sells his idea in the nick of time. (Episode: "Patty Hype")
5. ***Recognize employees' limits.*** In order to cut costs, Mr. Krab, the ultimate miser, charges workers for infractions like "existing" and "breathing." Squidward and SpongeBob complain and are fired, causing them to "dismantle the establishment," an objective they take literally. (Episode: "Squid of Strike")
6. ***Take a stand.*** Effective leaders know when values are being violated, ethics eroded, or spirits are crushed, and the leader is willing to draw a line in the sand and take a risk to do the right thing. Jellyfish Fields is threatened when a super-highway is about to be built. SpongeBob organizes a protest, but the highway wins, resulting in environmental decimation. However, SpongeBob helps the group "unpave" the highway and Jellyfish Fields is restored, with peace coming back to Bikini Bottom. (Episode: "SpongeBob's Last Stand")

SOURCES: Mekeisha Madden Toby, "'*SpongeBob SquarePants:* SpongeBob's Last Stand' Has Earth Day Message," *Detroit News*, April 22, 2010; Lucas Conley, "Leadership Secrets of SpongeBob SquarePants," *Fast Company*, September 2004, p. 45.

Contemporary Leadership

The concept of leadership evolves as the needs of organizations change. That is, the environmental context in which leadership is practiced influences which approach might be most effective, as well as what kinds of leaders are most admired by society. The technology, economic conditions, labor conditions, and social and cultural mores of the times all play a role. A significant influence on leadership styles in recent years is the turbulence and uncertainty of the environment. Ethical and economic difficulties, corporate governance concerns, globalization, changes in technology, new ways of working, shifting employee expectations, and significant social transitions have contributed to a shift in how we think about and practice leadership. Four approaches that are in tune with leadership for today's turbulent times are Level 5 leadership, servant leadership, authentic leadership, and interactive leadership, which has been associated with women's style of leading.

Level 5 Leadership

A study conducted by Jim Collins and his research associates identified the critical importance of what Collins calls *Level 5 leadership* in transforming companies from merely good to truly great organizations.[4] As described in his book *Good to Great: Why Some Companies Make the Leap . . . and Others Don't*,[5] Level 5 leadership refers to the highest level in a hierarchy of manager capabilities, as illustrated in Exhibit 11.1.

As reflected in the exhibit, a key characteristic of Level 5 leaders is an almost complete lack of ego (humility) coupled with a fierce resolve to do what is best for the organization (will). Having **humility** means being unpretentious and modest rather than arrogant and prideful. In contrast to the view of great leaders as larger-than-life personalities with strong egos and big ambitions, Level 5 leaders often seem shy and self-effacing. Although they accept full responsibility for mistakes, poor results, or failures, Level 5 leaders give credit for successes to other people. Qi Lu, described at the beginning of this chapter, demonstrates Level 5 qualities. Lu feels a strong sense of duty and loyalty, pouring his heart and soul into the mission rather than spending his energies promoting himself. On his last day of work at Yahoo, a problem came up with a database. Rather than leaving the problem for others, Lu worked side by side with his former employees to try to fix it. He finally left at midnight, when his network access was automatically cut off.[6]

Another good example of Level 5 leadership characteristics is Darwin E. Smith, former CEO of Kimberly-Clark.

KIMBERLY-CLARK

Few people have ever heard of Darwin Smith, who led Kimberly-Clark from 1971 to 1991—and that's probably just the way he wanted it. Smith was somewhat shy and awkward in social situations, and he was never featured in splashy articles in *Fortune* magazine or *The Wall Street Journal*. Yet anyone who interpreted his appearance and demeanor as a sign of ineptness soon learned differently. Smith demonstrated an aggressive determination to revive Kimberly-Clark, which at the time was a stodgy old paper company that had seen years of falling stock prices. When he took over, the company's core business was in coated paper. Convinced that this approach doomed the company to mediocrity, Smith took the controversial step of selling the company's paper mills and investing all its resources in consumer products such as Kleenex and Huggies diapers.

Over his 20 years as CEO, Smith turned Kimberly-Clark into the leading consumer paper products company in the world, beating rivals Scott Paper and Procter & Gamble. The company generated cumulative stock returns that were 4.1 times greater than those of the general market. When asked about his exceptional performance after his retirement, Smith said simply, "I never stopped trying to become qualified for the job."[7]

As the example of Darwin Smith illustrates, despite their personal humility, Level 5 leaders have a strong will to do whatever it takes to produce great and lasting results for their organizations. They are extremely ambitious for their companies rather than for themselves. This goal becomes highly evident in the area of succession planning. Level 5 leaders develop a solid corps of leaders throughout the organization, so that when they leave the company can continue to thrive and grow even stronger. Egocentric leaders, by contrast, often set their successors up for failure because it will be a testament to their own greatness if the company doesn't perform well without them. Rather than building an organization around "a genius with a thousand helpers," Level 5 leaders want everyone to develop to their fullest potential.

EXHIBIT 11.1

Level 5 Hierarchy

Level 1 – Individual	Level 2 – Team Member	Level 3 – Manager	Level 4 – Leader	Level 5 – Executive
Capable	Contributing	Competent	Effective	Level 5
Contributes talent, skills, knowledge	Contributes individually; works well in group	Manages team members and assets to reach set objectives	Stimulates high standards; champions dedication to vision	Builds excellence through dedication and humility

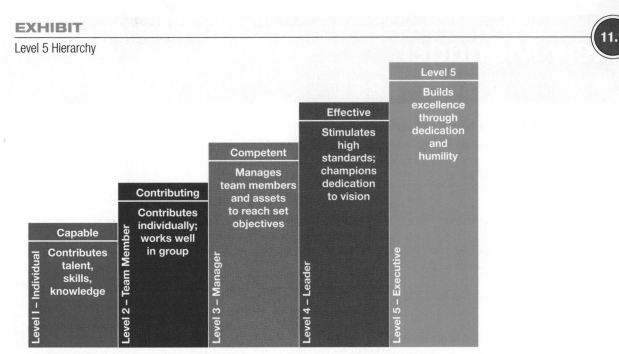

SOURCE: Based on Jim Collins, *Good to Great: Why Some Companies Make the Leap . . . and Others Don't* (New York: HarperCollins, 2001), p. 20.

Servant Leadership

When Jack Welch, long-time CEO of General Electric, speaks to MBA students, he reminds them that "any time you are managing people, your job is not about you, it's about them. It starts out about you as … an individual in a company," Welch says. "But once you get a leadership job, it moves very quickly to being about them."[8] Some leaders operate from the assumption that work exists for the development of the worker as much as the worker exists to do the work.[9] The concept of servant leadership, first described by Robert Greenleaf in 1970, has gained renewed interest in recent years as companies recover from ethical scandals and compete to attract and retain the best human talent.[10]

A **servant leader** transcends self-interest to serve others and the organization.[11] Servant leaders operate on two levels: for the fulfillment of their subordinates' goals and needs and for the realization of the larger purpose or mission of their organization. Servant leaders give things away—power, ideas, information, recognition, credit for accomplishments, even money. Servant leaders often work in the nonprofit world because it offers a natural way to apply their leadership drive and skills to serve others. But servant leaders also succeed in business. Harry Stine, founder of Stine Seed Company in Adel, Iowa, casually announced to his employees at the company's annual postharvest luncheon that they would each receive $1,000 for each year they had worked at the company. For some loyal workers, that amounted to a $20,000 bonus.[12]

What did your score on the "What's Your Personal Style" Self-Test questions on page 444 say about your humility? Go to the Ethical Dilemma, on page 473, that pertains to leadership for turbulent times.

Authentic Leadership

Another popular concept in leadership today is the idea of **authentic leadership**, which refers to individuals who know and understand themselves, who espouse and act consistent

New Manager Self-Test

What's Your Personal Style?

Ideas about effective leadership change over time. To understand your approach to leadership, think about your personal style toward others or toward a student group to which you belong, and then answer each item below as Mostly True or Mostly False for you.

	MOSTLY TRUE <<<	>>> MOSTLY FALSE
1. I am a modest, unassuming person.	______	______
2. When a part of a group, I am more concerned about how the group does than how I do.	______	______
3. I prefer to lead with quiet modesty rather than personal assertiveness.	______	______
4. I feel personally responsible if the team does poorly.	______	______
5. I act with quiet determination.	______	______
6. I resolve to do whatever needs doing to produce the best result for the group.	______	______
7. I am proactive to help the group succeed.	______	______
8. I facilitate high standards for my group's performance.	______	______

See It Online

Scoring and Interpretation: A recent view of leadership called Level 5 leadership says that the most successful leaders have two prominent qualities: humility and will. Give one point for each item marked Mostly True.

Humility: Items 1, 2, 3, 4

Will: Items 5, 6, 7, 8

Humility means a quiet, modest, self-effacing manner. A humble person puts group or organizational success ahead of personal success. *Will* means a quiet but fierce resolve to stay the course to achieve the group's desired outcome and to help the group succeed. The traits of humility and will are opposite the traditional idea of leadership as loud and self-centered. If you scored 3 or 4 on either humility or will, you are on track to Level 5 leadership, which says that ordinary people often make excellent leaders.

with higher order ethical values, and who empower and inspire others with their openness and authenticity.[13] To be authentic means being *real*, staying true to one's values and beliefs, and acting based on one's true self rather than emulating what others do. Authentic leaders inspire trust and commitment because they respect diverse viewpoints, encourage collaboration, and help others learn, grow, and develop as leaders. Tina Fey is one leader who has remained true to herself and her core values, in the rough-and-tumble world of show business, as shown in this Chapter's Benchmarking box, where she shares leadership lessons.

BENCHMARKING

Saturday Night Live

Tina Fey moved from improv artist to writer to head writer on Saturday Night Live. In the process, she learned from producer Lorne Michaels a number of leadership lessons:

1. To be a producer, one must discourage creativity. In show biz, everyone has lots of creativity and wants to show it off, whether it is sets, costumes, or props. It's wonderful to be surrounded by so much talent, but sometimes boundaries are needed. For example, you could have a situation where the script asks for a muffin on a white plate, but the prop person thinks it would be smarter to bring a Santa-shaped muffin in a silver tray. The producer has to find a kind way to explain that the character is Jewish, so a Santa theme isn't appropriate and how silver will reflect too brightly from the lights. And when actors come with their own "ideas" for a sketch, it usually means they want more air time, which isn't always a good idea. Questions work well here.
2. Be careful what you ask people to do. If you ask an actor to eat food newly chewed by someone else and they are turned off by it, the reply might be, "I don't think my character would do that." Think of actors as human beings and consider what you are asking them to do.
3. The show goes on not because it's ready, but because it's time for it to start: 11:30 P.M. No matter how great your writing and rehearsing have been, at some point you just have to let it go, accept it is good enough, and move on. You need to realize that you'll have some awesome sketches and some awful ones. That's part of the process, so just get used to it.
4. In hiring writers, make sure you have equal doses of Harvard types and scrappy Chicago improvisers. The diversity in the team is what brings out excellent comedy. With only Harvard writers, all the scenes would be parodies about the 1929 stock crash, with people wearing barrels. With only improvisers, you'd have entire shows with drag queens named Staci and Vicki screaming incessantly, "*You kiss your mutha with that face?*" Remember that Harvard is like Spock and Improv like Kirk. You need both.
5. Don't make any big decisions right at season end. Don't decide to buy a house, get married, change jobs, or anything else big during the intense letdown after a year of hard work.
6. You should not hire anyone unless you feel comfortable running into them in the hallway or copy room at 3 A.M. Don't hire creative but creepy.
7. Never tell crazy writers or actors they are crazy. Rather than be self-righteous, or just cutting them off (this has to be balanced with #1 above), ask lots of questions, such as: Why should your sketch go on four times longer than anyone else's?

© Kuzmik, Shutterstock

SOURCE: Tina Fey, "Lessons from Late Night," *The New Yorker* (March 11, 2011): 22–26.

Exhibit 11.2 outlines the key characteristics of authentic leaders, and each is discussed below.[14]

- ***Authentic leaders pursue their purpose with passion.*** To be authentic, leaders have to know the purpose of their leadership. Leaders who lead without a purpose can easily fall prey to greed and the desires of the ego. When leaders demonstrate a high level of passion and commitment to purpose, they inspire commitment from followers.
- ***Authentic leaders practice solid values.*** Authentic leaders have values that are shaped by their personal beliefs, and they stay true to them even under pressure. People come to know what the leader stands for, which inspires trust.
- ***Authentic leaders lead with their hearts as well as their heads.*** All leaders sometimes have to make tough choices, but authentic leaders maintain a compassion for others as well as the courage to make difficult decisions.
- ***Authentic leaders establish connected relationships.*** Authentic leaders build positive and enduring relationships, which makes followers want to do their best. In addition,

As a new manager, will your interpersonal style fit the contemporary leadership approaches described in the text? To find out, complete the New Manager Self-Test on page 447.

EXHIBIT 11.2

Components of Authentic Leadership

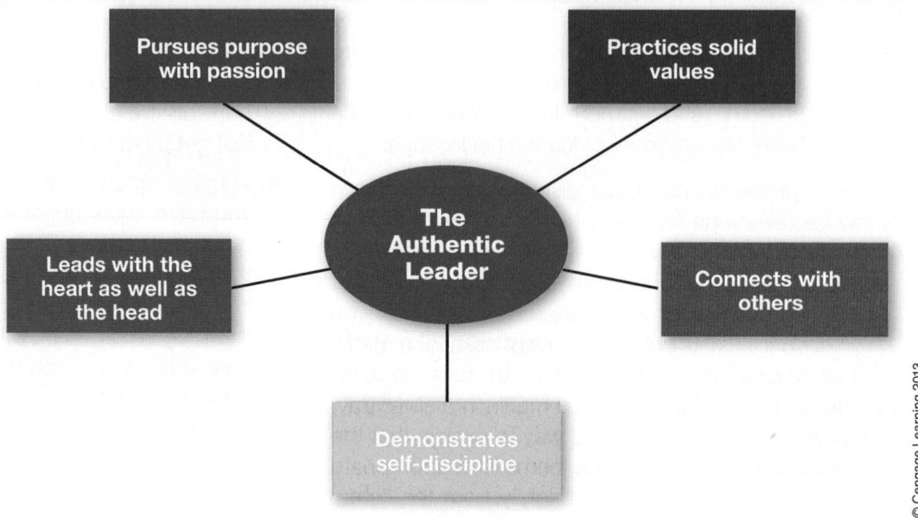

authentic leaders surround themselves with good people and work to help others grow and develop.

- ***Authentic leaders demonstrate self-discipline.*** A high degree of self-control and self-discipline keeps leaders from taking excessive or unethical risks that could harm others and the organization. When authentic leaders make mistakes, they openly admit them.

A leader who demonstrates many of the characteristics of authentic leadership is Michael Jordaan, CEO of South Africa's First National Bank (FNB). Jordaan has been described as being "comfortable in his own skin" and a person who has stayed true to his values. He believes in surrounding himself with the best people he can find, even people he considers better than him, because he isn't threatened by the abilities and successes of others. Jordaan works to make sure everyone feels like an important part of the team, and he is comfortable letting the person who knows the most about a specific situation take the lead. In addition, he is constantly seeking feedback so he can grow in his own leadership capabilities.[15] Research on the outcomes of authentic leadership is sparse, but advocates believe authentic leadership leads to better long-term organizational performance.[16]

Jin Lee/Bloomberg /Getty Images

ConceptConnection

The 2008 financial collapse put Debra Cafaro's leadership skills to the test. The CEO of Ventas, Inc., saw the housing crisis approaching and insisted the Louisville-based healthcare real estate investment trust build cash reserves. Although she wanted to project calmness and certainty when the economic downturn hit, Cafaro says that "in order to be authentic, I also had to acknowledge, 'I'm scared, too.'" Throughout the crisis, Cafaro operated as an **interactive leader**, one who, in her words, makes sure "we're working together, collaborating—marching in the same direction." She succeeded. Ventas not only survived the recession but is flourishing.

Gender Differences

Some of the general characteristics associated with Level 5 leaders and authentic leaders are also hallmarks of interactive leadership, which has been found to be associated with female leaders. **Interactive leadership** means that the leader favors a consensual and collaborative process, and influence derives from relationships rather than position power and formal authority.[17]

New Manager Self-Test

Personal Potentials

Instructions: Think back to how you typically behave toward others at work or in student groups. Please respond to the following items based on whether you frequently displayed each behavior.

	True	Somewhat	False
1. I am more devoted to my group's success than to my own.	_____	_____	_____
2. I act with quiet modesty rather than personal assertiveness.	_____	_____	_____
3. I come across as a simple, unassuming person.	_____	_____	_____
4. I act with quiet yet intense determination.	_____	_____	_____
5. I am relentless to help the group succeed.	_____	_____	_____
6. I pursue persistent high standards for my group's performance.	_____	_____	_____
7. My actions meet the needs of others before my own.	_____	_____	_____
8. I am always offering a helping hand to those around me.	_____	_____	_____
9. I give away credit and recognition to others.	_____	_____	_____
10. I encourage the growth of others, expecting nothing in return.	_____	_____	_____
11. I like to be of service to others.	_____	_____	_____
12. Giving makes me happier than receiving.	_____	_____	_____

Scoring and Interpretation: Compute your score for questions 1–6 with 3 points for each True, 2 points for each Somewhat, and 1 point for each False. **Total score for 1–6:_______.** Compute your score for questions 7–11 with 3 points for each True, 2 points for each Somewhat, and 1 point for each False. **Total score for 7–12:_______.** Your scores for these questions pertain to personal potentials for leaders that are described in the chapter. Your score for questions 1–6 pertain *Level 5 leadership humility and will.* A high score (15–18) would be closer to a Level 5 leader while a low score (6–10) might imply more orientation toward self-importance. Answers 1–3 pertain specifically to humility and answers 3–6 pertain to will. You may compute separate scores for humility and will to learn on which aspect you score higher. The total score for questions 7–12 is about *servant leadership*. A higher score (15–18) implies the ability to serve others in the role of leader. A lower score (6–10) would imply greater focus on serving self rather than others. Do you see any similarity between the concepts of humility and servant leadership? How do you feel about your scores on these dimensions? Are you attracted to the qualities of Level 5 and servant leadership or would you prefer a different approach to leadership?

SOURCE: Based On David W. Johnson and Frank P. Johnson, *Joining Together: Group Theory and Group Skills*, 8th ed. (New York: Allyn and Bacon, 2003), pp. 189–190.

Although both men and women can practice interactive leadership, research indicates that women's style of leadership is typically different from most men's and is particularly suited to today's organizations.[18] Using data from actual performance evaluations, one study found that when rated by peers, subordinates, and bosses, female managers scored significantly higher than men on abilities such as motivating others, fostering communication, and listening, as illustrated in Exhibit 11.3.[19] Another study of leaders and their followers in businesses, universities, and government agencies found that women were rated higher on social and emotional skills, which are crucial for interactive leadership.[20] Indeed, a recent review of thousands of 360-degree performance evaluations discovered that women outshone men in almost every leadership dimension measured. The exception was that women were typically rated as less visionary, which some researchers believe hinders female managers' career advancement despite their exceptional ratings on other leadership dimensions.[21]

One good example of an interactive leader is Nell Minow, cofounder of the Corporate Library, a provider of corporate governance research. For Minow, leadership means expanding one's definition of *we* as opposed to *them*. "I found generally that … the larger the group that you had included in the 'we,' the better off everybody was," she says. Minow is vitally concerned with problems and issues that affect her followers, and she strives to help people do the best they can do and learn as much as they can.[22] Men can be interactive leaders as well, as illustrated by the example of Pat McGovern, founder and chairman of IDG, a technology publishing and research firm that owns magazines such as *CIO*, *PC World*, and *Computerworld.* McGovern believes having personal contact with employees and letting them know they're appreciated is a primary responsibility of leaders.[23] The characteristics associated with interactive leadership are emerging as valuable qualities for both male and female leaders in today's workplace. Values associated with interactive leadership include personal humility, inclusion, relationship building, and caring.

11.3 EXHIBIT

Gender Differences in Leadership Behaviors

Leadership Ability	Who Does It Best?
Motivating Others	(Women rated higher)
Fostering Communication	(Women rated higher)
Producing High-quality Work	(Women rated higher)
Strategic Planning	(Women and men rated about equally)
Listening to Others	(Women rated higher)
Analyzing Issues	(Women and men rated about equally)

SOURCE: Data from Hagberg Consulting Group, Management Research Group, Lawrence A. Pfaff, Personnel Decisions International Inc., Advanced Teamware Inc., as reported in Rochelle Sharpe, "As Leaders, Women Rule," *BusinessWeek* (November 20, 2000): 75–84.

- A significant influence on leadership styles in recent years is the turbulence and uncertainty of the environment.
- Humility and will have recently emerged as important leadership qualities.
- One effective approach in today's environment is *Level 5 leadership*, which is characterized by an almost complete lack of ego (humility), coupled with a fierce resolve to do what is best for the organization (will).
- Having **humility** means being unpretentious and modest rather than arrogant and prideful.
- A **servant leader** is a leader who serves others by working to fulfill followers' needs and goals as well as to achieve the organization's larger mission.
- **Authentic leadership** refers to leadership by individuals who know and understand themselves, who espouse and act consistent with higher order ethical values, and who empower and inspire others with their openness and authenticity.
- Women leaders typically score significantly higher than men on abilities such as motivating others, fostering communication, and listening—skills that are based on humility and authenticity and are particularly suited to today's organizations.
- **Interactive leadership** is a leadership style characterized by values such as inclusion, collaboration, relationship building, and caring.
- Although interactive leadership is associated with women's style of leading, both men and women can be effective interactive leaders.

From Management to Leadership

Hundreds of books and articles have been written in recent years about the differences between management and leadership. Good management is essential in organizations, yet managers have to be leaders too, because distinctive qualities are associated with management and leadership that provide different strengths for the organization. As shown in Exhibit 11.4, management and leadership reflect two different sets of qualities and skills that frequently overlap within a single individual. A person might have more of one set of qualities than the other, but ideally a manager develops a balance of both manager and leader qualities.[24]

A primary distinction between management and leadership is that management promotes stability and order within the existing organizational structure and systems. This ensures that suppliers are paid, customers invoiced, products and services produced on time, and so forth. Leadership, on the other hand, promotes vision and change. Leadership means questioning the status quo so that outdated, unproductive, or socially irresponsible norms can be replaced to meet new challenges.

Consider the challenge Sergio Marchionne faces as the new CEO of Chrysler Group LLC. To revive the smallest of the Big Three automakers after its trip through bankruptcy, Marchionne needs excellent management skills to improve financial results, oversee operational details, make tough decisions, and work with managers to execute a new strategy. However, he also needs consummate leadership abilities to inspire people with a vision that can move Chrysler away from its troubled past to a brighter future, improve cooperation among departments and divisions, and rebuild sagging morale in the company.[25]

EXHIBIT
Leader and Manager Qualities

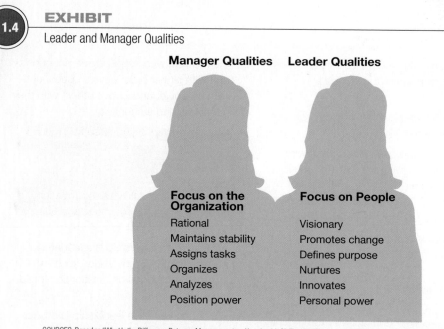

Manager Qualities	Leader Qualities
Focus on the Organization	**Focus on People**
Rational	Visionary
Maintains stability	Promotes change
Assigns tasks	Defines purpose
Organizes	Nurtures
Analyzes	Innovates
Position power	Personal power

SOURCES: Based on "What Is the Difference Between Management and Leadership?" *The Wall Street Journal Online*, http://guides.wsj.com/management/developing-a-leadership-style/what-is-the-difference-between-management-and-leadership (accessed June 28, 2009); and Genevieve Capowski, "Anatomy of a Leader: Where Are the Leaders of Tomorrow?" *Management Review* (March 1994): 12.

Leadership cannot replace management; it should be in addition to management. Good management is needed to help the organization meet current commitments, while good leadership is needed to move the organization into the future. Leadership's power comes from being built on the foundation of a well-managed organization.

- Leadership and management reflect two different sets of qualities and skills that provide different benefits for the organization.
- Management promotes stability and efficient organizing to meet current commitments, whereas leadership often inspires engagement and organizational change to meet new conditions.
- Both leadership and management are important to organizations, and people can learn to be good leaders as well as good managers.

Leadership Traits

Early efforts to understand leadership success focused on the leader's traits. **Traits** are the distinguishing personal characteristics of a leader, such as intelligence, honesty, self-confidence, and even appearance. The early research looked at leaders who had achieved a level of greatness, and hence was referred to as the *Great Man* approach. The idea was relatively simple: Find out what made these people great, and select future leaders who already exhibited the same traits or could be trained to develop them. Generally, early research found only a weak relationship between personal traits and leader success.[26]

EXHIBIT 11.5

Personal Characteristics of Leaders

Physical Characteristics	Personality	Work-Related Characteristics
Energy Physical stamina	Self-confidence Honesty and integrity Enthusiasm Desire to lead Independence	Achievement drive, desire to excel Conscientiousness in pursuit of goals Persistence against obstacles, tenacity
Intelligence and Ability	**Social Characteristics**	**Social Background**
Intelligence, cognitive ability Knowledge Judgment, decisiveness	Sociability, interpersonal skills Cooperativeness Ability to enlist cooperation Tact, diplomacy	Education Mobility

SOURCES: Based on Bernard M. Bass, *Bass & Stogdill's Handbook of Leadership: Theory, Research, and Managerial Applications*, 3rd ed. (New York: The Free Press, 1990), pp. 80–81; and S. A. Kirkpatrick and E. A. Locke, "Leadership: Do Traits Matter?" *Academy of Management Executive* 5, no. 2 (1991): 48–60.

In recent years, interest in examining leadership traits has reemerged. In addition to personality traits, physical, social, and work-related characteristics of leaders have been studied.[27] Exhibit 11.5 summarizes the physical, social, and personal leadership characteristics that have received the greatest research support. However, these characteristics do not stand alone. The appropriateness of a trait or set of traits depends on the leadership situation.

Effective leaders typically possess varied traits, and no single leader can have a complete set of characteristics that is appropriate for handling any problem, challenge, or opportunity that comes along. In addition, traits that are typically considered positive can sometimes have negative consequences, and traits sometimes considered negative can have positive consequences. For example, a highly dominant leader can run roughshod over others, but she can also command attention and respect and gain the high level of influence needed to accomplish an important goal.[28] Research has found that people high on dominance are usually rated as more competent and intelligent even when they are not, based simply on the confidence they display.[29]

Therefore, rather than just understanding their *traits*, the best leaders recognize and hone their *strengths*.[30] **Strengths** are natural talents and abilities that have been supported and reinforced with learned knowledge and skills and provide each individual with his or her best tools for accomplishment and satisfaction.[31] Every manager has a limited capacity; those who become good leaders are the ones who tap into their key strengths that can make a difference. Effective leadership isn't about having the "right" traits, but rather about finding the strengths that one can best exemplify and apply as a leader.

- **Traits** are distinguishing personal characteristics, such as intelligence, self-confidence, energy, and independence.
- **Strengths** are natural talents and abilities that have been supported and reinforced with learned knowledge and skills.

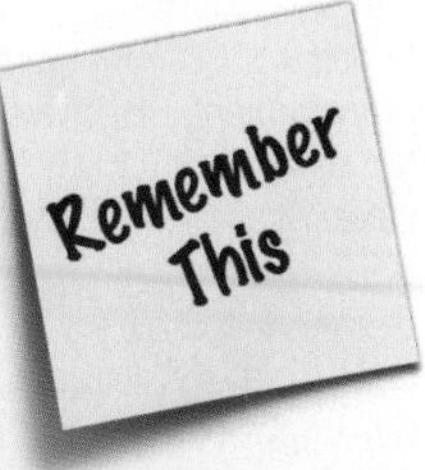

Behavioral Approaches

The inability to define effective leadership based solely on traits led to an interest in looking at the behavior of leaders and how it might contribute to leadership success or failure. Two basic leadership behaviors identified as important for leadership are attention to tasks and attention to people.

Task versus People

3

Two types of behavior that have been identified as applicable to effective leadership in a variety of situations and time periods are *task-oriented behavior* and *people-oriented behavior*.[32] Although they are not the only important leadership behaviors, concern for tasks and concern for people must be shown at some reasonable level. Thus, many approaches to understanding leadership use these *metacategories*, or broadly defined behavior categories, as a basis for study and comparison.

Important early research programs on leadership were conducted at The Ohio State University and the University of Michigan.[33] Ohio State researchers identified two major behaviors they called consideration and initiating structure. **Consideration** falls in the category of people-oriented behavior and is the extent to which the leader is mindful of subordinates, respects their ideas and feelings, and establishes mutual trust. **Initiating structure** is the degree of task behavior, that is, the extent to which the leader is task oriented and directs subordinate work activities toward goal attainment. Studies suggest that effective leaders may be high on consideration and low on initiating structure or low on consideration and high on initiating structure, depending on the situation.[34]

Research at the University of Michigan at about the same time also considered task- and people-oriented behaviors by comparing the behavior of effective and ineffective supervisors.[35] The most effective supervisors were those who established high performance goals and displayed supportive behavior toward subordinates. These were referred to as *employee-centered leaders*. The less-effective leaders were called *job-centered leaders*; these leaders tended to be less concerned with goal achievement and human needs and in favor of meeting schedules, keeping costs low, and achieving production efficiency.

Jennifer S. Altman / Contour by Getty Images

ConceptConnection

How has Clarence Otis, Jr.'s leadership style changed since he became Darden Restaurants' CEO? His experience has driven home the importance of **team management**. Otis (shown here in the Times Square Olive Garden) has found "it's less and less about getting the work done, and more and more about building the team." His team includes 174,000 employees working in the U.S.'s largest full-service restaurant operation. Darden's new headquarters was designed to facilitate teamwork among its brands—especially Olive Garden, Red Lobster, and Longhorn Steakhouse—by bringing 1,400 executives and support staff previously scattered in separate buildings under one roof for the first time.

The Leadership Grid

Building on the work of the Ohio State and Michigan studies, Blake and Mouton of the University of Texas proposed a two-dimensional theory called the Managerial Grid, which was later restated by Blake and McCanse as the **Leadership Grid**.[36] The model and five of its major management styles are depicted in Exhibit 11.6. Each axis on the grid is a nine-point scale, with 1 meaning low concern and 9 meaning high concern.

Team management (9, 9) often is considered the most effective style and is recommended for leaders because organization members work together to accomplish tasks. *Country club management* (1, 9) occurs when primary emphasis is given to people rather than to work outputs. *Authority-compliance management*

EXHIBIT 11.6

The Leadership Grid Figure

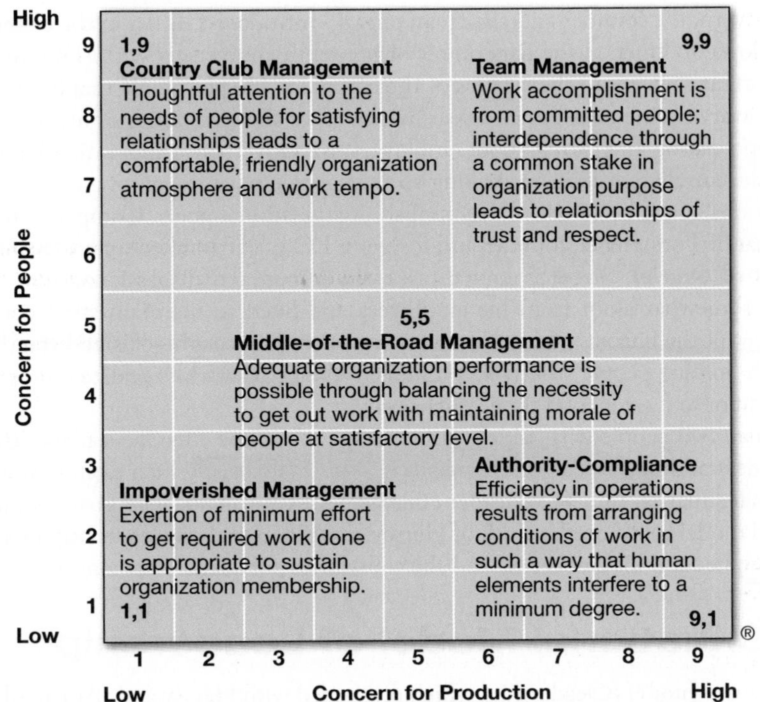

SOURCE: The Leadership Grid figure, Paternalism figure, and Opportunism figure from Robert R. Blake and Anne Adams McCanse, *Leadership Dilemmas-Grid Solutions* (formerly the Managerial Grid by Robert R. Blake and Jane S. Mouton) (Houston: Gulf Publishing Company, 1991), Grid figure, p. 29; Paternalism figure, p. 30; Opportunism figure, p. 31. Copyright © 1991 by Blake and Mouton, and Scientific Methods, Inc. Reproduced by permission of the owners.

(9, 1) occurs when efficiency in operations is the dominant orientation. *Middle-of-the-road management* (5, 5) reflects a moderate amount of concern for both people and production. *Impoverished management* (1, 1) means the absence of a management philosophy; managers exert little effort toward interpersonal relationships or work accomplishment.

- Two basic leadership behaviors identified as important for leadership are attention to tasks and attention to people.
- **Consideration** is the term used by researchers at The Ohio State University to describe the extent to which a leader is sensitive to subordinates, respects their ideas and feelings, and establishes mutual trust.
- **Initiating structure** is the term that describes the extent to which a leader is task oriented and directs subordinates' work activities toward goal accomplishment.
- Researchers at the University of Michigan used the terms *employee-centered leaders* and *job-centered leaders* to describe the same two basic leadership behaviors.
- The **leadership grid** is a two-dimensional leadership model that measures the leader's concern for people and concern for production to categorize the leader in one of five different leadership styles.

Contingency Approaches

3

Pat McGovern, the founder and chairman of IDG introduced earlier in the chapter, treats each employee to lunch at the Ritz on his or her tenth anniversary with IDG, to tell them how important they are to the success of the company. He personally thanks almost every person in every business unit once a year, which takes about a month of his time. In addition to appreciating and caring about employees, McGovern also shows that he believes in them by decentralizing decision making so that people have the autonomy to make their own decisions about how best to accomplish organizational goals. Compare McGovern's style to that of Tom Siebel, founder and former CEO of software company Siebel Systems (now part of Oracle). Siebel is known as a disciplined and dispassionate manager who remained somewhat aloof from his employees and liked to maintain strict control over every aspect of the business. He enforced a dress code, set tough goals and standards, and believed in holding people strictly accountable. "We go to work to realize our professional ambitions, not to have a good time," Siebel says.[37]

How can two people with widely different styles both be effective leaders? The answer lies in understanding **contingency approaches** to leadership, which explore how the organizational situation influences leader effectiveness. Contingency approaches include the situational model based on the work of Hersey and Blanchard, the leadership model developed by Fiedler and his associates, and the substitutes-for-leadership concept.

The Situational Model of Leadership

The **situational model** of leadership, which originated with Hersey and Blanchard, is an interesting extension of the behavioral theories summarized in the leadership grid (see Exhibit 11.6). This approach focuses a great deal of attention on the characteristics of followers in determining appropriate leadership behavior. The point of the situational model is that subordinates vary in readiness, which is determined by the degree of willingness and ability a subordinate demonstrates while performing a specific task. *Willingness* refers to a combination of confidence, commitment, and motivation, and a follower may be high or low on any of the three variables. *Ability* refers to the amount of knowledge, experience, and demonstrated skill a subordinate brings to the task. Effective leaders adapt their style according to the readiness level of the people they are managing. People low in readiness—because of little ability or training or insecurity—need a different leadership style than those who are high in readiness and have good ability, skills, confidence, and willingness to work.[38]

According to the situational model, a leader can adopt one of four leadership styles, as shown in Exhibit 11.7. The *telling style* is a highly directive style and involves giving explicit directions about how tasks should be accomplished. The *selling style* is one where the leader explains decisions and gives subordinates a chance to ask questions and gain clarity and understanding about work tasks. The *participating style* is one where the leader shares ideas with subordinates, gives them a chance to participate, and facilitates decision making. The fourth style, the *delegating style*, provides little direction and little support because the leader turns over responsibility for decisions and their implementation to subordinates.

Exhibit 11.7 summarizes the situational relationship between leader style and follower readiness. Follower readiness can be low, moderate, or high, as shown at the top of the exhibit. The telling style has the highest probability of successfully influencing low readiness followers who are unable or unwilling—because of poor ability and skills, little experience, or insecurity—to take responsibility for their own task behavior. The leader is specific, telling people exactly what to do, how to do it, and when. The selling and participating styles work for followers at moderate readiness levels. For example, followers might lack some education and experience for the job but have high confidence, interest, and willingness to learn. As shown in the exhibit, the selling style is effective in this situation because it

EXHIBIT 11.7

The Situational Model of Leadership

FOLLOWER READINESS

	LOW	MODERATE		HIGH
	Incapable and insecure followers ↓	Incapable but confident followers ↓	Capable but insecure followers ↓	Capable and confident followers ↓
Leadership Style	TELLING	SELLING	PARTICIPATING	DELEGATING
	Give specific instructions and supervise closely	Clarify and explain decisions as needed	Share ideas with followers and facilitate their decision making	Empower followers to make the decisions
Task Behaviors	High	High	Low	Low
Relationship Behaviors	Low	High	High	Low

SOURCE: From Phillips/Gully. *Organizational Behavior*, 1e. © 2012 South-Western, a part of Cengage Learning, Inc. Reproduced by permission. www.cengage.com/permissions.

involves giving direction but also includes seeking input from others and clarifying tasks rather than simply instructing that they be performed. When followers have the necessary skills and experience but are somewhat insecure in their abilities or lack high willingness, the participating style enables the leader to guide followers' development and act as a resource for advice and assistance. When followers demonstrate high readiness, that is, they have high levels of education, experience, and readiness to accept responsibility for their own task behavior, the delegating style can effectively be used. Because of the high readiness level of followers, the leader can delegate responsibility for decisions and their implementation to subordinates who have the skills, abilities, and positive attitudes to follow through. The leader provides a general goal and sufficient authority to do the task as followers see fit.

To apply the situational model, the leader diagnoses the readiness level of followers and adopts the appropriate style—telling, selling, participating, or delegating. For example, Jo Newton, an impulse import category leadership manager at Mars' Slough office near London, uses a primarily participative style. Newton and her team oversee how Mars candy products are displayed across thousands of stores throughout the United Kingdom. Most members of the team are at moderate to high readiness levels, so Newton doesn't try telling them what to do. "I like involving as many people as possible," she says. "I like people to come up with their own way of doing things, their own ideas, put their own stamp on something. I like to coach people as opposed to telling them things." Rather than giving the team directives, Newton advises them of the results the company wants, and then steps back, providing support and guidance as needed.[39] On the other hand, a leader taking over a new team of inexperienced or uncertain members would likely have to provide more direction with either a telling or selling style.

Fiedler's Contingency Theory

Whereas the situational model focused on the characteristics of followers, Fiedler and his associates looked at some other elements of the organizational situation to assess when one leadership style is more effective than another.[40] The starting point for Fiedler's theory is the extent to which the leader's style is task oriented or relationship (people) oriented.

AP Photo/Orlin Wagner

ConceptConnection

"Let's get going. Let's do something, let's move, and let's not be constrained by something that has happened in the past." That's how Edward Whitacre, Jr., General Motors' transitional CEO and chairman, described his leadership style. He faced a tough situation trying to restore the newly reorganized company's profitability so it could end government ownership. Whitacre used a **task-oriented style**, demanding quality and efficiency improvements and setting high standards. By the end of his brief tenure, GM had returned to profitability, paid back loans to U.S. and Canadian governments ahead of schedule, and begun the process of returning to private ownership.

Fiedler considered a person's leadership style to be relatively fixed and difficult to change; therefore, the basic idea is to match the leader's style with the situation most favorable for his or her effectiveness. By diagnosing leadership style and the organizational situation, the correct fit can be arranged.

Situation: Favorable or Unfavorable? The suitability of a person's leadership style is determined by whether the situation is favorable or unfavorable to the leader. The favorability of a leadership situation can be analyzed in terms of three elements: the quality of relationships between the leader and followers, the degree of task structure, and the extent to which the leader has formal authority over followers.[41]

A situation would be considered *highly favorable* to the leader when leader–member relationships are positive, tasks are highly structured, and the leader has formal authority over followers. In this situation, followers trust, respect, and have confidence in the leader. The group's tasks are clearly defined, involve specific procedures, and have clear, explicit goals. In addition, the leader has formal authority to direct and evaluate followers, along with the power to reward or punish. A situation would be considered *highly unfavorable* to the leader when leader–member relationships are poor, tasks are highly unstructured, and the leader has little formal authority. In a highly unfavorable situation, followers have little respect for or confidence and trust in the leader. Tasks are vague and ill-defined and lacking in clear-cut procedures and guidelines. The leader has little formal authority to direct subordinates and does not have the power to issue rewards or punishments.

Matching Leader Style to the Situation Combining the three situational characteristics yields a variety of leadership situations, ranging from highly favorable to highly unfavorable. When Fiedler examined the relationships among leadership style and situational favorability, he found the pattern shown in Exhibit 11.8. Task-oriented leaders are more effective when the situation is either highly favorable or highly unfavorable. Relationship-oriented leaders are more effective in situations of moderate favorability.

The task-oriented leader excels in the favorable situation because everyone gets along, the task is clear, and the leader has power; all that is needed is for someone to lead the charge and provide direction. Similarly, if the situation is highly unfavorable to the leader, a great deal of structure and task direction is needed. A strong leader will define task structure and establish strong authority. Because leader-member relations are poor anyway, a strong task orientation will make no difference in the leader's popularity. The following in-text example profiles two strong, task-oriented leaders who have emerged during the recent financial crisis.

U.S. TREASURY DEPARTMENT AND AMERICAN INTERNATIONAL GROUP

James Lambright is a U.S. Treasury Department official acting as chief investment officer for the Troubled Asset Relief Program (TARP). Executives of companies seeking bailout funds from TARP were vexed by his blunt, hard-nosed approach, but Lambright said he wasn't in the job to win a popularity contest. As he fielded call after call on New Year's Eve 2008, Lambright made it clear that executives had to do things his way or else.

When Citigroup's chief financial officer said he couldn't get some of the necessary waivers signed, Lambright reportedly said, "This is good news. This tells me you don't really need the money."

One of the largest recipients of bailout funds was American International Group (AIG), where Robert Benmosche now has one of the toughest jobs in corporate America. As the fourth CEO to lead AIG in 14 tumultuous months, Benmosche has to motivate tens of thousands of demoralized employees, placate Congress and government regulators, reassure shareholders, and soothe an angry public, all while trying to keep the company afloat and pay back TARP funds. Terms often used to describe Benmosche include blunt, decisive, tough, and aggressive. He has no compunction about upending cozy corporate traditions or making other unpopular decisions designed to cut costs, strengthen businesses, and restore financial stability.[42]

With industry analysts recently challenging AIG's long-term ability to survive, some observers question whether anyone can save AIG. However, Benmosche's tough, task-oriented approach is suitable for the difficult situation. Researchers at the University of Chicago who looked at CEOs in turnaround situations—where companies typically have high debt loads and a need to improve results in a hurry—found that tough-minded, task-focused characteristics such as analytical skills, a focus on efficiency, and setting high standards were more valuable leader qualities than were relationship skills such as good communication, listening, and teamwork.[43]

The relationship-oriented leader performs better in situations of intermediate favorability because human relations skills are important in achieving high group performance. In these situations, the leader may be moderately well liked, have some power, and supervise jobs that contain some ambiguity. A leader with good interpersonal skills can create a positive group atmosphere that will improve relationships, clarify task structure, and establish position power.

A leader, then, needs to know two things to use Fiedler's contingency theory. First, the leader should know whether he or she has a relationship- or task-oriented style. Second, the leader should diagnose the situation and determine whether leader–member relations, task structure, and position power are favorable or unfavorable.

EXHIBIT 11.8

How Leader Style Fits the Situation

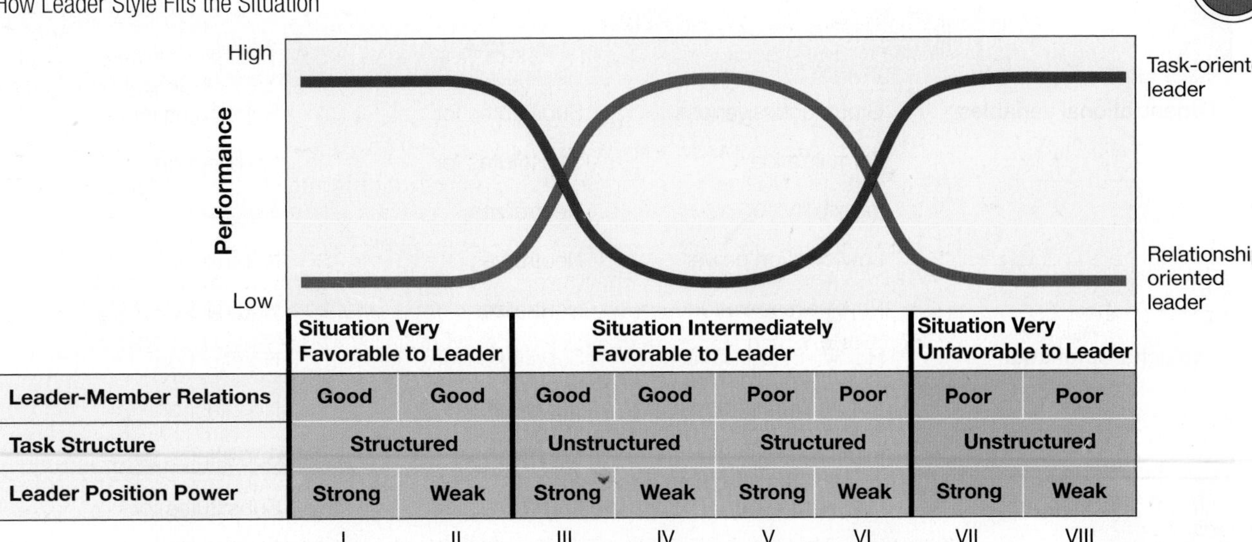

	Situation Very Favorable to Leader		Situation Intermediately Favorable to Leader				Situation Very Unfavorable to Leader	
Leader-Member Relations	Good	Good	Good	Good	Poor	Poor	Poor	Poor
Task Structure	Structured		Unstructured		Structured		Unstructured	
Leader Position Power	Strong	Weak	Strong	Weak	Strong	Weak	Strong	Weak
	I	II	III	IV	V	VI	VII	VIII

SOURCE: Based on Fred E. Fiedler, "The Effects of Leadership Training and Experience: A Contingency Model Interpretation," *Administrative Science Quarterly* 17 (1972): 455.

Fiedler believed fitting leader style to the situation can yield big dividends in profits and efficiency.[44] On the other hand, the model has also been criticized.[45] For one thing, some researchers have challenged the idea that leaders cannot adjust their styles as situational characteristics change. Despite criticisms, Fiedler's model has continued to influence leadership studies. Fiedler's research called attention to the importance of finding the correct fit between leadership style and the situation.

Substitutes for Leadership

The contingency leadership approaches considered so far focus on the leaders' style, the subordinates' nature, and the situation's characteristics. The final contingency approach suggests that situational variables can be so powerful that they actually substitute for or neutralize the need for leadership.[46] This approach outlines those organizational settings in which a leadership style is unimportant or unnecessary.

Exhibit 11.9 shows the situational variables that tend to substitute for or neutralize leadership characteristics. A **substitute** for leadership makes the leadership style unnecessary or redundant. For example, highly professional subordinates who know how to do their tasks do not need a leader who initiates structure for them and tells them what to do. A **neutralizer** counteracts the leadership style and prevents the leader from displaying certain behaviors. For example, if a leader has absolutely no position power or is physically removed from subordinates, the leader's ability to give directions to subordinates is greatly reduced.

Situational variables in Exhibit 11.9 include characteristics of the group, the task, and the organization itself. When followers are highly professional and experienced, both leadership styles are less important. People do not need much direction or consideration. With respect to task characteristics, highly structured tasks substitute for a task-oriented style, and a satisfying task substitutes for a people-oriented style. With respect to the organization itself, group cohesiveness substitutes for both leader styles. Formalized rules and

EXHIBIT 11.9

Substitutes and Neutralizers for Leadership

Variable		Task-Oriented Leadership	People-Oriented Leadership
Organizational variables	Group cohesiveness	Substitutes for	Substitutes for
	Formalization	Substitutes for	No effect on
	Inflexibility	Neutralizes	No effect on
	Low position power	Neutralizes	Neutralizes
	Physical separation	Neutralizes	Neutralizes
Task characteristics	Highly structured task	Substitutes for	No effect on
	Automatic feedback	Substitutes for	No effect on
	Intrinsic satisfaction	No effect on	Substitutes for
Group characteristics	Professionalism	Substitutes for	Substitutes for
	Training/experience	Substitutes for	No effect on

procedures substitute for leader task orientation. Physical separation of leader and subordinate neutralizes both leadership styles.

The value of the situations described in Exhibit 11.9 is that they help leaders avoid leadership overkill. Leaders should adopt a style with which to complement the organizational situation. Consider the work situation for bank tellers. A bank teller performs highly structured tasks, follows clearly written rules and procedures, and has little flexibility in terms of how to do the work. The head teller should not adopt a task-oriented style, because the organization already provides structure and direction. The head teller should concentrate on a people-oriented style to provide a more pleasant work environment. In other organizations, if group cohesiveness or intrinsic satisfaction meets employees' social needs, the leader is free to concentrate on task-oriented behaviors. The leader can adopt a style complementary to the organizational situation to ensure that both task needs and people needs of the work group will be met.

- A **contingency approach** is a model of leadership that describes the relationship between leadership styles and specific situations.
- One contingency approach is the **situational model**, which links the leader's behavioral style with the readiness level of followers.
- In general, a task-oriented leader style fits a low-readiness follower, and a relationship leader style fits a higher-readiness follower.
- In Fiedler's contingency theory, the suitability of a leader's style is determined by whether the situation is considered favorable or unfavorable to the leader.
- Task-oriented leaders are considered to perform better in either highly favorable or highly unfavorable situations.
- Relationship-oriented leaders are considered to perform better in situations of intermediate favorability.
- A **substitute** for leadership is a situational variable that makes a leadership style redundant or unnecessary.
- A **neutralizer** is a situational variable that counteracts a leadership style and prevents the leader from displaying certain behaviors.

Charismatic and Transformational Leadership

Research has also looked at how leadership can inspire and motivate people beyond their normal levels of performance. Some leadership approaches are more effective than others for bringing about high levels of commitment and enthusiasm. Two types with a substantial impact are charismatic and transformational.

Charismatic and Visionary Leadership

Charisma has been referred to as "a fire that ignites followers' energy and commitment, producing results above and beyond the call of duty."[47] The **charismatic leader** has the ability to inspire and motivate people to do more than they would normally do, despite obstacles and personal sacrifice. Followers are willing to put aside their own interests for the sake of the team, department, or organization. The impact of charismatic leaders is normally from (1) stating a lofty vision of an imagined future that employees identify with; (2) displaying an ability to understand and empathize with followers; and (3) empowering and trusting subordinates to accomplish results.[48] Charismatic leaders tend to be less predictable because they create an atmosphere of change, and they may be obsessed by visionary ideas that excite, stimulate, and drive other people to work hard.

Charismatic leaders include Mother Theresa, Sam Walton, Alexander the Great, Steve Jobs, David Koresh, Oprah Winfrey, Martin Luther King, Jr., and Osama bin Laden. Charisma can be used for positive outcomes that benefit the group, but it can also be used for self-serving purposes that lead to deception, manipulation, and exploitation of others. When charismatic leaders respond to organizational problems in terms of the needs of the entire group rather than their own emotional needs, they can have a powerful, positive influence on organizational performance.[49] As with the Level 5 and authentic leadership approaches we discussed earlier in the chapter, *humility* plays an important part in distinguishing whether a charismatic leader will work to benefit primarily the larger organization or use his or her gifts for ego-building and personal gain.[50]

Charismatic leaders are skilled in the art of *visionary leadership*. A **vision** is an attractive, ideal future that is credible yet not readily attainable. Vision is an important component of both charismatic and transformational leadership. Visionary leaders speak to the hearts of employees, letting them be part of something bigger than themselves. Where others see obstacles or failures, they see possibility and hope.

Charismatic leaders typically have a strong vision for the future, almost an obsession, and they can motivate others to help realize it.[51] These leaders have an emotional impact on subordinates because they strongly believe in the vision and can communicate it to others in a way that makes the vision real, personal, and meaningful. The Spotlight on Skills titled Are You a Charismatic Leader? provides a short quiz to help you determine whether you have the potential to be a charismatic leader.

Transformational versus Transactional Leadership

Transformational leaders are similar to charismatic leaders, but they are distinguished by their special ability to bring about innovation and change by recognizing followers' needs and concerns, providing meaning, challenging people to look at old problems in new ways, and acting as role models for the new values and behaviors. Transformational leaders inspire followers to believe not just in the leader personally but in their own potential to imagine and create a better future for the organization. Transformational leaders create significant change in both followers and the organization.[52]

Transformational leadership can be better understood in comparison to *transactional leadership*.[53] **Transactional leaders** clarify the role and task requirements of subordinates, initiate structure, provide appropriate rewards, and try to be considerate to and meet the social needs of subordinates. The transactional leader's ability to satisfy subordinates may improve productivity. Transactional leaders excel at management functions. They are hardworking, tolerant, and fair minded, and they take pride in keeping things running smoothly and efficiently. Transactional leaders often stress the impersonal aspects of performance, such as plans, schedules, and budgets. They have a sense of commitment to the organization and conform to organizational norms and values. Transactional leadership is important to all organizations, but leading change requires a different approach.

Transformational leaders have the ability to lead changes in the organization's mission, strategy, structure, and culture, as well as to promote innovation in products and technologies. Transformational leaders do not rely solely on tangible rules and incentives to control

SPOTLIGHT ON SKILLS

Are You a Charismatic Leader?

If you were the head of a major department in a corporation, how important would each of the following activities be to you? Answer "yes" or "no" to indicate whether you would strive to perform each activity.

1. Help subordinates clarify goals and how to reach them.
2. Give people a sense of mission and overall purpose.
3. Help get jobs out on time.
4. Look for the new product or service opportunities.
5. Use policies and procedures as guides for problem solving.
6. Promote unconventional beliefs and values.
7. Give monetary rewards in exchange for high performance from subordinates.
8. Command respect from everyone in the department.
9. Work alone to accomplish important tasks.
10. Suggest new and unique ways of doing things.
11. Give credit to people who do their jobs well.
12. Inspire loyalty to yourself and to the organization.
13. Establish procedures to help the department operate smoothly.
14. Use ideas to motivate others.
15. Set reasonable limits on new approaches.
16. Demonstrate social nonconformity.

The even-numbered items represent behaviors and activities of charismatic leaders. Charismatic leaders are personally involved in shaping ideas, goals, and direction of change. They use an intuitive approach to develop fresh ideas for old problems and seek new directions for the department or organization. The odd-numbered items are considered more traditional management activities, or what would be called *transactional leadership*. Managers respond to organizational problems in an impersonal way, make rational decisions, and coordinate and facilitate the work of others. If you answered "yes" to more even-numbered than odd-numbered items, you may be a potential charismatic leader.

SOURCES: Based on "Have You Got It?" a quiz that appeared in Patricia Sellers, "What Exactly Is Charisma?" *Fortune* (January 15, 1996): 68–75; Bernard M. Bass, *Leadership and Performance Beyond Expectations* (New York: Free Press, 1985); and Lawton R. Burns and Selwyn W. Becker, "Leadership and Managership," in S. Shortell and A. Kaluzny, eds., *Health Care Management* (New York: Wiley, 1986).

specific transactions with followers. They focus on intangible qualities such as vision, shared values, and ideas to build relationships, give larger meaning to diverse activities, and find common ground to enlist followers in the change process.[54] For example, when Michelle Rhee was chancellor of the District of Columbia public schools, she acted as a transformational leader in her efforts to revamp one of the most expensive, worst performing school systems in the country. She attacked the dysfunctional culture that rewards teachers for seniority rather than performance; revised systems and structures to slash bureaucracy; held school principals accountable for improving student performance; and focused people on a mission of putting the best interests of students first. Rhee quickly cut numerous administrative positions, fired teachers and principals who didn't meet performance standards, and closed underperforming schools. New procedures handsomely reward high-performing teachers; give principals more control over hiring, promoting, and firing; and put people on alert that low performance and complacency won't be tolerated. There is still a long way to go to fulfill the promise of making D.C. schools "the highest-performing urban school district in the nation," but Rhee brought new energy and movement to a long-stagnant system. About 85 percent of the students in the D.C. school system are African American, and many come from poor families. "We have a system that does wrong by poor kids of color," said Rhee. "If we're going to live up to our promise as a country . . . that has got to stop."[55]

Studies show that transformational leadership has a positive impact on follower development and follower performance. Moreover, transformational leadership skills can be learned and are not ingrained personality characteristics.[56] However, some personality traits may make it easier for a leader to display transformational leadership behaviors. For example, studies of transformational leadership have found that the trait of agreeableness, as discussed in the previous chapter, is often associated with transformational leaders.[57] In addition, transformational leaders are typically emotionally stable and positively engaged with the world around them, and they have a strong ability to recognize and understand others' emotions.[58] These characteristics are not surprising considering that these leaders accomplish change by building networks of positive relationships.

- A **charismatic leader** is a leader who has the ability to inspire and motivate people to transcend their expected performance, even to the point of personal sacrifice.
- Both charismatic and transformational leaders provide followers with an inspiring **vision**, an attractive, ideal future that is credible yet not readily attainable.
- A **transformational leader** is distinguished by a special ability to bring about innovation and change by creating an inspiring vision, shaping values, building relationships, and providing meaning for followers.
- A **transactional leader** clarifies subordinates' roles and task requirements, initiates structure, provides rewards, and displays consideration for followers.

Followership

No discussion of leadership is complete without a consideration of followership. Leadership matters, but without effective followers no organization can survive. People have different expectations of what constitutes a good follower versus a good leader. In studies asking people to rank the desired characteristics of leaders and followers, the top five qualities desired in a leader are that they be honest, competent, forward-looking, inspiring, and intelligent. For followers, the top five desired characteristics are that they be honest, competent, dependable, cooperative, and loyal. Other qualities highly valued in followers include intelligence, supportive attitude, caring, and maturity.[59] However, overall, many of the qualities that define a good follower are the same qualities as those possessed by a good leader. Leaders can develop an understanding of their followers and create the conditions that help them be most effective.[60]

One model of followership is illustrated in Exhibit 11.10. Robert E. Kelley conducted extensive interviews with managers and their subordinates and came up with five *follower styles*, which are categorized according to two dimensions, as shown in the exhibit.[61]

The first dimension is the quality of independent, **critical thinking** versus dependent, **uncritical thinking**. Independent critical thinkers are mindful of the effects of their own and others' behavior on achieving organizational goals. They can weigh the impact of their boss's and their own decisions and offer constructive criticism, creativity, and innovation. Conversely, a dependent, uncritical thinker does not consider possibilities beyond what he or she is told, does not contribute to the cultivation of the organization, and accepts the supervisor's ideas without thinking.

The second dimension of follower style is active versus passive behavior. An active follower participates fully in the organization, engages in behavior that is beyond the limits

EXHIBIT 11.10

Styles of Followership

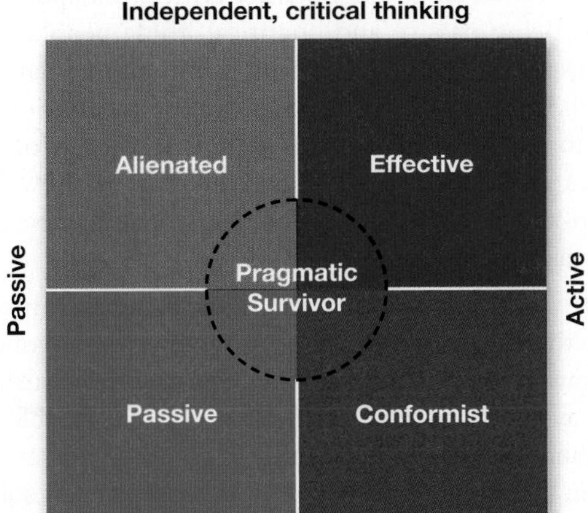

SOURCE: From *The Power of Followership* by Robert E. Kelley, p. 97, copyright © 1992 by Consultants to Executives and Organizations, Ltd. Used by permission of Doubleday, a division of Random House, Inc.

of the job, demonstrates a sense of ownership, and initiates problem solving and decision making. A passive follower, by contrast, is characterized by a need for constant supervision and prodding by superiors. Passivity is often regarded as laziness; a passive person does nothing that is not required and avoids added responsibility.

The extent to which an individual is active or passive and is a critical, independent thinker or a dependent, uncritical thinker determines whether the person will be an alienated follower, a passive follower, a conformist, a pragmatic survivor, or an effective follower, as illustrated in Exhibit 11.10:

1. The **alienated follower** is a passive, yet independent, critical thinker. Alienated employees are often effective followers who have experienced setbacks and obstacles, perhaps promises broken by their superiors. Thus, they are capable, but they focus exclusively on the shortcomings of their boss. Often cynical, alienated followers are able to think independently, but they do not participate in developing solutions to the problems or deficiencies they see. These people waste valuable time complaining about their boss without offering constructive feedback.
2. The **conformist** participates actively in a relationship with the boss but doesn't use critical thinking skills. In other words, a conformist typically carries out any and all orders regardless of the nature of the request. The conformist participates willingly, but without considering the consequences of what he or she is being asked to do—even at the risk of contributing to a harmful endeavor. A conformist is concerned only with avoiding conflict. This follower style might reflect an individual's overdependent attitude toward authority, yet it can also result from rigid rules and authoritarian environments that create a culture of conformity.
3. The **pragmatic survivor** has qualities of all four extremes—depending on which style fits with the prevalent situation. This type of person uses whatever style best benefits his or her own position and minimizes risk. Pragmatic survivors often emerge when an organization is going through desperate times and individuals find themselves doing whatever is needed to get themselves through the difficulty. Within any given

company, some 25 to 35 percent of people tend to be pragmatic survivors, avoiding risks and fostering the status quo.[62]

4. The **passive follower** exhibits neither critical, independent thinking nor active participation. Being passive and uncritical, these people show neither initiative nor a sense of responsibility. Their activity is limited to what they are told to do, and they accomplish things only with a great deal of supervision. Passive followers leave the thinking to the boss. Often, this style is the result of a micromanaging boss who encourages passive behavior. People learn that to show initiative, accept responsibility, or think creatively is not rewarded, and may even be punished by the boss, so they grow increasingly passive.
5. The **effective follower** is both a critical, independent thinker and active in the organization. Effective followers behave the same toward everyone, regardless of their position in the organization. They develop an equitable relationship with their leaders and do not try to avoid risk or conflict. These people are capable of self-management, discern strengths and weaknesses in themselves and their bosses, are committed to something bigger than themselves, and work toward competency, solutions, and positive impact.

Consider the night janitor at FAVI, a French copper-alloy foundry. While the janitor was cleaning one night, the phone rang and she answered it to discover that an important visitor to the company had been delayed and was now waiting at the airport without the promised ride to his hotel. (FAVI's CEO had left the airport when the visitor didn't arrive as expected.) What did the janitor do? She simply took the keys to one of the company cars, drove 90 minutes to pick up the visitor and deliver him to his hotel, then went back to finish the cleaning she had interrupted three hours earlier.[63] Effective followers recognize that they have power in their relationships with superiors; thus, they have the courage to manage upward, to initiate change, and to put themselves at risk or in conflict with the boss if they believe it serves the best interest of the team or organization.

- Leaders can accomplish nothing without effective followers.
- **Critical thinking** means thinking independently and being mindful of the effect of one's behavior on achieving goals.
- **Uncritical thinking** means failing to consider the possibilities beyond what one is told, accepting others' ideas without thinking.
- An **effective follower** is a critical, independent thinker who actively participates in the organization.
- An **alienated follower** is a person who is an independent, critical thinker but is passive in the organization.
- A **conformist** is a follower who participates actively in the organization but does not use critical thinking skills.
- A **passive follower** is one who exhibits neither critical independent thinking nor active participation.
- A follower who has qualities of all four follower styles, depending on which fits the prevalent situation, is called a **pragmatic survivor**.

Power and Influence

Both followers and leaders use power and influence to get things done in organizations.

Power is the potential ability to influence the behavior of others.[64] Sometimes the terms *power* and *influence* are used synonymously, but there are distinctions between the two.

Basically, **influence** is the effect a person's actions have on the attitudes, values, beliefs, or behavior of others. Whereas power is the capacity to cause a change in a person, influence may be thought of as the degree of actual change.

Power results from an interaction of leader and followers. Some power comes from an individual's position in the organization. Power may also come from personal sources, such as an individual's personal interests, goals, and values, as well as from sources such as access to information or important relationships. Followers as well as leaders can tap into a variety of power sources.

Michael A. Schwarz

ConceptConnection

"In business," says Daniel Amos, AFLAC chairman and CEO, "you should treat your employees like they can vote." The insurance company that Amos heads has been named to *Fortune*'s "100 Best Companies to Work For in America" for ten consecutive years. Amos (pictured here with the American Family Life Assurance Company [AFLAC] duck) influences employees using a combination of **reward power** and **referent power**. "You kind of try to kiss the babies and shake the hands and tell 'em you appreciate 'em and would like them to support you. You can do it like a dictator, but I'm not sure very many of them in the long run are successful."

Position Power

The traditional manager's power comes from the organization. The manager's position gives him or her the power to reward or punish subordinates to influence their behavior. Legitimate power, reward power, and coercive power are all forms of position power used by managers to change employee behavior.

Legitimate Power Power coming from a formal management position in an organization and the authority granted to it is called **legitimate power**. Once a person has been selected as a supervisor, most employees understand that they are obligated to follow his or her direction with respect to work activities. Subordinates accept this source of power as legitimate, which is why they comply. The story of Broadway's *Spiderman* is one where the producers did not exert their legitimate power, but instead let the director take charge, with disastrous results, as shown in this chapter's Business Blooper.

Reward Power Another kind of power, **reward power**, stems from the authority to bestow rewards on other people. Managers may have access to formal rewards such as pay increases or promotions. They also have at their disposal rewards such as praise, attention, and recognition. Managers can use rewards to influence subordinates' behavior.

Coercive Power The opposite of reward power is **coercive power**, which refers to the authority to punish or recommend punishment. Managers have coercive power when they have the right to fire or demote employees, criticize, or withdraw pay increases. If an employee does not perform as expected, the manager has the coercive power to reprimand him, put a negative letter in his file, deny him a raise, and hurt his chances for a promotion.

Personal Power

In contrast to the external sources of position power, personal power most often comes from internal sources, such as an individual's special knowledge or personal characteristics. Personal power is the primary tool of the leader, and it is becoming increasingly important

BUSINESS BLOOPER

Spiderman: Turn Off the Dark

Broadway musicals are supposed to cost a lot of money, but *Spiderman: Turn Off the Dark* has gone beyond imagination and become a superlative in ways the producers probably never intended. It has the biggest budget of any show, ever, on Broadway, at $75 million and counting, almost three times the next most expensive show, *Shrek*, at $25 million. And it's gotten arguably the worst reviews of a show that is still running.

How did a musical that credits Bono and The Edge as songwriters and the award-winning Julie Taymor (the *Lion King* on Broadway) as director turn in to a disaster so big even Spiderman would be at odds to solve it? It all began with successful producer Tony Adams, who had the vision and brought the U2 partners on board. But just as The Edge were signing the papers, Adams had a stroke and dropped dead. Adam's partner, David Garfinkle, took over. He was a competent entertainment attorney but had little experience as a producer, so he ceded creative control to Taymor, "a perfectionist whose aesthetic included never repeating herself." Unfortunately, Garfinkle did not follow Disney's lead in keeping Taymor under control when they collaborated on the extremely successful *Lion King* (which has grossed over $700 million), knowing her genius best flourishes under tight supervision. Veteran Broadway producer Jeffrey Seller noted, "Disney knew to stay on top of Julie to ensure they were all working toward the same goals. It paid off royally."

When Garfinkle couldn't raise enough money, he was replaced as lead producer by Michael Cohl, who claimed $30 million had already been wasted. Rather than see his job as reigning in Taymor, he saw his role as fund-raiser. Left on her own, Taymor hired top-dollar star designers for sets, costumes, and choreography, which made the budget soar even more. Taymor became obsessed with the special effects and flying sequences, which ended up taking months more to execute and involved some serious injuries of cast members. Bono saw problems, knowing that if the "wows" came from those effects and nothing else, not "from the soul or the heart, we will all think that we've failed."

Spiderman was pulling in $1 million per week in ticket sales, which barely covered the weekly running costs for this complex spectacle. The critics hated it. Safety violations continued to haunt the production, threatening shutdowns. Finally, in desperation, the producers fired Taymor, an act allegedly supported by Bono, and closed the show for three weeks in 2011 to rewrite and rehearse the new version. Most Broadway shows have three or four weeks of previews before opening night. *Spiderman*'s opening night was delayed six times, and the show finally opened in June 2011. The new director, Philip McKinley, is a former circus director, and people wondered whether he could get the lights up for *Turn Off the Dark*. Reviews have not been kind. Top critic Ben Brantley noted that part of the adrenaline rush of seeing the show is from worrying that flying actors might fall on top of you, but that the show itself went from an indecipherable mess (version 1.0) to a bore (2.0). Maybe *Spiderman* could learn lessons from the immensely popular and Tony-winning new musical, *The Book of Mormon*, whose entire $9 million budget was the amount *Spiderman* spent on sets, costumes, and shoes. Well, spiders do have more feet.

SOURCES: Kevin Flynn and Patrick Healy, "How the Numbers Add Up," *The New York Times*, June 23, 2011; Ben Brantley, "1 Radioactive bite, 8 legs and 183 previews," *The New York Times*, June 15, 2011; and Patrick Healy and Kevin Flynn, "A Broadway Superlative for All the Wrong Reasons," *The New York Times*, March 14, 2011.

as more businesses are run by teams of workers who are less tolerant of authoritarian management.[65] Two types of personal power are expert power and referent power.

Expert Power Power resulting from a person's special knowledge or skill regarding the tasks being performed is referred to as **expert power**. When someone is a true expert, others go along with recommendations because of his or her superior knowledge. Followers as well as leaders can possess expert power. For example, some managers lead teams in which members have expertise that the leader lacks. Some leaders at top management levels may lack expert power because subordinates know more about technical details than they do.

Referent Power **Referent power** comes from an individual's personal characteristics that command others' identification, respect, and admiration so they wish to emulate that individual. Referent power does not depend on a formal title or position. When employees admire a supervisor because of the way she deals with them, the influence is based on referent power. Referent power is most visible in the area of charismatic leadership. In social and religious movements, we often see charismatic leaders who emerge and gain a tremendous following based solely on their personal power.

Other Sources of Power

There are additional sources of power that are not linked to a particular person or position, but rather to the role an individual plays in the overall functioning of the organization. These important sources include personal effort, relationships with others, and information.

Personal Effort People who show initiative, work beyond what is expected of them, take on undesirable but important projects, and show interest in learning about the organization and industry often gain power as a result. Managers come to depend on particular subordinates, for instance, whom they know they can count on to take on a disagreeable job or put forth extra effort when it's necessary. However, these people aren't pushovers. Related to personal effort is the individual's willingness to be assertive in asking for what he or she wants and needs from superiors.

Network of Relationships People who are enmeshed in a network of relationships have greater power. A leader or employee with many relationships knows what's going on in the organization and industry, whereas one who has few interpersonal connections is often in the dark about important activities or changes. Developing positive associations with superiors or other powerful people is a good way to gain power, but people with the greatest power are those who cultivate relationships with individuals at all levels, both inside and outside the organization.

Information Information is a primary business resource, and people who have access to information and control over how and to whom it is distributed are typically powerful. To some extent, access to information is determined by a person's position in the organization. Top managers typically have access to more information than middle managers, who in turn have access to more information than lower-level supervisors or front-line employees.

Both leaders and followers can tap into these additional sources of power. Consider the following example.

MELLODY HOBSON, ARIEL INVESTMENTS

How did a poor African American girl growing up with a single mom in inner-city Chicago turn into one of the most recognized names in financial services? Intelligence, hard work, integrity, and a strong work ethic are part of the answer. But what really helped Mellody Hobson not only survive but thrive in the white male–dominated world of investing is her knack for tapping into and applying various sources of power.

Hobson, who is president of mutual fund company Ariel Investments, started at Ariel as a student intern and joined full time after college graduation. She immediately started networking, making friends and supporters that she's kept to this day. Hobson hangs out with celebrities like George Lucas and Ciara; enjoys talking with teachers and school children on Chicago's South Side; counts Warren Buffett, Dick Parsons, and Jamie Dimon among her friends; sits on the boards of Estée Lauder, Starbucks, and the Chicago Public Library; has hosted fundraisers for Barack Obama since his first Senate campaign; worked with Richard Daley to improve Chicago public schools; and loves mingling with Formula One race fans, where she cheers on Lewis Hamilton, the first black racer. "She finds a way to find a connection with virtually anyone," says David Geffen, cofounder of DreamWorks, where Hobson also sits on the board.

Hobson's networking skill has helped her achieve what she wants for herself and for Ariel Investments. Even when she was a 25-year-old new employee, Hobson was able to influence Ariel founder John Rogers and board members regarding a critical strategic decision—to strengthen Ariel as a brand focused on value investing by separating it from the Calvert Group, which focused on social investing (the two firms were involved in a joint venture). Rogers says he was initially shocked by Hobson's boldness, but Hobson used information, networking, hard work, and personal persuasion to convince him it was the right decision. "She went out and did a lot of heavy lifting and convinced our board and myself it was the right thing to do."[66]

Mellody Hobson had little formal power as a young Ariel employee, but she already understood how to gain power so she could accomplish goals. Successful leaders like Hobson take the time to build relationships both inside and outside the organization and to talk informally about important projects and priorities. All leaders need power to have an impact on their organizations. The next question is how leaders use their power to influence others, implement decisions, and facilitate change.

Interpersonal Influence Tactics

Leaders often use a combination of influence strategies, and people who are perceived as having greater power and influence typically are those who use a wider variety of tactics. One survey of a few hundred leaders identified more than 4,000 different techniques these people used to influence others.[67]

However, these tactics fall into basic categories that rely on understanding the principles that cause people to change their behavior and attitudes. Exhibit 11.11 lists seven principles for asserting influence. Notice that most of these involve the use of personal power rather than relying solely on position power or the use of rewards and punishments.[68]

1. ***Use rational persuasion.*** The most frequently used influence strategy is to use facts, data, and logical argument to persuade others that a proposed idea, request, or decision is appropriate. Using rational persuasion can often be highly effective because most people have faith in facts and analysis.[69] Rational persuasion is most successful when a leader has technical knowledge and expertise related to the issue at hand (expert power), although referent power is also used. That is, in addition to facts and figures, people also have to believe in the leader's credibility.
2. ***Make people like you.*** Recall our discussion of *likability* from the previous chapter. People would rather say yes to someone they like than to someone they don't. Effective leaders strive to create goodwill and favorable impressions. When a leader shows consideration and respect, treats people fairly, and demonstrates trust in others, people are more likely to want to help and support the leader by doing what he or she asks. In addition, most people like a leader who makes them feel good about themselves, so leaders should never underestimate the power of praise.
3. ***Rely on the rule of reciprocity.*** Leaders can influence others through the exchange of benefits and favors. Leaders share what they have—whether it is time, resources, services, or emotional support. The feeling among people is nearly universal that others should be paid back for what they do, in one form or another. This unwritten "rule of reciprocity" means that leaders who do favors for others can expect that others will do favors for them in return.[70]
4. ***Develop allies.*** Effective leaders develop networks of allies, people who can help the leader accomplish his or her goals. Leaders talk with followers and others outside of

EXHIBIT 11.11

Seven Interpersonal Influence Tactics for Leaders

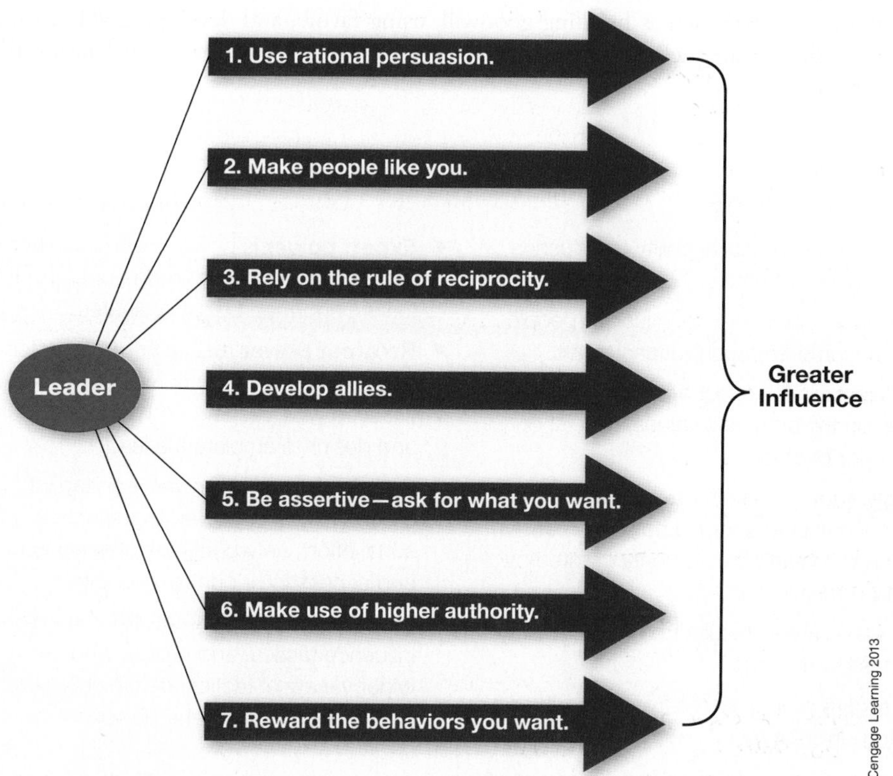
Leader
1. Use rational persuasion.
2. Make people like you.
3. Rely on the rule of reciprocity.
4. Develop allies.
5. Be assertive—ask for what you want.
6. Make use of higher authority.
7. Reward the behaviors you want.
Greater Influence

formal meetings to understand their needs and concerns as well as to explain problems and describe the leader's point of view. They strive to reach a meeting of minds with others about the best approach to a problem or decision.[71]

5. ***Ask for what you want.*** Another way to influence others is to make a direct and personal request. Leaders have to be explicit about what they want, or they aren't likely to get it. An explicit proposal is sometimes accepted simply because others have no better alternative. Also, a clear proposal or alternative will often receive support if other options are less well defined.
6. ***Make use of higher authority.*** Sometimes, to get things done, leaders have to use their formal authority, as well as gain the support of people at higher levels to back them up. However, research has found that the key to successful use of formal authority is to be knowledgeable, credible, and trustworthy—that is, to demonstrate expert and referent power as well as legitimate power. Managers who become known for their expertise, who are honest and straightforward with others, and who inspire trust can exert greater influence than those who simply issue orders.[72]
7. ***Reward the behaviors you want.*** Leaders can also use organizational rewards and punishments to influence others' behavior. The use of punishment in organizations is controversial, but negative consequences almost always occur for inappropriate or undesirable behavior. Leaders should not rely solely on reward and punishment as a means for influencing others, but combined with other tactics that involve the use of personal power, rewards can be highly effective.

Research indicates that people rate leaders as "more effective" when they are perceived to use a variety of influence tactics. But not all managers use influence in the same way. Studies have found that leaders in human resources, for example, tend to use softer, more subtle approaches such as building goodwill, using favors, and developing allies, whereas those in finance are inclined to use harder, more direct tactics such as formal authority and assertiveness.[73]

- **Power** is the potential ability to influence the behavior of others.
- All leaders use power to influence people and accomplish organizational goals.
- **Influence** is the effect a person's actions have on the attitudes, values, beliefs, or behavior of others.
- **Legitimate power** is power that stems from a manager's formal position in an organization and the authority granted by that position.
- **Reward power** results from the authority to bestow rewards.
- **Coercive power** stems from the authority to punish or recommend punishment.
- **Expert power** is power that results from a leader's special knowledge or skill in the tasks performed by subordinates.
- **Referent power** results from characteristics that command subordinates' identification with, respect and admiration for, and desire to emulate the leader.
- Both leaders and followers can tap into other sources of power, including personal effort, networks of relationships, and access to or control over information.
- Leaders use a wide range of interpersonal influence tactics, and people who use a wider variety of tactics are typically perceived as having greater power.

Discussion Questions

1. Do you think leadership style is fixed and unchangeable for a leader or flexible and adaptable? Discuss.
2. Suggest some personal traits that you believe would be useful to a business leader today. Are these traits more valuable in some situations than in others? How do you think traits differ from strengths?
3. In a study asking what people wanted from leaders versus followers, people ranked *maturity* number 8 for followers, but number 15 for leaders. What might account for people wanting a higher maturity level from followers?
4. If a male manager changes his behaviors to incorporate elements of interactive leadership more common to female managers, can he still be an "authentic" leader? Discuss.
5. Suggest the sources of power that would be available to a leader of a student government organization. What sources of power may not be available? To be effective, should student leaders keep power to themselves or delegate power to other students?
6. What skills and abilities does a manager need to lead effectively in a virtual environment? Do you believe a leader with a consideration style or an initiating-structure style would be more successful as a virtual leader? Explain your answer.
7. What is transformational leadership? Give examples of organizational situations that would call for transformational, transactional, or charismatic leadership.
8. How does Level 5 leadership differ from the concept of servant leadership? Do you believe anyone has the potential to become a Level 5 leader? Discuss.
9. Why do you think so little attention is given to followership compared to leadership in organizations?

Discuss how the role of an effective follower is similar to the role of a leader.

10. Do you think leadership is more important or less important in today's flatter, team-based organizations? Are some leadership styles better suited to such organizations as opposed to traditional hierarchical organizations? Explain.
11. Consider the leadership position of a senior partner in a law firm. What task, subordinate, and organizational factors might serve as substitutes for leadership in this situation?
12. Do you see yourself as having more leader qualities or more manager qualities? Do you think you will become a better leader or manager by developing the characteristics you already have or by trying to develop the characteristics you don't have? Discuss.

Self-Learning

Leadership Aptitude Questionnaire

Rate each of the following questions according to the following scale:

1 I am never like this.

2 I am rarely like this.

3 I am sometimes like this.

4 I am often like this.

5 I am always like this.

1. When I have a number of tasks or homework to do, I set priorities and organize the work around deadlines.
   1 2 3 4 5
2. Most people would describe me as a good listener.
   1 2 3 4 5
3. When I am deciding on a particular course of action for myself (such as hobbies to pursue, languages to study, which job to take, special projects to be involved in), I typically consider the long-term (three years or more) implications of what I would choose to do.
   1 2 3 4 5
4. I prefer technical or quantitative courses rather than those involving literature, psychology, or sociology.
   1 2 3 4 5
5. When I have a serious disagreement with someone, I hang in there and talk it out until it is completely resolved.
   1 2 3 4 5
6. When I have a project or assignment, I really get into the details rather than the "big picture" issues.
   1 2 3 4 5
7. I would rather sit in front of my computer than spend a lot of time with people.
   1 2 3 4 5
8. I try to include others in activities or discussions.
   1 2 3 4 5
9. When I take a course, I relate what I am learning to other courses I took or concepts I learned elsewhere.
   1 2 3 4 5
10. When somebody makes a mistake, I want to correct the person and let him or her know the proper answer or approach.
   1 2 3 4 5
11. I think it is better to be efficient with my time when talking with someone, rather than worry about the other person's needs, so that I can get on with my real work.
   1 2 3 4 5
12. I know my long-term vision of career, family, and other activities and have thought it over carefully.
   1 2 3 4 5
13. When solving problems, I would much rather analyze some data or statistics than meet with a group of people.
   1 2 3 4 5
14. When I am working on a group project and someone doesn't pull a fair share of the load, I am more likely to complain to my friends than confront the slacker.
   1 2 3 4 5
15. Talking about ideas or concepts can get me really enthused or excited.
   1 2 3 4 5
16. The type of management course for which this book is used is really a waste of time.
   1 2 3 4 5
17. I think it is better to be polite and not to hurt people's feelings.
   1 2 3 4 5
18. Data or things interest me more than people.
   1 2 3 4 5

Scoring and Interpretation

Subtract your scores for questions 6, 10, 14, and 17 from the number 6, and then add the total points for the following sections:

1, 3, 6, 9, 12, 15 Conceptual skills total score ______

2, 5, 8, 10, 14, 17 Human skills total score ______

4, 7, 11, 13, 16, 18 Technical skills total score ______

These skills are three abilities needed to be a good leader. Ideally, a leader should be strong (though not necessarily equal) in all three. Anyone noticeably weaker in any of the skills should take courses and read to build up that skill.

Group Learning

Assumptions about Leaders

Individually complete the sentences below.

1. A leader must always …
2. Leaders should never …
3. The best leader I ever had did …
4. The worst leader I ever had did …
5. When I am doing a good job as a leader, I …
6. I am afraid of leaders who …
7. I would follow a leader who …
8. I am repelled by leaders who …
9. Some people think they are good leaders, but they are not because they …
10. I want to be the kind of leader who …

In groups of four to six, discuss the following:

A. What did you learn about your own assumptions about leadership?

B. Trace those assumptions back to theories on leadership in this chapter.

C. What were common themes in your group?

Action Learning

Which Leadership Styles Are More Effective?

Step 1. Think about one situation in which a formal or informal leader was effective at motivating people, and another situation in which a leader was ineffective, perhaps demotivating people. When you have these situations firmly in mind, answer the following questions:

- What source or type of power was used by the effective leader? The ineffective leader?
- Did the effective leader emphasize a task-oriented or relationship-oriented style? Explain your rating. What about the ineffective leader?
- Did the effective leader come across as a humble person serving others or something larger than him- or herself, or did the leader seem ego centered and self-serving? What about the ineffective leader?

Step 2. Divide into groups of three to five students. Compare your answers and look for patterns that distinguish effective from ineffective leaders across your group members' experiences. What patterns do you find?

Step 3. Each group member should describe the leadership situation, with respect to its "favorability" or "readiness of followers." What relationship do you observe between the leadership situations and the style the leader used?

Step 4. Prepare to present your findings to the class and to participate in a discussion led by your instructor.

Ethical Dilemma

Too Much of a Good Thing?

Not long ago, Jessica Armstrong, vice president of administration for Delaware Valley Chemical, Inc., a New Jersey-based multinational company, made a point of stopping by department head Darius Harris's office and lavishly praising him for his volunteer work with an after-school program for disadvantaged children in a nearby urban neighborhood. Now she was about to summon him to her office so she could take him to task for dedication to the same volunteer work.

It was Carolyn Clark, Harris's secretary, who'd alerted her to the problem. "Darius told the community center he'd take responsibility for a fund-raising mass mailing. And then he asked me to edit the letter he'd drafted, make all the copies, stuff the envelopes, and get it into the mail—most of this on my own time," she reported, still obviously indignant. "When I told him, 'I'm sorry, but that's not my job,' he looked me straight in the eye and asked when I'd like to schedule my upcoming performance appraisal."

Several of Harris's subordinates also volunteered with the program. After chatting with them, Armstrong concluded most were volunteering out of a desire to stay on the boss's good side. It was time to talk to Harris.

"Oh, come on," responded Harris impatiently when Armstrong confronted him. "Yes, I asked for her help as a personal favor to me. But I only brought up the appraisal because I was going out of town, and we needed to set some time aside to do the evaluation." Harris went on to talk about how important working for the after-school program was to him personally. "I grew up in that neighborhood, and if it hadn't been for the people at the center, I wouldn't be here today," he said. Besides, even if he had pressured employees to help out—and he wasn't saying he had—didn't all the emphasis the company was putting on employee volunteerism make it okay to use employees' time and company resources?

After Harris left, Armstrong thought about the conversation. There was no question Delaware Valley actively encouraged employee volunteerism—and not just because it was the right thing to do. It was a chemical company with a couple of unfortunate accidental spills in its recent past that caused environmental damage and community anger.

Volunteering had the potential to help employees acquire new skills, create a sense of camaraderie, and play a role in recruiting and retaining talented people. But most of all, it gave a badly needed boost to the company's public image. Recently, Delaware Valley took every opportunity to publicize its employees' extracurricular community work on its Web site and in company publications. And the company created the annual Delaware Prize, which granted cash awards ranging from $1,000 to $5,000 to outstanding volunteers.

So now that Armstrong had talked with everyone concerned, just what was she going to do about the dispute between Darius Harris and Carolyn Clark?

What Would You Do?

1. Tell Carolyn Clark that employee volunteerism is important to the company and that although her performance evaluation will not be affected by her decision, she should consider helping Harris because it is an opportunity to help a worthy community project.
2. Tell Darius Harris that the employee volunteer program is just that: a volunteer program. Even though the company sees volunteerism as an important piece of its campaign to repair its tarnished image, employees must be free to choose whether to volunteer. He should not ask for the help of his direct reports with the after-school program.
3. Discipline Darius Harris for coercing his subordinates to spend their own time on his volunteer work at the community after-school program. This action will send a signal that coercing employees is a clear violation of leadership authority.

Case for Critical Analysis

Mountain West Health Plans, Inc.[74]

"Be careful what you wish for," thought Martin Quinn, senior vice president for service and operations for the Denver-based health insurance company, Mountain West Health Plans, Inc. When there was an opening for a new director of customer service last year due to Evelyn Gustafson's retirement, he'd seen it as the perfect opportunity to bring someone in to control the ever increasing costs of the labor-intensive department. He'd been certain he had found just the person in Erik Rasmussen, a young man in his late twenties with a shiny new bachelor's degree in business administration.

A tall, unflappable woman, Evelyn Gustafson consistently showed warmth and concern toward her mostly female, nonunionized employees as they sat in their noisy cubicles, fielding call after call about Mountain West's products, benefits, eligibility, and claims. Because she had worked her way up from a customer service representative position herself, she could look her subordinates right in the eye after they'd fielded a string of stressful calls and tell them she knew exactly how they felt. She did her best to offset the low pay by accommodating the women's needs with flexible scheduling, giving them frequent breaks, and offering plenty of training opportunities that kept them up to date in the health company's changing products and in the latest problem-solving and customer service techniques.

Her motto was: "Always put yourself in the subscriber's shoes." She urged representatives to take the time necessary to thoroughly understand the subscriber's problem and do their best to see that it was completely resolved by the call's completion. Their job was important, she told them. Subscribers counted on them to help them negotiate the often Byzantine complexities of their coverage. Evelyn's subordinates adored her, as demonstrated by the 10 percent turnover rate, compared to the typical 25 to 45 percent rate for customer service representatives. Mountain West subscribers were generally satisfied, although Quinn did hear some occasional grumbling about the length of time customers spent on hold.

However, whatever her virtues, Gustafson firmly resisted all attempts to increase efficiency and lower costs in a department where salaries accounted for close to 70 percent of the budget. That's where Erik Rasmussen came in. Upper-level management charged him with the task of bringing costs under control. Eager to do well in his first management position, the hard-working, no-nonsense young man made increasing the number of calls per hour each representative handled a priority. For the first time ever, the company measured the representatives' performance against statistical standards that emphasized speed, recorded the customer service calls, and used software that generated automated work schedules based on historical information and projected need. Efficient, not flexible, scheduling was the goal. In addition, the company cut back on training.

The results, Martin Quinn had to admit, were mixed. With more efficient scheduling and clear performance standards in place, calls per hour increased dramatically, and subscribers spent far less time on hold. The department's costs were finally heading downward, but department morale was spiraling downward as well, with the turnover rate currently at 30 percent and climbing. And Quinn was beginning to hear more complaints from subscribers who'd received inaccurate information from inexperienced representatives or representatives who sounded rushed.

It was time for Rasmussen's first performance review. Quinn knew the young manager was about to walk into his office ready to proudly recite the facts and figures that documented the department's increased efficiency. What kind of an evaluation was he going to give Rasmussen? Should he recommend some midcourse corrections?

Questions

1. How would you describe Evelyn Gustafson's leadership style? What were its strengths and weaknesses? What were the sources of her influence?
2. How would you describe Erik Rasmussen's leadership style as he tried to effect change? What are its strengths and weaknesses? What are the sources of his influence?
3. If you were Martin Quinn, would you recommend modifications in Erik Rasmussen's leadership style that you would like him to adopt? Do you think it will be possible for Rasmussen to make the necessary changes? If not, why not? If you do think change is possible, how would you recommend the desired changes be facilitated?

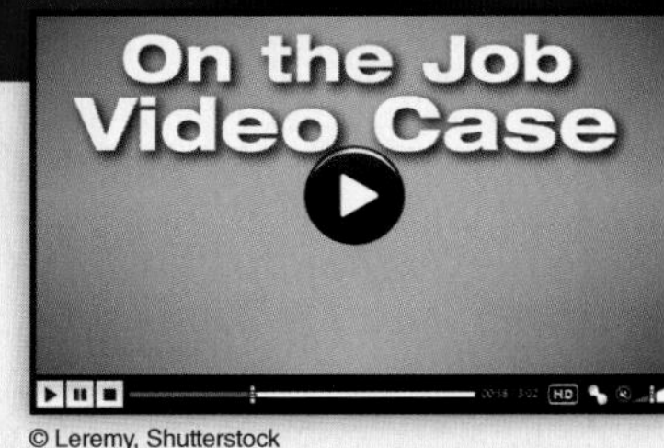

© Leremy, Shutterstock

Camp Bow Wow: Leadership

Some of the world's most iconic leaders have come from business. During the twentieth century, Henry Ford, Thomas J. Watson, Sr., Sam Walton, and Bill Gates made contributions that define how we live and work in the modern era. More recently, executives like Indra Nooyi, Oprah Winfrey, and Meg Whitman have reshaped leadership for a new century and inspired a generation of businesswomen in the process.

Heidi Ganahl, the 44-year-old founder of Camp Bow Wow, is among the most recent leaders to take the business world by storm. A little over a decade ago, while Ganahl was laying tile in her new pet-care facility in Boulder, Colorado, a powerful passion gripped the young entrepreneur and inspired confidence that her doggie day-care concept would catch on with pet owners. Today Camp Bow Wow ranks among the fastest-growing chains in America, with annual revenue of nearly $50 million.

As the owner of a wildly popular pet franchise, Ganahl is top dog to an increasing number of employees. "At Camp Bow Wow, leading a franchise company means leading 2,000 employees that work at camps, at Home Buddies, and at Bow Wow Behavior Buddies franchises," Ganahl said of her expanding pet care empire. One challenge Ganahl faces in leading so many talented people is getting everyone to follow a single business model. "One of the most important things about franchising is being able to duplicate and replicate the original business and, as it evolves, keep everybody on the same page, with all the facilities looking the same, the service the same, and the attributes of the brand the same," Ganahl said.

Although consistency and conformity are critical to the success of any chain, Camp Bow Wow seeks creative input from the franchisees who bought in to the system. To maintain a standard business template while encouraging fresh ideas, Ganahl keeps a door open for anyone who wants to meet and offer feedback. "I found that the best way to get people committed to a vision is to have an open-door policy and let people communicate their ideas and be part of the growth and execution of the brand," says the CEO. "If you do that, you'll come up with amazing things that you wouldn't have if you were not open to involving your team, franchisees, and staff." The policy has produced many visible improvements to the company, such as the new Tea Cup Pup Lounge, a play zone for small dogs. Originally recommended by a franchisee from Pittsburgh, the new play lounge has increased the safety and happiness of smaller pups that play at the camps.

Because franchise companies attract hundreds of independent business owners into the system, Ganahl has to work with many strong leaders. Sue Ryan, a Boulder businesswoman who bought one of Ganahl's original camp locations, says that the hand off of the business required two-way cooperation and respect, especially since the location had preestablished processes, goals, and staff. Despite some expected difficulties, Ganahl's approach made the transition as smooth as possible, and Ryan came away from the experience with a deep appreciation of Ganahl's leadership qualities. "She's very down to earth, so she doesn't bring a lot of ego to the table," Ryan said of Camp Bow Wow's founder. "Heidi knows what she has to offer and is confident with it, but she doesn't take it beyond there."

Another tricky part of Ganahl's job involves managing personal relationships. Heidi founded Camp Bow Wow with the help of family and friends, and many of these early contributors work at the corporate office today. "There's a line between friends, family, and business, and I've had a lot of friends and family join the company," Ganahl states. "It's difficult at times to hold folks accountable and to separate the business relationship from the family or friendship." She adds that the culture of a family business is very different from the culture of a franchise, but she insists that everyone in the organization is equally responsible for meeting the company's performance metrics and goals, regardless of personal connections.

Whether employees think of Heidi as boss, friend, or family, the Camp Bow Wow chief knows how to keep every individual focused on business. "We're all in this together, and we're all representing the brand," Ganahl states. "They're all on the front lines working with the customers and dogs; they are all a vital part of Camp Bow Wow."

Discussion Questions

1. Does Camp Bow Wow CEO Heidi Ganahl possess qualities associated with contemporary leadership?
2. In what way is Heidi Ganahl's leadership charismatic and visionary? Give examples.
3. Where does Heidi Ganahl's leadership fall on the Leadership Grid discussed in the chapter? Explain.

© VikaSuh, Shutterstock

Doomsday

The Reaper virus strikes Glasgow, Scotland, on April 3, 2008. It spreads and devastates the population throughout Scotland. Authorities seal off the borders and do not allow anyone to enter or leave the country. No aircraft flyovers are permitted. Social decay spreads, and cannibalistic behavior develops among the few remaining survivors. Eventually, no one is left alive in the quarantined area. The Reaper virus reemerges in 2032, this time in London, England. Classified satellite images show life in Glasgow and Edinburgh. Prime Minister John Hatcher (Alexander Siddig) and his assistant Michael Canaris (David O'Hara) assign the task of finding the cure to Security Chief Bill Nelson (Bob Hoskins).

Leadership This sequence starts at the beginning of DVD Chapter 4, "No Rules, No Backup," with a shot of the Department of Domestic Security emblem. The film cuts to Major Eden Sinclair (Rhona Mitra) standing in the rain smoking a cigarette while waiting for Chief Nelson. The sequence ends after Michael Canaris leaves the helicopter while saying to Sinclair, "Then you needn't bother coming back." He closes the helicopter's door. Major Sinclair blows her hair from her face while pondering his last statement. The film cuts to the helicopter lifting off the tarmac.

What to Watch for and Ask Yourself

- Assess the behavior of both Major Sinclair and Michael Canaris. Which leadership traits discussed earlier and shown in Exhibit 11.3 (page 450) does their behavior show?
- Apply the behavioral approaches to leadership discussed earlier in this chapter. Which parts apply to Sinclair and Canaris's behavior? Draw specific examples from the film sequence.
- Does this film sequence show any aspects of charismatic and transformational leadership? Draw some examples from the sequence.

© Pedro Nogueira, Shutterstock

Endnotes

1. Miguel Helft, "A Hired Gun for Microsoft, in Dogged Pursuit of Google," *The New York Times,* August 31, 2009, www.nytimes.com/2009/08/31/technology/internet/31search.html (accessed August 31, 2009).
2. Gary Yukl, "Managerial Leadership: A Review of Theory and Research," *Journal of Management* 15 (1989): 251–289.
3. James M. Kouzes and Barry Z. Posner, "The Credibility Factor: What Followers Expect from Their Leaders," *Management Review* (January 1990): 29–33.
4. James Collins, "Level 5 Leadership: The Triumph of Humility and Fierce Resolve," *Harvard Business Review* (January 2001): 67–76; James Collins, "Good to Great," *Fast Company* (October 2001): 90–104; A. J. Vogl, "Onward and Upward" (an interview with Jim Collins), *Across the Board* (September–October 2001): 29–34; and Jerry Useem, "Conquering Vertical Limits," *Fortune* (February 19, 2001): 84–96.
5. James Collins, *Good to Great: Why Some Companies Make the Leap and Others Don't* (New York: HarperBusiness, 2011).
6. Helft, "A Hired Gun for Microsoft."
7. Collins, "Level 5 Leadership."
8. Quoted in William J. Holstein, "The View's Still Great from the Corner Office," *The New York Times,* May 8, 2005.
9. Richard L. Daft and Robert H. Lengel, *Fusion Leadership: Unlocking the Subtle Forces That Change People and Organizations* (San Francisco: Berrett-Koehler, 1998).
10. Leigh Buchanan, "In Praise of Selflessness: Why the Best Leaders Are Servants," *Inc.* (May 2007): 33–35.
11. Robert K. Greenleaf, *Servant Leadership: A Journey into the Nature of Legitimate Power and Greatness* (Mahwah, NJ: Paulist Press, 1977).
12. Anne Fitzgerald, "Christmas Bonus Stuns Employees," *The Des Moines Register*, December 20, 2003.
13. Bill George, Peter Sims, Andrew N. McLean, and Diana Mayer, "Discovering Your Authentic Leadership," *Harvard Business Review* (February 2007): 129–138; and Bill George, *Authentic Leadership: Rediscovering the Secrets to Lasting Value.* (San Francisco: Jossey-Bass, 2003).
14. George, *Authentic Leadership*; and Bill George, "Truly Authentic Leadership," Special Report: America's Best Leaders, *U.S. News & World Report,* October 22, 2006, www.usnews.com/usnews/

news/articles/061022/30authentic.htm (accessed October 5, 2010).

15. "Authentic Leader with Courage; Becoming Authentic," *The Star* (June 23, 2010): 76.

16. *Ibid*

17. Judy B. Rosener, *America's Competitive Secret: Utilizing Women as a Management Strategy* (New York: Oxford University Press, 1995), pp. 129–135.

18. Alice H. Eagly and Linda L. Carli, "The Female Leadership Advantage: An Evaluation of the Evidence," *The Leadership Quarterly* 14 (2003): 807–834; Rosener, *America's Competitive Secret;* Judy B. Rosener, "Ways Women Lead," *Harvard Business Review* (November–December 1990): 119–125; Sally Helgesen, *The Female Advantage: Women's Ways of Leadership* (New York: Currency/ Doubleday, 1990); and Bernard M. Bass and Bruce J. Avolio, "Shatter the Glass Ceiling: Women May Make Better Managers," *Human Resource Management* 33, no. 4 (Winter 1994): 549–560.

19. Rochelle Sharpe, "As Leaders, Women Rule," *BusinessWeek* (November 20, 2000): 75–84.

20. Kevin S. Groves, "Gender Differences in Social and Emotional Skills and Charismatic Leadership," *Journal of Leadership and Organizational Studies* 11, no. 3 (2005): 30ff.

21. Herminia Ibarra and Otilia Obodaru, "Women and the Vision Thing," *Harvard Business Review* (January 2009): 62–70.

22. Adam Bryant, "Think 'We' for Best Results" (an interview with Nell Minow; Corner Office column), *The New York Times,* April 18, 2009, www.nytimes.com/2009/04/19/business/19corner.html (accessed April 27, 2009).

23. Leigh Buchanan, "Pat McGovern … For Knowing the Power of Respect," segment in "25 Entrepreneurs We Love," *Inc.* (April 2004): 110–147.

24. Gary Yukl and Richard Lepsinger, "Why Integrating the Leading and Managing Roles Is Essential for Organizational Effectiveness," *Organizational Dynamics* 34, no. 4 (2005): 361–375; and Henry Mintzberg, *Managing* (San Francisco: Berrett-Kohler Publishers, 2009).

25. Neal E. Boudette, "Fiat CEO Sets New Tone at Chrysler," *The Wall Street Journal,* June 21, 2009.

26. G. A. Yukl, *Leadership in Organizations* (Englewood Cliffs, NJ: Prentice Hall, 1981); and S. C. Kohs and K. W. Irle, "Prophesying Army Promotion," *Journal of Applied Psychology* 4 (1920): 73–87.

27. R. Albanese and D. D. Van Fleet, *Organizational Behavior: A Managerial Viewpoint* (Hinsdale, IL: The Dryden Press, 1983); and S. A. Kirkpatrick and E. A. Locke, "Leadership: Do Traits Matter?" *Academy of Management Executive* 5, no. 2 (1991): 48-60.

28. Timothy A. Judge, Ronald F. Piccolo, and Tomek Kosalka, "The Bright and Dark Sides of Leader Traits: A Review and Theoretical Extension of the Leader Trait Paradigm," *The Leadership Quarterly* 20 (2009): 855–875.

29. Reported in Robert Goodier, "Confidence Wins over Smarts," in "Head Lines: Men Are Choosy Too," *Scientific American Mind* (September 2009): 15.

30. Tom Rath and Barry Conchie, *Strengths Based Leadership* (Gallup Press, 2009); Marcus Buckingham and Donald O. Clifton, *Now, Discover Your Strengths* (New York: The Free Press, 2001), p. 12.

31. Buckingham and Clifton, *Now, Discover Your Strengths.*

32. Gary Yukl, Angela Gordon, and Tom Taber, "A Hierarchical Taxonomy of Leadership Behavior: Integrating a Half Century of Behavior Research," *Journal of Leadership and Organizational Studies* 9, no. 1 (2002): 13–32.

33. C. A. Schriesheim and B. J. Bird, "Contributions of the Ohio State Studies to the Field of Leadership," *Journal of Management* 5 (1979): 135–145; C. L. Shartle, "Early Years of the Ohio State University Leadership Studies," *Journal of Management* 5 (1979): 126–134; and R. Likert, "From Production- and Employee-Centeredness to Systems 1–4," *Journal of Management* 5 (1979): 147–156.

34. P. C. Nystrom, "Managers and the High-High Leader Myth," *Academy of Management Journal* 21 (1978): 325–331; and L. L. Larson, J. G. Hunt, and Richard N. Osborn, "The Great High-High Leader Behavior Myth: A Lesson from Occam's Razor," *Academy of Management Journal* 19 (1976): 628–641.

35. R. Likert, "From Production- and Employee-Centeredness to Systems 1–4."

36. Robert R. Blake and Jane S. Mouton, *The Managerial Grid III* (Houston, TX: Gulf, 1985).

37. Buchanan, "Pat McGovern . . . For Knowing the Power of Respect"; and Melanie Warner, "Confessions of a Control Freak," *Fortune* (September 4, 2000): 130–140.

38. This discussion is based on Paul Hersey and Ken Blanchard, "Revisiting the Life-Cycle Theory of Leadership," in "Great Ideas Revisited," *Training & Development* (January 1996): 42-47; Kenneth H. Blanchard and Paul Hersey, "Life-Cycle Theory of Leadership," in "Great Ideas Revisited," *Training & Development* (January 1996): 42-47; Paul Hersey, "Situational Leaders: Use the Model in Your Work," *Leadership Excellence* (February 2009): 12; and Paul Hersey and Kenneth H. Blanchard, *Management of Organizational Behavior: Utilizing Human Resources*, 4th ed. (Englewood Cliffs, NJ: Prentice Hall, 1982). The concept of *readiness* comes from Hersey, "Situational Leaders."

39. Jennifer Robison, "Many Paths to Engagement: How Very Different Management Styles Get the Same Great Results at Mars Incorporated," *Gallup Management Journal,* January 10, 2008, http://gmj.gallup.com/content/103513/Many- Paths-Engagement.aspx (accessed July 31, 2010).

40. Fred E. Fiedler, "Assumed Similarity Measures as Predictors of Team Effectiveness," *Journal of Abnormal and Social Psychology* 49 (1954): 381–388; F. E. Fiedler, *Leader Attitudes and Group Effectiveness* (Urbana, IL: University of Illinois Press, 1958); and F. E. Fiedler, *A Theory of Leadership Effectiveness* (New York: McGraw-Hill, 1967).

41. Fred E. Fiedler and M. M. Chemers, *Leadership and Effective Management* (Glenview, IL: Scott, Foresman, 1974).

42. Deborah Solomon, "Bailout Man Turns the Screws," *The Wall Street Journal,* April 7, 2009; Leslie Scism, Joann S. Lublin, and Liam Pleven, "AIG Chief: Loud Voice and a Listener's Ear," *The Wall Street Journal,* August 10, 2009; Francesco Guerrera, "AIG Tough Guy's Head-on Riposte," *Financial Times,* December 21, 2009; and Arthur D. Postal, "AIG's Long-Term Prospects Challenged as Industry Analysts Raise Red Flags," *National Underwriter Property & Casualty* (May 31, 2010): 6, 24.

43. Reported in George Anders, "Theory & Practice: Tough CEOs Often Most Successful, a Study Finds," *The Wall Street Journal*, November 19, 2007.
44. Fred E. Fiedler, "Engineer the Job to Fit the Manager," *Harvard Business Review* 43 (1965): 115–122; and F. E. Fiedler, M. M. Chemers, and L. Mahar, *Improving Leadership Effectiveness: The Leader Match Concept* (New York: Wiley, 1976).
45. R. Singh, "Leadership Style and Reward Allocation: Does Least Preferred Coworker Scale Measure Tasks and Relation Orientation?" *Organizational Behavior and Human Performance* 27 (1983): 178–197; and D. Hosking, "A Critical Evaluation of Fiedler's Contingency Hypotheses," *Progress in Applied Psychology* 1 (1981): 103–154.
46. S. Kerr and J. M. Jermier, "Substitutes for Leadership: Their Meaning and Measurement," *Organizational Behavior and Human Performance* 22 (1978): 375–403; and Jon P. Howell and Peter W. Dorfman, "Leadership and Substitutes for Leadership among Professional and Nonprofessional Workers," *Journal of Applied Behavioral Science* 22 (1986): 29–46.
47. Katherine J. Klein and Robert J. House, "On Fire: Charismatic Leadership and Levels of Analysis," *Leadership Quarterly* 6, no. 2 (1995): 183–198.
48. Jay A. Conger and Rabindra N. Kanungo, "Toward a Behavioral Theory of Charismatic Leadership in Organizational Settings," *Academy of Management Review* 12 (1987): 637–647; Jaepil Choi, "A Motivational Theory of Charismatic Leadership: Envisioning, Empathy, and Empowerment," *Journal of Leadership and Organizational Studies* 13, no. 1 (2006): 24ff; and William L. Gardner and Bruce J. Avolio, "The Charismatic Relationship: A Dramaturgical Perspective," *Academy of Management Review* 23, no. 1 (1998): 32–58.
49. Robert J. House and Jane M. Howell, "Personality and Charismatic Leadership," *Leadership Quarterly* 3, no. 2 (1992): 81–108; and Jennifer O'Connor, Michael D. Mumford, Timothy C. Clifton, Theodore L. Gessner, and Mary Shane Connelly, "Charismatic Leaders and Destructiveness: A Historiometric Study," *Leadership Quarterly* 6, no. 4 (1995): 529–555.
50. Rob Nielsen, Jennifer A. Marrone, and Holly S. Slay, "A New Look at Humility: Exploring the Humility Concept and Its Role in Socialized Charismatic Leadership," *Journal of Leadership and Organizational Studies* 17, no. 1 (February 2010): 33–44.
51. Robert J. House, "Research Contrasting the Behavior and Effects of Reputed Charismatic vs. Reputed Non-Charismatic Leaders," paper presented as part of a symposium, "Charismatic Leadership: Theory and Evidence," Academy of Management, San Diego, 1985.
52. Bernard M. Bass, "Theory of Transformational Leadership Redux," *Leadership Quarterly* 6, no. 4 (1995): 463–478; Noel M. Tichy and Mary Anne Devanna, *The Transformational Leader* (New York: John Wiley & Sons, 1986); James C. Sarros, Brian K. Cooper, and Joseph C. Santora, "Building a Climate for Innovation through Transformational Leadership and Organizational Culture," *Journal of Leadership and Organizational Studies* 15, no. 2 (November 2008): 145–158; and P. D. Harms and Marcus Crede, "Emotional Intelligence and Transformational and Transactional Leadership: A Meta-Analysis," *Journal of Leadership and Organizational Studies* 17, no. 1 (February 2010): 5–17.
53. The terms *transactional* and *transformational* come from James M. Burns, *Leadership* (New York: Harper & Row, 1978); and Bernard M. Bass, "Leadership: Good, Better, Best," *Organizational Dynamics* 13 (Winter 1985): 26–40.
54. Daft and Lengel, *Fusion Leadership*.
55. Jeff Chu, "The Iron Chancellor," *Fast Company* (September 2008): 112–143; Amanda Ripley, "Can She Save Our Schools?" *Time* (December 8, 2008): 36–44; and William McGurn, "Giving Lousy Teachers the Boot; Michelle Rhee Does the Once Unthinkable in Washington," *The Wall Street Journal*, July 27, 2010.
56. Taly Dvir, Dov Eden, Bruce J. Avolio, and Boas Shamir, "Impact of Transformational Leadership on Follower Development and Performance: A Field Experiment," *Academy of Management Journal* 45, no. 4 (2002): 735–744.
57. Robert S. Rubin, David C. Munz, and William H. Bommer, "Leading from Within: The Effects of Emotion Recognition and Personality on Transformational Leadership Behavior," *Academy of Management Journal* 48, no. 5 (2005): 845–858; and Timothy A. Judge and Joyce E. Bono, "Five-Factor Model of Personality and Transformational Leadership," *Journal of Applied Psychology* 85, no. 5 (October 2000): 751ff.
58. Rubin et al., "Leading from Within."
59. Augustine O. Agho, "Perspectives of Senior-Level Executives on Effective Followership and Leadership," *Journal of Leadership and Organizational Studies* 16, no. 2 (November 2009): 159–166; and James M. Kouzes and Barry Z. Posner, *The Leadership Challenge: How to Get Extraordinary Things Done in Organizations* (San Francisco: Jossey-Bass, 1990).
60. Barbara Kellerman, "What Every Leader Needs to Know About Followers," *Harvard Business Review* (December 2007): 84–91.
61. Robert E. Kelley, *The Power of Followership* (New York: Doubleday, 1992).
62. *Ibid.*, 117–118.
63. Vignette recounted in Isaac Getz, "Liberating Leadership: How the Initiative-Freeing Radical Organizational Form Has Been Successfully Adopted," *California Management Review* (Summer 2009): 32–58.
64. Henry Mintzberg, *Power In and Around Organizations* (Englewood Cliffs, NJ: Prentice Hall, 1983); and Jeffrey Pfeffer, *Power in Organizations* (Marshfield, MA: Pitman, 1981).
65. Jay A. Conger, "The Necessary Art of Persuasion," *Harvard Business Review* (May–June 1998): 84–95.
66. Jennifer Reingold, "The Unsinkable Mellody Hobson," *Fortune* (October 27, 2008): 148–157.
67. D. Kipnis, S. M. Schmidt, C. Swaffin-Smith, and I. Wilkinson, "Patterns of Managerial Influence: Shotgun Managers, Tacticians, and Politicians," *Organizational Dynamics* (Winter 1984): 58–67.
68. These tactics are based on Kipnis et al., "Patterns of Managerial Influence"; and Robert B. Cialdini, "Harnessing the Science of Persuasion," *Harvard Business Review* (October 2001): 72–79.
69. Kipnis et al., "Patterns of Managerial Influence"; and Jeffrey Pfeffer, *Managing with Power: Politics and Influence in Organizations* (Boston: Harvard Business School Press, 1992), chapter 13.
70. *Ibid.*
71. V. Dallas Merrell, *Huddling: The Informal Way to Management Success* (New York: AMACOM, 1979).

72. Robert B. Cialdini, *Influence: Science and Practice,* 4th ed. (Boston: Pearson Allyn & Bacon, 2000).

73. Harvey G. Enns and Dean B. McFarlin, "When Executives Influence Peers, Does Function Matter?" *Human Resource Management* 4, no. 2 (Summer 2003): 125–142.

74. Based on Gary Yukl, *Leadership in Organizations,* 4th ed. (Englewood Cliffs, NJ: Prentice Hall, 1998), pp. 66–67; and "Telephone Call Centers: The Factory Floors of the 21st Century," Knowledge @ Wharton Web site, April 10, 2002, http://knowledge.wharton.upenn.edu/index.cfm?fa=viewArticle&ID=540 (accessed September 20, 2010).

Chapter Outline

Motivating Employees

Learning Outcomes

After studying this chapter, you should be able to:

1. Define *motivation* and explain the difference between intrinsic and extrinsic rewards.
2. Identify and describe content theories of motivation based on employee needs.
3. Identify and explain process theories of motivation.
4. Describe the reinforcement perspective and how it can be used to motivate employees.
5. Explain social learning theory, including the concepts of vicarious learning, self-reinforcement, and self-efficacy.
6. Discuss major approaches to job design and how job design influences motivation.
7. Explain how empowerment heightens employee motivation.
8. Identify three elements of employee engagement, and describe some ways managers can create a work environment that promotes engagement.

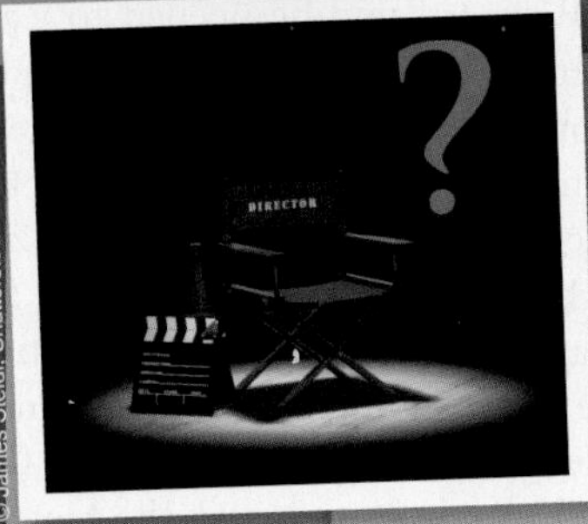

© James Steidl. Shutterstock

Are You Ready to Be a Manager?

Please circle your opinion below each of the following statements.

1 **At work, I am motivated by such things as a job well done or following an inspiring vision rather than merely by money and status.**

Mostly True | Mostly False

(See page 482, The Concept of Motivation [intrinsic versus extrinsic] and page 488, A Two-Factor Approach to Motivation.)

2 **I would be comfortable working in a place that offers flexibility in terms of hours and vacations.**

Mostly True | Mostly False

(See page 486, ERG Theory [flexible work schedules].)

3 **I like to be encouraged to set goals and then to receive feedback on how well I achieved those targets.**

Mostly True | Mostly False

(See page 492, Goal Setting.)

4 **I am able to learn new skills and behaviors when I have a positive role model.**

Mostly True | Mostly False

(See page 499, Social Learning Theory.)

5 **It is very motivating for me when I am empowered to do a more difficult job; this would include having information on the company's performance, being given enough power to carry out the assignment, and then being rewarded on my performance.**

Mostly True | Mostly False

(See page 505, Empowering People to Meet Higher Needs.)

When Carlos Ruiz took over as district sales manager in Bayamn, Puerto Rico, Mars Inc.'s oldest and largest market in that part of the world, he inherited a dispirited team of 15 salespeople who were just putting in their hours until quitting time. Turnover was high and performance was low. Within two years under his leadership, Ruiz's team was posting record numbers, and team members scored among the highest in the company on an employee engagement survey.[1] What made the difference? Ruiz excelled as a motivator. He gained people's trust by instituting rules that were fair, consistently applied, and tied to performance metrics. He went on sales calls with every team member and told them they were the experts and he needed to learn from them. He inspired people by telling them they weren't just selling boxes of candy bars; they were each running their own million-dollar business. "All of a sudden, their attitude towards their job [became], 'I'm valued here; I have a million-dollar business to take care of,' " Ruiz says.[2]

One secret for success in organizations is motivated and engaged employees. Most people begin a new job with energy and enthusiasm, but employees can lose their drive if managers fail in their role as motivators. Yet motivation is a challenge for managers because motivation arises from within employees and typically differs for each person. For example, Janice Rennie makes $350,000 a year selling residential real estate in Toronto; she attributes her success to the fact that she likes to listen carefully to clients and then find houses to meet their needs. Greg Storey is a skilled machinist who is challenged by writing programs for numerically controlled machines. After dropping out of college, he swept floors in a machine shop and was motivated to learn to run the machines. Frances Blais sells educational books and software. She is a top salesperson, but she doesn't care about the $50,000-plus commissions: "I'm not even thinking money when I'm selling. I'm really on a crusade to help children read well." In stark contrast, Rob Michaels gets sick to his stomach before he goes to work. Rob is a telephone salesperson who spends all day trying to get people to buy products they do not need, and the rejections are painful. His motivation is money; he earned $120,000 in the past year and cannot make nearly that much doing anything else.[3]

Rob is motivated by money; Janice, by her love of listening and problem solving; Frances, by the desire to help children read; and Greg, by the challenge of mastering numerically controlled machinery. Each person is motivated to perform, yet each has different reasons for performing. With such diverse motivations among individuals, how do managers find the right way to motivate employees toward common organizational goals?

This chapter reviews several approaches to employee motivation. First, we define motivation and the types of rewards managers use. Then, we examine several models that describe the employee needs and processes associated with motivation. We also look at the use of reinforcement for motivation, explain the concept of social learning, and examine how job design—changing the structure of the work itself—can affect employee satisfaction and productivity. Finally, we discuss the trend of empowerment and look at how managers imbue work with a sense of meaning by fostering employee engagement.

The Concept of Motivation

Most of us get up in the morning, go to school or work, and behave in ways that are predictably our own. We respond to our environment and the people in it with little thought as to why we work hard, enjoy certain classes, or find some recreational activities so much fun. Yet all these behaviors are motivated by something. **Motivation** refers to the forces either within or external to a person that arouse enthusiasm and persistence to pursue a certain course of action. Employee motivation affects productivity, and part of a manager's job is to channel motivation toward the accomplishment of organizational goals.[4] The study

New Manager Self-Test

Are You Engaged or Disengaged?

The term *employee engagement* is popular in the corporate world. To learn what engagement means, answer the following items twice—once for a course you both enjoyed and performed well in, and a second time for a course you did not enjoy and in which you performed poorly. Please mark a "1" to indicate whether each item is Mostly True or Mostly False for the course you enjoyed and performed well in, and a "2" to indicate whether each item is Mostly True or Mostly False for the course you did not enjoy and performed poorly in.

	MOSTLY TRUE <<<	>>> MOSTLY FALSE
1. I made sure to study on a regular basis.	______	______
2. I put forth effort.	______	______
3. I found ways to make the course material relevant to my life.	______	______
4. I found ways to make the course interesting to me.	______	______
5. I raised my hand in class.	______	______
6. I had fun in class.	______	______
7. I participated actively in small-group discussions.	______	______
8. I helped fellow students.	______	______

See It Online

Scoring and Interpretation: Engagement means that people involve and express themselves in their work, going beyond the minimum effort required. Engagement typically has a positive relationship with both personal satisfaction and performance. If this relationship was true for your classes, the number of "1s" in the Mostly True column will be higher than the number of "2s." You might expect a score of 6 or higher for a course in which you were engaged, and possibly 3 or lower if you were disengaged.

The challenge for a new manager is to learn to engage subordinates in the same way your instructors in your favorite classes were able to engage you. Teaching is similar to managing. What techniques did your instructors use to engage students? Which techniques can you use to engage people when you become a new manager?

SOURCE: Questions based on Mitchell M. Handelsman, William L. Briggs, Nora Sullivan, and Annette Towler, "A Measure of College Student Course Engagement," *Journal of Educational Research* 98 (January/February 2005): 184–191.

of motivation helps managers understand what prompts people to initiate action, what influences their choice of action, and why they persist in that action over time.

A simple model of human motivation is illustrated in Exhibit 12.1. People have *needs*—such as for recognition, achievement, or monetary gain—that translate into an internal tension that motivates specific behaviors with which to fulfill the need. To the extent that the behavior is successful, the person is rewarded in the sense that the need is satisfied. The reward also informs the person that the behavior was appropriate and can be used again in the future.

Rewards are of two types: intrinsic and extrinsic. **Intrinsic rewards** are the satisfactions a person receives in the process of performing a particular action. The completion of a complex task may bestow a pleasant feeling of accomplishment, or solving a problem that benefits

12.1 EXHIBIT
A Simple Model of Motivation

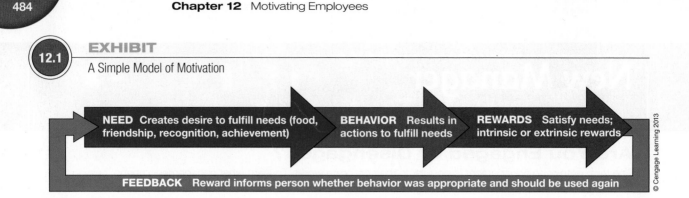

NEED Creates desire to fulfill needs (food, friendship, recognition, achievement)	**BEHAVIOR** Results in actions to fulfill needs	**REWARDS** Satisfy needs; intrinsic or extrinsic rewards

FEEDBACK Reward informs person whether behavior was appropriate and should be used again

others may fulfill a personal mission. Frances Blais sells educational materials for the intrinsic reward of helping children read well. **Extrinsic rewards** are given by another person, typically a manager, and include promotions, pay increases, and bonuses. They originate externally, as a result of pleasing others. Rob Michaels, who hates his sales job, nevertheless is motivated by the extrinsic reward of high pay. Although extrinsic rewards are important, good managers strive to help people achieve intrinsic rewards as well. The most talented and innovative employees are rarely motivated exclusively by rewards such as money and benefits, or even praise and recognition. Instead, they seek satisfaction from the work itself.[5] For example, at Google, people are motivated by an idealistic goal of providing "automated universal transference," which basically means unifying data and information around the world and totally obliterating language barriers via the Internet. People are energized by the psychic rewards they get from working on intellectually stimulating and challenging technical problems, as well as by the potentially beneficial global impact of their work.[6]

As a new manager, remember that people will be more engaged when they do things they really like. To reinforce this understanding, refer back to your answers on the New Manager Self-Test questionnaire on page 483.

The importance of motivation as illustrated in Exhibit 12.1 is that it can lead to behaviors that reflect high performance within organizations. Studies have found that high employee motivation goes hand in hand with high organizational performance and profits.[7] It is the responsibility of managers to find the right combination of motivational techniques and rewards to satisfy employees' needs and simultaneously encourage high work performance.

Some ideas about motivation, referred to as *content theories*, stress the analysis of underlying human needs and how needs can be satisfied in the workplace. *Process theories* concern the thought processes that influence behavior. They focus on how people seek rewards in work circumstances. *Reinforcement theories* and *social learning* focus on employee learning of desired work behaviors. In Exhibit 12.1, content theories focus on the concepts in the first box; process theories, on those in the second; and reinforcement and social learning theories, on those in the third.

- **Motivation** is the arousal of enthusiasm and persistence to pursue a certain course of action.
- All behaviors are motivated by something, such as the desire to fulfill needs for money, recognition, friendship, or a sense of accomplishment.
- **Intrinsic rewards** are the satisfactions a person receives in the process of performing a particular action.
- **Extrinsic rewards** are given by another person, such as a manager, and include pay increases, promotions, and praise.
- In addition to providing appropriate extrinsic rewards, good managers try to help people achieve intrinsic rewards from their work.

Content Perspectives on Motivation

Content theories emphasize the needs that motivate people. At any point in time, people have a variety of needs. These needs translate into an internal drive that motivates specific behaviors in an attempt to fulfill the needs. In other words, our needs are like a hidden catalog of the things we want and will work to get. To the extent that managers understand employees' needs, they can design reward systems to meet them and direct employees' energies and priorities toward attaining organizational goals.

The Hierarchy of Needs

Probably the most famous content theory was developed by Abraham Maslow.[8] Maslow's **hierarchy of needs theory** proposes that people are motivated by multiple needs and that these needs exist in a hierarchical order, as illustrated in Exhibit 12.2. Maslow identified five general types of motivating needs in order of ascendance:

1. ***Physiological needs.*** These most basic human physical needs include food, water, and oxygen. In the organizational setting, they are reflected in the needs for adequate heat, air, and base salary to ensure survival.
2. ***Safety needs.*** These needs include a safe and secure physical and emotional environment and freedom from threats—that is, for freedom from violence and for an orderly society. In the workplace, safety needs reflect the needs for safe jobs, fringe benefits, and job security. Managers at Burgerville, a regional restaurant chain based in Vancouver, Washington, discovered in a survey that health-care costs ranked as employees' top concern. After the firm began paying at least 90 percent of health-insurance premiums for hourly employees who worked at least 20 hours a week, turnover plunged, employees began working harder to get more hours (which are assigned based on performance), service improved, and sales increased.[9]
3. ***Belongingness needs.*** These needs reflect the desire to be accepted by one's peers, have friendships, be part of a group, and be loved. In the organization, these needs

EXHIBIT 12.2

Maslow's Hierarchy of Needs

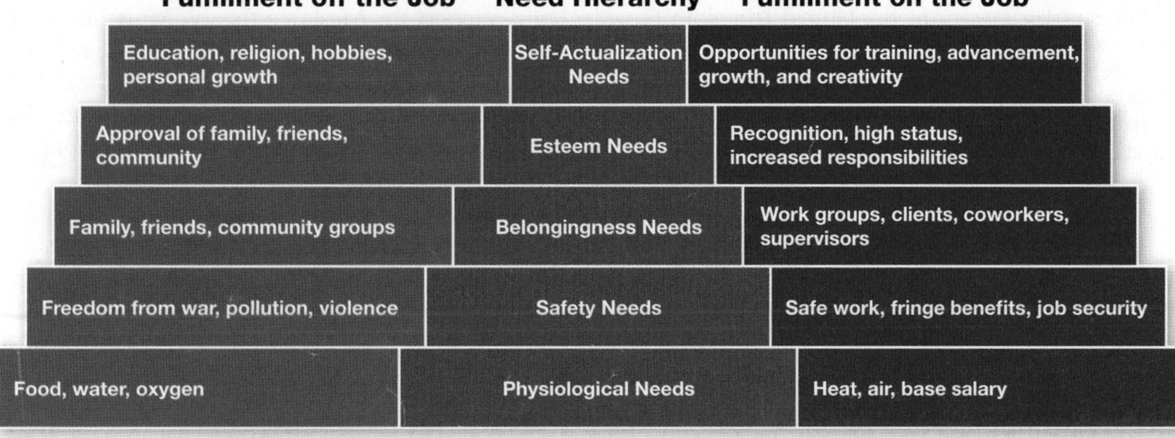

Najlah Feanny/Corbis

ConceptConnection

Gen-Yers, who, according to their managers, report for work with self-esteem to spare, often proceed directly from **existence needs** to **growth needs**. Once they're satisfied they're receiving fair pay, what younger employees want most is training. In fact, recent studies found that respondents chose training from a list of benefits three times more often than a cash bonus. There's a practical reason for this interest in personal growth. Gen-Yers know they need to acquire skills that will make them attractive job candidates. Unlike many of their elders, they don't expect to work for a single employer throughout their careers.

influence the desire for good relationships with coworkers, participation in a work group, and a positive relationship with supervisors.

4. ***Esteem needs.*** These needs relate to the desire for a positive self-image and to receive attention, recognition, and appreciation from others. Within organizations, esteem needs reflect a motivation for recognition, an increase in responsibility, high status, and credit for contributions to the organization. One example comes from Intuit, where Jennifer Lepird spent weeks working long, grueling hours on a big acquisition deal. Lepird was delighted to get a thank-you note from her manager, with a small gift certificate included, because it met her need to feel appreciated. "The fact that somebody took the time to recognize the effort made the long hours just melt away," she says.[10]
5. ***Self-actualization needs.*** These needs include the need for self-fulfillment, which is the highest need category. They concern developing one's full potential, increasing one's competence, and becoming a better person. Self-actualization needs can be met in the organization by providing people with opportunities to grow, be creative, and acquire training for challenging assignments and advancement.

As a new manager, recognize that some people are motivated primarily to satisfy lower-level physiological and safety needs, while others want to satisfy higher-level needs. Learn which lower- and higher-level needs motivate you by completing the Self-Learning on page 510.

According to Maslow's theory, low-order needs take priority—they must be satisfied before higher-order needs are activated. The needs are satisfied in sequence: Physiological needs come before safety needs, safety needs before social needs, and so on. A person desiring physical safety will devote his or her efforts to securing a safer environment and will not be concerned with esteem needs or self-actualization needs. Once a need is satisfied, it declines in importance and the next higher need is activated.

A study of employees in the manufacturing department of a major health care company in the United Kingdom provides some support for Maslow's theory. Most line workers said they worked at the company primarily because of the good pay, benefits, and job security. Thus, employees' lower-level physiological and safety needs were being met. When questioned about their motivation, employees indicated the importance of positive social relationships with both peers and supervisors (belongingness needs) and a desire for greater respect and recognition from management (esteem needs).[11]

ERG Theory

Clayton Alderfer proposed a modification of Maslow's theory in an effort to simplify it and respond to criticisms of its lack of empirical verification.[12] His **ERG theory** identified three categories of needs:

1. ***Existence needs.*** The needs for physical well-being.

2. ***Relatedness needs.*** The needs for satisfactory relationships with others.
3. ***Growth needs.*** The needs that focus on the development of human potential and the desire for personal growth and increased competence.

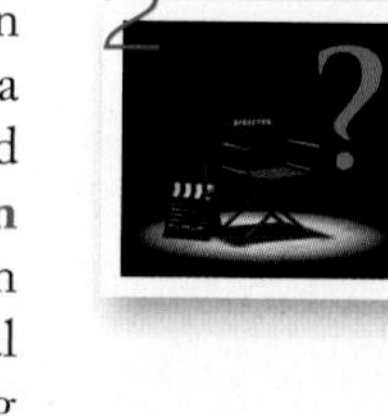

The ERG model and Maslow's need hierarchy are similar because both are in hierarchical form and presume that individuals move up the hierarchy one step at a time. However, Alderfer reduced the number of need categories to three and proposed that movement up the hierarchy is more complex, reflecting a **frustration-regression principle**, namely, that failure to meet a high-order need may trigger a regression to an already fulfilled lower-order need. Thus, a worker who cannot fulfill a need for personal growth may revert to a lower-order need and redirect his or her efforts toward making a lot of money. The ERG model therefore is less rigid than Maslow's need hierarchy, suggesting that individuals may move down as well as up the hierarchy, depending on their ability to satisfy needs. Need hierarchy theories explain why organizations find ways to recognize employees, encourage their participation in decision making, and give them opportunities to make significant contributions to the organization and society.

Many companies are finding that creating a humane work environment that allows people to achieve a balance between work and personal life is also a great high-level motivator. A few companies, such as J. A. Counter & Associates, take flexibility to the extreme, which enables employees to meet relatedness and personal growth needs.

J. A. COUNTER & ASSOCIATES

When profits began to fall at J. A. Counter & Associates, a $2.5 million insurance and investment advisory firm in New Richmond, Wisconsin, owner and CEO Linda Skoglund began implementing a series of changes to boost the bottom line. They worked, but they also hurt morale and left people fearful and distrustful of managers. So, Skoglund decided to try a new way of managing that had been developed by Cali Ressler and Jody Thompson when they were HR managers at Best Buy: a results-only work environment (ROWE).

Now, all employees at J.A. Counter can come and go as they please, without telling anyone where they are going or why, as long as they get their jobs done. If someone wants to take an afternoon off to attend a son's baseball game, no one is going to question her work ethic or commitment to her job. Some managers had a little trouble adjusting to the system. Mark Devereux, a senior investment advisor, found that his assistant Shannon Mehls was no longer at his beck and call. When he had an emergency, instead of dumping it on her, he had to handle the problem himself. "I had no idea how much I was creating fires until we started ROWE," Devereux says. He says he had "an 'aha' moment," and became more respectful of his assistant's time and skills. Mehls now sometimes helps Devereux with projects during off-hours, which never happened before ROWE, but she has the flexibility to manage her own time. She says employees now feel like "mini-entrepreneurs," managing their own schedules and focusing on results instead of just putting in 40 hours and getting a paycheck.[13]

Although not all managers would be comfortable working in a results-only work environment, there is evidence that people who have greater control over their work schedules are significantly less likely to suffer job burnout and are more highly committed to their employers, as shown in Exhibit 12.3. This idea is supported by a survey conducted at

EXHIBIT 12.3

The Motivational Benefits of Job Flexibility

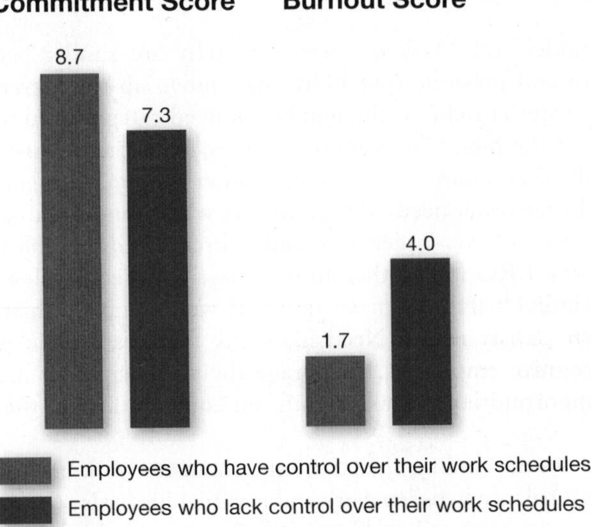

SOURCE: WFD Consulting data, as reported in Karol Rose, "Work-Life Effectiveness," *Fortune* (September 29, 2003): S1–S17.

Deloitte, which found that client service professionals cited workplace flexibility as a strong reason for wanting to stay with the firm. Another study at Prudential Insurance found that work-life satisfaction and work flexibility directly correlated to job satisfaction, organizational commitment, and employee retention.[14]

In the recent economic downturn, some companies found flexible options a great way to cut payroll costs while retaining and motivating valued employees. Sylvia Ann Hewlett, an economist and author of *Top Talent: Keeping Performance Up When Business Is Down*, points out that as companies expect more from employees while offering fewer financial incentives, managers can give people what many high-powered professionals crave the most: a chunk of free time. Accounting firm KPMG tried a program called Flexible Futures that offered employees in its British operations several options: (1) go to a four-day workweek and take a 20 percent pay cut; (2) choose a mini-sabbatical at 30 percent base pay; (3) opt for both of these; or (4) stay with their current employment arrangement. Over 80 percent of employees chose one of the flexible options. Other companies have implemented similar programs with great success.[15]

A Two-Factor Approach to Motivation

Frederick Herzberg developed another popular theory of motivation called the *two-factor theory*.[16] Herzberg interviewed hundreds of workers about times when they were highly motivated to work and other times when they were dissatisfied and unmotivated. His findings suggested that the work characteristics associated with dissatisfaction were quite different from those pertaining to satisfaction, which prompted the notion that two factors influence work motivation.

The two-factor theory is illustrated in Exhibit 12.4. The center of the scale is neutral, meaning that workers are neither satisfied nor dissatisfied. Herzberg believed that two entirely separate dimensions contribute to an employee's behavior at work. The first, called

EXHIBIT 12.4

Herzberg's Two-Factor Theory

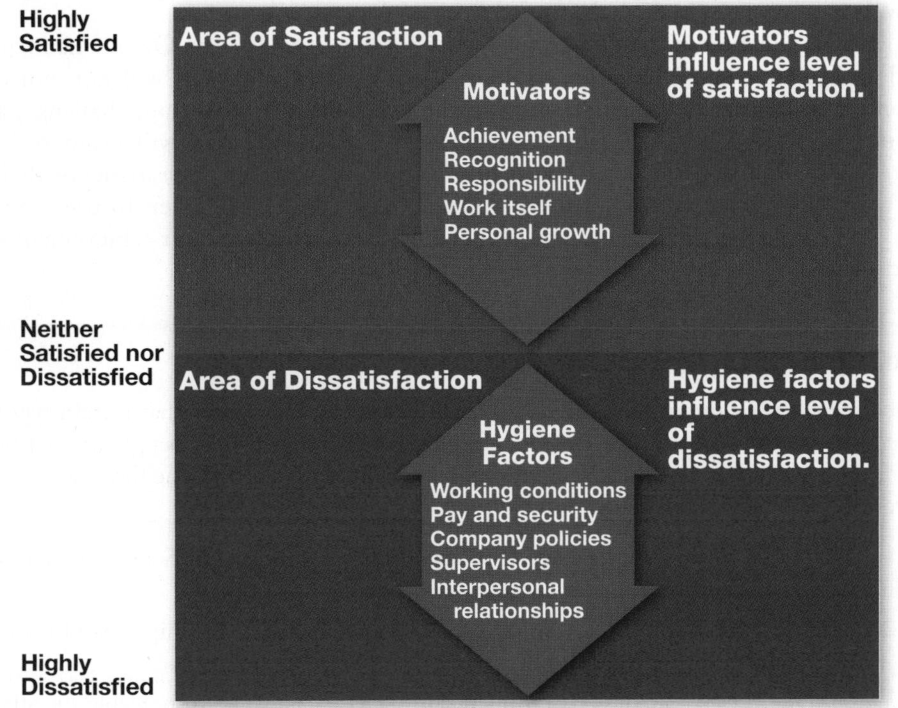

hygiene factors, involves the presence or absence of job dissatisfiers such as working conditions, pay, company policies, and interpersonal relationships. When hygiene factors are poor, work is dissatisfying. However, good hygiene factors simply remove the dissatisfaction; they do not in themselves cause people to become highly satisfied and motivated in their work.

The second set of factors does influence job satisfaction. **Motivators** focus on high-level needs and include achievement, recognition, responsibility, and opportunity for growth. Herzberg believed that when motivators are absent, workers are neutral toward work, but when motivators are present, workers are highly motivated and satisfied. Thus, hygiene factors and motivators represent two distinct factors that influence motivation. Hygiene factors work only in the area of dissatisfaction. Unsafe working conditions or a noisy work environment will cause people to be dissatisfied, but their correction will not lead to a high level of motivation and satisfaction. Motivators such as challenge, responsibility, and recognition must be in place before employees will be highly motivated to excel at their work.

Managers at Pizza Express, a chain of 350 restaurants across the United Kingdom, successfully apply the two-factor theory to meet employees' higher as well as lower-level needs. The company provides hygiene factors such as good salaries and benefits, including bonuses of up to 30 percent of annual salary, generous maternity and paternity leave, child-care vouchers, and free meals. It also implemented a program to meet higher-level needs for responsibility, achievement, and professional and personal growth. Local managers meet several times a year, sometimes for a social event such as visiting a cookery school or a fantastic restaurant; other times, to participate in making important company-level decisions. These motivators help keep restaurant managers engaged with their jobs rather than looking for greater satisfaction elsewhere. Consequently, the company has one of the lowest turnover rates in the industry.[17]

The implication of the two-factor theory for managers is clear. On one hand, providing hygiene factors will eliminate employee dissatisfaction but will not motivate workers to high achievement levels. On the other hand, recognition, challenge, and opportunities for personal growth are powerful motivators and will promote high satisfaction and performance. The manager's role is to remove dissatisfiers—that is, to provide hygiene factors sufficient to meet basic needs—and then to use motivators to meet higher-level needs and propel employees toward greater achievement and satisfaction.

Acquired Needs

The *acquired needs theory*, developed by David McClelland, proposes that certain types of needs are acquired during the individual's lifetime. In other words, people are not born with these needs but may learn them through their life experiences.[18] The three needs most frequently studied are these:

1. ***Need for achievement.*** The desire to accomplish something difficult, attain a high standard of success, master complex tasks, and surpass others.
2. ***Need for affiliation.*** The desire to form close personal relationships, avoid conflict, and establish warm friendships.
3. ***Need for power.*** The desire to influence or control others, be responsible for others, and have authority over others.

Early life experiences typically determine whether people acquire these needs. If children are encouraged to do things for themselves and receive reinforcement, they will acquire a need to achieve. If they are reinforced for forming warm human relationships, they will develop a need for affiliation. If they get satisfaction from controlling others, they will acquire a need for power.

For more than 20 years, McClelland studied human needs and their implications for management. People with a high need for *achievement* are frequently entrepreneurs. People who have a high need for *affiliation* are successful integrators, whose job is to coordinate the work of several departments in an organization.[19] Integrators include brand managers and project managers who must have excellent people skills. A high need for *power* often is associated with successful attainment of top levels in the organizational hierarchy. For example, McClelland studied managers at AT&T for 16 years and found that those with a high need for power were more likely to follow a path of continued promotion over time. More than half of the employees at the top levels had a high need for power. In contrast, managers with a high need for achievement but a low need for power tended to peak earlier in their careers and at a lower level. The reason is that achievement needs can be met through the task itself, but power needs can be met only by ascending to a level at which a person has power over others. Seth Priebatsch, who founded Scvngr, seems to be motivated by achievement, as shown in this chapter's Benchmarking box.

In summary, content theories focus on people's underlying needs and label those particular needs that motivate behavior. The hierarchy of needs theory, the ERG theory, the two-factor theory, and the acquired needs theory all help managers understand what motivates people. In this way, managers can design work to meet needs and hence elicit appropriate and successful work behaviors.

BENCHMARKING

Scvngr

How do you motivate smart but quirky employees? Workers so quirky, in fact, that some psychologists might call their behavior unstable and grandiose. If you are Highland Capital Partners and the quirky guy is 21-year-old Seth Priebatsch, who says he needs $750,000 to create a top-of-the-world game layer that will be a $1 billion a year venture, well, you say "yes." You let him work 96 hours in a row, crashing on a sleeping bag in his office. Priebatsch's pitch was successful and he went on to help start Scvngr in 2009. By 2010, it had 60 employees and $4 million from Google Ventures.

Scvnger is both a game and a game platform. Over 1,000 companies—including Zipcar, Warner Brothers, and Sony—pay it to create and manage challenges. The future is games, says Priebatsch. "The last decade was the decade where the social framework was built. The next decade will be the decade of games."

Priebatsch works relentlessly. Work is his "fun." He doesn't socialize or watch TV, and he is not motivated by wealth, "I'm not anti-money," he notes. "I like nice bikes, I like nice computers. I like that money is a representation of success, but the actual entity itself is not interesting for me. There is little that I would want that I don't have, and the things that I want money can't buy."

Really? Like what? Without hesitation, he replies, "I want to build the game layer on top of the world."

SOURCE: David Segal, "Just Manic Enough: Seeking the Perfect Entrepreneur," *The New York Times*, September 19, 2010.

- **Content theories** emphasize the needs that motivate people.
- The most well-known content theory is Maslow's **hierarchy of needs theory**, which proposes that people are motivated by five categories of needs—physiological, safety, belongingness, esteem, and self-actualization—that exist in a hierarchical order.
- **ERG theory** is a modification of the needs hierarchy and proposes three categories of needs: existence, relatedness, and growth.
- The **frustration-regression principle** is the idea that failure to meet a high-order need may cause a regression to an already satisfied lower-order need; thus, people may move down as well as up the need hierarchy.
- Giving employees more control over their work schedules and opportunities to contribute ideas are two ways managers meet people's higher-level needs.
- Best Buy and J. A. Counter & Associates have implemented a results-only work environment (ROWE), in which people can come and go as they please as long as they get their jobs done.
- One element of Herzberg's two-factor theory, **hygiene factors**, focuses on lower-level needs and involves the presence or absence of job dissatisfiers, including working conditions, pay, and company policies.
- Herzberg's second factor, **motivators**, influences job satisfaction based on fulfilling higher-level needs such as achievement, recognition, responsibility, and opportunities for personal growth.
- The *acquired needs theory* proposes that certain types of needs, including the need for achievement, need for affiliation, and need for power, are acquired during an individual's lifetime of experiences.

Process Perspectives on Motivation

Process theories explain how people select behavioral actions to meet their needs and determine whether their choices were successful. Important perspectives in this area include goal setting, equity theory, and expectancy theory.

Goal Setting

3

Recall from Chapter 5 our discussion of the importance and purposes of goals. Numerous studies have shown that specific, challenging targets significantly enhance people's motivation and performance levels.[20] You have probably noticed in your own life that you are more motivated when you have a specific goal, such as making an "A" on a final exam, losing 10 pounds before spring break, or earning enough money during the summer to buy a used car.

Goal-setting theory, described by Edwin Locke and Gary Latham, proposes that managers can increase motivation and enhance performance by setting specific, challenging goals, then helping people track their progress toward goal achievement by providing timely feedback. Key components of goal-setting theory include the following:[21]

- *Goal specificity* refers to the degree to which goals are concrete and unambiguous. Specific goals such as "visit one new customer each day," or "sell $1,000 worth of merchandise a week" are more motivating than vague goals such as "keep in touch with new customers" or "increase merchandise sales." For example, a lack of clear, specific goals is cited as a major cause of the failure of pay-for-performance incentive plans in many organizations.[22] Vague goals can be frustrating for employees.
- In terms of *goal difficulty*, hard goals are more motivating than easy ones. Easy goals provide little challenge for employees and don't require them to increase their output. Highly ambitious but achievable goals ask people to stretch their abilities and provide a basis for greater feelings of accomplishment and personal effectiveness. A study in Germany found that, over a three-year period, only employees who perceived their goals as difficult reported increases in positive emotions and feelings of job satisfaction and success.[23]
- *Goal acceptance* means that employees have to "buy into" the goals and be committed to them. Having people participate in setting goals is a good way to increase acceptance and commitment. At Aluminio del Caroni, a state-owned aluminum company in southeastern Venezuela, plant workers felt a renewed sense of commitment when top leaders implemented a *co-management* initiative that has managers and lower-level employees working together to set budgets, determine goals, and make decisions. "The managers and the workers are running this business together," said one employee who spends his days shoveling molten aluminum down a channel from an industrial oven to a cast. "It gives us the motivation to work hard."[24]
- Finally, the component of *feedback* means that people get information about how well they are doing in progressing toward goal achievement. It is important for managers to provide performance feedback on a regular, ongoing basis. However, self-feedback, where people are able to monitor their own progress toward a goal, has been found to be an even stronger motivator than external feedback.[25]

Why does goal setting increase motivation? For one thing, it enables people to focus their energies in the right direction. People know what to work toward, so they can direct their efforts toward the most important activities to accomplish the goals. Goals also energize behavior because people feel compelled to develop plans and strategies that keep them focused on achieving the target. Specific, difficult goals provide a challenge and encourage people to put forth high levels of effort. In addition, when goals are achieved, pride and satisfaction increase, contributing to higher motivation and morale.[26]

Equity Theory

Equity theory focuses on individuals' perceptions of how fairly they are treated compared with others. Developed by J. Stacy Adams, equity theory proposes that people are motivated to seek social equity in the rewards they receive for performance.[27]

According to equity theory, if people perceive their compensation as equal to what others receive for similar contributions, they will believe that their treatment is fair and equitable. People evaluate equity by a ratio of inputs to outcomes. Inputs to a job include education, experience, effort, and ability. Outcomes from a job include pay, recognition, benefits, and promotions. The input-to-outcome ratio may be arrived at by comparing one person to another in the work group, or to a perceived group average. A state of **equity** exists whenever the ratio of one person's outcomes to inputs equals the ratio of another's outcomes to inputs.

Inequity occurs when the input-to-outcome ratios are out of balance, such as when a new, inexperienced employee receives the same salary as a person with a high level of education or experience. Interestingly, perceived inequity also occurs in the other direction. Thus, if an employee discovers he or she is making more money than other people who contribute the same inputs to the company, the employee may feel the need to correct the inequity by working harder, getting more education, or considering lower pay. Studies of the brain have shown that people get less satisfaction from money they receive without having to earn it than they do from money they work to receive.[28] Perceived inequity creates tensions within individuals that motivate them to bring equity into balance.[29]

The most common methods for reducing a perceived inequity are these:

- ***Change work effort.*** A person may choose to increase or decrease his or her inputs to the organization. Individuals who believe they are underpaid may reduce their level of effort or increase their absenteeism. Overpaid people may increase effort on the job.
- ***Change outcomes.*** A person may change his or her outcomes. An underpaid person may request a salary increase or a bigger office. A union may try to improve wages and working conditions to be consistent with a comparable union whose members make more money.
- ***Change perceptions.*** Research suggests that people may change perceptions of equity if they are unable to change inputs or outcomes. They may artificially increase the status attached to their jobs or distort others' perceived rewards to bring equity into balance.
- ***Leave the job.*** People who feel inequitably treated may decide to leave their jobs rather than suffer the inequity of being under- or overpaid. In their new jobs, they expect to find a more favorable balance of rewards.

The implication of equity theory for managers is that employees indeed evaluate the perceived equity of their rewards compared to others'. Inequitable pay puts pressure on employees that is sometimes almost too great to bear. They attempt to change their work habits, try to change the system, or leave the job.[30] Consider Deb Allen, who went into the office on a weekend to catch up on work and found a document accidentally left on the copy machine. When she saw that some new hires were earning $200,000 more than their counterparts with more experience, and that "a noted screw-up" was making more than highly competent people, Allen began questioning why she was working on weekends for less pay than many others were receiving. Allen became so demoralized by the inequity that she quit her job three months later.[31]

In a recessionary environment, with corporate budgets under pressure, employees may be especially sensitive to inequity. For example, companies that received federal bailout funds and were sharply criticized for paying huge bonuses are struggling to find ways to keep rewarding the best people as they revise compensation plans. American International Group (AIG) is implementing a performance review ranking system, in which only 10 percent of employees can get a top ranking and receive high year-end incentive pay. Another

20 percent would be ranked in the second tier and 50 percent in the third, with each group receiving incentive pay commensurate with their rankings. A bottom group of 20 percent would receive minimal variable pay. New CEO Robert Benmosche, who has made compensation one of his top priorities as he struggles to keep AIG afloat, says the controversial system is a way to make sure people are paid competitively and equitably.[32]

Expectancy Theory

Expectancy theory suggests that motivation depends on individuals' expectations about their ability to perform tasks and receive desired rewards. Expectancy theory is associated with the work of Victor Vroom, although a number of scholars have made contributions in this area.[33]

Expectancy theory is concerned not with identifying types of needs but with the thinking process that individuals use to achieve rewards. For example, one interesting study of expectancy theory looked at patrol officer drug arrests in the midwestern United States. The research found that officers who produced the most drug arrests were more likely to have perceived that such arrests were a management priority and were rewarded by their organization, received specialized training to hone their skills related to drug interdiction, and perceived that they had sufficient time and resources to properly investigate suspected drug activity.[34]

Expectancy theory is based on the relationship among the individual's *effort*, the individual's *performance*, and the desirability of *outcomes* associated with high performance. These elements and the relationships among them are illustrated in Exhibit 12.5. The keys to expectancy theory are the expectancies for the relationships among effort, performance, and the value of the outcomes to the individual. Social media site Digg's popularity has fallen largely because its cadre of writer-members doesn't expect to have easy access when posting stories, as described in this chapter's Business Blooper.

E → P expectancy involves determining whether putting effort into a task will lead to high performance. For this expectancy to be high, the individual must have the ability, previous experience, and necessary equipment, tools, and opportunity to perform. Let's consider a simple sales example. If Paloma, a salesperson at the Diamond Gift Shop, believes that increased selling effort will lead to higher personal sales, we can say that she has a high E → P expectancy. However, if Paloma believes she has neither the ability nor the opportunity to achieve high performance, the expectancy will be low, and so will be her motivation.

P → O expectancy involves determining whether successful performance will lead to the desired outcome or reward. If the P → O expectancy is high, the individual will be

12.5 EXHIBIT
Major Elements of Expectancy Theory

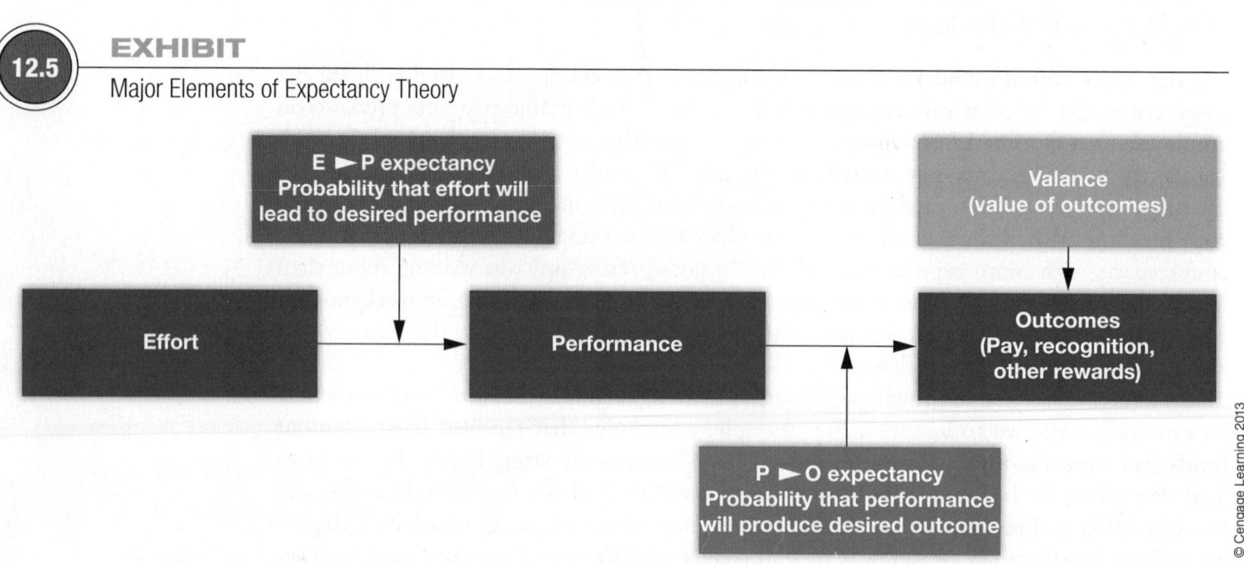

BUSINESS BLOOPER

Digg

When Kevin Rose started Digg in 2004, it was before Facebook was big and when Twitter wasn't even an idea yet; the social media site was novel, that is, a place for "social news" whose content would be chosen by citizen-editors. "There's no handful of editors in a smoke-filled room deciding which stories are important; the masses are deciding," Rose announced to *Business 2.0* magazine in 2006. That year, he was on the cover of *BusinessWeek* with the line, "How this kid made $60 million in 18 months." Google purportedly offered $200 million for Digg, but the deal fell through because of different management styles. But the heyday might be over. Unique U.S. users fell from 27.1 million monthly users in April 2010 to 13.7 million just three months later. Analysts say the reason is that users find it easier to post items on Facebook or Twitter. To post on Digg, the writer might have to spend six months voting on up to 200 articles a day to be able to build up enough social capital that other writers will endorse the new person's work. Most give up. Not surprising, because one recent issue had 20,000 stories submitted daily and only 200 made it to an accessible spot. Power Diggers had come to wield way too much power so that it was more like an exclusive membership club than some communal online experience. Such insularity goes against the grain of the open ethos of social media, which is likely the reason Digg has lost ground to Twitter and Facebook. Though a media darling a couple years ago, Digg may have lost its moment.

© Pixel 4 Images, Shutterstock

SOURCE: Todd Wasserman, "Can Digg Find its Way in the Crowd?" *The New York Times*, September 19, 2010.

more highly motivated. If the expectancy is that high performance will not produce the desired outcome, motivation will be lower. If Paloma believes that higher personal sales will lead to a pay increase, we can say that she has a high P → O expectancy. She might be aware that raises are coming up for consideration and talk with her supervisor or other employees to see whether increased sales will help her earn a better raise. If not, she will be less motivated to work hard.

Valence is the value of outcomes, or attraction to outcomes, for the individual. If employees do not value the outcomes that are available from high effort and good performance, motivation will be low. Likewise, if outcomes have a high value, motivation will be higher. If Paloma places a high value on the pay raise, valence is high, and she will have a high motivational force. On the other hand, if the money has low valence for Paloma, the overall motivational force will be low. For an employee to be highly motivated, all three factors in the expectancy model must be high.[35]

Expectancy theory attempts not to define specific types of needs or

Richard Levine / Alamy

ConceptConnection

According to **expectancy theory**, a reward that effectively motivates one individual doesn't necessarily work for another. So how can employers create attractive rewards that motivate all their employees, especially when economic conditions necessitate cuts in salary and benefits budgets? Many managers are turning to gift cards. One advantage is that they can be issued in virtually any denomination. But even more importantly, many gift cards allow the recipient to tailor a reward to his or her individual preference. A person can choose to splurge on some small luxury or use the card for essentials such as groceries.

As a new manager, how would you manage expectations and use rewards to motivate subordinates to perform well? Complete the New Manager Self-Test, on page 497, to learn more about your approach to motivating others.

rewards but only to establish that they exist and may be different for every individual. One employee might want to be promoted to a position of increased responsibility, and another might have high valence for good relationships with peers. Consequently, the first person will be motivated to work hard for a promotion, and the second, for the opportunity of a team position that will keep him or her associated with a group. Studies substantiate the idea that rewards need to be individualized to be motivating. A recent finding from the U.S. Department of Labor shows that the top reason people leave their jobs is because they "don't feel appreciated." Yet Gallup's analysis of 10,000 work groups in 30 industries found that making people feel appreciated depends on finding the right kind of reward for each individual. Some people prefer tangible rewards or gifts, whereas others place high value on words of recognition. In addition, some want public recognition, and others prefer to be quietly praised by someone they admire and respect.[36]

- **Process theories**, including goal-setting theory, equity theory, and expectancy theory, explain how people select behaviors with which to meet their needs and determine whether their choices were successful.
- **Goal-setting theory** proposes that specific, challenging goals increase motivation and performance when the goals are accepted by subordinates and these subordinates receive feedback to indicate their progress toward goal achievement.
- **Equity theory** focuses on individuals' perceptions of how fairly they are treated relative to others.
- A situation of **equity** exists when the ratio of one person's outcomes to inputs equals that of another's.
- **Expectancy theory** proposes that motivation depends on individuals' expectations about their ability to perform tasks and receive desired rewards.
- A person's **E → P expectancy** is the expectancy that putting effort into a given task will lead to high performance.
- **P → O expectancy** is the expectancy that high performance of a task will lead to the desired outcome.
- **Valence** is the value of outcomes (rewards) to the individual.

Reinforcement Perspective on Motivation

The reinforcement approach to employee motivation sidesteps the issues of employee needs and thinking processes described in the content and process theories. **Reinforcement theory** simply looks at the relationship between behavior and its consequences. It focuses on changing or modifying employees' on-the-job behavior through the appropriate use of immediate rewards and punishments.

Behavior modification is the name given to the set of techniques by which reinforcement theory is used to modify human behavior.[37] The basic assumption underlying behavior modification is the **law of effect**, which states that behavior that is positively reinforced tends to be repeated, and behavior that is not reinforced tends not to be repeated. **Reinforcement** is defined as anything that causes a certain behavior to be repeated or

New Manager Self-Test

Your Approach to Motivating Others

Think about situations in which you were in a student group or organization. Think about your informal approach as a leader and answer the items below. Indicate whether each item below is Mostly False or Mostly True for you.

	MOSTLY TRUE <<<	>>> MOSTLY FALSE
1. I ask the other person what rewards they value for high performance.	______	______
2. I reward people only if their performance is up to standard.	______	______
3. I find out whether the person has the ability to do what needs to be done.	______	______
4. I use a variety of rewards (treats, recognition) to reinforce exceptional performance.	______	______
5. I explain exactly what needs to be done for the person I'm trying to motivate.	______	______
6. I generously and publicly praise people who perform well.	______	______
7. Before giving somebody a reward, I find out what would appeal to that person.	______	______
8. I promptly commend others when they do a better-than-average job.	______	______

See It Online

Scoring and Interpretation: The items above represent two related aspects of motivation theory. For the aspect of *expectancy theory*, sum the points for Mostly True to the odd-numbered questions. For the aspect of *reinforcement theory*, sum the points for Mostly True for the even-numbered questions. Then enter your scores for your approach to motivation here:

Use of expectancy theory ________

Use of reinforcement theory ________

These two scores represent how you apply the motivational concepts of expectancy and reinforcement in your role as an informal leader. Three or more points on *expectancy theory* means you motivate people by managing expectations. You understand how a person's effort leads to performance and make sure that high performance leads to valued rewards. Three or more points for *reinforcement theory* means that you attempt to modify people's behavior in a positive direction with frequent and prompt positive reinforcement. New managers often learn to use reinforcements first, and as they gain more experience are able to apply expectancy theory.

SOURCES: These questions are based on D. Whetten and K. Cameron, *Developing Management Skills*, 5th ed. (Upper Saddle River, NJ: Prentice-Hall, 2002), pp. 302–303; and P. M. Podsakoff, S. B. Mackenzie, R. H. Moorman, and R. Fetter, "Transformational Leader Behaviors and Their Effects on Followers' Trust in Leader, Satisfaction, and Organizational Citizenship Behaviors," *Leadership Quarterly* 1, no. 2 (1990): 107–142.

inhibited. The four reinforcement tools are positive reinforcement, avoidance learning, punishment, and extinction, as summarized in Exhibit 12.6.

- **Positive reinforcement** is the administration of a pleasant and rewarding consequence following a desired behavior, such as praise for an employee who arrives on time or does a little extra work. Research shows that positive reinforcement does help to improve performance. Moreover, nonfinancial reinforcements such as positive feedback, social recognition, and attention are just as effective as financial incentives.[38] One study of employees at fast-food drive-through windows, for example, found that performance feedback and supervisor recognition had a significant effect on increasing the incidence of "up-selling," or asking customers to increase their order.[39] Montage Hotels & Resorts, known for its culture of gracious yet humble service, uses a variety of employee recognition programs to positively reinforce employees for providing exceptional service. CEO Alan J. Fuerstman says, "It's simple psychology. People commit more acts of kindness when they are appreciated for them."[40]
- **Avoidance learning** is the removal of an unpleasant consequence once a behavior is improved, thereby encouraging and strengthening the desired behavior. Avoidance learning is sometimes called *negative reinforcement*. The idea is that people will change a specific behavior to avoid the undesired result that behavior provokes. As a simple example, a supervisor who constantly reminds or nags an employee who is goofing off on the factory floor and stops the nagging when the employee stops goofing off is applying avoidance learning.
- **Punishment** is the imposition of unpleasant outcomes on an employee. Punishment typically occurs following undesirable behavior. For example, a supervisor may berate an employee for performing a task incorrectly. The supervisor expects that the negative outcome will serve as a punishment and reduce the likelihood of the behavior recurring. The use of punishment in organizations is controversial and often criticized because it fails to indicate the correct behavior. However, almost all managers report that they find it necessary to occasionally impose forms of punishment ranging from verbal reprimands to employee suspensions or firings.[41]

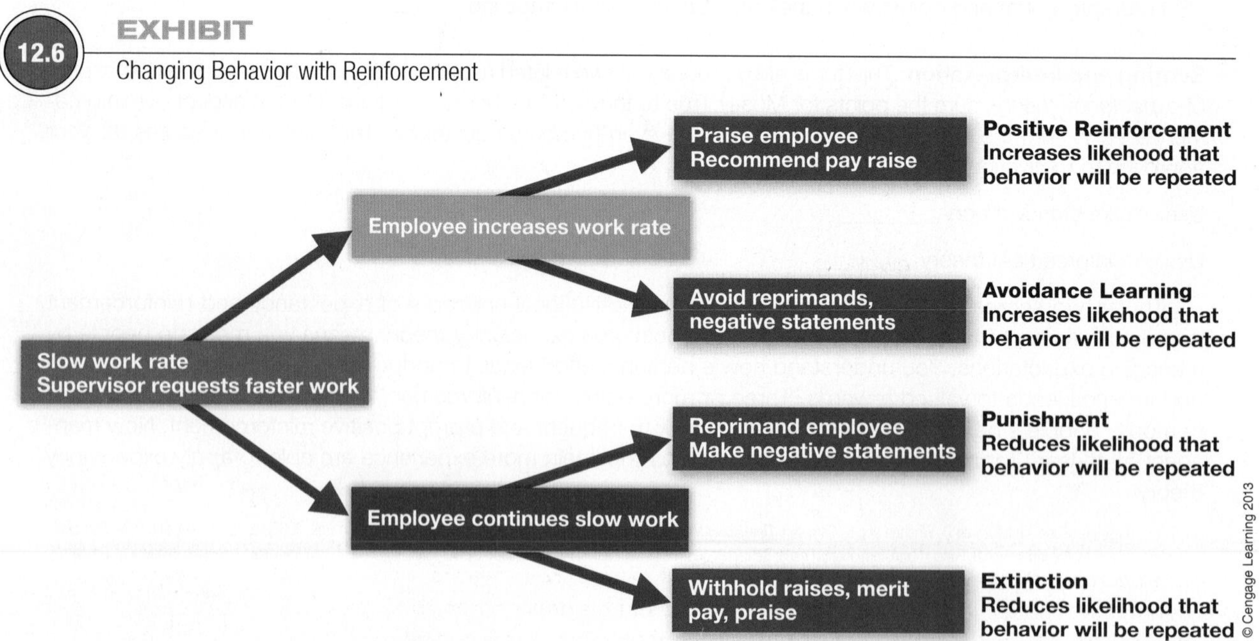

SOURCE: Based on Richard L. Daft and Richard M. Steers, *Organizations: A Micro/Macro Approach* (Glenview, IL: Scott, Foresman, 1986), p. 109.

- **Extinction** is the withholding of a positive reward. Whereas with punishment, the supervisor imposes an unpleasant outcome such as a reprimand, extinction involves withholding praise or other positive outcomes. With extinction, undesirable behavior is essentially ignored. The idea is that behavior that is not positively reinforced will gradually disappear. A *New York Times* reporter wrote a humorous article about how she learned to stop nagging and instead use reinforcement theory to shape her husband's behavior after studying how professionals train animals.[42] When her husband did something she liked, such as throw a dirty shirt in the hamper, she would use *positive reinforcement,* thanking him or giving him a hug and a kiss. Undesirable behaviors, such as throwing dirty clothes on the floor, on the other hand, were simply ignored, applying the principle of *extinction.*

Reward and punishment motivational practices based on the reinforcement theory dominate organizations. According to the Society for Human Resource Management, 84 percent of all companies in the United States offer some type of monetary or nonmonetary reward system, and 69 percent offer incentive pay, such as bonuses, based on an employee's performance.[43] However, in other studies, more than 80 percent of employers with incentive programs have reported that their programs are only somewhat successful or not working at all.[44] Despite the testimonies of organizations that enjoy successful incentive programs, criticism of these "carrot-and-stick" methods is growing, as discussed in the Spotlight on Skills titled The Carrot-and-Stick Controversy.

- **Reinforcement theory** is based on the relationship between a given behavior and its consequences.
- **Behavior modification** refers to the set of techniques by which reinforcement theory is used to modify human behavior.
- The **law of effect** asserts that positively reinforced behavior tends to be repeated, and unreinforced or negatively reinforced behavior tends to be inhibited.
- **Reinforcement** is anything that causes a certain behavior to be repeated or inhibited.
- **Positive reinforcement** is the administration of a pleasant and rewarding consequence following a desired behavior.
- Managers apply **avoidance learning**, called *negative reinforcement*, when they remove an unpleasant consequence once a behavior is improved.
- **Punishment** refers to the imposition of an unpleasant outcome following an undesirable behavior.
- **Extinction** refers to withholding positive rewards and essentially ignoring undesirable behavior.
- Carrot-and-stick motivational practices dominate organizations, but the use of rewards and punishments to shape people's behavior is controversial.

Social Learning Theory

Social learning theory is related to the reinforcement perspective, but it proposes that an individual's motivation can result not just from direct experience of rewards and punishments but also from the person's thoughts and beliefs and his or her observations of other people's behavior.[45] Three important elements of social learning theory related to motivation are vicarious learning, self-reinforcement, and self-efficacy.

SPOTLIGHT ON SKILLS

The Carrot-and-Stick Controversy

In some schools in New York City and Dallas, high school students get paid for doing well on advanced placement tests. Fourteen public schools in Washington are handing out checks for good grades, attendance, and behavior. Some elementary schools give students points or tokens for good performance that can be collected and redeemed for prizes. The use of such reward programs in schools is exploding, yet many psychologists and other researchers say such practices work in the short run but have damaging effects over the long term.

There's a raging debate, within both the field of education and businesses, about whether financial and other rewards really motivate the kind of behavior organizations want and need. A growing number of critics say no, arguing that carrot-and-stick approaches are a holdover from the Industrial Age and are inappropriate and ineffective in today's environment. Today's workplace demands innovation, creativity, and teamwork—behaviors that rarely are inspired by individual financial incentives. Reasons for criticism of carrot-and-stick approaches include the following:

1. ***Extrinsic rewards diminish intrinsic rewards.*** When people are motivated to seek an extrinsic reward, whether it is a bonus, an award, or the approval of a supervisor, generally they focus on the reward rather than on the work they do to achieve it. Thus, the intrinsic satisfaction people receive from performing their jobs actually declines. When people lack intrinsic rewards in their work, their performance stays just adequate to achieve the reward offered. In the worst case, employees may cover up mistakes or cheat to achieve the reward. One study found that teachers who were rewarded for increasing test scores frequently used various forms of cheating, for example.
2. ***Extrinsic rewards are temporary.*** Offering outside incentives may ensure short-term success, but not long-term high performance. In one study, when third-grade children were given toys and candy as rewards for reading, it actually diminished the time they later spent reading. When employees are focused only on the reward, they lose interest in their work. Without personal interest, the potential for exploration, creativity, and innovation disappears. Although the current deadline or goal may be met, better ways of working and serving customers will not be discovered, and the company's long-term success will be affected.
3. ***Extrinsic rewards assume people are driven by lower-level needs.*** Rewards such as bonuses, pay increases, and even praise presume that the primary reason people initiate and persist in behavior is to satisfy lower-level needs. However, behavior also is based on yearnings for self-expression and on feelings of self-esteem and self-worth. Typical individual incentive programs don't reflect and encourage the myriad behaviors that are motivated by people's need to express themselves and realize their higher needs for growth and fulfillment.

Today's organizations need employees who are motivated to think, experiment, and continuously search for ways to solve new problems. Alfie Kohn, one of the most vocal critics of carrot-and-stick approaches, offers the following advice to managers regarding how to pay employees: "Pay well, pay fairly, and then do everything you can to get money off people's minds." Indeed some evidence indicates that money is not primarily what people work for. Managers should understand the limits of extrinsic motivators and work to satisfy employees' higher, as well as lower, needs. To be motivated, employees need jobs that offer self-satisfaction in addition to a yearly pay raise.

SOURCES: Alfie Kohn, "Incentives Can Be Bad for Business," *Inc.* (January 1998): 93–94; A. J. Vogl, "Carrots, Sticks, and Self-Deception" (an interview with Alfie Kohn), *Across the Board* (January 1994): 39–44; Jeffrey Pfeffer, "Sins of Commission," *Business 2.0* (May 2004): 56; Lisa Guernsey, "Rewards for Students Under Microscope," *The New York Times*, March 3, 2009; and Alan Murray, "How Much Does Pay Matter?" *The Wall Street Journal*, March 10, 2010.

- **Vicarious learning**, or *observational learning*, occurs when an individual sees others perform certain behaviors and get rewarded for them. Young children often learn to behave well in school because they see that well-behaved children get more positive attention from the teacher, for example. Managers can enhance an individual's motivation to perform desired behaviors by ensuring that the individual (1) has a chance to observe the desirable behaviors; (2) accurately perceives the behaviors; (3) remembers the behaviors; (4) has the necessary skills to perform the behaviors; and (5) sees that the behaviors are rewarded by the organization.[46] Recall the discussion from Chapter 9 of on-the-job training. Managers typically pair a new employee with someone who models the type of behavior the organization wants. A key to vicarious motivation, though, is to make sure the learner knows that these behaviors are rewarded.

- **Self-reinforcement**, or self-control, refers to an individual motivating him or herself by setting goals and ways of reaching them and then providing positive reinforcement to him- or herself when goals are achieved. For example, students might motivate themselves to complete a dreaded term paper by 5:00 P.M. on Friday by focusing on the reward of a night on the town with friends. Managers can encourage self-reinforcement by enabling people to find intrinsic satisfaction in their jobs and giving people flexibility and autonomy to set goals and determine how to achieve them. At Meetup, a Web site company that helps people set up local groups for everything from sharing gardening tips to organizing political campaigns, managers found that giving employees autonomy caused most people to work harder because of self-reinforcement. CEO Scott Heiferman said, "We got more done in six weeks than in six months last year."[47]
- **Self-efficacy**, as defined in Chapter 10, is an individual's belief about his or her ability to successfully accomplish a specific task or outcome.[48] A famous quote from early automotive industrialist Henry Ford—"Whether you think that you can or think that you can't, you are usually right"—relates to the idea that our beliefs can shape our motivation. Managers increase self-efficacy by ensuring that people have the training, skills, and resources they need to perform well and by expressing confidence and trust in employees' abilities.

- **Social learning theory** proposes that an individual's motivation can result not just from direct experience of rewards and punishments but also from thoughts, beliefs, and observations of other people's behavior.
- **Vicarious learning** occurs when an individual sees others perform certain behaviors and get rewarded for them.
- The principle of **self-reinforcement** refers to an individual motivating him- or herself by setting goals and ways of reaching them and then providing positive reinforcement to him- or herself when goals are achieved.
- **Self-efficacy** is an individual's belief about his or her ability to successfully accomplish a specific task or outcome.

Job Design for Motivation

A *job* in an organization is a unit of work that a single employee is responsible for performing. A job could include writing tickets for parking violators in New York City, performing MRIs at Salt Lake Regional Medical Center, or doing long-range planning for the Fox television network. Jobs are an important consideration for motivation because performing their components may provide rewards that meet employees' needs. Managers need to know what aspects of a job provide motivation as well as how to compensate for routine tasks that have little inherent satisfaction. **Job design** is the application of motivational theories to the structure of work for improving productivity and satisfaction.

Job Enrichment

Recall from Chapter 1 the principles of scientific management, in which tasks are designed to be simple, repetitive, and standardized. This contributes to efficiency, but simplified jobs aren't typically effective as a motivational technique because they can be boring and routine. Thus, managers in many companies are redesigning simplified jobs into jobs that provide greater variety and satisfaction. One technique is to systematically rotate employees from one job to another to provide variety and stimulation, called *job rotation*. Another approach is to combine a series of small tasks into one new, broader job so that people perform a variety of activities, which is referred to as *job enlargement*.

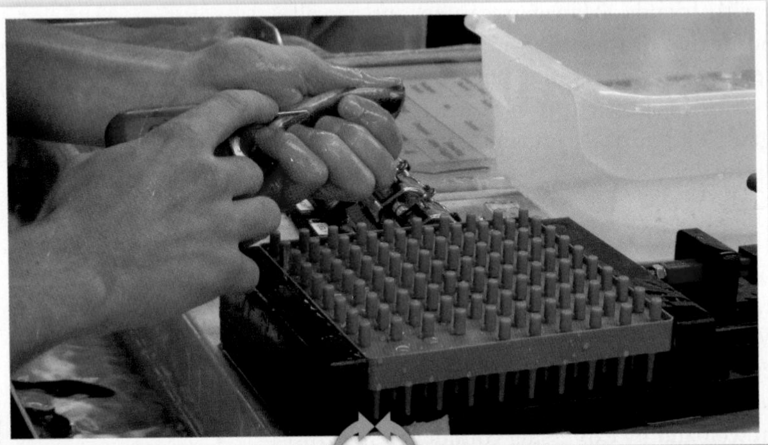

ConceptConnection

Inc. magazine and Winning Workplaces, a nonprofit consulting firm, named Biomark, Inc., one of the best small companies in the United States for 2010. A small, employee-owned company based in Boise, Idaho, Biomark produces electronic identification tags and detectors for fish and wildlife research. Innovative **job design** was a key reason Biomark won recognition. All employees—from receptionists to Dean Parks, an economist by profession and Biomark's president—learn how to go into the field to tag fish (shown here). Why? Parks believes cross-training and variety make for higher motivation and job satisfaction.

Overall, the trend is toward **job enrichment**, which means incorporating high-level motivators into the work, including responsibility, recognition, and opportunities for growth, learning, and achievement. In an enriched job, employees have control over the resources necessary for performing tasks, make decisions on how to do the work, experience personal growth, and set their own work pace. Research shows that when jobs are designed to be controlled more by employees than by managers, people typically feel a greater sense of involvement, commitment, and motivation, which in turn contribute to higher morale, lower turnover, and stronger organizational performance.[49]

Job Characteristics Model

One significant approach to job design is the job characteristics model developed by Richard Hackman and Greg Oldham.[50] Hackman and Oldham's research concerned **work redesign**, which is defined as altering jobs to increase both the quality of employees' work experience and their productivity. Hackman and Oldham's research into the design of hundreds of jobs yielded the **job characteristics model**, illustrated in Exhibit 12.7. The model consists of three major parts: core job dimensions, critical psychological states, and employee growth-need strength.

Core Job Dimensions Hackman and Oldham identified five dimensions that determine a job's motivational potential:

1. ***Skill variety.*** The number of diverse activities that compose a job and the number of skills used to perform it. A routine, repetitious assembly-line job is low in variety, whereas an applied research position that entails working on new problems every day is high in variety.
2. ***Task identity.*** The degree to which an employee performs a total job with a recognizable beginning and ending. A chef who prepares an entire meal has more task identity than a worker on a cafeteria line who ladles mashed potatoes.

EXHIBIT 12.7

The Job Characteristics Model

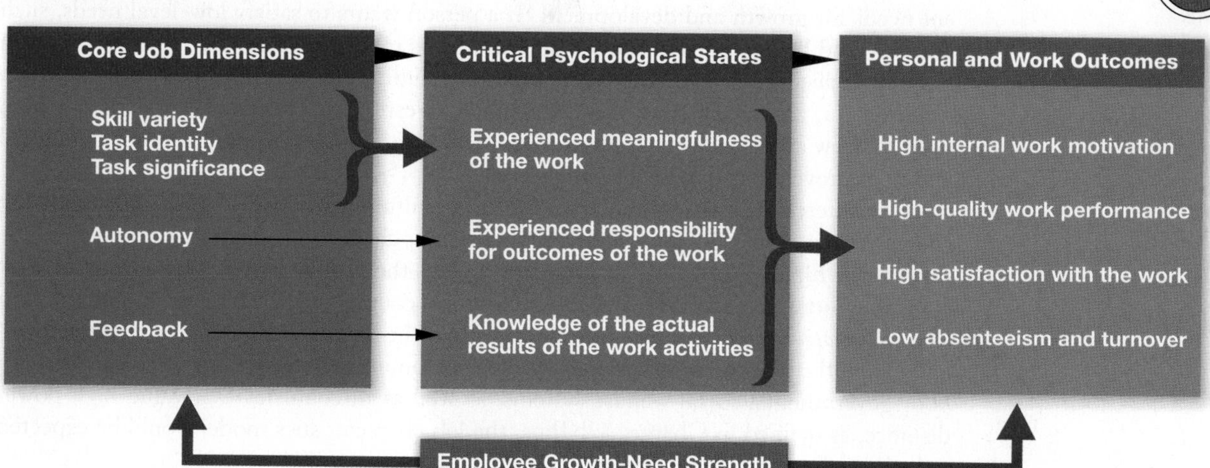

SOURCE: Adapted from J. Richard Hackman and G. R. Oldham, "Motivation through the Design of Work: Test of a Theory," *Organizational Behavior and Human Performance* 16 (1976): 256.

3. ***Task significance.*** The degree to which the job is perceived as important and having impact on the company or consumers. People who distribute penicillin and other medical supplies during times of emergencies would feel they have significant jobs.
4. ***Autonomy.*** The degree to which the worker has freedom, discretion, and self-determination in planning and carrying out tasks. A house painter can determine how to paint the house; a paint sprayer on an assembly line has little autonomy.
5. ***Feedback.*** The extent to which doing the job provides information back to the employee about his or her performance. Jobs vary in their ability to let workers see the outcomes of their efforts. A football coach knows whether the team won or lost, but a basic research scientist may have to wait years to learn whether a research project was successful.

The job characteristics model says that the more these five core characteristics can be designed into the job, the more the employees will be motivated and the higher will be performance, quality, and satisfaction.

Critical Psychological States The model posits that core job dimensions are more rewarding when individuals experience three psychological states in response to job design. In Exhibit 12.7, skill variety, task identity, and task significance tend to influence the employee's psychological state of *experienced meaningfulness of work.* The work itself is satisfying and provides intrinsic rewards for the worker. The job characteristic of autonomy influences the worker's *experienced responsibility.* The job characteristic of feedback provides the worker with *knowledge of actual results.* The employee thus knows how he or she is doing and can change work performance to increase desired outcomes.

Personal and Work Outcomes The impact of the five job characteristics on the psychological states of experienced meaningfulness, responsibility, and knowledge of actual results leads to the personal and work outcomes of high work motivation, high work performance, high satisfaction, and low absenteeism and turnover.

Employee Growth-Need Strength The final component of the job characteristics model is called *employee growth-need strength*, which means that people have different needs for growth and development. If a person wants to satisfy low-level needs, such as safety and belongingness, the job characteristics model has less effect. When a person has a high need for growth and development, including the desire for personal challenge, achievement, and challenging work, the model is especially effective. People with a high need to grow and expand their abilities respond favorably to the application of the model and to improvements in core job dimensions.

One interesting finding concerns the cross-cultural differences in the impact of job characteristics. Intrinsic factors such as autonomy, challenge, achievement, and recognition can be highly motivating in countries such as the United States. However, they may contribute little to motivation and satisfaction in a country such as Nigeria and might even lead to *demotivation*. A recent study indicates that the link between intrinsic characteristics and job motivation and satisfaction is weaker in economically disadvantaged countries with poor governmental social welfare systems, as well as in countries that value high power distance, as defined in Chapter 3.[51] Thus, the job characteristics model would be expected to be less effective in these countries.

- Jobs are an important consideration for motivation because performing their components may provide intrinsic rewards that meet employees' needs.
- **Job design** refers to applying motivational theories to the structure of work to improve motivation, productivity, and satisfaction.
- Most companies are moving away from simplified jobs and are using job rotation, job enlargement, and job enrichment to provide employees with greater variety, stimulation, and satisfaction.
- **Job enrichment** refers to incorporating high-level motivators such as achievement, recognition, and opportunities for growth, into the work.
- **Work redesign** means altering jobs to increase both the quality of employees' work experience and their productivity.
- The **job characteristics model** is a model of job design that considers core job dimensions, individuals' critical psychological states, and employee growth-need strength.

Innovative Ideas for Motivating

Despite the controversy over carrot-and-stick motivational practices discussed in the Spotlight on Skills box earlier in this chapter, organizations are increasingly using various types of incentive compensation as a way to motivate employees to higher levels of performance. For example, when Elise Lelon, owner of leadership-consulting firm The You Business, couldn't give pay raises in 2009 because of budget pressures, she created a generous lump-sum bonus program tied to the amount of revenue employees generated for the firm. "It gets their juices flowing and it helps the business grow," Lelon says.[52] Exhibit 12.8 summarizes several popular methods of incentive pay.

Go to the Ethical Dilemma, on page 512, that pertains to the use of incentive compensation as a motivational tool.

Variable compensation and forms of "at risk" pay such as bonus plans are key motivational tools that are becoming more common than fixed salaries at many companies. However, unless they are carefully designed, incentive plans can backfire, as evidenced by

EXHIBIT 12.8

New Motivational Compensation Programs

Program	Purpose
Pay for performance	Rewards individual employees in proportion to their performance contributions. Also called *merit pay.*
Gain sharing	Rewards all employees and managers within a business unit when predetermined performance targets are met. Encourages teamwork.
Employee stock ownership plan (ESOP)	Gives employees part ownership of the organization, enabling them to share in improved profit performance.
Lump-sum bonuses	Rewards employees with a one-time cash payment based on performance.
Pay for knowledge	Links employee salary with the number of task skills acquired. Workers are motivated to learn the skills for many jobs, thus increasing company flexibility and efficiency.
Flexible work schedule	*Flextime* allows workers to set their own hours. *Job sharing* allows two or more part-time workers to jointly cover one job. *Telecommuting*, sometimes called *flex-place,* allows employees to work from home or an alternative workplace.
Team-based compensation	Rewards employees for behavior and activities that benefit the team, such as cooperation, listening, and empowering others.
Lifestyle awards	Rewards employees for meeting ambitious goals with luxury items, such as high-definition televisions, tickets to big-name sporting events, and exotic travel.

recent problems in the mortgage and finance industries, where some people resorted to overly aggressive and even unethical behavior to earn huge bonuses. Numerous companies, including financial firms such as Morgan Stanley, Credit Suisse, and Goldman Sachs, as well as other organizations such as Home Depot, Verizon, and Aflac, are revising compensation plans to make sure incentives reward the desired behaviors.[53] One company that has been praised for an innovative approach to CEO compensation is Valeant Pharmaceuticals International. The unusual pay package designed by Valeant's board for new CEO Michael Pearson required that Pearson buy at least $3 million in stock, forgo routine annual equity grants, and hold many of his shares for years before selling. Experts are praising the deal for giving the CEO incentives to boost long-term value rather than shoot for short-term gains.[54]

Incentive programs can be effective if they are used appropriately and combined with motivational ideas that also provide people with intrinsic rewards and meet higher-level needs. Effective managers don't use incentive plans as the sole basis of motivation. The most effective motivational programs typically involve much more than money or other external rewards. Two recent motivational trends are empowering employees and creating an environment that promotes employee engagement.

Empowering People to Meet Higher Needs

One significant way managers can meet higher motivational needs is to shift power down from the top of the organization and share it with employees to enable them to achieve

goals. **Empowerment** is power sharing, the delegation of power or authority to subordinates in an organization.[55] Increasing employee power heightens motivation for task accomplishment because people improve their own effectiveness, choosing how to do a task and using their creativity.[56] Empowerment is one way managers promote self-reinforcement and self-efficacy, as defined in the discussion of social learning.

Empowering employees involves giving them four elements that enable them to act more freely to accomplish their jobs: information, knowledge, power, and rewards.[57]

1. ***Employees receive information about company performance.*** In companies where employees are fully empowered, all employees have access to all financial and operational information.
2. ***Employees have knowledge and skills to contribute to company goals.*** Companies use training programs and other development tools to help people acquire the knowledge and skills they need to contribute to organizational performance.
3. ***Employees have the power to make substantive decisions.*** Empowered employees have the authority to directly influence work procedures and organizational performance, such as through quality circles or self-directed work teams.
4. ***Employees are rewarded based on company performance.*** Organizations that empower workers often reward them based on the results shown in the company's bottom line. Organizations may also use other motivational compensation programs described in Exhibit 12.8 to tie employee efforts to company performance.

Many of today's organizations are implementing empowerment programs, but they are empowering workers to varying degrees. At some companies, empowerment means encouraging workers' ideas while managers retain final authority for decisions; at others it means giving employees almost complete freedom and power to make decisions and exercise initiative and imagination.[58] Current methods of empowerment fall along a continuum, as illustrated in Exhibit 12.9. The continuum runs from a situation in which front-line workers have almost no discretion, such as on a traditional assembly line, to full empowerment, where workers even participate in formulating organizational strategy.

Ann Johansson/Corbis

ConceptConnection

Heart patient Claudia Navarro (pictured left) and her physician, Dr. Leslie Saxon, talking here with a Medtronic, Inc., representative (right), could possibly find themselves invited to Medtronic's December holiday party. That's because the medical device manufacturer has a tradition of inviting doctors and patients to speak to employees at the annual gathering about how a Medtronic device—such as the defibrillator, wand, and programmer shown here—has affected their lives. It's one of the ways Medtronic managers heighten **employee engagement** by helping people realize the meaning of their work.

Giving Meaning to Work Through Engagement

In recent years, managers have focused on employee engagement, which puts less emphasis on extrinsic rewards such as pay and more emphasis on fostering an environment in which people feel valued and effective. Employee **engagement** means that people enjoy their jobs and are satisfied with their work conditions, contribute enthusiastically to meeting team and

EXHIBIT 12.9

A Continuum of Empowerment

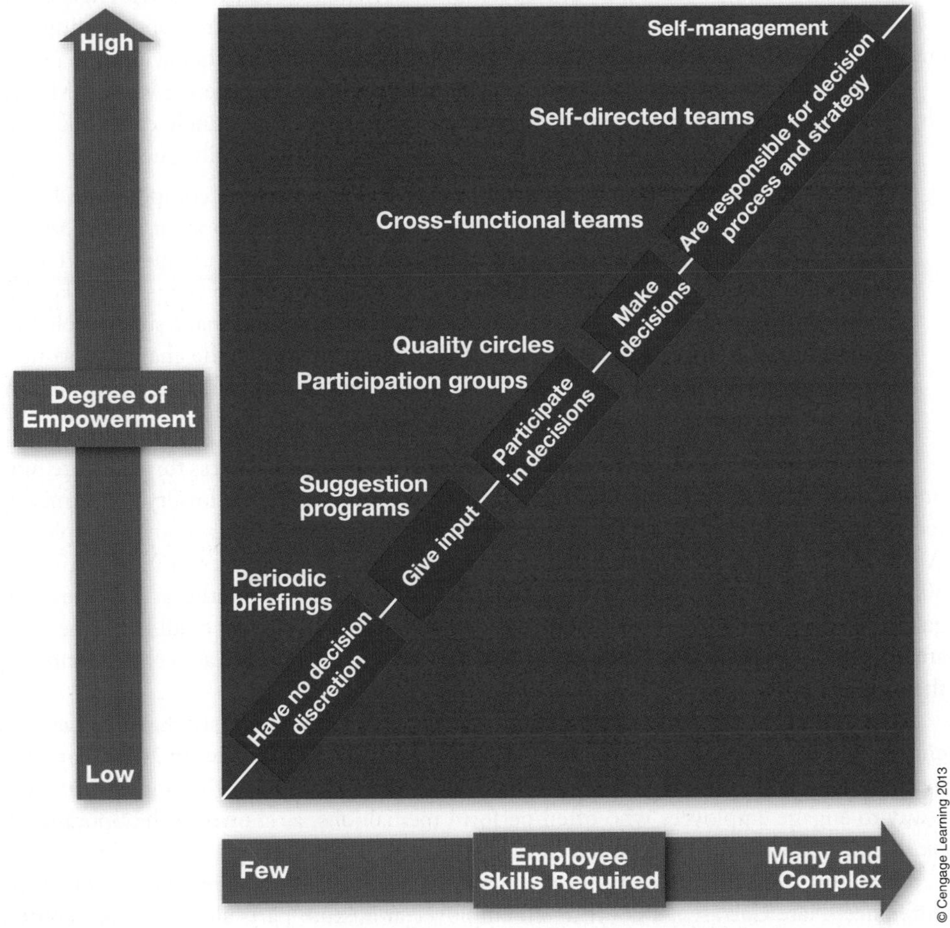

SOURCES: Based on Robert C. Ford and Myron D. Fottler, "Empowerment: A Matter of Degree," *Academy of Management Executive* 9, no. 3 (1995): 21–31; Lawrence Holpp, "Applied Empowerment," *Training* (February 1994): 39–44; and David P. McCaffrey, Sue R. Faerman, and David W. Hart, "The Appeal and Difficulties of Participative Systems," *Organization Science* 6, no. 6 (November–December 1995): 603–627.

organizational goals, and feel a sense of belonging and commitment to the organization. Fully engaged employees care deeply about the organization and actively seek ways to serve the mission.[59]

How do managers engage employees? Not by controlling and ordering them around, but by organizing the workplace in such a way that employees experience a sense of meaningfulness, connection, and growth.[60]

1. People experience a sense of *meaningfulness* when they believe they are working toward something of importance and have a chance to accomplish something that provides real value to the world. Good managers help people understand the purpose of their work, which contributes to feelings of pride and dignity. Kenexa, the leading human resources services company in the United States, uses psychologists and other scientists to study what motivates employees. One finding is that turnover is significantly lower among people who feel pride in their company and its mission than among those who don't.[61]

2. Engaged employees feel *connected* to the company, to one another, and to their managers. In a survey asking people what factors contribute to their engagement, 79 percent of people said "good relationships with coworkers" drove engagement to a high or very high extent. Even more, 91 percent, pointed to good relationships with their immediate supervisor as highly important.[62] It is the behavior of managers that makes the biggest difference in whether people feel engaged at work.[63] Managers promote engagement when they listen to employees, genuinely care about their concerns, and help them develop positive relationships with colleagues.
3. To be fully engaged, people need not only to feel that they are competent to handle what is asked of them, but also that they have the chance to *learn, grow, and advance*. Good managers help employees understand their own unique set of talents, skills, interests, attitudes, and needs; put people in jobs where they can make their best contribution and receive intrinsic rewards every day; and make sure people have what they need to perform well. In addition, they give people the chance to work on challenging projects, participate in high-quality training and learning programs, and provide opportunities for advancement within the organization.

Studies suggest that organizations with engaged employees have less turnover, are more productive and profitable, and enjoy greater employee and customer loyalty.[64] Alarmingly, recent surveys reflect low levels of engagement, particularly among Gen-Y employees. A survey of 7,500 workers found that 25 percent of Gen-Y employees in North America, 30 percent in the United Kingdom and Ireland, and 35 percent in Southeast Asia are disengaged.[65] Gallup's most recent semiannual survey found that 18 percent of all U.S. employees are *actively disengaged*.[66] Active disengagement means that people are actively undermining their organization's success.

Managers can assess the level of employee engagement and use strategies to facilitate engagement and improve performance. Morrison Management Specialists, which provides food, nutrition, and dining services to the health-care and senior-living industries, found a way to engage employees who often perform menial jobs, as shown in the Spotlight on Skills titled Morrison Management Specialists.

Sometimes, even simple changes in how managers treat employees can make all the difference. Nate Carrasco, a 26-year-old employee at an auto parts store, agrees. "Most of

SPOTLIGHT ON SKILLS

Morrison Management Specialists

Several years ago, executives at Morrison Management Specialists, which has 14,000 employees in 450 locations, decided to make employee engagement a top management priority. They started by making sure everyone understood the company's mission statement and five core values of trust, teamwork, customer focus, learning, and profit. The company's Web site address and ending for corporate e-mail addresses is *iammorrison.com*, which reinforces that every employee *is* the company.

Each year, top executives present an update of the company's direction and accomplishments to managers, who in turn hold conversations with employees throughout the organization to disseminate information about where the company stands and where it wants to go. Training sessions for hourly associates are organized under the title "Our Great Partnership" and strive to help people see how their everyday jobs tie in with the larger mission. A "People First" recognition program gives employees a chance to recognize one another for exceptional service. The company builds connections in other ways too, such as monthly meetings that give managers and employees a chance to discuss issues on a personal level.

SOURCE: Based on Maureen Soyars and Justin Brusino, "Essentials of Engagement: Contributions, Connections, Growth," *T&D* (March 2009): 62–65.

the time, [managers] only listen to what their bosses are saying. They need to come down to the employee level more and see what actually goes on, versus what their paperwork tells them."[67]

- Variable compensation and "at risk" pay have become key motivational tools, although these practices have been criticized in recent years for rewarding the wrong types of behavior.
- Employee empowerment and engagement are recent motivational trends that focus less on extrinsic rewards and more on creating a work environment that enables people to achieve intrinsic rewards and meet higher-level needs.
- **Empowerment** is the delegation of power and authority to subordinates in an organization.
- Empowering employees involves giving them information, knowledge, power, and rewards.
- Employee engagement has been one of the hottest topics in management in recent years.
- **Engagement** is an emotional and mental state in which employees enjoy their work, contribute enthusiastically to meeting goals, and feel a sense of belonging and commitment to the organization.
- Managers create an environment that promotes engagement by providing employees with a sense of meaning, a sense of connection, and a sense of competence and growth.
- The behavior of managers is the biggest factor in determining whether people feel motivated and engaged at work.

Discussion Questions

1. In response to security threats in today's world, the U.S. government federalized airport security workers. Many argued that simply making screeners federal workers would not solve the root problem: bored, low-paid, and poorly trained security workers have little motivation to be vigilant. How might these employees be motivated to provide the security that travel threats now demand?
2. One small company recognizes an employee of the month, who is given a parking spot next to the president's space near the front door. What theories would explain the positive motivation associated with this policy?
3. Using Hackman and Oldham's core job dimensions, compare and contrast the jobs of these two state employees: (1) Jared, who spends much of his time researching and debating energy policy to make recommendations that will eventually be presented to the state legislature and (2) Anise, who spends her days planting and caring for the flower gardens and grounds surrounding the state capitol building.
4. If an experienced executive assistant discovered that she made the same amount of money as a newly hired janitor, how do you think she would react? What inputs and outcomes might she evaluate to make this comparison?
5. Would you rather work for a supervisor high in need for achievement, affiliation, or power? Why? What are the advantages and disadvantages of each?
6. To keep people motivated in a tough economic environment, some companies have shifted from annual to semiannual bonuses. Do you think offering semiannual bonuses is a good way to motivate the kind of behaviors organizations need to survive the economic downturn? What might be some potential problems with this approach?
7. A survey of teachers found that two of the most important rewards were the belief that their work was important and a feeling of accomplishment. According to Maslow's theory, what needs do these rewards meet?

8. In the survey reported in question 7, the teachers also reported that pay and benefits were poor, yet they continue to teach. Use Herzberg's two-factor theory to explain this finding.
9. According to surveys, Gen-Y employees are the most disengaged of all workers, and 62 percent of employees under the age of 25 say they are unhappy with their jobs. What might be some reasons for this high level of dissatisfaction and disengagement among young people? As a manager, how might you enhance satisfaction and engagement for young employees?
10. How can empowerment lead to higher motivation of employees? Could a manager's empowerment efforts sometimes contribute to demotivation as well? Discuss.

Self-Learning

What Motivates You?[68]

Indicate how important each characteristic is to you. Answer according to your feelings about the most recent job you had or about the job you currently hold. Circle the number on the scale that represents your feeling—1 (very unimportant) to 7 (very important).

1. The feeling of self-esteem a person gets from being in that job

   1 2 3 4 5 6 7
2. The opportunity for personal growth and development in that job

   1 2 3 4 5 6 7
3. The prestige of the job inside the company (i.e., regard received from others in the company)

   1 2 3 4 5 6 7
4. The opportunity for independent thought and action in that job

   1 2 3 4 5 6 7
5. The feeling of security in that job

   1 2 3 4 5 6 7
6. The feeling of self-fulfillment a person gets from being in that position (i.e., the feeling of being able to use one's own unique capabilities, realizing one's potential)

   1 2 3 4 5 6 7
7. The prestige of the job outside the company (i.e., the regard received from others not in the company)

   1 2 3 4 5 6 7
8. The feeling of worthwhile accomplishment in that job

   1 2 3 4 5 6 7
9. The opportunity in that job to give help to other people

   1 2 3 4 5 6 7
10. The opportunity in that job for participation in the setting of goals

    1 2 3 4 5 6 7
11. The opportunity in that job for participation in the determination of methods and procedures

    1 2 3 4 5 6 7
12. The authority connected with the job

    1 2 3 4 5 6 7
13. The opportunity to develop close friendships in the job

    1 2 3 4 5 6 7

See It Online

Scoring and Interpretation

Score the exercise as follows to determine what motivates you:

Rating for question 5 = ________
Divide by 1 = ________ security
Rating for questions 9 and 13 = ________
Divide by 2 = ________ social
Rating for questions 1, 3, and 7 = ________
Divide by 3 = ________ esteem
Rating for questions 4, 10, 11, and 12 = ________
Divide by 4 = ________ autonomy
Rating for questions 2, 6, and 8 = ________
Divide by 3 = ________ self-actualization

Your instructor has national norm scores for presidents, vice presidents, and upper middle-level, lower middle-level, and lower-level managers with which you can compare your mean importance scores. How do your scores compare with the scores of managers working in organizations?

Group Learning

Work Versus Play

1. Form groups of three or four members. Answer this question: What drives you to expend energy on a play activity? For leisure, why do you choose the activities you do? (Don't discuss the particular activities, but rather *why* you choose them.) Select one of your group members as presenter.
2. Each group presents its main points to the class. The instructor will draw on the board a table, similar to the one below, based on information from the class presentations.

Activities	Outcome #1	Outcome #2	Outcome #3	Outcome #4	Outcome #5	Outcome #6
Example: #1 Soccer	High energy	Team bonding	Fitness			
#2						
#3						
#4						

3. Questions for class discussion:
   a. How can you build some of these motives for play into a work environment?
   b. What prevents you from making work more intrinsically motivating, as play is?
   c. Which motivation theories are relevant here?

SOURCE: Developed by Phil Anderson, University of St. Thomas, Minneapolis. Used with permission.

Action Learning

1. Interview four people who've had at least three jobs (maybe part-time) in their lives.
2. Ask them which jobs they liked the best and in which they worked the hardest. Why did they like that job and why did they work harder? Fill out the following table:
3.

Name of Person	Job #1		Job #2		Job #3	
	What They Liked About Job	What They Didn't Liked About Job	Liked	Didn't Like	Liked	Didn't Like
1. 2. 3. 4.						

4. Try to find patterns in the answers of the four people. Compare your outcomes to the motivation theories in this chapter. Which theories are confirmed or refuted based on your interviews? Did you see a connection between how much they like the job or particular tasks and how hard they work? Any patterns in motivation?
5. Your instructor may ask you to write a report on your findings or to meet in small groups to discuss patterns among all the interviewees. You would then be asked to either present your findings in class and/or write a group report.

Ethical Dilemma

To Renege or Not to Renege?[69]

Federico Garcia, vice president of sales for Puget Sound Building Materials, a company based in Tacoma, Washington, wasn't all that surprised by what company president Michael Otto and CFO James Wilson had to say during their meeting that morning.

Last year, launching a major expansion made sense to everyone at Puget, a well-established company that provided building materials as well as manufacturing and installation services to residential builders in the Washington and Oregon markets. Puget looked at the record new housing starts and decided it was time to move into the California and Arizona markets, especially concentrating on San Diego and Phoenix, two of the hottest housing markets in the country. Federico carefully hired promising new sales representatives and offered them hefty bonuses if they reached the goals set for the new territory over the following 12 months. All of the representatives had performed well, and three of them had exceeded Puget's goal—and then some. The incentive system he'd put in place had worked well. The sales reps were expecting handsome bonuses for their hard work.

Early on, however, it became all too clear that Puget had seriously underestimated the time it took to build new business relationships and the costs associated with the expansion, a mistake that was already eating into profit margins. Even more distressing were the most recent figures for new housing starts, which were heading in the wrong direction. As Michael said, "Granted, it's too early to tell if this is just a pause or the start of a real long-term downturn. But I'm worried. If things get worse, Puget could be in real trouble."

James looked at Federico and said, "Our lawyers built enough contingency clauses into the sales reps' contracts that we're not really obligated to pay those bonuses you promised. What would you think about not paying them?" Federico turned to the president, who said, "Why don't you think about it, and get back to us with a recommendation?"

Federico felt torn. On the one hand, he knew the CFO was correct. Puget wasn't, strictly speaking, under any legal obligation to pay out the bonuses, and the eroding profit margins were a genuine cause for concern. The president clearly did not want to pay the bonuses. But Federico had created a first-rate sales force that had done exactly what he'd asked them to do. He prided himself on being a man of his word, someone others could trust. Could he go back on his promises?

What Would You Do?

1. Recommend to the president that a meeting be arranged with the sales representatives entitled to a bonus and tell them that their checks were going to be delayed until the Puget's financial picture clarified. The sales reps would be told that the company had a legal right to delay payment and that it may not be able to pay the bonuses if its financial situation continues to deteriorate.
2. Recommend a meeting with the sales representatives entitled to a bonus and tell them the company's deteriorating financial situation triggers one of the contingency clauses in their contract so that the company won't be issuing their bonus checks. Puget will just have to deal with the negative impact on sales rep motivation.
3. Recommend strongly to the president that Puget pay the bonuses as promised. The legal contracts and financial situation don't matter. Be prepared to resign if the bonuses are not paid as you promised. Your word and a motivated sales team mean everything to you.

Case for Critical Analysis

Kimbel's Department Store[70]

Frances Patterson, Kimbel's CEO, looked at the latest "Sales by Manager" figures on her daily Web-based sales report. What did these up-to-the-minute numbers tell her about the results of Kimbel's trial of straight commission pay for its salespeople?

A regional chain of upscale department stores based in St. Louis, Kimbel's faces the challenge shared by most department stores these days: how to stop losing share of overall retail sales to discount store chains. A key component of the strategy the company formulated to counter this long-term trend

is the revival of great customer service on the floor, once a hallmark of upscale stores. Frances knows Kimbel's has its work cut out for it. When she dropped in on several stores incognito a few years ago, she was dismayed to discover that finding a salesperson actively engaged with a customer was rare. In fact, finding a salesperson when a customer wanted to pay for an item was often difficult.

About a year and a half ago, the CEO read about a quiet revolution sweeping department store retailing. At stores such as Bloomingdale's and Bergdorf Goodman, managers put all salespeople on straight commission. Frances decided to give the system a yearlong try in two area stores.

Such a plan, she reasoned, would be good for Kimbel's if it lived up to its promise of attracting better salespeople, improving their motivation, and making them more customer oriented. It could also potentially be good for employees. Salespeople in departments such as electronics, appliances, and jewelry, where expertise and highly personalized services paid off, had long worked solely on commission. But the majority of employees earned an hourly wage plus a meager 0.5 percent commission on total sales. Under the new scheme, all employees would earn a 7 percent commission on sales. When she compared the two systems, she saw that a new salesclerk in women's wear would earn $35,000 on $500,000 in sales, as opposed to only $18,000 under the old scheme.

Now, with the trial period about to end, Frances notes that while overall sales in the two stores have increased modestly, so also has employee turnover. When the CEO examined the sales-by-manager figures, it was obvious that some associates had thrived and others had not. Most fell somewhere in the middle.

For example, Juan Santore is enthusiastic about the change—and for good reason. He works in women's designer shoes and handbags, where a single item can cost upwards of $1,000. Motivated largely by the desire to make lots of money, he's a personable, outgoing individual with an entrepreneurial streak. Ever since the straight commission plan took effect, he has put even more time and effort into cultivating relationships with wealthy customers, and it shows. His pay has increased an average of $150 per week.

It's a different story in the lingerie department, where even luxury items have more modest price tags. The lingerie department head, Gladys Weinholtz, said salespeople in her department are demoralized. Several valued employees had quit, and most miss the security of a salary. No matter how hard they work, they cannot match their previous earnings. "Yes, they're paying more attention to customers," conceded Gladys, "but they're so anxious about making ends meet, they tend to pounce on the poor women who wander into the department." Furthermore, lingerie sales associates are giving short shrift to duties such as handling complaints or returns that don't immediately translate into sales. "And boy, do they ever resent the sales superstars in the other departments," said Gladys.

The year is nearly up. It's time to decide. Should Frances declare the straight commission experiment a success on the whole and roll it out across the chain over the next six months?

Questions

1. What theories about motivation underlie the switch from salary to commission pay?
2. What needs are met under the commission system? Are they the same needs in the shoes and handbag department as they are in lingerie? Explain.
3. If you were Frances Patterson, would you go back to the previous compensation system, implement the straight commission plan in all Kimbel's stores, or devise and test some other compensation method? If you decided to test another system, what would it look like?

aplia Aplia Highlights

Now use your Aplia homework to help you:

- Apply management theories in your life
- Assess your management skills
- Master management terms and concepts
- Apply your knowledge to real-world situations
- Analyze and solve challenging management problems

In order to take advantage of these elements, your instructor will need to have set up a course for your class within Aplia. Ask your instructor to contact his/her Cengage sales representative and Digital Solutions Manager to explore testing Aplia in your course this term.

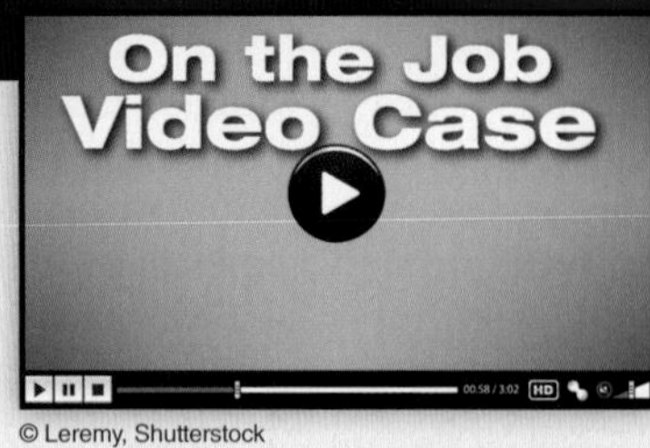

© Leremy, Shutterstock

LivingSocial Escapes: Motivating Employees

When today's young professionals look to catch a break from hectic city life, they look to LivingSocial Escapes. Founded in 2008 by Maia Josebachvili and Bram Levy, the social travel firm has earned high praise for its array of exciting outdoor adventures. Whether the moment calls for a lazy campfire gathering or a thrilling encounter with nature, expert guides at the East Coast trip service have a weekend getaway for any occasion.

LivingSocial Escapes offers a range of outdoor excursions. From whitewater rafting in the Poconos. to camping in the Catskills, the company's trips help customers escape the bubble and recapture their lust for life. The firm's passion for all things outdoors is rooted in the active lifestyles of founders Maia Josebachvili and Bram Levy. Josebachvili's adventure résumé includes such titles as "professional skydiver" and "mountain-bike racer." Levy's "outdoor cred" includes hikes in the Himalayas and scuba diving in Australia's Great Barrier Reef.

Not surprisingly, the business partners have a nontraditional approach to career development. Josebachvili's journey included a brief stint on Wall Street before launching LivingSocial Escapes. Levy, a former management consultant, joined LivingSocial Escapes because "it seemed like something fun to do." Levy says he figured he could "always come back to the safe world" if things didn't work out.

For the LivingSocial Escapes employees who work behind the scenes to deliver "Zen Escape Yoga Hikes" and "Boulder and Brew Tours," work motivation comes naturally. The company's managers, guides, and directors are driven by the freedom that only a start-up company can offer. "We gave everyone a lot of ownership in their cities," Josebachvili says. "We said every time you want to run a trip, you run it by us. We'd talk about it and we'd see if it works. Within a few months I was like, 'Okay, if you know it's going to work, don't come to us—you got this'. After a year, I felt really good about what they were doing."

Although his start-up is yet in early development, Levy says founding a company taught him important lessons about people and motivation. "When people are excited about something, they'll do virtually anything," Levy states. "We had employees across the country working for us for virtually no income and no stability, and merely because they enjoyed what we had to offer and they were having fun." As part of his training for new hires, Levy offers only the most basic outline of job responsibilities. "Think about the brand and what we're trying to develop," Levy tells new recruits. "Now take it and formulate what you think will be best and run with it."

Since 2008, the LivingSocial Escapes roster has grown to more than eight directors, 20 city managers, and dozens of adventure guides. Josebachvili claims that the company's directors, many of whom are in their mid-twenties, are excited about rapid expansion. "We're asking someone who's 23 years old to manage five different cities and city managers, as well as teams under the city managers." LivingSocial Escapes demands high commitment from teams, but if the company succeeds, employees can share in the financial rewards—even part-time guides get special bonuses if trips are profitable.

At this early stage, working for LivingSocial Escapes is not about stability or following a traditional career path: it's about adventure. "We're selling the nontraditional path," Levy states. "There are plenty of opportunities to have the stable career path that our parents' generation had and wants us to have as well. I think we're selling the opportunity to do something truly unique and different and have fun."

Discussion Questions

1. Which needs in Maslow's hierarchy are most important to the employees who work for LivingSocial Escapes, and how can managers use this information to develop a highly motivated workforce?
2. According to equity theory, how might a LivingSocial Escapes guide react if he or she feels underpaid or unappreciated?
3. What outcomes or rewards possess high valence for managers and guides who work at LivingSocial Escapes?

Biz Flix Video Case

Friday Night Lights (I)

The Odessa, Texas, passion for Friday night high school football comes through clearly in this cinematic treatment of H. G. (Buzz) Bissinger's well-regarded book of the same title.[71] Coach Gary Gaines (Billy Bob Thornton) leads the Permian High Panthers to the 1988 semifinals where it must compete against a team of much larger players. Fast-moving pace in the football sequences and a slower pace in the serious, introspective sequences give this film many fine moments.

Motivation This sequence starts with a panning shot of the Winchell's house. Coach Gaines says to Mike Winchell (Lucas Black), "Can you get the job done, Mike?" The sequence follows a harsh practice and Mike talking to his brother or sister from a telephone booth. The film continues with the Odessa-Permian versus Cooper football game.

What to Watch for and Ask Yourself

- This chapter defined motivation as "the forces either within or external to a person that arouse enthusiasm and persistence to pursue a certain course of action." Does Mike Winchell show the characteristics of this definition early in the sequence? Do you expect him to show any of the characteristics after the sequence ends and he returns to the team?
- Which needs discussed earlier in this chapter does Mike appear focused on early in the sequence? Which needs can become his focus later in the sequence? Review the hierarchy of needs theory and ERG theory sections earlier in the chapter for some suggestions.
- Apply the various parts of goal-setting theory to this sequence. Which parts of that theory appear in this sequence?

Endnotes

1. Jennifer Robison, "Many Paths to Engagement: How Very Different Management Styles Get the Same Great Results at Mars, Incorporated," *Gallup Management Journal,* January 10, 2008, http://gmj.gallup.com/content/103513/Many-Paths-Engagement.aspx (accessed January 10, 2008).
2. *Ibid.*
3. David Silburt, "Secrets of the Super Sellers," *Canadian Business* (January 1987): 54–59; "Meet the Savvy Supersalesmen," *Fortune* (February 4, 1985): 56–62; Michael Brody, "Meet Today's Young American Worker," *Fortune* (November 11, 1985): 90–98; and Tom Richman, "Meet the Masters. They Could Sell You Anything," *Inc.* (March 1985): 79–86.
4. Richard M. Steers and Lyman W. Porter, eds., *Motivation and Work Behavior,* 3rd ed. (New York: McGraw-Hill, 1983); Don Hellriegel, John W. Slocum, Jr., and Richard W. Woodman, *Organizational Behavior,* 7th ed. (St. Paul, MN: West, 1995), p. 170; and Jerry L. Gray and Frederick A. Starke, *Organizational Behavior: Concepts and Applications,* 4th ed. (New York: Macmillan, 1988), pp.104–105.
5. Carol Hymowitz, "Readers Tell Tales of Success and Failure Using Rating Systems," *The Wall Street Journal*, May 29, 2001.
6. Alan Deutschman, "Can Google Stay Google?" *Fast Company* (August 2005): 62–68.
7. See Linda Grant, "Happy Workers, High Returns," *Fortune* (January 12, 1998): 81; Elizabeth J. Hawk and Garrett J. Sheridan, "The Right Stuff," *Management Review* (June 1999): 43–48; Michael West and Malcolm Patterson, "Profitable Personnel," *People Management* (January 8, 1998): 28–31; Anne Fisher, "Why Passion Pays," *FSB* (September 2002): 58; and Curt Coffman and Gabriel Gonzalez-Molina, *Follow This Path: How the World's Great Organizations Drive Growth by Unleashing Human Potential* (New York: Warner Books, 2002).
8. Abraham F. Maslow, "A Theory of Human Motivation," *Psychological Review* 50 (1943): 370–396.
9. Sarah E. Needleman, "Burger Chain's Health-Care Recipe," *The Wall Street Journal*, August 31, 2009.
10. Telis Demos, "The Way We Work: Motivate without Spending Millions," *Fortune* (April 12, 2010): 37–38.
11. Sarah Pass, "On the Line," *People Management* (September 15, 2005): 38.
12. Clayton Alderfer, *Existence, Relatedness, and Growth* (New York: Free Press, 1972).
13. Scott Westcott, "Beyond Flextime: Trashing the Work Week," *Inc.* (August 2008): 30–31.
14. Karol Rose, "Work-Life Effectiveness," special advertising section, *Fortune* (September 29, 2003): S1–S17.
15. Sylvia Ann Hewlett, "Making Flex Time a Win–Win," *The New York Times*, December 19, 2009.

16. Frederick Herzberg, "One More Time: How Do You Motivate Employees?" *Harvard Business Review* (January 2003): 87–96.
17. Hashi Syedain, "Topped with Satisfaction," *People Management* (July 12, 2007), www.peoplemanagement.co.uk/pm/articles/2007/07/toppedwithsatisfaction.htm (accessed May 8, 2009); and PizzaExpress Web site, www.pizzaexpress.com (accessed May 8, 2009).
18. David C. McClelland, *Human Motivation* (Glenview, IL: Scott, Foresman, 1985).
19. David C. McClelland, "The Two Faces of Power," in *Organizational Psychology*, ed. D. A. Colb, I. M. Rubin, and J. M. McIntyre (Englewood Cliffs, NJ: Prentice Hall, 1971), pp. 73–86.
20. See Gary P. Latham and Edwin A. Locke, "Enhancing the Benefits and Overcoming the Pitfalls of Goal Setting," *Organizational Dynamics* 35, no. 4 (2006): 332–338; Edwin A. Locke and Gary P. Latham, "Building a Practically Useful Theory of Goal Setting and Task Motivation: A 35-Year Odyssey," *The American Psychologist* 57, no. 9 (September 2002): 705ff; Gary P. Latham and Edwin A. Locke, "Self-Regulation through Goal Setting," *Organizational Behavior and Human Decision Processes* 50, no. 2 (December, 1991): 212–247; G. P. Latham and G. H. Seijts, "The Effects of Proximal and Distal Goals on Performance of a Moderately Task," *Journal of Organizational Behavior* 20, no. 4 (1999): 421–428; P. C. Early, T. Connolly, and G. Ekegren, "Goals, Strategy Development, and Task Performance: Some Limits on the Efficacy of Goal Setting," *Journal of Applied Psychology* 74 (1989): 24–33; E. A. Locke, "Toward a Theory of Task Motivation and Incentives," *Organizational Behavior and Human Performance* 3 (1968): 157–189; and Gerard H. Seijts, Ree M. Meertens, and Gerjo Kok, "The Effects of Task Importance and Publicness on the Relation Between Goal Difficulty and Performance," *Canadian Journal of Behavioural Science* 29, no. 1 (1997): 54ff.
21. Locke and Latham, "Building a Practically Useful Theory of Goal Setting and Task Motivation."
22. Edwin A. Locke, "Linking Goals to Monetary Incentives," *Academy of Management Executive* 18, no. 4 (2005): 130–133.
23. Latham and Locke, "Enhancing the Benefits and Overcoming the Pitfalls of Goal Setting."
24. Brian Ellsworth, "Making a Place for Blue Collars in the Boardroom," *The New York Times*, August 3, 2005.
25. J. M. Ivanecevich and J. T. McMahon, "The Effects of Goal Setting, External Feedback, and Self-Generated Feedback on Outcome Variables: A Field Experiment," *Academy of Management Journal* 25, no. 2 (June 1982): 359–372; and G. P. Latham and E. A. Locke, "Self-Regulation through Goal Setting," *Organizational Behavior and Human Decision Processes* 50, no. 2 (1991): 212–247.
26. Gary P. Latham, "The Motivational Benefits of Goal-Setting," *Academy of Management Executive* 18, no. 4 (2004): 126–129.
27. J. Stacy Adams, "Injustice in Social Exchange," in *Advances in Experimental Social Psychology*, 2nd ed., ed. L. Berkowitz (New York: Academic Press, 1965); and J. Stacy Adams, "Toward an Understanding of Inequity," *Journal of Abnormal and Social Psychology* (November 1963): 422–436.
28. Daniel Yee, "Brain Prefers Working over Money for Nothing," *Cincinnati Post*, May 14, 2004.
29. Ray V. Montagno, "The Effects of Comparison to Others and Primary Experience on Responses to Task Design," *Academy of Management Journal* 28 (1985): 491–498; and Robert P. Vecchio, "Predicting Worker Performance in Inequitable Settings," *Academy of Management Review* 7 (1982): 103–110.
30. James E. Martin and Melanie M. Peterson, "Two-Tier Wage Structures: Implications for Equity Theory," *Academy of Management Journal* 30 (1987): 297–315.
31. Jared Sandberg, "Why You May Regret Looking at Papers Left on the Office Copier," *The Wall Street Journal*, June 20, 2006.
32. Serena Ng and Joann S. Lublin, "AIG Pay Plan: Rank and Rile; Insurer to Rate Workers on Scale, Compensate Accordingly," *The Wall Street Journal*, February 11, 2010.
33. Victor H. Vroom, *Work and Motivation* (New York: Wiley, 1964); B. S. Gorgopoulos, G. M. Mahoney, and N. Jones, "A Path-Goal Approach to Productivity," *Journal of Applied Psychology* 41 (1957): 345–353; and E. E. Lawler III, *Pay and Organizational Effectiveness: A Psychological View* (New York: McGraw-Hill, 1981).
34. Richard R. Johnson, "Explaining Patrol Officer Drug Arrest Activity through Expectancy Theory," *Policing* 32, no. 1 (2009): 6ff.
35. Richard L. Daft and Richard M. Steers, *Organizations: A Micro/Macro Approach* (Glenview, IL: Scott, Foresman, 1986).
36. Studies reported in Tom Rath, "The Best Way to Recognize Employees," *Gallup Management Journal* (December 9, 2004): 1–5; and Erin White, "Theory & Practice: Praise from Peers Goes a Long Way— Recognition Programs Help Companies Retain Workers as Pay Raises Get Smaller," *The Wall Street Journal*, December 19, 2005.
37. Alexander D. Stajkovic and Fred Luthans, "A Meta-Analysis of the Effects of Organizational Behavior Modification on Task Performance, 1975–95," *Academy of Management Journal* (October 1997): 1122–1149; H. Richlin, *Modern Behaviorism* (San Francisco: Freeman, 1970); and B. F. Skinner, *Science and Human Behavior* (New York: Macmillan, 1953).
38. Stajkovic and Luthans, "A Meta-Analysis of the Effects of Organizational Behavior Modification on Task Performance, 1975–95"; and Fred Luthans and Alexander D. Stajkovic, "Reinforce for Performance: The Need to Go Beyond Pay and Even Rewards," *Academy of Management Executive* 13, no. 2 (1999): 49–57.
39. Daryl W. Wiesman, "The Effects of Performance Feedback and Social Reinforcement on Up-Selling at Fast-Food Restaurants," *Journal of Organizational Behavior Management* 26, no. 4 (2006): 1–18.
40. Perry Garfinkel, "A Hotel's Secret: Treat the Guests Like Guests" (an interview with Alan J. Fuerstman), *The New York Times*, August 23, 2008.
41. Kenneth D. Butterfield and Linda Klebe Treviño, "Punishment from the Manager's Perspective: A Grounded Investigation and Inductive Model," *Academy of Management Journal* 39, no. 6 (December 1996): 1479–1512; and Andrea Casey, "Voices from the Firing Line: Managers Discuss Punishment in the Workplace," *Academy of Management Executive* 11, no. 3 (1997): 93–94.
42. Amy Sutherland, "What Shamu Taught Me About a Happy Marriage," *The New York Times*, June 25, 2006, www.nytimes.com/2006/06/25/fashion/25love.html?ex=1175659200&en=4c3d257c4d16e70d&ei=5070 (accessed April 2, 2007).
43. Amy Joyce, "The Bonus Question; Some Managers Still Strive to Reward Merit," *The Washington Post*, November 13, 2005.
44. Survey results from World at Work and Hewitt Associates, reported in Karen Kroll, "Benefits: Paying for Performance," *Inc.* (November 2004): 46; and Kathy Chu, "Firms Report Lackluster Results from Pay-for-Performance Plans," *The Wall Street Journal*, June 15, 2004.
45. Arthur Bandura, *Social Learning Theory* (Englewood Cliffs, NJ: Prentice Hall, 1977); T. R. V. Davis and F. Luthans, "A Social

Learning Approach to Organizational Behavior," *Academy of Management Review* 5 (1980): 281–290; and A. Bandura, *Self-Efficacy: The Exercise of Self-Control* (New York: W.H. Freeman, 1997).

46. Bandura, *Social Learning Theory*; and Davis and Luthans, "A Social Learning Approach to Organizational Behavior."

47. Heather Green, "How Meetup Tore Up the Rule Book," *BusinessWeek* (June 16, 2008): 88–89.

48. M. E. Gist, "Self-Efficacy: Implications for Organizational Behavior and Human Resource Management," *Academy of Management Review* (July 1987): 47; and Arthur Bandura, "Self-Efficacy," in V. S. Ramachaudran, ed., *Encyclopedia of Human Behavior*, vol. 4 (New York: Academic Press, 1994), pp. 71–81.

49. Christine M. Riordan, Robert J. Vandenberg, and Hettie A. Richardson, "Employee Involvement Climate and Organizational Effectiveness," *Human Resource Management* 44, no. 4 (Winter 2005): 471–488.

50. J. Richard Hackman and Greg R. Oldham, *Work Redesign* (Reading, MA: Addison-Wesley, 1980); and J. Richard Hackman and Greg Oldham, "Motivation through the Design of Work: Test of a Theory," *Organizational Behavior and Human Performance* 16 (1976): 250–279.

51. Xu Huang and Evert Van de Vliert, "Where Intrinsic Job Satisfaction Fails to Work: National Moderators of Intrinsic Motivation," *Journal of Organizational Behavior* 24 (2003): 157–179.

52. Sarah E. Needleman, "Business Owners Try to Motivate Employees; As Recession Lingers, Managers Hold Meetings and Change Hiring Practices to Alleviate Workers' Stress," *The Wall Street Journal*, January 14, 2010.

53. Aaron Lucchetti, "Morgan Stanley to Overhaul Pay Plan," *The Wall Street Journal*, December 29, 2009; Graham Bowley, "Credit Suisse Overhauls Compensation," *The New York Times*, October 21, 2009; Liam Pleven and Susanne Craig, "Deal Fees Under Fire Amid Mortgage Crisis; Guaranteed Rewards of Bankers, Middlemen Are in the Spotlight," *The Wall Street Journal*, January 17, 2008; Phred Dvorak, "Companies Seek Shareholder Input on Pay Practices," *The Wall Street Journal*, April 6, 2009; and Carol Hymowitz, "Pay Gap Fuels Worker Woes," *The Wall Street Journal*, April 28, 2008.

54. Joann S. Lublin, "Theory & Practice: Valeant CEO's Pay Package Draws Praise as Model," *The Wall Street Journal*, August 24, 2009.

55. Edwin P. Hollander and Lynn R. Offermann, "Power and Leadership in Organizations," *American Psychologist* 45 (February 1990): 179–189.

56. Jay A. Conger and Rabindra N. Kanungo, "The Empowerment Process: Integrating Theory and Practice," *Academy of Management Review* 13 (1988): 471–482.

57. David E. Bowen and Edward E. Lawler III, "The Empowerment of Service Workers: What, Why, How, and When," *Sloan Management Review* (Spring 1992): 31–39; and Ray W. Coye and James A. Belohav, "An Exploratory Analysis of Employee Participation," *Group and Organization Management* 20, no. 1 (March 1995): 4–17.

58. Robert C. Ford and Myron D. Fottler, "Empowerment: A Matter of Degree," *Academy of Management Executive* 9, no. 3 (1995): 21–31.

59. This definition is based on Mercer Human Resource Consulting's Employee Engagement Model, as described in Paul Sanchez and Dan McCauley, "Measuring and Managing Engagement in a Cross-Cultural Workforce: New Insights for Global Companies," *Global Business and Organizational Excellence* (November–December 2006): 41–50.

60. This section is based on Maureen Soyars and Justin Brusino, "Essentials of Engagement: Contributions, Connections, Growth," *T&D* (March 2009): 62–65; Kenneth W. Thomas, "The Four Intrinsic Rewards That Drive Employee Engagement," *Ivey Business Journal*, November–December 2009, www.iveybusinessjournal.com/article.asp?intArticle_id=867 (accessed November 24, 2009); and Cristina de Mello e Souza Wildermuth and Patrick David Pauken, "A Perfect Match: Decoding Employee Engagement—Part II: Engaging Jobs and Individuals," *Industrial and Commercial Training* 40, no. 4 (2008): 206–210.

61. Kate Rockwood, "The Employee Whisperer," *Fast Company* (November 2008): 72–73.

62. Soyars and Brusino, "Essentials of Engagement."

63. Theresa M. Welbourne, "Employee Engagement: Beyond the Fad and into the Executive Suite," *Leader to Leader* (Spring 2007): 45–51.

64. See J. K. Harter, F. L. Schmidt, and T. L. Hayes, "Business-Unit-Level Relationship between Employee Satisfaction, Employee Engagement, and Business Outcomes: A Meta-Analysis," *Journal of Applied Psychology* 87, no. 2 (2002): 268–279; Coffman and Gonzalez, *Follow This Path*; and A. M. Saks, "Antecedents and Consequences of Employee Engagement," *Journal of Managerial Psychology* 21, no. 7 (2006): 600–619.

65. "Employee Engagement Report 2008," BlessingWhite Web site, www.blessingwhite.com/eee__report.asp (accessed August 5, 2010).

66. Reported in "Many Employees Would Fire Their Boss," Gallup Organization news release, http://gmj.gallup.com/content/28867/Many-Employees-Would-Fire-Their-Boss.aspx (accessed August 6, 2010); and Leigh Woosley, "Rules of Disengagement: Gallup Poll Shows That More Than Half of Workers Are 'Checked Out,'" *Knight Ridder Tribune Business News*, June 11, 2006.

67. Rockwood, "The Employee Whisperer"; and quote from "Americans' Job Satisfaction Falls to Record Low," *USA Today*, January 5, 2010.

68. Lyman W. Porter, *Organizational Patterns of Managerial Job Attitudes* (New York: American Foundation for Management Research, 1964), pp. 17, 19. Used with permission.

69. Based on Doug Wallace, "The Company Simply Refused to Pay," *Business Ethics* (March–April 2000): 18; and Adam Shell, "Over-heated Housing Market Is Cooling," *USA Today*, November 2, 2005, www.usatoday.com/money/economy/housing/2005-11-01-real-estate-usat_x.htm.

70. Based on Cynthia Kyle, "Commissions Question—To Pay … Or Not to Pay?" *Michigan Retailer*, March 2003, www.retailers.com/news/retailers/03mar/mr0303 commissions.html (accessed March 8, 2006); "Opinion: Effective Retail Sales Compensation," *Furniture World Magazine* (March 7, 2006), www.furninfo.com /absolutenm/templates/NewsFeed.asp?articleid=6017 (accessed March 8, 2006); Terry Pristin, "Retailing's Elite Keep the Armani Moving Off the Racks," *The New York Times*, December 22, 2001; Francine Schwadel, "Chain Finds Incentives a Hard Sell," *The Wall Street Journal*, July 5, 1990; and Amy Dunkin, "Now Salespeople Really Must Sell for Their Supper," *BusinessWeek* (July 31, 1989): 50–52.

71. J. Craddock, ed., *VideoHound's Golden Movie Retriever* (Detroit, MI: Gale Cengage Learning, 2008), p. 368.

Chapter Outline

Communication Is the Manager's Job
- *What Is Communication?*
- *The Communication Process*

Communicating among People
- *Communication Channels*
- *Communicating to Persuade and Influence Others*
- *Gender Differences in Communication*
- *Nonverbal Communication*
- *Listening*

Organizational Communication
- *Formal Communication Channels*
- *Team Communication Channels*
- *Personal Communication Channels*

Workplace Communication
- *Crisis Communication*
- *Communication Technology*
- *Climate of Trust and Openness*

Managing Communication

Learning Outcomes

After studying this chapter, you should be able to:

1. Explain why communication is essential for effective management, and describe the communication process.
2. Describe the concept of channel richness, and explain how communication channels influence the quality of communication.
3. Understand how gender differences, nonverbal communication, and listening affect communication.
4. Explain the difference between formal and informal organizational communications and how to maximize the effectiveness of team communication.
5. Appreciate the role of personal communication channels in enhancing organizational communication.
6. Recognize the manager's role in managing crisis communication, using new communication technology, and creating a climate of trust.

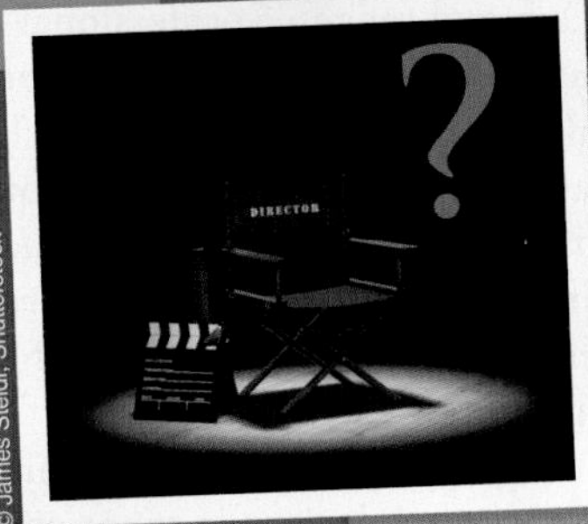

© James Steidl, Shutterstock

Are You Ready to Be a Manager?

Please circle your opinion below each of the following statements.

1 **When I am giving instructions to someone, I try to phrase them in way that will be understandable to that particular person.**

Mostly True Mostly False

(See page 523, The Communication Process.)

2 **When I have a message to deliver with emotional content, I know better than to send it via email. Face to face is the best, or if that's not possible, then telephone.**

Mostly True Mostly False

(See page 526, The Hierarchy of Channel Richness.)

3 **If I hope to persuade people, I know that I have to communicate with them often and easily.**

Mostly True Mostly False

(See page 528, Communicating to Persuade and Influence Others.)

4 **I could learn a lot about good communication from listening to women interact.**

Mostly True Mostly False

(See page 528, Gender Differences in Communication.)

5 **When someone else is talking, I focus on what the person is saying and try to find the underlying meaning rather than just preparing for my next air time.**

Mostly True Mostly False

(See page 530, Listening.)

When Brittany Sharkey, marketing coordinator for a Chicago consulting firm, decided to expand her personal network, she created a profile on LinkedIn, a business-oriented social networking site. After writing a compelling profile and adding connections, Sharkey joined 70 million registered users who use LinkedIn to expand their personal networks.[1] Personal networking, enhanced through social networking sites like LinkedIn, is an important skill for managers because it enables them to get things done more smoothly and rapidly than they could in isolation. Networking builds social, work, and career relationships that facilitate mutual benefit. How do managers build a personal network that includes a broad range of professional and social relationships? One key is to know how to communicate effectively. In fact, communication is a vital factor in every aspect of the manager's job.

Organizations in today's complex business environment depend on effective communication to ensure business success. A study by Watson Wyatt Worldwide found that companies with the most effective communication programs had a 47 percent higher total return to shareholders from 2002 to 2006 when compared with companies that had less effective communication.[2]

Not only does effective communication lead to better bottom-line results, but also much of a manager's time is spent communicating. Managers spend at least 80 percent of every working day in direct communication with others. In other words, 48 minutes of every hour is spent in meetings, on the telephone, communicating online, or talking informally while walking around. The other 20 percent of a typical manager's time is spent doing desk work, most of which is also communication in the form of reading and writing.[3]

This chapter explains why managers should make effective communication a priority. First, we examine communication as a crucial part of the manager's job and describe a model of the communication process. Next, we consider the interpersonal aspects of communication, including communication channels, persuasion, gender differences, listening skills, and nonverbal communication that affect managers' ability to communicate. Then, we look at the organization as a whole and consider formal upward, downward, and horizontal communications as well as personal networks and informal communications. Finally, we describe the manager's role in managing crisis communication, using new communication technology, and creating a climate of trust and openness.

UPI/Bill Greenblatt /Landov

ConceptConnection

As **communication champion** for Marriott International, CEO Bill Marriott gathers information and communicates the vision, values, and goals of the company. Here he stops to congratulate employees on the opening of a new Renaissance Grand Hotel in downtown St. Louis. In his blog, Marriott on the Move at *www.blogs.marriott.com*, the CEO opens communication with Marriott customers and employees and shares his views on current events and how they affect the company's mission.

Communication Is the Manager's Job

Exhibit 13.1 illustrates the crucial role of managers as communication champions. Managers gather important information from both inside and outside the organization and then distribute appropriate information to others who need it. Managers'

New Manager Self-Test

Are You Building a Personal Network?

How much effort do you put into developing connections with other people? Personal networks may help a new manager in the workplace. To learn something about your networking skills, answer the questions below. Please indicate whether each item is Mostly True or Mostly False for you in school or at work.

	MOSTLY TRUE <<<	>>> MOSTLY FALSE
1. I learn early on about changes going on in the organization and how they might affect my position or me.	______	______
2. I network as much to help other people solve problems as to help myself.	______	______
3. I am fascinated by other people and what they do.	______	______
4. I frequently use lunches to meet and network with new people.	______	______
5. I regularly participate in charitable causes.	______	______
6. I maintain a list of friends and colleagues to whom I send holiday greeting cards.	______	______
7. I maintain contact with people from previous organizations and school groups.	______	______
8. I actively give information to subordinates, peers, and my boss.	______	______

See It Online

Scoring and Interpretation: Give yourself 1 point for each item marked as Mostly True. A score of 6 or higher suggests active networking and a solid foundation on which to begin your career as a new manager. When you create a personal network, you become well connected to get things done through a variety of relationships. Having sources of information and support helps a new manager gain career traction. If you scored 3 or less, you may want to focus more on building relationships if you are serious about a career as a manager. People with active networks tend to be more effective managers and have broader impact on the organization.

communication is *purpose directed* in that it directs everyone's attention toward the vision, values, and desired goals of the team or organization and influences people to act in a way to achieve the goals. Managers facilitate *strategic conversations* by using open communication, actively listening to others, applying the practice of dialogue, and using feedback for learning and change. **Strategic conversation** refers to people talking across boundaries and hierarchical levels about the team or organization's vision, critical strategic themes, and the values that help achieve important goals.[4] For example, Campbell Soup CEO Doug Conant meets every six weeks with a group of 12 employees from across the company.

EXHIBIT 13.1

The Manager as Communication Champion

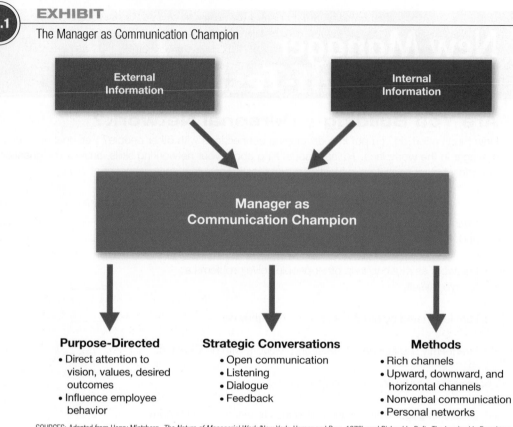

SOURCES: Adapted from Henry Mintzberg, *The Nature of Managerial Work* (New York: Harper and Row, 1973); and Richard L. Daft, *The Leadership Experience*, 3rd ed. (Cincinnati, OH: South-Western, 2005), p. 346.

During these lunch meetings, he asks for their opinions on what's going on in the business.[5] These strategic conversations allow Conant to regularly and actively solicit input from his employees and receive candid feedback.

Communication permeates every management function described in Chapter 1.[6] For example, when managers perform the planning function, they gather information; write letters, memos, and reports; and meet with other managers to formulate the plan. When managers lead, they communicate to share a vision of what the organization can be and motivate employees to help achieve it. When managers organize, they gather information about the state of the organization and communicate a new structure to others. The control function requires that managers obtain data about performance, compare it to plans and standards, and communicate any needed changes. Communication skills are a fundamental part of every managerial activity.

What Is Communication?

A professor at Harvard once asked a class to define communication by drawing pictures. Most students drew a manager speaking or typing on a computer keyboard. Some placed "speech balloons" next to their characters; others showed pages flying from a printer. "No," the professor told the class, "none of you has captured the essence of communication." He went on to explain that communication means "to share," not "to speak" or "to write."

Communication is the process by which information is exchanged and understood by two or more people, usually with the intent to motivate or influence behavior.

Communication is not just sending information. Honoring this distinction between *sharing* and *proclaiming* is crucial for successful management. A manager who does not listen is like a used-car salesperson who claims, "I sold a car—they just didn't buy it." Management communication is a two-way street that includes listening and other forms of feedback. Effective communication, in the words of one expert, occurs as follows:

> When two people interact, they put themselves into each other's shoes, try to perceive the world as the other person perceives it, and try to predict how the other will respond. Interaction involves reciprocal role-taking, the mutual employment of empathetic skills. The goal of interaction is the merger of self and other, a complete ability to anticipate, predict, and behave in accordance with the joint needs of self and other.[7]

It is the desire to share understanding that motivates executives to visit employees on the shop floor, hold small informal meetings, or interact with employees through a business blog. The information that managers gather from direct communication with employees shapes their understanding of the organization.

The Communication Process

Many people think communication is simple. After all, we communicate every day without even thinking about it. However, communication usually is complex, and the opportunities for sending or receiving the wrong messages are innumerable. No doubt, you have heard someone say, "But that's not what I meant!" Have you ever received directions you thought were clear and yet still got lost? How often have you wasted time on misunderstood instructions?

To better understand the complexity of the communication process, note the key elements outlined in Exhibit 13.2. Two essential elements in every communication situation are the sender and the receiver. The *sender* is anyone who wishes to convey an idea or concept to others, to seek information, or to express a thought or emotion. The *receiver* is the person to whom the message is sent. The sender **encodes** the idea by selecting symbols with which to compose a message. The **message** is the tangible formulation of the idea that is sent to the receiver. The message is sent through a **channel**, which is the communication carrier. The channel can be a formal report, a telephone call, an email message, or a face-to-face meeting. The receiver **decodes** the symbols to interpret the meaning of the

EXHIBIT 13.2

A Model of the Communication Process

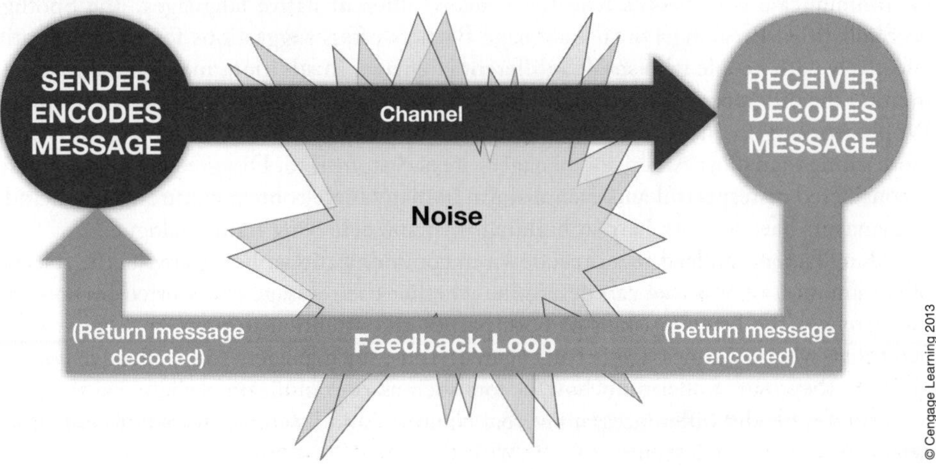

message. Encoding and decoding are potential sources for communication errors, because knowledge, attitudes, and background act as filters and create *noise* when translating from symbols to meaning. Finally, **feedback** occurs when the receiver responds to the sender's communication with a return message. Without feedback, the communication is *one-way*; with feedback, it is *two-way*. Feedback is a powerful aid to communication effectiveness, because it enables the sender to determine whether the receiver correctly interpreted the message.

- Effective managers build broad personal communication networks through which they accomplish their jobs.
- The manager's role as communication champion means to engage in purpose-driven strategic conversations via multiple channels.
- The term **channel** refers to the carrier of a communication, such as a phone call, blog, or text message.
- **Strategic conversation** refers to dialogue across boundaries and hierarchical levels about the team or organization's vision, critical strategic themes, and the values that help achieve important goals.
- **Communication** is the process by which information is exchanged and understood by two or more people.
- The **message** is the tangible formulation of an idea to be sent to a receiver.
- The sender **encodes** the idea by selecting symbols with which to compose a message and selecting a communication channel; the receiver **decodes** the symbols to interpret the meaning of the message.
- **Feedback** occurs when the receiver responds to the sender's communication with a return message.

Communicating among People

The communication model in Exhibit 13.2 illustrates the components of effective communication. Communications can break down if the sender and receiver do not encode or decode language in the same way.[8] We all know how difficult it is to communicate with someone who does not speak our language, and today's managers are often trying to communicate with people who speak many different native languages. The Spotlight on Skills titled Breaking Down Language Barriers offers suggestions for communicating effectively with people who speak a different language. In addition, managers should keep in mind the difference between high- and low-context cultures, as discussed in Chapter 3. People working in India, for example, have found that Indian communication is much more subtle than most American managers are accustomed to. Disagreeing with a superior is considered disrespectful and even disloyal in many high-context cultures, such as India, so managers have to work hard at building trust and achieving frank dialogue.[9]

Many factors can lead to a breakdown in communications. For example, the selection of communication channel can determine whether the message is distorted by noise and interference. The listening skills of both parties and attention to nonverbal behavior can determine whether a message is truly shared. Thus, for managers to be effective communicators, they must understand how factors such as communication channels, the ability to persuade, gender differences, nonverbal behavior, and listening all work to enhance or detract from communication.

SPOTLIGHT ON SKILLS

Breaking Down Language Barriers

In today's global business environment, odds are good you'll find yourself conversing with an employee, colleague, or customer who has limited skills in your native language. Here are some guidelines that will help you speak—and listen—more effectively.

1. ***Keep your message simple.*** Be clear about what you want to communicate, and keep to the point. Avoid slang. Using too many culturally narrow expressions, idioms, and colloquialisms or too much humor can cause your message to be totally lost in translation.
2. ***Select your words with care.*** Don't try to dazzle with your vocabulary. Choose simple words, and look for opportunities to use cognates—that is, words that resemble words in your listener's language. For example, *banco* in Spanish means "bank" in English. Assemble those simple words into equally simple phrases and short sentences. And be sure to avoid slang, jargon, and vague terminology such as *soon*, *often*, or *several*.
3. ***Pay close attention to nonverbal messages.*** Don't cover your mouth with your hand. Being able to see your lips helps your listener decipher what you are saying.
4. ***Speak slowly and carefully.*** In particular, avoid running words together. "Howyadoin?" won't make any sense to someone still struggling with the English language, for example.
5. ***Allow for pauses.*** If you're an American, your culture has taught you to avoid silence whenever possible. However, pauses give your listener time to take in what you have said, ask a question, or formulate a response.
6. ***Fight the urge to shout.*** Speaking louder doesn't make it any easier for someone to understand you. It also tends to be intimidating and could give the impression that you are angry.
7. ***Pay attention to facial expressions and body language, but keep in mind that the meaning of such cues can vary significantly from culture to culture.*** For example, Americans may view eye contact as a sign you're giving someone your full attention, but the Japanese consider prolonged eye contact rude.
8. ***Check for comprehension frequently and invite feedback.*** Stop from time to time and make sure you're being understood, especially if the other person laughs inappropriately, never asks a question, or continually nods and smiles politely. Ask the listener to repeat what you've said in his or her own words. If you find the other person hasn't understood you, restate the information in a different way instead of simply repeating yourself. Similarly, listen carefully when the non-native speaks, and offer feedback so the person can check your understanding of his or her message.

Effective multicultural communication isn't easy, but a small investment in clear communication will result in trust and improved productivity.

SOURCES: Marshall Goldsmith, "Crossing the Cultural Chasm," *BusinessWeek.com*, May 30, 2007, www.businessweek.com/careers/content/may2007/ca20070530_521679.htm (accessed April 8, 2008); WikiHow, "How to Communicate with a Non Native English Speaker," www.wikihow.com/Communicate-With-a-Non-Native-English-Speaker (accessed April 8, 2008); Sondra Thiederman, "Language Barriers: Bridging the Gap," www.thiederman.com/articles_detail.php?id=39 (accessed April 8, 2008); and Magellan Health Services, "Communicating with Non-native Speakers," www.magellanassist.com/mem/library/default.asp?TopicId=95&CategoryId=0&ArticleId=5 (accessed April 8, 2008).

Communication Channels

Managers have a choice of many channels through which to communicate. A manager may discuss a problem face-to-face, make a telephone call, use text messaging, send an email, write a memo or letter, or post an entry to a company blog, depending on the nature of the message. Research has attempted to explain how managers select communication channels to enhance communication effectiveness.[10] The research has found that channels differ in their capacity to convey information. Just as a pipeline's physical characteristics limit the kind and amount of liquid that can be pumped through it, a communication channel's physical characteristics limit the kind and amount of information that can be conveyed through it. The channels available to managers can be classified into a hierarchy based on information richness.

2

The Hierarchy of Channel Richness **Channel richness** is the amount of information that can be transmitted during a communication episode. The hierarchy of channel richness is illustrated in Exhibit 13.3. The capacity of an information channel is influenced by three characteristics: (1) the ability to handle multiple cues simultaneously; (2) the ability to facilitate rapid, two-way feedback; and (3) the ability to establish a personal focus for the communication. Face-to-face discussion is the richest medium, because it permits direct experience, multiple information cues, immediate feedback, and personal focus. Face-to-face discussions facilitate the assimilation of broad cues and deep, emotional understanding of the situation. Telephone conversations are next in the richness hierarchy. Although eye contact, posture, and other body language cues are missing, the human voice can still carry a tremendous amount of emotional information.

Electronic messaging, such email, instant messaging, and text messaging, is increasingly being used for messages that were once handled face-to-face or by telephone. However, in a survey by researchers at The Ohio State University, most respondents said they preferred the telephone or face-to-face conversation for communicating difficult news, giving advice, or expressing affection.[11] Because email messages lack both visual and verbal cues and don't allow for interaction and feedback, messages can sometimes be misunderstood. Using email to discuss disputes, for example, can lead to an escalation rather than a resolution of conflict.[12] "You should never engage in a disagreement electronically," says Don G. Lents, the chairman of Bryan Cave, an international law firm. "I tell our young lawyers, if you think you are going to have a difficult interaction with a colleague or a client, do it face-to-face so you can read the body language and other social signals."[13] Instant messaging and text messaging alleviate the problem of miscommunication to some extent by allowing for immediate feedback. **Instant messaging** (IM) allows users to see who is connected to a network and share shorthand messages or documents with them instantly. A growing number of managers are using IM, indicating that it helps people get responses faster and collaborate more smoothly.[14] Overreliance on email and IM can damage company communications because people stop talking to one another in a rich way that builds solid interpersonal relationships. However, some research indicates that electronic messaging can enable reasonably rich communication if the technology is used appropriately.[15] Organizations are also using videoconferencing that offers video capabilities to provide visual cues and greater channel richness.

13.3 **EXHIBIT**

A Continuum of Channel Richness

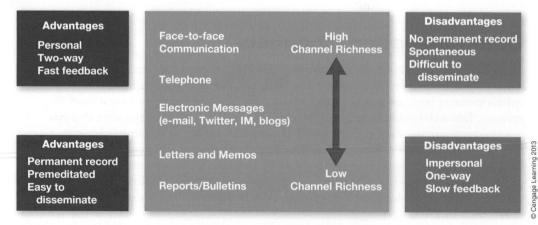

Advantages
Personal
Two-way
Fast feedback

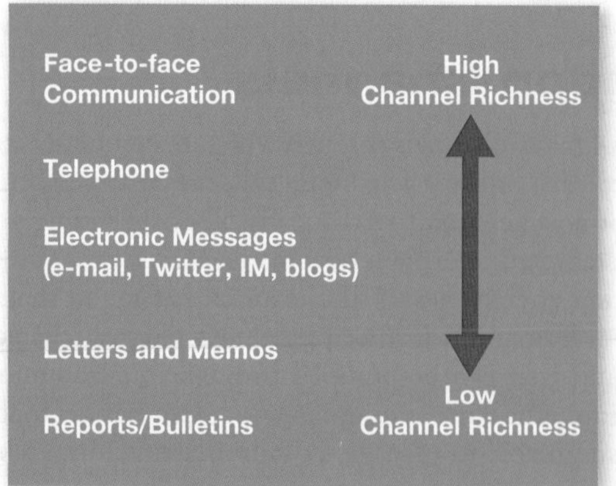

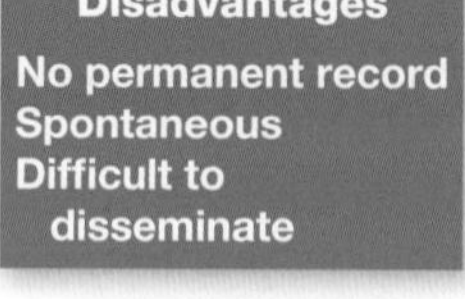

Advantages
Permanent record
Premeditated
Easy to disseminate

Disadvantages
Impersonal
One-way
Slow feedback

Still lower on the hierarchy of channel richness are written letters and memos. Written communication can be personally focused, but it conveys only the cues written on paper and is slower to provide feedback. Impersonal written media, including fliers, bulletins, and standard computer reports, are the lowest in richness. These channels are not focused on a single receiver, use limited information cues, and do not permit feedback.

Selecting the Appropriate Channel It is important for managers to understand that each communication channel has advantages and disadvantages and that each can be an effective means of communication in the appropriate circumstances.[16] Channel selection depends on whether the message is routine or nonroutine. *Nonroutine messages* typically are ambiguous, concern novel events, and involve great potential for misunderstanding. They often are characterized by time pressure and surprise. Managers can communicate nonroutine messages effectively by selecting rich channels. *Routine* messages are simple and straightforward. They convey data or statistics or simply put into words what managers already agree on and understand. Routine messages can be efficiently communicated through a channel lower in richness, such as a memo, email, IM, or Twitter. Written communications should be used when the communication is official and a permanent record is required.[17]

Brian Smith Photography

ConceptConnection

In the past, Kroma Makeup mailed out 200 sample kits of its custom-blended cosmetics every year, each one costing up to $200. Only about 10 percent of the recipients ever placed an order. Now, CEO Chris Tillet (pictured here with founder and wife Lee) sets up a desktop videoconference with potential customers; it includes a customized sales pitch and ample opportunity for two-way communication. The videoconference's **high degree of channel richness** allows Tillet to gauge the prospect's interest by observing **nonverbal cues**, such as facial expressions. Only if prospects appear interested does Tillet offer them a sample kit. Nearly every kit mailed results in a sale.

Managers at Innovative Beverage chose social networking and microblogging service Twitter as the preferred communication channel to send a routine message to customers following a customer-service glitch. When the company's drankbeverage.com site crashed after a surge of traffic following a segment on Fox News, Innovative Beverage quickly sent a "tweet" to consumers explaining that the company was working to resolve the problem. Peter Bianchi, Innovative's chief executive, says the site's 12-hour crash didn't appear to cause any lasting damage, and online sales peaked the day following the crash. "Twitter gave us an up-to-the-minute ability to take what would normally be a crisis situation and make it just another event," he said.[18]

The key is to select a channel to fit the message. During a major acquisition, one firm decided to send top executives to all major work sites of the acquired company, where most of the workers met the managers in person, heard about their plans for the company, and had a chance to ask questions. The results were well worth the time and expense of the personal face-to-face meetings because the acquired workforce saw their new managers as understanding, open, and willing to listen.[19] Communicating their nonroutine message about the acquisition in person prevented damaging rumors and misunderstandings. The choice of a communication channel can also convey a symbolic meaning to the receiver; in a sense, the medium becomes the message. The firm's decision to communicate face-to-face with the acquired workforce signaled to employees that managers cared about them as individuals.

Communicating to Persuade and Influence Others

3

Communication is not just for conveying information but also to persuade and influence people. Although communication skills have always been important to managers, the ability to persuade and influence others is even more critical today. Businesses are run largely by cross-functional teams that are actively involved in making decisions. Issuing directives is no longer an appropriate or effective way to get things done.[20]

To persuade and influence, managers have to communicate frequently and easily with others. Yet some people find interpersonal communication experiences unrewarding or difficult and thus tend to avoid situations where communication is required. The term **communication apprehension** describes this avoidance behavior and is defined as "an individual's level of fear or anxiety associated with either real or anticipated communication." With training and practice, managers can overcome their communication apprehension and become more effective communicators.

Effective persuasion doesn't mean telling people what you want them to do; instead, it involves listening, learning about others' interests and needs, and leading people to a shared solution.[21] Managers who forget that communication means *sharing*, as described earlier, aren't likely to be as effective at influencing or persuading others, as the founder and president of the executive coaching firm Valuedance learned the hard way.

VALUEDANCE

When Susan Cramm was asked by a client to help persuade the client's boss to support an initiative she wanted to launch, Cramm readily agreed. They scheduled a meeting with the boss, held a series of planning sessions where the two discussed the current situation at the client's firm, weighed the options, and decided on the best approach for launching the initiative. Filled with enthusiasm and armed with a PowerPoint presentation, Cramm was sure the client's boss would see things their way.

An agonizing 15 minutes later, she was out the door, PowerPoint presentation and all, having just had a lesson about the art of persuasion. What went wrong? Cramm had focused on the hard, rational matters and ignored the soft skills of relationship building, listening, and negotiating that are so crucial to persuading others. "Never did we consider the boss's views," Cramm said later about the planning sessions she and her client held to prepare for the meeting. "Like founding members of the 'it's all about me' club, we fell upon our swords, believing that our impeccable logic, persistence, and enthusiasm would carry the day."

With that approach, the meeting was over before it even began. The formal presentation shut down communications because it implied that Cramm had all the answers and the boss was just there to listen and agree.[22]

TAKE ACTION

Becoming an effective communicator may require you to overcome your fears and anxiety when communicating. Go to the Self-Learning, on pages 546–547, to assess your communication apprehension in a variety of communication settings.

As this example shows, people stop listening to someone when that individual isn't listening to them. By failing to show interest in and respect for the boss's point of view, Cramm and her client lost the boss's interest from the beginning, no matter how suitable the ideas they were presenting. To effectively influence and persuade others, managers have to show they care about how the other person feels. Persuasion requires tapping into people's emotions, which can be done only on a personal, rather than a rational, impersonal, level.

Gender Differences in Communication

To improve the effectiveness of workplace communication, managers should be aware of various factors that influence how people communicate. One important consideration is gender roles, the learned behaviors associated with being male or female. Deborah Tannen, author of *You Just Don't Understand: Women and Men in Conversation,* has spent three decades studying gender differences in communication. She found that men's talk tends to focus on hierarchy—competition for relative power—whereas women's tends to focus on connection—relative closeness or distance. Tannen says that a woman and a man may walk away from the same conversation asking different questions. He might wonder, *"Did that talk put me in a one-up or one-down position?"* whereas she might wonder, *"Did that talk bring us closer or push us farther apart?"*[23]

For most women, although certainly not all, talking means *conversation* and is primarily a language of rapport, a way to establish connections and negotiate relationships. Women use their unique conversational style to show involvement, connection, and participation, such as by seeking similarities and matching experiences with others. They tend to interrupt less than men do and work hard to keep a conversation going. For most men, on the other hand, talk is primarily a means to preserve independence and negotiate and maintain status in a hierarchy. Men tend to use verbal language to exhibit knowledge and skill, such as by telling stories, joking, or passing on information.[24] But all conversations and all relationships reflect a combination of hierarchy and connection. The two are not mutually exclusive but inextricably intertwined. All of us aspire to be powerful, and we all want to connect with others. Women's and men's conversational styles are simply different ways of reaching the same goals.[25]

Interestingly, some male managers may be shifting to a more female-oriented communication style in today's difficult economic environment because women's approach to leadership and communication may be more suited to inspiring employees and helping people pull together toward goals during difficult times. A report from McKinsey & Company, "Leadership Through the Crisis and After," notes that the kinds of behaviors executives say will help their companies through the crisis are most often practiced by female managers.[26] As discussed in Chapter 9, women typically score higher than men on abilities such as motivating others, fostering communication, and listening, abilities that are more important than ever when organizations are going through a tough time like a recession. With surveys reflecting that employee dissatisfaction is growing and confidence in leaders has plummeted to a ten-year low, both male and female managers are emphasizing more interactive communication to restore credibility and reinvigorate demoralized employees.

Grasping the different communication styles of men and women may help managers maximize every employee's talents and encourage both men and women to contribute more fully to the organization.

Nonverbal Communication

Managers should be aware that their body language—facial expressions, gestures, touch, and use of space—can communicate a range of messages, from enthusiasm, warmth, and confidence, to arrogance, indifference, and displeasure.[27] **Nonverbal communication** refers to messages sent through human actions and behaviors rather than through words.[28] Managers are watched, and their behavior, appearance, actions, and attitudes are symbolic of what they value and expect of others.

Most of us have heard the saying that "actions speak louder than words." Indeed, we communicate without words all the time, whether we realize it or not. Most managers are astonished to learn that words themselves carry little meaning. A significant portion of the shared understanding from communication comes from the nonverbal messages of facial expression, voice, mannerisms, posture, and dress. Consider the following example. During an interview about Facebook's new privacy policy with reporters from *The Wall Street Journal,* Mark Zuckerberg, Facebook's 26-year-old chief executive, sweated profusely and appeared shaken. As he defended the company's policy, so much sweat was dripping from his forehead that the interviewer suggested he take off his hoodie. Although his verbal responses provided plausible explanations for the new privacy policy, Zuckerberg's nonverbal cues suggested he was unprepared and lacked confidence in the new direction.[29]

Nonverbal communication occurs mostly face-to-face. One researcher found three sources of communication cues during face-to-face communication: the *verbal*, which are the actual spoken words; the *vocal*, which include the pitch, tone, and timbre of a person's voice; and *facial expressions*. According to this study, the relative weights of these three factors in message interpretation are as follows: verbal impact, 7 percent; vocal impact, 38 percent; and facial impact, 55 percent.[30] To some extent, we are all natural *face readers*, but facial expressions can be misinterpreted, suggesting that managers need to ask questions to make sure they're getting the right message. Managers can hone their skills at reading facial expressions and improve their ability to connect with and influence followers. Studies indicate that managers who seem responsive to the unspoken emotions of employees are more effective and successful in the workplace.[31]

Managers should take care to align their facial expressions and body language to support an intended message. When nonverbal signals contradict a manager's words, people become confused and may discount what is being said and believe the body language instead.[32] One manager who is a master at using body language to convey credibility and confidence is Steve Jobs of Apple. When he unveiled the iPhone at MacWorld 2007, Jobs fully faced the audience, made eye contact, kept his movements relaxed and natural, and stood tall. Through his body language, he communicated credibility, commitment, and honesty.[33]

Listening

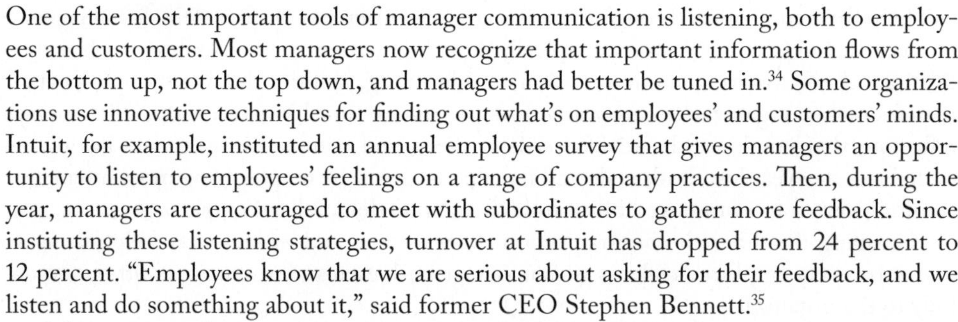

One of the most important tools of manager communication is listening, both to employees and customers. Most managers now recognize that important information flows from the bottom up, not the top down, and managers had better be tuned in.[34] Some organizations use innovative techniques for finding out what's on employees' and customers' minds. Intuit, for example, instituted an annual employee survey that gives managers an opportunity to listen to employees' feelings on a range of company practices. Then, during the year, managers are encouraged to meet with subordinates to gather more feedback. Since instituting these listening strategies, turnover at Intuit has dropped from 24 percent to 12 percent. "Employees know that we are serious about asking for their feedback, and we listen and do something about it," said former CEO Stephen Bennett.[35]

Managers are also tapping into the interactive nature of blogs to stay in touch with employees and customers. *Blogs*, running Web logs that allow people to post opinions, ideas, and information, provide a low-cost, always-fresh, real-time link between organizations and customers, employees, the media, and investors.[36] One estimate is that 16 percent of *Fortune* 500 companies use blogs to keep in touch with stakeholders.[37] Blogs give managers another way to get valuable feedback. Done correctly, listening is a vital link in the communication process, shown in Exhibit 13.2.

As a new manager, your social disposition gives others glimpses into your managerial style. Are you friendly and approachable? A good listener? Goal-oriented? Take the New Manager Self-Test, on page 531, to learn more about your social disposition.

Listening involves the skill of grasping both facts and feelings to interpret a message's genuine meaning. Only then can the manager provide the appropriate response. Listening requires attention, energy, and skill. Although about 75 percent of effective communication is listening, most people spend only 30 to 40 percent of their time listening, which leads to many communication errors.[38] One of the secrets of highly successful salespeople is that they spend 60 to 70 percent of a sales call letting the customer talk.[39] However, listening involves much more than just not talking. Many people do not know how to listen effectively. They concentrate on formulating what they are going to say next rather than on what is being said to them. Our listening efficiency, as measured by the amount of material understood and remembered by subjects 48 hours after listening to a 10-minute message, is, on average, no better than 25 percent.[40]

New Manager Self-Test

What Is Your Social Disposition?

How do you come across to others? What is your social disposition? To find out, please mark whether each item below is Mostly True or Mostly False for you.

	MOSTLY TRUE <<<	>>> MOSTLY FALSE
1. I want to climb the corporate ladder as high as I can.	_____	_____
2. I confront people when I sense a conflict.	_____	_____
3. People consider me cooperative and easy to work with.	_____	_____
4. I like to get right to the point.	_____	_____
5. I make quick decisions, usually without consulting others.	_____	_____
6. I make a real effort to understand other peoples' point of view.	_____	_____
7. I enjoy competing and winning.	_____	_____
8. I like to get to the bottom line.	_____	_____
9. I take a personal interest in people.	_____	_____

See It Online

Scoring and Interpretation: Give yourself 1 point for items 1, 2, 4, 5, 7, and 8 that you marked Mostly True and one point for items 3, 6, and 9 that you marked Mostly False. The questions pertain to whether your social disposition is one of being focused and driven toward personal success or whether you tend to come across as affable and friendly. If you scored 7 or higher, you are probably ambitious and goal oriented. A score of 3 or less would mean that you probably are empathic, ask questions, and enjoy collaborating with others.

A person with a driven disposition may be promoted to manager, but may not be a good listener, may fail to pick up on body language, or may not take time to engage in dialogue. A manager has to get things done through other people, and it helps to slow down, listen, build relationships, and take the time to communicate. Too much focus on your personal achievement may come across as uncaring. A new manager with a friendly disposition is often a good listener, makes inquiries, and experiences fewer communication mistakes.

SOURCE: Based on "Social Styles," in Paula J. Caproni, *Management Skills for Everyday Life: The Practical Coach*, 2nd ed. (Upper Saddle River, NJ: Prentice-Hall, 2005), pp. 200–203.

What constitutes good listening? Exhibit 13.4 gives ten keys to effective listening and illustrates a number of ways to distinguish a bad listener from a good listener. A good listener finds areas of interest, is flexible, works hard at listening, and uses thought speed to mentally summarize, weigh, and anticipate what the speaker says. Good listening means shifting from thinking about self to empathizing with the other person and thus requires a high degree of emotional intelligence, as described in Chapter 10.

13.4 EXHIBIT
Ten Keys to Effective Listening

Keys to Effective Listening	Poor Listener	Good Listener
1. Listen actively.	Is passive, laid back	Asks questions, paraphrases what is said
2. Find areas of interest.	Tunes out dry subjects	Looks for new learning
3. Resist distractions.	Is easily distracted; answers phone or sends text messages	Gives full attention, fights distractions, maintains concentration
4. Capitalize on the fact that thought is faster.	Tends to daydream	Mentally summarizes; weighs the evidence
5. Be responsive.	Avoids eye contact; is minimally involved	Nods and shows interest
6. Judge content, not delivery.	Tunes out if delivery is poor	Judges content; skips over delivery errors
7. Avoid premature judgment.	Has preconceptions	Does not judge until comprehension is complete
8. Listen for ideas.	Listens for facts	Listens to central themes
9. Work at listening.	Shows no energy; forgets what the speaker says	Works hard; exhibits active body state and eye contact
10. Exercise one's mind.	Resists difficult material in favor of light, recreational material	Uses heavier material as exercise for the mind

SOURCES: Adapted from Diann Daniel, "Seven Deadly Sins of (Not) Listening," http://www.cio.com/article/print/134801 (accessed April 8, 2008); Sherman K. Okum, "How to Be a Better Listener," *Nation's Business* (August 1975): 62; and Philip Morgan and Kent Baker, "Building a Professional Image: Improving Listening Behavior," *Supervisory Management* (November 1985): 34–38.

- **Channel richness** refers to the amount of information that can be transmitted during a communication episode.
- **Instant messaging** is electronic communication that allows users to see who is connected to a network and share information instantly.
- The ability to persuade others to behave in ways that help accomplish the vision and goals is crucial to good management.
- **Communication apprehension** is an individual's level of fear or anxiety associated with interpersonal communications.
- Gender roles, the learned behaviors associated with being male or female, directly influence communication.
- **Nonverbal communication** is communication that is transmitted through actions and behaviors rather than through words.
- **Listening** is the skill of receiving messages to accurately grasp facts and feelings to interpret the genuine meaning.

Organizational Communication

Another aspect of management communication concerns the organization as a whole. Organization-wide communications typically flow in three directions—downward, upward, and horizontally. Managers are responsible for establishing and maintaining formal channels of communication in these three directions. Managers also use informal channels, which means they get out of their offices and mingle with employees.

Formal Communication Channels

Formal communication channels are those that flow within the chain of command or task responsibility defined by the organization. The three formal channels and the types of information conveyed in each are illustrated in Exhibit 13.5.[41] Downward and upward communications are the primary forms of communication used in most traditional, vertically organized companies. However, many of today's organizations emphasize horizontal communication, with people continuously sharing information across departments and levels.

Electronic communication such as email and instant messaging have made it easier than ever for information to flow in all directions. For example, the U.S. Army uses technology to rapidly transmit communications about weather conditions and the latest intelligence on the insurgency to lieutenants in the field in Afghanistan and Iraq. Similarly, the U.S. Navy uses instant messaging to communicate within ships, across navy divisions, and even back to the Pentagon in Washington. "Instant messaging has allowed us to keep our crew members on the same page at the same time," says Lt. Cmdr. Mike Houston, who oversees the navy's communications program. "Lives are at stake in real time, and we're seeing a new level of communication and readiness."[42]

Downward Communication The most familiar and obvious flow of formal communication, **downward communication**, refers to the messages and information sent from top management to subordinates in a downward direction. Managers can communicate downward to employees in many ways. Some of the most common are through speeches, videos, blogs, podcasts, and company intranets.

EXHIBIT 13.5

Downward, Upward, and Horizontal Communication in Organizations

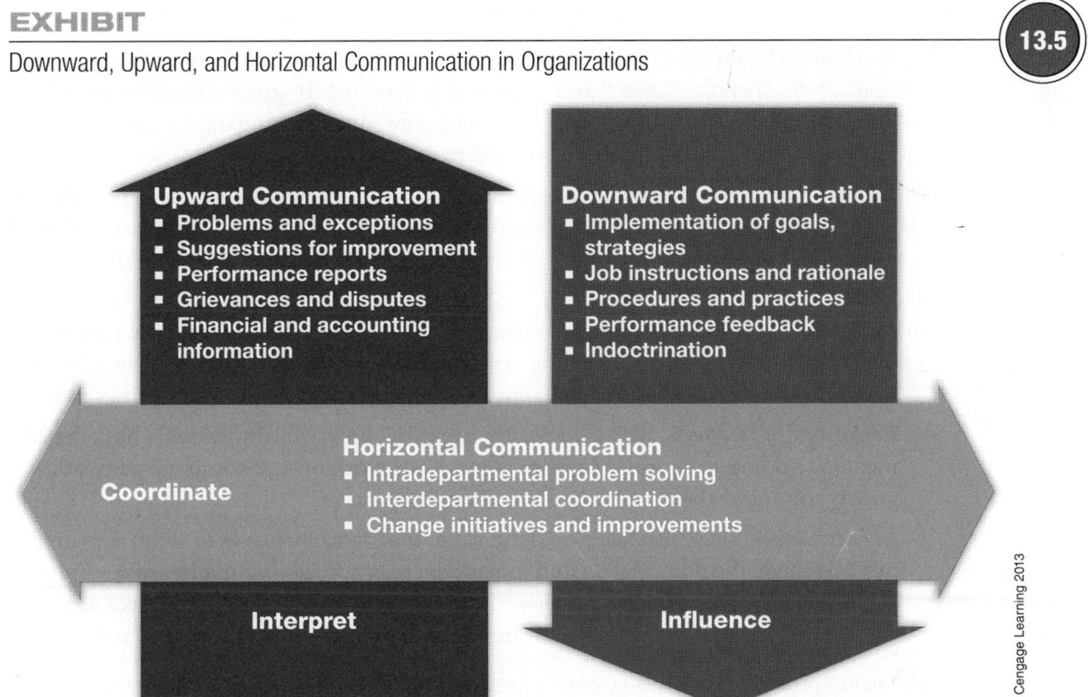

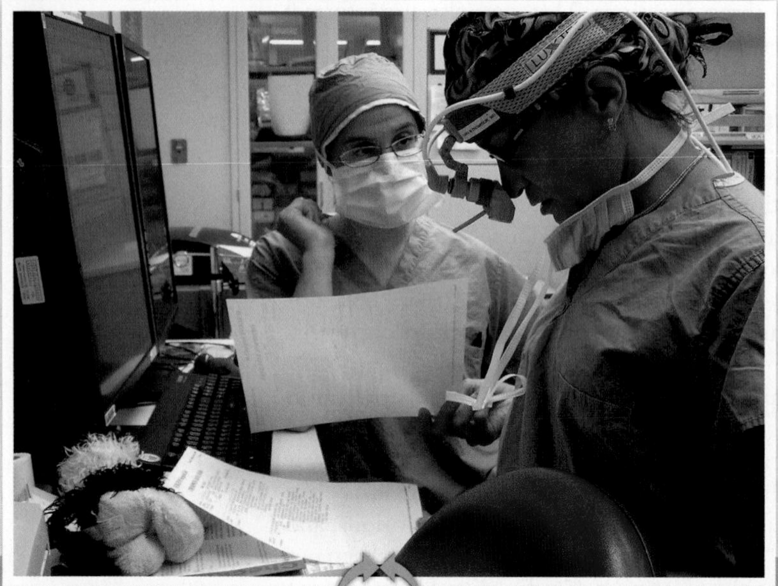

Photo by Lorna Benson, Minnesota Public Radio.org

ConceptConnection

When the Mayo Clinic formulated a strategic plan for the world-famous medical center, in 2007, the communications department experimented with a new way to facilitate **upward and downward communications**. They created "Let's Talk," an internal blog that allowed managers to use videos and blog posts to explain the plan. It also gave employees (such as the operating room staff pictured) a chance to give feedback. "The response was immediate and powerful," says manager Linda Donlin. By the time the plan was updated in 2010, using a Web site and blog to communicate with employees was a foregone conclusion.

It is impossible for managers to communicate with employees about everything that goes on in the organization, so they have to make choices about the important information to communicate.[43] Unfortunately, many U.S. managers could do a better job of effective downward communication. The results of one survey found that employees want open and honest communication about both the good and the bad aspects of the organization's performance. But when asked to rate their company's communication effectiveness on a scale of 0 to 100, the survey respondents' score averaged 69. In addition, a study of 1,500 managers, mostly at first and second management levels, found that 84 percent of these leaders perceive communication as one of their most important tasks, yet only 38 percent believe they have adequate communication skills.[44]

Managers can do a better job of downward communication by focusing on specific areas that require regular communication. Downward communication usually encompasses these five topics:

1. ***Goals and strategies.*** Communicating new strategies and goals provides information about specific targets and expected behaviors. It gives direction for lower levels of the organization. *Example:* "The new quality campaign is for real. We must improve product quality if we are to survive."
2. ***Job instructions and rationale.*** These directives indicate how to do a specific task and how the job relates to other organizational activities. *Example:* "Purchasing should order the bricks now so the work crew can begin construction of the building in two weeks."
3. ***Procedures and practices.*** These messages define the organization's policies, rules, regulations, benefits, and structural arrangements. *Example:* "After your first 90 days of employment, you are eligible to enroll in our company-sponsored savings plan."
4. ***Performance feedback.*** These messages appraise how well individuals and departments are doing their jobs. *Example:* "Joe, your work on the computer network has greatly improved the efficiency of our ordering process."
5. ***Indoctrination.*** These messages are designed to motivate employees to adopt the company's mission and cultural values and to participate in special ceremonies, such as picnics and United Way campaigns. *Example:* "The company thinks of its employees as family and would like to invite everyone to attend the annual picnic and fair on March 3."

A major problem with downward communication is *drop off*, the distortion or loss of message content. Although formal communications are a powerful way to reach all employees, much information gets lost—25 percent or so each time a message is passed from one person to the next. In addition, the message can be distorted if it travels a great distance from its originating source to the ultimate receiver. A tragic example is the following historical case.

> A reporter was present at a hamlet burned down by the U.S. Army 1st Air Cavalry Division in 1967. Investigations showed that the order from the division headquarters to the brigade was: "On no occasion must hamlets be burned down."
>
> The brigade radioed the battalion: "Do not burn down any hamlets unless you are absolutely convinced that the Viet Cong are in them."
>
> The battalion radioed the infantry company at the scene: "If you think there are any Viet Cong in the hamlet, burn it down."
>
> The company commander ordered his troops: "Burn down that hamlet."[45]

Information drop off cannot be completely avoided, but the techniques described in the previous sections can reduce it substantially. Using the right communication channel, consistency between verbal and nonverbal messages, and active listening can maintain communication accuracy as it moves down the organization.

Upward Communication Formal **upward communication** includes messages that flow from the lower to the higher levels in the organization's hierarchy. Most organizations take pains to build in healthy channels for upward communication. Employees need to air grievances, report progress, and provide feedback on management initiatives. Coupling a healthy flow of upward and downward communication ensures that the communication circuit between managers and employees is complete.[46] Five types of information communicated upward are the following:

1. ***Problems and exceptions.*** These messages describe serious problems with and exceptions to routine performance to make senior managers aware of difficulties. *Example:* "The printer has been out of operation for two days, and it will be at least a week before a new one arrives."
2. ***Suggestions for improvement.*** These messages are ideas for improving task-related procedures to increase quality or efficiency. *Example:* "I think we should eliminate step 2 in the audit procedure because it takes a lot of time and produces no results."
3. ***Performance reports.*** These messages include periodic reports that inform management how individuals and departments are performing. *Example:* "We completed the audit report for Smith & Smith on schedule but are one week behind on the Jackson report."
4. ***Grievances and disputes.*** These messages are employee complaints and conflicts that travel up the hierarchy for a hearing and possible resolution. *Example:* "The manager of operations research cannot get the cooperation of the Lincoln plant for the study of machine utilization."
5. ***Financial and accounting information.*** These messages pertain to costs, accounts receivable, sales volume, anticipated profits, return on investment, and other matters of interest to senior managers. *Example:* "Costs are 2 percent over budget, but sales are 10 percent ahead of target, so the profit picture for the third quarter is excellent."

You can polish your professional listening skills by completing the Action Learning on pages 548–549.

Smart managers make a serious effort to facilitate upward communication. For example, Mike Hall, CEO of Borrego Solar Systems, found an effective way to encourage his introverted engineers to speak up and submit ideas for improving the business. To get his staff to offer feedback and suggestions, Hall organized an internal contest he called the Innovation Challenge. All employees were encouraged to submit ideas about improving the business using the company intranet. Once all of the ideas were submitted, employees voted for their favorite idea, and the winner won $500 in cash. Nearly all of Borrego's employees participated in the contest. "We've been able to generate a lot of great ideas by tapping everyone's brains," Hall says.[47]

Horizontal Communication **Horizontal communication** is the lateral or diagonal exchange of messages among peers or coworkers. It may occur within or across departments. The purpose of horizontal communication is not only to inform but also to request support and coordinate activities. Horizontal communication falls into one of three categories:

1. ***Intradepartmental problem solving.*** These messages take place among members of the same department and concern task accomplishment. *Example:* "Kelly, can you help us figure out how to complete this medical expense report form?"
2. ***Interdepartmental coordination.*** Interdepartmental messages facilitate the accomplishment of joint projects or tasks. *Example:* "Bob, please contact marketing and production and arrange a meeting to discuss the specifications for the new subassembly. It looks like we might not be able to meet their requirements."
3. ***Change initiatives and improvements.*** These messages are designed to share information among teams and departments that can help the organization change, grow, and improve. *Example:* "We are streamlining the company travel procedures and would like to discuss them with your department." One organization that uses open communication to create positive change is Disney/Pixar, as described in the Spotlight on Skills titled Pixar and Disney.

Recall from Chapter 7 that many organizations build in horizontal communications in the form of task forces, committees, or even a matrix or horizontal structure to encourage coordination. At Chicago's Northwestern Memorial Hospital, two doctors created

SPOTLIGHT ON SKILLS

Pixar and Disney

How do you develop horizontal communication that allows creativity to be fostered? In mergers, this can be especially complex. When Disney bought Pixar, the fear was that the communication style and culture of Disney, which brought such box office bombs as "Chicken Little" and "Home on the Range," would prevail. The danger was that Pixar's immense creativity would be squelched by the button-down style of Disney. Instead, what the new entity produced was more brilliant than even Pixar had managed before. New movies included *Toy Story 3* as well as *Ratatouille* and *Wall-E.*

What was the secret? Pixar executive John Lasseter says it's not only about risk taking and management, but, perhaps more crucially, "It is about open communication at all times from top to bottom." In addition, Lasseter says it required the new company to use that communication to behave in the opposite way of any other company. Most studios want to do the safe thing, what they think will definitely work. "They want to guarantee success out there where there's a product, a movie. . . . And that's why Hollywood makes how many movies a year, and how many are actually good? Right?" asks Lasseter. It meant Lasseter had to fight against the numbers guys, who wanted to grind out one sequel after another. And if *Ratatouille* and *Wall-E* had been box office flops, Lasseter would not have the freedom he now has. Lucky for him and for us, Pixar succeed in those movies and was able to bring us *Up.*

SOURCE: James R. Stewart, "A Collision of Creativity and Cash, *The New York Times,* July 2, 2011, B1, B7.

a horizontal task force to reduce the incidence of hospital-borne infections. The infection epidemic that kills nearly 100,000 people a year is growing worse worldwide, but Northwestern reversed the trend by breaking down communication barriers. Infectious-disease specialists Lance Peterson and Gary Noskin launched a regular Monday morning meeting involving doctors and nurses, lab technicians, pharmacists, computer technicians, admissions representatives, and even the maintenance staff. The enhanced communication paid off. Over a three-year period, Northwestern's rate of hospital-borne infections plunged 22 percent and was roughly half the national average.[48]

Team Communication Channels

Team communication, a special form of horizontal communication, presents unique challenges for the manager. One important decision about the formation of a team is choosing the team's method of communicating, which influences both team performance and employee satisfaction.

Research into team communication has focused on two characteristics: the extent to which team communications are centralized and the nature of the team's task.[49] The relationship between these characteristics is illustrated in Exhibit 13.6. In a **centralized network**, team members must communicate through one individual to solve problems or make decisions. Centralized communication can be effective for large teams because it limits the number of people involved in decision making. The result is a faster decision that involves fewer people.[50] In a **decentralized network**, individuals can communicate freely with other team members. Members process information equally among themselves until all agree on a decision.[51]

In laboratory experiments, centralized communication networks achieved faster solutions for simple problems. Members could simply pass relevant information to a central person for a decision. Decentralized communications were slower for simple problems because information was passed among individuals until someone finally put the pieces together and solved the problem. However, for more complex problems, the decentralized communication network was faster. Because all necessary information was not restricted to one person, a pooling of information through widespread communications

EXHIBIT 13.6

Team Communication Networks

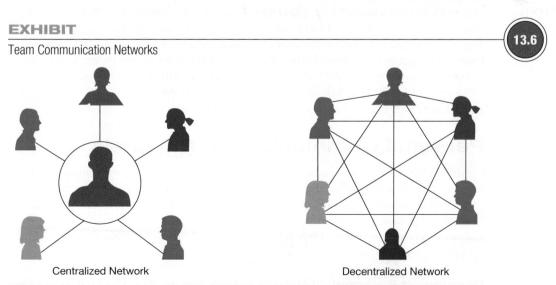

Centralized Network

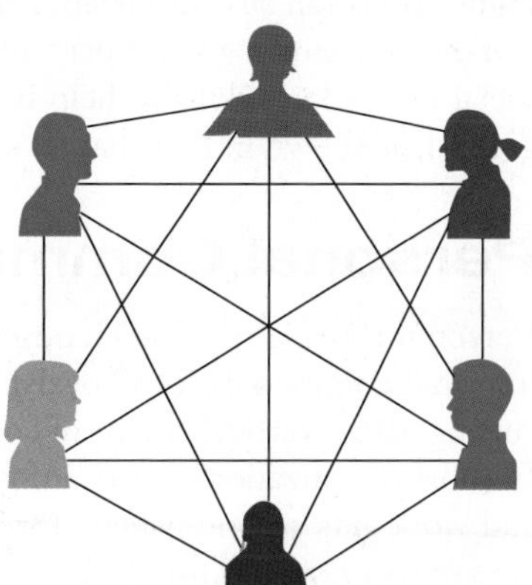

Decentralized Network

SOURCE: Joel Spolsky, "A Little Less Conversation," *Inc.* (February 2010): 28–29. Copyright 2010 by Mansueto Ventures LLC. Reproduced with permission of Mansueto Ventures LLC.

BENCHMARKING

U.S. Air Force

Can you run a war like a chat room? The U.S. Airforce is showing not only that you can, but now it's getting to be that you must. Once upon a time, military analysts were back-room technicians, tending towards the older side. The new generation are twenty-somethings, weaned on interactive games and computers, such as 25-year-old First Lieutenant Jamie Christopher, who used to make friends though Instant Messages and Facebook. Now she uses her social networking skills to hunt insurgents in Afghanistan. And she saves American lives. She and more than 4,000 other analysts (2,000 more will be added soon) study data from spy planes and drones to determine conditions, then communicate information to the troops on the ground. "2 poss children in fov," flashed her team to some Marines as they lined up for an air strike, letting them know there were possible innocents in the drone's view.

The analysts also study video feeds, scan images and listen to enemy conversations. In February of 2010, the team managed to alert troops to watch for about 300 roadside bombs. In one instance, analysts watched as a convoy came to a sudden stop, 500 feet from a bomb. Success. Gunnery Sergeant Sean M. Smothers likes the effectiveness of this new model. "To me, this whole operation was like a template for what we should be doing in the future," he says. Senior airmen will talk to the younger analysts, sometimes with important information and sometimes just to stay in touch. They even friend one another on Facebook. The networking has been so productive that higher-level commanders are going around normal military hierarchy and giving more control to the analysts. "If you want to act quickly," says US Air Force Intelligence leader Lt. Col. Jason M. Brown, "you've got to flatten things out and engage in the lowest possible levels."

SOURCE: Christopher Drew, "Military Taps Social Networking Skills"/The War Chatroom, *The New York Times*, June 8, 2010.

provided greater input into the decision. Similarly, the accuracy of problem solving was related to problem complexity. The centralized networks made fewer errors on simple problems but more errors on complex ones. Decentralized networks were less accurate for simple problems but more accurate for complex ones.[52]

The implication for organizations is as follows: In a highly competitive global environment, organizations typically use teams to deal with complex problems. When team activities are complex and difficult, all members should share information in a decentralized structure to solve problems. Teams need a free flow of communication in all directions.[53] Teams that perform routine tasks spend less time processing information, and thus communications can be centralized. Data can be channeled to a supervisor for decisions, freeing workers to spend a greater percentage of time on task activities. The U.S. military is using social networking skills to help its teams of analysts who work closely with troops on the ground, as shown in this chapter's Benchmarking box.

Personal Communication Channels

Personal communication channels exist outside the formally authorized channels. These informal communications coexist with formal channels but may skip hierarchical levels, cutting across vertical chains of command to connect virtually anyone in the organization. In most organizations, these informal channels are the primary way information spreads and work gets accomplished. Three important types of personal communication channels are *personal networks*, the *grapevine, and written communication.*

Developing Personal Communication Networks **Personal networking** refers to the acquisition and cultivation of personal relationships that cross departmental, hierarchical, and even organizational boundaries.[54] Successful managers consciously develop personal communication networks and encourage others to do so. In a communication network, people share information across boundaries and reach out to anyone who can further the goals of the team and organization. Exhibit 13.7 illustrates a communication network. Some people are central to the network while others play only a peripheral role. The key is that relationships are built across functional and hierarchical boundaries.

The value of personal networks for managers is that people who have more contacts have greater influence in the organization and get more accomplished. For example, in Exhibit 13.7, Sharon has a well-developed personal communication network, sharing information and assistance with many people across the marketing, manufacturing, and engineering departments. Contrast Sharon's contacts with those of Mike or Jasmine. Who do you think is likely to have greater access to resources and more influence in the organization? Here are a few tips from one expert networker for building a personal communication network:[55]

1. ***Build it before you need it.*** Smart managers don't wait until they need something to start building a network of personal relationships—by then, it's too late. Instead, they show genuine interest in others and develop honest connections.
2. ***Never eat lunch alone.*** People who excel at networking make an effort to be visible and connect with as many people as possible. Master networkers keep their social as well as business conference and event calendars full.
3. ***Make it win-win.*** Successful networking isn't just about getting what *you* want; it's also about making sure other people in the network get what *they* want.
4. ***Focus on diversity.*** The broader your base of contacts, the broader your range of influence. Build connections with people from as many different areas of interest as possible (both within and outside the organization).

Most of us know from personal experience that "who you know" sometimes counts for more than what you know. By cultivating a broad network of contacts, managers can significantly extend their influence and accomplish greater results.

EXHIBIT 13.7

An Organizational Communication Network

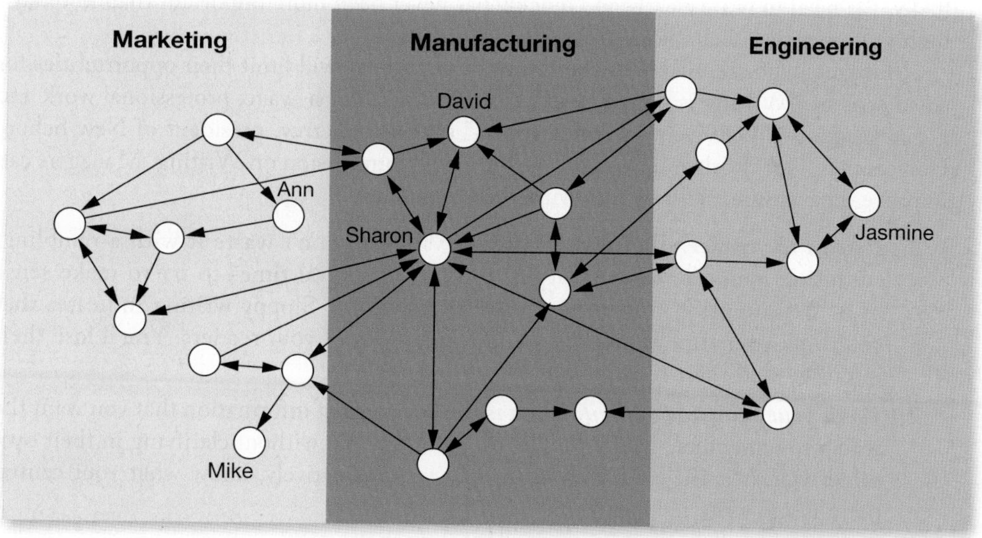

Marketing
Manufacturing
Engineering
David
Ann
Sharon
Jasmine
Mike

The Grapevine Although the word *gossip* has a negative connotation, it may actually be good for a company, especially during times of change, such as layoffs or downsizing. In fact, gossip can be an invaluable tool for managers. By paying attention to information from employees who are known for spreading office gossip, managers may be able to keep better tabs on what's happening in the workplace.[56] Gossip typically travels along the **grapevine**, an informal, person-to-person communication network that is not officially sanctioned by the organization.[57] The grapevine links employees in all directions, ranging from the CEO through middle management, support staff, and line employees. The grapevine will always exist in an organization, but it can become a dominant force when formal channels are closed. In such cases, the grapevine is actually a service because the information it provides helps makes sense of an unclear or uncertain situation. Employees use grapevine rumors to fill in information gaps and clarify management decisions. One estimate is that as much as 70 percent of all communication in a firm is carried out through its grapevine.[58] The grapevine tends to be more active during periods of change, excitement, anxiety, and sagging economic conditions. For example, a survey by professional employment services firm Randstad found that about half of all employees reported first hearing of major company changes through the grapevine.[59]

As a new manager, it is essential to build and nurture a personal communication network. Refer to the New Manager Self-Test on page 521 to determine the effectiveness of your networking skills.

Surprising aspects of the grapevine are its accuracy and its relevance to the organization. About 80 percent of grapevine communications pertain to business-related topics rather than personal gossip. Moreover, from 70 to 90 percent of the details passed through a grapevine are accurate.[60] Many managers would like the grapevine to be destroyed because they consider its rumors to be untrue, malicious, and harmful, which typically is not the case. Managers should be aware that almost five of every six important messages are carried to some extent by the grapevine rather than through official channels. In a survey of 22,000 shift workers in varied industries, 55 percent said they get most of their information via the grapevine.[61] Smart managers understand the company's grapevine. "If a leader has his ear to the ground, gossip can be a way for him to get a sense of what his employees are thinking or feeling," says Mitch Kusy, an organizational consultant, psychologist, and professor at Antioch University.[62] In all cases, but particularly in times of crisis, executives need to manage communications effectively so that the grapevine is not the only source of information.[63]

Written Communication Written communication skills are becoming increasingly important in today's collaborative workplace. "With the fast pace of today's electronic communications, one might think that the value of fundamental writing skills has diminished in the workplace," said Joseph M. Tucci, president and CEO of EMC Corporation. "Actually, the need to write clearly and quickly has never been more important than in today's highly competitive, technology-driven global economy."[64]

Managers who are unable to communicate in writing will limit their opportunities for advancement. "Writing is both a 'marker' of high-skill, high-wage, professional work and a 'gatekeeper' with clear equity implications," says Bob Kerrey, president of New School University in New York and chair of the National Commission on Writing. Managers can improve their writing skills by following these guidelines:[65]

1. ***Respect the reader.*** The reader's time is valuable; don't waste it with a rambling, confusing memo or email that has to be read several times to try to make sense of it. Pay attention to your grammar and spelling. Sloppy writing indicates that you think your time is more important than that of your readers. You'll lose their interest—and their respect.
2. ***Know your point and get to it.*** What is the key piece of information that you want the reader to remember? Many people just sit and write, without clarifying in their own mind what it is they're trying to say. To write effectively, know what your central point is and write to support it.

3. ***Write clearly rather than impressively.*** Don't use pretentious or inflated language, and avoid jargon. The goal of good writing for business is to be understood the first time through. State your message as simply and as clearly as possible.
4. ***Get a second opinion.*** When the communication is highly important, such as a formal memo to the department or organization, ask someone you consider to be a good writer to read it before you send it. Don't be too proud to take their advice. In all cases, read and revise the memo or email a second and third time before you hit the send button.

A former manager of communication services at consulting firm Arthur D. Little Inc. has estimated that around 30 percent of all business memos and emails are written simply to get clarification about an earlier written communication that didn't make sense to the reader.[66] By following these guidelines, you can get your message across the first time.

Remember This

- A communication channel that flows within the chain of command is called a **formal communication channel**.
- **Downward communication** refers to messages sent from top management down to subordinates; **upward communication** includes messages that flow from the lower to the higher levels in the organization's hierarchy.
- **Horizontal communication** is the lateral or diagonal exchange of messages among peers or coworkers and includes team communication.
- A **centralized network** is a team communication structure in which team members communicate through a single individual to solve problems or make decisions.
- A **decentralized network** is a team communication structure in which team members freely communicate with one another and arrive at decisions together.
- **Personal communication channels** exist outside formally authorized channels and include personal networks, the grapevine, and written communication.
- **Personal networking** refers to the acquisition and cultivation of personal relationships that cross departmental, hierarchical, and even organizational boundaries.
- The **grapevine** carries workplace gossip, a dominant force in organization communication when formal channels are closed.

Workplace Communication

Organizations with a high level of communication effectiveness develop strategies to manage crisis communication, use new communication technology, and create a climate of trust and openness.

Crisis Communication

A manager's skill at communicating becomes even more crucial during times of rapid change, uncertainty, or crisis. Over the past few years, the sheer number and scope of crises have made communication a more demanding job for managers. Consider the importance of communication in the success of Robert Dudley, appointed as CEO for BP in the midst of the 2010 oil spill crisis in the Gulf of Mexico. Dudley faced the massive task of helping BP survive the greatest environmental disaster in history, created when a rig drilling a well for BP exploded, killing 11 workers and causing hundreds of millions of gallons of oil to spew into the Gulf. Dudley entered his new role facing a myriad of challenges, all requiring superior communication skills: restoring trust among communities and the public, dealing with the costs and legal consequences of the oil spill, repairing damaged relationships with federal and state authorities, bolstering morale among BP employees, and winning back investors. His ability to communicate confidence, concern, and stability are critically important. "I can't think of any new chief executive of an oil company stepping into a more complicated situation," said Daniel Yergin, chairman of IHS Cambridge Energy Research Associates. "BP is going to be in a rebuilding mode, and the aftermath of the spill will go on for a long time."[67]

Managers can develop four primary skills for communicating in a crisis.[68]

- ***Stay calm, listen hard.*** Good crisis communicators don't allow themselves to be overwhelmed by the situation. Calmness and listening become more important than ever. Managers also learn to tailor their communications to reflect hope and optimism at the same time they acknowledge the current difficulties.
- ***Be visible.*** Many managers underestimate just how important their presence is during a crisis.[69] A manager's job is to step out immediately, both to reassure employees and respond to public concerns. Face-to-face communication with employees is crucial for letting people know that managers care about them and what they're going through.
- ***Get the awful truth out.***[70] Effective managers gather as much information as they can, do their best to determine the facts, and tell the truth to employees and the public as soon as possible. Getting the truth out quickly prevents rumors and misunderstandings. Toyota tried to hide some of the awful truth, which was a costly strategy, as shown in this chapter's Business Blooper.
- ***Communicate a vision for the future.*** People need to feel that they have something to work for and look forward to. Moments of crisis present opportunities for managers to communicate a vision of a better future and unite people toward common goals.

Ramin Talaie/Bloomberg/Getty Images

ConceptConnection

Shortly after eager customers such as Jeffrey Galvan (pictured here outside an Apple store) purchased the new iPhone 4, reports about the device's irritating tendency to drop calls surfaced. Former Apple CEO Steve Jobs got less than top marks for his **crisis communication skills** in handling this incident. Jobs insisted the problem didn't originate in the device's new integrated antenna design but rather was caused by the way users held the phone. After *Consumer Reports* faulted the antenna design, Jobs announced Apple would supply users with free cases to insulate the antenna—but only after complaining, "This has been blown so out of proportion that it's incredible."

Communication Technology

The rapidly changing digital environment is bringing sweeping changes to workplace communication. The global expansion of email continues at a swift pace with 21 percent growth in new customers from August 2008 to August 2009. Moreover, the use of other electronic communication services—such as Twitter and Facebook—jumped 31 percent in the same period.[71] This significant

BUSINESS BLOOPER

Toyota

"I hate to break it to you," wrote an executive at Toyota Corporation in an email in late 2009, "But we have a tendency for mechanical failure in accelerator pedals . . . on certain models." Three days later, after pressure from Congress and consumers, Toyota issued a recall on pedals that affected millions of vehicles. This was the culmination of four months of information gathering by federal regulators, who accused Toyota of deliberate efforts to hide defects from the government. Regulators had enough and issued a $16.4 million fine, saying Toyota had been "safety deaf" over the pedal issue. As a result of these and other safety issues, Toyota recalled a total of 20 million vehicles worldwide between 2009 and mid-2011, which tarnished the once seemingly unbeatable auto company.

SOURCE: Micheline Maynard, "Toyota Delayed a U.S. Recall, Documents Show," *The New York Times*, April 12, 2010.

increase in the use of social media signals a growing appetite among users for instant access and immediate sharing of information. Recognizing Twitter's potential for reaching thousands of people quickly, the CEO of Zappos.com uses the microblogging platform to connect with employees and customers in a friendly, personal way that has been highly effective, as described in the Spotlight on Skills titled Zappos.com.

Other companies also use social media to quickly communicate corporate news to customers. Domino's relied on the popularity of online communities to calm jittery customers after a damaging prank video was uploaded to YouTube showing two employees defacing pizzas and sandwiches. Domino's managers chose to respond with a viral video of their own. The video featured all of the elements of crisis communication described earlier in this chapter. The company president apologized and thanked the online community for bringing the issue to his attention. He announced that the wrongdoers would be prosecuted and outlined the steps Domino's was taking to ensure the episode would never happen again. By engaging in an online conversation about the crisis, Domino's demonstrated concern for its customers and squelched further rumors and fears.[72]

Popular collaboration tools, such as podcasts, blogs, and wikis, are also opening up opportunities for organizations to interact with employees and customers and improve collaboration among teams. General Motors launched an online public-relations campaign to rebuild trust with dealers and customers after emerging from bankruptcy protection. Part of the campaign includes GM's "Fastlane" blog, designed to give a more transparent glimpse into the workings of the tattered automaker.[73]

Climate of Trust and Openness

Perhaps the most important thing managers can do to enhance organizational communication is to create a *climate of trust and openness*. Open communication and dialogue can encourage people to communicate honestly with one another. Subordinates will feel free to transmit negative as well as positive messages to managers without fear of retribution. Efforts to develop interpersonal skills among employees can also foster openness, honesty, and trust.

Second, managers should develop and use *formal communication channels* in all directions. Scandinavian Designs uses two newsletters to reach employees. Dana Holding

SPOTLIGHT ON SKILLS

Zappos.com

Zappos.com CEO Tony Hsieh is dedicated to spreading the Zappos gospel to anyone who will listen. Zappos, an online shoe and clothing retailer, fosters a corporate culture dedicated to exceptional customer service and happiness. "At Zappos, our higher purpose is delivering happiness," Hsieh says. "Whether it's the happiness our customers receive when they get a new pair of shoes or the perfect piece of clothing, or the happiness they get when dealing with a friendly customer rep over the phone—these are all ways we bring happiness to people's lives.

Hsieh is an engaging communicator, giving one to four presentations a week. To strengthen his connection to employees and customers and build his leadership profile, Hsieh tapped into the potency of social media and began sending "tweets" to thousands of followers on Twitter. He is the number one Zappos Twitterer with over 10,000 followers and is ranked 42nd most followed of *all* Twitter users. "We're not really looking at short-term ROI [return on investment] in terms of sales. We're looking to form life-long relationships with our customers, and we think Twitter helps us do this," says Hsieh.

Hsieh followers include nearly 450 employees who find it a great way to meet up with each other after work and get to know each other from a different perspective. Employees are not required to Twitter and are not given any guidelines except to use their best judgment. Zappos does offer Twitter classes, but they are optional. "We're not really looking at Twitter as a way of driving additional traffic—it's really just a great way for employees and customers to see that we are real people, and it makes the relationship a lot more personal, which is what we ultimately want people to feel about the Zappos brand," says Hsieh.

SOURCES: Carmine Gallo, "Delivering Happiness the Zappos Way," *Businessweek Online*, May 12, 2009, http://www.businessweek.com/smallbiz/content/may2009/sb20090512_831040.htm (accessed August 12, 2010); and Brian Carter, "Twitter Marketing: An Interview with Zappos CEO Tony Hsieh," *The Inquistor*, August 28, 2008, http://www.inquisitr.com/2694/twitter-marketing-an-interview-with-zappos-ceo-tony-hsieh/ (accessed August 12, 2010).

Corporation developed the "Here's a Thought" board— called a HAT rack—to get ideas and feedback from workers. Other techniques include direct mail, bulletin boards, blogs, and employee surveys.

Third, managers should encourage the use of *multiple channels*, including both formal and informal communications. Multiple communication channels include written directives, face-to-face discussions, and the grapevine. For example, managers at GM's Packard Electric plant use multimedia, including a monthly newspaper, frequent meetings of employee teams, and an electronic news display in the cafeteria. Sending messages through multiple channels increases the likelihood that they will be properly received.

Fourth, the structure should *fit communication needs*. An organization can be designed to use teams, task forces, project managers, or a matrix structure as needed to facilitate the horizontal flow of information for coordination and problem solving. Structure should also reflect information needs. When team or department tasks are difficult, a decentralized structure should be implemented to encourage discussion and participation. It can be argued that Charlie Sheen and CBS do not share a climate of trust and openness, as shown in the Focus on Ethics titled Charlie Sheen and CBS.

SPOTLIGHT ON ETHICS

Charlie Sheen and CBS

How far does a network let its top star go before they cancel a profitable show? It is alright to get arrested for domestic violence because you choked your wife? How about partying with porn stars? Or perhaps being a drug addict but announcing to the world that you can rehab yourself? What pushed CBS over the edge, though, was when Charlie Sheen made some ugly anti-Semitic remarks about the *Two-and-a-Half* men producer, Chuck Lorre.

The decision to put some boundaries on Sheen will cost CBS plenty, about $250 million for the remainder of the 2011 season, after the series was cancelled in February of 2011. Considering the show costs a lot of money to produce, it means a net loss of $100 million. Such money often leads to sometimes quite unpleasant compromises in Hollywood, but CBS was firm, despite a flurry of even worse network bashing by Sheen. Within two months, Lorre announced that he was hoping to reboot the series without Sheen. Then in May of 2011, CBS said it was bringing in a replacement, Ashton Kutcher of *Punk'd* fame. Though die-hard fans are skeptical, one shouldn't forget that Charlie Sheen himself was a hit when he replaced Michael J. Fox in *Spin City*, and he won a Golden Globe for that role in 2000.

SOURCES: David Sanderson, "Replacement Parts, *Winnipeg Free Times*, May 28, 2011, p. E1; Kat Angus, "Lorre Eyes Reboot for 'Two and a Half Men,'" *Postmedia News*, May 2, 2011, p. D3; Tom Watkins, "Substance Abuse Is Ugly, Even for a Star," *Michigan Chronicle*, March 2–8, 2011, p. A5; Bill Carter, "Sheen Tantrum Likely to Cost in the Millions," *The New York Times*, February 26, 2011, B1 & B2.

- During a communication crisis, a manager should stay calm and listen carefully, reassure employees and the public, tell the truth, and communicate a vision for the future.
- Communication technology, such as social networking, creates new paths for communicating messages to a large group of employees and customers.
- If a manager creates a climate of trust and openness, employees will feel free to share both negative and positive messages.

Discussion Questions

1. Lee's Garage is an internal Walmart Web site that CEO H. Lee Scott uses to communicate with the company's 1.5 million U.S. employees. A public relations associate screens employee questions and Scott dictates his responses to an aide, who then posts them on the Web. What would you predict are the advantages and potential problems to this method of upper-level management's connecting with employees?
2. Describe the elements of the communication process. Give an example of each part of the model as it exists in the classroom during communication between teacher and students.
3. What communication channel would you select if you had to give an employee feedback about the way he mismanaged a call with a key customer? What channel would you use to announce to all employees the deadline for selecting new health-care plans? Explain your choices.
4. What are the characteristics of an effective listener? How would you rate yourself on those characteristics?
5. Some senior managers believe they should rely on written information and computer reports because these yield more accurate data than do face-to-face communications. Do you agree? Why or why not?

6. A survey conducted in 2008 by the Society for Human Resources Management found that 54 percent of human resources professionals had documented an uptick in gossip or rumors about recession-related downsizing or layoffs. As a manager, what communication strategies would you employ during a time of uncertainty in the workplace? What are the advantages and disadvantages of gossip during a time of uncertainty?
7. How does a climate of trust and openness improve organizational communication?
8. Assume you manage a small online business that sells herbal supplements. Without your knowledge, a disgruntled employee has posted damaging information about your company in the company's blog, including false information about dangerous ingredients in your best-selling supplement. What specific steps would you take to minimize the risk of this crisis?
9. Assume that you have been asked to design a training program to help managers become better communicators. What would you include in the program?
10. A study reported in the *Journal of Applied Psychology* found that people are more willing to lie and feel more justified doing so when using email than when using pen and paper, even if told their lie would be discovered. What might be some reasons for this? Should managers limit the use of email in their organizations? Discuss.

Self-Learning

Personal Assessment of Communication Apprehension[74]

The following questions are about your feelings toward communication with other people. Indicate the degree to which each statement applies to you by marking (5) Strongly agree, (4) Agree, (3) Undecided, (2) Disagree, or (1) Strongly disagree. There are no right or wrong answers. Many of the statements are similar to other statements. Do not be concerned about their similarities. Work quickly, and just record your first impressions.

Disagree Strongly ① ② ③ ④ ⑤ **Agree Strongly**

1. When talking in a small group of acquaintances, I am tense and nervous.

   1 2 3 4 5

2. When presenting a talk to a group of strangers, I am tense and nervous.

   1 2 3 4 5

3. When conversing with a friend or colleague, I am calm and relaxed.

   1 2 3 4 5

4. When talking in a large meeting of acquaintances, I am calm and relaxed.

   1 2 3 4 5

5. When presenting a talk to a group of friends or colleagues, I am tense and nervous.

   1 2 3 4 5

6. When conversing with an acquaintance or colleague, I am calm and relaxed.

   1 2 3 4 5

7. When talking in a large meeting of strangers, I am tense and nervous.

   1 2 3 4 5

8. When talking in a small group of strangers, I am tense and nervous.

   1 2 3 4 5

9. When talking in a small group of friends and colleagues, I am calm and relaxed.

   1 2 3 4 5

10. When presenting a talk to a group of acquaintances, I am calm and relaxed.

    1 2 3 4 5

11. When I am conversing with a stranger, I am calm and relaxed.

    1 2 3 4 5

12. When talking in a large meeting of friends, I am tense and nervous.

    1 2 3 4 5

13. When presenting a talk to a group of strangers, I am calm and relaxed.

    1 2 3 4 5

14. When conversing with a friend or colleague, I am tense and nervous.

    1 2 3 4 5

15. When talking in a large meeting of acquaintances, I am tense and nervous.

    1 2 3 4 5

16. When talking in a small group of acquaintances, I am calm and relaxed.

    1 2 3 4 5

17. When talking in a small group of strangers, I am calm and relaxed.

    1 2 3 4 5

18. When presenting a talk to a group of friends, I am calm and relaxed.

    1 2 3 4 5

19. When conversing with an acquaintance or colleague, I am tense and nervous.

    1 2 3 4 5

20. When talking in a large meeting of strangers, I am calm and relaxed.

    1 2 3 4 5

21. When presenting a talk to a group of acquaintances, I am tense and nervous.

    1 2 3 4 5

22. When conversing with a stranger, I am tense and nervous.

    1 2 3 4 5

23. When talking in a large meeting of friends or colleagues, I am calm and relaxed.

    1 2 3 4 5

24. When talking in a small group of friends or colleagues, I am tense and nervous.

    1 2 3 4 5

Scoring and Interpretation

This questionnaire permits computation of four subscores and one total score. Subscores relate to communication apprehension in four common situations—public speaking, meetings, group discussions, and interpersonal conversations. To compute your scores, add or subtract your scores for each item as indicated next.

Subscore/Scoring Formula: For each subscore, start with 18 points. Then add the scores for the plus (+) items and subtract the scores for the minus (−) items.

Public Speaking

18 + scores for items 2, 5, and 21; − scores for items 10, 13, and 18. Score = ______

Meetings

18 + scores for items 7, 12, and 15; − scores for items 4, 20, and 23. Score = ______

Group Discussions

18 + scores for items 1, 8, and 24; − scores for items 9, 16, and 17. Score = ______

Interpersonal Conversations

18 + scores for items 14, 19, and 22; − scores for items 3, 6, and 11. Score = ______

Total Score

Sum the four subscores for Total Score ______

This personal assessment provides an indication of how much apprehension (fear or anxiety) you feel in a variety of communication settings. Total scores may range from 24 to 120. Scores above 72 indicate that you are more apprehensive about communication than the average person. Scores above 85 indicate a high level of communication apprehension. Scores below 59 indicate a low level of apprehension. These extreme scores (below 59 and above 85) are generally outside the norm. They suggest that the degree of apprehension you may experience in any given situation may not be associated with a realistic response to that communication situation.

Scores on the subscales can range from a low of 6 to a high of 30. Any score above 18 indicates some degree of apprehension. For example, if you score above 18 for the public speaking context, you are like the overwhelming majority of people.

To be an effective communication champion, you should work to overcome communication anxiety. The interpersonal conversations create the least apprehension for most people, followed by group discussions, larger meetings, and then public speaking. Compare your scores with another student. What aspect of communication creates the most apprehension for you? How do you plan to improve it?

Group Learning

The following exercise will help you understand how "yes, but" statements are so familiar and how "yes, and" statements keep a dialogue or conversation going more effectively.

1. Form into pairs.
2. One person starts with a yes/no question relating to an "untrue" fact, asking about something which can be seen.
3. The other person affirms this statement (even if it is not actually true and might be ridiculous) and adds another yes/no question. You must be careful NOT to respond with a "Yes, but" answer.
4. Go through the questions and statements as quickly as you can.
5. The instructor will call time after several minutes.
6. The instructor will lead a discussion. How difficult was it to avoid the "yes, but" statements? What was the effect on doing "yes, and" continually?

Example of a possible dialogue:

"Is your hair green?"

"Yes and yesterday it was blue. Do you change the color of your hair on a daily basis?"

"Yes and I change my shirt/blouse daily. Did you tear a hole in your shirt at lunch today?

"Yes and it was very large. Did everyone notice?"

"Yes and I was very pleased with myself that I managed not to laugh. Are you going to buy a new shirt?

"Yes and I'm going to that new mall on the moon to do it. Do you go to the moon often?

"Yes and sometimes Mars as well. Can you breathe in the vacuum on the moon?"

"Yes and under water as well. Do you know how to breathe liquid nitrogen?"

SOURCES: Adapted by Steven S. Taylor (2007) from the work of Keith Johnstone, *Improvisation and the Theatre*, Theater Arts Book Publisher, 1987. Used with permission.

Action Learning

Listen Like A Pro

The fastest way to become a great listener is to act like a professional listener, such as a clinical psychologist. Therapists drop the need to interrupt or to express their own point of view in order to concentrate on the client's point of view. The therapist focuses intently and listens totally, drawing out information rather than thinking about a response.

Step 1. Divide into groups of four students. Within this group, each student selects one partner. Sit face-to-face with your partner, at a comfortable distance, and hold a steady gaze into your partner's left eye (not the nose or face, but the left eye)—use a soft gaze, not a hard stare.

Step 2. After you are comfortable with the eye contact, one partner should tell of an annoying experience over the last few days. The listener should maintain eye contact and can use facial expression, but should say nothing—just gaze into the pupil of the left eye. When the talker has finished, the partners should trade roles, with the previous listener now telling about an annoying experience and the new listener maintaining eye contact but not speaking.

Step 3. Discuss in your group how it felt to maintain eye contact and not to make any verbal response to what your partner was saying.

Step 4. Select a new partner in your group. The procedure is the same, with the speaker talking about the same annoyance. The only change is that the listener is to paraphrase what the speaker said after the speaker is finished. If the paraphrase is incorrect, the speaker can repeat the annoyance, and the listener can paraphrase a second time to be more accurate.

Step 5. Discuss in your group how it felt to maintain eye contact and to paraphrase what was said. How did paraphrasing affect your ability to concentrate on what the speaker was saying?

Step 6. Select another partner in your group. The procedure is the same; only this time instead of paraphrasing at the end, the listener is to ask five questions during the speaker's story. Each partner takes a turn as speaker and listener.

Step 7. Discuss in your group how it felt to ask questions. How did the questions affect your concentration on what the speaker was saying? In addition, discuss in your group the relative importance of each technique (eye contact, paraphrasing, and asking questions) for helping you maintain focus and listen like a professional. Your instructor may facilitate a class discussion about which listening techniques are more effective in various listening situations.

Ethical Dilemma

On Trial[75]

When Werner and Thompson, a Los Angeles business and financial management firm, offered Iranian-born Firoz Bahmania position as an accountant assistant one spring day in 2007, Bahmani felt a sense of genuine relief, but his relief was short-lived.

With his degree in accounting from a top-notch American university, he knew he was more than a little overqualified for the job. But time after time, he'd been rejected for suitable positions. His language difficulties were the reason most often given for his unsuccessful candidacy. Although the young man had grown up speaking both Farsi and French in his native land, he'd only begun to pick up English shortly before his arrival in the United States a few years ago. Impressed by his educational credentials and his quiet, courtly manner, managing partner Beatrice Werner overlooked his heavy accent and actively recruited him for the position, the only one available at the time. During his interview, she assured him he would advance in time.

It was clear to Beatrice that Firoz was committed to succeeding at all costs. But it soon also became apparent that Firoz and his immediate supervisor, Cathy Putnam, were at odds. Cathy was a seasoned account manager who had just transferred to Los Angeles from the New York office. Saddled with an enormous workload, she let Firoz know right from the start, speaking in her rapid-fire Brooklyn accent, that he'd need to get up to speed as quickly as possible.

Shortly before Cathy was to give Firoz his three-month probationary review, she came to Beatrice, expressed her frustration with Firoz's performance, and suggested that he be let go. "His bank reconciliations and financial report preparations are first-rate," Cathy admitted, "but his communication skills leave a lot to be desired. In the first place, I simply don't have the time to keep repeating the same directions over and over again when I'm trying to teach him his responsibilities. Then there's the fact that public contact is part of his written job description. Typically, he puts off making phone calls to dispute credit card charges or ask a client's staff for the information he needs. When he does finally pick up the phone . . . well, let's just say I've had more than one client mention how hard it is to understand what he's trying to say. Some of them are getting pretty exasperated."

"You know, some firms feel it's their corporate responsibility to help foreign-born employees learn English," Beatrice began. "Maybe we should help him find an English-as-a-second-language course and pay for it."

"With all due respect, I don't think that's our job," Cathy replied, with barely concealed irritation. "If you come to the United States, you should learn our language. That's what my mom's parents did when they came over from Italy. They certainly didn't expect anyone to hold their hands. Besides," she added, almost inaudibly, "Firoz's lucky we let him into this country."

Beatrice had mixed feelings. On one hand, she recognized that Werner and Thompson had every right to require someone in Firoz's position be capable of carrying out his public contract duties. Perhaps she had made a mistake in hiring him. But as the daughter of German immigrants herself, she knew firsthand both how daunting language and cultural barriers could be and that they could be overcome in time. Perhaps in part because of her family background, she had a passionate commitment to the firm's stated goals of creating a diverse workforce and a caring, supportive culture. Besides, she felt a personal sense of obligation to help a hard-working, promising employee realize his potential. What will she advise Cathy to do now that Firoz's probationary period is drawing to a close?

What Would You Do?

1. Agree with Cathy Putnam. Despite your personal feelings, accept that Firoz Bahmani is not capable of carrying out the accountant assistant's responsibilities. Make the break now, and give him his notice on the grounds that he cannot carry out one of the key stated job requirements. Advise him that a position that primarily involves paperwork would be a better fit for him.

2. Place Firoz with a more sympathetic account manager who is open to finding ways to help him improve his English and has the time to help him develop his assertiveness and telephone skills. Send Cathy Putnam to diversity awareness training.

3. Create a new position at the firm that will allow Firoz to do the reports and reconciliations for several account managers, freeing the account assistants to concentrate on public contact work. Make it clear that he will have little chance of future promotion unless his English improves markedly.

Case for Critical Analysis

Hunter-Worth[76]

Christmas was fast approaching. Just a short while ago, Chuck Moore, national sales manager for Hunter-Worth, a New York–based multinational toy manufacturer, was confident the coming holiday was going to be one of the company's best in years. At a recent toy expo, Hunter-Worth unveiled a new interactive plush toy that was cuddly, high tech, and tied into a major holiday motion picture expected to be a smash hit. Chuck had thought the toy would do well, but frankly, the level of interest took him by surprise. The buyers at the toy fair raved, and the subsequent pre-order volume was extremely encouraging. It had all looked so promising, but now he couldn't shake a sense of impending doom.

The problem in a nutshell was that the Mexican subsidiary that manufactured the toy couldn't seem to meet a deadline. Not only were all the shipments late so far, but they fell well short of the quantities ordered. Chuck decided to email Vicente Ruiz, the plant manager, about the situation before he found himself in the middle of the Christmas season with parents clamoring for a toy he couldn't lay his hands on.

In a thoroughly professional email that started with a friendly "Dear Vicente," Chuck inquired about the status of the latest order, asked for a production schedule for pending orders, and requested a specific explanation as to why the Mexican plant seemed to be having such difficulty shipping orders out on time. The reply appeared within the hour, but to his utter astonishment, it was a short message from Vicente's secretary. She acknowledged the receipt of his email and assured him the Mexican plant would be shipping the order, already a week late, in the next ten days.

"That's it," Chuck fumed. "Time to take this to Sato." He prefaced his original email and the secretary's reply with a terse note expressing his growing concern over the availability of what could well be this season's must-have toy. "Just what do I have to do to light a fire under Vicente?" he wrote. He then forwarded it all to his supervisors and friend, Michael Sato, the executive vice president for sales and marketing.

Next thing he knew, he was on the phone with Vicente—and the plant manager was furious. "Señor Moore, how dare you go over my head and say such things about me to my boss?" he sputtered, sounding both angry and slightly panicked. It seemed that Michael had forwarded Chuck's email to Hunter-Worth's vice president of operations, who had sent it on to the Mexican subsidiary's president.

That turn of events was unfortunate, but Chuck wasn't feeling all that apologetic. "You could have prevented all this if you'd just answered the questions I emailed you last week," he pointed out. "I deserved more than a form letter—and from your secretary, no less."

"My secretary always answers my emails," replied Vicente. "She figures that if the problem is really urgent, you would pick up the phone and talk to me directly. Contrary to what you guys north of the border might think, we do take deadlines seriously here. There's only so much we can do with the supply problems we're having, but I doubt you're interested in hearing about those." And Vicente hung up the phone without waiting for a response.

Chuck was confused and disheartened. Things were only getting worse. How could he turn the situation around?

Questions

1. Based on Vicente Ruiz's actions and his conversation with Chuck Moore, what differences do you detect in cultural attitudes toward communications in Mexico as compared with the United States? Is understanding these differences important? Explain.
2. What was the main purpose of Chuck's communication to Vicente? To Michael Sato? What factors should he have considered when choosing a channel for his communication to Vicente? Are they the same factors he should have considered when communicating with Michael Sato?
3. If you were Chuck, what would you have done differently? What steps would you take at this point to make sure the supply of the popular new toy is sufficient to meet the anticipated demand?

aplia Aplia Highlights

Now use your Aplia homework to help you:

- Apply management theories in your life
- Assess your management skills
- Master management terms and concepts
- Apply your knowledge to real-world situations
- Analyze and solve challenging management problems

In order to take advantage of these elements, your instructor will need to have set up a course for your class within Aplia. Ask your instructor to contact his/her Cengage sales representative and Digital Solutions Manager to explore testing Aplia in your course this term.

Plant Fantasies: Managing Communication

© Leremy, Shutterstock

Can companies really Twitter their way to profits? Is Facebook replacing face-to-face meetings? Do personal handwritten business letters have any place in the digital age? If Plant Fantasies is any indication, reports concerning the death of traditional business communication are greatly exaggerated. "In terms of emails and e-blasts and Facebook and tweeting, I don't do it," says Plant Fantasies owner Teresa Carleo. "I feel it's more significant and meaningful to make a connection with somebody." It's hard to argue with success: since founding Plant Fantasies in 1987, Carleo has become gardener to some of New York City's most prestigious property owners—including Donald Trump.

At first glance, Carleo's preference for traditional communication methods seems out of touch with twenty-first century technologies. Far from being neo-Luddites, however, the leaders at Plant Fantasies demand communication that works—and that means matching the right communication methods with the right business situations. For example, some tasks at Plant Fantasies involve installing and maintaining gardens. Other situations require collaboration with landscape designers. Still others involve speaking with clients. Not all communication channels are equally suited for each situation; tweeting may be effective in one situation yet hopelessly inappropriate within another setting.

According to Steve Martucci, the sales director for Plant Fantasies, nothing beats a personal meeting with clients. "When there's time, I think it's a great idea to always do face-to-face—it's good for the customer," the director states. "You want them to see you and remember you. You want them to see that you took the time to come there and that you didn't just shoot them an email in a cab going somewhere else."

According to Martucci, most new business at Plant Fantasies is generated by word of mouth. In the past, the sales director spent time and money on brochures and email marketing strategies. Martucci returned to face-to-face interaction after watching people ignore his electronic messages. "You need to meet people so they can put a face with a name," the sales director states. He also notes that email, while useful for some tasks, can eat up precious time. "Email is the best way to get the basic information across, but the back and forth for a conversation that would take a minute on the phone is a waste of time. I'd rather just make the phone call."

Although face-to-face interaction is preferred at Plant Fantasies, electronic communication is part of the company's overall communication strategy—especially when it comes to coordinating labor-oriented tasks. For example, if the company has 15 gardening jobs to fulfill in any given day, each job will require coordination of trucks, tools, plants, equipment, and laborers. To establish a daily agenda, Carleo sends a batch of email messages first thing in the morning. Then, as needed, landscape workers use cell phones and text messaging to address issues on site. "We all have Blackberrys, so we all do direct connect—which is very helpful because I have the trucks and people going around," Carleo explains.

To keep leaders on the same page at the office, Carleo hosts daily meetings. "I try to have a meeting at least once in my office." Carleo says. We talk and try to problem solve and throw ideas around." According to Martucci, the daily meetings are useful, and each member comes away with different perspectives. "We all listen differently. I'll go into meetings with Teresa, and she'll hear some of it and I'll hear other things—so we both take away different things from the meeting." Frequent contact is also important to Martucci, who admits being "a control freak" when it comes to staying connected with subordinates. "I always need to know what's going on, and I constantly check in. I don't think you can ever be too annoying," he said.

Despite the many digital communication technologies at her disposal, Teresa Carleo insists on making a personal connection with customers. After a friend's handwritten note recently touched her in a unique way, the Plant Fantasies founder decided to launch a personal letter writing campaign to clients. "I think I have a better chance of my customers opening that envelope than opening an e-blast," Carleo remarked. "Maybe I'm archaic, but my clients aren't 20 [years old]."

Discussion Questions

1. Using the concept of channel richness, explain why leaders at Plant Fantasies place a high value on face-to-face communication.
2. What impact might gender have on the communication styles of Teresa Carleo and Steve Martucci? Give examples.
3. Which of the three types of formal organizational communication would you expect to originate from Teresa Carleo and Steve Martucci, and why?

© VikaSuh, Shutterstock

Friday Night Lights (II)

The Odessa, Texas, passion for Friday night high school football comes through clearly in this cinematic treatment of H. G. (Buzz) Bissinger's well-regarded book of the same title.[77] Coach Gary Gaines (Billy Bob Thornton) leads the Permian High Panthers to the 1988 semifinals where it must compete against a team of much larger players. A fast-moving pace in the football sequences and a slower pace in the serious, introspective sequences give this film many fine moments.

Communication This sequence[78] begins with a shot of Coach Gaines and the team gathered around him during the half-time break. He starts his speech to the team by saying, "Well, it's real simple. You got two more quarters and that's it." It ends after Gaines says, "Boys, my heart is full. My heart's full."

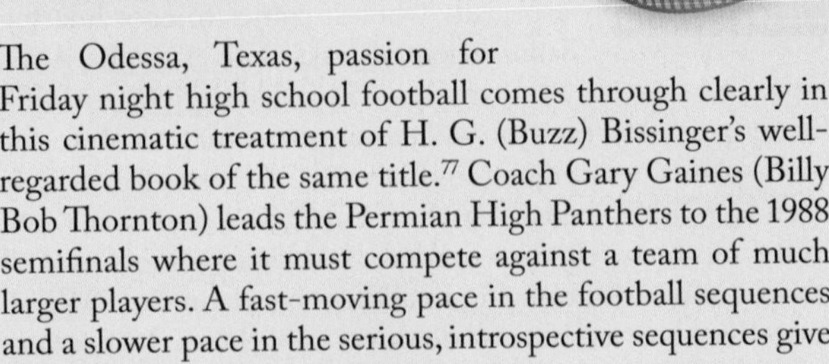

What to Watch for and Ask Yourself

- This chapter emphasized the speaker and the listener(s) in the communication process. Coach Gaines is the speaker, and team members and assistant coaches are listeners. Only Gaines spoke. Did he still meet the basic requirements of effective communication? Draw examples from his speech to support your conclusions.
- This chapter distinguished between purpose-directed communication and strategic conversation. Which of these communication types best fits this sequence? Draw examples from the sequence to make your point.
- Assess the effectiveness of this communication event. How do you expect team members and the assistant coaches to react in the second half of the game?

© Pedro Nogueira, Shutterstock

Endnotes

1. Liz Ryan, "Ten Ways to Use LinkedIn in your Job Search," *BusinessWeek,* June 25, 2010, www.businessweek.com/print/managing/content/jun2010/ca2010067_197297.htm (accessed July 26, 2010).
2. "Effective Communication Strategy Impacts Bottom Line," *Executive's Tax & Management Report* (January 2008): 15.
3. Henry Mintzberg, *The Nature of Managerial Work* (New York: Harper & Row, 1973).
4. Phillip G. Clampitt, Laurey Berk, and M. Lee Williams, "Leaders as Strategic Communicators," *Ivey Business Journal* (May–June 2002): 51–55.
5. Mina Kimes, "How Can I Get Candid Feedback from My Employees," *Fortune* (April 13, 2009): 24.
6. Fred Luthans and Janet K. Larsen, "How Managers Really Communicate," *Human Relations* 39 (1986): 161–178; and Larry E. Penley and Brian Hawkins, "Studying Interpersonal Communication in Organizations: A Leadership Application," *Academy of Management Journal* 28 (1985): 309–326.
7. D. K. Berlo, *The Process of Communication* (New York: Holt, Rinehart and Winston, 1960), p. 24.
8. Bruce K. Blaylock, "Cognitive Style and the Usefulness of Information," *Decision Sciences* 15 (Winter 1984): 74–91.
9. Gunjan Bagla, "Indiscreet Communication," *The Conference Board Review* (January–February 2009): 9–10.
10. Robert H. Lengel and Richard L. Daft, "The Selection of Communication Media as an Executive Skill," *Academy of Management Executive* 2 (August 1988): 225–232; Richard L. Daft and Robert H. Lengel, "Organizational Information Requirements, Media Richness and Structural Design," *Managerial Science* 32 (May 1986): 554–572; and Jane Webster and Linda Klebe Treviño, "Rational and Social Theories as Complementary Explanations of Communication Media Choices: Two Policy-Capturing Studies," *Academy of Management Journal* 38, no. 6 (1995): 1544–1572.
11. Research reported in "Email Can't Mimic Phone Calls," *Johnson City Press,* September 17, 2000.
12. Raymond E. Friedman and Steven C. Currall, "Email Escalation: Dispute Exacerbating Elements of Electronic Communication," http://papers.ssrn.com/sol3/papers.cfm?abstract_id=459429 (accessed September 21, 2010); Lauren Keller Johnson, "Does Email Escalate Conflict?" *MIT Sloan Management Review* (Fall 2002): 14–15; and Alison Stein Wellner, "Lost in Translation," *Inc. Magazine* (September 2005): 37–38.
13. Joe Sharkey, "Email Saves Time, but Being There Says More," *The New York Times,* January 26, 2010,

www.nytimes.com/2010/01/26/business/26road.html (accessed July 26, 2010).

14. Scott Kirsner, "IM Is Here. RU Prepared?" *Darwin Magazine* (February 2002): 22–24.

15. John R. Carlson and Robert W. Smud, "Channel Expansion Theory and the Experiential Nature of Media Richness Perceptions," *Academy of Management Journal* 42, no. 2 (1999): 153–170; R. Rice and G. Love, "Electronic Emotion," *Communication Research* 14 (1987): 85–108.

16. Ronald E. Rice, "Task Analyzability, Use of New Media, and Effectiveness: A Multi-Site Exploration of Media Richness," *Organizational Science* 3, no. 4 (November 1992): 475–500; and M. Lynne Markus, "Electronic Mail as the Medium of Managerial Choice," *Organizational Science* 5, no. 4 (November 1994): 502–527.

17. Richard L. Daft, Robert H. Lengel, and Linda Klebe Treviño, "Message Equivocality, Media Selection and Manager Performance: Implication for Information Systems," *MIS Quarterly* 11 (1987): 355–368.

18. Sarah E. Needleman, "Entrepreneurs 'Tweet' Their Way through Crises," *The Wall Street Journal Online*, September 15, 2009, http://online.wsj.com/article/SB125297893340910637.html?KEYWORDS=Entrepreneurs+Tweet +their+way+through+crises (accessed September 19, 2009).

19. Mary Young and James E. Post, "Managing to Communicate, Communicating to Manage: How Leading Companies Communicate with Employees," *Organizational Dynamics* (Summer 1993): 31–43.

20. Jay A. Conger, "The Necessary Art of Persuasion," *Harvard Business Review* (May–June 1998): 84–95.

21. *Ibid.*

22. Susan Cramm, "The Heart of Persuasion," *CIO* (July 1, 2005): 28–30.

23. Deborah Tannen, "He Said, She Said," *Scientific American Mind* (May–June, 2010): 55–59.

24. Deborah Tannen, *You Just Don't Understand: Women and Men in Conversation* (New York: Ballantine Books, 1991), p. 77.

25. Deborah Tannen, "He Said, She Said."

26. Study and surveys reported in Paul Harris, "Leadership Role Models Earn Trust and Profits," *T&D* (March 2010): 47–50.

27. Carol Kinsey Goman, "Body Language: Mastering the Silent Language of Leadership" (The Leadership Playlist column), *The Washington Post Online,* July 17, 2009, http://views.washingtonpost.com/leadership /leadership_playlist/2009/07/body-language-mastering-the-silent-language-of-leadership.html (accessed July 17, 2009).

28. I. Thomas Sheppard, "Silent Signals," *Supervisory Management* (March 1986): 31–33.

29. Carmine Gallo, "How to Stay Cool in the Hot Seat," *BusinessWeek,* June 22, 2010, www.businessweek.com/print/smallbiz/content/jun2010/sb20100622_820980.htm (accessed July 28, 2010).

30. Albert Mehrabian, *Silent Messages* (Belmont, CA: Wadsworth, 1971); and Albert Mehrabian, "Communicating without Words," *Psychology Today* (September 1968): 53–55.

31. Meridith Levinson, "How to Be a Mind Reader," *CIO* (December 1, 2004): 72–76; Mac Fulfer, "Non-verbal Communication: How to Read What's Plain as the Nose . . .," *Journal of Organizational Excellence* (Spring 2001): 19–27; Paul Ekman, *Emotions Revealed: Recognizing Faces and Feelings to Improve Communication and Emotional Life* (New York: Time Books, 2003).

32. Goman, "Body Language: Mastering the Silent Language of Leadership."

33. *Ibid.*

34. C. Glenn Pearce, "Doing Something about Your Listening Ability," *Supervisory Management* (March 1989): 29–34; and Tom Peters, "Learning to Listen," *Hyatt Magazine* (Spring 1988): 16–21.

35. Kelley Holland, "Under New Management; The Silent May Have Something to Say," *The New York Times*, November 5, 2006.

36. Debbie Weil, *The Corporate Blogging Book* (New York: Penguin Group, 2006), p. 3.

37. *Fortune* 500 Business Blogging Wiki, www.socialtext.net/bizblogs/index.cgi (accessed July 26, 2010).

38. M. P. Nichols, *The Lost Art of Listening* (New York: Guilford Publishing, 1995).

39. "Benchmarking the Sales Function," a report based on a study of 100 salespeople from small, medium, and large businesses, conducted by Ron Volper Group, White Plains, New York, as reported in "Nine Habits of Highly Effective Salespeople," *Inc.com*, June 1, 1997, http://www.inc .com/articles/1997/06/12054.html (accessed September 23, 2010).

40. Gerald M. Goldhaber, *Organizational Communication*, 4th ed. (Dubuque, IA: Brown, 1980), p. 189.

41. Richard L. Daft and Richard M. Steers, *Organizations: A Micro/Macro Approach* (New York: Harper Collins, 1986); and Daniel Katz and Robert Kahn, *The Social Psychology of Organizations*, 2nd ed. (New York: Wiley, 1978).

42. Greg Jaffe, "Tug of War: In the New Military, Technology May Alter Chain of Command," *The Wall Street Journal*, March 30, 2001; and Aaron Pressman, "Business Gets the Message," *The Industry Standard* (February 26, 2001): 58–59.

43. Phillip G. Clampitt, Robert J. DeKoch, and Thomas Cashman, "A Strategy for Communicating about Uncertainty," *Academy of Management Executive* 14, no. 4 (2000): 41–57.

44. Reported in Louise van der Does and Stephen J. Caldeira, "Effective Leaders Champion Communication Skills," *Nation's Restaurant News* (March 27, 2006): 20.

45. J. G. Miller, "Living Systems: The Organization," *Behavioral Science* 17 (1972): 69.

46. Michael J. Glauser, "Upward Information Flow in Organizations: Review and Conceptual Analysis," *Human Relations* 37 (1984): 613–643; and "Upward/Downward Communication: Critical Information Channels," *Small Business Report* (October 1985): 85–88.

47. Darren Dahl, "Pipe Up People! Rounding Up Staff," *Inc.* (February, 2010): 80–81.

48. Thomas Petzinger, "A Hospital Applies Teamwork to Thwart an Insidious Enemy," *The Wall Street Journal*, May 8, 1998.

49. E. M. Rogers and R. A. Rogers, *Communication in Organizations* (New York: Free Press, 1976); and A. Bavelas and D. Barrett, "An Experimental Approach to Organization Communication," *Personnel* 27 (1951): 366–371.

50. Joel Spolsky, "A Little Less Conversation," *Inc.* (February, 2010): 28–29.

51. This discussion is based on Daft and Steers, *Organizations.*

52. Bavelas and Barrett, "An Experimental Approach"; and M. E. Shaw, *Group Dynamics: The Psychology of Small Group Behavior* (New York: McGraw-Hill, 1976).

53. Richard L. Daft and Norman B. Macintosh, "A Tentative Exploration into the Amount and Equivocality of Information Processing in Organizational Work Units," *Administrative Science Quarterly* 26 (1981): 207–224.

54. This discussion of informal networks is based on Rob Cross, Nitin Nohria, and Andrew Parker, "Six Myths about Informal Networks," *MIT Sloan Management Review* (Spring 2002): 67–75; and Rob Cross and Laurence Prusak, "The People Who Make Organizations Go—or Stop," *Harvard Business Review* (June 2002): 105–112.

55. Tahl Raz, "The 10 Secrets of a Master Networker," *Inc.* (January 2003).

56. Stephanie Armour, "Office Gossip Has Never Traveled Faster, Thanks to Tech," *USA Today,* November 1, 2007, www.usatoday .com /tech/webguide/internetlife/2007-09-09-office-gossip-technology_n .htm (accessed March 28, 2008).

57. Keith Davis and John W. Newstrom, *Human Behavior at Work: Organizational Behavior*, 7th ed. (New York: McGraw-Hill, 1985).

58. Suzanne M. Crampton, John W. Hodge, and Jitendra M. Mishra, "The Informal Communication Network: Factors Influencing Grapevine Activity," *Public Personnel Management* 27, no. 4 (Winter 1998): 569–584.

59. Survey results reported in Jared Sandberg, "Ruthless Rumors and the Managers Who Enable Them," *The Wall Street Journal*, October 29, 2003.

60. Donald B. Simmons, "The Nature of the Organizational Grapevine," *Supervisory Management* (November 1985): 39–42; and Davis and Newstrom, *Human Behavior.*

61. Barbara Ettorre, "Hellooo. Anybody Listening?" *Management Review* (November 1997): 9.

62. Eilene Zimmerman, "Gossip Is Information by Another Name," *The New York Times*, February 3, 2008, www.nytimes .com/2008/02/03/jobs/03career.html?scp=1&sq=Gossip%20 Is%20Information%20by%20Another%20Name&st=cse (accessed February 3, 2008).

63. Lisa A. Burke and Jessica Morris Wise, "The Effective Care, Handling, and Pruning of the Office Grapevine," *Business Horizons* (May–June 2003): 71–74; "They Hear It through the Grapevine," cited in Michael Warshaw, "The Good Guy's Guide to Office Politics," *Fast Company* (April–May 1998): 157–178; and Carol Hildebrand, "Mapping the Invisible Workplace," *CIO Enterprise*, section 2 (July 15, 1998): 18–20.

64. The National Commission on Writing, "Writing Skills Necessary for Employment, Says Big Business," September 14, 2004, www.writingcommission.org/pr/writing_for_employ.html (accessed April 8, 2008).

65. Based on Michael Fitzgerald, "How to Write a Memorable Memo," *CIO* (October 15, 2005): 85–87; and Jonathan Hershberg, "It's Not Just What You Say," *Training* (May 2005): 50.

66. Mary Anne Donovan, "Email Exposes the Literacy Gap," *Workforce* (November 2002): 15.

67. Julia Werdigier and Jad Mouawad, "Road to New Confidence at BP Runs Through U.S.," *The New York Times*, July 26, 2010, www.nytimes.com/2010/07/27/business/27dudley.html?_r=1&sq=BP%20Hayward&st=cse&adxnnl=1&scp=7&adxnnlx=1280315332-P6V 5i9wUaL40EYFeOSH52w (accessed July 27, 2010).

68. This section is based on Leslie Wayne and Leslie Kaufman, "Leadership, Put to a New Test," *The New York Times*, September 16, 2001; Ian I. Mitroff, "Crisis Leadership," *Executive Excellence* (August 2001): 19; Jerry Useem, "What It Takes," *Fortune* (November 12, 2001): 126–132; Andy Bowen, "Crisis Procedures That Stand the Test of Time," *Public Relations Tactics* (August 2001): 16; and Matthew Boyle, "Nothing Really Matters," *Fortune* (October 15, 2001): 261–264.

69. Stephen Bernhut, "Leadership, with Michael Useem," *Ivey Business Journal* (January–February 2002): 42–43.

70. Mitroff, "Crisis Leadership."

71. Jessica E. Vascellaro, "Why Email No Longer Rules," *The Wall Street Journal Online*, October 12, 2009, http://online.wsj.com/article/SB10001424052970203803904574431151489408372.html (accessed October 15, 2009).

72. Richard S. Levick, "Domino's Discovers Social Media," *BusinessWeek*, April 21, 2009, www.businessweek.com/print/managing/content/apr2009/ca20090421_555468.htm (accessed April 21, 2009).

73. John D. Stoll, "Repair Job: GM Urges, 'Tell Fritz'" *The Wall Street Journal Online*, July 20, 2009, http://online.wsj.com/article/SB124804822336763843.html?mod=djem_jiewr_LD (accessed July 27, 2010).

74. J. C. McCroskey, "Measures of Communication-Bound Anxiety," *Speech Monographs* 37 (1970): 269–277; J. C. McCroskey and V. P. Richmond, "Validity of the PRCA as an Index of Oral Communication Apprehension," *Communication Monographs* 45 (1978): 192–203; J. C. McCroskey and V. P. Richmond, "The Impact of Communication Apprehension on Individuals in Organizations," *Communication Quarterly* 27 (1979): 55–61; J. C. McCroskey, *An Introduction to Rhetorical Communication* (Englewood Cliffs, NJ: Prentice Hall, 1982).

75. Mary Gillis, "Iranian Americans," *Multicultural America,* www.everyculture.com/multi/Ha-La/Iranian-Americans.html (accessed September 19, 2006); and Charlene Marmer Solomon, "Managing Today's Immigrants," *Personnel Journal* 72, no. 3 (February 1993): 56–65.

76. Based on Harry W. Lane, *Charles Foster Sends an Email* (London, Ontario: Ivey Publishing, 2005); Frank Unger and Roger Frankel, *Doing Business in Mexico: A Practical Guide on How to Break into the Market* (Council on Australia Latin America Relations and the Department of Foreign Affairs and Trade, 2002): 24–27; and Ignacio Hernandez, "Doing Business in Mexico—Business Etiquette," MexGrocer.com, www.mexgrocer.com/business-in-mexico.html (accessed September 18, 2006).

77. J. Craddock, ed., *VideoHound's Golden Movie Retriever* (Detroit, MI: Gale, Cengage Learning, 2008), p. 368.

78. "This sequence is heavily based on DVD Chapter 27, "Half-Time." However, we edited in scenes from other parts of the film to reduce the number of identifiable talents to whom we must pay a fee. If you have seen this film, then you will know that this exact sequence does not exist at any point in the film."

Chapter Outline

Why Teams at Work?
- *What Is a Team?*
- *The Dilemma of Teams*

How to Make Teams Effective
- *Model of Team Effectiveness*
- *Effective Team Leadership*

Types of Teams
- *Formal Teams*
- *Self-Directed Teams*

Innovative Uses of Teams
- *Virtual Teams*
- *Global Teams*

Team Characteristics
- *Size*
- *Diversity*
- *Member Roles*

Team Processes
- *Stages of Team Development*
- *Team Cohesiveness*
- *Team Norms*

Managing Team Conflict
- *Types of Conflict*
- *Balancing Conflict and Cooperation*
- *Causes of Conflict*
- *Styles to Handle Conflict*
- *Negotiation*

Work Team Effectiveness
- *Productive Output*
- *Satisfaction of Members*
- *Capacity to Adapt and Learn*

Leading Teams

Learning Outcomes

After studying this chapter, you should be able to:

1. Identify the types of teams in organizations.
2. Discuss some of the problems and challenges of teamwork.
3. Identify roles within teams and the type of role you could play to help a team be effective.
4. Explain the general stages of team development.
5. Identify ways in which team size and diversity of membership affects team performance.
6. Explain the concepts of team cohesiveness and team norms and their relationship to team performance.
7. Understand the causes of conflict within and among teams and how to reduce conflict.
8. Describe the different characteristics and consequences of task conflict versus relationship conflict.
9. Define the outcomes of effective teams and how managers can enhance team effectiveness.

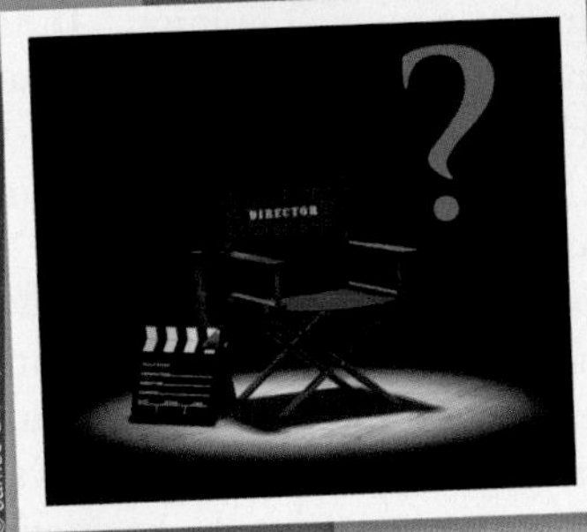

Are You Ready to Be a Manager?

Please circle your opinion below each of the following statements.

1 I am energized when I work in a productive team.

Mostly True | Mostly False

(See page 560, What Is a Team?)

2 I am able to have honest and tactful discussions with "free riders" on my team.

Mostly True | Mostly False

(See page 560, The Dilemma of Teams.)

3 I am able to share information and power with others and also admit when I don't know something.

Mostly True | Mostly False

(See page 563, Effective Team Leadership.)

4 When I join a new team, I spend time observing the norms of this group before I take any actions or make comments.

Mostly True | Mostly False

(See page 576, Team Norms.)

5 I know that some conflict is good in a team, to prevent "groupthink," and I am able to help resolve conflict by assertively and collaboratively addressing the issues.

Mostly True | Mostly False

(See page 578, Managing Team Conflict.)

When Tasty Catering co-owner and CEO Thomas Walter first read *Good to Great*, by Jim Collins, he knew he wanted his company to be more like the "great" ones Collins described. How did he make that happen? He turned strategic decision making over to teams of front-line employees from all across the company—chefs and accountants, clerical workers and drivers, supervisors and servers. Walter formed two strategy teams—one conducts all its meetings in English, the other in Spanish, which is the first language for about a third of Tasty Catering's workforce. "It puts all of us on an even playing field," said Anna Wollin, an account executive. "I had been with the company less than a year, and my opinion was as important as an owner's opinion." The strategy teams redrew the organization chart from a traditional departmental structure to a collection of small cross-functional teams arranged in a circle around the customer. Day-to-day management decisions are still made by the owners, but teams make many of their own choices about how best to manage their work and accomplish goals.[1]

Teams have become the primary way in which many companies accomplish their work, from the assembly line to the executive suite. Many people get their first management experience in a team setting, and you will probably sometimes have to work in a team as a new manager. Teams have real advantages, but it can sometimes be tough to work in a team. You may have already experienced the challenges of teamwork as a student, where you've had to give up some of your independence and rely on the team to perform well in order to earn a good grade.

Good teams can be highly productive, but teams aren't always successful. In a survey of manufacturing organizations, about 80 percent of respondents said they used some kind of teams, but only 14 percent of those companies rated their teaming efforts as highly effective. Just over half of the respondents said their efforts were only "somewhat effective," and 15 percent considered their efforts not effective at all.[2]

This chapter focuses on teams and their applications within organizations. We first look at why organizations use teams, discuss the dilemma of teamwork, and provide an overview of what makes an effective team. We define various types of teams, explore the stages of team development, and examine how characteristics such as size, cohesiveness, diversity, and norms influence team effectiveness. We also discuss how individuals can make contributions to teams, look at techniques for managing team conflict, and describe how negotiation can facilitate cooperation and teamwork. The final section of the chapter focuses on the outcomes of effective work teams within organizations. Teams are a central aspect of organizational life, and the ability to manage them is a vital component of manager and organization success.

Why Teams at Work?

Why aren't organizations just collections of individuals going their own way and doing their own thing? Clearly, teamwork provides benefits or companies wouldn't continue to use this structural mechanism. To understand the value of teamwork, consider the following recent situation: Trapped underground after a copper mine collapsed in San José, Chile, 33 miners had little food, scant water, dusty conditions, and frayed nerves. The situation could have led to chaos, but these men quickly perceived that teamwork offered them the best chance to survive. The miners organized into several teams in charge of critical activities such as communication with rescue workers, the transport of supplies from above ground, rationing and distribution of food, managing health concerns, and securing the mine to prevent further rock falls. Leaders emerged who helped the teams coordinate their activities and maintain a sense of solidarity as days stretched into weeks and weeks into

New Manager Self-Test

How Do You Like to Work?

Your approach to your job or schoolwork may indicate whether you thrive on a team. Answer the questions below about your work preferences. Please answer whether each item below is Mostly True or Mostly False for you.

	MOSTLY TRUE <<<	>>> MOSTLY FALSE
1. I prefer to work on a team rather than do individual tasks.	______	______
2. Given a choice, I try to work by myself rather than face the hassles of group work.	______	______
3. I enjoy the personal interaction when working with others.	______	______
4. I prefer to do my own work and let others do theirs.	______	______
5. I get more satisfaction from a group victory than an individual victory.	______	______
6. Teamwork is not worthwhile when people do not do their share.	______	______
7. I feel good when I work with others, even when we disagree.	______	______
8. I prefer to rely on myself rather than others to do an assignment.	______	______

See It Online

Scoring and Interpretation: Give yourself 1 point for each odd-numbered item you marked Mostly True and 1 point for each even-numbered item you marked Mostly False. An important part of a new manager's job is to be both part of a team and to work alone. These items measure your preference for group work. Teamwork can be both frustrating and motivating. If you scored 2 or fewer points, you definitely prefer individual work. A score of 7 or above suggests that you prefer working in teams. A score of 3 to 6 indicates comfort working alone and in a team. A new manager needs to do both.

SOURCE: Based on Eric M. Stark, Jason D. Shaw, and Michelle K. Duffy, "Preference for Group Work, Winning Orientation, and Social Loafing Behavior in Groups," *Group & Organization Management* 32, no. 6 (December 2007): 699–723.

months. Experts agree that teamwork and leadership were key to the miners' survival, and consultants, academics, and government officials are looking at the events that unfolded underground for lessons not only in integrity and courage but also in teamwork, coordination, and leadership.[3]

Most of us will never face the kind of crisis situation these 33 miners endured and the urgent need to work together for our very survival. Yet organizations are by their very nature made up of various individuals and groups that have to work together and coordinate their activities to accomplish objectives. Much work in organizations is *interdependent*, which means that individuals and departments rely on other individuals and departments for information or resources to accomplish their work. When tasks are highly interdependent, a team can be the best approach to ensuring the level of coordination, information sharing, and exchange of materials necessary for successful task accomplishment.

What Is a Team?

1

A **team** is a unit of two or more people who interact and coordinate their work to accomplish a common goal for which they are committed and hold themselves mutually accountable.[4] At Cirque du Soleil, the CEO, chief operating officer, chief financial officer, and vice president of creation function as a top management team to develop, coordinate, and oversee acrobatic troupes that travel to approximately 100 cities on four continents a year. Google assembles teams of three or four employees to assess new ideas and recommend whether they should be implemented. And at the Ralston Foods plant in Sparks, Nevada, teams of production workers handle all team hiring, scheduling, quality, budgeting, and disciplinary issues.[5]

The definition of a team has four components. First, two or more people are required. Second, people in a team have regular interaction. People who do not interact (e.g., when standing in line at a lunch counter or riding in an elevator) do not compose a team. Third, people in a team share a performance goal, whether it is to design a new smartphone, build an engine, or complete a class project. Fourth, people in a team are committed to the goal and hold themselves mutually accountable for performance.

Although a *team* is a *group* of people, these two terms are not interchangeable. An employer, a teacher, or a coach can put together a *group* of people and never build a *team*. The team concept implies a sense of shared mission and collective responsibility. Exhibit 14.1 lists the primary differences between groups and teams. One example of a true team comes from the military, where U.S. Navy surgeons, nurses, anesthesiologists, and technicians make up eight-person forward surgical teams that operated for the first time ever in combat during Operation Iraqi Freedom. These teams were scattered over Iraq and were able to move to new locations and be set up within an hour. With a goal of saving the 15 to 20 percent of wounded soldiers and civilians who will die unless they receive critical care within 24 hours, members of these teams smoothly coordinated their activities to accomplish a critical shared mission.[6]

2

The Dilemma of Teams

If you've been in a class where the instructor announced that part of the grade would be based on a team project, you probably heard a few groans. The same thing happens in organizations. Some people love the idea of teamwork, others hate it, and many people

EXHIBIT 14.1

Differences between Groups and Teams

Group	Team
• Has a designated strong leader	• Shares or rotates leadership roles
• Holds individuals accountable	• Holds team accountable to each other
• Sets identical purpose for group and organization	• Sets specific team vision or purpose
• Has individual work products	• Has collective work products
• Runs efficient meetings	• Runs meetings that encourage open-ended discussion and problem solving
• Measures effectiveness indirectly by influence on business (such as financial performance)	• Measures effectiveness directly by assessing collective work
• Discusses, decides, delegates work to individuals	• Discusses, decides, shares work

SOURCE: Adapted from Jon R. Katzenbach and Douglas K. Smith, "The Discipline of Teams," *Harvard Business Review* (March–April 1995): 111–120.

have both positive and negative emotions about working as part of a team. There are three primary reasons teams present a dilemma for many people:

- ***We have to give up our independence.*** When people become part of a team, their success depends on the team's success; therefore, they must depend on how well other people perform, not just on their own individual initiative and actions. Most people are comfortable with the idea of making sacrifices to achieve their own individual success, yet teamwork demands that they make sacrifices for *group* success.[7] The idea is that each person should put the team first, even if at times it hurts the individual. Many employees, particularly in individualistic cultures such as the United States, have a hard time appreciating and accepting that concept. Some cultures, such as Japan, have had greater success with teams because traditional Japanese culture values the group over the individual.
- ***We have to put up with free riders.*** Teams are sometimes made up of people who have different work ethics. The term **free rider** refers to a team member who attains benefits from team membership but does not actively participate in and contribute to the team's work. You might have experienced this frustration in a student project team, where one member put little effort into the group project but benefited from the hard work of others when grades were handed out. Free riding is sometimes called *social loafing* because some members do not exert equal effort.[8]
- ***Teams are sometimes dysfunctional.*** Some companies have had great success with teams, but there are also numerous examples of how teams in organizations fail spectacularly.[9] "The best groups will be better than their individual members, and the worst groups will be worse than the worst individual," says organizational psychologist Robert Sutton.[10] A great deal of research and team experience over the past few decades have produced significant insights into what causes teams to succeed or fail. The evidence shows that how teams are managed plays the most critical role in determining how well they function.[11] Exhibit 14.2 lists five dysfunctions that are common in teams and describes the contrasting desirable characteristics that effective team leaders develop.

EXHIBIT 14.2

Five Common Dysfunctions of Teams

Dysfunction	Effective Team Characteristics
Lack of Trust—People don't feel safe to reveal mistakes, share concerns, or express ideas.	**Trust**—Members trust one another on a deep emotional level; feel comfortable being vulnerable with one another.
Fear of Conflict—People go along with others for the sake of harmony; don't express conflicting opinions.	**Healthy Conflict**—Members feel comfortable disagreeing and challenging one another in the interest of finding the best solution.
Lack of Commitment—If people are afraid to express their true opinions, it's difficult to gain their true commitment to decisions.	**Commitment**—Because all ideas are put on the table, people can eventually achieve genuine buy-in around important goals and decisions.
Avoidance of Accountability—People don't accept responsibility for outcomes; engage in finger-pointing when things go wrong.	**Accountability**—Members hold one another accountable rather than relying on managers as the source of accountability.
Inattention to Results—Members put personal ambition or the needs of their individual departments ahead of collective results.	**Results Orientation**—Individual members set aside personal agendas; focus on what's best for the team. Collective results define success.

SOURCES: Based on Patrick Lencioni, *The Five Dysfunctions of a Team* (New York: John Wiley & Sons, 2002); and P. Lencioni, "Dissolve Dysfunction: Begin Building Your Dream Team," *Leadership Excellence* (October 2009): 20.

- A **team** is unit of two or more people who interact and coordinate their work to accomplish a goal for which they are committed and hold themselves mutually accountable.
- Organizations as diverse as Cirque du Soleil, Ralston Foods, and the United States Navy use teams to perform tasks that are highly interdependent and require a high level of coordination.
- Teams present a dilemma for most people because individual success depends on how well others perform, there are common dysfunctions that afflict teams, and there is a potential for free riders.
- A **free rider** is a person who benefits from team membership but does not make a proportionate contribution to the team's work.
- Five common dysfunctions of teams are lack of trust, fear of conflict, lack of commitment, avoidance of accountability, and inattention to results.
- How teams are managed makes the biggest difference in determining how well they function.

How to Make Teams Effective

Smoothly functioning teams don't just happen. Stanford sociologist Elizabeth Cohen studied group work among young school children and found that only when teachers took the time to define roles, establish norms, and set goals did the groups function effectively as a team.[12] In organizations, effective teams are built by managers who take specific actions to help people come together and perform well as a team.

Some of the factors associated with team effectiveness are illustrated in Exhibit 14.3. Work team effectiveness is based on three outcomes—productive output, personal satisfaction, and the capacity to adapt and learn.[13] *Satisfaction* pertains to the team's ability to meet the personal needs of its members and hence maintain their membership and commitment. *Productive output* pertains to the quality and quantity of task outputs as defined by team goals. *Capacity to adapt and learn* refers to the ability of teams to bring greater knowledge and skills to job tasks and enhance the potential of the organization to respond to new threats or opportunities in the environment.

14.3 EXHIBIT

Work Team Effectiveness Model

Model of Team Effectiveness

The model of team effectiveness in Exhibit 14.3 provides a structure for the remainder of this chapter. The factors that influence team effectiveness begin with the organizational context.[14] The organizational context in which the team operates is described in other chapters and includes such matters as overall leadership, strategy, environment, culture, and reward systems. Within that context, managers define teams. Important team characteristics are the type of team, the team structure, and team composition. Managers must decide when to create permanent teams within the formal structure and when to use a temporary task team. The diversity of the team in terms of task-related knowledge and skills can have a tremendous impact on team processes and effectiveness. In addition, diversity in terms of gender and race affect a team's performance.[15] Team size and roles also are important.

These team characteristics influence processes internal to the team, which, in turn, affect output, satisfaction, and the team's contribution to organizational adaptability. Good team leaders understand and manage stages of team development, cohesiveness, norms, and conflict to build an effective team. These processes are influenced by team and organizational characteristics and by the ability of members and leaders to direct these processes in a positive manner.

REUTERS/Tim Shaffer

ConceptConnection

West Philly Hybrid X, the only high school team to enter the 2010 Progressive Insurance Automotive X Prize Competition, turned in an impressive performance. Challenged to design a 100-mile-per-gallon, alternative-energy car, the team from inner-city Philadelphia was one of 21 out of 111 original entrants to survive the first round, beating out MIT and Tesla Motors. Leader and former teacher Simon Hauger (pictured above, lifting the car hood) believes in **sharing power**. "I put the students at the center," he says. "The kids are empowered to make big decisions and think creatively. And teenagers, we've found, always think outside the box."

Effective Team Leadership

Team leaders play an important role in shaping team effectiveness. In addition to managing internal processes, there are three specific ways in which leaders contribute to team success:[16]

- ***Rally people around a compelling purpose.*** It is the leader's responsibility to articulate a clear, compelling purpose and direction, one of the key elements of effective teams. This ensures that everyone is moving in the same direction rather than floundering around wondering why the team was created and where it's supposed to be going. Research has found that leaders who can focus people on a clear mission and goals are important to the success of all teams and are particularly critical to the effectiveness of virtual teams.[17]
- ***Share power.*** Good team leaders embrace the concept of teamwork in deeds as well as words. This means sharing power, information, and responsibility. It requires that the leader have faith that team members will make good decisions, even if those decisions might not be the ones the leader would make. Craig Williams, vice president of Walmart's Global People Division, described one manager who would go through agenda items at team meetings one by one, asking for discussion but often showing annoyance, and then make all the decisions himself. Good team leaders often let a different member run the meeting each time, perhaps based on who is most familiar or most affected by the topic being discussed.[18] Effective meetings are essential to effective teamwork. The Spotlight on Skills titled How to Run a Great Meeting gives some tips for running a dynamic, productive meeting.
- ***Admit ignorance.*** Often, people appointed to lead teams find that they don't know nearly as much as their teammates know. Good team leaders aren't afraid to admit their

Go to the Self-Learning, on pages 586–587, that pertains to effective versus ineffective teams.

ignorance and ask for help. This serves as a *fallibility model* that lets people know that lack of knowledge, problems, concerns, and mistakes can be discussed openly without fear of appearing incompetent. Although it's hard for many managers to believe, admitting ignorance and being willing to learn from others can earn the respect of team members faster than almost any other behavior.

- Team leaders pay attention to stages of team development, team size and diversity, and other processes to build an effective team.
- Three specific ways leaders contribute to team success are by rallying people around a compelling purpose, sharing power and responsibility, and admitting their imperfections and shortcomings.

Types of Teams

Organizations use many types of teams. Some are created as part of the organization's formal structure and others are designed to increase employee participation.

Formal Teams

Formal teams are created by the organization as part of the formal organization structure. Two common types of formal teams are vertical and horizontal, which typically represent vertical and horizontal structural relationships, as described in Chapter 7. These two types of teams are illustrated in Exhibit 14.4.

EXHIBIT 14.4 Horizontal and Vertical Teams in an Organization

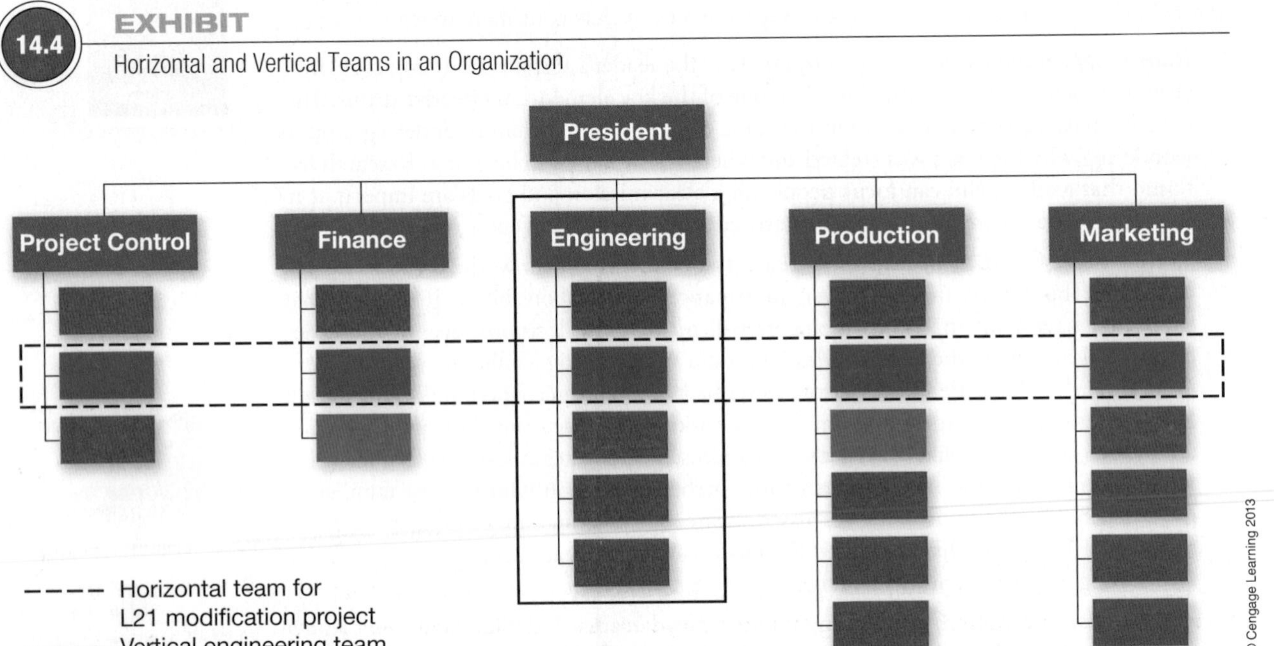

SPOTLIGHT ON SKILLS

How to Run a Great Meeting

A survey in the United States and Britain found that people spend an average of 5.6 hours a week in meetings, yet 69 percent of respondents considered most of that time wasted. Meetings can be excellent avenues to solving problems, sharing information, and achieving shared goals, but good meetings don't just happen. Here are some tips on how to make meetings worthwhile and productive.

Prepare in Advance

Advance preparation is the single most important tool for running an efficient, productive meeting.

- ***Define the purpose.*** Is the meeting's purpose to share information, draw on participants' expertise and skills, elicit their commitment to a project, or coordinate the efforts required to accomplish a specific task? The leader needs to be clear about what the purpose is. If a meeting isn't essential, don't have it.
- ***Invite the right people.*** Meetings fail when too many, too few, or the wrong people are involved. Don't let the meeting get too big, but make sure everyone with a contribution to make or a stake in the topic is represented.
- ***Prepare an agenda and identify the expected outcome.*** Distributing a simple list of the topics to be discussed lets people know what to expect. If the meeting is for exploration only, say so. A lack of decision making can be frustrating if participants expect action to be taken.

Bring out the Best during the Meeting

During the meeting, certain techniques will bring out the best in people and ensure a productive session:

- ***Start on time, state the purpose, and review the agenda.*** Starting on time has symbolic value because it tells people that the topic is important and that the leader values their time. Begin by stating the meeting's explicit purpose and clarifying what should be accomplished by its conclusion.
- ***Establish ground rules.*** Outlawing cell phones, handhelds, and laptops can make sure people aren't distracted. Other rules concern how people should interact, such as emphasizing equal participation and respectful listening.
- ***Create involvement.*** Good leaders draw out the silent and control the talkative so that the meeting isn't dominated by one or two assertive people. In addition, they encourage a free flow of ideas, provoke discussion with open-ended questions, and make sure everyone feels heard.
- ***Keep it moving.*** Allowing participants to waste time by getting into discussions of issues not on the agenda is a primary reason people hate meetings. Move the meeting along as needed to meet time constraints.

Attend to the End as Much as the Beginning

Review and follow-up is important to summarize and implement agreed-upon points.

- ***End with a call to action.*** Summarize the discussion, review any decisions made, and make sure everyone understands his or her assignments.
- ***Follow up swiftly.*** Send a short memo to summarize the meeting's key accomplishments, outline agreed-upon activities, and suggest schedules for implementation.

SOURCES: Based on Antony Jay, *How to Run a Meeting* (Boston, MA: Harvard Business Review Classics, 2009); Beth Bratkovic, "Running an Effective Meeting," *Government Finance Review* (April 2007): 58–60; Phred Dvorak, "Corporate Meetings Go Through a Makeover," *The Wall Street Journal*, March 6, 2006; Richard Axelrod, Emily M. Axelrod, Julie Beedon, and Robert Jacobs, "Creating Dynamic, Energy-Producing Meetings," *Leader to Leader* (Spring 2005): 53–58; and Howard M. Guttman, "Leading Meetings 101: Transform Them from Dull to Dynamic," *Leadership Excellence* (July 2009): 18.

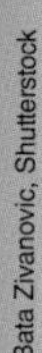

Vertical Team A **vertical team** is composed of a manager and his or her subordinates in the formal chain of command. Sometimes called a *functional team* or a *command team*, the vertical team may in some cases include three or four levels of hierarchy within a functional department. Typically, the vertical team includes a single department in an organization. A financial analysis department, a quality control department, an accounting department, and a human resource department are all vertical or command teams. Each is created by the organization to attain specific goals through members' joint activities and interactions.

Horizontal Team A **horizontal team** is composed of employees from about the same hierarchical level but from different areas of expertise.[19] A horizontal team is drawn from several departments, is given a specific task, and may be disbanded after the task is completed. Horizontal teams include cross-functional teams, committees, and special-purpose teams.

As described in Chapter 7, a *cross-functional team* is a group of employees from different departments formed to deal with a specific activity and existing only until the task is completed. Sometimes called a *task force*, the team might be used to create a new product in a manufacturing organization or a new history curriculum in a university. Georgetown Preparatory School used a task force to develop a flu preparedness plan some years ago, and was one of the few schools that was ready when the H1N1 (swine flu) outbreak hit in the winter of 2009. Georgetown began thinking about a flu preparedness plan during the earlier avian flu scare. To share knowledge and responsibility all across the school community, leaders put together a team made up of teachers, coaches, administrators, support staff, and outside consultants. The result was FluPrep, a plan that makes everyone aware of what they can do individually and collectively to combat seasonal influenza, as well as to learn about and prepare for other, more deadly health threats. The team addressed a number of difficult questions, such as how to encourage "responsible absence," whether to track foreign travel of students and staff, at what point the school would close should an outbreak occur, and how to use distance learning.[20]

Another good example comes from Jet Blue, discussed in the Spotlight on Skills titled JetBlue, which used a task force to improve how the airline handles "irregular operations," such as severe weather.

SPOTLIGHT ON SKILLS

JetBlue

All airlines face the problem of unpredictable weather, and how effectively they manage and recover from these events dramatically affect performance and customer satisfaction. JetBlue suffered a serious customer satisfaction crisis when severe snowstorms paralyzed New York airports in February 2007. Rather than canceling flights, JetBlue loaded the planes and hoped for a break in the weather. Unfortunately, some passengers were trapped on planes for nearly ten hours.

Managers put together a task force made up of crew schedulers, systems operators, dispatchers, reservations agents, and other employees to revise how the airline handled and recovered from irregular operations. At the first meeting, they presented a simulated emergency and asked the team to map out how they would respond. As team members went through the process, they began to spot problems. Ultimately, the "irregular operations strike force" identified more than 1,000 process flaws, which were narrowed down to 85 critical ones. The task force spent nine months in intense meetings working out solutions.

The effort paid off, dramatically improving both JetBlue's regular on-time performance and its recovery time from major events such as storms.

SOURCE: Dan Heath and Chip Heath, "Blowing the Baton Pass," *Fast Company* (July–August 2010): 46–48.

When several departments are involved, and many views have to be considered, tasks are best served with a horizontal, cross-functional team, such as those at JetBlue and Georgetown Preparatory School.

Another type of horizontal team, a **committee**, is generally long lived and may be a permanent part of the organization's structure. Membership is often decided by a person's title or position rather than by personal expertise. A committee needs official representation, compared with selection for a cross-functional team, which is based on personal qualifications for solving a problem. Committees typically are formed to deal with tasks that recur regularly. For example, a grievance committee handles employee grievances; an advisory committee makes recommendations in the areas of employee compensation and work practices; a worker-management committee may be concerned with work rules, job design changes, and suggestions for work improvement.

Special-purpose teams, sometimes called *project teams*, are created outside the formal organization structure to undertake a project of special importance or creativity.[21] The International House of Pancakes (IHOP) created a special-purpose team to identify software and processes for making sure IHOP managers get regular, up-to-date, and reliable information from its restaurants around the country.[22] Cisco Systems used a special-purpose team to create a new multimedia device called the Cius that combines features of the iPad, Kindle, and BlackBerry.[23] A special-purpose team still is part of the formal organization and has its own reporting structure, but members perceive themselves as a separate entity.

Self-Directed Teams

Some teams are designed to increase the participation of workers in decision making and the conduct of their jobs, with the goal of improving performance. Employee involvement started out simply with techniques such as information sharing with employees or asking employees for suggestions about improving the work. Gradually, companies moved toward greater autonomy for employees, which ultimately led to self-directed teams.[24]

Self-directed teams typically consist of 5 to 20 multiskilled workers who rotate jobs to produce an entire product or service or at least one complete aspect or portion of a product or service (e.g., engine assembly, insurance claim processing). The central idea is that the teams themselves, rather than managers or supervisors, take responsibility for their work, make decisions, monitor their own performance, and alter their work behavior as needed to solve problems, meet goals, and adapt to changing conditions.[25]

Self-directed teams are permanent teams that typically include the following elements:

- The team includes employees with several skills and functions, and the combined skills are sufficient to perform a major organizational task. A team may include members from the foundry, machining, grinding, fabrication, and sales departments, with members cross-trained to perform one another's jobs. The team eliminates barriers among departments, enabling excellent coordination to produce a product or service.
- The team is given access to resources such as information, equipment, machinery, and supplies needed to perform the complete task.
- The team is empowered with decision-making authority, which means that members have the freedom to select new members, solve problems, spend money, monitor results, and plan for the future.[26] Self-directed teams can enable employees to feel challenged, find their work meaningful, and develop a stronger sense of identity with the organization.

- **Formal teams** are created by organizations as part of the formal organization structure.
- A **vertical team** is composed of a manager and his or her subordinates in the formal chain of command.
- A **horizontal team** is made up of employees from about the same hierarchical level but from different areas of expertise.
- Horizontal teams include cross-functional teams, committees, and special-purpose teams.
- A *cross-functional team,* sometimes called a task force, is a group of employees from different departments who deal with a specific activity and exist as a team only until the task is completed.
- A **committee** is a long-lasting, sometimes permanent team created as part of the formal organization structure to deal with tasks that occur regularly.
- **Special-purpose teams** are teams created outside the formal structure to undertake a project of special importance, such as developing a new product like the Cius multimedia device from Cisco Systems.
- A **self-directed team** consists of multiskilled employees who rotate jobs to produce an entire product or service, often led by an elected team member.
- Self-directed teams take responsibility for their work, make decisions, monitor their own performance, and alter their work behavior as needed to solve problems and meet goals.

Innovative Uses of Teams

Some exciting new approaches to teamwork have resulted from advances in information technology, shifting employee expectations, and the globalization of business. Two types of teams that are increasingly being used are virtual teams and global teams.

Virtual Teams

A **virtual team** is made up of geographically or organizationally dispersed members who are linked primarily through advanced information and telecommunications technologies.[27] Although some virtual teams are made up of only organizational members, virtual teams often include contingent workers, members of partner organizations, customers, suppliers, consultants, or other outsiders. Team members use e-mail, instant messaging, telephone and text messaging, wikis and blogs, videoconferencing, and other technology tools to collaborate and perform their work, although they might also sometimes meet face-to-face. Many virtual teams are cross-functional teams that emphasize solving customer problems or completing specific projects. Others are permanent self-directed teams.

With virtual teams, team membership may change fairly quickly, depending on the tasks to be performed.[28] One of the primary advantages of virtual teams is the ability to rapidly assemble the most appropriate group of people to complete a complex project, solve a particular problem, or exploit a specific strategic opportunity. Virtual teams present unique challenges. Exhibit 14.5 lists some critical areas managers should address when leading virtual teams. Each of these areas is discussed in more detail below:[29]

- ***Using technology to build relationships*** is crucial for effective virtual teamwork. Leaders first select people who have the right mix of technical, interpersonal, and communication

EXHIBIT 14.5

What Effective Virtual Team Leaders Do

Practice	How It's Done
Use Technology to Build Relationships	• Bring attention to and appreciate diverse skills and opinions • Use technology to enhance communication and trust • Ensure timely responses online • Manage online socialization
Shape Culture through Technology	• Create a psychologically safe virtual culture • Share members' special experience/strengths • Engage members from cultures where they may be hesitant to share ideas
Monitor Progress and Rewards	• Scrutinize electronic communication patterns • Post targets and scorecards in virtual work space • Reward people through online ceremonies, recognition

SOURCES: Based on Table 1, Practices of Effective Virtual Team Leaders, in Arvind Malhotra, Ann Majchrzak, and Benson Rosen, "Leading Virtual Teams," *Academy of Management Perspectives* 21, no. 1 (February 2007): 60–69; and Table 2, "Best Practices" Solutions for Overcoming Barriers to Knowledge Sharing in Virtual Teams, in Benson Rosen, Stacie Furst, and Richard Blackburn, "Overcoming Barriers to Knowledge Sharing in Virtual Teams," *Organizational Dynamics* 36, no. 3 (2007): 259–273.

skills to work in a virtual environment, and then make sure they have opportunities to know one another and establish trusting relationships. Encouraging online social networking, where people can share photos and personal biographies, is one key to virtual team success. One recent study suggests that higher levels of online communication increase team cohesiveness.[30] Leaders also build trust by making everyone's roles, responsibilities, and authority clear from the beginning, by shaping norms of full disclosure and respectful interaction, and by providing a way for everyone to stay up-to-date. In a study of which technologies make virtual teams successful, researchers found that round-the-clock virtual work spaces, where team members can access the latest versions of files, keep track of deadlines and timelines, monitor one another's progress, and carry on discussions between formal meetings, got top marks.[31]

- ***Shaping culture through technology*** involves creating a virtual environment in which people feel safe to express concerns, admit mistakes, share ideas, acknowledge fears, or ask for help. Leaders reinforce a norm of sharing all forms of knowledge, and they encourage people to express "off-the-wall" ideas and ask for help when it's needed. Team leaders set the example by their own behavior. Leaders also make sure they bring diversity issues into the open and educate members early on regarding possible cultural differences that could cause communication problems or misunderstandings in a virtual environment.
- ***Monitoring progress and rewarding members*** means that leaders stay on top of the project's development and make sure everyone knows how the team is progressing toward meeting goals. Posting targets, measurements, and milestones in the virtual workspace can make progress explicit. Leaders also provide regular feedback, and they reward both individual and team accomplishments through avenues such as virtual award ceremonies and recognition at virtual meetings. They are liberal with praise and congratulations, but criticism or reprimands are handled individually rather than in the virtual presence of the team.

SPOTLIGHT ON SKILLS

Nokia

In a study of 52 virtual teams in 15 leading multinational companies, London Business School researchers found that Nokia's teams were among the most effective, even though they were made up of people working in several different countries, across time zones and cultures. What makes Nokia's teams so successful?

Nokia managers are careful to select people who have a collaborative mind-set, and they form many teams with volunteers who are highly committed to the task or project. The company also tries to make sure some members of a team have worked together before, providing a base for trusting relationships. Making the best use of technology is critical. In addition to a virtual work space that team members can access 24 hours a day, Nokia provides an online resource where virtual workers are encouraged to post photos and share personal information. With the inability of members to get to know each other one of the biggest barriers to effective virtual teamwork, encouraging and supporting social networking has paid off for Nokia.

SOURCE: Pete Engardio, "A Guide for Multinationals: One of the Greatest Challenges for a Multinational Is Learning How to Build a Productive Global Team," *BusinessWeek* (August 20, 2007): 48–51; and Lynda Gratton, "Working Together … When Apart," *The Wall Street Journal*, June 18, 2007.

As the use of virtual teams grows, there is growing understanding of what makes them successful. Some experts suggest that managers solicit volunteers as much as possible for virtual teams, and interviews with virtual team members and leaders support the idea that members who truly want to work as a virtual team are more effective.[32] At Nokia, a significant portion of its virtual teams is made up of people who volunteered for the task, as shown in the Spotlight on Skills titled Nokia.

Global Teams

As the example of Nokia shows, virtual teams are also sometimes global teams. **Global teams** are cross-border work teams made up of members of different nationalities whose activities span multiple countries.[33] Some global teams are made up of members who come from different countries or cultures and meet face-to-face, but many are virtual global teams whose members remain in separate locations around the world and conduct their work electronically.[34] For example, at one global software company, teams of software developers coordinate their work electronically so that the team is productive around the clock. Team members in London code a project and transmit the code each evening to members in the United States for testing. U.S. team members then forward the code they've tested to Tokyo for debugging. The next morning, the London team members pick up with the code debugged by their Tokyo colleagues, and another cycle begins.[35]

Global teams present enormous challenges for team leaders, who have to bridge gaps of time, distance, and culture.[36] In some cases, members speak different languages, use different technologies, and have different beliefs about authority, communication, decision making, and time orientation. For example, in some cultures, such as the United States, communication is explicit and direct, whereas in many other cultures meaning is embedded in the way the message is presented. U.S.-based team members are also typically highly focused on "clock time" and tend to follow rigid schedules, whereas many other cultures have a more relaxed, cyclical concept of time. These different cultural attitudes can affect work pacing, team communications, decision making, the perception of deadlines, and other issues, and provide rich soil for misunderstandings. No wonder when the executive council of *CIO* magazine asked global chief information officers to rank their greatest challenges, managing virtual global teams ranked as the most pressing issue.[37] "You need to be intensely international" to help global teams succeed, said Greg Caltabiano, CEO of chip-designer Teknovus Inc. (now part of Broadcom Corporation). "You have to chip away at 'we versus them.'"[38]

Organizations using global teams invest the time and resources to adequately educate employees and find ways to encourage cross-cultural understanding. At Teknovus, Caltabiano sent U.S. employees on short visits to the company's Asian offices and required that all new overseas hires spend time in the United States.[39] Managers working with global teams make sure all team members appreciate and understand cultural differences, are focused on clear goals, and understand their roles and responsibilities. For a global team to be effective, all team members must be willing to deviate somewhat from their own values and norms, adopt a global mind-set, and establish new norms for the team.[40] As with virtual teams, carefully selecting team members, building trust, and sharing information are critical to success.

- A **virtual team** is a team made up of members who are geographically or organizationally dispersed, rarely meet face-to-face, and interact to accomplish their work primarily using advanced information and telecommunications technologies.
- A **global team** is made up of employees who come from different countries and whose activities span multiple countries.
- Many global teams are virtual teams, but some global teams meet face-to-face.

Team Characteristics

After deciding the type of team to use, the next issue of concern to managers is designing the team for greatest effectiveness. Team characteristics of particular concern are size, diversity, and member roles.

Size

More than 30 years ago, psychologist Ivan Steiner examined what happened each time the size of a team increased, and he proposed that team performance and productivity peaked at about five—a quite small number. He found that adding additional members beyond five caused a decrease in motivation, an increase in coordination problems, and a general decline in performance.[41] Since then, numerous studies have found that smaller teams perform better, although most researchers say it's impossible to specify an optimal team size. One recent investigation of team size based on data from 58 software development teams found that the best-performing teams ranged in size from three to six members.[42]

Teams need to be large enough to incorporate the diverse skills needed to complete a task, enable members to express good and bad feelings, and aggressively solve problems. However, they should also be small enough to permit members to feel an intimate part of the team and to communicate effectively and efficiently. In general, as a team increases in size, it becomes harder for each member to interact with and influence the others. Subgroups often form in larger teams and conflicts among them can occur. Turnover and absenteeism are higher because members feel less like an important part of the team.[43]

Although the Internet and advanced technologies are enabling larger groups of people to work more effectively in virtual teams, one study found that members of smaller virtual teams participated more actively, were more committed to the team, were more focused on team goals, and had higher levels of rapport than larger virtual teams.[44] Large projects can be split into components and assigned to several smaller teams to keep the benefits of small size. At Amazon.com, CEO Jeff Bezos established a "two-pizza rule." If a team gets so large that members can't be fed with two pizzas, it should be split into smaller teams.[45]

Diversity

Because teams require a variety of skills, knowledge, and experience, it seems likely that heterogeneous teams would be more effective than homogeneous ones. In general, research supports this idea, showing that diverse teams produce more innovative solutions to problems.[46] Diversity in terms of functional area and skills, thinking styles, and personal characteristics is often a source of creativity. In addition, diversity may contribute to a healthy level of disagreement that leads to better decision making.

Research studies have confirmed that both functional diversity and demographic diversity can have a positive impact on work team performance.[47] Although racial, national, and ethnic diversity can hinder team interaction and performance in the short term, with effective leadership, the problems fade over time.[48]

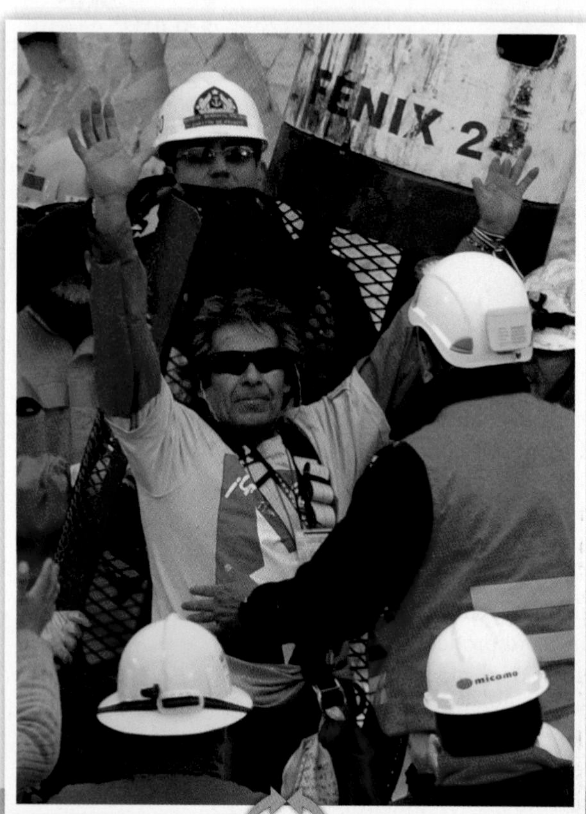

MARTIN BERNETTI/AFP/Getty Images

ConceptConnection

After a 2010 copper mine collapse in Chile, 33 miners spent 69 days confined to 600 square feet while awaiting rescue. A critical factor contributing to their survival was that they organized themselves into teams. Each individual had a role to play. For example, Mario Gómez (pictured), at 63 the oldest of the miners, played a **socioemotional role**. A deeply religious man, he created a buddy system by organizing the miners into groups of three, encouraged the miners to pray, and counseled them as needed.

Member Roles

For a team to be successful over the long run, it must be structured to both maintain its members' social well-being and accomplish its task. In successful teams, the requirements for task performance and social satisfaction are met by the emergence of two types of roles: task specialist and socioemotional.[49]

People who play a **task specialist role** spend time and energy helping the team reach its goal. They often display the following behaviors:

- ***Initiate ideas.*** Propose new solutions to team problems.
- ***Give opinions.*** Offer opinions on task solutions; give candid feedback on others' suggestions.
- ***Seek information.*** Ask for task-relevant facts.
- ***Summarize.*** Relate various ideas to the problem at hand; pull ideas together into a summary perspective.
- ***Energize.*** Stimulate the team into action when interest drops.[50]

People who adopt a **socioemotional role** support team members' emotional needs and help strengthen the social entity. They display the following behaviors:

- ***Encourage.*** Are warm and receptive to others' ideas; praise and encourage others to draw forth their contributions.

- ***Harmonize.*** Reconcile group conflicts; help disagreeing parties reach agreement.
- ***Reduce tension.*** Tell jokes or in other ways draw off emotions when group atmosphere is tense.
- ***Follow.*** Go along with the team; agree to other team members' ideas.
- ***Compromise.*** Will shift own opinions to maintain team harmony.[51]

The Group Learning, on page 587, gives you a chance to evaluate and discuss various team member roles and behaviors.

Teams with mostly socioemotional roles can be satisfying, but they also can be unproductive. At the other extreme, a team made up primarily of task specialists will tend to have a singular concern for task accomplishment. This team will be effective for a short period of time but will not be satisfying for members over the long run. Effective teams have people in both task specialist and socioemotional roles. A well-balanced team will do best over the long term because it will be personally satisfying for team members as well as permit the accomplishment of team tasks.

- Issues of particular concern to managers for team effectiveness are selecting the right type of team for the task, balancing the team's size and diversity, and ensuring that both task and social needs are met.
- Small teams are typically more productive and more satisfying to their members than are large teams.
- Jeff Bezos established a "two-pizza rule" at Amazon.com: If a team gets so large that members can't be fed with two pizzas, it is split into smaller teams.
- The **task specialist role** is a team role in which an individual devotes personal time and energy to helping the team accomplish its activities and reach its goal.
- The **socioemotional role** is a team role in which an individual provides support for team members' emotional needs and helps strengthen social unity.

Team Processes

Now we turn our attention to internal team processes. Team processes pertain to those dynamics that change over time and can be influenced by team leaders. In this section, we discuss stages of development, cohesiveness, and norms. The fourth type of team process, conflict, will be covered in the next section.

Stages of Team Development

After a team has been created, it develops through distinct stages.[52] New teams are different from mature teams. Recall a time when you were a member of a new team, such as a fraternity or sorority pledge class, a committee, or a small team formed to do a class assignment. Over time the team changed. In the beginning, team members had to get to know one another, establish roles and norms, divide the labor, and clarify the team's task. In this way, each member became part of a smoothly operating team. The challenge for leaders is to understand the stages of development and take action that will lead to smooth functioning.

Research findings suggest that team development is not random but evolves over definitive stages. One useful model for describing these stages is shown in Exhibit 14.6. Each stage confronts team leaders and members with unique problems and challenges.[53]

EXHIBIT 14.6
Five Stages of Team Development

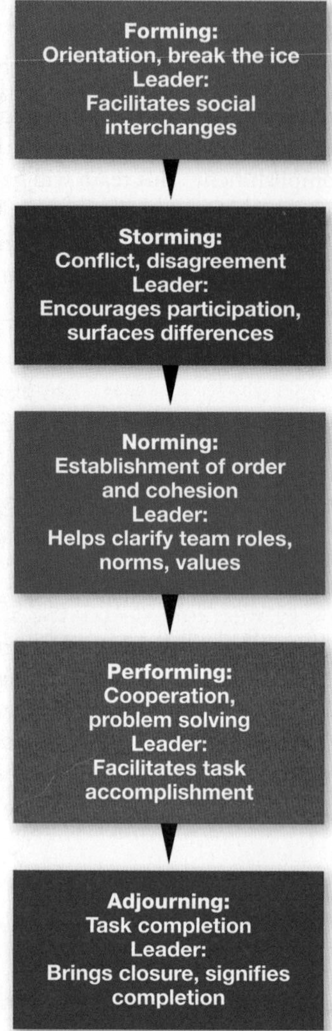

SOURCES: Based on the stages of small group development in Bruce W. Tuckman, "Developmental Sequence in Small Groups," *Psychological Bulletin* 63 (1965): 384–399; and B. W. Tuckman and M. A. Jensen "Stages of Small Group Development Revisited," *Group and Organizational Studies* 2 (1977): 419–427.

Forming The **forming** stage of development is a period of orientation and getting acquainted. Members break the ice and test one another for friendship possibilities and task orientation. Uncertainty is high during this stage, and members usually accept whatever power or authority is offered by either formal or informal leaders. During this initial stage, members are concerned about things such as "What is expected of me?" "What behavior is acceptable?" "Will I fit in?" During the forming stage, the team leader should provide time for members to get acquainted with one another and encourage them to engage in informal social discussions.

Storming During the **storming** stage, individual personalities emerge. People become more assertive in clarifying their roles and what is expected of them. This stage is marked by conflict and disagreement. People may disagree over their perceptions of the team's goals or how to achieve them. Members may jockey for position, and coalitions or subgroups based on common interests may form. Unless teams can successfully move beyond this stage, they may get bogged down and never achieve high performance. During the storming stage, the team leader should encourage participation by each team member. Members should propose ideas, disagree with one another, and work through the uncertainties and conflicting perceptions about team tasks and goals.

Norming During the **norming** stage, conflict is resolved, and team harmony and unity emerge. Consensus develops on who has the power, who are the leaders, and what are members' roles. Members come to accept and understand one another. Differences are resolved, and members develop a sense of team cohesion. During the norming stage, the team leader should emphasize unity within the team and help to clarify team norms and values.

Performing During the **performing** stage, the major emphasis is on problem solving and accomplishing the assigned task. Members are committed to the team's mission. They are coordinated with one another and handle disagreements in a mature way. They confront and resolve problems in the interest of task accomplishment. They interact frequently and direct their discussions and influence toward achieving team goals. During this stage, the leader should concentrate on managing high task performance. Both socioemotional and task specialist roles contribute to the team's functioning.

Adjourning The **adjourning** stage occurs in committees and teams that have a limited task to perform and are disbanded afterward. During this stage, the emphasis is on wrapping up and gearing down. Task performance is no longer a top priority. Members may feel heightened emotionality, strong cohesiveness, and depression or regret over the team's disbandment. At this point, the leader may wish to signify the team's disbanding with a ritual or ceremony, perhaps giving out plaques and awards to signify closure and completeness.

These five stages typically occur in sequence, but in teams that are under time pressure, they may occur quite rapidly. The stages may also be accelerated for virtual teams. For example, at McDevitt Street Bovis, a large construction management firm, bringing people together for a couple of days of team building helps teams move rapidly through the forming and storming stages.

McDEVITT STREET BOVIS

Rather than the typical construction project characterized by conflicts, frantic scheduling, and poor communications, McDevitt Street Bovis wants its collection of contractors, designers, suppliers, and other partners to function like a true team—putting the success of the project ahead of their own individual interests.

The team-building process at Bovis is designed to take teams to the performing stage as quickly as possible by giving everyone an opportunity to get to know one another; explore the ground rules; and clarify roles, responsibilities, and expectations. The team is first divided into separate groups that may have competing objectives—such as the clients in one group, suppliers in another, engineers and architects in a third, and so forth—and asked to come up with a list of their goals for the project. Although interests sometimes vary widely in purely accounting terms, common themes almost always emerge. By talking about conflicting goals and interests, as well as what all the groups share, facilitators help the team gradually come together around a common purpose and begin to develop shared values that will guide the project. After jointly writing a mission statement for the team, each party says what it expects from the others, so that roles and responsibilities can be clarified. The intensive team-building session helps take members quickly through the forming and storming stages of development. "We prevent conflicts from happening," says facilitator Monica Bennett. Leaders at McDevitt Street Bovis believe building better teams builds better buildings.[54]

Team Cohesiveness

Another important aspect of the team process is cohesiveness. **Team cohesiveness** is defined as the extent to which members are attracted to the team and motivated to remain in it.[55] Members of highly cohesive teams are committed to team activities, attend meetings, and are happy when the team succeeds. Members of less cohesive teams are less concerned about the team's welfare. High cohesiveness is normally considered an attractive feature of teams.

Determinants of Team Cohesiveness Several characteristics of team structure and context influence cohesiveness. First is *team interaction*. When team members have frequent contact, they get to know one another, consider themselves a unit, and become more committed to the team.[56] Second is the concept of *shared goals*. If team members agree on purpose and direction, they will be more cohesive. Third is *personal attraction to the team*, meaning that members have similar attitudes and values and enjoy being together.

Two factors in the team's context also influence group cohesiveness. The first is the *presence of competition*. When a team is in moderate competition with other teams, its cohesiveness increases as it strives to win. Finally, *team success* and the favorable evaluation of the team by outsiders add to cohesiveness. When a team succeeds in its task and others in the organization recognize the success, members feel good, and their commitment to the team will be high.

Consequences of Team Cohesiveness The outcome of team cohesiveness can fall into two categories—morale and productivity. As a general rule, morale is higher in cohesive teams because of increased communication among members, a friendly team climate, maintenance of membership because of commitment to the team, loyalty, and member participation in team decisions and activities. High cohesiveness has almost uniformly good effects on the satisfaction and morale of team members.[57]

With respect to the productivity of the team as a whole, research findings suggest that teams in which members share strong feelings of connectedness and generally positive interactions tend to perform better.[58] Thus, a friendly, positive team environment contributes to productivity as well as member satisfaction. Other research, however, indicates that the degree of productivity in cohesive teams may depend on the relationship between management and the work team. One study surveyed more than 200 work teams and correlated job performance with their cohesiveness.[59] Highly cohesive teams were more productive when team members felt management support and less productive when they sensed management hostility and negativism.

Team Norms

A **team norm** is an informal standard of conduct that is shared by team members and guides their behavior.[60] Norms are valuable because they provide a frame of reference for what is expected and acceptable.

Norms begin to develop in the first interactions among members of a new team.[61] Exhibit 14.7 illustrates four common ways in which norms develop. Sometimes, the first behaviors that occur in a team set a precedent. For example, at one company, a team leader began his first meeting by raising an issue and then "leading" team members until he got the solution he wanted. The pattern became ingrained so quickly into an unproductive team norm that members dubbed meetings the "Guess What I Think" game.[62] Other influences on team norms include critical events in the team's history, as well as behaviors, attitudes, and norms that members bring with them from outside the team.

EXHIBIT 14.7

Four Ways Team Norms Develop

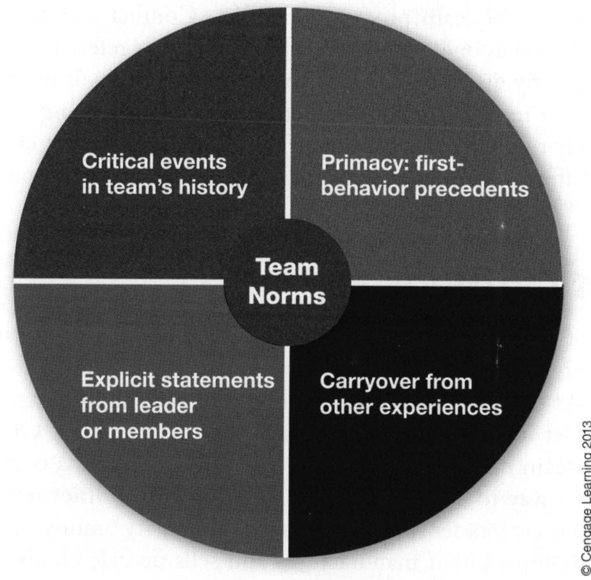

Team leaders play an important role in shaping norms that will help the team be effective. For example, research shows that when leaders have high expectations for collaborative problem solving, teams develop strong collaborative norms.[63] Making explicit statements about the desired team behaviors is a powerful way leaders influence norms. Explicit statements symbolize what counts and thus have considerable impact. When he was CEO of Ameritech, Bill Weiss established a norm of cooperation and mutual support among his top leadership team by telling them bluntly that if he caught anyone trying to undermine the others, the guilty party would be fired.[64]

- The **forming** stage of team development is a period of orientation and getting acquainted.
- **Storming** is the stage of team development in which individual personalities and roles emerge, along with resulting conflicts.
- **Norming** refers to the stage of development in which conflicts are resolved and team harmony and unity emerge.
- The **performing** stage is the stage in which members focus on problem solving and accomplishing the team's assigned task.
- **Adjourning** is the stage during which members of temporary teams prepare for the team's disbandment.
- **Team cohesiveness** refers to the extent to which team members are attracted to the team and motivated to remain a part of it.
- Morale is almost always higher in cohesive teams, and cohesiveness can also contribute to higher productivity.
- A **team norm** is an informal standard of conduct that is shared by team members and guides their behavior.

Managing Team Conflict

5 The final characteristic of team process is conflict. Conflict can arise among members within a team or between one team and another. **Conflict** refers to antagonistic interaction in which one party attempts to block the intentions or goals of another.[65] Whenever people work together in teams, some conflict is inevitable. Bringing conflicts out into the open and effectively resolving them is one of the team leader's most challenging, yet most important, jobs. Effective conflict management has a positive impact on team cohesiveness and performance.[66]

Types of Conflict

Two basic types of conflict that occur in teams are task conflict and relationship conflict.[67] **Task conflict** refers to disagreements among people about the goals to be achieved or the content of the tasks to be performed. Two shop foremen might disagree over whether to replace a valve or let it run despite the unusual noise it is making. Or two members of a top management team might disagree about whether to acquire a company or enter into a joint venture as a way to expand globally. **Relationship conflict** refers to interpersonal incompatibility that creates tension and personal animosity among people. For example, in one team at a company that manufactures and sells upscale children's furniture, team members found their differing perspectives and working styles to be a significant source of conflict during crunch times. Members who needed peace and quiet were irked at those who wanted music playing in the background. Compulsively neat members found it almost impossible to work with those who liked working among stacks of clutter.[68]

In general, research suggests that task conflict can be beneficial because it leads to better decision making and problem solving. On the other hand, relationship conflict is typically associated with negative consequences for team effectiveness.[69] One study of top management teams, for example, found that task conflict was associated with higher decision quality, greater commitment, and more decision acceptance, whereas the presence of relationship conflict significantly reduced those same outcomes.[70]

Balancing Conflict and Cooperation

There is evidence that mild conflict can be beneficial to teams.[71] A healthy level of conflict helps to prevent *groupthink*, as discussed in Chapter 6, in which people are so committed to a cohesive team that they are reluctant to express contrary opinions. When people in work teams go along simply for the sake of harmony, problems typically result. Thus, a degree of conflict leads to better decision making because multiple viewpoints are expressed. Lack of such conflict got Dell Computer in trouble, as shown in this chapter's Business Blooper.

However, conflict that is too strong, focused on personal rather than work issues, or not managed appropriately can be damaging to the team's morale and productivity. Too much conflict can be destructive, tear relationships apart, and interfere with the healthy exchange of ideas and information.[72] Team leaders have to find the right balance between conflict and cooperation, as illustrated in Exhibit 14.8. Too little conflict can decrease team performance because the team doesn't benefit from a mix of opinions and ideas—even disagreements—that might lead to better solutions or prevent the team from making mistakes. At the other end of the spectrum, too much conflict outweighs the team's cooperative efforts and leads to a decrease in employee satisfaction and commitment, hurting team performance. A moderate amount of conflict that is managed appropriately typically results in the highest levels of team performance.

Go to the Ethical Dilemma, on page 588, that pertains to team cohesiveness and conflict.

BUSINESS BLOOPER

Dell Computer

The University of Texas's math department was having trouble with its Dell computers, but the company's excuse was that the school had put undue burden on the machines by trying to do complex math problems. Huh? A three-year lawsuit's unsealed documents show awareness by employees that millions of computers sold were faulty, putting businesses, and even patients in hospitals, at risk. Groupthink and conflict-avoidance teams doubtless helped keep up the façade at Dell. Customer support employees sent emails such as this one: "We need to avoid all language indicating the boards were bad or had 'issues' per our discussions this morning." Salespeople were told, "Don't bring this to the customer's attention proactively," and "Emphasize uncertainty."

The bigger they are, the harder they fall. "Dell, as a company, was the model everyone focused on 10 years ago," said Harvard professor David B. Yoffie. "But when you combine missing a variety of shifts in the industry with management turmoil, it's hard not to have the shine come off your reputation."

SOURCE: Ashlee Vance, "Suit over Faulty Computers Highlights Dell's Decline," *The New York Times*, June 29, 2010.

Causes of Conflict

Several factors can lead to conflict:[73] One of the primary causes is competition over resources such as money, information, or supplies. When individuals or teams must compete for scarce or declining resources, conflict is almost inevitable. In addition, conflict often occurs simply because people are pursuing differing goals. Goal differences are natural in organizations. Individual salespeople's targets may put them in conflict with one another or with the sales manager. Moreover, the sales department's goals might conflict with those of manufacturing, and so forth.

Conflict may also arise from communication breakdowns. Poor communication can occur in any team, but virtual and global teams are particularly prone to communication

EXHIBIT 14.8

Balancing Conflict and Cooperation

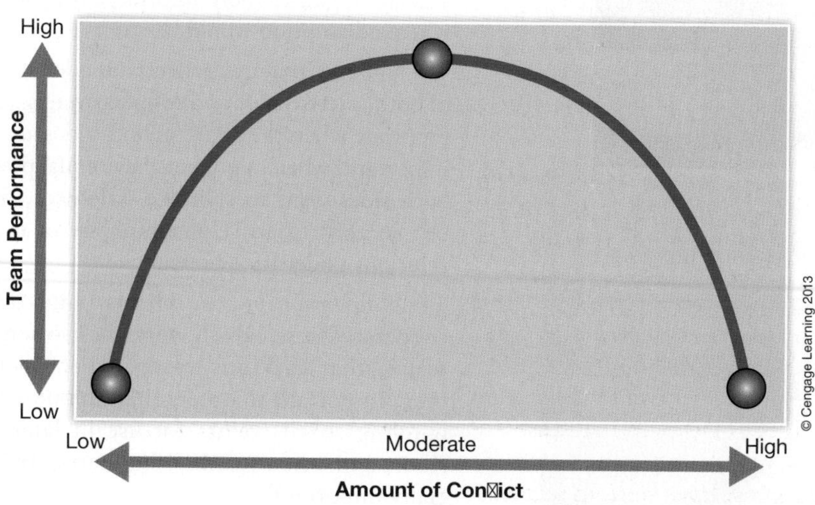

breakdowns. For one thing, trust issues can be a major source of conflict in virtual teams if members feel that they are being left out of important communication interactions.[74] In addition, the lack of nonverbal cues in virtual interactions leads to more misunderstandings. The importance of nonverbal cues is demonstrated by a story from TRW Automotive, a global manufacturer of automotive chassis and safety systems. As part of a program to teach team dynamics and leadership skills, two TRW instructors decided to videotape a Brazilian team as members worked together on a specific problem. Because neither instructor spoke Portuguese, they debated about whether to require the team to conduct the meeting in English but eventually decided that allowing members to use their first language would produce more natural communication dynamics. Interestingly, the instructors found that they could discern all the important team dynamics without understanding a single word, simply by observing tone of voice, body posture, changes in the pace of speech, who took charge of the white board and when, and so forth. This dramatic illustration of the role of nonverbal cues in effective communication led TRW to begin training virtual team leaders in how to build trust and improve communication in the absence of these nonverbal cues.[75]

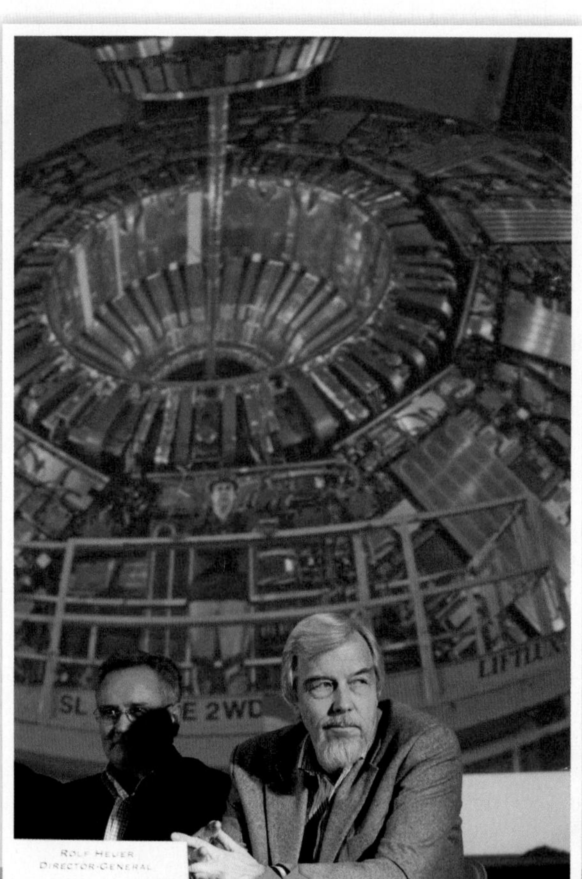

AP Photo/Keystone, Laurent Gillieron

ConceptConnection

Just who's running the Large Hadron Collider (LHC) project, an international $6 billion particle accelerator designed to simulate the universe's birth by producing high-energy proton collisions? The answer: everyone. Built at CERN, the European particle laboratory near Geneva, LHC involves 10,000 scientists and engineers working in hundreds of institutions. Because participants recognize they need everyone's cooperation to succeed, they've adopted a **collaborative style of handling conflicts**. Each research group is a democratic collective; those collectives appoint members to negotiate with other groups. "The top guy," notes CERN's "top guy," Director General Rolf-Dieter Heuer, "can only convince the other guys to do what he wants them to do."

Styles to Handle Conflict

Teams as well as individuals develop specific styles for dealing with conflict, based on the desire to satisfy their own concern versus the other party's concern. A model that describes five styles of handling conflict is in Exhibit 14.9. The two major dimensions are the extent to which an individual is assertive versus cooperative in his or her approach to conflict.[76]

1. The *competing style* reflects assertiveness to get one's own way and should be used when quick, decisive action is vital on important issues or unpopular actions, such as during emergencies or urgent cost cutting.
2. The *avoiding style* reflects neither assertiveness nor cooperativeness. It is appropriate when an issue is trivial, when there is no chance of winning, when a delay to gather more information is needed, or when a disruption would be costly.
3. The *compromising style* reflects a moderate amount of both assertiveness and cooperativeness. It is appropriate when the goals on both sides are equally important, when opponents have equal power and both sides want to split the difference, or when people need to arrive at temporary or expedient solutions under time pressure.
4. The *accommodating style* reflects a high degree of cooperativeness, which works best when people realize that they are wrong, when an issue is more important to others than to oneself, when building social credits for use in later discussions, and when maintaining harmony is especially important.

EXHIBIT 14.9

A Model of Styles to Handle Conflict

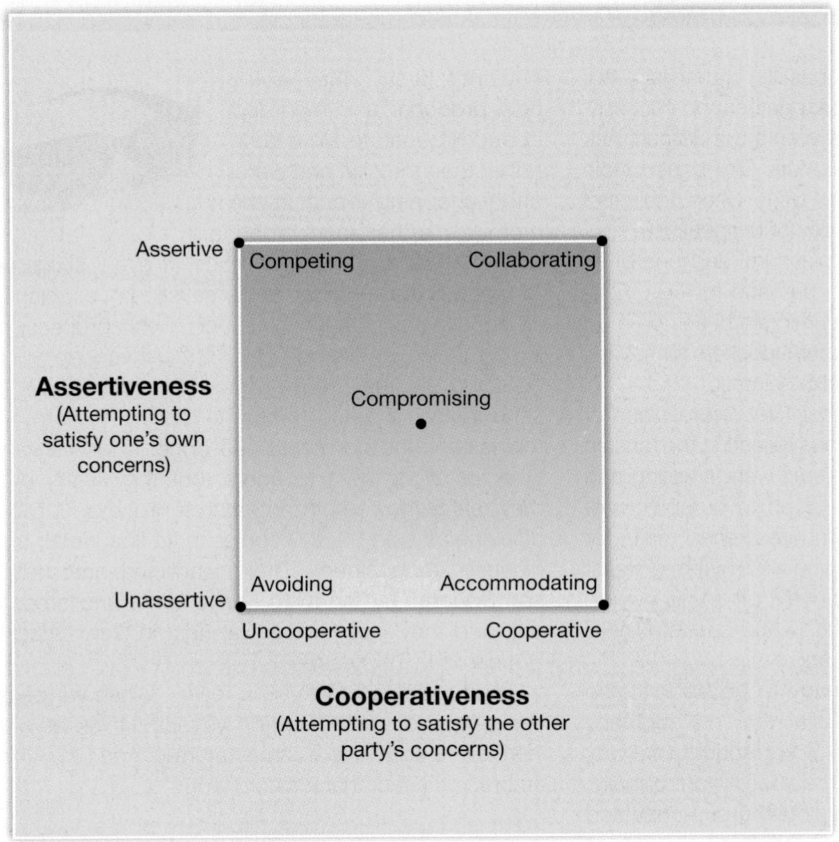

SOURCE: Adapted from Kenneth Thomas, "Conflict and Conflict Management," in *Handbook of Industrial and Organizational Behavior*, ed. M. D. Dunnette (New York: John Wiley, 1976), p. 900.

5. The *collaborating style* reflects both a high degree of assertiveness and cooperativeness. The collaborating style enables both parties to win, although it may require substantial bargaining and negotiation. The collaborating style is important when both sets of concerns are too important to be compromised, when insights from different people need to be merged into an overall solution, and when the commitment of both sides is needed for a consensus. The indie-rock band The Strokes learned to negotiate their differences and ended up with a successful new album, as described in this chapter's Benchmarking box.

Effective team members vary their style to fit the specific situation. Each of the five styles is appropriate in certain cases. These styles of handling conflict are especially useful when an individual disagrees with others. But what does a manager or team leader do when a conflict erupts among others within a team or among teams for which the manager is responsible?

Research suggests the use of superordinate goals, mediation, and negotiation for resolving conflicts among people or departments:

- ***Superordinate goals.*** The larger objective that cannot be attained by a single party is called a **superordinate goal.**[77] It is similar to the concept of vision. A powerful vision often compels people to overcome conflicts and cooperate for the greater good. Similarly, a superordinate goal requires the cooperation of conflicting team members for achievement. People must pull together. To the extent that employees can be focused

As a new manager, appreciate that some conflict can be healthy, but don't let conflict reduce the team's effectiveness and well-being. Take the New Manager Self-Test on page 583 to learn about your personal style for handling conflict.

BENCHMARKING

The Strokes

Forming a rock band has its challenges, but keeping that rock band together and successful at the same time is even more difficult. Ask the Strokes, the New York City–based indie band that burst on the scene 9/11/01, when their first album was released and also the day of unspeakable horrors. That album, *This Is It*, went platinum, and one of its tracks, "Last Night," is still in high demand for DJs. Getting to that point had included cramming in buses on tour, sharing beds, and living "in each other's pockets for several years straight," said lead guitarist Nick Valensi.

Their next recording experience, *First Impressions of Earth*, was not as successful, perhaps reflecting the tension the group was experiencing. Problems were erupting and lives were changing, causing the group to be splintered. After their rise to stardom, they endured rehab stints for both frontman Julian Casablancas and also rhythm guitarist Albert Hammond, Jr. Casablancas went off on his own to record and tour. Valensi, Casablancas and bassist Nicolai Fraiture got married and had children.

Five years later, they were ready to go back to the studio and work together again. But they realized they needed a new way to interact, a new equilibrium, in a way that each member's voice would be heard more equally. Casablanca sees it as a way to maintain group unity and calls it "Operation Make Everyone Satisfied." How does it work? Firstly, they got a new producer and recorded in bucolic upstate New York rather than the city, and were often chopping wood in the mornings rather than ordering in bagels. They did many versions of every song, waiting for each band member to be satisfied. Casablancas intentionally stayed away for much of this process, believing his style was a roadblock. "I'm just very opinionated," he says. But they kept on recording, with Casablancas sending in lyrics and tracks he did on his own and listening to what the others had done. It took a very long time for all of them to agree, but they finally did, and they realize how important such a process is. Did it pay off? *Angles* sold 90,000 copies in its first week, the third highest-selling album. Their headlining dates at Madison Square Garden (with Kanye West and others) sold out, and they'll perform at Jazzfest in New Orleans and Bonnaroo in Tennessee.

And they learned to be a team. "When we became a band," says drummer Fabrizio Moretti, "I think we were trying hard to seem like it came naturally. And I think now we embrace the fact that it's hard work."

SOURCES: Keith Caulfield, "Over the Counter," *Billboard*, April 9, 2011, p. 33; Melena Ryzik, Different Strokes, *The New York Times*, March 13, 2011, pp. AR1 & AR20.

on team or organization goals, the conflict will decrease because they see the big picture and realize they must work together to achieve it.

- ***Mediation.*** Using a third party to settle a dispute is referred to as **mediation**. A mediator could be a supervisor, a higher-level manager, an outside consultant, or someone from the human resource department. The mediator can discuss the conflict with each party and work toward a solution. If a solution satisfactory to both sides cannot be reached, the parties might be willing to turn the conflict over to the mediator and abide by his or her solution.

Negotiation

One distinctive type of conflict management is **negotiation**, whereby people engage in give-and-take discussions and consider various alternatives to reach a joint decision that is acceptable to both parties. Negotiation is used when a conflict is formalized, such as between a union and management.

Types of Negotiation Conflicting parties may embark on negotiation from different perspectives and with different intentions, reflecting either an *integrative* approach or a *distributive* approach.

New Manager Self-Test

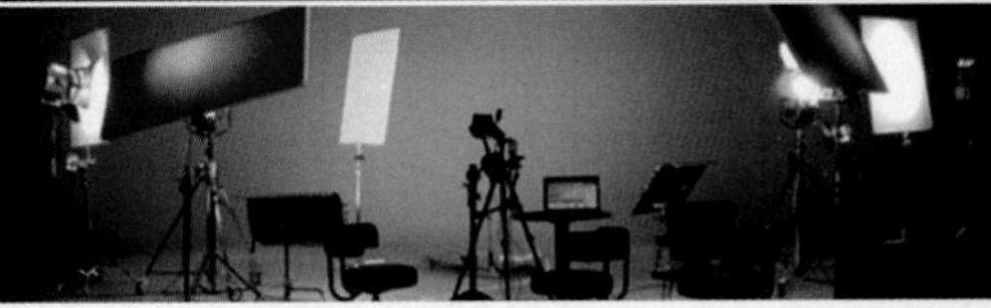

Managing Conflict

Conflicting opinions and perspectives occur in every team. The ability to handle conflict and disagreement is one mark of a successful new manager. To understand your approach to managing conflict, think about disagreements you have had with people on student teams or in other situations, then answer each of the following items as Mostly True or Mostly False for you.

	MOSTLY TRUE <<<	>>> MOSTLY FALSE
1. I typically assert my opinion to win a disagreement.	______	______
2. I often suggest solutions that combine others' points of view.	______	______
3. I prefer not to argue with team members.	______	______
4. I raise my voice to get other people to accept my position.	______	______
5. I am quick to agree when someone makes a good point.	______	______
6. I tend to keep quiet rather than argue with other people.	______	______
7. I stand firm in expressing my viewpoints during a disagreement.	______	______
8. I try to include other people's ideas to create a solution they will accept.	______	______
9. I like to smooth over disagreements so people get along.	______	______

See It Online

Scoring and Interpretation: Three categories of conflict-handling strategies are measured in this instrument: competing, accommodating, and collaborating. By comparing your scores you can see your preferred conflict-handling strategy.

Give yourself 1 point for each item marked Mostly True.

Competing: Items 1, 4, 7

Accommodating: Items 2, 5, 8

Collaborating: Items 3, 6, 9

For which conflict-handling strategy do you score highest? New managers may initially be accommodating to get along with people until they size up the situation. A too strong competing style may prevent subordinates from having a say in important matters. The collaborating style tries for a win–win solution and has the long-run potential to build a constructive team. How would your strategy differ if the other people involved in a disagreement were family members, friends, subordinates, or bosses?

Integrative negotiation is based on a win–win assumption, in that all parties want to come up with a creative solution that can benefit both sides. Rather than viewing the conflict as a win–lose situation, people look at the issues from multiple angles, consider trade-offs, and try to "expand the pie" rather than divide it. With integrative negotiation, conflicts are managed through cooperation and compromise, which fosters trust and positive long-term relationships. **Distributive negotiation**, on the other hand, assumes the "size of the pie" is fixed and each party attempts to get as much of it as they can. One side wants to win, which means the other side must lose. With this win–lose approach, distributive negotiation is competitive and adversarial rather than collaborative, and does not typically lead to positive long-term relationships.[78]

Most experts emphasize the value of integrative negotiation for today's collaborative business environment. That is, the key to effectiveness is to see negotiation not as a zero-sum game but as a process for reaching a creative solution that benefits everyone.[79]

Rules for Reaching a Win-Win Solution Achieving a win–win solution through integrative negotiation is based on four key strategies:[80]

1. ***Separate the people from the problem.*** For successful integrative negotiation, people stay focused on the problem and the source of conflict rather than attacking or attempting to discredit each other.
2. ***Focus on interests, not current demands.*** Demands are what each person wants from the negotiation, whereas interests are why they want them. Consider two sisters arguing over the last orange in the fruit bowl. Each insisted she should get the orange and refused to give up (demands). If one sister had asked the other *why* she wanted the orange (interests), the sisters would have discovered that one wanted to eat it and the other wanted the peel to use for a project. By focusing on interests, the sisters would be able to arrive at a solution that gave each what she wanted.[81] *Demands* create yes-or-no obstacles to effective negotiation, whereas *interests* present problems that can be solved creatively.
3. ***Generate many alternatives for mutual gain.*** Both parties in an integrative negotiation come up with a variety of options for solving the problem and engage in give-and-take discussions about which alternatives can get each side what it wants.
4. ***Insist that results be based on objective standards.*** Each party in a negotiation has its own interests and would naturally like to maximize its outcomes. Successful negotiation requires focusing on objective criteria and maintaining standards of fairness rather than using subjective judgments about the best solution.

- **Conflict** refers to antagonistic interaction in which one party attempts to block the intentions or goals of another.
- Some conflict, particularly task conflict, can be beneficial to teams.
- **Task conflict** is conflict that results from disagreements about the goals to be achieved or the content of the tasks to be performed.
- **Relationship conflict** results from interpersonal incompatibility that creates tension and personal animosity among people.
- Causes of conflict include competition over resources, goal differences, and communication breakdowns.
- Teams and individuals use a variety of styles for dealing with conflict, including the competing style, the avoiding style, the compromising style, the accommodating style, and the collaborating style and each can be effective under certain circumstances.
- Focusing people on a **superordinate goal**, which means a larger objective that cannot be obtained by a single individual, is one way team leaders can resolve conflicts.
- **Mediation** is the process of using a third party to settle a dispute.
- **Negotiation** is a conflict management strategy whereby people engage in give-and-take discussions and consider various alternatives to reach a joint decision that is acceptable to both parties.
- **Integrative negotiation** is a collaborative approach that is based on a win-win assumption, whereby the parties want to come up with a creative solution that benefits both sides of the conflict.
- **Distributive negotiation** is a competitive and adversarial approach in which each party strives to get as much as it can, usually at the expense of the other party.

Work Team Effectiveness

Teams are the building blocks of today's organizations, but teams do not always live up to their potential or to the dreams managers have for them. In this section, we look at the positive outcomes of effective teams. By assessing teams in terms of productive output, personal satisfaction, and the capacity to adapt and learn, managers can better identify actions that will enhance work team effectiveness.[82]

Productive Output

One aspect of effectiveness relates to whether the team's output (such as decisions, products, or services) meets the requirements of customers or clients in terms of quality, quantity, and timeliness. An IBM team made up of members in the United States, Germany, and the United Kingdom, for example, used collaboration software as a virtual meeting room to solve a client's technical problem resulting from Hurricane Katrina within the space of just a few days.[83]

Effective teams can unleash enormous energy and creativity from employees. **Social facilitation** refers to the tendency for the presence of others to enhance one's motivation and performance. Simply being in the presence of other people has an energizing effect.[84] This benefit of teams is often lost in virtual and global teams because people are working in isolation from their teammates. Good virtual team leaders build in communication mechanisms that keep people interacting.

Satisfaction of Members

Another important question is whether the team experience contributes to the well-being, personal satisfaction, and development of its members. Effective teams provide multiple opportunities for people to satisfy their individual needs and to develop both personally and professionally.[85] As described in Chapter 12, employees have needs for belongingness and affiliation, and working in teams can help meet these needs. Participative teams can also reduce boredom, increase individuals' feeling of dignity and self-worth, and contribute to skill development because the whole person is employed. At Radius, a Boston restaurant, for example, two-person kitchen teams have full responsibility for their part of a meal, which gives them a greater sense of accomplishment and importance and enables them to expand their culinary and organizational skills.[86] People who have a satisfying team environment cope better with stress, enjoy their jobs, and have a higher level of organizational commitment.

Capacity to Adapt and Learn

Coordination is the key to successful teamwork. A professor of management at Santa Clara University analyzed 14 years of National Basketball Association results and found that teams that had played together longer won more games. By playing together over a period of time, members learned to anticipate their teammates' moves, coordinate their activities, and adapt their behavior to defeat the competition.[87] Consider that at the 2008 Beijing Summer Olympics, the USA men's 4 × 100 relay team expected to win gold but instead was disqualified for a humiliating baton drop during the qualifying heats. What happened? The runners had practiced baton passes a million times—but not with each other. Thus, their ability to coordinate their actions was lacking.[88]

The same thing can happen in work teams. When team activities are effectively coordinated, members learn to anticipate one another's actions and respond appropriately. Over time, effective teams learn from experience and use that learning to revitalize and regenerate themselves, smoothly adapting to shifting organizational and competitive demands.[89]

- Work team effectiveness is assessed based on three outcomes: productive output, team member satisfaction, and capacity to adapt and learn.
- **Social facilitation** is the tendency for the presence of other people to influence an individual's motivation and performance.
- An analysis of 14 years of National Basketball Association results found that teams that had played together longer won more games.

Discussion Questions

1. Volvo went to self-directed teams to assemble cars because of the need to attract and keep workers in Sweden, where pay raises are not a motivator (high taxes) and many other jobs are available. Are these factors good reasons for using a team approach? Discuss.
2. Discuss how the dilemmas of teamwork might be intensified in a virtual team. What dilemmas do you feel when you have to do class assignments as part of a team? Discuss.
3. Suppose you are the leader of a team that has just been created to develop a new registration process at your college or university. How can you use an understanding of the stages of team development to improve your team's effectiveness?
4. Imagine yourself as a potential member of a team responsible for designing a new package for a breakfast cereal. Do you think interpersonal skills would be equally important if the team is organized face-to-face versus a virtual team? Why or why not? Might different types of interpersonal skills be required for the two types of teams? Be specific.
5. If you were the leader of a special-purpose team developing a new computer game and conflicts arose related to power and status differences among team members, what would you do? How might you use the various conflict-resolution techniques described in the chapter?
6. Experts say that for teams to function well, members have to get to know one another in some depth. What specifically would you do to facilitate this in a co-located team? What about in a global virtual team?
7. When you are a member of a team, do you adopt a task specialist or socioemotional role? Which role is more important for a team's effectiveness?
8. Some people argue that the presence of an outside threat correlates with a high degree of team cohesion. Would you agree or disagree? Explain your answer.
9. Do you believe that admitting ignorance is a good way for a team leader to earn respect? Would this cause some people to disrespect the leader and question his or her suitability for team leadership? Discuss.
10. In one company, 40 percent of its workers and 20 percent of its managers resigned during the first year after reorganizing into teams. What might account for this dramatic turnover? How might managers ensure a smooth transition to teams?

Self-Learning

This and That: Best Team—Worst Team[90]

Think of two teams of which you were a member—the best and the worst in terms of personal satisfaction and team performance. These teams could come from any area in your experience—for example, athletic team, student club, class team, work team, project team, church committee, or volunteer organization. List below the specific behaviors of the teams that made them the best and worst for you.

Best team behaviors: ______________________________

Worst team behaviors: ______________________________

In class: (1) Sit in a small group of three to five students. Each student tells the brief story of his or her best and worst team experiences. (2) After all stories are heard, one team member writes on a flipchart (or blackboard) two headings—"More of This" and "Less of That." Under "This," write team member suggestions for positive behaviors that make for effective teamwork. Under "That," write team member suggestions for negative behaviors that prevent effective teamwork. (3) After brainstorming items, each group condenses each list to five key behaviors the group considers most important. (4) After the lists are finalized, students can walk around the classroom and review all lists. (5) Discuss answers to the following questions either in your group or as a class.

1. What is the most important behavior for This and for That?
2. What factors influence the presence of This or That behaviors on a team?
3. What personal changes would you need to make as a team member to demonstrate more of This?
4. What personal changes would you need to make as a team member to demonstrate less of That?
5. How might a team leader be able to attain more of This on a team and less of That?

Group Learning

Teams on TV

1. Form into groups of three to five members. As a group, choose a TV show where teams are central to the plot. Examples include: *The Office, Parks & Recreation, Law & Order (any of them), CSI, 30 Rock,* etc. Make sure the instructor agrees with your choice of TV show.
2. Watch several shows (make sure group members watch the same shows) and study team behavior. Use the Member Roles on pages 574–575 of this textbook and also the Stages of Team Development on pages 575–577. Take notes on which characters perform which role(s) and what stages of development the group is in during a particular show.
3. As a group, come to an agreement on which roles and stages were present in those shows.
4. Your instructor will tell you whether to prepare either a group presentation or group paper on your findings.
5. What did you learn about teams from this assignment? Were there some surprises?

Action Learning

Team Feedback Exercise

Step 1. Divide into groups of three to four students. Think back to recent experiences working in a team, either at work or school. Write down your answers to the following questions.

What behaviors by other team members did you most appreciate?

____

____

What behaviors of other team members did you least appreciate?

____

____

What do you think the team members appreciated about you?

____

____

What actions of yours might the team members have appreciated least?

____

____

Step 2. Take turns sharing your answers with other members of your group. Make notes about common themes for answers to each of the above questions. What is the single most important theme for each of the answers above?

Step 3. What are the implications of the answers for you as a member of a future team? How might you change your behavior to make a larger contribution to a team?

Ethical Dilemma

One for All and All for One?[91]

Melinda Asbel watched as three of her classmates filed out of the conference room. Then she turned back to the large wooden table and faced her fellow members (a student and three faculty members) of the university's judiciary committee.

The three students—Joe Eastridge, Brad Hamil, and Lisa Baghetti—had just concluded their appeal against a plagiarism conviction stemming from a group project for an international marketing course. Melinda, who happened to be in the class with the students on trial, remembered the day the professor, Hank Zierden, had asked Joe, Brad, and Lisa, along with the group's leader, Paul Colgan, to stay after class. She happened to walk by the classroom a half hour later to see four glum students emerge. Even though Paul had a chagrined expression on his face, Joe was the one who looked completely shattered. It didn't take long for word to spread along the ever-active grapevine that Paul had admitted to plagiarizing his part of the group paper.

At the hearing, the students recounted how they'd quickly and unanimously settled on Paul to lead the group. He was by far the most able student among them, someone who managed to maintain a stellar GPA even while taking a full course load and holding down a part-time job. After the group worked together for weeks analyzing the problem and devising a marketing plan, Paul assigned a section of the final paper to each member. With the pressure of all those end-of-the-semester deadlines bearing down on them, everyone was delighted when Paul volunteered to write the company and industry background, the section that typically took the most time to produce. Paul gathered in everyone's contributions, assembled them into a paper, and handed out the final draft to the other members. They each gave it a quick read. They liked what they saw and thought they had a good chance for an A.

Unfortunately, as Paul readily admitted when Professor Zierden confronted them, he had pulled the section he'd contributed directly off the Internet. Pointing out the written policy he had distributed at the beginning of the semester stating that each group member was equally responsible for the final product, the professor gave all four students a zero for the project. The group project and presentation counted for 30 percent of the course grade.

Joe, Brad, and Lisa maintained they were completely unaware that Paul had cheated. "It just never occurred to us Paul would ever need to cheat," Brad said. They were innocent bystanders, the students argued. Why should they be penalized? Besides, the consequences weren't going to fall on each of them equally. Although Paul was suffering the embarrassment of public exposure, the failing group project grade would only put a dent in his solid GPA. Joe, on the other hand, was already on academic probation. A zero probably meant he wouldn't make the 2.5 GPA he needed to stay in the business program.

At least one of the faculty members of the judiciary committee supported Professor Zierden's actions. "We're assigning more and more group projects because increasingly that's the way these students are going to find themselves working when they get real jobs in the real world," he said. "And the fact of the matter is that if someone obtains information illegally while on the job, it's going to put the whole corporation at risk for being sued, or worse."

Even though she could see merit to both sides, Melinda was going to have to choose. If you were Melinda, how would you vote?

What Would You Do?

1. Vote to exonerate the three group project members who didn't cheat. You're convinced they had no reason to suspect Paul Colgan of dishonesty. Exonerating them is the right thing to do.
2. Vote in support of Hank Zierden's decision to hold each individual member accountable for the entire project. The professor clearly stated his policy at the beginning of the semester, and the students should have been more vigilant. The committee should not undercut a professor's explicit policy.
3. Vote to reduce each of the three students' penalties. Instead of a zero, each student will receive only half of the possible total points for the project, which would be an F. You're still holding students responsible for the group project, but not imposing catastrophic punishment. This compromise both undercuts the professor's policy and punishes "innocent" team members to some extent, but not as severely.

Case for Critical Analysis

Calgary Oil Shale Technologies, Inc.[92]

When Martin Bouchard took over as president and CEO of Calgary Oil Shale Technologies, Inc. (COST), one of his top goals was to introduce teams as a way of solving the morale and productivity problems at the company's Alberta field operations site. COST is a subsidiary of an international oilfield services company. The subsidiary specializes in supplying technology and data management to optimize the recovery of oil from oil shale formations in Alberta, Colorado, and Utah. Oil shale is sedimentary rock containing a high proportion of organic matter that can be converted into crude oil or natural gas. With the price of crude oil skyrocketing and world supplies limited, energy companies in Canada and the United States were making a big push to recover hydrocarbons trapped in oil shale and slow-forming oil formations. Through its proprietary logging technology, COST could distinguish oil-bearing rock layers and help energy companies gain higher productivity from oil shale production.

COST used highly trained professionals, such as geologists, geophysicists, and engineers, to handle the sophisticated technology. They also used skilled and semiskilled labor to run the company's field operations. The two groups regularly clashed, and when one engineer's prank sent a couple of operations workers to the emergency room, the local press had a field day publishing articles about the conflict. The company hired Algoma Howard, a First Nations descendant, to develop a teamwork program to improve productivity and morale at the Calgary facility. Howard previously had had great success using teams as a way to bring people together, enable them to understand one another's problems and challenges, and coordinate their efforts toward a common goal. The idea was to implement the program at other COST locations after the pilot project.

In Alberta, Howard had a stroke of luck in the form of Carlos Debrito, a long-time COST employee who was highly respected at the Alberta office and was looking for one final challenging project before he retired. Debrito had served in just about every possible line and staff position at COST over his 26-year career, and he understood the problems workers faced on both the technical and field sides of the business. Howard was pleased when Debrito agreed to serve as leader for the Alberta pilot program.

The three functional groups at the Alberta site included operations, made up primarily of hourly workers who operated and maintained the logging equipment; the "below ground" group, consisting of engineers, geologists, and geophysicists who determined where and how to dig or drill; and a group of equipment maintenance people who were on call. Howard and Debrito decided the first step was to get these different groups talking to one another and sharing ideas. They instituted monthly "fireside chats," optional meetings to which all employees were invited. The chats were held in the cafeteria during late afternoon, and people could have free coffee or tea and snacks brought by Howard and Debrito. The idea was to give employees a chance to discuss difficult issues and unresolved problems in a relaxed, informal setting. The only people who showed up at the first meeting were a couple of engineers who happened to wander by the cafeteria and see the snack table. Debrito opened the meeting by folding out a cardboard "fireplace" and pulling four chairs around it for the small group to talk. Word quickly spread of the silly "fireplace" incident (and the free food), and more and more people gradually began to attend the meetings. Early sessions focused primarily on talking about what the various participants saw as "their" group's needs, as well as the problems they experienced in working with the "other" groups. One session almost came to fisticuffs until Debrito loudly announced that someone needed to go out and get another log for the fire, breaking the tension and moving things along. During the next session, Debrito and Howard worked with the group to come up with "rules of engagement," including guidelines such as "focus on the issue, not the person," "lose the words *us* and *them*," and "if you bring it up, you have to help solve it."

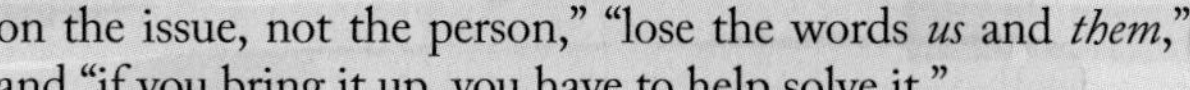

Within about six months, the fireside chats had evolved into lively problem-solving discussions focused on issues that all three groups found important. For example, a maintenance worker complained that a standard piece of equipment failed repeatedly due to cold weather and sand contamination. Debrito listened carefully and then drew a maintenance engineer into the discussion. The engineer came up with a new configuration better suited to the conditions, and downtime virtually disappeared.

The next step for Howard and Debrito was to introduce official "problem-busting" teams. These temporary teams included members from each of the three functional areas and from various hierarchical levels, and each was assigned a team leader, which was typically a respected first-line supervisor. Team leaders were carefully trained in team building, shared-leadership, and creative problem-solving techniques. The teams were asked to evaluate a specific problem identified in a fireside chat and then craft and implement a solution. The teams were disbanded when the problem was solved. CEO Martin Bouchard authorized the teams to address problems within certain cost guidelines without seeking management approval.

Despite the camaraderie that had developed during the fireside chats, some delicate moments occurred when engineers resented working with field personnel and vice versa. In addition, some managers felt disempowered by the introduction of problem-busting teams. They had seen their role as that of problem solver. Now, they were asked to share responsibility and support decisions that might come from the lowest-level workers in the company. Building commitment and trust among lower-level employees wasn't easy either. Howard suggested to Debrito that they use a "connection ladder" that she had observed used in a hospital nursing team. The idea is for the leader to identify where each team member is in terms of connection/disconnection with the process to determine what approach can help move the person from indifference toward commitment. Over time, and with Debrito's and Howard's continuing guidance, the problem-busting teams eventually began to come together and focus on a number of chronic problems that had long been ignored.

About a year and a half into the team-building program, the entire workforce in Alberta was organized into permanent cross-functional teams that were empowered to make their own decisions and elect their own leaders. By this time, just about everyone was feeling comfortable working cross-functionally, and within a few months, things were really humming. The professional and hourly workers got along so well that they decided to continue the fireside chat sessions after work, either in the cafeteria with snacks provided by volunteers or at a local bar. Some tensions between the groups remained, of course, and at one of the chats an operations worker jokingly suggested that the team members should duke it out once a week to get rid of the tensions so they could focus all their energy on their jobs. Several others joined in the joking, and eventually, the group decided to square off in a weekly hockey game. For the opening game, Howard served as goalie on one side and Debrito as goalie on the other. Implementation of teams at the Alberta facility was deemed by management to be a clear success. Productivity and morale were soaring and costs continued to decline.

The company identified the Colorado office as the next facility where Algoma Howard and her leadership team needed to introduce the cross-functional teams that had proven so successful in Alberta. Howard's team felt immense pressure from top management to get the team-based productivity project up and running smoothly and quickly in Colorado. Top executives believed the lessons learned in Alberta would make implementing the program at other sites less costly and time-consuming. However, when Howard and her team attempted to implement the program at the Colorado facility, things did not go well. Because people were not showing up for the fireside chats, Howard's team, feeling pressed for time, made attendance mandatory. Ground rules were set by the leadership team at the beginning, based on the guidelines developed in Alberta, and the team introduced specific issues for discussion, again using the information they had gleaned from the early freewheeling Alberta sessions as a basis. However, the meetings still produced few valuable ideas or suggestions.

When it came time to form problem-busting teams, Howard thought it might be a good idea to let the groups select their own leaders, as a way to encourage greater involvement and commitment among the Colorado workers. The leaders were given the same training that had been provided in Alberta. However, although a few of the problem-busting teams solved important problems, none of them showed the kind of commitment and enthusiasm Howard had seen in Alberta. In addition, the Colorado workers refused to participate in softball games and other team-building exercises that her team developed for them. Howard finally convinced some workers to join in a softball game by bribing them with free food and beer, but the first game ended with a fight between two operations workers and a group of engineers.

"If I just had a Carlos Debrito in Colorado, things would go a lot more smoothly," Howard thought. "These workers don't trust us the way workers in Alberta trusted him." It seemed that no matter how hard Howard and her team tried to make the project work in Colorado, morale continued to decline, and conflicts between the different groups of workers actually seemed to increase.

Questions

1. Algoma Howard and Carlos Debrito phased in permanent cross-functional teams in Alberta. What types of teams are the "fireside chats" and "problem-busting teams"? Through what stage or stages of team development did these groups evolve?
2. What role did Carlos Debrito play in the success of the Alberta team-based productivity project? What leadership approach did he employ to help reduce conflict between labor and the professionals? Do you agree with Algoma Howard that if she just had a Carlos Debrito in Colorado, the project would succeed? Explain your answer.
3. What advice would you give Algoma Howard and her team for improving the employee-involvement climate, containing costs, and meeting production goals at the Colorado facility?

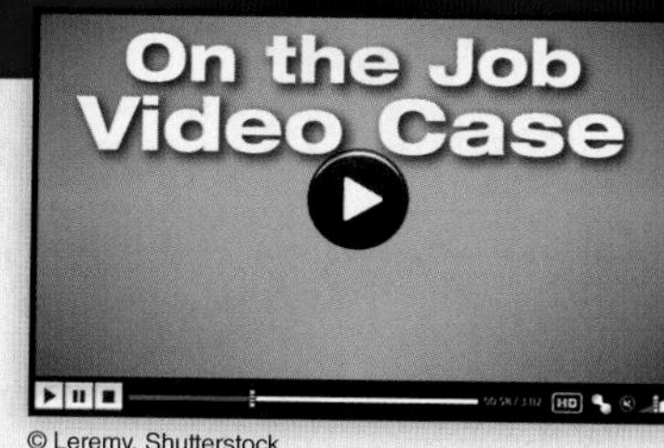

© Leremy, Shutterstock

Holden Outerwear: Leading Teams

"I like the word *team* because it brings people together," says Mikey LeBlanc, professional snowboarder and founder of Holden Outerwear. The Portland resident launched Holden in 2002 to support his snowboarding addiction, and today LeBlanc's company produces some of the most interesting designs ever to appear on slopes.

With their stylish zippers, fit cuts, and leather shoulders and snaps, Holden technical garments have more in common with urban skate wear than with traditional ski suits. Recreational snowboarders wear Holden Outerwear because the collections are sleek and fashionable; experts like Holden because the performance outerwear promotes the right state of mind for taming mountains.

When asked about the advantages of his company's team development process, LeBlanc waxes philosophical. "You can watch an NBA team that has a superstar who doesn't work well with anyone, or you can watch a great team that works together. That's what we're trying to have here at Holden," LeBlanc says. The soft-spoken snowboarding pro adds that working in teams is necessary for practical and inspirational reasons. "It can't be just one person because you get spread too thin, and the inspiration of design would be lost," he states.

Nikki Brush, a design and development manager at Holden, shares LeBlanc's perspective. Her appreciation of teams was an evolution, however. Brush says her first work-group experiences in college were anything but inspirational: one student would cut a pattern, another person would cut fabric, and still another would have to sew—but no one took ownership of the project. Things changed when Brush entered the workforce and received a team assignment that proved to be transformative. "It was the first time I really felt like I worked with someone as a team, because we were both on the same page," Brush remembers. "I trusted her, she trusted me, and in the long run it made us so much better as designers—and more effective at delivering the product." The experience taught Brush that teams make a difference when individual members hustle, take ownership, and collaborate on shared goals.

Holden's use of teams is something that emerged out of necessity. For much of the company's brief history, managers worked independently on design projects—a preference that offered ultimate control over the process. But as the company grew, LeBlanc needed more designers, and he began looking to outside freelancers for help. For the first time, Holden managers formed virtual teams to produce new apparel lines, and many of the team members were outside contractors. LeBlanc states that the transition was exciting and harrowing at the same time: "Bringing new people in is always really scary. You're opening up your secrets, and you're opening up the way you do your process." He likens the experience to inviting guests for the holidays. "Bringing someone in is like bringing someone home for Thanksgiving dinner—it's like a family here," Holden's owner says with characteristic earnestness.

As for Nikki Brush, she remembers being the "guest" invited over for the holidays. The young designer was a freelancer when Holden's design chief first contacted her. In a matter of months, she designed one of the most popular pieces of a new Holden collection. Today she is a full time manager at the company. "What I bring is my strong attention to detail, as far as both development and design go," Brush says.

The switch from freelancer to in-house manager has been positive for Nikki Brush, although her role on the team has changed. "Freelancing is interesting because you're not invested in the company, and you don't know 100 percent where they've been or where they're going," she says. Even so, she is happier working inside the firm. Not only does she now know where Holden is going, but she helps set the course.

Discussion Questions

1. Is Design Manager Nikki Brush a part of a *group*, or part of a *team?* Explain the difference.
2. What type of team did Nikki Brush participate in when she was a freelancer? What type of team does she participate in as a full-time employee at Holden?
3. What are potential disadvantages of teams for Holden's apparel designers? What can managers do to help avoid these downsides?

Welcome Home, Roscoe Jenkins

Hollywood talk-show host Roscoe Jenkins (Martin Lawrence) returns to his Georgia home for his parents' 50th wedding anniversary. Cultures clash between the big-city Roscoe and other family members. The culture clash becomes even more severe because of the presence of his upper-class fiancée, Bianca Kittles (Joy Bryant), who does not understand this family and feels superior to them.

Conflict: It Can Sneak Up on You This sequence starts with Roscoe and his brother, Sheriff Otis Jenkins (Michael Clarke Duncan), carrying a tub of fish and ice from Monty's butcher shop to Sheriff Jenkins's pickup truck. It follows the baseball game during which Roscoe hit a ball that struck Mama Jenkins (Margaret Avery) in the head. This sequence ends after Sheriff Jenkins knocks out his brother. The film continues with Roscoe walking down a dirt road. Betty (Mo'Nique) approaches in her car.

What to Watch for and Ask Yourself

- Based on your understanding of a team as described in this chapter, do Roscoe Jenkins and his brother, Sheriff Otis Jenkins, form a team in this film sequence? Why or why not?
- This chapter defined conflict as "antagonistic interaction in which one party attempts to block the intentions or goals of another." Does the interaction in this film sequence show this definition in action? Give examples from the sequence.
- Which conflict-handling style best fits the behavior shown in this film sequence? Give some examples from the sequence.

Endnotes

1. "A Company of 'Level 5' Leaders," *Inc.* (June 2010): 87–88.
2. Industry Week/Manufacturing Performance Institute's Census of Manufacturers for 2004, reported in Traci Purdum, "Teaming, Take 2," *Industry Week* (May 2005): 41–43.
3. Matt Moffett, "Trapped Miners Kept Focus, Shared Tuna—Foiled Escape, Bid to Organize Marked First Two Weeks Underground in Chile," *The Wall Street Journal*, August 25, 2010; and "Lessons on Leadership and Teamwork—From 700 Meters Below the Earth's Surface," Universia Knowledge @ Wharton, September 22, 2010, www.wharton.universia.net/index.cfm?fa=viewArticle&id=1943&language=english (accessed September 29, 2010).
4. Carl E. Larson and Frank M. J. LaFasto, *TeamWork* (Newbury Park, CA: Sage, 1989); J. R. Katzenbach and D. K. Smith, *The Wisdom of Teams* (Boston, MA: Harvard Business School Press, 1993); and Dawn R. Utley and Stephanie E. Brown, "Establishing Characteristic Differences between Team and Working Group Behaviors," *Institute of Industrial Engineers Annual Conference Proceedings* (2010): 1–6.
5. Telis Demos, "Cirque du Balancing Act," *Fortune* (June 12, 2006): 114; Daniel R. Kibbe and Jill Casner-Lotto, "Ralston Foods: From Greenfield to Maturity in a Team-Based Plant, *Journal of Organizational Excellence* (Summer 2002): 57–67.
6. "'Golden Hour' Crucial Time for Surgeons on Front Line," *Johnson City Press*, April 1, 2003.
7. Study by G. Clotaire Rapaille, reported in Karen Bernowski, "What Makes American Teams Tick?" *Quality Progress* 28, no. 1 (January 1995): 39–42.
8. Avan Jassawalla, Hemant Sashittal, and Avinash Malshe, "Students' Perceptions of Social Loafing: Its Antecedents and Consequences in Undergraduate Business Classroom Teams," *Academy of Management Learning and Education* 8, no.1 (2009): 42-54; and Robert Albanese and David D. Van Fleet, "Rational Behavior in Groups: The Free-Riding Tendency," *Academy of Management Review* 10 (1985): 244–255.
9. David H. Freedman, "The Idiocy of Crowds" (What's Next column), *Inc. Magazine* (September 2006): 61–62.
10. Quoted in Jason Zweig, "The Intelligent Investor: How Group Decisions End Up Wrong-Footed," *The Wall Street Journal*, April 25, 2009.
11. "Why Some Teams Succeed (and So Many Don't)," *Harvard Management Update* (October 2006): 3–4; Frederick P. Morgeson, D. Scott DeRue, and Elizabeth P. Karam, "Leadership in Teams: A Functional Approach to Understanding Leadership Structure and Processes," *Journal of Management* 36, no. 1 (January 2010): 5–39; and Patrick Lencioni, "Dissolve Dysfunction: Begin Building Your Dream Team," *Leadership Excellence* (October 2009): 20.
12. Reported in Jerry Useem, "What's That Spell? Teamwork!" *Fortune* (June 12, 2006): 65–66.

13. Eric Sundstrom, Kenneth P. DeMeuse, and David Futrell, "Work Teams," *American Psychologist* 45 (February 1990): 120–133; and Morgeson et al., "Leadership in Teams."

14. Deborah L. Gladstein, "Groups in Context: A Model of Task Group Effectiveness," *Administrative Science Quarterly* 29 (1984): 499–517. For an overview of research on team effectiveness, see John Mathieu, M. Travis Maynard, Tammy Rapp, and Lucy Gilson, "Team Effectiveness 1997–2007: A Review of Recent Advancements and a Glimpse into the Future," *Journal of Management* 34, no. 3 (June 2008): 410–476.

15. Sujin K. Horwitz and Irwin B. Horwitz, "The Effects of Team Diversity on Team Outcomes: A Meta-Analytic Review of Team Demography," *Journal of Management* 33, no. 6 (December 2007): 987–1015; and Dora C. Lau and J. Keith Murnighan, "Demographic Diversity and Faultlines: The Compositional Dynamics of Organizational Groups," *Academy of Management Review* 23, no. 2 (1998): 325–340.

16. Based on J. Richard Hackman, *Leading Teams: Setting the Stage for Great Performances* (Boston, MA: Harvard Business School Press, 2002), p. 62; Lee G. Bolman and Terrence E. Deal, "What Makes a Team Work?" *Organizational Dynamics* (August 1992): 34–44; Amy Edmondson, Richard Bohmer, and Gary Pisano, "Speeding Up Team Learning," *Harvard Business Review* (October 2001): 125–132; and Jeanne M. Wilson, Jill George, and Richard S. Wellings, with William C. Byham, *Leadership Trapeze: Strategies for Leadership in Team-Based Organizations* (San Francisco: Jossey-Bass, 1994), p. 14.

17. Aparna Joshi, Mila B. Lazarova, and Hui Liao, "Getting Everyone on Board: The Role of Inspirational Leadership in Geographically Dispersed Teams," *Organization Science* 20, no. 1 (January–February 2009): 240–252.

18. Howard M. Guttman, "Leading Meetings 101: Transform Them from Dull to Dynamic," *Leadership Excellence* (July 2009): 18.

19. Thomas Owens, "Business Teams," *Small Business Report* (January 1989): 50–58.

20. Margaret Frazier, "Flu Prep," *The Wall Street Journal*, March 25–26, 2006.

21. Susanne G. Scott and Walter O. Einstein, "Strategic Performance Appraisal in Team-Based Organizations: One Size Does Not Fit All," *Academy of Management Executive* 15, no. 2 (2001): 107–116.

22. Mathew Schwartz, "From Short Stack to Competitive Advantage: IHOP's Pursuit of Data Quality," *Business Intelligence Journal* 11, no. 3 (Third Quarter, 2006): 46–51.

23. John Murawski, "Cisco Unveils 'Business Tablet,'" *McClatchy-Tribune Business News,* June 30, 2010.

24. James H. Shonk, *Team-Based Organizations* (Homewood, IL: Business One Irwin, 1992); and John Hoerr, "The Payoff from Teamwork," *BusinessWeek* (July 10, 1989): 56–62.

25. Ruth Wageman, "Critical Success Factors for Creating Superb Self-Managing Teams," *Organizational Dynamics* (Summer 1997): 49–61.

26. Thomas Owens, "The Self-Managing Work Team," *Small Business Report* (February 1991): 53–65.

27. The discussion of virtual teams is based on Phillip L. Hunsaker and Johanna S. Hunsaker, "Virtual Teams: A Leader's Guide," *Team Performance Management* 14, no. 1–2 (2008): 86; Wayne F. Cascio and Stan Shurygailo, "E-Leadership and Virtual Teams," *Organizational Dynamics* 31, no. 4 (2002): 362–376; Anthony M. Townsend, Samuel M. DeMarie, and Anthony R. Hendrickson, "Virtual Teams: Technology and the Workplace of the Future," *Academy of Management Executive* 12, no. 3 (August 1998): 17–29; and Deborah L. Duarte and Nancy Tennant Snyder, *Mastering Virtual Teams* (San Francisco: Jossey-Bass, 1999).

28. Jessica Lipnack and Jeffrey Stamps, "Virtual Teams: The New Way to Work," *Strategy & Leadership* (January–February 1999): 14–19.

29. This discussion is based on Arvind Malhotra, Ann Majchrzak, and Benson Rosen, "Leading Virtual Teams," *Academy of Management Perspectives* 21, no. 1 (February 2007): 60–69; Benson Rosen, Stacie Furst, and Richard Blackburn, "Overcoming Barriers to Knowledge Sharing in Virtual Teams," *Organizational Dynamics* 36, no. 3 (2007): 259–273; Marshall Goldsmith, "Crossing the Cultural Chasm; Keeping Communication Clear and Consistent with Team Members from Other Countries Isn't Easy, Says Author Maya Hu-Chan," *Business Week Online,* May 31, 2007, www.businessweek.com/careers/content/may2007/ca20070530_521679.htm (accessed August 24, 2007); and Bradley L. Kirkman, Benson Rosen, Cristina B. Gibson, Paul E. Tesluk, and Simon O. McPherson, "Five Challenges to Virtual Team Success: Lessons from Sabre, Inc.," *Academy of Management Executive* 16, no. 3 (2002): 67–79.

30. Darl G. Kolb, Greg Prussia, and Joline Francoeur, "Connectivity and Leadership: The Influence of Online Activity on Closeness and Effectiveness," *Journal of Leadership and Organizational Studies* 15, no. 4 (May 2009): 342–352.

31. Ann Majchrzak, Arvind Malhotra, Jeffrey Stamps, and Jessica Lipnack, "Can Absence Make a Team Grow Stronger?" *Harvard Business Review* 82, no. 5 (May 2004): 131.

32. Lynda Gratton, "Working Together … When Apart," *The Wall Street Journal*, June 18, 2007; Kirkman et al., "Five Challenges to Virtual Team Success."

33. Vijay Govindarajan and Anil K. Gupta, "Building an Effective Global Business Team," *MIT Sloan Management Review* 42, no. 4 (Summer 2001): 63–71.

34. Charlene Marmer Solomon, "Building Teams Across Borders," *Global Workforce* (November 1998): 12–17.

35. Carol Saunders, Craig Van Slyke, and Douglas R. Vogel, "My Time or Yours? Managing Time Visions in Global Virtual Teams," *Academy of Management Executive* 18, no. 1 (2004): 19–31.

36. This discussion is based on Jeanne Brett, Kristin Behfar, and Mary C. Kern, "Managing Multicultural Teams," *Harvard Business Review* (November 2006): 84-91; and Saunders et al., "My Time or Yours?"

37. Richard Pastore, "Global Team Management: It's a Small World After All," *CIO,* January 23, 2008, www.cio.com/article/174750/Global_Team_Management_It_s_a_Small_World_After_All (accessed May 20, 2008).

38. Quoted in Phred Dvorak, "Frequent Contact Helps Bridge International Divide" (Theory & Practice column), *The Wall Street Journal*, June 1, 2009.

39. Dvorak, "Frequent Contact Helps Bridge International Divide."

40. Sylvia Odenwald, "Global Work Teams," *Training and Development* (February 1996): 54–57; Frank Siebdrat, Martin Hoegl, and Holger Ernst, "How to Manage Virtual Teams," *MIT Sloan Management Review* (Summer 2009): 63–68; and Debby Young, "Team Heat," *CIO* (September 1, 1998): 43–51.

41. Reported in Jia Lynn Yang, "The Power of Number 4.6," part of a special series, "Secrets of Greatness: Teamwork," *Fortune* (June 12, 2006): 122.

42. Martin Hoegl, "Smaller Teams—Better Teamwork: How to Keep Project Teams Small," *Business Horizons* 48 (2005): 209–214.

43. For research findings on group size, see Erin Bradner, Gloria Mark, and Tammie D. Hertel, "Team Size and Technology Fit: Participation, Awareness, and Rapport in Distributed Teams," *IEEE Transactions on Professional Communication* 48, no. 1 (March 2005): 68–77; M. E. Shaw, *Group Dynamics*, 3rd ed. (New York: McGraw-Hill, 1981); G. Manners, "Another Look at Group Size, Group Problem-Solving and Member Consensus," *Academy of Management Journal* 18 (1975): 715–724; and Hoegl, "Smaller Teams—Better Teamwork."

44. Bradner, Mark, and Hertel, "Team Size and Technology Fit: Participation, Awareness, and Rapport in Distributed Teams."

45. Yang, "The Power of Number 4.6."

46. Warren E. Watson, Kamalesh Kumar, and Larry K. Michaelsen, "Cultural Diversity's Impact on Interaction Process and Performance: Comparing Homogeneous and Diverse Task Groups," *Academy of Management Journal* 36 (1993): 590–602; Gail Robinson and Kathleen Dechant, "Building a Business Case for Diversity," *Academy of Management Executive* 11, no. 3 (1997): 21–31; and David A. Thomas and Robin J. Ely, "Making Differences Matter: A New Paradigm for Managing Diversity," *Harvard Business Review* (September–October 1996): 79–90.

47. D. van Knippenberg and M. C. Schippers, "Work Group Diversity," *Annual Review of Psychology* 58 (2007): 515–541; J. N. Cummings, "Work Groups: Structural Diversity and Knowledge Sharing in a Global Organization," *Management Science* 50, no, 3 (2004): 352–364; J. Stuart Bunderson and Kathleen M. Sutcliffe, "Comparing Alternative Conceptualizations of Functional Diversity in Management Teams: Process and Performance Effects," *Academy of Management Journal* 45, no. 5 (2002): 875–893; and Marc Orlitzky and John D. Benjamin, "The Effects of Sex Composition on Small Group Performance in a Business School Case Competition," *Academy of Management Learning and Education* 2, no. 2 (2003): 128–138.

48. Watson et al. "Cultural Diversity's Impact on Interaction Process and Performance"; and D. C. Hambrick, S. C. Davison, S. A. Snell, and C. C. Snow, "When Groups Consist of Multiple Nationalities: Towards a New Understanding of the Implications," *Organization Studies* 19, no. 2 (1998): 181–205.

49. R. M. Belbin, *Team Roles at Work* (Oxford: Butterworth Heinemann, 1983); Tony Manning, R. Parker, and G. Pogson, "A Revised Model of Team Roles and Some Research Findings," *Industrial and Commercial Training* 38, no. 6 (2006): 287–296; George Prince, "Recognizing Genuine Teamwork," *Supervisory Management* (April 1989): 25–36; and K. D. Benne and P. Sheats, "Functional Roles of Group Members," *Journal of Social Issues* 4 (1948): 41–49.

50. Robert A. Baron, *Behavior in Organizations*, 2nd ed. (Boston: Allyn & Bacon, 1986).

51. *Ibid.*

52. Kenneth G. Koehler, "Effective Team Management," *Small Business Report* (July 19, 1989): 14–16; and Connie J. G. Gersick, "Time and Transition in Work Teams: Toward a New Model of Group Development," *Academy of Management Journal* 31 (1988): 9–41.

53. Bruce W. Tuckman and Mary Ann C. Jensen, "Stages of Small-Group Development Revisited," *Group and Organizational Studies* 2 (1977): 419–427; and Bruce W. Tuckman, "Developmental Sequences in Small Groups," *Psychological Bulletin* 63 (1965): 384–399. See also Linda N. Jewell and H. Joseph Reitz, *Group Effectiveness in Organizations* (Glenview, IL: Scott, Foresman, 1981).

54. Thomas Petzinger Jr., "Bovis Team Helps Builders Construct a Solid Foundation" *The Wall Street Journal*, March 21, 1997.

55. Shaw, *Group Dynamics.*

56. Daniel C. Feldman and Hugh J. Arnold, *Managing Individual and Group Behavior in Organizations* (New York: McGraw-Hill, 1983).

57. Amanuel G. Tekleab, Narda R. Quigley, and Paul E. Tesluk, "A Longitudinal Study of Team Conflict, Conflict Management, Cohesion, and Team Effectiveness," *Group & Organization Management* 34, no. 2 (April 2009): 170–205; Dorwin Cartwright and Alvin Zander, *Group Dynamics: Research and Theory*, 3rd ed. (New York: Harper & Row, 1968); and Elliot Aronson, *The Social Animal* (San Francisco: W. H. Freeman, 1976).

58. Marcial Losada and Emily Heaphy, "The Role of Positivity and Connectivity in the Performance of Business Teams," *American Behavioral Scientist* 47, no. 6 (February 2004): 740–765,

59. Stanley E. Seashore, *Group Cohesiveness in the Industrial Work Group* (Ann Arbor, MI: Institute for Social Research, 1954).

60. J. Richard Hackman, "Group Influences on Individuals," in *Handbook of Industrial and Organizational Psychology*, ed., M. Dunnette (Chicago: Rand McNally, 1976).

61. The following discussion is based on Daniel C. Feldman, "The Development and Enforcement of Group Norms," *Academy of Management Review* 9 (1984): 47–53.

62. Wilson et al., *Leadership Trapeze*, p. 12.

63. Simon Taggar and Robert Ellis, "The Role of Leaders in Shaping Formal Team Norms," *The Leadership Quarterly* 18 (2007): 105–120.

64. Geoffrey Colvin, "Why Dream Teams Fail," *Fortune* (June 12, 2006): 87–92.

65. Stephen P. Robbins, *Managing Organizational Conflict: A Nontraditional Approach* (Englewood Cliffs, NJ: Prentice Hall, 1974).

66. Tekleab et al., "A Longitudinal Study of Team Conflict, Conflict Management, Cohesion, and Team Effectiveness."

67. Based on K. A. Jehn, "A Multimethod Examination of the Benefits and Determinants of Intragroup Conflict," *Administrative Science Quarterly* 40 (1995): 256–282; and K. A. Jehn, "A Qualitative Analysis of Conflict Types and Dimensions in Organizational Groups," *Administrative Science Quarterly* 42 (1997): 530–557.

68. Linda A. Hill, "A Note for Analyzing Work Groups," *Harvard Business School Cases,* August 28, 1995; revised April 3, 1998, Product # 9-496-026, ordered at http://hbr.org/search/linda+a+hill/4294934969/.

69. A. Amason, "Distinguishing the Effects of Functional and Dysfunctional Conflict on Strategic Decision Making: Resolving a Paradox for Top Management Teams," *Academy of Management Journal* 39, no. 1 (1996): 123–148; Jehn, "A Multimethod Examination of the Benefits and Determinants of Intragroup Conflict"; and K. A. Jehn and E. A. Mannix, "The Dynamic Nature of Conflict: A Longitudinal Study of Intragroup Conflict and Group Performance, *Academy of Management Journal* 44 (2001): 238–251.

70. Amason, "Distinguishing the Effects of Functional and Dysfunctional Conflict on Strategic Decision Making."

71. Dean Tjosvold, Chun Hui, Daniel Z. Ding, and Junchen Hu, "Conflict Values and Team Relationships: Conflict's Contribution to Team Effectiveness and Citizenship in China," *Journal of Organizational Behavior* 24 (2003): 69–88; C. De Dreu and E. Van de Vliert, *Using Conflict in Organizations* (Beverly Hills, CA: Sage, 1997); and Kathleen M. Eisenhardt, Jean L. Kahwajy, and L. J. Bourgeois III, "Conflict and Strategic Choice: How Top Management Teams Disagree," *California Management Review* 39, no. 2 (Winter 1997): 42–62.

72. Koehler, "Effective Team Management"; and Dean Tjosvold, "Making Conflict Productive," *Personnel Administrator* 29 (June 1984): 121.

73. This discussion is based in part on Richard L. Daft, *Organization Theory and Design* (St. Paul, MN: West, 1992), chapter 13; and Paul M. Terry, "Conflict Management," *The Journal of Leadership Studies* 3, no. 2 (1996): 3–21.

74. Yuhyung Shin, "Conflict Resolution in Virtual Teams," *Organizational Dynamics* 34, no. 4 (2005): 331–345.

75. Holly Duckworth, "How TRW Automotive Helps Global Teams Perform at the Top of Their Game," *Global Business and Organizational Excellence* (November–December 2008): 6–16.

76. This discussion is based on K. W. Thomas, "Towards Multidimensional Values in Teaching: The Example of Conflict Behaviors," *Academy of Management Review* 2 (1977): 487.

77. Robbins, *Managing Organizational Conflict*.

78. "Negotiation Types," *The Negotiation Experts,* June 9, 2010, http://www .negotiations.com/articles/negotiation types/ (accessed September 28, 2010).

79. Rob Walker, "Take It or Leave It: The Only Guide to Negotiating You Will Ever Need," *Inc.* (August 2003): 75–82.

80. Based on Roger Fisher and William Ury, *Getting to Yes: Negotiating Agreement Without Giving In* (New York: Penguin, 1983).

81. This familiar story has been reported in many publications, including "The Six Best Questions to Ask Your Customers," Marketing and Distribution Company Limited, www.madisco .bz/articles/The%20Six%20Best%20Questions%20to%20 Ask%20Your%20Customers.pdf (accessed September 28, 2010).

82. Based in part on Hill, "A Note for Analyzing Work Groups."

83. "Big and No Longer Blue," *The Economist* (January 21–27, 2006): 26.

84. R. B. Zajonc, "Social Facilitation," *Science* 149 (1965): 269–274; and Miriam Erez and Anit Somech, "Is Group Productivity Loss the Rule or the Exception? Effects of Culture and Group-Based Motivation," *Academy of Management Journal* 39, no. 6 (1996): 1513–1537.

85. Claire M. Mason and Mark A. Griffin, "Group Task Satisfaction; The Group's Shared Attitude to Its Task and Work Environment," *Group and Organizational Management* 30, no. 6 (2005): 625–652.

86. Gina Imperato, "Their Specialty? Teamwork," *Fast Company* (January–February 2000): 54–56.

87. Reported in Scott Thurm, "Theory & Practice: Teamwork Raises Everyone's Game—Having Employees Bond Benefits Companies More Than Promoting 'Stars,'" *The Wall Street Journal*, November 7, 2005.

88. Dan Heath and Chip Heath, "Blowing the Baton Pass."

89. Hill, "A Note for Analyzing Work Groups."

90. Based on James W. Kinneer, "This and That: Improving Team Performance," in *The 1997 Annual: Volume 2, Consulting* (San Francisco: Pfeiffer, 1997), pp. 55–58.

91. Based on Ellen R. Stapleton, "College to Expand Policy on Plagiarism," *The Ithacan Online*, April 12, 2001, www.ithaca. edu/ithacan/articles/0104/12/news/0college_to_e.htm (accessed April 12, 2001).

92. Based on Michael C. Beers, "The Strategy That Wouldn't Travel," *Harvard Business Review* (November–December 1996): 18–31; Cathy Olofson, "Can We Talk? Put Another Log on the Fire," *Fast Company* (December 19, 2007), www.fastcompany .com/magazine/28/minm.html (accessed September 3, 2008); Karen Blount, "How to Build Teams in the Midst of Change," *Nursing Management* (August 1998): 27–29; and Erin White, "How a Company Made Everyone a Team Player," *The Wall Street Journal,* August 13, 2007.

PART 6

Controlling

Launched as an opera house in 1912, the Nederlander Organization has become one of the most esteemed entertainment management companies in America. The firm's music division, Nederlander Concerts, showcases premier rock and pop performances at prestigious venues such as the Los Angeles Greek Theatre, the San Jose Civic, and the Santa Barbara Bowl.

Nederlander's small-to-mid-sized venues host some of the biggest names in show business, from U2 and Pearl Jam, to Jimmy Buffet and 30 Seconds to Mars. Fans pay higher prices for Nederlander shows, as the thrill of watching bands rock out in intimate settings beats the mega-crowd mayhem of stadium concerts.

To make profits on venues with 5,000 or fewer seats, Nederlander's financial managers must keep tight control over revenues and costs. Revenues come from ticket sales, concert sponsorships, merchandise, and concessions. Costs include payroll, energy expenses, daily operations, and the price of securing popular touring artists.

Nederlander's annual budget, created at the start of each year, provides an important financial map against which all costs and revenues are measured. In addition, each Nederlander event has its own P&L (profit and loss) statement. By comparing monthly financial statements against the annual budget, managers are able to track progress toward financial targets while keeping an eye on expenses.

"The show must go on" is the motto of the entertainment world. Yet without savvy financial managers and effective controls, the curtain would fall on companies like Nederlander.

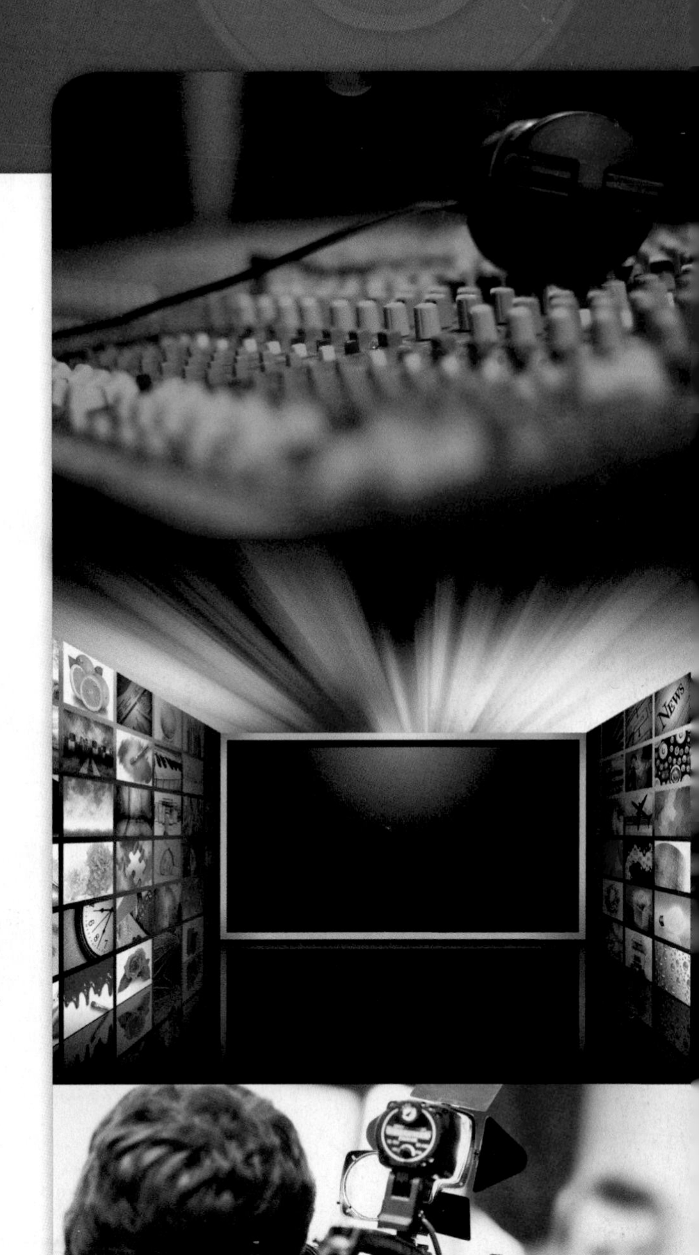

Chapter Outline

The Meaning of Control
- *Choosing Standards and Measures*
- *The Balanced Scorecard*

Feedback Control Model
- *Steps of Feedback Control*
- *Application to Budgeting*

Financial Control
- *Financial Statements*

The Changing Philosophy of Control
- *Hierarchical versus Decentralized Approaches*
- *Open-Book Management*

Total Quality Management
- *TQM Techniques*
- *TQM Success Factors*

Trends in Quality Control
- *International Quality Standards*

Managing Quality and Performance

Learning Outcomes

After studying this chapter, you should be able to:

1. Define organizational control and explain why it is a key management function.
2. Explain the benefits of using the balanced scorecard to track performance and control of the organization.
3. Explain the four steps in the control process.
4. Discuss the use of financial statements and budgeting as management controls.
5. Contrast the hierarchical and decentralized methods of control.
6. Identify the benefits of open-book management.
7. Describe the concept of total quality management and major TQM techniques, such as quality circles, benchmarking, Six Sigma principles, reduced cycle time, and continuous improvement.
8. Identify current trends in quality control, including ISO 9000 and corporate governance, and discuss their impact on organizations.

© James Steidl, Shutterstock

Are You Ready to Be a Manager?

Please circle your opinion below each of the following statements.

1 I enjoy keeping track of my own or my team's progress and like to keep statistics on how well we are doing.

Mostly True | Mostly False

(See page 600, Managing Quality and Performance.)

2 In my own life, I judge my success not only by how much money I do or can earn, but also by how much I learn and the quality of my relationships.

Mostly True | Mostly False

(See page 603, The Balanced Scorecard.)

3 I set goals for myself each week and then look and see how well I met my own goals.

Mostly True | Mostly False

(See page 606, Measure Actual Performance.)

4 I have a budget for myself and know this is a tool to help me make better decisions about how to use my resources.

Mostly True | Mostly False

(See page 608, Application to Budgeting.)

5 When I'm working on a project, I try to find someone who's done something similar and been very successful and I try to learn from that person how I can be even more effective.

Mostly True | Mostly False

(See page 619, Benchmarking.)

Ask avid sports fans about their favorite players, and they'll likely rattle off some key statistics about their performance. Take fans of the L.A. Lakers' Kobe Bryant, for example. Anyone who closely follows this NBA basketball star can easily recite statistics that highlight his on-court performance: points per game, rebounds, assists, three-pointers, and steals. Although Bryant's statistics are important throughout the season, they take on greater significance during post-season championship games when competition is fiercest. Consider Bryant's performance during the final game of the NBA Championship in 2010, when the Lakers beat the Boston Celtics 83–79 to win their 16th championship. During this close game, Kobe Bryant made just 6 of 24 shots, but he nailed a big jumper with five minutes to play. In the fourth quarter, Bryant hit 8 of 9 free throws and nabbed 15 rebounds in the final minutes. "I had to do something," said Bryant. "Whoever won the rebounds won each game, so I was trying to get in there and make as many as I could."[1]

All sports coaches and team managers track player statistics, such as number of rebounds, and use that data to make important decisions such as which players to play, trade, or sit on the bench. Does tracking player performance and overall team statistics result in more wins during the season? Some coaches believe it does. In fact, some NBA teams are hiring employees whose sole responsibility is to collect data about team and player performance. Half the league's teams have at least one statistician who analyzes team and player data. Many of these teams are among the NBA's best. The 15 teams who have invested heavily in statistics—and tracking player performance—have won 59.3 percent of their games. The 15 teams without such analysts have won only 40.7 percent of their games.[2]

© VITO PALMISANO

ConceptConnection

Shortly after its introduction of kombucha, Honest Tea, a Bethesda, Maryland-based bottled organic beverage company, faced an unanticipated **organizational control** issue. A drink with a small but fervent following, kombucha is a vinegary, fermented tea that purportedly bestows various health benefits. In June 2010, testing revealed that the drink's alcoholic content often exceeded government standards for nonalcoholic beverages; consequently, all producers voluntarily recalled the item. When Honest Tea managers ran tests on the same batch, levels were inconsistent, reported CEO and cofounder Seth Grossman (left). By using a new process that ensured lower, more stable alcohol levels, they got Honest Kombucha back on store shelves by August.

As a manager, you will also use a variety of measures to monitor performance. Many of these measures will include control issues, including controlling work processes, regulating employee behavior, setting up basic systems for allocating financial resources, developing human resources, analyzing financial performance, and evaluating overall profitability.

This chapter introduces basic mechanisms for controlling the organization. We begin by summarizing the objectives of the control process and the use of the balanced scorecard to measure performance. Then we discuss the four steps in the control process and methods for controlling financial performance, including the use of budgets and financial statements. The next sections examine the changing philosophy of control, today's approach to total quality management, and trends such as ISO certification and corporate governance.

The Meaning of Control

It seemed like a perfect fit. In the chaotic aftermath of Hurricane Katrina, the American Red Cross needed private-sector help to respond to the hundreds of thousands of people seeking emergency aid. Staffing company Spherion Corporation had the expertise to hire and train temporary workers fast, and the company had a good track record working with the Red Cross. Yet Red Cross officials soon noticed something odd: an unusually large number of Katrina victim money orders, authorized by employees at the Spherion-staffed

New Manager Self-Test

What Is Your Attitude Toward Organizational Regulation and Control?

Managers have to control people for organizations to survive, yet this control should be the right amount and type. Companies are often less democratic than the society of which they are a part. Think honestly about your beliefs about the regulation of other people and answer each item that follows as Mostly True or Mostly False.

	MOSTLY TRUE <<<	>>> MOSTLY FALSE
1. I believe people should be guided more by feelings and less by rules.	______	______
2. I think employees should be on time to work and to meetings.	______	______
3. I believe efficiency and speed are not as important as letting every-one have their say when making a decision.	______	______
4. I think employees should conform to company policies.	______	______
5. I let my significant other make the decision and have his or her way most of the time.	______	______
6. I like to tell other people what to do.	______	______
7. I am more patient with the least capable people.	______	______
8. I like to have things running "just so."	______	______

See It Online

Scoring and Interpretation: Give yourself 1 point for each Mostly True answer to the odd-numbered questions and 1 point for each Mostly False answer to the even-numbered questions. A score of 6 or above suggests you prefer decentralized control for other people in organizations. A score of 3 or less suggests a preference for more control and bureaucracy in a company. Enthusiastic new managers may exercise too much of their new control and get a negative backlash. However, too little control may mean less accountability and productivity. The challenge for new managers is to strike the right balance for the job and people involved.

SOURCE: Adapted from J. J. Ray, "Do Authoritarians Hold Authoritarian Attitudes?" *Human Relations* 29 (1976): 307–325.

call center, were being cashed near the call center itself—in Bakersfield, California, far from the hurricane-ravaged area. A federal investigation found that some call-center employees were issuing money orders to fake hurricane victims and cashing the orders for themselves. Fortunately, the fraud was discovered quickly, but the weak control systems that allowed the scam to occur got both the Red Cross and Spherion into a public relations and political mess.[3]

A lack of control can have repercussions that damage an organization's health, hurt its reputation, and threaten its future. One area in which many managers are implementing stronger controls is employee use of the Internet and e-mail, as described in the Spotlight on Skills box titled Cyberslackers Beware: Big Brother Is Watching.

SPOTLIGHT ON SKILLS

Cyberslackers Beware: Big Brother Is Watching

Ryan Elmore, owner of Pepper Jack's Neighborhood Grill, was shocked when he learned what his employees were doing when he left the restaurant. After installing networked cameras that he could access through an online service, Elmore discovered that his employees were sending text messages, giving free meals to friends, and taking multiple cigarette breaks each hour. "I couldn't believe it," says Elmore. "You may trust your employees, but you don't know what happens when you walk out that door."

As Elmore learned, a whole host of distractions can reduce employee productivity. Today's managers find that instant access to technology is the main culprit behind the increase in "cyberslackers," people who spend part of their workday sending personal e-mails and text messages, posting on Facebook, or downloading music and videos that hog available bandwidth and sometimes introduce viruses. In addition, it takes just a few bad apples engaging in harmful and possibly illegal activities, such as harassing other employees over the Web, to cause serious problems for their employers. So it's not surprising that the use of sophisticated software to both block employees' access to certain sites and monitor their Internet and e-mail use has grown exponentially.

A certain degree of vigilance is clearly warranted. However, enlightened managers strive for a balanced approach that protects the organization's interests while maintaining a positive, respectful work environment. Surveillance overkill can sometimes cost more than it saves, and it can also have a distinctly negative impact on employee morale. At the very least, employees may feel as though they're not being treated as trustworthy, responsible adults.

Here are some guidelines for creating an effective but fair "acceptable use policy" for workplace Internet use.

- ***Make sure employees understand that they have no legal right to privacy in the workplace.*** The courts so far have upheld an organization's right to monitor any and all employee activities on computers purchased by an employer for work purposes.
- ***Create a written Internet policy.*** Make sure you clearly state what qualifies as a policy violation by giving clear, concrete guidelines for acceptable use of e-mail, the Internet, and any other employer-provided hardware or software. For example, spell out the types of Web sites that are never to be visited while at work and what constitutes acceptable e-mail content. Are employees ever permitted to use the Web for personal use? If so, specify what they can do, for how long, and whether they need to confine their personal use to lunchtime or breaks. List the devices you'll be checking and tell them the filtering and monitoring procedures you have in place. Get employees to sign a statement saying they've read and understand the policy.
- ***Describe the disciplinary process.*** Give people a clear understanding of the consequences of violating the organization's Internet and electronic use policy. Make sure they know the organization will cooperate if a criminal investigation arises.
- ***Review the policy at regular intervals.*** You'll need to modify your guidelines as new technologies and devices appear.

Managers should remember that monitoring e-mail and Internet use doesn't have to be an all-or-nothing process. Some organizations use continuous surveillance; others screen only when they believe a problem exists, or they disseminate a policy and leave enforcement to the honor system. Look carefully at your workforce and the work they're doing, and assess your potential liability and security needs. Then come up with a policy and monitoring plan that makes sense for your organization.

SOURCES: Jennifer Alsever, "Being Big Brother," *FSB* (October, 2008): 43; Lorraine Cosgrove Ware, "People Watching," *CIO* (August 15, 2005): 24; "Employee E-mail and Internet Usage Monitoring: Issues and Concerns," Technical Resource Group Web site, www.picktrg.com/pubs/EmployeeMonitoring_WP062804.pdf; Pui-Wing Tam, Erin White, Nick Wingfield, and Kris Maher, "Snooping E-Mail by Software Is Now a Workplace Norm," *The Wall Street Journal*, March 9, 2005; and Ann Sherman, "Firms Address Worries over Workplace Web Surfing," *Broward Daily Business Review* (May 17, 2006): 11.

Organizational control refers to the systematic process of regulating organizational activities to make them consistent with the expectations established in plans, targets, and standards of performance. In a classic article on the control function, Douglas S. Sherwin summarizes the concept as follows: "The essence of control is action which adjusts operations to predetermined standards, and its basis is information in the hands of managers."[4] Thus, effectively controlling an organization requires information about performance standards and actual performance, as well as actions taken to correct any deviations from the standards. To effectively control an organization, managers need to decide what information is essential, how they will obtain that information, and how they can and should respond to it. Having the correct data is essential. Managers decide which standards, measurements, and metrics are needed to effectively monitor and control the organization and set up systems for obtaining that information. For example, Shenzhen Hepalink, a Chinese pharmaceutical company, generates more than 300 pages of data for each batch of heparin (blood-thinning agent) it produces for the United States in order to guarantee quality and safety. "The products we make are directly injected into people's blood streams," says Li Li, Shenzhen Hepalink's chairman. "So we have great responsibilities." China's drug industry has come under increasing scrutiny following a series of deaths and illnesses due to contaminants. For Shenzhen Hepalink, organizational control is vital to ensuring confidence in the safety of its drugs.[5]

Choosing Standards and Measures

Most organizations focus on measuring and controlling financial performance, such as sales, revenue, and profit. Yet managers increasingly recognize the need to also measure intangible aspects of performance to manage the value-creating activities of the contemporary organization.[6] British Airways, for example, measures its performance in key areas of customer service because its strategy is to compete on superior service in an industry dominated by companies that compete on price. Underpinning this strategy is a belief that delivery of excellent service will result in higher levels of customer retention and profitability. Thus, British Airways measures and controls areas of customer service that have the greatest impact on a customer's service experience, including in-flight service, meal rating, baggage claim, and executive club membership.[7] Instead of relying only on financial measures to judge the company's performance, British Airways uses a number of different operational measures to track performance and control the organization.

The Group Learning, on pages 625–626, will give you a chance to practice developing a control system that includes rules to guide behavior and statistics for measuring performance.

The Balanced Scorecard

Like British Airways, many firms are now taking a more balanced perspective of company performance, integrating various dimensions of control that focus on markets and customers as well as employees and financials.[8] Managers recognize that relying exclusively on financial measures can result in short-term, dysfunctional behavior. Nonfinancial measures provide a healthy supplement to the traditional financial measures, and companies are investing significant sums in developing more balanced measurement systems as a result.[9] The **balanced scorecard** is a comprehensive management control system that balances traditional financial measures with operational measures relating to a company's critical success factors.[10]

A balanced scorecard contains four major perspectives, as illustrated in Exhibit 15.1: financial performance, customer service, internal business processes, and the organization's capacity for learning and growth.[11] Within these four areas, managers identify key performance metrics the organization will track. The *financial performance* perspective reflects a concern that the organization's activities contribute to improving short- and long-term financial performance. It includes traditional measures such as net income and return on investment. *Customer service* indicators measure things such as how customers view the organization, as well as customer retention and satisfaction. Popularity doesn't always mean high customer satisfaction ratings. For example, 500 million people use Facebook. But a survey conducted by ForeSee Results found that among the 30 Web sites it tracks, Facebook ranked second from the bottom for customer satisfaction. It was also among the lowest 5 percent of all 223 companies ForeSee tracks.[12] *Business process* indicators focus on production and operating statistics, such as order fulfillment or cost per order.

The final component of the balanced scorecard looks at the organization's *potential for learning and growth*, focusing on how well resources and human capital are being managed

EXHIBIT 15.1
The Balanced Scorecard

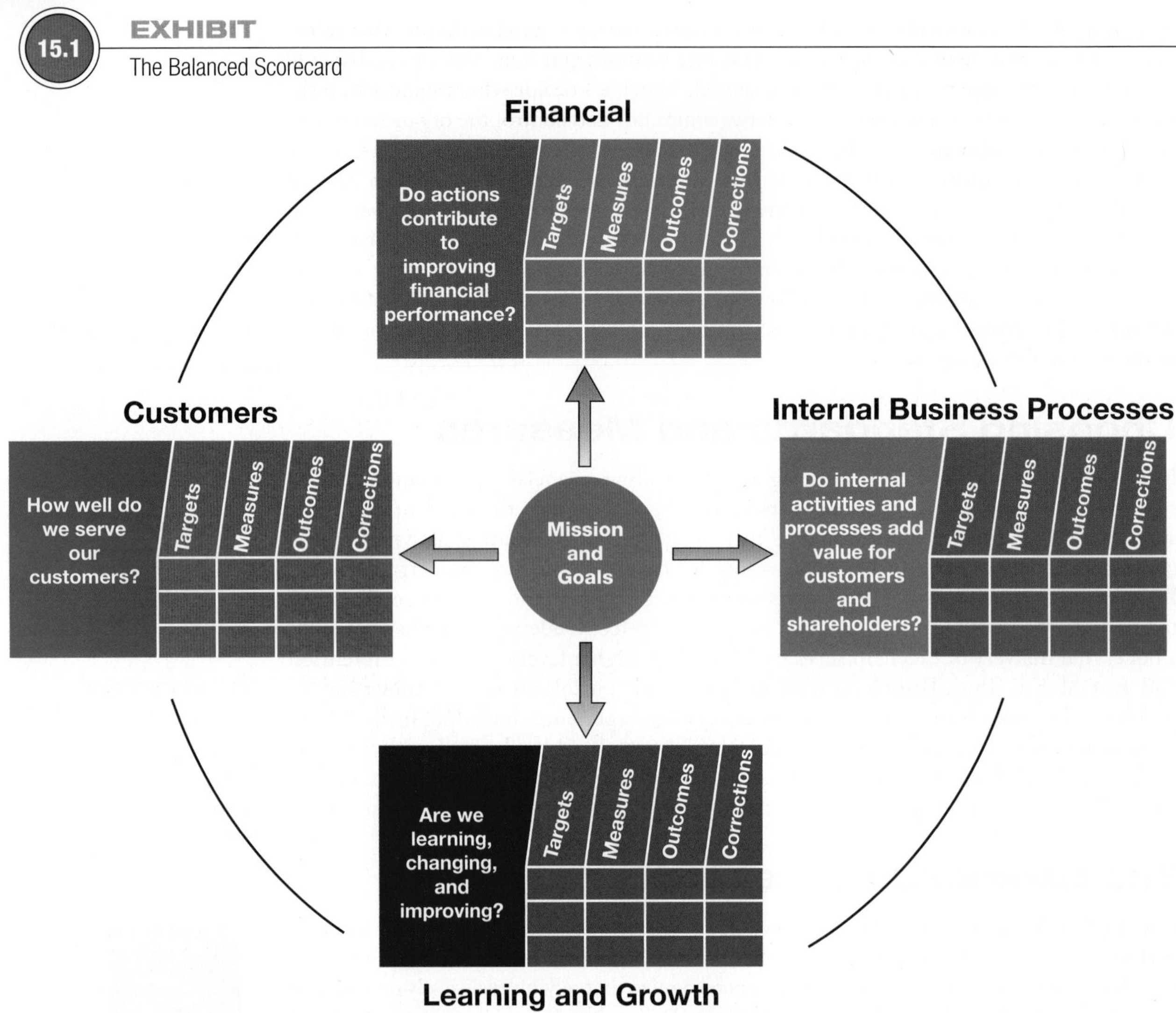

SOURCES: Based on Robert S. Kaplan and David P. Norton, "Using the Balanced Scorecard as a Strategic Management System," *Harvard Business Review* (January– February 1996): 75–85; and Chee W. Chow, Kamal M. Haddad, and James E.Williamson, "Applying the Balanced Scorecard to Small Companies," *Management Accounting* 79, no. 2 (August 1997): 21–27.

for the company's future. Metrics may include things such as employee retention and the introduction of new products. The components of the scorecard are designed in an integrative manner, as illustrated in Exhibit 15.1.

Managers record, analyze, and discuss these various metrics to determine how well the organization is achieving its strategic goals. The balanced scorecard is an effective tool for managing and improving performance only if it is clearly linked to a well-defined organizational strategy and goals.[13] At its best, use of the scorecard cascades down from the top levels of the organization so that everyone becomes involved in thinking about and discussing strategy.[14] The scorecard has become the core management control system for many organizations, including well-known organizations such as Bell Emergis (a division of Bell Canada), Exxon Mobil Corp., CIGNA (insurance), Hilton Hotels, and even some units of the U.S. federal government.[15] As with all management systems, the balanced scorecard is not right for every organization in every situation. The simplicity of the system causes some managers to underestimate the time and commitment that is needed for the approach to become a truly useful management control system. If managers implement the balanced scorecard using a *performance measurement* orientation rather than a *performance management* approach that links targets and measurements to corporate strategy, use of the scorecard can actually hinder or even decrease organizational performance.[16]

- Statistical measurement is an important part of achieving high performance.
- **Organizational control** is the systematic process through which managers regulate organizational activities to meet planned goals and standards of performance.
- Most organizations measure and control performance using quantitative financial measures.
- Increasingly, organizations are measuring less-tangible aspects of performance in addition to financial measures.
- A **balanced scorecard** is a comprehensive management control system that balances traditional financial measures with measures of customer service, internal business processes, and the organization's capacity for learning and growth.

Feedback Control Model

All well-designed control systems involve the use of feedback to determine whether performance meets established standards. Managers need feedback, for example, in each of the four categories of the balanced scorecard. British Airways ties its use of the balanced scorecard to a feedback control model. Scorecards are used as the agenda for monthly management meetings. Managers focus on the various elements of the scorecard to set targets, evaluate performance, and guide discussion about what further actions need to be taken.[17] In this section, we examine the key steps in the feedback control model and then look at how the model applies to organizational budgeting.

Steps of Feedback Control

Managers set up control systems that consist of the four key steps illustrated in Exhibit 15.2: Establish standards, measure performance, compare performance to standards, and make corrections as necessary.

EXHIBIT 15.2

Feedback Control Model

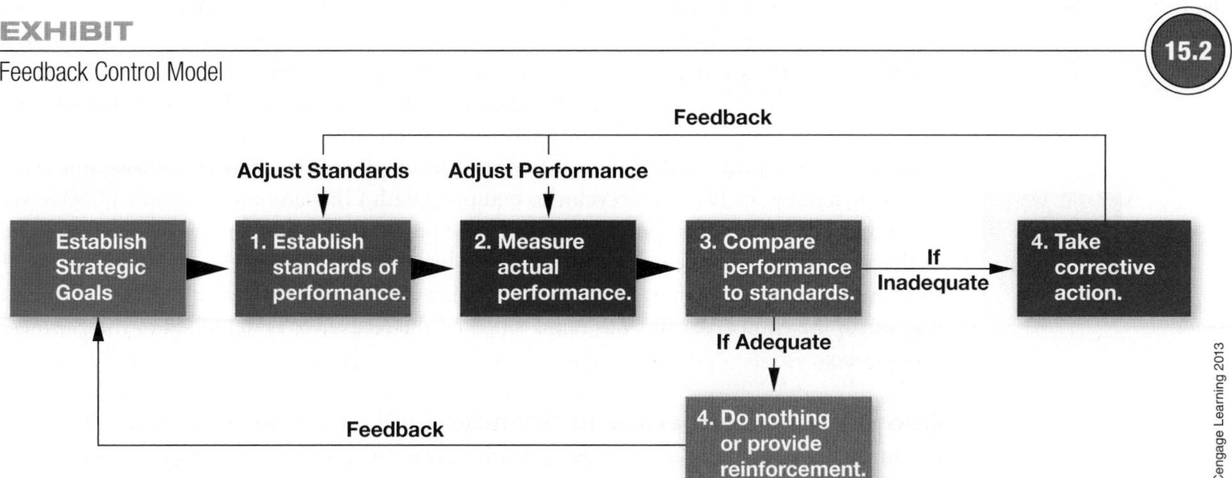

Establish Standards of Performance Within the organization's overall strategic plan, managers define goals for organizational departments in specific, operational terms that include a *standard of performance* against which to compare organizational activities. A standard of performance could include "reducing the reject rate from 15 to 3 percent," "increasing the corporation's return on investment to 7 percent," or "reducing the number of accidents to one per each 100,000 hours of labor." Managers should carefully assess what they will measure and how they will define it. In the auto industry, crash test ratings provide a standard of performance established by the National Highway Traffic Safety Administration. When crash test ratings are below standard, managers rethink design and manufacturing processes to improve crash test results. Although Daimler's ultra-tiny Smart ForTwo car won a Five Star rating for driver protection, it won just a Three Star rating for passenger protection, indicating the need for improved passenger safety features.[18]

Tracking such measures as customer service, employee involvement, or, for auto manufacturers, crash test results, is an important supplement to traditional financial and operational performance measurement, but many companies have a hard time identifying and defining nonfinancial measurements.[19] To effectively evaluate and reward employees for the achievement of standards, managers need clear standards that reflect activities that contribute to the organization's overall strategy in a significant way. Standards should be defined clearly and precisely so employees know what they need to do and can determine whether their activities are on target.[20]

Ryan McVay/Photodisc/Jupiter Images

ConceptConnection

Is it possible to make scientific discovery efficient? Managers at pharmaceuticals company Wyeth (now part of Pfizer Inc.) think so. They devised a streamlined research and development system driven by ambitious, quantifiable **standards of performance**. Managers routinely **compare performance to standards** and issue automated scorecards for each individual. Wyeth ties compensation to accomplishment of these all-or-nothing targets. So far, the approach has yielded impressive results. With no additional investment, Wyeth has seen the number of new drugs that emerge from the early discovery phase increase fourfold.

Measure Actual Performance Most organizations prepare formal reports of quantitative performance measurements that managers review daily, weekly, or monthly. These measurements should be related to the standards set in the first step of the control process. For example, if sales growth is a target, the organization should have a means of gathering and reporting sales data. If the organization has identified appropriate measurements, regular review of these reports helps managers stay aware of whether the organization is doing what it should. Technology is aiding many organizations in measuring performance. For example, GPS tracking devices installed on government-issued vehicles are helping many communities reduce waste and abuse, in part by catching employees shopping, working out at the gym, or otherwise loafing while on the clock. Although some claim this technology is intrusive, city officials say tracking the whereabouts of government employees has deterred abuses and saved taxpayers money. In Denver, 76 vehicles equipped with GPS units were driven 5,000 fewer miles than the unequipped fleet during the same period the year before, indicating the value of this type of quantitative measure.[21] Retailer Metropark USA was evidently only looking at its sales figures rather than other measures (such as whether the expensive store environment was worth the extra cost) and was blind-sided by the recession, as described in the Business Blooper box.

3

Compare Performance to Standards The third step in the control process is comparing actual activities to performance standards. When managers read computer

BUSINESS BLOOPER

Metropark USA Clothing

Development of a new clothing company with high-end, expensive duds for ages 20–35 unraveled when Metropark USA went bankrupt in early 2011 and was forced to close all of its 69 stores in 21 states. One of their consultants noted, "Not that the concept is wrong, but the concept is narrow and has high sensitivity to economic and credit risk," partly because people in that age group are not at their "peak earning power," as they might be 10 or 20 years later. Resources were put in to make the stores have the "high energy of a night club," but why wouldn't shoppers just go straight to a club, if that's what they really wanted? Started in 2005, the chain went public in 2008, with strong sales in previous years and goals to open 300 stores nationwide. But with the economic collapse of 2008, the target buyers found themselves already overborrowed and credit cards were suddenly hard to get. Not to mention the unemployment rate for twenty-somethings skyrocketed. Not having a job can be a real curtailment to buying clothes in a clubby environment.

SOURCE: Hang Nguyen, "Clothing Retailer Going out of Business," *McClathy-Tribune Business News*, May 12, 2011.

reports or walk through the plant, they identify whether actual performance meets, exceeds, or falls short of standards. Typically, performance reports simplify such comparisons by placing the performance standards for the reporting period alongside the actual performance for the same period and by computing the variance—that is, the difference between each actual amount and the associated standard. To correct the problems that most require attention, managers focus on variances.

When performance deviates from a standard, managers must interpret the deviation. They are expected to dig beneath the surface and find the cause of the problem. If the sales goal is to increase the number of sales calls by 10 percent and a salesperson achieved an increase of 8 percent, where did she fail to achieve her goal? Perhaps several businesses on her route closed, additional salespeople were assigned to her area by competitors, or she needs training in making cold sales calls more effectively. Managers should take an inquiring approach to deviations to gain a broad understanding of factors that influence performance. Effective management control involves subjective judgment and employee discussions, as well as objective analysis of performance data. Nick Sarillo has figured out an effective way to monitor employee performance, as described in the Spotlight on Skills titled Nick's Pizza & Pub.

Take Corrective Action Managers also determine what changes, if any, are needed. One example comes from Walmart. When customers expressed growing fears about food safety, Walmart managers decided to take corrective action and purchase produce, meat, and seafood only from suppliers accredited by private-inspection offices. They selected GlobalG.A.P., the biggest private regulator, to certify that food products sold in Walmart stores met high safety standards. GlobalG.A.P. includes limits on pesticide residue, a ban on nonessential animals around packing houses, and restrictions on the use of fertilizers. These standards, higher than those required by the U.S. Food and Drug Administration, increase shelf price but boost consumer confidence through high safety standards.[22]

SPOTLIGHT ON SKILLS

Nick's Pizza & Pub

Nick Sarillo started Nick's Pizza & Pub because he couldn't find a decent place in his Chicago suburb to take his three kids to eat. And he also wanted to prove people wrong who told him employees wouldn't work hard, or they would steal. He knew they were wrong and he finally figured out how to create a system that engaged the best parts of his workers. He calls his system "Trust" and Track," because he trains workers in correct procedures, then trusts the employees to do the right thing while tracking their performance. But he knows he needs a solid system. For example, after this business took off from the half-price Mondays and Tuesdays, he set up a pizza assembly line of 18 mostly high-schoolers. Then he set up a checklist of everything that needed to be done by 4:00 P.M. and had employees turn over laminated "ops cards" in the time-card slots, one for each task. The cards are red on top and green on the bottom. When all the cards show green, it means everything is done.

He also has a system for giving feedback on performance and it involves three types:

1. ***Feedback loop, for new employees.*** At the end of a shift, the supervisor will ask the trainee what was done well and what could have been done better. The trainee answers and the supervisor responds, hence the feedback loop term.
2. ***Performance feedback,*** also at shift's end, when the shift supervisor describes something done well and something that could be improved.
3. ***Direct feedback,*** is in the moment, commenting on what has just been done, good or bad. Managers are given a great deal of training and role playing to know how to give high-quality feedback.

Sarillo's control system works. He's now in two locations, Elgin and Crystal Lake. Industry average for profits is around 6 percent, while Nick's is about 14 percent and sometimes as high as 18 percent. Yearly sales are $7 million. That's a lot of pizza slices.

SOURCE: Bo Burlingham, "Lessons from a Blue-Collar Millionaire," *Inc. Magazine,* (February 2010): 57–63.

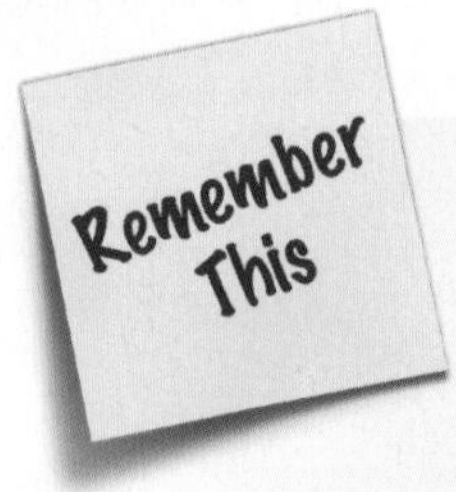

- The feedback control model involves using feedback to determine whether performance meets established standards.
- Well-designed control systems include four key steps: establish standards, measure performance, compare performance to standards, and make corrections as necessary.

Application to Budgeting

Go to the Self Learning, on page 625, that pertains to budgetary control.

Budgetary control, one of the most commonly used methods of managerial control, is the process of setting targets for an organization's expenditures, monitoring results and comparing them to the budget, and making changes as needed. As a control device, budgets are reports that list planned and actual expenditures for cash, assets, raw materials, salaries, and other resources. In addition, budget reports usually list the variance between the budgeted and actual amounts for each item.

A budget is created for every division or department within an organization, no matter how small, as long as it performs a distinct project, program, or function. The fundamental unit of analysis for a budget control system is called a responsibility center. A **responsibility center** is defined as any organizational department or unit under the supervision of a single person who is responsible for its activity.[23] A three-person appliance sales office in Watertown, New York, is a responsibility center, as is a quality control department, a marketing department, and an entire refrigerator manufacturing plant. The manager of each unit has budget responsibility. Top managers use budgets for the company as a whole, and middle managers traditionally focus on the budget performance of their department or division. Budgets that managers typically use include expense budgets, revenue budgets, cash budgets, and capital budgets.

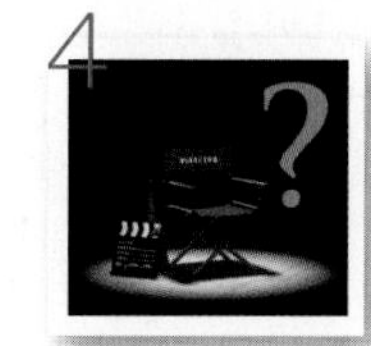

Expense Budget An **expense budget** includes anticipated and actual expenses for each responsibility center and for the total organization. An expense budget may show all types of expenses or may focus on a particular category, such as materials or research and development expenses. When actual expenses exceed budgeted amounts, the difference signals the need for managers to identify possible problems and take corrective action if needed. The difference may arise from inefficiency, or expenses may be higher because the organization's sales are growing faster than anticipated. Conversely, expenses below budget may signal exceptional efficiency or possibly the failure to meet some other standards, such as a desired level of sales or quality of service. Either way, expense budgets help identify the need for further investigation but do not substitute for it.

Revenue Budget A **revenue budget** lists forecasted and actual revenues of the organization. In general, revenues below the budgeted amount signal a need to investigate the problem to see whether the organization can improve revenues. In contrast, revenues above budget would require determining whether the organization can obtain the necessary resources to meet the higher than expected demand for its products or services. Managers then formulate action plans to correct the budget variance.

Cash Budget The **cash budget** estimates receipts and expenditures of money on a daily or weekly basis to ensure that an organization has sufficient cash to meet its obligations. The cash budget shows the level of funds flowing through the organization and the nature of cash disbursements. If the cash budget shows that the firm has more cash than necessary to meet short-term needs, the company can arrange to invest the excess to earn interest income. In contrast, if the cash budget shows a payroll expenditure of $20,000 coming at the end of the week, but only $10,000 in the bank, the organization must borrow cash to meet the payroll.

Capital Budget The **capital budget** lists planned investments in major assets such as buildings, heavy machinery, or complex information technology systems, often involving expenditures over more than a year. Capital expenditures not only have a large impact on future expenses, but they also are investments designed to enhance profits. Therefore, a capital budget is necessary to plan the impact of these expenditures on cash flow and profitability. Controlling involves not only monitoring the amount of capital expenditures but also evaluating whether the assumptions made about the return on the investments are holding true. Managers can evaluate whether continuing investment in particular projects is advisable, as well as whether their procedures for making capital expenditure decisions are adequate. Some companies, including Boeing, Merck, Shell, United Technologies, and Whirlpool, evaluate capital projects at several stages to determine whether they are still in line with the company's strategy.[24]

Budgeting is an important part of organizational planning and control. Many traditional companies use **top-down budgeting**, which means that the budgeted amounts for the coming year are literally imposed on middle- and lower-level managers.[25] These managers set departmental budget targets in accordance with overall company revenues and expenditures specified by top executives. Although the top-down process provides some advantages, the movement toward employee empowerment, participation, and learning means that many organizations are adopting **bottom-up budgeting**, a process in which lower-level managers anticipate their departments' resource needs and pass them up to top management for approval.[26] Companies of all kinds are increasingly involving line managers in the budgeting process. At the San Diego Zoo, scientists, animal keepers, and other line managers use software and templates to plan their department's budget needs because, as CFO Paula Brock says, "Nobody knows that side of the business better than they do."[27] Each of the 145 zoo departments also does a monthly budget close and reforecast so that resources can be redirected as needed to achieve goals within budget constraints. Thanks to the bottom-up process, for example, the zoo was able to quickly redirect resources to protect its valuable exotic bird collection from an outbreak of a highly infectious bird disease without significantly damaging the rest of the organization's budget.[28]

- Budgetary control, one of the most commonly used forms of managerial control, is the process of setting targets for an organization's expenditures, monitoring results and comparing them to the budget, and making changes as needed.
- A **responsibility center** is any organizational department or unit under the supervision of a single person who is responsible for its activity.
- An **expense budget** outlines the anticipated and actual expenses for a responsibility center.
- A **revenue budget** lists forecasted and actual revenues of the organization.
- The **cash budget** estimates receipts and expenditures of money on a daily or weekly basis to ensure that an organization has sufficient cash to meet its obligations.
- A budget that plans and reports investments in major assets to be depreciated over several years is called a **capital budget**.
- Many companies use **top-down budgeting**, which means that the budgeted amounts for the coming year are literally imposed on middle- and lower-level managers.
- On the other hand, **bottom-up budgeting** involves lower-level managers anticipating their department's budget needs and passing them up to top management for approval.

Financial Control

In every organization, managers need to watch how well the organization is performing financially. Not only do financial controls tell whether the organization is on sound financial footing, but they also can be useful indicators of other kinds of performance problems. For example, a sales decline may signal problems with products, customer service, or sales force effectiveness.

Financial Statements

Financial statements provide the basic information used for financial control of an organization. Two major financial statements—the balance sheet and the income statement—are the starting points for financial control.

The **balance sheet** shows the firm's financial position with respect to assets and liabilities at a specific point in time. An example of a balance sheet is presented in Exhibit 15.3.

EXHIBIT 15.3
Balance Sheet

New Creations Landscaping Consolidated Balance Sheet December 31, 2012					
Assets			**Liabilities and Owners' Equity**		
Current assets:			Current liabilities:		
Cash	$ 25,000		Accounts payable	$200,000	
Accounts receivable	75,000		Accrued expenses	20,000	
Inventory	500,000		Income taxes payable	30,000	
Total current assets		$ 600,000	Total current liabilities		$ 250,000
Fixed assets:			Long-term liabilities:		
Land	250,000		Mortgages payable	350,000	
Buildings and fixtures	1,000,000		Bonds outstanding	250,000	
			Total long-term liabilities		$ 600,000
Less depreciation	200,000		Owners' equity:		
Total fixed assets		1,050,000	Common stock	540,000	
			Retained earnings	260,000	
			Total owners' equity		800,000
Total assets		$1,650,000	Total liabilities and net worth		$1,650,000

The balance sheet provides three types of information: assets, liabilities, and owners' equity. *Assets* are what the company owns, and they include *current assets* (those that can be converted into cash in a short time period) and *fixed assets* (such as buildings and equipment that are long term in nature). *Liabilities* are the firm's debts, including both *current debt* (obligations that will be paid by the company in the near future) and *long-term debt* (obligations payable over a long period). *Owners' equity* is the difference between assets and liabilities and is the company's net worth in stock and retained earnings.

The **income statement**, sometimes called a profit-and-loss statement, or P&L for short, summarizes the firm's financial performance for a given time interval, usually one year. A sample income statement is shown in Exhibit 15.4. Some organizations calculate the income statement at three-month intervals during the year to see whether they are on target for sales and profits. The income statement shows revenues coming into the organization from all sources and subtracts all expenses, including cost of goods sold, interest, taxes, and depreciation. The *bottom line* indicates the net income—profit or loss—for the given time period.

Today, many U.S. organizations are under tremendous pressure to improve the bottom line. One response has been to cut the workforce and ask remaining employees to perform multiple tasks. "I used to have one copy editor, one rewrite editor, two event managers, a designer, and several writers and salespeople," said Cynthia Good, founder and CEO of *Pink*, an online publication for young female managers. Now, Good has just a few people working at *Pink*, and each individual does multiple jobs.[29] Corporate recruiters say versatility has become a sought-after quality in employees as companies continue battling a tough economy. A survey by consulting firm Accenture PLC reveals that many companies are still hiring, but they're looking for people with diverse skills and the ability to adapt quickly.[30]

EXHIBIT 15.4

Income Statement

New Creations Landscaping Income Statement For the Year Ended December 31, 2012		
Gross sales	$3,100,000	
Less sales returns	200,000	
Net sales		$2,900,000
Less expenses and cost of goods sold:		
Cost of goods sold	2,110,000	
Depreciation	60,000	
Sales expenses	200,000	
Administrative expenses	90,000	2,460,000
Operating profit		440,000
Other income		20,000
Gross income		460,000
Less interest expense	80,000	
Income before taxes		380,000
Less taxes	165,000	
Net income		$ 215,000

- Financial statements provide the basic information used for financial control of an organization.
- The **balance sheet** shows the firm's financial position with respect to assets and liabilities at a specific point in time.
- The **income statement** summarizes the firm's financial performance for a given time interval.

The Changing Philosophy of Control

Managers' approach to control is changing in many of today's organizations. In connection with the shift to employee participation and empowerment, many companies are adopting a *decentralized* rather than a *hierarchical* control process. Hierarchical control and decentralized control represent different philosophies of corporate culture, which was discussed in Chapter 2. Most organizations display some aspects of both hierarchical and decentralized control, but managers generally emphasize one or the other, depending on the organizational culture and their own beliefs about control. One organization that does not seem to have enough of either kind of control is Air India, described in the Business Blooper box.

Hierarchical versus Decentralized Approaches

Hierarchical control involves monitoring and influencing employee behavior through extensive use of rules, policies, hierarchy of authority, written documentation, reward

BUSINESS BLOOPER

Air India

Former United Airlines pilot Bob Haygooni lasted at Air India only 16 months. Maybe it was when he visited the cockpit and found the other pilots had used old newspaper to completely cover the windshield of the plane, to keep the sun out. "All you had in the cockpit was this yellowish glow, as the light permeated the newspaper," he said, noting it was a visibility hazard he'd never before encountered in his 30 years of flying. Turns out, this was completely normal at Air India. And Haygooni was not alone in leaving the airline. Passengers have departed in droves because of delayed flights and substandard customer service. Once the only airline in the country, now it lags behind three of the country's commercial airlines: Jet Airways, IndiGo, and Kingfisher, leaving Air India with less than 15 percent of the domestic air travel market. PR executive Harjiv Singh thinks all Indians should boycott the airline. He was a loyal customer in Air India's business class but now flies Continental or a European airline. Air India seems to be in a class of its own regarding troubles. Peter Harbison, Executive of the Center for Asia Pacific Aviation, singled out the airline as a prime example of government mismanagement. "There are other state-owned airlines in other emerging-market countries that have similar problems," he said. "But I can't think of one as bad as Air India."

© Pixel 4 Images, Shutterstock

SOURCE: Heather Timmons, "Pilots Join Crows Who Won't Fly Air India," *International Herald Tribune*, May 26, 2011.

systems, and other formal mechanisms.[31] In contrast, decentralized control relies on cultural values, traditions, shared beliefs, and trust to foster compliance with organizational goals. Managers operate on the assumption that employees are trustworthy and willing to perform effectively without extensive rules and close supervision.

Exhibit 15.5 contrasts the use of hierarchical and decentralized methods of control. Hierarchical methods define explicit rules, policies, and procedures for employee behavior. Control relies on centralized authority, the formal hierarchy, and close personal supervision. Responsibility for quality control rests with quality control inspectors and supervisors rather than with employees. Job descriptions generally are specific and task related, and managers define minimal standards for acceptable employee performance. In exchange for meeting the standards, individual employees are given extrinsic rewards such as wages, benefits, and possibly promotions up the hierarchy. Employees rarely participate in the control process, with any participation being formalized through mechanisms such as grievance procedures. With hierarchical control, the organizational culture is somewhat rigid, and managers do not consider culture a useful means of controlling employees and the organization. Technology often is used to control the flow and pace of work or to monitor employees, such as by measuring the number of minutes employees spend on phone calls or how many keystrokes they make at the computer.

Hierarchical control techniques can improve a company's bottom line by reducing employee misconduct, such as employee theft, which on average equals 7 percent of revenues according to the Association of Certified Fraud Examiners. During bleak economic times, employee theft increases, and two-thirds of executives expect it to rise in the next few years. New sleuthing technology has increased internal controls by enabling managers to continuously monitor employee behavior. Valenti Management, which owns 129 Wendy's and Chili's franchises, installed fingerprinting scanners on its cash registers, providing a foolproof method to tie all actions at the cash register to specific employees.[32]

EXHIBIT 15.5

Hierarchical and Decentralized Methods of Control

	Hierarchical Control	Decentralized Control
Basic Assumptions	People are incapable of self-discipline and cannot be trusted. They need to be monitored and controlled closely.	People work best when they are fully committed to the organization.
Actions	Uses detailed rules and procedures; formal control systems.	Features limited use of rules; relies on values, group and self-control, selection, and socialization.
	Uses top-down authority, formal hierarchy, position power, quality control inspectors.	Relies on flexible authority, flat structure, expert power; everyone monitors quality.
	Relies on task-related job descriptions.	Relies on results-based job descriptions; emphasizes goals to be achieved.
	Emphasizes extrinsic rewards (pay, benefits, status).	Emphasizes extrinsic and intrinsic rewards (meaningful work, opportunities for growth).
	Features rigid organizational culture; distrust of cultural norms as means of control.	Features adaptive culture; culture recognized as means for uniting individual, team, and organizational goals for overall control.
Consequences	Employees follow instructions and do *just* what they are told.	Employees take initiative and seek responsibility.
	Employees feel a sense of indifference toward work.	Employees are actively engaged and committed to their work.
	Employee absenteeism and turnover is high.	Employee turnover is low.

SOURCES: Based on Naresh Khatri, Alok Bavega, Suzanne A. Boren, and Abate Mammo, "Medical Errors and Quality of Care: From Control to Commitment," *California Management Review* 48, no. 3 (Spring, 2006): 118; Richard E. Walton, "From Control to Commitment in the Workplace," *Harvard Business Review* (March–April 1985): 76–84; and Don Hellriegel, Susan E. Jackson, and John W. Slocum, Jr., *Management*, 8th ed. (Cincinnati, Ohio: South-Western, 1999), p. 663.

Decentralized control is based on values and assumptions that are almost opposite to those of hierarchical control. Rules and procedures are used only when necessary. Managers rely instead on shared goals and values to control employee behavior. The organization places great emphasis on the selection and socialization of employees to ensure that workers have the appropriate values needed to influence behavior toward meeting company goals. No organization can control employees 100 percent of the time, and self-discipline and self-control are what keep workers performing their jobs up to standard. Empowerment of employees, effective socialization, and training all can contribute to internal standards that provide self-control.

With decentralized control, power is more dispersed and is based on knowledge and experience as much as position. The organizational structure is flat and horizontal, as discussed in Chapter 7, with flexible authority and teams of workers solving problems and making improvements. Everyone is involved in quality control on an ongoing basis. Job descriptions generally are results based, with an emphasis more on the outcomes to be achieved than on the specific tasks to be performed. Managers use not only extrinsic rewards such as pay but also the intrinsic rewards of meaningful work and the opportunity to learn and grow. Technology is used to empower employees by giving them the information they need to make effective decisions, work together, and solve problems. People are rewarded for team and organizational success as well as their individual performance, and the emphasis is on equity among employees. Employees participate in a wide range

SPOTLIGHT ON SKILLS

United States Army

The United States Army recently decided to invite more than 140,000 members of the Army's online forums to begin a massive collaborative project—rewriting seven of the field manuals that give instructions and guidelines on all aspects of Army life. This initiative, using the same software behind the online encyclopedia Wikipedia, was a significant cultural shift for the Army. The field manuals, written for a couple of hundred years by specialists in colleges and research centers, are now being written by battle-tested soldiers.

The program allows Army personnel from privates to generals to go online and collaboratively rewrite seven field manuals. The goal, say the officers behind the effort, is to tap more of the experience and advice from today's field soldiers. The guides touch on topics that rank-and-file soldiers have had to master because of the wars in Iraq and Afghanistan, including desert operations, unmanned aircraft systems operations, and movements of an infantry rifle platoon within a Stryker brigade combat team.

This shift has caused some within the Army to fear the loss of control that comes with empowering anyone along the chain of command to contribute. Many in the Army have been suspicious about the idea, questioning whether every soldier should have equal right to "create doctrine," said Colonel Charles J. Burnett, the director of the Army's Battle Command Knowledge System. "We've gotten the whole gamut of responses from black to white," he said. "'The best thing since sliced bread' to 'the craziest idea I have ever heard.'"

SOURCE: Noam Cohen, "Care to Write Army Doctrine? If You Have ID, Log Right On," *The New York Times*, August 14, 2009.

of areas, including setting goals, determining standards of performance, governing quality, and designing control systems.

With decentralized control, the culture is adaptive, and managers recognize the importance of organizational culture for uniting individual, team, and organizational goals for greater overall control. Ideally, with decentralized control, employees will pool their areas of expertise to arrive at procedures that are better than managers could come up with working alone. In a startling break from its hierarchical culture, the U.S. Army chose an innovative decentralized approach to developing its field manuals, driven by a desire to embrace technology, break down barriers, and streamline processes, as shown in the Spotlight on Skills titled United States Army. This program provides one illustration of a shift toward decentralized control within the U.S. Army. In this case, the Army seems willing to accept some loss of control so that the field manuals can provide the most relevant and useful instructions to soldiers on the front lines.

As a new manager, will you tend to watch things closely or give others freedom to perform? Complete the New Manager Self-Test, on page 617, to get some feedback on your own approach to control.

Open-Book Management

One important aspect of decentralized control in many organizations is open-book management. An organization that promotes information sharing and teamwork admits employees throughout the organization into the loop of financial control and responsibility to encourage active participation and commitment to goals. **Open-book management** allows employees to see for themselves—through charts, computer printouts, meetings, and so forth—the financial condition of the company. Second, open-book management shows the individual employee how his or her job fits into the big picture and affects the financial future of the organization. Finally, open-book management ties employee rewards to the company's overall success. With training in interpreting the financial data, employees can see the interdependence and importance of each function. If they are rewarded according to performance, they become motivated to take responsibility for their entire team or function rather than merely their individual jobs.[33] Cross-functional communication and cooperation are also enhanced.

The goal of open-book management is to get every employee thinking and acting like a business owner. To get employees to think like owners, management provides them with the same information owners have: what money is coming in and where it is going. Open-book management helps employees appreciate why efficiency is important to the organization's success as well as their own.

Managers in some countries have more trouble running an open-book company because prevailing attitudes and standards encourage confidentiality and even secrecy concerning financial results. Many businesspeople in countries such as China, Russia, and India, for example, are not accustomed to publicly disclosing financial details, which can present problems for multinational companies operating there.[34] Exhibit 15.6 lists a portion

EXHIBIT 15.6

International Opacity Index: Which Countries Have the Most Secretive Economies?

Country	2007–2008 Opacity Score	2005–2006 Score
Nigeria	57	60
Venezuela	48	50
Saudi Arabia	47	52
China	45	48
India	44	44
Indonesia	41	56
Russia	41	45
Mexico	37	43
Taiwan	34	33
South Korea	31	35
South Africa	26	32
Japan	25	26
United States	23	21
Canada	22	24
Germany	17	27
Ireland	16	25
Singapore	14	28
Hong Kong	12	19
Finland	9	17

The higher the opacity score, the more secretive the national economy, meaning that prevailing attitudes and standards discourage openness regarding financial results and other data.

SOURCE: Joel Kurtzman and Glenn Yago, "Opacity Index, 2007–2008: Measuring Global Business Risks," published by Milken Institute (April 2008), http://www.milkeninstitute.org/pdf/2008OpacityIndex.pdf (accessed June 16, 2008).

New Manager Self-Test

What Is Your Control Approach?

As a new manager, how will you control your work unit? What is your natural control approach? Please answer whether each item below is Mostly True or Mostly False for you.

	MOSTLY TRUE <<<	>>> MOSTLY FALSE
1. I find myself losing sight of long-term goals when there is a short-term crisis.	______	______
2. I prefer complex to simple problems and projects.	______	______
3. I am good at mapping out steps needed to complete a project.	______	______
4. I make most decisions without needing to know an overall plan.	______	______
5. I keep my personal books and papers in good order.	______	______
6. I prefer tasks that challenge my thinking ability.	______	______
7. I think about how my behavior relates to outcomes I desire.	______	______
8. I like to be part of a situation where results are measured and count for something.	______	______

See It Online

Scoring and Interpretation: Control systems are designed and managed via a manager's "systems" thinking. Systems thinking considers how component parts of system interact to achieve desired goals. Systems thinking means seeing the world in an organized way and thinking about underlying cause-and-effect relationships. Give yourself 1 point for each Mostly True answer to items 2, 3, and 5–8 and 1 point for each Mostly False answer to items 1 and 4. A score of 6 or above means that you appear to have a natural orientation toward systems thinking and control. You see the world in an organized way and focus on cause-and-effect relationships that produce outcomes. If you scored 3 or less, you probably are not very focused on control issues and relationships. You may not be interested or have the time to understand complex relationships. As a new manager, you may have to put extra effort into understanding control relationships to produce the outcomes you and the organization desire.

of a recent *Opacity Index*, which offers some indication of the degree to which various countries are open regarding economic matters. The higher the rating, the more opaque, or hidden, the economy of that country. In the partial index in Exhibit 15.6, Nigeria has the highest opacity rating at 57, and Finland the lowest at 9. The United States has an opacity rating of 23. In countries with higher ratings, financial figures are typically closely guarded and managers may be discouraged from sharing information with employees and the public. Globalization is beginning to have an impact on economic opacity in various countries by encouraging a convergence toward global accounting standards that support more accurate collection, recording, and reporting of financial information. Thus, most countries have improved their ratings over the past few years. Indonesia, Singapore, and Ireland all show significant decreases in opacity since the 2005–2006 ratings, for example.

- The philosophy of control has shifted to reflect changes in leadership methods.
- **Hierarchical control** involves monitoring and influencing employee behavior through extensive use of rules, policies, hierarchy of authority, written documentation, reward systems, and other formal mechanisms.
- With **decentralized control**, the organization fosters compliance with organizational goals through the use of organizational culture, group norms, and a focus on goals rather than rules and procedures.
- **Open-book management** allows employees to see for themselves the financial condition of the organization and encourages them to think and act like business owners.

Total Quality Management

Another popular approach based on a decentralized control philosophy is **total quality management (TQM)**, an organization-wide effort to infuse quality into every activity in a company through continuous improvement. Managing quality is a concern for every organization. Ford, for example, vows that its new compact and subcompact vehicles will have substantially fewer problems during their first three months on the road than models from other automakers. According to Ford Vice President of Global Quality Bennie Fowler, Ford will keep the number of quality problems (called "things gone wrong") at 800 per 1,000 vehicles (there can be more than one thing wrong per vehicle), well below the industry average (even Honda struggles to get below 1,000). The company is working hard to regain customer confidence after lagging behind foreign competitors such as Toyota and Honda.[35] It hopes that an emphasis on total quality management will recapture confidence by U.S. consumers.

TQM became attractive to U.S. managers in the 1980s because it had been successfully implemented by Japanese companies such as Toyota, Canon, and Honda, which were gaining market share and an international reputation for high quality. The Japanese system was based on the work of such U.S. researchers and consultants as Deming, Juran, and Feigenbaum, whose ideas attracted U.S. executives after the methods were tested overseas.[36] The TQM philosophy focuses on teamwork, increasing customer satisfaction, and lowering costs. Organizations implement TQM by encouraging managers and employees to collaborate across functions and departments, as well as with customers and suppliers, to identify areas for improvement, no matter how small. Each quality improvement is a step toward perfection and meeting a goal of zero defects. Quality control becomes part of the day-to-day business of every employee, rather than being assigned to specialized departments.

TQM Techniques

The implementation of total quality management involves the use of many techniques, including quality circles, benchmarking, Six Sigma principles, reduced cycle time, and continuous improvement.

Quality Circles A **quality circle** is a group of 6 to 12 volunteer employees who meet regularly to discuss and solve problems affecting the quality of their work.[37] At a set time during the workweek, the members of the quality circle meet, identify problems, and try to find solutions. Circle members are free to collect data and take surveys. Many companies train people in team building, problem solving, and statistical quality control. The reason for using quality circles is to push decision making to an organization level at which recommendations can be made by the people who do the job and know it better than anyone else.

Benchmarking Introduced by Xerox in 1979, benchmarking is now a major TQM component. **Benchmarking** is defined as "the continuous process of measuring products, services, and practices against the toughest competitors or those companies recognized as industry leaders to identify areas for improvement."[38] The key to successful benchmarking lies in analysis. Starting with its own mission statement, a company should honestly analyze its current procedures and determine areas for improvement. As a second step, a company carefully selects competitors worthy of copying. For example, Xerox studied the order fulfillment techniques of L.L.Bean, the Freeport, Maine, mail-order firm, and learned ways to reduce warehouse costs by 10 percent. Companies can emulate internal processes and procedures of competitors but must take care to select companies whose methods are compatible. Once a strong, compatible program is found and analyzed, the benchmarking company can then devise a strategy for implementing a new program.

Six Sigma Six Sigma quality principles were first introduced by Motorola in the 1980s and were later popularized by General Electric, where former CEO Jack Welch praised Six Sigma for quality and efficiency gains that saved the company billions of dollars. Based on the Greek letter *sigma*, which statisticians use to measure how far something deviates from perfection, **Six Sigma** is a highly ambitious quality standard that specifies a goal of no more than 3.4 defects per million parts. That essentially means being defect free 99.9997 percent of the time.[39] However, Six Sigma has deviated from its precise definition to become a generic term for a quality-control approach that takes nothing for granted and emphasizes a disciplined and relentless pursuit of higher quality and lower costs. The discipline is based on a five-step methodology referred to as *DMAIC* (Define, Measure, Analyze, Improve, and Control, pronounced "deMay-ick" for short), which provides a structured way for organizations to approach and solve problems.[40]

Effectively implementing Six Sigma requires a major commitment from top management, because Six Sigma involves widespread change throughout the organization. At Honeywell, for example, all employees are expected to understand Six Sigma fundamentals. Six Sigma provides a common language among employees, complements efforts to remove fat from the organization, and supports efforts to "get it right the first time." Honeywell explains its dedication to Six Sigma and what it means to reach this high level of performance with these examples:

- If your water heater operated at Four Sigma (not Six), you would be without hot water for more than 54 hours each year. At Six Sigma, you would be without hot water for less than two minutes a year.
- If your cell phone operated at Four Sigma, you would be without service for more than four hours a month. At Six Sigma, it would be about nine seconds a month.

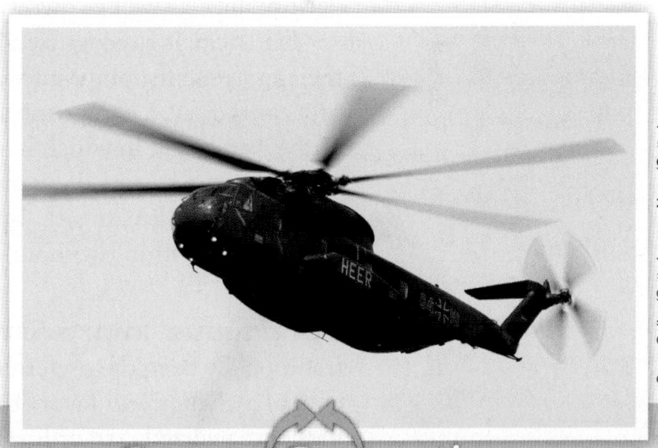

Sean Gallup/Getty Images News/Getty Images

ConceptConnection

Rockwell Collins Deutschland, a German manufacturer of aircraft avionics and precision mechanisms for satellites, landed a 2007 contract to upgrade its country's military transport helicopters. Because the company had only recently become a subsidiary of Rockwell Collins, an aviation electronics and information technology corporation headquartered in Cedar Rapids, Iowa, its employees got a crash course in the parent company's *Lean Electronics* program, which combines principles and methods of **continuous improvement** and **Six Sigma.** Applying Lean Electronics allowed the subsidiary not only to find better ways of producing the helicopters but also to streamline and optimize their processes, resulting in $2.85 million in annual savings.

15.7
EXHIBIT
The Importance of Quality Improvement Programs

99 Percent Amounts to:	Six Sigma Amounts to:
117,000 pieces of lost first-class mail per hour	1 piece of lost first-class mail every two hours
800,000 mishandled personal checks each day	3 mishandled checks each day
23,087 defective computers shipped each month	8 defective computers shipped each month
7.2 hours per month without electricity	9 seconds per month without electricity

SOURCE: Based on data from *Statistical Abstract of the United States*, U.S. Postal Service, as reported in Tracy Mayor, "Six Sigma Comes to IT: Targeting Perfection," *CIO* (December 1, 2003): 62–70.

- A Four Sigma process will typically result in one defective package of product for every three truckloads shipped. A Six Sigma process means one defective package for every 5,350 truckloads.[41]

Exhibit 15.7 lists some additional statistics that illustrate why Six Sigma is important for both manufacturing and service organizations.

Reduced Cycle Time Cycle time has become a critical quality issue in today's fast-paced world. **Cycle time** refers to the steps taken to complete a company process, such as making an airline reservation, processing an online order, or opening a retirement fund. The simplification of work cycles, including dropping barriers between work steps and among departments and removing worthless steps in the process, enables a TQM program to succeed. Even if an organization decides not to use quality circles or other techniques, substantial improvement is possible by focusing on improved responsiveness and acceleration of activities into a shorter time. Reduction in cycle time improves overall company performance as well as quality.[42]

L.L.Bean is a recognized leader in cycle time control. Workers used flowcharts to track their movements, pinpoint wasted motions, and completely redesign the order-fulfillment process. Today, a computerized system breaks down an order based on the geographic area of the warehouse in which items are stored. Items are placed on conveyor belts, where electronic sensors re-sort the items for individual orders. After orders are packed, they are sent to a FedEx facility on site. Improvements such as these have enabled L.L.Bean to process most orders within two hours after the order is received.[43]

Continuous Improvement In North America, crash programs and designs have traditionally been the preferred method of innovation. Managers measure the expected benefits of a change and favor the ideas with the biggest payoffs. In contrast, Japanese companies have realized extraordinary success from making a series of mostly small improvements. This approach, called **continuous improvement**, or *kaizen*, is the implementation of a large number of small, incremental improvements in all areas of the organization on an ongoing basis. In a successful TQM program, all employees learn that they are expected to contribute by initiating changes in their own job activities. The basic philosophy is that improving things a little bit at a time, all the time, has the highest probability of success. Innovations can start simple, and employees can build on their success in this unending process. Here's how one auto parts plant benefited from a TQM and continuous improvement philosophy.

The idea of continuous improvement is what international development leader SNV is doing to change the way businesses view and deal with poverty around the world, as shown in the Benchmarking box.

BENCHMARKING

Inclusive Business

"Business cannot succeed in societies that fail," is the premise for the alliance between the international development agency SNV and the World Business Council for Sustainable Development, which has worked in ten countries to create something called "inclusive business," bringing together aid and trade in developing countries. The idea is to reduce or eliminate poverty. For many years, governments and agencies saw poverty as an economic issue, requiring solutions of macroeconomic growth and trickle-down benefits. In more recent thinking, the development community realizes poverty is a social disease, as well, and SNV took the lead in enhancing "inclusive business" growth, collaborating so that both micro- and macro-economic strategies are employed and that the private sectors can have interventions bringing together all levels of the society toward value creation.

One of the SNV programs involves the Bolivian dairy-product company, Delizia, which saw its production volume increase from 360,000 to 900,000 liters per month, as a result of this initiative. To do this, SNV worked with the individual milk suppliers, helping them to become partners in the supply chain and to secure needed financing from local banks. They were able to build hydroponic greenhouses and ensure better feed for the cattle. Now, there is more trust between the company and suppliers, with productivity up 29 percent and family incomes up by 42 percent, to an average of $269 per month. Also, the largest corn producer in Ecuador, PRONACA, was taking only 30 percent of its corn or maize from small growers, so SNV started a project with PRONACA and small-scale farms to offer training in quality control, new and tested technologies, and access to credit. This meant PRONACA was able to buy 300 percent more corn from the small-scale producers than it had in the past, which greatly enriched the growers' lives. The small-scale farmers increased their incomes 350 percent from the subsistence level of $72 per month to over $250. So, PRONACA and the small-scale farmers benefited. As SNV executive Reintje van Haeringen says, "Inclusive Business is about bringing success to both business and poor people. Everybody wins."

© Kuzmik, Shutterstock

SOURCES: Robert de Jongh et al. , "Inclusive Business, Creating Value in Latin America," Netherlands Development Organisation SNV and World Business Council for Sustainable Development (WBSCD), March 16, 2011, pp. 1–92; and Reintje van Haeringen, personal communication, May 2011.

DANA CORPORATION'S PERFECT CIRCLE PRODUCTS FRANKLIN STEEL PRODUCTS PLANT

The Dana Corporation's Perfect Circle Products Franklin Steel Products plant in Franklin, Kentucky, was named one of *Industry Week* magazine's ten Best North American Manufacturing Facilities a record-setting six times. Despite operating in a high-volume, high-mix environment, churning out thousands of different auto parts and after-market products, Dana Franklin maintained a 99 percent on-time delivery rate to customers. In addition, customer complaints and reject rates were exceptionally low.

These results were amazing accomplishments for the plant's small workforce (just 44 production and management personnel), especially considering that some of the equipment they used was more than 50 years old. Yet the philosophy at the plant was that with each unit produced, with each hour, with each day and each week, the plant would get just a little bit better. Plant manager Tim Parys said the plant "sort of adopted the Japanese philosophy in that the worst that the equipment ever runs is the day that you put it on the floor."

In addition to continuous improvement on the plant floor, typically two or three active Six Sigma initiatives were underway at any time in the Franklin plant. Almost everyone working there achieved a Six Sigma green belt or black belt. The company regularly held four-day *kaizen* events, in which team members selected from the entire workforce would focus on eliminating wasteful materials, activities, and processes. Production technician Ronnie Steenbergen believed *kaizen* enabled the factory to squeeze out tremendous improvements from its "old machines."[44]

15.8 EXHIBIT

Quality Program Success Factors

Positive Factors	Negative Factors
• Tasks make high skill demands on employees.	• Management expectations are unrealistically high.
• TQM serves to enrich jobs and motivate employees.	• Middle managers are dissatisfied about loss of authority.
• Problem-solving skills are improved for all employees.	• Workers are dissatisfied with other aspects of organizational life.
• Participation and teamwork are used to tackle significant problems.	• Union leaders are left out of QC discussions.
• Continuous improvement is a way of life.	• Managers wait for big, dramatic innovations.

TQM Success Factors

Despite its promise, total quality management does not always work. A few firms have had disappointing results. In particular, Six Sigma principles might not be appropriate for all organizational problems, and some companies have expended tremendous energy and resources for little payoff.[45] Many contingency factors (listed in Exhibit 15.8) can influence the success of a TQM program. For example, quality circles are most beneficial when employees have challenging jobs; participation in a quality circle can contribute to productivity because it enables employees to pool their knowledge and solve interesting problems. TQM also tends to be most successful when it enriches jobs and improves employee motivation. In addition, when participating in the quality program improves workers' problem-solving skills, productivity is likely to increase. Finally, a quality program has the greatest chance of success in a corporate culture that values quality and stresses continuous improvement as a way of life, as at the Dana Franklin plant just described.

- **Total quality management (TQM)** is an organization-wide effort to infuse quality into every activity in a company through continuous improvement.
- The TQM philosophy focuses on teamwork, increasing customer satisfaction, and lowering costs.
- **Quality circles** offer one technique for implementing total quality management and include a group of 6 to 12 volunteer employees who meet regularly to discuss and solve problems affecting the quality of their work.
- Another option for tracking quality is **benchmarking**, the continuous process of measuring products, services, and practices against major competitors or industry leaders.
- **Six Sigma** is a quality control approach that emphasizes a relentless pursuit of higher quality and lower costs.
- A reduction in **cycle time**, the steps that are taken to complete a company process, improves overall company performance as well as quality.
- **Continuous improvement**, or *kaizen,* is the implementation of a large number of small, incremental improvements in all areas of the organization on an ongoing basis.

Trends in Quality Control

Many companies are responding to changing economic realities and global competition by reassessing organizational management and processes—including control mechanisms. Some of the major trends in quality and financial control include international quality standards, economic value-added and market value-added systems, activity-based costing, and increased corporate governance.

International Quality Standards

One impetus for total quality management in the United States is the increasing significance of the global economy. Many countries have adopted a universal benchmark for quality management practices, **ISO 9000 standards**, which represent an international consensus of what constitutes effective quality management as outlined by the International Organization for Standardization.[46] Hundreds of thousands of organizations in 157 countries, including the United States, have been certified against ISO 9000 standards to demonstrate their commitment to quality. Europe continues to lead in the total number of certifications, but the greatest number of new certifications in recent years has been in the United States. One of the more interesting organizations to become ISO certified was the Phoenix, Arizona, Police Department's Records and Information Bureau. In today's environment, where the credibility of law enforcement agencies has been called into question, the bureau wanted to make a clear statement about its commitment to quality and accuracy of information provided to law enforcement personnel and the public.[47] ISO certification has become the recognized standard for evaluating and comparing companies on a global basis, and more U.S. companies are feeling the pressure to participate to remain competitive in international markets. In addition, many countries and companies require ISO certification before they will do business with an organization.

Corporate Governance Many organizations have moved toward increased control from the top in terms of corporate governance. Traditionally defined as the ways in which an organization safeguards the interests of shareholders, the term **corporate governance** has been expanded to refer to the framework of systems, rules, and practices by which an organization ensures accountability, fairness, and transparency in its relationship with all stakeholders, including investors, employees, customers, and the general public.[48]

Concerns over corporate governance came to the forefront some years ago in light of the failure of top executives and corporate directors to provide adequate oversight and control at failed companies such as Enron, HealthSouth, Adelphia Communications, and WorldCom. In some cases, financial reporting systems were manipulated to produce false results and hide internal failures. In response, the U.S. government enacted the Sarbanes-Oxley Act of 2002, often referred to as SOX, which requires several types of reforms, including better internal monitoring to reduce the risk of fraud,

AP Photo/Paul Sakuma, file

ConceptConnection

Mark Hurd (left) was praised for turning around a troubled Hewlett-Packard as chairman and CEO. But in 2010, Hurd resigned under pressure after an investigation exonerated him of sexual harassment charges but uncovered an alleged $20,000 in falsified expense reports. Some argued Hurd's ouster was an example of **overcontrol**. Said Hurd's chief champion—and, as it turns out, future employer—Oracle CEO Larry Ellison (right), "The HP board just made the worst personnel decision since the idiots on the Apple board fired Steve Jobs many years ago." Others felt the HP board had been guilty of **undercontrol** because it hadn't exercised enough oversight of Hurd.

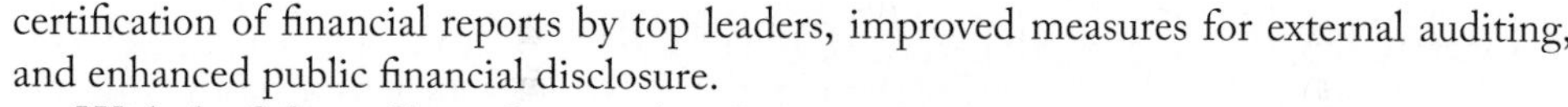

certification of financial reports by top leaders, improved measures for external auditing, and enhanced public financial disclosure.

With the failure of large firms such as Lehman Brothers and Bear Stearns in 2008, corporate governance again became a hot topic. Lax oversight likely contributed both to the failure of these firms and to a worldwide economic crisis. "I don't think there's any question that a dramatic failure of corporate governance was a central issue of the crisis," said Phil Angelides, chairman of the Financial Crisis Inquiry Commission appointed by the U.S. Congress. Global regulators from 27 countries recently imposed new rules and restraints on financial institutions designed to limit risk taking and increase oversight.[49] In addition, the U.S. Securities and Exchange Commission now requires that companies justify their board structure in proxy statements to ensure that boards are designed in a way to provide needed oversight of management actions.[50]

As a new manager, find a balance between oversight and control on the one hand and mutual trust and respect on the other. Go to the Ethical Dilemma, on pages 627, that pertains to new workplace control issues.

Although undercontrol is a significant problem, overcontrol of employees can be damaging to an organization as well. Managers might feel justified in monitoring e-mail and Internet use, as described in the Spotlight on Skills earlier in this chapter, for example, yet employees often resent and feel demeaned by close monitoring that limits their personal freedom and makes them feel as if they are constantly being watched. Excessive control of employees can lead to demotivation, low morale, lack of trust, and even hostility among workers. Managers have to find an appropriate balance, as well as develop and communicate clear policies regarding workplace monitoring. Although oversight and control are important, good organizations also depend on mutual trust and respect among managers and employees.

- As global business expands, many companies have adopted a universal benchmark for quality management practices, including **ISO 9000 standards**, which represent an international consensus of what constitutes effective quality management as outlined by the International Organization for Standardization.
- Many organizations are moving toward increased control from the top in terms of **corporate governance**, which refers to the framework of systems, rules, and practices by which an organization ensures accountability, fairness, and transparency in the firm's relationship with stakeholders.

Discussion Questions

1. You're a manager who employs a participative control approach. You've concluded that corrective action is necessary to improve customer satisfaction, but first you need to convince your employees that the problem exists. What kind of evidence do you think employees will find more compelling: quantitative measurements or anecdotes from your interactions with customers? Explain your answer.
2. Describe the advantages of using a balanced scorecard to measure and control organizational performance. Suppose you created a balanced scorecard for Walmart. What specific customer service measures would you include?
3. In bottom-up budgeting, lower-level managers anticipate their departments' resource needs and pass them up to top management for approval. Identify the advantages of bottom-up budgeting.
4. Most companies have policies that regulate employees' personal use of work computers during work hours. Some even monitor employee e-mails and track the Web sites that have been visited. Do you consider this type of surveillance an invasion of privacy? What are

the advantages of restricting employee use of the Internet and e-mail at work?

5. Think of a class you've taken in the past. What standards of performance did your professor establish? How was your actual performance measured? How was your performance compared to the standards? Do you think the standards and methods of measurement were fair? Were they appropriate to your assigned work? Why or why not?
6. Some critics argue that Six Sigma is a collection of superficial changes that often result in doing a superb job of building the wrong product or offering the wrong service. Do you agree or disagree? Explain.
7. What types of analysis can managers perform to help them diagnose a company's financial condition? How might a review of financial statements help managers diagnose other kinds of performance problems as well?
8. Why is benchmarking an important component of total quality management (TQM) programs? Do you believe a company could have a successful TQM program without using benchmarking?
9. How might activity-based costing provide better financial control tools for managers of a company such as Kellogg that produces numerous food products?
10. What is ISO certification? Why would a global company like General Electric want ISO certification?

Self-Learning

Is Your Budget in Control?

By the time you are in college, you are in charge of at least some of your own finances. How well you manage your personal budget may indicate how well you will manage your company's budget on the job. Respond to the following statements to evaluate your own budgeting habits. If the statement doesn't apply directly to you, respond the way you think you would behave in a similar situation.

1. I spend all my money as soon as I get it. Yes No
2. At the beginning of each week (or month, or term), I write down all my fixed expenses. Yes No
3. I never seem to have any money left over at the end of the week (or month). Yes No
4. I pay all my expenses, but I never seem to have any money left over for fun. Yes No
5. I am not putting any money away in savings right now; I'll wait until after I graduate from college. Yes No
6. I can't pay all my bills. Yes No
7. I have a credit card, but I pay the balance in full each month. Yes No
8. I take cash advances on my credit card. Yes No
9. I know how much I can spend on eating out, movies, and other entertainment each week. Yes No
10. I pay cash for everything. Yes No
11. When I buy something, I look for value and determine the best buy. Yes No
12. I lend money to friends whenever they ask, even if it leaves me short of cash. Yes No
13. I never borrow money from friends. Yes No
14. I am putting aside money each month to save for something that I really need. Yes No

Scoring and Interpretation

"Yes" responses to statements 2, 9, 10, 13, and 14 point to the most disciplined budgeting habits; "yes" responses to 4, 5, 7, and 11 reveal adequate budgeting habits; "yes" responses to 1, 3, 6, 8, and 12 indicate the poorest budgeting habits. If you have answered honestly, chances are you'll have a combination of all three. Look to see where you can improve your budgeting.

Group Learning

Create a Group Control System

Step 1. Form into groups of three to five students. Each group will assume that another student group has been given an assignment of writing a major paper that will involve research by individual group members that will be integrated into the final paper. Each group member has to do his or her part.

Step 2. Your assignment is to develop a list of rules and identify some statistics by which to control the behavior of members in that group. Brainstorm and discuss potential rules to govern member behavior and consequences for breaking those rules.

Step 3. First, select the five rules you think are most important for governing group member behavior. Consider the following situations that rules might cover: arriving late for a meeting; missing a meeting; failing to complete a work assignment; disagreements about desired quality of work; how to resolve conflicts about paper content; differences in participation, such as one person doing all the talking and someone else talking hardly at all; how to handle meetings that start late; the use of an agenda and handling deviations from the agenda; and any other situation that your group thinks a rule should cover.

Rules you determine are important	List statistics that could be developed to measure the behavior and group outcomes.	How will you know if the group is following the rule and performing as expected?
1.		
2.		
3.		
4.		
5.		

Step 4. Now consider what statistics could be developed to measure the behavior and outcome of the group pertaining to those five rules. What kinds of things could be counted to understand how the group is performing and whether members are following the rules?

Step 5. Discuss the following questions: Why are rules important as a means of control? What are the advantages and disadvantages of having many rules (hierarchical control) versus few rules (decentralized control) for a student group? How can statistics help a group ensure appropriate behavior and a high-quality product?

Step 6. Be prepared to present your conclusions to the class.

Action Learning

Schoolwork Standards

1. Interview four students besides yourself, students not taking this same course right now. Make sure two of them are top grade-earners and two are about average. Tell the students you will keep their information confidential, that you will only be reporting results in a paper you will write, and that you will not divulge any names. Then stick to that promise.
2. Ask them questions about how they study, how much they read, how do they manage to work on and finish a project or paper, how they feel about grades, and so on.
3. Determine whether they use any of the control mechanisms described in this chapter: Feedforward, concurrent, and feedback.
4. Have they developed standards for their work? Do they compare the actual performance to the standard? What happens when the performance is less than expected, for example, they don't get as high a grade as expected?
5. Write a report for your instructor, comparing the top students to the others. Make sure you don't mention the students' names in your report, but that you keep them anonymous.
6. Your instructor may lead a class discussion on the findings. Again, do not mention anyone's names. If you want to talk about your own experiences as a student, that would be fine.

Ethical Dilemma

The Wages of Sin?[51]

Chris Dykstra, responsible for loss prevention at Westwind Electronics, took a deep breath before he launched into making his case for the changes he was proposing in the company's shoplifting policy. He knew convincing Ross Chenoweth was going to be a hard sell. Ross, the president and CEO, was the son of the founder of the local, still family-owned consumer electronics chain based in Phoenix, Arizona. He'd inherited not only the company but also his father's strict moral code.

"I think it's time to follow the lead of other stores," Chris began. He pointed out that most other retailers didn't bother calling the police and pressing charges unless the thief had shoplifted merchandise worth more than $50 to $100. In contrast, Westwind currently had the zero-tolerance policy toward theft that Ross's father had put in place when he started the business. Chris wanted to replace that policy with one that prosecuted only individuals between 18 and 65, who had stolen more than $20 worth of goods and who had a previous history of theft at Westwind. In the case of first-time culprits under 18 or over 65, he argued for letting them off with a strict warning regardless of the value of their ill-gotten goods. Repeat offenders would be arrested.

"Frankly, the local police are getting pretty tired of having to come to our stores every time a teenager sticks a CD in his jacket pocket," Chris pointed out. "And besides, we just can't afford the costs associated with prosecuting everyone." Every time he pressed charges against a shoplifter who'd made off with a $10 item, Westwind lost money. The company had to engage a lawyer and pay employees overtime for their court appearances. In addition, Chris was looking at hiring more security guards to keep up with the workload. Westwind was already in a battle it was losing at the moment with the mass retailers who were competing all too successfully on price, so passing on the costs of its zero-tolerance policy to customers wasn't really an option. "Let's concentrate on catching dishonest employees and those organized theft rings. They're the ones who are really hurting us," Chris concluded.

There was a long pause after Chris finished his carefully prepared speech. Ross thought about his recently deceased father, both an astute businessman and a person for whom honesty was a key guiding principle. If he were sitting here today, he'd no doubt say that theft was theft, that setting a minimum was tantamount to saying that stealing was acceptable just as long as you don't steal too much. He looked at Chris. "You know, we've both got teenagers. Is this really a message you want to send out, especially to kids? You know as well as I do that there's nothing they like better than testing limits. It's almost an invitation to see whether you can beat the system." But then Ross faltered as he found himself glancing at the latest financial figures on his desk—another in a string of quarterly losses. If Westwind went under, a lot of employees would be looking for another way to make a living. In his heart, he believed in his father's high moral standards, but he had to ask himself: Just how moral could Westwind afford to be?

What Would You Do?

1. Continue Westwind's zero-tolerance policy toward shoplifting. It's the right thing to do—and it will pay off in the end in higher profitability because the chain's reputation for being tough on crime will reduce overall losses from theft.
2. Adopt Chris Dykstra's proposed changes and show more leniency to first-time offenders. It is a more cost-effective approach to the problem than the current policy, plus it stays close to your father's original intent.
3. Adopt Chris Dykstra's proposed changes with an even higher limit of $50 or $100, which is still less than the cost of prosecution. In addition, make sure the policy isn't publicized. That way you'll reduce costs even more and still benefit from your reputation for prosecuting all shoplifters.

Case for Critical Analysis

Lincoln Electric[52]

Imagine having a management system that is so successful—the Lincoln Management System—that other businesses benchmark their own systems by it. That is the situation of Ohio-based Lincoln Electric. For a number of years, other companies have tried to figure out Lincoln Electric's secret—how management coaxes maximum productivity and quality from its workers, even during difficult financial times. Lately, however, Lincoln Electric has been trying

to solve a mystery of its own: Why is the company having such difficulty exporting a management system abroad that has worked so well at home?

Lincoln Electric is a leading manufacturer of welding products, welding equipment, and electric motors, with more than $1 billion in sales and 6,000 workers worldwide. The company's products are used for cutting, manufacturing, and repairing other metal products. Although it is now a publicly traded company, members of the Lincoln family still own more than 60 percent of the stock.

Lincoln uses a diverse control approach. Tasks are precisely defined, and individual employees must exceed strict performance goals to achieve top pay. The incentive and control system is powerful. Production workers are paid on a piece-rate basis, plus merit pay based on performance. Employees also are eligible for annual bonuses, which fluctuate according to the company's profits, and they participate in stock purchase plans. A worker's bonus is based on four factors: work productivity, work quality, dependability, and cooperation with others. Some factory workers at Lincoln have earned more than $100,000 a year.

However, the Lincoln system succeeds largely because of an organizational culture based on openness and trust, shared control, and an egalitarian spirit. To begin with, the company has earned employee trust with its no-layoff policy. In fact, the last time it laid off anyone was in 1951. Although the line between managers and workers at Lincoln is firmly drawn, managers respect the expertise of production workers and value their contributions to many aspects of the business. The company has an open-door policy for all top executives, middle managers, and production workers, and regular face-to-face communication is encouraged. Workers are expected to challenge management if they believe practices or compensation rates are unfair. Most workers are hired right out of high school, then trained and cross-trained to perform different jobs. Some eventually are promoted to executive positions, because Lincoln believes in promoting from within. Many Lincoln workers stay with the company for life.

One of Lincoln's founders felt that organizations should be based on certain values, including honesty, trustworthiness, openness, self-management, loyalty, accountability, and cooperativeness. These values continue to form the core of Lincoln's culture, and management regularly rewards employees who manifest them. Because Lincoln so effectively socializes employees, they exercise a great degree of self-control on the job. Each supervisor oversees 100 workers, and less tangible rewards complement the piece-rate incentive system. Pride of workmanship and feelings of involvement, contribution, and esprit de corps are intrinsic rewards that flourish at Lincoln Electric. Cross-functional teams, empowered to make decisions, take responsibility for product planning, development, and marketing. Information about the company's operations and financial performance is openly shared with workers throughout the company.

Lincoln emphasizes anticipating and solving customer problems. Sales representatives are given the technical training they need to understand customer needs, help customers understand and use Lincoln's products, and solve problems. This customer focus is backed by attention to the production process through the use of strict accountability standards and formal measurements for productivity, quality, and innovation for all employees. In addition, a software program called Rhythm helps streamline the flow of goods and materials in the production process.

Lincoln's system worked so well in the United States that senior executives decided to extend it overseas. Lincoln built or purchased 11 plants in Japan, South America, and Europe, with plans to run the plants from the United States using Lincoln's expertise with management control systems. Managers saw the opportunity to beat local competition by applying manufacturing control incentive systems to reduce costs and raise production in plants around the world. The results were abysmal and nearly sunk the company. Managers at international plants failed to meet their production and financial goals every year—they exaggerated the goals sent to Lincoln's managers to receive more resources, especially during the recession in Europe and South America. Many overseas managers had no innate desire to increase sales, and workers were found sleeping on benches because not enough work was available. The European labor culture was hostile to the piece-work and bonus control system. The huge losses in the international plants, which couldn't seem to adopt Lincoln's vaunted control systems, meant the company would have to borrow money to pay U.S. workers' bonuses, or forgo bonuses for the first time in Lincoln's history. Top managers began to wonder: Had they simply done a poor job of applying the Lincoln Management System to other cultures, or was it possible that it simply wasn't going to work abroad?

Questions

1. Does Lincoln follow a hierarchical or decentralized approach to management? Explain your answer and give examples.
2. Based on what you've just read, what do you think makes the Lincoln System so successful in the United States?
3. What is the problem with transporting Lincoln's control systems to other national cultures? What suggestions would you make to Lincoln's managers to make future international manufacturing plants more successful?
4. Should Lincoln borrow money and pay bonuses to avoid breaking trust with its U.S. workers? Why or why not?

aplia Aplia Highlights

Now use your Aplia homework to help you:

- Apply management theories in your life
- Assess your management skills
- Master management terms and concepts
- Apply your knowledge to real-world situations
- Analyze and solve challenging management problems

In order to take advantage of these elements, your instructor will need to have set up a course for your class within Aplia. Ask your instructor to contact his/her Cengage sales representative and Digital Solutions Manager to explore testing Aplia in your course this term.

1.

2. It took years to establish the culture

3. Because they are a threat to other cultures Managers need to have a plan a start off small and build the culture

4. No, it will put them in more debt.

Barcelona Restaurant Group: Managing Quality and Performance

© Leremy, Shutterstock

"We're a chain that's not a chain," Andy Pforzheimer says of his Barcelona Restaurant Group, a collection of seven wine and tapas bars located throughout Connecticut and Atlanta, Georgia. Launched in 1995 by Pforzheimer and business partner Sasa Mahr-Batuz, Barcelona is the restaurant of choice for diners who crave flavorful European tapas, sophisticated modern ambience, and the largest collection of Spanish wines of any restaurant group in the country.

An entrepreneur and renowned chef, Pforzheimer began cooking his own meals in high school as a way to control his weight for the school wrestling squad. While a freshman in college, he routinely cooked dinners for black-tie events. At age 19, while studying under a chef in France, Pforzheimer learned a restaurant philosophy that would guide his management decisions throughout his career: "The French chef used to say, 'Restaurants are very simple things: good food, good service, reasonable price.' He's right, and I'll throw in good location and management that pays attention to how they're running the business. That's it—it's really not that complicated."

But Barcelona is not just about good food: it's about a dining experience. Pforzheimer estimates that food makes up 50 percent of the total Barcelona experience, and the rest is comprised of important intangibles: the music, the lighting, the clientele, the atmospherics, and the conversation with managers and wait staff. "Quality in a restaurant is about lots of tiny details," Pforzheimer says. Barcelona's owner notes that managing a restaurant's performance entails managing food quality, wait times, hospitality, bussing, restrooms, prices, and more. For Barcelona to be successful, each employee must deliver his part of the total experience night after night.

To ensure consistent quality across the board, Barcelona uses five "feedback loops" that gauge restaurant performance. First, Barcelona participates in a Secret Shoppers program in which restaurant reviewers make four unannounced monthly visits to Barcelona locations. During the outings, the covert shoppers rate Barcelona on 120 aspects of the dining experience. "We started doing it a few years ago with one or two shops per month, and we've increased the frequency because it's really effective," states Barcelona COO Scott Lawton. "We're actually finding out details on things that are important to us." Second, Barcelona offers a credit card rewards network in which customers get meal discounts and airline miles in return for offering survey feedback. Third, the company issues comment cards in the check presenter, and owners read through all comments. Fourth, the chain receives e-mails from friends and family, and every e-mail addressed to Barcelona goes directly to Pforzheimer. Finally, surveillance cameras allow owners to monitor all work areas from any computer.

Although Barcelona's feedback loops provide good quantitative data, the owners and general managers are the true eyes and ears of the company. Pforzheimer and his leadership teams walk the floor constantly to advise wait staff and gather feedback from customers. On one occasion, a Cuban customer complained that the bar's mojitos had lost their zing after the restaurant switched to inexpensive $9 dollar rum. The customer suggested using Castillo brand rum, informing management that it was inexpensive yet perfect for mojitos. Managers followed the customer's advice, and now Barcelona serves great tasting mojitos at lower expense. According to Pforzheimer, this tactic of management by walking around has led to similar improvements in menu choices, recipes, music, artwork, and more.

And although managing costs is important, Barcelona refuses to sacrifice quality to pinch a few pennies. "The fine line that we walk," says Scott Lawton, "is determining how can we give the very best product and the very best service and still make a good profit. It doesn't have to be the best profit, but it has to be a good profit."

There's plenty at stake if Barcelona fails to control its performance. Pforzheimer notes that disappointing one's customers is the quickest way to kill a business. However, failure is about more than losing money: it's also about losing face.

"What's at stake is my business and my self-respect," says the restaurateur. "Making people happy is what motivates chefs." Pforzheimer says if he can't do that, he wouldn't be able to stay in the restaurant business.

Discussion Questions

1. How do managers at Barcelona control the company's financial performance?
2. What is the "balanced scorecard" approach to measuring corporate performance, and in what ways does Barcelona utilize this approach?
3. List the four steps of the feedback control model and describe an instance where Barcelona followed this process to improve its performance.

In Bruges

Hit man Ray (Colin Farrell) botches the simple job of murdering a priest in a confessional. The "botch" occurs when a bullet passes through the priest's body into a young boy's head. Deeply troubled, Ray and fellow hit man Ken (Brendan Gleeson) go to the beautiful medieval Flemish city of Bruges, Belgium. Ken engages in tourist activities, which Ray finds highly boring. Various characters, such as an American dwarf actor and a beautiful woman selling drugs on a film set, add color and interest to this film.

Customer Focus This sequence has two parts that are separated by a title slide that reads "And another interaction for the ticket seller." Watch Part I up to the title slide and pause the film. Answer the first two questions. Restart the film sequence and play to the end. Answer the third question.

Part I. This sequence starts as Ken enters the tower to buy a ticket. It ends after he asks the ticket seller (Rudy Blomme) whether he is happy. This sequence follows the discussion about the city of Bruges between Ken and Ray.

Part II. This sequence begins as Ken and Harry Waters (Ralph Fiennes) approach the bell tower. It follows their discussion over beers about where Harry should shoot Ken. The ticket seller tells Ken that the tower is closed because a visitor had a heart attack. This sequence ends after Harry's interaction with the ticker seller. The film continues with various scenes based on the plaza.

What to Watch for and Ask Yourself

- Ken is the customer, and the ticket seller responds to him as a customer. Do you perceive the ticket seller as having a customer focus as emphasized in this chapter? Why or why not?
- The ticket seller will interact with Ken and Harry Waters in Part II of this film sequence. Do you predict that the ticket seller's customer approach could result in negative results for him? Why or why not?
- Part II offers a lesson in customer focus. What did the ticket seller fail to understand about his customers?

Endnotes

1. "Playoff Gameday," NBA Web site, www.nba.com/lakers/news/100617_gameday_celtics.html (accessed September 23, 2010).
2. David Biderman, "Are Statheads the NBA's Secret Weapon?" *The Wall Street Journal*, March 12, 2010, http://online.wsj.com/article/NA_WSJ_PUB:SB10001424052 748704869304575109723724933264.html (accessed August 24, 2010).
3. Yochi J. Dreazen, "More Katrina Woes: Incidents of Fraud at Red Cross Centers," *The Wall Street Journal*, October 19, 2005.
4. Douglas S. Sherwin, "The Meaning of Control," *Dunn's Business Review* (January, 1956).
5. Gordon Fairclough, "In China, a Contrast in Drug Supply," *The Wall Street Journal Asia*, March 10, 2008.
6. "On Balance," a *CFO* Interview with Robert Kaplan and David Norton, *CFO* (February 2001):73–78; and Bill Birchard, "Intangible Assets + Hard Numbers = Soft Finance," *Fast Company* (October 1999): 316–336.
7. Andy Neely and Mohammed Al Najjar, "Management Learning Not Management Control: The True Role of Performance Measurement," *California Management Review* 48, no. 3 (Spring 2006): 105 ff.
8. This discussion is based on a review of the balanced scorecard in Richard L. Daft, *Organization Theory and Design*, 7th ed. (Cincinnati, OH: South-Western, 2001), pp. 300–301.
9. Neely and Al Najjar, pp. 105 and 112.
10. Robert Kaplan and David Norton, "The Balanced Scorecard: Measures That Drive Performance," *Harvard Business Review* (January–February 1992): 71–79; and Chee W. Chow, Kamal M. Haddad, and James E. Williamson, "Applying the Balanced Scorecard to Small Companies," *Management Accounting* 79, no. 2 (August 1997): 21–27.
11. Based on Kaplan and Norton, "The Balanced Scorecard"; Chow, Haddad, and Williamson, "Applying the Balanced Scorecard"; and Cathy Lazere, "All Together Now," *CFO* (February 1998): 28–36.
12. Arik Hesseldahl, "Facebook: Popularity Unpopular," *BusinessWeek Online*, August 12, 2010, www.businessweek.com/magazine/content/10_34/b4192086028904.htm (accessed August 24, 2010).
13. Geert J. M. Braam and Edwin J. Nijssen, "Performance Effects of Using the Balanced Scorecard: A Note on the Dutch Experience," *Long Range Planning* 37 (2004): 335–349; Kaplan and

Norton, "The Balanced Scorecard"; and Cam Scholey, "Strategy Maps: A Step-by-Step Guide to Measuring, Managing, and Communicating the Plan," *Journal of Business Strategy* 26, no. 3 (2005): 12–19.

14. Nils-Göran Olve, Carl-Johan Petri, Jan Roy, and Sofie Roy, "Twelve Years Later: Understanding and Realizing the Value of Balanced Scorecards," *Ivey Business Journal Online*, May–June 2004, www.iveybusinessjournal.com/article.asp?intArticle_ID=487 (accessed October 4, 2010); Eric M. Olson and Stanley F. Slater, "The Balanced Scorecard, Competitive Strategy, and Performance," *Business Horizons* (May–June 2002): 11–16; and Eric Berkman, "How to Use the Balanced Scorecard," *CIO* (May 15, 2002): 93–100.

15. *Ibid.*; and Brigitte W. Schay, Mary Ellen Beach, Jacqueline A. Caldwell, and Christelle LaPolice, "Using Standardized Outcome Measures in the Federal Government," *Human Resource Management* 41, no. 3 (Fall 2002): 355–368.

16. Braam and Nijssen, "Performance Effects of Using the Balanced Scorecard."

17. Olve et al., "Twelve Years Later: Understanding and Realizing the Value of Balanced Scorecards."

18. Peter Valdes-Dapena, "Tiny Smart Car Gets Crash Test Kudos," *Fortune* (May 14, 2008), http://money.cnn.com/2008/05/14/autos/smart_fortwo_iihs_crash_test/index.htm (accessed May 14, 2008).

19. Richard E. Crandall, "Keys to Better Performance Measurement," *Industrial Management* (January–February 2002): 19–24; Christopher D. Ittner and David F. Larcker, "Coming Up Short on Nonfinancial Performance Measurement," *Harvard Business Review* (November 2003): 88–95.

20. Crandall, "Keys to Better Performance Measurement."

21. Frank Eltman, "Tracking Systems Help Cities Monitor Employees, Save," *The Tennessean*, November 16, 2007.

22. John W. Miller, "Private Food Standards Gain Favor," *The Wall Street Journal,* March 11, 2008.

23. Sumantra Ghoshal, *Strategic Control* (St. Paul, MN: West, 1986), Chapter 4; and Robert N. Anthony, John Dearden, and Norton M. Bedford, *Management Control Systems*, 5th ed. (Homewood, IL: Irwin, 1984).

24. John A. Boquist, Todd T. Milbourn, and Anjan V. Thakor, "How Do You Win the Capital Allocation Game?" *Sloan Management Review* (Winter 1998): 59–71.

25. Anthony, Dearden, and Bedford, *Management Control Systems.*

26. Participation in budget setting is described in a number of studies, including Neil C. Churchill, "Budget Choice: Planning versus Control," *Harvard Business Review* (July–August 1984): 150–164; Peter Brownell, "Leadership Style, Budgetary Participation, and Managerial Behavior," *Accounting Organizations and Society* 8 (1983): 307–321; and Paul J. Carruth and Thurrell O. McClandon, "How Supervisors React to 'Meeting the Budget' Pressure," *Management Accounting* 66 (November 1984): 50–54.

27. Tim Reason, "Budgeting in the Real World," *CFO* (July 2005): 43–48.

28. Ibid.

29. Bridget Mintz Testa, "Multiskilled Employees Sought as Versatility Becomes a Workplace Virtue," *Workforce Management Online*, September 2010, www.workforce.com/section/recruiting- staffing/feature/multiskilled- employees-sought-versatility-becomes-a/index.html (accessed October 4, 2010).

30. Ibid.

31. William G. Ouchi, "Markets, Bureaucracies, and Clans," *Administrative Science Quarterly* 25 (1980): 129–141; and B. R. Baligia and Alfred M. Jaeger, "Multinational Corporations: Control Systems and Delegation Issues," *Journal of International Business Studies* (Fall 1984): 25–40.

32. Michelle Conlin, "To Catch a Corporate Thief," *BusinessWeek* (February 16, 2009): 52.

33. Perry Pascarella, "Open the Books to Unleash Your People," *Management Review* (May 1998): 58–60.

34. Mel Mandell, "Accounting Challenges Overseas," *World Trade* (December 1, 2001): 48–50.

35. Matthew Dolan and Jeff Bennett, "Corporate News: Ford Vows to Build Higher-Quality Small Cars," *The Wall Street Journal*, August 12, 2008.

36. A. V. Feigenbaum, *Total Quality Control: Engineering and Management* (New York: McGraw-Hill, 1961); John Lorinc, "Dr. Deming's Traveling Quality Show," *Canadian Business* (September 1990): 38–42; Mary Walton, *The Deming Management Method* (New York: Dodd-Meade & Co., 1986); and J. M. Juran and Frank M. Gryna, eds., *Juran's Quality Control Handbook,* 4th ed. (New York: McGraw-Hill, 1988).

37. Edward E. Lawler III and Susan A. Mohrman, "Quality Circles after the Fad," *Harvard Business Review* (January–February 1985): 65–71; and Philip C. Thompson, *Quality Circles: How to Make Them Work in America* (New York: AMACOM, 1982).

38. D. J. Ford, "Benchmarking HRD," *Training and Development* (July1993): 37–41.

39. Tracy Mayor, "Six Sigma Comes to IT: Targeting Perfection," *CIO* (December 1, 2003): 62–70; Hal Plotkin, "Six Sigma: What It Is and How to Use It," *Harvard Management Update* (June 1999): 3–4; Tom Rancour and Mike McCracken, "Applying 6 Sigma Methods for Breakthrough Safety Performance," *Professional Safety* 45, no. 10 (October 2000): 29–32; G. Hasek, "Merger Marries Quality Efforts," *Industry Week* (August 21, 2000): 89–92; and Lee Clifford, "Why You Can Safely Ignore Six Sigma," *Fortune* (January 22, 2001): 140.

40. Dick Smith and Jerry Blakeslee "The New Strategic Six Sigma," *Training & Development* (September 2002): 45–52; Michael Hammer and Jeff Goding, "Putting Six Sigma in Perspective," *Quality* (October 2001): 58–62; and Mayor, "Six Sigma Comes to IT."

41. Jack Bouck, "Creating a Customer-Focused Culture: The Honeywell Experience," *Industrial Management*, (November/December, 2007): 11.

42. Philip R. Thomas, Larry J. Gallace, and Kenneth R. Martin, *Quality Alone Is Not Enough* (New York: American Management Association, 1992).

43. Kate Kane, "L.L. Bean Delivers the Goods," *Fast Company* (August–September 1997): 104–113.

44. George Taninecz, "Change for the Better," *Industry Week* (October 2004): 49–50; and "Dana Corporation Earns Record Sixth *Industry Week* 10 Best Plants Award," *PR Newswire* (September 27, 2004): 1.

45. Clifford, "Why You Can Safely Ignore Six Sigma"; and Hammer and Goding, "Putting Six Sigma in Perspective."

46. Syed Hasan Jaffrey, "ISO 9001 Made Easy," *Quality Progress* 37, no. 5 (May 2004): 104; Frank C. Barnes, "ISO 9000 Myth and Reality: A Reasonable Approach to ISO 9000," *SAM Advanced Management Journal* (Spring 1998): 23–30;

and Thomas H. Stevenson and Frank C. Barnes, "Fourteen Years of ISO 9000: Impact, Criticisms, Costs, and Benefits," *Business Horizons* (May–June 2001): 45–51.

47. David Amari, Don James, and Cathy Marley, "ISO 9001 Takes On a New Role—Crime Fighter," *Quality Progress* 37, no. 5 (May 2004): 57ff.

48. *"Corporate Governance,"* Business Dictionary Web site, www.businessdictionary.com/definition/corporate-governance.html (accessed September 16, 2010); *"Words to Understand: Corporate Governance Models,"* Gruppo Hera Italy Web site, http://eng.gruppohera.it/group/hera_ondemand/words_understand/page23.html (accessed September 16, 2010); and "Corporate Governance Issues in 2009," *The Corporate Eye*, March 10, 2009, www.corporate-eye.com/blog/2009/03/corporate-governance-issues-2009 (accessed September 16, 2010).

49. Damian Paletta and David Enrich, "Banks Get New Restraints," *The Wall Street Journal*, September 13, 2010.

50. Joann S. Lublin, "Lead Directors Gain Clout to Counterbalance Strong CEOs," *The Wall Street Journal*, September 13, 2010.

51. Based on Michael Barbaro, "Some Leeway for the Small Shoplifter," *The New York Times*, July 13, 2006.

52. Based on Herb Greenberg, "Why Investors May Do Well with Firms That Avoid Layoffs," *The Wall Street Journal*, September 9, 2006; Mark Gottlieb, "Feeding the Dragon," *Industry Week* 251, no. 1 (February 2002): 54–55; Donald Hastings, "Lincoln Electric's Harsh Lessons from International Expansion," *Harvard Business Review* (May–June 1999): 3–11; and Joseph Maciariello, "A Pattern of Success: Can This Company Be Duplicated?" *Drucker Management* 1, no. 1 (Spring 1997): 7–11.

Appendix A

Managing Small Business Start-ups

Do You Think Like an Entrepreneur?[1]

An entrepreneur faces many demands. Do you have the proclivity to start and build your own business? To find out, consider the extent to which each of the following statements characterizes your behavior. Please answer each of the following items as Mostly True or Mostly False for you.

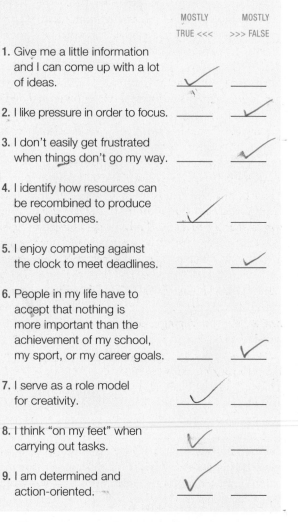

	MOSTLY TRUE <<<	MOSTLY >>> FALSE
1. Give me a little information and I can come up with a lot of ideas.	_____	_____
2. I like pressure in order to focus.	_____	_____
3. I don't easily get frustrated when things don't go my way.	_____	_____
4. I identify how resources can be recombined to produce novel outcomes.	_____	_____
5. I enjoy competing against the clock to meet deadlines.	_____	_____
6. People in my life have to accept that nothing is more important than the achievement of my school, my sport, or my career goals.	_____	_____
7. I serve as a role model for creativity.	_____	_____
8. I think "on my feet" when carrying out tasks.	_____	_____
9. I am determined and action-oriented.	_____	_____

SCORING AND INTERPRETATION: *Each question pertains to some aspect of improvisation, which is a correlate of entrepreneurial intentions. Entrepreneurial improvisation consists of three elements. Items 1, 4, and 7 pertain to creativity or ingenuity, the ability to produce novel solutions under constrained conditions. Items 2, 5, and 8 pertain to working under pressure or stress, the ability to excel under pressure-filled circumstances. Items 3, 6, and 9 pertain to action or persistence, the determination to achieve goals and solve problems in the moment. If you answered Mostly True to at least two of three questions for each subscale, or six of nine for all the questions, then consider yourself an entrepreneur in the making, with the potential to manage your own business. If you scored 1 or fewer Mostly True on each subscale, or 3 or fewer for all nine items, then you might want to consider becoming a manager by working for someone else.*

Many people dream of starting their own business. Some decide to start a business because they're inspired by a great idea or want the flexibility that comes from being self-employed. Others decide to go into business for themselves after they get laid off or find their opportunities limited in big companies. Interest in entrepreneurship and small business is at an all-time high. At college campuses across the United States, ambitious courses, programs, and centers teach the fundamentals of starting a small business. Entrepreneurs have access to business incubators, support networks, and online training courses. The enormous growth of franchising gives beginners an escorted route into a new business. In addition, the Internet opens new avenues for small business formation.

Today, the fastest-growing segment of small business in both the United States and Canada is in one-owner operations, or *sole proprietorships*.[2] Sole proprietorships in the United States reached an all-time high of 19.5 million in 2004, the most recent year with statistics available.[3] After the crash of the dot-com boom, many of these entrepreneurs are finding opportunities in low-tech businesses such as landscaping, child care, and janitorial services. Overall, since the 1970s, the number of businesses in the United States economy has been growing faster than the labor force.[4]

However, running a small business is difficult and risky. The U.S. Small Business Administration (SBA) reports that about 30 percent of small businesses fail within two years of opening, and 56 percent fold after four years.[5] For high-tech businesses, the failure rate is even higher. Research indicates that the chances are only 6 in 1 million that an idea for a high-tech business eventually turns into a successful public company.[6] Despite these risks, people are entering the world of entrepreneurship at an unprecedented rate. In 2006, an estimated 649,700 new businesses were established in the United States, while an estimated 564,700 closed their doors for good.[7] Small-business formation is the primary process by which an economy recreates and reinvents itself,[8] and the turbulence in the small-business environment is evidence of a shifting but thriving U.S. economy.

What Is Entrepreneurship?

Entrepreneurship is the process of initiating a business venture, organizing the necessary resources, and assuming the associated risks and rewards.[9] An **entrepreneur** is someone who engages in entrepreneurship. An entrepreneur recognizes a viable idea for a business product or service and carries it out by finding and assembling the necessary resources—money, people, machinery, location—to undertake the business venture. Entrepreneurs also assume the risks and reap the rewards of the business. They assume the financial and legal risks of ownership and receive the business's profits.

A good example of entrepreneurship is Jeff Fluhr, who dropped out of Stanford during his first year of graduate school to launch StubHub, a leading Internet player in the burgeoning market of ticket reselling, an industry that may be doing as much as $10 billion a year in volume. Hardworking and persistent, Fluhr struggled to raise money during the early days of the business, a time when many investors had been stung by the dot-com crash. His tenacity paid off as he convinced executives from Viacom Inc., Home Box Office, and Madison Square Garden to invest in his plan to reinvent the online ticket-resale industry. StubHub gives consumers access to high-demand concert, theater, and sporting events that are usually unavailable because promoters now reserve large blocks of tickets for fan-club members, season-ticket holders, and sponsors. StubHub allows sellers to list tickets at StubHub—free of charge—and sell them either by auction or at a fixed price. The company's two call centers receive approximately 2,500 calls a day and sell more than $200 million worth of tickets annually.[10] Fluhr, who comes from a family of entrepreneurs, was willing to take the risks and is now reaping the rewards of entrepreneurship.

Successful entrepreneurs have many different motivations, and they measure rewards in different ways. One study classified small-business owners in five different categories, as illustrated in Exhibit A.1. Some people are *idealists*, who like the idea of working on something that is new, creative, or personally meaningful. *Optimizers* are rewarded by the personal satisfaction of being business owners. Entrepreneurs in the *sustainer* category like the chance to balance work and personal life and often don't want the business to grow too large, while *hard workers* enjoy putting in the long hours and dedication to build a larger, more profitable business. The *juggler* category includes entrepreneurs who like the chance a small business gives them to handle everything themselves. These high-energy people thrive on the pressure of paying bills, meeting deadlines, and making payroll.[11]

Compare the motivation of Paula Turpin to that of Greg Littlefield. Turpin borrowed a few thousand dollars to start a hair salon, Truly Blessed Styles, in Shirley, New York. She does all the cutting, styling, and coloring herself, while her mother helps schedule appointments and keeps the books. Turpin likes the flexibility and freedom of working for herself. Although she hopes to expand by adding beauty supplies, she doesn't want the headaches of managing a large business. Greg Littlefield quit his management job and started a cleaning service because he reasoned that it would never lack customers. From the beginning, when he was working two part-time jobs and cleaning buildings by himself at night, Littlefield had plans for expansion. Within a decade, Littlefield's firm, Professional Facilities Management, grew into a 900-employee company providing a range of services including housekeeping, landscaping, minor maintenance, and security services.[12] Greg Littlefield reflects the motivation of a *hard worker*, whereas Paula Turpin's motivation is more that of a *sustainer*.

EXHIBIT A.1

Five Types of Small-Business Owners

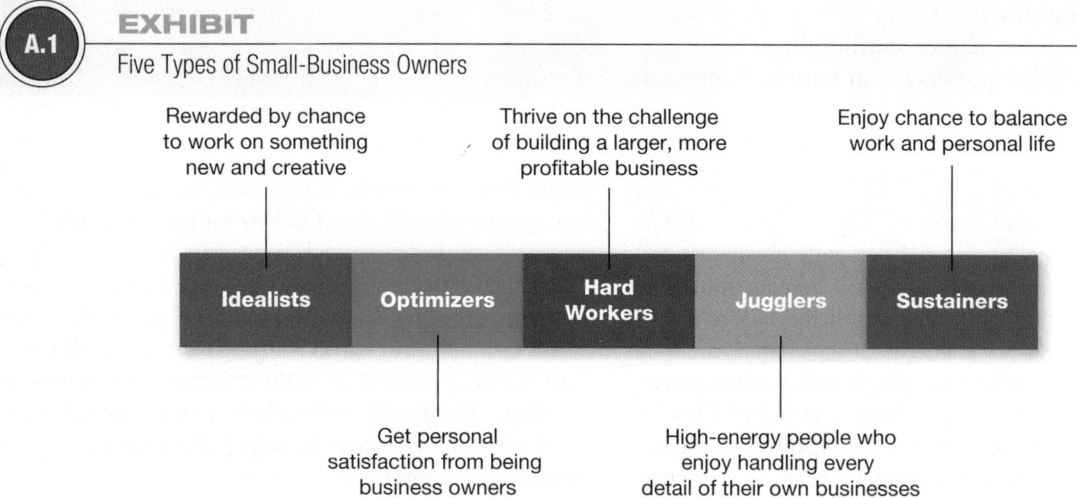

Source: Based on a study conducted by Yankelovich Partners for Pitney Bowes in Mark Henricks, "Type-Cast," *Entrepreneur* (March 2000): 14–16.

Sometimes people start new businesses when they lose their jobs due to corporate downsizing. The major layoffs in the early 2000s provided just the push some latent entrepreneurs needed to strike out on their own. Some experts think an economic downturn is actually the best time to start a business. For one thing, a downturn opens up lots of opportunities because people are looking for lower costs and better ways of doing things. The economic climate also enables the new business to hire good people, forces the entrepreneur to keep costs in line, and provides the time needed to build something of lasting value rather than struggling to keep pace with rapid growth.[13]

Entrepreneurship Today

Not so long ago, scholars and policy makers worried about the potential of small business to survive. The turbulence in the technology sector and the demise of many dot-com start-ups heightened concerns about whether small companies can compete with big business. However, entrepreneurship and small business, including high-tech start-ups, are vital, dynamic, and increasingly important parts of the U.S. economy. Small businesses represent 99.7 percent of all firms and employ about half of all private-sector employees. In addition, small businesses have generated 60 percent to 80 percent of new jobs annually over the last decade.[14]

Entrepreneurship in other countries is also booming. The list of entrepreneurial countries around the world, shown in Exhibit A.2, is intriguing. A project monitoring entrepreneurial activity around the world

EXHIBIT

Entrepreneurial Countries Around the World

Country	Percentage of Individuals Age 18 to 64 Active in Starting or Managing a New Business, 2007
Thailand	47.4
Peru	39.0
Colombia	33.6
Venezuela	24.9
China	24.6
Argentina	24.1
Dominican Republic	23.2
Brazil	22.4
Chile	21.4
Iceland	19.8
Greece	18.7
Uruguay	18.5
Ireland	16.8
Portugal	15.4
Hong Kong	15.0

Source: Table 1, "Prevalence Rates of Entrepreneurial Activity Across Countries, 2007," in Niels Bosma, Kent Jones, Erkko Autio, and Jonathan Levie, *Global Entrepreneurship Monitor 2007 Executive Report* (Babson College and the London Business School), March 14, 2008. Permission to reproduce this table has been kindly granted by the copyright holders. The GEM is an international consortium comprising 42 countries in 2007. Our thanks go to the authors, researchers, funding bodies, and other contributors who have made this possible.

reports that an estimated 47.4 percent of adults age 18 to 64 in Thailand are either starting up or managing new enterprises. The percentage in Peru is 39 percent; in Colombia, 33.6 percent. China and Argentina also show higher rates of entrepreneurial activity than the U.S. rate of 14.1 percent. China's boost in entrepreneurial activity continues to increase due to the rapid expansion of the Chinese economy, especially in the big cities.[15]

Definition of Small Business

The U.S. Small Business Administration defines a small business as "one that is independently owned and operated and which is not dominant in its field of operation."[16] Exhibit A.3 gives a few examples of how the SBA defines small business for a sample of industries.

However, the definition of small business is currently under revision in response to concerns from small-business owners. After nationwide public hearings, the SBA determined that standards should be changed in light of shifting economic and industry conditions. Redefining small-business size standards is a daunting task, but SBA leaders agree that the standards need to be more flexible in today's world. The SBA's definition has been revised a number of times over the years to reflect changing economic conditions.[17]

Exhibit A.3 also illustrates general categories of businesses most entrepreneurs start: manufacturing, retail, and Internet services. Additional categories of small businesses are construction, hospitality, communications, finance, and real estate.

Impact of Entrepreneurial Companies

The impact of entrepreneurial companies on the U.S. economy is astonishing. According to the Small Business Administration, businesses with fewer than 500 employees represent 99.7 percent of all firms with employees in the United States, employ more than 50 percent of the nation's nonfarm private sector workers, and generate more than 50 percent of the nation's nonfarm gross domestic product. In addition, small businesses represent 97 percent of America's exporters and produce 28.6 percent of all export value.[18] In 2000, the status of the SBA administrator was elevated to a cabinet-level position in recognition of the importance of small business in the U.S. economy.[19]

Inspired by the growth of companies such as eBay, Google, and Amazon.com, entrepreneurs are still flocking to the Internet to start new businesses. In addition, demographic and lifestyle trends create new opportunities in areas such as environmental services, lawn care, computer maintenance, children's markets, fitness, and

EXHIBIT A.3

Examples of SBA Definitions of Small Business

Manufacturing	
Soft-drink manufacturing	Number of employees does not exceed 500
Electronic computer manufacturing	Number of employees does not exceed 1,000
Prerecorded CD, tape, and record producing	Number of employees does not exceed 750
Retail (Store and Nonstore)	
Sporting goods stores	Average annual receipts do not exceed $6.5 million
Electronic auctions	Average annual receipts do not exceed $23.0 million
Convenience stores	Average annual receipts do not exceed $6.5 million
Miscellaneous Internet Services	
Internet service providers	Average annual receipts do not exceed $23.0 million
Web search portals	Average annual receipts do not exceed $6.5 million
Internet publishing and broadcasting	Number of employees does not exceed 500

Source: U.S. Small Business Administration, *Table of Small-Business Size Standards Matched to North American Industry Classification System Codes* (www.sba.gov/idc/groups/public/documents/sba_homepage/serv_sstd_tablepdf.pdf) (accessed June 23, 2008).

home health care. Entrepreneurship and small business in the United States is an engine for job creation and innovation.

- **Job Creation**. Researchers disagree over what percentage of new jobs is created by small business. Research indicates that the *age* of a company, more than its size, determines the number of jobs it creates. In other words, virtually *all* new jobs in recent years have come from new companies, which include not only small companies but also new branches of huge, multinational organizations.[20] However, small companies still are thought to create a large percentage of new jobs in the United States. The SBA reports that small businesses create 65 percent or more of America's new jobs. Jobs created by small businesses give the United States an economic vitality no other country can claim. However, as reflected in Exhibit A.2 earlier in this appendix (page 638), entrepreneurial economic activity is dramatically expanding in other countries as well.
- **Innovation**. According to Cognetics, Inc., a research firm run by David Birch that traces the employment and sales records of some 9 million companies, new and smaller firms have been responsible for 55 percent of the innovations in 362 different industries and 95 percent of all radical innovations. In addition, fast-growing businesses, which Birch calls *gazelles*, produce twice as many product innovations per employee as do larger firms. Small firms that file for patents typically produce 13 to 14 times more patents per employee than large patenting firms.[21] Among the notable products for which small businesses can be credited are WD-40, the jet engine, and the shopping cart.

Who Are Entrepreneurs?

The heroes of American business—Henry Ford, Steve Jobs, Sam Walton, Bill Gates, Oprah Winfrey, Larry Page, Sergey Brin—are almost always entrepreneurs. Entrepreneurs start with a vision. Often they are unhappy with their current jobs and see an opportunity to bring together the resources needed for a new venture. However, the image of entrepreneurs as bold pioneers probably is overly romantic. A survey of the CEOs of the nation's fastest-growing small firms found that these entrepreneurs could be best characterized as hardworking and practical, with great familiarity with their market and industry.[22] For example, Jason Goldberg, T-Mobile USA's former strategic-planning director, grew frustrated with the flood of unqualified candidates he received from popular job boards, so he created Jobster as a new approach to online recruiting. Jobster takes advantage of the referring power of a social network, meaning that every job candidate is recommended by a trusted reference. Job recruiters reduce their risk of hiring an unknown candidate when they hire someone who comes with a referral. Striking a nerve with the hiring community, Jobster has signed 475 corporate clients since its launch in 2005, and its roster of clients is growing 30 percent every year.[23]

Diversity of Entrepreneurs

Entrepreneurs often have backgrounds and demographic characteristics that distinguish them from other people. Entrepreneurs are more likely to be the first-born within their families, and their parents are more likely to have been entrepreneurs. In addition, immigrants are more likely to start small businesses than native-born Americans.[24] Consider former veterinarian Salvador Guzman, who moved from Mexico to become a busboy in a friend's Mexican restaurant in Nashville, Tennessee. Energized by the opportunities to succeed in the United States as an entrepreneur, Guzman started his own restaurant with three partners and a savings of $18,000, joining more than 2.4 million self-employed immigrants in the United States. Now he owns 14 restaurants and the first Spanish-language radio station in Tennessee.[25]

Entrepreneurship offers opportunities for individuals who may feel blocked in established corporations. Women-owned and minority-owned businesses may be the emerging growth companies of the next decade. In 2005, women owned 6.5 million U.S. businesses that generated $950.6 billion in revenues and employed more than 7 million workers. In Canada as well, women entrepreneurs are thriving. Since 1989, the rate of small businesses started by women in Canada grew 60 percent faster than the growth in the number of small businesses started by men.[26] Statistics for minorities in the United States are also impressive, with minorities owning 4.1 million firms that generated $694 billion in revenues and employed 4.8 million people.[27] The number of new firms launched by minorities is growing about 17 percent a year, with African American businesses growing at a rate of about 26 percent a year. African American males between the ages of 25 and 35 start more businesses than any other group in the country. Moreover, the face of entrepreneurship for the future will be increasingly diverse. When Junior Achievement (an organization that

EXHIBIT A.4

A Glimpse of Tomorrow's Entrepreneurs

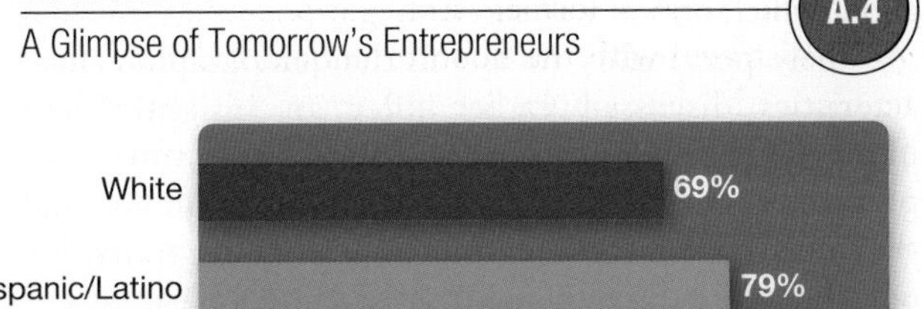

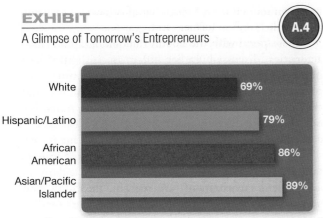

Percentage of teenagers polled by Junior Achievement who said they want to start their own business

Source: Junior Achievement Survey results reported in Cora Daniels, "Minority Rule," *FSB* (December 2003–January 2004): 65–66.

educates young people about business) conducted a poll of teenagers ages 13 to 18, it found a much greater interest among minorities than whites in starting a business, as shown in Exhibit A.4.[28]

The types of businesses launched by minority entrepreneurs are also increasingly sophisticated. The traditional minority-owned mom-and-pop retail store or restaurant is being replaced by firms in industries such as financial services, insurance, and media. For example, Pat Winans, an African American who grew up in a Chicago ghetto, started Magna Securities, a successful institutional brokerage firm in New York City, with just $5,000. Ed Chin, a third-generation Chinese American, founded AIS Corporation to offer small and midsized companies the kind of sophisticated insurance packages usually available only to large companies. Chin originally found a niche by catering to the Asian marketplace, but word of mouth has helped his company expand beyond that market.[29]

Personality Traits

A number of studies have investigated the personality characteristics of entrepreneurs and how they differ from successful managers in established organizations. Some suggest that entrepreneurs in general want something different from life than do traditional managers. Entrepreneurs seem to place high importance on being free to achieve and maximize their potential. Some 40 traits are identified as being associated with entrepreneurship, but 6 have special importance.[30] These characteristics are illustrated in Exhibit A.5.

Internal Locus of Control. The task of starting and running a new business requires the belief that you can make things come out the way you want. The entrepreneur not only has a vision but also must be able to plan to achieve that vision and believe it will happen. An **internal locus of control** is the belief by individuals that their future is within their control and that external forces have little influence. For entrepreneurs, reaching goals for the future is seen as being in the hands of the individual. Many people, however, feel that the world is highly uncertain and that they are unable to make things come out the way they want. An **external locus of control** is the belief by individuals that their future is not within their control but rather is influenced by external forces. Entrepreneurs are individuals who are convinced they can make the difference between success

EXHIBIT A.5

Characteristics of Entrepreneurs

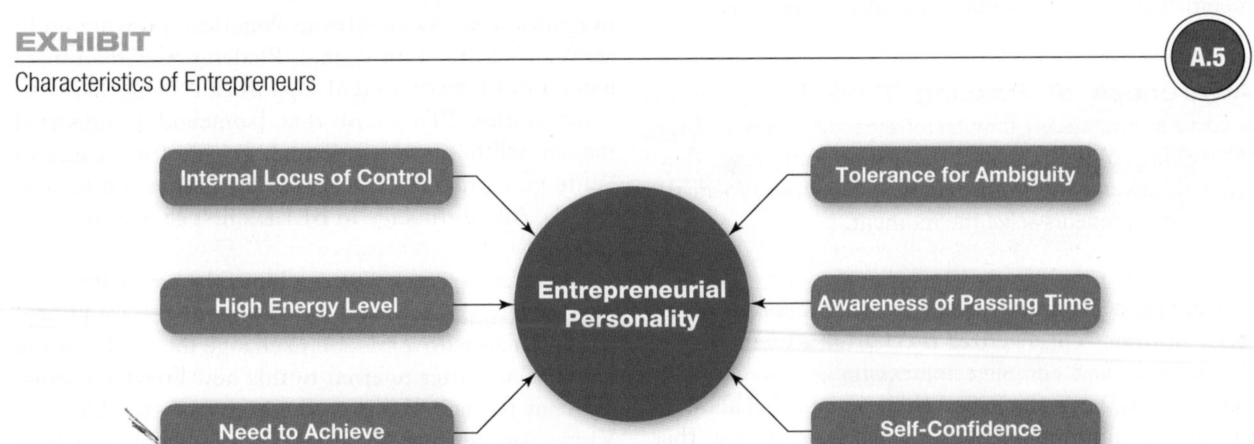

Source: Adapted from Charles R. Kuehl and Peggy A. Lambing, *Small Business: Planning and Management* (Ft. Worth, TX: Dryden Press, 1994): 45.

and failure; hence, they are motivated to take the steps needed to achieve the goal of setting up and running a new business.

High Energy Level. A business start-up requires great effort. Most entrepreneurs report struggle and hardship. They persist and work incredibly hard despite traumas and obstacles. A survey of business owners reported that half worked 60 hours or more per week. Another reported that entrepreneurs worked long hours, but that beyond 70 hours little benefit was gained. New business owners work long hours, with only 23 percent working fewer than 50 hours, which is close to a normal workweek for managers in established businesses.

Need to Achieve. Another human quality closely linked to entrepreneurship is the **need to achieve**, which means that people are motivated to excel and pick situations in which success is likely.[31] People who have high achievement needs like to set their own goals, which are moderately difficult. Easy goals present no challenge; unrealistically difficult goals cannot be achieved. Intermediate goals are challenging and provide great satisfaction when achieved. High achievers also like to pursue goals for which they can obtain feedback about their success.

Self-Confidence. People who start and run a business must act decisively. They need confidence about their ability to master the day-to-day tasks of the business. They must feel sure about their ability to win customers, handle the technical details, and keep the business moving. Entrepreneurs also have a general feeling of confidence that they can deal with anything in the future; complex, unanticipated problems can be handled as they arise.

Awareness of Passing Time. Entrepreneurs tend to be impatient; they feel a sense of urgency. They want things to progress as if there is no tomorrow. They want things moving immediately and seldom procrastinate. Entrepreneurs seize the moment.

Tolerance for Ambiguity. Many people need work situations characterized by clear structure, specific instructions, and complete information. **Tolerance for ambiguity** is the psychological characteristic that allows a person to be untroubled by disorder and uncertainty. This trait is important because few situations present more uncertainty than starting a new business. Decisions are made without clear understanding of options or certainty about which option will succeed.

These personality traits and the demographic characteristics discussed earlier offer an insightful but imprecise picture of the entrepreneur. Successful entrepreneurs come in all ages, from all backgrounds, and they may have a combination of personality traits. No one should be discouraged from starting a business because he or she doesn't fit a specific profile. One review of small business suggests that the three most important traits of successful entrepreneurs, particularly in a turbulent environment, are realism, flexibility, and passion. Even the most realistic entrepreneurs tend to underestimate the difficulties of building a business, so they need flexibility and a passion for their idea to survive the hurdles.[32]

Social Entrepreneurship: An Innovative Approach to Small Business

In today's shifting business and social environment, a new breed of entrepreneur has emerged—the **social entrepreneur**. Social entrepreneurs are leaders who are committed to both good business and positive social change. They create new business models that meet critical human needs and solve important problems that remain unsolved by current economic and social institutions.[33] Consider Earl Martin Phalen, who founded Building Educated Leaders for Life (BELL) out of his Boston living room in 1992 to provide after-school and summer support services to low-income students in grades K–6. As an African American growing up in the state's foster-care system, Phalen understood firsthand how the right kind of support can change lives and communities. "To know that [somebody] supported me, and all of a sudden, it took my life from going to jail to going to Yale," he says of his motivation to start BELL. All 20 students in BELL's first class went on to college.[34]

Social entrepreneurship combines the creativity, business smarts, passion, and hard work of the traditional entrepreneur with a mission to change the world for the better. One writer referred to this new breed as a cross between Richard Branson, the high-powered CEO of Virgin Airlines, and Mother Teresa, a Catholic nun who dedicated her life to serving the poor.[35] Social entrepreneurs have a primary goal of improving society rather than maximizing profits, but they also emphasize solid business results, high performance standards, and accountability for results. The organizations created by social entrepreneurs may or may not make a profit, but the bottom line for these companies is always social betterment rather than economic return. For entrepreneur Peter Thum, founder of Ethos Water, the purpose of his business was to sell expensive bottled water in the West in stores like Starbucks and donate part of the profits to clean-water initiatives in developing countries such as Honduras and Kenya. By 2010, Ethos will give more than $10 million a year to nonprofits that fund safe-water projects.[36]

Social entrepreneurship is not new, but the phenomenon has blossomed over the past 20 or so years. Exact figures for the number of social entrepreneurs are difficult to verify, but estimates number in the tens of thousands working around the world. The innovative organizations created by social entrepreneurs are defying the traditional boundaries between business and welfare.[37] One good illustration is Homeboy Industries, a company that started 12 years ago in a converted warehouse in Los Angeles. With 18 employees, Homeboy emphasizes rehabilitation of former gang members over revenue. The silk-screening part of the business generated $1.1 million in 2008, and the bakery produced another $3 million in revenue. Jesuit priest and founder Reverend Gregory Boyle explains that the "cash-producing part of the business brings in enough to pay for the free services." These services include therapy for former gang members, housing assistance, job development, counseling, and tattoo-removal treatments. Boyle's goal is to hire and train the neighborhood's young men to break the cycle of gangs, crime, and imprisonment.[38]

Launching an Entrepreneurial Start-Up

Whether one starts a socially oriented company or a traditional for-profit small business, the first step in pursuing an entrepreneurial dream is to come up with a viable idea and then plan like crazy. Once someone has a new idea in mind, a business plan must be drawn up and decisions must be made about legal structure, financing, and basic tactics, such as whether to start the business from scratch and whether to pursue international opportunities from the start.

Starting with the Idea

To some people, the idea for a new business is the easy part. They do not even consider entrepreneurship until they are inspired by an exciting idea. Other people decide they want to run their own business and set about looking for an idea or opportunity. Exhibit A.6 shows the most important reasons that people start a new business and the source of new business ideas. Note that 37 percent of business founders got their idea from an in-depth understanding of the industry, primarily because of past job experience. Interestingly, almost as many—36 percent—spotted a market niche that wasn't being filled.[39] After Camille Young decided to develop a healthier lifestyle and diet, she became frustrated trying to find organic food in Jersey City. Young explains, "I had to go to Manhattan to find organic food. It was annoying that Jersey City didn't even have a juice bar. Then I started thinking, Why don't I open one?" To fill this market niche, she opened two BaGua Juice stores that sell a variety of nutritious smoothies to health-conscious consumers.[40]

EXHIBIT 

Sources of Entrepreneurial Motivation and New Business Ideas

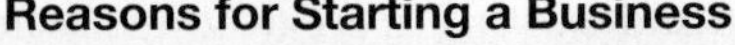

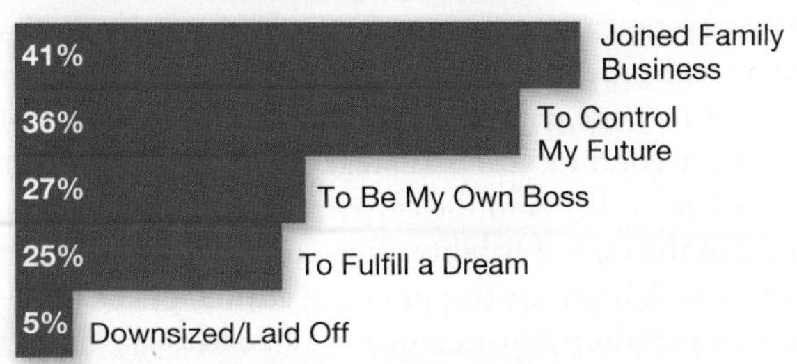

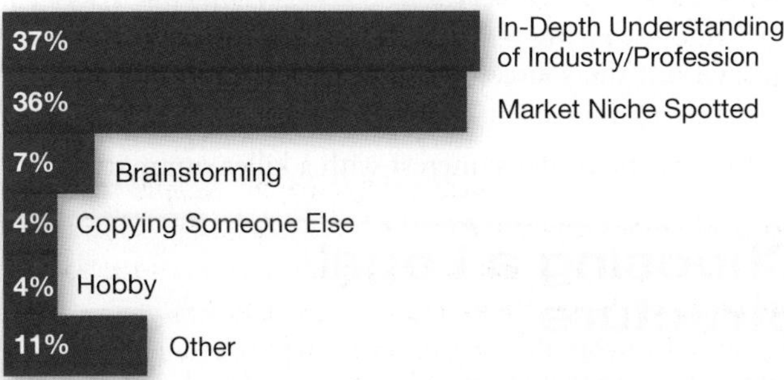

Source: 1994 Inc. 500 Founder's Survey. Copyright 1994 and 2001 by Mansueto Ventures LLC. Reproduced with permission of Mansueto Ventures LLC in the format Textbook via Copyright Clearance Center.

The trick for entrepreneurs is to blend their own skills and experience with a need in the marketplace. Acting strictly on one's own skills may produce something no one wants to buy. On the other hand, finding a market niche that the entrepreneur does not have the ability to fill doesn't work either. Both personal skill and market need typically must be present.

Writing the Business Plan

Once an entrepreneur is inspired by a new business idea, careful planning is crucial. A **business plan** is a document that specifies the business details prepared by an entrepreneur prior to opening a new business. Planning forces the entrepreneur to carefully think through the issues and problems associated with starting and developing the business. Most entrepreneurs have to borrow money, and a business plan is absolutely critical for persuading lenders and investors to participate in the business. Studies show that small businesses with a carefully thought-out, written business plan are much more likely to succeed than those without one.[41] To attract the interest of venture capitalists or other potential investors, the entrepreneur should keep the plan crisp and compelling.

The details of a business plan may vary, but successful business plans generally share several characteristics.[42] They:

- demonstrate a clear, compelling vision that creates an air of excitement;
- provide clear and realistic financial projections;
- profile potential customers and the target market;
- include detailed information about the industry and competitors;
- provide evidence of an effective entrepreneurial management team;
- pay attention to good formatting and clear writing;
- are short—no more than 50 pages;
- highlight critical risks that may threaten business success;
- spell out the sources and uses of start-up funds and operating funds; and
- capture the reader's interest with a killer summary.

Choosing a Legal Structure

Before entrepreneurs begin a business, and perhaps again as it expands, they must choose an appropriate legal structure for the company. The three basic choices are proprietorship, partnership, or corporation.

Sole Proprietorship. A **sole proprietorship** is defined as an unincorporated business owned by an individual for profit. Proprietorships make up the majority of businesses in the United States. This form is popular because it is easy to start and has few legal requirements. A proprietor has total ownership and control of the company and can make all decisions without consulting anyone. However, this type of organization also has drawbacks. The owner has unlimited liability for the business, meaning that if someone sues, the owner's personal as well as business assets are at risk. Also, financing can be harder to obtain because business success rests on one person's shoulders.

Partnership. A **partnership** is an unincorporated business owned by two or more people. Partnerships, like proprietorships, are relatively easy to start. Two friends may reach an agreement to start a graphic arts company. To avoid misunderstandings and make sure the business is well planned, it is wise to draw up and sign a formal partnership agreement with the help of an attorney. The agreement specifies how partners are to share responsibility and resources and how they will contribute their expertise. The disadvantages of partnerships are the unlimited liability of the partners and the disagreements that almost always occur among strong-minded people. A poll by *Inc.* magazine illustrated the volatility of partnerships. Fifty-nine percent of respondents considered partnerships a bad business move, citing reasons such as partner problems and conflicts. Partnerships often dissolve within five years. Respondents who liked partnerships pointed to the equality of partners (sharing of workload and emotional and financial burdens) as the key to a successful partnership.[43]

Corporation. A **corporation** is an artificial entity created by the state and existing apart from its owners. As a separate legal entity, the corporation is liable for its actions and must pay taxes on its income. Unlike other forms of ownership, the corporation has a legal life of its own; it continues to exist regardless of whether the owners live or die. And the corporation, not the owners, is sued in the case of liability. Thus, continuity and limits on owners' liability are two principal advantages of forming a corporation. For example, a physician can form a corporation so that liability for malpractice will not affect his or her personal assets. The major disadvantage of the corporation is that it is expensive and complex to do the paperwork required to incorporate the business and to keep the records required by law. When proprietorships and partnerships are successful and grow large, they often incorporate to limit liability and to raise funds through the sale of stock to investors.

Arranging Financing

Most entrepreneurs are particularly concerned with financing the business. A few types of businesses can still be started with a few thousand dollars, but starting a business usually requires coming up with a significant amount of initial funding. An investment is required to acquire labor and raw materials and perhaps a building and equipment. High-tech businesses, for example, typically need from $50,000 to $500,000 just to get through the first six months, even with the founder drawing no salary.[44]

Many entrepreneurs rely on their own resources for initial funding, but they often have to mortgage their homes, depend on credit cards, borrow money from a bank, or give part of the business to a venture capitalist.[45] Exhibit A.7 summarizes the most common sources of start-up capital for entrepreneurs. The financing decision initially involves two options—whether to obtain loans that must be repaid (debt financing) or whether to share ownership (equity financing).

Debt Financing. Borrowing money that has to be repaid at a later date to start a business is referred to as **debt financing.** One common source of debt financing for a start-up is to borrow from family and friends. Increasingly, entrepreneurs are using their personal credit cards as a form of debt financing. Another common source is a bank loan. Banks provide some 25 percent of all financing for small business. Sometimes entrepreneurs can obtain money from a finance company, wealthy individuals, or potential customers. A typical source of funds for businesses with high potential is through **angel financing.** Angels are wealthy individuals, typically with business experience and contacts, who believe in the idea for the start-up and are willing to invest their personal funds to help the business get started. Significantly, angels also provide advice and assistance as the entrepreneur is developing the company. The entrepreneur wants angels who can make business contacts, help find talented employees, and serve as all-around advisors.

Another form of loan financing is provided by the Small Business Association (SBA). Staples, which started with one office-supply store in Brighton, Massachusetts, in 1986, got its start toward rapid growth with the assistance of SBA financing. Today, Staples is North America's largest operator of office superstores, with 1,738 retail outlets in the United States and Canada, a thriving international presence in 27 countries, and $27 billion in sales.[46] SBA financing is especially helpful for people without substantial assets, providing an opportunity for single parents, minority-group members, and others with a good idea but who might be considered high risk by a traditional bank. The percentage of SBA loans to women, Hispanics, African Americans, and Asian Americans has increased significantly in recent years.[47]

EXHIBIT A.7

Sources of Start-Up Capital for Entrepreneurs

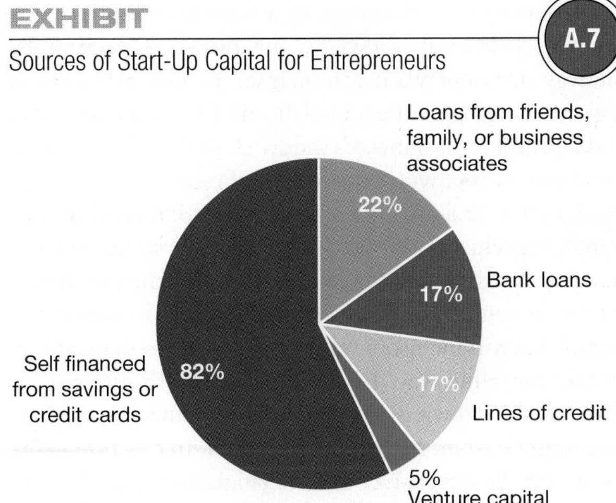

Source: Jim Melloan, "The Inc. 5000," *Inc.* (September 1, 2006): 187. Copyright 2006 by Mansueto Ventures LLC.

Equity Financing. Any money invested by owners or by those who purchase stock in a corporation is considered equity funds. **Equity financing** consists of funds that are invested in exchange for ownership in the company.

A **venture capital firm** is a group of companies or individuals that invests money in new or expanding businesses for ownership and potential profits. This form of capital is a potential for businesses with high earning and growth possibilities. Venture capitalists are particularly interested in high-tech businesses such as biotechnology, innovative online ventures, or telecommunications because they have the potential for high rates of return on investment.[48] The venture capital firm Lighthouse Capital Partners, for example, provided some of the early funding for Netflix, the online DVD rental service.[49] Venture capitalists also usually provide assistance, advice, and information to help the entrepreneur prosper. A growing number of minority-owned venture capital firms, such as

Provender Capital, founded by African American entrepreneur Fred Terrell, are ensuring that minorities have a fair shot at acquiring equity financing.[50]

Tactics for Becoming a Business Owner

Aspiring entrepreneurs can become business owners in several different ways. They can start a new business from scratch, buy an existing business, or start a franchise. Another popular entrepreneurial tactic is to participate in a business incubator.

Start a New Business. One of the most common ways to become an entrepreneur is to start a new business from scratch. This approach is exciting because the entrepreneur sees a need for a product or service that has not been filled before and then sees the idea or dream become a reality. Ray Petro invested his $50,000 life savings and took out a $25,000 loan to launch Ray's Mountain Bike Indoor Park after learning from other mountain-biking enthusiasts of their frustration with not being able to ride during the winter months. Taryn Rose started her shoe company, Taryn Rose International, after searching for stylish shoes that wouldn't destroy her feet while working long hours as an orthopedic surgeon.[51] The advantage of starting a business is the ability to develop and design the business in the entrepreneur's own way. The entrepreneur is solely responsible for its success. A potential disadvantage is the long time it can take to get the business off the ground and make it profitable. The uphill battle is caused by the lack of established clientele and the many mistakes made by someone new to the business. Moreover, no matter how much planning is done, a start-up is risky, with no guarantee that the new idea will work. Some entrepreneurs, especially in high-risk industries, develop partnerships with established companies that can help the new company get established and grow. Others use the technique of outsourcing—having some activities handled by outside contractors—to minimize the costs and risks of doing everything in-house.[52] For example, Philip Chigos and Mary Domenico are building their children's pajama business from the basement of their two-bedroom apartment, using manufacturers in China and Mexico to produce the goods and partnering with a local firm to receive shipments, handle quality control, and distribute finished products.[53]

Buy an Existing Business. Because of the long start-up time and the inevitable mistakes, some entrepreneurs prefer to reduce risk by purchasing an existing business. This direction offers the advantage of a shorter time to get started and an existing track record. The entrepreneur may get a bargain price if the owner wishes to retire or has other family considerations. Moreover, a new business may overwhelm an entrepreneur with the amount of work to be done and procedures to be determined. An established business already has filing systems, a payroll tax system, and other operating procedures. Potential disadvantages are the need to pay for goodwill that the owner believes exists and the possible existence of ill will toward the business. In addition, the company may have bad habits and procedures or outdated technology, which may be why the business is for sale.

Buy a Franchise. Franchising is perhaps the most rapidly growing path to entrepreneurship. The International Franchise Association reports that the country's 909,253 franchise outlets account for about $2.3 trillion in annual sales and are the source of 21 million jobs, 15.3 percent of all U.S. private-sector jobs.[54] **Franchising** is an arrangement by which the owner of a product or service allows others to purchase the right to distribute the product or service with help from the owner. The franchisee invests his or her money and owns the business but does not have to develop a new product, create a new company, or test the market. Franchises exist for weight-loss clinics, pet-sitting services, sports photography, bakeries, janitorial services, auto-repair shops, real-estate offices, and numerous other types of businesses, in addition to the traditional fast-food outlets. Exhibit A.8 lists the top ten fastest-growing franchises, including the type of business, the number of outlets, and the initial franchise costs. Initial franchise fees don't include the other start-up costs the entrepreneur will have to cover.

The powerful advantage of a franchise is that management help is provided by the owner. For example, Subway does not want a franchisee to fail. Subway has regional development agents who do the research to find good locations for Subway's sandwich outlets. The Subway franchisor also provides two weeks of training at company headquarters and ongoing operational and marketing support.[55] Franchisors provide an established name and national advertising to stimulate demand for the product or service. Potential disadvantages are the lack of control that occurs when franchisors want every business managed in exactly the same way. In some cases, franchisors require that franchise owners use certain contractors or suppliers that might cost more than others would. In addition, franchises can be expensive, and the high start-up costs are followed with monthly payments to the franchisor that can run from 2 percent to 15 percent of gross sales.[56]

Entrepreneurs who are considering buying a franchise should investigate the company thoroughly. The

EXHIBIT

Top Ten Fastest-Growing Franchises for 2008

Franchise	Type of Business	Number of Outlets	Franchise Costs
7–11	Convenience store	5,580	Varies
Subway	Submarine sandwich restaurant	21,344	$15,000
Dunkin' Donuts	Doughnut shop	5,451	$40,000–80,000
Pizza Hut	Pizza restaurant	4,757	$25,000
McDonald's	Hamburger restaurant	11,772	$45,000
Sonic Drive-in Restaurant	Drive-in hamburger restaurant	2,655	$45,000
KFC Corp.	Fast food chicken restaurant	4,287	$25,000
Intercontinental Hotels	Middle market lodging	2,541	Varies
Dominos Pizza	Pizza delivery	4,571	$25,000
RE/MAX Int'l	Real estate agency	4,315	$12,500–25,000

Source: Based on data 2008 Fastest-Growing Franchises, Entrepreneur.com, www.entrepreneur.com/franzone/fastestgrowing/index.html (accessed June 23, 2008).

prospective franchisee is legally entitled to a copy of franchisor disclosure statements, which include information on 20 topics, including litigation and bankruptcy history, identities of the directors and executive officers, financial information, identification of any products the franchisee is required to buy, and from whom those purchases must be made. The entrepreneur also should talk with as many franchise owners as possible, because they are among the best sources of information about how the company really operates.[57] Exhibit A.9 lists

EXHIBIT

Sample Questions for Choosing a Franchise

Questions about the Entrepreneur	Questions about the Franchisor	Before Signing the Dotted Line
1. Will I enjoy the day-to-day work of the business?	1. What assistance does the company provide in terms of selection of location, setup costs, and securing credit; day-to-day technical assistance; marketing; and ongoing training and development?	1. Do I understand the risks associated with this business, and am I willing to assume them?
2. Do my background, experience, and goals make this opportunity a good choice for me?	2. How long does it take the typical franchise owner to start making a profit?	2. Have I had an advisor review the disclosure documents and franchise agreement?
3. Am I willing to work within the rules and guidelines established by the franchisor?	3. How many franchises changed ownership within the past year, and why?	3. Do I understand the contract?

Source: Based on Thomas Love, "The Perfect Franchisee," *Nation's Business* (April 1998): 59–65; and Roberta Maynard, "Choosing a Franchise," *Nation's Business* (October 1996): 56–63.

some specific questions entrepreneurs should ask about themselves and the company when considering buying a franchise. Answering such questions can improve the chances for a successful career as a franchisee.

Participate in a Business Incubator. An attractive option for entrepreneurs who want to start a business from scratch is to join a business incubator. A **business incubator** typically provides shared office space, management-support services, and management and legal advice to entrepreneurs. Incubators also give entrepreneurs a chance to share information with one another about local business, financial aid, and market opportunities. A recent innovation is the *virtual incubator*, which does not require that people set up on-site. These virtual organizations connect entrepreneurs with a wide range of experts and mentors and offer lower overhead and cost savings for cash-strapped small-business owners. Christie Stone, cofounder of Ticobeans, a coffee distributor in New Orleans, likes the virtual approach because it gives her access to top-notch advice while allowing her to keep her office near her inventory.[58]

The concept of business incubators arose about two decades ago to nurture start-up companies. Business incubators have become a significant segment of the small-business economy, with approximately 1,400 in operation in North America and an estimated 5,000 worldwide.[59] The incubators that are thriving are primarily not-for-profits and those that cater to niches or focus on helping women or minority entrepreneurs. These incubators include those run by government agencies and universities to boost the viability of small business and spur job creation. The great value of an incubator is the expertise of a mentor, who serves as advisor, role model, and cheerleader, and ready access to a team of lawyers, accountants, and other advisors. Incubators also give budding entrepreneurs a chance to network and learn from one another.[60] "The really cool thing about a business incubator is that when you get entrepreneurial people in one place, there's a synergistic effect," said Tracy Kitts, vice president and chief operating officer of the national Business Incubation Association. "Not only do they learn from staff, they learn tons from each other, and this really contributes to their successes."[61]

Starting an Online Business

Many entrepreneurs are turning to the Internet to expand their small businesses or launch a new venture. In fact, 12.1 percent of sole proprietors are engaging in e-commerce, up from 9.4 percent in 2005, according to a survey of 1,235 businesses.[62] Anyone with an idea, a personal computer, access to the Internet, and the tools to create a Web site can start an online business. These factors certainly fueled Ashley Qualls's desire to create a Web site that has become a destination for millions of teenage girls. Starting at age 15, Ashley launched Whateverlife.com with a clever Web site, an $8 domain name, and a vision to provide free designs (hearts, flowers, celebrities) for MySpace pages. Her hobby exploded into a successful business with advertising revenue of more than $1 million so far. Ashley's motivation to start Whateverlife.com was fueled by an opportunity to turn a rewarding hobby into a thriving online business.[63]

Additional incentives for starting an online business include low overhead and the ability to work from home or any location. These are some of the incentives that motivated Landy Ung to launch 8coupons.com, a business that sends discount coupons directly to users' mobile phones via text messages. She and her boyfriend, Wan His Yuan, run the business from their 500-square-foot studio apartment, meaning headquarters is, effectively, their couch. Ung and Yuan have put $30,000 into the business, and operating costs remain low. The business demands many hours of hard work and diligence, however, frequently keeping both up until 3 A.M.[64]

Entrepreneurs who aspire to start online businesses follow the usual steps required to start a traditional business: identify a profitable market niche, develop an inspiring business plan, choose a legal structure, and determine financial backing. Beyond that, they need to be unusually nimble, persistent in marketing, savvy with technology, and skillful at building online relationships. Several steps required to start an online business are highlighted here.

- **Find a market niche**. To succeed in the competitive online market, aspiring entrepreneurs need to identify a market niche that isn't being served by other companies. Online businesses experience success when they sell unique, customized, or narrowly focused products or services to a well-defined target audience.
- **Create a professional Web site**. Online shoppers have short attention spans, so a Web site should entice them to linger. To improve customers' online experience, Web sites should be easy to navigate, intuitive, and offer menus that are easy to read and understand. Even "small-time" sites need "big-time" designs and should avoid common mistakes such as typos, excessively large files that are slow to load, too much information, and sensory overload.[65] FragranceNet.com competes with big-time competitors, with a Web site that clearly communicates its value proposition (designer brands at discount prices), easy navigation, and superior customer service.[66]

- **Choose a domain name**. A domain name gives a company an address on the Web and a unique identity. Domain names should be chosen carefully and be easy to remember, pronounce, and spell. How is a domain name selected? The options for creating a domain name are many and include (1) using the company name (dell.com), (2) creating a domain name that describes your product or service (1-800-Flowers.com), or (3) choosing a domain name that doesn't have a specific meaning and provides options for expanding (Google.com).[67]
- **Build online relationships**. In a storefront business, business owners develop loyal customer relationships through personal attention and friendly service. In the virtual business world, however, business owners connect with customers primarily through an online experience. Creating a positive, online relationship with customers requires time and resources, as Marla Cilley, owner of FlyLady.net, discovered. Cilley cultivated a cultlike following to her Internet business by sharing personal encouragement and housecleaning advice to middle-aged homemakers who call themselves FlyLadies. Her adoring customers send her nearly 5,000 grateful messages each day. She hired a team of six off-site readers to respond to each one. Through positive customer experiences and shared testimonials, Cilley continues to grow her self-help empire.[68] This demanding process of responding to thousands of e-mails helps FlyLady.com develop a loyal following and strong customer relationships.

Managing a Growing Business

Once an entrepreneurial business is up and running, how does the owner manage it? Often the traits of self-confidence, creativity, and internal locus of control lead to financial and personal grief as the enterprise grows. A hands-on entrepreneur who gave birth to the organization loves perfecting every detail. But after the start-up, continued growth requires a shift in management style. Those who fail to adjust to a growing business can be the cause of the problems rather than the solution.[69] In this section, we look at the stages through which entrepreneurial companies move, and then consider how managers should carry out their planning, organizing, leading, and controlling.

Stages of Growth

Entrepreneurial businesses go through distinct stages of growth, with each stage requiring different management skills. The five stages are illustrated in Exhibit A.10.

1. *Start-up*. In this stage, the main problems are producing the product or service and obtaining

EXHIBIT A.10

Five Stages of Growth for an Entrepreneurial Company

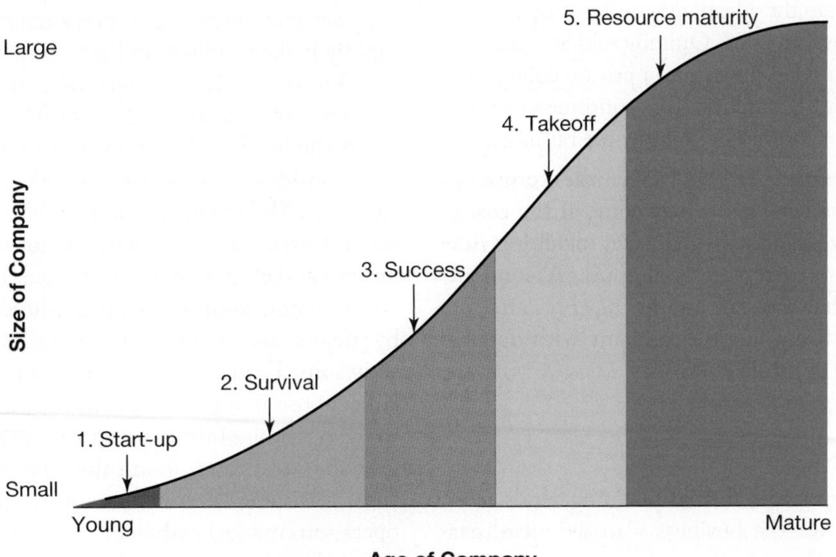

Source: Based on Neil C. Churchill and Virginia L. Lewis, "The Five Stages of Small Business Growth," *Harvard Business Review* (May–June 1993): 30–50.

customers. Several key issues facing managers are: Can we get enough customers? Will we survive? Do we have enough money? Burt's Bees was in the start-up stage when Roxanne Quimby was making candles and personal care products by hand from the beeswax of Burt Shavitz's bees and selling them at craft fairs in Maine.

2. *Survival.* At this stage, the business demonstrates that it is a workable business entity. It produces a product or service and has sufficient customers. Concerns here involve finances—generating sufficient cash flow to run the business and making sure revenues exceed expenses. The organization will grow in size and profitability during this period. Burt's Bees reached $3 million in sales by 1993, and Quimby moved the business from Maine to North Carolina to take advantage of state policies that helped her keep costs in line.
3. *Success.* At this point, the company is solidly based and profitable. Systems and procedures are in place to allow the owner to slow down if desired. The owner can stay involved or consider turning the business over to professional managers. Quimby chose to stay closely involved with Burt's Bees, admitting that she's a bit of a control freak about the business.
4. *Takeoff.* Here the key problem is how to grow rapidly and finance that growth. The owner must learn to delegate, and the company must find sufficient capital to invest in major growth. This period is pivotal in an entrepreneurial company's life. Properly managed, the company can become a big business. However, another problem for companies at this stage is how to maintain the advantages of "smallness" as the company grows. In 2003, Quimby sold 80 percent of Burt's Bees to AEA Investors, a private equity firm, for more than $175 million. She continued as CEO and focuses on continuing to grow the business.
5. *Resource maturity.* At this stage, the company's substantial financial gains may come at the cost of losing its advantages of small size, including flexibility and the entrepreneurial spirit. A company in this stage has the staff and financial resources to begin acting like a mature company with detailed planning and control systems.

Planning

In the early start-up stage, formal planning tends to be nonexistent except for the business plan described earlier in this chapter. The primary goal is simply to remain alive. As the organization grows, formal planning usually is not instituted until the success stage. Recall from Chapter 1 that planning means defining goals and deciding on the tasks and use of resources needed to attain them. Chapters 5 and 6 describe how entrepreneurs can define goals and implement strategies and plans to meet them. It is important that entrepreneurs view their original business plan as a living document that evolves as the company grows or the market changes.

One planning concern for today's small businesses is the need to be Web savvy. For many small companies today, their Web operations are just as critical as traditional warehouse management or customer-service operations. The growing importance of e-business means entrepreneurs have to plan and allocate resources for Internet operations from the beginning and grow those plans as the company grows. Of the small companies that have Web sites, more than half say the site has broken even or paid for itself in greater efficiency, improved customer relationships, or increased business.[70]

Organizing

In the first two stages of growth, the organization's structure is typically informal, with all employees reporting to the owner. Around the third stage—success—functional managers often are hired to take over duties performed by the owner. A functional organization structure will begin to evolve, with managers in charge of finance, manufacturing, and marketing. Another organizational approach is to use outsourcing, as described earlier. Method, a company launched by two 20-something entrepreneurs to develop a line of nontoxic cleaning products in fresh scents and stylish packaging, contracted with an industrial designer for the unique dish-soap bottle and uses contract manufacturers in every region of the country to rapidly make products and get them to stores.[71]

During the latter stages of entrepreneurial growth, managers must learn to delegate and decentralize authority. If the business has multiple product lines, the owner may consider creating teams or divisions responsible for each line. The organization must hire competent managers and have sufficient management talent to handle fast growth and eliminate problems caused by increasing size. As an organization grows, it might also be characterized by greater use of rules, procedures, and written job descriptions. For example, Tara Cronbaugh started a small coffeehouse in a college town, but its success quickly led to the opening of three additional houses. With the rapid growth, Cronbaugh found that she needed a way to ensure consistency across operations. She put together an operations manual with detailed rules, procedures, and job descriptions so managers and employees at each coffeehouse would be following the same pattern.[72] Chapters 7 through 9 discuss organizing in detail.

Leading

The driving force in the early stages of development is the leader's vision. This vision, combined with the leader's personality, shapes corporate culture. The leader can signal cultural values of service, efficiency, quality, or ethics. Often entrepreneurs do not have good people skills but do have excellent task skills in either manufacturing or marketing. By the success stage of growth, the owner must either learn to motivate employees or bring in managers who can. Rapid takeoff is not likely to happen without employee cooperation. The president of Foreign Candy Company of Hull, Iowa, saw his company grow rapidly when he concentrated more on employee needs and less on financial results. He made an effort to communicate with employees, conducted surveys to learn how they were feeling about the company, and found ways to involve them in decision making. His shift in leadership style allowed the company to enter the takeoff stage with the right corporate culture and employee attitudes to sustain rapid growth.

Leadership also is important because many small firms have a hard time hiring qualified employees. Labor shortages often hurt small firms that grow rapidly. A healthy corporate culture can help attract and retain good people.[73] Chapters 10 through 14 present the dynamics of leadership.

Controlling

Financial control is important in each stage of the entrepreneurial firm's growth. In the initial stages, control is exercised by simple accounting records and by personal supervision. By stage 3—success—operational budgets are in place, and the owner should start implementing more structured control systems. During the takeoff stage, the company will need to make greater use of budgets and standard cost systems and use computer systems to provide statistical reports. These control techniques will become more sophisticated during the resource maturity stage.

As Amazon.com grew and expanded internationally, for example, entrepreneur and CEO Jeff Bezos needed increasingly sophisticated control mechanisms. Bezos hired a computer-systems expert to develop a system to track and control all of the company's operations.[74] Control is discussed in Chapter 15.

Summary

- *Entrepreneurship* is the process of initiating a business, organizing the necessary resources, and assuming the associated risks and rewards. Entrepreneurship plays an important role in the economy by stimulating job creation, innovation, and opportunities for minorities and women. An entrepreneur recognizes a viable idea for a business product or service and combines the necessary resources to carry it out. Entrepreneurs may be classified as *idealists*, *optimizers*, *sustainers*, *hard workers*, or *jugglers*.
- The Small Business Administration defines a *small business* as "one that is independently owned and operated and which is not dominant in its field of operation." The U.S. economy is ripe for entrepreneurial ventures, but entrepreneurial activity is also booming in other countries, with some of the highest rates in developing nations.
- Entrepreneurs place high importance on being free to achieve and maximize their potential. An entrepreneurial personality includes the traits of internal locus of control, high energy level, need to achieve, tolerance for ambiguity, awareness of passing time, and self-confidence.
- A new breed of entrepreneur, the *social entrepreneur*, is committed to both good business and positive social change. Social entrepreneurs sometime blur the line between business and social activism because they combine the creativity, business smarts, passion, and hard work of the traditional entrepreneur with a mission to improve the world.
- A business plan is a document specifying the business details prepared by an entrepreneur prior to opening a new business. Businesses with carefully written business plans are more likely to succeed than those without them. Small businesses may be organized as sole proprietorships, partnerships, or corporations. Initial funding for a small business may come from debt financing, borrowing money that has to be repaid, or equity financing, funds that are invested in exchange for ownership.
- Small businesses generally proceed through five stages of growth: start-up, survival, success, takeoff, and resource maturity. The management functions of planning, organizing, leading, and controlling should be tailored to each stage of growth.

Discussion Questions

1. You are interested in being your own boss and have the chance to buy a franchise office-supply store that is for sale in your city. You will need outside investors to help pay the franchise fees and other start-up costs. How will you determine whether this is a good entrepreneurial opportunity and make your decision about buying the store?
2. Over the past 20 years, entrepreneurship has been the fastest-growing course of study on campuses throughout the country. However, debate continues about whether you can teach someone to be an entrepreneur. Do you think entrepreneurship can be taught? Why or why not?
3. Why would small-business ownership have great appeal to immigrants, women, and minorities?
4. Consider the six personality characteristics of entrepreneurs. Which two traits do you think are most like those of managers in large companies? Which two are least like those of managers in large companies?
5. How would you go about deciding whether you wanted to start a business from scratch, buy an existing business, or buy into a franchise? What information would you collect and analyze?
6. Many entrepreneurs say they did little planning, perhaps scratching notes on a legal pad. How is it possible for them to succeed?
7. What personal skills do you need to keep your financial backers feeling confident in your new business? Which skills are most useful when you're dealing with more informal sources such as family and friends versus receiving funds from stockholders, a bank, or a venture capital firm? Would these considerations affect your financing strategy?
8. Many people who are successful at the start-up stage of a business are not the right people to carry the venture forward. How do you decide whether you're better suited to be a serial entrepreneur (start the business and then move on to start another) or whether you can guide the venture as it grows and matures?
9. How does starting an online business differ from starting a small business such as a local auto-repair shop or delicatessen? Is it really possible for businesses that operate totally in cyberspace to build close customer relationships? Discuss.
10. Do you think entrepreneurs who launched new businesses on their own after deciding to leave jobs versus those who have been forced to leave jobs as a result of downsizing are likely to have different traits? Which group is more likely to succeed? Why?

Self Learning

What's Your Entrepreneurial IQ?

Rate yourself on the following 15 behaviors and characteristics, according to the following scale.

① = Strongly disagree

② = Disagree

③ = Agree

④ = Strongly agree

1. I am able to translate ideas into concrete tasks and outcomes.
   1 2 3 4
2. When I am interested in a project, I tend to need less sleep.
   1 2 3 4
3. I am willing to make sacrifices to gain long-term rewards.
   1 2 3 4
4. Growing up, I was more of a risk taker than a cautious child.
   1 2 3 4
5. I often see trends, connections, and patterns that are not obvious to others.
   1 2 3 4
6. I have always enjoyed spending much of my time alone.
   1 2 3 4
7. I have a reputation for being stubborn.
   1 2 3 4
8. I prefer working with a difficult but highly competent person to working with someone who is congenial but less competent.
   1 2 3 4

9. As a child, I had a paper route, a lemonade stand, or another small enterprise.
   1 2 3 4
10. I usually keep New Year's resolutions.
   1 2 3 4
11. I'm not easily discouraged, and I persist when faced with major obstacles.
   1 2 3 4
12. I recover quickly from emotional setbacks.
   1 2 3 4
13. I would be willing to dip deeply into my nest egg—and possibly lose all I had saved—to go it alone.
   1 2 3 4
14. I get tired of the same routine day in and day out.
   1 2 3 4
15. When I want something, I keep the goal clearly in mind.
   1 2 3 4

Scoring and Interpretation

Total your score for the 15 items. If you tallied 50–60 points, then you have a strong entrepreneurial IQ. A score of 30–50 indicates good entrepreneurial possibilities. Your chances of starting a successful entrepreneurial business are good if you have the desire and motivation. If you scored below 30, you probably do not have much entrepreneurial potential.

Go back over each question, thinking about changes you might make to become more or less entrepreneurial, depending on your career interests.

Ethical Dilemma

Closing the Deal

As the new, heavily recruited CEO of a high-technology start-up backed by several of Silicon Valley's leading venture capitalists, Chuck Campbell is flying high—great job, good salary, stock options, and a chance to be in on the ground floor and build one of the truly great twenty-first-century organizations. Just a few days into the job, Chuck participated in a presentation to a new group of potential investors for funding that could help the company expand marketing, improve its services, and invest in growth. By the end of the meeting, the investors had verbally committed $16 million in funding.

But things turned sour pretty fast. As Chuck was leaving about 9 P.M., the corporate controller, Betty Mars, who just returned from an extended leave, cornered him. He was surprised to find her working so late, but before he could even open his mouth, Betty blurted out her problem: The numbers Chuck had presented to the venture capitalists were flawed. "The assumptions behind the revenue growth plan are absolutely untenable," she said. "Not a chance of ever happening." Chuck was stunned. He told Betty to get on home and he'd stay and take a look at the figures.

At 11 P.M., Chuck was still sitting in his office wondering what to do. His research showed that the numbers were indeed grossly exaggerated, but most of them were at least statistically possible (however remote that possibility was). However, what really troubled him was that the renewal income figure was just flat-out false—and it was clear that one member of the management team who participated in the presentation knew it was incorrect all along. To make matters worse, it was the renewal income figure that ultimately made the investment so attractive to the venture capital firm. Chuck knew what was at stake—no less than the life or death of the company itself. If he told the truth about the deceptive numbers, the company's valuation would almost certainly be slashed and the $16 million possibly canceled.

What Would You Do?

1. Say nothing about the false numbers. Of course, the company will miss the projections and have to come up with a good explanation, but isn't that par for the course among fledgling high-tech companies? Chances are the whole thing will blow over without a problem.
2. Go ahead and close the deal, but come clean later. Explain that the controller had been on an extended leave of absence, and because you had been on the job only a few days, you had not had time to personally do an analysis of the numbers.
3. Take swift action to notify the venture capitalists of the truth of the situation—and start cleaning house to get rid of people who would knowingly lie to close a deal.

Source: Adapted from Kent Weber, "The Truth Could Cost You $16 Million," *Business Ethics* (March–April 2001): 18.

Case for Critical Analysis

Emma's Parlor

Emma Lathbury's shoulders sagged as she flipped the cardboard sign hanging in the window of her tearoom's front door from "Open" to "Closed." The normally indefatigable 52-year-old owner of Emma's Parlor was bone tired. Any doubts she'd harbored about the wisdom of seriously considering some major changes in her business were fast disappearing.

She hadn't felt this weary since she'd left nursing in the early 1990s. After years of working as an intensive care nurse—with its grueling hours, emotionally draining work, and lack of both respect and autonomy—she'd developed a bad case of burnout. At the time, she was convinced she could walk away from a secure, if difficult, profession and figure out a way of making a living that suited her high-energy, outgoing personality. Then one day, she noticed an 1870s-vintage Gothic Revival cottage for sale in the small Illinois farming community near where she'd grown up, and the answer to her dilemma came to her with a startling clarity. She'd get the financing, buy the house, and open up a cozy Victorian tearoom. Emma was certain she could make it work.

And she had. Her success was due in part to her unintentionally perfect timing. Specialty teas had taken off during the 1990s, with no end in sight to their current double-digit annual growth rate. But the solid performance of Emma's Parlor also owed a good deal to its owner's hard work and all those 60- and 70-hour weeks she'd put in, which was more fun when she worked for herself. She'd personally chosen the precise shades of purple and plum for the cottage's exterior, hung the lace curtains, selected the fresh flowers that graced the small circular tables, hired the staff, and tracked down and tested recipes for the finger sandwiches, scones, jams, and Battenburg cake that earned her glowing reviews in numerous guidebooks and a national reputation. Quickly realizing that special events were key to attracting customers, she organized and publicized fanciful gatherings that drew everyone from children toting their favorite stuffed animals to an Alice-in-Wonderland affair; to women dressed in their best outfits, complete with big floppy hats; to a Midwest version of a royal garden party. The tearoom, which now employed about 20 people, was nearly always completely booked.

Most of all, the former nurse developed a real expertise when it came to teas, becoming particularly fascinated by the medicinal benefits of herbal teas. She started by conducting evening workshops on the efficacy of organic teas in treating everything from a simple upset stomach to menopausal distress. Eventually, she began blending her own Emma's Parlor Organic Teas and selling them to retail stores, restaurants, and individuals over the Web. As more and more publicity pointed to the benefits of tea, her Web-based business flourished, generating slightly less revenue than she was realizing from the tearoom. The profit margins were higher.

Despite the fulfillment she found in running her own business, it was getting too big for her to handle. Emma was beginning to experience the all-too-familiar symptoms of burnout. After she locked the front door, she made herself a soothing cup of rosebud tea, kicked off her sensible shoes, and sat down to review her options. Maybe she could drop the tearoom and focus on the Internet business or vice versa. She could try to master the fine art of delegation and turn Emma's Parlor over to an experienced restaurant manager, or she could take herself out of the picture by selling the tearoom outright. Then again, she could simply close the restaurant or the Internet business.

Questions

1. At what business stage is Emma's Parlor? At what stage is her Web-based organic tea business? What synergies exist between the two businesses? How critical do you think those synergies are to the success of each business?
2. How does Emma Lathbury fit the profile of the typical entrepreneur? Which of those traits are likely to continue to serve her well, and which might be counterproductive at this stage of her business?
3. After listing the pros and cons for each of Emma's options and considering her personality, which course of action would you recommend?

Sources: Based on Alison Stein Wellner, "Business Was Booming But the Richardsons Were Seriously Burned Out," *Inc. Magazine* (April 2006): 52–54; Mark Blumenthal, "Total Tea Sales in U.S. Forecast for $10 Billion in 2010," *HerbalGram* (2004): 61–62; and TeaMap Tearoom Directory (www.teamap.com).

Endnotes

1. Based on Keith M. Hmieleski and Andrew C. Corbett, "Proclivity for Improvisation as a Predictor of Entrepreneurial Intentions," *Journal of Small Business Management* 44(1) (January 2006): 45–63; and "Do You Have an Entrepreneurial Mind?" *Inc.com* (October 19, 2005).
2. Elizabeth Olson, "They May Be Mundane, But Low-Tech Businesses Are Booming," *New York Times*, April 28, 2005 (www.nytimes.com/2005/04/28/business/28sbiz.html?_r=1&scp=1&sq=They%20May%20Be%20Mundane,%20But%20Low-Tech%20Businesses%20Are%20

Booming&st=cse&oref=slogin); and "CIBC Report Predicts Canada Will Be Home to One Million Women Entrepreneurs By 2010," *Canada NewsWire* (June 28, 2005): 1.

3. U.S. Small Business Administration (www.sba.gov).
4. John Case, "Where We Are Now," *Inc.* (May 29, 2001): 18–19.
5. Amy E. Knaup, "Survival and Longevity in the Business Employment Dynamics Database," *Monthly Labor Review,* 128(5) (May 2005): 50–56; and Brian Headd, "Redefining Business Success: Distinguishing Between Closure and Failure," *Small Business Economics,* 21(1) (August 2003): 51–61.
6. Reported in "Did You Know?" in J. Neil Weintraut, "Told Any Good Stories Lately?" *Business 2.0* (March 2000): 139–140.
7. U.S. Small Business Administration (www.sba.gov).
8. John Case, "Who's Looking at Start-Ups?" *Inc.* (May 29, 2001): 60.
9. Donald F. Kuratko and Richard M. Hodgetts, *Entrepreneurship: A Contemporary Approach,* 4th ed. (Fort Worth, TX: Dryden Press, 1998): 30.
10. Steve Stecklow, "StubHub's Ticket to Ride," *Wall Street Journal,* January, 17, 2006.
11. Study conducted by Yankelovich Partners, reported in Mark Henricks, "Type-Cast," *Entrepreneur* (March 2000): 14–16.
12. Olson, "Low-Tech Businesses Are Booming."
13. Norm Brodsky, "Street Smarts: Opportunity Knocks," *Inc.* (February 2002): 44–46; and Hilary Stout, "Start Low," *Wall Street Journal,* May 14, 2001.
14. U.S. Small Business Administration (www.sba.gov).
15. Global Entrepreneurship Monitor, "Table 2: Prevalence Rates of Entrepreneurial Activity Across Countries, 2007," *2007 GEM Tables and Figures,* Babson College and the London Business School, March 14, 2008 (www.gemconsortium.org/about.aspx?page=pub_gem_global_reports).
16. U.S. Small Business Administration (www.sba.gov).
17. Thuy-Doan Le Bee, "How Small Is Small? SBA Holds Hearings to Decide," *Sacramento Bee,* June 29, 2005.
18. U.S. Small Business Administration (www.sba.gov).
19. Barbara Benham, "Big Government, Small Business," *Working Woman* (February 2001): 24.
20. Research and statistics reported in "The Job Factory," *Inc.* (May 29, 2001): 40–43.
21. Ian Mount, "The Return of the Lone Inventor," *FSB* (March 2005): 18; Office of Advocacy, U.S. Small Business Administration (www.sba.gov/advo).
22. John Case, "The Origins of Entrepreneurship," *Inc.* (June 1989): 51–53.
23. Jeanette Borzo, "Taking on the Recruiting Monster," *Business 2.0* (January–February 2007): 44.
24. Kauffman Foundation (www.kauffman.org).
25. "Small Business Ambassador," *FSB* (February 2007): 28.
26. U.S. Small Business Administration (www.sba.gov); "CIBC Report Predicts Canada Will Be Home to One Million Women Entrepreneurs by 2010," *Canada NewsWire* (June 28, 2005): 1.
27. U.S. Small Business Administration (www.sba.gov).
28. Statistics reported in Cora Daniels, "Minority Rule," *FSB* (December 2003–January 2004): 65–66; Elizabeth Olson, "New Help for the Black Entrepreneur," *New York Times,* December 23, 2004; and David J. Dent, "The Next Black Power Movement," *FSB* (May 2003): 10–13.
29. Ellyn Spragins, "Pat Winans" profile, and Cora Daniels, "Ed Chin" profile, in "The New Color of Money," *FSB* (December 2003–January 2004): 74–87.
30. This discussion is based on Charles R. Kuehl and Peggy A. Lambing, *Small Business: Planning and Management,* 3rd ed. (Ft. Worth, TX: Dryden Press, 1994).
31. David C. McClelland, *The Achieving Society* (New York: Van Nostrand, 1961).
32. Paulette Thomas, "Entrepreneurs' Biggest Problems—and How They Solve Them," *Wall Street Journal* (March 17, 2003).
33. Definition based on Albert R. Hunt, "Social Entrepreneurs: Compassionate and Tough-Minded," *Wall Street Journal* (July 13, 2000); David Puttnam, "Hearts Before Pockets," *New Statesman* (February 9, 2004): 26; and Christian Seelos and Johanna Mair, "Social Entrepreneurship: Creating New Business Models to Serve the Poor," *Business Horizons* 48 (2005): 241–246.
34. Cheryl Dahle, "Filling the Void: The 2006 Social Capitalist Award Winners," *Fast Company* (January–February 2006): 50–61.
35. Puttnam, "Hearts Before Pockets."
36. Jessica Harris, "Ethics in a Bottle," *FSB* (November 2007): 44.
37. Cheryl Dahle, "The Change Masters," *Fast Company* (January 2005): 47–58; David Bornstein, *How to Change the World: Social Entrepreneurs and the Power of New Ideas* (Oxford: Oxford University Press, 2004).
38. James Flanigan, "Small Businesses Offer Alternatives to Gang Life," *New York Times,* March 20, 2008 (www.nytimes.com/2008/03/20/business/smallbusiness/20edge.html) (accessed June 23, 2008).
39. Leslie Brokaw, "How to Start an *Inc.* 500 Company," *Inc.* 500 (1994): 51–65.
40. Interview with Phaedra Hise, "A Chance to Prove My Worth," *FSB* (February 2007): 26.
41. Paul Reynolds, "The Truth About Start-Ups," *Inc.* (February 1995): 23; Brian O'Reilly, "The New Face of Small Businesses," *Fortune* (May 2, 1994): 82–88.
42. Based on Ellyn E. Spragins, "How to Write a Business Plan That Will Get You in the Door," *Small Business Success* (November 1990); Linda Elkins, "Tips for Preparing a Business Plan," *Nation's Business* (June 1996): 60R–61R; Carolyn M. Brown, "The Do's and Don'ts of Writing a Winning Business Plan," *Black Enterprise* (April 1996): 114–116; and Kuratko and Hodgetts, *Entrepreneurship,* 295–397. For a clear, thorough, step-by-step guide to writing an effective business plan, see Linda Pinson and Jerry Jinnett, *Anatomy of a Business Plan,* 5th ed. (Virginia Beach, VA: Dearborn, 2001).
43. The INC. FAXPOLL, *Inc.* (February 1992): 24.
44. Duncan MacVicar, "Ten Steps to a High-Tech Start-Up," *Industrial Physicist* (October 1999): 27–31.
45. "Venture Capitalists' Criteria" *Management Review* (November 1985): 7–8.
46. "Staples Makes Big Business from Helping Small Businesses," *SBA Success Stories* (www.sba.gov/successstories.html) (accessed on March 12, 2004); Staples (www.staples.com/sbd/content/about/media/overview.html) (accessed July 16, 2008).

47. Elizabeth Olson, "From One Business to 23 Million," *New York Times*, March 7, 2004 (http://query.nytimes.com/gst/fullpage.html?res=9C03E6D6113FF934A35750C0A9629CB63) (accessed July 16, 2008).

48. "Where the Venture Money Is Going," *Business 2.0* (January–February 2004): 98.

49. Gary Rivlin, "Does the Kid Stay in the Picture?" *New York Times*, February 22, 2005.

50. Dent, "The Next Black Power Movement."

51. Kristen Hampshire, "Roll With It," *FSB* (November 2005): 108–112; Jennifer Maxwell profile in Betsy Wiesendanger, "Labors of Love," *Working Woman* (May 1999): 43–56; Jena McGregor, Taryn Rose profile in "25 Top Women Business Builders," *Fast Company* (May 2005): 67–75.

52. Wendy Lea, "Dancing with a Partner," *Fast Company* (March 2000): 159–161.

53. Matt Richtel, "Outsourced All the Way," *New York Times*, June 21, 2005 (www.nytimes.com).

54. International Franchise Association (www.franchise.org/) (accessed June 23, 2008).

55. Quinne Bryant, "Who Owns 20+Subway Franchises?" *Business Journal of Tri-Cities Tennessee/Virginia* (August 2003): 42–43.

56. For a current discussion of the risks and disadvantages of owning a franchise, see Anne Fisher, "Risk Reward," *FSB* (December 2005–January 2006): 44.

57. Anne Field, "Your Ticket to a New Career? Franchising Can Put Your Skills to Work in Your Own Business," in *Business Week Investor: Small Business* section, *BusinessWeek* (May 12, 2003): 100+; and Roberta Maynard, "Choosing a Franchise," *Nation's Business* (October 1996): 56–63.

58. Darren Dahl, "Getting Started: Percolating Profits." *Inc.* (February 2005): 38.

59. 2006 figures from the National Business Incubation Association (www.nbia.org/resource_center/bus_inc_facts/index.php/) (accessed July 16, 2008).

60. Oringel, "Sowing Success."

61. Laura Novak, "For Women, a Recipe to Create a Successful Business," *New York Times*, June 23, 2007 (www.nytimes.com/2007/06/23/business/smallbusiness/23cocina.html?_r=1&sq=Laura%20Novak,%20â€œFor%20Women,%20a%20Recipe%20to%20Create%20a%20Successful%20Business&st=cse&adxnnl=1&oref=slogin&scp=1&adxnnlx=1225894278=APkyZ4kswGDrm3QtejIg6A) (accessed June 23, 2008).

62. Sue Shellenbarger, "The Job That Follows You Wherever You May Roam," *Wall Street Journal* online (http://online.wsj.com/public/us) (accessed July 10, 2008).

63. Chuck Salter, "Girl Power," *Fast Company* (September, 2007): 104.

64. Ellen Simon, "Starting Simple," *Miami Herald*, November 13, 2007.

65. Jason R. Rich, *Unofficial Guide to Starting a Business Online*, 2nd ed. (New York: Wiley, 2006): 116.

66. Ellen Reid Smith, *e-loyalty: How to Keep Customers Coming Back to Your Website* (New York: HarperCollins, 2000): 19.

67. Ibid, 127.

68. Susan G. Hauser, "Nagging for Dollars," *FSB* (September 2007): 76.

69. Carrie Dolan, "Entrepreneurs Often Fail as Managers," *Wall Street Journal*, May 15, 1989.

70. George Mannes, "Don't Give Up on the Web," *Fortune* (March 5, 2001): 184B–184L.

71. Bridgett Finn, "Selling Cool in a Bottle," *Business 2.0* (December 1, 2003) (http://money.cnn.com/magazines/business2/business2_archive/2003/12/01/354202/index.htm) (accessed November 5, 2008).

72. Amanda Walmac, "Full of Beans," *Working Woman* (February 1999): 38–40.

73. Udayan Gupta and Jeffery A. Tannenbaum, "Labor Shortages Force Changes at Small Firms," *Wall Street Journal*, May 22, 1989; "Harnessing Employee Productivity," *Small Business Report* (November 1987): 46–49; and Molly Kilmas, "How to Recruit a Smart Team," *Nation's Business* (May 1995): 26–27.

74. Saul Hansell, "Listen Up! It's Time for a Profit: A Front Row Seat as Amazon Gets Serious," *New York Times*, May 20, 2001.

360-degree feedback A process that uses multiple raters, including self-rating, to appraise employee performance and guide development.

A

accountability The fact that the people with authority and responsibility are subject to reporting and justifying task outcomes to those above them in the chain of command.

achievement culture A results-oriented culture that values competitiveness, personal initiative, and achievement.

adaptability culture A Culture that is characterized by values that support a company's ability to interpret and translate signals from the environment into new behavior responses.

adjourning The stage of team development in which members prepare for the team's disbandment.

administrative model A decision-making model that describes how managers actually make decisions in situations characterized by nonprogrammed decisions, uncertainty, and ambiguity.

administrative principles A subfield of the classical management perspective that focuses on the total organization rather than the individual worker, delineating the management functions of planning, organizing, commanding, coordinating, and controlling.

affirmative action A policy requiring employers to take positive steps to guarantee equal employment opportunities for people within protected groups.

alienated follower A person who is an independent, critical thinker but is passive in the organization.

ambidextrous approach Incorporating structures and processes that are appropriate for both the creative impulse and for the systematic implementation of innovations.

ambiguity A condition in which the goals to be achieved or the problem to be solved is unclear, alternatives are difficult to define, and information about outcomes is unavailable.

angel financing Financing provided by a wealthy individual who believes in the idea for a start-up and provides personal funds and advice to help the business get started.

application form A device for collecting information about an applicant's education, previous job experience, and other background characteristics.

assessment center A technique for selecting individuals with high managerial potential based on their performance on a series of simulated managerial tasks.

attitude A cognitive and affective evaluation that predisposes a person to act in a certain way.

attributions Judgments about what caused a person's behavior—either characteristics of the person or of the situation.

authentic leadership Leadership by individuals who know and understand themselves, who act consistently with higher order ethical values, and who empower and inspire others with their openness and authenticity.

authoritarianism The belief that power and status differences should exist within the organization.

authority The formal and legitimate right of a manager to make decisions, issue orders, and allocate resources to achieve organizationally desired outcomes.

avoidance learning The removal of an unpleasant consequence when an undesirable behavior is corrected.

B

balance sheet A financial statement that shows the firm's financial position with respect to assets and liabilities at a specific point in time.

balanced scorecard A comprehensive management control system that balances traditional financial measures with measures of customer service, internal business processes, and the organization's capacity for learning and growth.

behavior modification The set of techniques by which reinforcement theory is used to modify human behavior.

behavioral sciences approach A subfield of the humanistic management perspective that applies social science in an organizational context, drawing from economics, psychology, sociology, and other disciplines.

behaviorally anchored rating scale (BARS) A rating technique that relates an employee's performance to specific job-related incidents.

benchmarking The continuous process of measuring products, services, and practices against major competitors or industry leaders.

Big Five personality factors Dimensions that describe an individual's extroversion, agreeableness, conscientiousness, emotional stability, and openness to experience.

bottom of the pyramid (BOP) A concept that proposes corporations can alleviate poverty and other social ills, as well as make significant profits, by selling to the world's poor.

bottom-up budgeting A budgeting process in which lower-level managers budget their departments' resource needs and pass them up to top management for approval.

bounded rationality The concept that people have the time and cognitive ability to process only a limited amount of information on which to base decisions.

brainstorming A technique that uses a face-to-face group to spontaneously suggest a broad range of alternatives for decision making.

bureaucratic organizations A subfield of the classical management perspective that emphasizes management on an impersonal, rational basis through such elements as clearly defined authority and responsibility, formal record-keeping, and separation of management and ownership.

business incubator An innovation that provides shared office space, management support services, and management advice to entrepreneurs.

business plan A document specifying the business details prepared by an entrepreneur prior to opening a new business.

C

capital budget A budget that plans and reports investments in major assets to be depreciated over several years.

cash budget A budget that estimates and reports cash flows on a daily or weekly basis to ensure that the company has sufficient cash to meet its obligations.

centralization The location of decision authority near top organizational levels.

centralized network A team communication structure in which team members communicate through a single individual to solve problems or make decisions.

ceremony A planned activity at a special event that is conducted for the benefit of an audience.

certainty The situation in which all the information the decision maker needs is fully available.

chain of command An unbroken line of authority that links all individuals in the organization and specifies who reports to whom.

change agent An OD specialist who contracts with an organization to facilitate change.

changing The intervention stage of organization development in which individuals experiment with new workplace behavior.

channel The carrier of a communication.

channel richness The amount of information that can be transmitted during a communication episode.

charismatic leader A leader who has the ability to motivate subordinates to transcend their expected performance.

chief ethics officer A company executive who oversees ethics and legal compliance.

classical model A decision-making model based on the assumption that managers should make logical decisions that will be in the organization's best economic interests.

classical perspective A management perspective that emerged during the nineteenth and early twentieth centuries that emphasized a rational, scientific approach to the study of management and sought to make organizations efficient operating machines.

coaching A method of directing, instructing, and training a person with the goal to develop specific management skills.

coalition An informal alliance among managers who support a specific goal.

code of ethics A formal statement of the organization's values regarding ethics and social issues.

coercive power Power that stems from the authority to punish or recommend punishment.

cognitive dissonance A condition in which two attitudes, or a behavior and an attitude, conflict.

collectivism A preference for a tightly knit social framework in which individuals look after one another and organizations protect their members' interests.

committee A long-lasting, sometimes permanent team in the organization structure created to deal with tasks that recur regularly.

communication The process by which information is exchanged and understood by two or more people, usually with the intent to motivate or influence behavior.

communication apprehension An individual's level of fear or anxiety associated with interpersonal communications.

compensation Monetary payments (wages, salaries) and nonmonetary goods/commodities (benefits, vacations) used to reward employees.

compensatory justice The concept that individuals should be compensated for the cost of their injuries by the party responsible and also that individuals should not be held responsible for matters over which they have no control.

competitive advantage What sets the organization apart from others and provides it with a distinctive edge in the marketplace.

competitors Other organizations in the same industry or type of business that provide goods or services to the same set of customers.

conflict Antagonistic interaction in which one party attempts to thwart the intentions or goals of another.

conformist A follower who participates actively in the organization, but does not use critical thinking skills.

consideration A type of leader behavior that describes the extent to which the leader is sensitive to subordinates, respects their ideas and feelings, and establishes mutual trust.

consistency culture A culture that values and rewards a methodical, rational, orderly way of doing things.

content theories A group of theories that emphasize the needs that motivate people.

contingency approach A model of leadership that describes the relationship between leadership styles and specific organizational situations.

contingency plans Plans that define company responses to specific situations, such as emergencies, setbacks, or unexpected conditions.

contingency view An extension of the humanistic perspective in which the successful resolution of organizational problems is thought to depend on managers' identification of key variations in the situation at hand.

contingent workers People who work for an organization, but not on a permanent or full-time basis, including temporary placements, contracted professionals, or leased employees.

continuous improvement The implementation of a large number of small, incremental improvements in all areas of the organization on an ongoing basis.

continuous process production Mechanization of the entire workflow and nonstop production, such as in chemical plants or petroleum refineries.

coordination The quality of collaboration across departments.

core competence A business activity that an organization does particularly well in comparison to competitors.

corporate governance The system of governing an organization to ensure accountability, fairness, and transparency in the organization's relationships with stakeholders.

corporate social responsibility The obligation of organization management to make decisions and take actions that will enhance the welfare and interests of society as well as the organization.

corporate university An in-house training and education facility that offers broad-based learning opportunities for employees.

corporation An artificial entity created by the state and existing apart from its owners.

countertrade The barter of products for other products rather than their sale for currency.

creativity The generation of novel ideas that might meet perceived needs or offer opportunities for the organization.

critical thinking Thinking independently and being mindful of the effect of one's behavior on achieving goals.

cross-functional team A group of employees from various functional departments that meet as a team to resolve mutual problems.

cultural competence The ability to interact effectively with people of different cultures.

cultural intelligence (CQ) A person's ability to use reasoning and observation skills to interpret unfamiliar gestures and situations and devise appropriate behavioral responses.

cultural leader A manager who uses signals and symbols to influence corporate culture.

culture The set of key values, beliefs, understandings, and norms that members of an organization share.

culture change A major shift in the norms, values, attitudes, and mind-set of the entire organization.

culture shock Feelings of confusion, disorientation, and anxiety that result from being immersed in a foreign culture.

customer relationship management (CRM) Systems that help companies keep in close touch with customers, collect and manage customer data, and collaborate with customers to provide the most valuable products and services.

customers People and organizations in the environment that acquire goods or services from the organization.

cycle time The steps taken to complete a company process.

D

debt financing Borrowing money that has to be repaid at a later date in order to start a business.

decentralization The location of decision authority near lower organizational levels.

decentralized control The use of organizational culture, group norms, and a focus on goals, rather than rules and procedures, to foster compliance with organizational goals.

decentralized network A team communication structure in which team members freely communicate with one another and arrive at decisions together.

decentralized planning Managers work with planning experts to develop their own goals and plans.

decision A choice made from available alternatives.

decision making The process of identifying problems and opportunities and then resolving them.

decision styles Differences among people with respect to how they perceive problems and make decisions.

decode To translate the symbols used in a message for the purpose of interpreting its meaning.

delegation The process managers use to transfer authority and responsibility to positions below them in the hierarchy.

departmentalization The basis on which individuals are grouped into departments, and departments into the total organization.

descriptive An approach that describes how managers actually make decisions rather than how they should make decisions according to a theoretical ideal.

devil's advocate A decision-making technique in which an individual is assigned the role of challenging the assumptions and assertions made by the group, to prevent premature consensus.

diagnosis The step in the decision-making process in which managers analyze underlying causal factors associated with the decision situation.

digital technology The use of the Internet and other digital processes to conduct or support business operations.

discretionary responsibility Organizational responsibility that is voluntary and guided by the organization's desire to make social contributions not mandated by economics, law, or ethics.

discrimination The hiring or promoting of applicants based on criteria that are not job relevant.

disruptive innovation Innovations in products, services, or processes that radically change competition in an industry, such as the advent of CDs or digital cameras.

distributive justice The concept that different treatment of people should not be based on arbitrary characteristics. In the case of substantive differences, people should be treated differently in proportion to the differences among them.

distributive negotiation A competitive and adversarial negotiation approach in which each party strives to get as much as it can, usually at the expense of the other party.

diversity All the ways in which employees differ.

diversity training Special training designed to educate employees about the importance of diversity, make people aware of their own biases, and teach them skills for communicating and working in a diverse workplace.

divisional structure An organization structure in which departments are grouped based on similar organizational outputs.

downward communication Messages sent from top management down to subordinates.

E

E → P expectancy Expectancy that putting effort into a given task will lead to high performance.

economic dimension The dimension of the general environment representing the overall economic health of the country or region in which the organization operates.

economic forces Forces that affect the availability, production, and distribution of a society's resources among competing users.

effective follower A critical, independent thinker who actively participates in the organization.

effectiveness The degree to which the organization achieves a stated goal.

efficiency The use of minimal resources—raw materials, money, and people—to produce a desired volume of output.

electronic brainstorming Bringing people together in an interactive group over a computer network to suggest alternatives; sometimes called *brainwriting*.

emotion A mental state that arises spontaneously rather than through conscious effort and is often accompanied by physiological changes.

employee network groups Groups based on social identity, such as gender or race, and organized by employees to focus on concerns of employees from that group.

employment test A written or computer-based test designed to measure a particular attribute such as intelligence or aptitude.

empowerment The delegation of power and authority to subordinates.

encode To select symbols with which to compose a message.

engagement A situation in which employees enjoy their work, contribute enthusiastically to meeting goals, and feel a sense of belonging and commitment to the organization.

entrepreneur Someone who recognizes a viable idea for a business product or service and carries it out.

entrepreneurship The process of initiating a business venture, organizing the necessary resources, and assuming the associated risks and rewards.

equity A situation that exists when the ratio of one person's outcomes to inputs equals that of another's.

equity financing Financing that consists of funds that are invested in exchange for ownership in the company.

equity theory A process motivation theory that focuses on individuals' perceptions of how fairly they are treated relative to others.

ERG theory A modification of the needs hierarchy theory that proposes three categories of needs: existence, relatedness, and growth.

escalating commitment Continuing to invest time and resources in a failing decision.

ethical dilemma A situation that arises when all alternative choices or behaviors are deemed undesirable because of potentially negative consequences, making it difficult to distinguish right from wrong.

ethics The code of moral principles and values that governs the behaviors of a person or group with respect to what is right or wrong.

ethics committee A group of executives assigned to oversee the organization's ethics by ruling on questionable issues and disciplining violators.

ethics training Training programs to help employees deal with ethical questions and values.

ethnocentrism A cultural attitude marked by the tendency to regard one's own culture as superior to others.

ethnorelativism The belief that groups and subcultures are inherently equal.

euro A single European currency that replaced the currencies of 16 European nations.

exit interview An interview conducted with departing employees to determine the reasons for and thoughts about their termination.

expectancy theory A process theory that proposes that motivation depends on individuals' expectations about their ability to perform tasks and receive desired rewards.

expense budget A budget that outlines the anticipated and actual expenses for a responsibility center.

expert power Power that stems from special knowledge of or skill in the tasks performed by subordinates.

exporting A market entry strategy in which the organization maintains its production facilities within its home country and transfers its products for sale in foreign countries.

extinction The withholding of a positive reward.

extrinsic reward A reward given by another person.

F

fast-cycle team A multifunctional team that is provided with high levels of resources and empowerment to accomplish an accelerated product development project.

feedback A response by the receiver to the sender's communication.

femininity A cultural preference for relationships, cooperation, group decision making, and quality of life.

flat structure A management structure characterized by an overall broad span of control and relatively few hierarchical levels.

force-field analysis The process of determining which forces drive and which resist a proposed change.

formal communication channel A communication channel that flows within the chain of command or task responsibility defined by the organization.

formal team A team created by the organization as part of the formal organization structure.

forming The stage of team development characterized by orientation and acquaintance.

franchising An arrangement by which the owner of a product or service allows others to purchase the right to distribute the product or service with help from the owner.

free rider A person who benefits from team membership, but does not make a proportionate contribution to the team's work.

frustration-regression principle The idea that failure to meet a high-order need may cause a regression to an already satisfied lower-order need.

functional structure The grouping of positions into departments based on similar skills, expertise, and resource use.

fundamental attribution error The tendency to underestimate the influence of external factors on another's behavior and to overestimate the influence of internal factors.

G

general environment The layer of the external environment that affects the organization indirectly.

glass ceiling Invisible barrier that separates women and minorities from top management positions.

global outsourcing Engaging in the international division of labor so as to obtain the cheapest sources of labor and supplies regardless of country; also called *offshoring*.

global team A work team made up of members of different nationalities whose activities span multiple countries; may operate as a virtual team or meet face-to-face.

globalization The extent to which trade and investments, information, ideas, and political cooperation flow between countries.

goal A desired future state that the organization attempts to realize.

goal-setting theory A motivation theory in which specific, challenging goals increase motivation and performance when the goals are accepted by subordinates and these subordinates receive feedback to indicate their progress toward goal achievement.

grapevine An informal, person-to-person communication network of employees that is not officially sanctioned by the organization.

groupthink The tendency of people in groups to suppress contrary opinions.

H

halo effect A type of rating error that occurs when an employee receives the same rating on all dimensions regardless of his or her performance on individual ones.

Hawthorne studies A series of experiments on worker productivity, begun in 1924 at the Hawthorne plant of Western Electric Company in Illinois, which attributed employees' increased output to managers' better treatment of them during the study.

hero A figure who exemplifies the deeds, character, and attributes of a strong corporate culture.

hierarchical control The use of rules, policies, hierarchy of authority, reward systems, and other formal devices to influence employee behavior and assess performance.

hierarchy of needs theory A content theory that proposes that people are motivated by five categories of needs—physiological, safety, belongingness, esteem, and self-actualization—that exist in a hierarchical order.

high-context culture A culture in which communication is used to enhance personal relationships.

high-performance culture A culture based on a solid organizational mission or purpose that uses shared adaptive values to guide decisions and business practices and to encourage individual employee ownership of both bottom-line results and the organization's cultural backbone.

horizontal communication The lateral or diagonal exchange of messages among peers or coworkers.

horizontal linkage model An approach to product change that emphasizes shared development of innovations among several departments.

horizontal team A formal team composed of employees from about the same hierarchical level but from different areas of expertise.

human capital The economic value of the knowledge, experience, skills, and capabilities of employees.

human relations movement A movement in management thinking and practice that emphasizes satisfaction of employees' basic needs as the key to increased worker productivity.

human resource management (HRM) Activities undertaken to attract, develop, and maintain an effective workforce within an organization.

human resource planning The forecasting of human resource needs and the projected matching of individuals with expected job vacancies.

human resources perspective A management perspective that suggests jobs should be designed to meet higher-level needs by allowing workers to use their full potential.

humility Being unpretentious and modest rather than arrogant and prideful.

hygiene factors Factors that involve the presence or absence of job dissatisfiers, including working conditions, pay, company policies, and interpersonal relationships.

I

idea champion A person who sees the need for and champions productive change within the organization.

idea incubator An in-house program that provides a safe harbor where ideas from employees throughout the organization can be developed without interference from company bureaucracy or politics.

implementation The step in the decision-making process that involves using managerial, administrative, and persuasive abilities to translate the chosen alternative into action.

income statement A financial statement that summarizes the firm's financial performance for a given time interval; sometimes called a *profit-and-loss statement*.

individualism A preference for a loosely knit social framework in which individuals are expected to take care of themselves.

individualism approach The ethical concept that acts are moral when they promote the individual's best long-term interests.

influence The effect a person's actions have on the attitudes, values, beliefs, or behavior of others.

infrastructure A country's physical facilities that support economic activities.

initiating structure A type of leader behavior that describes the extent to which the leader is task oriented and directs subordinate work activities toward goal attainment.

instant messaging (IM) Electronic communication that allows users to see who is connected to a network and share information instantly.

integrative negotiation A collaborative approach to negotiation that is based on a win–win assumption, whereby the parties want to come up with a creative solution that benefits both sides of the conflict.

interactive leadership A leadership style characterized by values such as inclusion, collaboration, relationship building, and caring.

interim manager A manager who is not affiliated with a specific organization, but works on a project-by-project basis or provides expertise to organizations in a specific area.

internal environment The environment that includes the elements within the organization's boundaries.

international dimension Portion of the external environment that represents events originating in foreign countries, as well as opportunities for U.S. companies in other countries.

international management The management of business operations conducted in more than one country.

intrinsic reward The satisfaction received in the process of performing an action.

intuition The immediate comprehension of a decision situation based on past experience but without conscious thought.

involvement culture A culture that places high value on meeting the needs of employees and values cooperation and equality.

ISO 9000 Standards A set of standards that represent an international consensus of what constitutes effective quality management, as outlined by the International Organization for Standardization.

J

job analysis The systematic process of gathering and interpreting information about the essential duties, tasks, and responsibilities of a job.

job characteristics model A model of job design that comprises core job dimensions, critical psychological states, and employee growth-need strength.

job description A concise summary of the specific tasks and responsibilities of a particular job.

job enrichment A job design that incorporates achievement, recognition, and other high-level motivators into the work.

job evaluation The process of determining the value of jobs within an organization through an examination of job content.

job satisfaction A positive attitude toward one's job.

job specification An outline of the knowledge, skills, education, and physical abilities needed to adequately perform a job.

joint venture A variation of direct investment in which an organization shares costs and risks with another firm to build a manufacturing facility, develop new products, or set up a sales and distribution network.

justice approach The ethical concept that moral decisions must be based on standards of equity, fairness, and impartiality.

L

labor market The people available for hire by the organization.

large-group intervention An approach that brings together participants from all parts of the organization (and may include key outside stakeholders as well) to discuss problems or opportunities and plan for major change.

law of effect The assumption that positively reinforced behavior tends to be repeated, and unreinforced or negatively reinforced behavior tends to be inhibited.

leadership The ability to influence people toward the attainment of organizational goals.

leadership grid A two-dimensional leadership theory that measures the leader's concern for people and for production.

learning A change in behavior or performance that occurs as the result of experience.

legal-political dimension The dimension of the general environment that includes federal, state, and local government regulations and political activities designed to influence company behavior.

legitimate power Power that stems from a formal management position in an organization and the authority granted to it.

line authority A form of authority in which individuals in management positions have the formal power to direct and control immediate subordinates.

listening The skill of receiving messages to accurately grasp facts and feelings in order to interpret the genuine meaning.

locus of control The tendency to place the primary responsibility for one's success or failure either within oneself (internally) or on outside forces (externally).

long-term orientation A greater concern for the future and high value on thrift and perseverance.

low-context culture A culture in which communication is used to exchange facts and information.

M

Machiavellianism The tendency to direct much of one's behavior toward the acquisition of power and the manipulation of other people for personal gain.

management The attainment of organizational goals in an effective and efficient manner through planning, organizing, leading, and controlling organizational resources.

managing diversity Creating a climate in which the potential advantages of diversity for organizational or group performance are maximized, while the potential disadvantages are minimized.

market entry strategy An organizational strategy for entering a foreign market.

masculinity A cultural preference for achievement, heroism, assertiveness, work centrality, and material success.

mass production Long production runs used to manufacture a large volume of products with the same specifications.

matching model An employee selection approach in which the organization and the applicant attempt to match each other's needs, interests, and values.

matrix approach An organization structure that uses functional and divisional chains of command simultaneously in the same part of the organization.

matrix boss The product or functional boss responsible for one side of the matrix.

mediation The process of using a third party to settle a dispute.

mentor A higher-ranking, senior organizational member who is committed to providing upward mobility and support to a protégé's professional career.

mentoring When an experienced employee guides and supports a less experienced employee.

merger The combining of two or more organizations into one.

message The tangible formulation of an idea to be sent to a receiver.

mission The organization's reason for existence.

mission statement A broadly stated definition of the organization's basic business scope and operations that distinguishes it from similar types of organizations.

modular approach The process by which a manufacturing company uses outside suppliers to provide large components of the product, which are then assembled into a final product by a few workers.

monoculture A culture that accepts only one way of doing things and one set of values and beliefs.

moral-rights approach The ethical concept that moral decisions are those that best maintain the rights of those people affected by them.

motivation The arousal, direction, and persistence of behavior.

motivators Factors that influence job satisfaction based on fulfillment of high-level needs such as achievement, recognition, responsibility, and opportunity for growth.

multicultural teams Teams made up of members from diverse national, racial, ethnic, and cultural backgrounds.

Myers–Briggs Type Indicator (MBTI) Personality test that measures a person's preference for introversion vs. extroversion, sensation vs. intuition, thinking vs. feeling, and judging vs. perceiving.

N

natural dimension The dimension of the general environment that includes all elements that occur naturally on earth, including plants, animals, rocks, and natural resources such as air, water, and climate.

need for change A disparity between existing and desired performance levels.

need to achieve A human quality linked to entrepreneurship, in which people are motivated to excel and pick situations in which success is likely.

negotiation A conflict management strategy whereby people engage in give-and-take discussions and consider various alternatives to reach a joint decision that is acceptable to both parties.

neutralizer A situational variable that counteracts a leadership style and prevents the leader from displaying certain behaviors.

new-venture fund A fund providing resources from which individuals and groups can draw to develop new ideas, products, or businesses.

new-venture team A unit separate from the mainstream of the organization that is responsible for initiating and developing innovations.

nondirective interview An approach in which the interviewer asks broad, open-ended questions and permits the applicant to talk freely with minimal interruption.

nonprogrammed decision A decision made in response to a situation that is unique, is poorly defined and largely unstructured, and has important consequences for the organization.

nonverbal communication A communication transmitted through actions and behaviors rather than through words.

normative An approach that defines how a decision maker should make decisions and provides guidelines for reaching an ideal outcome for the organization.

norming The stage of team development in which conflicts developed during the storming stage are resolved, and team harmony and unity emerge.

O

on-the-job training (OJT) A type of training in which an experienced employee "adopts" a new employee to teach him or her how to perform job duties.

open innovation Extending the search for and commercialization of new ideas beyond the boundaries of the organization.

open-book management Sharing financial information and results with all employees in the organization.

operational goals Specific, measurable results expected from departments, work groups, and individuals within the organization.

operational plans Plans developed at the organization's lower levels that specify action steps toward achieving operational goals and that support tactical planning activities.

opportunity A situation in which managers see potential organizational accomplishments that exceed current goals.

organization A social entity that is goal directed and deliberately structured.

organization chart The visual representation of an organization's structure.

organization development (OD) The application of behavioral science techniques to improve an organization's health and effectiveness through its ability to cope with environmental changes, improve internal relationships, and increase learning and problem-solving capabilities.

organization structure The framework in which the organization defines how tasks are divided, resources are deployed, and departments are coordinated.

organizational behavior An interdisciplinary field dedicated to the study of how individuals and groups tend to act in organizations.

organizational change The adoption of a new idea or behavior by an organization.

organizational citizenship Work behavior that goes beyond job requirements and contributes as needed to the organization's success.

organizational commitment Loyalty to and heavy involvement in one's organization.

organizational control The systematic process through which managers regulate organizational activities to make them consistent with expectations established in plans, targets, and standards of performance.

organizational environment All elements existing outside the organization's boundaries that have the potential to affect the organization.

organizing The management function concerned with assigning tasks, grouping tasks into departments, and allocating resources to departments.

outsourcing Contracting out selected functions or activities of an organization to other organizations that can do the work more cost efficiently.

P

P → O expectancy Expectancy that successful performance of a task will lead to the desired outcome.

panel interview An interview in which the candidate meets with several interviewers who take turns asking questions.

partnership An unincorporated business owned by two or more people.

passive follower A person who exhibits neither critical independent thinking nor active participation.

pay-for-performance Incentive pay that ties at least part of compensation to employee effort and performance.

people change A change in the attitudes and behaviors of a few employees in the organization.

perception The cognitive process people use to make sense out of the environment by selecting, organizing, and interpreting information.

perceptual defense The tendency of perceivers to protect themselves by disregarding ideas, objects, or people that are threatening to them.

perceptual distortions Errors in perceptual judgment that arise from inaccuracies in any part of the perceptual process.

perceptual selectivity The process by which individuals screen and select the various stimuli that vie for their attention.

performance The organization's ability to attain its goals by using resources in an efficient and effective manner.

performance appraisal The process of observing and evaluating an employee's performance, recording the assessment, and providing feedback to the employee.

performing The stage of team development in which members focus on problem solving and accomplishing the team's assigned task.

permanent team A group of participants from several functions who are permanently assigned to solve ongoing problems of common interest.

personal communication channels Communication channels that exist outside the formally authorized channels and do not adhere to the organization's hierarchy of authority.

personal networking The acquisition and cultivation of personal relationships that cross departmental, hierarchical, and even organizational boundaries.

personality The set of characteristics that underlie a relatively stable pattern of behavior in response to ideas, objects, or people in the environment.

plan A blueprint specifying the resource allocations, schedules, and other actions necessary for attaining goals.

planning The management function concerned with defining goals for future organizational performance and deciding on the tasks and resources needed to attain them.

pluralism An environment in which the organization accommodates several subcultures, including employees who would otherwise feel isolated and ignored.

point–counterpoint A decision-making technique in which people are assigned to express competing points of view.

political forces The influence of political and legal institutions on people and organizations.

political instability Events such as riots, revolutions, or government upheavals that affect the operations of an international company.

political risk A company's risk of loss of assets, earning power, or managerial control due to politically based events or actions by host governments.

positive reinforcement The administration of a pleasant and rewarding consequence following a desired behavior.

power The potential ability to influence others' behavior.

power distance The degree to which people accept inequality in power among institutions, organizations, and people.

practical approach The ethical concept that sidesteps debates about what is right, good, or just, and bases decisions on prevailing standards of the profession and the larger society, taking the interests of all stakeholders into account.

pragmatic survivor A follower who has qualities of all four follower styles, depending on which fits the prevalent situation.

prejudice The tendency to view people who are different as being deficient.

pressure group An interest group that works within the legal-political framework to influence companies to behave in socially responsible ways.

problem A situation in which organizational accomplishments have failed to meet established goals.

procedural justice The ethical concept that rules should be clearly stated and consistently and impartially enforced.

process theories A group of motivation theories that explain how employees select behaviors with which to meet their needs and determine whether their choices were successful.

product change A change in the organization's product or service outputs.

programmed decision A decision made in response to a situation that has occurred often enough to enable decision rules to be developed and applied in the future.

project manager A person responsible for coordinating the activities of several departments on a full-time basis for the completion of a specific project; it also refers to a manager responsible for a temporary work project that involves the participation of people from various functions and levels of the organization.

projection The tendency to see one's own personal traits in other people.

punishment The imposition of an unpleasant outcome following undesirable behavior.

Q

quality circle A group of 6 to 12 volunteer employees who meet regularly to discuss and solve problems affecting the quality of their work.

quantitative perspective A management perspective that emerged after World War II and applies mathematics, statistical techniques, and other computer technology to facilitate management decision making, particularly for massive and complex problems.

R

realistic job preview A recruiting approach that gives applicants all pertinent and realistic information about the job and the organization.

recruiting The activities or practices that define the desired characteristics of applicants for specific jobs.

reengineering The radical redesign of business processes to achieve dramatic improvements in cost, quality, service, and speed.

referent power Power that results from characteristics that command subordinates' identification with, respect and admiration for, and desire to emulate the leader.

refreezing The reinforcement stage of organization development in which individuals acquire a desired new skill or attitude and are rewarded for it by the organization.

reinforcement Anything that causes a given behavior to be repeated or inhibited.

reinforcement theory A motivation theory based on the relationship between a given behavior and its consequences.

relationship conflict Interpersonal incompatibility that creates tension and personal animosity.

responsibility The duty to perform the task or activity an employee has been assigned.

responsibility center An organizational unit under the supervision of a single person who is responsible for its activity.

revenue budget A budget that identifies the forecasted and actual revenues of the organization.

reward power Power that results from the authority to bestow rewards on other people.

rightsizing Intentionally reducing the company's workforce to the point where the number of employees is deemed to be right for the company's current situation.

risk A situation in which a decision has clear-cut goals and good information is available, but the future outcomes associated with each alternative are subject to chance.

risk propensity The willingness to undertake risk with the opportunity of gaining an increased payoff.

role A set of expectations for one's behavior.

role ambiguity Uncertainty about what behaviors are expected of a person in a particular role.

role conflict Incompatible demands of different roles.

S

satisficing To choose the first solution alternative that satisfies minimal decision criteria, regardless of whether better solutions are presumed to exist.

scenario building Looking at trends and discontinuities and imagining possible alternative futures, to build a framework within which unexpected future events can be managed.

scientific management A subfield of the classical management perspective that emphasizes scientifically determined changes in management practices as the solution to improving labor productivity.

selection The process of determining the skills, abilities, and other attributes a person needs to perform a particular job.

self-confidence General assurance in one's own ideas, judgment, and capabilities.

self-directed teams A group of multiskilled employees who rotate jobs to produce an entire product or service, often led by an elected team member.

self-reinforcement Motivating oneself by setting goals and ways of reaching them and then providing positive reinforcement when goals are achieved.

self-serving bias The tendency to overestimate the contribution of internal factors to one's successes and the contribution of external factors to one's failures.

servant leader A leader who works to fulfill subordinates' needs and goals as well as to achieve the organization's larger mission.

service technology Intangible outputs and direct contact between employees and customers.

short-term orientation A concern with the past and present and a high value on meeting social obligations.

situational model A contingency approach to leadership that links the leader's behavioral style with the task readiness of subordinates.

Six Sigma A quality control approach that emphasizes a relentless pursuit of higher quality and lower costs.

skunkworks A separate, small, informal, highly autonomous, and often secretive group that focuses on breakthrough ideas for the business.

slogan A phrase or sentence that succinctly expresses a key corporate value.

small-batch production A type of manufacturing technology that involves the production of goods in batches of one or a few products designed to customer specification.

social entrepreneur An entrepreneurial leader who is committed to both good business and changing the world for the better.

social facilitation The tendency for the presence of others to influence an individual's motivation and performance.

social forces The aspects of a culture that guide and influence relationships among people—their values, needs, and standards of behavior.

social learning theory Proposes that an individual's motivation can result not just from direct experience of rewards and punishments but also from thoughts, beliefs, and observations of other people's behavior.

sociocultural dimension The dimension of the general environment representing the demographic characteristics, norms, customs, and values of the population within which the organization operates.

socioemotional role A role in which the individual provides support for team members' emotional needs and social unity.

sole proprietorship An unincorporated business owned by an individual for profit.

span of management The number of employees reporting to a supervisor; also called *span of control.*

special-purpose team A team created outside the formal organization to undertake a project of special importance or creativity.

staff authority A form of authority granted to staff specialists in their area of expertise.

stakeholder Any group within or outside the organization that has a stake in the organization's performance.

stereotype A rigid, exaggerated, irrational belief associated with a particular group of people.

stereotype threat A psychological experience of a person who, when engaged in a task, is aware of a stereotype about his or her identity group, suggesting that he or she will not perform well on that task.

stereotyping The tendency to assign an individual to a group or broad category and then attribute generalizations about the group to the individual.

storming The stage of team development in which individual personalities and roles emerge along with resulting conflicts.

story A narrative based on true events and repeated frequently and shared among organizational employees.

strategic conversation Dialogue across boundaries and hierarchical levels about the team or organization's vision, critical strategic themes, and the values that help achieve important goals.

strategic goals Broad statements of where the organization wants to be in the future; pertain to the organization as a whole rather than to specific divisions or departments.

strategic management The set of decisions and actions used to formulate and implement strategies that will provide a competitively superior fit between the organization and its environment so as to achieve organizational goals.

strategic plans The action steps by which an organization intends to attain strategic goals.

strategy The plan of action that prescribes resource allocation and other activities for dealing with the environment, achieving a competitive advantage, and attaining organizational goals.

strategy execution The stage of strategic management that involves the use of managerial and organizational tools to direct resources toward achieving strategic outcomes.

strategy formulation The stage of strategic management that involves the planning and decision making that lead to the establishment of the organization's goals and of a specific strategic plan.

strengths Natural talents and abilities that have been supported and reinforced with learned knowledge and skills.

stress A physiological and emotional response to stimuli that place physical or psychological demands on an individual.

stretch goal A reasonable yet highly ambitious, compelling goal that energizes people and inspires excellence.

structured interview An interview that uses a set of standardized questions that are asked of every applicant.

substitute A situational variable that makes a leadership style unnecessary or redundant.

subsystems Parts of a system that depend on one another for their functioning.

superordinate goal A goal that cannot be reached by a single party.

suppliers People and organizations that provide the raw materials the organization uses to produce its output.

survey feedback A type of OD intervention in which questionnaires on organizational climate and other factors are distributed among employees and their results reported back to them by a change agent.

sustainability Economic development that generates wealth and meets the needs of the current population while preserving the environment for the needs of future generations.

SWOT analysis Analysis of the strengths, weaknesses, opportunities, and threats (SWOT) that affect organizational performance.

symbol An object, act, or event that conveys meaning to others.

synergy The concept that the whole is greater than the sum of its parts.

system A set of interrelated parts that function as a whole to achieve a common purpose.

systems thinking Seeing both the distinct elements of a system or situation and the complex and changing interaction among those elements.

T

tactical goals Goals that define the outcomes that major divisions and departments must achieve for the organization to reach its overall goals.

tactical plans Plans designed to help execute major strategic plans and to accomplish a specific part of the company's strategy.

tall structure A management structure characterized by an overall narrow span of management and a relatively large number of hierarchical levels.

task conflict Disagreements among people about the goals to be achieved or the content of the tasks to be performed.

task environment The layer of the external environment that directly influences the organization's operations and performance.

task force A temporary team or committee formed to solve a specific short-term problem involving several departments.

task specialist role A role in which the individual devotes personal time and energy to helping the team accomplish its task.

team A unit of two or more people who interact and coordinate their work to accomplish a specific goal.

team building A type of OD intervention that enhances the cohesiveness of departments by helping members learn to function as a team.

team cohesiveness The extent to which team members are attracted to the team and motivated to remain in it.

team norm A standard of conduct that is shared by team members and guides their behavior.

team-based structure Structure in which the entire organization is made up of horizontal teams that coordinate their activities and work directly with customers to accomplish the organization's goals.

technical complexity The degree to which complex machinery is involved in the production process, to the exclusion of people.

technological dimension The dimension of the general environment that includes scientific and technological advancements in the industry and society at large.

technology change A change that pertains to the organization's production process.

telecommuting Using computers and telecommunications equipment to perform work from home or another remote location.

tolerance for ambiguity The psychological characteristic that allows a person to be untroubled by disorder and uncertainty.

top leader In a matrix structure, the overseer of both the product and functional chains of command, responsible for the entire matrix.

top-down budgeting A budgeting process in which middle- and lower-level managers set departmental budget targets in accordance with overall company revenues and expenditures specified by top management.

total quality management (TQM) A concept that focuses on managing the total organization to deliver quality to customers. Four significant elements of TQM are employee involvement, focus on the customer, benchmarking, and continuous improvement.

traits Distinguishing personal characteristics, such as intelligence, values, and appearance.

transactional leader A leader who clarifies subordinates' roles and task requirements, initiates structure, provides rewards, and displays consideration for subordinates.

transformational leader A leader distinguished by a special ability to bring about innovation and change.

two-boss employees In a matrix structure, employees who report to two supervisors simultaneously.

Type A behavior Behavior pattern characterized by extreme competitiveness, impatience, aggressiveness, and devotion to work.

Type B behavior Behavior pattern that lacks Type A characteristics and includes a more balanced, relaxed lifestyle.

U

uncertainty The situation that occurs when managers know which goals they wish to achieve, but information about alternatives and future events is incomplete.

uncertainty avoidance A value characterized by people's intolerance for uncertainty and ambiguity, and resulting support for beliefs that promise certainty and conformity.

uncritical thinking Failing to consider the possibilities beyond what one is told; accepting others' ideas without thinking.

unfreezing The stage of organization development in which participants are made aware of problems, to increase their willingness to change their behavior.

upward communication Messages transmitted from the lower to the higher levels in the organization's hierarchy.

utilitarian approach The ethical concept that moral behaviors produce the greatest good for the greatest number.

V

valence The value or attraction a specific reward or outcome has for an individual.

venture capital firm A group of companies or individuals that invests money in new or expanding businesses, for ownership and potential profits.

vertical team A formal team composed of a manager and his or her subordinates in the organization's formal chain of command.

vicarious learning Occurs when an individual sees others perform certain behaviors and get rewarded for them.

virtual network structure An organization structure that disaggregates major functions to separate companies that are brokered by a small headquarters organization.

virtual team A team made up of members who are geographically or organizationally dispersed, rarely meet face-to-face, and do their work using advanced information technologies.

virtue ethics approach The ethical concept that says moral behavior stems from personal virtues. If a manager develops good character traits and learns to overcome negative traits, he or she will make ethical decisions based on personal virtue.

vision An attractive, ideal future that is credible, yet not readily attainable.

W

wage and salary surveys Surveys that show what other organizations pay incumbents in jobs that match a sample of "key" jobs selected by the organization.

whistle-blowing The disclosure by an employee of illegal, immoral, or illegitimate practices by the organization.

work redesign The altering of jobs to increase both the quality of employees' work experience and their productivity.

work sample test A method for evaluating frontline-position applicants' performance in completing simulated tasks that are a part of the job.

work specialization The degree to which organizational tasks are subdivided into individual jobs; also called *division of labor*.

H

I

J

K

P

Q

R

S

Subject Index